Trager's The Law of Journalism and Mass Communication

Eighth Edition

For our families and mentors

Trager's The Law of Journalism and Mass Communication

Eighth Edition

Victoria Smith Ekstrand

The University of North Carolina at Chapel Hill

Caitlin Ring Carlson

Seattle University

Erin Coyle

Temple University

Susan Dente Ross

Washington State University

Amy Reynolds

Kent State University

Los Angeles | London | New Delhi
Singapore | Washington DC | Melbourne

FOR INFORMATION:

SAGE Publications, Inc.
2455 Teller Road
Thousand Oaks, California 91320
E-mail: order@sagepub.com

SAGE Publications Ltd.
1 Oliver's Yard
55 City Road
London, EC1Y 1SP
United Kingdom

SAGE Publications India Pvt. Ltd.
Unit No. 323-333, Third Floor, F-Block
International Trade Tower
Nehru Place, New Delhi 110 019
India

SAGE Publications Asia-Pacific Pte. Ltd.
18 Cross Street #10-10/11/12
China Square Central
Singapore 048423

Printed in the United States of America

Library of Congress Control Number: 2023905144

ISBN: 9781071857922

Acquisitions Editor: Charles Lee

Editorial Assistant: Enawamre Ogar

Production Editor: Astha Jaiswal

Copy Editor: Diane DiMura

Typesetter: diacriTech

Cover Designer: Candice Harman

Marketing Manager: Victoria Velasquez

This book is printed on acid-free paper.

23 24 25 26 27 10 9 8 7 6 5 4 3 2 1

BRIEF CONTENTS

DETAILED CONTENTS

LIST OF FEATURES

Chapter 9   Electronic Media Regulation: From Radio to the Internet

Cases for Study

Red Lion Broadcasting Co., Inc. v. Federal Communications Commission

Federal Communications Commission v. Prometheus Radio Project

International Law

Advertising to Children

Points of Law

Section 315 of the Communications Act of 1934

Real World Law

The FCC Commissioners

Modernization of the FCC

Low Power FM Radio Stations

COVID-19 Issues in an Era of "Cord Cutting"

Online Video Distributors

America's Digital Divide

Social Media Platforms as Public Forums

Chapter 10   Obscenity and Indecency: Social Norms and Legal Standards

Cases for Study

Federal Communications Commission v. Pacifica Foundation

Federal Communications Commission v. Fox Television Stations, Inc.

International Law

Kenya Moves to Ban All Online Pornography

Points of Law

The *Miller* Test

Real World Law

Sexting and Teens

Technology and Parental Control

Chapter 11   Intellectual Property: Protecting and Using Intangible Creations

Cases for Study

Matal v. Tam

Google LLC v. Oracle America, Inc.

Points of Law

The 1976 Copyright Act

Exclusive Rights in Copyrighted Works

Infringing Copyright

PREFACE

This book is intended and designed primarily to serve those planning to work in journalism, public relations, advertising or marketing in new, social or traditional media. Our goal is to offer a truly readable overview of the laws of journalism and mass communication and situate the most significant aspects of that law within the social and political contexts that give them meaning. We focus sharply on the legal issues related to gathering and disseminating information in today's multimedia age that we believe are most relevant to professional communicators.

Our unique approach to "The Law of Journalism and Mass Communication" developed in response to the way we teach and the way we believe people learn. We see the law as the shifting product of specific decisions at distinct times in particular places. As such, the law is best understood when we see and feel its effects on real people in routine conflicts and through the actions of our government as well as our friends, neighbors and families.

Our hope is that "The Law of Journalism and Mass Communication" is both approachable and interesting, grounded in the traditions and rules of law but also chock-full of fresh facts and new examples that bring the law to life today. We incorporate the latest court and legislative rulings and turn attention toward the events outside of courts and beyond the judiciary to illustrate how the law works in the real world for people living their lives each day. If we have succeeded, you will find this volume both educational and interesting.

FEATURES

In this eighth edition of "The Law of Journalism and Mass Communication," readers will discover a wealth of new content—from the U.S. Supreme Court, federal and state courts, Congress, executive agencies, federal and state policymakers and advisory groups, and media organizations and allies. Readers also will discover more than 60 new photographs and dozens of charts, graphs and tables to illustrate key trends or issues. More tightly focused breakout boxes in **International Law**, **Points of Law** and **Real World Law** highlight contemporary examples of the law in action or emphasize central concepts of law as well as intersections with international law and policy. They serve to supplement the principal discussion and to underscore important tests, breathe life into the facts and widen the lens through which we view the law.

At the end of each chapter, there is a **Glossary** of key terms along with two **Cases for Study**, which allow readers to engage directly with significant, often landmark, decisions to build upon the legal analysis and commentary of each chapter of "The Law of Journalism and Mass Communication."

ORGANIZATION AND COVERAGE

We have refreshed the look, feel and flow of many of the chapters in this edition to provide a clearer path through sometimes fast-expanding areas of the law and to offer new examples to guide better understanding of legal complexities. Among the more notable changes in this eighth edition of "The Law of Journalism and Mass Communication," readers will find an increased emphasis in each chapter on the historical, theoretical and constitutional foundations of the legal topic as a point of departure for examination of legal evolutions, alterations and current challenges. The authors believe this grounding is especially beneficial in areas of rapid legal change. It helps readers navigate the abundance of legal decisions and details to concentrate on the core concepts and principles that endure and embody the rule of law. We hope these alterations aid comprehension and retention of the material as they facilitate classroom activities, creativity and discussion.

In each chapter, the **Emerging Law** section has been updated to reflect the most pressing issues within each area of law. These sections cover topics such as nonconsensual pornography, social media regulation, book banning in K–12 schools, and "greenwashing" practices in marketing. Each chapter benefits from unique updates that are as timely as possible. More precisely, the first chapter offers a revised tone and approach to the introduction of communication law that takes current pressures on democratic governance and eroding trust in democracy into consideration. Chapter 1 also includes an updated overview of the U.S. Supreme Court and the inclusion of the case *U.S. v. Alvarez*, which has implications for protecting false speech under the First Amendment in the age of mis- and disinformation. It also includes a new Points of Law section on the tribal court system. Chapter 2 has been reorganized to begin by addressing the role of theory in the development of First Amendment doctrine. The discussion of the marketplace of ideas, self-governance, autonomy and self-fulfillment and critical perspectives, including critical race theory, have been added. Chapter 2 also includes a discussion of the changing media landscape along with a new Real World Law section focused on mask mandates, COVID-19 and the First Amendment.

Building from the foundations of the preceding chapters, Chapter 3 on speech distinctions moves chronologically through the U.S. Supreme Court's evolving definitions of speech categories and their First Amendment protection. A new section on Harassment, Cyberstalking and Cyberbullying has been added along with a discussion of incitement regarding the January 6, 2021, insurrection on the nation's Capitol. The discussion of hate speech has been updated to address international efforts to regulate this content online. The recent Supreme Court ruling in *Mahanoy Area School District v. B.L.* has been added to the section on school speech, along with a Real World Law box regarding public school teachers' use of students' preferred pronouns.

New cases and examples sharpen Chapter 4 on libel and emotional distress. Several Real World Law boxes have been added or updated here to address issues surrounding the president and defamation, fake news and disinformation and contemporary threats to our conception of actual malice. Chapter 5 on libel defenses includes updated cases and examples along with a revised section on states' Anti-SLAPP protections.

Chapter 6 on privacy provides a crisper summary of constitutional privacy and presents electronic privacy and U.S. Supreme Court decisions early on as a basis for new case law and statutes. The chapter offers a more detailed overview on privacy and data protection based on new case law. A new map detailing state laws addressing student athlete's name, image and likeness rights also has been added.

Chapter 7 on information gathering includes new cases and examples to illustrate issues ranging from right of access to right to record. A section on access to government records has been expanded, along with a section regarding the laws governing drone use. The privacy section in this chapter also has been expanded to include more information about The Health Insurance Portability and Accountability Act. A new International Law Box on threats and harassment of journalists has been added. A new case, *Van Buren v. United States* is now excerpted at the close of the chapter.

Chapter 8 has been updated with new cases and examples that reflect changes in media coverage of trials. Special attention has been paid to how courts have both utilized and regulated online access to court proceedings and how use of social media may interfere with fair trial rights. New maps detailing camera access to courts and juvenile age of jurisdiction and transfer to adult court have been added.

Chapter 9 on electronic media regulation has been updated to include a new section regarding gender and racial diversity of broadcast radio and television ownership, particularly in light of the Supreme Court's recent ruling in *FCC v. Prometheus Radio Project,* which has been added as a case for study at the close of the chapter. An in-depth discussion of Section 230 and its impact has also been included, along with a section on emerging state laws regarding social media regulation and the government's failed attempts to use anti-trust regulation to limit the influence of social media and other technology companies.

A more detailed explanation of the relationship between obscenity laws and LGBTQ rights has been added to the discussion of the history of obscenity law in Chapter 10. Indecency on streaming services and the government's lack of jurisdiction are also discussed, along with recent cases challenging Allow States and Victims to Fight Online Sex Trafficking Act. The **Emerging Law** section discusses state regulation of nonconsensual pornography, with a focus on deepfaked material.

Chapter 11 now begins by connecting intellectual property to student experiences with remix culture. Relevant new legislation such as the Protect Lawful Streaming Act and the Trademark Modernization Act are included as is a discussion of the roll out of the Copyright Alternative in Small-Claims Enforcement Act, which should make it easier for copyright holders to bring claims forward. Real World Law sections on NFTs have been added along with a discussion of trademarking social media hashtags. The case, *Google LLC v. Oracle America Inc.* has been added to the cases for study section at the end of the chapter.

The final chapter, Chapter 12, on advertising has been reorganized to reflect what we are calling the "3Cs of advertising law: Commercial Speech, Consumer Protection, and Corporate Political Speech." The chapter's revised introduction now reflects the growing importance of data mining in the lifeblood of the U.S. advertising economy. Several new Real World Law sections cover prominent issues such as false advertising for COVID treatments, regulation of content produced by student influencers, and the Consumer Financial Protection Bureau. A Section about gun advertising has been added along with an expansion of the discussion of the FTC's role in managing mis- and disinformation on social media platforms.

In this eighth edition of "The Law of Journalism and Mass Communication," you will discover a new breadth, diversity and dynamism of material intended to provide the tools for direct engagement with the law. As in the past, we have made every effort to ensure that this edition is lively and full of the most recent legal and policy decisions, the cutting-edge research in the field and the social, technological and economic influences upon them that transform the work and the products of professional communicators. Despite all the revisions, updates and new content, we believe this text will feel familiar to our longtime adopters. We hope you will find it in good order. As Aristotle once said, "Good law is good order."

DIGITAL RESOURCES

To supplement this text, we provide a wide range of online materials through a SAGE Edge companion website, located at **http://edge.sagepub.com/medialaw8e**. The site includes both student learning aids and teaching tools. The following resources have been updated and revised to enhance use of this new edition.

Password-protected **Instructor Resources** include the following:

- A **Microsoft® Word test bank** containing multiple-choice, true/false, short-answer and essay questions for each chapter. The test bank provides you with a diverse range of prewritten options as well as the opportunity for editing any question and/or inserting your own personalized questions to assess students' progress and understanding.

- Editable, chapter-specific Microsoft® **PowerPoint® slides** that offer you complete flexibility to create a multimedia presentation for your course that highlights the content and features you wish to emphasize.

- **Lecture notes** that summarize key concepts on a chapter-by-chapter basis to help you with preparation for lectures and class discussions.

- Lively and stimulating **class activities** that may be used to reinforce active, in-class learning. The activities include both individual and group opportunities.

- **Tables and figures** that may be downloaded for use in assignments, handouts and presentations.

- **Sample course syllabi** with suggested models for structuring your course that give you options to customize your course to your exact needs.

- **Links to professional resources**.

Our **Student Study Site** is completely open-access and offers a wide range of additional features:

- Mobile-friendly **eFlashcards** that reinforce understanding of key terms and concepts outlined in the chapters.

- Mobile-friendly **web quizzes** that allow for independent assessment of progress made in learning course material.

- **Links to professional resources** that guide students to materials that reinforce chapter concepts and facilitate research.

- An archive of **cases in media law** that provides the opportunity to read many of the legal decisions that construct "The Law of Journalism and Mass Communication."

ACKNOWLEDGMENTS

For almost five decades, Robert Trager has been a leading voice in media law education. As the founding author of this book, "The Law of Journalism and Mass Communication," he has helped to guide students in the study of media. We wish to acknowledge and thank Bob—more affectionately known as "Trager" to us. We honor his continuing wisdom, guidance and support in the publication of this edition, which now bears his name on the masthead. Thank you, Trager, for lighting the path so many of us now walk.

This book has been a collaborative effort not only among its authors but also between us and the community we serve. The knowledge, insights and comments of a large and expanding group of people have helped us update and improve this book. We offer our deep respect and gratitude to all those who have shaped our understanding of the field, gently pointed out our faults of commission or omission and reinforced the strengths of this edition of "The Law of Journalism and Mass Communication." You have been more generous than we might reasonably expect.

Beyond the friends, families, students, mentors and colleagues who have encouraged and supported us in uncounted ways, we extend special thanks to all the anonymous reviewers who provided valuable feedback or, perhaps, favored our text among other books in the field. We also thank the talented editors, designers and staff at CQ Press/SAGE who helped bring this new edition to you.

Finally, and most importantly, we thank you, our readers.

The authors and SAGE also gratefully acknowledge the contributions of the following reviewers:

REVIEWERS

Julie Roosa, Iowa State University
Patrick McGrail, Jacksonville State University
Judith G. Curtis, University of North Carolina - Pembroke
Angela Anima-Korang, East Texas Baptist University
James Carviou, Missouri Western State University
Gilbert Martinez, Texas State University
Amanda Reid, University of North Carolina at Chapel Hill
Ivan Saperstein, Seton Hall University
Michael Berry, King's College
Roger Soenksen, James Madison University

ABOUT THE AUTHORS

Victoria Smith Ekstrand is an associate professor at the UNC Hussman School of Journalism and Media and is currently serving the UNC Graduate School as the Caroline H. and Thomas S. Royster Distinguished Professor for Graduate Education, where she leads UNC's premier doctoral fellows from across campus. She has been a media law and free expression scholar for more than two decades. Before that, she worked as a senior executive for The Associated Press at its headquarters in New York City.

Caitlin Ring Carlson is an associate professor in communication and media at Seattle University and the former head of the Association for Education in Journalism and Mass Communication Law and Policy Division. She teaches courses in media law, gender equality and freedom of expression and media systems. Her research focuses on media law and policy as they pertain to new media, freedom of expression, and social justice. Her first book, "Hate Speech," was published by MIT Press in 2021. Before earning her PhD at the University of Colorado, she worked as a public relations practitioner.

Erin Coyle is an associate professor in journalism at the Temple University Klein College of Media and Communication. She teaches courses in media law and ethics, reporting, writing, and media history. Her research focuses on freedom of expression, access to government information and officials and free press–fair trial and privacy rights. While earning her PhD at the University of North Carolina at Chapel Hill, she served on the First Amendment Law Review. Before entering graduate school, she worked as a journalist covering government affairs.

Susan Dente Ross is professor of English at Washington State University. Onetime head of the Association for Education in Journalism and Mass Communication Law Division, she is a Fulbright scholar whose work on freedom of speech and press seeks greater global equity and justice for the disempowered. She writes on law, policy and media's role in conflict transformation and reconciliation. A former owner/editor of a community newspaper, she continues to publish creative nonfiction.

Amy Reynolds is dean of the College of Communication and Information at Kent State University. Her research focuses on dissent, First Amendment history and media sociology. She has written or edited seven books. Prior to becoming a dean, she was a journalism professor at Louisiana State University and Indiana University. Before earning her PhD at the University of Texas, she worked as a reporter, producer and editor at newspapers and television stations.

Amy Coney Barrett was confirmed as a U.S. Supreme Court justice in 2020. She was approved by the U.S. Senate, 55–43.

Supreme Court nominee Ketanji Brown Jackson testifies during her Senate Judiciary Committee confirmation hearing on Capitol Hill in Washington. She was confirmed by the U.S Senate, 53–47, in April 2022.

THE RULE OF LAW

Law in a Changing Communication and Political Environment

CHAPTER OUTLINE

Rule of Law

Body of the Law
Constitutions
Statutes
Common Law
Equity Law
Administrative Law
Executive Orders

Structure of the Judicial System
Court Jurisdiction
Trial Courts
Courts of Appeal
The U.S. Supreme Court

Processes of the Law
Civil Suits
Summary Judgment

Finding and Reading Case Law
Briefing Cases
Analyzing *Marbury v. Madison*

Cases for Study
- *Marbury v. Madison*
- *U.S. v. Alvarez*

LEARNING OBJECTIVES

1.1 Define rule of law and explain the role of law in society.

1.2 Describe the six original sources that create laws of journalism and mass communication.

1.3 Describe the structure of the U.S. judicial system and how cases move through the appeals process.

1.4 Find and feel comfortable using legal research resources.

1.5 Understand how to read and brief a case.

RULE OF LAW

In 2020, then-U.S. Attorney General Bill Barr addressed college students in Michigan, and told them the rule of law "is the lynchpin of American freedom." As the nation's top lawyer in the country, he said its "essence" is that "whatever rule you apply to in one case must be the same rule you would apply to similar cases," and that it "requires the law be clear, that it be communicated to the public, and that we respect its limits."[1] Not long after his speech, however, a federal judge accused Barr and the U.S. Justice Department of hiding how they decided that former President Trump should not be charged with obstructing special counsel Robert Mueller's investigation of Russian interference in the 2016 presidential election.[2]

In 2021, Katie Wright, mother of Daunte Wright, a 20-year-old biracial man who was shot and killed during a traffic stop by a Minnesota police officer, questioned Americans' faith in the rule of law. "The last few days everybody has asked me what we want, what do we want to see happen. Everybody keeps saying 'justice.' But unfortunately, there's never going to be justice for us. Justice would bring our son home to us. Knocking on the door with his big smile. Coming in the house. Sitting down. Eating dinner with us. . . . I do want accountability—100 percent accountability. But even then, when that happens, if that even happens, we're still going to bury our son. . . . So when people say 'justice,' I just shake my head."[3]

For an increasing number of Americans, this kind of disconnect between the rule of law and what some scholars term a rule *by* law, reveals yet more evidence of growing concerns about trust in U.S. democracy and the rule of law. As one legal scholar put it, "there are a lot of tough questions surrounding this one little phrase, the rule of law."[4]

The ancient Greek philosopher Aristotle said people are basically self-interested; they pursue their own interests in preference to the collective good or the cause of justice. However, self-interest is ultimately shortsighted and self-destructive. A lumber company that seeks only to generate the greatest immediate profit ultimately deforests the timberlands it depends on.[5] Astute people therefore recognize that personal interests and short-term goals must sometimes give way to broader or longer-term objectives. Everyone benefits when people adopt a system of rules to promote a balance between gain and loss, between cost and benefit and between personal and universal concerns. Aristotle called this balance the "golden mean." Human interests are served and justice is best achieved when a society adopts a system of law to balance conflicting human objectives and allow people to live together successfully.[6]

Belief in the power of law to promote this balance and restrain human injustice is the foundation of the U.S. Constitution and the **rule of law**. Quoting President John Adams, the U.S. Supreme Court said the notion that "our government is a government of laws, not of men" is central to our constitutional nature.[7] "Stripped of all technicalities, [the rule of law] means that government in all its actions is bound by rules fixed and announced beforehand—rules which make it possible to foresee with fair certainty how [government] will use its coercive powers in given circumstances, and to plan . . . on the basis of this knowledge."[8]

In essence, laws establish a contract that governs interactions among residents and between the people and their government. Legal rules establish the boundaries of acceptable behavior and empower government to punish violations. The rule of law limits the power of government because it prohibits government from infringing on the rights and liberties of the people. This system constrains the actions of both the people and the government to enhance liberty, freedom and justice for all.

But the strength of the rule of law is only as effective as the trust and faith placed in it by citizens.[9] And trust in government institutions, which includes the legal system, has been declining in the United States since the 1960s. Only about one-quarter of Americans in 2021 said they could trust their government to do what is right just about always (2%) or most of the time (22%), according to the Pew Research Center. That is down significantly from the beginnings of the survey in 1958, when 75 percent of Americans thought they could trust their government always or most of the time. Additionally, about two-thirds of Americans in 2020 reported thinking that their political system needed major changes or reform.[10]

And laws, of course, are not the only way that citizens govern interactions among themselves and their government. Democratic norms and unwritten rules occur throughout government operations and local communities, and concerns about the erosion of such norms has grown in recent years, particularly during the Trump administration, but also dating as far back as the 1970s.[11] In the digital age, the increasing power of technology and corporate influence on American life led Harvard Law professor Lawrence Lessig to posit that the lives of U.S. citizens are increasingly regulated by four forces: law, social norms, the market and architecture (mostly digital technologies at this point).[12] Each one of these forces acts to regulate media and depending on the situation, may hold more power over it. While technology continues to impact and challenge laws in the U.S. and worldwide, law remains a dominant organizing force in and among societies.

In 1964, as the United States expanded what many then believed was an illegal military action in Vietnam, Harvard legal scholar Lon Fuller articulated what would become a foundational understanding of the rule of law. In Fuller's view, the rule of law was a set of standards that established norms and procedures to encourage consistent, neutral decision making equally for all. Fuller's formal, conceptual definition has been criticized because it does not provide specific guidance to those drafting, interpreting or applying the law.[13] As one legal scholar noted, the rule of law is created through its application. It "cannot be [understood] in the abstract."[14] Additionally, some critical studies of law characterize the labeling of "neutral" legal principles and doctrines as problematic. These scholars see the law as often interdeterminate and a product of those who hold power.[15]

For Fuller, the rule of law established eight "desiderata," or desired outcomes, to guide how laws should be created and employed. The rule of law requires laws to be (1) general and not discriminatory, (2) widely known and disseminated, (3) forward-looking in their application rather than retroactive, (4) clear and specific, (5) self-consistent and complementary of each other, (6) capable of being obeyed, (7) relatively stable over time and (8) applied and enforced in ways that reflect their underlying intent.

As a mechanism for ordering human behavior, the law functions best when it makes clear, comprehensible and consistent distinctions between legal and illegal behavior. People can only obey laws that they know about and understand. Good laws must be publicly disseminated and sufficiently clear and precise to properly inform citizens of when and how the laws apply (as well as when they do not).

INTERNATIONAL LAW
FOUR FOUNDATIONS OF THE RULE OF LAW

The World Justice Project has articulated four foundations of the rule of law based on internationally accepted universal standards. Accordingly, a system of the rule of law exists when:

1. All individuals and private entities are accountable under the law.
2. The laws are fair, clear, public and stable.
3. The processes by which the laws are enacted, administered and enforced are open, robust and timely for all.
4. Those who apply the law are competent, ethical, independent, neutral and diverse.[16]

Many argue that any movement toward a universal rule of law is a form of imperialism that tramples the unique priorities of individual nations and limits the freedom of different peoples to create distinct, culturally appropriate systems of law.[17]

Vague laws fail to define their terms or are unclear. They are unacceptable because people may avoid participating in legal activities out of uncertainty over whether their actions are illegal. This tramples people's freedom. In 2018, the U.S. Supreme Court by a vote of 5–4 struck down a provision of the Immigration and Nationality Act[18] as unconstitutionally vague.[19] The law practically required the deportation of any immigrant convicted of an "aggravated felony" or "crime of violence." The Court reasoned that applying the provision's imprecise language "necessarily devolves into guesswork and intuition, invites arbitrary enforcement and fails to provide fair notice,"[20] all of which violate the basic tenets of due process. These core elements of due process, Justice Neil M. Gorsuch wrote in concurrence, are foundational to the Constitution's original meaning and basic to the rule of law.[21]

INTERNATIONAL LAW
U.S. RULE OF LAW DOES NOT RANK FIRST

An international index ranks the United States 27th among 139 countries in how citizens experience the rule of law.[22] The World Justice Project report put the United States behind the Nordic countries, the Czech Republic and Japan but well ahead of Afghanistan, Cambodia and Venezuela. Overall, the World Justice Project noted that deterioration in the rule of law is spreading worldwide.

The study found relative weaknesses in the U.S. respect for equal treatment of citizens and absence of discrimination, and the timeliness and impartiality of criminal justice.

Clear laws define their terms and detail their application in order to limit government officials' **discretion**. Clear laws advance the rule of law by reducing the ability of officials to apply legal rules differently to their friends and foes. "True freedom requires the rule of law and justice, and a judicial system in which the rights of some are not secured by the denial of rights to others," one observer noted.[23]

Good laws accomplish their objectives with minimum infringement on the freedoms and liberties of the people. Well-tailored laws advance specific government interests or prevent particular harms without punishing activities that pose no risk to society. A law that sought to limit noisy disturbances of residential neighborhoods at night, for example, would be poorly tailored and **overbroad** if it prohibited all discussion out of doors, anywhere at any time.

The rule of law requires the law to be internally consistent, logical and relatively stable. To ensure slow evolution rather than rapid revolution of legal rules, judges in U.S. courts interpret and apply laws based upon the **precedents** established by other court rulings. Precedent, or **stare decisis**, is the legal principle that tells courts to stand by what courts have decided previously. As the U.S. Supreme Court has written, "[T]he very concept of the rule of law underlying our own Constitution requires such continuity over time that a respect for precedent is, by definition, indispensable."[24] The principle holds that subsequent court decisions should adhere to the example and reasoning of earlier decisions in similar factual situations. Reliance on precedent is the heart of the common law (discussed later) and encourages predictable application of the law. The Supreme Court's 2022 decision to overrule *Roe v. Wade*, however, raised questions among some commentators about whether the current Court is committed to the principles of stare decisis. A Congressional report in 2018 found that the Court has reversed itself only 141 times, or on average, less than once a year since 1851.[25]

Although the application of prior rulings promotes the rule of law by increasing the consistency and uniformity of legal decision making,[26] it does not always happen. Sometimes precedents are unclear or seem to conflict. Then the rule of law can be ambiguous.[27] Especially where constitutional values are at issue, courts may "not allow principles of stare decisis to block correction of error," the California Supreme Court said.[28]

In 2010, for example, a "bitterly divided" U.S. Supreme Court ruled 5–4 in *Citizens United v. Federal Election Commission* that certain federal limits on campaign finance violated the Constitution. Observers noted that the decision made "sweeping changes in federal election law"[29] and "represented a sharp doctrinal shift."[30] Some said the Court had ignored binding precedent. Others argued that "the central principle which critics of this ruling find most offensive . . . has been affirmed by decades of Supreme Court jurisprudence."[31] Thus, the conflict centered less on *whether* to apply precedent and more on *which* precedents to apply.

BODY OF THE LAW

The laws of the United States have grown in number and complexity as American society has become increasingly diverse and complicated. Many forms of communication and the laws that govern them today did not exist in the 1800s. Technology has been a driving force for change in the law of journalism and mass communication. U.S. law also has developed in response to social, political, philosophical and economic changes. Employment and advertising laws, for example, emerged and multiplied as the nation's workforce shifted and the power of corporations grew. Legislatures create new laws to reflect evolving understandings of individual rights, liberties and responsibilities. Even well-established legal concepts, such as libel—harm to another's reputation—have evolved to reflect new realities of the role of communication in society and the power of mass media to harm individuals.

The laws of journalism and mass communication generally originate from six sources.

Constitutions

Statutes

Common Law

Equity Law

Administrative Law

Executive Orders

Constitutions

Constitutional law establishes the nature, functions and limits of government. The U.S. Constitution, the fundamental law of the United States, was framed in 1787 and ratified in 1789. Each of the states also has a constitution. These constitutions define the structure of government and delegate and limit government power to protect certain fundamental human rights. "Constitutions are checks upon the hasty action of the majority," said President William Howard Taft in 1911. "They are self-imposed restraints of a whole people upon a majority of them to secure sober action and a respect for the rights of the minority."[32]

Given the legacy of British religious oppression and the revolution against the Crown that formed this country, it should not be surprising that the U.S. Constitution protects individual liberties sometimes at the expense of much larger groups. The First Amendment, for example, generally protects an individual's right to speak very offensively, while laws in other countries are far more likely to punish hate speech, name-calling, denial of the Holocaust, criticism of government officials, anti-religious speech and much more.

The U.S. Constitution establishes the character of government, organizes the federal government and provides a minimum level of individual rights and privileges throughout the country. It creates three separate and coequal branches of government—the executive, the legislative and the judicial—and designates the functions and responsibilities of each. The executive branch oversees government and administers, or executes, laws. The legislative branch enacts laws, and the judicial branch interprets laws and resolves legal conflicts.

POINTS OF LAW
THE THREE BRANCHES OF FEDERAL GOVERNMENT

The Executive

The president, the cabinet and the administrative agencies execute laws.

The Legislative

The Senate and the House of Representatives pass laws.

The Judicial

The three levels of courts review laws and adjudicate disputes.

Separation of government into branches provides checks and balances within government to support the rule of law. For example, "restrictions derived from the separation of powers doctrine prevent the judicial branch from deciding **political questions** . . . that revolve around policy choices and value determinations" because the Constitution gives the legislative and executive branches express authority to make political decisions.[33] This does not necessarily mean that the judiciary is immune from politics. An increasingly polarized political climate has raised the stakes for judicial appointments and elections. A 2019 study by two Harvard researchers indicated that as nominations to the U.S. Supreme Court become more contentious, partisan rhetoric about the courts can change public perceptions of the court's role as immune from political questions.[34]

The **Supremacy Clause** of the Constitution establishes the Constitution as the supreme law of the land and resolves conflicts among laws by establishing that all state laws must give way to federal law, and state or federal laws that conflict with the Constitution are invalid. In a similar way, some federal laws preempt state laws, which in turn may preempt city statutes. Here, too, a changing political climate can affect debate about the Supremacy Clause and the balance of state and national legislative power. In recent years, some state legislatures have introduced bills attempting to increase their power over immigration,[35] telecommunication policy[36] and gun ownership.[37] This tension is always present in U.S. law, but is often elevated during times of social change and political partisanship.

As the bedrock of the law, the Constitution is relatively difficult to change. There are two ways to amend the Constitution. The first and only method actually used is for both chambers of Congress to pass a proposed constitutional amendment by a two-thirds vote in each. The second method is for two-thirds of the state legislatures to vote for a Constitutional Convention, which then proposes one or more amendments. All amendments to the Constitution also must be ratified by three-fourths of the state legislatures. When Mississippi recently became the last state to ban slavery by ratifying the Thirteenth Amendment to the Constitution, the vote was only symbolic. The needed three-fourths of states ratified the amendment in 1865.[38]

In many ways, state constitutions are distinct and independent from the U.S. Constitution they mirror. Under the principle of **federalism**, states are related to, yet independent of, the federal government and each other. Federalism encourages experimentation and variety in government. Each state has freedom to structure its unique form of government and to craft state constitutional protections that exceed the rights granted by the U.S. Constitution. For example, the U.S. Constitution says nothing about municipalities; states create and determine the authority of cities or towns. While the federal right to privacy exists only through the U.S. Supreme Court's interpretation of the protections afforded by the Fourth Amendment to the Constitution, Washington state's constitution contains an explicit privacy clause that protects individuals from disturbances of their private affairs.[39]

Congress has approved only 33 of the thousands of proposed amendments to the U.S. Constitution, and the states have ratified only 27 of these. The first 10 amendments to the Constitution, which form the Bill of Rights, were ratified in 1791 after several states called for increased constitutional protection of individual liberties. In fewer than 500 words, the Bill of Rights expressly guarantees fundamental rights and limits government power. For example, the First Amendment (see Chapter 2) prevents government from abridging the people's right to speak and worship freely. State constitutions are amended by a direct vote of the people.

Statutes

The U.S. Constitution explicitly delegates the power to enact statutory laws to the popularly elected legislative branch of government. City, county, state and federal legislative bodies enact **statutory law**. Like constitutions, statutes are written down; both types of law are called **black-letter law**, meaning formally enacted, written law that is available in legal reporters or other documents.

INTERNATIONAL LAW
U.S. COURTS MAY (OR MAY NOT) APPLY INTERNATIONAL LAWS

It may seem strange, but U.S. courts do not have a certain and fixed method for dealing with international laws. Judges and academics have debated the topic for decades because the Constitution does not clearly establish how foreign laws should be applied in cases decided in the United States. Once a rather theoretical question, exploding global commerce and communications give this topic increased urgency and impact.

The Constitution delegates exclusive power over war and foreign relations to the Congress and the president.[40] The Constitution's Supremacy Clause establishes three sources of law: the Constitution itself, "laws made in pursuance" to the Constitution and "Treaties."[41] Because laws can be adopted only through action of the U.S. Senate or state legislatures, some argue that U.S. courts need not recognize the law of other nations.[42]

Others claim that the Constitution's establishment of the courts[43] implicitly conveys the responsibility to incorporate international law as enforceable common law when they generally and consistently rely upon it to guide decisions.[44] Thus, if courts use international law, it binds. But what if some U.S. states do and others do not?

The resulting uncertainty can create inconsistency in the application of the law and undermine the rule of law.

Legislatures make laws to respond to—or predict and attempt to prevent—social problems. Statutory law may be very specific to define the legal limits of particular activities. All criminal laws are statutes, for example. Statutes also establish the rules of copyright, broadcasting, advertising and access to government meetings and information. Statutes are formally adopted through a public process and are meant to be clear and stable. They are written down in statute books and codified, which means they are compiled into topics by codes, and anyone can find and read them in public repository libraries.

Laws can change. Even the U.S. Constitution—the foundational contract between the U.S. government and the people—can be changed through amendment. Other laws—statutes, regulations and rules—may be repealed or amended by the federal, state and local bodies that adopted them, and they may be interpreted or invalidated by the courts. In its landmark 1803 ruling in *Marbury v. Madison* (excerpted at the end of this chapter), the Supreme Court established the courts' power to interpret laws. The Court held that "[i]t is emphatically the province and duty of the judicial department to say what the law is. Those who apply the rule to particular cases must of necessity expound and interpret that rule."[45]

When the language of a statute is unclear, imprecise or ambiguous, courts determine the law's meaning and application through a process called statutory **construction**. Statutes may be difficult to interpret because they fail to define key terms. When a statute suggests more than one meaning, courts generally look to the law's preamble, or statement of purpose, for guidance on how the legislature intended the law to apply. Courts may use legislative committee reports, debates and public statements to guide their statutory interpretation.

Courts tend to engage in **strict construction**, which narrowly defines laws according to their literal meaning and clearly stated intent. The effort to interpret laws according to the "plain meaning" of the words—the **facial meaning** of the law—limits any tendency courts might have to rewrite laws through creative or expansive interpretation. This **deference** to legislative intent reflects courts' recognition that the power to write laws lies with the publicly elected legislature (see Figure 1.1).

In 2020, the 117th U.S. Congress seated its most diverse group of new members. According to the Pew Research Center, almost a quarter of voting members (23%) of the U.S. House of Representatives and Senate are racial or ethnic minorities. There has been a long-running trend toward higher numbers of non-white lawmakers on Capitol Hill: This was the sixth Congress to break the record set by the one before it.

Courts may invalidate state statutes that conflict with federal laws, or city statutes that conflict with either state or federal law. However, courts try to interpret the plain meaning of a statute to avoid conflicts with other laws, including the Constitution. Courts review the constitutionality of a statute only as a last resort. When engaging in constitutional review,

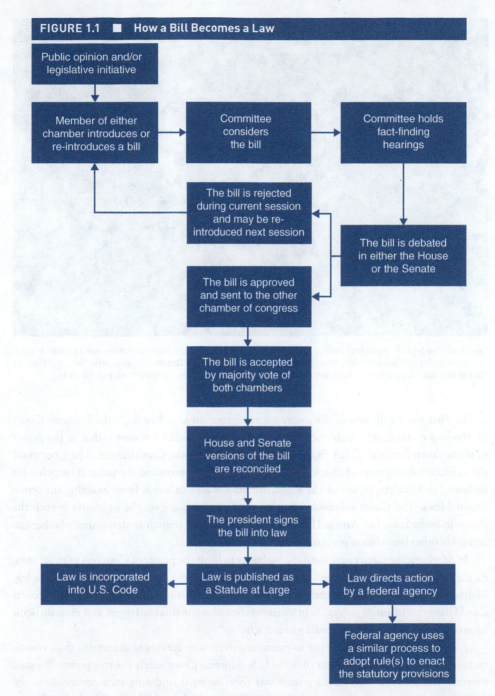

FIGURE 1.1 ■ How a Bill Becomes a Law

Public opinion and/or legislative initiative

Member of either chamber introduces or re-introduces a bill

Committee considers the bill

Committee holds fact-finding hearings

The bill is rejected during current session and may be re-introduced next session

The bill is debated in either the House or the Senate

The bill is approved and sent to the other chamber of congress

The bill is accepted by majority vote of both chambers

House and Senate versions of the bill are reconciled

The president signs the bill into law

Law is incorporated into U.S. Code

Law is published as a Statute at Large

Law directs action by a federal agency

Federal agency uses a similar process to adopt rule(s) to enact the statutory provisions

courts generally attempt to preserve any portions of the law that can be upheld without violating the general intent of the statute. For example, the U.S. Supreme Court struck down the Communications Decency Act[46] without undermining the balance of the comprehensive Telecommunications Act of 1996 (see Chapter 9).

Known as "The Squad," these four Democratic members of the U.S. House of Representatives were elected in 2018: Ayanna Pressley of Massachusetts, Ilhan Omar of Minnesota, Alexandria Ocasio-Cortez of New York, and Rashida Tlaib of Michigan. All are said to represent the diversity of young progressives in the left wing of the party.

In what some call "one of the greatest legal events" in U.S. history,[47] the Supreme Court in *Marbury v. Madison*[48] established the Court's power of **judicial review**—that is, the power to strike down laws the Court finds to be in conflict with the Constitution. The Court said the constitutional system of checks and balances implicitly provided the judicial branch with authority to limit the power of the legislative branch and to bar it from enacting unconstitutional laws. The Court acknowledged that the Constitution gave the legislative branch the power to make laws, but Article III empowered the judicial branch to determine whether the actions of other branches of government were unconstitutional.

In *Marbury*, the Court gave itself the authority to limit the power of Congress to enact laws. As the final arbiters of law in the United States, the courts must ensure that actions of the legislative and executive branches conform to the U.S. Constitution, *Marbury* held. "Why courts should have this ultimate power . . . in a democratic order remains the largest and most difficult issue of constitutional law," according to one scholar.[49]

Judicial review allows all courts to examine government actions to determine their constitutionality. However, courts other than the U.S. Supreme Court rarely use this power. If a state supreme court determined that a statute was constitutional under its state constitution, the decision could be appealed to the U.S. Supreme Court, which could decide that the law did not meet the standards set by the U.S. Constitution.

Historically, the Supreme Court has used its power of judicial review sparingly and rarely struck down laws as unconstitutional. For more than half a century after *Marbury*, the Court did not use its power as chief interpreter of the Constitution. As a general rule, the Court will defer to the lawmaking authority of the executive and legislative branches of government by interpreting laws in ways that do not conflict with the Constitution. Nonetheless, it has invalidated numerous acts of Congress.

Common Law

The **common law** is judge-made law. Most common law is found at the state level, although there is some remaining federal common law. Judges create the common law when they rely on legal custom, tradition and prior court decisions to guide their decisions in pending cases. Common law often arises in situations not covered expressly by statutes when judges base their ruling on precedent and legal **doctrines** established in similar cases. For example, under common law, judges may treat print publishers and online distributors of threatening communications differently (see Chapter 3).

The common law is not written down in one place. It consists of a vast body of legal principles created from hundreds of years of dispute resolution that reaches past the founding of this country back to England. For centuries prior to the settlement of the American colonies, English courts "discovered" the doctrines people had used throughout time to resolve disagreements. Judges then applied these "common" laws to guide court decisions. The resulting decisions, and the reasoning that supported them, was known as English common law. It became the foundation of U.S. common law. Common law principles are sometimes adopted into statute by legislators. This was the case with the "fair use" doctrine in copyright law, which was enshrined in federal copyright law in 1976.

Eventually, common law grew beyond the problem-solving principles of the common people. Today, U.S. common law rests on the presumption that prior court rulings, or precedent, should guide future courts. The essence of precedent, stare decisis, is that courts should follow each other's guidance. Once a higher court has established a principle relevant to a certain set of facts, fairness requires lower courts to try to apply the same principle to similar facts. This establishes consistency and stability in the law.

REAL WORLD LAW
PRECEDENT IS A CORNERSTONE OF THE RULE OF LAW

In a 2018 dissenting opinion, Justice Elena Kagan wrote:

> The idea that today's Court should stand by yesterday's decisions is a foundation stone of the rule of law. It promotes the evenhanded, predictable and consistent development of legal doctrine. It fosters respect for and reliance on judicial decisions. And it contributes to the actual and perceived integrity of the judicial process by ensuring that decisions are founded in the law rather than in the proclivities of individuals.[50]

Under the rule of stare decisis, the decision of a higher court, such as the U.S. Supreme Court, establishes a precedent that binds lower court rulings. A binding precedent of the U.S. Supreme Court constrains all lower federal courts throughout the country, and the decisions of each circuit court of appeals bind the district courts in that circuit. Similarly, lower state courts must follow the precedents of their own state appellate and supreme courts. However, courts from different and coequal jurisdictions do not establish binding precedent upon their peers. Courts in Rhode Island are not bound to follow precedents established in Wyoming, and federal district courts are not bound to apply precedents established by appellate courts in other federal circuits. In fact, different federal appellate courts sometimes hand down directly conflicting decisions. To avoid such conflicts, however, courts often look to each other's decisions for guidance.

Applying precedent is not clear cut. After all, the common law must be discovered through research in the thousands of court decisions collected into centuries of volumes, called court reporters. Sometimes, multiple lines of precedent seem to converge and suggest different outcomes.[51] Then a court must choose.

Even when stare decisis is clear and its power most direct, lower courts may decide not to adhere to precedent. At the risk of the judges' credibility, courts may simply ignore precedent. Courts also may depart from precedent with good reason. Courts examining a new but similar question may decide to **modify precedent**—that is, to alter the precedent to respond to changed realities. Thus, the U.S. Supreme Court might find that contemporary attitudes and practices no longer support a precent more than 20 years old permitting government to maintain the secrecy of computer compilations of public records.[52]

Courts also may **distinguish from precedent** by asserting that factual differences between the current case and the precedent case outweigh similarities. For example, the Supreme Court 40-plus years ago distinguished between newspapers and broadcasters in terms of any right of public access.[53] The Court said the public has a right to demand that broadcasters provide diverse content on issues of public importance because broadcasters use the public airwaves. The Court did not apply that reasoning when it later considered virtually the same question as applied to newspapers. Newspapers, the Court said, are independent members of the press with a protected right to control their content. The Supreme Court similarly has said "common-sense distinctions" differentiate advertising, which the courts call commercial speech, from other varieties of speech.[54]

Finally, courts very occasionally will **overturn precedent** outright and reject the fundamental premise of an earlier decision. This is a radical step and generally occurs only to remedy past errors or to reflect a fundamental rethinking of the law. In the Supreme Court's decision in *Janus*, the Court overruled a 30-year-old Court precedent that had required public employees to pay their "fair share" of union dues even if the employees chose not to join the union.[55] The Court said an older case had been poorly reasoned, produced inconsistent outcomes and violated nonmembers' right to be free from government-compelled subsidies of private speech on matters of public concern.

Equity Law

Equity law is a second form of law made by judges when they apply general principles of ethics and fairness to determine the proper remedy for a legal harm. When a court orders someone to stop using your trademark in addition to paying fines that cover the costs of actual damages caused, the order recognizes that continued use might force you out of business or associate you with products of lesser quality. Such a ruling represents the application of equity law to achieve a just result.

Equity law is intended to provide fair remedies for various harms that are not addressed in other forms of law or because fairness will not be achieved fully or at all through the rigid application of strict rules. No specific, black-letter laws dictate equity. Rather, judges use their conscience and discretion to decide what is fair and issue decrees to ensure that justice is achieved. Thus, restraining orders that require paparazzi to stay a certain distance away from celebrities are a form of equity law. An injunction in 1971 that temporarily prevented The New York Times and The Washington Post from publishing stories based on the Pentagon Papers was another form of equity relief. While the law of equity is related to common law, the rules of equity law are more flexible and are not governed by precedent.

Administrative Law

Constitutions and legislatures delegate authority to executives and to specialized executive branch agencies to make the decisions and create the rules that form **administrative law.** Administrative agencies, such as the Federal Election Commission or the Federal Trade Commission, create the rules, regulations, orders and decisions that execute, or carry out, laws enacted by Congress.

Administrative law may represent the largest proportion of contemporary law in the United States. An alphabet soup of state and federal administrative agencies—such as the Federal Communications Commission, which oversees interstate electronic communication—provides both legislative and judicial functions. These agencies adopt orders, rules and regulations with the force of law to implement the laws enacted by Congress and signed by the president.

The authority, or even the existence, of administrative agencies can change. Legislatures may adopt or amend laws to revise the responsibilities of administrative agencies. Thus, when Congress adopted the Telecommunications Act of 1996, it substantially revised the responsibilities of the FCC, originally authorized by the Communications Act of 1934.

Administrative agencies enforce the administrative rules they adopt. They conduct hearings in which they interpret their rules, grant relief, resolve disputes and levy fines or penalties. Courts generally have the power to hear appeals to the decisions of administrative agencies after agency appeal procedures are exhausted. Then courts engage in regulatory construction and judicial review. Courts generally defer to the judgment of expert administrative agencies and void agency rules and actions only when the agency clearly has exceeded its authority, violated its rules and procedures, or provided no evidence to support its ruling.

In 2015, however, the U.S. Supreme Court refused to defer to administrative interpretations of the meaning of the Affordable Care Act's precise terms.[56] The Court said the "task to determine the correct reading" of the law fell to the Court itself when, as in this case, Congress did not intend to delegate the authority to "fill in the statutory gaps" to the administrative agency.[57] Carefully parsing the meaning of the key phrases in the contested section of the law and "bearing in mind . . . that the words of a statute must be read in their context and with a view to their place in the overall statutory scheme,"[58] the Court affirmed the ruling of the Fourth Circuit Court of Appeals and found the law constitutional.[59] In *West Virginia v. EPA*, the U.S. Supreme Court in 2022 held that agencies can't take action on anything the Court considers a "major question" without clear Congressional approval, no matter how much expertise the agency has and regardless of congressional intent.[60]

Many saw the Court's actions in both cases as signaling a movement away from deference to administrative agency judgments. Some said the Court's shift reinforced the rule of law by counterbalancing any tendency for the new administrative agency leaders appointed by each incoming president to alter the interpretation of administrative laws.[61]

Executive Orders

Government executives, such as the president, may issue **executive orders** (EO) to create another source of law. Presidents Barack Obama, Donald Trump and Joe Biden have used executive orders to achieve policy objectives when Congress failed to act. Their executive orders prompted frequent outcry from political opponents and protests that each was circumventing the express authority of Congress, in violation of the rule of law.

Executive Orders of Recent U.S. Presidents				
	Time Period	Total	No./Yr.	Exec. Order No.
William J. Clinton	**Total**	**364**	**46**	**12834–13197**
	Term I	200	50	12834–13033
	Term II	164	41	13034–13197
George W. Bush	**Total**	**291**	**36**	**13198–13488**
	Term I	173	43	13198–13370
	Term II	118	30	13371–13488
Barack Obama	**Total**	**276**	**35**	**13489–13764**
	Term I	147	37	13489–13635
	Term II	129	32	13636–13764
Donald J. Trump	**Total**	**220**	**55**	**13765–13984**
Joseph R. Biden (2021)	Total	108	50	13985 – 14092

Source: Washington–Biden, The American Presidency Project, presidency.proxied.lsit.ucsb.edu/data/orders.php.

The president, governors and mayors do not have unlimited power to issue executive orders. The Supreme Court long has held that executive orders must fall within the inherent powers of the executive to have the force of law.[62] The Court has said executive orders must arise from the president's explicit power under Article II, Section 2 of the Constitution, his role as commander in chief, or his responsibility to ensure that laws are properly executed. If the delegation of power to the executive is not clear, the authority to issue executive orders falls into what Justice Robert H. Jackson once called a "zone of twilight" ambiguity.[63] However, the limits to the power to issue executive orders are largely informal and primarily a matter of self-restraint and tradition.[64]

Early in 2019, for example, the American Civil Liberties Union and 16 states filed separate lawsuits in federal court in California challenging President Trump's executive order declaring a national emergency to build a wall along the southern border.[65] The ACLU argued that the executive order unconstitutionally usurped the authority of Congress to control spending. A U.S. district court and the U.S. Circuit Court of Appeals for the Ninth Circuit ruled against the Trump administration,[66] and the U.S. Supreme Court announced it would hear the case in 2020. In 2021, President Joe Biden terminated the order with his own executive order, and the Supreme Court cancelled hearing arguments in the case.[67]

Former President Trump's 2017 executive order banning Muslims from the U.S. was also challenged by protestors and courts.[68] Titled "Protecting the Nation From Foreign Terrorist Entry into the United States," the EO was initially blocked by courts,[69] but a later version of the order was upheld by the U.S. Supreme Court.[70] The EO was also revoked in January 2021 by President Biden.

Some executive orders are routine. For example, each president of the United States issues orders that determine what types of records will be open and which will be classified as secret, how long they will remain secret and who has access to them. Changes in these rules not only affect the operations of the executive agencies that create the documents, they also affect the ability of citizens to oversee and review the actions of their government (see Chapter 7).

STRUCTURE OF THE JUDICIAL SYSTEM

A basic understanding of the structure of the court system in the United States is fundamental to an appreciation of the functioning of the law. Trial courts, or federal district courts, do fact-finding, apply the law and settle disputes. Courts of appeal, including federal circuit courts and supreme courts in each system, review how lower courts applied the law. Through their judgments, courts can hand down equitable remedies, reshape laws or even throw out laws as unconstitutional.

Court Jurisdiction

An independent court system operates in each state, the District of Columbia and the federal government. The military and the U.S. territories, such as Puerto Rico, also have court systems.

Each of these court systems operates under the authority of the relevant constitution. For example, the U.S. Constitution requires the establishment of the Supreme Court of the United States and authorizes Congress to establish other courts it deems necessary to the proper functioning of the federal judiciary. **Jurisdiction** refers to a court's authority to hear a case. Every court has its own jurisdiction—that is, its own geographic or topical area of responsibility and authority.

In 2017, the U.S. Supreme Court reiterated its recognition of two types of court jurisdiction: general and specific.[71] Typically, the site or location of general jurisdiction is an individual's home or a corporation's headquarters. Given general jurisdiction, a court may hear any claim against that defendant. To be heard in a forum of specific jurisdiction, a suit must relate to the defendant's contacts with that forum. In libel, for example, the standard has been that any court in any locale where the alleged libel could be seen or heard would have jurisdiction.[72] A court may dismiss a lawsuit outside of its jurisdiction.

POINTS OF LAW
TRIBAL COURTS

The Indian Reorganization Act of 1934 gave Native American tribes in the United States the right to enact their own laws and establish their own formal tribal courts. Today, there are about 400 tribal justice systems in the United States.[73] Some tribes have blended judicial systems, combining elements of both Western and native systems. Others prefer traditional dispute resolution based entirely on tribal customs. In 2020, the U.S. Supreme Court ruled that about half of Oklahoma is within a Native American reservation.[74] The decision meant the state could no longer prosecute crimes on such territory—only the tribal courts or federal government could do so. In 2022, the high court narrowed that decision, ruling that Oklahoma could prosecute crimes committed against Native Americans by non- Native Americans on a reservation.[75]

New technologies present new challenges to the determination of jurisdiction. Consider online libel. Given that statements published online are potentially seen anywhere, any court might claim jurisdiction (see Chapter 5). Then the plaintiff might initiate the lawsuit in any court and would likely file the suit in the court expected to render a favorable decision. In a broad ruling that could limit **forum shopping**, the practice of seeking the most favorable court to hear your case, the U.S. Supreme Court held that unless there is a substantial link between the forum of the court and the source of injury, a company may only be sued "at home."[76] Following a detailed discussion of jurisdiction, the Court unanimously held that a national newspaper's "home" is in one of only two places: where the company is incorporated or the main location of its business.[77]

As access to the internet becomes accepted as an essential public utility (in principle if not yet in law),[78] nations struggle individually and collectively to determine who has legal jurisdiction over international online disputes.[79] The U.S. Supreme Court test to establish specific jurisdiction often applies to such online disputes and requires courts to find that (1) the defendant intentionally acted inside the jurisdiction of the court, (2) the plaintiff's claim arose from that activity and (3) it is reasonable for the court to exercise jurisdiction.[80]

POINTS OF LAW

THREE-PART TEST FOR SPECIFIC COURT JURISDICTION[81]

1. The defendant purposefully conducted activities in the jurisdiction of the court.
2. The plaintiff's claim arose out of the defendant's activities within that jurisdiction.
3. It is constitutionally reasonable for the court to exercise jurisdiction.

The U.S. Constitution spells out the areas of jurisdiction of the federal courts. Within their geographic regions, federal courts exercise authority over cases that relate to interstate or international controversies or that interpret and apply federal laws, treaties, or the U.S. Constitution. Thus, federal courts hear cases involving copyright laws. The federal courts also decide cases in which the federal government is a party, such as when the states bring suit against presidential directives extending protections for undocumented immigrants.[82] Cases involving controversies between states, between citizens of different states, or between a state and a citizen of another state also are heard in federal courts. Thus, a libel suit brought by a resident of Pennsylvania against a newspaper in California would be heard in federal court.

Trial Courts

The state, federal and specialized court systems in the United States are organized similarly; most court systems have three tiers. At the lowest level, trial courts are the courts where nearly all cases begin. Each state contains at least one of the nation's 94 trial-level federal courts, which are called district courts. Trial courts reach decisions by finding facts and applying existing law to them. They are the only courts to use juries. They do not establish precedents. Some judges view the routine media coverage of legal actions taking place in trial courts as a threat to the fairness of trials (see Chapter 8). Some judges also fear that media coverage will cast their court in disrepute and reduce public trust in the judicial system.

Courts of Appeal

Anyone who loses a case at trial may appeal the decision. However, courts of appeal generally do not make findings of fact or receive new evidence in the case. Only in rare cases do courts of appeal review case facts **de novo**, a phrase meaning "new" or "over again." Instead, appellate courts review the legal process of the lower court. Courts of appeal examine the procedures and tests used by the lower court to determine whether **due process** was carried out—that is, whether the proper law was applied and whether the judicial process was fair and appropriate.

Decisions in appellate courts are based primarily on detailed written arguments, or briefs, and on short oral arguments from the attorneys representing each side of the case. Individuals and organizations that are not parties to the case, called amicus curiae ("friends of the court"), may receive court permission to submit a brief called an **amicus brief**.

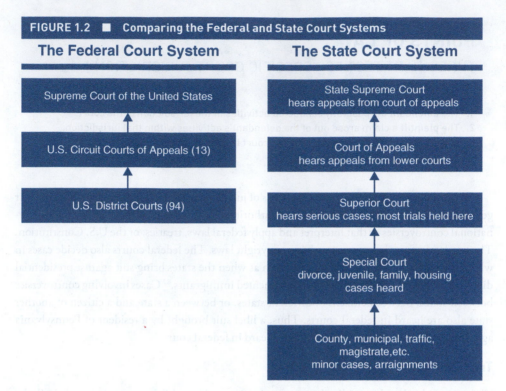

FIGURE 1.2 ■ Comparing the Federal and State Court Systems

The Federal Court System

Supreme Court of the United States

U.S. Circuit Courts of Appeals (13)

U.S. District Courts (94)

The State Court System

State Supreme Court
hears appeals from court of appeals

Court of Appeals
hears appeals from lower courts

Superior Court
hears serious cases; most trials held here

Special Court
divorce, juvenile, family, housing
cases heard

County, municipal, traffic,
magistrate,etc.
minor cases, arraignments

Most court systems have two levels of appellate courts: the intermediate courts of appeal and the supreme court. In the federal court system, there are 13 intermediate-level appellate courts, called circuit courts. A panel of three judges hears all except the most important cases in the federal circuit courts of appeal. Only rarely do all the judges of the circuit court sit **en banc** to hear an appeal. *En banc* literally means "on the bench" but is used to mean "in full court." Twelve of the federal circuits represent geographic regions (see Figure 1.3). For example, the U.S. Court of Appeals for the Ninth Circuit bears responsibility for the entire West Coast, Hawaii and Alaska, and the U.S. Court of Appeals for the D.C. Circuit covers the District of Columbia. The 13th circuit, the U.S. Court of Appeals for the Federal Circuit, handles specialized appeals. In addition, separate, specialized federal courts handle cases dealing with the armed forces, international trade or veterans' claims, among other things (See Table 1.1.).

Courts of appeal may **affirm** the decision of the lower court with a majority opinion, which means they ratify or uphold the prior ruling and leave it intact. They also may **overrule** the lower court, reversing the previous decision. Any single judge or minority of the court may write a **concurring opinion** agreeing with the result reached by the court opinion but presenting different reasoning, legal principles or issues. Judges who disagree with the opinion of the court may write a **dissenting opinion**, critiquing the majority's reasoning or judgment and providing the basis for the divergent conclusion.

Majority decisions issued by courts of appeal establish precedent for lower courts within their jurisdiction. Their rulings also may be persuasive outside their jurisdiction. If only a plurality of the judges hearing a case supports the opinion of the lower court, the decision does

FIGURE 1.3 ■ U.S. Circuit Courts of Appeal

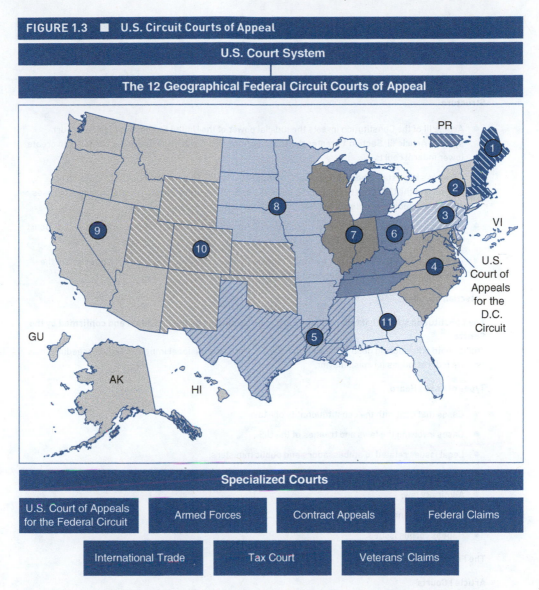

U.S. Court System

The 12 Geographical Federal Circuit Courts of Appeal

Specialized Courts

| U.S. Court of Appeals for the Federal Circuit | Armed Forces | Contract Appeals | Federal Claims |

| International Trade | Tax Court | Veterans' Claims |

not establish binding precedent. Similarly, dissenting and concurring opinions do not have the force of law, but they often influence subsequent court reasoning.

Courts of appeal also **remand**, or send back, decisions to the lower court to establish a more detailed record of facts or to reconsider the case. A decision to remand a case may not be appealed. Courts of appeal often remand cases when they believe that the lower court did not fully explore issues in the case and needs to develop a more complete record of evidence as the basis for its decision.

A circuit court of appeals decision must be signed by at least two of the three sitting judges and is final. The losing party may ask the court to reconsider the case or may request a rehearing en banc. Such requests are rarely granted. Losing parties also may appeal the verdict of any intermediate court of appeals to the highest court in the state or to the U.S. Supreme Court.

TABLE 1.1 ■ Comparing Federal and State Courts

The federal government, and each state government, has its own court system.

The Federal Court System

Structure

- Article III of the Constitution invests the judicial power of the United States in the federal court system. Article III, Section 1 creates the U.S. Supreme Court and gives Congress authority to create lower federal courts.

- Congress has established 13 U.S. Courts of Appeals, 94 U.S. District Courts, the U.S. Court of Claims and the U.S. Court of International Trade. U.S. Bankruptcy Courts handle bankruptcy cases. Magistrate Judges handle some District Court matters.

- Parties may appeal a decision of a U.S. District Court, the U.S. Court of Claims and/or the U.S. Court of International Trade to a U.S. Court of Appeals.

- A party may ask the U.S. Supreme Court to review a decision of the U.S. Court of Appeals, but the Supreme Court usually is under no obligation to do so.

Selection of Judges

The Constitution states that federal judges are to be nominated by the President and confirmed by the Senate.
Judges hold office during good behavior, typically, for life. Congressional impeachment proceedings may remove federal judges for misbehavior.

Types of Cases Heard

- Cases that deal with the constitutionality of a law;
- Cases involving the laws and treaties of the U.S.;
- Legal issues related to ambassadors and public ministers;
- Disputes between two or more states;
- Admiralty law;
- Bankruptcy; and
- Habeas corpus issues.

The Federal Court System

Article I Courts

Congress created several Article I, or legislative courts, that do not have full judicial power. Article I courts are:

- U.S. Court of Appeals for Veterans Claims
- U.S. Court of Appeals for the Armed Forces
- U.S. Tax Court

(Continued)

TABLE 1.1 ■ Comparing Federal and State Courts (*Continued*)

The State Court System

Structure

- The Constitution and laws of each state establish the state courts. Most states have a Supreme Court, an intermediate Court of Appeals, and state trial courts, sometimes referred to as Circuit or District Courts.
- States usually have courts that handle specific legal matters, e.g., probate court (wills and estates); juvenile court; family court; etc.
- Parties dissatisfied with the decision of the trial court may take their case to the intermediate Court of Appeals.
- Parties have the option to ask the highest state court to hear the case.
- Only certain cases are eligible for review by the U.S. Supreme Court.

Selection of Judges

State court judges are selected in a variety of ways, including

- election,
- appointment for a given number of years,
- appointment for life and
- combinations of these methods, e.g., appointment followed by election.

Types of Cases Heard

- Most criminal cases, probate (involving wills and estates)
- Most contract cases, tort cases (personal injuries), family law (marriages, divorces, adoptions), etc.

State courts are the final arbiters of state laws and constitutions. Their interpretation of federal law or the U.S. Constitution may be appealed to the U.S. Supreme Court.

Source: United States Courts, www.uscourts.gov/about-federal-courts/court-role-and-structure; www.uscourts.gov/aboutfederal-courts/court-role-and-structure/comparing-federal-state-courts.

The U.S. Supreme Court

Established in 1789, the Supreme Court of the United States functions primarily as an appellate court, although the Constitution establishes the Court's **original jurisdiction** in a few specific areas. In general, Congress has granted lower federal courts jurisdiction in these same areas, so almost no suits begin in the U.S. Supreme Court. Instead, the Court hears cases on appeal from all other federal courts, federal regulatory agencies and state supreme courts.

Cases come before the Court either on direct appeal from the lower court or through the Court's grant of a **writ of certiorari**. Certain federal laws, such as the Bipartisan Campaign Reform Act,[83] guarantee a direct right of appeal to the U.S. Supreme Court. More often, the Court grants a writ of certiorari for compelling reasons, such as when a case poses a novel or pressing legal question. The Court often grants certiorari to cases in which different U.S. circuit courts of appeal have issued conflicting opinions. The Court may consider whether an issue is ripe for consideration, meaning that the case presents a real and present controversy rather than a hypothetical concern. In addition, the Court may reject some petitions as **moot** because the controversy is no longer "live." Mootness may be an issue, for example, when a student who has challenged school policy graduates before the case is resolved. The Court sometimes accepts cases that appear to be moot if it believes the problem is likely to arise again.

The Court's Makeup

The chief justice of the United States and eight associate justices make up the Supreme Court. The president nominates and the Senate confirms the chief justice as well as the other eight members of the Court, who sit "during good behavior"[84] for life or until retirement. This gives the president considerable influence over the Court's political ideology. (See Table 1.2.)

TABLE 1.2 ■ The U.S. Supreme Court at a Glance, 2022			
Justice	**Born**	**Nominating President**	**Year Appointed**
Chief Justice John G. Roberts Jr.	1955	George W. Bush	2005
Associate Justice Clarence Thomas	1948	George H. W. Bush	1991
Associate Justice Sonia Sotomayor	1954	Barack Obama	2009
Associate Justice Neil M. Gorsuch	1967	Donald Trump	2017

Justice	Born	Nominating President	Year Appointed
Associate Justice Samuel A. Alito Jr.	1950	George W. Bush	2006
Associate Justice Elena Kagan	1960	Barack Obama	2010
Associate Justice Brett M. Kavanaugh	1965	Donald Trump	2018
Associate Justice Amy Coney Barrett	1972	Donald Trump	2020
Associate Justice Ketanji Brown Jackson	1970	Joe Biden	2022

Photos source: SupremeCourt.gov.

Supreme Court of the United States justices, Fall 2022

Fred Schilling, Collection of the Supreme Court of the United States

After the Senate failed to give President Obama's Supreme Court nominee a confirmation vote after the death of Supreme Court justice Antonin Scalia, President Trump took office and nominated conservative Neil Gorsuch, who took the vacant seat in 2017. Justice Anthony Kennedy's retirement in 2018 and the death of Justice Ruth Bader Ginsburg in 2020 changed the balance of the Court. The 2018 confirmation of Brett Kavanaugh and the 2020 confirmation of Amy Coney Barrett, both nominated by President Trump, shifted the Court toward the conservative end and made Chief Justice John Roberts the swing vote. Kavanaugh's confirmation hearings were especially contentious because of testimony by Professor Christine Blasey, who accused him of sexual assault. Coney Barrett's confirmation hearings featured questions about her pro-life views, the Affordable Care Act and her stance on climate change. Most observers argue these new justices will change the direction of American jurisprudence for decades.

In 2022, President Biden nominated Ketanji Brown Jackson, the first Black woman to be nominated for the Court, after Justice Steven Breyer announced his retirement. Brown Jackson was formerly a Supreme Court law clerk, a public defender, a federal district court judge, a federal appeals court judge and vice chair of the U.S. Sentencing Commission. While Jackson's appointment will not change the balance of the Court, she will be joining Justices Elena Kagan and Sonia Sotomayor, the first Latino justice appointed to the Court, on the liberal side of the Court, and observers expect her dissents to receive notice.[85] Overall, the Court still leans right with Justices Alito, Thomas, Gorsuch, Kavanaugh and Coney Barrett in the conservative majority, along with Chief Justice Roberts—though Roberts has from time to time joined the liberals in some opinions.

INTERNATIONAL LAW
JUDICIAL SELECTION PROCESSES NEED TO SUPPORT RULE OF LAW

The World Justice Project's Rule of Law Index identified problematic trends in the judicial selection process in the United States over the last few years. Noting that judicial selection is an essential bulwark of the rule of law, particularly as related to judicial independence and accountability, the report highlighted significant differences in the U.S. process and that of most Western democratic nations.

While the United States allows almost anyone to become a judge, other countries require judges to meet certain standards for age, legal education and legal experience. In addition, most countries allow executives to appoint judges only from a list created by an independent body, which is not the case in the United States. This raises questions of judicial independence. Finally, very few countries allow public election of judges, while most states elect at least some judges. Elections make judges more accountable but also affect judicial outcomes, according to studies.

"Independence versus accountability is that tension that just runs throughout the judicial process. . . . But obviously the more independent you make the judges then in a certain sense the less accountable they can be."[86]

Chief Justice John Roberts now is the justice closest to the center of the Court. A conservative, the chief justice tries to develop agreement across the Court by encouraging narrow rulings.

Justices Samuel Alito, Clarence Thomas, Brett Kavanaugh, Neil Gorsuch and Amy Coney Barrett create a staunch conservative bloc in the Court.[87] Conservative justices, in general, want to reduce the role of the federal government, including the Supreme Court. They tend to favor a narrow, or close, reading of the Constitution that relies more heavily on original intent than on contemporary realities. These justices have propelled the Court's rightward shift on business, campaign finance and race.[88]

The demographics of the Supreme Court have important symbolic significance even if they do not directly influence the Court's rulings. Throughout history, U.S. Supreme Court justices have been overwhelmingly married, male, white and Protestant. Today, the Court is more diverse than in the past. Four female justices (one Hispanic) and two African American justices sit on the current Court, but the Court that is the final arbiter of the law in this country does not reflect the diversity of the U.S. population. Court membership overrepresents certain educational backgrounds and religious faiths. Four of the sitting justices graduated from Yale Law School and four from Harvard. While 24 percent of the U.S. population is Roman Catholic, six members of the Court (67%), including the chief justice, profess to this faith.[89] No Supreme Court justice has self-identified as other than heterosexual and cisgender.

REAL WORLD LAW

SCALIA SAID RULES, HISTORY SHOULD GUIDE COURT INTERPRETATIONS

After serving almost 30 years on the Court, Justice Antonin Scalia was one of the longest-seated justices in the Supreme Court's history when he died in 2016.[90] His views shaped many areas of contemporary mass communication law as well as the rule of law.

Justice Scalia relied on originalism and clear rules to constrain the discretion of judges. Originalists argue that the Constitution's meaning should be determined by how the text was understood at the time it was adopted, "a historical criterion that is conceptually . . . separate from the preferences of the judge himself,"[91] Justice Scalia said. He argued that the Supreme Court should "curb—even reverse—the tendency of judges to imbue authoritative texts with their own policy preferences."

Clearly delineated and consistently applied rules are necessary, he said, to "provide greater certainty in the law and hence greater predictability and greater respect for the rule of law."[92] Concrete rules are preferable to multipart tests or balancing, he said, because "when . . . I adopt a general rule . . . I not only constrain lower courts, I constrain myself as well."[93] The predictability of clear rules helps "enhance the legitimacy of decisions . . . [and] embolden the decision maker to resist the will of a hostile majority," one observer said.[94]

Granting Review. Petitioners may ask the Supreme Court for a writ of certiorari if the court of appeals or the highest state court denies them a hearing or issues a verdict against them. Writs are granted at the discretion of the Court. All seated justices consider a writ, which is granted only if at least four justices vote to hear the case. This is called the rule of four.

Neither the decision to grant nor the decision to deny a writ of certiorari indicates anything about the Court's opinion regarding the merits of the lower court's ruling. Denial of certiorari generally means that the justices do not think the issue is sufficiently important or timely to decide. In recent years, an average of 8,200 petitions have been filed with the Court, which grants fewer than 1 percent of them.[95] Petitions filed are accompanied by the required fee of $300. The vast majority of petitions are filed without the fee—often by prisoners who cannot pay the required filing fee.

Reaching Decisions. Once the Court agrees to hear a case, the parties file written briefs outlining the facts and legal issues in the case and summarizing their legal arguments. The justices review the briefs prior to oral argument in the case, which generally lasts one hour. The justices may sit silently during oral argument, or they may pepper the attorneys with questions.

Following oral argument, the justices meet in a private, closed conference to take an initial vote on the outcome. Discussion begins with the chief justice and proceeds around the table in order of descending seniority of the associate justices. Then voting proceeds from the most junior member of the Court and ends with the chief justice. The chief justice or the most senior justice in the majority determines who will draft the majority opinion.

This 1885 lithograph shows "Our Overworked Supreme Court."

"Our overworked Supreme Court" by Joseph Ferdinand Keppler. Published by Keppler & Schwarzmann, December 9, 1885, via SupremeCourt.gov

A majority of the justices must agree on a point of law for the Court to establish binding precedent. Draft opinions are circulated among the justices, and negotiations may attempt to shift votes. It may take months for the Court to achieve a final decision, which is then announced on decision day.

Two other options exist for the Supreme Court. It may issue a **per curiam opinion**, which is an unsigned opinion by the Court as a whole. Although a single justice may draft the opinion, that authorship is not made public. Per curiam opinions often do not include the same thorough discussion of the issues found in signed opinions. The Supreme Court also may resolve a case by issuing a **memorandum order**. A memorandum order simply announces the vote of the Court without providing an opinion. This quick and easy method to dispense with a case has become more common with the Court's growing tendency to issue fewer signed opinions. More recently, the Court has come under criticism for increasing use of the **shadow docket**, a nickname for actions by the Court that do not go through the full opinion process. These cases comprise emergency orders and summary decisions that do not include information about how each justice voted or why a majority came to a certain conclusion.[96]

The ideological leanings of the individual justices, and of the Court as a whole, come into play in the choice of cases granted review and the ultimate decisions of the Court.[97] The U.S. Supreme Court relies on a wide range of sources to guide its interpretation of the Constitution. **Originalists** and **textualists** seek the meaning of the Constitution primarily in its explicit text, the historical context in which the document developed and the recorded history of its deliberation and original meaning. Some justices look beyond the text to discover how best to apply the Constitution today. Their interpretation relies more expressly on deep-seated personal and societal values, ethical and legal concepts, and the evolving interests of a shifting society. The Court's reasoning at times also builds on international standards, treaties or conventions, such as the Universal Declaration of Human Rights, or the decisions of courts outside the United States as well as state and other federal courts.

PROCESSES OF THE LAW

Although each court or case follows a somewhat idiosyncratic path, similar patterns of judicial process emerge. In a criminal matter, the case starts when a government agency investigates a possible crime. After gathering evidence, the government arrests someone for a crime, such as distributing false and misleading advertising through the internet. The standard of evidence needed for an arrest or to issue a search warrant is known as **probable cause**, which is more than mere suspicion.

The case then goes before a **grand jury** or a judge. Unlike trial juries (also called petit juries), grand juries do not determine guilt. Grand juries hear the state's evidence and determine whether that evidence establishes probable cause to believe that a crime has been committed. A grand jury may be convened on the county, state or federal level. If the case proceeds without a grand jury, the judge makes a probable cause determination at a preliminary hearing. If the state fails to establish probable cause, the case may not proceed. If probable cause is found, the person is indicted (see Figure 1.4).

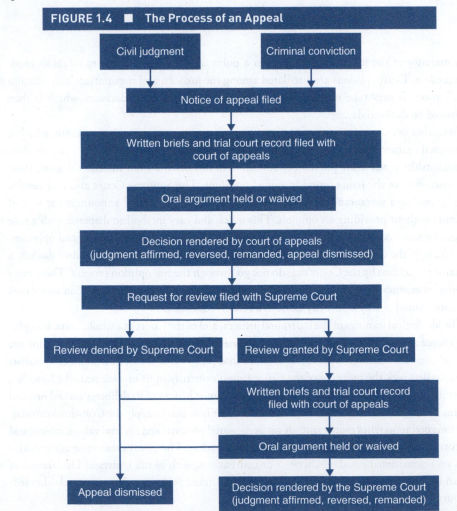

FIGURE 1.4 ■ The Process of an Appeal

Civil judgment → Criminal conviction

Notice of appeal filed

Written briefs and trial court record filed with court of appeals

Oral argument held or waived

Decision rendered by court of appeals (judgment affirmed, reversed, remanded, appeal dismissed)

Request for review filed with Supreme Court

Review denied by Supreme Court | Review granted by Supreme Court

Written briefs and trial court record filed with court of appeals

Oral argument held or waived

Appeal dismissed | Decision rendered by the Supreme Court (judgment affirmed, reversed, remanded)

Then the case moves to a court arraignment, where the defendant is formally charged and pleads guilty or not guilty. A plea bargain may be arranged in which the defendant pleads guilty to reduced charges or an agreed-upon sentence. Plea bargains account for almost 95 percent of all felony convictions in the United States.[98] If a not-guilty plea is entered, the case usually proceeds to trial. The judge may set bail.

Proof beyond a reasonable doubt is required to establish guilt in a criminal trial. A guilty verdict prompts a sentencing hearing. A criminal sentence may include jail or prison time and a fine or fines.

Civil Suits

Civil cases generally involve two private individuals or organizations asking the courts to settle a conflict. The person who files a civil complaint or sues is the **plaintiff**. The person responding to the suit is the **defendant**. The civil injury one person or organization inflicts on another is called a tort. **Tort** law provides the means for the injured party to establish fault and receive compensation.

The majority of communication and media lawsuits are civil suits in which the plaintiff must prove their case by the preponderance of evidence. This standard of proof is lower than in criminal cases.

Civil suits begin when the plaintiff files a pleading with the clerk of court. To receive a damage award, a plaintiff generally must show that the harm occurred, that the defendant caused the harm and that the defendant was at fault, meaning the defendant acted either negligently or with malicious intent. Under a **strict liability** standard, the plaintiff does not need to demonstrate fault on the part of the defendant in order to win the suit. Strict liability applies in cases involving inherently dangerous products or activities. Under strict liability, the individual who produced the product or took the action is liable for all resulting harms.

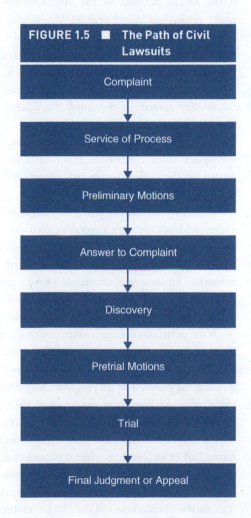

FIGURE 1.5 ■ The Path of Civil Lawsuits

- Complaint
- Service of Process
- Preliminary Motions
- Answer to Complaint
- Discovery
- Pretrial Motions
- Trial
- Final Judgment or Appeal

At a court hearing, the defendant may answer the complaint by filing a countersuit, by denying the charge, by filing a **motion to dismiss** or by filing a motion for **summary judgment** (see next page). A motion to dismiss, or **demurrer**, asks a court to reject a complaint because it is legally insufficient. For example, a defendant may admit that it distributed a story but argue that the story did not cause any legally actionable harm to the plaintiff. If the court grants the motion to dismiss, the plaintiff may appeal.

Before a case goes to trial, the disputing parties may agree to an out-of-court settlement. When this occurs, there is no public record of the outcome of the case. Out-of-court resolutions often prohibit the parties from discussing the terms of the settlement. In the 2019 settlement of the lawsuit former San Francisco 49ers quarterback Colin Kaepernick brought against the NFL, for example, a confidentiality agreement prevented the disclosure of any settlement details.[99]

Sometimes a judge will settle a civil case through a court conference. Civil suits are settled by the parties before trial almost 97 percent of the time.[100]

If the two sides do not settle, they begin to gather evidence through a process called **discovery**. In trying to build a case, one or both parties may issue a **subpoena**, which is a legal

Colin Kaepernick of the San Francisco 49ers takes a knee during the national anthem in Charlotte, N.C., in 2016. He settled his collusion lawsuit against the NFL in 2019.

Michael Zagaris/San Francisco 49ers/Getty Images

command for someone, sometimes a media professional, to appear and testify in court or turn over evidence, such as outtakes or notes. Citizens are legally obligated to comply with subpoenas, and the judge may punish noncompliance with a contempt of court citation, fines or jail.

If the parties do not reach a settlement, the case may proceed to a jury trial, which is required if either party requests it. To form a jury, the court summons individuals from a local pool, called the **venire**, that is usually based on voters' rolls. The locality where the court hears the suit is called the **venue**. The lawyers and judge select jurors through a process of questioning called **voir dire**, which literally means "to speak the truth."

While the theoretical goal is to seat an impartial jury for the trial, attorneys on both sides hope to gain advantage through the juror selection process. Attorneys may challenge potential jurors "for cause," such as when a prospective juror knows a party in the suit. They also may eliminate a limited number of potential jurors through **peremptory challenges**, in which they need not show a reason for the rejection. Expert consulting on jury selection, witness preparation, media interactions and the like help attorneys shape the jury and public messaging about the trial.

After evidence is presented at trial, the judge instructs the jury on how to apply the law to the case. Then the jury deliberates. If the jury cannot reach a verdict, the judge may order a new trial with a new jury. When a jury reaches a verdict, the judge generally enters it as the judgment of the court. However, the judge may overturn the verdict if it is contrary to the law. A successful plaintiff usually will be awarded damages.

Either party may appeal the judgment of the court. For example, if a party believes the jury was not properly instructed on the law, they may appeal on the basis of violation of due process. It can take years and cost hundreds of thousands of dollars to appeal a case. The person who challenges the decision of the court is called the petitioner or **appellant**. The respondent to the appeal, or the **appellee**, wants the verdict to be affirmed.

Summary Judgment

When parties ask a court to dismiss a case, they file a motion for summary judgment asking the judge to decide the case on the basis of pretrial submissions when neither party disputes the underlying facts.[101] A summary judgment results in a legal determination by a court *without* a full trial and avoids the cost of trial and the risk of loss to the moving party.

A court's summary judgment may be issued based on the merits of the case as a whole or on specific issues critical to the case. In a libel case, this may occur when a plaintiff is clearly unable to meet one or more elements of the burden of proof, such as the falsity of the published material (see Chapter 4). If the judge determines evidence supports an uncontested conclusion that one party should win the case, the judge hands down a summary judgment in that party's favor.

Summary judgment may be granted at several points in litigation, but usually prior to trial. The U.S. Supreme Court has said that courts considering motions for summary judgment "must view the facts and inferences to be drawn from them in the light most favorable to the opposing party."[102] In libel cases, this means that courts must take into account the burden the plaintiff is required to meet at trial. The Court created this obstacle to summary judgment because the nonmoving party loses the opportunity to present their case when a judge grants summary judgment to the opposing side.[103] Media defendants sometimes seek summary judgments to protect themselves from the high costs of frivolous lawsuits intended to harass, intimidate, or affect content.[104]

For decades, courts would dismiss a case only if "no set of facts" could support the plaintiff's claim.[105] But the U.S. Supreme Court changed this standard when it decided two cases, *Bell Atlantic v. Twombly* in 2007[106] and *Ashcroft v. Iqbal* in 2009.[107] What is known as the *Twombly/Iqbal* test says a court will dismiss a case if the plaintiff cannot state a plausible claim. That requires a court to determine "exactly where plausibility falls in that gray area between possible and probable."[108] It is more difficult for plaintiffs to present plausible facts to support their claim than it is simply to show that no set of facts could prove the claim, which means that courts applying the *Twombly/Iqbal* test dismiss a case more readily. Courts continue to disagree what "plausible" means in this context.

Finding And Reading the Case Law

This textbook provides an introduction and overview to key areas of the law of journalism and mass communication. Many students will wish, or their professors will require them, to supplement this text with research in primary legal sources. Primary sources are the actual documents that make up the law (e.g., statutes, case decisions, administrative rules and committee reports). Legal research often begins in secondary sources that analyze, interpret and discuss the primary documents. Perhaps the most useful secondary sources for beginning researchers in communication law are "American Jurisprudence" (2nd, ed.), "Corpus Juris Secundum" and "Media Law Reporter." The first two are legal encyclopedias that summarize legal subjects and reference relevant cases and legal articles. "Media Law Reporter" provides both topical summaries and excerpts of key media law cases organized by subject. However, "Media Law Reporter" is not comprehensive. It contains only the cases selected by the editors to highlight prominent issues in media law. Law review articles provide invaluable scholarship and references to contemporary legal topics. However, primary source research in administrative, legislative and court documents is necessary to thoroughly research a legal topic.

The main reading room in the U.S. Supreme Court Library.
SupremeCourt.gov

This text cannot provide a detailed explanation of how to navigate these complex and diverse legal materials. However, access to primary legal materials is available online and in databases such as Westlaw and Nexis Universe.

The notes at the end of this book contain citations to many of the important cases in the law of journalism and mass communication. These legal citations provide the names of the parties in the case, the number of the volume in which the case is reported, the abbreviated name of the official legal reporter (or book) in which the case appears, the page of the reporter on which the case begins and the year in which the case was decided. For example, a citation might look like this: *FEC v. Wisconsin Right to Life, Inc.*, 551 U.S. 449, 534 (2007) (Souter, J., dissenting)." This citation shows that the first party, the Federal Election Commission, filed an appeal from a decision in favor of the second party, Wisconsin Right to Life, Inc. The decision in this case striking down a ban on issue advertising prior to elections or primaries can be found in the U.S. Reports collection, which contains U.S. Supreme Court opinions. The case appears in volume 551 (the number *before* the name of the reporter), beginning on page 449 (the number *after* the name of the reporter). The case was decided in 2007 (the number in parentheses). In addition, the page number following the comma tells you precisely what page of the decision is referenced, and the parentheses at the end indicate that the reference comes from a dissenting opinion by Justice David Souter.

This chapter shows that the law of journalism and mass communication contains many terms and concepts that may be unfamiliar to the general reader. Key definitions at the end of the chapter and in the glossary at the back of the book should help you navigate opinions for lawyers trained in legal terminology and doctrines. At first, it may be difficult to grasp the meaning and importance of a case. With practice, however, anyone can learn the language and read case law with relative ease.

The following steps will help you read the law more quickly and with better comprehension. You will understand the law far better and more easily if you give yourself sufficient time to use these three steps:

1. ***Preread the case.*** Prereading identifies the *structure* of the decision, the various *rules or doctrines* that underlie the court's reasoning, and the *outcome* of the case. These three elements highlight the most important elements of the court's reasoning. To preread, quickly skim

   a. The topic sentence of each paragraph to get the gist of the opinion and identify its most important sections

   b. The first few paragraphs of the opinion, which should establish the parties, the issues and the history of the case

   c. The last few paragraphs of the opinion to understand the **holding** (which is the legal principle taken from the decision of the court) or to get a summary of the outcome of the case

2. ***Skim the entire case.*** Scan the entire case and mark the start of key sections of the case for more careful reading.

3. ***Read carefully the sections you have identified as important.*** Underline or highlight as you go. You may want to take note of the following:

   a. ***The issue.*** Knowing the issue in the case helps you know which elements of the history and facts are significant. In this text, the chapter titles generally signal the issue on which the case excerpt will focus. The case itself also often includes language that identifies the issue. Such language includes, "The question before the Court is whether . . ." and "The issue in this case is . . ."

   b. ***The facts.*** Identify which facts are central to the issue by asking yourself whether the dispute in the case is about a question of fact (e.g., what happened) or a question of law (e.g., which test, doctrine or category of speech is relevant). A libel decision that turns on the identity of the individual whose reputation was harmed would represent a question of fact, making related facts central to the holding.[109]

  c. *The case history.* The circumstances surrounding a decision often are pivotal to the issue before the court. Sometimes the relevant history is one of shifting legal doctrine, as when the court gradually affords commercial speech greater constitutional protection.[110] Sometimes the important context is factual, as when the court protects defamatory comments situated within a generally accurate portrayal of the violent oppression of Blacks during the civil rights movement.[111]

  d. *The common law rule.* The rule is the heart of the decision; it is the common law developed in this case. It relates to the holding but is the more general rule applied here and applicable to other cases. To identify the rule, ask whether the court has created a new test, engaged in balancing, or applied an established doctrine in a new way. What are the elements of the rule, and what are its exceptions?

  e. *The analysis.* Here the court applies the rule to the facts. In libel law, for example, public officials must prove actual malice to win their suit. How does the court apply this element of the test?

Careful reading of the law is the first stage in conducting legal research and positions you well to write case briefs, which summarize the key elements of a court decision.

Briefing Cases

Case briefs simplify and clarify a court's opinions by selecting the five most important elements of the decision. Briefs focus on key elements and set aside content that does not directly inform the court's decision.

The five components of a case brief are often referred to as FIRAC. They are Facts, Issue, Rule of Law, Analysis and Conclusion (or holding).

  1. *The Facts.* The facts summary should include all the information needed to understand the issue and the decision of the court. The facts statement consists of a brief but inclusive discussion of what happened in the legal dispute before it reached this court. It should include who the parties are, what happened in the trial court, and the basis for appeal. What happened between the parties that gave rise to the case? Who initiated the lawsuit? What was the substance of the complaint, and what type of legal action was brought? What was the defense? What did other courts reviewing the case decide? What legal errors provide the basis for the appeal?

  2. *The Issue.* Here, one sentence summarizes the specific question decided by the court in this case. The issue should be phrased as a single question that can be answered "yes" or "no."

  3. *The Rule of Law.* The rule of law states, preferably in one sentence, the precedent established by this decision that will bind lower courts.

4. *The Analysis.* This section, also called the *rationale*, details how and why the court reached its decision. In this section, it is important to discuss the details of the court's reasoning and how it creates new law. Consider whether it establishes a new test, clarifies existing legal distinctions, defines a new category, or highlights changing realities that affect the law. A thorough analysis must describe the reasoning for all the opinions in the decision and highlight the specific points on which concurring and dissenting opinions diverge from the opinion of the court.

5. *The Conclusion.* This is a simple declarative statement of the holding reached by the present court. What did the court decide, and did it affirm, remand or reverse? Provide the vote of the court if it is an appellate court.

Analyzing *Marbury v. Madison*

The following case brief previews the first case excerpted at the end of this chapter.

FACTS: William Marbury was one of President John Adams' 42 "midnight appointments" on the eve of his departure from the White House. The necessary paperwork and procedures to secure his and several other appointments were completed, but Secretary of State John Marshall—himself a midnight appointee—failed to deliver Marbury's commission. Upon assuming the presidency, Thomas Jefferson ordered his secretary of state—James Madison—not to deliver the commission. Under authority of the Judiciary Act of 1789, Marbury sued to ask the Supreme Court to order Madison, through a writ of mandamus, to deliver the commission. A writ of mandamus is a court order requiring an individual or organization either to perform or to stop a particular action.

ISSUE: Does the Supreme Court have the power to review acts of Congress and declare them void if they violate the Constitution?

RULE of LAW: Under Article VI, Section 2 of the U.S. Constitution, the Supreme Court is implicitly given the power to review acts of Congress and to strike them down as void if they are "repugnant" to the Constitution.

ANALYSIS: A commission signed by the president and sealed by the secretary of state is complete and legally binding. Denial of Marbury's commission violates the law, creating a governmental obligation to remedy the violation. A writ of mandamus is such a remedy. The Constitution is the "supreme law of the land" (Art. VI). As such, it is "superior" and "fundamental and paramount." It establishes "certain limits" on the power of the government it creates, including the power of Congress. The Constitution also establishes that "[it] is emphatically the province and duty of the judicial department to say what the law is." The Supreme Court, therefore, must determine the law that applies in a specific case and decide the case according to the law. If the Court finds that "ordinary" statutory law conflicts with the dictates of the Constitution, the "fundamental" constitutional law must govern. Accordingly, "a legislative act contrary to the Constitution is not law," and the Court must strike it down to give the Constitution its due weight.

Under Article III of the Constitution, Congress has the power to regulate the appellate jurisdiction, but not the original jurisdiction, of the Supreme Court. The Court's original jurisdiction is defined completely and exclusively by Article III and cannot be altered except by amendment of the Constitution. Through the Judiciary Act of 1789, Congress *added* to the original jurisdiction of the Court. Being outside the power given to Congress by the Constitution, this act is illegitimate. Because the power of mandamus was not granted to the Court by the Constitution either, the Court does not have the power to order mandamus on behalf of Marbury.

The Court held the provision of the Judiciary Act unconstitutional and declared the mandamus void.

CONCLUSION: Marshall, C.J. 6–0. Yes. Relying heavily on the inherent "logical reasoning" of the Constitution, rather than on any explicit text, the Court dismissed the case for lack of jurisdiction but found that Congress' grant of original power of mandamus to the Court violated the separation of power established in Article III of the Constitution.

KEYTERMS

administrative law	holding
affirm	judicial review
amicus brief	jurisdiction
appellant	memorandum order
appellee	modify precedent
black-letter law	moot
common law	motion to dismiss
concurring opinion	original jurisdiction
constitutional law	originalists
construction	overbroad laws
defendant	overrule
deference	overturn precedent
demurrer	per curiam opinion
de novo	peremptory challenge
discovery	plaintiff
discretion	political questions
dissenting opinion	precedent
distinguish from precedent	probable cause
doctrines	remand
due process	rule of law
en banc	shadow docket
equity law	stare decisis
executive orders	statutory law
facial meaning	strict construction
federalism	strict liability
forum shopping	subpoena
grand jury	summary judgment

Supremacy Clause	venire
textualists	venue
tort	voir dire
vague laws	writ of certiorari

CASES FOR STUDY
THINKING ABOUT THEM

The first case excerpt is from *Marbury v. Madison*, the decision in which the Supreme Court established its own power of judicial review. A central question resolved by the Supreme Court in *Marbury v. Madison* was whether, under the Constitution, the Court had authority to void duly enacted laws that it deemed to violate the U.S. Constitution.

The second case excerpt is from *U.S. v. Alvarez*, a case in which the Supreme Court struck down a federal law that made it a crime to lie about receiving a Congressional medal of honor. The Court deemed the law to be unconstitutional under the First Amendment because it failed a legal test known as strict or "exacting scrutiny," which requires the government to show a compelling interest in the regulation and that the regulation be least restrictive. This test is covered in more detail in Chapter 2. The Court ruled that while the government had a compelling interest in protecting the military's honor with the regulation, the law was overbroad and not the least restrictive alternative. The Court said the government could likely protect the integrity of the military awards system by creating a database of medal winners accessible and searchable on the internet. Furthermore, the Court said that while some forms of lying are not protected by the First Amendment (for instance, perjury or fraud), most lying is handled by "counterspeech," the notion that more speech is the remedy for speech that is false. The counterspeech doctrine is also covered in more detail in Chapter 2. The case is a good example of the court's reliance on an open marketplace of ideas to counter falsehoods. It also demonstrates how courts deal with a government regulation on speech that is overbroad.

MARBURY V. MADISON
SUPREME COURT OF THE UNITED STATES 5 U.S. 137 (1803)

CHIEF JUSTICE JOHN MARSHALL delivered the Court's opinion:

. . . The constitution vests the whole judicial power of the United States in one supreme court, and such inferior courts as congress shall, from time to time, ordain and establish. This power is expressly extended to all cases arising under the laws of the United States; and consequently, in some form, may be exercised over the present case; because the right claimed is given by a law of the United States.

In the distribution of this power it is declared that "the supreme court shall have original jurisdiction in all cases affecting ambassadors, other public ministers and consuls, and those in which a state shall be a party. In all other cases, the supreme court shall have appellate jurisdiction."

It has been insisted at the bar, that as the original grant of jurisdiction to the supreme and inferior courts is general, and the clause, assigning original jurisdiction to the supreme court, contains no negative or restrictive words; the power remains to the legislature, to assign original jurisdiction to that court in other cases than those specified in the article which has been recited; provided those cases belong to the judicial power of the United States.

If it had been intended to leave it to the discretion of the legislature to apportion the judicial power between the supreme and inferior courts according to the will of that body, it would certainly have been useless to have proceeded further than to have defined the judicial power, and the tribunals in which it should be vested. The subsequent part of the section is . . . entirely without meaning, if such is to be the construction. If congress remains at liberty to give this court appellate jurisdiction, where the constitution has declared their jurisdiction shall be original; and original jurisdiction where the constitution has declared it shall be appellate; the distribution of jurisdiction, made in the constitution, is form without substance. . . .

It cannot be presumed that any clause in the constitution is intended to be without effect; and therefore such a construction is inadmissible, unless the words require it. . . .

When an instrument organizing fundamentally a judicial system, divides it into one supreme, and so many inferior courts as the legislature may ordain and establish; then enumerates its powers, and proceeds so far to distribute them, as to define the jurisdiction of the supreme court by declaring the cases in which it shall take original jurisdiction, and that in others it shall take appellate jurisdiction, the plain import of the words seems to be, that in one class of cases its jurisdiction is original, and not appellate; in the other it is appellate, and not original. If any other construction would render the clause inoperative, that is an additional reason for rejecting such other construction, and for adhering to their obvious meaning. .

To enable this court then to issue a mandamus, it must be shown to be an exercise of appellate jurisdiction, or to be necessary to enable them to exercise appellate jurisdiction.

It has been stated at the bar that the appellate jurisdiction may be exercised in a variety of forms, and that if it be the will of the legislature that a mandamus should be used for that purpose, that will must be obeyed. This is true; yet the jurisdiction must be appellate, not original.

It is the essential criterion of appellate jurisdiction, that it revises and corrects the proceedings in a cause already instituted, and does not create that case. Although, therefore, a mandamus may be directed to courts, yet to issue such a writ to an officer for the delivery of a paper, is in effect the same as to sustain an original action for that paper, and therefore seems not to belong to appellate, but to original jurisdiction. Neither is it necessary in such a case as this, to enable the court to exercise its appellate jurisdiction.

The authority, therefore, given to the supreme court, by the act establishing the judicial courts of the United States, to issue writs of mandamus to public officers, appears not to be warranted by the constitution; and it becomes necessary to enquire whether a jurisdiction, so conferred, can be exercised.

The question, whether an act, repugnant to the constitution, can become the law of the land, is a question deeply interesting to the United States; but, happily, not of an intricacy proportioned to its interest. It seems only necessary to recognise certain principles, supposed to have been long and well established, to decide it.

That the people have an original right to establish, for their future government, such principles as, in their opinion, shall most conduce to their own happiness, is the basis, on which the whole American fabric has been erected. The exercise of this original right is a very great exertion; nor can it, nor ought it to be frequently repeated. The principles, therefore, so established, are deemed fundamental. And as the authority, from which they proceed, is supreme, and can seldom act, they are designed to be permanent.

This original and supreme will organizes the government, and assigns to different departments their respective powers. It may either stop here; or establish certain limits not to be transcended by those departments.

The government of the United States is of the latter description. The powers of the legislature are defined, and limited; and that those limits may not be mistaken, or forgotten, the constitution is written. To what purpose are powers limited, and to what purpose is that limitation committed to writing; if these limits may, at any time, be passed by those intended to be restrained? The distinction between a government with limited and unlimited powers is abolished, if those limits do not confine the persons on whom they are imposed, and if acts prohibited and acts allowed are of equal obligation. It is a proposition too plain to be contested, that the constitution controls any legislative act repugnant to it; or, that the legislature may alter the constitution by an ordinary act.

Between these alternatives there is no middle ground. The constitution is either a superior, paramount law, unchangeable by ordinary means, or it is on a level with ordinary legislative acts, and like other acts, is alterable when the legislature shall please to alter it.

If the former part of the alternative be true, then a legislative act contrary to the constitution is not law: if the latter part be true, then written constitutions are absurd attempts, on the part of the people, to limit a power in its own nature illimitable.

Certainly all those who have framed written constitutions contemplate them as forming the fundamental and paramount law of the nation, and consequently the theory of every such government must be, that an act of the legislature repugnant to the constitution is void.

This theory is essentially attached to a written constitution, and is consequently to be considered by this court as one of the fundamental principles of our society. It is not therefore to be lost sight of in the further consideration of this subject.

If an act of the legislature, repugnant to the constitution, is void, does it, notwithstanding its invalidity, bind the courts, and oblige them to give it effect? Or, in other words, though it be not law, does it constitute a rule as operative as if it was a law? This would be to overthrow in fact what was established in theory; and would seem, at first view, an absurdity too gross to be insisted on. It shall, however, receive a more attentive consideration.

It is emphatically the province and duty of the judicial department to say what the law is. Those who apply the rule to particular cases, must of necessity expound and interpret that rule. If two laws conflict with each other, the courts must decide on the operation of each. So if a law be in opposition to the constitution; if both the law and the constitution apply to a particular case, so that the court must either decide that case conformably to the law, disregarding the constitution; or conformably to the constitution, disregarding the law; the court must determine which of these conflicting rules governs the case. This is of the very essence of judicial duty.

If then the courts are to regard the constitution; and the constitution is superior to any ordinary act of the legislature; the constitution, and not such ordinary act, must govern the case to which they both apply.

Those then who controvert the principle that the constitution is to be considered, in court, as a paramount law, are reduced to the necessity of maintaining that courts must close their eyes on the constitution, and see only the law.

This doctrine would subvert the very foundation of all written constitutions. It would declare that an act, which, according to the principles and theory of our government, is entirely void, is yet, in practice, completely obligatory. It would declare, that if the legislature shall do what is expressly forbidden, such act, notwithstanding the express prohibition, is in reality effectual. It would be giving to the legislature a practical and real omnipotence with the same breath which professes to restrict their powers within narrow limits. It is prescribing limits, and declaring that those limits may be passed at pleasure.

That it thus reduces to nothing what we have deemed the greatest improvement on political institutions—a written constitution, would of itself be sufficient, in America where written constitutions have been viewed with so much reverence, for rejecting the construction. But the peculiar expressions of the constitution of the United States furnish additional arguments in favour of its rejection.

The judicial power of the United States is extended to all cases arising under the constitution. Could it be the intention of those who gave this power, to say that, in using it, the constitution should not be looked into? That a case arising under the constitution should be decided without examining the instrument under which it arises?

This is too extravagant to be maintained. . . .

[I]t is apparent, that the framers of the constitution contemplated that instrument, as a rule for the government of courts, as well as of the legislature.

Why otherwise does it direct the judges to take an oath to support it? This oath certainly applies, in an especial manner, to their conduct in their official character. How immoral to impose it on them, if they were to be used as the instruments, and the knowing instruments, for violating what they swear to support!

The oath of office, too, imposed by the legislature, is completely demonstrative of the legislative opinion on the subject. It is in these words, "I do solemnly swear that I will administer justice without respect to persons, and do equal right to the poor and to the rich; and that I will faithfully and impartially discharge all the duties incumbent on me as according to the best of my abilities and understanding, agreeably to the constitution, and laws of the United States."

Why does a judge swear to discharge his duties agreeably to the constitution of the United States, if that constitution forms no rule for his government? If it is closed upon him, and cannot be inspected by him?

If such be the real state of things, this is worse than solemn mockery. To prescribe, or to take this oath, becomes equally a crime.

It is also not entirely unworthy of observation, that in declaring what shall be the supreme law of the land, the constitution itself is first mentioned; and not the laws of the United States generally, but those only which shall be made in pursuance of the constitution, have that rank.

Thus, the particular phraseology of the constitution of the United States confirms and strengthens the principle, supposed to be essential to all written constitutions, that a law repugnant to the constitution is void; and that courts, as well as other departments, are bound by that instrument.

The rule must be discharged.

U.S. V ALVAREZ (2012)

JUSTICE KENNEDY announced the judgment of the Court and delivered an opinion, in which THE CHIEF JUSTICE, JUSTICE GINSBURG, and JUSTICE SOTOMAYOR join:

Lying was his habit. Xavier Alvarez, the respondent here, lied when he said that he played hockey for the Detroit Red Wings and that he once married a starlet from Mexico. But when he lied in announcing he held the Congressional Medal of Honor, respondent ventured onto new ground; for that lie violates a federal criminal statute, the Stolen Valor Act of 2005.

In 2007, respondent attended his first public meeting as a board member of the Three Valley Water District Board. The board is a governmental entity with headquarters in Claremont, California. He introduced himself as follows: "I'm a retired marine of 25 years. I retired in the year 2001. Back in 1987, I was awarded the Congressional Medal of Honor. I got wounded many times by the same guy." None of this was true. For all the record shows, respondent's statements were but a pathetic attempt to gain respect that eluded him. The statements do not seem to have been made to secure employment or financial benefits or admission to privileges reserved for those who had earned the Medal.

Respondent was indicted under the Stolen Valor Act for lying about the Congressional Medal of Honor at the meeting. The United States District Court for the Central District of California rejected his claim that the statute is invalid under the First Amendment. Respondent pleaded guilty to one count, reserving the right to appeal on his First Amendment claim. The United States Court of Appeals for the Ninth Circuit, in a decision by a divided panel, found the Act invalid under the First Amendment and reversed the conviction. This Court granted certiorari. 565 U. S. (2011).

. . .

It is right and proper that Congress, over a century ago, established an award so the Nation can hold in its highest respect and esteem those who, in the course of carrying out the "supreme and noble duty of contributing to the defense of the rights and honor of the nation," have acted with extraordinary honor. And it should be uncontested that this is a legitimate Government objective, indeed a most valued national aspiration and purpose. This does not end the inquiry, however. Fundamental constitutional principles require that laws enacted to honor the brave must be consistent with the precepts of the Constitution for which they fought.

The Government contends the criminal prohibition is a proper means to further its purpose in creating and awarding the Medal. When content-based speech regulation is in question, however, exacting scrutiny is required. Statutes suppressing or restricting speech must be judged by the sometimes inconvenient principles of the First Amendment. By this measure, the statutory provisions under which respondent was convicted must be held invalid, and his conviction must be set aside.

I

Respondent's claim to hold the Congressional Medal of Honor was false. There is no room to argue about interpretation or shades of meaning. On this premise, respondent violated §704(b); and, because the lie concerned the Congressional Medal of Honor, he was subject to an enhanced penalty under subsection (c). Those statutory provisions are as follows:

"(b) FALSE CLAIMS ABOUT RECEIPT OF MILITARY

DECORATIONS OR MEDALS.––Whoever falsely represents himself or herself, verbally or in writing, to have been awarded any decoration or medal authorized by Congress for the Armed Forces of the United States

. . . shall be fined under this title, imprisoned not more than six months, or both.

"(c) ENHANCED PENALTY FOR OFFENSES INVOLVING CONGRESSIONAL MEDAL OF HONOR.––

"(1) IN GENERAL.––If a decoration or medal involved in an offense under subsection (a) or (b) is a Congressional Medal of Honor, in lieu of the punishment provided in that subsection, the offender shall be fined under this title, imprisoned not more than 1 year, or both."

Respondent challenges the statute as a content-based suppression of pure speech, speech not falling within any of the few categories of expression where content-based regulation is permissible. The Government defends the statute as necessary to preserve the integrity and purpose of the Medal, an integrity and purpose it contends are compromised and frustrated by the false statements the statute prohibits. It argues that false statements "have no First Amendment value in themselves," and thus "are protected only to the extent needed to avoid chilling fully protected speech." Although the statute covers respondent's speech, the Government argues that it leaves breathing room for protected speech, for example speech which might criticize the idea of the Medal or the importance of the military. The Government's arguments cannot suffice to save the statute. . . .

III

The probable, and adverse, effect of the Act on freedom of expression illustrates, in a fundamental way, the reasons for the Law's distrust of content-based speech prohibitions.

The Act by its plain terms applies to a false statement made at any time, in any place, to any person. It can be assumed that it would not apply to, say, a theatrical performance. Still, the sweeping, quite unprecedented reach of the statute puts it in conflict with the First Amendment. Here the lie was made in a public meeting, but the statute would apply with equal force to personal, whispered conversations within a home. The statute seeks to control and suppress all false statements on this one subject in almost limitless times and settings. And it does so entirely without regard to whether the lie was made for the purpose of material gain.

Permitting the government to decree this speech to be a criminal offense, whether shouted from the rooftops or made in a barely audible whisper, would endorse government authority to compile a list of subjects about which false statements are punishable. That governmental power has no clear limiting principle. Our constitutional tradition stands against the idea that we need Oceania's Ministry of Truth [from George Orwell's novel, "1984"]. Were this law to be sustained, there could be an endless list of subjects the National Government or the States could single out. Where false claims are made to effect a fraud or secure moneys or other valuable considerations, say offers of employment, it is well established that the Government may restrict speech without affronting the First Amendment. But the Stolen Valor Act is not so limited in its reach. Were the Court to hold that the interest in truthful discourse alone is sufficient to sustain a ban on speech, absent any evidence that the speech was used to gain a material advantage, it would give government a broad censorial power unprecedented in this Court's cases or in our constitutional tradition. The mere potential for the exercise of that power casts a chill, a chill the First Amendment cannot permit if free speech, thought, and discourse are to remain a foundation of our freedom. . . .

IV

The previous discussion suffices to show that the Act conflicts with free speech principles. But even when examined within its own narrow sphere of operation, the Act cannot survive. In assessing content-based restrictions on protected speech, the Court has not adopted a freewheeling approach, but rather has applied the "most exacting scrutiny." Although the objectives the Government seeks to further by the statute are not without significance, the Court must, and now does, find the Act does not satisfy exacting scrutiny.

The Government is correct when it states military medals "serve the important public function of recognizing and expressing gratitude for acts of heroism and sacrifice in military service," and also " 'foste[r] morale, mission accomplishment and esprit de corps' among service members." General George Washington observed that an award for valor would "cherish a virtuous ambition in . . . soldiers, as well as foster and encourage every species of military merit." Time has not diminished this idea. In periods of war and peace alike public recognition of valor and noble sacrifice by men and women in uniform reinforces the pride and national resolve that the military relies upon to fulfill its mission. . . . The Government's interest in protecting the integrity of the Medal of Honor is beyond question. But to recite the Government's compelling interests is not to end the matter. The First Amendment requires that the Government's chosen restriction on the speech at issue be "actually necessary" to achieve its interest. There must be a direct causal link between the restriction imposed and the injury to be prevented.

The link between the Government's interest in protecting the integrity of the military honors system and the Act's restriction on the false claims of liars like respondent has not been shown. Although appearing to concede that "an isolated misrepresentation by itself would not tarnish the meaning of military honors," the Government asserts it is "common sense that false representations have the tendency to dilute the value and meaning of military awards." It must be acknowledged that when a pretender claims the Medal to be his own, the lie might harm the Government by demeaning the high purpose of the award, diminishing the honor it confirms, and creating the appearance that the Medal is awarded more often than is true. Furthermore, the lie may offend the true holders of the Medal. From one perspective it insults their bravery and high principles when falsehood puts them in the unworthy company of a pretender.

Yet these interests do not satisfy the Government's heavy burden when it seeks to regulate protected speech. The Government points to no evidence to support its claim that the public's general perception of military awards is diluted by false claims such as those made by Alvarez. . . .The lack of a causal link between the Government's stated interest and the Act is not the only way in which the Act is not actually necessary to achieve the Government's stated interest. The Government has not shown, and cannot show, why counterspeech would not suffice to achieve its interest. The facts of this case indicate that the dynamics of free speech, of counterspeech, of refutation, can overcome the lie. Respondent lied at a public meeting. . . . Once the lie was made public, he was ridiculed online, his actions were reported in the press, and a fellow board member called for his resignation. There is good reason to believe that a similar fate would befall other false claimants. Indeed, the outrage and contempt expressed for respondent's lies can serve to reawaken and reinforce the public's respect for the Medal, its recipients, and its high purpose. The acclaim that recipients of the Congressional Medal of Honor receive also casts doubt on the proposition that the public will be misled by the claims of charlatans or become cynical of those whose heroic deeds earned them the Medal by right.

The remedy for speech that is false is speech that is true. This is the ordinary course in a free society. The response to the unreasoned is the rational; to the uninformed, the enlightened; to the straight-out lie, the simple truth. The theory of our Constitution is "that the best test of truth is the power of the thought to get itself accepted in the competition of the market." The First Amendment itself ensures the right to respond to speech we do not like, and for good reason. Freedom of speech and thought flows not from the beneficence of the state but from the inalienable rights of the person. And suppression of speech by the government can make exposure of falsity more difficult, not less so. Society has the right and civic duty to engage in open, dynamic, rational discourse. These ends are not well served when the government seeks to orchestrate public discussion through content-based mandates.

Expressing its concern that counterspeech is insufficient, the Government responds that because "some military records have been lost . . . some claims [are] unverifiable." This proves little, however; for without verifiable records, successful criminal prosecution under the Act would be more difficult in any event. So, in cases where public refutation will not serve the Government's interest, the Act will not either. In addition, the Government claims that "many [false claims] will remain unchallenged." The Government provides no support for the contention. And in any event, in order to show that public refutation is not an adequate alternative, the Government must demonstrate that unchallenged claims undermine the public's perception of the military and the integrity of its awards system. This showing has not been made.

It is a fair assumption that any true holders of the Medal who had heard of Alvarez's false claims would have been fully vindicated by the community's expression of outrage, showing as it did the Nation's high regard for the Medal. The same can be said for the Government's interest. The American people do not need the assistance of a government prosecution to express their high regard for the special place that military heroes hold in our tradition. Only a weak society needs government protection or intervention before it pursues its resolve to preserve the truth. Truth needs neither handcuffs nor a badge for its vindication.

In addition, when the Government seeks to regulate protected speech, the restriction must be the "least restrictive means among available, effective alternatives." There is, however, at least one less speech-restrictive means by which the Government could likely protect the integrity of the military awards system. A Government-created database could list Congressional Medal of Honor winners. Were a database accessible through the Internet, it would be easy to verify and expose false claims. It appears some private individuals have already created databases similar to this, and at least one database of past winners is online and fully searchable. The Solicitor General responds that although Congress and the Department of Defense investigated the feasibility of establishing a database in 2008, the Government "concluded that such a database would be impracticable and insufficiently comprehensive." Without more explanation, it is difficult to assess the Government's claim, especially when at least one database of Congressional Medal of Honor winners already exists.

The Government may have responses to some of these criticisms, but there has been no clear showing of the necessity of the statute, the necessity required by exacting scrutiny.

* * *

The Nation well knows that one of the costs of the First Amendment is that it protects the speech we detest as well as the speech we embrace. Though few might find respondent's statements anything but contemptible, his right to make those statements is protected by the Constitution's guarantee of freedom of speech and expression. The Stolen Valor Act infringes upon speech protected by the First Amendment.

The judgment of the Court of Appeals is affirmed.

It is so ordered.

DISSENT

JUSTICE ALITO, with whom JUSTICE SCALIA and JUSTICE THOMAS join, dissenting:

Only the bravest of the brave are awarded the Congressional Medal of Honor, but the Court today holds that every American has a constitutional right to claim to have received this singular award. The Court strikes down the Stolen Valor Act of 2005, which was enacted to stem an epidemic of false claims about military decorations. These lies, Congress reasonably concluded, were undermining our country's system of military honors and inflicting real harm on actual medal recipients and their families.

Building on earlier efforts to protect the military awards system, Congress responded to this problem by crafting a narrow statute that presents no threat to the freedom of speech. The statute reaches only knowingly false statements about hard facts directly within a speaker's personal knowledge. These lies have no value in and of themselves, and proscribing them does not chill any valuable speech.

By holding that the First Amendment nevertheless shields these lies, the Court breaks sharply from a long line of cases recognizing that the right to free speech does not protect false factual statements that inflict real harm and serve no legitimate interest. I would adhere to that principle and would thus uphold the constitutionality of this valuable law.

. . .

Congress passed the Stolen Valor Act in response to a proliferation of false claims concerning the receipt of military awards. For example, in a single year, *more than 600* Virginia residents falsely claimed to have won the Medal of Honor. An investigation of the 333 people listed in the online edition of Who's Who as having received a top military award revealed that fully a third of the claims could not be substantiated. When the Library of Congress compiled oral histories for its Veterans History Project, 24 of the 49 individuals who identified themselves as Medal of Honor recipients had not actually received that award. The same was true of 32 individuals who claimed to have been awarded the Distinguished Service Cross and 14 who claimed to have won the Navy Cross. Notorious cases brought to Congress' attention included the case of a judge who falsely claimed to have been awarded *two* Medals of Honor and displayed counterfeit medals in his courtroom; a television network's military consultant who falsely claimed that he had received the Silver Star; and a former judge advocate in the Marine Corps who lied about receiving the Bronze Star and a Purple Heart.

. . .

As Congress recognized, the lies proscribed by the Stolen Valor Act inflict substantial harm. In many instances, the harm is tangible in nature: Individuals often falsely represent themselves as award recipients in order to obtain financial or other material rewards, such as lucrative contracts and government benefits. An investigation of false claims in a single region of the United States, for example, revealed that 12 men had defrauded the Department of Veterans Affairs out of more than $1.4 million in veteran's benefits. In other cases, the harm is less tangible, but nonetheless significant. The lies proscribed by the Stolen Valor Act tend to debase the distinctive honor of military awards. And legitimate award recipients and their families have expressed the harm they endure when an imposter takes credit for heroic actions that he never performed. One Medal of Honor recipient described the feeling as a " 'slap in the face of veterans who have paid the price and earned their medals.'"

. . .

Because a sufficiently comprehensive database is not practicable, lies about military awards cannot be remedied by what the plurality calls "counterspeech." Without the requisite database, many efforts to refute false claims may be thwarted, and some legitimate award recipients may be erroneously attacked. In addition, a steady stream of stories in the media about the exposure of imposters would tend to increase skepticism among members of the public about the entire awards system. This would only exacerbate the harm that the Stolen Valor Act is meant to prevent.

. . .

Allowing the state to proscribe false statements in these areas also opens the door for the state to use its power for political ends. Statements about history illustrate this point. If some false statements about historical events may be banned, how certain must it be that a statement is false before the ban may be upheld? And who should make that calculation? While our cases prohibiting viewpoint discrimination would fetter the state's power to some degree, the potential for abuse of power in these areas is simply too great.

In stark contrast to hypothetical laws prohibiting false statements about history, science, and similar matters, the Stolen Valor Act presents no risk at all that valuable speech will be suppressed. The speech punished by the Act is not only verifiably false and entirely lacking in intrinsic value, but it also fails to serve any instrumental purpose that the First Amendment might protect. Tellingly, when asked at oral argument what truthful speech the Stolen Valor Act might chill, even respondent's counsel conceded that the answer is none.

* * *

The Stolen Valor Act is a narrow law enacted to address an important problem, and it presents no threat to freedom of expression. I would sustain the constitutionality of the Act, and I therefore respectfully dissent.

In 2020, demonstrators protested the death of George Floyd in New York City. Protests erupted in at least 140 cities across the United States, prompting the National Guard to be activated in at least 21 states.

Gabriele Holtermann/ Sipa via AP Images

THE FIRST AMENDMENT

Speech and Press Freedoms in Theory and Reality

CHAPTER OUTLINE

Theoretical Foundations and History of the First Amendment
The Marketplace of Ideas
The Principle of Self-Governance
Self-Governance and the Press Clause
Autonomy and Self-Fulfillment
Critical Perspectives and the Role of Theory in Law

Technology and the First Amendment

How Courts Interpret the First Amendment

When Government Restrains First Amendment Freedoms

How the Supreme Court Reviews Laws Affecting First Amendment Rights
Content-Based Laws
Content-Neutral Laws

Protections and Boundaries for Different Categories of Speech
Political Speech
Government Speech
Compelled Speech
Election Speech
Anonymous Speech

Protections for Assembly and Association
Private Property as a Public Forum
Funding as Forum
Associating Freely

Emerging Law

Cases for Study
- *New York Times Co. v. United States*
- *Reed v. Town of Gilbert*

LEARNING OBJECTIVES

2.1   Define and explain the major theories of the First Amendment and the impact of U.S. History on the First Amendment.

2.2   Describe the impact of technology on the First Amendment and legal doctrine.

2.3   Explain how courts evaluate and interpret First Amendment claims.

2.4   Identify and Explain How Courts evaluate First Amendment claims regarding government restrictions of the press.

2.5   Explain how the courts evaluate the wording of statutes regulating speech.

2.6   Describe and define the boundaries of political speech, government speech, compelled speech, election speech and anonymous speech.

2.7   Explain and apply public forum doctrine and the growing interest in associational rights.

In January 2021, former President Donald Trump was banned from Twitter, and Republicans across the United States expressed concern that Americans' online speech rights were under attack.[1] At the same time, Democrats argued that Americans were regularly fed a sea of dangerous online mis- and disinformation, leading not only to the Jan. 6, 2021, attack on the U.S. Capitol, but also to lagging vaccination rates in the wake of the COVID-19 pandemic and the rise of the deadly Delta variant.[2] The current landscape of free expression in the United States is one of increasing politicization and polarization, causing scholars and commentators to worry that democracy itself is at risk or already failing.[3]

The entrance of digital media has upended many assumptions about our speech and press freedoms as they previously existed in the offline world. As platforms like Instagram, Facebook and Twitter increasingly dominate the speech landscape, more questions have arisen about content moderation, the First Amendment-protected practice of corporations deciding whether users are abiding by the platforms' terms of service (TOS). Those TOS often prescribe the acceptable conditions for online speech and the behavior of users. While most users express harmless opinions and musings on life, some posts are more incendiary and violate the TOS. In recent years, platforms have had to decide what to do about online speech that serves up violence, harassment or mis- and disinformation. In some cases, platforms flag or censor such posts; in other cases, platforms have chosen to "deplatform" users themselves by restricting them from using their service.

Platforms moderate using both human and artificial intelligence, but the practice invariably raises new questions: Should the platforms wield such power in a free society? What responsibility should platforms have to host truthful information, particularly information that serves the public welfare? How transparent should that process be? And, for our purposes, what role does the First Amendment play in these disputes, and is our societal relationship to the principles and history of free expression and speech changing? Scholars across disciplines are taking a closer look at all of these questions.[4]

This chapter begins to explore this shifting landscape by first looking back at the history and theoretical foundations of the First Amendment. It also begins to explore some of the current pressure points as these principles and doctrines face new challenges in the digital age.

THEORETICAL FOUNDATIONS AND HISTORY OF THE FIRST AMENDMENT

The history of the First Amendment and free expression in the United States has always been a history of boundaries. It is also a history of exchange, as some rights expand while others contract, depending on social conditions. In the wake of new social problems and new technologies that challenge free expression or the welfare of the Republic, the law has always tried to balance the interests of speakers against other important societal interests. Often, those values conflict. While Americans frequently invoke the legacy and romance of U.S. free speech practices—"You can't do that! It's my free speech right to say that!"—the law often tells a different story. There have always been narrow "carveouts" to the First Amendment. Indeed, the entire study of media law in this textbook is a study of those carefully constructed exceptions.

It is important to understand that the First Amendment is first and foremost *a protection from government attempts to censor speech*. This legal principle is known as **state action**. The government—whether local, state or federal—must be in some way attempting to violate your First Amendment rights for you to claim them in court. So when private actors—be they your parents or the corporations that run the sites and social media apps you use—regulate your speech, the First Amendment is generally not a shield to those restrictions. If your parents say you cannot speak at the dinner table, you do not have a First Amendment right to challenge them—although you may still argue with them!

As a nation, we often favor and rely on these normative processes of speech and debate to solve our disputes rather than on the law and the First Amendment. This is what democracies and courts prefer, as painful and emotional as those debates sometimes become. Given our recent political divides, however, more of these disputes are landing in court. But the principle of state action remains: There is no First Amendment claim, generally speaking, without evidence of state action.

State action is rooted in the words of the First Amendment, which includes only 45 words. "Congress shall make no law respecting an establishment of religion, or prohibiting the free exercise thereof; or abridging the freedom of speech, or of the press; or the right of the people peaceably to assemble, and to petition the government for a redress of grievances." Since the adoption of the Bill of Rights in 1791, thousands of articles, books and legal cases have tried to interpret the First Amendment and define the boundaries of the six freedoms it protects.[5]

It's important for media law students to look to the *actual* words of the First Amendment. A *literal* interpretation of the First Amendment would completely ban Congress, and only Congress, from "abridging" the freedom of speech or of the press in any way. Think about it. The first words of the First Amendment are "CONGRESS shall make NO law . . ." This would imply the First Amendment applies ONLY to Congress and that it can't make ANY law. But that is not the case. In 1925, the U.S. Supreme Court said the First Amendment applied to state legislatures as well as to Congress.[6] Supreme Court decisions also make clear that although the First Amendment says government "shall make no law," the First Amendment's ban is *not* absolute.[7] Again, this textbook is an exploration of all those narrowly tailored exceptions.

Additionally, it's helpful to think of the First Amendment as either a set of five freedoms from government intervention or a series of "negative rights." The First Amendment doesn't affirmatively state that you have free speech. It simply says you are protected *from* government interference in (or state action against) your speech, press, religious establishment and practice, petition and assembly. This is part of what makes the current debates about online free expression so interesting and challenging. In many cases today, restrictions on speech are coming from private actors—from platforms like Instagram or from corporations who control citizen employment—and not directly from government (though there may be some indirect connections, which we'll address later).

POINTS OF LAW

THE NEGATIVE RIGHTS OF THE FIRST AMENDMENT

Unlike other western democracies, the United States frames its free expression rights as freedom from the government ("negative rights") rather than statements of citizen rights ("positive rights"). The First Amendment lists five freedoms from government intervention (six if you count the exercise and establishment of religion separately). The speech and press provisions are known as the "free expression clause" and are the main focus of this textbook. The five freedoms are as follows:

- Speech
- Press
- Religion (establishment and exercise)
- Petition
- Assembly

The emphasis on government involvement in citizen speech rights is a direct result of our early colonial experience. Historians of the First Amendment generally agree that the First Amendment was intended to prevent the U.S. government from adopting the types of suppressive laws that flourished in England following the introduction of the printing press in 1450. Beginning in the early 1500s, the British Crown controlled all presses in England through its licensing power. King Henry VIII and the Roman Catholic Church sought to suppress challenges to their power by outlawing critical views as heresy (criticism of the church) or sedition (challenges to government). They jointly imposed a strict system of licensing of printers and prior review of all publications.

Review before printing enabled the king's officers to ban disfavored authors and ideas. Printers suspected of publishing outlawed texts faced fines, prison, torture or even execution. In exchange for lucrative monopoly printing contracts, licensed printers reported and attacked unlicensed printers and destroyed their presses, but unlicensed texts continued to appear.

The Marketplace of Ideas

In 1643, the power of prior review shifted from the king's officers to the British Parliament. Authors and publishers protested government censorship and developed theories to justify press freedom. In 1644, English poet John Milton's unlicensed "Areopagitica" argued that an open **marketplace of ideas** advanced the interests of society and humankind. Milton, who was angered by church and state attempts to destroy his pamphlet advocating divorce, said the free exchange of ideas was vital to the discovery of truth. He also wrote that censors invariably fail at their task, and that once disclosed, evils and falsehoods are nearly impossible to control. He wrote, famously,

> Though all the winds of doctrine were let loose to play upon the earth, so Truth be in the field, we do injuriously by licensing and prohibiting to misdoubt her strength. Let her and Falsehood grapple; who ever knew Truth put to the worse in a free and open encounter?[8]

Milton's concept of the "marketplace of ideas" grew in popularity and was advanced by 18th century enlightenment philosopher John Stuart Mill. In his treatise *On Liberty*, Mill argued against censorship and for the free flow of ideas. Mill believed that the competition of ideas was what would lead to separating falsehoods from fact.[9] He argued it was necessary that falsehoods be allowed to roam in the marketplace of ideas, if not just for the competition but also because falsehoods *sometimes* became truths. Under marketplace theory, we must actually know falsehoods to have a basis for comparison and the determination of truth.[10]

The marketplace of ideas remains a guiding principle in nearly all First Amendment decisions to this day. It has been understood as the freedom needed for ideas to be exchanged, free from government interference, in order for the best and most productive ideas to emerge. In *Abrams v. United States*, Justice Oliver Wendell Holmes wrote a dissenting opinion that has been often quoted since: ". . . the best test of truth is the power of the thought to get itself accepted in the competition of the market, and that truth is the only ground upon which their wishes safely can be carried out."[11] It is often the reason that courts seek to keep the speech landscape as open as possible with minimal interference from government.

As a theory for free expression and the First Amendment, however, the marketplace of ideas rests on several assumptions receiving more attention, including notions of equal access to the marketplace. In recent years, theories of the U.S. Constitution as purely a limit on government power—not as a provider of personal liberties—have challenged the notion that an unregulated marketplace of ideas achieves truth or good democratic outcomes.[12] Marketplace theory can be used justify First Amendment protections for political lies, "socially worthless untruths" or mis- and disinformation, and new technological forms of "cheap and abundant robotic speech" (e.g., Siri).[13] Marketplace proponents have historically argued that such low-value speech will eventually be corrected by the marketplace, which is preferable to interference from the courts or the government.

But some critics of marketplace theory argue if the U.S. Constitution is solely a check on government, it has no proactive role in addressing imbalances of power among collective speakers (social media, major media corporations, the internet) who may overwhelm and dangerously mislead society. A hands-off approach to liars and deliberate disinformation is justified by the notions that all "truths" are partial; the identity of speakers does not determine the value of their speech and government may not establish preferred orthodoxies.[14] These are important and ongoing discussions at a time in which disinformation has threatened public health and led to violence against the state.

The Principle of Self-Governance

In 1694, the British Parliament failed to renew the Licensing Act, which required texts be reviewed before publication, and this official **prior restraint** of publications ended. But for the next 100 years, the British government enacted and enforced laws that punished immoral, illegal or dangerous speech after the fact. Political thinkers of the day generally did not view punishment after the fact as censorship because it allowed people to speak and publish and held them accountable for the harms their speech was believed to cause, such as sedition, **defamation** (criticism of individuals) and blasphemy (sacrilegious speech about God).

The British licensed presses in the colonies, and government censors previewed publications until the 1720s. The crime of **seditious libel** made it illegal to publish anything harmful to the reputation of a colonial governor. At that time, truth was not a defense because truthful criticism still harmed the governor's reputation, and the governor had a legal right to be compensated for that harm.

The Founders' experiences with regulations by the British Crown, including a series of Stamp Acts that created new taxes on newspapers, ultimately led to the drafting and passage of the First Amendment in the Bill of Rights. The Founders relied heavily on the importance of self-governance for the new nation. In England, sovereignty rested with the king. In contrast, James Madison wrote that "In the United States the case is altogether different. The People, not the Government, possess the absolute sovereignty."[15] Madison saw "free communication among the people" as a critical part of that self-governance, the "only effectual guardian of every other right."[16]

Proponents of self-governance theory see the right of free expression under the First Amendment as flowing from the government's grant of that right. French political philosopher Jean-Jacques Rousseau advanced the idea of a social contract between the people and their government in which the people limit some individual freedoms for a government that advances the collective interest.[17] Rousseau said all people are born free and equal but need the constraints of morality and law to become civilized and nonviolent. Accordingly, people form a social contract in which they remain sovereign and retain their human rights. Therefore, government censorship can never be justified.

Alexander Meiklejohn, an early 20th-century philosopher and educator, is often identified as one of the leading proponents of self-governance theory. He argued that the First Amendment was the key to democratic rule; unless self-governing citizens had access to information and opinions about issues about which they must decide, democracy could not flourish. In this sense, citizen participation in political issues was critical. He famously wrote:

> "The First Amendment, then, is not the guardian of unregulated talkativeness. It does not require that, on every occasion, every citizen shall take part in public debate. Nor can it give assurance that everyone shall have opportunity to do so. . . . What is essential is not that everyone shall speak, but that everything worth saying shall be said."[18]

Self-Governance and the Press Clause

British legal scholar Sir William Blackstone described the prevailing understanding of a free press under common law in the mid-18th century.[19] He wrote,

> The liberty of the press is indeed essential to the nature of a free state, but this consists in laying no *previous* restraints upon publications, and not in freedom from censure for criminal matter when published. Every freeman has an undoubted right to lay what sentiments he pleases before the public, to forbid this is to destroy the freedom of the press, but if he publishes what is improper, mischievous or illegal, he must take the consequences of his own temerity.[20]

Blackstone's view of freedom of the press and of British licensing, taxation and common law restraints on speech and press traveled to the American colonies.[21] With growing independence, however, the colonies attempted to dismantle some British common law traditions. In the case of John Peter Zenger, this publisher of a newspaper in New York clearly had broken the sedition law by printing criticism of colonial Gov. William Cosby. Cosby jailed Zenger to stop the publications. Arguing for the defense, Andrew Hamilton said no one should be jailed for publishing truthful and fair criticism of government. The jury agreed and acquitted Zenger in 1734 despite the contrary common law.

Very few trials for seditious libel followed. However, the struggle to define the acceptable limits of free speech and a free press continued in colonial legislatures that used their power to question, convict, jail and fine those who published criticism of the legislature of breach of parliamentary privilege.

This mixed history shaped First Amendment freedoms of speech and of the press. The Constitution's framers understood both the British tradition of punishment for sedition, blasphemy and libel, and the colonists' growing enthusiasm for increasingly free debate and self-governance. It seems clear the authors of the First Amendment intended to provide a ban on prior restraints. Less clear is whether they intended to eliminate the common law regarding sedition, blasphemy and libel.[22] Also unclear is the Framers' intent for the press clause as part of the First Amendment, although scholars point out that press rights were included in many state constitutions prior to the passage of the Bill of Rights. Most of these statements affirm the idea that the press received important protection independent of other expressive rights and emphasized that the right was to limit targeted government restrictions of the press.[23]

As the 18th century ended, U.S. laws continued to punish criticism of government. Seven years after the adoption of the First Amendment, the Sedition Act imposed heavy fines and jail time on individuals who stirred up public emotions or expressed malicious views against the government. More than a dozen prosecutions and convictions under the Alien and Sedition Acts targeted outspoken publishers and political opponents of President John Adams.[24] The Alien and Sedition Acts expired without the U.S. Supreme Court reviewing their constitutionality, but more than 150 years later, Justice William J. Brennan said that "the court of history" clearly found the Sedition Act unconstitutional.[25]

The press, then and now, plays a unique role in the execution of self-governance. In the 1970s, Professor Vincent Blasi proposed his "checking value" theory of the First Amendment, the idea that a critical purpose of free expression is to serve as a "check" on government power. Blasi argued that the colonial pamphleteers, the earliest members of the U.S. press, "organized much of their political thought around the need they perceived to check the abuse of governmental power."[26] The press, under this extension of self-governance theory, plays an important role in holding government officials accountable to the people and serves as the "**Fourth Estate**." In this way, the press is seen as an unofficial fourth branch of government, serving as part of the checks and balances system of representative government in the U.S.

Autonomy and Self-Fulfillment

By the late 1600s, English philosopher and political theorist John Locke argued that government censorship was an improper exercise of power.[27] Locke first said that all people have fundamental natural rights, including life, personal liberty and self-fulfillment. Freedom of expression is central to these natural rights. Government has no innate rights or authority, and its power derives solely through a grant from the people. Government actions outside the sphere of power granted by the people are illegitimate. The people do not give government the power over their natural human rights. Accordingly, government censorship is always illegitimate. Locke's vision of government was revolutionary.

Students often readily identify with the idea of free expression as flowing from within and from the identities they craft for themselves on campus. Law professor C. Edwin Baker developed a "liberty theory" of free speech arguing that "the First Amendment protects a broad realm of nonviolent, noncoercive, expressive activity," serving two primary values, self-fulfillment and self-realization.[28] Baker wrote:

> "The liberty model holds that the free speech clause protects not a marketplace, but rather an arena of individual liberty from certain types of government restrictions. Speech or self-expressive conduct is protected not as a means to achieve a collective good but because of its value to the individual."[29]

Another legal scholar, Thomas Emerson, proposed that individual protections for free expression can actually benefit the larger society by offering it a type of "safety valve."

> The argument that the process of open discussion, far from causing society to fly apart, stimulates forces that lead to greater cohesion ... Stated in narrower and perhaps cruder terms, the position is that allowing dissidents to expound their views enables them to 'let off steam.' The classic example is the Hyde Park (London) meeting where any person is permitted to say anything he wishes to whatever audience he can assemble. This results in a release of energy, a lessening of frustration, and a channeling of resistance into courses consistent with law and order. It operates, in short, as a catharsis throughout the body politic.[30]

Critics of autonomy and self-fulfillment as the primary basis for free expression point out that while such arguments have personal appeal—we can all relate to wanting and needing personal freedom of expression to pursue our goals or blow off steam—such personal expression can present problems for social welfare and a democratic state. Probably the best and most recent example is the speech of those associated with the anti-vaccination movement. To the extent that the First Amendment protects the speech of "anxi-vaxxers" and their personal desire to reject modern medicine and vaccines, their speech has also placed society at risk of dangerous infection.[31]

Critical Perspectives and the Role of Theory in Law

In science, theories are designed to predict reactions under certain conditions. Within the law, theories play a different but related role. Legal theories in a democracy are used to justify judicial decision making and doctrine related to human behavior that serves (or doesn't serve) democracy. When judges make decisions in First Amendment cases, they are aided by precedent but also by these theories of free expression. From that combination of precedent and theory, judges arrive at **legal doctrine**, a rule or set of rules or principles that are followed within a particular legal field. The marketplace of ideas, self-governance and autonomy/self-fulfillment reflect some of the more popular theories mentioned in First Amendment case law. These discussions, often found in **dicta**, form the background against which precedent and legal doctrine are developed and later followed in subsequent cases. Dicta include parts of a decision that are not part of the law but often influence and contextualize legal doctrine.

Some legal scholars are critical of this paradigm because it often relies on jurists with long-standing power and influence to establish which theories and doctrine are the ones that help establish new precedent. Critical race theory, a perspective most notably advanced by law professor Kimberlé Crenshaw and discussed primarily in law schools, has received renewed attention and debate in recent years. Crenshaw and others argue that such choices are inherently political and serve status quo perspectives, keeping longstanding power structures in place. Critical race theory (CRT) especially challenges "the ways in which race and racial power are constructed and represented in American legal culture and more generally in American society as a whole."[32] CRT has received increasing attention with the passage of at least 18 state anti-CRT laws or executive orders banning discussion about the theory in public schools.[33] Opponents and scholars have argued that CRT has never been taught in public schools and that these new statutes ban virtually any discussion about how racism has impacted the country. Critics say the new laws violate the First Amendment by silencing discussion about the nation's history.[34]

Legal scholars who study the First Amendment from this perspective argue that a strict adherence to marketplace theory, for instance, allows hate speech to flourish and creates a marketplace of intimidation and trauma in its wake.[35] First Amendment case law does not rely on this perspective. Marketplace theory is particularly prominent in First Amendment legal doctrine, and opponents of CRT argue that carving out exceptions for hate speech in the United States would not only be extremely difficult, but would also censor the sources of hate that need to be seen to be addressed.[36] CRT proponents counter that the rise of domestic terrorists and white supremacists in the United States is in part due to the structures that have fueled it, such as unbridled protections for hate speech.[37] Hate speech is addressed in fuller detail in Chapter 3.

INTERNATIONAL LAW
ARTICLE 19, INTERNATIONAL FREE EXPRESSION AND THE PANDEMIC

Passed by the United Nations in 1948, the Universal Declaration of Human Rights (UDHR) established that fundamental human rights be universally protected for the first time. Article 19 of the UDHR serves as the bedrock for free expression rights worldwide. It states,

"Everyone has the right to freedom of opinion and expression; this right includes freedom to hold opinions without interference and to seek, receive and impart information and ideas through any media and regardless of frontiers."[38]

Articles 20 and 21 protect the freedom of assembly and the right to "take part in the government of his country."

One barometer of international internet freedom is the Google transparency report. In 2019, the report listed the United States as third most restrictive in online censorship among the leading 20 industrialized nations.[39] Article19.org, a group devoted to measuring free expression worldwide, produces a yearly report on government censorship. Its 2021 report revealed that rather than focusing on controlling COVID-19, many governments used the pandemic as an excuse to suppress critical information, implement states of emergency without proper limits, and place unreasonable and unnecessary restrictions on the media. The group wrote that "by presenting a false choice between human rights and public health, governments have used a cunning tactic to shut down public discussion and scrutiny of their decisions."[40]

TECHNOLOGY AND THE FIRST AMENDMENT

In 1791, when the First Amendment was adopted, speaking to crowds in town squares and the printed word—the press—was *the* medium of mass communication. Printing of pamphlets, posters, books and newspapers was the primary means to distribute your message, and the masses reached were small. The largest 18th-century newspapers had circulations of no more than 200 or so readers. Word of mouth—speech—remained essential to spreading timely information.

Today, the First Amendment faces a very different reality. New media—motion pictures, radio, television, telephone, cable, the internet, Alexa—provide new types, reach, modes and uses of communication. As consumers of media also become producers of that content, the lines between press and speech, between information and entertainment, also blur, creating complications for the marketplace of ideas and the principles of self-governance and self-fulfillment, as well as for the law.

REAL WORLD LAW
WHAT'S PUBLICATION?

When an employee clicks "like" on a Facebook post, is that speech or press?

A U.S. district court in Virginia ruled that Facebook "likes" are not expression protected by the First Amendment.[41] Two sheriff's employees were fired after they clicked "like" on the campaign Facebook page of their boss's election opponent. They sued, saying the termination violated their free speech rights, but the district court rejected their challenge.

On appeal, the Fourth Circuit Court of Appeals disagreed.[42] It wrote,

On the most basic level, clicking on the "like" button literally published the statement that the User "likes" something, which is itself a substantive statement. . . . That a user may use a single mouse click to produce the message that he likes the page instead of typing the same message with several individual keystrokes is of no constitutional significance.

Liking a political candidate's campaign page communicates the user's approval of the candidate and supports the campaign by associating the user with it. In this way, it is the internet equivalent of displaying a political sign in one's front yard, which the Supreme Court has held is substantive speech.[43]

The nature of U.S. media keeps changing. Six companies now control the bulk of communications (cell, cable, films, news) across the United States.[44] These include Comcast, News Corp, Disney, Time Warner, CBS and Viacom. Some of these companies create content, some distribute it and some do both, making the lines ever more blurred. This arrangement has concerned scholars and policymakers who worry that too much power in too few hands creates an environment for easy censorship and threatens access to diverse voices and content—as well as democracy itself.[45] Others contend that the internet has improved access for marginalized communities and voices, offering new ways for diverse voices to be heard.[46]

Amid this change, new companies are gaining ground and altering the very nature of the U.S. media market. For example, Netflix buys content from traditional media, but it now also creates and sells its own content. In 2021, Amazon announced plans to buy movie giant MGM. Some media providers, like AT&T, who made plans to buy and feature content, have changed their plans. Fewer owners controlling more diverse media present challenges to the Court's carefully drawn distinctions and the assumption that competition ensures an open marketplace of ideas.[47]

But some scholars have suggested that the threat to the marketplace of ideas today is less about ownership control than it is about increasing "noise" in that marketplace. Siva Vaidhyanathan, a media studies scholar from the University of Virginia, says media consolidation is better told as a tale of three layers.[48] At the ground level are the cable and telecommunication companies like Comcast, AT&T, T-Mobile and Verizon, controlling the media pipelines and flooding our lives with data and content. At the second layer, the Google–Facebook duopoly represents "two of the most valuable companies in the world and the masters of our attention."[49] Nearly every other media company depends on Google and Facebook and platforms like them to be seen and monetized through tracking, a fact that gives these platforms extraordinary control over not just entertainment, but also state messaging in the case of some authoritarian governments around the world. At the third level are the content providers, who must pay close attention to the second level in order to sustain their business models. This includes the work of traditional news media, who now rely on social media for their content to be seen and for their livelihood. This has created an environment ripe for "clickbait," content often designed less to inform and more to make users want to click, a phenomenon that seemingly works against principles of the marketplace of ideas and democratic governance.

Some members of Congress are seeking to create more competition in the marketplace by introducing bills to break up the monopolistic hold of the second layer, the platforms, with antitrust law proposals. As of 2021, these bills were still pending. (See more on this in Chapter 9.) In the meantime, the second layer wields enormous power, by controlling not only what content is seen but by default, what content is monetized. They dominate rather than distribute, leaving a media landscape of both "concentration and cacophony."[50]

For its part, the U.S. Supreme Court has struggled to decide whether and how the First Amendment protects new media.[51] For a time, the Court generally treated each medium differently on the grounds that each presented unique First Amendment capabilities. In 1949, for example, one justice argued that "the moving picture screen, the radio, the newspaper, the handbill, the sound truck and the street corner orator have differing natures, values, abuses and dangers. Each, in my view, is a law unto itself."[52] The Court accepted regulatory differences "justified by some special characteristic of the press"[53] or by specific distinctions among the media. Government could regulate broadcasters differently from newspapers because broadcasters act as trustees of scarce public airwaves.[54] Unique regulations on cable operators did not violate the First Amendment, the Court said, because cable threatened the survival of free over-the-air broadcasts.[55]

By the 1990s, however, the court understood that the internet was fast becoming the cornerstone of the American news and entertainment landscape. In 1997, the U.S. Supreme Court ruled in *Reno v. ACLU* that the internet deserved the same high level of First Amendment protection awarded to newspapers. Nearly 20 years later in *North Carolina v. Packingham*, the Court wrote that "websites can provide perhaps the most powerful mechanisms available to a private citizen to make his or her voice be heard."[56] Quoting the earlier *Reno* case, the Court wrote that the internet allows users to "become a town crier with a voice that resonates farther than it could from any soapbox."[57]

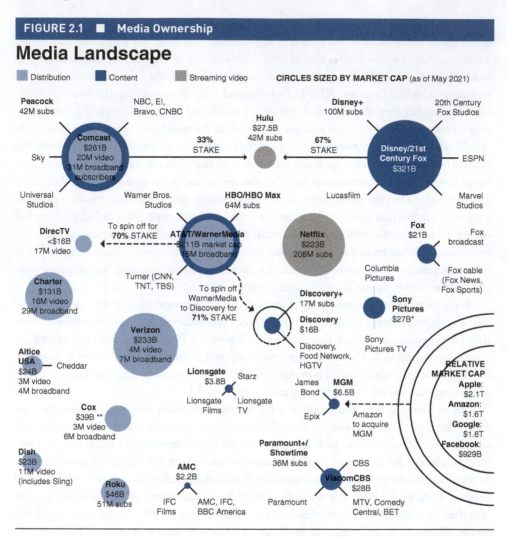

FIGURE 2.1 ■ Media Ownership

Media Landscape

Rani Molla, "Media landscape", Vox.com, May 27, 2021, https://www.vox.com/2018/1/23/16905844/media-landscape-verizonamazon-comcast-disney-fox-relationships-chart

HOW COURTS INTERPRET THE FIRST AMENDMENT

The mixed legacy of British common law and the fast-changing nature of communications create obstacles to a consistent, stable interpretation of the Constitution. Textualists assert that the First Amendment's own words are the most concrete and unwavering explanation of its meaning, but the Constitution is more than 230 years old. It obviously says nothing about whether court orders requiring WikiLeaks to disclose the source of its access to confidential government documents would "abridge" the freedom of "the press" or whether Facebook "likes" are a protected part of First Amendment "freedom of speech."[58]

Some justices look to history, seeking the **original intent** of the Framers of the Constitution, to help them determine whether occupying the streets of Ferguson, Mo., or wearing bandanas and carrying AR-15 rifles at a Texas protest are protected speech.[59] Unfortunately, the authors of the First Amendment left scant records to indicate what they meant by "the freedom of speech, or of the press."

Other justices view the Constitution as a living document and argue that the ambiguity of constitutional language is its greatest strength. To them, a clear understanding of what the words of the First Amendment meant in 1791 would rarely be relevant today. At the time the Constitution was written, for example, women did not have the right to vote and African Americans were considered to be 3/5 of a person. For these justices, the Constitution is an evolving document. Others argue that such a malleable understanding of the Constitution gives the U.S. Supreme Court too much power and poses a threat to legal predictability.

To reach decisions, the U.S. Supreme Court often weighs the constitutional interests on one side of a case against the competing interests on the other side. When courts make decisions by weighing the specific facts on each side of the case, their reasoning is called **ad hoc balancing**. No clear rule dictates the weight of interests in ad hoc balancing. Instead, judges determine which side has greater constitutional merit.

Courts also use categories of speech to reach some First Amendment decisions. The Supreme Court has defined several speech categories, such as political speech and commercial speech, to guide the appropriate First Amendment application. Simply put, the Court's categories give some kinds of speech a lot of protection; some, less; others, none at all. When speech falls into one of these categories, the courts do not balance the value of the speech against society's interests. Using this approach, the courts' central question is whether a specific act of expression falls within a fully protected, less protected or unprotected class.

Decades ago in *Chaplinsky v. New Hampshire*,[60] the Court first noted that "certain well-defined and narrowly limited classes of speech . . . are no essential part of any exposition of ideas, and are of such slight social value as a step to truth" that government may prevent and punish this speech without violating the First Amendment. In *Chaplinsky*, the Court did not fully develop the different "narrow" categories of speech, but subsequent rulings make clear that political speech enjoys full constitutional protection, while fighting words and obscenity are unprotected categories. The First Amendment also does not prohibit laws that punish blackmail, extortion, perjury, false advertising and disruptive speech in the public school classroom, for example. These exceptions are covered in more detail in subsequent chapters.

When the category of speech is less clearly defined, the courts generally balance the nature of the speech against any competing societal values using what is called **categorical balancing**. For example, pornography is not a legal category of speech. To determine whether certain pornographic images deserve constitutional protection, courts must balance the right to freedom of sexual expression against the harms it causes in the specific circumstances of the case.[61] Judges do this on a case-by-case basis.

The U.S. Supreme Court used balancing in *Lane v. Franks* to rule that the First Amendment protects the right of public employees to testify in court on matters of public concern.[62] Weighing the interest of a government agency to control the speech of its employees against the right of the person to testify in court, the Court first clarified the boundary between government and private speech. "When public employees make statements pursuant to their official duties, the employees are not speaking as citizens for First Amendment purposes"[63] but are speaking for

George Washington presiding over debate at the Constitutional Convention in 1787.
Everett Collection Inc/Alamy Stock Photo

the government, the Court wrote. The First Amendment protection for government employee speech depends on that distinction as well as on the public value of the speech. In *Lane*, the value of public testimony about government corruption outweighed the government interest in stopping it.

The Supreme Court sidestepped an opportunity to decide the amount of First Amendment protection given to false speech when it considered whether a federal law that made it a crime to lie about being awarded U.S. military honors violated the Constitution.[64] In its decision in *United States v. Alvarez* striking down the Stolen Valor Act, which is excerpted in Chapter 1, only four justices held that the First Amendment absolutely protects false statements. Reasoning for this plurality, Justice Anthony Kennedy argued that speech may be excluded from First Amendment protection only in the rare and extreme circumstances of the "historic categories" that pose a grave and imminent threat. False claims about military awards do not. Congress later amended the Stolen Valor Act to make it illegal to profit from such lies.[65]

The Ninth Circuit Court of Appeals later distinguished between false action and lies to rule that the First Amendment did not prevent government from punishing the wearing of unearned military medals.[66] The First Amendment protected only false claims of military honors.

Similarly, the Sixth Circuit Court of Appeals found an Ohio law prohibiting "false statements" during a political campaign unconstitutional.[67] The court reasoned that "the First Amendment protects the 'civic duty' to engage in public debate, with a preference for counteracting lies with more accurate information, rather than by restricting lies." The First

Amendment directs government not to restrict speech, and as the Supreme Court established, the "fixed star in our constitutional constellation" is that the government may not "prescribe what shall be orthodox in politics."[68]

WHEN GOVERNMENT RESTRAINS FIRST AMENDMENT FREEDOMS

The U.S. Supreme Court has established one bedrock principle: Freedom of speech and of the press cannot coexist with prior restraint. Prior restraints stop speech before it is spoken and halt presses before they print. They are the essence of censorship. But in today's world of Instagram and Snapchat, how should government step in to avoid the harms speech may cause?

The Court's modern understanding of prior restraint originated in 1931.[69] In *Near v. Minnesota*, the Court said that prior restraint, especially any outright ban on expression, is the least tolerable form of government intervention in the speech marketplace.[70] The case began after the publisher of a Minneapolis newspaper printed charges that city officials allowed Jewish gangsters to run gambling, bootlegging and racketeering businesses across the city. When the publisher could not show that the attacks were true and published with good intent, the court shut down the paper under a state public nuisance law that punished publication of "scandalous or defamatory material."

On review, the Supreme Court ruled that the permanent ban on future issues of the newspaper was unconstitutional. The Court said the First Amendment stands as a nearly absolute barrier to classic prior restraints. Government prohibitions before publication are unacceptable unless the government can show that the action is essential to avoid a very narrow list of harms, such as the disclosure of military movements.

POINTS OF LAW
SUPREME COURT'S DOCTRINE IN *NEAR V. MINNESOTA*

In its 1931 decision in *Near v. Minnesota*, the U.S. Supreme Court established that government
- prior restraints on publication are unconstitutional
- EXCEPT when a communication is
  - obscene,
  - incites violence and the overthrow of government,
  - or reveals military secrets
- *and* the government makes a specific showing that a prior restraint is justified.

In all other cases, government may punish communications only after the fact.[71]

In *Near*, the Supreme Court held that the First Amendment placed a heavy, but not absolute, burden on government prior restraints. While the "liberty of speech, and of the press, is not an absolute right, . . . [t]he fact that the liberty . . . may be abused by miscreant purveyors of scandal does not make any the less necessary the immunity from previous restraint in dealing with official misconduct."[72] The Court said prior restraints may be permissible but only in "exceptional cases. When a nation is at war . . . [n]o one would question but that a government might prevent actual obstruction to its recruiting service or the publication of the sailing dates of transports or the number and location of troops." It said that the government also could prevent the publication of obscenity, incitements to violence and overthrow of government and "words that may have all the effect of force."[73]

In 1971, the U.S. Supreme Court ruled in *New York Times Co. v. United States* (excerpted at the end of this chapter) that a court order preventing publication of news stories based on leaked Pentagon reports was an unconstitutional prior restraint.[74] The New York Times had begun a series of news stories based on a top-secret Department of Defense study of the then-ongoing U.S. involvement in Vietnam. The Nixon administration asked for a court **injunction** to stop the publication of the so-called Pentagon Papers report on the status of the war. The government said publication threatened national security and the safety of U.S. troops. The district court agreed and enjoined publication.

Dr. Daniel Ellsberg (left), the U.S. Defense Department consultant who leaked the Pentagon Papers, speaks to reporters after his 1971 arraignment on charges of illegal possession of the classified documents.

Associated Press

Many compared the WikiLeaks posting of more than 90,000 classified U.S. military documents on the war in Afghanistan in 2010 to the publication of the Pentagon Papers during the Vietnam War.[75] Both leaks hinged on media providing greater transparency and credibility to information about an ongoing and controversial war involving U.S. troops.[76] However, the Pentagon Papers documents were at least three years old and were released as U.S. troops began to withdraw from Vietnam; some WikiLeaks material was only a few weeks old and appeared as the war in Afghanistan was ramping up.[77] Former U.S. army analyst Chelsea Manning served six years in military custody for her role in leaking hundreds of thousands of documents and cables to Wikileaks. Wikileaks Founder Julian Assange has been charged under the Espionage Act. In late 2021, the United Kingdom's High Court ruled that Assange could be extradited to the U.S. to face the charges.

Acting with unusual speed in the case of the Pentagon Papers, the U.S. Supreme Court said the injunction violated the Constitution because the government had not shown that the ban was essential to prevent "direct, immediate and irreparable damage to our Nation or its people."[78] The Court said, "[A]ny system of prior restraints of expression comes to this Court bearing a heavy presumption against its constitutional validity"[79] The Court decision left open the possibility that prior restraints might be constitutional if the government could meet this very rigorous test.

Five years later, in *Nebraska Press Association v. Stuart*, the Court said prior restraints are generally unconstitutional because they pose too great a risk that government will censor ideas it disfavors and distort the marketplace of ideas.[80] The Court said that if "a threat of criminal or civil sanctions after publication 'chills' speech, prior restraint 'freezes' it." Prohibited prior restraints have three elements: (1) government oversight over whole categories of speech, content or publications; (2) government determination of acceptable content; and (3) government power to stop content before it reaches the public.

The First Amendment poses its greatest obstacle to direct prior restraints on the news media because every moment of a ban on reporting causes direct harm to the First Amendment rights of both the media and the public.[81] Yet news organizations report that policies imposed on government agencies, the "management" of reporters through government public relations offices and calls by government officials to punish or remove journalists all have the effect of prior restraint.[82] The government says it has the power to control the flow of information from its employees and to classify information.

Prior restraints usually arise in the form of court orders that stop speech or publication. For example, the Supreme Court long ago said a state court injunction preventing the scheduled broadcast of an investigative news report was unconstitutional; indefinite delay of news was unacceptable under the First Amendment.[83] As another court noted, "News delayed is news denied."[84] The Supreme Court decision involved CBS News' intended broadcast of undercover footage of a South Dakota meatpacking plant. Although the broadcast relied on "calculated misdeeds" and might cause significant harm to the meatpacking company, the Court ruled that the "most extraordinary remedy" of an injunction was unwarranted because it was not essential.

In 2020, the Trump administration tried to stop the publication of a memoir by John Bolton, Trump's former national security adviser, titled "The Room Where it Happened."[85] The book details Bolton's 17 months as Trump's national security adviser. In it, Bolton called Trump incompetent and unfit for office. The Trump administration not only sought to stop the publication of the book, but it also looked to extend its injunction against the publisher and any downstream bookseller, claiming that Bolton did not obtain the proper security clearance for such a book. A federal judge ruled that the publication could proceed, writing that it was too late to stop the book, given that thousands of copies had already been distributed around the globe.[86] The judge left open the possibility that Bolton could be held responsible for violating the established rules of pre-publication clearance for those with access to classified information. The Justice Department closed its investigation into the book in 2021.[87]

POINTS OF LAW
WHAT IS A PRIOR RESTRAINT?

A prior restraint is good, old, garden-variety censorship. Prior restraint exists when

1. any government body or representative
2. reviews speech or press *prior* to distribution and
3. stops the dissemination of ideas *before* they reach the public.

The Supreme Court has called prior restraint "the most serious and the least tolerable infringement on First Amendment rights."[88]

The U.S. Supreme Court has held that a prior restraint on the media can be justified only when there is clear and convincing evidence that the speech will cause great and certain harm that cannot be addressed by less intrusive measures or when the speaker clearly engaged in criminal activity to obtain the information being banned.[89] The ban on prior restraints does not prohibit laws that silence discussion of particular topics, such as threats to national security. Judges' orders prohibiting trial participants from discussing ongoing trials also generally are acceptable. Laws that limit use of copyrighted material are mandated by the Constitution, and laws that criminalize obscenity are accepted. Police also may legally prevent the speech involved when individuals conspire to commit a crime or to incite violence.

Yale professor Jack Balkin has argued that prior restraints look different in the digital age. Today, prior restraints are imposed by what Balkin calls the "infrastructure of free expression"—that is, the digital pipelines and platforms that host and control such expression. Rather than stopping speakers or publishers, the government today can attempt to regulate speech through control over digital networks, search engines, payment systems and advertisers creating a type of digital prior restraint, mostly through the use of subpoenas and warrants for information. (See Chapter 9 for more about these topics.)[90]

People in favor of and against a mask mandate for Cobb County schools gather and protest ahead of the school board meeting in August 2021 in Marietta, Ga. (Ben Gray/Atlanta Journal-Constitution via AP)

REAL WORLD LAW

DO MASK MANDATES DURING A PANDEMIC VIOLATE THE FIRST AMENDMENT?

The short answer is "no."

In 2020 and 2021, a handful of plaintiffs across the United States claimed their civil liberties were threatened when several states began to impose mask mandates during the COVID-19 pandemic.[91] Under the Tenth Amendment, power that isn't assigned to the federal government is reserved to the states. Because mask mandates aren't anywhere in the federal codes, states can impose mask requirements. These cases were dismissed by the courts, however, governors in Texas and Florida have issued executive orders banning local mask mandates, and those orders have been the subject of ongoing court challenges at the time of publication.

Constitutional rights are also subject to the government's authority to protect the health, safety and welfare of the community.[92] In 1905, the U.S. Supreme Court upheld a smallpox vaccination requirement in Cambridge, Mass. In *Jacobson v. Massachusetts*, the Court ruled that the requirement was constitutional. The court wrote that it was "the inherent right of every freeman to care for his own body and health in such way as to him seems best," but the court added, "[t]here are manifold restraints to which every person is necessarily subject for the common good. On any other basis, organized society could not exist with safety to its members."[93]

In July 2020, a court in Palm Beach, Florida, refused to block a mask mandate ordered by the county. Citing the *Jacobson* case, judge John S. Kastrenakes wrote "the right to be free from governmental intrusion does not automatically or completely shield an individual's conduct from regulation."[94] In another case in 2020, Minnesota federal district court judge Patrick J. Schlitz said such claims were "meritless" because they do "not implicate the First Amendment at all" and even if they did, the Minnesota order requiring masks would "easily pass muster under *U.S. v. O'Brien*" and the *Jacobson* case. Schlitz wrote that mask wearing was not "inherently expressive," and even if it was, the order was unrelated to the suppression of speech.[95]

HOW THE SUPREME COURT REVIEWS LAWS AFFECTING FIRST AMENDMENT RIGHTS

The U.S. Supreme Court does not view all government actions that appear to restrain freedom of speech in advance as prior restraints. The Court decides the constitutionality of laws by drawing a number of distinctions. It first determines whether a law involves speech at all. Minimum-wage regulations and laws that prevent monopolies fall within the power of Congress to regulate commerce.[96] The Court generally presumes that these **laws of general application** are constitutional. The Supreme Court reviews challenges to such laws under its least rigorous or minimum review, called **rational review**. Under rational review, a law is constitutional if government can show it serves a rational purpose. Laws reviewed under minimum scrutiny must be reasonable and serve a legitimate government purpose to be constitutional.

When government actions do affect the freedom of speech and press protected by the First Amendment, the Supreme Court first determines whether the law targets the ideas expressed or aims at some goal unrelated to the content of the message. The Court calls the first type of law **content based** and the second **content neutral**. Content-based laws regulate what is being said; they single out certain messages or types of speech for particular treatment. Laws that prohibit the "desecration" of the U.S. flag are content based.[97] Content-neutral laws restrict where, when and how ideas are expressed. Also called **time/place/manner laws**, content-neutral restrictions often advance public interests unrelated to speech.

Content-Based Laws

The U.S. Supreme Court generally presumes content-based laws are unconstitutional. Like prior restraints, laws that punish expression of specific ideas after the fact pose a serious threat of government censorship. To stop government regulation of disfavored ideas, the Supreme Court applies its most rigorous test to determine whether content-based laws are constitutional. The toughest standard of review, **strict scrutiny**, finds laws that apply different treatment to different types of speech unconstitutional unless they use (1) the least restrictive means (2) to advance a compelling government interest.

Laws employ the least restrictive means only if they are extremely narrowly tailored to their goals and affect the smallest possible amount of protected speech. The Supreme Court generally finds that a law is least restrictive if the government has no other reasonable method to achieve its goals that would be less harmful to free speech rights. To pass strict scrutiny, laws also must directly advance a compelling or paramount government interest. The Court has said a **compelling interest** is an interest of the highest order that relates to core constitutional concerns or the most significant functions of government. Compelling government interests include national security, the electoral process and public health and safety.

In *Simon & Schuster v. Crime Victims Board*, for example, the Supreme Court struck down a New York law that required convicted criminals to turn over the profits of publications that made even passing reference to their crimes.[98] The state said the money would compensate crime victims, increase victim compensation and decrease the "fruits" of crime. Simon & Schuster had published a true-crime autobiography of a Mafia figure and challenged the law on the grounds that it targeted specific content for punishment by the government. The Supreme Court found the law content-based law and said it advanced a compelling government interest, but it also punished writings that deserved full First Amendment protection.[99] The law was unconstitutional because it did not use the least restrictive means to achieve its goal.

POINTS OF LAW
STRICT SCRUTINY

The U.S. Supreme Court has said content-based laws are constitutional only if they pass strict scrutiny. To pass strict scrutiny, a law must

1. be necessary and
2. employ the least restrictive means
3. to advance a compelling government interest.

Strict scrutiny is the most rigorous test used by the courts to determine whether a law is constitutional. Few laws pass this test.

Content-Neutral Laws

Laws that impose speech restrictions to advance legitimate government interests without targeting particular viewpoints or content generally are constitutional. Many laws that limit noise in school zones are content neutral and constitutional.[100] The Supreme Court applies **intermediate scrutiny** to such laws and finds them constitutional if they restrict speech as little as necessary to advance an important government interest unrelated to speech. Content-neutral laws generally regulate the non-speech elements of messages, such as the location, time of day or volume. If content-neutral laws advance a legitimate government goal and do not favor particular views, the Court generally finds them constitutional even if they reduce the method, location or quantity of speech.

The U.S. Supreme Court established its foundational First Amendment test for content-neutral laws in its review of the conviction of David Paul O'Brien for burning his draft card during an anti–Vietnam War protest. O'Brien violated a federal law that made it a crime to knowingly destroy a draft card. The government said the law aided the functioning of the draft and the U.S. military and protected the national security.[101] O'Brien argued that the law was unconstitutional on its face (see Chapter 1) and infringed his freedom of speech.

In *United States v. O'Brien*, the Supreme Court disagreed and upheld O'Brien's conviction.[102] Looking at the actual words of the law—a type of review called statutory construction (see Chapter 1)—the Supreme Court said the statute served a substantial government interest in ensuring the operation of the military draft and caused only minimal harm to O'Brien's speech. The law was content neutral because it did not target disfavored viewpoints and was narrowly tailored because it left O'Brien free to express his opposition to the draft in other ways. Finally, the Court said the government could constitutionally place a small burden on **symbolic expression**—the combination of speech and action represented by draft-card burning.

The decision produced a new three-part test for incidental regulations of speech, known as the ***O'Brien* test**. Under the *O'Brien* test, courts find a law content neutral and constitutional if the law (1) is unrelated to the suppression of speech, (2) advances an important or substantial government interest and (3) is narrowly tailored to achieve that interest while only incidentally restricting protected speech. If the Court finds a law is not directed at the content of speech and does not target ideas disfavored by government, it generally passes the first prong. Then the Court must find the law serves an **important or substantial government interest**. A government interest is important when it is weighty or significant, more than merely convenient or reasonable. Laws intended to serve government goals unrelated to content tend to meet this standard, such as regulating the sizes of commercial or political signs in a municipality or requiring notice to a town for an annual parade.

The third part of the *O'Brien* test, sometimes called the narrow-tailoring standard, requires a law to "fit" its purpose. A law "fits" when it advances the government interest without imposing an unnecessary burden on speech.[103] The calculation is not precise. Narrowly tailored laws must be clear and not give officials unlimited discretion.[104] They need not be the best fit, however. Historically, most laws reviewed under *O'Brien* intermediate scrutiny have been upheld.

David P. O'Brien (second from left), 19, was among several young men on the courthouse steps in Boston in 1967 burning their draft cards in protest to the Vietnam War.

Bettmann/Getty Images

The Court applied the *O'Brien* test to uphold a regulation requiring New York City employees to control the volume and sound mix of performers in Central Park.[105] Performers said the rule unconstitutionally allowed the city to control their expression even when it served no important government interest. The Court, however, said the city's complete control of sound was a narrowly tailored means for the city to protect nearby (wealthy) residents from disturbance. *Ward v. Rock Against Racism* established that *O'Brien* requires only a loose fit. A law is narrow tailored if the government interest would suffer without a law that serves the interest reasonably well.

In *Hill v. Colorado*, the Court held that a state law creating moving, non-protest zones around people entering abortion clinics was a valid, narrowly tailored, content-neutral restriction that directly advanced the government's important interest in protecting the public from harassment.[106] But in 2014 in *McCullen v. Coakley*, the Court held that a fixed, 35-foot buffer zone around clinics was an unconstitutional prior restraint.[107] The Supreme Court said the fixed zone imposed a serious burden on individuals seeking to "counsel" women because it was not narrowly tailored to promote "public safety, patient access to health care, and unobstructed use of public sidewalks and roadways." The difference rested on the Court's conclusion that permanent buffer zones made it "substantially more difficult" to engage in one-on-one conversations.

Courts prior to 2015 generally reviewed statutes that regulated signs to protect community safety and aesthetics under *O'Brien* and found them content neutral and constitutional.[108] In *Reed v. Town of Gilbert*, the U.S. Supreme Court changed this when it unanimously struck down a sign ordinance that established nearly two dozen categories of signs (e.g., church, temporary directional, political), each with its own restrictions.[109] In *Reed*, the Court said the law was content based on its face because it "applie[d] to particular speech because of the topic discussed or the idea or message expressed."[110] Regulations that "draw distinctions based on the message . . . [or that] defin[e] regulated speech by particular subject matter . . . [or] by its function or purpose . . . are subject to strict scrutiny."[111]

POINTS OF LAW

O'BRIEN INTERMEDIATE SCRUTINY

The Supreme Court generally applies some form of intermediate scrutiny to content-neutral laws that incidentally affect the freedom of speech. A law is constitutional under *O'Brien* intermediate scrutiny if it falls within the power of government and

1. advances an important or substantial government interest
2. that is unrelated to suppression of speech and
3. is narrowly tailored to only incidentally restrict First Amendment freedoms.[112]

The Court held that laws that make content distinctions, regardless of the law's purpose, are always content based.[113] A law that differentiates between different types of messages cannot be viewed as content neutral even if it serves an important purpose unrelated to speech content. The purpose of the law becomes relevant only after a court decides that the law does *not* make content distinctions, the *Reed* Court said. The Supreme Court then applied strict scrutiny, its most rigorous review, and found the town of Gilbert's sign law unconstitutional.

Some said the *Reed* holding marked an "important change in First Amendment doctrine," shifted the nature of content-neutral review and "imperil[ed] hundreds, even perhaps thousands, of local, state and federal laws that make subject matter or viewpoint distinctions."[114] In the year following the decision, four U.S. circuit courts of appeal struck down laws that likely would have survived pre-*Reed* intermediate scrutiny.[115] A representative decision of the U.S. Appeals Court for the Seventh Circuit concluded that, under *Reed*, "[a]ny law distinguishing one kind of speech from another by reference to [the] meaning [of the speech] now requires a compelling justification" rather than merely the important government interest required for content-neutral restrictions to be found constitutional under *O'Brien*.[116] However, some researchers found that though *Reed* has been "consequential," it has not changed the doctrine in this area as much as feared. Indeed, that same study concluded that many circuit courts have worked to narrow *Reed's* interpretation.[117]

The Court itself cautioned against reading *Reed* too narrowly in a 2022 decision, *City of Austin v. Reagan National Advertising*.[118] In that case, the city of Austin had an ordinance that allowed "on premises" signs (signs connected to a physical advertiser location) but restricted "off premises" signs (signs without a physical advertiser location). Owners of pre-existing off-premises signs were also prohibited from converting them to digital signs. When Austin denied Reagan National's application to convert signs to digital advertising, the advertising company sued saying the regulation violated the First Amendment. The U.S. Supreme Court reversed the Fifth Circuit, which ruled that under *Reed*, the regulation was unconstitutional. In a 6–3 decision, Justice Sotomayor, writing for the Court, said the Austin ordinance does not "single out any topic or subject matter for differential treatment," like in *Reed*.[119] Because the city's distinction rests only on location, rather than on content, Sotomayor concluded, it is not subject to strict scrutiny. The Court remanded the case back to the lower courts for reconsideration and a fuller determination of whether the regulation meets the intermediate scrutiny test.

POINTS OF LAW

INTERMEDIATE SCRUTINY AFTER *REED V. TOWN OF GILBERT*

Following the Supreme Court's ruling in *Reed v. Town of Gilbert*, courts should follow this two-step process to determine whether to apply intermediate scrutiny to laws affecting speech.[120] Intermediate scrutiny should be applied only if

1. the law does not distinguish between categories or types of speech and
2. the law's purpose is not related to the viewpoint or content of the speech.

PROTECTIONS AND BOUNDARIES FOR DIFFERENT CATEGORIES OF SPEECH

Despite its overall aversion for content-based restrictions on speech, the Court itself has, over time, created a hierarchy of speech categories that range from high-value speech, such as political speech, to low-value speech, such as indecent speech. Both levels of speech are protected by the First Amendment to a greater or lesser degree, but it is clear from a century of case law that some kinds of speech receive more protections from the Court than others. This section will cover high-value political speech and some of its offshoots. Chapter 3 covers some lower-value speech categories such as indecency, and Chapter 12 covers commercial speech, a speech category given an intermediate level of protection by the Court.

Political Speech

Political speech lies at the "core of what the First Amendment is designed to protect."[121] The U.S. Supreme Court has said political speech involves any "communication concerning political change."[122] This encompasses ballots and voting, electioneering speeches and lobbying, campaign spending and yard signs, political advertisements, cartoons and blogs, petitions and buttons and maybe even protests. Believing that political speech is integral to democratic government, the Court generally has used strict scrutiny to review laws that seem to infringe on political speech.[123] Many forms of art—including literature, music, dance, film, plays and visual art—are also at the core of First Amendment protections.

In 2018, the Supreme Court ruled that a Minnesota state ban on wearing political insignia or slogans inside a polling place on Election Day violated the First Amendment.[124] The Court struck down the law as poorly tailored to fit the "special purpose" of the polling place as "an island of calm." The Court accepted that government could exclude "some forms of advocacy" from the polls but said the loosely drafted Minnesota statute presented "riddles" that encouraged "haphazard interpretations." "[I]f a State wishes to set its polling places apart as areas free of partisan discord, it must employ a more discernible approach than the one Minnesota has offered here," the Court concluded.[125]

Another lawsuit began when an anti-abortion group planned a billboard campaign claiming that a candidate for the U.S. House of Representatives backed taxpayer-funded abortion because he supported the Affordable Care Act. The candidate sought a court order to block the ads as false, and the anti-abortion group challenged the constitutionality of the state law prohibiting lies in campaign ads. The Sixth Circuit Court of Appeals allowed the candidate to sue for defamation,[126] but he could not prove the defamatory statement was made with knowledge that it was false or reckless disregard for its truth, which is required for public officials to win a libel suit (see Chapter 4).

On remand from the Supreme Court,[127] the Sixth Circuit Court found the law unconstitutional because its content-based restriction on core political speech was not narrowly tailored to advance the state's compelling interest in preserving the integrity of its elections.[128] Despite the

Sixth Circuit's ruling, today 38 states have laws directly targeting false statements in the context of local and national elections.[129]

Despite the Supreme Court's position that political speech deserves the highest level of constitutional protection, news organizations and government may punish employees whose political expression violates their policies. In an older ruling, the Washington State Supreme Court held that the First Amendment protection of editorial autonomy allows newspapers in Washington to prohibit reporters from engaging in political activity.[130]

Government Speech

When we talk about free expression and the First Amendment, we usually think about the speech of private citizens. Private citizens generally enjoy maximum First Amendment protections. But if you have friends or family members who work for either the state or federal government—for instance, a family member in the military—you likely know that while they retain their First Amendment rights, their ability to speak is more highly regulated because of their important responsibilities. Additionally, the government itself can be a speaker. This section addresses both of these unique situations.

Courts have attempted to distinguish the ability of government to control the speech of its employees from the freedom of individuals who work in government to engage in protected speech outside of their employment. Government employees do not lose their personal freedom of speech when they accept government work,[131] but the government has the authority to classify sensitive materials and control their distribution, especially in the name of national security. The government also may impose codes of silence and control the content of employee speech and work products to advance governmental interests.[132]

The U.S. Supreme Court has held that government control of employee speech extends only to speech directly related to government employment.[133] The Court struck down the portion of a federal law requiring nongovernmental organizations to disseminate specific messages as a condition of receiving federal funding.[134] The Court said the law unconstitutionally sought "to leverage funding to regulate speech outside the contours of the program itself."[135]

In *Garcetti v. Ceballos*, the Supreme Court clarified the distinction between speech *as* a government employee and independent speech *of* a government employee.[136] The Court said the First Amendment did not prohibit government from limiting or punishing an employee's inappropriate work-related expression. The case involved a county attorney's transfer and denial of promotion after he reported alleged inaccuracies in a sheriff's affidavit. The attorney said the actions unconstitutionally punished his protected speech; the government countered that the attorney's report was punishable employee speech. In a 5–4 ruling, the Supreme Court agreed with the government and said the government has authority "over what [expression] the employer itself has commissioned or created."[137]

Then, in 2016, the Supreme Court ruled that the First Amendment prevented a city police department from demoting an employee in order to stop the employee's "overt involvement" in a political campaign.[138] After a police officer reported seeing a detective picking up a campaign sign for a mayoral candidate opposing the chief of police, the chief demoted the detective. The Supreme Court said the purpose of obtaining the political sign was immaterial to its decision.

It ruled that the police department's intention to punish protected individual, political activity was sufficient to demonstrate that it had violated the First Amendment.

In another case involving a complaint of attempted retaliatory firing by a city council, the Supreme Court denied that the action violated the Constitution and described the employee's claim as "an ordinary workplace grievance." The unanimous Court held that the right of employees to petition for redress must be balanced "against the government's interest . . . in the effective and efficient management of its internal affairs."[139] The government's need to manage its affairs "requires proper restraints on the invocation of rights by employees."[140]

In a decision involving mandatory union payments by public employees, the Supreme Court said that the state of Illinois could not require workers hired by Medicaid clients and funded through that federal program to pay union dues if they chose not to join the union.[141] The Court reasoned that these health care workers were not full-fledged government employees. Two years later, with only eight members sitting on the Court, the justices split evenly on whether government agencies could compel their own employees to contribute to unions that used the funding to support political or ideological causes the employees disfavored.[142]

In 2017, the Supreme Court made clear that courts should use "great caution before extending government-speech precedents . . . [because] private speech could be passed off as government speech [and] silence[d] simply [by] affixing a government seal of approval."[143] The following year, the Second Circuit Court of Appeals rejected the argument that simply granting a vendor permit to an Italian-food truck, Wandering Dago, turned the vendor's speech into government speech. The appeals court held that the Constitution prevented the state from refusing to grant a permit to the vendor simply because it found the name to be an offensive, ethnic slur.[144]

Many of these rulings turn on somewhat obscure distinctions between the government's own speech and efforts to regulate private speech. In *Walker v. Texas Division, Sons of Confederate Veterans*, the Supreme Court waded directly into this "muddy" and "befuddling area of the law"[145] to establish "the outer bounds of the government-speech doctrine."[146] The case involved a Texas Department of Motor Vehicles denial of a specialty license plate bearing the image of a Confederate battle flag. The department refused to permit the plate because it was an "offensive" symbol of "hate."[147] The Court majority in *Walker* upheld the state's authority to control the content of the "quasi-government" speech on license plates because it bore a clear link to the government. Government, like private citizens, has the right to be free from association with unwanted messages.

The *Walker* majority relied on the Supreme Court's reasoning in *Pleasant Grove v. Summum*, which held that government could select the monuments it displays in its parks.[148] A religious group raised a First Amendment challenge to a city's decision not to post the group's "Seven Aphorisms" on a permanent monument.[149] In reviewing the case, the Supreme Court first said that various limitations inherent to public displays make it impractical for government to accommodate all speakers. The Court concluded "that the City's decision to accept certain privately donated monuments while rejecting respondent's is best viewed as a form of government speech . . . not subject to the Free Speech Clause."[150] The selected speakers effectively extended government speech and were subject to government control of content.

Writing in dissent in *Walker*, Justice Samuel Alito said the plates, designed and paid for by private individuals, represented private speech.[151] Along with the three other conservative justices then on the Supreme Court, he acknowledged that government had a small part in the speech but expressed doubt that vanity messages on license plates were government speech at all because they played no role in governmental functions or policies.

In 2019, *Manhattan Community Access Corp. v. Halleck* asked the U.S. Supreme Court to decide whether a municipally created and licensed company with some government-appointed directors violated the Constitution when it rejected programming for its public access channels that it deemed offensive.[152] The Second Circuit Court of Appeals had ruled that cable operator was a state actor and "the electronic version of the public square"[153] that violated the First Amendment when it refused to broadcast a film criticizing Manhattan Community Access Corp.[154]

The Supreme Court disagreed.[155] Writing for the majority in a sharply divided 5–4 decision, Justice Brett Kavanaugh concluded that the First Amendment did not apply; the cable company was not a state actor because it did not perform "a function traditionally exclusively performed by the state."[156] Providing a forum for speech is not an exclusive governmental function, and "a private entity who opens its property for speech by others is not transformed by that fact alone into a state actor," the Court concluded.[157]

The majority and dissent agreed that New York state law extensively regulates cable operators, limiting their "editorial discretion and in effect requir[ing them] to operate almost like a common carrier."[158] Still, the majority said this did not make the cable company a state actor subject to the First Amendment.[159] Justice Sotomayor disagreed sharply and said the state essentially appointed the cable company as its "agent" to provide the public forum.[160] She and three others said the Court's ruling "risks sowing confusion among the lower courts about how and when government outsourcing will render any abuses that follow beyond the reach of the Constitution."[161]

Some said the Court's decision affirmed the foundational concept that "private firms [are] not bound by the First Amendment."[162] Others said it reinforced fears about the impact of newly appointed Supreme Court justices on civil liberties.[163] One legal expert said the Court had given Facebook "carte blanche to allow hate speech or [to] delete hate speech."[164]

Compelled Speech

The U.S. Supreme Court has said, "The right to speak and the right to refrain from speaking are complementary components of the broader concept of individual freedom of mind."[165] Accordingly, government may not force citizens to express ideas with which they disagree. This is known in First Amendment law as the **compelled speech** doctrine. The First Amendment not only limits government censorship; it also prevents the government from punishing citizens for refusing to "articulate, advocate, or adhere" to what a government might compel citizens to say or do.[166]

More than 75 years ago, the Supreme Court issued a foundational ruling when students who were Jehovah's Witnesses challenged the then-mandatory flag salute and Pledge of Allegiance in schools as a violation of their religious beliefs. The Supreme Court agreed.[167] Despite the important role of public schools in teaching students civic values and responsibilities,[168] schools may not indoctrinate students into particular ideologies, the Court said.[169] "No official, high or petty, can prescribe what shall be orthodox in politics, nationalism, religion or other matters of opinion or force citizens to confess by word or act their faith therein."[170]

Forty years later, the Court extended that freedom to license plates. A married couple, also Jehovah's Witnesses, challenged a New Hampshire law requiring all license plates to bear the state slogan, "Live Free or Die." In violation of state law, the couple covered up the slogan because they found it "morally, ethically, religiously and politically abhorrent." The Supreme Court struck down the law, saying it required citizens to promote the state's ideological message on their own property. Individuals have a constitutional right "to refrain from speaking" and "not to be coerced by the state into advertising a slogan" that violates their beliefs.[171]

In 2018, the Supreme Court said the First Amendment prevented the state of California from forcing state-licensed "crisis pregnancy centers" to notify clients that public family-planning services were available.[172] The Court rejected the notion that noncommercial professional speech was a discrete category with its own First Amendment rules and declined to consider the case under its compelled speech or government-speech precedents. Instead, it found that the law would fail both strict and intermediate scrutiny because its numerous exemptions failed to fit the state's asserted interest in informing low-income women about state-supported services. The challenged law mandated that licensed centers inform patients of some state-sponsored services, including contraception and abortion, and required unlicensed centers to disclose their lack of licensing.

That same year, the Supreme Court's narrow ruling in *Masterpiece Cakeshop v. Colorado Civil Rights Commission* found that Colorado violated the First Amendment rights of a baker when it found him guilty of violating the state's anti-discrimination law by refusing to bake a wedding cake for a same-sex couple.[173] The case pitted the government's desire to prevent discrimination against the First Amendment's mandate that government not require individuals to express ideas to which they object. The Court found that the state's punishment of the baker was unconstitutional because it did not treat the baker's sincere religious concerns—core elements of his freedoms of speech and association—with the neutrality and care they were due. Instead, the state's hostility to the baker's beliefs violated the "fixed star" of the Constitution that government may not take sides in matters of religion.[174]

Election Speech

More than a decade ago, Congress passed the Bipartisan Campaign Reform Act (BCRA), banning "soft money" contributions to national political parties and imposing limits on the amount and source of funds candidates may accept and spend. The law limited individual spending and prohibited corporate (including nonprofit and union) funding of political messages during a certain period prior to an election. In *Citizens United v. Federal Election Commission*, the Supreme Court found the law's well-established restrictions on corporate and union election spending facially unconstitutional.[175] The Court reasoned that the BCRA's requirements that political donors be disclosed adequately addressed the government's concern that unrestricted corporate election spending might lead to political corruption. Direct limits on how corporations and unions could fund campaigns violated the First Amendment. Courts have applied *Citizens United* to strike down numerous restrictions on political spending.[176]

Then in *McCutcheon v. FEC*, the Court struck down another piece of the BCRA, removing the cap on total individual political contributions.[177] The Court said the aggregate limit reduced an individual's ability to participate in the political process without advancing the government's interest in preventing corruption. "Congress may target only a specific type of corruption— 'quid pro quo' corruption," or bribery, [178] Chief Justice John Roberts wrote for the Court.

REAL WORLD LAW

POST–CITIZENS UNITED: OUTSIDE DONORS SHAPE POLITICAL CAMPAIGNS

More than two decades after the Supreme Court's landmark decision in *Citizens United v. Federal Election Commission* [179] deregulated many areas of campaign financing, dozens of scholarly articles each year examine its impact on freedom of speech, elections, corporations, democracy and more.

One report found that the total amount of money in presidential elections increased more than 1,200 percent from $225 million in 1980 to nearly $3 billion in 2012.[180] That figure increased to $4.1 billion in the 24 months of the 2019-2020 election cycle.[181]

Initial increases were fueled by individual donors, but since 2012, "the amount of outside spending from ideological groups" has topped all other categories. At the same time, candidates and their campaigns are spending less, meaning that outside spending plays an increasing role in elections.

One empirical study found that "removing bans on . . . outside spending increase[d] the electoral success of Republican candidates and [led] to ideologically more conservative state legislatures" but neither increased "ideological polarization" nor decreased attention to "the public good."[182]

Many scholars and activists continue to write about either overturning *Citizens United* or amending the Constitution to change the balance of power in elections.[183]

When the state of Colorado sought to apply state campaign finance disclosure requirements to a film about the impact of political advocacy groups on state politics, the film's producer, Citizens United, sued.[184] Citizens United argued that its film was not "electioneering communication" under the law and the law violated its First Amendment freedoms. On appeal, the Tenth Circuit Court of Appeals said it could find no legitimate basis to distinguish between the advocacy group's movies on political subjects and "legitimate press functions."[185] The First Amendment, it said, required film producers to be exempt from disclosure requirements.

The Supreme Court also has ruled that government may refuse to assist employee political contributions.[186] The Court employed rational review to uphold an Idaho state ban on the use of government payroll deductions for political contributions. The majority reasoned that the Constitution imposed no affirmative obligation on government to facilitate such political activities and the ban advanced the state's interest in avoiding the appearance of partisan political activity.

In 2019 hearings before Congress, Rep. Alexandria Ocasio-Cortez, D-NY, criticized the nation's "fundamentally broken" campaign finance laws under which, she said, it's "super legal . . . to be a pretty bad guy."

Sipa via AP Images

Anonymous Speech

The Supreme Court has said anonymous political speech has an "honorable tradition" that "is a shield from the tyranny of the majority."[187] In *McIntyre v. Ohio Elections Commission*, a 1995 case involving the distribution of anonymous leaflets, the Court found that anonymous speech was "an aspect of the freedom of speech protected by the First Amendment."[188] In another case involving a state ban on anonymous campaign literature, the Court said the state's interest in preventing fraud and political influence was sufficiently important, but the law was not narrowly tailored. A long line of cases protects anonymous political speech.[189]

In 2010, the Supreme Court suggested that citizens engaged in the political process do not have an absolute right to keep their identities secret.[190] A citizen referendum sought to repeal a Washington state law granting new rights to same-sex domestic partners. The state open records law (see Chapter 7) required release of the names of people who endorsed the referendum, but referendum supporters argued that disclosure violated their First Amendment right to anonymous political speech and increased the threat of reprisals. The Supreme Court applied strict scrutiny and ruled that public disclosure of the petitioners' names was substantially related to the important government interest in preserving the integrity of balloting and elections. On remand, the lower court ruled that the First Amendment did not protect anonymity even when disclosure might facilitate harassment.[191]

The protection sometimes afforded anonymous political speech does not extend generally to a broad right to anonymity. In an illustrative case, the Ninth Circuit Court of Appeals denied a request from online review site Glassdoor, Inc. to **quash** a subpoena requiring the company to disclose the identity of people criticizing a government contractor whose business was under investigation.[192] The government initially sought identifying information on 125 posts but narrowed the request to eight critical reviews. Federal law generally requires online service providers to disclose customer communications and records when the government shows reasonable grounds to believe they are relevant to an ongoing criminal investigation.[193] Here, the circuit court reasoned that citizens, like journalists, do not have a First Amendment right not to testify in a grand jury investigation (see Chapter 8).[194] In contrast, a federal district court in Texas struck down a subpoena seeking subscriber data on five Twitter accounts implicated in alleged cyber harassment.[195]

REAL WORLD LAW
RIGHT TO SPEAK ANONYMOUSLY LIKELY FAILS TO PROTECT YOUR DATA

Government requests to social media for confidential subscriber information are becoming ubiquitous. One company that measures such requests reported that U.S. government requests for anonymous subscriber information to Google increased 510 percent since 2010; Requests to Facebook increased 364 percent since 2013.[196]

In a case involving a private chat app, a federal judge approved a subpoena request filed by victims of the August 2017 car attack at a Charlottesville white-rights protest to disclose the identities of those using Discord to organize the rally.[197] Violence at the rally caused one death and more than three dozen injuries. The judge said the user identification could be disclosed to the court, though not the public, because the interest in prosecuting criminal conspiracy outweighed any claimed user right to anonymous speech.[198] Citing privacy provisions under the Stored Communications Act, the judge denied a subpoena to access the content of users' Discord messages.

PROTECTIONS FOR ASSEMBLY AND ASSOCIATION

People across the United States assemble daily to exchange ideas on public street corners and in town parks, in elementary school cafeterias and university lecture halls. Each of these gatherings occurs in what the U.S. Supreme Court calls a **public forum**. The concept of public forums recognizes the long and central role of public oratory in the United States. The idea is that a lot of government property is essentially held in trust for use by the public; it is the public's space.

An early Supreme Court decision involved a challenge to a city ordinance prohibiting the distribution of pamphlets in city streets and parks. It explained the concept as follows:

> Wherever the title of streets and parks may rest, they have immemorially been held in trust for the use of the public and, time out of mind, have been used for purposes of assembly, communicating thoughts between citizens and discussing public questions. Such use of the streets and public places has, from ancient times, been a part of the privileges, immunities, rights and liberties of citizens.[199]

The people have a First Amendment right to use public forum property to express them-selves free from fear of government censorship or punishment.[200] The Court has ruled that the Constitution allows Nazis, Vietnam War protesters, civil rights activists and the homeless to march and assemble in public places.[201]

In 2011 in *Snyder v. Phelps*, the Supreme Court ruled that even "outrageous" speech on a public sidewalk about a public issue cannot be punished.[202] The father of a Marine killed in the Iraq War had sought damages from Westboro Baptist Church members for harm caused by their picketing at his son's funeral with signs reading "Thank God for dead soldiers" and "Fag troops." But the Court held that the First Amendment protects public picketing even when the messages "fall short of refined social or political commentary." The people's right to speak and assemble in public forums is not absolute; it is balanced against other considerations and must be compatible with the normal activity in that place.

The Supreme Court has established a hierarchy of three types of public forums according to the nature of the place, its primary activities and the history of public access.[203] Lands his-torically intended for public use—such as parks, streets and sidewalks adjacent to many public buildings—are **traditional public forums**.[204] The public has a general and presumed right to use these places for expression. Thus, in 2013, the Sixth Circuit Court of Appeals struck down Michigan's 94-year-old ban on "begging in a public place." The court said begging is a protected form of speech and the state could not ban from a traditional public forum "an entire category of activity that the First Amendment protects."[205]

Government may set up rules, hours and policies to facilitate use of traditional public forums. Rules that close public parks after dark or require permits for gatherings are constitu-tional if they are fairly applied and content neutral, meaning they are tailored to their purpose and do not discriminate because of the content of the group's ideas or politics. Appeals courts have found restrictions on rallies on a town lawn[206] and disorderly gatherings in public places[207] unconstitutional because they prohibited more protected speech than necessary to serve the town objectives. Government must demonstrate a compelling interest to ban all expressive activities or assembly in a traditional public forum.

The Supreme Court has held that government may ban public picketing and protests from traditional public forums to protect core privacy, safety or health interests. The Court upheld a ban on targeted picketing outside a doctor's residence and no-protest buffer zones outside abor-tion clinics.[208]

The primary purpose of public schools and university classrooms, high school newspapers and fairgrounds is not to serve public assembly or speech. Yet they may provide ideal settings for public expression. When government chooses to allow public use of these spaces, it creates **designated or limited public forums**,[209] and government may limit their public use.

The government may restrict the times and manners of public use of a designated pub-lic forum to ensure that public assemblies do not conflict with the property's primary func-tion. Government may impose well-tailored, reasonable, content-neutral licensing and usage regulations. In general, the Supreme Court reviews regulations of designated, or limited, pub-lic forums under intermediate scrutiny, balancing the citizen right of free expression against the primary function of the facility. When the government facility is operating as a public forum, government officials do not have unfettered discretion over its use and may not make content-based discriminations among users.[210] Public access cannot be denied entirely without a compelling reason.

Two decades after the Fourth Circuit Court of Appeals described interactive, online services as "a forum for a true diversity of political discourse, unique opportunities for cultural development and myriad avenues for intellectual activity,"[211] the U.S. Supreme Court in 2017 adopted language that evoked public forum analysis.[212] "While in the past there may have been difficulty in identifying the most important places (in a spatial sense) for the exchange of views, today the answer is clear. It is cyberspace . . . and social media in particular," the Court said.[213] Early in 2019, the Fourth Circuit Court of Appeals picked up the language to rule that a Virginia official violated the First Amendment by banning a constituent from the official's Facebook page.[214]

In 2019, the U.S. Court of Appeals for the Second Circuit ruled that former President Trump violated the First Amendment when he blocked seven followers on Twitter.[215] The Second Circuit ruled that on Twitter, the president acted in a government capacity when he blocked users and that his account constituted a public forum. Blocking such users was a type of viewpoint discrimination, according to the court.[216] Trump's administration appealed the ruling to the U.S. Supreme Court, which vacated the decision because the issues were moot under the new Biden administration.[217] (This case is discussed in more detail in Chapter 9.)

President Donald Trump holds a Bible as he visits outside St. John's Church across Lafayette Park from the White House in June 2020, in Washington. Part of the church was set on fire during protests that month.

AP Photo/Patrick Semansky

REAL WORLD LAW
CONTROLLING SPACE TO LIMIT PROTEST?

In 2018, the National Park Service proposed new rules that would limit significantly gatherings around the White House and the National Mall, limit the number of people who could gather without a permit and prohibit demonstrations around most memorials "to preserve an atmosphere of contemplation."[218] One change would reduce the area for public demonstrations adjacent to the White House by 80 percent and "would all but prohibit civic gatherings" there.[219] Another would require demonstrators to pay for permits to "cover some of the costs" of administration, which the park service previously funded.

The park service said the rules had not been updated in more than a decade and needed revision to reduce complexity and address increased public demonstrations in Washington, D.C. The number of applications for protest permits decreased 31 percent between 2010 and 2017, according to an American Civil Liberties Union study.

After the death of George Floyd in 2020, peaceful demonstrators gathered in Lafayette Square Park across from the White House. The park is managed by the National Park Service. Without provocation, former President Trump and Attorney General William Barr directed federal authorities to fire tear gas, pepper spray, rubber bullets and flash bombs into the crowd. The ACLU filed a lawsuit on behalf of the protestors, alleging the protestors' First and Fourth Amendment rights had been violated. A district court allowed the First Amendment claims to proceed in the case but dismissed claims for monetary compensation and for an order to prevent future attacks.[220]

Some government property simply is not available for public use. **Nonpublic forums** exist where public access, assembly and speech would conflict with the proper functioning of the government service and where there is no history of public access. Courts generally defer to the government to determine when government property is off limits. In nonpublic forums, government behaves more like a private property owner and controls the space to achieve government objectives. Military bases, prisons, post office walkways, utility poles, airport terminals and private mailboxes are all nonpublic forums.[221] Government may exclude the entire public or certain speakers or messages from nonpublic forums on the basis of a reasonable or rational, viewpoint-neutral interest.[222]

Private Property as a Public Forum

Public forums, sometimes, though rarely, exist on private property. When private property replaces or functions as a traditional public space, it may be treated as a public forum. The law in this area is unclear. However, when the open area of an enclosed shopping mall or a large private parking lot is used widely for public assembly and expression, the Supreme Court has said the private property owner sometimes may be required to allow public gatherings and free expression.[223]

When an online private forum becomes a public forum is an open legal question because of the nature of social media. Social media platforms are run by private companies, and as such, those companies are legally permitted to dictate the rules for users in their service agreements. While users have First Amendment rights online, First Amendment claims against social media are generally limited because there is no state action. Cases like *Knight v. Trump*, however, are beginning to raise questions about the extent to which social media can retain their status as private forums. (This topic is addressed in more detail in Chapter 9.)

POINTS OF LAW
WHERE CAN I SPEAK?

The Supreme Court has designated three types of public property as held in trust for the public to provide "the liberty to discuss *publicly* and truthfully all matters of public concern without prior restraint or fear of subsequent punishment."[224] The Court's public forum doctrine establishes the following:[225]

- *Traditional public forums* include areas historically used and created for public use or expressive activity.
- *Limited/designated public forums* exist when government permits public use under specific conditions of spaces with other primary purposes, such as school buildings.
- *Nonpublic forums* arise when government property has a primary purpose that is incompatible with public use (e.g., inside the Pentagon or a prison).
- *Private forums* are not owned by the government and serve the purposes of private individuals or corporations (e.g., a private home, a company's building, a platform like Instagram). The First Amendment generally does not apply for speakers other than the private owner in such spaces unless the space is used for used widely for public purposes.

Funding as Forum

Sometimes government funds that subsidize expression create something like a public forum. If government funding supports broad speech and associational activities, the government generally may not discriminate on the basis of the ideas expressed.[226] Government spending may not, for example, disfavor large newspapers, general interest magazines or commercial publications.[227] Government allocation of benefits and costs must be content neutral and evenhanded. When a program provided free legal services to welfare recipients, for example, the Supreme Court held that it could not refuse services to people challenging existing welfare laws.[228]

Many government funding programs have the express purpose of discriminating among applicants according to the ideas they express. The National Endowment for the Arts, for example, funds artists based on the value and quality of submitted artistic proposals. NEA grants are designed to advance the NEA's objectives, not to create a public forum for art. Accordingly, the NEA may choose not to fund art it disfavors or finds indecent or offensive.[229] The same is true of book purchases for public school libraries. School libraries are not public forums for all printed materials; they provide curriculum- and age-appropriate materials to school students. Therefore, library choices based on the school-age appropriateness of books do not violate the Constitution.[230]

Associating Freely

Sometimes viewed as a "derivative" right "associated" with free speech,[231] the right to freedom of association has developed somewhat separately from freedom of speech precedents. Some researchers have viewed cases and scholarship on associational rights as "remarkably thin" and "neglected."[232] Several U.S. Supreme Court rulings established that government generally cannot force private organizations to include individuals or to support messages with which they disagree.[233] In one famous case, organizers of the large, annual St. Patrick's Day parade in Boston refused to allow an LGBTQ alliance to participate. The alliance sued, arguing that its exclusion from the parade violated its freedom of speech. The trial court agreed. Because the parade had no expressive purpose, the court said, forced inclusion of alliance members in the event would cause no harm to the parade organizer's First Amendment rights.

A unanimous Supreme Court reversed. The Court said it was unnecessary to the alliance's message that it participate in the organizer's event. The alliance could reach the desired audience in a number of ways that would not infringe on the organizer's freedom of association and speech. The Court said, "Whatever the reason [for excluding the group], it boils down to the choice of a speaker not to propound a particular point of view, and that choice is presumed to lie beyond the government's power of control."[234] An LGBTQ alliance participated in Boston's St. Patrick's Day parade for the first time in 2015.[235]

EMERGING LAW

The nation's growing political divide has highlighted the problems with **gerrymandering**, a practice in which electoral districts are drawn "with the purpose of giving one political group an advantage over another, a practice which often results in districts with bizarre or strange shapes."[236] Several cases have been heard by courts to address, among other constitutional issues, whether the First Amendment is implicated in the practice of gerrymandering.

Several Supreme Court cases presenting challenges to the constitutionality of state electoral redistricting put freedom of association center stage. In 2018, the Supreme Court decided both *Abbott v. Perez* and *Gill v. Whitford*, which respectively challenged Texas and Wisconsin electoral redistricting as a violation of freedom of voter association and the Fourteenth Amendment right to equal protection.[237] In both cases, challengers said the new districting, which created an "efficiency gap" in favor of Republican voters, was unconstitutional because it diluted the power of an individual Democratic voter.[238]

Reviewing statewide evidence against the equal protection challenge, the Supreme Court in *Abbott* upheld the Texas redistricting because the plaintiffs had failed to show the individual voter harm or clear discriminatory legislative intent needed to support a voter dilution challenge. In *Gill*, the Court remanded the challenge to Wisconsin's redistricting for more detailed fact finding.[239] Both majority dicta and a four-justice dissent encouraged a fuller presentation of the First Amendment issues. Writing for the dissent, Justice Elena Kagan said the existing statewide evidence might be sufficient for a freedom of association challenge because a statewide "gerrymander weakens [the Democratic party's] capacity to perform all its functions . . . [and]

has burdened the ability of like-minded people across the State to affiliate in a political party and carry out that organization's activities and objects."[240]

In 2019, the U.S. Supreme Court heard *Rucho v. Common Cause*, a case involving voters and other plaintiffs from North Carolina and Maryland, who filed suits challenging their states' congressional districting maps as unconstitutional partisan gerrymanders. The plaintiffs included First Amendment claims. The Supreme Court ruled that while the district courts had said such claims could proceed, there was no "clear" and "manageable" way of distinguishing permissible from impermissible partisan motivation on the part of the states to influence associational rights of the plaintiffs.[241] The Court struck down these claims. Overall, the court ruled that partisan gerrymandering claims present political questions beyond the reach of the federal courts.

KEYTERMS

ad hoc balancing

categorical balancing

compelled speech

compelling interest

content based

content neutral

defamation

designated or limited public forum

dicta

Fourth Estate

gerrymandering

important government interest

injunction

intermediate scrutiny

laws of general application

legal doctrine

marketplace of ideas

nonpublic forum

O'Brien test

original intent

prior restraint

public forum

quash

rational review

seditious libel

state action

strict scrutiny

symbolic expression

time/place/manner laws

traditional public forum

CASES FOR STUDY
THINKING ABOUT THEM

The first of this chapter's two case excerpts examines the First Amendment protection from prior restraints on the press. In *New York Times Co. v. United States*, the U.S. Supreme Court provided expedited review of a federal injunction against war reporting by The Times and The Washington Post based on leaked classified documents. The Court's careful delineation of the government's limited ability to exercise prior restraint on speech underscored the importance of the separation of powers and reaffirmed that the government has very limited authority over the press. The second excerpt, *Reed v. Town of Gilbert*, presents the Supreme Court's 2015 decision articulating what some believe is a new understanding of which laws are reviewed under strict scrutiny because they are defined as content based. Although the justices reach a unanimous decision, they do not all endorse the majority's definition of content-based laws or its automatic application of strict scrutiny to such laws.

The two case excerpts explore two fundamental approaches to understanding the First Amendment. One Supreme Court decision establishes the extent and limits of the First Amendment's protection from government prior restraint on the press. The other redefines the basic distinction between laws that regulate on the basis of content and those that do not. As you read these case excerpts, keep the following questions in mind:

- What justification does the Court offer in *New York Times Co. v. United States* for the First Amendment's nearly absolute ban on prior restraints?
- In *Reed v. Town of Gilbert*, why do the justices disagree on the definition of content neutrality?
- What do the two decisions indicate about the power of the First Amendment to limit government regulations of "the press" and of the people's right to speak through signs?
- Does the Court use the same level of scrutiny in both cases? How do you know?

NEW YORK TIMES CO. V. UNITED STATES
SUPREME COURT OF THE UNITED STATES 403 U.S. 713 (1971)

PER CURIAM OPINION:

We granted certiorari in these cases in which the United States seeks to enjoin the New York Times and the Washington Post from publishing the contents of a classified study entitled "History of U.S. Decision-Making Process on Viet Nam Policy."

"Any system of prior restraints of expression comes to this Court bearing a heavy presumption against its constitutional validity." The Government "thus carries a heavy burden of showing justification for the imposition of such a restraint." The [lower courts] held that the Government had not met that burden. We agree.

The judgment of the Court of Appeals for the District of Columbia Circuit is therefore affirmed. The order of the Court of Appeals or the Second Circuit is reversed, and the case is remanded with directions to enter a judgment affirming the judgment of the District Court for the Southern District of New York. The stays entered June 25, 1971, by the Court are vacated. The judgments shall issue forthwith.

So ordered.

JUSTICE HUGO BLACK, with whom JUSTICE WILLIAM DOUGLAS joined, concurring:

I adhere to the view that the Government's case against the Washington Post should have been dismissed, and that the injunction against the New York Times should have been vacated without oral argument when the cases were first presented to this Court. I believe that every moment's continuance of the injunctions against these newspapers amounts to a flagrant, indefensible, and continuing violation of the First Amendment. . . .

In the First Amendment, the Founding Fathers gave the free press the protection it must have to fulfill its essential role in our democracy. The press was to serve the governed, not the governors. The Government's power to censor the press was abolished so that the press would remain forever free to censure the Government. The press was protected so that it could bare the secrets of government and inform the people. Only a free and unrestrained press can effectively expose deception in government. And paramount among the responsibilities of a free press is the duty to prevent any part of the government from deceiving the people and sending them off to distant lands to die of foreign fevers and foreign shot and shell. In my view, far from deserving condemnation for their courageous reporting, the New York Times, the Washington Post, and other newspapers should be commended for serving the purpose that the Founding Fathers saw so clearly. In revealing the workings of government that led to the Vietnam War, the newspapers nobly did precisely that which the Founders hoped and trusted they would do. . . .

The word "security" is a broad, vague generality whose contours should not be invoked to abrogate the fundamental law embodied in the First Amendment. The guarding of military and diplomatic secrets at the expense of informed representative government provides no real security for our Republic. The Framers of the First Amendment, fully aware of both the need to defend a new nation and the abuses of the English and Colonial governments, sought to give this new society strength and security by providing that freedom of speech, press, religion, and assembly should not be abridged. . . .

JUSTICE WILLIAM DOUGLAS, with whom JUSTICE HUGO BLACK joined, concurring:

. . . It should be noted at the outset that the First Amendment provides that "Congress shall make no law . . . abridging the freedom of speech, or of the press." That leaves, in my view, no room for governmental restraint on the press. . . .

The dominant purpose of the First Amendment was to prohibit the widespread practice of governmental suppression of embarrassing information. It is common knowledge that the First Amendment was adopted against the widespread use of the common law of seditious libel to punish the dissemination of material that is embarrassing to the powers-that-be. The present cases will, I think, go down in history as the most dramatic illustration of that principle. . . .

Secrecy in government is fundamentally antidemocratic, perpetuating bureaucratic errors. Open debate and discussion of public issues are vital to our national health. On public questions there should be "uninhibited, robust, and wide-open" debate. . . .

JUSTICE WILLIAM BRENNAN, concurring:

. . . The error that has pervaded these cases from the outset was the granting of any injunctive relief whatsoever, interim or otherwise. The entire thrust of the Government's claim throughout these cases has been that publication of the material sought to be enjoined "could," or "might," or "may" prejudice the national interest in various ways. But the First Amendment tolerates absolutely no prior judicial restraints of the press predicated upon surmise or conjecture that untoward consequences may result. Our cases, it is true, have indicated that there is a single, extremely narrow class of cases in which the First Amendment's ban on prior judicial restraint may be overridden. Our cases have thus far indicated that such cases may arise only when the Nation "is at war," during which times "[n]o one would question but that a government might prevent actual obstruction to its recruiting service or the publication of the dates of transports or the number and location of troops." Even if the present world situation were assumed to be tantamount to a time of war, or if the power of presently available armaments would justify even in peacetime the suppression of information that would set in motion a nuclear holocaust, in neither of these actions has the Government presented or even alleged that publication of items from or based upon the material at issue would cause the happening of an event of that nature. "[T]he chief purpose of [the First Amendment's] guaranty [is] to prevent previous restraints upon publication." Thus, only governmental allegation and proof that publication must inevitably, directly, and immediately cause the occurrence of an event kindred to imperiling the safety of a transport already at sea can support even the issuance of an interim restraining order. . . . Unless and until the Government has clearly made out its case, the First Amendment commands that no injunction may issue. . . .

JUSTICE POTTER STEWART, with whom JUSTICE BYRON WHITE joined, concurring:

. . . If the Constitution gives the Executive a large degree of unshared power in the conduct of foreign affairs and the maintenance of our national defense, then, under the Constitution, the Executive must have the largely unshared duty to determine and preserve the degree of internal security necessary to exercise that power successfully. It is an awesome responsibility, requiring judgment and wisdom of a high order. I should suppose that moral, political, and practical considerations would dictate that a very first principle of that wisdom would be an insistence upon avoiding secrecy for its own sake. For when everything is classified, then nothing is classified, and the system becomes one to be disregarded by the cynical or the careless, and to be manipulated by those intent on self-protection or self-promotion. I should suppose, in short, that the hallmark of a truly effective internal security system would be the maximum possible disclosure, recognizing that secrecy can best be preserved only when credibility is truly maintained. . . .

JUSTICE BYRON WHITE, with whom JUSTICE POTTER STEWART joined, concurring:

I concur in today's judgments, but only because of the concededly extraordinary protection against prior restraints enjoyed by the press under our constitutional system. I do not say that in no circumstances would the First Amendment permit an injunction against publishing information about government plans or operations. . . . But I nevertheless agree that the United States has not satisfied the very heavy burden that it must meet to warrant an injunction against publication in these cases, at least in the absence of express and appropriately limited congressional authorization for prior restraints in circumstances such as these. . . .

CHIEF JUSTICE WARREN BURGER, dissenting:

. . . As I see it, we have been forced to deal with litigation concerning rights of great magnitude without an adequate record, and surely without time for adequate treatment either in the prior proceedings or in this Court. . . .

I agree generally with Mr. Justice Harlan and Mr. Justice Blackmun, but I am not prepared to reach the merits.

JUSTICE JOHN HARLAN, with whom CHIEF JUSTICE WARREN BURGER and JUSTICE HARRY BLACKMUN join, dissenting:

. . . The power to evaluate the "pernicious influence" of premature disclosure is not, however, lodged in the Executive alone. I agree that, in performance of its duty to protect the values of the First Amendment against political pressures, the judiciary must review the initial Executive determination to the point of satisfying itself that the subject matter of the dispute does lie within the proper compass of the President's foreign relations power. . . . Moreover, the judiciary may properly insist that the determination that disclosure of the subject matter would irreparably impair the national security be made by the head of the Executive Department concerned. . . .

But, in my judgment, the judiciary may not properly go beyond these two inquiries and re-determine for itself the probable impact of disclosure on the national security. . . .

JUSTICE HARRY BLACKMUN, dissenting:

. . . The First Amendment, after all, is only one part of an entire Constitution. . . . Each provision of the Constitution is important, and I cannot subscribe to a doctrine of unlimited absolutism for the First Amendment at the cost of downgrading other provisions. First Amendment absolutism has never commanded a majority of this Court. What is needed here is a weighing, upon properly developed standards, of the broad right of the press to print and of the very narrow right of the Government to prevent. Such standards are not yet developed.

REED V. TOWN OF GILBERT
SUPREME COURT OF THE UNITED STATES 135 S. CT. 2218 (2015)

JUSTICE CLARENCE THOMAS delivered the Court's opinion:

The town of Gilbert, Arizona (or Town), has adopted a comprehensive code governing the manner in which people may display outdoor signs (Sign Code or Code). The Sign Code identifies various categories of signs based on the type of information they convey, then subjects each category to different restrictions. One of the categories is "Temporary Directional Signs Relating to a Qualifying Event," loosely defined as signs directing the public to a meeting of a nonprofit group. The Code imposes more stringent restrictions on these signs than it does on signs conveying other messages. We hold that these provisions are content-based regulations of speech that cannot survive strict scrutiny.

The Sign Code prohibits the display of outdoor signs anywhere within the Town without a permit, but it then exempts 23 categories of signs from that requirement. These exemptions include everything from bazaar signs to flying banners. Three categories of exempt signs are particularly relevant here.

The first is "Ideological Sign[s]." This category includes any "sign communicating a message or ideas for noncommercial purposes that is not a Construction Sign, Directional Sign, Temporary Directional Sign Relating to a Qualifying Event, Political Sign, Garage Sale Sign, or a sign owned or required by a governmental agency." Of the three categories discussed here, the Code treats ideological signs most favorably, allowing them to be up to 20 square feet in area and to be placed in all "zoning districts" without time limits.

The second category is "Political Sign[s]." This includes any "temporary sign designed to influence the outcome of an election called by a public body." The Code treats these signs less favorably than ideological signs. The Code allows the placement of political signs up to 16 square feet on residential property and up to 32 square feet on nonresidential property, undeveloped municipal property, and "rights-of-way." These signs may be displayed up to 60 days before a primary election and up to 15 days following a general election.

The third category is "Temporary Directional Signs Relating to a Qualifying Event." This includes any "Temporary Sign intended to direct pedestrians, motorists, and other pass-ersby to a 'qualifying event.'" A "qualifying event" is defined as any "assembly, gathering, activity, or meeting sponsored, arranged, or promoted by a religious, charitable, community service, educational, or other similar non-profit organization." The Code treats temporary directional signs even less favorably than political signs. Temporary directional signs may be no larger than six square feet. They may be placed on private property or on a public right-of-way, but no more than four signs may be placed on a single property at any time. And, they may be displayed no more than 12 hours before the "qualifying event" and no more than 1 hour afterward.

Petitioners Good News Community Church (Church) and its pastor, Clyde Reed, wish to advertise the time and location of their Sunday church services. The Church is a small, cash-strapped entity that owns no building, so it holds its services at elementary schools or other locations in or near the Town. In order to inform the public about its services, which are held in a variety of different locations, the Church began placing 15 to 20 temporary signs around the Town, frequently in the public right-of-way abutting the street. The signs typically displayed the Church's name, along with the time and location of the upcoming service. Church members would post the signs early in the day on Saturday and then remove them around midday on Sunday. The display of these signs requires little money and man-power, and thus has proved to be an economical and effective way for the Church to let the community know where its services are being held each week.

This practice caught the attention of the Town's Sign Code compliance manager, who twice cited the Church for violating the Code. The first citation noted that the Church exceeded the time limits for displaying its temporary directional signs. The second citation referred to the same problem, along with the Church's failure to include the date of the event on the signs. Town officials even confiscated one of the Church's signs, which Reed had to retrieve from the municipal offices.

Reed contacted the Sign Code Compliance Department in an attempt to reach an accom-modation. His efforts proved unsuccessful. The Town's Code compliance manager informed the Church that there would be "no leniency under the Code" and promised to punish any future violations.

Shortly thereafter, petitioners filed a complaint . . . arguing that the Sign Code abridged their freedom of speech in violation of the First and Fourteenth Amendments. The District Court denied the petitioners' motion for a preliminary injunction. The Court of Appeals for the Ninth Circuit affirmed, holding that the Sign Code's provision regulating temporary directional signs did not regulate speech on the basis of content. . . . It then remanded for the District Court to determine in the first instance whether the Sign Code's distinctions among temporary directional signs, political signs, and ideological signs nevertheless constituted a content-based regulation of speech. . . .

On remand, the District Court granted summary judgment in favor of the Town. The Court of Appeals again affirmed, holding that the Code's sign categories were content neutral. The court concluded that "the distinctions between Temporary Directional Signs, Ideological Signs, and Political Signs . . . are based on objective factors relevant to Gilbert's creation of the specific exemption from the permit requirement and do not otherwise consider the substance of the sign.". . . [T]he Court of Appeals concluded that the Sign Code is content neutral. As the court explained, "Gilbert did not adopt its regulation of speech because it disagreed with the message conveyed" and its "interests in regulat[ing] temporary signs are unrelated to the content of the sign." Accordingly, the court believed that the Code was "content-neutral as that term [has been] defined by the Supreme Court." In light of that determination, it applied a lower level of scrutiny to the Sign Code and concluded that the law did not violate the First Amendment.

We granted certiorari, and now reverse.

The First Amendment, applicable to the States through the Fourteenth Amendment, prohibits the enactment of laws "abridging the freedom of speech." Under that Clause, a government, including a municipal government vested with state authority, "has no power to restrict expression because of its message, its ideas, its subject matter, or its content." Content-based laws—those that target speech based on its communicative content—are presumptively unconstitutional and may be justified only if the government proves that they are narrowly tailored to serve compelling state interests.

Government regulation of speech is content based if a law applies to particular speech because of the topic discussed or the idea or message expressed. This commonsense meaning of the phrase "content based" requires a court to consider whether a regulation of speech "on its face" draws distinctions based on the message a speaker conveys. Some facial distinctions based on a message are obvious, defining regulated speech by particular subject matter, and others are more subtle, defining regulated speech by its function or purpose. Both are distinctions drawn based on the message a speaker conveys, and, therefore, are subject to strict scrutiny.

Our precedents have also recognized a separate and additional category of laws that, though facially content neutral, will be considered content-based regulations of speech: laws that cannot be "justified without reference to the content of the regulated speech," or that were adopted by the government "because of disagreement with the message [the speech] conveys." Those laws, like those that are content based on their face, must also satisfy strict scrutiny.

The Town's Sign Code is content based on its face. It defines "Temporary Directional Signs" on the basis of whether a sign conveys the message of directing the public to church or some other "qualifying event." It defines "Political Signs" on the basis of whether a sign's message is "designed to influence the outcome of an election." And it defines "Ideological Signs" on the basis of whether a sign "communicat[es] a message or ideas" that do not fit within the Code's other categories. It then subjects each of these categories to different restrictions.

The restrictions in the Sign Code that apply to any given sign thus depend entirely on the communicative content of the sign. . . . [T]he Church's signs inviting people to attend its worship services are treated differently from signs conveying other types of ideas. On its face, the Sign Code is a content-based regulation of speech. We thus have no need to consider the government's justifications or purposes for enacting the Code to determine whether it is subject to strict scrutiny.

In reaching the contrary conclusion, the Court of Appeals offered several theories to explain why the Town's Sign Code should be deemed content neutral. None is persuasive.

The Court of Appeals first determined that the Sign Code was content neutral because the Town "did not adopt its regulation of speech [based on] disagree[ment] with the message conveyed," and its justifications for regulating temporary directional signs were "unrelated to the content of the sign." In its brief to this Court, the United States similarly contends that a sign regulation is content neutral—even if it expressly draws distinctions based on the sign's communicative content—if those distinctions can be "'justified without reference to the content of the regulated speech.'"

But this analysis skips the crucial first step in the content-neutrality analysis: determining whether the law is content neutral on its face. A law that is content based on its face is subject to strict scrutiny regardless of the government's benign motive, content-neutral justification, or lack of "animus toward the ideas contained" in the regulated speech. We have thus made clear that "[i]llicit legislative intent is not the sine qua non of a violation of the First Amendment," and a party opposing the government "need adduce no evidence of an improper censorial motive." Although "a content-based purpose may be sufficient in certain circumstances to show that a regulation is content based, it is not necessary." In other words, an innocuous justification cannot transform a facially content-based law into one that is content neutral.

That is why we have repeatedly considered whether a law is content neutral on its face before turning to the law's justification or purpose. Because strict scrutiny applies either when a law is content based on its face or when the purpose and justification for the law are content based, a court must evaluate each question before it concludes that the law is content neutral and thus subject to a lower level of scrutiny.

The Court of Appeals and the United States misunderstand our decision in Ward [v. Rock Against Racism]. [It] had nothing to say about facially content-based restrictions because it involved a facially content-neutral ban on the use, in a city-owned music venue, of sound amplification systems not provided by the city. In that context, we looked to governmental motive, including whether the government had regulated speech "because of disagreement" with its message, and whether the regulation was "'justified without reference to the content of the speech.'" But Ward's framework "applies only if a statute is content neutral." Its rules thus operate "to protect speech," not "to restrict it."

The First Amendment requires no less. Innocent motives do not eliminate the danger of censorship presented by a facially content-based statute. . . . That is why the First Amendment expressly targets the operation of the laws—i.e., the "abridg[ement] of speech"—rather than merely the motives of those who enacted them. "The vice of content-based legislation . . . is not that it is always used for invidious, thought-control purposes, but that it lends itself to use for those purposes."

For instance, . . . one could easily imagine a Sign Code compliance manager who disliked the Church's substantive teachings deploying the Sign Code to make it more difficult for the Church to inform the public of the location of its services. Accordingly, we have repeatedly "rejected the argument that 'discriminatory . . . treatment is suspect under the First Amendment only when the legislature intends to suppress certain ideas.'"

The Court of Appeals next reasoned that the Sign Code was content neutral because it "does not mention any idea or viewpoint, let alone single one out for differential treatment." It reasoned that, for the purpose of the Code provisions, "[i]t makes no difference which candidate is supported, who sponsors the event, or what ideological perspective is asserted."

The Town seizes on this reasoning, insisting that "content based" is a term of art that "should be applied flexibly" with the goal of protecting "viewpoints and ideas from government censorship or favoritism." In the Town's view, a sign regulation that "does not censor or favor particular viewpoints or ideas" cannot be content based. The Sign Code allegedly passes this test because its treatment of temporary directional signs does not raise any concerns that the government is "endorsing or suppressing 'ideas or viewpoints,'" and the provisions for political signs and ideological signs "are neutral as to particular ideas or viewpoints" within those categories.

This analysis conflates two distinct but related limitations that the First Amendment places on government regulation of speech. Government discrimination among viewpoints—or the regulation of speech based on "the specific motivating ideology or the opinion or perspective of the speaker"—is a "more blatant" and "egregious form of content discrimination." But it is well established that "[t]he First Amendment's hostility to content-based regulation extends not only to restrictions on particular viewpoints, but also to prohibition of public discussion of an entire topic."

Thus, a speech regulation targeted at specific subject matter is content based even if it does not discriminate among viewpoints within that subject matter. For example, a law banning the use of sound trucks for political speech—and only political speech—would be a content-based regulation, even if it imposed no limits on the political viewpoints that could be expressed. The Town's Sign Code likewise singles out specific subject matter for differential treatment, even if it does not target viewpoints within that subject matter. Ideological messages are given more favorable treatment than messages concerning a political candidate, which are themselves given more favorable treatment than messages announcing an assembly of like-minded individuals. That is a paradigmatic example of content-based discrimination.

Finally, the Court of Appeals characterized the Sign Code's distinctions as turning on "the content-neutral elements of who is speaking through the sign and whether and when an event is occurring." That analysis is mistaken on both factual and legal grounds.

To start, the Sign Code's distinctions are not speaker based. The restrictions for political, ideological, and temporary event signs apply equally no matter who sponsors them. If a local business, for example, sought to put up signs advertising the Church's meetings, those signs would be subject to the same limitations as such signs placed by the Church. And if Reed had decided to display signs in support of a particular candidate, he could have made those signs far larger—and kept them up for far longer—than signs inviting people to attend his church services. If the Code's distinctions were truly speaker based, both types of signs would receive the same treatment.

In any case, the fact that a distinction is speaker based does not, as the Court of Appeals seemed to believe, automatically render the distinction content neutral. Because "[s]peech restrictions based on the identity of the speaker are all too often simply a means to control content," we have insisted that "laws favoring some speakers over others demand strict scrutiny when the legislature's speaker preference reflects a content preference." Thus, a law limiting the content of newspapers, but only newspapers, could not evade strict scrutiny simply because it could be characterized as speaker based. Likewise, a content-based law that restricted the political speech of all corporations would not become content neutral just because it singled out corporations as a class of speakers....

Nor do the Sign Code's distinctions hinge on "whether and when an event is occurring." The Code does not permit citizens to post signs on any topic whatsoever within a set period leading up to an election, for example. . . .

And, just as with speaker-based laws, the fact that a distinction is event based does not render it content neutral. . . . A regulation that targets a sign because it conveys an idea about a specific event is no less content based than a regulation that targets a sign because it conveys some other idea. Here, the Code singles out signs bearing a particular message: the time and location of a specific event. This type of ordinance may seem like a perfectly rational way to regulate signs, but a clear and firm rule governing content neutrality is an essential means of protecting the freedom of speech, even if laws that might seem "entirely reasonable" will sometimes be "struck down because of their content-based nature."

Because the Town's Sign Code imposes content-based restrictions on speech, those provisions can stand only if they survive strict scrutiny, "which requires the Government to prove that the restriction furthers a compelling interest and is narrowly tailored to achieve that interest." Thus, it is the Town's burden to demonstrate that the Code's differentiation between temporary directional signs and other types of signs, such as political signs and ideological signs, furthers a compelling governmental interest and is narrowly tailored to that end. The Town cannot do so. It has offered only two governmental interests in support of the distinctions the Sign Code draws: preserving the Town's aesthetic appeal and traffic safety. Assuming for the sake of argument that those are compelling governmental interests, the Code's distinctions fail as hopelessly underinclusive.

Starting with the preservation of aesthetics, temporary directional signs are "no greater an eyesore," than ideological or political ones. Yet the Code allows unlimited proliferation of larger ideological signs while strictly limiting the number, size, and duration of smaller directional ones. The Town cannot claim that placing strict limits on temporary directional signs is necessary to beautify the Town while at the same time allowing unlimited numbers of other types of signs that create the same problem.

The Town similarly has not shown that limiting temporary directional signs is necessary to eliminate threats to traffic safety, but that limiting other types of signs is not. The Town has offered no reason to believe that directional signs pose a greater threat to safety than do ideological or political signs. If anything, a sharply worded ideological sign seems more likely to distract a driver than a sign directing the public to a nearby church meeting.

In light of this underinclusiveness, the Town has not met its burden to prove that its Sign Code is narrowly tailored to further a compelling government interest. . . .

Our decision today will not prevent governments from enacting effective sign laws. The Town asserts that an "'absolutist'" content-neutrality rule would render "virtually all distinctions in sign laws . . . subject to strict scrutiny," but that is not the case. Not "all distinctions" are subject to strict scrutiny, only content-based ones are. Laws that are content neutral are instead subject to lesser scrutiny.

The Town has ample content-neutral options available to resolve problems with safety and aesthetics. For example, its current Code regulates many aspects of signs that have nothing to do with a sign's message: size, building materials, lighting, moving parts, and portability. And on public property, the Town may go a long way toward entirely forbidding the posting of signs, so long as it does so in an evenhanded, content-neutral manner. Indeed, some lower courts have long held that similar content-based sign laws receive strict scrutiny, but there is no evidence that towns in those jurisdictions have suffered catastrophic effects.

We acknowledge that a city might reasonably view the general regulation of signs as necessary because signs "take up space and may obstruct views, distract motorists, displace alternative uses for land, and pose other problems that legitimately call for regulation." At the same time, the presence of certain signs may be essential, both for vehicles and pedestrians, to guide traffic or to identify hazards and ensure safety. A sign ordinance narrowly tailored to the challenges of protecting the safety of pedestrians, drivers, and passengers—such as warning signs marking hazards on private property, signs directing traffic, or street numbers associated with private houses—well might survive strict scrutiny. The signs at issue in this case, including political and ideological signs and signs for events, are far removed from those purposes. As discussed above, they are facially content based and are neither justified by traditional safety concerns nor narrowly tailored.

We reverse the judgment of the Court of Appeals and remand the case for proceedings consistent with this opinion.

It is so ordered.

JUSTICE SAMUEL ALITO, with whom JUSTICE ANTHONY KENNEDY and JUSTICE SONIA SOTOMAYOR joined, concurring:

I join the opinion of the Court but add a few words of further explanation.

As the Court holds, what we have termed "content-based" laws must satisfy strict scrutiny. Content-based laws merit this protection because they present, albeit sometimes in a subtler form, the same dangers as laws that regulate speech based on viewpoint. Limiting speech based on its "topic" or "subject" favors those who do not want to disturb the status quo. Such regulations may interfere with democratic self-government and the search for truth.

As the Court shows, the regulations at issue in this case are replete with content-based distinctions, and as a result they must satisfy strict scrutiny. This does not mean, however, that municipalities are powerless to enact and enforce reasonable sign regulations. . . .*

In addition to regulating signs put up by private actors, government entities may also erect their own signs consistent with the principles that allow governmental speech. They may put up all manner of signs to promote safety, as well as directional signs and signs pointing out historic sites and scenic spots.

Properly understood, today's decision will not prevent cities from regulating signs in a way that fully protects public safety and serves legitimate esthetic objectives.

Of course, content-neutral restrictions on speech are not necessarily consistent with the First Amendment. Time, place, and manner restrictions "must be narrowly tailored to serve the government's legitimate, content-neutral interests." But they need not meet the high standard imposed on viewpoint- and content-based restrictions.

JUSTICE STEPHEN BREYER, concurring:

I join JUSTICE KAGAN's separate opinion. Like JUSTICE KAGAN, I believe that categories alone cannot satisfactorily resolve the legal problem before us. The First Amendment requires greater judicial sensitivity both to the Amendment's expressive objectives and to the public's legitimate need for regulation than a simple recitation of categories, such as "content discrimination" and "strict scrutiny," would permit. In my view, the category "content discrimination" is better considered . . . as a rule of thumb, rather than as an automatic "strict scrutiny" trigger, leading to almost certain legal condemnation.

To use content discrimination to trigger strict scrutiny sometimes makes perfect sense. There are cases in which the Court has found content discrimination an unconstitutional method for suppressing a viewpoint. And there are cases where the Court has found content discrimination to reveal that rules governing a traditional public forum are, in fact, not a neutral way of fairly managing the forum in the interest of all speakers. In these types of cases, strict scrutiny is often appropriate, and content discrimination has thus served a useful purpose.

But content discrimination, while helping courts to identify unconstitutional suppression of expression, cannot and should not always trigger strict scrutiny. To say that it is not an automatic "strict scrutiny" trigger is not to argue against that concept's use. I readily concede, for example, that content discrimination, as a conceptual tool, can sometimes reveal weaknesses in the government's rationale for a rule that limits speech. . . . I also concede that, whenever government disfavors one kind of speech, it places that speech at a disadvantage, potentially interfering with the free marketplace of ideas and with an individual's ability to express thoughts and ideas that can help that individual determine the kind of society in which he wishes to live, help shape that society, and help define his place within it.

Nonetheless, in these latter instances to use the presence of content discrimination automatically to trigger strict scrutiny and thereby call into play a strong presumption against constitutionality goes too far. That is because virtually all government activities involve speech, many of which involve the regulation of speech. Regulatory programs almost always require content discrimination. And to hold that such content discrimination triggers strict scrutiny is to write a recipe for judicial management of ordinary government regulatory activity. . . .

I recognize that the Court could escape the problem by watering down the force of the presumption against constitutionality that "strict scrutiny" normally carries with it. But, in my view, doing so will weaken the First Amendment's protection in instances where "strict scrutiny" should apply in full force.

The better approach is to generally treat content discrimination as a strong reason weighing against the constitutionality of a rule where a traditional public forum, or where viewpoint discrimination, is threatened, but elsewhere treat it as a rule of thumb, finding it a helpful, but not determinative legal tool, in an appropriate case, to determine the strength of a justification. I would use content discrimination as a supplement to a more basic analysis, which, tracking most of our First Amendment cases, asks whether the regulation at issue works harm to First Amendment interests that is disproportionate in light of the relevant regulatory objectives. Answering this question requires examining the seriousness of the harm to speech, the importance of the countervailing objectives, the extent to which the law will achieve those objectives, and whether there are other, less restrictive ways of doing so. . . .

Here, regulation of signage along the roadside, for purposes of safety and beautification is at issue. There is no traditional public forum nor do I find any general effort to censor a particular viewpoint. Consequently, the specific regulation at issue does not warrant "strict scrutiny." Nonetheless, for the reasons that JUSTICE KAGAN sets forth, I believe that the Town of Gilbert's regulatory rules violate the First Amendment. I consequently concur in the Court's judgment only.

JUSTICE ELENA KAGAN, with whom JUSTICE RUTH BADER GINSBURG and JUSTICE STEPHEN BREYER joined, concurring:

Countless cities and towns across America have adopted ordinances regulating the posting of signs, while exempting certain categories of signs based on their subject matter. For example, some municipalities generally prohibit illuminated signs in residential neighborhoods, but lift that ban for signs that identify the address of a home or the name of its owner or occupant. In other municipalities, safety signs such as "Blind Pedestrian Crossing" and "Hidden Driveway" can be posted without a permit, even as other permanent signs require one. Elsewhere, historic site markers—for example, "George Washington Slept Here"—are also exempt from general regulations. And similarly, the federal Highway Beautification Act limits signs along interstate highways unless, for instance, they direct travelers to "scenic and historical attractions" or advertise free coffee.

Given the Court's analysis, many sign ordinances of that kind are now in jeopardy. Says the majority: When laws "single[] out specific subject matter," they are "facially content based"; and when they are facially content based, they are automatically subject to strict scrutiny. And although the majority holds out hope that some sign laws with subject-matter exemptions "might survive" that stringent review, the likelihood is that most will be struck down. After all, it is the "rare case[] in which a speech restriction withstands strict scrutiny." To clear that high bar, the government must show that a content-based distinction "is necessary to serve a compelling state interest and is narrowly drawn to achieve that end."

So on the majority's view, courts would have to determine that a town has a compelling interest in informing passersby where George Washington slept. . . . The consequence—unless courts water down strict scrutiny to something unrecognizable—is that our communities will find themselves in an unenviable bind: They will have to either repeal the exemptions that allow for helpful signs on streets and sidewalks, or else lift their sign restrictions altogether and resign themselves to the resulting clutter.

Although the majority insists that applying strict scrutiny to all such ordinances is "essential" to protecting First Amendment freedoms, I find it challenging to understand why that is so. This Court's decisions articulate two important and related reasons for subjecting content-based speech regulations to the most exacting standard of review. The first is "to preserve an uninhibited marketplace of ideas in which truth will ultimately prevail." The second is to ensure that the government has not regulated speech "based on hostility—or favoritism—towards the underlying message expressed." Yet the subject-matter exemptions included in many sign ordinances do not implicate those concerns. . . .

We apply strict scrutiny to facially content-based regulations of speech, in keeping with the rationales just described, when there is any "realistic possibility that official suppression of ideas is afoot." That is always the case when the regulation facially differentiates on the basis of viewpoint. It is also the case (except in non-public or limited public forums) when a law restricts "discussion of an entire topic" in public debate.

Indeed, the precise reason the majority applies strict scrutiny here is that "the Code singles out signs bearing a particular message: the time and location of a specific event." We have stated that "[i]f the marketplace of ideas is to remain free and open, governments must not be allowed to choose 'which issues are worth discussing or debating.'" And we have recognized that such subject-matter restrictions, even though viewpoint-neutral on their face, may "suggest[] an attempt to give one side of a debatable public question an advantage in expressing its views to the people." Subject-matter regulation, in other words, may have the intent or effect of favoring some ideas over others. When that is realistically possible—when the restriction "raises the specter that the Government may effectively drive certain ideas or viewpoints from the marketplace"—we insist that the law pass the most demanding constitutional test.

But when that is not realistically possible, we may do well to relax our guard so that "entirely reasonable" laws imperiled by strict scrutiny can survive.

This point is by no means new. . . . Our cases have been far less rigid than the majority admits in applying strict scrutiny to facially content-based laws—including in cases just like this one [when] the law's enactment and enforcement revealed "not even a hint of bias or censorship. . . ." The majority could easily have taken [that] tack here.

The Town of Gilbert's defense of its sign ordinance—most notably, the law's distinctions between directional signs and others—does not pass strict scrutiny, or intermediate scrutiny, or even the laugh test. . . . The absence of any sensible basis for [the law's] distinctions dooms the Town's ordinance under even the intermediate scrutiny that the Court typically applies to "time, place, or manner" speech regulations. Accordingly, there is no need to decide in this case whether strict scrutiny applies to every sign ordinance in every town across this country containing a subject-matter exemption.

I suspect this Court and others will regret the majority's insistence today on answering that question in the affirmative. . . . Because I see no reason why such an easy case calls for us to cast a constitutional pall on reasonable regulations quite unlike the law before us, I concur only in the judgment.

In 2019, leading rappers like Dr. Dre (left) and Snoop Dogg waited for the U.S. Supreme Court to decide whether lyrics protesting police violence against black men were punishable threats or protected free speech.

Jeff Kravitz/FilmMagic/Getty Images

SPEECH DISTINCTIONS

Disruptive Speech, Student Speech, and Media Harm

CHAPTER OUTLINE

Disruptive Speech
From a Bad Tendency to a Clear and Present Danger
From Clear and Present Danger to Incitement
True Threats
Harassment, Cyberstalking and Cyberbullying
Fighting Words
Hate Speech
Offensive Speech

Symbolic Speech
Burning Speech

Do Media Incite Harm?
Physical Harms
Negligence
Harmful Images
Other Harms

Speech in K–12 Schools
Public Forum Analysis
The *Tinker* Test
The *Fraser* Approach
The *Hazelwood* Test
Choosing the Proper Test

Campus Speech
Student Fees and Speech
Student Publications at Universities
Professional Standards and Student Speech
Speech Codes

Emerging Law

Cases for Study
- *Mahanoy Area School District v. B.L.*
- *Elonis v. United States*

LEARNING OBJECTIVES

3.1   Assess when disruptive speech falls into one of the categories of unprotected speech, including Incitement, True Threats, Harassment, or Fighting Words.

3.2   Determine when symbolic speech is and is not protected by the First Amendment.

> **3.3** Recognize situations that may and may not result in negligence suits against members of the media.
>
> **3.4** Apply the appropriate legal test to determine when non-university-student speech is and is not permitted on and off school premises.
>
> **3.5** Understand when university student speech may be restricted.
>
> **3.6** Recognize efforts by state legislatures and school boards to restrict access to controversial materials and chill student speech.

Not all speech is protected by the First Amendment. Courts and legislatures have, over time, carved out certain categories of expression that are unprotected. Incitement to violence, true threats, fighting words, and harassment are unprotected because of their tendency to cause immediate harm or a breach of the peace. Others, such as false advertising, are not protected because they mislead consumers and have little value within public discourse. Blackmail, perjury, and obscenity are also categories of unprotected speech.

The reasons for not extending First Amendment protection to certain forms of expression vary. This chapter focuses on how courts determine the boundaries of protected speech, particularly for expression at the fringes of Frist Amendment protection.

One of these areas is disruptive speech. Some disruptive speech, such as **hate speech** and other vulgar or offensive speech is protected by the First Amendment. However, expression that incites violence or threatens or harasses others is exempt from First Amendment protection. This chapter will explore how these categories were established and the justifications behind this approach.

We'll also look at potentially harmful speech that appears in mass media outlets and explore the responsibility content providers and journalists have to consider these harms. Finally, we'll explore First Amendment protection for speech in K–12 schools and on college campuses.

DISRUPTIVE SPEECH

Contrary to the childhood chant, words *can* hurt you. Speakers—sometimes intentionally, sometimes not—disrupt organized activities or offend, denigrate or degrade people. People call each other names; they hurl hateful insults and epithets at each other. They threaten; they harass. They fill public meetings and public streets with dissent and discontent. The words and images they use alienate people, cause fear and increase conflict.

The U.S. Supreme Court has developed several tests to help it and other courts decide when unpopular or disturbing speech must be protected and when it may be punished. The Court has said free expression is not protected if it causes imminent harm or plays "no essential part of any exposition of ideas, and [is] of such slight social value as a step to truth that any benefit that may be derived from [it] is clearly outweighed by the social interest in order and morality."[1] No bright lines define the boundaries of this category. The border between protected and unprotected speech is not fixed. The Court's tests afford leeway in response to changing circumstances.

From a Bad Tendency to a Clear and Present Danger

When does speech cross the line from protected expression into unprotected incitement to violence? The answer to that question has evolved over the last century. In 1919, Justice Oliver Wendell Holmes wrote for a unanimous U.S. Supreme Court that government had both a right and a duty to prevent speech that presented a "**clear and present danger**" to the nation.[2] This doctrine established that restrictions on First Amendment Rights would be upheld if they were necessary to prevent an extremely serious and imminent harm. The case of *Schenck v. United States* began when Charles Schenck, a Socialist Party member, mailed anti-draft pamphlets to men in Philadelphia. The pamphlets encouraged readers to reject the government's pro-war philosophy and oppose U.S. participation in World War I. Schenck was convicted of violating the Espionage Act of 1917, which was enacted to unify the nation behind the war effort.

In affirming Schenck's conviction, the Supreme Court said the mailing had a "tendency" that could endanger national security. Justice Holmes said ordinarily harmless words may become criminal during times of war because of the heightened danger they pose: "It is a question of proximity and degree."[3] Common sense indicates that "the most stringent protection of free speech would not protect a man in falsely shouting fire in a theatre and causing a panic."[4] Nor would it protect an individual in a military recruitment office falsely shouting, "I have a bomb."

Under the Espionage Act, a unanimous Court affirmed other convictions for anti-war protests, speeches and pamphlets the Court said might tend to endanger the nation. In one case, the Court upheld a 10-year prison term for publishing writings that questioned the constitutionality of the draft and the merits of the war.[5] The Court said the publications presented "a little breath [that] would be enough to kindle a flame" of unrest.[6] The Court also upheld the conviction of a speaker who told Socialist Party conventioneers, "You are fit for something better than slavery and cannon fodder."[7] The jury relied on the speaker's court testimony that he abhorred the war to demonstrate both his intent and the likelihood he would harm the war effort.

The Court also used this so-called bad-tendency standard to uphold a Sedition Act conviction of five friends whose pamphlets criticized U.S. interference in the Russian Revolution and encouraged strikes at U.S. munitions factories.[8] The leaflets told workers to oppose "the hypocrisy of the United States and her allies." This time writing in dissent, Justice Holmes said the "surreptitious publishing of a silly leaflet by an unknown man" did not pose a sufficiently grave and imminent danger to permit punishment.[9] The First Amendment requires government to protect diverse and loathsome opinions, he wrote, "unless they so imminently threaten immediate interference with the lawful and pressing purposes of the law that an immediate check is required to save the country."[10] This Holmes dissent in *Abrams v. United States* transformed his interpretation of the First Amendment and the clear and present danger test.

The Court relied on the clear and present danger test for 50 years, most often to affirm punishment of communists.[11] During the Red Scare of the 1920s, the Court affirmed the conviction of an immigrant for publication and distribution of Socialist Party literature urging the rise of socialism in the United States.[12] Without evidence that the pamphlets caused any harm or disruption, the Supreme Court in *Gitlow v. New York* upheld the conviction for criminal anarchy and advocacy to overthrow the government, saying that the pamphlets lit a "revolutionary spark" that might ignite a "sweeping and destructive conflagration."[13] The majority said the writings "endanger[ed] the foundations of organized government and threaten[ed] its overthrow by unlawful means."[14]

Now writing in dissent, Justice Holmes declared, "Every idea is an incitement" and most ideas "should be given their chance and have their way" in the dialogue of a free and democratic society.[15] The mere dissemination of ideas does not endanger the nation.

The majority of the Court did not embrace Holmes' view, but its *Gitlow* decision expanded free speech protection by establishing the doctrine of incorporation. The **incorporation doctrine** applies the Fourteenth Amendment's due process clause to limit the power of state and local governments to abridge the Bill of Rights.[16] In other words, incorporation prevents the states, as well as the federal government, from abridging protected First Amendment rights.

In the years leading up to U.S. involvement in World War II, the Supreme Court used the clear and present danger test to uphold the conviction of a labor activist for participating in meetings of the Communist Labor Party.[17] In *Whitney v. California*, the Court accepted without evidence that the Communist party was violent and ruled that the First Amendment did not bar California from making it a crime to belong to a group that advocated violence. Mere party membership was sufficient to pose an imminent threat that was "relatively serious."[18] Writing in concurrence, Justice Louis Brandeis said a clear and present danger existed when previous conduct suggested a group *might contemplate* advocacy of immediate serious violence.[19]

During the anti-communist frenzy of the 1950s, the Court used the clear and present danger test to uphold a federal law that required labor union officers to swear they were not communists.[20] In dissent, Justice Hugo Black said the test did not sufficiently protect unpopular political speech or association from overzealous regulation: "Too often it is fear which inspires such passions, and nothing is more reckless or contagious. In the resulting hysteria, popular indignation tars with the same brush all those who have ever been associated with any member of the group under attack."[21]

Members of the Court increasingly questioned the ability of the clear and present danger test to protect radical speech. In several cases, the Court ruled that regulation of speech is unconstitutional if it does not address a problem more severe than abstract expressions about revolt and is not narrowly tailored to avoid infringing on protected speech.[22] While it is constitutional to regulate speech that advocates illegal action, government may not punish the mere expression of radical ideas. This doctrine was established in *Brandenburg v. Ohio*, a case involving incitement.

From Clear and Present Danger to Incitement

In 1969, the U.S. Supreme Court determined that the clear and present danger test was inadequate.[23] In *Brandenburg v. Ohio*, the Court adopted a new test that drew a bright-line distinction between advocating violence as an abstract concept and inciting imminent violence when it ruled that the First Amendment protects the right to advocate but not to incite, or provoke, immediate violence.[24]

The case involved Clarence Brandenburg, a television repairman and Ku Klux Klan leader, who spoke to a dozen KKK members in the woods of rural Ohio. Brandenburg made vague threats to take "revengeance" against various government leaders, and his racist speech was later televised. Brandenburg was convicted under state criminal conspiracy law of attempting to violently overthrow government. He said the conviction violated his right of free speech.

The Supreme Court struck down Brandenburg's conviction, holding that the First Amendment protected people's right to advocate abhorrent ideas. Brandenburg's anti-Semitic and racist comments were highly offensive, the Court said, but "[m]ere advocacy of the use of force or violence does not remove speech from the protection of the First Amendment."[25] To protect the expression of abstract ideas about the necessity of violence from government intrusion, the Court established a test named after the case. The *Brandenburg* test permits government to punish the advocacy of violence only by showing that the advocacy was (1) intended to and (2) likely to incite imminent (3) lawless action.[26]

POINTS OF LAW
THE *BRANDENBURG* INCITEMENT TEST

In *Brandenburg v. Ohio*, the U.S. Supreme Court established a two-pronged test to determine when it is constitutional for government to punish illegal encouragement of violence.[27]
  The test holds that speech may be punished if

1. It is directed to inciting or producing imminent lawless action
     AND
2. Is likely to produce such action.

  Under *Brandenburg*, punishable incitement exists if the facts show that intent, likelihood, and imminence are probable and that the violence is so immediate that no other action would address the harm. The Court has not clearly defined these three elements.[28]

In a second case, *Hess v. Indiana*, Gregory Hess used profanity at an anti–Vietnam War rally after sheriff's officers moved demonstrators out of the street. On appeal, the U.S. Supreme Court overturned Hess' conviction for disorderly conduct. The First Amendment protected his speech that was not intended to, and not likely to, provoke an imminent violation of the law.[29] The Court held that unless a speaker so inflamed a crowd that people responded with immediate, illegal acts, the speech was protected.

Under *Brandenburg*, the incitement does not have to be explicit, but two recent U.S. Supreme Court decisions[30] raise the bar needed for government to show that prosecution is reasonable because a communication is sufficiently likely to be "directed to inciting or producing imminent lawless action and is likely to incite or produce such action."[31] Relying on *Bell Atlantic v. Twombly* and *Ashcroft v. Iqbal*, the Court said charges should be dismissed if judges' "common sense" and judicial experience indicated that (1) the preliminary facts (2) did not make a plausible showing (3) that the necessary elements of the crime were met.[32]

In a 2017 decision, the Sixth Circuit Court of Appeals applied the *Twombly/Iqbal* standard to dismiss an incitement suit brought against President Donald Trump for telling a crowd at a campaign rally to "get 'em out of here." He was referring to protesters at the event.[33] After President Trump's comment, members of the crowd pushed and shoved the protesters as they exited, and the protesters sued the president for damages for "inciting to riot."

A court may dismiss a charge of incitement using the plausibility standard if the court's common-sense interpretation of the preliminary facts establishes that intent, likelihood and imminence are unlikely to be shown. The government's showing of these key elements must rely on facts alone, not on "legal conclusion[s]" that may be incorrect.[34] The facts must present a case that is more than speculative; it must be "plausible on its face" and provide a "reasonable" basis for the court to believe that it is "more than a sheer possibility" that the defendant is liable.[35]

Former President Trump's speech to a group of supporters immediately before the January 6, 2021, insurrection on the U.S. Capitol led the House of Representatives to bring forth an article of impeachment charging former President Trump with "incitement to insurrection." According to the article, President Trump's false claims about the 2020 presidential election results and his statements to the crowd, including "if you don't fight like hell you're not going to have a country anymore" encouraged—and foreseeably resulted in—lawless action at the Capitol.[36] Five people, including one police officer, died when a mob of President Trump's supporters stormed the Capitol Building while lawmakers certified the election results in favor of President Biden. The Senate acquitted the former president on the impeachment charges.

A large group of pro-Trump protestors stormed the U.S. Capitol Building on January 6, 2021

When applied to claims that media content provokes violence, the incitement test requires a showing that exposure to the media content would cause immediate violent or unlawful activity. Despite the ubiquity of social media, that is nearly impossible to prove. When seeing, reading or hearing media material, a person must process the information before taking action. There generally is time to prevent a person from committing violent acts. The incitement test also requires proof that media content is likely to cause a reasonable person to act illegally. Rarely will a court find that a reasonable person would commit violence in response to media content.

Intimidation and Threats

When speech crosses certain lines, the government may restrict messages that are sufficiently detrimental to important competing interests. A decade and a half ago, the U.S. Supreme Court created a category of speech it called **true threats**, which refers to expression that is directed toward an individual or historically identified group with the intent of causing fear or harm. The case involved three cross burnings, one at a KKK rally and two in the yard of a Black family. In *Virginia v. Black*, the Court ruled that the First Amendment allows states to punish individuals who set crosses ablaze with the intent to intimidate.[37] The Court said laws may constitutionally target a specific subset of fighting words, such as cross burnings, that is so "inextricably intertwined" with a clear and pervasive history of violence that it constitutes a threat. The Court said a burning cross is an instrument of racial terror and imminent violence whose power to intimidate overshadows free speech concerns. In *R.A.V. v. City of St. Paul*, the Court struck down a law that unconstitutionally targeted a subset of speech the city found particularly offensive.[38]

Writing for the majority in *Virginia v. Black*, Justice Sandra Day O'Connor reasoned that despite the inextricable connection between cross burnings and the KKK's "reign of terror in the South," history alone does not transform offensive speech into unprotected threats. Here the cross burning involved an intent to intimidate, which may be punished. For speech to become a punishable threat, a speaker must (1) direct the threat toward one or more individuals (2) with the intent of causing the listener(s) (3) to fear bodily harm or death.[39] In this case, cross burning was constitutionally punishable because the intimidation was intended to create pervasive fear of violence in the targeted individual or group. In dissent, Justice Clarence Thomas said the law punished only illegal acts and was unrelated to First Amendment concerns: "Those who hate cannot terrorize and intimidate to make their point."

In 2015, the Supreme Court remanded the First Amendment question of when social media posts constitute true threats punishable by law.[40] The case of *Elonis v. United States* involved a Pennsylvania man convicted of making Facebook threats to his estranged wife and law enforcement officers. Anthony Elonis said he did not intend any threats and was composing "therapeutic" rap lyrics to express his depression and frustration after his wife took their children and left him.[41] At trial, Elonis' wife testified that she was terrified by the posts, had filed a protective order against him, and feared for her life and that of her children. The jury convicted Elonis.

On appeal, the Third Circuit Court of Appeals identified both a subjective and an objective element to threats.[42] The subjective element involves the speaker's knowing communication of an

National Network to End Domestic Violence Vice President Paulette Sullivan Moore speaks with reporters about victims' rights after arguments in the case of Anthony Elonis

intention to cause harm. The objective standard means that a reasonable person would view the communication as a threat. The court affirmed the conviction on the grounds that the lyrics clearly met the objective standard.

But the Supreme Court disagreed. A conviction for a true threat cannot rely on the recipient's perception and the speaker's mere negligence, it said.[43] Conviction for making a threat, like any criminal conviction, requires a showing that the defendant intended to commit the crime or knew that a reasonable person would perceive the communication as a threat.[44] "Wrongdoing must be conscious to be criminal. . . . [T]his principle is as universal and persistent in mature systems of law as belief in freedom of the human will," the Court said.[45]

On remand, the Third Circuit reviewed the trial court's instructions to the jury, which said that a threat exists when a reasonable communicator would understand the receiver would perceive a threat. The court concluded that the instructions met the Supreme Court's requirement and reaffirmed Elonis's conviction.[46] Elonis was released in 2016 after serving 44 months in jail.

POINTS OF LAW
TEST FOR A TRUE THREAT

In 2003, the U.S. Supreme Court decision in *Virginia v. Black* held that punishment of true threats is acceptable under the Constitution given both speaker intent and a reasonable person's objective response.[47] In *United States v. Elonis*, the Court affirmed the test. A threat may be punished without violating the First Amendment if the speaker

1. directs the message to an individual or group,
2. intends to threaten, and
3. knows a reasonable recipient will perceive a threat.[48]

While many courts apply both elements two and three,[49] others use only one to rule that a threat may be punished.[50] Despite this inconsistency, the U.S. Supreme Court has denied three certiorari requests to review cases that posed the question of what the proper standard should be.[51]

Questions related to the role of assessing a speaker's intent in determining whether expression meets the definition for a true threat was at the forefront of a recent Kansas Supreme Court ruling. Here, the court overturned the convictions of two men who had been charged under Kansas' criminal threats statute.[52] One of the men had threatened a police officer by telling the officer's son that he would find his father "in a ditch." The other man was convicted of threatening to burn down his elderly mother's home and kill her. The Kansas Supreme Court reversed the lower court's convictions and said that the state's criminal threats statute was overbroad because it left room for statements made without the intent to cause fear or violence to be considered punishable threats.[53] In 2020, the U.S. Supreme Court declined to review a challenge to this case.[54]

Answering questions about a speaker's intent can be particularly difficult when potential threats appear online or in other media content. The Pennsylvania Supreme Court upheld the conviction of Jamal Knox, who performed under the name Mayhem Mal, for terrorist threats toward police officers for his rap song, "Fuck the Police."[55] The song, posted widely through Facebook and YouTube, names two Pittsburgh police officers and ends with the phrase "Let's kill these cops cuz they don't do us no good."[56] The named officers said the lyrics made them "nervous," and one quit the police force. Defense attorneys argued that the rap song was pure political speech that "no reasonable person familiar with rap music would have interpreted as a true threat of violence." Knox said the song was written from his rap persona and he had no intention to threaten or harm the officers. The state's high court ruled that Knox intended to threaten and intimidate. The U.S. Supreme Court declined to review the case in 2019.[57]

Several prominent rappers, including Chance the Rapper, submitted an amicus brief to the Supreme Court urging them to reconsider the conviction of Mayhem Mal for song lyrics that allegedly threatened police

Given the difficulty of determining a speaker's intent, particularly online, some states have developed additional criteria to evaluate threats. In 2020, the Colorado Supreme Court established its own standard for assessing whether statements made online constitute a true threat.[58] That court held that "a true threat is a statement that, considered in context and under the totality of the circumstances, an intended or foreseeable recipient would reasonably perceive as a serious expression of intent to commit an act of unlawful violence."[59] This diverges from the current true threats test, which does not consider the context of the expression or the circumstances surrounding it.

Online Harassment, Cyberstalking, and Cyberbullying

Threats against individuals can be part of the larger phenomenon of online harassment. Online harassment, which is also called cyberharassment, is the term used to refer to a broad category of behaviors that involve repeated or severe online expression amounting to a "course of conduct" targeted at a particular person or group that causes substantial emotional distress and/or fear of bodily harm.[60] One type of online harassment is cyberstalking, which generally refers to a pattern of threatening or malicious behaviors by a single perpetrator who uses electronic means to stalk their victim.[61] Cyberstalking occurs between individuals and does not include general communications about the victim. For example, repeated private messages targeted at a victim would qualify as cyberstalking, but posts about a victim on a public social media account would not. Most states have laws prohibiting cyberharassment and cyberstalking. However, some of these laws have been successfully challenged on First Amendment grounds.[62] In 2017, the Illinois Supreme Court struck down the state's cyberstalking law as unconstitutional. The court said that the law was overbroad and restricted more protected speech than was necessary. Other states have also had to revise their cyberstalking laws to ensure they were narrowly drawn.[63] At issue in many of these instances is the extent to which the laws target constitutionally protected speech or unprotected speech such as true threats.[64]

The term "cyberbullying" refers to the "willful and repeated harm inflicted through the use of computers, cell phones, and other electronic devices" and is usually used in reference to the online behavior of school-age children and young adults. According to the Cyberbullying Research Center, 48 states have bullying laws that specifically address cyberbullying or electronic harassment by individuals under 18.[65]

Notably, online harassment, cyberstalking, and cyberbullying laws are extremely difficult to enforce, particularly when anonymous online posters are involved. In addition, these crimes present substantial jurisdictional issues, and police departments often do not have the bandwidth or resources necessary to thoroughly investigate violations of federal and state online harassment and cyberstalking statutes.[66]

Fighting Words

The First Amendment protects people's right to vent anger in words. However, when expression directed at an individual causes immediate harm or triggers a violent response, it may be considered fighting words.

This category of unprotected speech was initially carved out by the U.S. Supreme Court in 1942 in *Chaplinsky v. New Hampshire*.[67] This case established that the government may punish speech that provokes a violent reaction from a listener. When residents complained that Walter Chaplinsky was distributing Jehovah's Witness pamphlets on the streets, a group of people became restless. A police officer warned Chaplinsky to stop because he was disturbing the peace, and later another officer detained him. The officer and Chaplinsky encountered the first officer, who warned Chaplinsky again, and Chaplinsky called the officer a "goddamned racketeer" and a "damned Fascist." Chaplinsky was convicted under a state law that defined disturbing the peace as publicly calling someone "any offensive, derisive or annoying word . . . or name . . . with intent to deride, offend or annoy."

In its landmark decision, the U.S. Supreme Court upheld the conviction, ruling that the First Amendment did not protect narrow categories of speech that make no contribution to the discussion of ideas or the search for truth. The Court said Chaplinsky's comments were unprotected **fighting words** that "by their very utterance inflict injury or tend to incite immediate breach of peace."[68]

In 1949, the Supreme Court heard the case of a priest who was arrested for disorderly conduct when his anti-Semitic and pro-Fascist comments to a sympathetic audience riled a group outside the assembly hall to violence. Illinois courts upheld his conviction, ruling that the law punished only unprotected fighting words that "stir[] the public to anger, invite[] dispute, bring[] about a condition of unrest, . . . create[] a disturbance or . . . molest[] the inhabitants in the enjoyment of peace and quiet by arousing alarm."[69]

The U.S. Supreme Court reversed, reasoning that "a function of free speech under our system of government is to *invite* dispute."[70] The Court in *Terminiello v. Chicago* said speech "may indeed best serve its high purpose when it induces a condition of unrest, creates dissatisfaction with conditions as they are or even stirs people to anger."[71] The First Amendment protects such speech "unless shown likely to produce a clear and present danger of a serious substantive evil that rises far above public inconvenience, annoyance or unrest."[72] Subsequent Supreme Court rulings[73] have confirmed that the Constitution permits government to prohibit only those face-to-face comments that are inherently likely to trigger an immediate reaction of disorder or violence. For example, in 2022, the Sixth Circuit Court of Appeals said that even profane speech directed at police could not be considered fighting words unless the circumstances created a situation where violence was likely to occur. In this instance, a man came to the attention of local law enforcement for wearing a T-shirt to the Clark County Fair in Ohio that said, "Fuck the Police." He eventually changed, but complaints about his attire had already prompted police to intervene. Ultimately, the man was arrested and removed from the fairgrounds. While being escorted from the premises by six officers, he said, "Fucking thugs with guns that don't uphold the United States Constitution. Fuck all you. You dirty rat bastards."[74] He also called the cops "fucking thugs with badges" and "motherfuckers."[75]

The charges against the man were eventually dropped and the Sixth Circuit ruled that his statements did not constitute unprotected fighting words because the circumstances did not create a situation where violence was likely. In the past, the U.S. Supreme Court and the Sixth Circuit Court of Appeals have both said that police officers are expected to exercise greater restraint in their response than the average citizen.[76] The First Amendment requires that police tolerate coarse criticism.[77]

POINTS OF LAW
FIGHTING WORDS

Under the U.S. Supreme Court's fighting words doctrine, the First Amendment does not protect words that

1. include a direct personal insult addressed to an individual and
2. are inherently likely to provoke violence.

In the United States, even the most offensive words in the English language are protected by the First Amendment unless they tend to cause immediate acts of violence. In 2021, the Fourth Circuit Court of Appeals vacated the conviction and sentence of a man who used the n-word during a bizarre altercation with employees and civilians at the Quantico Marine Corps Exchange.[78] The Fourth Circuit Court of Appeals said that in the trial, the government failed to show that anyone reacted violently to the man's use of the term and therefore the statement did not constitute fighting words. This, the Fourth Circuit judges said, differed greatly from a 2020 case in which the Connecticut Supreme Court upheld the conviction of a white man who repeatedly used the n-word to threaten the Black officer who had ticketed him.[79] Here, the defendant repeatedly used the slur, stepped toward the officer in an aggressive and threatening manner, and warned him to "remember Ferguson," where an African American man had died at the hands of a white man only three weeks before.[80] Connecticut's highest court upheld the defendant's conviction, explaining that the repeated use of the ugly epithet along with the defendant's use of other threatening and abusive words, his menacing invocation of Ferguson, his offensive and irate body language, and the officer's recognition of this as a threat established that the defendant had used fighting words likely to provoke a violent reaction.[81]

As these cases demonstrate, in the United States, even the most offensive language is protected by the First Amendment unless it provokes an immediate violent reaction. As a result, use of the fighting words doctrine today is fairly limited.[82]

Hate Speech

Unless hate speech falls into one of the unprotected categories of speech outlined earlier in this chapter, such as incitement, true threats, harassment, or fighting words, it is protected by the First Amendment. In fact, hate speech is not a legal term. However, it is commonly understood as expression that seeks to malign people based on their fixed identity characteristics, such as their race, ethnicity, national origin, religion, gender, gender identity, sexual orientation, age, or disability. Hate speech can include spoken words, such as slurs and epithets, as well as symbols and images.

Neo Nazis, Alt-Right, and White Supremacists encircle counter protestors during the United the Right Rally in Charlottesville, Va. in 2017

Hate speech differs from hate crimes. Hate crimes are criminal acts that are motivated by prejudice against a victim or victims because of their identity characteristics. If a criminal act is designated as a hate crime, it often carries additional penalties such as an increased prison sentence. Hate speech may be used during the commission of a hate crime but the terms are not synonymous with one another.

For centuries, hate speech has been used by people in power to dehumanize minority racial or ethnic groups in order to make violence against them more palatable. Ascribing undesirable traits to members of certain groups and comparing them to animals are two specific ways hate speech can fuel bias-motivated violence and genocide. For example, before the Holocaust, Jewish people were referred to as "rats" or "vermin." The genocide in Rwanda in the mid-1990s was preceded by a radio campaign that painted the ethnic minority group, the Tutsis, as inyenzi or cockroaches. More recently, military forces in Myanmar used Facebook to execute a targeted campaign of hate speech against the Rohingya Muslims. The violence sparked by this effort included rape, murder, and arson and has led to the exodus of 700,000 Rohingya from the country. A 2018 Study by Reuters and UC Berkley found thousands of Facebook posts calling Rohingya or other Muslims dogs, maggots, or rapists.

Given the potential harm hate speech can cause, many other democracies prohibit incitement to hatred, both in person and online. Citing concerns about the impact on human dignity and the psychological damage hate speech can cause, these countries have enacted criminal and civil legislation that allows victims of hate speech to seek legal recourse. In the United States, courts and legislatures have long held that it is necessary to tolerate even the most hateful expression to preserve our democracy. Justifications like those offered in Chapter 2 such as the marketplace of ideas, political self-governance, and personal liberty are often cited as the reasons hate speech is protected. Many prominent scholars have also expressed concerns about the misuse of hate speech laws against the people they were designed to protect and instead call for counterspeech as a remedy.[83] For example, Mike Love, a Black man, was sentenced to a 23-month jail term for violating the state's ethnic intimidation law when he called several undercover police officers "white boys" and "fucking crackers" and told them to "get off the corner" prior to an altercation.[84] While the idea that white people can be the victim of racism seems antithetical to the concept, this case demonstrates how laws designed to protect racial, ethnic, and religious minorities might be co-opted by whites and used against members of those groups. To be considered constitutional, anti-bias and anti-hate-speech laws cannot punish certain forms of racist speech and not others. As a result, these laws have generally been considered unconstitutional by U.S. Courts.

The primary Supreme Court decision dealing with a hate speech law, *R.A.V. v. City of St. Paul*, involved several white teenage boys who, late one night, made a crude wooden cross from a broken chair and set it ablaze in the yard of a Black family.[85] They were convicted of violating a local statute that punished the display of symbols—such as a burning cross—that aroused "anger, alarm or resentment in others on the basis of race, color, creed, religion or gender." The Minnesota Supreme Court upheld the conviction, reasoning that the bias-motivated crime statute punished only unprotected fighting words.

A unanimous U.S. Supreme Court reversed, but the justices did not agree on why. Five justices said the law was too narrow, or **underinclusive**, because it punished only a specific subset of fighting words that the government found particularly objectionable. Thus, the law imposed unconstitutional **viewpoint-based discrimination** because it punished certain forms of racist speech (cross burnings) but not others. The remaining four justices said the law was overbroad; it punished too much speech, not too little. They said the law unconstitutionally went beyond fighting words to punish speech that did not arise in face-to-face encounters and whose only harm was to prompt "generalized reactions" of hurt or offense.

In explaining its reasoning, the *R.A.V.* Court said:

> It is not true that "fighting words" have at most a "de minimus" expressive content, or that their content is in all respects "worthless and undeserving of constitutional protection"; sometimes they are quite expressive indeed. We have not said that they constitute "no part of the expression of ideas," but only that they constitute "no essential part of any expression of ideas." . . . [T]he unprotected features of [fighting] words are, despite their verbal character, essentially a "nonspeech" element of communication.[86]

Since *R.A.V.*, most efforts to tailor a constitutional hate speech ordinance have failed. Supreme Court decisions make the precise level of protection the Constitution affords fighting words unclear. They suggest that speech loses its constitutional protection when the speaker intends to provoke violence or incite immediate unrest in a targeted individual or group. The Supreme Court has shied away from using the fighting words category to judge the constitutionality of laws that attempt to regulate highly volatile speech and instead has examined the reach of the law. The Court has struck down laws that attempt to punish specific types of offensive speech on the grounds that the laws are not sufficiently narrowly tailored to prevent intrusion on protected speech.

A hooded member of the Ku Klux Klan sets a cross on fire

In response to the Supreme Court's clear position that hate speech ordinances are unconstitutional, some victims of hate speech have tried to use relevant tort laws to sue their perpetrators for emotional distress. As we'll see in Chapter 4, the Supreme Court overturned Albert Snyder's successful emotional distress claim against the leader of the Westboro Baptist Church for picketing his son's military funeral with signs that said "God hates f*gs" and "Thank God for dead soldiers." In an 8–1 decision the Supreme Court said that if the speech in question relates to a matter of public concern, which in this case was the question of whether members of the LGBTQ community should be able to openly serve in the military, it cannot be grounds for an emotional distress claim.

However, when the government is the speaker, it cannot be compelled into using hateful words or images. In 2015, the Supreme Court ruled that states have the right to block confederate flag license plates.[87] At issue in this instance was Texas's decision to deny the Sons of Confederate Veterans request to feature the confederate flag on their specialty license plate. In a 5–4 ruling, the Supreme Court rejected the argument that the license plates were a nonpublic government forum because Texas was not simply managing government property, but instead was engaging in expressive conduct.

In recent decades, questions about the U.S. government's treatment of hate speech have been eclipsed by concerns about how social media platforms regulate hateful content. As private virtual spaces, social media platforms are not required to extend First Amendment protection to hate speech. The terms of service users sign act as a contract between an individual and a company such as Facebook, Twitter, or TikTok. To retain the privilege of posting on a particular site, users must adhere to the community guidelines set by the social media organization. Platforms may discipline users that violate community standards or terms of service by removing offending content or accounts. However, the U.S. government will rarely intervene. Section 230 of the Communications Decency Act (CDA) states that providers of interactive computer services in the U.S., such as ISPs or social media companies, shall not be treated as publishers and, therefore, are not responsible for what third parties do on their sites. The CDA is discussed in more detail in Chapter 5.

To deal with the problem of hate speech, social media platforms use a combination of automatic detection and community flagging to identify and remove problematic content from their sites. Automatic detection uses sophisticated algorithms and artificial intelligence to locate and remove hate speech, while community flagging relies on users to identify potential hate speech, which is then reviewed either by artificial intelligence or human content moderators. Although Facebook's Community Standards Enforcement report indicates that the company took action on 31.5 million pieces of hateful content in Q2 of 2021,[88] documents released by Facebook whistleblower Frances Haugen show that amount is likely representative of only 3 to 5 percent of the hate speech currently on Facebook.

The company has also come under fire for its engagement-based formula, which instructs the newsfeed algorithm to prioritize extreme viewpoints to keep users on the platform longer.[89] This engagement translates directly into advertising dollars. In her October 2021 testimony to the U.S. Congress, Haugen, who was part of Facebook's Civic Integrity Department, testified about how the company's engagement-based formula helps sensational content, such as posts that feature rage, hate, or misinformation, gain traction.

INTERNATIONAL LAW
INTERNATIONAL APPROACHES TO LIMITING ONLINE HATE

While the US takes an essentially hands-off approach to the regulation of hate speech in social media content, in 2017, Germany passed the Network Enforcement Law, or NetzDG, which requires social media companies with more than two million users to remove or block access to reported content that violates restrictions against hate speech included in the German Criminal Code. Companies must remove "obvious hate speech" within 24 hours of receiving a notification or risk a €50 million fine.[90] Proponents of this law believe it is necessary to motivate companies like Facebook, Twitter, and others to act more aggressively to stem the tide of hate flowing from their sites. Those who disagree with the law feel it goes too far in limiting expression and will result in the removal of legal and permitted content on these sites.[91] Following Germany's lead, France's Parliament passed a law requiring social media networks to remove obviously hateful content or risk a fine.[92] The law also requires social media sites to create a new button to make it easier for users to report abuse.

In addition to creating legal parameters to address hate speech on social media, many social media companies have established cooperative agreements with governments to address the issue. After the 2019 attack on two Mosques in New Zealand, global leaders met with executives from Facebook, Google, Twitter, and other companies to compile a set of guidelines known as the "Christchurch Call," which sought to enact measures against extreme, violent, and hateful rhetoric online.[93] For the past several years, the European Commission has been working directly with social media organizations including Facebook, Twitter, and YouTube to combat the spread of hateful content in Europe. The result of that effort has been the creation of the "Code of Conduct on Countering Illegal Hate Speech Online." A 2021 report on the initiative indicated that since the implementation of the Code of Conduct, "IT companies are now assessing 81 percent of flagged content within 24 hours and 62.5 percent of the content deemed to be illegal hate speech is removed, which is lower than in previous years."[94]

Offensive Speech

Although many different types of speech offend or cause discomfort, mental anguish or suffering, the U.S. Supreme Court has said the First Amendment protects our right to express ourselves in our own words. In *Cohen v. California*,[95] Paul Robert Cohen appealed his conviction for disturbing the peace for opposing the Vietnam War by wearing a jacket bearing the phrase "Fuck the Draft" in the Los Angeles courthouse. Cohen said the First Amendment protected his pure political speech. The Supreme Court agreed. Although court officials have broad authority to maintain decorum, they cannot punish speech that does not disrupt the court's functioning simply because they find the words offensive.

The Supreme Court went further in *Cohen* and said the First Amendment protected both the content and the feelings expressed through a message. Meaningful protection for free speech goes beyond the "cognitive content" to protect the "emotive function" of a message, the Court said. It is not simply *what* you say but *how* you say it that enjoys constitutional protection. As Justice John Harlan famously wrote, "One man's vulgarity is another's lyric." [96]

Decades after Paul Robert Cohen became famous as the voice of free speech and anti–Vietnam War protest, he said his renown was accidental. He appealed his case to the U.S. Supreme Court because he wanted to avoid serving 30 days in jail.

Reprinted by permission of Advertising Archives

SYMBOLIC SPEECH

Much expression that might anger or upset people does not cross the line into incitement, fighting words or threats. Sometimes it does not even take the form of words. Nonverbal expression, in the form of burning flags, wearing armbands or marching through the public streets, is what the U.S. Supreme Court has called symbolic speech. The Court has said symbolic speech deserves First Amendment protection in some cases, but it has rejected "the view that an apparently limitless variety of conduct can be labeled speech whenever the person engaging in the conduct intends thereby to express his idea."[97] Only actions that are "closely akin to 'pure speech'" are viewed as symbolic speech.[98]

Some of the most vehement and heated debate in the 1960s involved symbolic speech. Amid the civil rights movement and protests against the Vietnam War, the Court held that the Constitution protected the rights of protest groups to express the most radical and unpopular political ideas. However, there were limits, and the line between protected political protest and illegal activity, incitement or fighting words was not always obvious.

Burning Speech

In the first of these cases (which is discussed in Chapter 2), the Supreme Court affirmed the power of government to punish David O'Brien for burning his draft card in violation of a federal law intended to facilitate the military draft. The *O'Brien* ruling established intermediate scrutiny as the standard of judicial review of content-neutral laws that incidentally infringed protected speech. In affirming O'Brien's conviction, the Court focused on why the government had enacted the law (intent) and how the law operated (effect) while acknowledging the expressive content of the public destruction of a draft card.[99]

Fast-forward 20 years, and the Court reviewed a case in which Gregory Lee Johnson had been convicted, sentenced to a year in prison and fined $2,000 for burning the American flag during a protest at the Republican National Convention in Dallas. In *Texas v. Johnson*, the Supreme Court used strict scrutiny to strike down a Texas law that made it a crime to desecrate the flag.[100] The state of Texas said its ban on flag desecration preserved an important symbol of national unity and prevented breach of the peace. Johnson argued that the law violated his right to free speech. The Supreme Court agreed. Finding flag burning to be a form of symbolic speech, the Court struck down the Texas law as unconstitutionally content based.

A sharply divided Supreme Court held that the law failed to pass strict scrutiny because it served no compelling interest. The state's interest in preserving the sanctity of the flag represented an unconstitutional attempt to punish ideas government disliked. The law's sole purpose was to prohibit expression the state found offensive. "If there is a bedrock principle underlying the First Amendment," Justice William Brennan wrote for the Court, "it is that the government may not prohibit the expression of an idea simply because society finds the idea itself offensive or disagreeable."[101] The law was unconstitutional because it neither served a compelling interest nor used the least intrusive means to advance its goals.

The Constitution also generally protects exaggeration, hyperbole and excess in speech by looking to the context to determine whether the words should be taken on their face. For example, the Court said an anti-war protester's comment to fellow marchers that "we'll take the fucking street later" did not present the clear and present danger of violence required under the incitement test because it was unlikely to prompt any immediate action.[102]

DO MEDIA INCITE HARM?

A series of Federal Trade Commission reports on violent entertainment marketed to children consistently cites research establishing "that exposure to violence in entertainment media alone does not cause a child to commit a violent act."[103] Although there is little agreement on how exposure to television, video game, music and movie violence influences youth aggression,[104] some news articles have suggested connections exist between exposure to these media to mass murders.[105] Lawsuits have claimed that injury resulted from imitating the violence in movies like "Natural Born Killers" and video games like "Doom," and courts have been asked to determine the level of media responsibility.[106]

Physical Harms

One lawsuit decades ago began when 13-year-old Ronny Zamora shot and killed his 83-year-old neighbor. Zamora's parents sued, claiming the television networks had failed to exercise "ordinary care to prevent their son from being impermissibly stimulated, incited and instigated to duplicate the atrocities he viewed on television."[107] A federal district court said the networks did not have a duty to stop showing violent programs and could not be held responsible for the teen's actions. To dictate a limit on violent content would violate the First Amendment rights of the networks and the public, the court held.[108]

If a court uses the incitement test when a member of the media is sued for causing physical harm, the plaintiff rarely wins. Plaintiffs generally fail to convince courts that media intentionally encouraged people to harm themselves or others. One case of media incitement involved a Hustler magazine article titled "Orgasm of Death," describing autoerotic asphyxiation. The parents of a 14-year-old boy who hanged himself with a copy of Hustler open to the story sued Hustler. The Fifth Circuit Court of Appeals said Hustler was not liable and did not incite the boy's actions.[109] The magazine not only did not urge readers to perform the act described; it repeatedly warned against it.

Courts have not found that media incited violence even when media knew criminal activity might be related to their content. For example, two decades ago Paramount Pictures continued distributing the movie "The Warriors" despite knowledge of two killings near California theaters that showed the film. When a teenager was stabbed and killed by another youth after leaving "The Warriors," the

The violent images and play of video games, such as "Call of Duty," generate public and legislative concern.

DigitalTrends.com

murdered boy's father sued Paramount. The Massachusetts Supreme Court held that the film's fictional portrayal of gang warfare did not constitute incitement because it did not advocate violent or unlawful acts.[110]

In a rare ruling of its kind, the Fourth Circuit Court of Appeals held a book publisher liable because it intended for criminals to buy and use the book "Hit Man: A Technical Manual for Independent Contractors" as a how-to for murder.[111] After a killer mimicked the book's detailed instructions to murder a woman, her son and the son's nurse, the court said the First Amendment did not protect Paladin Press because it encouraged, aided and abetted a crime. "[E]very court that has addressed the issue" agrees the First Amendment does not necessarily prevent finding a mass medium liable for assisting a crime, even if that aid "takes the form of the spoken or written word."[112] Paladin Press settled the case for $5 million.[113]

Negligence

Plaintiffs suing the media for causing physical harm often argue that the media negligently distributed material that led to injury or death. When such suits are based on the tort of **negligence** the plaintiff must show that the media defendant had a duty of due care, the defendant breached that duty, and the breach caused the plaintiff's injury. Although lawsuits have proliferated, courts rarely find the media negligent and liable for violent content.[114]

For example, one court found NBC was not negligent when a girl was raped after the network aired the film "Born Innocent." Four days after the film aired, a 9-year-old was attacked and raped on a San Francisco beach in a manner similar to central events in the film. The girl's parents sued NBC, claiming it was negligent in showing the movie when children could watch it. A state appellate court said the First Amendment barred any finding that NBC had a duty of care to the girl.[115] To do otherwise, the court said, would cause NBC to engage in self-censorship.

Foreseeability

To determine a defendant's duty of care, courts often ask whether the defendant should have foreseen that its product messages would cause harm. If a reasonable person would not foresee the harm, there was no duty.

Soldier of Fortune magazine ads promoting "GUN FOR HIRE . . . All jobs considered" preceded two murder attempts, one of which was successful. A federal district court rejected the magazine's argument that the First Amendment protected its right to publish the ads.[116] The court said free speech is not absolute, and a jury could find the ads "had a substantial probability of ultimately causing harm to some individuals."[117] The magazine had a duty of due care because it was foreseeable that the ads could lead to physical injury.

However, Soldier of Fortune could not foresee harm from an ad that read, "EX-MARINES—67–69 'Nam Vets, Ex-DI, weapons specialist—jungle warfare, pilot, M.E., high risk assignments, U.S. or overseas."[118] In response to the ad, Robert Black paid John Wayne Hearn $10,000 to kill Black's wife. After Sandra Black's murder, her mother and son sued the magazine. The appellate court said the magazine had "no duty to refrain from publishing a facially innocuous classified advertisement when the ad's context—at most—made its message ambiguous."[119]

In a third case, a federal appellate court said Soldier of Fortune was obligated to determine whether the language of an ad, on its face, created an unreasonable risk of causing violent crime.[120]

The Sixth Circuit Court of Appeals held that video game manufacturers have no duty to protect against an individual's independent decision to kill.[121] Parents of a 14-year-old video game player who shot three of his peers at their high school sued video game producers, claiming the negligent distribution of violent video games made them liable for alleged harms to the couple's son and his victims. The court held there was insufficient proof that the game producers should have foreseen that their products could prompt the shooting.[122] Even if the gameplay involved shootings, it is "simply too far a leap from shooting characters on a video screen . . . to shooting people in a classroom," the court said.[123]

Proximate Cause. If a defendant's actions led to the plaintiff's injury, the defendant caused the injury. But unless the defendant's action was the **proximate cause** of the harm, courts will not hold the defendant liable. To determine proximate cause, courts decide whether there is a direct relationship between the defendant's action and the plaintiff's injury. Courts often refuse to find proximate cause if there is a weak linkage between the defendant's action and the subsequent injury.

In one case, a mother sued the manufacturer of "Dungeons & Dragons"[124] on the grounds that her son committed suicide when he lost touch with reality because of the game. A federal appellate court said the suicide was independent of the gameplay. Both the loss of reality and the decision to commit suicide were intervening events. Similarly, when a teenager committed suicide while listening to an Ozzy Osbourne album that includes the song "Suicide Solution," the teenager's parents sued. A California appellate court said the connection between the suicide and the song's lyrics was too tenuous to show proximate cause.[125]

POINTS OF LAW
MEDIA LIABILITY FOR NEGLIGENCE

To win a lawsuit for injury caused by media negligence, the plaintiff must prove breach of media's duty of care because the content presented

1. reasonably foreseeable harm or
2. proximate (directly related) cause of the harm.

The U.S. Supreme Court weighed in when it struck down a California law.[126] In *Brown v. Entertainment Merchants Association*, a video game merchants' group challenged a state law that prohibited sale of violent video games to minors and required package labeling of violent content.[127] The law targeted only violent video games that (1) appealed to deviant or morbid interests, (2) were patently offensive under contemporary community standards, and (3) lacked serious artistic or other value (see discussion of related obscenity standards in Chapter 10). The state said the law was intended to advance the important government interest in preventing psychological harm to minors.

But the Supreme Court said the law unconstitutionally singled out video games from other media because of the games' interactivity and attractiveness to children.[128] In *Brown*, the Court refused to create a new category of disfavored speech for video game violence. It said violent video games deserve full First Amendment protection and California's attempt to do otherwise was both "unprecedented and mistaken."[129]

Reviewing the law under strict scrutiny, the Court found it facially unconstitutional. "It is difficult to distinguish politics from entertainment and dangerous to try. . . . Like the protected books, plays and movies that preceded them, video games communicate ideas and even social messages. . . . That suffices to confer First Amendment protection."[130]

In his concurring opinion, Justice Samuel Alito urged care when sweeping new technologies under the media umbrella. He wrote:

In considering the application of unchanging constitutional principles to new and rapidly evolving technology, this Court should proceed with caution. . . . We should not jump to the conclusion that new technology is fundamentally the same as some older thing with which we are familiar. And we should not hastily dismiss the judgment of legislators, who may be in a better position than we are to assess the implications of new technology.[131]

In a rare decision after *Brown*, the Alabama Supreme Court allowed a civil lawsuit brought by the families of two murdered police officers to proceed against the makers of a video game. In the underlying case, the Alabama court upheld a 17-year-old's conviction and death sentence for killing the officers during his arrest for carjacking.[132] The teen used the defense that his extensive play of "Grand Theft Auto" had caused posttraumatic stress and prompted the killings.[133] The officers' families wanted to hold the game makers liable.

Rather than holding media companies accountable for the impact of their content, some victims have sued social media companies for their conduct, claiming that the platforms' failure to act constituted negligence. Three separate victims of sex trafficking who became entangled with their abusers on Facebook sued the company for negligence.[134] The Supreme Court of Texas dismissed all of the negligence claims, citing the immunity from liability offered by Section 230.[135] Under that statute, computer service providers are not responsible for what third parties say and do on their sites and thus are not legally required to protect their users from the malicious or objectionable activity of other users. Plaintiffs in a somewhat similar case against Twitter also had their negligence claims dismissed by a California District Court because of Section 230, which is discussed in greater detail in Chapter 5.[136]

Harmful Images

The U.S. Supreme Court used its review of a federal statute making it a crime to profit from "depictions of animal cruelty"[137] to reaffirm its power to define categories of speech and to determine which are, and are not, fully protected by the First Amendment. In *United States v. Stevens*, the Supreme Court said Congress did not have the power to prohibit images of animal cruelty because the Constitution fully protects even violent and deeply disturbing images.[138]

In reviewing the conviction of Robert J. Stevens for compiling and selling videotapes of dogfights in violation of the Animal Crush Video Prohibition Act, the Court said it is possible "there are some categories of speech that have been historically unprotected [that] have not yet been specifically identified or discussed . . . in our case law. But if so, there is no evidence that 'depictions of animal cruelty' is among them."[139] Neither Congress nor the Supreme Court has "freewheeling authority to declare new categories of speech outside the scope of the First Amendment," the Court said. It found the law substantially overbroad and struck it down because it infringed fully protected speech.[140]

Other Harms

Any person or company involved with preparing or publishing news, entertainment and advertising may be sued for any number of legal claims. Media are not exempt when laws, such as contract laws, apply generally to any competent adult. Thus, when media make contractual agreements, they may be sued for breaching a contract.

For example, when documentary filmmakers interviewed an art critic for their film about censorship, the filmmakers signed a contract stating that the interview would not be distributed beyond a single British channel. After the film won numerous awards and was selected to open a prestigious festival, the critic sued. The filmmakers argued that the contract did not apply because they used only brief portions of the interview in the film. The court interpreted the contract to prevent reuse of the unedited interview footage, so the documentary with only interview excerpts could be exhibited wherever the producer wanted.[141]

The U.S. Supreme Court's 2018 decision in *Masterpiece Cakeshop v. Colorado Civil Rights Commission* underscores why neutral laws of general applicability apply to individuals and media firms alike.[142] The case involved a ruling of the Colorado Civil Rights Commission that a baker violated the state's anti-discrimination law by refusing to bake a wedding cake for a same-sex couple. The baker said the wedding violated his profound religious beliefs and his choice not to bake the cake was protected by the First Amendment. The Court said it was "unexceptional" that the government's power to enact anti-discrimination laws "protect[s] gay persons . . . [and] other classes of individuals in acquiring whatever products and services they choose on the same terms and conditions as are offered to other members of the public."[143] However, the Court struck down the law **as applied** because of the hostility officials showed toward the baker during an early hearing on the issue. The Supreme Court will revisit this question when it hears the case of a Colorado web designer who has refused to create websites for gay weddings. Experts hope the ruling in that case will provide a clear answer to whether public accommodation laws that compel artists to speak violate the free speech clause of the First Amendment.[144]

In another recent decision, the Supreme Court ruled that a prior criminal conviction cannot justify government suppression of speech that does not meet either the *Brandenburg* or the *Cohen* standard. The Court ruled in *State v. Packingham* that a North Carolina law barring sex offenders from using social media websites like Facebook and Twitter was unconstitutional.[145]

SPEECH IN SCHOOLS

There is nothing in the wording of the First Amendment to suggest that it protects the rights of minors, public school students or campus media differently from the rights of others. However, U.S. society has asserted unique interests in protecting and educating its youth. Sometimes courts have accepted the idea that the nation's interest in developing its youth outweighs the free speech rights of public school students. Courts have struggled to determine both how and where to draw the line between advancing the important concerns of parents and educators and protecting the sometimes-conflicting rights of students to freedom of speech and association.

More than 75 years ago, the U.S. Supreme Court applied its doctrine that "[t]he right to speak and the right to refrain from speaking are complementary components of the broader concept of individual freedom of mind"[146] to students. Public school students who were Jehovah's Witnesses challenged the mandatory flag salute and Pledge of Allegiance in school as a violation of their religious beliefs. In *West Virginia State Board of Education v. Barnette*, the Court agreed.[147] Despite the important role of public schools in teaching students civic values and responsibilities,[148] schools may not indoctrinate students into particular ideologies, the Court said.[149] In *Barnette*, the Court held that "[i]f there is any fixed star in our constitutional constellation, it is that no official, high or petty, can prescribe what shall be orthodox in politics, nationalism, religion or other matters of opinion or force citizens to confess by word or act their faith therein."[150]

Public Forum Analysis

The courts have used several different approaches to determine when student press and speech are protected. In many cases, the U.S. Supreme Court has viewed public schools and universities—including school-sponsored events, publications, funding and physical spaces—as limited public forums. Under public forum doctrine, and applying the *O'Brien* test (discussed in Chapter 2), schools may impose reasonable content-neutral time, place and manner regulations on student speech activities to advance educational objectives. What this means in practice is that schools and universities may adopt regulations to advance educational goals even if the rules incidentally limit students' and teachers' freedom of speech. School officials generally may not dictate the content of student speech except to prevent speech that would directly undermine the school's educational mission. Courts have upheld public school restrictions on students' clothing, the hours school facilities may be used by outsiders, the school-related expression of teachers, and the content of school-sponsored student speech and publications.

In several other approaches, the Court looked to the age, impressionability and maturity of the students; the location of the expression; the content of the speech; and the specific educational goals of the institution to determine the case outcome. Political turbulence and social unrest play a part. As one Court observer noted, sometimes "the very concept of academic freedom is under fire."[151] Such case-specific decisions do not provide clear rules of law. The variety of tests yields different outcomes among primary, secondary and postsecondary schools as well as between a high school newspaper and a university student's speech during an open public debate.

REAL WORLD LAW

PRONOUN POLICIES IN PUBLIC SCHOOLS

In certain parts of the country, schools have enacted policies designed to respect students' gender identities by requiring teachers and staff to use gender nonconforming students' chosen names, pronouns and honorifics.[152] However, some teachers have resisted these mandates, even though the U.S. Departments of Education and Justice have said that under Title IX, transgender and other gender nonconforming students have the right to be treated according to their gender identity.[153]

Teachers who have refused to adhere to these new pronoun policies claim that they violate their First Amendment rights to free expression and free exercise of religion.[154] School administrators have responded to these refusals by disciplining and, in some instances, terminating the contracts of teachers who ignore the stated policy.

A handful of the teachers fired for refusing to use students' preferred names and pronouns have taken legal action against school administrators, asserting that the policies violate their constitutional and statutory rights. To date, courts have heard three cases brought by teachers who objected to the policy even though the students' parents and medical professionals had signed off on changes to official school records.[155]

In one case, a district court ruled that a teacher could not be penalized for speaking out against the policy at a public school board meeting.[156] However, in another case, the court held that that addressing students in a classroom is not a matter of public concern and is part of the teacher's role as a public employee.[157] Therefore the school was justified in firing the teacher for failing to adhear to the neutral policy. The question of whether teachers can claim a religious exception to this policy remains unanswered. Moving forward, courts will likely use the "third-party harm principle" to consider the magnitude and likelihood of the harm caused by having teachers exempted from policies requiring them to use students preferred pronouns.[158]

The *Tinker* Test

If *Barnette* declared students' fundamental freedom from indoctrination, *Tinker v. Des Moines Independent Community School District* established school classes as a site that is "peculiarly the marketplace of ideas" where speech may be regulated only to prevent a "substantial disruption" to school activities.[159] The U.S. Supreme Court's *Tinker* test, as it is known, arose from a 1969 decision involving symbolic anti-war protest in school.

When a brother and sister in middle school and high school wore black armbands, a popular protest to the Vietnam War, they were suspended for violating a new policy prohibiting black armbands. The students did not disrupt classes, and they sued, claiming the suspensions violated their right to free speech.

In what some call "the most important Supreme Court case in history protecting the constitutional rights of students,"[160] the Court in *Tinker* agreed with the students. The Court held that the symbolic expression of the armbands was "akin to pure speech" and fully protected under the First Amendment.[161] When novel or deviant issues are expressed, the First Amendment must weigh heavily in favor of the expression and against the bureaucratic urge to suppress, the Court said. The Constitution does not allow officials to suppress student expression that is unpleasant or discomfiting.[162] Under the First Amendment, it is "unmistakable" that individuals do not "shed their constitutional rights to freedom of speech or expression at the schoolhouse gate."[163] Unless student expression substantially disrupts the school's educational activities, school administrators lack authority to regulate the speech, the Court said.[164]

The Tinkers (Lorena, Paul and Mary Beth, left to right) speak with the press in 1969 after learning the U.S. Supreme Court upheld the teens' right to wear anti-war armbands in school.

Bettmann/Getty Images

For nearly four decades, the rule was clear: Only when speech inside or adjacent to the school during school hours disrupts school activities may it be punished.[165] Then the Court's ruling in *Morse v. Frederick* seemed to muddy the test. In *Morse*, the Court held that the "substantial disruption" rule established in *Tinker* was not limited to speech during school hours or in the school building.[166]

The *Morse* case began when high school senior Joseph Frederick displayed a banner reading "Bong Hits 4 Jesus" during a school field trip. Frederick said he did it for a laugh and to get himself on TV. The school's principal, Deborah Morse, did not find it humorous and told him to remove the banner. When he refused, she tore down the sign and suspended him for violating a school policy that banned the advocacy of illegal drug use. Frederick sued, alleging that the principal had violated his right to free speech.

The district court sided with the principal, but the Ninth Circuit Court of Appeals reversed, ruling that school officials may not "punish and censor non-disruptive" speech by students at school-sponsored events simply because they object to the message. In a 5–4 ruling, the U.S. Supreme Court sided with the principal. The Court ruled that school officials may prohibit messages that advocate illegal drug use without running afoul of the First Amendment. For the majority, Chief Justice John Roberts wrote that students' First Amendment protection does not extend to speech that directly contravenes an important school policy. The Court reasoned that the "special environment" and the educational mandate of the schools permitted officials to prohibit student speech that raises a "palpable" danger to established school anti-drug policy.[167] The sanction was constitutional because it punished advocacy of illegal drug use.

In 2021, the Supreme Court revisited the question about whether the First Amendment prohibits public school officials from regulating off-campus student speech.[168] In the case, *Mahanoy Area School District v. B.L.*, a student challenged her suspension from the cheerleading team because of the content of a post on Snapchat. B.L. had tried out for the varsity cheerleading squad but failed to make the team and was placed on junior varsity. In response, she posted a snap to her story that included a photo of her and a friend with middle fingers raised and the caption "Fuck school fuck softball fuck cheer fuck everything."[169] The post was seen by about 250 people and prompted coaches to suspend B.L. from the team for one year for violating team and school rules. B.L. challenged the suspension as a violation of her First Amendment rights.

In an 8–1 opinion, the Supreme Court ruled that the school's decision to suspend B.L. for her social media post violated her First Amendment rights. Writing for the majority, Justice Stephen Bryer restated the three circumstances in which the Court had previously said schools may regulate student speech, respectively citing *Bethel, Morse,* and *Hazelwood*. These include indecent, lewd, or vulgar speech uttered during an assembly on school grounds; speech promoting illegal drug use uttered during a class trip; and speech that others may perceive as official communications from the school, such as content appearing in a school-sponsored newspaper.[170]

Justice Bryer went on to identify three features of off-campus speech that distinguish schools' efforts to regulate it from their efforts to regulate on-campus speech. First, this form of expression falls squarely within the zone of parental, rather than school-related, responsibility. Second, these posts can happen at any time of day and thus courts should be more skeptical of a school's efforts to regulate off-campus speech, for doing so may mean the student cannot engage in that kind of speech at all. Third, schools are nurseries of democracy and thus have an interest in protecting even unpopular speech.[171]

Applying these, Justice Bryer acknowledged that B.L.'s comments were made off school grounds outside of school hours and, as such, she was speaking in circumstances where her parents, not the school, had responsibility. Moreover, the Supreme Court disagreed with the Third Circuit Court of Appeals and said that *Tinker* did apply but that B.L.'s speech did not cause "substantial disruption" or threaten harm to the rights of others.[172]

Writing in concurrence, Justice Samuel Alito said that the regulation of many types of off-premises student speech raises serious First Amendment concerns, and school officials should proceed cautiously before venturing into this territory.[173] Justice Thomas was the sole dissenter in the case arguing that the decision disregards the 150 years of history supporting the coach.[174]

The *Fraser* Approach

Decades ago, the U.S. Supreme Court was asked to determine the limits of students' right to profane or offensive speech in public schools. The case of *Bethel School District v. Fraser* involved a speech by Matthew Fraser nominating a classmate for student government.[175] Employing a number of metaphors for male sexual prowess, Fraser addressed nearly 600 high school students, including some 14-year-olds, who were required to attend the school-sponsored assembly. The assistant principal said the speech violated a school policy prohibiting obscene speech that "materially and substantially interferes with the educational process." She suspended Fraser and prohibited his selection as graduation speaker.

Fraser challenged the action as a violation of his First Amendment rights. On review, the Supreme Court upheld the school's decision. The Court said that when student speech occurs during a school-sponsored event, the student's liberty of speech may be curtailed to protect the school's educational purpose, especially when young students are in the audience. This is particularly true if the forum for the student speech suggests that the student is speaking for the school. The *Fraser* decision held that eliminating vulgarity and profanity from school events advanced the duty of schools to "inculcate . . . habits and manners of civility."[176] Rather than view student First Amendment rights as paramount, the Court said it was "perfectly appropriate" for a school to impose student sanctions to disassociate the school from speech that threatened its core purpose.

The *Hazelwood* Test

Two years later, the U.S. Supreme Court reaffirmed school authority over school-sanctioned activities and speech. In this case, students in the journalism class at Hazelwood East High School in St. Louis, Mo., published a student newspaper, Spectrum, under the supervision of a faculty adviser who reviewed the content. The principal also reviewed each issue before publication, but school policy said students enjoyed freedom of "responsible" speech.

After the principal removed two pages of the newspaper that included one story about teen pregnancy at the school and a second about the impact of divorce on students at the school, student editors sued. The principal said the targeted stories invaded the privacy of students and parents interviewed and contained material inappropriate for younger students. Other inoffensive stories were also eliminated by removal of the pages to expedite printing before the school year ended. The trial court rejected the students' challenge, but the court of appeals reversed, saying the school could edit the newspaper's content only to avoid legal liability, not to advance grammatical, journalistic or social values.

In *Hazelwood School District v. Kuhlmeier*, the Supreme Court again reversed and said school administrators, not student reporters and editors, have authority to determine the appropriate content of a school-sponsored student newspaper.[177] When a school creates and supervises a forum for student speech, such as a student assembly or a teacher-supervised student newspaper, the school endorses that speech and is not only permitted but required to control the content to achieve educational goals, the Court said.[178] Schools must exercise their supervisory function to promote a positive educational environment in all "school-sponsored . . . expressive activities that students, parents and members of the public might reasonably perceive to bear the imprimatur of the school."[179] In a footnote, however, the Court made clear that the decision did not apply to the university student press.[180]

In an effort to counteract the impact of the *Hazelwood* decision, which allows school administrators to interfere with student publications, students have worked with the Student Press Law Center on a grassroots effort to change state laws to better recognize student press freedom. Since the initiative began, 15 states have adopted the New Voices Laws, which ensure that student media can only be censored if that media is libelous or slanderous, contains an unwarranted invasion of privacy, violates state or federal law or incites students to disrupt the orderly operation of a school.[181]

POINTS OF LAW
COURT REVIEW OF NON-UNIVERSITY-STUDENT SPEECH

U.S. Supreme Court decisions generally approach non-university-student speech cases in one of three ways:

1. Is the speech disruptive? If the speech disrupts the functioning of the public school or violates the rights and interests of other students, it may be regulated under *Tinker*.[182]
2. Is the speech of low value? If the speech is lewd or if it conflicts with the school's pedagogical goals or public values, it may be regulated under *Fraser*.[183]
3. Is the speech sponsored by the school or perceived to reflect the school's official position and endorsement? If the speech is closely associated with the school's activities, curriculum or policies, it may be regulated under *Hazelwood*.[184]

Choosing the Proper Test

Despite the guidance offered by the Supreme Court in *Mahanoy*, there is still uncertainty about when *Tinker* applies and when *Fraser*, *Hazelwood* or *O'Brien* should dictate the outcome. For example, the Second Circuit Court of Appeals limited the application of *Tinker* to "a student's personal expression . . . [that] happens to occur on the school premises." It applied *Hazelwood* to rule that a middle school had authority to ban a class president from a scheduled speech unless she deleted a closing religious blessing because the speech constituted school-sponsored expression.[185]

The Third Circuit Court of Appeals applied forum analysis to find unconstitutional an elementary school ban on student nondisruptive distribution of materials from nonschool organizations.[186] In another case, the Third Circuit relied on *Fraser* to find that a middle school student had a good likelihood of winning a challenge to the school's prohibition of breast-cancer-awareness bracelets reading "i ♥ boobies! (KEEP A BREAST)."[187] The school had said the bracelets were "lewd, vulgar, profane or plainly offensive." But the court said they likely were protected speech because they were nondisruptive and discussed an important social issue.

The Tenth Circuit used *Tinker* as the basis for ruling that school officials did not violate the First Amendment when they prevented high school students from distributing rubber fetus dolls in school.[188] And, again applying *Tinker*, the Fourth Circuit upheld student punishment for wearing a Confederate flag T-shirt to school because "school officials could reasonably forecast" that the shirt "would materially and substantially disrupt the work and discipline of the school."[189]

Although determining which test applies when remains fluid, in general, rules limiting student expression in and about public schools or school policies likely are constitutional if the policies neither (1) limit expressive content that is compatible with the school's educational priorities nor (2) target specific content without a strong educational justification.

The Supreme Court has refused to grant university administrators "the same degree of deference" it grants to high school administrators to regulate student expression[190] because college students are "less impressionable than younger students"[191] and because the special characteristics of public schools require that students' rights are "not automatically coextensive with the rights of adults in other settings."[192] The Court generally protects the free speech and free press rights of university students as an essential part of their educational experience. The university and, to some degree, its faculty control the content of the curriculum. Otherwise, university policies and procedures generally must provide a neutral platform for broad discussion of issues.[193]

Campus Speech

The U.S. Supreme Court has established that universities have a greater obligation to create and maintain forums for broad public discussion than do the public schools. In *Papish v. Board of Curators of the University of Missouri*, the Supreme Court established that "the mere dissemination of ideas—no matter how offensive to good taste—on a state university campus may not be shut off in the name alone of 'conventions of decency.'"[194] The Court said the university violated the First Amendment rights of 32-year-old journalism graduate student Barbara Papish when it expelled her for distributing an underground campus newspaper that contained a political cartoon depicting policemen raping the Statue of Liberty and the Goddess of Justice, and an article under the title, "M—f— Acquitted."

The Supreme Court has distinguished universities from public schools and held that a university's "mission is well served if students have the means to engage in dynamic discussions of philosophical, religious, scientific, social and political subjects in their extracurricular campus life outside the lecture hall."[195] As a consequence, public universities not only may but must support all messages without regard to content to enhance wide-open extracurricular debate and free speech interests.[196] Despite this charge, some public university activities either intentionally or inadvertently restrict the right to freedom of expression. For example, in recent years some universities have enacted policies that limit student speech to certain "zones" on campus, require advance authorization from the university and impose a vague nondiscrimination/nonharassment policy that prohibits "unwelcome" speech and "suggestive or insulting gestures or sounds."[197]

REAL WORLD LAW
THE FREE SPEECH CLIMATE ON U.S. COLLEGE CAMPUSES

In recent years, tension has emerged as public universities seek to uphold their commitment to free expression and robust intellectual debate alongside a desire to reduce harm to students from historically marginalized groups. U.S. colleges and universities have traditionally been primarily white, hetero-normative spaces, which can make learning and thriving difficult for marginalized students.[198] In response to these conditions, students and administrators have created "safe spaces," designated environments in which students can explore ideas and express themselves in a context with well-understood ground rules for conversations. "Trigger warnings" are also used to let students know that upcoming material may be upsetting for some.

Students have also become less tolerant of the idea that universities must provide a platform for controversial speakers. At Middlebury College in Vermont, students shouted down a discussion between one of their professors and Charles Murray, an author and political scientist whose books argue that marginalized groups are disadvantaged because they cannot compete with intellectually, psychologically, and morally superior white men. The Young Americas Foundation canceled a speech by conservative pundit Ann Coulter at the University of California Berkley over fears that protests against her speech would turn violent.

John Ellison, Dean of Students at the University of Chicago, directly addressed the issue in a letter to the incoming freshmen class that said intellectual safe spaces and trigger warnings would no longer exist on campus, and controversial speakers would no longer be canceled. According to the Foundation for Individual Rights in Education's (FIRE) annual campus free speech survey, 66 percent of students report some level of acceptance for speaker shout-downs and 23 percent consider it acceptable for people to use violence to stop certain speech.[199] About 80 percent of students reported censoring their viewpoints at their colleges at least some of the time.[200]

FIRE argues that this data demonstrates a substantial threat to free expression on U.S. college campuses.[201] According to FIRE, the emergence of free speech zones, the shouting down of controversial speakers on campus, the removal of confederate monuments, and speech codes are all evidence that students' and professors' right to free expression is under attack. Legal scholar and Georgetown University professor Alexander Tsesis disagrees noting that hate speakers are generally not inviting intellectual debate or seeking political dialogue, but instead silencing people through intimidation and limiting the marketplace of ideas on college campuses. The goals of democratic self-governance or self-expression, he says, do not require that we extend protection to speech that diminishes the sense of security for those targeted.[202]

Student Fees and Speech

Almost 25 years ago, the U.S. Supreme Court held that public universities must fund student groups on the basis of content-neutral policies.[203] When a university's funding "program [is] designed to facilitate private speech," the funding creates a public forum that prohibits university control of the content of the speech.[204] Writing in concurrence, Justice David Souter said the power of school authorities "to limit expressive freedom of students . . . is confined to high schools, whose students and their schools' relation to them are different and at least arguably distinguishable from their counterparts in college education."[205] Consequently, neither university administrators nor students who contribute fees for student activities may discriminate among student groups because of the ideas they express.[206]

The Supreme Court recently reshaped this concept when it ruled in *Christian Legal Society v. Martinez* that a California law school could deny funding and other benefits to an explicitly religious student group whose members were required to sign a statement of faith.[207] The school's failure to recognize Christian Legal Society as an official student group denied the group access to university recruitment fairs, bulk emails and posting on school bulletin boards—benefits that clearly implicate First Amendment rights. Yet the Court said the law school's denial based on its requirement that recognized student groups be open to "all comers" was a reasonable, viewpoint-neutral means to advance school interests in nondiscriminatory access for students. Alternative, non-university means of communication "reduce[d] the importance of [university] channels" in reaching law school students and adequately protected the group's speech interests.[208]

In what some saw as a radical expansion of *Tinker*, the Court relied on it to defer to the judgment of law school administrators "in light of the special characteristics of the school environment."[209] Writing in dissent, Justice Samuel Alito concluded that after the decision there is "no freedom for expression that offends prevailing standards of political correctness in our country's institutions of higher learning."[210]

Student Publications at Universities

Although student fees or university allocations generally fund student newspapers and yearbooks in whole or in part, the Supreme Court generally has viewed campus publications as forums for student expression in which universities may not control content. "Colleges and universities are supposed to be bastions of unbridled inquiry and expression," as one writer put it, "but they probably do as much to repress speech as any other institution in young people's lives."[211] The author said a recent study found that only about one-third of students and fewer than 1 in 5 faculty members strongly agreed that it is "safe to hold unpopular positions on campus."

When Kansas State University officials confiscated a student yearbook they said contained some objectionable content, the en banc Sixth Circuit Court of Appeals ruled that the confiscation violated students' First Amendment rights.[212] Declining to apply *Hazelwood* because a university "yearbook [must] be analyzed as a limited public forum—rather than [the] nonpublic forum" of a high school newspaper, the court said the university had neither the need nor the authority to control the content of speech in the student yearbook.[213]

Despite the asserted differences between high schools and universities, some courts apply *Hazelwood* to review restrictions on university-subsidized and -approved publications.[214] One case began when a dean at Governors State University in Illinois required her preapproval of content before publication of the student newspaper. Student editors sued, claiming the action violated their First Amendment rights. The Seventh Circuit Court of Appeals, using *Hazelwood*, held that the student newspaper was a limited-purpose public forum beyond the control of the university's administration.

The Ninth Circuit Court of Appeals found that editors of a conservative student newspaper at Oregon State University had a legitimate First Amendment claim to nondiscriminatory access to campus to distribute their publication.[215] The case involved an independent student newspaper distributed through campus newspaper boxes. Under a new unwritten policy allegedly intended to clean up campus, university employees removed this newspaper's distribution boxes, leaving those for USA Today and others. A written OSU policy established most of the campus as a public forum. The Ninth Circuit held that university constraints on free speech in the campus public forum were subject to the most stringent scrutiny. It held that the university's "standardless policy" unconstitutionally, purposefully and arbitrarily singled out the independent newspaper.

Some university administrators try to influence the content of student media by pressuring faculty or staff advisers. In a recent example, the top editors of the University of Georgia's student newspaper resigned en masse, claiming nonstudent managers hired to oversee The Red and Black had interfered with their editorial autonomy.[216] A memo on content guidelines circulating among the paper's publishing board questioned the journalistic value of "content that catches people or organizations doing bad things." Within days of the student walkout, the university reiterated its support of student control of content and reinstated the student editors.[217]

In an earlier fight over university student newspaper content, a federal district court ruled that the First Amendment did not prohibit Kansas State University from removing and reassigning the adviser of The Collegian.[218] The adviser was dismissed amid controversy over the newspaper's coverage of campus diversity issues and events.[219] Student editors and the adviser sued, claiming that the adviser's removal was unconstitutional censorship. The head of the journalism school said a content analysis of the newspaper supported the adviser's removal,[220] and university administrators said budget concerns drove the decision.[221]

Professional Standards and Student Speech

Several court decisions establish greater latitude for colleges to punish speech by students. In *Tatro v. University of Minnesota*, the Minnesota Supreme Court upheld university sanctions on a student for "satirical commentary and violent fantasy" she posted on Facebook about a school cadaver.[222] Students in anatomy lab were required to sign a policy that allowed only "respectful and discreet" comments about cadavers. On Facebook, the student said she liked working with cadavers because it provided opportunity for "lots of aggression to be taken out" with an embalming knife that she wanted to use to "stab a certain someone in the throat."[223] In response, the student received an F in the lab, was placed on probation and was required to have a psychiatric examination. She sued, arguing that the sanctions violated her freedom of speech.[224] The university said it had authority to regulate any student speech "reasonably related to legitimate pedagogical concerns."

Rather than rely on established tests to review the case, the state supreme court held that the university's action did not violate the First Amendment because the rules were "narrowly tailored and directly related to established professional conduct standards."[225] The court said the core mission of the university program was to instill professional standards of ethics and behavior in its students.[226] Therefore, the university could "constitutionally regulate off-campus conduct that violate[s] specific professional obligations," although it could not "regulate a student's personal expression at any time, in any place, for any claimed curriculum-based reason."[227]

Although the Minnesota court in *Tatro* emphasized the narrowness of its ruling, a growing number of federal appeals courts has upheld the authority of colleges to punish or even expel college students, especially graduate students, for speech that violates the "professional standards" of their chosen field.[228] These courts recognize that greater latitude is provided to college student speech than to the free expression of less mature students[229] but split on whether to apply *Hazelwood* to these university speech cases.[230]

In the mid-1960s, Mario Savio, leader of the Berkeley Free Speech Movement, participates in massive student protests at the University of California, Berkeley that set off the free speech movement nationwide.

AP Photo/Robert W. Klein

The Ninth Circuit Court of Appeals also crafted its own test to review sanctions on university student speech related to professional standards. In *Oyama v. University of Hawaii*, the Ninth Circuit affirmed the constitutionality of the university's effective expulsion of a student based on his unprofessional and inappropriate speech.[231] The student was denied a student teacher placement because he made disparaging remarks about students with disabilities and said he favored consensual sexual relations with children. The student sued, saying the punishment violated his First Amendment rights.

The Ninth Circuit said *Hazelwood* did not apply.[232] It relied heavily on *Tatro* and found the university's punishment constitutional because it "related directly to defined and established professional standards, was narrowly tailored to serve the University's foundational mission of evaluating [student] suitability for teaching and reflected reasonable professional judgment."[233]

The Eighth Circuit Court of Appeals relied squarely on *Hazelwood* in deciding *Keefe v. Adams*.[234] After Craig Keefe posted angry comments on Facebook that made a fellow nursing student "extremely uncomfortable and nervous," school administrators removed Keefe from the nursing program for "behavior unbecoming of the profession and transgression of professional boundaries."[235] Turning *Hazelwood* on its head, the Eighth Circuit said a "university may have an even stronger interest in the content of its curriculum and imposing academic discipline than did the high school at issue in Hazelwood."[236] The court ruled that "college administrators and educators in a professional school have discretion to require compliance with recognized standards of the profession, both on and off campus, so long as their actions are reasonably related to legitimate pedagogical concerns."[237]

The Supreme Court denied certiorari in *Keefe*,[238] allowing this and other rulings to stand that "leave[] college students with diminished free-speech protection in all forums . . . if their speech can be deemed unprofessional" even when it does not substantially disrupt school activities,[239] according to experts.

Speech Codes

In what some call a concession to political correctness[240] and others consider an important step toward a more safe, tolerant and inclusive society,[241] universities across the United States began adopting and strengthening campus speech codes in the 1980s.[242] The codes vary widely but generally prohibit harassment, bigotry and discrimination on campus. Courts found the speech codes that targeted offensive or disfavored speech unconstitutional because they reduced exchange of ideas based on content.[243] As one federal district court wrote, "The Supreme Court has consistently held that statutes punishing speech or conduct solely on the grounds that they are unseemly or offensive are unconstitutionally overbroad."[244] Nonetheless, campus hate speech codes continue to be adopted.[245] The universities argue that the codes are essential to protect civil discourse and advance their educational missions.

More recently, universities have revised and adopted anti-discrimination and anti-harassment policies that may implicate free speech.[246] The rules implement federal Title VII civil rights prohibitions against workplace harassment, hostile work environments[247] and discrimination.[248] In one case, the University of Wisconsin defended its Design for Diversity by asserting that Title VII required it to regulate hostile academic environments. The federal district court disagreed and held that Title VII does not supersede the First Amendment.[249] The University of Michigan recently settled a suit challenging the school's harassment and bullying policies. The University agreed to revise the definition of terms used in the policies and abolish its Bias Response Team online resource which allowed students to file a report if they felt affected by "incidents of bias."[250]

Faculty language that provokes student protest and outrage has led some universities to examine the boundary between faculty First Amendment freedoms and university priorities to provide a setting conducive to education and equity for all.[251] In 2021, the University of Rochester suspended a professor for his repeated use of the n-word in a class discussion about whether the term should be used in in academic contexts.[252] That same year, Columbia University declined to punish a professor for using the word while quoting a scene from the film "8 Mile."[253] Legal scholars Randall Kennedy and Eugene Volokh have raised concerns about how making certain words taboo infringes on educators' right to free expression, as well as their academic freedom.[254] Other academics have condemned the use of slurs in the classroom noting that there is usually little benefit to using racial epithets and the fact that students find the comments offensive is reason enough in most cases not to use them.[255]

EMERGING LAW

In the past, the U.S. Supreme Court has said students' free speech rights prevented schools from removing books from the school library simply because someone might find them offensive.[256] Over the objections of a library review committee, a school board removed 10 books from school libraries because some board members found them "objectionable," "anti-American, anti-Christian, anti-[Semitic] and just plain filthy."[257] Several students sued, and the Supreme Court said the book removal violated the First Amendment.

Although K–12 schools must ensure that curriculum is age appropriate and of good quality, schools may not constitutionally remove library books to placate a hypersensitive few. When the readings are optional, individual student freedom of choice prevails. The Court said that "access [to controversial materials] prepares students for active and effective participation in the pluralistic, often contentious society in which they will soon be adult members."[258] Decisions to remove books may not be made "in a narrowly partisan or political manner"[259] and are more likely to be constitutional if they advance a curricular purpose.

Despite the Supreme Court's position on this issue, efforts to remove books, particularly those with themes focused on anti-racism, anti-Semitism and LGBTQ issues, have increased in recent years. For example, in 2022, a Tennessee school board voted unanimously to remove the Pulitzer prize winning Holocaust novel, *Maus*, from its curriculum.[260] In Pennsylvania, student protests convinced the Central York School Board to reverse its decision to ban anti-racism books and other resources, which included a children's book about Rosa Parks, Malala Yousafzai's autobiography, and CNN's Sesame Street town hall on racism.[261]

A school board in Tennesse adopted an order to remove the graphic novel "Maus" by Art Spiegelman from school libraries

The removal of anti-racist resources in schools is part of a larger trend among school boards and state legislatures to ban the teaching of critical race theory (CRT). Critical race theory originated in the 1970s as a legal framework to explore the racial inequities and differential outcomes that persisted after the civil rights movement. Legal scholars like Derek Bell, Kimberlé Crenshaw and Richard Delgado began writing about how racism was embedded into laws and policies which shape social institutions ranging from the criminal justice system to the education system to the housing market. Critical race theory does not blame white people for the past but asks them to share the responsibility for dismantling these oppressive systems. Critical race theory is generally taught to students in law or graduate school.

In 2021, the term critical race theory was co-opted by political pundits to challenge the teaching of anti-racist concepts and ideas such as white privilege or implicit bias in U.S. classrooms. To date, 14 states have passed laws that prohibit discussion or trainings that suggest that the U.S. is inherently racist, as well as any discussions about conscious and unconscious bias, privilege, discrimination and oppression. Dozens of other states have introduced or plan to introduce similar legislation. State school boards in Florida, Georgia, Utah and Alabama have also introduced new guidelines barring CRT-related discussions. Florida, has passed a law that limits discussion of LGBTQ issues in schools.[262]

Proponents of this type of legislation claim that it gives parents more control over what their children are taught in school. Opponents, however, fear that it creates a **chilling effect** on what educators are willing to discuss in the classroom and further marginalizes racial minorities and members of the LGBTQ community.[263]

KEYTERMS

as applied

chilling effect

clear and present danger

fighting words

hate speech

incorporation doctrine

negligence

proximate cause

true threat

underinclusive

viewpoint-based discrimination

CASES FOR STUDY
THINKING ABOUT THEM

The two case excerpts that follow highlight the U.S. Supreme Court's attempts to balance the First Amendment freedom of speech with concerns for educational goals and personal safety. Both cases help identify the parameters of First Amendment protection: The first, *Mahanoy*, clarifies when schools might constitutionally regulate students' speech on social media. The second, *Elonis*, helps define when words that express ideas, even in artistic form, may lose constitutional protection because they threaten others and engender fear.

- Consider what each decision, as well as the two taken together, demonstrates about the different categories of speech in the U.S. Supreme Court's jurisprudence.
- In these two decisions defining the extent of First Amendment freedoms, does the Supreme Court focus on the nature of the speech, the intent of the law, the impact of the regulation, or something else to reach its conclusion?
- To what extent does the Supreme Court's decision in *Mahanoy* turn on the category of speech, the type of speaker, the location of speech, or other factors involved?
- Does *Elonis* provide a workable definition of true threats and a clear test to determine when such speech is unprotected?

MAHANOY AREA SCHOOL DISTRICT V. B.L.
SUPREME COURT OF THE UNITED STATES 594 US (2021)

JUSTICE BREYER delivered the Court's opinion:

A public high school student used, and transmitted to her Snapchat friends, vulgar language and gestures criticizing both the school and the school's cheerleading team. The student's speech took place outside of school hours and away from the school's campus. In response, the school suspended the student for a year from the cheerleading team. We must decide whether the Court of Appeals for the Third Circuit correctly held that the school's decision violated the First Amendment. Although we do not agree with the reasoning of the Third Circuit panel's majority, we do agree with its conclusion that the school's disciplinary action violated the First Amendment.

B. L. (who, together with her parents, is a respondent in this case) was a student at Mahanoy Area High School, a public school in Mahanoy City, Pennsylvania. At the end of her freshman year, B. L. tried out for a position on the school's varsity cheerleading squad and for right fielder on a private softball team. She did not make the varsity cheerleading team or get her preferred softball position, but she was offered a spot on the cheerleading squad's junior varsity team. B. L. did not accept the coach's decision with good grace, particularly because the squad coaches had placed an entering freshman on the varsity team.

That weekend, B. L. and a friend visited the Cocoa Hut, a local convenience store. There, B. L. used her smartphone to post two photos on Snapchat, a social media application that allows users to post photos and videos that disappear after a set period of time. B. L. posted the images to her Snapchat "story," a feature of the application that allows any person in the user's "friend" group (B. L. had about 250 "friends") to view the images for a 24 hour period.

The first image B. L. posted showed B. L. and a friend with middle fingers raised; it bore the caption: "Fuck school fuck softball fuck cheer fuck everything." The second image was blank but for a caption, which read: "Love how me and [another student] get told we need a year of jv before we make varsity but tha[t] doesn't matter to anyone else?" The caption also contained an upside-down smiley-face emoji.

B. L.'s Snapchat "friends" included other Mahanoy Area High School students, some of whom also belonged to the cheerleading squad. At least one of them, using a separate cellphone, took pictures of B. L.'s posts and shared them with other members of the cheerleading squad. One of the students who received these photos showed them to her mother (who was a cheerleading squad coach), and the images spread. That week, several cheerleaders and other students approached the cheerleading coaches "visibly upset" about B. L.'s posts. Questions about the posts persisted during an Algebra class taught by one of the two coaches.

After discussing the matter with the school principal, the coaches decided that because the posts used profanity in connection with a school extracurricular activity, they violated team and school rules. As a result, the coaches suspended B. L. from the junior varsity cheerleading squad for the upcoming year. B. L.'s subsequent apologies did not move school officials. The school's athletic director, principal, superintendent, and school board, all affirmed B. L.'s suspension from the team. In response, B. L., together with her parents, filed this lawsuit in Federal District Court. . .

. . . We have made clear that students do not "shed their constitutional rights to freedom of speech or expression," even "at the school house gate." But we have also made clear that courts must apply the First Amendment "in light of the special characteristics of the school environment." One such characteristic, which we have stressed, is the fact that schools at times stand in loco parentis, i.e., in the place of parents.

This Court has previously outlined three specific categories of student speech that schools may regulate in certain circumstances: (1) "indecent," "lewd," or "vulgar" speech uttered during a school assembly on school grounds, speech, uttered during a class trip, that promotes "illegal drug use," and (3) speech that others may reasonably perceive as "bear[ing] the imprimatur of the school," such as that appearing in a school-sponsored newspaper.

Finally, in Tinker, we said schools have a special interest in regulating speech that "materially disrupts classwork or involves substantial disorder or invasion of the rights of others." These special characteristics call for special leeway when schools regulate speech that occurs under its supervision.

Unlike the Third Circuit, we do not believe the special characteristics that give schools additional license to regulate student speech always disappear when a school regulates speech that takes place off campus. The school's regulatory interests remain significant in some off-campus circumstances. The parties' briefs, and those of amici, list several types of off-campus behavior that may call for school regulation. These include serious or severe bullying or harassment targeting particular individuals; threats aimed at teachers or other students; the failure to follow rules concerning lessons, the writing of papers, the use of computers, or participation in other online school activities; and breaches of school security devices, including material maintained within school computers.

Even B. L. herself and the amici supporting her would redefine the Third Circuit's off-campus/on-campus distinction, treating as on campus: all times when the school is responsible for the student; the school's immediate surroundings; travel en route to and from the school; all speech taking place over school laptops or on a school's website; speech taking place during remote learning; activities taken for school credit; and communications to school email accounts or phones. And it may be that speech related to extracurricular activities, such as team sports, would also receive special treatment under B. L.'s proposed rule.

We are uncertain as to the length or content of any such list of appropriate exceptions or carveouts to the Third Circuit majority's rule. That rule, basically, if not entirely, would deny the off-campus applicability of Tinker's highly general statement about the nature of a school's special interests. Particularly given the advent of computer-based learning, we hesitate to determine precisely which of many school-related off-campus activities belong on such a list. Neither do we now know how such a list might vary, depending upon a student's age, the nature of the school's off-campus activity, or the impact upon the school itself. Thus, we do not now set forth a broad, highly general First Amendment rule stating just what counts as "off campus" speech and whether or how ordinary First Amendment standards must give way off campus to a school's special need to prevent, e.g., substantial disruption of learning-related activities or the protection of those who make up a school community.

We can, however, mention three features of off-campus speech that often, even if not always, distinguish schools' efforts to regulate that speech from their efforts to regulate on-campus speech. Those features diminish the strength of the unique educational characteristics that might call for special First Amendment leeway.

First, a school, in relation to off-campus speech, will rarely stand in loco parentis. The doctrine of in loco parentis treats school administrators as standing in the place of students' parents under circumstances where the children's actual parents cannot protect, guide, and discipline them. Geographically speaking, off-campus speech will normally fall within the zone of parental, rather than school-related, responsibility.

Second, from the student speaker's perspective, regulations of off-campus speech, when coupled with regulations of on-campus speech, include all the speech a student utters during the full 24-hour day. That means courts must be more skeptical of a school's efforts to regulate off-campus speech, for doing so may mean the student cannot engage in that kind of speech at all. When it comes to political or religious speech that occurs outside school or a school program or activity, the school will have a heavy burden to justify intervention.

Third, the school itself has an interest in protecting a student's unpopular expression, especially when the expression takes place off campus. America's public schools are the nurseries of democracy. Our representative democracy only works if we protect the "marketplace of ideas." This free exchange facilitates an informed public opinion, which, when transmitted to lawmakers, helps produce laws that reflect the People's will. That protection must include the protection of unpopular ideas, for popular ideas have less need for protection. Thus, schools have a strong interest in ensuring that future generations understand the working in practice of the well-known aphorism, "I disapprove of what you say, but I will defend to the death your right to say it." (Although this quote is often attributed to Voltaire, it was likely coined by an English writer, Evelyn Beatrice Hall.)

Given the many different kinds of off-campus speech, the different potential school-related and circumstance-specific justifications, and the differing extent to which those justifications may call for First Amendment leeway, we can, as a general matter, say little more than this: Taken together, these three features of much off-campus speech mean that the leeway the First Amendment grants to schools in light of their special characteristics is diminished. We leave for future cases to decide where, when, and how these features mean the speaker's off-campus location will make the critical difference. This case can, however, provide one example. . .

Although we do not agree with the reasoning of the Third Circuit's panel majority, for the reasons expressed above, resembling those of the panel's concurring opinion, we nonetheless agree that the school violated B. L.'s First Amendment rights. The judgment of the Third Circuit is therefore affirmed.

It is so ordered.

JUSTICE ALITO, with whom JUSTICE GORSUCH joins, concurring:

. . . There are more than 90,000 public school principals in this country and more than 13,000 separate school districts. The overwhelming majority of school administrators, teachers, and coaches are men and women who are deeply dedicated to the best interests of their students, but it is predictable that there will be occasions when some will get carried away, as did the school officials in the case at hand. If today's decision teaches any lesson, it must be that the regulation of many types of off-premises student speech raises serious First Amendment concerns, and school officials should proceed cautiously before venturing into this territory.

JUSTICE THOMAS, dissenting:

Disregarding these important issues, the majority simply posits three vague considerations and reaches an outcome.

A more searching review reveals that schools historically could discipline students in circumstances like those presented here. Because the majority does not attempt to explain why we should not apply this historical rule and does not attempt to tether its approach to anything stable, I respectfully dissent. . . .

The Court transparently takes a common-law approach to today's decision. In effect, it states just one rule: Schools can regulate speech less often when that speech occurs off campus. It then identifies this case as an "example" and "leav[es] for future cases" the job of developing this new common-law doctrine. But the Court's foundation is untethered from anything stable, and courts (and schools) will almost certainly be at a loss as to what exactly the Court's opinion today means.

Perhaps there are good constitutional reasons to depart from the historical rule, and perhaps this Court and lower courts will identify and explain these reasons in the future. But because the Court does not do so today, and because it reaches the wrong result under the appropriate historical test, I respectfully dissent.

ELONIS V. UNITED STATES

SUPREME COURT OF THE UNITED STATES 135 S. CT. 2001 (2015)

CHIEF JUSTICE JOHN ROBERTS delivered the Court's opinion:

Federal law makes it a crime to transmit in interstate commerce "any communication containing any threat . . . to injure the person of another." 18 U. S. C. § 875(c). Petitioner was convicted of violating this provision under instructions that required the jury to find that he communicated what a reasonable person would regard as a threat. The question is whether the statute also requires that the defendant be aware of the threatening nature of the communication, and—if not—whether the First Amendment requires such a showing.

Anthony Douglas Elonis was an active user of the social networking web site Facebook. . . . . In May 2010, Elonis' wife of nearly seven years left him, [and] . . . Elonis began "listening to more violent music" and posting self-styled "rap" lyrics . . . [that] included graphically violent language and imagery. This material was often interspersed with disclaimers that the lyrics were "fictitious," with no intentional "resemblance to real persons." Elonis posted an explanation to another Facebook user that "I'm doing this for me. My writing is therapeutic."

Elonis' co-workers and friends viewed the posts in a different light. Around Halloween of 2010, Elonis posted a photograph of himself and a co-worker at a "Halloween Haunt" event at the amusement park where they worked. In the photograph, Elonis was holding a toy knife against his co-worker's neck, and in the caption Elonis wrote, "I wish." . . . [The] chief of park security was a Facebook "friend" of Elonis, saw the photograph, and fired him.

In response, Elonis posted a new entry on his Facebook page:

"Moles! Didn't I tell y'all I had several? Y'all sayin' I had access to keys for all the f***in' gates. That I have sinister plans for all my friends and must have taken home a couple. Y'all think it's too dark and foggy to secure your facility from a man as mad as me? You see, even without a paycheck, I'm still the main attraction. Whoever thought the Halloween Haunt could be so f***in' scary?" . . .

Elonis' posts frequently included crude, degrading, and violent material about his soon-to-be ex-wife. Shortly after he was fired, Elonis posted an adaptation of a satirical sketch that he and his wife had watched together. In the actual sketch, called "It's Illegal to Say . . .," a comedian explains that it is illegal for a person to say he wishes to kill the President, but not illegal to explain that it is illegal for him to say that. When Elonis posted the script of the sketch, however, he substituted his wife for the President. The posting was part of the basis for Count Two of the indictment, threatening his wife:

"Hi, I'm Tone Elonis.

Did you know that it's illegal for me to say I want to kill my wife? . . .

It's one of the only sentences that I'm not allowed to say. . . .

Now it was okay for me to say it right then because I was just telling you that it's illegal for me to say I want to kill my wife. . . .

Um, but what's interesting is that it's very illegal to say I really, really think someone out there should kill my wife. . . .

But not illegal to say with a mortar launcher.

Because that's its own sentence. . . .

I also found out that it's incredibly illegal, extremely illegal to go on Facebook and say something like the best place to fire a mortar launcher at her house would be from the cornfield behind it because of easy access to a getaway road and you'd have a clear line of sight through the sun room. . . .

Yet even more illegal to show an illustrated diagram [of the house]. . . ."

The details about the home were accurate. At the bottom of the post, Elonis included a link to the video of the original skit, and wrote, "Art is about pushing limits. I'm willing to go to jail for my Constitutional rights. Are you?"

After viewing some of Elonis' posts, his wife felt "extremely afraid for [her] life." A state court granted her a three-year protection-from-abuse order against Elonis (essentially, a restraining order). Elonis referred to the order in another post on his "Tone Dougie" page, also included in Count Two of the indictment:

"Fold up your [protection-from-abuse order] and put it in your pocket.

Is it thick enough to stop a bullet?

Try to enforce an Order

that was improperly granted in the first place

Me thinks the Judge needs an education

on true threat jurisprudence

And prison time 'll add zeros to my settlement . . .

And if worse comes to worse

I've got enough explosives to take care of the State Police and the Sheriff's Department."

At the bottom of this post was a link to the Wikipedia article on "Freedom of speech." . . . That same month, . . . Elonis posted [this] entry . . .:

"That's it, I've had about enough

I'm checking out and making a name for myself

Enough elementary schools in a ten mile radius to initiate the most heinous school shooting ever imagined

And hell hath no fury like a crazy man in a Kindergarten class

The only question is . . . which one?"

A grand jury indicted Elonis for making threats to injure . . . in violation of 18 U. S. C. §875(c). In the District Court, Elonis moved to dismiss the indictment for failing to allege that he had intended to threaten anyone. The District Court denied the motion, holding that Third Circuit precedent required only that Elonis "intentionally made the communication, not that he intended to make a threat." At trial, Elonis testified that his posts emulated the rap lyrics of the well-known performer Eminem . . . In Elonis' view, he had posted "nothing . . . that hasn't been said already." The Government presented as witnesses Elonis' wife and co-workers, all of whom said they felt afraid and viewed Elonis' posts as serious threats.

Elonis requested a jury instruction that "the government must prove that he intended to communicate a true threat." The District Court denied that request. The jury instructions instead informed the jury that

> "A statement is a true threat when a defendant intentionally makes a statement in a context or under such circumstances wherein a reasonable person would foresee that the statement would be interpreted by those to whom the maker communicates the statement as a serious expression of an intention to inflict bodily injury or take the life of an individual."

The Government's closing argument emphasized that it was irrelevant whether Elonis intended the postings to be threats—"it doesn't matter what he thinks." A jury convicted Elonis . . . [and] sentenced [him] to three years, eight months' imprisonment and three years' supervised release.

Elonis renewed his challenge to the jury instructions in the Court of Appeals, contending that the jury should have been required to find that he intended his posts to be threats. The Court of Appeals disagreed, holding that the intent required by Section 875(c) is only the intent to communicate words that the defendant understands, and that a reasonable person would view as a threat.

We granted certiorari.

. . . This statute requires that a communication be transmitted and that the communication contain a threat. It does not specify that the defendant must have any mental state with respect to these elements. In particular, it does not indicate whether the defendant must intend that his communication contain a threat.

Elonis argues that the word "threat" itself in Section 875(c) imposes such a requirement. According to Elonis, every definition of "threat" or "threaten" conveys the notion of an intent to inflict harm. . . . For its part, the Government argues that Section 875(c) should be read in light of its neighboring provisions . . . [that] expressly include a mental state requirement of an "intent to extort." According to the Government, the[se] express "intent to extort" requirements . . . should preclude courts from implying an unexpressed "intent to threaten" requirement in Section 875(c).

. . . The most we can conclude from the language of Section 875(c) and its neighboring provisions is that Congress meant to proscribe a broad class of threats in Section 875(c), but did not identify what mental state, if any, a defendant must have to be convicted. . . .

The fact that the statute does not specify any required mental state, however, does not mean that none exists. We have repeatedly held that "mere omission from a criminal enactment of any mention of criminal intent" should not be read "as dispensing with it." This rule of construction reflects the basic principle that "wrongdoing must be conscious to be criminal." . . . The "central thought" is that a defendant must be "blameworthy in mind" before he can be found guilty. . . . Although there are exceptions, the "general rule" is that a guilty mind is "a necessary element in the indictment and proof of every crime." We therefore generally "interpret[] criminal statutes to include broadly applicable scienter requirements, even where the statute by its terms does not contain them."

This is not to say that a defendant must know that his conduct is illegal before he may be found guilty. The familiar maxim "ignorance of the law is no excuse" typically holds true. Instead, our cases have explained that a defendant generally must "know the facts that make his conduct fit the definition of the offense," even if he does not know that those facts give rise to a crime. . . .

[I]n *United States v. X-Citement Video* (1994), we considered a statute criminalizing the distribution of visual depictions of minors engaged in sexually explicit conduct. We rejected a reading of the statute which would have required only that a defendant knowingly send the prohibited materials, regardless of whether he knew the age of the performers. We held instead that a defendant must also know that those depicted were minors, because that was "the crucial element separating legal innocence from wrongful conduct."

When interpreting federal criminal statutes that are silent on the required mental state, we read into the statute "only that *mens rea* which is necessary to separate wrongful conduct from 'otherwise innocent conduct.'" . . .

Section 875(c), as noted, requires proof that a communication was transmitted and that it contained a threat. . . . The parties agree that a defendant under Section 875(c) must know that he is transmitting a communication. But communicating *something* is not what makes the conduct "wrongful." Here "the crucial element separating legal innocence from wrongful conduct" is the threatening nature of the communication. The mental state requirement must therefore apply to the fact that the communication contains a threat.

Elonis' conviction, however, was premised solely on how his posts would be understood by a reasonable person. Such a "reasonable person" standard is a familiar feature of civil liability in tort law, but is inconsistent with "the conventional requirement for criminal conduct—*awareness* of some wrongdoing." Having liability turn on whether a "reasonable person" regards the communication as a threat—regardless of what the defendant thinks—"reduces culpability on the all-important element of the crime to negligence," and we "have long been reluctant to infer that a negligence standard was intended in criminal statutes." Under these principles, "what [Elonis] thinks" does matter.

The Government is at pains to characterize its position as something other than a negligence standard, emphasizing that its approach would require proof that a defendant "comprehended [the] contents and context" of the communication. . . . Elonis can be convicted, the Government contends, if he himself knew the contents and context of his posts, and a reasonable person would have recognized that the posts would be read as genuine threats. That is a negligence standard.

In light of the foregoing, Elonis' conviction cannot stand. The jury was instructed that the Government need prove only that a reasonable person would regard Elonis' communications as threats, and that was error. Federal criminal liability generally does not turn solely on the results of an act without considering the defendant's mental state. That understanding "took deep and early root in American soil" and Congress left it intact here: Under Section 875(c), "wrongdoing must be conscious to be criminal." . . .

Our holding makes clear that negligence is not sufficient to support a conviction under Section 875(c), contrary to the view of nine Courts of Appeals. . . . The judgment of the United States Court of Appeals for the Third Circuit is reversed, and the case is remanded for further proceedings consistent with this opinion.

It is so ordered.

JUSTICE ALITO, concurring in part and dissenting in part:

. . . The Court's disposition of this case is certain to cause confusion and serious problems. . . . The Court holds that the jury instructions in this case were defective because they required only negligence in conveying a threat. But the Court refuses to explain what type of intent was necessary. Did the jury need to find that Elonis had the *purpose* of conveying a true threat? Was it enough if he *knew* that his words conveyed such a threat? Would *recklessness* suffice? The Court declines to say. Attorneys and judges are left to guess. . . .

This Court has not defined the meaning of the term "threat" in §875(c), but in construing the same term in a related statute, the Court distinguished a "true 'threat'" from facetious or hyperbolic remarks. In my view, the term "threat" in §875(c) can fairly be defined as a statement that is reasonably interpreted as "an expression of an intention to inflict evil, injury, or damage on another." Conviction under §875(c) demands proof that the defendant's transmission was in fact a threat, *i.e.*, that it is reasonable to interpret the transmission as an expression of an intent to harm another. In addition, it must be shown that the defendant was at least reckless as to whether the transmission met that requirement. . . . I would hold that a defendant may be convicted under §875(c) if he or she consciously disregards the risk that the communication transmitted will be interpreted as a true threat. . . .

There remains the question whether interpreting §875(c) to require no more than recklessness with respect to the element at issue here would violate the First Amendment. . . .

Elonis argues that the First Amendment protects a threat if the person making the statement does not actually intend to cause harm. . . .

Elonis also claims his threats were constitutionally protected works of art. Words like his, he contends, are shielded by the First Amendment because they are similar to words uttered by rappers and singers in public performances and recordings. . . . But context matters. "Taken in context," lyrics in songs that are performed for an audience or sold in recorded form are unlikely to be interpreted as a real threat to a real person. Statements on social media that are pointedly directed at their victims, by contrast, are much more likely to be taken seriously. . . .

Threats of violence and intimidation are among the most favored weapons of domestic abusers, and the rise of social media has only made those tactics more commonplace. A fig leaf of artistic expression cannot convert such hurtful, valueless threats into protected speech. . . .

We have sometimes cautioned that it is necessary to "exten[d] a measure of strategic protection" to otherwise unprotected false statements of fact in order to ensure enough "'breathing space'" for protected speech. A similar argument might be made with respect to threats. But we have also held that the law provides adequate breathing space when it requires proof that false statements were made with reckless disregard of their falsity. Requiring proof of recklessness is similarly sufficient here.

Finally, because the jury instructions in this case did not require proof of recklessness, I would vacate the judgment below and remand for the Court of Appeals to decide in the first instance whether Elonis' conviction could be upheld under a recklessness standard.

JUSTICE THOMAS, dissenting:

We granted certiorari to resolve a conflict in the lower courts over the appropriate mental state for threat prosecutions under 18 U. S. C. §875(c). . . . Rather than resolve the conflict, the Court casts aside the approach used in nine Circuits and leaves nothing in its place.

Lower courts are thus left to guess at the appropriate mental state for §875(c). All they know after today's decision is that a requirement of general intent will not do. But they can safely infer that a majority of this Court would not adopt an intent-to-threaten requirement, as the opinion carefully leaves open the possibility that recklessness may be enough.

This failure to decide throws everyone from appellate judges to everyday Facebook users into a state of uncertainty. . . . Because the Court of Appeals properly applied the general-intent standard, and because the communications transmitted by Elonis were "true threats" unprotected by the First Amendment, I would affirm the judgment below. . . .

Because §875(c) criminalizes speech, the First Amendment requires that the term "threat" be limited to a narrow class of historically unprotected communications called "true threats." To qualify as a true threat, a communication must be a serious expression of an intention to commit unlawful physical violence, not merely "political hyperbole"; "vehement, caustic, and sometimes unpleasantly sharp attacks"; or "vituperative, abusive, and inexact" statements. It also cannot be determined solely by the reaction of the recipient, but must instead be "determined by the interpretation of a *reasonable* recipient familiar with the context of the communication," lest historically protected speech be suppressed at the will of an eggshell observer. There is thus no dispute that, at a minimum, §875(c) requires an objective showing: The communication must be one that "a reasonable observer would construe as a true threat to another." And there is no dispute that the posts at issue here meet that objective standard. . . .

Our default rule in favor of general intent applies with full force to criminal statutes addressing speech. Well over 100 years ago, this Court considered a conviction under a federal obscenity statute that punished anyone "'who shall knowingly deposit, or cause to be deposited, for mailing or delivery,'" any "'obscene, lewd, or lascivious book, pamphlet, picture, paper, writing, print, or other publication of an indecent character.'" In that case, as here, the defendant argued that, even if "he may have had . . . actual knowledge or notice of [the paper's] contents" when he put it in the mail, he could not "be convicted of the offence . . . unless he knew or believed that such paper could be properly or justly characterized as obscene, lewd, and lascivious." The Court rejected that theory . . .

Applying ordinary rules of statutory construction, I would read §875(c) to require proof of general intent. To "know the facts that make his conduct illegal" under §875(c), a defendant must know that he transmitted a communication in interstate or foreign commerce that contained a threat. . . . A defendant like Elonis, however, who admits that he "knew that what [he] was saying was violent" but supposedly "just wanted to express [him]self," acted with the general intent required under §875(c), even if he did not know that a jury would conclude that his communication constituted a "threat" as a matter of law. . . .

Requiring general intent in this context is not the same as requiring mere negligence. . . . [T]he defendant must *know*—not merely be reckless or negligent with respect to the fact—that he is committing the acts that constitute the . . . offense.

But general intent requires *no* mental state (not even a negligent one) concerning the "fact" that certain words meet the *legal* definition of a threat. . . .

Elonis also insists that we read an intent-to-threaten element into §875(c) in light of the First Amendment. But our practice of construing statutes "to avoid constitutional questions . . . is not a license for the judiciary to rewrite language enacted by the legislature." . . .

Elonis does not contend that threats are constitutionally protected speech, nor could he: "From 1791 to the present, . . . our society . . . has permitted restrictions upon the content of speech in a few limited areas," true threats being one of them. Instead, Elonis claims that only *intentional* threats fall within this particular historical exception. . . .

Elonis also insists that our precedents require a mental state of intent when it comes to threat prosecutions under §875(c). . . .

We generally have not required a heightened mental state under the First Amendment for historically unprotected categories of speech. For instance, the Court has indicated that a legislature may constitutionally prohibit "'fighting words,' those personally abusive epithets which, when addressed to the ordinary citizen, are, as a matter of common knowledge, inherently likely to provoke violent reaction," without proof of an intent to provoke a violent reaction. Because the definition of "fighting words" turns on how the "ordinary citizen" would react to the language, this Court has observed that a defendant may be guilty of a breach of the peace if he "makes statements likely to provoke violence and disturbance of good order, even though no such eventuality be intended," and that the punishment of such statements "as a criminal act would raise no question under [the Constitution]." . . . I see no reason why we should give threats pride of place among unprotected speech.

Montgomery, Ala., police commissioner L.B. Sullivan (second from right) sued The New York Times for libel in the 1960s. The U.S. Supreme Court decision in *New York Times Co. v. Sullivan* is one of the most important legal cases in the history of U.S. constitutional law.

Bettmann/Getty Images

4 LIBEL AND EMOTIONAL DISTRESS

The Plaintiff's Case

Defamation law is intended to protect an individual's reputation. It allows people with besmirched reputations the opportunity to file claims against the responsible parties. People or companies may file claims to impugn or clear reputations, deter criticism, and retain defendant.

CHAPTER OUTLINE

A Brief History

The Elements of Libel: The Plaintiff's Case
Statement of Fact
Publication
Identification
Defamation
Falsity
Fault
Actual Malice

Emotional Distress

Intentional Infliction of Emotional Distress
Intentional or Reckless
Extreme and Outrageous
Severe Emotional Distress
Actual Malice
Matters of Public Concern

Negligent Infliction of Emotional Distress

Emerging Law

Cases for Study
- *New York Times Co. v. Sullivan*
- *Hustler Magazine, Inc. v. Falwell*

LEARNING OBJECTIVES

4.1   Review the brief history of libel law.

4.2   Apply the elements a plaintiff must prove to win a libel case.

4.3   Examine what may be considered emotional distress.

4.4   Explain the elements of intentional infliction of emotional distress.

4.5   Describe the elements of negligent infliction of emotional distress.

4.6   Consider how emerging law could change libel and emotional distress claims.

Defamation law is intended to protect an individual's reputation. It allows people who believe their reputations have been injured to file claims against the responsible parties. People or companies may file suits to attempt to repair reputations, deter criticism, and restrain defendants from making further defamatory comments. Plaintiffs often seek monetary **damages**. After a Kentucky teenager sought more than $500 million in damages from eight media defendants in 2020, CNN, NBC, and The Washington Post settled defamation suits addressing coverage of the teenager's encounter with an indigenous man that was recorded in a viral video.[1] A federal court granted five other media defendants' motions for summary judgment.[2] After the 2020 U.S. Presidential elections, voting machine companies also filed suits seeking more than a billion dollars from individuals and media organizations accused of harming the companies' reputations by challenging the fairness of the election.[3] For nearly 60 years, First Amendment precedent has made famous people and government leaders' defamation cases against media defendants hard to win. Two U.S. Supreme Court Justices, however, recently have indicated it may be time to reconsider that standard,[4] which also is applied in intentional infliction of emotional distress claims that famous people or government leaders file.

This chapter reviews the elements a plaintiff must prove to win defamation claims. This chapter also reviews what a plaintiff must prove to win an intentional or a negligent infliction of emotional distress claim.

The idea that a person's reputation is valuable and worth protecting is centuries old. Throughout the course of Western civilization, people have closely associated reputation with one's ability to participate in social and economic life.[5] Former U.S. Supreme Court Chief Justice William Rehnquist wrote that the rights of persons to protect their own reputation against unjustified and wrongful harm "reflects no more than our basic concept of the essential dignity and worth of every human being—a concept at the root of any decent system of ordered liberty."[6]

According to the U.S. Supreme Court, the common law of slander and libel is designed to achieve society's "pervasive and strong interest in preventing and redressing attacks upon reputation."[7] The challenge becomes "balanc[ing] the State's interest in compensating private individuals for injury to their reputation against the First Amendment interest in protecting this type of expression."[8]

One important consideration in libel claims is truth. Centuries ago, truthful statements that damaged reputation could be libelous. That is no longer the case. The U.S. Supreme Court recognizes that libel lawsuits may have chilling effects, deterring people from taking on risks of publishing information that could harm others' reputations. A libel plaintiff, the party who initiates lawsuits, thus, cannot recover damages from a media defendant without proving allegedly defamatory speech of public concern is false.[9]

The word "defamation" generally refers to false communication about another person that damages that person's reputation or brings them into disrepute. Both slander and libel are forms of defamation. Historically, people associated "slander" with spoken words that damage reputation and "libel" with written defamation. The laws governing each are similar but distinct. The distinction between libel and slander is largely an historical artifact. Slander lawsuits rarely emerge today because most spoken word claims arise in the context of mass media.

The general purpose of libel laws is to allow people who are defamed to restore their reputations. When a successful plaintiff is awarded damages, three objectives are served: The plaintiff is compensated for their reputational and other losses, the defendant is punished, and the defendant and others are discouraged from committing the same kind of libelous conduct in the future. Thus, a societal benefit may result, particularly if as much attention is given to setting the record straight as was given to the reputation-damaging remarks.

A BRIEF HISTORY

Western civilization's earliest recorded prosecution for reputation-damaging remarks is arguably the trial and execution of Socrates in 399 BCE. In response to charges of slandering Greek gods and corrupting Athens youth, the philosopher was brought before a public court. He admitted his "slanderous" teachings and, by a vote of 277 to 224, was found guilty. Socrates accepted his execution to dramatize the primacy of the life of the mind and the need for freedom of thought.[10]

The word "libel" means "little book" in Latin. The legal term comes from the ancient Roman practice of publishing booklets that one Roman used to defame another. Although ancient Greek as well as Roman law contributed to the development of libel law in Western societies, the English common law is where American libel law finds its most significant roots.

In 15th century England, one of two courts heard defamation complaints: the court of common law or the court of the Star Chamber. The court of the Star Chamber evolved from the meetings of the king's royal council. Established in 1487, it was named after the star painted on the ceiling of the room in which it met. In the early 1600s, the court of the Star Chamber declared libel a criminal offense because it tended to cause a breach of the peace. If the libel was "against a magistrate, or other public person, it [was] a greater offence."[11] The court of the Star Chamber generally viewed written defamation as more serious than spoken. Penalties for defamation included the possibility that the defamer "may be punished by fine and imprisonment, and if the case be exorbitant, by pillory and loss of his ears."[12] The Star Chamber was disbanded in 1641, and common law courts resumed their jurisdiction over defamation cases.[13]

Eighteenth-century English judge Sir William Blackstone and his "Commentaries on the Law of England" played a major role in the development of law in the United States. Libel law was no exception. Punishment for defamation was consistent with the concept of freedom of the press. A free press, Blackstone wrote, "consists in laying no previous restraints upon publications, and not in freedom from censure for criminal matter when published."[14] Anyone can express his sentiments to the public, he added, "but if he publishes what is improper, mischievous, or illegal, he must take the consequences of his own temerity."[15]

Those consequences were to take the form of damages. As a chief justice of the U.S. Supreme Court later described, "Defamation law developed not only as a means of allowing an individual to vindicate his good name, but also for the purpose of obtaining redress for harm caused by such statements."[16]

That legal principle was brought to the American colonies and into the states after independence. But England also provided America with legal theories that were less desirable in a republic committed to individual freedoms. Among them was the concept of seditious libel. At various times throughout American history, authorities have been especially sensitive to criticism of the government. In response, laws have been passed to criminalize such expression. For example, the **Sedition Act of 1798** made it a federal crime to write "any false, scandalous and malicious" statements against either the president or Congress.[17] Under the act, anyone "opposing or resisting any law of the United States, or any act of the President of the United States," could be imprisoned for up to two years. The act also made it illegal to "write, print, utter, or publish" anything that criticized the president or Congress. While the act permitted a defendant to escape penalty by proving the truth of the writing, and juries were permitted to decide critical questions of law and fact, the law was intended to silence critics of political powers.

Echoing Blackstone, John Marshall, chief justice of the United States between 1801 and 1835, defended the Sedition Act. He argued it was consistent with the First Amendment because it did not impose a prior restraint.[18] "It is known to all," he wrote, that those who publish libels or who "libel the government of the state" may "be both sued and indicted."[19] Among the act's opponents was James Madison, the principal author of the First Amendment: "It would seem a mockery to say that no laws should be passed preventing publications from being made, but that laws might be passed punishing them in case they should be made."[20] Madison and his supporters ultimately prevailed. The act expired in 1801.

Most state defamation statutes that criminalized publishing truthful statements about public officials subsequently have been found unconstitutional.[21] Some states still recognize criminal libel laws. In New Hampshire, persons may be found guilty of a misdemeanor if they purposely communicate to another person information they know is false and "know will tend to expose any other living person to public hatred, contempt or ridicule."[22] Robert Freese, a New Hampshire man, recently was charged twice with misdemeanor libel. First, he was arrested for a Craigslist post calling a life coach's business "a scam" and accusing the coach of "being involved in a road rage incident and distributing heroin." Freese pleaded guilty and was fined almost $1500. More recently, Freese was arrested after posting online that a retiring police officer was "the dirtiest" and "most corrupt cop" that Freese "had the displeasure of knowing." In the second case, charges were dropped after the state attorney general determined the police lacked evidence Freese made the statements with knowledge they were not true.[23]

In 2018, Freese filed a complaint stating the New Hampshire criminal libel law "violates the First Amendment because it criminalizes defamatory speech" and violates the Fourteenth Amendment due to vagueness. A district court dismissed the claim.[24] In 2022, a U.S. Court of Appeals for the First Circuit panel found the law did not violate the First Amendment because the U.S. Supreme Court has allowed criminalizing false statements made with **actual malice**, knowledge of falsity or reckless disregard for the truth.[25] The First Circuit panel also determined the law "provides reasonably clear guidelines" for its application, thus it was not vague. In fact, the law adopts the state common law defamation standards that have been applied in civil cases for more than a century.[26]

In a concurring opinion, Circuit Judge O. Rogeriee Thompson acknowledged the "troubling seditious-criminal-libel historical context" for criminal defamation laws. Thompson stated such laws "have their genesis in undemocratic systems that criminalized any speech criticizing public officials." Criminal defamation laws could be "weaponized by a person who disagrees with whatever speech has been uttered," Thomson wrote. These laws are susceptible to abuse, as they may be used to stiffle speech. Criminal defamation laws, thus, "cannot be reconciled with our democratic ideals of robust debate and uninhibited free speech." This is particularly true when criminal defamation laws are applied to punish defendants who lack money to pay damages in civil libel cases.[27] The following sections explore the elements of civil libel claims.

THE ELEMENTS OF LIBEL: THE PLAINTIFF'S CASE

Libel is a tort governed by state law, with some protection under the First Amendment, which is discussed later in this chapter. Just as defamation was recognized first as a harm committed by the spoken word and later as one that could also be committed through writing, the opportunities for libelous speech have increased exponentially with the development of communication technologies. Because of the ease and speed of communicating in today's digital age, possibilities for libel are on the rise.

Libel law serves to check the power of the media by opening its newsgathering and decision-making processes to public scrutiny and accountability. Although the best cure for bad speech may be more speech,[28] contemporary American society is often unwilling to rely only on corrective speech as a remedy for false and damaging statements to reputations. Libel law is one of the checks and balances in that process. The right of individuals to be secure in their reputations is weighed against the rights of others to be heard on issues of importance. Libel cases are emerging as means to address misinformation.[29]

Unlike in the era of common law libel, when the defendant was required to prove that a defamatory statement was true, the **burden of proof**—the requirement for a party to a case to demonstrate one or more claims by the presentation of evidence—is now on the **plaintiff**, the party who initiates a lawsuit.[30] To win, the plaintiff must prove that all of the required elements apply to the allegedly libelous material. Each of these elements requires definition and explanation.

POINTS OF LAW

THE PLAINTIFF'S LIBEL CASE

1. A statement of fact,
2. That is published,
3. That is of and concerning the plaintiff,
4. That is defamatory,
5. That is false,
6. That causes damage (or harm) and
7. For which the defendant is at fault.

Statement of Fact

To be libelous, a statement must make an **assertion of fact**, which may be proven true or false. In 2021, a U.S. Surgeon General Advisory statement recognized people have been exposed to facts, opinions, rumors, myths and misinformation about COVID-19. As people increasingly have turned to social media for information, correcting misinformation has grown more challenging. The statement recommended journalists provide more context and rely on a broader range of credible sources. The statement also recommended governments help people distinguish between facts and opinions.[31]

The dictionary defines a **fact** as "a piece of information presented as having objective reality"[32] and opinion as "a view, judgment or appraisal formed in the mind about a particular matter" or "a belief stronger than impression and less strong than positive knowledge."[33] Understanding the difference between fact and opinion is important because an expression of opinion cannot be libelous.

A federal district court in Illinois recently decided the title of a blogger's article about pet food did not contain allegations of fact. The title, "Caught Again," did not provide enough specificity to be considered a precise and verifiable fact. The headline was vague and hyperbolic. The article's assertion that the company "lost" that certification was considered opinion, an interpretation of the company's giving up that status in 2017. The court, however, allowed to proceed a claim addressing the blogger's misidentifying the manufacturer of cat food that consumers reported had made two cats sick.[34]

How can you tell the difference between fact and opinion? If you write that in October 2021 the U.S. unemployment rate was 4.6 percent, you are offering a precise assertion of fact that can be proven true or false. If you write that you think the U.S. unemployment rate is too high, that is opinion. Opinion is not libelous because an opinion cannot be false. Falsity is another requirement of the plaintiff's libel case. (The opinion defense is explained in detail in Chapter 5.) For now, it is enough to understand that whether material can be considered an expression of opinion requires a rigorous analysis.

Publication

For a statement to be libelous, the plaintiff must show that the statement was **published**, made to more than the plaintiff and defendant. To satisfy this standard, only one person in addition to the defendant and subject of the allegedly defamatory statement must have seen or heard the information in question. A group text message could meet this standard. When information is presented through mass media, including social media, publication is presumed.

Defamation law makes important distinctions between original publications and republications. The single publication rule indicates that printing or distributing multiple copies of a single edition of a newspaper, book or magazine or article in an online publication can only serve as the basis for one defamation claim.[35] The republication rule indicates that providing that same information in a new edition to a new audience may lead to a separate defamation claim.[36] The Sixth Circuit Court of Appeals explained "the test of whether a statement has been republished is if the speaker has affirmatively reiterated it in an attempt to reach a new audience that that statement's prior dissemination did not encompass."[37]

Republication

Repeating libelous information is as potentially harmful to someone's reputation as publishing it in the first place. Thus, the person who republishes can be held just as responsible as the originator. Republishing libelous information is seen as a new publication in the eyes of the law. This is true even when careful attribution occurs. The law's rationale is to prevent individuals or the media from freely committing defamation simply by attributing the libelous material to another source.

Context is key when determining whether publishing a hyperlink to an original piece may be considered a single publication or a **republication**.[38] In 2021, a Fourth Circuit Court of Appeals panel addressed this issue in a defamation case addressing false allegations that a Russian-born academic was a Russian spy who had an affair with a U.S. Army general. Two judges reasoned the republication rule did not apply to a New York Times hyperlink in one article to another New York Times article.[39] The hyperlink served as a reference for the newspaper's audience; "a mere hyperlink, without more, cannot constitute republication."[40] Dissenting in part, another judge reasoned that "context matters"; the hyperlink to a "provocative phrase" made the hyperlink more like "clickbait" intended to attract more people to read the original article.[41]

Also in 2021, a federal judge in New York indicated that the purpose for including a hyperlink in a newspaper article was not relevant when considering whether publishing a hyperlink should be considered republication of defamatory content. Simply using a hyperlink to call attention to an earlier article without restating defamatory content was not considered republication. In New York, "republication may occur when a publisher makes changes to material already published on a website, or add[s] substantive material to allegedly defamatory content on a website."[42]

On the other hand, in 2021, an Eighth Circuit Court of Appeals panel found a defamation complaint against a reporter and Hearst Magazine Media adequately alleged a tweeted hyperlink could constitute republication. The court reasoned that the complaint "sufficiently alleges" the reporter "presented material to a new audience," encouraging them to read an article about Congressman Devin Nunes. The reporter knew that article was the basis of a defamation claim when the reporter provided a hyperlink to the article in a tweet.[43] The Eighth Circuit declined to hear an appeal en banc.[44]

Rep. Devin Nunes sued Hearst Media and reporter Ryan Lizza, alleging that Lizza's Esquire Magazine article and tweet hurt his reputation.

J. Scott Applewhite/Associated Press

In an age of rapidly changing communication technologies, the republication rule could seem at odds with the wish to promote the free flow of ideas—a tenet of the First Amendment. Section 230 of the **Communications Decency Act**, the part of the 1996 Tele-communications Act that largely attempted to regulate internet content, the fair report privilege, the neutral reportage defense and the wire service defense, all discussed in Chapter 5, confront this issue.

Vendors and Distributors. Publisher liability in libel is determined by whether publishers are or should be aware of the material they disseminate, possibly including a presumption that they have read and edited the content. To prove publication, a libel plaintiff must show not just that libelous material was published; the plaintiff must also identify a specific person, group, or business responsible for the publication. Among those who are granted a republication exception are vendors and distributors. For example, booksellers like Amazon.com, libraries, and newsstands are not publishers of the works they stock. They cannot be sued for libel based on the works they make available because they do not control the content of those products.

Before passage of the Communications Decency Act more than 20 years ago, internet service providers were regarded as both publishers[45] and distributors of information that others published.[46] This issue was resolved when Section 230 of the CDA was tested by a libel claim against AOL (then America Online, Inc.).[47]

Kenneth Zeran claimed AOL injured his reputation by not quickly removing false information about him. His claim arose after an anonymous AOL user posted an advertisement for T-shirts with images and a slogan glorifying the 1995 Oklahoma City bombing. The ad included Zeran's telephone number. Zeran said he had no knowledge of the ad. "By its plain language, Section 230 creates a federal immunity to any cause of action that would make service providers liable for information originating with a third-party user of that service," the First Circuit Court of Appeals noted.[48] The court said Section 230 prevents courts from considering an ISP a publisher[49] because Congress recognized that to do so would create an "obvious chilling effect" on speech.[50]

Nearly a decade after the *Zeran* decision, the First Circuit Court of Appeals ruled that the definition of "provider of an interactive computer service" includes service providers who do not directly connect their users to the internet.[51] Unlike AOL in the *Zeran* case, the defendant here only managed a series of websites. The court reasoned that narrowing protection only to services that provide internet access undermined congressional intent and held that Section 230 immunity should be broadly construed.[52]

In 2020, the Second Circuit Court of Appeals found Section 230 could not protect Joy Reid, a cable media personality, against a defamation claim addressing two inaccurate social media posts. One post attributed racist remarks to Roslyn La Liberte, a woman "passionate about this country's immigration policies" who spoke at a city council meeting in Simi Valley, Calif. Another juxtaposed a photo showing La Liberte with her mouth open and her hand at her throat in front of a minority teenager with a historic image showing a white woman "screaming execrations at a Black child trying to go to school" in Arkansas in the 1950s.[53]

Joy Reid, host of MSNBC's "The Reidout" was sued for defamation in social media posts.
Theo Wargo/Getty Images

The appellate court explained that Section 230 immunity did not provide Reid with immunity for the two posts Reid authored. Considering Reid wrote both posts, Reid was not considered a publisher of "information *provided by another content provider*."[54] (Section 230 as a defense is discussed in detail in Chapter 5.)

INTERNATIONAL LAW
LIABILITY FOR PUBLISHING THIRD-PARTY COMMENTS ON SOCIAL MEDIA

News media organizations changed how Facebook users could interact with their public Facebook pages in Australia in 2021. CNN blocked access to their pages in Australia. Others stopped permitting comments on their pages.[55]

Those changes followed Dylan Voller's attempt to sue some of Australia's largest news media for defamation by third-party comments posted on news media public pages and government leaders' plans to change the country's defamation laws. In 2016 and 2017, news media posted content about Voller being mistreated in a juvenile detention facility, and news media did not block third-party comments on their pages.[56] To determine whether his defamation case could proceed, three courts considered whether the news media acted as publishers.[57]

First, a Supreme Court of South Wales primary judge found news media use of a Facebook page "encourages and facilitates visits by third-party users to a media outlet's own website." The number of posted comments could increase the visibility of the Facebook page, direct more viewers to the websites of the news media and increase media revenues. Each organization had a Facebook page administrator who could prevent, block or hide comments by third-party posters, and they could anticipate which stories "would be expected to draw adverse comments about the person who was the subject of the news story."[58]

The Court of Appeals also found the news organizations were publishers. News media cited a 1982 court opinion that indicates publishers "must have been instrumental to, or a participant in," communication, and the news media argued they simply administered a page on which others posted comments.[59] The Court of Appeals, however, cited a 2013 opinion stating that internet platform providers that hosted a discussion forum "had encouraged and facilitated" postings and, thus, were "participants in their publication."[60]

In 2021, a majority of the High Court of Australia dismissed appeals from the lower court's judgment and affirmed that "facilitating, encouraging and thereby assisting the posting of comments" on the public Facebook pages of news media made the news media publishers of the third-party comments. Rather than accept the news media claims that publishers must intentionally make material available, the court cited a 2018 opinion finding that "All that is required is a voluntary act of participation in the communication of a defamatory statement."[61]

In 2021, Australian Prime Minister Scott Morrison announced plans to introduce legislation that would require social media companies to take down material that a person complained was defamatory.[62]

Unknown Publisher/Anonymous Speech.   Sometimes material is published, but the speaker is unknown. A hallmark of the internet and interaction through some mobile applications and social media is anonymous communication. The ability to speak anonymously can allow ideas and viewpoints that otherwise might remain unexpressed to enter the marketplace of ideas by reducing the fear of reprisal. "Under our constitution, anonymous pamphleteering is not a pernicious, fraudulent practice, but an honorable tradition of advocacy and of dissent," U.S. Supreme Court Justice Antonin Scalia once wrote, "Anonymity is a shield from the tyranny of the majority."[63] As Chapter 2 notes, the Supreme Court has recognized a First Amendment right to anonymous speech. But what happens when the wish to protect anonymous speech collides with the imperative of holding people accountable for libelous expression?

Generally speaking, state courts have taken multiple approaches to "unmasking" anonymous posters on the internet in libel cases. One of the most used approaches was developed in _Dendrite v. John Doe #3_.[64] In that case, a court in New Jersey held that the plaintiff must present the court with **prima facie**, "on its face," evidence sufficient to prove the plaintiff has a case that can withstand a motion to dismiss. A **motion to dismiss** is a formal request to the court to dismiss a case. A defendant often files this motion immediately after a plaintiff files suit, although it may be filed at any time during legal proceedings by either party. Grounds for dismissing a lawsuit are determined by each jurisdiction's laws. If the plaintiff's case can withstand a motion to dismiss, then the court likely would be confronted with balancing the First Amendment rights of the anonymous speaker against the strength of the prima facie case and the need to disclose the anonymous speaker.[65]

Two recent cases in California illustrate how the *Dendrite* holding may be applied. In one case, Yelp, Inc. petitioned an appeals court to overturn a court order that required the company to produce documents that Yelp argued would reveal the identity of an anonymous reviewer.[66] The court agreed that Yelp had standing to assert a First Amendment right on behalf of its anonymous reviewer, but it also said the plaintiff succeeded in making a prima facie showing that the Yelp review in question was actionable. A prima facia showing, based on looking at evidence on its face, is considered a sufficient showing of evidence to establish a fact unless substantially contradictory evidence is presented. The prima facie showing established that the plaintiff was entitled to discovery of the reviewer's identity because the review could constitute defamation.[67]

Another case involved the Glassdoor job recruiting and review website. A software and email archiving company filed a defamation lawsuit against several unnamed individuals based on critical reviews posted on Glassdoor's website.[68] ZL Technologies, Inc. subpoenaed Glassdoor records to identify and provide contact information for the anonymous posters and Glassdoor resisted. The trial court denied ZL's motion to compel Glassdoor to provide the information, noting that the defendants had a First Amendment right to remain anonymous.[69] An appeals court disagreed. In addition to applying *Dendrite* and holding that ZL Technologies had made a prima facie showing of an actionable claim, the appeals court added a new requirement. The court said that reasonable efforts must be made to notify the anonymous defendants before they are unmasked to give them an opportunity to respond.[70]

Most cases that apply a second commonly used approach ultimately expose a defendant's identity.[71] The Delaware Supreme Court has held that a defamation plaintiff must "satisfy a summary judgment standard before obtaining the identity of an anonymous defender." Under a summary judgment standard, a judge must view certain points in the light most favorable to the defendant and make a judgment from that perspective. The Delaware Supreme Court wrote, "Indeed, there is reason to believe that many defamation plaintiffs bring suit merely to unmask the identities of anonymous critics. . . . The goals of this new breed of libel action are largely symbolic, the primary goal being to silence John Doe and others like him."[72]

Courts in the Tenth Circuit most commonly use a four-part balancing test to weigh one party's First Amendment privilege to not disclose information against another party's necessity for discovery.[73] A trial court first must consider the validity of the claimed privilege, then a court may consider "(1) the relevance of the evidence; (2) the necessity of receiving the information sought; (3) whether the information is available from other sources; and (4) the nature of the information."[74]

Virginia takes a different approach. To unmask anonymous users, plaintiffs must show they have a legitimate, good faith basis to claim an actionable offense within the court's jurisdiction, and the identity of the anonymous speaker is central to advancing their case.[75] Most other state courts have rejected this standard because it does not offer the speaker sufficient First Amendment protection.

Identification

A libel plaintiff is required to show that they were the specific person whose reputation was harmed or, possibly, that they were a member of a small group that was defamed. Addressing **identification**, early common law asked whether the statement was "of and concerning" the plaintiff—a standard still employed.[76] This test asks whether the allegedly defamatory statement reasonably refers to the plaintiff. People can be identified by name, by title, through photographic images, or within a context in which their identity can be inferred. Someone other than the plaintiff and the defendant must recognize that the content is about the plaintiff. In addition, the intention of the publisher is not critical to this determination; a publisher may not have intended to implicate the plaintiff, but identification might have occurred, nonetheless.

Two police officers involved in a deadly shooting sued Seattle City Council member Kshama Sawant for defamation.

Genna Martins /San Francisco Chronicle via Getty Images

In 2021, the Ninth Circuit Court of Appeals addressed whether Seattle City Council member Kshama Sawant plausibly identified two police officers involved in the shooting of a Black man when she called for accountability. Calling the shooting "just a blatant murder at the hands of the police," Sawant said, "We need justice on the individual actions and we need to turn the tide on the systemic police brutality and racial profiling."[77] A district court had dismissed the case on grounds her statements were not "of and concerning" the police officers. The appeals court, however, reasoned that her language "can reasonably be understood as referring to the officers" involved in the shooting, audience members knew the plaintiffs were involved in the shooting and audience members understood her remarks "to refer to" both officers. The appeals court reversed the district court's dismissal and remanded the case.[78]

Group Identification

In some circumstances, libel law allows any member of a group to sue when the entire group has been libeled. The key is whether in libeling the group, the information is also "of and concerning" the specific individual bringing the lawsuit. In general, the smaller the group, the more likely it is that its individual members have been identified. According to one authority, "It is not possible to set definite limits as to the size of the group or class, but the cases in which recovery [of damages] has been allowed usually have involved numbers of 25 or fewer."[79]

A court will evaluate each situation on its specific facts. Some rulings in this category indicate that if a group has fewer than 25 members, any one of them could file a successful libel claim, depending on the libelous material in question. As a group grows in size, the inclusiveness of the language that allegedly libeled its members becomes a factor.[80]

The Supreme Court of Nebraska recently addressed a group libel claim involving approximately 70 percent of tanning salons known to be in Omaha and Lincoln, Neb., between 2015 and 2017. During that period, the salons claimed a cancer education and prevention campaign named "The Bed is Dead" made false and defamatory statements that were of and concerning the salons. The court found there was not sufficient evidence that people either understood the statements or should have understood the statements as referring to the salons or as intended to refer to the salons.[81]

The U.S. District Court for the Eastern District of Kentucky recently considered whether a teenager could be identified in Washington Post articles related to a 2019 viral video showing an interaction between Nathan Phillips, an indigenous man, and Nicholas Sandmann, a Kentucky high school student wearing a "Make America Great Again" ("MAGA") hat. Sandmann was at the front of a group of his high school classmates in Washington, DC, when Phillips approached the students while singing and beating a drum. The court found that Sandmann could not be identified in articles that did not name Sandmann and were not accompanied with his photograph. References to "hat wearing teens," "the teens, "teens and other participants," "a few people, "those who should listen most closely," "students," and "boys in MAGA caps" do not identify Sandmann.[82]

Defamation

Another element in the plaintiff's case involves the allegedly libelous content itself. For the plaintiff to win, the material at issue must be **defamatory**, harmful to reputation.[83] The challenge is defining and establishing a standard of defamation. The standard begins with the premise that when reputation is damaged, defamation occurs.

Some words by themselves may qualify as defamatory. Some kinds of statements convey such defamatory meaning that they are considered to be defamatory as a matter of law. This is **libel per se**, a statement whose injurious nature is apparent on its face and requires no further proof.[84] Libel per se typically involves accusations of criminal activity, unethical activity or practice, unprofessional behavior or immoral actions (sometimes called moral turpitude, which is conduct contrary to community standards).[85]

For example, in 2021, a California appeals court categorized as libel per se statements in emails, social media posts, and a letter to the editor alleging elected officials arranged for a developer to receive a public contract in exchange for the officials receiving jobs and a donation to a cause they supported. The statements accused the plaintiffs of improper professional conduct. "Any reasonable reader would understand the publications to be asserting facts harmful to their reputations, without external information," the court said.[86] The trial court had not erred in denying the defendant's motions to strike the defamation claim as a strategic lawsuit against public participation (see Chapter 5).

In 2021, a court of appeals in Louisiana affirmed a trial court's award of $15,000 damages in a defamation per se case. That case addressed podcasts and social media posts falsely alleging a female was a prostitute engaged in sex trafficking whose family sold her to the man she would marry. In Louisiana, words that falsely accuse a person of being involved in criminal conduct are considered defamatory per se. The Louisiana Supreme Court declined to hear the case.[87]

In 2020, the U.S. District Court for the Southern District of Iowa determined that police officers' statements that a police officer "had lost it and was taking medication for those out of touch with reality" were slander per se. Those statements related to "mental attributes such as disease or insanity" and challenged the plaintiff's professional competence. The court did not grant summary judgment in the officer's defamation case.[88]

The New York Supreme Court recently held that HIV infection fell under the "loathsome disease" category of libel per se. A model posed for photos on an unrelated topic, and two years later, her image was sold to Getty Images, which then licensed one of the photos to the New York City Division of Human Rights (DHR). The DHR used the image in print and digital ads about HIV/AIDS that read, "I AM POSITIVE (+)" and "I HAVE RIGHTS" along with additional information. The appeals court noted that while it did not consider HIV loathsome, it acknowledged that people who suffer from an HIV diagnosis are often ostracized and targets of discrimination. The court granted summary judgment for defamation per se.[89]

POINTS OF LAW
DISTINGUISHING DEFAMATORY FROM NONDEFAMATORY STATEMENTS

Distinguishing defamatory from nondefamatory statements is more art than science. Within various contexts, the following definitions of "defamatory" have been offered:

- Words or images that are false and injurious to another;
- Words or images that expose another person to hatred, contempt or ridicule;
- Words or images that tend to harm the reputation of another so as to lower them in the estimation of the community or deter third persons from associating or dealing with them;[90]
- Words or images that subject a person to the loss of goodwill or confidence from others;[91]
- Words or images that subject a person to scorn or ridicule;
- Words or images that tend to expose persons to hatred, contempt or aversion, or tend to induce an evil opinion of them in the minds of a substantial number of people in the community; or
- Words or images that tend to prejudice someone in the eyes of a substantial and respectable minority of the community.[92]

Whatever the standard, courts traditionally have said that the matter must be viewed from the perspective of "right-thinking" people.[93]

The Eighth Circuit Court of Appeals recently found that Facebook posts falsely asserting the president of a governing body for darts tournaments had lied and manipulated a situation were capable of defamatory meaning.[94] The Fourth Circuit Court of Appeals, however, found a twelve-second clip from a documentary was misleading but not capable of defamatory meaning. The clip was edited in a way that made a journalist's complex question about doing away with gun background checks appear to stump members of the Virginia Citizens Defense League (VCDL), a Second Amendment advocacy organization. The court reasoned "the essential message that VCDL members failed to respond instantly to a complex question is simply not defamatory."[95]

President Donald Trump (left) faced defamation allegations from former "The Apprentice" contestant Summer Zervos (right).

AP Photos/Pablo Martinez Monsivais

Ringo H.W. Chiu

REAL WORLD LAW
THE PRESIDENT AND DEFAMATION

Presidents have raised important questions about whether a sitting president has immunity from civil litigation while in office.

In 2019, a New York appeals court held that the Supremacy Clause does not shield the U.S. president from state civil court actions when there is no conflict with federal law.[96] That decision followed a 2018 New York appeals court decision that a defamation lawsuit against President Donald Trump brought by Summer Zervos, a former contestant on "The Apprentice," could proceed. President Trump's lawyers argued that the president cannot be sued for unofficial acts while in office. [97]

The New York court disagreed and applied the U.S. Supreme Court decision in *Clinton v. Jones* as precedent.[98] That case involved a sexual harassment lawsuit brought against then-President Bill Clinton while he was in office. The Supreme Court held in *Clinton* that a sitting president does not have temporary immunity from civil litigation while in office.[99]

On further appeal in 2019, the decision to let the case proceed was upheld. A five-justice panel wrote, "We reject defendant President Trump's argument that the Supremacy Clause of the United States Constitution prevents a New York State court—and every other state court in the country—from exercising its authority under its state constitution."[100]

The court held that his statements were clearly susceptible to defamatory meaning and cited precedent for defamation claims maintained against people who call purported victims of sexual assault liars.[101]

In March 2021, a New York appellate court allowed a defamation suit against Donald Trump to proceed after he had left the office of president.[102] Almost eight months later, Summer Zervos, a former contestant on "The Apprentice," entered an agreement to end that lawsuit after Trump's attorney declared their intention to countersue Zervos for chilling Trump's free speech rights.[103]

In October 2020, a federal district court rejected government arguments that an American journalist who sued Trump for defamation was suing a federal government employee for statements within the scope of his employment. The case addresses E. Jean Carroll's claim that Trump defamed her by saying she falsely accused him of raping her in the 1990s. The court reasoned the president is not an employee of the federal government and Trump's comments about her allegations lacked any relationship to the president's official duties.[104] In 2022, a federal district court rejected Trump's attempt to assert a new defense and countersue under New York's anti-SLAPP statute.[105]

In another case, a federal court dismissed adult film actress Stephanie Clifford's lawsuit against Trump on grounds that an allegedly defamatory tweet about her was rhetorical hyperbole (see Chapter 5).[106]

Article headlines can occasionally be the source of successful libel claims. As with captions and teasers, their abbreviated nature and shortened message may still be interpreted in a defamatory way. Harvard Law School Professor Laurence Lessig recently described a practice of using a shocking headline "to entice readers to click on a particular article" with awareness doing so could harm an identified person's reputation as "clickbait defamation."[107] Whether the headline is "of and concerning" the plaintiff becomes material—as do the other elements of the plaintiff's case.

A federal court in Tennessee recently denied a motion for summary judgment in a case addressing an allegedly defamatory headline and its use of the word scam. After country-music artist Daryle Singletary died, the owner of a recording company indicated fans could download a previously unreleased song sung by Singletary with proceeds benefitting Singletary's family. FoxNews.com published a headline, "Daryle Singletary's new single is a scam, not benefiting his widow and kids, business partner says." The federal court found a jury could consider that headline to convey a defamatory meaning, and the content of the article did not nullify the defamatory meaning. The court stated the plaintiff "could be held up to public hatred, contempt, or ridicule for perpetrating a scam, especially one that involves the misuse of a recording of a recently deceased person and purportedly collecting donations on behalf of a grieving family."[108]

Article illustrations and photographs can also result in libel if they are juxtaposed in a way that creates a defamatory impression. A New York court held that an archived crime scene photo used as a visual with an article about gang violence was capable of defamatory meaning. The photo of a 10-year-old boy looking over yellow police tape at a crime scene was placed underneath the headline "Call to Get Tougher on Gang Activities." The appeals court said that the juxtaposition of the photo and the text could create a defamatory impression and that connecting a person to a serious crime like gang activity constitutes libel per se.[109]

In contrast with libel per se is **libel per quod**, which is actionable as defamation only when the plaintiff introduces additional facts to show defamation. Libel per quod arises when the matter by itself does not appear to be defamatory, but knowledge of additional information would damage the plaintiff's reputation.[110] An example of libel per quod would be a news article in which the plaintiff was reported to have visited 123 Main Street. By itself, the report is not defamatory. But if most readers are aware this is a place to buy and sell heroin, then the report would have accused the plaintiff of involvement in illegal activity.

Among the challenges for a court is deciding what the words or images at issue in a libel case mean and whether they can be considered defamatory. Whether they are actionable cannot simply be determined according to whether they harmed the plaintiff's reputation. The allegedly libelous matter may conceivably harm reputation without rising to the level of defamation. Thus, another element of defamation that plaintiffs must show is that the material "is reasonably capable of sustaining defamatory meaning."[111] A judge decides whether the words constituting the statement at issue are capable of conveying defamatory meaning. If so, the case may move to trial to determine whether, in fact, the words did convey a defamatory meaning.

Business Reputation

While businesses and corporations do not have reputations in the same sense that individuals do, they can suffer reputational harm that can impair their ability to conduct business. In addition, individuals within businesses and corporations may have a legitimate libel claim when criticism of the business falsely implies wrongdoing on their part.[112]

Trade Libel. **Trade libel** is defamatory material that pertains to criticism of products rather than criticism of people or businesses. When it applies to food products, it is sometimes colloquially called "veggie libel." These are state laws that became popular in the 1990s. In one of the most famous cases, a group of Texas cattlemen sued Oprah Winfrey for remarks she made about mad cow disease. During that time, international media had reported on the disease after several people in the United Kingdom died from eating infected beef. An episode of "The Oprah Winfrey Show" titled "Dangerous Food" explored the topic of diseased beef. Although neither Texas nor any of the plaintiffs was mentioned, the Texas Beef Group and several other Texas-based cattle companies filed suit. They claimed the show's producers "intentionally edited . . . much of the factual and scientific information that would have calmed the hysteria it knew one guest's false exaggerations would create."[113] The plaintiffs added that this "malicious" treatment "caused markets to immediately" crash and they suffered damages as a result.[114] When Winfrey commented during the show that the information about tainted beef had "just stopped me cold from eating another burger,"[115] the flames were fanned. The plaintiffs sought $100 million in damages. Winfrey won at trial and on appeal. The Texas cattlemen were unable to meet the burden of proof.[116]

Texas cattlemen sued Oprah Winfrey for remarks she made about mad cow disease.

Jordan Strauss/Invision/AP

A series of reports by ABC News that called a processed meat product "pink slime" were the focus of a recent trade libel suit brought by Beef Products, Inc. (BPI). The company sought $1.2 billion in damages under South Dakota's "veggie libel" law. BPI says it was defamatory to call its "lean finely textured beef," made from raw chunks of meat and fat beef trimmings, "pink slime," a term that originated from a U.S. Department of Agriculture (USDA) microbiologist.[117]

BPI's product was used by many fast-food chains and sold by large grocery store chains. ABC News reports said the product was made with "low grade" meat, including scraps and waste, and was supposedly made partially from connective animal tissue. BPI maintained that the product was made from muscle, or meat. The public pressured fast-food chains to eliminate the textured beef product, and BPI's revenues plummeted, resulting in the closure of three of its processing plants and the loss of 700 jobs.[118]

ABC argued that the use of the term "pink slime" was protected expression of opinion and sought to have the complaint dismissed. A South Dakota court held that "the use of the term pink slime with a food product can be reasonably interpreted as implying that the food product is not meat and is not fit to eat, which are objective facts which can be proven." The court allowed the lawsuit to move forward[119] against ABC, news anchor Diane Sawyer and one ABC news correspondent. BPI recently settled out of court. ABC News did not retract or apologize for its report, noting that the company reached "an amicable resolution" with BPI.[120]

The Seventh Circuit Court of Appeals noted in 2021 that most states have adopted different approaches for defamation of a person, a corporation, or a product. Under a

Restatement of Torts, which reports on state interpretations of common law, a plaintiff must demonstrate a defendant communicated "an injurious falsehood" about a product the communicator knew to be false or made with reckless disregard as to its truth. Some states recognize that if a competitor does not believe their product is better than a rival's products, a competitor may make comparisons between the quality of those products "if the comparison does not contain false assertions of specific unfavorable facts" about the rival's products.[121]

REAL WORLD LAW
FAKE NEWS AND DISINFORMATION

Fake news and disinformation are globally significant concepts.[122] Fake news is misinformation, or false information intentionally conveyed with intention to mislead.[123] According to Merriam-Webster, the term was generally used in the 19th century by local newspapers to identify misinformation. In the 16th century, people used the term "false news."[124] The Nazis used the German equivalent "Lügenpresse" in the 1930s to advance their propaganda campaigns.[125]

Political actors and movements around the globe have breathed new life into the phrase fake news in an attempt to undermine public confidence in mainstream news media and advance their own political agendas. Others correctly use the term to identify misleading false information, propaganda and fake social media accounts designed to spread misinformation. Facebook and Twitter now report regularly on how they are trying to stop the spread of fake news from fake accounts and profiles on their platforms.[126]

A recent European Commission report explained disinformation as false, inaccurate or misleading information that was designed and spread for profit or to cause harm.[127] Merriam Webster defines disinformation as deliberately spreading false information to influence public opinion or conceal truth.[128]

In 2020, an attorney for Smartmatic USA Corp., an election technology company, sent Fox News a 20-page letter asserting the television network had engaged in a disinformation campaign against the election technology company. The letter warned the company would file a defamation claim and demanded a retraction of dozens of false and defamatory misleading assertions the network published and republished in relation to the U.S. 2020 election.[129] Fox News subsequently showed an election technology expert fact-checking multiple points the network previously had conveyed about Smartmatic.[130]

In 2021, Smartmatic sued Fox News, three of the network's anchors and two of the network's frequent guest commentators for defamation and disparagement. Seeking at least $2.7 billion in damages, Smartmatic accused the defendants of casting the company and its software as villains in a disinformation campaign designed to gain favors from the Trump administration and to attract more viewers. Smartmatic also filed similar defamation suits against Newsmax and One America News Network.[131]

A second company, Dominion Voting Systems, Inc., sued Fox News for conveying multiple false assertions that harmed the company's reputation. That suit seeks at least $1.6 billion in damages for false and defamatory claims related to a conspiracy theory that the U.S. 2020 election was rigged.[132]

Falsity

For a statement to be libelous, it must be false, meaning not true. The plaintiff is responsible for demonstrating that the statement at issue is false rather than the defendant proving the statement is true.

Historically, this was reversed: The burden of proof to show a statement is true was placed on the defendant. Libel law in the United States now clearly places the burden of proof regarding **falsity** on the plaintiff. The U.S. Supreme Court has emphatically reinforced this aspect of libel law. In *Philadelphia Newspapers, Inc. v. Hepps*, Justice Sandra Day O'Connor emphasized the importance of protecting and encouraging the free flow of information and ideas:

> We believe that the Constitution requires us to tip [the scales] in favor of protecting free speech. . . . The burden of proving truth upon media defendants who publish speech of public concern deters such speech because of the fear that liability will unjustifiably result. . . . Because such a "chilling" effect would be antithetical to the First Amendment's protection of true speech on matters of public concern . . . a plaintiff must bear the burden of showing that the speech at issue is false before recovering damages for defamation from a media defendant. To do otherwise could only result in a deterrence of the speech which the Constitution makes free.[133]

The burden of proof of falsity occasionally serves as a deterrent to potential plaintiffs. The requirement to delve deeply into the allegedly libelous statement and refute its veracity is sometimes so distasteful that would-be plaintiffs choose not to file libel claims in the first place.

Substantial Truth

Libel law provides some latitude with regard to falsity. Minor error or discrepancy does not necessarily make a statement false. As long as the statement is substantially true, it cannot meet the standard for falsity and therefore cannot be libelous. The U.S. Supreme Court said that **substantial truth** "would absolve a defendant even if she cannot justify every word of the alleged defamatory matter; it is sufficient if the substance of the charge is proved true, irrespective of the slight inaccuracy in the details. . . . Minor inaccuracies do not amount to falsity so long as the substance, the gist, the sting of the libelous charge can be justified."[134]

For example, CNN's 2019 coverage of the first impeachment of President Trump repeated a lawyer's statement that his client would testify that California Congressman Devin Nunes and three of his aides had traveled to Europe and Nunes met with a former Ukrainian prosecutor regarding Biden. Derek Harvey, a senior advisor to Nunes, was named in that report. Harvey sued CNN for defamation and indicated he had traveled to Malta and Libya—not to Europe—with Nunes. In 2021, the U.S. District Court for the District of Maryland held Harvey could not show the statement was materially false. "Falsity does not require absolute precision," the court stated. "Minor inaccuracies do not amount to falsity provided that the substance or gist is justified."[135]

Libel by Implication. While individual statements may be factually accurate, taken together they sometimes may paint a different picture. Through implication or innuendo, one can create libelous messages. In a case dismissed by a Washington state appeals court, a crane operator sued a newspaper for what he said was implied in headlines. After an accident, Seattle Post-Intelligencer headlines read, "Operator in crane wreck has history of drug abuse" and "Man completed mandated rehab program after his last arrest in 2000." The crane operator's tests for drugs after the accident were negative. He filed several claims including libel, although he admitted that there were no false statements in the newspaper. Still, he claimed "defamation by implication" due to the juxtaposing of true statements in a way that created a false impression.[136]

An Iowa Supreme Court ruling stated that if a true fact is not properly and thoroughly explained it can become defamatory if, when read in a particular way, it carries false implications.[137] In another case, in 2021, an Eighth Circuit Court of Appeals panel applied Iowa law. The panel found a reasonable reader could draw false and defamatory implications from a magazine article that falsely implied Congressman Nunes "conspired with others to hide [his family] farm's use of undocumented labor." The statements at issue in defamation by implication claims must be considered within the context of an entire article. The court reasoned that a reasonable reader could understand that statement in the context of the article's main theme that suggests "Nunes and his family hid the farm's move to Iowa—the 'politically explosive' secret." The Eighth Circuit declined to hear an appeal en banc.[138]

Libel by implication can also happen through the juxtaposition of images. The Third Circuit Court of Appeals concluded that the juxtaposition of a photo did create a defamatory impression in a case that involved a Philadelphia firefighter who appeared in a picture next to a story about a sex scandal within the city's fire department. The court decided that a reasonable person could conclude that the inclusion of the firefighter's picture and name juxtaposed to the story would incorrectly implicate him in the sex scandal.[139]

The Ninth Circuit Court of Appeals unanimously decided in favor of an unidentified performer in the pornography industry after a stock photo of her appeared within a story about a female performer testing positive for HIV, which temporarily shut down the porn industry in California. The unidentified performer was one of the most popular soft porn actresses on the internet. While the story text noted that the unidentified performer who tested positive was new to the industry, the court held that the photo juxtaposition resulted in a reasonable implication that the statements in the story referred to the model/actress used in the stock photo, even though she was not named.[140]

Fault

To support a libel claim, a plaintiff must show that the defendant was at **fault**, or responsible, in making public the allegedly false and defamatory statement of fact. Prior to *New York Times Co. v. Sullivan*, fault was not an element of common law libel. That landmark case eliminated the concept of libel as a no-fault tort, and subsequent U.S. Supreme Court cases explained what level of fault is used in libel suits.[141] As a general rule, public officials and public figures must prove actual malice as a standard of fault, and **private figures**, people who are neither famous nor serving as public officials, must prove negligence.

New York Times Co. v. Sullivan

One of the most important legal cases in the history of American constitutional law is a libel case, *New York Times Co. v. Sullivan*.[142] The U.S. Supreme Court's ruling in that case has had monumental impact, not just on journalism but on democracy and society as a whole.

THE NEW YORK TIMES, TUESDAY, MARCH 29, 1960

Heed Their Rising Voices

> "The growing movement of peaceful mass demonstrations by Negroes is something new in the South, something understandable.... Let Congress heed their rising voices, for they will be heard."
>
> —New York Times editorial
> Saturday, March 19, 1960

AS the whole world knows by now, thousands of Southern Negro students are engaged in widespread non-violent demonstrations in positive affirmation of the right to live in human dignity as guaranteed by the U. S. Constitution and the Bill of Rights. In their efforts to uphold these guarantees, they are being met by an unprecedented wave of terror by those who would deny and negate that document which the whole world looks upon as setting the pattern for modern freedom...

In Orangeburg, South Carolina, when 400 students peacefully sought to buy doughnuts and coffee at lunch counters in the business district, they were forcibly ejected, tear-gassed, soaked to the skin in freezing weather with fire hoses, arrested en masse and herded into an open barbed-wire stockade to stand for hours in the bitter cold.

In Montgomery, Alabama, after students sang "My Country, 'Tis of Thee" on the State Capitol steps, their leaders were expelled from school, and truckloads of police armed with shotguns and tear-gas ringed the Alabama State College Campus. When the entire student body protested to state authorities by refusing to re-register, their dining hall was padlocked in an attempt to starve them into submission.

In Tallahassee, Atlanta, Nashville, Savannah, Greensboro, Memphis, Richmond, Charlotte, and a host of other cities in the South, young American teenagers, in face of the entire weight of official state apparatus and police power, have boldly stepped forth as protagonists of democracy. Their courage and amazing restraint have inspired millions and given a new dignity to the cause of freedom.

Small wonder that the Southern violators of the Constitution fear this new, non-violent brand of freedom fighter... even as they fear the upswelling right-to-vote movement. Small wonder that they are determined to destroy the one man who, more than any other, symbolizes the new spirit now sweeping the South—the Rev. Dr. Martin Luther King, Jr., world-famous leader of the Montgomery Bus Protest. For it is his doctrine of non-violence which has inspired and guided the students in their widening wave of sit-ins; and it is this same Dr. King who founded and is president of the Southern Christian Leadership Conference—the organization which is spearheading the surging right-to-vote movement. Under Dr. King's direction the Leadership Conference conducts Student Workshops and Seminars in the philosophy and techniques of non-violent resistance.

Again and again the Southern violators have answered Dr. King's peaceful protests with intimidation and violence. They have bombed his home almost killing his wife and child. They have assaulted his person. They have arrested him seven times—for "speeding," "loitering" and similar "offenses." And now they have charged him with "perjury"—a *felony* under which they could imprison him for *ten years*. Obviously, their real purpose is to remove him physically as the leader to whom the students and millions of others—look for guidance and support, and thereby to intimidate *all* leaders who may rise in the South. Their strategy is to behead this affirmative movement, and thus to demoralize Negro Americans and weaken their will to struggle. The defense of Martin Luther King, spiritual leader of the student sit-in movement, clearly, therefore, is an integral part of the total struggle for freedom in the South.

Decent-minded Americans cannot help but applaud the creative daring of the students and the quiet heroism of Dr. King. But this is one of those moments in the stormy history of Freedom when men and women of good will must do more than applaud the rising-to-glory of others. The America whose good name hangs in the balance before a watchful world, the America whose heritage of Liberty these Southern Upholders of the Constitution are defending, is *our* America as well as theirs...

We must heed their rising voices—yes—but we must add our own.

We must extend ourselves above and beyond moral support and render the material help so urgently needed by those who are taking the risks, facing jail, and *even death* in a glorious re-affirmation of our Constitution and its Bill of Rights.

We urge you to join hands with our fellow Americans in the South by supporting, with your dollars, this combined appeal for all three needs—the defense of Martin Luther King—the support of the embattled students—and the struggle for the right-to-vote.

Your Help Is Urgently Needed . . . NOW!!

Stella Adler
Raymond Pace Alexander
Harry Van Arsdale
Harry Belafonte
Julie Belafonte
Dr. Algernon Black
Marc Blitzstein
William Branch
Marlon Brando
Mrs. Ralph Bunche
Diahann Carroll

Dr. Alan Knight Chalmers
Richard Coe
Nat King Cole
Cheryl Crawford
Dorothy Dandridge
Ossie Davis
Sammy Davis, Jr.
Ruby Dee
Dr. Philip Elliott
Dr. Harry Emerson Fosdick

Anthony Franciosa
Lorraine Hansbury
Rev. Donald Harrington
Nat Hentoff
James Hicks
Mary Hinkson
Van Heflin
Langston Hughes
Morris Iushewitz
Mahalia Jackson
Mordecai Johnson

John Killens
Eartha Kitt
Rabbi Edward Klein
Hope Lange
John Lewis
Viveca Lindfors
Carl Murphy
Don Murray
John Murray
A. J. Muste
Frederick O'Neal

L. Joseph Overton
Clarence Pickett
Shad Polier
Sidney Poitier
A. Philip Randolph
John Raitt
Elmer Rice
Jackie Robinson
Mrs. Eleanor Roosevelt
Bayard Rustin
Robert Ryan

Maureen Stapleton
Frank Silvera
Hope Stevens
George Tabor
Rev. Gardner C.
    Taylor
Norman Thomas
Kenneth Tynan
Charles White
Shelley Winters
Max Youngstein

We in the south who are struggling daily for dignity and freedom warmly endorse this appeal

Rev. Ralph D. Abernathy
(Montgomery, Ala.)

Rev. Fred L. Shuttlesworth
(Birmingham, Ala.)

Rev. Kelley Miller Smith
(Nashville, Tenn.)

Rev. W. A. Dennis
(Chattanooga, Tenn.)

Rev. C. K. Steele
(Tallahassee, Fla.)

Rev. Matthew D. McCollom
(Orangeburg, S.C.)

Rev. William Holmes Borders
(Atlanta, Ga.)

Rev. Douglas Moore
(Durham, N.C.)

Rev. Wyatt Tee Walker
(Petersburg, Va.)

Rev. Walter L. Hamilton
(Norfolk, Va.)

I. S. Levy
(Columbia, S.C.)

Rev. Martin Luther King, Sr.
(Atlanta, Ga.)

Rev. Henry C. Bunton
(Memphis, Tenn.)

Rev. S.S. Seay, Sr.
(Montgomery, Ala.)

Rev. Samuel W. Williams
(Atlanta, Ga.)

Rev. A. L. Davis
(New Orleans, La.)

Mrs. Katie E. Whickham
(New Orleans, La.)

Rev. W. H. Hall
(Hattiesburg, Miss.)

Rev. J. E. Lowery
(Mobile, Ala.)

Rev. T. J. Jemison
(Baton Rouge, La.)

COMMITTEE TO DEFEND MARTIN LUTHER KING AND THE STRUGGLE FOR FREEDOM IN THE SOUTH

312 West 125th Street, New York 27, N.Y. UNiversity 6-1700

Chairmen: A. Philip Randolph, Dr. Gardner C. Taylor; *Chairmen of Cultural Division:* Harry Belafonte, Sidney Poitier; *Treasurer:* Nat King Cole; *Executive Director:* Bayard Rustin; *Chairmen of Church Division:* Father George B. Ford, Rev. Harry Emerson Fosdick, Rev. Thomas Kilgore, Jr., Rabbi Edward E. Klein; *Chairman of Labor Division:* Morris Iushewitz

Please mail this coupon TODAY!

Committee To Defend Martin Luther King
and
The Struggle For Freedom In The South
312 West 125th Street, New York 27, N.Y.
UNiversity 6-1700

I am enclosing my contribution of $_____ for the work of the Committee.

Name _____

Address _____

City _____ Zone ____ State ____

☐ I want to help   ☐ Please send further information

Please make checks payable to:
Committee to Defend Martin Luther King

The New York Times "advertorial" that prompted L.B. Sullivan's libel lawsuit against the newspaper.

Originally published in The New York Times, March 29, 1960

The circumstances of *New York Times Co. v. Sullivan* arose within the context of the civil rights movement of the 1960s. African American groups seeking racial equality under the law frequently engaged in nonviolent marches in Southern states. These events were minimized or ignored by the local Southern press but were covered elsewhere, including frequently in The New York Times.

Against that backdrop, a coalition of civil rights leaders purchased space in The New York Times for a full-page statement. Carrying the headline "Heed Their Rising Voices," the "advertorial" made charges against officials in Southern states who they claimed used violent and illegal methods to suppress the marches. Although the gist of the statement was factually accurate, there were some errors of fact. Asserting he had been defamed, L.B. Sullivan, the police commissioner of Montgomery, Ala., filed a libel claim against the Times and some of the civil rights leaders who had purchased the newspaper space.

Although Sullivan was not identified by name in the statement, he maintained that it was "of and concerning" him. The ad criticized public officials who used illegal tactics and violence to counter peaceful demonstrations. Sullivan maintained that the statements implicated him. He and his attorneys were able to file a libel claim in Alabama because several copies of the paper had been circulated in Montgomery County. A trial court quickly ruled in Sullivan's favor, awarding him $500,000 in damages. The Alabama Supreme Court upheld both the verdict and the award.

The New York Times appealed the case to the U.S. Supreme Court, arguing that because Sullivan was a public official, a higher standard should be applied. The case came at a critical time both in the history of the civil rights movement and for The New York Times, which could have suffered crippling financial damage if the judgment against it was affirmed. In a landmark ruling that rewrote U.S. libel law, the Court ruled 9–0 in favor of the Times, reversing the judgment of the Alabama Supreme Court.

The Court's decision in *Sullivan* was based on the premise that readily punishing a media organization for publishing criticism of government officials was contrary to "the central meaning of the First Amendment," an argument that for the first time applied the protections of the First Amendment to libel law. The Court's decision rested on the principle that media defendants did not have sufficient protection from libel suits. Awarding victories to libel plaintiffs too easily, the Court reasoned, threatened to choke off the free flow of information that is essential to the maintenance of a democratic society. Fear of making even minor errors would result in a chilling effect on the media, unduly restricting press freedom. Moreover, this freedom was especially important when it came to criticism of the government and government officials. This kind of political speech is a core First Amendment value.[143] To allow libel plaintiffs who are government officials to be successful without a showing of fault would be tantamount to reinstituting seditious libel—prohibiting criticism of the government.

REAL WORLD LAW

CONTEMPORARY THREATS TO *NEW YORK TIMES CO. V. SULLIVAN*

Between 2019 and 2022, the U.S. Supreme Court declined multiple opportunities to reconsider applying the actual malice standard to public figures. In three cases, Justices wrote concurring or dissenting opinions suggesting the Court should revisit this standard.[144]

In 2022, Justice Clarence Thomas wrote the Court should reconsider applying the actual malice standard to public figures when he dissented from the Court's decision not to hear *Coral Ridge Ministries Media, Inc. v. Southern Poverty Law Center* (SPLC), a case that involved the SPLC's designation of a religious group as a "hate group."[145]

Thomas would have heard that case, which shows "*New York Times* and its progeny have allowed media organizations and interest groups to cast false aspersions on public figures with near impunity." Thomas stated that the Court has not shown the actual malice standard fits with the original understandings of the First and Fourteenth Amendments.[146]

Justice Neil Gorsuch and Justice Thomas wrote dissenting opinions in 2021 when the Court declined to hear *Berisha v. Lawson*, a case that asked the Court to reconsider the application of actual malice to public figures. The case addressed a book's portrayal of Shkelzen Berisha as an international arms dealer who had run-ins with the Albanian mafia.[147]

Justice Gorsuch indicated the U.S. Supreme Court departed from the original meaning of press freedom (see Chapter 1) when it established the application of actual malice for public officials in 1964 in *New York Times Co. v. Sullivan*. Recognizing the media landscape had dramatically changed since 1964, Gorsuch stated the Court would benefit from reconsidering the actual malice standard. Multiple news organizations, which engaged in fact-checking, have closed. Yet, social media allows people to easily spread falsehoods and rumors.[148]

Gorsuch explained that the Supreme Court initially adopted the actual malice standard with reasoning that "tolerating the publication of *some* false information was a necessary and acceptable cost to pay to ensure truthful statements vital to democratic self-government were not inadvertently suppressed." The actual malice standard, however, has evolved "into an effective immunity from liability."[149]

Justice Thomas stated that the application of actual malice to renowned figures "bears no relation to the text, history, or structure of the Constitution." Thomas reasoned that the Court should reconsider the actual malice standard to provide public figures "the protection the First Amendment requires."[150]

Thomas explained that lies harm people regardless of whether they are public or private figures. For example, he described a shooting at a pizza shop that followed false rumors the shop was "the home of a Satanic child sex abuse ring involving top Democrats." He also reminded the Court of Kathrine McKee, who had accused comedian Bill Cosby of rape, to state "surely this Court should not remove a woman's right to defend her reputation in court simply because she accuses a powerful man of rape."[151]

In a concurring opinion in *McKee v. Cosby* in 2019, Thomas called for the Court to reconsider *New York Times Co. v. Sullivan*. Thomas argued that the landmark ruling has no basis in the Constitution as understood by the framers. "*New York Times* and the Court's decisions extending it were policy-driven decisions masquerading as constitutional law," Thomas wrote.[152]

Thomas's opinion appeared in his concurrence to the Court's decision not to hear an appeal in McKee's defamation lawsuit against Cosby. Lower courts determined that McKee is a limited-purpose public figure for defamation purposes. She said Cosby raped her. Cosby called her a liar.[153]

"Although the Court [in *New York Times Co. v. Sullivan*] held that its newly minted actual-malice rule was required by the First and Fourteenth Amendments," Thomas wrote, "it made no attempt to base that rule on the original understanding of those provisions. . . . There are sound reasons to question whether either the First or Fourteenth Amendment, as originally understood, encompasses an actual-malice standard for public figures or otherwise displaces vast swaths of state defamation law."[154]

Central to different defamation lawsuits against comedian Bill Cosby in several states are his public statements that several of his alleged victims of sexual assault lied when they accused him.

Gilbert Carrasquillo/Getty Images

For Sullivan to win his case, Justice William Brennan, Jr. wrote, the police commissioner would have to prove that The New York Times published the editorial-advertisement knowing it contained false information or with reckless disregard for its truth. This new standard of fault, Brennan wrote, is "actual malice," a statement made knowing it is false or with reckless disregard for its truth. Media defendants must have some room for error—"breathing space."[155] After this ruling, plaintiffs who are public officials must prove that defamatory content is published with actual malice—a new level of fault.

Justice Brennan explained: "We consider this case against the background of a profound national commitment to the principle that debate on public issues should be uninhibited, robust, and wide-open."[156] This debate should be open not just to members of the press but also to members of the public.[157] If libel plaintiffs were not required to show actual malice before they could win libel suits, such debate would be unduly limited because of self-censorship by both the public and the press, he wrote.[158] The Supreme Court's opinion emphasized that when people enter government service, they assume roles in which their job performance is rightly scrutinized and often criticized. Thus, the open debate the Court sought to protect "may well include vehement, caustic, and sometimes unpleasantly sharp attacks on government and public officials."[159]

Furthermore, because public officials have easy access to the news media, they have an avenue by which to correct reputational harm they may have suffered. Thus, they must meet a more difficult standard than the one applied to cases involving private plaintiffs.[160]

The opinion emphasized that the First Amendment permitted—even encouraged—an aggressive press. This was especially true with regard to the media's role as a "watchdog" in democratic society, keeping an eye on those in government. Allowing libel suits to proceed too easily would damage democracy. Referring to the consequences of large damage awards against newspapers, Brennan wrote, "Whether or not a newspaper can survive a succession of such judgments, the pall of fear and timidity imposed upon those who would give voice to public criticism is an atmosphere in which the First Amendment freedoms cannot survive."[161]

Enjoying added protection from lawsuits in public official libel cases, the news media were more aggressive in the wake of the *Sullivan* case. In the years immediately following the ruling, aggressive coverage of events such as the civil rights movement, the Vietnam War, and the Watergate scandal followed.[162]

New York Times Co. v. Sullivan "constitutionalized" libel law. The decision gave new meaning to the phrase "freedom of the press." Restricting the flow of information, as the Supreme Court observed was possible under prior libel standards, is antithetical to the First Amendment.

Actual Malice

"Actual malice" is defined as knowledge of falsity or reckless disregard for the truth. Although the examination of this concept began within the discussion of *New York Times Co. v. Sullivan*, additional scrutiny is required given the developments that followed the landmark ruling.

Knowledge of Falsity

Knowledge of falsity is nothing more than lying—publishing information with awareness it is false. Knowledge of falsity is uncommon in the news media, where truth and accuracy are universal standards. Intentionally distorted representation may rise to the level of knowledge of falsity. During the 1964 presidential campaign, for example, some people questioned Republican Party nominee Sen. Barry Goldwater's fitness for office. Fact magazine's publisher asked hundreds of psychiatrists to analyze Goldwater's mental condition in a questionnaire. He received a variety of responses but published only those that reflected poorly on the senator. When Goldwater sued for libel, the Second Circuit Court of Appeals concluded that the publisher's conduct qualified as knowledge of falsity.[163]

Does knowingly changing the quoted statements of an interview subject also qualify as knowledge of falsity? Reporter Janet Malcolm did just that in articles published in The New Yorker. The articles were based on more than 40 hours of taped interviews with psychoanalyst Jeffrey Masson. The U.S. Supreme Court noted that in those hours of recorded interviews, no statements identical to the challenged passages appeared. In its decision, the Court ruled that while readers presume that words within quotation marks are verbatim reproductions of what the interviewee said, it would be unrealistic for the law to require the press to meet such a standard. Justice Anthony Kennedy wrote, "A deliberate alteration of the words uttered by a plaintiff does not equate with knowledge of falsity . . . unless the alteration results in a material change in the meaning conveyed by the statement."[164] Absent an alteration that changes the meaning, the words remain substantially true. Courts today often refer to the outcome in the *Masson* case as the material change of meaning doctrine.

In 2014, the U.S. Supreme Court further clarified the material change of meaning doctrine in a case involving a former pilot who sued an airline for defamation after the airline reported his "suspicious" behavior to the Transportation Security Administration.[165] The Aviation and Transportation Security Act (ATSA) has an immunity provision for reporting suspicious behavior to the TSA. In a 6–3 vote, the Supreme Court said the ATSA provided immunity to the airline unless the disclosure to the ATSA was made with actual malice. The court applied the *New York Times Co. v. Sullivan* actual malice standard and wrote that immunity applied unless the statements to the ATSA were materially false.[166] Writing for the majority, Justice Sonia Sotomayor said that to accept the plaintiff's demand for precise wording in reporting suspicious behavior to the ATSA "would vitiate the purpose of ATSA immunity," and that "baggage handlers, flight attendants, gate agents and other airline employees who report suspicious behavior to the [A]TSA should not face financial ruin if, in the heat of a potential threat, they fail to choose their words with exacting care."[167]

Reckless Disregard for the Truth. **Reckless disregard for the truth** may be thought of as highly irresponsible journalism, such as publishing information with serious doubts about whether the information could be correct. In its *New York Times Co. v. Sullivan* ruling, the U.S. Supreme Court made it clear that the failure by the newspaper in that case to check the advertisement against its own records did not rise to the level of reckless disregard considering that credible sources appeared to have shown support for the advertisement's messages. A few years later, the Court considered two cases simultaneously that added to the understanding of reckless disregard. In the first, a weekly magazine, The Saturday Evening Post, published an article in 1963 about an attempt to fix a 1962 college football game. The magazine's source claimed he had been "patched" into a telephone conversation between the athletic director at the University of Georgia, Wally Butts, and the head football coach at the University of Alabama, Paul "Bear" Bryant. Moreover, the source claimed that in the call he heard the two men arranging the fix. The source, George Burnett, said he took careful notes of the conversation.

The Saturday Evening Post based its article on Burnett's recollection but never asked to see his notes. No effort was made by the magazine to corroborate the information with other sources, nor were other potential sources of information consulted, such as football experts, game films, or witnesses. Burnett's credibility also went unchecked. It turned out he had a criminal record. As Justice John Marshall Harlan II wrote for the Court, "In short, the evidence is ample to support a finding of highly unreasonable conduct constituting an extreme departure from the standards of investigation and reporting ordinarily adhered to by responsible publishers." The Court indicated that the lack of responsibility by The Saturday Evening Post clearly qualified as conduct that rises to the level of reckless disregard for the truth.[168]

In the second case, a retired major general, Edwin Walker, sued the Associated Press (AP) for its reports on his role in incidents surrounding efforts to keep the peace at the University of Mississippi when it was enrolling its first Black student in 1962. The AP reported that Walker had taken command of a violent crowd of protesters and had personally led a charge against federal marshals sent there to enforce a court decree and to assist in preserving order. The report also described Walker as encouraging rioters to use violence and giving them technical advice on combating the effects of tear gas. These false statements were distributed to several other media outlets.[169]

Edwin Walker stands between U.S. Marshals in 1962 after the University of Mississippi admitted its first Black student.

Paul Slade/Paris Match via Getty Images

In distinguishing the two cases, the Supreme Court cited one significant factor: "The evidence showed that the Butts story was in no sense 'hot news,' and the editors of the magazine recognized the need for a thorough investigation of the serious charges. . . . In contrast to the

Butts article, the dispatch which concerns us in *Walker* was news which required immediate dissemination. . . . Considering the necessity for rapid dissemination, nothing in this series of events gives the slightest hint of a severe departure from accepted publishing standards."[170]

Thus, the urgency of a story has a significant bearing on whether the methods used by the news media defendant exhibit reckless disregard for the truth. The Court is willing to allow the news media some wiggle room when there is deadline pressure. In addition, the reliability of a story's source and the believability of the information are factors in the judgment.

POINTS OF LAW
"RECKLESS DISREGARD" CRITERIA

- *Urgency of the story.* Is there time to check the information?
- *Source reliability.* Is the source trustworthy?
- *Number of sources.* Is there more than one source?
- *Story believability.* Is further examination necessary?

The following year, the U.S. Supreme Court further developed its reckless disregard standard. The Court admitted that "reckless disregard" cannot be summarized in a single definition; "There must be sufficient evidence to permit the conclusion that the defendant in fact entertained serious doubts as to the truth of his publication," according to the Court. "Publishing with such doubts shows reckless disregard for the truth or falsity and demonstrates actual malice."[171]

In determining the publisher's state of mind, the Supreme Court infused an element of subjectivity. The Court said the purpose of the actual malice standard was to emphasize free expression. If it erred in its definition of reckless disregard, the Court said it would do so on the side that enhanced rather than chilled expression.

Four decades ago, the Supreme Court ruled that a defendant's state of mind is relevant and can be considered as evidence.[172] Ten years later, the Court held that reckless disregard does not necessarily need to focus on any single lapse by the defendant. It could rest on an evaluation of the record as a whole—the more mistakes that are made, the more readily a court may conclude that a defendant acted with reckless disregard. The case involved an Ohio newspaper that acted with actual malice when it failed to interview the one witness who could have verified its story about alleged corruption in a local election for a judgeship. The newspaper did not listen to a tape it had been told would exonerate the plaintiff, a tape that the plaintiff delivered to the newspaper at the newspaper's request. An editorial the newspaper published prior to the libelous report indicated the editor had already decided to publish the allegations at issue regardless of evidence to the contrary. Discrepancies in the testimony of the defendant's own witnesses supported the idea that the defendant had failed to conduct a complete investigation with the deliberate intent of avoiding the truth. They acted with **purposeful avoidance of the truth**, publishing information when there are obvious doubts about the accuracy of information and not taking obvious steps to check its accuracy.[173]

Conceptually, reckless disregard for the truth, rather than knowledge of falsity, is more commonly present in actual malice libel claims. The reliability of sources, the believability of information, and the reporting process are still key considerations when courts consider actual malice claims today.

Based upon a review of email exchanges, electronic files, and testimony about a newspaper reporter's newsgathering process, the Supreme Court of North Carolina found a former North Carolina State Bureau of Investigation special agent provided clear and convincing evidence of reckless disregard for the truth in her claims that The News & Observer published six false and defamatory statements about her. The court explained that evidence sufficiently indicated the reporter and newspaper published those statements "with serious doubts as to the truth of the statements or a high degree of awareness of probable falsity."[174]

Challenging the reporter's credibility, the state high court noted that electronic files and email messages reporter Mandy Locke shared with colleagues indicated she had started reporting on special agent Beth Desmond's work for a series of articles on problems in the North Carolina State Bureau of Investigation.[175]

Locke's report on Desmond's testimony in a first-degree murder trial addressed photographs an attorney had taken of bullets Desmond had examined for that trial. The defendant sought a mistrial based in part on what the photographs portrayed. Desmond told Locke the photographs did not accurately show what she had observed when analyzing bullets under a microscope.[176]

Desmond and independent experts told Locke that analysis needed to be based upon observing bullets under a microscope. Desmond told Locke that Desmond's supervisor had observed the bullets under a microscope and reached the same conclusions as Desmond. Locke, however, did not interview Desmond's supervisor.[177]

After reviewing email exchanges and testimonies from four independent experts who stated they did not make defamatory statements The News & Observer attributed to them, the court reasoned it would not have made sense for those experts to have made the statements attributed to them.[178]

The state high court determined that evidence suggests the newspaper published the statements about Desmond "with serious doubts as to the truth of the statements or a high degree of awareness of probable falsity." The court concluded that the newspaper's publication of inaccurate statements stemmed from a "purposeful avoidance of the truth." The court declined to rehear the case in 2020.[179]

Public Officials. *New York Times Co. v. Sullivan* also established that not only is the content of the allegedly libelous material important, so is the nature of the plaintiff. The ruling said the standard of fault for public official plaintiffs is actual malice. Private figures, on the other hand, are usually required to show some lesser, easier-to-prove level of fault, typically negligence.

"It is clear that the public official designation applies at the very least to those among the hierarchy of government employees who have or appear to have to the public substantial responsibility for or control over the conduct of governmental affairs," wrote Justice Brennan.[180] The U.S. Supreme Court defined public officials as people the public is justified in wanting to know about because they serve the public. Information about them may relate to the officials' qualifications, conduct and character. Not all individuals paid by the government for their work will meet the criteria.

Conversely, one can meet the public official standard without being a government employee. For example, the U.S. Supreme Court held that a libel plaintiff in New Hampshire hired by three elected county commissioners to supervise a county-owned public recreation facility is a public official. "Where a position in government has such apparent importance that the public has an independent interest in the qualifications and performance of the person who holds it, beyond the general public interest in the qualifications, conduct and performance of all government employees, both elements we identified in *New York Times* are present, and the *New York Times* malice standards apply," the Court wrote.[181]

In 2021, the Supreme Court of Georgia found a part-time public defender was a public official in a defamation case addressing an ACLU blog post about the public defender's official conduct. The court reasoned the public defender was appointed to the position to provide public defense services in misdemeanor cases, and he was responsible for determining whether defendants in misdemeanor cases should receive public defender services due to inability to pay.[182]

A person usually remains a public official even after leaving a position that includes substantial responsibility for or control over the conduct of governmental affairs, as long as the allegedly libelous material pertains to the person's conduct while in that post. The U.S. Supreme Court has said that it is possible, though rare, for the passage of time to erode the public's interest in the official's conduct in office. In these unusual circumstances, the actual malice standard would no longer apply.[183]

Public Figures. In two cases decided after *New York Times Co. v. Sullivan*, the U.S. Supreme Court determined that public figures also must prove actual malice. The Court determined this in *Curtis Publishing Co. v. Butts* and *Associated Press v. Walker*, the two cases described previously and considered simultaneously by the Court. Chief Justice Earl Warren wrote, "To me, differentiation between public figures and 'public officials' and the adoption of separate standards of proof for each has no basis in law, logic, or First Amendment policy. Increasingly in this country, the distinctions between governmental and private sectors are blurred."[184] This is perhaps even more true in the 2020s than in the 1960s. One reason a higher level of fault is required of public officials is that they typically have access to the media to correct damage to their reputation. **Public figures** are plaintiffs who are in the public spotlight, usually voluntarily, who must prove the defendant acted with actual malice to win damages. Warren wrote:

"Public figures," like "public officials," often play an influential role in ordering society. And surely as a class these "public figures" have as ready access as "public officials" to the mass media of communication, both to influence policy and to counter criticism of their views and activities. Our citizenry has a legitimate and substantial interest in the conduct of such persons, and freedom of the press to engage in uninhibited debate about their involvement in public issues and events is as crucial as it is in the case of "public officials." The fact that they are not amenable to the restraints of the political process only underscores the legitimate and substantial nature of the interest, since it means that public opinion may be the only instrument by which society can attempt to influence their conduct.[185]

While the Court determined in the *Butts* and *Walker* decisions in 1967 that public figures should meet the same standard of fault as public officials, the Court identified more specific categories of public figures in subsequent cases.

All-Purpose Public Figures. The U.S. Supreme Court has defined categories of public figures required to prove actual malice as the standard of fault if they sue for libel. In *Gertz v. Robert Welch, Inc.*, the Court said that some people "occupy positions of such persuasive power and influence that they are deemed public figures for all purposes."[186] An **all-purpose public figure** is anyone a court labels to be public under all circumstances. They occupy positions of such persuasive power and influence as to be deemed public figures for all purposes. That is, no matter the context, the individual's name is widely recognizable to at least some segments of the public. In the *Gertz* ruling, Justice Lewis Powell echoed Justice Brennan's *New York Times Co. v. Sullivan* rationale, noting that an individual who seeks government office must accept "certain necessary consequences of that involvement in public affairs. He runs the risk of closer public scrutiny than might otherwise be the case."[187] He then added the key declaration: "Those classed as public figures stand in a similar position."[188]

Because the Supreme Court has said that a public figure is someone with widespread fame or notoriety, the individual's prominence is important in determining public figure status. Some courts add an additional requirement: The person must also have written or spoken about a broad range of issues. These are people who have acquired some degree of fame outside the public official sphere—"celebrities," for example. This could include not only those in the entertainment field but also some athletes, activists, religious leaders, and business leaders. All-purpose public figure libel plaintiffs are required to prove actual malice.

Limited-Purpose Public Figures. More common than all-purpose public figures are those people who have attained public figure status only within a narrow set of circumstances. These people, in the words of the Court, "have thrust themselves to the forefront of particular public controversies in order to influence the resolution of the issues involved." Like an all-purpose public figure, a **voluntary limited-purpose public figure** invites attention and comment. An individual may be a limited-purpose public figure within a particular community or a particular field.[189]

Unlike an all-purpose public figure, a limited-purpose public figure's prominence may apply only to a narrowly drawn context. Merely being an executive within a prominent and influential company, for example, does not by itself make one an all-purpose public figure. Professionals are typically not all-purpose public figures, but under certain circumstances, they can be limited-purpose public figures. For example, voluntary use of controversial or unorthodox techniques may be enough to confer limited-purpose public figure status. Publicly defending such methods or adopting other controversial stands also tends to bring about limited-purpose public figure status. A doctor who had written extensively on health issues as a newspaper columnist, who had authored several journal articles on the subject, and who had appeared on at least one nationally broadcast television program discussing health and nutrition issues was held to be a limited-purpose public figure for a limited range of issues—those pertaining to health and nutrition.[190]

A District of Columbia Court of Appeals panel recently found owners of a Russian business conglomerate were limited-purpose public figures. The case addressed a reference to the business owners in political research on potential ties between the Trump campaign and Russia. The court recognized a strong public interest in political and commercial relationships between the United States, the Russian government and Russian oligarchs. As a topic of intense national and international discussion, the topic was a public controversy. Records showed the plaintiffs were involved in litigation more than a decade earlier and subjects of multiple news stories during the decade preceding the publication of political research the business owners claimed defamed them. The U.S. Supreme Court declined to review the case in 2021.[191]

An individual may assume limited-purpose public figure status within small publics but may revert to being a private figure in larger spheres. For example, a university professor may be a public figure on campus and in the adjacent academic community but a private person beyond those boundaries. The professor's public figure status is context specific.

Although the groundwork had already been established,[192] another series of rulings by the U.S. Supreme Court more precisely articulated who qualifies as a public figure. In one case, a man had been in the news 16 years prior to a false characterization in a book, but he had not voluntarily thrust himself into the public eye. The Supreme Court ruled he was not a public figure.[193] In another case, when a wealthy and well-known socialite sued for libel over a report about her behavior that led to divorce, the Court said she was a private figure because her involvement in the divorce was not voluntary.[194] In a third case, the Court held that a scientist who had received federal grants and who had published papers in scientific journals was a private figure. The defendant claimed the scientist had become a public figure through the notoriety of his libel suit. The Court ruled that libel defendants cannot, in effect, create a public figure through the defamation claim itself or media coverage of it.[195]

POINTS OF LAW
PLAINTIFFS AND STANDARD OF FAULT[196]

Category of Plaintiff	Standard of Fault	How to Identify
Public Officials	Actual Malice	Government employees who have substantial responsibility for or control over the conduct of governmental affairs People who do not work for the government but are implicated when the public has an independent interest in their qualifications and performance (e.g., government contractors) Not ALL government employees—based on the public importance of position

Category of Plaintiff	Standard of Fault	How to Identify
All-Purpose Public Figures	Actual Malice	A person a court labels to be public under all circumstances People who occupy positions of pervasive power and influence Sometimes an additional requirement that the person has commented publicly about a broad range of issues Common examples—celebrities, professional athletes, activists, businesses and religious leaders
Limited-Purpose Public Figures	Actual Malice	People who have attained public status only within a narrow set of circumstances, such as being involved in a public controversy People who have received attention and comment by engaging or participating in a matter of public controversy and trying to affect the controversy Most common category
Private Figures	Negligence, but Sometimes Actual Malice	All those who do not qualify as public figures or limited purpose public figures Standard of fault depends on state law, typically negligence Strict liability OK in some cases involving private individuals and private speech

In some cases, defendants attempt **bootstrapping**, the forbidden practice of a defendant claiming that the plaintiff is a public figure solely on the basis of the statement that is the reason for the lawsuit. Bootstrapping occurs when media defendants "attach" themselves to the protection of the actual malice standard by citing media coverage of the plaintiff as evidence that the plaintiff is a public figure. Courts have noted that the public controversy at issue must have existed prior to the publication upon which the defamation claim is based in order for the plaintiff to be categorized as a public figure.[197] Courts attempt to carefully decide which came first: the controversy or the allegedly libelous story about the controversy.

Just as media are not permitted to bootstrap themselves onto their own material to strengthen their defense, a plaintiff may not avoid the actual malice standard by claiming that the attention was unwanted. The proper question for a court is not whether the plaintiff volunteered for the publicity but whether the plaintiff volunteered for an activity from which publicity would foreseeably arise.

Even if an individual is not active in a particular field of endeavor, presence within that field may satisfy a court's limited-purpose public figure requirements. One court explains, if a person has "chosen to engage in a profession which draws him regularly into regional and national view and leads to fame and notoriety in the community . . . he invites general public discussion. . . . If society chooses to direct massive public attention to a particular sphere of activity, those who enter that sphere inviting such attention overcome the *Times* standard."[198]

Drawing public attention to matters of public concern almost always results in a court making some kind of public figure determination because of the significance of the Supreme Court's

Gertz precedent. For example, after more than 20 other women had come forward with public accusations of sexual assault against comedian Bill Cosby, Kathrine McKee told the New York Daily News that Cosby raped her in 1974. The Daily News subsequently published an article describing McKee's account of the alleged rape. Cosby's attorney emailed the Daily News a letter refuting McKee's claims.[199]

McKee alleged that the attorney also leaked the letter to other media. Within hours, she claimed, various news organizations reported on the letter. McKee said this harmed her reputation and that her dispute with Cosby was a matter of private concern. A federal district court disagreed and dismissed McKee's defamation lawsuit, holding that she was a limited-purpose public figure who could not show actual malice.[200] The First Circuit Court of Appeals upheld the trial court ruling. "[T]he web of sexual assault allegations implicating Cosby, an internationally renowned comedian commonly referred to as America's Dad, constitutes a public controversy. . . . By purposefully disclosing to the public her own rape accusation against Cosby via an interview with a reporter, McKee thrust herself to the forefront of this controversy, seeking to influence its outcome."[201] The U.S. Supreme Court declined to hear the case in 2019.[202]

Involuntary Public Figures.   In *Gertz*, the U.S. Supreme Court also suggested that there may be a third category: involuntary public figures. An **involuntary limited-purpose public figure** "becomes a public figure through no purposeful action of his own." These are people who do not necessarily thrust themselves into public controversies voluntarily but are drawn into specific issues.[203] An individual could be drawn into a matter of public controversy through unforeseen or unintended circumstances, becoming a public figure through no purposeful action. The Court added, however, that the occurrence of such public figures is "exceedingly rare."[204] Cases surface only occasionally where plaintiffs are declared involuntary public figures.[205]

Losing Public Figure Status.   It is theoretically possible for one-time public figures or officials to revert to private status with the passage of time, but courts have been inconsistent in their application of this concept. One consideration is whether the person's role in a particular matter remains in the public consciousness or is of public concern. To return to private status, plaintiffs would likely need to demonstrate that they are no longer subjects of public concern and that their libel claims are not connected to events or controversies of which the public remains aware.

A Texas court of appeals opinion recently held a small-town police chief was a public figure less than two years after he resigned from his position. He sued a newspaper for inaccurately running his mugshot with an article about a man with the same first and last name who was charged with manufacturing and delivering a controlled substance. The subject matter of this defamation case addressed his fitness as a police officer and police chief. The court also noted a previous Fifth Circuit Court of Appeals case indicated a person had not returned to private figure status almost six years after leaving public office.[206]

Private Figures.   A libel plaintiff who does not qualify as a public official or public figure is considered a **private figure**. Private figures usually do not have to prove actual malice as the level of fault. Typically, they need to show only that the libel defendant acted with negligence.

While the definition of negligence varies from state to state, it is easier to prove than actual malice. **Negligence** is the failure to exercise reasonable or ordinary care. No single definition clearly establishes what constitutes negligence in news reporting. Media operate according to a variety of professional standards, especially as new forms of media continue to emerge. What is "acceptable" for social media may not be for television news reporting. Unlike professions in medicine or law, no single authoritative code of conduct guides reporters, public relations practitioners, or even the late-night comedians who increasingly discuss news events. Examples of negligence may include, but are not limited to, relying on a single or anonymous source, making careless misstatements about the contents of documents, failing to follow established internal practices and policies and making errors when taking notes or quoting sources.

Ohio courts recently applied a negligence standard in a case addressing a television station's coverage of a robbery on its newscast, website and Facebook page. The station showed an image of two males and a female directly under the headline "Robbers Put Gun to Child's Head and Steal Hoverboard." A station employee found the image in a law enforcement media report that indicated the people photographed "may have been involved" in the crime. The station argued that its report was based on details from a reliable source, a law enforcement media information report. A trial court granted summary judgment, reasoning a reasonable person would not find the statement defamatory. An Ohio appellate court reversed, finding a question of fact remained about whether the station "acted reasonably to ensure the accuracy of its reporting," and the Ohio Supreme Court declined to review the case in 2021.[207]

The Nature of the Statement. Whether a plaintiff is considered an all-purpose or limited-purpose public figure in a libel suit can depend on the nature of the material being published—specifically whether it relates to a matter of public concern. In a case that reached the U.S. Supreme Court, a credit reporting agency issued a credit report that erroneously reported the bankruptcy filing of a Vermont construction contractor. The credit report had been sent to five subscribers who, by agreement, could not repeat the information. The contractor sued for libel. The U.S. Supreme Court upheld a lower court ruling that the contractor was a private figure because the statement about its supposed bankruptcy was not a matter of public concern.[208] The Court wrote that the status of the speaker, the purpose of the speech, the nature of the statement and the size of the audience are relevant in determining matters of public concern.[209]

Additionally, in its 5–4 decision in *Dun & Bradstreet, Inc. v. Greenmoss Builders, Inc.*, the Supreme Court explored the question of whether **strict liability** could apply in private defamation claims involving non-media defendants. Under a strict liability standard, the plaintiff does not need to demonstrate fault on the part of the defendant in order to win the suit. The Court held that if a defendant's statement did not involve a matter of public concern, then presumed punitive damages could be awarded without a showing of actual malice.[210]

Generally speaking, a majority of lower court decisions involving libel in the private person–private information context have concluded that states can impose liability without fault in line with the Court's *Dun & Bradstreet* decision. In a federal district court in Oregon, the application of strict liability to a libel case raised questions about bloggers and their status as media defendants.[211] Kevin Padrick, a senior executive with Obsidian Finance Group, sued blogger

Crystal Cox for criticisms she posted about him and Obsidian on her personal, issue-specific website www.obsidianfinancesucks.com, as well as on some third-party websites. Cox suggested, among other things, that Padrick and Obsidian committed fraud, were corrupt and paid off the media and politicians, as well as that Padrick had hired a hit man to kill her.[212]

The court rejected Cox's claim that she was a media defendant. The court determined Cox to be a private figure because she provided no evidence of education in journalism, no connections with established news organizations, and no adherence to basic journalistic standards. The court also held that her post about Obsidian Finance did not involve matters of public concern.[213] A jury awarded damages of $1 million to Obsidian Finance and $1.5 million to Padrick.

Cox filed a motion for a new trial, arguing that the jury instructions misstated the law and that the verdict was excessive. That motion was denied. Subsequently, both Cox and Obsidian appealed to the Ninth Circuit Court of Appeals. The circuit court agreed with First Amendment scholar Eugene Volokh, who argued that Cox was entitled to the same protection afforded media defendants in the *Gertz* case. He said the court must apply at least a negligence standard of fault and that the speech at issue was a matter of public concern.[214]

The Ninth Circuit decision held that bloggers are entitled to the protection provided by *Gertz* when a blog post involves a matter of public concern. Rejecting the notion that First Amendment protection applies only to trained and credentialed journalists, the panel quoted the U.S. Supreme Court's ruling in *Citizens United v. Federal Election Commission*: "We have consistently rejected the proposition that the institutional press has any constitutional privilege beyond that of other speakers. . . . As the Supreme Court has accurately warned, a First Amendment distinction between the institutional press and other speakers is unworkable. . . . In defamation cases, the public-figure status of a plaintiff and the public importance of the statement at issue—not the identity of the speaker—provide the First Amendment touchstones."[215]

EMOTIONAL DISTRESS

Sometimes people who bring a libel lawsuit will also claim a harm that does not simply involve reputation. A news story could cause emotional distress, serious mental anguish, even though it is not defamatory. Or a libelous story injuring a plaintiff's reputation might also upset them emotionally. There are two categories of emotional distress suits. First, **intentional infliction of emotional distress** involves extreme and outrageous intentional or reckless conduct causing plaintiffs to endure severe emotional harm; public official and public figure plaintiffs must show the defendant acted with actual malice. Second, **negligent infliction of emotional distress** addresses a careless breach of a duty that causes the plaintiff severe emotional harm.

Just as a libel defendant may act with actual malice—that is, intentionally or recklessly publishing false material—so may an intentional or reckless act or statement cause emotional distress. A **reckless** action is taken with no consideration of the legal harms that might result. Also, being **negligent**—an act or statement made by mistake or without anticipating the possible harm the act or statement could cause—may inflict emotional distress, just as a negligently published article may defame someone. Emotional distress cases sometimes are called "emotional injury" or "mental distress" suits.

The law defines **emotional distress** as serious mental or emotional pain and suffering or mental anguish.[216] Plaintiffs must show the emotional injury is very serious or severe and that they experienced considerable mental pain or anguish.[217] Merely feeling upset, angry, embarrassed or resentful is not enough to win a lawsuit based on infliction of emotional distress.[218] Emotions such as severe disappointment or an intense feeling of shame or humiliation may cause the extreme mental pain the emotional distress tort requires.[219]

INTENTIONAL INFLICTION OF EMOTIONAL DISTRESS

Intentional or reckless conduct that is extreme and outrageous and causes severe emotional harm can be grounds for a successful lawsuit.[220] The key to intentional infliction of emotional distress (IIED) is that the defendant's actions must have been **outrageous**, actions a civilized society considers intolerable and beyond all bounds of decency.[221]

Intentional or Reckless

A plaintiff suing for IIED must prove the defendant acted in a way that **intentionally**—willfully or purposely—or **recklessly**—deliberate in its disregard of potential distress—caused severe emotional distress. The conduct may be considered willful, wanton, or reckless.[222]

In 2021, a federal district court denied a motion to dismiss an IIED claim that stated the plaintiff had not plausibly demonstrated defendants acted for the sole purpose of causing emotional distress. The plaintiff, a marketing executive for an insurance company, asserted that a marketing company and its owner targeted her and made false statements about her, seeking revenge for claiming the company had "fabricated invoices." The court reasoned that those "allegations support an inference" that one reason for the defendants' actions was to cause emotional distress. At trial, a plaintiff would be required to provide more evidence that defendants acted with a purpose of causing emotional distress.[223] In 2022, however, a federal district court granted a motion to dismiss part of the claim regarding statements the plaintiff had not shown to be false.[224]

When plaintiffs cannot prove defendants intentionally caused emotional distress, they may be able to prove recklessness. In a recent opinion, the U.S. Court of Appeals for the Second Circuit explained that disregarding a substantial likelihood for conduct to cause emotional distress could be considered recklessness. Engaging in conduct with knowledge of a person's susceptibility to emotional harm also may constitute recklessness.[225]

Extreme and Outrageous

Media defendants win most IIED cases primarily because courts do not find the media acted in a manner that is extreme in degree and outrageous in character. Courts may describe **outrageous** conduct as so extreme "as to go beyond all possible bounds of decency, and to be regarded as atrocious, and utterly intolerable in a civilized community."[226] Courts also may consider conduct outrageous when a defendant has knowledge a plaintiff was especially susceptible to harm by such conduct.[227]

In West Virginia, a court dismissed a defamation and IIED case against HBO and comedian John Oliver for statements made on an episode of "Last Week Tonight with John Oliver." Oliver made several critical comments about the coal industry and said that an official government investigation contradicted coal company owner Robert Murray's view that an earthquake had caused a mine collapse. The court dismissed the IIED claim on several grounds, including that the plaintiffs did not prove the statements were highly offensive and outrageous.[228]

Usually, insults or impolite comments do not amount to outrageous conduct, nor do words that cause annoyance. The high standard plaintiffs must meet—the defendant's conduct must be beyond all possible bounds of decency—is meant to prevent lawsuits being filed over mere insults, annoying comments and other remarks that are aggravating but not outrageous.[229]

In 2020, a federal district court in Massachusetts dismissed a law student's defamation and IIED case against a legal website for statements made in an article. The article criticized a judge's treatment of a law student and called the student a "little brat" who "made a series of dumb mistakes." The court held the speech was unkind and insulting, but not extreme or outrageous.[230]

Joel and Mary Rich recently settled an IIED case they filed against Fox News in 2018. The case addressed the network's coverage of a conspiracy theory about their son Seth's 2016 murder.

Matt Miller/The Washington Post via Getty Images

Fox News recently settled an IIED case the Rich family brought against Fox News, a reporter for the network, and a guest commentator for the network.[231] The settlement followed a Second Circuit Court of Appeals finding that the Riches stated a plausible IIED claim addressing extreme and outrageous conduct, plausibly amounting to "a campaign of emotional torture."[232]

Seth Rich, the son of Joel and Mary Rich, was killed in a robbery when the 27-year-old was working for the Democratic National Committee in 2016. His parents objected to a conspiracy theory alleging Seth was killed because he had leaked DNC emails to Wikileaks. Although law enforcement found no support for the conspiracy theory, a reporter and a guest commentator for Fox News sought to share the story via mainstream media.[233]

Over a six-month period, a reporter and guest commentator contacted the Riches and arranged to have a source, identified as an independent private investigator, meet with the family. The reporter and commentator told their source "an anonymous FBI investigator had seen emails between Seth and Wikileaks." Their source became the named source in a Fox News story suggesting Seth could have leaked the emails "because—as his father said—he wanted to make a difference in the world."[234] Fox News retracted the story five days later.[235]

The appeals court found the Rich family plausibly could prove outrageousness due to knowledge of their susceptibility to emotional distress. Through communication with the family, the defendants learned that the family was grieving. The family also had made a public statement that the conspiracy theory was hurting them.[236]

A federal district court in Virginia also recently found a defendant plausibly alleged conduct of website owners, operators and authors was "outrageous and intolerable." The website owners, operators and authors had falsely portrayed Brennan Gilmore, a man who recorded a vehicle hitting protestors at the 2017 "Unite the Right" rally, as a "deep state operative who conspired to orchestrate violence." The court, however, dismissed the IIED claim because Gilmore did not allege the conduct caused sufficiently severe emotional distress.[237]

Severe Emotional Distress

Proving severe emotional distress was caused by the defendant's action or expression requires proving more than having feelings of mild annoyance or embarrassment. In 2021, the Georgia Court of Appeals held a female had not sufficiently demonstrated she endured severe emotional distress as a result of a text message falsely stating she had a sexually transmitted infection (STI). She provided an affidavit stating she endured embarrassment, depression, anxiety, weight loss, hair loss and suicidal thoughts after her former companion sent a text message alleging she had an STI. The court determined there was not sufficient evidence that she experienced severe emotional distress because she had not sought medical care for those symptoms. "The law intervenes only where the distress inflicted is so severe that no reasonable [person] could be expected to endure it," the court reasoned. The court declined to reconsider the case.[238]

In addition to proving that intentional or reckless actions or statements were extreme and outrageous and caused severe emotional distress, a famous person suing for IIED also must prove actual malice.[239]

Actual Malice

The U.S. Supreme Court requires public figures to prove actual malice in addition to the tort's other elements. As discussed earlier in this chapter, in *New York Times Co. v. Sullivan*, the Supreme Court defined "actual malice" as publishing with knowledge of falsity or a reckless disregard for the truth.[240] After the Rev. Jerry Falwell sued Larry Flynt and *Hustler* magazine for intentional infliction of emotional distress, the Court extended its actual malice ruling to IIED cases in *Hustler Magazine, Inc. v. Falwell*.[241] Flynt published what he claimed was a parody of a Campari advertising campaign. At the time, Campari, a liquor manufacturer, published ads in which celebrities discussed their "first time," an obvious double entendre about tasting Campari and having sex.

In Flynt's satire, Falwell, the leader of a national organization named the Moral Majority, described his "first time" as being with his mother in an outhouse. The magazine portrayed Falwell, who was known for speaking out against immorality, as a hypocrite for engaging in immoral activities. Hustler included a disclaimer saying "ad parody—not to be taken seriously," and the magazine's table of contents cited the page as "Fiction—Ad and Personality Parody."

Falwell sued Flynt for libel, appropriation and intentional infliction of emotional distress. A federal district court jury rejected the libel claim because the satire was so outlandish no one would believe it was a statement of fact, but the jury said Flynt intentionally inflicted emotional distress. The jury awarded Falwell $100,000 in compensatory damages and $100,000 in punitive damages.[242] A federal appellate court affirmed, saying the satire was outrageous and intentionally published.[243]

Jerry Falwell talks about his first time.*

FALWELL: My first time was in an outhouse outside Lynchburg, Virginia.

INTERVIEWER: Wasn't it a little cramped?

FALWELL: Not after I kicked the goat out.

INTERVIEWER: I see. You must tell me all about it.

FALWELL: I never *really* expected to make it with Mom, but then after she showed all the other guys in town such a good time, I figured, "What the hell!"

INTERVIEWER: But your mom? Isn't that a bit odd?

FALWELL: I don't think so. Looks don't mean that much to me in a woman.

INTERVIEWER: Go on.

FALWELL: Well, we were drunk off our God-fearing asses on Campari, ginger ale and soda—that's called a Fire and Brimstone—at the time. And Mom looked better than a Baptist whore with a $100 donation.

INTERVIEWER: Campari in the crapper with Mom . . . how interesting. Well, how was it?

FALWELL: The Campari was great, but Mom passed out before I could come.

INTERVIEWER: Did you ever try it again?

FALWELL: Sure . . .

lots of times. But not in the outhouse. Between Mom and the shit, the flies were too much to bear.

INTERVIEWER: We meant the Campari.

FALWELL: Oh, yeah. I always get sloshed before I go out to the pulpit. You don't think I could lay down all that bullshit *sober*, do you?

© 1983—Imported by Campari U.S.A. New York, NY. 48°proof Spirit Apéritif (Liqueur)

Campari, like all liquor, was made to mix you up. It's a light, 48-proof, refreshing spirit, just mild enough to make you drink too much before you know you're schnockered. For your first time, mix it with orange juice. Or maybe some white wine. Then you won't remember anything the next morning. *Campari. The mixable that smarts.*

CAMPARI You'll never forget your first time.

*"AD PARODY—NOT TO BE TAKEN SERIOUSLY"

The ad parody that prompted Jerry Falwell to sue Larry Flynt and Hustler magazine.

But the U.S. Supreme Court reversed that decision, holding that as a public figure Falwell had to present proof that a false statement of fact was made with actual malice.[244] The Court found that, as satire, the First Amendment protected the magazine's Campari ad. Biting, even hurtful, humor is the stock-in-trade of satirical works, the Court found, and it was simply not possible to create a constitutionally valid distinction between political cartoons and satires and the arguably tasteless Campari ad spoof. If juries were permitted to award damages for such satires, the Court warned, jurors could decide what was outrageous based on their political leanings, which would violate the First Amendment.[245]

Not all parodies and satires were protected, the *Falwell* Court said. A public figure or public official who could prove that a satire included a false statement of fact published with actual malice could win a lawsuit for IIED. Because the jury in this case had found there were no factual statements in the piece—it was just a parody—Falwell could not successfully sue for IIED.[246]

The Court also suggested Falwell might have used the IIED tort as a replacement for his rejected libel claim. The Court reasoned that if public figures had to prove actual malice to win libel cases, they should carry that burden for IIED as well.[247]

Matters of Public Concern

In 2011, the U.S. Supreme Court again ruled that an IIED claim infringed the First Amendment. The Court said in *Snyder v. Phelps* that speech about matters of public concern, even "particularly hurtful" expression, is protected against an IIED lawsuit.[248] In *Snyder v. Phelps*, protesters from Westboro Baptist Church in Kansas picketed the funeral of a Marine killed in action in Iraq. Westboro's 75 congregants, most of whom were church founder Fred Phelps' family members, believed "God hates and punishes the United States for its tolerance of homosexuality, particularly in America's military," according to the Court.[249] The group expressed its views by picketing, frequently near military funerals.

Phelps and six of his family members picketed 1,000 feet from the Marine's hometown Catholic church for 30 minutes before the funeral. They displayed signs saying, for example, "God Hates the USA/Thank God for 9/11," "Thank God for Dead Soldiers" and "Pope in Hell." Only the tops of the signs were visible to those in the funeral procession as it passed close to the protesters. Later that evening, while watching a televised news report about the demonstration, the Marine's father, Albert Snyder, saw what the signs said.[250]

Snyder sued for IIED and other torts. He said several of the signs, such as those saying "You're Going to Hell" and "God Hates You," were directed at him. The jury granted a multimillion-dollar award for the IIED and other claims. Phelps appealed. The Fourth Circuit Court of Appeals reversed, holding that the First Amendment protected Westboro's statements because they dealt with matters of public concern, could not be proven false and were hyperbole.[251]

The U.S. Supreme Court agreed with the appellate court. Westboro's signs related to matters of public concern, and as *New York Times Co. v. Sullivan* emphasized, the First Amendment stands for "a profound national commitment to the principle that debate on public issues should be uninhibited, robust, and wide-open," the Court ruled. Citing *Hustler Magazine, Inc. v. Falwell*, the Court said the First Amendment may be a defense against an IIED claim.[252]

Westboro Baptist Church members in front of the U.S. Supreme Court building as the Court hands down its *Snyder v. Phelps* decision.

Chip Somodevilla/Getty Images

In response to the *Snyder* decision, Congress adopted a law forbidding protests two hours before or after a military funeral and demonstrations closer than 300 feet from such funerals with a possible award of $50,000 in statutory damages.[253]

The Court did not decide whether expression directed to a private individual or during disorderly demonstrations would be protected against an IIED claim even if the content addressed matters of public concern. The Court said it did not consider whether the Marine's father was a public or private figure. Had he been found a public figure, he would have had to prove actual malice, as the Court said in *Falwell*. But in *Snyder*, the Court said the Westboro picketers were aiming their expression at the general public, not at Albert Snyder or his family. Because the expression was about matters of public concern and was directed toward a broad audience, the speech was protected regardless of what elements Snyder had to prove to win an IIED lawsuit.[254]

In 2021, an unpublished Second Circuit Court of Appeals opinion indicated the First Amendment barred an intentional infliction of emotional distress claim addressing a Connecticut television news report that described the conduct of a man arrested for allegedly following a woman as stalking. Affirming a district court's dismissal of the claim, the appeals court described the news reports as substantially true discussions of public affairs. The U.S. Supreme Court declined to review the case.[255]

NEGLIGENT INFLICTION OF EMOTIONAL DISTRESS

If one person carelessly causes another emotional harm, the injured person may sue using a tort called negligent infliction of emotional distress (NIED). The law asks whether defendants should have anticipated that their careless actions would injure the plaintiffs. More formally, a plaintiff suing for NIED must prove (1) the defendant had a duty to use due care, (2) the defendant negligently breached that duty, (3) the breach caused the plaintiff's injury, and (4) the breach was the proximate cause of the plaintiff's severe emotional distress.[256]

In an unpublished 2019 decision, the Sixth Circuit Court of Appeals found a memoir author failed to adequately state a claim for negligent infliction of emotional distress against the publisher of the Fifty Shades trilogy. The memoir author claimed she suffered from hair loss and lesions due to stress from believing the trilogy was based on her work without her permission. The Sixth Circuit, however, explained the author had not shown the publisher owed her any **duty of care**.[257] A duty of due care means the defendant should have foreseen that negligence could cause harm to the person or people to whom they owed a duty. Breaching the duty means the defendant did not act as a reasonable person would.

Causing the plaintiff's emotional distress means the defendant's actions were the direct reason the plaintiff was emotionally harmed. This may be called "cause-in-fact." **Proximate cause** is the law's way of asking if it is reasonable to conclude the defendant caused the plaintiff's injury. NIED suits against the media often turn on the proximate cause question. Courts usually find that actions taken by a media organization are only tangentially related to the plaintiff's injury. If the connection between what the organization did and how the plaintiff was injured is too indirect to find the mass medium responsible, the plaintiff cannot prove proximate cause.

Courts in some states require plaintiffs to show a degree of physical harm.[258] The harm may be that the defendant physically injured (or even just touched) the plaintiff, caused emotional harm or caused emotional harm resulting in physical symptoms.[259] The plaintiff's challenge is convincing courts that an emotional distress claim is real. Courts see the NIED tort as caught between two important concerns. The law wants to compensate people whose emotional injuries are caused by others' negligence. Judges, however, want to avoid suits for trivial or fraudulent emotional harm claims.[260] These competing interests have "caused inconsistency and incoherence in the law," one court said.[261]

In 2021, the Eleventh Circuit Court of Appeals dismissed a negligent infliction of emotional distress claim filed against Twitter, Google and Facebook. Victims of a shooting at a Florida night club and family members of victims of that shooting claimed the media platforms helped the shooter access radical jihadist and ISIS-sponsored content.[262]

The Eleventh Circuit explained that negligent infliction of emotional distress in Florida requires proving proximate cause as well as actual harm. Under Florida law, harm may be deemed proximate if human foresight "would lead one to expect that similar harm is likely to be substantially caused" by an act or omission. The court said that how the state would apply that rule of law to third-party actions when the applicable doctrine was not made clear.[263]

POINTS OF LAW

IIED AND NIED

Plaintiff's Case (IIED)*
   Defendant's intentional or reckless conduct

- was extreme and outrageous—beyond the bounds of decency tolerated in civilized society;
- involved actual malice if plaintiff is a public official or public figure; and
- caused plaintiff's severe emotional distress.

---

*If the expression is about matters of public concern and directed toward a broad audience, the First Amendment may protect the expression against an IIED claim.

Plaintiff's Case (NIED)

- Defendant had a duty to use care;
- defendant negligently breached that duty;
- the breach caused the plaintiff's injury; and
- the breach was the proximate cause of the plaintiff's severe emotional distress.

NIED suits against the media usually fail, although plaintiffs have successfully sued for NIED when the media have put them in harm's way. For example, after a woman had been physically attacked, but before the assailant was apprehended by police, a newspaper published the woman's name and address. After the newspaper published the article, the assailant terrorized his victim several more times. A Missouri appellate court upheld the victim's NIED suit.[264]

EMERGING LAW

As electronic media has made it easier for people to immediately share digital content with vast audiences around the globe, courts have considered significant questions about defamation, intentional infliction of emotional distress and negligent infliction of emotional distress law.

Courts have seen a surge of defamation cases in which plaintiffs seek not only damages but also a court order (called injunctive relief) to stop future publication of defamatory content.[265] As part of a libel suit Project Veritas filed against The New York Times in 2020, a New York judge prohibited The New York Times from publishing documents a lawyer prepared for Project Veritas. In 2021, a judge also required the newspaper to turn over physical copies of the documents and destroy electronic copies.[266] On appeal, the paper was not required to turn over documents or destroy electronic copies, but the paper was not allowed to publish the documents.[267] A subsequent appellate review issued a stay, allowing the newspaper to publish excerpts from Project Veritas attorney memos.[268]

The bar for an injunction is very high because of concerns about prior restraint. The First Circuit Court of Appeals recently considered whether a court could impose a permanent injunction when prior defamatory claims are likely to be repeated.[269] On appeal, the court vacated the permanent injunction, writing that it could not survive the "scrutiny that the Constitution demands for prior restraints on speech."[270] The court stated, "By its very nature, defamation is an inherently contextual tort."[271]

In 2022, a federal judge in Georgia granted a permanent injunction related to a defamation, intentional infliction of emotional distress, and false light invasion of privacy case. The order prohibits YouTuber TashaK and TashaK's production company from publishing or republishing false and defamatory assertions about Grammy-winning musician Cardi B.[272] The injunction followed a jury award of almost $4 million in damages to Cardi B. TashaK immediately appealed the district court's confirmation of the jury verdict.[273] The Eleventh Circuit Court of Appeals dismissed that appeal, reasoning the appeal was filed before the district court's judgment was final.[274] Tasha K then declared her intention to file another appeal later in 2022.[275]

Musician Cardi B sought and received a permanent injunction to prevent TashaK and the YouTuber's production company from publishing or republishing false and defamatory statements about Cardi B.

Nicholas Hunt/Getty Images

Also in 2022, the U.S. Supreme Court declined to reconsider whether public figure defamation plaintiffs must prove actual malice in *Coral Ridge Ministries Media, Inc. v. Southern Poverty Law Center*. Justice Thomas wrote a dissenting opinion, explaining he would hear the case to revisit the actual malice standard.[276] Between March 17 and June 7, the Court had rescheduled the case eleven times, moving the case from one Justice's private conferences to another's private conferences before the Justices discussed the case.[277]

Coral Ridge Ministries Media, Inc. alleged it was defamed when the Southern Poverty Law Center (SPLC) listed the religious organization on a "Hate Map." In 2021, the Eleventh Circuit Court of Appeals found a federal district court had not erroneously concluded the religious organization failed to prove the SPLC acted with actual malice. Considering the SPLC website explains hate groups are "organizations that have beliefs or practices that attack or malign an entire class of people, typically for their immutable characteristics," the Eleventh Circuit found it hard to conceive the SPLC use of that term based on the religious group's opposition of homosexual conduct would be misleading. Coral Ridge Ministries Media, Inc. also did not prove the SPLC "doubted the truth of its designation," the court said.[278]

In 2021, the U.S. Supreme Court declined to hear two defamation claims that involved questions about actual malice. *Tah v. Global Witness Publishing, Inc.* addressed two former Liberian officials' complaint that an international human rights organization published false and defamatory statements suggesting the officials accepted bribes. The District of Columbia Circuit Court of Appeals had affirmed a district court's dismissal of the defamation complaint due to the officials' failure to plausibly demonstrate the statements were published with actual malice.[279]

A District of Columbia Circuit majority opinion did not perceive allegations the human rights organization's investigation was based on a preconceived storyline to be sufficient evidence of actual malice. Nor did the majority opinion consider allegations of publishing the report with ill will to be evidence of actual malice. The majority also reasoned that omitting from the report that the officials denied allegations of bribery was not evidence of publishing with a "high degree of awareness of probably falsity." The majority explained the implications that such factors could infer actual malice would have significant implications for investigative journalism.[280]

In the U.S. Supreme Court's denial of a second case, Justices Thomas and Gorsuch proposed the nation's highest court should reconsider the actual malice standard now that social media allows users to instantly become public figures, to spread false information without fact-checking its accuracy and to spread disinformation.[281]

Comments made during confirmation hearings before the U.S. Senate suggest atleast two other recently confirmed Justices might be open to reconsidering *New York Times Co. v. Sullivan.* Justice Amy Coney Barrett did not list *Sullivan* among "super-precedents that could not be overturned," and she declined to comment on Justice Thomas's criticism of the actual malice standard. Justice Elena Kagan said, "The Framers of the Constitution did not understand the First Amendment as extending to libelous speech."[282] When asked about this precedent in 2022, Justice Ketanji Brown Jackson stated criteria for overturning precedent without indicating how she would apply the criteria to consider this precedent.[283]

Media lawyer Matthew Schafer has challenged assertions that the actual malice standard should be reconsidered. Schafer asserted there is historical support for the precedent, and overturning *Sullivan* would seem more likely "to chill reputable news organizations while doing little to deter bad actors operating anonymously on the internet."[284]

Courts have considered media defendants' uses of social media, email and other emerging technologies when evaluating whether defendants acted with actual malice.[285] For example, in 2021, the Eighth Circuit Court of Appeals allowed to proceed Congressman Devin Nunes's libel claim addressing a reporter's tweet about an article that was the basis of a libel suit. The libel claim provided notification that the article contained false and defamatory information, which might be considered evidence of reckless disregard. Reasoning it might be plausible to believe reporter Ryan Lizza "engaged in the purposeful avoidance of the truth," an Eighth Circuit panel remanded this part of the case for further proceedings.[286] The Eighth Circuit declined to hear an appeal en banc.[287]

In 2021, the Supreme Court of Rhode Island indicated NBC 10 WJAR did not act with purposeful avoidance of the truth when reporting on a parking ticket scandal. A nightly newscast indicated police officers had issued significantly more parking tickets in the districts of two council members who had opposed a police union proposal. A police captain named in the story claimed the station published false and defamatory assertions of fact about him with reckless disregard for the truth.[288]

The news report was based on information received from an anonymous source and a former police officer the reporter believed were credible sources. The reporter had tried calling the captain to confirm the story, but was not able to reach the captain. The Supreme Court of Rhode Island indicated that nothing in the record indicated the reporter's reliance on those sources or reasons for finding them credible were reckless "or that he had any serious doubts about the veracity of what they were relating to him."[289]

The chief of police at that time told the reporter the captain was not involved in the scandal.[290] The court cited precedent indicating mere denials related to a political issue are too common to provide clear and convincing evidence of likely errors or serious doubts. The court, thus, affirmed a lower court's grant of a motion of summary judgment for the defendant.[291]

The plaintiff in that case also filed intentional infliction of emotional distress and negligent infliction of emotional distress claims. Affirming a lower court's grant of a motion of summary judgment for the defendant on those claims as well, the Supreme Court of Rhode Island cited a basic principle of media law, "one may not breathe life into an otherwise doomed defamation claim by re-baptizing it as a different cause of action."[292]

Other recent cases have clarified that some states do not allow plaintiffs to receive damages for IIED in claims when they may receive damages under defamation or other laws. For example, the Fifth Circuit Court of Appeals stated in 2021 that Texas considers IIED to be "a gap-filler tort," which means a plaintiff cannot recover damages for IIED when a plaintiff could recover damages under another area of law, such as recovering damages for harm to reputation under defamation law.[293] The Second Circuit Court of Appeals also indicated that in New York IIED may be invoked in circumstances under which other laws would not allow recovery of damages.[294] In 2020, however, a U.S. District Court for the District of Massachusetts stated "[A] failed defamation claim cannot be recycled as a tort claim for negligent or intentional infliction of emotional distress."[295]

KEYTERMS

actual malice	defamatory
all-purpose public figures	duty of care
assertion of fact	emotional distress
bootstrapping	falsity
burden of proof	fault
Communications Decency Act	identification
damages	intentional infliction of emotional distress
defamation plaintiff's case	involuntary public figure

knowledge of falsity
libel by implication
libel per quod
libel per se
limited-purpose public figure
motion to dismiss
negligence
negligent
negligent infliction of emotional distress
outrageous and extreme conduct

prima facie
private figure
publication
public figures
purposeful avoidance of the truth
reckless
reckless disregard for the truth
republication
Sedition Act of 1798
substantial truth

CASES FOR STUDY
THINKING ABOUT THEM

The two case excerpts that follow are considered landmark cases about both libel and intentional infliction of emotional distress. As you read these case excerpts, keep the following questions in mind:

- How do the two decisions help define the meaning of actual malice as it applies to public officials and public figures?
- What are the important concepts that each of these decisions adds to laws about libel and intentional infliction of emotional distress?
- According to the U.S. Supreme Court in *New York Times Co. v. Sullivan* and in *Hustler Magazine, Inc. v. Falwell*, how does libel law implicate the First Amendment?
- What approach does the Supreme Court take in trying to balance First Amendment rights against the right not to be emotionally harmed and to protect your reputation?

NEW YORK TIMES CO. V. SULLIVAN
SUPREME COURT OF THE UNITED STATES 376 U.S. 254 (1964)

JUSTICE WILLIAM BRENNAN, Jr. delivered the Court's opinion:

We are required in this case to determine for the first time the extent to which the constitutional protections for speech and press limit a State's power to award damages in a libel action brought by a public official against critics of his official conduct.

Respondent L.B. Sullivan is one of the three elected Commissioners of the City of Montgomery, Alabama. He testified that he was "Commissioner of Public Affairs and the duties are supervision of the Police Department, Fire Department, Department of Cemetery and Department of Scales." He brought this civil libel action against the four individual petitioners, who are Negroes and Alabama clergymen, and against petitioner the New York Times Company, a New York corporation which publishes the New York Times, a daily newspaper. A jury in the Circuit Court of Montgomery County awarded him damages of $500,000, the full amount claimed, against all the petitioners, and the Supreme Court of Alabama affirmed. . . .

Of the 10 paragraphs of text in the advertisement, the third and a portion of the sixth were the basis of respondent's claim of libel. . . .

It is uncontroverted that some of the statements contained in the two paragraphs were not accurate descriptions of events which occurred in Montgomery. Although Negro students staged a demonstration on the State Capitol steps, they sang the National Anthem and not "My Country, 'Tis of Thee." Although nine students were expelled by the State Board of Education, this was not for leading the demonstration at the Capitol, but for demanding service at a lunch counter in the Montgomery County Courthouse on another day. Not the entire student body, but most of it, had protested the expulsion, not by refusing to register, but by boycotting classes on a single day; virtually all the students did register for the ensuing semester. . . .

Because of the importance of the constitutional issues involved, we granted the separate petitions for certiorari of the individual petitioners and of the Times. We reverse the judgment. We hold that the rule of law applied by the Alabama courts is constitutionally deficient for failure to provide the safeguards for freedom of speech and of the press that are required by the First and Fourteenth Amendments in a libel action brought by a public official against critics of his official conduct. We further hold that under the proper safeguards the evidence presented in this case is constitutionally insufficient to support the judgment for respondent. . . .

The publication here was not a "commercial" advertisement . . . [that] communicated information, expressed opinion, recited grievances, protested claimed abuses, and sought financial support on behalf of a movement whose existence and objectives are matters of the highest public interest and concern. That the Times was paid for publishing the advertisement is as immaterial in this connection as is the fact that newspapers and books are sold. . . . Any other conclusion would discourage newspapers from carrying "editorial advertisements" of this type, and so might shut off an important outlet for the promulgation of information and ideas by persons who do not themselves have access to publishing facilities—who wish to exercise their freedom of speech even though they are not members of the press. . . . To avoid placing such a handicap upon the freedoms of expression, we hold that, if the allegedly libelous statements would otherwise be constitutionally protected from the present judgment, they do not forfeit that protection because they were published in the form of a paid advertisement. . . .

The general proposition that freedom of expression upon public questions is secured by the First Amendment has long been settled by our decisions. The constitutional safeguard, we have said, "was fashioned to assure unfettered interchange of ideas for the bringing about of political and social changes desired by the people. . . ."

. . . The First Amendment, said Judge Learned Hand, "presupposes that right conclusions are more likely to be gathered out of a multitude of tongues, than through any kind of authoritative selection. To many this is, and always will be, folly; but we have staked upon it our all." . . . Thus we consider this case against the background of a profound national commitment to the principle that debate on public issues should be uninhibited, robust, and wide-open, and that it may well include vehement, caustic, and sometimes unpleasantly sharp attacks on government and public officials. The present advertisement, as an expression of grievance and protest on one of the major public issues of our time, would seem clearly to qualify for the constitutional protection. The question is whether it forfeits that protection by the falsity of some of its factual statements and by its alleged defamation of respondent. . . .

That erroneous statement is inevitable in free debate, and . . . it must be protected if the freedoms of expression are to have the "breathing space" that they "need . . . to survive. . . ."

Injury to official reputation affords no more warrant for repressing speech that would otherwise be free than does factual error. . . .

If neither factual error nor defamatory content suffices to remove the constitutional shield from criticism of official conduct, the combination of the two elements is no less inadequate. . . .

. . . A rule compelling the critic of official conduct to guarantee the truth of all his factual assertions—and to do so on pain of libel judgments virtually unlimited in amount—leads to a comparable "self-censorship." Allowance of the defense of truth, with the burden of proving it on the defendant, does not mean that only false speech will be deterred. . . . The constitutional guarantees require, we think, a federal rule that prohibits a public official from recovering damages for a defamatory falsehood relating to his official conduct unless he proves that the statement was made with "actual malice"—that is, with knowledge that it was false or with reckless disregard of whether it was false or not. . . .

. . . As Madison said, "the censorial power is in the people over the Government, and not in the Government over the people." It would give public servants an unjustified preference over the public they serve, if critics of official conduct did not have a fair equivalent of the immunity granted to the officials themselves. . . .

We hold today that the Constitution delimits a State's power to award damages for libel in actions brought by public officials against critics of their official conduct. Since this is such an action, the rule requiring proof of actual malice is applicable. . . .

Applying these standards, we consider that the proof presented to show actual malice lacks the convincing clarity which the constitutional standard demands, and hence that it would not constitutionally sustain the judgment for respondent under the proper rule of law. . . .

Finally, there is evidence that the Times published the advertisement without checking its accuracy against the news stories in the Times' own files. The mere presence of the stories in the files does not, of course, establish that the Times "knew" the advertisement was false, since the state of mind required for actual malice would have to be brought home to the persons in the Times' organization having responsibility for the publication of the advertisement. . . .

The judgment of the Supreme Court of Alabama is reversed and the case is remanded to that court for further proceedings not inconsistent with this opinion.

Reversed and remanded.

HUSTLER MAGAZINE, INC. V. FALWELL
SUPREME COURT OF THE UNITED STATES 485 U.S. 46 (1988)

CHIEF JUSTICE WILLIAM REHNQUIST delivered the Court's opinion:

Petitioner Hustler Magazine, Inc., is a magazine of nationwide circulation. Respondent Jerry Falwell, a nationally known minister who has been active as a commentator on politics and public affairs, sued petitioner and its publisher, petitioner Larry Flynt, to recover damages for invasion of privacy, libel, and intentional infliction of emotional distress. . . .

The inside front cover of the November 1983 issue of Hustler Magazine featured a "parody" of an advertisement for Campari Liqueur that contained the name and picture of respondent and was entitled "Jerry Falwell talks about his first time." This parody was modeled after actual Campari ads that included interviews with various celebrities about their "first times." Although it was apparent by the end of each interview that this meant the first time they sampled Campari, the ads clearly played on the sexual double entendre of the general subject of "first times." Copying the form and layout of these Campari ads, Hustler's editors chose respondent as the featured celebrity and drafted an alleged "interview" with him in which he states that his "first time" was during a drunken incestuous rendezvous with his mother in an outhouse. The Hustler parody portrays respondent and his mother as drunk and immoral, and suggests that respondent is a hypocrite who preaches only when he is drunk. In small print at the bottom of the page, the ad contains the disclaimer, "ad parody—not to be taken seriously." The magazine's table of contents also lists the ad as "Fiction; Ad and Personality Parody."

[Falwell sued. He failed on the libel and privacy claims.] The jury ruled for respondent on the intentional infliction of emotional distress claim. . . .

On appeal, the United States Court of Appeals for the Fourth Circuit affirmed the judgment against petitioners. . . .

At the heart of the First Amendment is the recognition of the fundamental importance of the free flow of ideas and opinions on matters of public interest and concern. . . . We have therefore been particularly vigilant to ensure that individual expressions of ideas remain free from governmentally imposed sanctions. . . .

The sort of robust political debate encouraged by the First Amendment is bound to produce speech that is critical of those who hold public office or those public figures who are "intimately involved in the resolution of important public questions or, by reason of their fame, shape events in areas of concern to society at large." . . . Such criticism, inevitably, will not always be reasoned or moderate; public figures as well as public officials will be subject to "vehement, caustic, and sometimes unpleasantly sharp attacks." . . .

Of course, this does not mean that any speech about a public figure is immune from sanction in the form of damages. Since *New York Times Co. v. Sullivan*, we have consistently ruled that a public figure may hold a speaker liable for the damage to reputation caused by publication of a defamatory falsehood, but only if the statement was made "with knowledge that it was false or with reckless disregard of whether it was false or not." False statements of fact are particularly valueless; they interfere with the truth-seeking function of the marketplace of ideas, and they cause damage to an individual's reputation that cannot easily be repaired by counterspeech, however persuasive or effective. But even though falsehoods have little value in and of themselves, they are "nevertheless inevitable in free debate," and a rule that would impose strict liability on a publisher for false factual assertions would have an undoubted "chilling" effect on speech relating to public figures that does have constitutional value. "Freedoms of expression require 'breathing space.'" This breathing space is provided by a constitutional rule that allows public figures to recover for libel or defamation only when they can prove both that the statement was false and that the statement was made with the requisite level of culpability. . . .

Generally speaking, the law does not regard the intent to inflict emotional distress as one which should receive much solicitude, and it is quite understandable that most if not all jurisdictions have chosen to make it civilly culpable where the conduct in question is sufficiently "outrageous." But in the world of debate about public affairs, many things done with motives that are less than admirable are protected by the First Amendment. . . .

[Although] a bad motive may be deemed controlling for purposes of tort liability in other areas of the law, we think the First Amendment prohibits such a result in the area of public debate about public figures.

Were we to hold otherwise, there can be little doubt that political cartoonists and satirists would be subjected to damages awards without any showing that their work falsely defamed its subject. . . .

. . . Several famous examples of this type of intentionally injurious speech were drawn by Thomas Nast, probably the greatest American cartoonist to date, who was associated for many years during the post–Civil War era with Harper's Weekly. In the pages of that publication Nast conducted a graphic vendetta against William M. "Boss" Tweed and his corrupt associates in New York City's "Tweed Ring." It has been described by one historian of the subject as "a sustained attack which in its passion and effectiveness stands alone in the history of American graphic art." . . .

Despite their sometimes caustic nature, from the early cartoon portraying George Washington as an ass down to the present day, graphic depictions and satirical cartoons have played a prominent role in public and political debate. . . .

Respondent contends, however, that the caricature in question here was so "outrageous" as to distinguish it from more traditional political cartoons. There is no doubt that the caricature of respondent and his mother published in Hustler is at best a distant cousin of the political cartoons described above, and a rather poor relation at that. If it were possible by laying down a principled standard to separate the one from the other, public discourse would probably suffer little or no harm. But we doubt that there is any such standard, and we are quite sure that the pejorative description "outrageous" does not supply one. "Outrageousness" in the area of political and social discourse has an inherent subjectiveness about it which would allow a jury to impose liability on the basis of the jurors' tastes or views, or perhaps on the basis of their dislike of a particular expression. An "outrageousness" standard thus runs afoul of our longstanding refusal to allow damages to be awarded because the speech in question may have an adverse emotional impact on the audience. . . .

We conclude that public figures and public officials may not recover for the tort of intentional infliction of emotional distress by reason of publications such as the one here at issue without showing in addition that the publication contains a false statement of fact which was made with "actual malice," *i.e.*, with knowledge that the statement was false or with reckless disregard as to whether or not it was true. This is not merely a "blind application" of the *New York Times* standard, it reflects our considered judgment that such a standard is necessary to give adequate "breathing space" to the freedoms protected by the First Amendment.

Here it is clear that respondent Falwell is a "public figure" for purposes of First Amendment law. The jury found against respondent on his libel claim when it decided that the Hustler ad parody could not "reasonably be understood as describing actual facts about [respondent] or actual events in which [he] participated." The Court of Appeals interpreted the jury's finding to be that the ad parody "was not reasonably believable," and in accordance with our custom we accept this finding. Respondent is thus relegated to his claim for damages awarded by the jury for the intentional infliction of emotional distress by "outrageous" conduct. But, for reasons heretofore stated, this claim cannot, consistently with the First Amendment, form a basis for the award of damages when the conduct in question is the publication of a caricature such as the ad parody involved here. The judgment of the Court of Appeals is accordingly . . .

Comedian Sacha Baron Cohen won the dismissal of a $95 million defamation lawsuit by former U.S. Senate Candidate, Roy Moore, who claimed he was tricked into being portrayed as a pedophile on Cohen's Showtime series "Who Is America?"

5

LIBEL
Defenses and Privileges

CHAPTER OUTLINE

Truth

Anti-SLAPP Protection

Fair Report Privilege

Opinion
Letters to the Editor and Online Comments
Rhetorical Hyperbole Parody and Satire

Section 230 Immunity

Other Defenses
Neutral Reportage
Wire Service Defense
Single-Publication Rule
The Libel-Proof Plaintiff

Additional Defense Considerations
Summary Judgment
Motion to Dismiss for Actual Malice
Jurisdiction
Statutes of Limitations
Retractions

Emerging Law

Cases for Study
- *Milkovich v. Lorain Journal Co.*
- *Dallas Morning News v. Tatum*

LEARNING OBJECTIVES

5.1 Determine when truth can function as a defense for libel.

5.2 Compare federal courts interpretations of various states' Anti-SLAPP legislation.

5.3 Apply the concepts of absolute and qualified privilege to questions regarding newsgathering.

5.4 Analyze whether a statement is a false fact or a protected opinion using the Ollman Test.

5.5 Evaluate when computer service providers can rely on Section 230 immunity as a defense for libel.

> **5.6** Assess when credible accusations may or may not be subject to libel suits.
>
> **5.7** Be familiar with how elements of the legal system such as jurisdictions, statutes of limitations and summary judgement may influence outcomes in libel cases.
>
> **5.8** Analyze recent developments in the application of the single-publication rule.

Plaintiffs in a libel lawsuit must prove all the elements explained in Chapter 4 to have a chance for their claim to prevail. When plaintiffs fail to prove even one element of a libel claim, they lose. Even if plaintiffs are able to prove each element of a libel claim, that may not be sufficient to win. Parties sued for libel can use many defenses, any of which has the potential to be successful, depending on the circumstances of the case. There is one important difference between the plaintiff's case and the defendant's challenges: Although the plaintiff must prove every element of their case, a successful defendant needs only one suitable defense.

Fortunately for libel defendants, there are multiple defenses and privileges in place to protect their communication. Statements that are true or are pure opinion cannot be grounds for successful libel suits. There are also laws in place to minimize frivolous lawsuits aimed at silencing public discourse. Reporting that draws on government documents and proceedings is also considered protected expression. In this chapter, we will explore each of the defenses for libel in detail.

TRUTH

Defending a libel suit may consist of merely taking the elements of the plaintiff's case, explained in Chapter 4, and proving their opposite. A libel defendant may be able to demonstrate that there is no liability for publishing the statement at issue if it is not defamatory, it was not published or the plaintiff was not identified. Truth or substantial truth is the appropriate counterargument to the plaintiff's claim that the material at issue is false.

Truth is sometimes viewed as the most basic and ironclad of all libel defenses. As noted in Chapter 4, the plaintiff is responsible for demonstrating that the statement at issue is false rather than the defendant proving the statement is true. A minor error or discrepancy does not necessarily make a statement false. As long as the statement is substantially true, it cannot meet the standard for falsity and therefore cannot be libelous.

As part of a defense strategy, a libel defendant may attempt to demonstrate to a court that it conducted itself in a responsible way in gathering and reporting the news. The defendant is then more likely to garner support for its argument that it should not be found at fault, or legally responsible for committing libel. The media defendant, for example, may need to disprove the plaintiff's claim that its employees acted with reckless disregard for the truth or that they were negligent.

In attempting to prove that a libel defendant acted with reckless disregard, a plaintiff is likely to attempt to build a case bit by bit, demonstrating a series of irresponsible or careless acts in the newsgathering and publishing process. Courts have said that no single element is sufficient to prove clearly and convincingly that a defendant acted with reckless disregard, but each can be used as evidence to build a case.

News media libel defendants want to strengthen their position by showing as many of the following as possible:

- They thoroughly investigated the story.

- They conducted interviews with credible people who had knowledge of facts related to the story, including the subject of the story.

- They did not solely rely on previously published material.

- They did not solely rely on biased stories.

- Their reporting was careful, systematic and painstaking.

- They sought multiple viewpoints, which were included in the story when possible.

- They showed a willingness to retract or correct a story when facts warranted such action.

- If applicable, there was a demonstrable deadline.

In addition to defending a libel case on the elements, those accused of libel have several defenses at their disposal that may not directly correspond with any specific element of the plaintiff's case.

Attorney Gloria Allred (right) represented several women suing comedian Bill Cosby for defamation after he called them liars for alleging sexual misconduct or assault. Central to their claims is the notion of truth.

Marcus Ingram/Getty Images

ANTI-SLAPP PROTECTION

Chilling speech is the goal of some defamation lawsuits. In those cases, libel law is used not as a shield against threatened harms or as a means of correcting them, but as a weapon to prevent speech from occurring in the first place. **SLAPPs** (strategic lawsuits against public participation),[1] are lawsuits whose purpose is to harass critics into silence, which suppresses the critics'

First Amendment rights. For example, a news media outlet publishes a story critical of a large corporation. That corporation sues the media outlet for libel, even though the corporation knows it cannot win on the elements. The lawsuit is really meant to discourage or silence any further criticism by forcing the media outlet into court where it must pay high attorney's fees and spend time defending itself. This would be a SLAPP.

Plaintiffs rarely win these cases. Noting that SLAPPs are often used to suppress First Amendment rights, a majority of states have enacted anti-SLAPP legislation.[2] Generally, **anti-SLAPP laws** allow defendants to make a motion to strike a lawsuit because it involves a matter of public concern. Plaintiffs have the burden to show that they will prevail in the lawsuit; otherwise, the suit is dismissed. If a defendant prevails, some anti-SLAPP laws allow them to collect attorney's fees from the plaintiff.

Courts have generally upheld the constitutionality of anti-SLAPP laws. However, there have been a few instances where state Supreme Courts struck down anti-SLAPP laws by holding that the laws violated a plaintiff's right to a jury trial.[3] The Washington and Minnesota state supreme courts struck down the laws on their face, meaning that none of the other provisions within the anti-SLAPP laws survived. In response, the Washington state legislature passed a statute in 2021 that addressed the previous law's deficits and restored the defense against defamation claims for speakers and publishers.[4]

Other states, such as New York and California, have recently amended their decades-old anti-SLAPP legislation to provide more robust protection from meritless lawsuits. In 2020, New York extended their anti-SLAPP statute to apply to any communication in a public place or a public forum in connection with an issue of public interest.[5] This new language also expands the level of fault that plaintiffs need to prove from gross irresponsibility to actual malice, regardless of whether they are a private citizen, so long as the issue at hand is a matter of public interest.[6]

For example, a New York District Court said that the state's revised anti-SLAPP statute imposed an actual malice statute on former Alaskan Governor Sarah Palin, who had sued The New York Times for defamation over an editorial that linked her campaign material to the shooting of Representative Gabby Giffords.[7] The court held that the editorial qualified as speech on a matter of public interest, and therefore, the statute imposed an actual malice burden on Palin.[8] Ultimately, Palin was unable to prove that The New York Times had acted with actual malice and therefore she lost her case.[9]

Currently, 31 states, the District of Columbia, and one U.S. territory (Guam) either have enacted an anti-SLAPP statute or have state courts that recognize anti-SLAPP protections as a matter of case law. State courts consider new anti-SLAPP statutes as they emerge.

Sarah Palin, former vice presidential candidate.

Alex Wong/Getty Images

In the past few years, some plaintiffs have brought anti-SLAPP claims in federal court, and the outcome is mixed.[10] The primary question in many of these cases is whether anti-SLAPP laws conflict with the **Federal Rules of Civil Procedure,** which are the general rules that govern all civil proceedings in the U.S. district courts. The Federal Rules of Civil Procedure date back to the 1930s. Some federal courts have determined that these rules prevent the application of state-law protections like those provided by anti-SLAPP laws.[11]

Never was the circuit courts' split on this issue more evident than during a two-week period in July 2020 when the Ninth and Second Circuit Courts came to completely different conclusions in their application of anti-SLAPP statutes in federal court. The Ninth Circuit Court of Appeals said that state-level anti-SLAPP laws are applicable in federal actions when it granted former President Trump's anti-SLAPP motion against Stephanie Clifford, an adult film star who goes by the stage name Stormy Daniels.[12] Clifford lost her defamation lawsuit against former President Trump in a federal court in California. The court ordered her to pay the president nearly $300,000 in legal fees because of his anti-SLAPP motion. The Ninth Circuit Court of Appeals upheld the application of California's anti-SLAPP law and the financial judgment against Clifford. The state's anti-SLAPP law requires that the plaintiff pay the defendant's legal costs when a defendant succeeds on an anti-SLAPP motion in California.[13]

MSNBC Host Joy Reid

Theo Wargo/Staff/Getty

Two weeks after this decision from the Ninth Circuit Court of Appeals, the Second Circuit Court of Appeals rejected the application of California's anti-SLAPP law in a case involving tweets from journalist Joy Reid about Roslyn La Liberte. At issue were two tweets from Reid showing a photo of La Liberte appearing to scream at a teenager during a 2018 city council meeting to oppose California's sanctuary state law. Reid posted the photo and attributed racist remarks to La Liberte, remarks which the teenager in question eventually refuted, noting that their altercation ended in a hug. In their ruling, the Second Circuit Court of Appeals said that they disagreed with the Ninth Circuit Court of Appeals' ruling that California's anti-SLAPP statute and the Federal Rules can exist side by side without conflict.[14]

The D.C. Circuit Court ruled similarly that a federal court could not apply a state or locality's anti-SLAPP provisions because applying both the Federal Rules and the anti-SLAPP statute was too burdensome on courts.[15] Even though the D.C. Circuit Court did not apply the D.C. anti-SLAPP statute, it still found that the defamation claim brought by the son of current Palestinian leader Mahmoud Abbas should be dismissed because his case was not based on factual representations.[16]

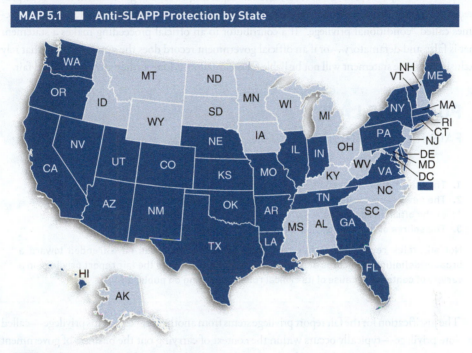

MAP 5.1 ■ Anti-SLAPP Protection by State

 States with anti-SLAPP protection

States without anti-SLAPP protection

In addition to the D.C. Circuit, the Fifth Circuit and Eleventh Circuit Courts of Appeals have also rejected the use of state anti-SLAPP laws, while the First and Ninth Circuits have consistently held that state-level anti-SLAPP laws are applicable in federal actions. Given these different applications of anti-SLAPP statutes in various federal courts, legal experts thought this issue was ripe for hearing by the U.S. Supreme Court.[17] However, the Supreme Court has consistently elected not to take cases involving state anti-SLAPP laws.[18] In 2018, the Supreme Court declined to hear a Tenth Circuit Court case out of New Mexico that rejected the application of that state's anti-SLAPP law in federal court.[19] In 2020, Congressman Steve Cohen of Tennessee reintroduced a bill to the U.S. House of Representatives that would create federal anti-SLAPP protections.[20] However, there has been little movement on the proposed legislation since its introduction. For now, the application of state anti-SLAPP laws in federal courts varies based on the different circuit court jurisdictions.

FAIR REPORT PRIVILEGE

An open society demands that members of the public have access to information relating to government proceedings. Citizens in a participatory democracy are entitled to such information.[21] The fair report privilege is based on the idea that keeping citizens informed about matters of public interest is sometimes more important than avoiding incidental damage to individual reputations. Under the **fair report privilege**, accurate and fair reporting of official government records or proceedings provides protection from defamation and related claims. Fair report privilege is also sometimes called "conditional privilege." If a contributor to an official proceeding makes a statement that is false and defamatory—or if an official government record does the same—reports that rely exclusively on the statement will not be liable for defamation as long as they are accurate and fair.

POINTS OF LAW
FAIR REPORT PRIVILEGE

1. The information must come from an "official" government record or proceeding.
2. The news report must fairly and accurately reflect information from the public record or the official proceeding.
3. The source of the statement should be clearly noted in the news report.

Not all states recognize the fair report privilege. Recent cases have trended toward a broader definition of records and proceedings and have upheld the fair report privilege in a variety of contexts because of its critical role in reporting on public affairs.

The justification for the fair report privilege stems from another privilege. This privilege—called absolute privilege—typically occurs within the context of carrying out the business of government and grants immunity from liability. **Absolute privilege** provides a complete exemption from liability for defamation because the statement was relevant to, pertinent to, and made during official government proceedings. It exists so that people participating in various government arenas, for example legislatures and courts, can communicate information without the fear of being sued for libel.

The fair report privilege is a qualified or conditional extension of absolute privilege. The condition or qualification to absolute privilege, as noted above, is that official records must be accurately and fairly reported. The fair report privilege covers officials and proceedings in the executive, judicial and legislative branches of state, local and federal governments and, often, private individuals communicating with the government. Media accounts of judicial proceedings, including testimony, depositions, attorney arguments, trials, verdicts, opinions and orders—those aspects that are typically open or available to the public—are usually covered. Also, documents that relate to the judicial branch are typically included under the fair report privilege.

For example, a Pennsylvania state court applied the fair report privilege to an article about a convicted drug dealer, even though there was a minor discrepancy between the news account and the court record. The newspaper said the plaintiff owned the car in which he was arrested, but the court report stated that the plaintiff was actually a passenger. The court said the fact difference was minor and immaterial.[22] A New York court came to a similar conclusion when it held that minor inaccuracies, including when those errors are about the precise legal significance of court orders and filings, are protected by the state's fair report privilege.[23]

Law enforcement agencies are also covered by the fair report privilege, including reports of police activity. For example, a former Belleville, Ill., police chief sued the local newspaper for libel after the newspaper reported that he was the subject of a rape investigation. A three-judge panel of the state appellate court unanimously dismissed the case, ruling that the newspaper was protected by the fair report privilege because its article was a fair and accurate report based on a local prosecutor's comments.[24]

Not every statement by a police officer is privileged. Privilege is generally determined on a case-by-case fact basis with different outcomes in different states. One state supreme court, for example, refused to apply the fair report privilege to statements made by a police officer to a reporter during an interview.[25] The court ruled that the officer's participation in the interview and his remarks were not considered to be part of his official duties—a key determinant in deciding whether the privilege applies.

In South Carolina, a court held that the fair report privilege applied to an email the sheriff's department sent to a newspaper and was not limited to official records and press releases. In Michigan, a U.S. district court applied the privilege to unofficial statements made to the press by police officers.[26] The Sixth Circuit Court of Appeals, applying Tennessee law, upheld a summary judgment in favor of a local TV news station that produced a story based on a ride-along with the U.S. Marshals Service during which the marshals erroneously arrested an individual with the same name as the fugitive. A day after the ride-along, the station aired its report of the arrest. Although the arrest itself was in error, the court held that the television report was a fair and accurate account of an official government action. Because the station didn't know the marshals had arrested the wrong person, the court found no evidence of actual malice to overcome the privilege.[27]

A Massachusetts court did not recognize the fair report privilege in the "BAG MEN" case. In the manhunt that ensued after the 2013 Boston Marathon bombing, the New York Post published a picture of two young men who attended the Boston Marathon on the front page under the headline "BAG MEN."[28] The New York Post argued that the fair report privilege applied because the photograph it used came from an FBI email. The court said the article had not fairly and accurately reported the information, so the fair report privilege did not apply. The case was ultimately settled out of court.[29]

Various media outlets, including the celebrity gossip website TMZ, accurately reported information from a press conference held by the attorney general of New York. In that press conference and in a subsequent press release, the attorney general discussed the arrest of a woman for her alleged involvement in a drug and prostitution ring. TMZ's headline for its story read, "Super Bowl Prostitution Bust Was Asian Invasion."

The problem: The attorney general indicted and arrested the wrong person, and the woman identified by TMZ and others sued for defamation and other claims. A federal district court in New Jersey dismissed the claims under fair report privilege. The court held that the media defendants accurately reported the information from the attorney general's press conference and press release, even though the attorney general presented inaccurate information.[30] The Third Circuit Court of Appeals upheld the application of the fair report privilege, noting that privilege does not hinge on the accuracy of the underlying official statement or document.[31]

Over the past several years, fair report privilege decisions tend to uphold the privilege in a broad variety of contexts. The Second Circuit Court of Appeals upheld the dismissal of a case against The New York Times, which published allegations of sexual misconduct based on records derived from an Equal Employment Opportunity Commission Complaint and sex discrimination and retaliation suit.[32] The article in question, "At the Justice Dept.'s Death Penalty Unit, Accusations of Favoritism, Gender Bias and Unwanted Groping," detailed complaints about the former chief of the U.S. Department of Justice's Capital Case Section. The Second Circuit held that because the Times' reporting was based on specific court proceedings and seven declarations filed in those proceedings, the fair report privilege applied.

Even when potentially defamatory statements are included in lawsuits, the media outlets that report the information from the lawsuit are generally protected by the fair report privilege. In 2019, the Eleventh Circuit Court of Appeals ruled that an Associated Press story accurately reported information from a lawsuit that verified Sports Performance Lab's sale of performance-enhancing drugs to Major League Baseball (MLB) players.[33] Responding to an MLB investigation into the sale of illegal performance-enhancing drugs, DNA Labs filed a suit against MLB, alleging that the investigation interfered with their business operations. In that suit, DNA Labs provided details about a supplement they sold which was derived from elk antler tissue and contained a growth hormone. When the Associated Press reported that the hormone in question was on the MLB's list of banned substances, the owner of DNA Labs sued the AP for defamation, along with ESPN and USA Today, who had republished the AP's story. Because the information came directly from litigation materials, all three media outlets were protected by the fair report privilege.

However, courts have not been so quick to extend the fair report privilege to attorneys' statements about their clients' defamatory allegations via traditional and social media. The Texas State Supreme Court reversed a lower court decision in a suit brought by the Downtown Aquarium in Houston against the Animal Legal Defense Fund (ALDF).[34] The ALDF sued the Aquarium for violating the endangered species act by keeping four Bengal tigers in poor conditions. The same day it filed the suit, the ALDF sent a press release about the issue to local media and shared several related posts on their Facebook page. The Aquarium sued for defamation and the ALDF claimed that it was protected by the fair report privilege since the information was based on official judicial proceedings. However, the Texas State Supreme Court said that the social media posts and other media statements didn't play a formal role in the judicial process. Statements by attorneys to media promoting client's allegations are not related to facilitating the proper administration of the justice system. Therefore, the Court refused to extend the fair report privilege to those statements.[35]

The fair report privilege has been extended to include hyperlinks to other news articles that cite an official proceeding.[36] For example, casino magnate Sheldon Adelson sued a political group for defamation based on its online petition that encouraged then-presidential candidate Mitt Romney to reject financial contributions from Adelson because his money was "tainted" and "dirty."[37] The Second Circuit Court of Appeals upheld the Nevada Supreme Court's ruling that a hyperlink to an Associated Press story, which described a sworn declaration made in a lawsuit by an ex-employee against Adelson's company, was sufficient to invoke the fair report privilege. The circuit court upheld the dismissal of Adelson's defamation claim.[38]

Legal experts say that the fair report privilege is critical to reporting on public affairs and its broader application by the courts is a significant development. They note that New York and California have the largest bodies of case law about the fair report privilege and that other states are increasingly looking at those decisions as precedents.[39] Even so, different outcomes—including the failure to recognize the fair report privilege—occur in different states and court systems.[40] As noted earlier, not all states recognize the fair report privilege.[41]

OPINION

Justice Louis Brandeis wrote early in the 20th century, "[F]reedom to think as you will and speak as you think are means indispensable to the discovery and spread of political truth."[42] Historically, the common law provided a fair comment and criticism privilege to afford legal immunity for the honest expression of opinion on matters of legitimate public interest based on a true or privileged statement of fact.[43] Today, holding and expressing opinions is a right guaranteed by the First Amendment. "Under the First Amendment there is no such thing as a false idea. However pernicious an opinion may seem, we depend for its correction not on the conscience of judges and juries but on the competition of other ideas," wrote U.S. Supreme Court Justice Lewis Powell in *Gertz* (also discussed in Chapter 4).[44]

Although the *Gertz* decision constitutionalized the opinion defense, it did not provide specific guidance on how to apply it. Even today, after subsequent cases have offered guidance, the foundational difficulty comes in attempting to distinguish statements of fact from statements of opinion. Stating an opinion involves far more than attaching "In my opinion," "I believe" or similar qualifiers to a statement. More than 35 years ago, the D.C. Circuit Court of Appeals began to develop the attributes of opinion. That court articulated a four-part test to determine whether a statement was one of fact or an expression of opinion.[45] Not all of the test's elements needed to be satisfied; rather, the answers to its questions were to be evaluated in total.

REAL WORLD LAW
FAIR COMMENT AND CRITICISM

Fair comment and criticism is a common law privilege that protects critics from lawsuits brought by individuals in the public eye. Historically, the fair comment and criticism privilege was incorporated into the common law to afford legal immunity for the honest expression of opinion on matters of legitimate public interest based on a true or privileged statement of fact.[46] Comment was generally privileged when it addressed a matter of public concern, was based on true or privileged facts, represented the actual opinion of the speaker and was not made solely for the purpose of causing harm.[47] The privilege of fair comment applied only to an expression of opinion and not to a false statement of fact, whether it was expressly stated or implied from an expression of opinion.[48] As the U.S. Supreme Court has stated, "The privilege of 'fair comment' was the device employed to strike the appropriate balance between the need for vigorous public discourse and the need to redress injury to citizens wrought by invidious or irresponsible speech."[49] Practically speaking, this common law defense is rarely used today because the stronger constitutional opinion defense that first emerged in *Gertz*[50] and was subsequently clarified in *Milkovich*[51] (discussed later in the chapter) offers more protection.

Named for the case from which it stems, *Ollman v. Evans*,[52] the *Ollman* test appeared to provide a sound and relatively straightforward instrument, in four parts, to assess opinion:

1. Is the statement verifiable—can the statement be proved either true or false? Opinion is indirectly linked to the falsity/truth element of libel. That is, if a statement cannot be proved true or false, then it may satisfy the legal definition of an expression of opinion.

2. What is the common usage or meaning of the words?

3. What is the journalistic context in which the statement occurs? This element is especially important for the media. It provides added weight for an opinion defense when the material in question appears in a part of a publication (or, e.g., a broadcast or website) traditionally reserved for opinions—for example, the op-ed pages, personal columns, social media or blogs. The statement must be considered within the material taken as a whole. The language of an entire opinion column, for example, may signal that a specific statement, standing alone, which would appear to be factual, is actually an expression of opinion.

4. What is the broader social context into which the statement fits? For example, was the statement at issue made within a context or in a place where the expression of opinions is common or expected? Or was it made within a context in which statements are presumed to be statements of fact?

Soon after the *Ollman* test was established, courts granted opinion a wide berth of protection. Newsweek magazine, for example, was vindicated in publishing a reference to a false accusation that a former South Dakota governor had sexually assaulted a teenage girl. The words appeared to some people to constitute a statement of fact, but the court found them to be "imprecise, unverifiable" and "presented in a forum where spirited writing is expected and involves criticism of the motives and intentions of a public official."[53] Other plaintiffs who sued because they were called unscrupulous charlatans, neo-Nazis, sleazebags, and ignorant and spineless politicians lost their cases because courts determined these charges to be expressions of opinion rather than statements of fact.[54]

In 1898, a well-known stage act, the Cherry Sisters, lost their libel lawsuit because the fair comment and criticism privilege protected a bad review that appeared in an Iowa newspaper.

Photo courtesy of The History Center

Six years after the D.C. Circuit Court created the *Ollman* test, the U.S. Supreme Court reframed what had appeared to be a nearly absolute opinion defense. The case involved a high school wrestling team that brawled with a competing team during a match. Several people were injured. After a hearing, the coach of one team was censured and his team was placed on probation. A lawsuit was filed in an attempt to prevent the team probation.

At a hearing, the coach, Michael Milkovich, denied that he had incited the brawl. In the next day's newspaper, a local sports columnist wrote that Milkovich, along with a school superintendent, misrepresented the truth in an effort to keep the team off probation. "Anyone who attended the meet . . . knows in his heart that [they] lied at the hearing after each having given his solemn oath to tell the truth," the column read. "But they got away with it." The columnist added that the episode provided a lesson for the student body: "If you get in a jam, lie your way out."[55]

The coach sued for libel. After 15 years and several appeals, the Ohio Court of Appeals held that the column was constitutionally protected opinion, but the U.S. Supreme Court reversed.[56] The Court rejected the broad application of the concept that there is "no such thing as a false idea." "[T]his passage has become the opening salvo in all arguments for protection from defamation actions on the ground of opinion, even though [the original] case did not remotely concern the question," Chief Justice William Rehnquist wrote for the Court.[57] The passage from *Gertz* was not intended to create a wholesale defamation exemption for anything that might be labeled opinion. "Not only would such an interpretation be contrary to the tenor and context of the passage, but it would also ignore the fact that expressions of 'opinion' may often imply an assertion of objective fact," according to the Court.[58]

Chief Justice Rehnquist wrote that facts can disguise themselves as opinions. Merely embedding statements of fact in a column does not transform those statements into expressions of opinion. They remain statements of fact and, if false, may be the basis of a libel suit. Whether the material is verifiable—whether it can be proved true or false—is paramount. The Supreme Court said the key question in this case was whether a reasonable reader could conclude that the statements in the column implied that Milkovich had lied in the judicial proceeding. The Court believed that such an implication had been made and ruled for Milkovich. Even though the material was in a column and thus satisfied the "journalistic context" part of the *Ollman* test, the Court said it was not opinion.[59]

Since the *Milkovich* decision (excerpted at the end of the chapter), courts have provided First Amendment protection to two broad categories of opinion: (1) statements that are not provably false and (2) statements that "cannot reasonably [be] interpreted as stating actual facts."[60]

For example, the Supreme Court of Texas recently dismissed a defamation lawsuit against The Dallas Morning News on grounds that it was opinion based on true facts.[61] The lawsuit originated after the paper ran a column suggesting that the parents of a teenager who committed suicide had acted deceptively when they omitted that information from his obituary. The court noted that the column did include an implication of defamatory content and the writer did not follow journalistic ethical standards, yet the implication in the column was true and therefore protected as opinion.[62] This case, *Dallas Morning News v. Tatum*, (excerpted at the end of this chapter), illustrates how courts apply *Milkovich* and analyze defamatory meaning and statements of fact and opinion.

For example, courts disagreed with CNN's claim that an op-ed article about Russian interference in the 2016 presidential election and the potential involvement of President Trump and his staff in allowing similar tampering with the 2020 election was pure opinion.[63] The article said, "The Trump campaign assessed the potential risks and benefits of again seeking Russia's help in 2020 and has decided to leave that option on the table."[64] CNN argued that the statement was pure opinion, but in applying *Ollman*, the court determined that the statement about whether the campaign had assessed the potential risks and benefits of seeking Russia's help in 2020 had a precise meaning and was capable of being proven true or false. The text of the statement was factual, the court said, despite the article being published in the opinion section.

POINTS OF LAW
POST-*MILKOVICH* OPINION DEFENSE

1. Verifiability: Can the statement be proven true or false? This can include an analysis of the meaning of words. If a statement cannot be proven true or false, then it is likely protected opinion. If a statement is proven true or is opinion based on true facts, then it is not actionable.
2. Context: Consideration of general context, including the work at issue and where the work appears.
3. From *Milkovich*[45]: If a statement cannot reasonably be interpreted as an actual fact, then it is opinion. Opinion includes rhetorical hyperbole and loose, figurative language.

A statement that fails either test—verifiability or context—is called an opinion.

The opinion defense even protects derogatory opinions when they are based on disclosed facts. In 2020, the Third Circuit Court of Appeals affirmed the dismissal of a lawsuit filed by a 12-year-old Trump supporter who claimed that a Newsweek article had defamed him.[66] The young man, referred to by his initials, C.M., in court documents, was one of two children featured in an article called "Trump's Mini-Mess." The article talked about interviews C.M. and another minor had done with media personalities and other political candidates in which they expressed support for Trump initiatives like building a wall on the border of Mexico. The article referred to an interview C.M. had done with Alex Jones of Infowars, in which C.M. talked about Jones' attack on journalist Megyn Kelly. After laying out the facts, the Newsweek article included a quote from journalism professor, Todd Gitlin, who said that the "kids were being weaponized" and that the hard right was using interviews like the one C.M. did to camouflage "defending raw racism and sexual abuse." The Third Circuit said that the professor's statements were pure opinion that appeared after the statements of facts in the article and did not imply any undisclosed facts. Although the professor's opinions were forceful, that does not strip them of their First Amendment protection.

Letters to the Editor and Online Comments

The approach that courts take to applying protection to online comments is based primarily on earlier cases that focused on letters to the editor of a newspaper. Letters to the editor are typically viewed as expressions of opinion rather than statements of fact. For that reason, historically, newspapers and magazines have won most cases based on the publication of such letters. Courts have sought to provide protection for the publication of letters, often viewing them as part of an open forum for the general public. In many cases in which letters to the editor were not protected as opinion, courts have held that those letters combined opinion and facts.[67]

Today, courts generally offer the same protection for opinions published on opinion blogs or review websites, such as Yelp, as well as comments that appear below news articles or on social media platforms. The location of a letter or comment within a publication is likely to have a significant bearing in determining whether it qualifies as opinion. This stems directly from the "journalistic context" element of the *Ollman* test. By appearing within a section of a publication that is clearly set aside for the expression of opinions—including opinions from readers—a letter (versus an article) or an online comment (that appears below an article) or even a review is much more likely to be viewed by a court as an expression of opinion. The same is true in the context of publication of comments on specific websites and social media platforms.

Twitter CEO and SpaceX and Tesla Founder, Elon Musk

PHILIP PACHECO/Contributor/Getty

Entrepreneur Elon Musk won his case against a British cave explorer who Musk had called "pedo guy" on Twitter.[68] Musk argued that Twitter was a world of unfiltered opinion and therefore his comments would be understood by the reader as just that, opinion.[69] In another case, a New York trial court dismissed a libel case on the grounds that criticism published on an online review website amounted to pure opinion and did not include provable defamatory facts. In that case, a medical doctor sued over comments that claimed she was "a terrible doctor" and was "mentally unstable and has poor skills." The court held that the comments were opinion in the context of the internet and said that anonymous comments on the web "can be understood as a platform for 'unsupported and often baseless assertions of opinion' rather than fact."[70]

An appellate court in California affirmed the dismissal of a libel case against the Gizmodo tech blog. In that case, the plaintiff challenged an article that criticized him for overhyping his startups and new tech products. Gizmodo's use of the word "scam" was central to the plaintiff's argument, but the court looked at the article as a whole and said it was opinion that had "the tone and style of a sarcastic product or movie review." The court also noted that Gizmodo allowed readers to draw their own conclusions about the plaintiff's products through links to product source materials.[71]

Rhetorical Hyperbole, Parody and Satire

If the material on which a libel claim is based is so outrageous that no reasonable person could believe it, then a plaintiff cannot show damage to their reputation. The most infamous example of this is from *Hustler Magazine, Inc. v. Falwell*,[72] discussed in Chapter 4.

The U.S. Supreme Court first recognized rhetorical hyperbole as protected speech—and therefore a libel defense—when a developer sued the publisher of a newspaper after the newspaper printed articles reporting that some people characterized the developer's negotiating tactics as blackmail.[73] The developer argued that the word "blackmail" implied that the developer had committed the crime of blackmail. The Supreme Court rejected the developer's argument, holding that the word "blackmail" was defamatory when reported because "even the most careless reader must have perceived that the word was no more than rhetorical hyperbole, a vigorous epithet used by those who considered [the developer's] negotiating position extremely unreasonable."[74]

MSNBC Host Rachel Maddow
Theo Wargo/Staff/Getty

Hyperbole, or rhetorical hyperbole, is a figure of speech that uses extreme exaggeration to make a point or show emphasis. Journalist and cable television host Rachel Maddow recently prevailed in a lawsuit against her for statements she made about One American News (OAN) employee Kristian Rouz.[75] Maddow's MSNBC show ran a segment about Rouz's work as a freelancer for Sputnik News, a Russian state-financed news organization that played a role in Russia's interference in the 2016 U.S. presidential election. Maddow said that "at the same time [Rouz] works for Trump's favorite—One America News team—he is also being paid by the

Russian government to produce government-funded pro-Putin propaganda for a Russian propaganda outfit called Sputnik."[76] She went on to say that OAN "really literally is paid Russian propaganda." OAN's parent company Herring Networks sued Maddow for defamation. Upon hearing the case, the Ninth Circuit Court of Appeals ruled that a reasonable person would understand Maddow's statement that OAN reports Russian propaganda was an "obvious exaggeration," cushioned within an undisputed news story.[77]

Similar to rhetorical hyperbole, satire or parody meant to be humorous or offer social commentary is often not libelous. For example, in 2021 a federal judge dismissed a $95 million lawsuit filed by former U.S. Senate Candidate Roy Moore against comedian Sacha Baron Cohen.[78] Moore had appeared as a guest on Cohen's Showtime series, "Who Is America" under the auspices of receiving an award. On the show, Cohen, playing a fictional Israeli anti-terrorism expert, demonstrated a wand-like device which he claimed was a pedophile detector. When Cohen waved the wand over Moore, it beeped, implying that he was a pedophile. The judge who dismissed the case said that the segment was "clearly a joke" and that no reasonable viewer would see it differently. The judge also said that the consent agreement Moore signed before the interview barred him from bringing legal claims, despite the fact that Cohen misrepresented the nature of the program and interview.[79]

SECTION 230 IMMUNITY

Section 230 of the federal Communications Decency Act (CDA) of 1996[80] is critical to the functioning of the internet.[81] As mentioned in Chapter 4, Section 230 offers immunity to websites in libel claims, although the protection is not absolute. Section 230 generally provides legal protection to website operators and internet service providers when issues arise from content created by others. For 20 years, courts have rejected attempts to limit the application of Section 230 to only "traditional" ISPs like Verizon or AT&T. Instead, they have extended protection to the many diverse entities commonly called "interactive computer service providers."[82] Under this broader definition, websites and other interactive services that rely on user-generated content, information provided from third-party RSS feeds, or reader comments also may receive immunity from libel claims under Section 230. This broader definition includes social media platforms like YouTube, Facebook and Twitter as well as review websites like Yelp.

The key to determining whether Section 230 protects against a libel claim is to identify the source of the content and the extent to which the ISP interacted directly with the content. For example, courts have ruled that when bloggers allow third parties to add readers' comments or other materials to their blogs, then Section 230 protects them. What is less clear is whether those who edit comments or selectively publish reader comments also would fall under Section 230 immunity.[83]

In 2011, a California state court considered whether Facebook qualified for immunity under Section 230 for its "Sponsored Story" advertising system. Five plaintiffs sued Facebook for placing their usernames and profile pictures in Sponsored Stories on friends' Facebook pages. For example, plaintiff Angel Fraley "liked" Rosetta Stone's Facebook profile in order to receive a free software demonstration. Subsequently, Fraley's friends' Facebook pages showed a Sponsored Story advertisement with the Rosetta Stone logo and her "like" for Rosetta Stone.[84]

Facebook argued that it is protected under Section 230 because it is an "interactive computer service" with content provided by third parties. But, the court disagreed in the context of the Sponsored Story feature, saying that because Facebook creates and develops the commercial content without user consent, Facebook is not immune. "Although Facebook meets the definition of an interactive computer service under the CDA … it also meets the statutory definition of an information content provider. . . . Furthermore, [the fact that members] are information content providers does not preclude [Facebook] from also being an information content provider by helping develop at least in part the information posted in the form of Sponsored Stories."[85] In this case, the court is making a clear distinction between content creation and distribution.

In California, Courtney Love won the first Twitter libel case to ever go before a jury because the plaintiff could not prove actual malice.

Scott Dudelson/Getty Images

A ruling by the Sixth Circuit Court of Appeals further extends Section 230 protection if the operator of a website creates or adds content to a post that is potentially libelous. In a case that involved TheDirty.com, a U.S. district court in Kentucky held that the website was not immune from liability for potentially defamatory comments third-party posters made on the website. TheDirty.com is a popular website that allows users to "anonymously upload comments, photographs, and video, which [the website owner] then selects and publishes along with his own distinct, editorial comments. In short, the website is a user-generated tabloid primarily targeting non-public figures."[86]

The Sixth Circuit panel reversed the lower court decision, holding that the website owner's additional comments did not materially contribute to the defamatory content of the third-party statements. According to this ruling, Section 230 immunity remained even if an ISP encouraged defamatory posts, selected the defamatory posts for publication and/or "adopted or ratified" the defamatory posts through its own comments.[87] This is called the "material contribution test," which means that a website operator does not forgo Section 230 immunity unless the operator "materially contributes" to the defamatory content produced by the users.[88]

Although Section 230 is a robust defense for ISPs and information content providers, it is far from ironclad. In 2016, the Ninth Circuit Court of Appeals refused to grant immunity under Section 230 to Internet Brands, Inc. in a case that involved the Model Mayhem networking website it operated for people in the modeling industry. The plaintiff in the case, identified as Jane

Doe, posted her information to the site and was then contacted by two men posing as talent scouts who lured her to a fake audition where they drugged her, raped her and recorded the rape for sale and distribution as pornography. Doe sued Internet Brands under a California law that requires a warning of harm when a person has a "special relationship to either the person whose conduct needs to be controlled or . . . to the foreseeable victim of that conduct."[89] Doe asserted that Internet Brands knew its website was being used by sexual predators and failed to warn users. "The duty to warn allegedly imposed by California law would not require Internet Brands to remove any user content or otherwise affect how it publishes or monitors such content," according to the Ninth Circuit. "Any alleged obligation to warn could have been satisfied without changes to the content posted by the website's users and without conducting a detailed investigation. Internet Brands could have given a warning to Model Mayhem users, perhaps by posting a notice on the website or by informing users by email what it knew."[90] This ruling applies only under state law in California.

Recently, questions have arisen about whether Section 230 protects social media and other internet platforms from liability when their algorithms target users with a recommendation for third party content. The Supreme Court will weigh in on the issue when hears the case *Gonzalez v. Google*, which was filed by the family of a woman killed during an ISIS attack in Paris in 2015.[91] The family claims that YouTube's algorithms are responsible for recommending video content that aided in ISIS recruiting practices that made the attack possible. In its ruling on the case, the Ninth Circuit Court of Appeals said that Section 230 protected these kinds of recommendations as long as the provider's algorithm treated content on its own website similarly.[92]

POINTS OF LAW

DOES SECTION 230 IMMUNITY APPLY?

Section 230[93] immunity applies to internet service providers and websites if
- the ISP/website is a content distributor, not a content creator; or
- the ISP/website did not interact directly with the content.
  Section 230 immunity also applies when
- ISPs/websites correct, edit, add or remove content—so long as they do not substantially alter the meaning of the content;
- ISPs/websites solicit or encourage users to submit content;
- ISPs/websites pay a third party to create or submit content—so long as they do not substantially alter the meaning of the content; or
- ISPs/websites provide forms or drop-downs to facilitate content submission by users—so long as the forms and drop-downs are neutral.

OTHER DEFENSES

Neutral Reportage

As explained in Chapter 4, someone who repeats libelous information is potentially as responsible as the originator of that same information. Republication is not a valid libel defense. But that longtime rule of libel law was loosened somewhat by the doctrine of neutral reportage.

Neutral reportage is a defense accepted in some jurisdictions that provides First Amendment protection for reporting of an accusation made by a responsible and prominent organization, even when it turns out the accusation was false and libelous. The doctrine recognizes the importance of the First Amendment principle of the free flow of information and suggests that accusations made by one individual about another should be available to the public. In some circumstances, the news value lies not in whether the accusation is true but simply in the fact that the accusation was made or who made it. According to neutral reportage, the news media should not be restrained from merely reporting an accusation as long as the reporting is done in a fair, objective, and balanced (i.e., neutral) manner. Even if the publisher of the reported accusations has serious doubts about their veracity, the neutral reportage doctrine could provide a successful defense.

The neutral reportage defense was established in 1977 and applied only to cases involving public figures.[94] Since then, the scope of that application has sometimes expanded beyond public figures, although courts have not uniformly embraced neutral reportage. Its recognition has been spotty. The U.S. Supreme Court has not heard a neutral reportage case, so individual state and federal districts determine how to handle neutral reportage.[95] While neutral reportage remains an option in the libel defendant's arsenal, the inconsistent manner in which courts have accepted it makes its application in a specific case questionable. Much depends on how a court in a given jurisdiction may have ruled on neutral reportage previously. The neutral reportage defense has received renewed attention recently because of the #MeToo movement and the trend of people making allegations, typically on social media, of sexual misconduct by public figures. Legal experts note that both the fair report privilege and neutral reportage may protect media reporting on #MeToo allegations that have emerged on social media, but only in limited situations and depending on jurisdiction.[96]

Courts' willingness to accept neutral reportage claims will likely be put to the test in the ongoing case against Fox Corporation for statements made on Fox News about Smartmatic voting machines. As discussed in Chapter 4, Smartmatic has sued Fox for $2.7 billion in damages for what it says are the 100 false statements Fox News personalities made claiming that Smartmatic was responsible for fixing, rigging, and ultimately, stealing the 2020 U.S. election.[97] In their motion to dismiss the suit, Fox said that it fairly reported and commented on compelling allegations about what it described as a hotly contested election.[98]

POINTS OF LAW
NEUTRAL REPORTAGE

The First Amendment is a defense in a libel case in some jurisdictions if the following apply:
- The story is newsworthy and related to a public controversy.
- The accusation is made by a responsible person or group.
- The charge is about a public official, public figure or public organization.
- The story is accurate, containing denials or other views.
- The reporting is neutral.

Wire Service Defense

The wire service defense is related to the neutral reportage doctrine. It provides a defense for republication on the condition that the reporting meets certain standards. The wire service defense reflects and acknowledges the extent to which news media are dependent on news services, such as the Associated Press, particularly for nonlocal news. To expect verification of every report is unreasonable. This defense holds that the accurate republication of a story provided by a reputable news agency does not constitute fault as a matter of law. The wire defense is available to libel defendants if four factors are met: (1) The defendant received material containing the defamatory statements from a reputable newsgathering agency, (2) the defendant did not know the story was false, (3) nothing on the face of the story reasonably could have alerted the defendant that it may have been incorrect, and (4) the original wire service story was republished without substantial change.

The wire service defense has succeeded even when a newspaper published a story that relied on past wire service articles[99] and when a network affiliate broadcast news reports of its parent network.[100] Like the neutral reportage privilege, the wire service defense has been accepted only in a limited number of jurisdictions.

Single-Publication Rule

Another issue related to republication is the availability of an article subsequent to its initial publication. Does the republication of a work weeks, months or years after its original publication constitute a publication, therefore subjecting it to additional, separate libel claims? Traditionally the answer to this question has been no. The **single-publication rule** limits libel victims to only one cause of action even with republications of the libel in the same outlet, which is common in mass media and online. The rule holds that the entire edition of a newspaper or magazine is a single publication. Subsequent sales or reissues are not new publications. Courts across the United States also apply the single-publication rule to online publications and social media.[101] Generally, courts do not consider shares, links, or re-tweets to be republication unless the post involves content changes that create a new libel. However, a recent decision from the Eighth Circuit Court of Appeals, which is discussed in the Emerging Law section at the end of the chapter, suggests that resharing the link to defamatory content may be grounds to bring a new claim.

POINTS OF LAW
THE WIRE SERVICE DEFENSE

The wire service defense may be applied in some jurisdictions as long as the following are present:

1. The defendant received material containing the defamatory statements from a reputable newsgathering agency.
2. The defendant did not know the story was false.
3. Nothing on the face of the story reasonably alerted the defendant that it may have been incorrect.
4. The original wire service story was republished without substantial change.

The Libel-Proof Plaintiff

When an individual's reputation is already so bad that additional false accusations could not harm it further, the individual may be unable to win a defamation suit. Under these circumstances, a libel defendant may be able to invoke the concept of the **libel-proof plaintiff**, which is a plaintiff whose reputation is deemed to be so damaged that additional false statements of and concerning that person cannot cause further harm. The U.S. Supreme Court has held that states are free to adopt the doctrine as they see fit.[102]

Since the concept was first articulated as a libel defense,[103] two different ways to implement it have emerged.

One application of the libel-proof concept occurs when any reputational harm to the plaintiff caused by a false accusation only incrementally adds to the already damaged reputation. Suppose, for example, that an individual is identified in an article as a thief, child molester and tax evader. If all of those charges are true, does it make any difference if the article also falsely identifies the individual as a kidnapper? Not likely—in such a case, the publisher could probably win, arguing that the single false statement causes negligible (or incremental) harm beyond what already exists and therefore is not grounds for a libel suit. The plaintiff is libel-proof.

In 2020, the Supreme Court of New York dismissed a case brought by former Major League Baseball player Lenny Dykstra, who the court deemed a libel-proof plaintiff.[104] Dykstra sued his former New York Mets teammate Ron Darling Jr. for statements made in Darling's memoir, "108 Stitches: Loose Threads, Ripping Yarns, and the Darndest Characters from My Time in the Game." The book includes a story about Dykstra making racist comments to pitcher Dennis "Oil Can" Boyd during game three of the 1986 World Series. The court was presented with evidence, much of which came from Dykstra's own autobiography, which showed that he was infamous for being racist, misogynist, and anti-gay, as well as a sexual predator, a drug-abuser, a thief, and an embezzler. Dykstra had a reputation of being willing to do anything to benefit himself and his team, including using steroids and blackmailing umpires. In applying the libel-proof plaintiff doctrine, the court found that the publication of Darling's book did not expose Dykstra to any further "public contempt, ridicule, aversion or disgrace."[105]

Major League Baseball Player, Lenny Dykstra

Ron Vesely/Contributor/Getty

Like other common law libel privileges, the acceptance of this part of the doctrine has not been universal. In an early ruling, the D.C. Circuit Court of Appeals rejected the libel-proof plaintiff doctrine. A journalist described the founder of an organization as a racist, fascist, anti-Semitic neo-Nazi. The defense argued that previous publications had already so irreparably tarnished the plaintiff's reputation that the libel-proof doctrine should apply. In an opinion written by then-Judge

Antonin Scalia, the court rejected the claim, ruling that "we cannot envision how a court would go about determining that someone's reputation had already been 'irreparably' damaged—i.e., that no new reader could be reached by the freshest libel."[106] In writing that no matter how bad one's reputation is, it can always be worsened, Scalia offered an analogy: "It is shameful that Benedict Arnold was a traitor; but he was not a shoplifter to boot, and one should not have been able to make that charge while knowing its falsity with impunity."[107]

Courts may also recognize a second way to apply the libel-proof doctrine—libel plaintiffs with tarnished reputations with regard to a particular issue are libel-proof only with respect to that issue. Libel claims pursued in this context present the question of whether previous publicity and the issue before the court are within the same framework.

INTERNATIONAL LAW
INTERNATIONAL JURISDICTION IN LIBEL ACTIONS

Because U.S. libel law is more protective of defendants than are laws in other countries, U.S. citizens have historically been more susceptible to libel verdicts against them in foreign courts. International plaintiffs have been known to engage in "libel tourism," shopping for a country other than the United States in which to file a libel claim.

U.S. law prohibits libel tourism by preventing federal courts from enforcing a foreign libel judgment against an American journalist, author, or publisher if it is inconsistent with the First Amendment. The law also allows individuals who have a foreign judgment levied against them to demonstrate that it is not enforceable in the United States.[108]

What about libel actions that cross the U.S. borders? The Texas Supreme Court held that a Mexican recording artist living in Texas could sue TV Azteca because the Mexican multimedia company intentionally targeted the Texas market and it was not unreasonable or burdensome for TV Azteca to have to comply with the laws of the jurisdiction in which it does business and in which the Mexican recording artist lived.[109]

For example, a plaintiff challenged a newspaper report that he had tested positive for drug use. In this 40-year-old decision, the court found that although the report was incorrect, the plaintiff was libel-proof regarding this specific issue because he had previously admitted using drugs.[110] Had the new report falsely damaged his reputation regarding a topic unrelated to drug use, the libel-proof plaintiff doctrine could not have been invoked. The plaintiff still had a positive reputation to protect in other areas.

ADDITIONAL DEFENSE CONSIDERATIONS

Summary Judgment

A libel defendant can ask a court to dismiss a lawsuit by filing a motion for summary judgment. As noted in Chapter 1, a summary judgment is just what the name implies: A judge promptly decides certain elements of a case and grants the motion to dismiss the case. It can occur at any of several points in litigation but usually occurs prior to trial.

A judge may issue a summary judgment on grounds that there is no genuine dispute about any material fact. With libel, this generally means a plaintiff is clearly unable to meet at least one element in their burden of proof. On numerous occasions, the U.S. Supreme Court said that when considering motions for summary judgment, courts "must view the facts and inferences to be drawn from them in the light most favorable to the opposing party."[111] Particularly in libel cases, this means that courts must take into account the burden the plaintiff must meet at trial. The rationale behind this view is that if the summary judgment is granted, the plaintiff's opportunity to prove a case ends, but if a defendant's motion for summary judgment is denied, the defendant still has an opportunity to prove their case at trial.[112]

Summary judgments can be important tools for protecting free expression, particularly in an environment in which plaintiffs have harassed the media by filing frivolous lawsuits (e.g., see the description of SLAPPs earlier in this chapter). One federal judge wrote that summary procedures are essential in First Amendment cases. Free debate is at stake if the harassment succeeds. One purpose of the *New York Times Co. v. Sullivan* actual malice principle, the judge wrote, is to prevent people from being discouraged in the full and free exercise of their First Amendment rights.[113]

Motion to Dismiss for Actual Malice

Until 1979, summary judgment was a preferred method of dealing with libel cases involving actual malice. When the defense submitted a motion for summary judgment—based on the contention that the plaintiff could not prove actual malice—the judge would either grant or deny it. If granted, the case was over. In 1979, the U.S. Supreme Court cast doubt on the appropriateness of summary judgment in libel cases because any examination of actual malice "calls a defendant's state of mind into question."[114] Although some lower courts took the admonition to heart—using it as a basis for denying summary judgment—motions for summary judgment are still granted more often than not. In 1986, the Court ruled that in determining whether to grant motions for summary judgment, trial judges should decide whether public plaintiffs who file lawsuits claiming they have been libeled can meet the actual malice standard by "clear and convincing evidence." If not, summary judgment should be granted.[115]

This issue was revisited by the U.S. Supreme Court more than a decade ago. In 2007, the Supreme Court significantly changed the standard for the motion to dismiss in *Bell Atlantic Corp. v. Twombly*.[116] Two years later, it affirmed its decision in *Ashcroft v. Iqbal*.[117] Under *Twombly* and *Iqbal*, judges should use "judicial common sense" to determine the plausibility of a claim and the sufficiency of the evidence. The Supreme Court justified the change by noting the increasing legal costs to defendants. One study suggested that more motions to dismiss have succeeded in courts since *Twombly* and *Iqbal* in many different areas of the law.[118]

In 2012, two federal appeals courts applied *Twombly* and *Iqbal* to actual malice proceedings. The First Circuit Court of Appeals dismissed a case involving a political candidate's complaint that a political attack ad defamed him. The court said that the use of "actual malice buzzwords" was not sufficient to make a claim and that the candidate must "lay out enough facts from which [actual] malice might reasonably be inferred."[119] The Fourth Circuit Court of Appeals granted a motion to dismiss a case involving NASCAR driver Jeremy Mayfield, who sued NASCAR for reporting that he tested positive for recreational or performance-enhancing drugs. Mayfield said NASCAR knew the test result was a false positive because he was taking prescription medication at the time. The court said Mayfield's evidence was insufficient.[120]

In 2016, the Eleventh Circuit Court of Appeals joined six other circuits in holding that the standard from *Twombly* and *Iqbal* applies to the actual malice element in defamation cases.[121] Legal experts now consider *Twombly* and *Iqbal* another form of defense for defamation claims, but note that motions to dismiss remain uncommon.[122] This was the standard used to dismiss a 2020 case against Fox News, which was sued by Karen McDougal for statements Tucker Carlson made about her on air. During his show, "Tucker Carlson Tonight," Carlson accused McDougal of extorting former President Trump out of approximately $150,000 in exchange for her silence about an

NASCAR driver Jeremy Mayfield.

Todd Warshaw/Stringer/Getty Images

alleged affair between her and the president. McDougal sued for defamation. In her claim, McDougal said that she had sufficiently pleaded actual malice based on the allegations that Carlson was personally and politically biased in favor of President Trump and would therefore ignore the truth to publish a story in support of the president. McDougal cited 47 favorable tweets Carlson posted by President Trump as evidence of Carlson's bias. In applying the legal standard from *Twombly* and *Iqbal*, the District Court found that McDougal's claim was pure speculation and the tweets were not indicative of a close personal relationship sufficient to establish actual malice. Therefore, the case was dismissed.[123]

Jurisdiction

A court may dismiss a lawsuit on the grounds that the court lacks jurisdiction. Traditionally in libel, the standard has been that wherever the material in question could be seen or heard, a court in any of those locales would have jurisdiction.[124] Thus, a plaintiff could go "forum shopping" in an attempt to find a jurisdiction most favorable to their case.

Given that statements published on the internet can potentially be seen anywhere, any court could claim jurisdiction. A plaintiff could initiate the lawsuit in any court, including those that might be most favorable. But early in the 21st century, significant restrictions were placed on this practice. The Fourth Circuit Court of Appeals applied a three-pronged test for determining the exercise of jurisdiction: (1) whether the defendant purposefully conducted activities in the state, (2) whether the plaintiff's claim arises out of the defendant's activities there, and (3) whether the exercise of jurisdiction would be constitutionally reasonable.[125]

To understand the test, it is helpful to examine the circumstances surrounding the case in which it was first applied. Two Connecticut newspapers were investigating conditions of confinement at a Virginia prison. The story was relevant in Connecticut because some of the overflow prison population in Connecticut was being transferred to a Virginia facility. Articles that included content critical of the Virginia prison and its management appeared in the newspaper in both its print and online editions. The Virginia prison warden sued in federal court in Virginia, claiming that the online content was seen in Virginia and had defamed him there. The appeals court ruled that because the newspapers did not direct their website content to a Virginia audience, courts there had no jurisdiction. The court carefully reviewed the articles and determined they were aimed at a local (Connecticut) audience.[126] Placing content online, the court ruled, is not sufficient by itself to subject a person to the jurisdiction in another state just because the information could be accessed there.[127] Otherwise, a person who places information on the internet could be sued anywhere the information could be accessed. The bottom line, according to this ruling, is that jurisdiction rests where the publication's intended audience is located.

Statutes of Limitations

Statutes of limitations apply for virtually all crimes and civil actions. Charges of most criminal activity and civil actions can be filed only during a limited time after the alleged violation of the law. Courts do not like old claims. While not a defense per se, delay in filing a libel lawsuit can work to the benefit of a defendant, sometimes requiring dismissal where the lawsuit is barred by the statute of limitations.

In libel, the length of statutes of limitations is one, two, or three years, depending on the state. The clock begins ticking on the date the material was made available to the public. With some printed publications, this can be prior to the date of publication on the cover. Many monthly magazines, for example, are mailed to subscribers and appear on newsstands or online well before the official publication date.

Statutes of limitations arguments have arisen in the context of adding new defendants to libel lawsuits as well as to the filing of anti-SLAPP motions.[128] The single-publication rule also applies to statutes of limitations. The reissue of a printed publication or a post online does not restart the statute of limitations calendar as a truly new publication would. A modification to a website—when the modification is unrelated to the allegedly defamatory statement—does not amount to a new publication. For purposes of libel claims and statutes of limitations, the date of publication remains the date on which the material was originally posted.

Retractions

While not a libel defense per se, retractions and corrections published to correct content can play a role in helping libel defendants by mitigating the damage to the plaintiff that resulted from the libelous publication. The degree to which a retraction is offered promptly, is displayed prominently, and is plainly stated will likely help the defendant's cause. The rationale is that a retraction can help reduce the damage to the plaintiff's reputation; the defendant therefore should be required to pay less in damages.

MAP 5.2 ■ Length of Statutes of Limitations in Libel Actions

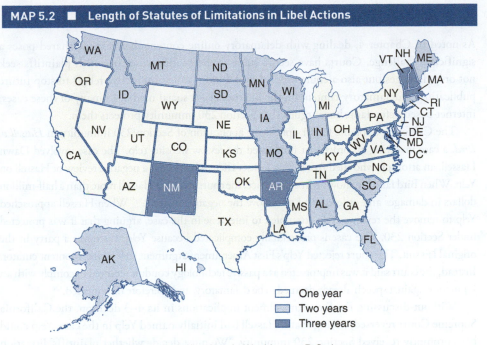

☐ One year
◼ Two years (light)
◼ Three years (dark)

* The statute of limitations in libel actions in Washington, D.C., is one year.

While issuing a retraction is certainly the responsible action to undertake, doing so may work against the defendant if the offended party files a lawsuit. Depending on their wording, retractions may be viewed as an admission of guilt. Consequently, libel defense attorneys may advise against issuing them in the first place. In part as a response to this paradox, a majority of states have adopted **retraction statutes**, which are state laws that limit the damages a plaintiff may receive if the defendant has issued a retraction of the material at issue. Retraction statutes are meant to discourage the punishment of any good-faith effort of admitting a mistake. Increasingly, these laws prevent plaintiffs from recovering some damages after publication of a retraction.[129] Retraction statutes vary in their strength and coverage.[130] The protection they offer differs in many ways, from prohibitions on punitive damages to restricting damages to out-of-pocket losses.[131] Most of these statutes look favorably on media defendants who issue retractions. Rather than penalizing media organizations that indirectly acknowledge some degree of negligence, these statutes offer a kind of compensation by reducing their obligation to pay damages.

Some retraction statutes have been found unconstitutional. The Arizona Supreme Court, for example, ruled that the retraction statute in that state violated the state constitution.[132] The law limited plaintiffs to recovering only special damages when retractions were published.[133] But the Arizona Constitution holds that "[t]he right of action to recover damages for injuries shall never be abrogated, and the amount recovered shall not be subject to any statutory limitation."[134] Because the law conflicted with the Arizona Constitution, it did not survive judicial scrutiny. Although a retraction or correction of a news report in Arizona may no longer immunize a libel defendant from all punitive damage claims, it may serve to reduce those damages.

EMERGING LAW

As noted in Chapter 4, dealing with defamatory online content that is easily shared poses a significant challenge. Courts have seen a surge of defamation cases in which plaintiffs seek not only damages but also a court-ordered prohibition (called injunctive relief) to stop future publication of defamatory content on the internet or via social media. In many of these cases, internet-based defendants have argued that Section 230 immunity protects them.

The California Supreme Court upheld the application of Section 230 immunity in *Hassell v. Bird*, a case involving an order that implicated the review website Yelp. The case involved Dawn Hassell, an attorney, who sued Ava Bird, a former client who posted a negative review of Hassell on Yelp. When Bird failed to show up in court twice, the court awarded Hassell more than a half-million dollars in damages and ordered Bird to remove the negative reviews.[135] When Hassell approached Yelp to remove the reviews, Yelp attempted to intervene in the case, arguing that it was protected under Section 230. The case is procedurally complicated because Yelp was never a party in the original lawsuit. The court rejected Yelp's First Amendment argument that it was a content curator. Instead, the court said it was unprotected as a passive technology conduit required to comply with an injunction against speech already deemed to be defamatory, and therefore unprotected.[136]

Without discussing the First Amendment implications in its 4–3 decision, the California Supreme Court reversed, noting that if Hassell had initially named Yelp in the case, Yelp could have promptly received Section 230 immunity. "We must decide whether plaintiffs' litigation strategy allows them to accomplish indirectly what Congress has clearly forbidden them to achieve directly. We believe the answer is no."[137] Because of the close 4–3 decision, legal experts caution against reading long-term implications into the ruling.[138] Experts say the practice of excluding internet-based content distributors from libel lawsuits to try to avoid questions of Section 230 immunity could continue.

In addition to issues regarding Section 230, the application of the single-publication rule to hyperlinks is also posing problems for defamation defendants. There is now a split between the Fourth and Eighth Circuit Courts of Appeals regarding whether resharing a link amounts to republication. When the Fourth Circuit Court of Appeals was asked to hear a case about statements that had been republished after the one-year statute of limitations, it held that hyperlinking did not amount to republication.[139] At issue here were statements made by Stefan Halper about Svetlana Lokhova, a Russian academic who Halper claimed was a Russian spy who had an affair with General Michael Flynn as part of a collusion plot between President Trump and Russian intelligence. Lokhova asked the court to consider shared links and third-party tweets containing the alleged defamatory statements as new publications that fell within the one-year time frame for the statute of limitations. The Fourth Circuit declined and said that hyperlinks were reference tools used to direct readers to previous publications. Therefore, the court saw "no principled reason for holding a hyperlink distinct from a traditional reference, such as a footnote, for purposes of republication."[140] This case confirmed that new links and re-tweets of old stories were not enough to create a new case and restart the statute of limitations period.

Later that year, the Eighth Circuit Court of Appeals ruled that Esquire magazine journalist Ryan Lizza's tweet containing a link to a story at the center of an earlier defamation suit amounted to a "republication."[141] The story, "Milking the System," accused California

Congressman Devin Nunes' family of relying on labor from undocumented immigrants at their Iowa dairy operation. Lizza's tweet said, "I noticed that Devin Nunes is in the news. If you're interested in a strange tale about Nunes, small-town Iowa, the complexities of immigration policy, a few car chases, and lots of cows, I've got a story for you."[142] It also included a link to the original story, which was the subject of a defamation suit Nunes had brought against Lizza that had been dismissed in August 2020.

The Eighth Circuit examined the *Lokhova* case and concluded that the Fourth Circuit did not categorically hold that hyperlinking to an original publication never constituted republication. The Eighth Circuit said that the single-publication rule was not intended to apply to separate aggregate publications on different occasions. If the same defamatory statement is published in the morning and evening editions of a newspaper, each edition is a single publication and thus, two separate defamation suits may be filed. This is because each publication reaches a new audience, and therefore, the repetition warrants a separate case. Applying that logic to Lizza's tweet containing the link to the original article, the Eighth Circuit characterized the post as a republication that revived Nunes' original libel claim by exposing a new audience to the story. The case has now been remanded back to the district court.[143]

Given the apparent discrepancy between the Circuit Courts of Appeals on this issue, it is possible that the Supreme Court may soon weigh in to clarify when and how the single-publication rule applies to reshares of links to potentially defamatory material. Until then, journalists and social media users should pause before resharing links to content that may be defamatory.

KEYTERMS

absolute privilege	neutral reportage
anti-SLAPP laws	retraction statutes
fair report privilege	single-publication rule
Federal Rules of Civil Procedure	SLAPP (strategic lawsuit against public
libel-proof plaintiff	participation)

CASES FOR STUDY
THINKING ABOUT THEM

One of the case excerpts that follow is from the U.S. Supreme Court. The other is from the Supreme Court of Texas. At the center of each is the libel defense of opinion. As you read these case excerpts, keep the following questions in mind:

● How does the *Milkovich* decision help define the meaning of opinion? Did it expand or narrow the definition of opinion?

● *Dallas Morning News v. Tatum* offers an example of how a state court determines defamatory meaning and statements of fact. What was most important to its conclusion that the column was opinion?

● How did the *Dallas Morning News* case apply the *Milkovich* precedent?

MILKOVICH V. LORAIN JOURNAL CO.

SUPREME COURT OF THE UNITED STATES 497 U.S. 1 (1990)

CHIEF JUSTICE WILLIAM REHNQUIST delivered the Court's opinion:

Respondent J. Theodore Diadiun authored an article in an Ohio newspaper implying that petitioner Michael Milkovich, a local high school wrestling coach, lied under oath in a judicial proceeding about an incident involving petitioner and his team which occurred at a wrestling match. Petitioner sued Diadiun and the newspaper for libel, and the Ohio Court of Appeals affirmed a lower court entry of summary judgment against petitioner. This judgment was based in part on the grounds that the article constituted an "opinion" protected from the reach of state defamation law by the First Amendment to the United States Constitution. We hold that the First Amendment does not prohibit the application of Ohio's libel laws to the alleged defamations contained in the article.

This case is before us for the third time in an odyssey of litigation spanning nearly 15 years. Petitioner Milkovich, now retired, was the wrestling coach at Maple Heights High School in Maple Heights, Ohio. In 1974, his team was involved in an altercation at a home wrestling match with a team from Mentor High School. Several people were injured. In response to the incident, the Ohio High School Athletic Association (OHSAA) held a hearing at which Milkovich and H. Don Scott, the Superintendent of Maple Heights Public Schools, testified. Following the hearing, OHSAA placed the Maple Heights team on probation for a year and declared the team ineligible for the 1975 state tournament. OHSAA also censured Milkovich for his actions during the altercation. Thereafter, several parents and wrestlers sued OHSAA in the Court of Common Pleas of Franklin County, Ohio, seeking a restraining order against OHSAA's ruling on the grounds that they had been denied due process in the OHSAA proceeding. Both Milkovich and Scott testified in that proceeding. The court over-turned OHSAA's probation and ineligibility orders on due process grounds.

The day after the court rendered its decision, respondent Diadiun's column appeared in the News-Herald, a newspaper which circulates in Lake County, Ohio, and is owned by respondent Lorain Journal Co. The column bore the heading "Maple beat the law with the 'big lie,'" beneath which appeared Diadiun's photograph and the words "TD Says." The carryover page headline announced ". . . Diadiun says Maple told a lie." The column contained the following passages:

> . . . [A] lesson was learned (or relearned) yesterday by the student body of Maple Heights High School, and by anyone who attended the Maple-Mentor wrestling meet of last Feb. 8.
>
> A lesson which, sadly, in view of the events of the past year, is well they learned early.
>
> It is simply this: If you get in a jam, lie your way out.
>
> If you're successful enough, and powerful enough, and can sound sincere enough, you stand an excellent chance of making the lie stand up, regardless of what really happened.
>
> The teachers responsible were mainly head Maple wrestling coach, Mike Milkovich, and former superintendent of schools H. Donald Scott.
>
> . . .
>
> Anyone who attended the meet, whether he be from Maple Heights, Mentor, or impartial observer, knows in his heart that Milkovich and Scott lied at the hearing after each having given his solemn oath to tell the truth.

But they got away with it.

Is that the kind of lesson we want our young people learning from their high school administrators and coaches?

I think not.[144]

Petitioner commenced a defamation action against respondents in the Court of Common Pleas of Lake County, Ohio, alleging that the headline of Diadiun's article and the nine passages quoted above "accused plaintiff of committing the crime of perjury, an indictable offense in the State of Ohio, and damaged plaintiff directly in his life-time occupation of coach and teacher, and constituted libel *per se*." The action proceeded to trial, and the court granted a directed verdict to respondents on the ground that the evidence failed to establish the article was published with "actual malice" as required by *New York Times Co. v. Sullivan.* The Ohio Court of Appeals for the Eleventh Appellate District reversed and remanded, holding that there was sufficient evidence of actual malice to go to the jury. The Ohio Supreme Court dismissed the ensuing appeal for want of a substantial constitutional question, and this Court denied certiorari.

On remand, relying in part on our decision in *Gertz v. Robert Welch, Inc.* (1974), the trial court granted summary judgment to respondents on the grounds that the article was an opinion protected from a libel action by "constitutional law," and alternatively, as a public figure, petitioner had failed to make out a *prima facie* case of actual malice. The Ohio Court of Appeals affirmed both determinations. On appeal, the Supreme Court of Ohio reversed and remanded. The court first decided that petitioner was neither a public figure nor a public official under the relevant decisions of this Court. The court then found that "the statements in issue are factual assertions as a matter of law, and are not constitutionally protected as the opinions of the writer. . . . The plain import of the author's assertions is that Milkovich, *inter alia*, committed the crime of perjury in a court of law." This Court again denied certiorari.

Meanwhile, Superintendent Scott had been pursuing a separate defamation action through the Ohio courts. Two years after its Milkovich decision, in considering Scott's appeal, the Ohio Supreme Court reversed its position on Diadiun's article, concluding that the column was "constitutionally protected opinion." Consequently, the court upheld a lower court's grant of summary judgment against Scott.

The *Scott* court decided that the proper analysis for determining whether utterances are fact or opinion was set forth in the decision of the United States Court of Appeals for the District of Columbia Circuit in *Ollman v. Evans* (1984). Under that analysis, four factors are considered to ascertain whether, under the "totality of circumstances," a statement is fact or opinion. These factors are: (1) "the specific language used"; (2) "whether the statement is verifiable"; (3) "the general context of the statement"; and (4) "the broader context in which the statement appeared." The court found that application of the first two factors to the column militated in favor of deeming the challenged passages actionable assertions of fact. That potential outcome was trumped, however, by the court's consideration of the third and fourth factors. With respect to the third factor, the general context, the court explained that "the large caption 'TD Says' . . . would indicate to even the most gullible reader that the article was, in fact, opinion." As for the fourth factor, the "broader context," the court reasoned that because the article appeared on a sports page—"a traditional haven for cajoling, invective, and hyperbole"—the article would probably be construed as opinion.

Subsequently, considering itself bound by the Ohio Supreme Court's decision in *Scott*, the Ohio Court of Appeals in the instant proceedings affirmed a trial court's grant of summary judgment in favor of respondents, concluding that "it has been decided, as a matter of law, that the article in question was constitutionally protected opinion." The Supreme Court of Ohio dismissed petitioner's ensuing appeal for want of a substantial constitutional question. We granted certiorari, to consider the important questions raised by the Ohio courts' recognition of a constitutionally required "opinion" exception to the application of its defamation laws. We now reverse. . . .

Respondents would have us recognize, in addition to the established safeguards discussed above, still another First-Amendment-based protection for defamatory statements which are categorized as "opinion" as opposed to "fact." For this proposition they rely principally on the following dictum from our opinion in *Gertz*:

> "Under the First Amendment there is no such thing as a false idea. However pernicious an opinion may seem, we depend for its correction not on the conscience of judges and juries but on the competition of other ideas. But there is no constitutional value in false statements of fact."

Judge Friendly appropriately observed that this passage "has become the opening salvo in all arguments for protection from defamation actions on the ground of opinion, even though the case did not remotely concern the question." Read in context, though, the fair meaning of the passage is to equate the word "opinion" in the second sentence with the word "idea" in the first sentence. Under this view, the language was merely a reiteration of Justice Holmes' classic "marketplace of ideas" concept. . . . ("[T]he ultimate good desired is better reached by free trade in ideas . . . the best test of truth is the power of the thought to get itself accepted in the competition of the market").

Thus, we do not think this passage from *Gertz* was intended to create a wholesale defamation exemption for anything that might be labeled "opinion." . . . [The "marketplace of ideas" origin of this passage "points strongly to the view that the 'opinions' held to be constitutionally protected were the sort of thing that could be corrected by discussion"]. Not only would such an interpretation be contrary to the tenor and context of the passage, but it would also ignore the fact that expressions of "opinion" may often imply an assertion of objective fact.

If a speaker says, "In my opinion John Jones is a liar," he implies a knowledge of facts which lead to the conclusion that Jones told an untruth. Even if the speaker states the facts upon which he bases his opinion, if those facts are either incorrect or incomplete, or if his assessment of them is erroneous, the statement may still imply a false assertion of fact. Simply couching such statements in terms of opinion does not dispel these implications; and the statement, "In my opinion Jones is a liar," can cause as much damage to reputation as the statement, "Jones is a liar." As Judge Friendly aptly stated: "[It] would be destructive of the law of libel if a writer could escape liability for accusations of [defamatory conduct] simply by using, explicitly or implicitly, the words 'I think.'" It is worthy of note that, at common law, even the privilege of fair comment did not extend to "a false statement of fact, whether it was expressly stated or implied from an expression of opinion."

. . . [R]espondents do not really contend that a statement such as, "In my opinion John Jones is a liar," should be protected by a separate privilege for "opinion" under the First Amendment. But they do contend that in every defamation case the First Amendment mandates an inquiry into whether a statement is "opinion" or "fact," and that only the latter statements may be actionable. They propose that a number of factors developed by the lower courts (in what we hold was a mistaken reliance on the *Gertz* dictum) be considered in deciding which is which. But we think the "'breathing space'" which "'freedoms of expression require in order to survive'" is adequately secured by existing constitutional doctrine without the creation of an artificial dichotomy between "opinion" and fact.

Foremost, we think [precedent] stands for the proposition that a statement on matters of public concern must be provable as false before there can be liability under state defamation law, at least in situations, like the present, where a media defendant is involved. Thus, unlike the statement, "In my opinion Mayor Jones is a liar," the statement, "In my opinion

Mayor Jones shows his abysmal ignorance by accepting the teachings of Marx and Lenin," would not be actionable. [Precedent] ensures that a statement of opinion relating to matters of public concern which does not contain a provably false factual connotation will receive full constitutional protection. . . .

We are not persuaded that, in addition to these protections, an additional separate constitutional privilege for "opinion" is required to ensure the freedom of expression guaranteed by the First Amendment. The dispositive question in the present case then becomes whether a reasonable factfinder could conclude that the statements in the Diadiun column imply an assertion that petitioner Milkovich perjured himself in a judicial proceeding. We think this question must be answered in the affirmative. As the Ohio Supreme Court itself observed, "The clear impact in some nine sentences and a caption is that [Milkovich] 'lied at the hearing after ... having given his solemn oath to tell the truth.'" This is not the sort of loose, figurative, or hyperbolic language which would negate the impression that the writer was seriously maintaining that petitioner committed the crime of perjury. Nor does the general tenor of the article negate this impression.

We also think the connotation that petitioner committed perjury is sufficiently factual to be susceptible of being proved true or false. A determination whether petitioner lied in this instance can be made on a core of objective evidence by comparing, *inter alia*, petitioner's testimony before the OHSAA board with his subsequent testimony before the trial court. As the *Scott* court noted regarding the plaintiff in that case, "Whether or not H. Don Scott did indeed perjure himself is certainly verifiable by a perjury action with evidence adduced from the transcripts and witnesses present at the hearing. Unlike a subjective assertion, the averred defamatory language is an articulation of an objectively verifiable event." So too with petitioner Milkovich.

[Previous] decisions . . . establishing First Amendment protection for defendants in defamation actions surely demonstrate the Court's recognition of the Amendment's vital guarantee of free and uninhibited discussion of public issues. But there is also another side to the equation; we have regularly acknowledged the "important social values which underlie the law of defamation," and recognized that "[s]ociety has a pervasive and strong interest in preventing and redressing attacks upon reputation." . . .

We believe our decision in the present case holds the balance true. The judgment of the Ohio Court of Appeals is reversed, and the case is remanded for further proceedings not inconsistent with this opinion.

Reversed.

DALLAS MORNING NEWS V. TATUM
SUPREME COURT OF TEXAS 554 S.W.3D 614 (2018)

JUSTICE JEFFREY V. BROWN delivered the Court's opinion:

Words—so innocent and powerless as they are, as standing in a dictionary, how potent for good and evil they become in the hands of one who knows how to combine them.

—Nathaniel Hawthorne

In this libel-by-implication case, we must determine whether the defamatory meanings the Tatums allege are capable of arising from the words that Steve Blow combined in a column that The Dallas Morning News published.[145] We conclude that the column is reasonably capable of meaning that the Tatums acted deceptively and that the accusation of deception is reasonably capable of defaming the Tatums. However, as we further conclude that the accusation is an opinion, we reverse the court of appeals' judgment and reinstate the trial court's summary judgment for petitioners Steve Blow and The Dallas Morning News. . . .

Paul Tatum was the son of John and Mary Ann Tatum. At seventeen years old, Paul was a smart, popular, and athletic high-school student. By every indication, he was a talented young man with a bright future. One mid-May evening, Paul, driving alone, crashed his parents' vehicle on his way home from a fast-food run. The vehicle's airbag deployed, and the crash was so severe that investigators later discovered Paul's eyelashes and facial tissue at the scene. The crash's cause has never been conclusively established and no evidence suggests that Paul was intoxicated or otherwise under the influence of any substance when the crash occurred.

Paul found his way home on foot. He began drinking and he called a friend. The phone call indicated to the friend that Paul was behaving erratically. The friend, concerned, traveled to Paul's house to see him in person. The friend found Paul at the Tatums' house in a confused state and holding one of the Tatum family's firearms. The friend left the room . . . to report Paul's irrational behavior to [his] parent, who was waiting in a car outside the Tatums' house. Soon after, the friend heard a gunshot. Paul had killed himself.

In the wake of Paul's death, the Tatums discovered medical literature positing a link between traumatic brain injury and suicide. The Tatums concluded that the car accident caused irrational and suicidal ideations in Paul, which in turn led to his death. . . . Paul's mother, a mental-health professional, had never noticed any suicidal tendencies in Paul. By her account, and by all others, Paul was a normal, healthy, and mentally stable young man. For the Tatums, these observations underscored the plausibility of their theory that Paul's car crash generated a brain injury that led to his suicide.

. . . [T]he Tatums sought to memorialize Paul by writing an obituary, which they published by purchasing space in The Dallas Morning News. The obituary stated that Paul died "as a result of injuries sustained in an automobile accident." The Tatums chose this wording to reflect their conviction that Paul's suicide resulted from suicidal ideation arising from a brain injury rather than from any undiagnosed mental illness. The Dallas Morning News published the obituary on May 21, 2010. More than 1,000 people attended Paul's funeral.

Steve Blow is a columnist for The Dallas Morning News. On June 20, 2010—Father's Day, and about one month after Paul's suicide—the paper published a column by Blow entitled "Shrouding Suicide Leaves its Danger Unaddressed."

The column characterized suicide as the "one form of death still considered worthy of deception." While it did not refer to the Tatums by name, it quoted from Paul's obituary and referred to it as "a paid obituary in this newspaper." Although those who knew Paul already knew the truth, the column revealed what the obituary left out: Paul's death "turned out to have been a suicide." After providing another example of an undisclosed suicide, the column went on to lament that "we, as a society, allow suicide to remain cloaked in such secrecy, if not outright deception." The reason we should be more open, according to the column, is that "the secrecy surrounding suicide leaves us greatly underestimating the danger there" and that "averting our eyes from the reality of suicide only puts more lives at risk." The reason we are not open about suicide, the column speculated, is that "we don't talk about the illness that often underlies it—mental illness." . . . Blow wrote that we should not feel embarrassed by suicide and that "the last thing I want to do is put guilt on the family of suicide victims." The column concluded with an exhortation: "Awareness, frank discussion, timely intervention, treatment—those are the things that save lives. Honesty is the first step."

Blow drafted the column without attempting to contact the Tatums and the paper published it without letting the Tatums know that it was going to print. Those who knew the Tatums immediately recognized that the obituary the column referenced was Paul's. . . .

The Tatums filed suit. They alleged libel and libel per se against Blow and the paper. In particular, the Tatums alleged the column defamed them by its "gist." . . . The News filed a motion for traditional and no-evidence summary judgment. The News asserted several traditional grounds. Among them were that the column was not reasonably capable of a defamatory meaning and that the column was an opinion. Without specifying why, the trial court granted the News's motion.

The Tatums appealed. The court of appeals . . . reversed and remanded the Tatums' claims that were based on libel and libel per se. . . .

It held the column was not an opinion because "the column's gist that the Tatums were deceptive when they wrote Paul's obituary is sufficiently verifiable to be actionable in defamation." The News's defenses based on fair comment, official proceedings, truth, substantial truth, actual malice, and negligence fared no better. Thus, the court of appeals rejected every possible ground on which the trial court might have based its grant of summary judgment.

The News petitioned this Court for review. It argues that the court of appeals was wrong on four fronts: the column is not reasonably capable of defamatory meaning; it is non-actionable opinion; it is substantially true; and the court of appeals did not properly analyze actual malice.

IIDefamation is a tort, the threshold requirement for which is the publication of a false statement of fact to a third party. The fact must be defamatory concerning the plaintiff, and the publisher must make the statement with the requisite degree of fault. And in some cases, the plaintiff must also prove damages. . . .

Texas recognizes the common-law rule that defamation is either per se or per quod. . . .

In a defamation case, the threshold question is whether the words used "are reasonably capable of a defamatory meaning." In answering this question, the "inquiry is objective, not subjective." But if the court determines the language is ambiguous, the jury should determine the statement's meaning. If a statement is not verifiable as false, it is not defamatory. Similarly, even when a statement *is* verifiable as false, it does not give rise to liability if the "entire context in which it was made" discloses that it is merely an opinion masquerading as a fact.

Both the U.S. Constitution and the Texas Constitution "robustly protect freedom of speech," and the Texas Constitution expressly acknowledges a cause of action for defamation. . . .

III"Meaning is the life of language." Thus, the first question in a libel action is whether the words used are "reasonably capable of a defamatory meaning." In answering it, the "inquiry is objective, not subjective." We note that the question involves two independent steps. The first is to determine whether the meaning the plaintiff alleges is reasonably capable of arising from the text of which the plaintiff complains. . . . The second step is to answer whether the meaning—if it is reasonably capable of arising from the text—is reasonably capable of defaming the plaintiff.

In the typical defamation case, the determination of what a publication means involves little beyond browsing the publication's relevant portions in search of the defamatory content of which the plaintiff complains. That is, defamatory meanings are ordinarily transmitted the same way that other meanings are—explicitly. But this is not the typical defamation case. Rather, the Tatums allege that the column defames them by its "gist."

. . . [F]or clarity, we introduce the following terms. To begin, "textual defamation" refers to the common-law concept of defamation per se, that is, defamation that arises from the statement's text without reference to any extrinsic evidence. On the other hand, "extrinsic defamation" refers to the common-law concept of defamation per quod, which is to say, defamation that *does* require reference to extrinsic circumstances. . . . This case concerns, in part, the distinction between textual defamation and extrinsic defamation.

Extrinsic defamation occurs when a statement whose textual meaning is innocent becomes defamatory when considered in light of "other facts and circumstances sufficiently expressed before" or otherwise known to the reader. The requirements for proving an extrinsic-defamation case—including the torts professor's perennial favorites of innuendo, inducement, and colloquium—are somewhat technical. Only two are of interest here. First, it must be remembered that an extrinsically defamatory statement *requires* extrinsic evidence to be defamatory at all.

Textual defamation occurs when a statement's defamatory meaning arises from the words of the statement itself, without reference to any extrinsic evidence. The ordinary textual defamation involves a statement that is explicitly defamatory. Explicit textual-defamation cases share two common attributes. First, none necessarily involve any extrinsic evidence. Thus, none necessarily involve extrinsic defamation. Second, the defamatory statement's literal text and its communicative content align—what the statement *says* and what the statement *communicates* are the same. In other words, the defamation is both *textual* and *explicit*. . . . When a publication's text implicitly communicates a defamatory statement, we refer to the plaintiff's theory as "defamation by implication."

In a defamation-by-implication case, the defamatory meaning arises from the statement's text, but it does so implicitly. Defamation by implication is not the same thing as textual defamation. Rather, it is a subset of textual defamation. . . .

. . . [A] defendant may be liable for a "publication that gets the details right but fails to put them in the proper context and thereby gets the story's 'gist' wrong.." . . Thus, [our prior cases] recognize that a plaintiff can rely on an entire publication to prove that a defendant has implicitly communicated a defamatory statement.

However, and of special importance in this case, there is no reason that implicit meanings must arise only from an entire publication or not at all. . . .

[W]e acknowledge that in a textual-defamation case, a plaintiff may allege that meaning arises in one of three ways. First, meaning may arise explicitly. . . . Second, meaning may arise implicitly as a result of the article's entire gist. . . . Third, as in this case, the plaintiff may allege that the defamatory meaning arises implicitly from a distinct portion of the article rather than from the article's as-a-whole gist. As other courts have recognized, the distinction between "as-a-whole" gist and "partial" implication is important.

. . . Accordingly, we use the following terms. "Gist" refers to a publication or broadcast's main theme, central idea, thesis, or essence. . . . [We] use "gist" in its colloquial sense. In this usage, publications and broadcasts typically have a single gist.

"Implication," on the other hand, refers to the inferential, illative, suggestive, or deductive meanings that may emerge from a publication or broadcast's discrete parts. . . . "Defamation by implication," as a subtype of textual defamation, covers both "gist" and "implication."

The difference between gist and implication is especially important in two contexts. The first relates to the substantial-truth doctrine. "A broadcast with specific statements that err in the details but that correctly convey the gist of a story is substantially true." . . . We have never held, nor do we today, that a true implication—as opposed to a true gist—can save a defendant from liability for publishing an otherwise factually defamatory statement. Second, the difference between gist and implication matters when considering the requirements that the U.S. Constitution imposes on defamation law.

By nature, defamations by implication require construction. . . . Thus, to determine whether a defamation by implication has occurred, the question is the same as it is for defamatory content generally: is the publication "reasonably capable" of communicating the defamatory statement? But to whose "reason" does "reasonably capable" refer?

Sometimes we have said that "reasonably capable" requires us to construe a publication "based upon how a person of ordinary intelligence *would* perceive it." . . . The "would" standard recognizes that gist, in particular, is the type of implication that no reasonable reader would fail to notice. But the "would" standard falls short when applied to implications. Not all readers will pick up on all reasonable implications in all publications. In fact, it seems apparent that *no* reader *would* internalize every implication from a single article—or even a single sentence.

. . . Instead, when the plaintiff claims defamation by implication, the judicial task is to determine whether the meaning the plaintiff alleges arises from an objectively reasonable reading. . . . Even reasonable readers do not internalize every single implication that a publication conveys. . . . So in an implication case, the judicial role is not to map out every single implication that a publication is capable of supporting. Rather, the judge's task is to determine whether the implication the plaintiff alleges is among the implications that the objectively reasonable reader would draw. . . .

Meanings sometimes terminate in ambiguities. And because defamation involves meaning, ambiguity is often an issue in defamation cases. . . .

Questions of meaning and ambiguity recur in three different types. First, if a court determines that a statement is capable of defamatory meaning and *only* defamatory meaning—that it is unambiguous—then the jury plays no role in determining the statement's meaning. Second, courts sometimes determine that a statement is capable of at least one defamatory and at least one non-defamatory meaning. . . . Third, a court may determine that the statement is not capable of any defamatory meanings. . . .

Our point in reciting these black-letter applications of our defamation law is to emphasize that the analytical framework for considering ambiguities does not evaporate simply because the plaintiff alleges an implicit meaning. . . .

The potential chilling effect is especially strong in defamation-by-implication cases. Unlike explicit statements, publishers cannot be expected to foresee every implication that may reasonably arise from a certain publication. To avoid this chilling effect, the *First Amendment* "imposes a special responsibility on judges whenever it is claimed that a particular communication is [defamatory]." For appellate judges, one of these responsibilities is to comply with the "requirement of independent appellate review reiterated" in *New York Times v. Sullivan* as a matter of "federal constitutional law." Although *Sullivan* emphasized the "actual malice" requirement that applies when the plaintiff, defendant, or subject matter are sufficiently "public," we recognize that its reasoning extends to the *First Amendment* concerns that defamation by implication raises.

The Constitution requires protection beyond that which the "objectively reasonable reader" standard provides. . . .

One way of cabining the dangers that defamation by implication poses would be to subsume the constitutional question within the question of meaning. However, we see no reason for thinking that either the U.S. Constitution or the Texas Constitution has anything to do with what a word in its everyday usage *means*. . . . We cannot solve the constitutional challenges that the tort of defamation by implication presents simply by heightening our standard of meaning. Doing so would be to swim against the current of our traditional jurisprudence that favors "plain meaning." Consequently, we reject a heightened standard of "meaning" as a workable limit on the chilling effect that defamation by implication poses.

A second category of protection disallows defamation by implication, whether altogether or in certain contexts. Some states have taken this approach. . . . Our cases allow public figures—and by extension, private figures, to bring cases alleging defamation by implication. These precedents prevent us from relying on wholesale rejection of defamation by implication to protect the freedoms that the *First Amendment* enshrines.

Still other courts have taken a third path by suggesting that defamatory implications might presumptively constitute opinion in some contexts. We reject the view that implications are opinions, either necessarily or presumptively. Publishers cannot avoid liability for defamatory statements simply by couching their implications within a subjective opinion. Thus, after the U.S. Supreme Court's landmark decision in *Milkovich v. Lorain Journal Co.*, the opinion inquiry seeks to ascertain whether a statement is "verifiable," not whether it manifests a personal view. But no court can decide whether a statement is verifiable until the court decides what the statement *is*—that is, until it conducts an inquiry into the publication's meaning. Of course, implications may frequently turn out to be non-verifiable opinions, but we disagree that implications are presumptively opinion simply by virtue of being implicit. So we see little hope that asking a court to decide from the outset whether a statement is an opinion will limit the number of defamation-by-implication claims that reach a jury.

A fourth and final limit is to rely on or adjust the culpability standards that *Sullivan* lays out. . . . [W]e decline to recognize "culpability" as a limit on our meaning inquiry.

In place of these tests, we believe the D.C. Circuit was correct when it stated the following limit on the inquiry into meaning:

> [I]f a communication, viewed in its entire context, merely conveys materially true facts from which a defamatory inference can reasonably be drawn, the libel is not established. But if the communication, by the particular manner or language in which the true facts are conveyed, supplies additional, affirmative evidence suggesting that the defendant *intends* or *endorses* the defamatory inference, the communication will be deemed capable of bearing that meaning.

Thus, a plaintiff who seeks to recover based on a defamatory implication—whether a gist or a discrete implication—must point to "additional, affirmative evidence" within the publication itself that suggests the defendant "intends or endorses the defamatory inference." . . .

First, the evidence of intent must arise from the publication itself. In considering whether the publication demonstrates such an intent, the court must, as always, "evaluate the publication as a whole rather than focus on individual statements." . . .

Second, in consonance with our precedent and in accord with the judiciary's traditional role when considering plain meaning, the intent or endorsement inquiry "is objective, not subjective." . . . [T]he question is whether the publication indicates by its plain language that the publisher intended to convey the meaning that the plaintiff alleges.

Third, the rule may vary in application depending on the type of defamation that the plaintiff alleges. It does not apply in cases of explicit defamation because when the defendant speaks explicitly, the court indulges the presumption that the defendant intended the communicatory content that he conveyed. . . .

Finally, in a discrete-implication case, it becomes especially relevant for the court to apply the requirement that the publication's text demonstrates the publisher's intent to convey the meaning the plaintiff alleges. In applying the requirement, courts must bear its origin in mind. The especially rigorous review that the requirement implements is merely a reflection of the "underlying principle" that obligates "judges to decide when allowing a case to go to a jury would, in the totality of the circumstances, endanger *first amendment* freedoms."

At the time of summary judgment, the Tatums' live petition alleged that the column defamed them by implicitly communicating the following "gist":

> [The Tatums] created a red herring in the obituary by discussing a car crash in order to conceal the fact that Paul's untreated mental illness—ignored by Plaintiffs—resulted in a suicide that Plaintiffs cannot come to terms with. Defendants led their readers to believe it is people like Plaintiffs—and their alleged inability to accept that their loved ones suffer from mental illness—who perpetuate and exacerbate the problems of mental illness, depression, and suicide.

From this paragraph we discern that the Tatums construe the column to mean that:

- The Tatums acted deceptively in publishing the obituary;
- Paul had a mental illness, which the Tatums ignored and which led to Paul's suicide; and
- The Tatums' deception perpetuates and exacerbates the problem of suicide in others.

None of these meanings appear in the column's explicit text. Nor do they depend on any extrinsic evidence. Thus, while the Tatums allege a textual defamation, their claim rests on defamation by implication rather than on explicit meaning.

The column's gist has nothing to do with the Tatums. Rather, the column's gist is that our society ought to be more forthcoming about suicide and that by failing to do so, our society is making the problem of suicide worse, not better. So none of the meanings the Tatums allege arise from the column's gist.

As to the first meaning the Tatums allege, we agree that the column's text supports the discrete implication that the Tatums acted deceptively. The standard is whether an objectively reasonable reader would draw the implication that the Tatums allege. Here, the gist of Blow's column is that bereaved families often do society a disservice by failing to explicitly mention when suicide is the cause of death. Blow holds up the Tatums as an example of the very phenomenon that his column seeks to discourage. Blow would have no reason to mention the Tatums' obituary except to support his point that suicide often goes undiscussed. . . . Here, an objectively reasonable reading must end with the conclusion that Blow points to the Tatums as one illustration of his thesis that suicide is often "shrouded in secrecy." . . . [W]e conclude that the publication's text objectively demonstrates an intent to convey that the Tatums were deceptive.

But we do not agree that the second and third meanings the Tatums allege are implications that an objectively reasonable reader would draw.

The second alleged meaning rests on the premise that the column means that Paul had a mental illness. We do not agree that the column conveys that meaning. Though the column does say that "mental illness" "often" underlies suicide, the column does so immediately after citing the statistic that suicide is "the third-leading cause of death among young people." The author's use of the word "often" means the column does not logically entail that all suicides are the result of mental illness. And we think the space between the discussion of the Tatums and the discussion of mental illness negates the inferential construction that the Tatums allege—especially since the reference to mental illness follows a citation to a population-level statistic rather than the example paragraphs . . . [W]e conclude that the second meaning the Tatums allege does not arise from an objectively reasonable reading of the column.

Nor does their third. The column declares that "the last thing I want to do is put guilt on the family of suicide victims." An objectively reasonable reader must conclude that the column is about our society as a whole, not about the Tatums in particular. Blow wrote the column to affect future conduct, not to direct blame at any particular family (including the Tatums) for past conduct.

Because the column is "reasonably capable" of communicating the meaning that the Tatums were deceptive, the next question is whether that meaning is "reasonably capable" of defaming the Tatums. We conclude that it is.

. . . We agree with the Tatums and with the court of appeals that the column's accusation of deception is "reasonably capable" of injuring the Tatums' standing in the community. . . . Thus, the accusation is reasonably capable of being defamatory. "Deception" and "honesty" are antonyms. Blow's statement accusing the Tatums of the first is capable of impeaching their character for the second.

We conclude that of the defamatory meanings the Tatums allege, the only one capable of arising from Blow's column is the implicit statement that the Tatums acted deceptively. However, "statements that are not verifiable as false" are not defamatory. And even when a statement is verifiable, it cannot give rise to liability if "the entire context in which it was made" discloses that it was not intended to assert a fact. A statement that fails either test—verifiability or context—is called an opinion.

The News, of course, denies that it has accused the Tatums of deception. But even if the column explicitly levied that accusation, the News argues that the deception in this case is inherently unverifiable. The Tatums' mental states in the hours following Paul's death simply cannot be factually verified. Unlike in *Milkovich*, which involved perjury, no "core of objective evidence" exists from which a jury could draw any conclusions about the Tatums' mental states. The News also argues that the column's context clearly discloses that it contains opinions, and that even if the accusation is capable of verification, it is protected because it is among the opinions that the column contains.

The Tatums contend that the charge of deception is verifiable. The accusation turns on whether the Tatums drafted the obituary with a deceptive mental state. Though the News argues this makes the accusation unverifiable, the law determines mental states all the time. Defamation, the very body of law at issue, has developed a robust process for determining whether a defendant's mental state constitutes actual malice. It cannot be the case, the Tatums argue, that defamation law can ascertain a defendant's mental state but not a plaintiff's. As for context, the Tatums argue that "a reasonable reader . . . would conclude that Blow is making objectively verifiable assertions regarding the Tatums and their deliberate misrepresentations of fact in the Obituary." Thus, in the Tatums' view, the statement is both verifiable and contextually stated as a fact.

. . . "[S]tatements that are not verifiable as false cannot form the basis of a defamation claim." However, *Milkovich* requires courts to focus not only "on a statement's verifiability," but also on "the entire context in which it was made." And even when a statement *is* verifiable as false, it does not give rise to liability if the "entire context in which it was made" discloses that it is merely an opinion masquerading as fact. ("[*Milkovich* protects] statements that cannot 'reasonably [be] interpreted as stating actual facts.' . . ." [second alteration in original] (citations omitted). Thus, statements that cannot be verified, as well as statements that cannot be understood to convey a verifiable fact, are opinions. Whether a statement is an opinion is a question of law. Finally, the type of writing at issue, though not dispositive, must never cease to inform the reviewing court's analysis.

The column's context manifestly discloses that any implied accusation of deception against the Tatums is opinion. Thus, we need not decide whether the accusation is wholly verifiable.

The column does not implicitly accuse the Tatums of being deceptive people in the abstract or by nature. Instead, it accuses them of a single, understandable act of deception, undertaken with motives that should not incite guilt or embarrassment. And it does so using language that conveys a personal viewpoint rather than an objective recitation of fact. The first sentence begins "So I guess," the column uses various versions of "I think" and "I understand," and near the column's close Blow states "the last thing I want to do is put guilt on the family of suicide victims." This first-person, informal style indicates that the format is subjective rather than objective. Nor does the column imply any undisclosed facts. The Tatums list several "exculpatory" facts that they say Blow should have included in the column. But Blow did not imply that he had personal knowledge that any of the facts the Tatums assert were false. Instead, he compared a quotation from the obituary against an account of Paul's suicide. These two accounts diverged, which Blow noted. Any speculation as to *why* the accounts diverged—if it appears in the column at all—was reasonably based on these disclosed facts. Thus, the column's words indicate that the statement is an opinion. The column's title does the same. The column as a whole, though it includes facts, argues in support of the opinion that the title conveys—society ought to be more frank about suicide. It is an opinion piece through and through.

The court of appeals ignored the column's context, opting instead to focus on decontextualized words which it—not Blow—emphasized. . . . [U]nder our precedent recognizing *Milkovich*'s joint tests, the accusation is not actionable.

Blow's column is an opinion because it does not, in context, defame the Tatums by accusing them of perpetrating a morally blameworthy deception. But to the extent that the column states that the Tatums acted deceptively, it is true. Implicit defamatory meanings—like explicit defamatory statements—are not actionable if they are either true or substantially true. . . .

The statement at issue, which arises implicitly, is that the Tatums acted deceptively when they published the obituary. . . . In our view, the statement that the Tatums were deceptive is both literally and substantially true.

The statement is literally true because the Tatums' obituary is deceptive. It leads readers to believe something that is not true. It states that Paul died from injuries arising from a car accident when in fact Paul committed suicide. . . . The Tatums respond that they earnestly believed that the obituary was true. But the Tatums' beliefs, however sincere, do not make the obituary's message any less deceptive. Indeed, the Tatums argue that Blow should have included all kinds of background facts about the Tatums' beliefs concerning traumatic brain injuries, cause of death, and other matters. But the Tatums themselves did not include any of this information in Paul's obituary. The Tatums cannot argue both that the obituary was true without this background information and that the column is false for failing to include it.

The Tatums also respond that deception implies intentionality. We agree. But the Tatums plainly and intentionally omitted from the obituary the crucial fact that Paul committed suicide. Their motive with regard to the omission is immaterial to whether the obituary is deceptive. . . .

The column does not accuse the Tatums of being deceptive people in general, but instead of buckling to the current societal pressure to avoid disclosing suicide when it occurs. And to the extent that readers thought less of the Tatums after reading the column, it would be because they concluded on their own that the Tatums acted deceptively, not because they decided to believe the column's implied assertion to that effect. . . .

The Tatums respond that a literally truthful column would have included many caveats beyond the fact that the Tatums did not intend to deceive. These facts all relate to whether the Tatums' view of Paul's death was reasonable or scientifically justified. . . .

Blow's column was callous, certainly, but it was not false.

The publication of Blow's column may have run afoul of certain journalistic, ethical, and other standards. But the standards governing the law of defamation are not among them. Accordingly, we reverse the judgment of the court of appeals and reinstate the trial court's summary judgment in favor of petitioners Steve Blow and The Dallas Morning News, Inc.

JUSTICE JEFFREY S. BOYD, joined by JUSTICE DEBRA LEHRMANN and JUSTICE JAMES BLACKLOCK, concurring:

I imagine it's no surprise by now that many courts and commentators have complained that defamation law is a "quagmire," lacks "clarity and certainty," is "overly confusing" and "convoluted," leaves courts "hopelessly and irretrievably confused," and "has spawned a morass of case law in which consistency and harmony have long ago disappeared." I'm afraid [part] of the Court's opinion in this case—in which the Court addresses whether Steve Blow's column was reasonably capable of a defamatory meaning—tends to prove their point. . . . I fear its effort to advance the law by introducing new terminology and addressing concepts unnecessary to this decision only makes things worse.

The Court begins its twenty-five-page analysis by introducing the new labels "textual defamation" and "extrinsic defamation" for what courts have always called "defamation per se" and "defamation per quod." . . . Textual defamation by implication involves the publication's gist, which may arise implicitly because of the article's as-a-whole gist . . . but only if it is reasonably capable of a defamatory meaning, which does not mean it is or is not ambiguous, but does mean it is capable of at least one defamatory meaning. . . . Or defamation by implication may arise from a partial or discrete implication, which really means the gist of a part of the article (but the Court doesn't call that a gist), to which implication the substantial-truth doctrine does not apply. . . . But regardless of whether the defamation by implication arises from the as-a-whole gist or a discrete implication, the decision whether it is reasonably capable of a defamatory meaning must not exert too great a chilling effect on *First Amendment* activities—a particular concern in implication cases. So the plaintiff has an especially rigorous burden in such cases . . . [and] the court must conduct an especially vigorous review to confirm the defendant's intent to convey the meaning the plaintiff alleges.

Got it?

. . . I'm not yet ready to scrap our convoluted principles. I can accept the idea that defamation law must be fairly complicated due to its "frequent collision . . . with the overriding constitutional principles of free speech and free press." Despite its "technical complexity," defamation law has "shown remarkable stamina in the teeth of centuries of acid criticism," which "may reflect one useful strategy for a legal system forced against its ultimate better judgment to deal with dignitary harms." But we should always do our best to reduce the confusion, or, at least, avoid adding to it.

The question in this case is pretty simple: For summary-judgment purposes, was Blow's column reasonably capable of a defamatory meaning? We need not—and the Court does not—announce any new substantive legal principles to decide that issue. . . .

I agree that the Tatums provided some evidence that Blow's column was reasonably capable of conveying the defamatory meaning that the Tatums published a deceptive obituary. I also agree, however, that if the column expressed that assertion, it expressed it as Blow's opinion, not as a fact. Because the column only expressed a potentially defamatory opinion, the Tatums cannot recover for defamation, and we need not also consider whether Blow's opinion was correct or substantially true. . . .

In a recent U.S. Supreme Court ruling about cellphone privacy, Chief Justice John Roberts remarked, "The proverbial visitor from Mars might conclude [cellphones] were an important feature of human anatomy."[1]

Pixelfit/istock.com

6

PROTECTING PRIVACY

Conflicts Among the Press, the Government and the Right to Privacy

CHAPTER OUTLINE

Constitutional Right to Privacy

Privacy Torts

Intrusion
>   Plaintiff's Case
>   Defenses

False Light
>   Plaintiff's Case
>   Defenses

Appropriation
>   Commercialization and Right of Publicity
>   Plaintiff's Case
>   Defenses

Private Facts
>   Plaintiff's Case
>   First Amendment Defense

Privacy and Data Protection

Emerging Law

Cases for Study
- *Cox Broadcasting Corp. v. Cohn*
- *Carpenter v. United States*

LEARNING OBJECTIVES

6.1   Review the constitutional right to privacy relevant to controlling access to information.

6.2   Explain the four privacy torts and to what they apply.

6.3   Describe the elements of a plaintiff's intrusion claim.

6.4   Apply the elements of a plaintiff's false light claim.

6.5   Differentiate between right of privacy and right of publicity-based appropriation claims.

6.6   Identify the elements of a plaintiff's private facts claim and relevant First Amendment privileges.

6.7   Recognize data protection standards related to information privacy.

6.8   Discuss how emerging trends are protecting privacy and publicity rights.

Individuals often strive to shape their identities by choosing which information and images they share with others. When such personal data or images are shared with larger audiences, serious emotional distress and monetary damage may result from individuals losing control over how their personal details or images are presented to others. Such harmful conduct may be considered invasions of privacy. When government actors make unwarranted intrusions to access private areas or personal data, violations of constitutional privacy may occur.

Torts may be applied to address other invasions of privacy. For example, privacy torts address invasions of privacy resulting from intrusion upon private life, widely publicizing private information in a highly offensive manner, using a person's identity for the communicators' benefit without consent, and misportraying individuals. Communicators must consider whether the First Amendment could protect such publicity and whether applying laws to punish that publicity could infringe upon free speech or press rights. It is important for communicators to understand risks and rights related to accessing private places and publicizing personal information or images. They also must recognize how others may access and use data communicators share or collect via the internet, apps or digital devices.

Although libel has been recognized for more than 400 years, the notion that courts or legislatures should protect privacy rights is only about 130 years old.[2] In 1890, two Boston lawyers—Samuel Warren and his law partner, then-future U.S. Supreme Court Justice Louis Brandeis—wrote "The Right to Privacy" for the Harvard Law Review.[3] Warren and Brandeis knew that no statutes shielded people's private lives; the lawyers contended that the common law should recognize privacy rights.[4] They argued that human dignity required protecting individual privacy.[5]

In the 20th century, the U.S. Supreme Court formally recognized a constitutional right to privacy. During the seven decades after the Warren and Brandeis article, a few state courts accepted a common law right of privacy, and several other states adopted privacy laws.[6] In recent decades, federal agencies and state legislatures have started to play a greater role in protecting privacy. Today, the Federal Trade Commission has the power to police companies' data security practices, it enforces various laws that address data security and personal privacy, and it is exploring issuing rules that could address data security and company's collection of information.[7] States also have enacted data privacy laws that address how companies may use consumers' data.[8]

Louis D. Brandeis and his law partner Samuel Brandeis wrote an 1890 essay calling upon judges to recognize a legal right to privacy in the United States.

Harris & Ewing. Library of Congress (LC-USZ62-31230)

CONSTITUTIONAL RIGHT TO PRIVACY

The word "privacy" is not included in the U.S. Constitution. The constitutional right to privacy is grounded in the founders' recognition of important personal liberties. Founding Father and second President John Adams recalled in his papers that it was the British writs of assistance, or generic court orders, during colonial times that allowed British officers to conduct random searches of shops, warehouses and private homes. President Adams suggested that public outrage over this practice "helped spark the Revolution itself" and is the reason for the Fourth Amendment.[9] That amendment protects "the right of the people to be secure in their persons, houses, papers, and effects, against unreasonable searches and seizures."[10]

The Third and Fifth Amendments also protect different aspects of privacy.[11] Fifty years ago, in *Griswold v. Connecticut*, the U.S. Supreme Court said the word "liberty" in the Fourteenth Amendment—"[N]or shall any State deprive any person of life, liberty, or property, without due process of law"—also includes personal privacy.[12] In *Griswold*, the Supreme Court struck down a state's ban on the use of birth control, noting that it violated the privacy rights of married people. The Court said that a right to privacy was implicit in the various amendments previously mentioned, as well as the Ninth Amendment and even the First Amendment's "freedom to associate and privacy in one's associations."[13]

Most Americans associate the U.S. Supreme Court's 7–2 *Roe v. Wade* decision with abortion rights.[14] In coming to its judgment in *Roe*, the Court also affirmed the qualified constitutional protection for personal privacy established in *Griswold*. Justice Harry Blackmun wrote for the Court:

> This right to privacy, whether it be founded in the Fourteenth Amendment's concept of personal liberty and restrictions upon state action, as we feel it is, or, as the District Court determined, in the Ninth Amendment's reservation of rights to the people, is broad enough to encompass a woman's decision whether or not to terminate her pregnancy.[15]

In *Roe*, the Court emphasized that the right of personal privacy is qualified and must be weighed against important state interests in regulation.[16]

In *Whalen v. Roe*, a case addressing New York state's collection of the names and addresses of persons to whom doctors prescribed certain medications that had lawful and unlawful uses, the U.S. Supreme Court addressed privacy in relation to the Fourteenth Amendment. The unanimous Court described two kinds of interests in cases addressing protecting privacy. First, **informational privacy** "is the individual interest in avoiding disclosure of personal matters," Justice John Paul Stephens wrote. Second, he described **decisional privacy** as "the interest in independence in making certain kinds of important decisions."[17] The Court determined the state collection of patients' names and addresses and the potential for unwanted disclosures of this information did not pose a serious threat to informational or decisional privacy. Nonetheless, the Court acknowledged "the threat to privacy implicit in the accumulation of vast amounts of personal information in computerized data banks or other massive government files."[18]

In a plurality decision in *Planned Parenthood of Southeastern Pennsylvania v. Casey,* Justices Sandra Day O'Connor, Anthony Kennedy, and David Souter addressed Fourteenth Amendment protection for decisional privacy in relation to abortion. As the Due Process Clause of the Fourteenth Amendment protects liberty, the Justices reasoned the Fourteenth Amendment protects the "personal decision" whether to terminate a pregnancy.[19] Affirming *Roe,* the plurality stated: "These matters, involving the most intimate and personal choices a person may make in a lifetime, choices central to personal dignity and autonomy, are central to the liberty protected by the Fourteenth Amendment."[20]

The earliest U.S. Supreme Court case that explored Fourth Amendment privacy-related protections focused on property and not people. Fourth Amendment cases often hinge on what constitutes a search under the law. Judges issue **search warrants**, legal orders issued to authorize law enforcement to search locations and seize items. A valid search warrant must be based on **probable cause**—sufficient information and facts to think a crime was committed based on reliable information and facts.

In 1928, the Court held that an electronic eavesdropping device did not amount to a search under the Fourth Amendment because placing the device did not involve physical entry into the defendant's home.[21] Justice Brandeis dissented, writing that "every unjustifiable intrusion by the Government upon the privacy of the individual, whatever the means employed," was an unconstitutional search under the Fourth Amendment.[22]

In the 1960s, the Court's approach shifted. In *Silverman v. United States,* the U.S. Supreme Court held that it was a search when federal officers eavesdropped on defendants by using a microphone placed through the wall of a home. This search, the Court held, violated the Fourth Amendment.[23] In *Katz v. United States,* the defendant was convicted of illegal betting over a telephone line in a public phone booth. The government recorded his phone conversations without a warrant, which led to his conviction. The Supreme Court threw out that evidence, calling it a Fourth Amendment violation. In his concurrence, Justice John Marshall Harlan II wrote, "[A] person has a constitutionally protected reasonable expectation of privacy," and "electronic as well as physical intrusion into a place that is in this sense private may constitute a violation of the Fourth Amendment."[24]

Courts have recognized Justice Harlan's concurrence in *Katz* as the Harlan "reasonable expectation of privacy test." The test requires that an individual have an actual expectation of privacy and that society is prepared to recognize this as reasonable.[25] In a recent case, Chief Justice John Roberts wrote, "Justice Harlan's concurrence profoundly changed our Fourth Amendment jurisprudence."[26]

POINTS OF LAW
CONSTITUTIONAL RIGHT TO PRIVACY

- The U.S. Constitution protects from governmental invasion of privacy.
- Protection comes from the First, Third, Fourth, Fifth, Ninth and Fourteenth Amendments.

- The U.S. Supreme Court has said personal privacy rights are qualified and not absolute (see *Griswold v. Connecticut*).[27]
- Justice John Harlan's "reasonable expectation of privacy" test from *Katz* establishes a Fourth Amendment right to privacy when
  1. a person has an actual expectation of privacy that
  2. society recognizes as reasonable.[28]

More than thirty years ago, the Court said a search of a public employee's desk and filing cabinet did not violate their Fourth Amendment rights.[29] Courts have said the First Amendment does not bar private employers from examining email messages on an employee's computer because the company's interest in preventing illegal activity or unprofessional comments outweighs an employee's privacy interest.[30]

Just over a decade ago, in *City of Ontario v. Quon*, the U.S. Supreme Court unanimously held that government employers may see public employees' text messages sent and received on government-issued equipment if the searches have a legitimate work-related purpose and public employees have been told not to expect privacy.[31] The case involved a police officer who used a department-issued pager to communicate with fellow officers. When the city audited officers' pagers, it found one officer had exchanged sexually explicit text messages with both his wife and his mistress. The officer claimed the city violated his reasonable expectation of privacy. The Court said even if the officer did have a reasonable expectation of privacy, the city's search of his pager did not violate it. Although the Court said its ruling was narrowly applied to the case facts, subsequent cases have applied the ruling to government-issued computers and other communication technologies.[32]

Today, many challenges to privacy involve communication via new technologies. Recent U.S. Supreme Court cases have tackled questions about how courts should apply decades-old precedents to technology that did not exist at the time of those decisions. For example, the Court held that the government must have a search warrant to use a thermal imaging device on a home because use of this technology constituted a search.[33] In *United States v. Jones*, the Supreme Court unanimously held that physically mounting a GPS transmitter on a car amounts to a search and violates the Fourth Amendment.[34]

In *Riley v. California*, a unanimous Supreme Court said law enforcement may not search a person's cellphone without a warrant. The decision involved convictions of two suspects for criminal activity based on evidence found on their cellphones—one a smartphone, the other a flip phone. The government argued that searching a cellphone found on a person at the time of arrest fell under the "incident to arrest" exception, which allows for a search of a person without a warrant at the time of an arrest. Writing for the Court, Chief Justice Roberts said the "incident to arrest" exception does not apply to a cellphone:

> Modern cellphones, as a category, implicate privacy concerns far beyond those implicated by the search of a cigarette pack, a wallet, or a purse. Cellphones differ in both a quantitative and a qualitative sense from other objects that might be kept on an arrestee's person.[35]

Privacy concerns also may arise when government attempts to access data stored outside personal electronic devices. In *Carpenter v. United States* (excerpted at the end of this chapter), the Supreme Court in extended Fourth Amendment protection to cell-site location information (CSLI), produced when your cellphone connects to your carrier's wireless network through a cell tower.[36] As required under the Stored Communications Act, the police obtained a subpoena, or court order, to get months of Timothy Carpenter's CSLI. Police then used CSLI to connect Carpenter to various robbery crime scenes. He was convicted, largely because of the CSLI.[37]

Writing for the majority in a 5–4 decision, Chief Justice Roberts said using a subpoena to obtain CSLI is not enough—instead, this constitutes a search under the Fourth Amendment and requires a search warrant. "The seismic shifts in digital technology that made possible the tracking of not only Carpenter's location but also everyone else's, not for a short period but for years and years [is] unlike the nosy neighbor who keeps an eye on comings and goings," he wrote. Wireless carriers "are ever alert, and their memory is nearly infallible."[38]

Graham Hughes/Alamy Stock Photo

In *Carpenter*, the Court noted that the case did not fit neatly with existing precedents, specifically two cases decided in the 1970s: *United States v. Miller* and *Smith v. Maryland*.[39] The Court held in both cases that an individual has no expectation of privacy in bank and phone company records kept by third parties (e.g., the bank or phone company).[40] Called the **third-party doctrine**, the concept holds that people who voluntarily give information to third parties, such as banks, phone companies or internet service providers, forfeit any reasonable expectation of privacy.

The Supreme Court rejected the application of the third-party doctrine to CSLI in *Carpenter*:

We decline to extend *Smith* and *Miller*[.] . . . Given the unique nature of cell phone location records, the fact that the information is held by a third party does not by itself overcome the user's claim to *Fourth Amendment* protection. . . . Although [CSLI] records are generated for commercial purposes, that distinction does not negate Carpenter's anticipation of privacy in his physical location. . . . [T]he time-stamped data provides an intimate window into a person's life, revealing not only his particular movements, but through them his "familial, political, professional, religious, and sexual associations." These location records "hold for many Americans the privacies of life." . . . [C]ell phone tracking is remarkably easy, cheap, and efficient compared to traditional investigative tools. With just the click of a button, the Government can access each carrier's deep repository of historical location information at practically no expense.[41]

The Court noted that the decision in *Carpenter* does not overturn *Miller* and *Smith* or the section of the Stored Communications Act that allowed law enforcement to obtain most records with a subpoena. The decision should be applied narrowly to CSLI rather than all third-party records. In four separate dissents, the four dissenting justices disagreed on why the majority was in error. Justices Anthony Kennedy and Samuel Alito argued primarily that the third-party doctrine should apply.[42] Justice Clarence Thomas said the framers of the U.S. Constitution did not intend privacy to be incorporated into the Fourth Amendment in the way the Court has done so over the years, particularly in its application of the *Katz* "reasonable expectation of privacy."[43] Justice Neil Gorsuch said property law precedents provide a better avenue for determining privacy concerns with new technologies.[44]

PRIVACY TORTS

The dictionary defines privacy as "freedom from unauthorized intrusion" and the "state of being let alone and able to keep certain especially personal matters to oneself."[45] This common definition of privacy reflects the evolution of privacy law, whether constitutional or based on state statutes or common law precedents. Sixty years ago, William Prosser, a torts expert and law school dean, suggested that states should divide privacy law into four categories: intrusion, false light, appropriation and private facts.[46] Intrusion is defined as physically or technologically disturbing another's reasonable expectation of privacy. False light is the privacy tort that involves making persons seem to be someone they are not in the public eye. Appropriation is generally using a person's name, picture or voice without permission for commercial purposes. Private facts is publicizing highly offensive, true private information that is not newsworthy or lawfully obtained from a public record. Courts and state legislatures adopted and continue to use Prosser's categories, but not all states allow plaintiffs to sue for each of the four privacy torts. Additionally, the appropriation tort currently includes two different torts: commercialization and right to publicity.

Only living individuals may sue for three of the privacy torts: intrusion, private facts and false light.[47] Similar to a person's reputation in a libel case, privacy is considered a personal right. The dead do not have personal privacy rights. Also, businesses, associations, unions and other groups generally do not have personal privacy rights, thus they most often cannot sue for a privacy tort.[48] Only individuals may sue for appropriation in many states. But a few states allow businesses and nonprofit organizations to bring appropriation lawsuits. Additionally, in many states, the right of publicity is extended to heirs.

Intrusion

While many of the U.S. Supreme Court cases discussed earlier focus on limits to government intrusions, it is important to consider the news media have utilized some invasive techniques to report on issues of public concern. What limits exist for investigative newsgathering techniques that can include, for example, hidden microphones and cameras?

Invasive newsgathering techniques may amount to **intrusion upon seclusion**, physically or technologically disturbing another's reasonable expectation of privacy.[49] (Information-gathering techniques that may be classified as intrusion are discussed further in Chapter 7.) The intrusion tort is intended to ensure people retain their dignity by preventing unwanted encroachment into an individual's personal physical space and private affairs. New York and Virginia have refused to recognize the intrusion tort.[50]

Recent Federal Aviation Administration rules have made it easier for businesses to fly light-weight drones.

mailfor/istock.com

Plaintiff's Case

Journalists may be sued for intrusion if they intentionally interfere with another person's solitude or meddle in the person's private concerns in a way that would be highly offensive to a **reasonable person**, which is the law's version of an average member of a community. The intrusion may be physical, such as entering someone's house without permission; technological, such as using a geolocation device; or sensory, such as striving to see or overhear private affairs.[51]

Reasonable Expectation of Privacy. An intrusion upon seclusion may occur when an intentional intrusion interferes with a person's interest in "solitude or seclusion" related to that person or their private affairs.[52] In 2020, the Ninth Circuit Court of Appeals found four plaintiffs had standing to sue Facebook for intrusion upon seclusion based on the company's use of plug-ins on third-party sites to track the plaintiffs' browsing histories. The court reasoned the plaintiffs had adequately shown they had a reasonable expectation of privacy when they logged off Facebook. The court identified the relevant question as "whether a user would reasonably expect that Facebook would have access" to their data when they were not logged onto Facebook. The court also considered whether the collected data was sensitive and whether the tracking practice violated social norms.[53]

Journalists might infringe upon a reasonable expectation of privacy to obtain information by intentionally entering private property without permission. Anyone who does so has committed intrusion, an act similar to trespass (discussed in Chapter 7). Trespass is both a crime and a tort. A trespasser may be sued for intrusion in a civil claim. Intrusion occurs only if a person has a reasonable expectation of privacy.[54] For example, people have a reasonable expectation that others will not enter their private property, such as a house or apartment, without consent.

That may not be the case for private land to which the public has access. In a lawsuit involving Google's Street View feature, which provides searchable panoramic street views, a couple sued Google for intrusion. Street View showed the couple's house and swimming pool. The couple said the pictures could be obtained only by driving up the private street on which their home is located, a street marked as "Private Road, No Trespassing." However, no reasonable person would be highly offended by Google's entry onto the road, the Third Circuit Court of Appeals said, because guests and delivery trucks entered the road and saw what Street View's pictures showed.[55]

Ordinarily, there is not a reasonable expectation of privacy on public streets and sidewalks and in public parks where people can be seen or overheard. However, there may be circumstances when people do have a reasonable expectation of privacy in public places. For example, the U.S. Supreme Court upheld a Colorado law that created an eight-foot bubble around individuals entering a health care facility.[56] The statute made it illegal to approach within eight feet of a person going into an abortion clinic—the law's primary focus—to hand out a leaflet, display a sign or interact without the person's consent. The law applied within a 100-foot radius around a health care facility's entrance. In *Hill v. Colorado*, the Court said the law was neither content nor viewpoint based. Therefore, the Court did not apply a strict scrutiny standard. The state needed to show only a substantial interest. The Court said Colorado's interests in public health and in protecting the rights of individuals to avoid unwanted communication met the intermediate scrutiny test. Colorado's law implies that people entering health clinics have a reasonable expectation of privacy.

Journalists should not assume people involved in a news event occurring on public property lack a reasonable expectation of privacy. For example, an automobile accident victim reasonably expected discussions with emergency personnel to be private even if medical treatment took place on the side of a public road, a court held.[57]

It is not always easy to determine whether property is private or public. Taxpayers own government land, but they may not always be permitted on the property. A federal district court ruled that police could arrest reporters entering a naval base without permission to cover protests.[58]

Intrusion suits also have been brought based on news reporters finding information in **public records**, which are government records that are available for people to inspect. Courts have held that there is no reasonable expectation of privacy in public records or publicly recorded court proceedings.[59]

Intentional Physical or Technological Intrusion. The more technology develops, the more ways intrusion can occur. For example, at least 44 states have enacted laws addressing a variety of concerns, including privacy protection, with unmanned aircraft systems or drones.[60] Using tracking devices or hacking also may be considered intrusive. In 2020, a California appellate court allowed a fitness and health celebrity's intrusion upon seclusion claim to proceed against a magazine group that conceded it was illegal for a private eye to use a tracking device to help a tabloid get photographs of the celebrity.[61] Almost a year later, a federal court in Washington, D.C., allowed a businessman's intrusion claim to proceed against public relations contractors. The claim alleged the defendants were part of a conspiracy related to hacking into a private computer. The court said such an intrusion "would represent an intentional intrusion on the victim's private affairs" and such an intrusion "would be highly offensive to a reasonable person."[62]

Older technology, such as a camera's telephoto lens, also can intrude. In one case, a woman's sister-in-law, husband, and children visited her home after she disappeared. They swam in the home's pool, surrounded by a seven-foot-high fence, while a CBS television network cameraman stood on a neighbor's porch and videotaped them using a telephoto lens. A federal district court permitted the family to sue CBS for intrusion, saying:

> We find that the plaintiffs' allegations that they were swimming in the backyard pool of a private home surrounded by a seven-foot privacy fence are sufficient to allege both that they believed they were in a secluded place and that the activity was private.[63]

In 2021, appellate courts in Florida and California addressed intrusion claims involving camera recordings of private residential property. A Florida appellate court found homeowners were likely to succeed on an intrusion upon seclusion claim addressing a 25-foot-high surveillance camera that could record over a six-foot-high privacy fence. The court recognized a reasonable expectation of privacy for the property surrounding a residence. "There is a material difference between occasionally viewing the activities within a neighbor's backyard that are observable without peering over a privacy fence and erecting a camera to see over a privacy fence to thereafter surveil and record those activities on a consistent basis," the court said.[64]

In 2021, a California appellate court affirmed a lower court's finding that any intrusion from iPhone and Nest security cameras recording part of a neighbor's backyard was insubstantial when most recordings of conversations were barely audible and the plaintiffs could barely be seen in video recordings. Audio recordings primarily were audible when people were talking loudly enough to reduce reasonable expectations of privacy. Evidence indicated the cameras were posted due to "legitimate safety concerns" related to resident comedian Kathy Griffin's "status as a public figure and past death threats and stalking," the court said.[65]

A California appellate court recently found that cameras posted due to comedian Kathy Griffin's safety concerns did not intrude upon neighbors' privacy rights.

Vivien Killilea / Getty Images

Highly Offensive to a Reasonable Person. A plaintiff also must show that a reasonable person would find the intrusion into the plaintiff's solitude or private affairs highly offensive. In 2020, the Ninth Circuit Court of Appeals explained this requires considering several factors. Those include "the likelihood of serious harm to the victim, the degree and setting of the intrusion," motives and objectives for an intrusion and social norms. A plaintiff must demonstrate the intrusion is not acceptable.[66]

Defenses

Consent is the only defense for an intrusion suit based on trespass in nearly all cases. Newsworthiness is not a defense because publishing is not an element of the tort. Intrusion happens in the newsgathering process. However, the Ninth Circuit Court of Appeals said a story's newsworthiness may reduce the intrusion's offensiveness.[67] This is important because a plaintiff must prove the intrusion was highly offensive.

POINTS OF LAW
INTRUSION UPON SECLUSION

Plaintiff's Case
- A reasonable expectation of privacy and
- An intentional intrusion on privacy
- That would be highly offensive to a reasonable person

Defense
- Consent

Consent. People cannot claim a reasonable expectation of privacy or seclusion has been intruded upon if they gave consent for someone to be on their private property. For example, a restaurant owner allowed a television news crew to videotape a health inspector evaluating the restaurant. After the station ran an unflattering story, the restaurant sued for intrusion. Because a trial jury found that the restaurant owner had given the television crew consent to enter the premises, an appeals court rejected the restaurant's claim.[68] Consent can also be implied. For example, if a journalist enters private property and the property owner responds to the reporter's questions, there is implied consent to remain and continue the interview.[69]

False Pretenses. Using false pretenses to enter private property is a long-standing reporting technique. Courts are not in agreement, but have said reporters sometimes can deceptively gain entry without invading privacy. In one case, a producer for the ABC television network program "Primetime Live" sent seven people, posing as patients and equipped with hidden cameras, to eye clinics owned by Dr. J. H. Desnick. "Primetime Live" used portions of the hidden video recordings in a story it aired suggesting that Desnick's clinics performed unnecessary cataract surgery. Desnick sued ABC for intrusion and other torts. The clinics were open to anyone who wanted an eye examination, the Seventh Circuit Court of Appeals said. The people posing as patients were allowed into the clinics, just like anyone else. The people posing as patients meant to deceive, but that did not invalidate consent to enter, the court held.[70]

The Seventh Circuit noted that people sometimes use deception to enter private or semiprivate premises. For example, a restaurant owner might refuse entry to a food critic known to write harsh reviews. But restaurant critics usually do not identify themselves to the owner when they enter. The court said this deception does not negate the restaurant owner's consent. The court said this analysis might not apply to someone using false pretenses to enter for no substantive reason, for example someone who pretends to be a utilities meter reader to enter a private home. In contrast, the hypothetical restaurant critic—and the people posing as eye clinic patients—had valid reasons to be on private property, the court said.

In a different case, a photographer dressed in hospital apparel recorded a video of emergency room personnel treating a man who had a bad reaction to a drug. He asked the patient to sign a release form. The photographer said the video would be used to train hospital personnel. The patient signed the release. After the video ran on a cable program, "Trauma: Life in the ER," the patient sued for intrusion and other claims. A court agreed that the patient had a reasonable expectation of privacy in a hospital emergency room. The court said the photographer's deception invalidated the patient's consent.[71]

Entering a home or office using false pretenses may provide grounds for an intrusion suit. At least one court said that combining false pretenses with surreptitious image and audio recording after entering a home was intrusive. To investigate a person practicing medicine without a license, a Life magazine reporter and a photographer claimed to be patients and were admitted to the man's home. The reporter had a microphone in her purse, and the photographer used a small, concealed camera to take pictures. A federal appellate court ignored the false pretenses question and focused on the surreptitious reporting. The court said people have a reasonable expectation of privacy in their homes. Even though a person might expect a visitor to repeat what is seen and heard in the house, it is not expected that "what is heard and seen will be transmitted by photograph or recording . . . to the public at large."[72] The court added, "The First Amendment is not a license to trespass, to steal, or to intrude by electronic means into the precincts of another's home or office."[73]

Most states have laws making it illegal to pretend to be a law enforcement officer. In some states, it is unlawful to pretend to be any public servant.[74]

False Light

False light is a privacy tort that involves making a person seem in the public eye to be someone they are not. A misleading story, social media post, or YouTube video that misrepresents a person's character may be grounds for a false light suit.[75] False light often involves the misattribution of a person's actions or beliefs. Typically, a false light tort does not require a plaintiff to show injury to reputation, although California sees false light and libel as such close relatives that a false light plaintiff must prove reputational injury.[76] Some states do not recognize false light because this tort is so similar to libel. They also say false light is so vague it encroaches on First Amendment rights.[77] Courts in other states allow a plaintiff to sue for both defamation and false light based on the same facts.

False light addresses harm to privacy interests. In 2022, a federal district court dismissed a false light claim that addressed a plaintiff's public professional life. World champion Russian chess player Nona Gaprindashvili, the first female to be recognized as an International Chess Grandmaster, filed false light and defamation claims against Netflix. The case addresses a miniseries, "The Queen's Gambit." During a scene set in 1968, a fictional chess tournament announcer accurately described her as a world champion then inaccurately stated she had "never faced men." The court dismissed the false light claim with prejudice because she had not proven the statements about her public professional life intruded into her private life, but the court did not dismiss the defamation claim.[78] Netflix settled the defamation claim.[79]

Plaintiff's Case

Most states recognizing false light require a plaintiff to prove (1) the material was published, (2) the plaintiff was identified, (3) the published material was false or created a false impression, (4) the statements or pictures put the plaintiff in a false light that would be highly offensive to a reasonable person and (5) the defendant acted with actual malice—they knew the material was false or recklessly disregarded its falsity.[80] Only individual persons can bring a false light suit.[81]

Publication. The false light tort requires material to have been widely distributed to the public generally or to a large segment of the community.[82] Generally, communication to a few people does not amount to publication for the false light tort, although courts in a few states allow publication to be proved by dissemination to just one person or a few people.[83] For these courts, that smaller group must have a special relationship with the plaintiff so the plaintiff would be highly offended if the group saw or heard the publication.[84]

Identification. Plaintiffs must prove the material in question was about them. The courts of some states, such as California, define identification for false light just as they do for libel. It is sufficient for one or more people to say the communication identified the plaintiff.[85] Most courts hold that because the publication requirement means many people must be exposed to the story, a large segment of the public must reasonably believe the false material refers to the plaintiff.

In 1962, Nona Gaprindashvili was the first female International Chess Grandmaster. A federal court dismissed Nona Gaprindashvili's false light claim against Netflix, addressing how the world chess champion was mentioned in "The Queen's Gambit."

ITAR-TASS News Agency / Alamy Stock Photo

Falsity. Published material supporting a false light suit must be false or imply false information. If the publication is true and does not create a false implication, it cannot be grounds for a false light suit even if the material emotionally upsets the plaintiff. Minor errors ordinarily do not make a story sufficiently incorrect to meet the falsity standard.

Some courts hold that true facts can lead to false implications if the defendant intended that result. For example, The New York Times published a story implying that a businessman named Robert Howard might be using an alias and really was another person, Howard Finkelstein, a convicted felon. The story included only true statements: Records showed that Finkelstein used the name Robert Howard; Howard denied he was Finkelstein, yet rumors circulated saying he might be. A jury found that the reporter did not libel Howard because the story did not absolutely say he was Finkelstein. A federal appellate court said the story's implication that the businessman might be the felon could sustain a false light suit.[86] Still, there must be a clear connection between the statements leading to a false light suit and the implied falsehood the plaintiff claims.

Highly Offensive to a Reasonable Person. At a false light trial, the **fact finder**—the jury, if there is one, or the judge assesses the facts presented as evidence in each case—must determine whether the published material would be highly offensive to a reasonable person. Defining "highly offensive" is a very subjective task. A Federal court in Arizona recently found that an exotic dance club's use of models' photographs in online advertisements without the models' consent was a significant misrepresentation of the models. The court reasoned that falsely implying the models endorsed, or possibly stripped, at such a club could be highly offensive to a reasonable person.[87]

Some legal scholars try to clarify the term "highly offensive" by using three categories: embellishment, distortion and fictionalization.[88] These are not legal categories, but they can help to recognize a circumstance that could potentially give rise to a false light claim.

A story is embellished when false material is added to otherwise true facts. For example, a series of newspaper columns told a true story of a mother giving up a baby for adoption, the baby being adopted, a court giving the natural father custody four years later, and the father hiring a psychologist to help the child adjust to a new home. One column falsely said the psychologist "has readily admitted that she sees her job as doing whatever the natural parents instruct her to do." The plaintiff said the writer knew that statement was false. An Illinois appellate court determined a jury could find it highly offensive to a reasonable person to suggest a psychologist would ignore her professional commitments.[89]

Distortion occurs when facts are omitted or the context in which material is published makes an otherwise accurate story appear false. For example, a member of the Solana Beach, California, City Council recently filed a false light claim to address a campaign advertisement that quoted language from an almost decade-old certificate of appreciation a council member had signed. Omitting the fact that the language came from that certificate when using the quote in the context of a campaign advertisement implied the council member endorsed a candidate running for office. Used in other circumstances, the quote might not have led to a lawsuit.[90]

Fictionalization is taking real facts and making them fiction. This can result in a false light claim when a person's name or other identifying characteristics, for example, are part of a largely fictional piece. In one case, a supermarket tabloid newspaper published a picture of 97-year-old Arkansas resident Nellie Mitchell to illustrate a story with the headline, "Pregnancy Forced Granny to Quit Work at Age 101." The story was a fictional account of an Australian woman who left her paper route at the age of 101 because she became pregnant during an extramarital affair with a rich client. Mitchell, in fact, delivered newspapers in her hometown for nearly 50 years. Mitchell won her false light suit and, after the newspaper's appeals, was awarded $1 million in damages.[91]

Fault. Decades ago, the U.S. Supreme Court decided two false light cases: *Time, Inc. v. Hill* and *Cantrell v. Forest City Publishing Co.* Both cases involved private individual plaintiffs, not public officials or public figures, and the Court held that they had to prove actual malice to win.

The Hill family sued Time, Inc., publisher of Life magazine, for a story and photographs about a play's account of the family's experience of being held hostage for 19 hours by escaped convicts. The convicts did not harm the Hills, and the family later said they were treated with respect. The play portrayed a fictional Hilliard family held hostage, beaten and verbally abused by escaped convicts. The Hills claimed that the text and accompanying photographs suggested the convicts treated the real Hill family as ruthlessly as the fictional hostages and this put the family in a false light. The Hills sued and won.[92]

The U.S. Supreme Court reversed, saying the jury should have been told that the Hills could win only if they proved actual malice. The First Amendment protects the press from being sued for negligent misstatements when reporting stories of public interest, the Court reasoned.[93]

Seven years after *Hill*, the U.S. Supreme Court again said a private plaintiff had to prove actual malice. In *Cantrell v. Forest City Publishing Co.*, the Supreme Court upheld a jury verdict in the Cantrell family's favor because the trial judge correctly told the jury to apply the actual malice standard. The case involved a feature in the Cleveland Plain Dealer newspaper about the impact of a bridge collapse on a small community in West Virginia. The article and accompanying photographs featured the Cantrell family and highlighted their abject poverty. The Court said there was sufficient evidence to show that portions of the article were false and were published with knowing falsity or reckless disregard for the truth.[94]

POINTS OF LAW
FALSE LIGHT

Plaintiff's Case
- Publication of
- false facts
- about the identified individual
- that would be highly offensive to a reasonable person
- with actual malice, for both private and public plaintiffs (although a few state courts only require negligence for private plaintiffs) in cases involving matters of public interest.[95]

Defense
- Libel defenses

Courts in at least 11 states follow the Supreme Court precedents in *Hill* and *Cantrell*, requiring false light plaintiffs to show actual malice.[96] For example, the Tenth Circuit Court of Appeals recently affirmed a lower court's dismissal of a case addressing a Sports Illustrated series on the Oklahoma State University football program. A supporter of the team sued Time, Inc., and two Sports Illustrated reporters for false light after an article alleged he overpaid players for work they did or paid players for work they did not do.[97] The reporters interviewed dozens of football players, coaches and administrators to investigate the university's efforts to recruit and attain football players. Prior to publication, they re-interviewed some sources to check accuracy, fact-checked the article and had lawyers read the article. They "were thorough in their investigation, editing, and review," the court said; the plaintiff could not prove actual malice with convincing clarity.[98]

Some state courts are divided on requiring private persons to prove actual malice in false light cases. Courts in at least five states and the District of Columbia have applied *Gertz v. Robert Welch, Inc.* (discussed in Chapter 4) to false light cases. They have suggested that the U.S. Supreme Court would apply *Gertz* today if it heard another false light appeal.[99] These state courts would require only that a private individual prove negligence in a false light suit, not actual malice. For example, in 2022, a federal court in Tennessee dismissed a false light claim one social media user filed against another due to failure to demonstrate the defendant acted negligently regarding the falsity of statements made about the plaintiff.[100]

Defenses

Not all state courts recognize the false light tort, and parts of the tort remain in flux. Many courts say that if false light plaintiffs prove all elements of their cases, media defendants may use the libel defenses discussed in Chapter 5 to defeat the claim.[101] For example, media defendants can utilize the fair report privilege.[102] People with absolute privilege if sued for libel— certain public officials and others involved in judicial proceedings or government meetings—also have absolute privilege in false light suits. Truth is also defense in a false light suit.[103] Only a few courts have decided whether opinion is a defense for a false light claim, and they disagree.[104]

More recently, some appellate courts have also applied anti-SLAPP statutes to false light claims. As noted in Chapter 5, anti-SLAPP laws generally allow a defendant to make a motion to strike a lawsuit because it involves a matter of public concern. The plaintiff has the burden to show that they will prevail in the lawsuit, otherwise the suit is dismissed. If a defendant prevails, some anti-SLAPP laws allow them to collect attorney's fees from the plaintiff.[105]

In 2020, the Supreme Court of Nevada said the state's ant-SLAPP statute applied to a false light, defamation and intentional and negligent emotional distress lawsuit. The case addressed articles published on the Veterans in Politics International, Inc. website and sent in an email chain. The case also addressed comments made in a phone conversation.[106]

The state appellate court affirmed a lower court's dismissal of the claims addressing the articles but did not dismiss the claims addressing comments made via phone. Nevada's statute applies to statements communicated in "a place open to the public" or an open forum. Sending the statements to approximately 50,000 email subscribers was "akin to a radio or television broadcast or newsletter," the court stated. The phone conversation, however, did not meet that standard. The court noted a lawyer's conduct in court and judicial transparency were matters of public interest. The court also considered the statements in the article, which were "truthful or made without knowledge of [their] falsehood," to be provided in good faith.[107]

In recent years, rapper 50 Cent has filed multiple lawsuits in multiple jurisdictions to protect his right of publicity.

Pictorial Press, Ltd./Alamy Stock Photo

Appropriation

Appropriation includes two different torts: **commercialization** and the **right of publicity**. Many people do not want their names or pictures to be in advertisements because they want to remain private. Generally using a person's name, picture or voice without permission for commercial or trade purposes is appropriation, an area of privacy tort law.[108] The Supreme Court has decided only one appropriation case (*Zacchini v. Scripps-Howard Broadcasting Co.*, discussed later in this section), and that case predates many of the modern technologies and media platforms to which the Supreme Court has since given First Amendment protection.[109]

State courts take a range of approaches to resolve appropriation cases, often based on whether the alleged appropriation arises in a commercial context (see Chapter 12) or another First Amendment context. The courts often apply strict scrutiny, rather than a balancing of interests, when reviewing cases involving the media (see Chapter 3). However, many courts apply a balancing approach to resolve some right of publicity claims.[110] Before addressing these issues, the next section will define the commercialization and right of publicity torts as well as what plaintiffs are required to prove.

Commercialization and Right of Publicity

The appropriation tort that protects people who want privacy is called "commercialization" or "misappropriation." Commercialization, the word this chapter uses, prohibits using another person's name or likeness for commercial purposes without permission. No state has refused to allow appropriation suits, although courts in some states have not yet ruled on the issue.[111]

Some people, however, want their names and pictures to be publicized, and they want to control when, how and where their names and pictures will be used for advertising and other commercial purposes. They also want to be paid for giving their permission for their identities to be used. Courts often refer to this part of the appropriation tort as the "right of publicity."[112] This appropriation tort protects celebrities' rights to have their names, pictures, likenesses, voices and identities used for commercial or trade purposes only with permission.

New York state adopted the country's first appropriation law in 1903.[113] Two years later, Georgia became the first state to recognize appropriation as a common law privacy tort. A federal appeals court judge, Jerome Frank, first used the phrase "right of publicity" nearly 70 years ago.[114] The court ruled that professional baseball players had a right to earn money when their names were used on baseball cards. Courts generally find that people have both a right to protect their privacy and a right to decide when their name or picture may or may not be used commercially by others.[115] The commercial value of a celebrity's name or picture, though, will be much greater than that of a relatively unknown individual. Courts also have said a right of publicity could be transferred, as a car can be sold, but the right of privacy cannot.

Although both commercialization and the right of publicity prevent the use of someone's name, picture, likeness, voice or identity for advertising or other commercial purposes without permission, they differ in two important ways. First, commercialization protects an individual's dignity connected with personal privacy, while the right of publicity protects the monetary value of using a well-known individual's name, likeness and picture. Second, courts generally consider commercialization a personal right, one that does not survive a person's death. The right of publicity may be considered a property right. In many states, the right of publicity survives death.[116] Just as people may determine who gets their cars after they die—through wills or by state law—people may choose who will control their rights of publicity after death.[117]

In many states, the right of publicity survives death. In 2021, New York first recognized **post-mortem rights of publicity**, referring to persons' abilities to control the commercial use of their names, pictures, likenesses, voices and identities after death. Those rights last 40 years after death for persons who lived in New York.[118] In some states, the right may last for 20 to 100 years, depending on the state, as long as the right is used.[119] Nebraska does not have a time limit.[120]

Several state legislatures have explored efforts to extend or alter the right of publicity **post-mortem**. Maryland, Massachusetts and New Hampshire recently failed to extend the application of their statutes to 70 years beyond death, but Indiana lawmakers passed an amendment to the state's existing statute to apply 100 years beyond death.[121] Federal courts have recently resolved issues of jurisdiction related to post-mortem rights of publicity. For example, in 2021, the U.S. Tax Court stated that musician Michael Jackson's legal interests and rights are determined under California law, where he lived at the time of his death.[122] Similar cases have applied the law of the state of primary residence of the celebrity at the time of death.[123]

A recently proposed Louisiana House Bill, which was not approved, would have recognized a right of publicity as a property right protected against commercial uses of a person's name, voice, signature, photograph, image or likeness without permission, regardless of whether a person resided in Louisiana. The bill would have created a post-mortem right of publicity for 70 years after death.[124] The publicity rights also would have extended to any digital replica, "a computer-generated or electronic reproduction of an individual's likeness or voice that intentionally depicts the likeness or voice of the individual."[125]

Plaintiff's Case

To win a commercialization or right of publicity case, plaintiffs must prove their names or likenesses were used for commercial purposes without permission. Plaintiffs must also show commercial uses were of and concerning them and were widely distributed.

Name or Likeness. Appropriation occurs most obviously when a person's name, picture or likeness—clearly identifying the person—is used commercially without permission. Having the same name that is used in an advertisement is usually not enough to show identification. Something in the ad must show the ad was of and concerning that plaintiff.[126]

A name can sometimes be the primary basis of a claim. For example, Hasbro and Fox News anchor Harris Faulkner recently settled a case in New Jersey after Faulkner accused the toy maker of violating her right of publicity. A New Jersey court refused to dismiss Faulkner's claim, based largely on the use of her name. Hasbro had named a toy hamster from its "Littlest Pet Shop" line Harris Faulkner. Legal experts predicted that arguments claiming the hamster looked like Faulkner would probably fail but suggested that Faulkner had a strong claim on a name-based right of publicity.[127]

It is not sufficient that the commercial use only hints at the plaintiff's identity or may remind some people of the plaintiff.[128] Rather, there must be reasonable grounds for identifying the plaintiff. For example, in a recent case involving the rapper 50 Cent, a court held that his

Fox News anchor Harris Faulkner; Hasbro's Harris Faulkner hamster.

Mike Coppola/Getty Images

Courtesy of Hasbro

likeness was invoked for commercial purposes when a website posted, reproduced and screened photos of the rapper in its masthead. The court said that even though the images were of poor visual quality, visitors to the website could still see that the pictures were of 50 Cent.[129]

A court in Illinois dismissed a right of publicity case brought by a Guinness World Records record holder against Wendy's. The fast-food chain ran a kid's meal promotion that included Guinness-themed toys, one of which was a hacky sack. An accompanying card listed Guinness facts about the footbag, including this: "How many times in a row can you kick this footbag without it hitting the ground? Back in 1997, Ted Martin made his world record of 63,326 kicks in a little less than nine hours!"[130] The court said that the use of Martin's name on the instruction card did not amount to an endorsement and did not violate Martin's right of publicity. Rather, the instruction card was part of a product, not an advertisement, and it never suggested that Martin endorsed anything. The Seventh Circuit Court of Appeals upheld the dismissal, noting that the Illinois right of publicity law does not apply to the use of a person's name when it truthfully identifies a person as an author or performer.[131]

Generally, courts have held that names and associated information widely available to the public are not protected by right of publicity. For example, the Eighth Circuit Court of Appeals ruled that an online fantasy baseball league operator could use Major League Baseball players' names and statistics without MLB's permission.[132] The court said the information was widely available in the public domain, making it factual rather than personal to the players.

What about the use of a private person's name without consent in generic online advertising? Although their names were not used, two plaintiffs in Illinois sued several internet companies that offer online reports about people using information compiled from public records and other sources. The companies, including Intelius, pay internet search engines to advertise their people-search reports. When a user on one of these websites types a person's name into the search engine, the first and last name of the person being searched will appear in the defendants' advertisements through an automated process. The defendant companies designed the ads to look as if they contained valuable information about the searched-for person, including items like criminal record, divorce record, background checks and bankruptcy. The district court dismissed the right of publicity claim because the advertisements failed to identify the specific plaintiffs in the case, as opposed to identifying anyone who shared their same names.[133]

Voice. Individuals' voices are protected against commercial use without consent. Further, advertisers may not use **sound-alikes** without permission or a disclaimer. A sound-alike is someone whose voice sounds like another person's voice. For commercial use, sound-alikes require permission or a disclaimer. For example, singer and actress Bette Midler refused to allow Ford Motor Co. to use her hit recording "Do You Want to Dance?" in a commercial. Ford's advertising agency then hired a member of Midler's backup singing group to imitate Midler's rendition of the song. After the radio commercial aired, several people told Midler they thought she had performed in the ad, which failed to say Midler was not the singer. Midler sued Ford and its advertising agency. A federal appellate court said they appropriated part of Midler's identity.[134]

POINTS OF LAW
APPROPRIATION

Plaintiff's Case
- Using a person's name, image, likeness, voice or identity
- for advertising or other commercial uses
- without permission.

Defenses
- Newsworthiness
- First Amendment
- Incidental use
- Mass media advertising
- Consent

Identity. People have characteristics beyond their face or voice that the appropriation tort protects. Game show host Vanna White sued Samsung Electronics for appropriation after the company ran a series of magazine ads showing its products in futuristic settings. A robot standing by a "Wheel of Fortune"-style letter board wore an evening gown, jewelry and a long blond wig. A federal appellate court said the ad appropriated White's identity, even though it did not use her name, image or voice.[135]

Actors impersonating celebrities in noncommercial or non-advertising situations, such as in a satire or parody, are not appropriating the celebrities' likenesses or voices. The First Amendment protects such expression.[136] But the Vanna White case shows that protection does not extend to impersonations in advertisements or other commercial situations. The appellate court specifically rejected Samsung's contention that the robot ad was meant as a satire.[137]

In 2021, actor Sacha Baron Cohen sued a Massachusetts corporation for using a photograph of Cohen's character Borat with two thumbs up on a commercial billboard advertising cannabis.

Jason Merritt /Getty Images

Commercial Use or Appropriation. The right of publicity protects famous people against unapproved uses of their names and likenesses to advertise or promote services or goods. For example, in 2021, actor Sacha Baron Cohen sued a Massachusetts corporation for $ 9 million for using his image without permission on a commercial billboard advertising cannabis. The billboard featured a photograph of Cohen's character Borat.[138] Both sides agreed to dismiss the case in 2022.[139]

Two recent cases help to clarify when names may be considered used for commercial uses. Both cases address uses of a specific person's name in relation to products that provide information about named persons. In 2021, a federal court in Washington declined to dismiss a case in which Whitepages Inc. used a plaintiff's name in an online "free preview, as an enticement to purchase [Whitepages'] subscription services" for background reports.[140]

In 2021, a federal court in California explained that the "use of a person's name and likeness to promote a product (other than which pertains to the person themselves) is the essence of an appropriation of one's name or likeness."[141] The Court granted a motion to dismiss a claim two people filed against Thomson Reuters Corp. for using their names, likenesses and personal information in dossiers provided through CLEAR. That online platform allows people to input a person's name to search for information about that person then pay to access information. Thomson Reuters Corp. neither suggested the plaintiffs endorsed CLEAR nor used their names or likenesses in advertisements for CLEAR. The court reasoned the plaintiffs' identities were not being appropriated or used to advertise the product.[142]

In 2021, the Sixth Circuit Court of Appeals addressed the use of one's likeness when the court considered whether Redbubble, Inc., an Australian-based online retailer, could be liable for violating Ohio's right-of-publicity statute. Ohio's statute provides a persona may not be used without consent "in connection with a product, advertising a product, or soliciting the purchase of a product." Ohio State University claimed Redbubble violated the school's rights of publicity when third-party artists used Redbubble's platform to sell items displaying the likeness of football coach Urban Meyer. He had assigned his publicity right to the university when serving as the university's head football coach. The appeals court determined that Redbubble actively advertises and markets products sold in its marketplace and "directs consumers to purchase those products," thus the court reversed a district court's entry of summary judgment for Redbubble.[143] For discussion of the trademark claim in this case, see Chapter 11.

Consent. People may provide permission for their names, images, likenesses or identities to be used for specific commercial uses. Providing permission for a specific entity to use one's image for one use does not equate to providing permission to use the image for other uses. Two recent cases addressing strip club uses of photographs for promotional purposes shed light on the importance of consent.

Models with no connection to a strip club recently sued a club owner for using their images to advertise a club on Facebook without consent from the models. Although the models had allowed certain entities to use their images for specific business uses, a federal court noted in 2020 that this strip club was not among those entities. The strip club owner had used the images without the models' consent. "The right of publicity protects a person's ability to control how their likeness is used," the court said.[144]

A second case similarly addressed the use of photographs of models, actresses and businesswomen to promote strip clubs without their consent. A district court granted summary judgment for the defendants, reasoning that models who filed claims under New York law, within its one-year statute of limitations, had signed contracts granting "the releasee unlimited rights to use the images at issue." On appeal, the models argued the defendants did not have written consent from the models or anyone else, and the release agreements did not extend to the defendants. Because the club and its contractors agreed the releases did not extend to them, the Second Circuit Court of Appeals court reasoned that defendants lacked written consent to use the images for promotional purposes. In 2021, the Second Circuit reversed the summary judgment and remanded the case.[145]

Defenses

Even if plaintiffs can prove that their names or likenesses were used for commercial purposes without permission, there are several defenses for appropriation.

Newsworthiness. Newsworthiness is a common defense. Media publish newsworthy material despite having a commercial purpose.[146] Courts have defined the word "newsworthy" broadly, in relation to matters of public interest. The newsworthiness defense sometimes shows up in unlikely cases.

The U.S. Supreme Court has heard only one appropriation case and rejected a television station's claim of a newsworthiness defense to a right of publicity suit when a local newscast showed an entertainment act in its entirety without consent or compensation.[147] The television station recorded and subsequently broadcast all 15 seconds of human cannonball Hugo Zacchini's act, including the most critical part—his flight from the cannon to the net. The Court said that people who saw the entire act on television were less likely to attend the performance in person and focused on the economic value of his act.

> There is no doubt that entertainment, as well as news, enjoys First Amendment protection. It is also true that entertainment itself can be important news. . . . But, it is important to note that neither the public nor [the television station] will be deprived of the benefit of [Zacchini's] performance as long as his commercial stake in his act is appropriately recognized.[148]

The television station's First Amendment rights were not more important than protecting Zacchini's financial interest in his performance, the Court said.[149]

The U.S. Supreme Court said human cannonball Hugo Zacchini could win an appropriation lawsuit against a television station that aired his performance in its entirety.

Bettmann/Getty Images

REAL WORLD LAW
DOES NEWSWORTHINESS APPLY TO DOCUDRAMAS?

In 2021, a New York appellate court addressed the application of newsworthiness to a made-for-television movie, based on a true story, that dramatizes a matter of public interest.[150]

Christopher Porco, who had been convicted of murdering his father and attempting to kill his mother, argued that Lifetime Entertainment Services was violating his right of privacy by using his name and likeness in the movie, "Romeo Killer: The Chris Porco Story," and promotional materials for the movie. Porco's case addressed a conflict between his privacy rights and First Amendment protection for conveying newsworthy events and matters of public interest.[151]

In a 2021 memorandum order, an appellate court explained that courts previously had avoided "a fatal conflict with the free dissemination of thoughts, ideas, newsworthy events, and matters of public interest guaranteed by the First Amendment" by recognizing the statutory provisions "do not apply to reports of newsworthy events on matters of public interest, even if the reports were produced with profit in mind." The movie could be considered newsworthy because facts about the crime, investigation and trial were of public interest. [152]

To show the newsworthiness defense would not protect the movie, Porco would have to show the movie is "materially and substantially fictitious," wherein "a knowing fictionalization amounts to an all-pervasive use of imaginary incidents, culminating in a biography that is nothing more than an attempt to trade on the persona of the plaintiff."[153]

Although the movie is at times fictionalized, providing fictional dialogue, scenes and names and using composite characters, the movie "presents a broadly accurate depiction" of the matters of public interest. The creators clarified the movie is "a dramatization," "based on a true story," with fictionalized information and events. They did not inaccurately suggest the blend of factual and fictional information was a true account. The court, thus, concluded the account was not "so infected with fiction, dramatization or embellishment that it cannot be said to fulfill the purpose of the newsworthiness exception."[154]

New York has not recognized rights of privacy under common law. Rather, the legislature recognized narrowly constructed statutory rights that protect a person's picture, name or portrait, providing narrow protection against nonconsensual uses for advertising purposes only. The appellate court determined none of the promotional or advertising materials for the movie suggested Porco endorsed the movie, and the promotions and advertisements "were ancillary to the protected use in the film."[155]

First Amendment. First Amendment defenses in right of publicity cases are common today, particularly in the context of news or artistic works, such as movies and video games. Over the years, courts have also considered whether commercial products—such as posters, dolls, T-shirts and games—have First Amendment protection.[156] A California appellate court recently found celebrity billionaire Kieu Hoang could not demonstrate a likelihood to win a right of publicity claim based on his name, image and identity being used in a news article posted on the BBC Vietnamese Facebook Page. The article described matters of public interest, Hoang's international business experience and "a sickening culture" in Vietnam and China. "The right of publicity cannot, consistent with the First Amendment, be a right to control the celebrity's image by censoring disagreeable portrayals," the court stated. "[T]he First Amendment dictates that the right to comment on, parody, lampoon, and make other expressive uses of the celebrity image must be given broad scope."[157]

Courts most often have decided posters do not have First Amendment protection. Courts have said the First Amendment protects selling posters with pictures of newsworthy individuals or events, such as a poster with a picture of former San Francisco 49ers quarterback Joe Montana celebrating the team's 1990 Super Bowl victory.[158] Courts drew a distinction between merchandise exploiting celebrities' names or likenesses and posters conveying newsworthy information of public interest. Courts, however, found appropriation when posters of singer Elvis Presley and professional wrestlers were distributed without permission.[159]

Billionaire Kieu Hoang recently sued a journalist for violating his right of publicity and other claims.

Tim Pannell/The Forbes Collection/Getty Images

The question of First Amendment protection versus right of publicity arises most frequently when a well-known person is used in an artistic work. For example, recently, a federal judge in New York ruled that hip-hop star Pitbull did not violate actress Lindsay Lohan's right of publicity by including the line "I'm tiptoein', to keep flowin', I got it locked up, like Lindsay Lohan" in his hit song "Give Me Everything." Rather, the song is a work of art protected by the First Amendment.[160]

One approach used to resolve this kind of conflict is the **artistic relevance test** (see Chapter 11). More courts today apply the **transformative use test**, which determines whether the First Amendment protects a work that uses a person's name, picture, likeness, voice or identity for artistic purposes against a right of publicity suit.[161] The California Supreme Court proposed the transformative use test to distinguish protected artistic expression about celebrities from expression that encroaches on the right of publicity in a case involving the Three Stooges. The First Amendment protects a work that adds enough new elements to the original to transform it. Changing the original by giving it a new meaning or a different message justifies First Amendment protection. Transformative works may be satires, news reports, fictional works, social criticism or video games.

In the California Supreme Court case, an artist created a charcoal sketch of the Three Stooges, transferred the sketch to T-shirts and lithographs and sold thousands. A company owning the Three Stooges' publicity rights sued.[162] The California court acknowledged the conflict between the artist's First Amendment right to express himself and the right of celebrities to protect their property and financial interests in their images. The court concluded, "When artistic expression takes the form of a literal depiction or imitation of a celebrity for commercial gain, directly trespassing on the right of publicity without adding significant expression beyond that trespass," the celebrity's rights outweigh First Amendment protections.[163] The court found that the Three Stooges drawing was a "literal, conventional" depiction of the three men, with no discernible transformative elements. Because the drawing did not transform the Three Stooges' pictures, it had no First Amendment protection.

In 2020, a federal court denied a motion for summary judgment in a right of publicity claim addressing the nonconsensual use of a man's tattoo on a Cardi B album cover. The designer who created the cover said he copied and pasted an image of a tattoo on the back of the plaintiff onto the back of a model. The designer explained manipulating the size of the tattoo, but the court noted "significant elements" were "virtually unchanged." The use was not considered transformative. To be considered a transformative use, the court stated, "the revised image must have significant transformative or creative elements to make it something more than mere likeness or imitation."[164] In 2022, without addressing this defense, a jury found the man's likeness was not misappropriated.[165]

Courts have heard several cases that test the application of the transformative use test to video games. The earliest and most prominent cases settled for $60 million after a lengthy appeals process in the Ninth Circuit Court of Appeals. They involved three college athletes who filed **class action lawsuits** against the video game company Electronic Arts, the National Collegiate Athletic Association and the Collegiate Licensing Company (now known as IMG College Licensing).[166] Class action lawsuits are filed by individuals acting on behalf of a larger group with a common legal interest, such as similar injuries caused by the same product. A decade ago, Ed O'Bannon, the star of UCLA's 1995 championship basketball team, and Sam Keller, former quarterback from Arizona State University and the University of Nebraska, argued in a U.S. district court in California that EA's NCAA-themed video games violated their right of publicity because their likenesses were used without compensation.[167] The players noted that the video games depicted every distinctive characteristic of them except their names. At the same time, former Rutgers quarterback Ryan Hart made the same claim in a U.S. district court in New Jersey.[168]

In both cases, EA argued that its First Amendment rights trumped the players' right of publicity. Although the facts in both cases are nearly identical and both courts applied the transformative use test, the two courts came to different decisions. In California, the court applied the transformative use test and held that EA's use of Keller was not transformative and did not deserve First Amendment protection. In New Jersey, the court ruled in favor of EA and criticized the California decision, which it suggested "[il]logically . . . consider[ed] the setting in which the character sits . . . yet ignore[d] the remainder of the game."[169] The Third Circuit Court of Appeals eventually reversed the New Jersey district court's summary judgment decision.[170]

Both cases settled out of court with agreements to pay millions of dollars to the student athletes named in the class action suits.[171]

On the heels of the settlements, 10 former college football and basketball players filed a similar right of publicity lawsuit in federal court against major broadcast companies, athletic conferences and licensers. Former Vanderbilt University football player Javon Marshall was the lead plaintiff in the lawsuit, which sought damages for the misappropriation of the names, images and likenesses of college athletes in broadcasts and advertisements without their consent.[172] In 2016, the Sixth Circuit Court of Appeals affirmed a Tennessee district court ruling, which dismissed the case and noted that a common law right of publicity does not exist in that state.[173]

Recently, the NCAA appealed the Ninth Circuit's decision in the O'Bannon case to the U.S. Supreme Court, arguing the case was wrongly decided, but the Supreme Court declined to hear it. The NCAA's interest in the ruling stemmed from additional claims that the organization's rules violate antitrust laws by not allowing student athletes compensation for the use of their names and likenesses.[174] The NCAA recently changed its policies about compensation for uses of student athlete names, images and likenesses. (See the Emerging Law section of this chapter.)

In 2019, a federal court in Pennsylvania granted Gears of War video game developers' motion for summary judgment in a right of publicity case filed by "Hard Rock Hamilton," a former professional wrestler and football player. In the video game series, a character named Augustus Cole is a soldier and former professional athlete, who played a fictional game. Cole and Hamilton have "broadly similar faces, hair styles, races, skin tones, and large, muscular body builds" and similar-sounding voices. Cole, however, has a distinct personality unlike Hamilton's personality. The series also includes a series of **avatars** that allow players to transform Cole with costumes and skins that differ from Hamilton's. Avatars are icons or images that represent a person in a video game or other computer-generated content. "There are sufficient creative differences between the two characters to satisfy the Transformative Use standard," the court said. The court also noted the series places Cole in a "profoundly transformative context" as a solider fighting "formerly subterranean reptilian humanoids" on a fictional planet.[175]

In 2020, a federal in Pennsylvania also granted Epic Games, Inc.'s motion for summary judgment in a right of privacy and publicity case musician and musical performer Leo Pellegrino filed. Pellegrino asserted the video game company used his Signature Move in Fortnite, the Phone It In emote, in which a character sways its knees, hips and upper body while playing a saxophone. The court noted that Fortnite avatars with the Phone It In emote do "not bear a strong resemblance" or have similar appearances to Pellegrino. As the avatars equipped with the emote have distinct identities from Pellegrino, the memorandum opinion concludes the "use of Pellegrino's likeness is sufficiently transformative" to receive First Amendment protection that outweighs the asserted rights to privacy and publicity.[176]

In 2021, a federal district court in Nevada granted a motion to dismiss a right of publicity claim filed against Walt Disney Studios Motion Pictures, finding the transformative use defense applied. The claim alleges that Disney violated the right to publicity for Evel Knievel, a motorcycle daredevil who performed spectacular jumps from the 1960s to the 1980s, using his likeness for the character Duke Caboom in Toy Story 4. The cartoon action figure rides a motorcycle, called the "Duke Caboom Stunt Cycle," yet feels insecure "about his stuntman abilities."[177]

Musician and musical performer Leo Pellegrino sued Epic Games for using his likeness with the Phone It In emote.
Roberta Parkin/Getty Images

While the court found the character reminiscent of Evel Knievel, the character was "not a literal depiction" of the famous stuntman. For example, their names, clothing and hair colors and styles differed. At most, the court explained, Evel Knievel "is one of the raw materials from" which Duke Caboom was created, and the character was "not an attempt to imitate Evel Knievel." The court stated, "the creative elements of Duke Caboom predominate the action figure," and the marketability and economic value of the character "cannot be said to derive from Evel Knievel."[178]

The transformative use test also provides protection for artists. Nearly two decades ago, the California Supreme Court used the test to rule that a comic book artist transformed images of two musicians, Johnny and Edgar Winter.[179] The California Supreme Court said, "An artist depicting a celebrity must contribute something more than a merely trivial variation" of the celebrity's image. The artist "must create something recognizably his own" for a court to find "significant transformative elements" in the artist's work.[180]

Another way to balance the First Amendment and the right of publicity is the **predominant use test**. This test is applied to determine whether uses of a name or picture was more for commercial purposes or protected expression. The question is whether a person's name or image is used more for commercial purposes or substantive expression. The Missouri Supreme Court applied this test in ruling that a comic book creator named a character "Antonio 'Tony Twist' Twistelli" more to sell the comics than for free speech purposes. In the comic, Twistelli was portrayed as an organized crime leader. A real Tony Twist, a former professional hockey player, sued for misuse of his name. A jury awarded $15 million in damages, and the state's high court affirmed the ruling.[181]

Courts have long held that the First Amendment protects using celebrities' names in biographies and fiction, including movies and television programs. Although this was part of appropriation law long before the California Supreme Court used the transformative use test, the reasons are similar. Books, news stories, movies and television programs add transformative elements by putting the names in a context. For example, a movie called "Panther," combining fact and fiction, portrayed several members of the Black Panther Party, a political group active in the 1960s and 1970s that promoted Black power and social activism. Bobby Seale, a prominent member of the Black Panthers, sued. A federal district court rejected Seale's appropriation claim, saying the First Amendment protected using his name in the film.[182]

Ads for the Media. Another First Amendment-based appropriation defense holds that mass media may run advertisements for themselves without consent when using the names and likenesses of public figures if those figures were part of their original content. Courts recognized this defense when a magazine, Holiday, ran ads for itself in two other publications. One ad urged people to subscribe, and the other ad suggested advertising agencies place their clients' ads in Holiday. Both ads included pictures of actress Shirley Booth that Holiday had published in one of its issues. Booth sued under New York's appropriation law. The state's highest court said that to stay in business and to use its First Amendment rights, the magazine had to attract subscribers and advertisers. Illustrating the magazine's content and quality by showing what it publishes did not violate Booth's rights, the court concluded. Holiday magazine won the suit in part because it did not suggest Booth endorsed the magazine.[183]

Former Chicago Bulls star Michael Jordan more recently sued a grocery store chain based on a magazine ad in which Jewel Food Stores congratulated him for being inducted into the Basketball Hall of Fame. The Seventh Circuit Court of Appeals found that because the grocery store logo was prominently featured along with its marketing slogan then linked in the ad text to Jordan, it constituted image advertising. The case was remanded to the lower court, but the Seventh Circuit said a First Amendment defense would not apply in the case.[184]

Consent. The best appropriation defense is consent. That is why professional photographers use releases—contracts prepared by lawyers and signed by all parties involved—when taking pictures for advertisements or other commercial use. Oral consent can be a defense, but proving it can be difficult if plaintiffs claim they did not give permission.[185] Also, the law does not allow certain people to give consent, such as minors and those who are not mentally or emotionally capable of agreeing. And consent is limited to the agreement's terms. Consent to use a picture in an ad through 2023, for example, does not allow its use in 2025. Similarly, if a person gives consent to use a picture in a smartphone ad, the picture cannot be used to advertise shoes. If a person gives sweeping consent—to use a picture at any time in the future in any advertisement—a court likely will hold that the agreement is more limited than indicated.

Consent most often is explicit; people agree to allow their names to be used. But consent may also be implied. For example, a man sued the owner of a smartphone app that would send the user's contacts a text message invitation to join the app. The invitation included the user's name so people invited to join could see who sent the message. The man argued that including his name in the text message invitation exceeded the scope of his consent. The app did not allow him to view the text message invitation before the app sent it. A court in Illinois held that because the man decided to use the app to send the text messages, a reasonable user would understand his name was necessary for the invitation process to work.[186]

Incidental Use. The use of a person's name or likeness may be incidental to a work's primary purpose. Incidental use typically arises in appropriation claims and not right of publicity claims. A court could rule that a person's name or likeness was used so briefly that the purpose was not to make a profit or gain commercial benefit. For example, a name applied to a fictional terrorist in a comic book appeared in 1 of 116 panels spanning 24 pages. A person who said the comic book applied his name to the terrorist sued under New York's appropriation law. A federal district court said the name's use was incidental to the comic book's primary purpose and could not sustain a privacy suit.[187]

In a recent case, an Ohio couple sued Amazon.com and others for false light and appropriation for the use of their engagement photo on the cover of a self-published novel. The novel was a satirical, erotic account of a married woman's fascination with New England Patriots player Rob Gronkowski, titled "A Gronking to Remember." The court observed that the novel was alleged to be "less than tasteful" and "offensive."[188] The book was the butt of jokes on late-night talk shows before the 2014 Super Bowl and received some national media attention. The author of the self-published novel argued that his use of the photo on the cover was incidental. The district court disagreed.

> This argument confuses and misstates the issue in this case—it would be relevant if the plaintiff in the case were Rob Gronkowski, a public figure. The incidental use doctrine applies, however, only to persons with celebrity or other notorious status—which plaintiffs did not have.[189]

Rather, the couple argued that the novel's author appropriated their engagement photo "for his own commercial benefit." On appeal, the Sixth Circuit Court of Appeals held that the couple was not able to demonstrate the commercial value of their image to the corporate defenders in the case and granted Amazon and the other publishers summary judgment.[190]

Private Facts

A court first recognized the private facts tort in 1927.[191] Only four states have not recognized this tort. The Supreme Court of Indiana first recognized the tort in 2022, stating "Recognition of this tort is especially important today, as private information is more easily accessed and disseminated—particularly in ways that can reach a large audience."[192] The private facts tort is intended to protect a person's dignity and peace of mind by discouraging giving widespread publicity to intimate facts. If private facts are publicized, a jury may award monetary damages to compensate for the resulting emotional injury.[193] Courts recognize a First Amendment defense to a private facts lawsuit.[194]

Plaintiff's Case

Journalists and others can be sued for the **private facts** tort if they publicize truthful private information that is not of legitimate public concern and is highly offensive to a reasonable person.[195]

Publicity. Publicity in the private facts tort is not the same as publication in a libel suit. In libel, publication to a third party, someone other than the plaintiff and defendant, is sufficient. For the private facts tort, most courts require **widespread publicity**, making material available to a lot of people or the general public.[196] Revealing intimate information in the media will meet the definition of publicity.[197] Some courts hold that revealing private facts to small groups of people who have a special relationship with the plaintiff is sufficient. This could include the plaintiff's fellow workers, church members, colleagues in a social organization or neighbors.[198]

Private, Intimate Facts. Intimate facts are those sensitive details a person would not want the community to know. Private facts suits, for example, could relate to a person's financial condition,[199] medical information[200] or domestic difficulties[201] when the subject has not made such information widely available to others. Often, private facts suits concern sexual activities.[202]

POINTS OF LAW
PRIVATE FACTS

Plaintiff's Case
- Publicizing
- private, intimate facts
- that would be highly offensive to a reasonable person
- and are not of legitimate concern to the public.

Defenses
- Conditional First Amendment Privilege: Truthful reporting of information on a matter of public significance when that information was lawfully obtained from public records

---

Not all facts about a person are private. Information in a public record, such as a court filing or an arrest record, is public information. Facts are not private if a person made them public. Information told to a few close relatives or friends remains private, and people may define their own circles of intimacy, according to courts.[203]

For example, in 2020, a federal court in Illinois considered whether a plaintiff's transgender status was a private fact when a supervisor disclosed that medical information to a few co-workers at a correctional facility. The defense indicated the information was not private because three co-workers knew or suspected this information. The court rejected that argument, reasoning the argument suggested the plaintiff's status was not widely known and the defendant had "revealed concrete information that had previously remained private." The court did not grant the defense motion to dismiss the private facts claim.[204]

If a person reveals intimate facts publicly, the private facts tort does not limit the media from publishing the information. For example, a friendship between two high school girls deteriorated into a bitter feud. The first girl accused the second of being pregnant, and that girl teased the first about her Jewish heritage, seeking psychological counseling and having plastic surgery. The second girl's family self-published a book about the feud. The book included school, police and legal documents connected with the situation. The first girl sued for private facts, among other torts. She claimed the book included "1) excerpts and summaries from her Myspace.com webpage; 2) three statements related to her Jewish ancestry; 3) her enrolment (sic) at [a university]; 4) two statements regarding Plaintiff's decision to seek professional psychological care or counseling; 5) Plaintiff's transfer from one high school to another under a superintendent's agreement; and 6) two statements regarding plastic surgery on Plaintiff's nose."[205] The court held that categories 1, 2, 3 and 5 were not private. The plaintiff wrote on her Myspace page that she sought psychological help and agreed that she could not conceal what she posted there. As to plastic surgery, the court said it "questions whether this matter is truly private: cosmetic surgery on one's face is by its nature exposed to the public eye."[206]

Recently, people have questioned whether victims of nonconsensual pornography or "revenge porn" can win private facts lawsuits. Legal experts say a private facts lawsuit is hard to win in revenge porn cases because often the victim initially shared the explicit image with someone, usually a friend or sexual partner. Many courts have found that the act of voluntarily sharing the image makes it no longer private.[207] Many organizations, like the Cyber Civil Rights Initiative, are fighting revenge porn by appealing to state legislatures. In 2021, 48 states, the District of Columbia, Guam and Puerto Rico had laws that criminalized revenge porn.[208]

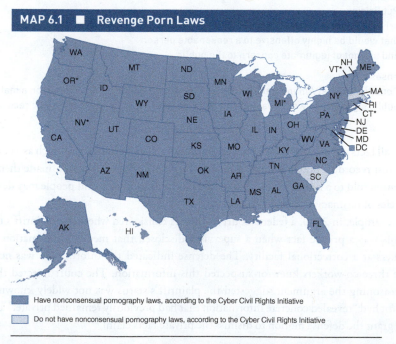

MAP 6.1 ■ Revenge Porn Laws

■ Have nonconsensual pornography laws, according to the Cyber Civil Rights Initiative

☐ Do not have nonconsensual pornography laws, according to the Cyber Civil Rights Initiative

All states except Massachusetts and South Carolina have revenge porn laws, according to the Cyber Civil Rights Initiative.

Highly Offensive to a Reasonable Person. The question before a court hearing a private facts case is would it outrage the community's notions of decency if the intimate information were published?[209] In 2022, the Supreme Court of Indiana explained this type of disclosure "must be one that offends society's accepted, communal norms and social mores." A plaintiff must prove that a reasonable person would feel "seriously aggrieved by" the disclosure.[210]

Legitimate Public Concern. A plaintiff cannot win a private facts lawsuit if the information is **newsworthy**, or of legitimate public concern. The media help determine what is newsworthy through their reporting behaviors. Courts give the media considerable leeway to determine what is newsworthy. Stories about crimes, suicides, divorces, catastrophes, diseases and other topics may include intimate information people do not want published. If newsworthy, however, these private facts cannot be the basis of a successful private facts suit.[211]

Many courts have said the First Amendment will not protect publicizing highly intimate facts unless they are of public concern. In defining newsworthiness, courts have distinguished between information the public is entitled to know and facts publicized for a morbid or sensational reason. In 2021, a federal court in Florida dismissed a private facts claim Alan Grayson, a former congressional candidate, filed against political groups and individuals. The case addressed the disclosure of multiple facts, including the candidate's employment of a congressional staffer and call for a reporter to be arrested, during his 2018 campaign. The court said, "A political candidate's domestic turmoil, congressional activities, and interactions with the media are undoubtedly subjects of legitimate news interest." The court explained the way a political candidate conducts his professional and personal life "is of value and concern to the voting public."[212]

Several courts have taken a slightly different approach to defining newsworthiness about people involuntarily put in the public eye. These courts determine whether there is a logical connection between the news event and the private facts. Well-known people are inherently more newsworthy than others. Even celebrities, though, have a right to keep private facts that would be highly embarrassing if publicized.

For example, in part based on a private facts claim, actress Pamela Anderson Lee and rock musician Bret Michaels successfully prevented distribution of their sex tape.[213] More recently, former professional wrestler Hulk Hogan, whose real name is Terry Bollea, sued Gawker Media for reporting on and showing excerpts of a sex tape that showed him having sex with the wife of a friend, Todd Clem, who is a radio shock jock named Bubba the Love Sponge. Clem made the recording and gave Gawker the tape; the media outlet did not pay for it. Bollea sued Clem and his wife for invasion of privacy and settled out of court after Clem acknowledged that Bollea did not know his sexual encounter was being recorded. Bollea also sued Gawker for invasion of privacy, seeking $100 million in damages.[214]

Initially, the case focused on whether issuing an injunction to prevent the publication of the tape was appropriate under the First Amendment. In ruling on the injunction, the judge wrote that Hogan's public discussions—with TMZ, on The Howard Stern Show and in his autobiography—about his many affairs showed that the subject was not truly private and that reporting on the sex tape was a matter of public concern.[215]

Hulk Hogan
John Pendygraft/Tampa Bay Times via AP

When Bollea's privacy lawsuit went before a jury, he argued that his celebrity status as Hulk Hogan should not deprive him of privacy protections, that he did not know the sexual encounter was being recorded, that Gawker did not seek his permission to publish the video and that Gawker was not a journalism site but rather was acting solely for its own commercial gain. The jury found in favor of Bollea, determining that the publication of the sex tape was offensive and not a matter of legitimate public concern. It recommended awarding $140 million in both actual and punitive damages, an award later upheld by a judge. Privacy law experts say it is more common for juries, rather than judges, to determine newsworthiness, which has recently resulted in larger jury verdicts in privacy cases.[216]

Nick Denton, Gawker's CEO, appealed the Bollea verdict and later declared personal bankruptcy, as did Gawker Media. In late 2016, Gawker and Bollea settled the invasion of privacy lawsuit for $31 million, ending the appeals process, and Gawker was sold. The new owner of Gawker.com took down the article involved in the litigation and initially shut down the site. The new owner relaunched Gawker.com in 2021.[217]

Many legal experts suggest that Gawker and Denton might have prevailed on appeal based on First Amendment grounds but that the legal fight would be too costly after the revelation that billionaire Peter Thiel, the founder of PayPal, was financing Bollea's lawsuit.[218]

Newsworthiness can be a defense to a private facts suit. In the past, media defendants had the burden of showing that the facts were of legitimate public interest, and some courts continue to put the newsworthiness burden on the defendant. Other courts require the plaintiff in a private facts suit to prove that the intimate facts were not newsworthy.

In one example, a newspaper reported that a student body president was transgender. Toni Diaz, born Antonio Diaz, underwent sex reassignment surgery before entering a community college. Elected student body president, she charged school administrators with mishandling student funds. A local newspaper columnist wrote of Diaz, "Now I realize, that in these times, such a matter is no big deal, but I suspect his female classmates in P.E. 97 may wish to make other showering arrangements." Diaz, who had told only close relatives and friends of her operation, sued the paper and columnist.[219]

A court ruled that Diaz, as plaintiff, had to prove the private facts were not newsworthy because putting the burden on the media could lead to self-censorship. The court ruled that Diaz could show it was not newsworthy to publish remarks about her gender and that her gender had no connection with her ability to be student body president.[220]

When a news media outlet publishes a **mug shot**, the police photograph of an arrested person's face, it is considered newsworthy and not a violation of privacy. Mug shots are usually considered public records, not private facts. In recent years, dozens of for-profit mug shot websites have emerged, posting publicly available mug shots for widespread viewing. Some of the websites charge people money to have their photographs removed.[221] At least fourteen states have passed laws prohibiting companies that publish mug shots from charging fees to remove or correct information.[222]

Several plaintiffs have also filed various privacy-related lawsuits against these websites. A federal court in Pennsylvania dismissed one lawsuit but left open the question of whether mug shot websites constitute a form of a news report.[223] A district court in Illinois decided in a right of publicity claim that Mugshots.com and its second website, Unpublisharrest.com, which removed listings from Mugshots.com for a fee, were commercial enterprises not entitled to First Amendment protection.[224]

Some private facts plaintiffs have argued that the passage of time may mean that information is no longer of legitimate concern to the public. Either the plaintiff was newsworthy many years before the media published the intimate information, or the private facts relate to events that happened long ago. Courts have rejected this contention, saying that newsworthiness does not disappear over time.[225]

First Amendment Defense

One way to balance privacy interests against First Amendment interests is to focus on the source of the information. Should the press lose a private facts suit if the intimate information came from a public record? The U.S. Supreme Court has recognized a conditional First Amendment privilege that protects publishing truthful information of public significance lawfully obtained from public records, unless punishing the media would serve a compelling state interest. Court decisions have not held that the First Amendment always will protect publishing truthful information taken from public records, but the Supreme Court has not yet found a compelling state interest that overrides the press's First Amendment rights.[226]

Truthfully Reported. In *Florida Star v. B.J.F.*, for example, the Supreme Court held that the First Amendment protected a newspaper that truthfully published the name of a rape victim, reasoning that violent crime is a publicly significant topic.[227] A woman identified as B.J.F. reported to a Florida sheriff's department that she had been robbed and sexually assaulted. The sheriff's department prepared an incident report that identified B.J.F. by her full name and placed the report in its pressroom, which was open to the public. An inexperienced reporter for The Florida Star saw the report, and the paper published a brief story on the case, including B.J.F.'s full name. This was contrary to the paper's policy of not naming rape victims. B.J.F. sued the sheriff's department and The Florida Star under a state law making it illegal for media to publish the name of a sexual assault victim. The sheriff's department settled before trial, and B.J.F. won her case against the newspaper, a result that was upheld by a Florida appellate court.[228]

The newspaper appealed the case to the U.S. Supreme Court, which reversed, holding that the First Amendment protects a newspaper that publishes truthful information lawfully obtained from public records, provided no compelling state interest requires otherwise. Although protecting the identity of a sexual assault victim could serve a compelling state interest, the Court said, three factors worked against that conclusion. First, the government itself supplied the information. Second, the state law forbidding names from being published had no exceptions, even if the community already knew the victim's name. Third, the state law applied only to the media, allowing others to disseminate a victim's name. Under these circumstances, the Court said, the right to a free press outweighed the state's interest in preventing publication of B.J.F.'s name.[229]

Information in government records available to the public cannot be considered private. Facts presented in public meetings also are not secret. Unless a judge seals a record, making it unavailable, court records are public. When government records are not publicly accessible, they may not be considered public records in a private facts lawsuit. Similarly, not all publicly accessible places are "public." For example, publishing a picture and a conversation obtained by entering a private hospital room may not be protected even if other parts of the hospital generally are open to the public.[230]

Lawfully Obtained.   In three decisions, the U.S. Supreme Court ruled that when the press had legally obtained truthful information from public records, the press was not liable for publishing private facts. Nearly 50 years ago in *Cox Broadcasting Corp. v. Cohn*, excerpted at the end of this chapter, the Court said for the first time that truthful information lawfully obtained from a public court record could not be the basis of a private facts lawsuit.[231]

The case involved the rape and murder of a 17-year-old female in Georgia. At a court proceeding some months after the crime, a reporter covering the incident learned the name of the victim from indictments filed against six defendants and reported her name. The victim's father sued the television station for broadcasting her name. He won at trial and again on the television station's appeal to the Georgia Supreme Court. But the U.S. Supreme Court reversed, noting that the First Amendment protects the press against a private facts tort if the information is obtained from generally available public records.

In a separate case originating in Oklahoma, news media violated a juvenile court judge's order by publishing the name and picture of an 11-year-old boy charged with second-degree murder for shooting a railroad employee. Reporters were in the courtroom when the juvenile appeared, and the court put his name on the public record. Photographers took pictures as the minor left the courthouse. The Supreme Court said the press had lawfully obtained information available to the public and held that the First Amendment prohibits punishing the press for revealing information taken from public records.[232]

In another case, newspaper reporters who were monitoring a police scanner in West Virginia responded to a crime scene and learned from witnesses and investigators the name of a 14-year-old boy charged with killing a classmate. State prosecutors obtained an indictment against the press for publishing the boy's name in violation of a state law. The Supreme Court, however, ruled in favor of the newspaper, reasoning that the First Amendment protects news reports where journalists have lawfully obtained truthful information from publicly available sources. The Court said protecting the minor's privacy was not a compelling reason to restrict the freedom of the press.[233]

Matter of Public Significance. The Supreme Court has also held that the First Amendment sometimes protects publication of private information even where it was not lawfully obtained by a source—so long as the media were not involved in illegally acquiring the information—and the information relates to a matter of public significance, or is newsworthy.[234]

In *Bartnicki v. Vopper* (discussed further in Chapter 7), the Court said the media were not liable for publishing an intercepted cellphone conversation between two labor negotiators discussing a matter of public significance. Punishing the media for publishing information they obtained without acting illegally would not further a compelling government interest, the Court said.[235]

PRIVACY AND DATA PROTECTION

Today, people's concerns about privacy persist alongside additional threats from marketers, **data brokers** and other businesses that surveil consumers and amass personally identifiable information. These brokers collect, store, aggregate, analyze and sell billions of pieces of personal data from nearly every U.S. consumer. Data brokers analyze and repackage the information they collect for sale for marketing or risk mitigation purposes or for people searches.[236]

Data is collected many ways, including via our online communications, financial transactions and WiFi connected devices. Many smartphone applications send users' sensitive information to advertisers and third-party data collectors.[237] U.S. courts have allowed websites and advertisers to put cookies—technology that tracks what websites people visit—on computers.[238] State and international governments have enacted comprehensive data privacy laws. Congress and federal agencies have recognized privacy rights within certain realms, such as information stored and shared via credit reports.[239]

The California Consumer Privacy Act of 2018, effective from 2020 to 2022, provided consumers with rights to request and receive information about business collection of categories of personal information and purposes for which that information would be used. That law gave consumers the right to know what information companies collect about them, why they are collecting data, and with whom they are sharing data. It also made it difficult to share or sell data about children younger than 16, and it makes it easier for consumers to sue companies after a data breach.[240]

In 2020, voters approved a proposition to establish the California Privacy Protection Agency, which has authority to enforce consumer privacy law in that state. The legislature also amended the state's consumer privacy protection statute to require businesses that collect personal information to inform consumers whether their information is sold or shared. Businesses also must disclose categories of information that will be collected and purposes for which the information will be collected or used. And, businesses are instructed not to collect personal information for other purposes. The amendment goes into effect in 2023.[241]

In 2021, three additional states passed or amended legislation relevant to online data privacy. For example, the governor of Colorado signed into law the Colorado Privacy Act, which is similar to Virginia's Consumer Data Privacy Protection Act and California's Consumer Privacy Act and Consumer Privacy Rights Act. When Colorado's law goes into effect in 2023, the law will apply to businesses, other than financial institutions, that collect or process consumer data and either operate in Colorado or target Colorado residents.[242]

The Colorado law also recognizes data privacy rights for consumers to opt out of the processing of personal data for certain purposes. Those purposes include using data for targeted advertising, selling personal data or profiling consumers. Consumers also will have rights to access collected personal data, correct inaccuracies and have data deleted.[243] In 2022, Connecticut passed a law that will provide consumers with similar rights as of July 2023.[244]

In 2021, Virginia's legislature passed the Virginia Consumer Data Privacy Protection Act, which also provides rights to opt out of having personal data sold to third parties or processed for targeted advertising. The statute limits the collection of personal data to purposes disclosed to consumers and considered "adequate, relevant, and reasonably necessary" to purposes for which data are processed. The statute also requires "meaningful privacy notice." Data controllers must disclose whether they share data with third parties. If they sell or process information for targeted advertising, they need to "clearly and conspicuously disclose" this and indicate how consumers may opt out.[245]

The act also prevents processing sensitive data about a consumer without consent. In 2022, however, legislation was proposed to allow sensitive data to be processed without consumer consent if data is only used for marketing, advertising, fundraising or similar uses "related to outreach, communications, or information sharing" without producing legal or other significant effects for consumers.[246] Utah enacted a law with similar consumer privacy protections in 2022. The Utah Consumer Privacy Act will provide consumers with rights to opt out of having sensitive for-profit entities process their personal data at the end of 2023.[247]

The Nevada Privacy of Information Collected on the Internet Act pertains to operators of websites and online services for commercial purposes. The law requires operators who collect and maintain information about Nevada residents to notify consumers about collection of certain types of personally identifiable information, including names, addresses, contact information and social security numbers. Operators must notify consumers about the types of third parties that may receive consumer information. Operators also must indicate how consumers may review and request changes to information collected and shared.[248] Nevada recently passed an amendment that allows consumers to opt out of the sale of their personal information and extends the law to data brokers.[249]

MAP 6.2 ■ Consumer Privacy Laws

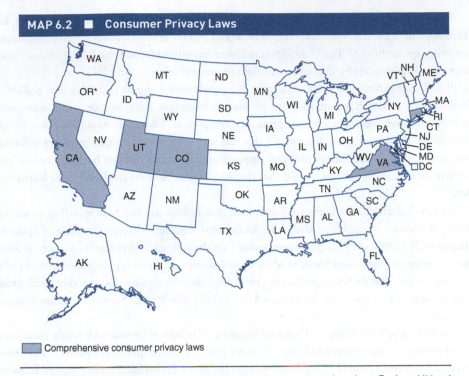

Comprehensive consumer privacy laws

As of April 2022, five U.S. states had approved comprehensive consumer privacy laws. Twelve additional states had active consumer privacy legislation, according to IAPP U.S. State Privacy Legislation Tracker.

Privacy law scholar Woodrow Hartzog noted that existing state data privacy laws are narrow in scope. While laws allow opting out of data collection, sales, sharing and surveillance, technology does not always make those options feasible. "Our current privacy laws are not working. They were not designed to confront the likes of Amazon and Facebook. They do not tackle the massive power that bigger businesses wield over our everyday lives when they use tools of surveillance and discrimination," Hartzog stated.[250] Bills proposed in Massachusetts, New York, Oklahoma and Washington could provide consumers with more protection by requiring companies to get consumers consent, or have consumers opt-in to such practices. States also are addressing privacy rights related to surveillance using biometric features or collecting **biometric data**. This type of information relates to personal characteristics, such as fingerprints or unique facial features, that may be used to identify an individual.[251]

The Illinois Biometric Information Privacy Act (BIPA) generally prevents any private entity from collecting, capturing, purchasing or obtaining a person's biometric identifier or information. To do so, several things must happen. A company or business must inform people (1) that biometric information will be collected and stored; (2) the purpose for which the information is collected, stored and used; and (3) the amount of time in which the information will be collected, stored and used. An entity also must receive consent. BIPA also prevents any private entity with biometric identifiers or information from selling, leasing, trading or profiting from that information. The law also generally does not allow disclosing or disseminating biometric identifiers or information without consent from the person whose biometric information has been collected.[252]

Congress has provided topic-specific legislation, such as the **Fair Credit Reporting Act** (FCRA), which addresses the accuracy, fairness and privacy of information stored in consumer reporting agency files.[253] The U.S. Supreme Court recently addressed the FCRA in cases with important implications for data collectors with inaccurate information.[254]

The U.S. Supreme Court ruled in favor of a people search engine in *Spokeo, Inc. v. Robins*. Spokeo's online search engine contains personal information about people for its users, who include employers seeking to evaluate prospective employees. Thomas Robins filed a class action suit against Spokeo after he determined that the search engine contained incorrect information that misrepresented his marital and employment status and inflated both his income and his level of education. Robins argued that the inaccuracies violated the Fair Credit Reporting Act.[255]

In a 6–2 decision, the Supreme Court held that Robins did not have standing to sue for damages because he could not show that he suffered "concrete" harm as a result of Spokeo's alleged FCRA violation.[256] Legal experts noted that the ruling could extend to numerous other statutes used in class action lawsuits when those lawsuits are based on alleged technical violations of the law that do not cause harm. They added that the decision did not give much guidance for other cases involving the increased risk to individuals when personal data are misused or incorrect.[257]

In 2021, the U.S. Supreme Court addressed a class action lawsuit addressing inaccurate credit reporting agency reports. Sergio Ramirez filed the class action suit against TransUnion after a car salesman refused to sell Ramirez a car because a TransUnion report flagged Ramirez as a potential terrorist or drug trafficker. More than 8,000 people joined the lawsuit alleging TransUnion compiled lists of personal and financial information in credit reports that indicated their names matched names the Treasury Department Office of Foreign Assets Control (OFAC) listed as potential criminals. A jury had awarded the plaintiffs about $8 million in statutory damages and $52 million in punitive damages, and the Ninth Circuit Court of Appeals called TransUnion's handling of the OFAC information reckless.[258]

In a 5–4 decision, the Supreme Court held that plaintiffs, who could show third-party businesses received their reports, had standing to sue TransUnion. The majority opinion found harm from being labeled a potential terrorist was sufficiently close "to the harm from a false and defamatory statement" for those plaintiffs to show they "suffered a concrete injury." The plaintiffs whose reports were not disseminated to third-party businesses, however, could not demonstrate "concrete harm." Risk of injury was not sufficient for plaintiffs to have standing to sue.[259]

The dissenting justices stated that erroneously indicating law-abiding citizens were potential terrorists or drug traffickers violated the FCRA. As the Act provides people with rights to have accuracy in credit-reporting, the dissenting justices indicated "each class member established a violation of his or her privacy rights."[260] Justice Elena Kagan wrote that concreteness of harm includes real harm or a "risk of real harm."[261]

The Federal Trade Commission (FTC) has addressed privacy violations as unfair trade practices. The FTC is the chief federal agency that protects consumer privacy and enforces federal privacy laws. The FTC recently issued a substantive report about consumer privacy protection and called on companies to adopt its recommended best practices. The FTC report suggested that at all stages of product development, companies build in consumer privacy protections, including consumer data security, limited data collection and retention, and procedures to promote data accuracy. The report also recommended giving consumers the option to control how they share their information and the ability to choose a "Do Not Track" mechanism. The FTC also encouraged companies to strive toward transparency in how they collect and use consumer information.[262] Current federal and state privacy laws do not sufficiently protect American consumers, according to the FTC. The burden of understanding websites' privacy policies falls upon online users who must read user agreements and try to ensure their own privacy.[263]

The FTC recently issued a report on data brokers to educate the public about how these companies use, maintain and disseminate the personal data they collect. The report noted that none of the nine major data brokers obtained their data directly from consumers. Instead, the data originated from both public and private sources, online and offline. Information collected included Social Security numbers, interest in health issues, voter records, viewed news reports, social media posts, information from travel websites and transaction data from retailers.[264] The FTC said consumers could benefit from the data these brokers collect and analyze but found little transparency in the industry. Additionally, the report said these brokers unnecessarily store consumer data indefinitely, which can increase security risks for consumers (e.g., increased risk of identity theft).[265]

The FTC also has received and adjudicated complaints related to consumer privacy. In 2021, the FTC and Zoom Video Communications, Inc., finalized a settlement for claims the video conferencing company misled consumers about how much security Zoom provided for meetings. The FTC order prohibits Zoom from misrepresenting security features or collection and use of information, including names, addresses, contact information, social security numbers and recorded content or transcripts. The order also requires implementation of a comprehensive security program.[266]

INTERNATIONAL LAW
GLOBAL DATA PROTECTION REGULATION IN THE EU AND CHINA

As companies interact with corporations and consumers around the globe, it is increasingly important to understand data privacy regulations from other countries.

Recently, the European Union implemented a new framework for consumer data protection. The Global Data Protection Regulation (GDPR) significantly changed how companies handle consumer privacy and gave EU citizens the right to control their own data. Data privacy experts have hailed the GDPR as one of the most powerful data privacy laws in the world. The GDPR requires companies to explain how they store and use consumers' personal data, allows people to request companies delete their personal data and allows people to object to their personal data being used for direct marketing purposes.[267]

The GDPR expands the concept of the "right to be forgotten." An EU Court of Justice (in essence, a "supreme court" for the European Union) decision that required Google to unlink articles from its searches that people claimed are irrelevant or no longer accurate.[268] Since 2014, this "right to be forgotten" has resulted in more than three million URL delisting requests to Google, which has approved about 55 percent of those.[269]

In 2021, China enacted the Personal Information Protection Law of the P.R.C. (PIPL), which is similar to the GDPR. PIPL applies to data processing inside and outside China. The law provides Chinese people with rights pertaining to their personal information. Those rights include prohibiting processing, reviewing and copying, correcting and deleting, and requesting explanations of processing rules. Individuals may sue organizations that reject requests to exercise those rights.[270]

EMERGING LAW

The U.S. Supreme Court addressed implicit constitutional rights to privacy in 2022 when the Court overturned *Roe v. Wade* and *Planned Parenthood of Southeastern Pennsylvania v. Casey*. Courts, legislators and the FTC have addressed other privacy or publicity rights. The NCAA and legislators also have recognized publicity rights for student-athletes.

In May 2022, Politico published a leaked draft opinion in *Dobbs v. Jackson Women's Health Organization*. The draft majority opinion stated that five U.S. Supreme Court justices supported overturning *Roe* because the Constitution neither explicitly refers to abortion nor privacy. Any implicit constitutional right must be rooted in U.S. history and tradition. The draft opinion indicated five justices did not believe the right to have an abortion existed before the 20th century.[271]

In the *Dobbs* opinion published in June of 2022, a 6–3 majority of the Court focused on textualism and history to overrule *Roe* and *Casey*. Justice Samuel Alito wrote for the majority that the Constitution does not mention abortion. Alito stated that *Roe* grounded the right to an abortion in a right to privacy. *Roe* connected privacy rights to five amendments that do not include the word privacy. The Court's interpretation of "personal privacy" has "conflated two very different meanings" of privacy—informational privacy, shielding personal information against government disclosure, and decisional privacy, making "personal decisions without governmental interference,"—although only decisional privacy was relevant to abortion, Alito stated.[272]

Noting *Casey* focused on liberty rather than privacy, the majority distinguished the right to abortion from other rights that the Court has recognized "fall within the Fourteenth Amendment's protection of liberty."[273] The Due Process Clause has been interpreted to recognize certain liberties "deeply rooted in this Nation's history and tradition" as implicit rights, but Alito stated American law did not recognize the right to abortion until the latter part of the 20th century.[274] The majority concluded there is no constitutional right to an abortion, thus the people and their elected representatives could determine whether to recognize a right to abortion.[275] Leading organizations of American historians, however, noted the final opinion, which mentioned history 67 times, misinterpreted history and traditions and "established a flawed and troubling precedent."[276]

Privacy rights for data stored on electronic devices are not absolute. In 2021, the First Circuit Court of Appeals stated that U.S. Customs and Border Patrol and U.S. Immigration and Customs Enforcement policies did not violate the Fourth Amendment. The polices allowed warrantless searches of electronic devices at the U.S. border. As the Ninth and Eleventh Circuits had previously determined, the First Circuit found basic border searches of electronic devices "may be performed without reasonable suspicion." As the Eleventh Circuit also had determined, the First Circuit decided advanced border searches of electronic devices may be performed without a warrant or probable cause. The balancing of Fourth Amendment interests favors the government, the court stated, when privacy concerns are "tempered by the fact that such searches are taking place at the border, where the Government's interest in preventing the entry of unwanted persons and effects is at its zenith."[277]

The **Telephone Consumer Protection Act of 1991** (TCPA), a federal law that now prohibits most robocalls to cell phones and home phones, is intended to protect individuals against intrusive telemarketing. In 2014, Noah Duguid received several text notifications that someone was trying to access his Facebook account, although Duguid neither had a Facebook account nor provided the social media company with his phone number. Duguid filed a class action lawsuit alleging Facebook violated the TCPA by storing phone numbers in a database and programming equipment to send automated text messages. A federal court granted a motion to dismiss the case on grounds Facebook did not send text messages to randomly and sequentially generated numbers.[278]

The Ninth Circuit reversed, holding the TCPA applied when numbers were stored to be called and dialed automatically. In 2021, the Supreme Court unanimously reversed the Ninth Circuit decision. The Court held that under the TCPA an auto dialer must have "capacity to use a random or sequential number generator." The Court rejected Duguid's argument that the narrow interpretation would "unleash a torrent of robocalls."[279]

Facebook and TikTok, a popular social media application, recently settled class action privacy suits. Meta, the parent company of Facebook, agreed to settle a data privacy lawsuit for $90 million. That case addressed allegations the social media platform used cookies and plug-ins to track and save information about users' online activities even after users logged out of Facebook.[280] A federal court recently approved a $92 million settlement of multiple class action claims filed against TikTok. The lawsuits claimed TikTok violated federal laws and Illinois and California laws by collecting personal data and biometric data.[281] More than a handful of states have passed laws that address biometric identification.[282]

Following state efforts to provide consumer data privacy protection, the FTC and members of Congress considered threats to consumer privacy in 2022. The Federal Trade Commission invited public comments on needs for new rules related to commercial surveillance and data security.[283] Members of Congress circulated a draft bill intended to provide more comprehensive data privacy protection in the United States. If approved, the law would provide more protection for children, limit targeted advertising and provide a duty of loyalty to limit the collection, processing and transfer of data.[284]

As technology makes it easier to create digital replicas of individual identities or deep fakes (see Chapter 10), members of Congress and state legislatures have considered how to protect rights computer-generated simulations may harm. A 2021 amendment to Hawaii privacy law makes it a crime to intentionally create, disclose or threaten to disclose images or videos that use persons' likenesses to make them appear as if they were nude or engaged in sexual conduct.[285]

New York Civil Rights Law similarly protects privacy rights for persons who, through digital alteration of images or videos, appear to perform sex acts they did not perform.[286] New York Civil Rights Law also protects publicity rights against computer-generated or digitally manipulated sound recordings or audio-visual works that inaccurately indicate persons performed other recordings or works.[287]

In a right of publicity case, Karen Hepp, a newscaster who hosts Good Day Philadelphia in Pennsylvania, sued several social media companies after a photograph taken with neither her knowledge nor her consent was used online without her permission. The photograph was used in a Reddit post linked to an Imgur post. The photograph appeared on Facebook in an advertisement for a dating app. She asserted the uses violated her right of publicity. The district court dismissed the claims, finding all three companies were immune from liability under Section 230 of the Communications Decency Act, as that act applies to intellectual property.[288]

The Third Circuit Court of Appeals affirmed dismissal of the claims against Reddit and Imgur on grounds of lack of jurisdiction but reversed and remanded the dismissal of the claim against Facebook under Section 230 (see Chapter 5). One part of Section 230 says the statute shall not "be construed to limit or expand any law pertaining to intellectual property." The court noted that *Zacchini v. Scripps-Howard Broadcasting Company* explained the right of publicity as a property right "closely analogous to" two types of intellectual property rights, patent and copyright, that protect against "unjust enrichment by the theft of good will." The Third Circuit found publicity rights also are similar to trademarks, thus the intellectual property exception to Section 230 prevented Facebook from being immune from liability.[289]

Publicity rights also may be recognized through contracts. The NCAA and lawmakers recently have reconsidered NCAA student-athletes' rights to benefit from uses of their names, images and likenesses. A 2021 interim NCAA Name Image and Likeness (NIL) policy states that student-athletes benefiting from uses of their names, images or likenesses should follow state laws and report activities to the colleges or universities where they play sports. Benefits cannot include pay-for-play or recruiting inducements from schools. Under the interim policy, other benefits received while following state laws will not make college athletes ineligible for NCAA athletics.

The NCAA policy is written to expire when federal legislation or a new NCAA policy passes.[290] In 2020 and 2021, multiple bills were introduced in the U.S. House and Senate and in state legislatures. By 2023, more than half of the U.S. states will have laws in effect that recognize student-athlete rights to benefit from uses of their names, images or likenesses.[291]

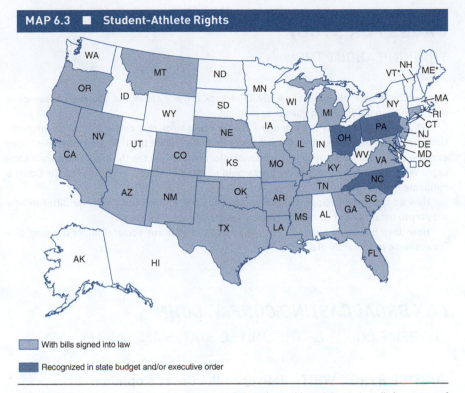

MAP 6.3 ■ Student-Athlete Rights

☐ With bills signed into law

☐ Recognized in state budget and/or executive order

At least 26 U.S. states will have laws that recognize student-athlete rights to benefit from uses of their names, images or likenesses by 2023, according to the Business of College Sports.

Business of College Sports Name, Image and Likeness Legislation by State tracker

KEYTERMS

appropriation

artistic relevance test

avatar

biometric data

class action lawsuit

commercialization

data broker

decisional privacy

disclosure of private facts

fact finder

Fair Credit Reporting Act

false light

highly offensive to a reasonable person

informational privacy

intrusion upon seclusion

mug shot

newsworthy

post-mortem (After death)

predominant use test

private facts

probable cause

public record

reasonable person

right of publicity

search warrant

sound-alike

third-party doctrine

transformative use test

widespread publicity

CASES FOR STUDY
THINKING ABOUT THEM

The two case excerpts that follow are landmark privacy cases. As you read these case excerpts, keep the following questions in mind:

Why does the majority in *Carpenter v. United States* think that cell-site location information should not be covered by the third-party doctrine? Might the U.S. Supreme Court also exclude other categories of data or personal information from the third-party doctrine concept? Why do you think these categories would or should be excluded, based on the Court's rationale in *Carpenter*?

How do the two decisions in *Cox Broadcasting Corp. v. Cohn* and *Carpenter* differ in how they try to balance the right of privacy against other important rights?

How does the Court suggest technology has changed our societal understanding of a "reasonable expectation of privacy"?

COX BROADCASTING CORP. V. COHN
SUPREME COURT OF THE UNITED STATES 420 U.S. 469 (1975)

JUSTICE BYRON WHITE delivered the Court's opinion:

The issue before us in this case is whether, consistently with the First and Fourteenth Amendments, a State may extend a cause of action for damages for invasion of privacy caused by the publication of the name of a deceased rape victim which was publicly revealed in connection with the prosecution of the crime.

In August 1971, appellee's 17-year-old daughter was the victim of a rape and did not survive the incident. Six youths were soon indicted for murder and rape. Although there was substantial press coverage of the crime and of subsequent developments, the identity of the victim was not disclosed pending trial, perhaps because of Ga. Code Ann. § 26-9901 (1972), which makes it a misdemeanor to publish or broadcast the name or identity of a rape victim. In April 1972, some eight months later, the six defendants appeared in court. Five pleaded guilty to rape or attempted rape, the charge of murder having been dropped. The guilty pleas were accepted by the court, and the trial of the defendant pleading not guilty was set for a later date.

In the course of the proceedings that day, appellant Wassell, a reporter covering the incident for his employer, learned the name of the victim from an examination of the indictments which were made available for his inspection in the courtroom. That the name of the victim appears in the indictments and that the indictments were public records available for inspection are not disputed. Later that day, Wassell broadcast over the facilities of station WSB-TV, a television station owned by appellant Cox Broadcasting Corp., a news report concerning the court proceedings. The report named the victim of the crime and was repeated the following day.

In May 1972, appellee brought an action for money damages against appellants, relying on § 26-9901 and claiming that his right to privacy had been invaded by the television broadcasts giving the name of his deceased daughter. Appellants admitted the broadcasts but claimed that they were privileged under both state law and the First and Fourteenth Amendments. The trial court, rejecting appellants' constitutional claims and holding that the Georgia statute gave a civil remedy to those injured by its violation, granted summary judgment to appellee as to liability, with the determination of damages to await trial by jury.

On appeal, the Georgia Supreme Court, in its initial opinion, held that the trial court had erred in construing § 26-9901 to extend a civil cause of action for invasion of privacy and thus found it unnecessary to consider the constitutionality of the statute.... Upon motion for rehearing the Georgia court countered the argument that the victim's name was a matter of public interest and could be published with impunity by relying on § 26-9901 as an authoritative declaration of state policy that the name of a rape victim was not a matter of public concern. This time the court felt compelled to determine the constitutionality of the statute and sustained it as a "legitimate limitation on the right of freedom of expression contained in the First Amendment." The court could discern "no public interest or general concern about the identity of the victim of such a crime as will make the right to disclose the identity of the victim rise to the level of First Amendment protection."

. . . . [W]e conclude that we have jurisdiction to review the judgment of the Georgia Supreme Court rejecting the challenge under the First and Fourteenth Amendments to the state law authorizing damage suits against the press for publishing the name of a rape victim whose identity is revealed in the course of a public prosecution. . . .

Georgia stoutly defends both § 26-9901 and the State's common-law privacy action challenged here. Its claims are not without force, for powerful arguments can be made, and have been made, that however it may be ultimately defined, there *is* a zone of privacy surrounding every individual, a zone within which the State may protect him from intrusion by the press, with all its attendant publicity. Indeed, the central thesis of the root article by Warren and Brandeis, The Right to Privacy, was that the press was overstepping its prerogatives by publishing essentially private information and that there should be a remedy for the alleged abuses.

More compellingly, the century has experienced a strong tide running in favor of the so-called right of privacy. In 1967, we noted that "[it] has been said that a 'right of privacy' has been recognized at common law in 30 States plus the District of Columbia and by statute in four States." We there cited the 1964 edition of Prosser's Law of Torts. The 1971 edition of that same source states that "[in] one form or another, the right of privacy is by this time recognized and accepted in all but a very few jurisdictions." Nor is it irrelevant here that the right of privacy is no recent arrival in the jurisprudence of Georgia, which has embraced the right in some form since 1905 when the Georgia Supreme Court decided the leading case of *Pavesich v. New England Life Ins. Co.*

These are impressive credentials for a right of privacy, but we should recognize that we do not have at issue here an action for the invasion of privacy involving the appropriation of one's name or photograph, a physical or other tangible intrusion into a private area, or a publication of otherwise private information that is also false although perhaps not defamatory. The version of the privacy tort now before us—termed in Georgia "the tort of public disclosure"—is that in which the plaintiff claims the right to be free from unwanted publicity about his private affairs, which, although wholly true, would be offensive to a person of ordinary sensibilities. Because the gravamen of the claimed injury is the publication of information, whether true or not, the dissemination of which is embarrassing or otherwise painful to an individual, it is here that claims of privacy most directly confront the constitutional freedoms of speech and press. The face-off is apparent, and the appellants urge upon us the broad holding that the press may not be made criminally or civilly liable for publishing information that is neither false nor misleading but absolutely accurate, however damaging it may be to reputation or individual sensibilities. In this sphere of collision between claims of privacy and those of the free press, the interests on both sides are plainly rooted in the traditions and significant concerns of our society. Rather than address the broader question whether truthful publications may ever be subjected to civil or criminal liability consistently with the First and Fourteenth Amendments, or to put it another way, whether the State may ever define and protect an area of privacy free from unwanted publicity in the press, it is appropriate to focus on the narrower interface between press and privacy that this case presents, namely, whether the State may impose sanctions on the accurate publication of the name of a rape victim obtained from public records—more specifically, from judicial records which are maintained in connection with a public prosecution and which themselves are open to public inspection. We are convinced that the State may not do so.

In the first place, in a society in which each individual has but limited time and resources with which to observe at first hand the operations of his government, he relies necessarily upon the press to bring to him in convenient form the facts of those operations. Great responsibility is accordingly placed upon the news media to report fully and accurately the proceedings of government, and official records and documents open to the public are the basic data of governmental operations. Without the information provided by the press, most of us and many of our representatives would be unable to vote intelligently or to register opinions on the administration of government generally. With respect to judicial proceedings in particular, the function of the press serves to guarantee the fairness of trials and to bring to bear the beneficial effects of public scrutiny upon the administration of justice.

Appellee has claimed in this litigation that the efforts of the press have infringed his right to privacy by broadcasting to the world the fact that his daughter was a rape victim. The commission of crime, prosecutions resulting from it, and judicial proceedings arising from the prosecutions, however, are without question events of legitimate concern to the public and consequently fall within the responsibility of the press to report the operations of government.

The special protected nature of accurate reports of judicial proceedings has repeatedly been recognized. This Court, in an opinion written by MR. JUSTICE DOUGLAS, has said:

"A trial is a public event. What transpires in the court room is public property. If a transcript of the court proceedings had been published, we suppose none would claim that the judge could punish the publisher for contempt. And we can see no difference though the conduct of the attorneys, of the jury, or even of the judge himself, may have reflected on the court. *Those who see and hear what transpired can report it with impunity.* There is no special perquisite of the judiciary which enables it, as distinguished from other institutions of democratic government, to suppress, edit, or censor events which transpire in proceedings before it."

The developing law surrounding the tort of invasion of privacy recognizes a privilege in the press to report the events of judicial proceedings. The Warren and Brandeis article noted that the proposed new right would be limited in the same manner as actions for libel and slander where such a publication was a privileged communication: "the right to privacy is not invaded by any publication made in a court of justice . . . and (at least in many jurisdictions) reports of any such proceedings would in some measure be accorded a like privilege."

The Restatement of Torts, § 867, embraced an action for privacy. . . . According to this draft, ascertaining and publishing the contents of public records are simply not within the reach of these kinds of privacy actions.

Thus, even the prevailing law of invasion of privacy generally recognizes that the interests in privacy fade when the information involved already appears on the public record. The conclusion is compelling when viewed in terms of the First and Fourteenth Amendments and in light of the public interest in a vigorous press. The Georgia cause of action for invasion of privacy through public disclosure of the name of a rape victim imposes sanctions on pure expression—the content of a publication—and not conduct or a combination of speech and nonspeech elements that might otherwise be open to regulation or prohibition. The publication of truthful information available on the public record contains none of the indicia of those limited categories of expression, such as "fighting" words, which "are no essential part of any exposition of ideas, and are of such slight social value as a step to truth that any benefit that may be derived from them is clearly outweighed by the social interest in order and morality."

By placing the information in the public domain on official court records, the State must be presumed to have concluded that the public interest was thereby being served. Public records by their very nature are of interest to those concerned with the administration of government, and a public benefit is performed by the reporting of the true contents of the records by the media. The freedom of the press to publish that information appears to us to be of critical importance to our type of government in which the citizenry is the final judge of the proper conduct of public business. In preserving that form of government, the First and Fourteenth Amendments command nothing less than that the States may not impose sanctions on the publication of truthful information contained in official court records open to public inspection.

We are reluctant to embark on a course that would make public records generally available to the media but forbid their publication if offensive to the sensibilities of the supposed reasonable man. Such a rule would make it very difficult for the media to inform citizens about the public business and yet stay within the law. The rule would invite timidity and self-censorship and very likely lead to the suppression of many items that would otherwise be published and that should be made available to the public. At the very least, the First and Fourteenth Amendments will not allow exposing the press to liability for truthfully publishing information released to the public in official court records. If there are privacy interests to be protected in judicial proceedings, the States must respond by means which avoid public documentation or other exposure of private information. Their political institutions must weigh the interests in privacy with the interests of the public to know and of the press to publish. Once true information is disclosed in public court documents open to public inspection, the press cannot be sanctioned for publishing it. In this instance, as in others, reliance must rest upon the judgment of those who decide what to publish or broadcast.

Appellant Wassell based his televised report upon notes taken during the court proceedings and obtained the name of the victim from the indictments handed to him at his request during a recess in the hearing. Appellee has not contended that the name was obtained in an improper fashion or that it was not on an official court document open to public inspection. Under these circumstances, the protection of freedom of the press provided by the First and Fourteenth Amendments bars the State of Georgia from making appellants' broadcast the basis of civil liability.

Reversed.

CHIEF JUSTICE WARREN BURGER concurs in the judgment:

JUSTICE LEWIS POWELL, Jr., concurring, with whom JUSTICE WILLIAM DOUGLAS joins. . . .

JUSTICE WILLIAM DOUGLAS, concurring in the judgment:

I agree that the state judgment is "final," and I also agree in the reversal of the Georgia court. On the merits, the case for me is on all fours with *New Jersey State Lottery Comm'n v. United States.* For the reasons I stated in my dissent from our disposition of that case, there is no power on the part of government to suppress or penalize the publication of "news of the day."

JUSTICE WILLIAM REHNQUIST, dissenting:

Because I am of the opinion that the decision which is the subject of this appeal is not a "final" judgment or decree, as that term is used in 28 U. S. C. § 1257, I would dismiss this appeal for want of jurisdiction. . . .

CARPENTER V. UNITED STATES

SUPREME COURT OF THE UNITED STATES 138 S. CT. 2206 (2018)

CHIEF JUSTICE JOHN ROBERTS delivered the Court's opinion:

This case presents the question whether the Government conducts a search under the *Fourth Amendment* when it accesses historical cell phone records that provide a comprehensive chronicle of the user's past movements.

There are 396 million cell phone service accounts in the United States—for a Nation of 326 million people. Cell phones perform their wide and growing variety of functions by connecting to a set of radio antennas called "cell sites." Although cell sites are usually mounted on a tower, they can also be found on light posts, flagpoles, church steeples, or the sides of buildings. . . .

Cell phones continuously scan their environment looking for the best signal, which generally comes from the closest cell site. Most modern devices, such as smartphones, tap into the wireless network several times a minute whenever their signal is on, even if the owner is not using one of the phone's features. Each time the phone connects to a cell site, it generates a time-stamped record known as cell-site location information (CSLI). The precision of this information depends on the size of the geographic area covered by the cell site. The greater the concentration of cell sites, the smaller the coverage area. As data usage from cell phones has increased, wireless carriers have installed more cell sites to handle the traffic. That has led to increasingly compact coverage areas, especially in urban areas.

Wireless carriers collect and store CSLI for their own business purposes, including finding weak spots in their network. . . . In addition, wireless carriers often sell aggregated location records to data brokers, without individual identifying information of the sort at issue here. While carriers have long retained CSLI for the start and end of incoming calls, in recent years phone companies have also collected location information from the transmission of text messages and routine data connections. Accordingly, modern cell phones generate increasingly vast amounts of increasingly precise CSLI.

In 2011, police officers arrested four men suspected of robbing a series of Radio Shack and (ironically enough) T-Mobile stores. . . . The suspect identified 15 accomplices who had participated in the heists and gave the FBI some of their cell phone numbers; the FBI then reviewed his call records to identify additional numbers that he had called around the time of the robberies.

Based on that information, the prosecutors applied for court orders under the Stored Communications Act to obtain cell phone records for petitioner Timothy Carpenter and several other suspects. That statute, as amended in 1994, permits the Government to compel the disclosure of certain telecommunications records. . . . Federal Magistrate Judges issued two orders directing Carpenter's wireless carriers—MetroPCS and Sprint—to disclose [CSLI] ... during the four-month period when the string of robberies occurred. . . . Altogether the Government obtained 12,898 location points cataloging Carpenter's movements—an average of 101 data points per day.

Carpenter was charged with six counts of robbery and an additional six counts of carrying a firearm during a federal crime of violence. Prior to trial, Carpenter . . . argued that the Government's seizure of the records violated the Fourth Amendment because they had been obtained without a warrant supported by probable cause. The District Court denied the motion.

At trial . . . FBI agent Christopher Hess . . . produced maps that placed Carpenter's phone near four of the charged robberies. In the Government's view, the location records clinched the case. . . . Carpenter was convicted on all but one of the firearm counts and sentenced to more than 100 years in prison.

The Court of Appeals for the Sixth Circuit affirmed. The court held that Carpenter lacked a reasonable expectation of privacy in the location information collected by the FBI because he had shared that information with his wireless carriers. Given that cell phone users voluntarily convey cell-site data to their carriers as "a means of establishing communication," the court concluded that the resulting business records are not entitled to Fourth Amendment protection. . . .

The Fourth Amendment protects "[t]he right of the people to be secure in their persons, houses, papers, and effects, against unreasonable searches and seizures." The "basic purpose of this Amendment" . . . "is to safeguard the privacy and security of individuals against arbitrary invasions by governmental officials."

. . . For much of our history, Fourth Amendment search doctrine was "tied to common-law trespass" and focused on whether the Government "obtains information by physically intruding on a constitutionally protected area." More recently, the Court has recognized that "property rights are not the sole measure of Fourth Amendment violations." In [*Katz*], we established that "the Fourth Amendment protects people, not places," and expanded our conception of the Amendment to protect certain expectations of privacy as well. . . .

[The Fourth] Amendment seeks to secure "the privacies of life" against "arbitrary power." . . . [A] central aim of the Framers was "to place obstacles in the way of a too permeating police surveillance."

We have kept this attention to Founding-era understandings in mind when applying the Fourth Amendment to innovations in surveillance tools. . . .

[I]n *Riley*, the Court recognized the "immense storage capacity" of modern cell phones in holding that police officers must generally obtain a warrant before searching the contents of a phone. . . .

The case before us involves the Government's acquisition of wireless carrier cell-site records revealing the location of Carpenter's cell phone whenever it made or received calls. This sort of digital data—personal location information maintained by a third party—does not fit neatly under existing precedents. Instead, requests for cell-site records lie at the intersection of two lines of cases, both of which inform our understanding of the privacy interests at stake.

The first set of cases addresses a person's expectation of privacy in his physical location and movements. [W]e [have] considered the Government's use of a "beeper" to aid in tracking a vehicle through traffic. . . . The Court concluded [in *Knotts*] that the "augment[ed]" visual surveillance did not constitute a search because "[a] person traveling in an automobile on public thoroughfares has no reasonable expectation of privacy in his movements from one place to another." . . .

This Court in *Knotts*, however, was careful to distinguish between the rudimentary tracking facilitated by the beeper and more sweeping modes of surveillance. . . . Significantly, the Court reserved the question whether "different constitutional principles may be applicable" if "twenty-four hour surveillance of any citizen of this country [were] possible."

Three decades later, the Court considered more sophisticated surveillance of the sort envisioned in *Knotts* and found that different principles did indeed apply. In *United States v. Jones* . . . the Court decided the case based on the Government's physical trespass of the vehicle. At the same time, five Justices agreed that related privacy concerns would be raised by, for example, "surreptitiously activating a stolen vehicle detection system" in Jones's car to track Jones himself, or conducting GPS tracking of his cell phone. Since GPS monitoring of a vehicle tracks "every movement" a person makes in that vehicle, the concurring Justices concluded that "longer term GPS monitoring in investigations of most offenses impinges on expectations of privacy"—regardless whether those movements were disclosed to the public at large.

In a second set of decisions, the Court has drawn a line between what a person keeps to himself and what he shares with others. We have previously held that "a person has no legitimate expectation of privacy in information he voluntarily turns over to third parties." . . . As a result, the Government is typically free to obtain such information from the recipient without triggering Fourth Amendment protections.

This third-party doctrine largely traces its roots to *Miller*. While investigating Miller for tax evasion, the Government subpoenaed his banks, seeking several months of canceled checks, deposit slips, and monthly statements. The Court rejected a Fourth Amendment challenge to the records collection. For one, Miller could "assert neither ownership nor possession" of the documents; they were "business records of the banks." For another, the nature of those records confirmed Miller's limited expectation of privacy, because the checks were "not confidential communications but negotiable instruments to be used in commercial transactions," and the bank statements contained information "exposed to [bank] employees in the ordinary course of business." . . .

Three years later, *Smith* applied the same principles in the context of information conveyed to a telephone company. . . .

The question we confront today is how to apply the Fourth Amendment to a new phenomenon: the ability to chronicle a person's past movements through the record of his cell phone signals. Such tracking partakes of many of the qualities of the GPS monitoring we considered in *Jones*. Much like GPS tracking of a vehicle, cell phone location information is detailed, encyclopedic, and effortlessly compiled.

At the same time, the fact that the individual continuously reveals his location to his wireless carrier implicates the third-party principle of *Smith* and *Miller*. But while the third-party doctrine applies to telephone numbers and bank records, it is not clear whether its logic extends to the qualitatively different category of cell-site records. After all, when *Smith* was decided in 1979, few could have imagined a society in which a phone goes wherever its owner goes, conveying to the wireless carrier not just dialed digits, but a detailed and comprehensive record of the person's movements.

We decline to extend *Smith* and *Miller* to cover these novel circumstances. Given the unique nature of cell phone location records, the fact that the information is held by a third party does not by itself overcome the user's claim to *Fourth Amendment* protection. Whether the Government employs its own surveillance technology as in *Jones* or leverages the technology of a wireless carrier, we hold that an individual maintains a legitimate expectation of privacy in the record of his physical movements as captured through CSLI. The location information obtained from Carpenter's wireless carriers was the product of a search. . . .

A person does not surrender all *Fourth Amendment* protection by venturing into the public sphere.... Prior to the digital age, law enforcement might have pursued a suspect for a brief stretch, but doing so "for any extended period of time was difficult and costly and therefore rarely undertaken." For that reason, "society's expectation has been that law enforcement agents and others would not—and indeed, in the main, simply could not—secretly monitor and catalogue every single movement of an individual's car for a very long period."

Allowing government access to cell-site records contravenes that expectation.... [L]ike GPS monitoring, cell phone tracking is remarkably easy, cheap, and efficient compared to traditional investigative tools. With just the click of a button, the Government can access each carrier's deep repository of historical location information at practically no expense.

In fact, historical cell-site records present even greater privacy concerns than the GPS monitoring of a vehicle we considered in *Jones*.... A cell phone faithfully follows its owner beyond public thoroughfares and into private residences, doctor's offices, political head-quarters, and other potentially revealing locales.... Accordingly, when the Government tracks the location of a cell phone it achieves near perfect surveillance, as if it had attached an ankle monitor to the phone's user.

Moreover, the retrospective quality of the data here gives police access to a category of information otherwise unknowable.... Critically, because location information is continu-ally logged for all of the 400 million devices in the United States—not just those belonging to persons who might happen to come under investigation—this newfound tracking capacity runs against everyone....

Whoever the suspect turns out to be, he has effectively been tailed every moment of every day for five years, and the police may—in the Government's view—call upon the results of that surveillance without regard to the constraints of the Fourth Amendment. Only the few without cell phones could escape this tireless and absolute surveillance.

The Government and Justice Kennedy contend, however, that the collection of CSLI should be permitted because the data is less precise than GPS information....

While the records in this case reflect the state of technology at the start of the decade, the accuracy of CSLI is rapidly approaching GPS-level precision. As the number of cell sites has proliferated, the geographic area covered by each cell sector has shrunk, particularly in urban areas. In addition, with new technology measuring the time and angle of signals hitting their towers, wireless carriers already have the capability to pinpoint a phone's loca-tion within 50 meters.

Accordingly, when the Government accessed CSLI from the wireless carriers, it invaded Carpenter's reasonable expectation of privacy in the whole of his physical movements.

The Government's primary contention to the contrary is that the third-party doctrine governs this case....

The Government's position fails to contend with the seismic shifts in digital technology that made possible the tracking of not only Carpenter's location but also everyone else's, not for a short period but for years and years. Sprint Corporation and its competitors are not your typical witnesses. Unlike the nosy neighbor who keeps an eye on comings and goings, they are ever alert, and their memory is nearly infallible. There is a world of difference between the limited types of personal information addressed in *Smith* and *Miller* and the exhaustive chronicle of location information casually collected by wireless carriers today. The Government thus is not asking for a straightforward application of the third-party doc-trine, but instead a significant extension of it to a distinct category of information....

The Court has in fact already shown special solicitude for location information in the third-party context. In *Knotts*, the Court relied on *Smith* to hold that an individual has no rea-sonable expectation of privacy in public movements that he "voluntarily conveyed to anyone who wanted to look." But when confronted with more pervasive tracking, five Justices agreed [in *Jones*] that longer term GPS monitoring of even a vehicle traveling on public streets constitutes a search. Justice Gorsuch wonders why "someone's location when using a phone" is sensitive, and Justice Kennedy assumes that a person's discrete movements "are not particularly private." Yet this case is not about "using a phone" or a person's movement at a particular time. It is about a detailed chronicle of a person's physical presence compiled every day, every moment, over several years. Such a chronicle implicates privacy concerns far beyond those considered in *Smith* and *Miller*.

. . . Cell phone location information is not truly "shared" as one normally understands the term. In the first place, cell phones and the services they provide are "such a pervasive and insistent part of daily life" that carrying one is indispensable to participation in modern society. Second, a cell phone logs a cell-site record by dint of its operation, without any affirmative act on the part of the user beyond powering up. Virtually any activity on the phone generates CSLI, including incoming calls, texts, or e-mails and countless other data connections that a phone automatically makes when checking for news, weather, or social media updates. Apart from disconnecting the phone from the network, there is no way to avoid leaving behind a trail of location data. As a result, in no meaningful sense does the user voluntarily "assume[] the risk" of turning over a comprehensive dossier of his physical movements.

We therefore decline to extend *Smith* and *Miller* to the collection of CSLI. Given the unique nature of cell phone location information, the fact that the Government obtained the information from a third party does not overcome Carpenter's claim to Fourth Amendment protection. The Government's acquisition of the cell-site records was a search within the meaning of the Fourth Amendment.

Our decision today is a narrow one. . . . We do not disturb the application of *Smith* and *Miller* or call into question conventional surveillance techniques and tools, such as security cameras. Nor do we address other business records that might incidentally reveal location information. Further, our opinion does not consider other collection techniques involving foreign affairs or national security. As Justice Frankfurter noted when considering new innovations in airplanes and radios, the Court must tread carefully in such cases, to ensure that we do not "embarrass the future."

Having found that the acquisition of Carpenter's CSLI was a search, we also conclude that the Government must generally obtain a warrant supported by probable cause before acquiring such records. . . .

At some point, the dissent should recognize that CSLI is an entirely different species of business record—something that implicates basic Fourth Amendment concerns about arbitrary government power much more directly than corporate tax or payroll ledgers. When confronting new concerns wrought by digital technology, this Court has been careful not to uncritically extend existing precedents. . . .

This is certainly not to say that all orders compelling the production of documents will require a showing of probable cause. The Government will be able to use subpoenas to acquire records in the overwhelming majority of investigations. We hold only that a warrant is required in the rare case where the suspect has a legitimate privacy interest in records held by a third party.

Further, even though the Government will generally need a warrant to access CSLI, case-specific exceptions may support a warrantless search of an individual's cell-site records under certain circumstances. . . .

As a result, if law enforcement is confronted with an urgent situation, such fact-specific threats will likely justify the warrantless collection of CSLI. Lower courts, for instance, have approved warrantless searches related to bomb threats, active shootings, and child abductions. Our decision today does not call into doubt warrantless access to CSLI in such circumstances. While police must get a warrant when collecting CSLI to assist in the mine-run criminal investigation, the rule we set forth does not limit their ability to respond to an ongoing emergency. . . .

We decline to grant the state unrestricted access to a wireless carrier's database of physical location information. In light of the deeply revealing nature of CSLI, its depth, breadth, and comprehensive reach, and the inescapable and automatic nature of its collection, the fact that such information is gathered by a third party does not make it any less deserving of Fourth Amendment protection. The Government's acquisition of the cell-site records here was a search under that Amendment.

The judgment of the Court of Appeals is reversed, and the case is remanded for further proceedings consistent with this opinion.

It is so ordered.

JUSTICE ANTHONY KENNEDY, with whom JUSTICE CLARENCE THOMAS and JUSTICE SAMUEL ALITO join, dissenting.[292]

This case involves new technology, but the Court's stark departure from relevant *Fourth Amendment* precedents and principles is, in my submission, unnecessary and incorrect, requiring this respectful dissent.

The new rule the Court seems to formulate puts needed, reasonable, accepted, lawful, and congressionally authorized criminal investigations at serious risk in serious cases, often when law enforcement seeks to prevent the threat of violent crimes. . . .

The Court has twice held that individuals have no Fourth Amendment interests in business records which are possessed, owned, and controlled by a third party. This is true even when the records contain personal and sensitive information. So when the Government uses a subpoena to obtain, for example, bank records, telephone records, and credit card statements from the businesses that create and keep these records, the Government does not engage in a search of the business's customers within the meaning of the Fourth Amendment.

. . . Cell-site records, however, are no different from the many other kinds of business records the Government has a lawful right to obtain by compulsory process. Customers like petitioner do not own, possess, control, or use the records, and for that reason have no reasonable expectation that they cannot be disclosed pursuant to lawful compulsory process. . . .

In concluding that the Government engaged in a search, the Court unhinges Fourth Amendment doctrine from the property-based concepts that have long grounded the analytic framework that pertains in these cases. In doing so it draws an unprincipled and unworkable line between cell-site records on the one hand and financial and telephonic records on the other. According to today's majority opinion, the Government can acquire a record of every credit card purchase and phone call a person makes over months or years without upsetting a legitimate expectation of privacy. But, in the Court's view, the Government crosses a constitutional line when it obtains a court's approval to issue a subpoena for more than six days of cell-site records in order to determine whether a person was within several hundred city blocks of a crime scene. That distinction is illogical and will frustrate principled application of the Fourth Amendment in many routine yet vital law enforcement operations.

It is true that the Cyber Age has vast potential both to expand and restrict individual freedoms in dimensions not contemplated in earlier times. . . .

Here the only question necessary to decide is whether the Government searched anything of Carpenter's when it used compulsory process to obtain cell-site records from Carpenter's cell phone service providers. This Court's decisions in *Miller* and *Smith* dictate that the answer is no, as every Court of Appeals to have considered the question has recognized. . . .

Based on *Miller* and *Smith* . . . it is well established that subpoenas may be used to obtain a wide variety of records held by businesses, even when the records contain private information. Credit cards are a prime example. State and federal law enforcement, for instance, often subpoena credit card statements to develop probable cause to prosecute crimes ranging from drug trafficking and distribution to healthcare fraud to tax evasion. . . . Subpoenas also may be used to obtain vehicle registration records, hotel records, employment records, and records of utility usage, to name just a few other examples.

. . . In my respectful view the majority opinion misreads this Court's precedents, old and recent, and transforms *Miller* and *Smith* into an unprincipled and unworkable doctrine. . . .

The Court appears . . . to read *Miller* and *Smith* to establish a balancing test. For each "qualitatively different category" of information, the Court suggests, the privacy interests at stake must be weighed against the fact that the information has been disclosed to a third party. When the privacy interests are weighty enough to "overcome" the third-party disclosure, the Fourth Amendment's protections apply.

That is an untenable reading of *Miller* and *Smith*. . . .

[T]he Court maintains, cell-site records are "unique" because they are "comprehensive" in their reach; allow for retrospective collection; are "easy, cheap, and efficient compared to traditional investigative tools"; and are not exposed to cell phone service providers in a meaningfully voluntary manner. But many other kinds of business records can be so described. Financial records are of vast scope. Banks and credit card companies keep a comprehensive account of almost every transaction an individual makes on a daily basis. "With just the click of a button, the Government can access each [company's] deep repository of historical [financial] information at practically no expense." And the decision whether to transact with banks and credit card companies is no more or less voluntary than the decision whether to use a cell phone. Today, just as when *Miller* was decided, "'it is impossible to participate in the economic life of contemporary society without maintaining a bank account.'" But this Court, nevertheless, has held that individuals do not have a reasonable expectation of privacy in financial records. . . .

Technological changes involving cell phones have complex effects on crime and law enforcement. Cell phones make crimes easier to coordinate and conceal, while also providing the Government with new investigative tools that may have the potential to upset traditional privacy expectations. How those competing effects balance against each other, and how property norms and expectations of privacy form around new technology, often will be difficult to determine during periods of rapid technological change. . . . Congress weighed the privacy interests at stake and imposed a judicial check to prevent executive overreach. The Court should be wary of upsetting that legislative balance and erecting constitutional barriers that foreclose further legislative instructions. . . . The Court's decision runs roughshod over the mechanism Congress put in place to govern the acquisition of cell-site records and closes off further legislative debate on these issues.

The Court says its decision is a "narrow one." But its reinterpretation of *Miller* and *Smith* will have dramatic consequences for law enforcement, courts, and society as a whole. . . .

The Court's decision also will have ramifications that extend beyond cell-site records to other kinds of information held by third parties, yet the Court fails "to provide clear guidance to law enforcement" and courts on key issues raised by its reinterpretation of *Miller* and *Smith*. . . .

This case should be resolved by interpreting accepted property principles as the baseline for reasonable expectations of privacy. Here the Government did not search anything over which Carpenter could assert ownership or control. Instead, it issued a court-authorized subpoena to a third party to disclose information it alone owned and controlled. That should suffice to resolve this case. . . .

These reasons all lead to this respectful dissent.

U.S. Supreme Court Justice Amy Coney Barrett wrote the majority opinion in *Van Buren v. United States*, excerpted at the end of the chapter. That case considered whether the Computer Fraud and Abuse Act covered a law enforcement officer's search in a license plate database for non-law enforcement purposes.

Erin Schaff/*The New York Times* via AP Pool

7 GATHERING INFORMATION

Opportunities and Obstacles

CHAPTER OUTLINE

Brief Overview of Access

First Amendment Right of Access
Access to Public and Quasi-Public Places
Right to Record

Statutory Right of Access
Access to Federal Records
Access to State Records
Access to Federal and State Meetings
Face-to-Face and Participant Recording

Statutory Limits to Access
Trespass and Ag-Gag Laws
Drone Laws
Exemptions to Open Records
Exemptions to Open Meetings
Limits Placed on Access to Personally Identifiable Information
Covert Recording or Intercepting "Wire" Communications

Other Limits to Gathering Information
Harassment and Stalking
Fraud and Misrepresentation
Problems With Sources and Confidentiality

Emerging Law

Cases for Study
- *U.S. Department of Justice v. Reporters Committee for Freedom of the Press*
- *Van Buren v. United States*

LEARNING OBJECTIVES

7.1   Identify general rights of access.

7.2   Explain the First Amendment right of access.

7.3   Describe statutory right of access to information and places.

7.4   List the statutory limits to access information and places.

7.5   Appraise other limits to gathering information.

7.6   Discuss how communication professionals' information-gathering rights are changing.

Citizens and journalists need access to information and places to scrutinize powerful officials and to participate in democratic societies. Yet, global press freedom has decreased in recent years as citizens and journalists have faced declining trust in journalism and threats of arrest when attempting to record and report information.[1] Laws have provided some rights for individuals to access government-held information and proceedings, but access rights are not absolute. Recording rights may vary from place to place as well as according to which equipment is being used and how that equipment is used. It is important to consider circumstances under which government actors may deny requests for records, to attend meetings or to record interactions. It is also important to consider circumstances under which using technology to record people or interactions could be unlawful.

BRIEF OVERVIEW OF ACCESS

While the Constitution authorizes Congress to keep some records secret, courts have a history of openness (see Chapter 8). Still, no law ensures openness of information from the executive branch. The first Congress in 1789 adopted only a "housekeeping" statute that empowered federal departments to establish their own rules and policies for keeping and sharing documents.[2] Few questions about access to government information presented themselves until World War II ended and the Cold War spread global distrust.[3] Congress enacted its first substantive records law, the Administrative Procedure Act of 1946, to give federal officials discretion to make records public except "for good cause" or "in the public interest."[4] The law generally enabled federal government agencies to keep all unpublished records secret. News leaders advocated for more access to government information and proceedings for citizens and journalists to scrutinize government activity.[5]

In a mid-1960s case involving a ban on travel to Cuba, the U.S. Supreme Court held that weighty national security considerations required that "the right to speak and publish does not carry with it the unrestrained right to gather information."[6] Congress enacted the Freedom of Information Act (called FOIA, pronounced foy-yuh) in 1966.[7] The law created a presumption of access to all official executive agency records unless the material met the requirements of at least one of nine exemptions. In the 1970s, two federal laws established access to meetings of federal advisory committees[8] and policymaking bodies,[9] and the Privacy Act protected seven types of agency-held personal information from this openness.[10]

U.S. Supreme Court rulings on public access relate to specific laws and particular government information, institutions and events. The Court has never defined precise parameters of a First Amendment right of access to government information, but the Court, in 1972, said freedom of the press would be "eviscerated" without some protection for gathering information.[11] A few years later, the Court explained that "the public's interest in knowing about its government is protected by the guarantee of a free press, but the protection is indirect. The Constitution itself is neither a Freedom of Information Act nor an official secrets act."[12] Many other countries have official secrets laws to protect state secrets and information related to national security.

Some states adopted **"sunshine laws,"** laws for access to government information and meetings, much earlier than Congress enacted FOIA. Many states enacted open-records and open-meetings laws between the 1950s and 1970s.[13] In the five following decades, both federal and state legislatures have amended laws to respond to the changing nature of recordkeeping in the electronic age[14] and passed exemptions[15] that create significant differences in what state and federal government information and proceedings people may access.[16] Some state laws have been modeled after FOIA. When interpreting those laws, state courts may look to Supreme Court opinions for guidance. For example, a 2021 Supreme Court of Alaska opinion addressing access to law enforcement records cited *U.S. Department of Justice v. Reporters Committee for Freedom of the Press*,[17] excerpted at the end of this chapter.[18]

Since the 9/11 terrorist attacks, courts have struggled to reconcile the need for national security with the uncertain First Amendment guarantee of government openness.[19] A recent study found that, in most states, "open records laws are riddled with loopholes while the government agencies meant to enforce them are often toothless and underfunded."[20] One state records act includes 43 exemptions, and dozens of exemptions may be found in other state laws.[21] In contrast, while the 2015 USA Freedom Act restored post–9/11 anti-terrorism provisions, it also increased public access to the government's national security apparatus. For example, Section 402 of the act required the federal government to declassify and release "significant" opinions of the secret proceedings of the Foreign Intelligence Surveillance (FISA) Court that reviews the legality of national security operations. Nonetheless, many FISA Court opinions have not been released (see Chapter 8).[22]

FIRST AMENDMENT RIGHT OF ACCESS

While legal scholars and media advocates indicate that the First Amendment should be understood to protect rights to gather information and report news,[23] the Supreme Court has not clearly defined the First Amendment right of access to government information and institutions. The court has said merely that newsgathering plays an important role in advancing First Amendment interests.[24]

Although some courts have consistently ruled that no explicit newsgathering right exists under the First Amendment, the First Circuit Court of Appeals recognized in 2020 that secretly recording police officers performing their duties in public spaces is a type of newsgathering "within the scope of the First Amendment."[25] Government, however, has "no obligation to permit a type of newsgathering that would interfere with police officers' ability to do their jobs," the court said.[26]

Several circuit courts of appeal have found a First Amendment right of public access to governmental proceedings.[27] For example, in 2019 the Ninth Circuit Court of Appeals applied a test established to generally support a public right of access to judicial proceedings (see discussion of the *Press-Enterprise* test in Chapter 8). The court said the First Amendment right to access governmental proceedings includes "a right to hear the sounds of executions" in addition to viewing executions "in their entirety."[28]

First Amendment access rights, however, do not extend to information about specific drugs, personnel and procedures used in executions. In 2019, the Ninth Circuit reasoned that information was not "part of any official record of the execution proceeding."[29] Almost two years later, the Ninth Circuit remanded a case involving two Idaho death row inmates' First and Fourteenth Amendment claims involving the state's refusal to disclose which lethal injection drugs the inmates would receive. The court stated the inmates' "First Amendment claims appear squarely foreclosed by our caselaw." The law did not require the inmates to learn specifically which lethal injection drugs they would receive when they knew the range of drugs Idaho's execution protocol allowed.[30] In a similar case in Alabama, the Eleventh Circuit Court of Appeals held that the public enjoyed a common law right of access to the death-penalty protocol.[31]

Photographers stand away from police while photographing an officer holding down a protester during a Black Lives Matter protest in Boston in 2020.

Joseph Prezioso/AFP via Getty Images

The First Amendment does not provide a right to access all government property or proceedings nor does it protect the press or public against liability for violating rules of general applicability.[32] In 2021, the Seventh Circuit Court of Appeals ruled the governor of Wisconsin had not violated two journalists' First Amendment rights by excluding them from press conferences. Applying forum analysis (see Chapter 2), the court reasoned that press conferences were not public fora. Because the criteria applied to exclude some journalists were viewpoint neutral, meaning they were not based upon the journalists' views, the journalists' First Amendment rights were not violated, the court said.[33] Long-standing bans on the reporting of military troop locations and movements also withstand scrutiny as do policies on "pool reporting" and embedding reporters with the military.[34]

Access to Public and Quasi-Public Places

A complex array of statutes and court precedents establish protections for access to public and quasi-public spaces. Public sidewalks, public parks and some public properties constitute First

Amendment public forums established for public use, with some limitations (see Chapter 2). Government may restrict access to these to ensure the proper functioning of public services and to protect public safety. Accordingly, police and other public safety officials may order individuals, including journalists, to stay away from a crime scene or other event on public land or in public forums, but they may not apply policies in an arbitrary or discriminatory fashion. Police may arrest anyone who disobeys a lawful order and interferes with police functions.[35]

Recent court decisions turn on fact determinations of the nature of the location involved. Some government lands and buildings, such as military bases, prisons and polling sites, are not broadly open to the public. A representative case involved two separate arrests of individuals for photographing Customs and Border Protection (CBP) operations at the U.S.–Mexico border.[36] The plaintiffs argued that CBP policies ban photography from "large swaths" of public streets and sidewalks adjacent to border entry points. The Ninth Circuit Court of Appeals remanded the case to determine, among other things, whether CBP regulations violate First Amendment rights in traditional public forums.[37]

In 2020, a federal court granted a permanent injunction against a New York law applied to communications in traditional public forums, on public streets or sidewalks. The law deemed as a misdemeanor calling aloud, shouting or holding or displaying signs or placards about the conduct of a trial, character of a court or jury or calling for any action related to a trial within 200 feet of a courthouse. Although protecting the integrity of the judicial process and shielding trial participants from such influence were compelling interests, the law was not necessary to serve those interests, the court said.[38]

In 2022, the Second Circuit determined that New York law, which allowed any person protesting a trial within 200 feet of a courthouse to be held in criminal contempt, was facially valid and could pass strict scrutiny. The court, however, stated it was unconstitutional to apply that law to punish a person for protesting "the correct principles of the legal system, unconnected to any specific trial" in a non-intrusive and non-disruptive manner. Thus, the court vacated the injunction and remanded the case for the district court to enjoin enforcement of the law to punish any non-disruptive and non-intrusive protest not connected to a specific trial.[39]

When the Third Circuit Court of Appeals reviewed Pennsylvania's law requiring people to remain 10 feet away from polls unless voting, it saw the law as a limit on information gathering that could interfere with the primary purpose of the polling place. In reviewing both the logic and experience of public access to the polls, the Third Circuit said (1) openness might reduce voter fraud but also discourage some people from voting and (2) the secrecy of the ballot had increased through time. The court concluded that both elements supported the limit on public access to the polls.[40]

A recent federal district court ruling allowed the U.S. National Park Service to ban observers from the annual cull of buffalo from Yellowstone. The court reasoned that the culls historically had been closed to the public and closures were narrowly tailored to protect the safety of workers and the public. "Viewing the culling of bison is not protected First Amendment speech or activity." Even if it applied the First Amendment, the court said, it would find the park was a nonpublic forum and the ban was content-neutral.[41]

Some seemingly public property may at times be closed to the public. In one case, the Wisconsin Supreme Court upheld a photojournalist's conviction for disorderly conduct for circumventing a roadblock, then jumping a fence to take pictures of an airplane crash at a publicly owned airport. Officers had limited access to authorized personnel, but the journalist refused to leave or stop taking pictures. The court rejected the argument that the First Amendment requires news media access to emergency sites. Access was restricted, not denied, the court said, and journalists who followed the airport's media guidelines were taken to the crash site.[42]

Some of the estimated 900 bison culled from Yellowstone in 2015 awaiting slaughter in the Stephens Creek Capture Facility in Montana.

Jim Peaco (CC-BY-2)

The U.S. Court of Appeals for the District of Columbia has recognized a public interest in assuring that journalists are not excluded from covering the White House or its press conferences. The First Amendment interest in receiving a White House press pass is a liberty interest that cannot be denied without fair notice, as required under the Fifth Amendment. Decisions to not grant journalists press passes "must be based on compelling governmental interests," such as protecting the safety of the president.[43] Yet, in recent years, White House officials revoked multiple correspondents' hard passes, which provided access to the White House and its events. A federal district court enjoined the White House from revoking a CNN reporter's hard pass after he refused to yield a microphone during a press conference.[44] In 2020, the U.S. Court of Appeals for the District of Columbia reasoned the White House had to provide fair notice about conduct that could lead to suspending a journalist's hard pass.[45]

The nature of communication was central to a recent case addressing filming on land administered by the National Park Service. An independent filmmaker recently was charged with a misdemeanor for filming segments of a commercial film in the Colonial National Historic Park without obtaining a National Park Service permit or paying filming fees. In 2019, the filmmaker argued that the federal law requiring commercial filmmakers to seek a permit and pay fees to film in federal parks was unconstitutional. In 2021, a D.C. District Court judge determined the content-based regulations were unconstitutionally overbroad, as they were applied to traditional public forums and designated public forums. The judge issued an injunction that prohibited the National Park Service from enforcing the permit and fee requirements.[46]

Jim Acosta, CNN White House chief correspondent, returned to the White House after a federal judge ordered the White House to reinstate his hard pass.

Alex Wong/Getty Images News

In 2022, the D.C. Circuit Court of Appeals vacated the injunction and described the district court's reasoning as "flawed." The court recognized the First Amendment protects filmmaking, but "speech-protective rules of a public forum apply only to communicative activity." The court explained that filmmakers do not "seek to communicate with others" where they are filming scenes in parks; filmmakers engage in communicative activities to create speech. "There is no historical right of access to government property in order to create speech," the court stated.[47] Thus, the court assessed the regulation of commercial filmmaking as if it occurred in a nonpublic forum. The restrictions were deemed reasonable and viewpoint neutral, although the regulations do not require attaining permits or paying fees for "news-gathering activities."[48]

Right to Record

It generally is legal to record whatever can be viewed or heard on or from public property, but the recording of some events may be restricted under certain circumstances. In 2021, a North Carolina judge sentenced a newspaper editor to five days in jail after a journalist used an audio recorder during a murder trial, when recording was not allowed.[49] After a developer challenged a Tennessee township planning commission's refusal to allow video recording of a meeting, the Third Circuit Court of Appeals stated that forbidding video recording did not meaningfully restrict the developer's First Amendment right of access to a public meeting.[50]

When reporters previously challenged the Maryland Legislature's ban on recording legislative sessions, the state appeals court said that although newsgathering enjoys some First

Amendment protection, banning recorders does not infringe on that right.[51] It called the ban "a mere inconvenience."[52] Similar reasoning guides the U.S. Supreme Court, the federal court system and state judiciaries that continue to limit or prohibit cameras in courtrooms, as explained in Chapter 8.[53]

In recent years, conflicts with law enforcement over the right to record officers' actions have increased. Police have detained or arrested people recording anything from large public protests to traffic stops and confiscated or destroyed their footage. Most U.S. circuit courts of appeals have concluded that the First Amendment protects individuals from punishment for recording police activity in public.[54] But interpretations of such rights may vary by location and according to circumstances.

In 2021, the Tenth Circuit Court of Appeals declined to decide whether a citizen had a First Amendment right to record police in public spaces.[55] Identifying a split among circuits as to whether such a First Amendment right exists, the court stated a right to record police was not clearly established in 2014 when officers briefly detained and searched a man's tablet after the man lied about recording police officers using force during an arrest in Denver.[56]

In 2020, the First Circuit Court of Appeals recognized a limited First Amendment right to secret and nonconsensual recording of police officers carrying out their official duties in traditional public fora, including public parks, sidewalks and roadsides.[57] The right to record police performing their duties in public spaces could be restricted, however, if recording interferes with police duties. When the court previously reviewed the arrest of a woman who sat in her car and used her cellphone to film a traffic stop, the court said the First Amendment protected her right to peacefully and nondisruptively record public police activity.[58] Three years earlier, the court had ruled that the First Amendment requires police to justify an arrest for recording by showing that filming hindered performance of their duties.[59]

Applying similar reasoning, the Fifth Circuit Court of Appeals upheld charges against a man who refused repeated orders to stop recording police when recording interfered with performance of their duties.[60] The man was a member of a community group in Austin, Texas, dedicated to holding police officers accountable for misconduct. At two separate events the same evening, several officers told the man he was "interfering" with their official actions because he did not stay an arm's length away from them. He said he remained farther away than the required arm's length. The court, however, ruled that the officers were immune from liability for violating his First Amendment rights because he repeatedly disobeyed the officers' orders to step back.

Recent state court decisions have reached different conclusions about First Amendment rights concerning recording police or other public officials. The Supreme Court of Hawaii recently affirmed the MauiTime publisher's broad First Amendment and state constitutional rights to be protected from arrest for disorderly conduct and disobeying a police officer for filming traffic stops in public.[61] In 2020, however, the Court of Appeals of Georgia rejected a man's claims that a deputy sheriff arrested him for recording a dispute on private property when the man had a First Amendment right to record.[62] The court affirmed the deputy sheriff had qualified immunity at the time of the man's arrest for obstructing law enforcement when the man refused to leave despite the deputy's instructions to leave.

Photographers stay more than an arm's length away from police arresting a protester during a 2020 Black Lives Matter protest.

Timothy A. Clary/Getty Images

Government may impose limitations on filming, recording or photographing in public or private locations.[63] For example, a Pennsylvania court found a policy that forbade filming in the lobby and interior of a police station was narrowly tailored to serve important government interests, including ensuring "safety, security and privacy" of law enforcement, informants and crime victims.[64]

STATUTORY RIGHT OF ACCESS

In an 1822 letter addressing public education in Kentucky, James Madison articulated the need for people to receive information in a democratic society. "Knowledge will forever govern ignorance," he wrote, "and a people who mean to be their own governors must arm themselves with the power which knowledge gives."[65] Yet, the size and complexity of government did not prompt citizens to seek laws that require public access to records and proceedings until the 20th century. Legislators then developed laws that obligate government to open its business to the public.[66]

Today, two sets of laws—at both the federal and state levels—establish boundaries for public access to government meetings and records. (Access to judicial proceedings and records is addressed separately in Chapter 8.) Other statutes determine particular conditions under which recordings (audio or video) are permitted. The following provides an introduction to general principles and concepts advanced by these laws. Federal and state laws, however, differ in significant ways, and professional communicators should become familiar with the laws where they work.

Access to Federal Records

More than 55 years ago, Congress passed the **Freedom of Information Act**, a federal law that requires records held by federal government agencies be made available to the public, with the intention of allowing anyone access to records held by federal executive branch agencies.[67] The law established that "disclosure, not secrecy, is the dominant objective," according to the U.S. Supreme Court.[68] Exemptions and exclusions that allow government to withhold information must be interpreted narrowly to afford the greatest possible access. The Open Government Act of 2007 modified the law to clarify its exemptions,[69] to specify its application to electronic records[70] and to limit fees and response times.[71] The federal FOIA Improvement Act of 2016 mandates a "presumption of openness" that permits agencies to withhold records only if it is "reasonably foreseeable" that disclosure would harm one of the interests protected by FOIA's exemptions.[72] In a recent FOIA case, a federal district court admonished the General Services Administration for releasing emails but not their supporting attachments. The court said "GSA's blinkered literalism, distinguishing emails from email attachments, is at odds with the agency's 'duty to construe a FOIA request liberally.'"[73]

The language of FOIA provides access to "agency records," which raises two questions: (1) What is an agency? and (2) What is a record? Under the law, "agency" is defined as "any executive department, military department, government corporation, government-controlled corporation or other establishment in the executive branch of the government, including the Executive Office of the President or any independent regulatory agency." This includes all federal executive offices, such as the Office of Management and Budget.[74]

The law excludes the White House itself, including the president's closest advisers and their staffs. It also excludes Congress, the federal courts and the myriad of quasi-executive organizations that receive federal funding but are not under the direct control of the federal government—for example, the Corporation for Public Broadcasting.[75] Covered government entities include cabinet-level departments, such as Defense, Homeland Security and Justice; regulatory agencies, such as the Federal Communications Commission and the Securities and Exchange Commission; and others, such as NASA and the U.S. Postal Service.

The Lenexa Federal Records Center in Kansas is a major holding facility for federal government documents.

National Archives

Neither the text of FOIA nor its **legislative history**, Congressional reports and records of debate about proposed legislation, defines "record."[76] Courts have interpreted the act to apply to all tangible or fixed items that (a) document government actions and (b) may be reproduced. Thus, computer files, paper reports, films, videotapes, photographs and audio recordings are records under the law. A record already exists; it is not something government might compile.

While the definitions of agency and record are relatively clear, the criteria necessary to link an agency and a record for something to qualify as an "agency record" remain in dispute. The "statutory silence"[77] on the precise definition of covered agency records leaves courts to construe this key legal phrase.[78] "The use of the word agency as a modifier demonstrates that Congress contemplated some relationship between an agency and the record requested," the U.S. Supreme Court said.[79] In Senate hearings, the term "agency record" was assumed to include "all papers which an agency preserves in the performance of its functions."[80] The key is that the record pertains to the agency's functions.

In a decision shortly after the law's passage, a federal court of appeals ruled that a congressional transcript held by the CIA was not a covered agency record.[81] The agency's mere possession of a document did not transform it into an agency record.[82] Nonetheless, FOIA requests disclose a vast array of information. They have led government to release data related to NASA mishaps,[83] design deficiencies in the Hubble Space Telescope, dangers to local communities from nuclear weapons plants, hazardous lead levels in wines, misuse of government resources and emails exchanged between regulators and industries they regulate.[84]

POINTS OF LAW
RECORDS UNDER FOIA

In light of the Freedom of Information Act's unclear definition of agency record, courts have developed the following criteria:

- A record is anything in a fixed form (video, audio, digital or paper).
- An agency record must be part of the legitimate conduct of the agency's official duties.
- An agency record likely is any document created and possessed by the agency.
- A record possessed but not created by an agency may not be an agency record.
- An agency is not required to create a record that does not exist or to obtain a record not under agency control.

Requesting a record from a federal government agency is relatively easy. (Obtaining the record may not be.) FOIA requests may be made by telephone, email or mail. Agencies enjoy some discretion on whether to release records, so it may help to begin with a friendly telephone call to identify the record holder and perhaps obtain the records without further effort.[85] A written request helps record the date of the request, the precise records requested and the agency's responses, all of which are essential if you later sue the agency to obtain the records.

Requests should be as specific as possible because the agency has the option to charge for records searches or duplication fees at cost unless the agency waives fees. FOIA provides for fee waivers for news media and fee reductions for nonprofit organizations. Some records requesters, however, find requests for fee waivers may trigger lengthy delays. Many federal agency websites offer instructions on how to file FOIA requests. The Reporters Committee for Freedom of the Press also provides a useful online guide,[86] with an online FOIA letter generator[87] and step-by-step help with letter preparation.

Agencies have 20 working days, excluding weekends and holidays, to respond to FOIA requests. "Respond" does not mean comply, but the D.C. Circuit Court of Appeals held that the agency "must at least indicate within the relevant time period the scope of the documents it will produce and the exemptions it will claim with respect to any withheld documents."[88] Appeals may be filed for unreasonable delays, and denials may be challenged in federal court. Recent research found the number of FOIA lawsuits was increasing in part due to delayed responses to records requests.[89] One request for records from the National Archives and Records Administration was at least 25 years old in 2019.[90]

The law's presumption of access places the burden of proof on the agency to show why any delay or nondisclosure is valid. To prepare for potential appeals, it is important to keep track of the date on which a request is submitted, when responses are received, what responses are received and what records, if any, are released. It is also important to note which exemption, if any, is cited when records are not disclosed. The agency must cite the specific exemption that justifies nondisclosure and must limit nondisclosure to only those narrow portions of the requested records that qualify.

Within 90 days of receiving an agency denial of a records request, a requester may submit an appeal in writing.[91] The written appeal should explain why the requester disagrees with the denial and include information that supports that belief. After receiving the appeal, an agency has 20 working days to respond, and the agency may receive an additional 10 working days. If the agency still does not disclose the requested records, the requester may file a lawsuit. Individual reporters and news organizations filed almost 700 FOIA cases between 2001 and 2020.[92] More than half of those cases were filed during the Trump administration, with media filing 122 FOIA suits in 2020 alone.

A national security and cybersecurity reporter filed a FOIA lawsuit after the Central Intelligence Agency (CIA) declined to process his request for records "related to CIA use of poison for covert operations." The CIA responded that processing the request was beyond the agency's scope. The agency subsequently revised its policies to forbid not processing FOIA requests related to acts beyond the agency's "primary mission" and released some documents. The reporter, however, alleged the CIA had a pattern of refusing to process requests, "had not demonstrated the sufficiency of its searches" and had not sufficiently justified "its withholdings and redactions." A federal district court granted the CIA's motion for summary judgment and dismissed the case.[93]

In 2021, the U.S. Circuit Court of Appeals for the District of Columbia affirmed the district court's dismissal for several reasons.[94] A revised CIA policy had responded to the reporter's complaints about a previous pattern of refusing to process record requests deemed beyond the agency's primary mission. The CIA also had "sufficiently searched its operational files," the circuit court said. Providing a document that explained the locations searched and the terms subject matter experts used to find records demonstrated the CIA's search was "reasonably calculated to uncover all relevant documents."[95] Noting the U.S. Supreme Court previously held the National Security Information Act of 1947 allows the CIA to "exempt its operational files" from disclosure under FOIA,[96] the court accepted the CIA explanation it had performed a line-by-line review of records and released "all reasonably segregable, non-exempt information."[97]

Courts have allowed federal agencies essentially to say, "We don't have to tell you if we have the documents." This nonreply response is called a **"Glomar" response**, taken from the CIA's refusal to disclose whether it had information related to the rumored involvement of Howard Hughes' Glomar Explorer in U.S. attempts to recover a lost Soviet submarine. Some states followed the federal government's use of Glomar responses.[98] Requesters sometimes overcome a Glomar response by showing a federal official publicly acknowledged a record's existence. Buzzfeed used this approach to challenge a Glomar response to its request for data about U.S. payments to Syrian rebels after President Donald Trump tweeted about "payments to Syrian rebels." A district court considered that tweet an acknowledgement, but the U.S. Court of Appeals for the District of Columbia ruled in 2021 the tweet "was not an official acknowledgment of the existence" or nonexistence of CIA records.[99]

Almost 30 years ago, Congress passed the **Electronic Freedom of Information Act (EFOIA)**, a 1996 amendment to FOIA that applies the law to electronically stored information and extends FOIA to computer records.[100] The law established that computer searches to retrieve records do not constitute creation of a new record, a justification some agencies had used to deny access to electronic records. EFOIA requires agencies to deliver documents in "any form or format requested" that is "readily reproducible by the agency."[101]

EFOIA requires federal agencies to create a FOIA section on their websites and to provide "electronic reading rooms" filled with online copies of records, policy statements, administrative opinions and general indexes of frequently sought documents.[102] The law does not define general index. In 2020, the Fourth Circuit Court of Appeals was not persuaded that an index of permits and applications created pursuant to the Endangered Species Act was insufficient due to organization by animal species.[103] EFOIA encourages agencies to provide expedited access to records when the requester can demonstrate a compelling safety or public interest need for rapid access. Following EFOIA, many states adopted specific provisions to ensure and improve electronic access to state records.[104]

REAL WORLD LAW

SAMPLE FOIA REQUEST LETTER[105]

Agency Head [or Freedom of Information Act Officer]

Name of Agency

Address of Agency

City, State, Zip Code

Re: Freedom of Information Act Request

Date

Dear _____ :

This is a request under the Freedom of Information Act.

I request that a copy of the following documents [or documents containing the following information] be provided to me: [identify the documents or information as specifically as possible].

In order to help to determine my status to assess fees, you should know that I am [insert a suitable description of the requester and the purpose of the request].

[Sample requester descriptions:

1. a representative of the news media affiliated with the _____ [newspaper, magazine, television station, etc.], and this request is made as part of newsgathering and not for a commercial use.
2. affiliated with an educational, nonprofit or noncommercial scientific institution, and this request is made for a scholarly, public service or scientific purpose and not for a commercial use.
3. an individual seeking information for personal use and not for a commercial use.
4. affiliated with a private corporation and am seeking information for use in the company's business.]

[Optional] I am willing to pay fees for this request up to a maximum of $_____. If you estimate that the fees will exceed this limit, please inform me prior to providing copies of the requested records.

[Optional] I request a waiver of all fees for this request. Disclosure of the requested information is in the public interest because it is likely to contribute significantly to public understanding of the operations or activities of the government and is not primarily in my commercial interest. [Include a specific explanation.]

Thank you for your consideration of this request.

Sincerely,

Name

Address

City, State, Zip Code

Telephone number [Optional]

Access to State Records

Each state and the District of Columbia has an access-to-information/open records statute. Some follow the model of FOIA; others look very different. In Texas, for example, a state agency has only 10 days to comply with a request.[106] The tradition of state open records is deeper in some states than the federal tradition. As early as 1849, Wisconsin provided for inspection of public records. State open-records laws tend to be intended to promote government accountability. Illinois links the right of access to enabling "people to fulfill their duties of discussing public issues fully and freely" and making "informed political judgments."[107]

Because there is so much state-to-state variation in open-records laws, sometimes called **freedom of information laws** (FOILs), characterizing them broadly is virtually impossible. Even those that appear similar may differ in their details. Generally speaking, however, some observations are helpful:

- State agencies are not required to create or acquire records in response to a request.
- Few states require agencies to produce record indexes.
- Some states require that requesters be state residents.

- Many states have exemptions similar to those of FOIA.

- Most state open-records laws cover electronic and computer-stored records, but some states do not require that records be transformed into a user-friendly format.

- Some state open-records laws cover the legislature, executive branch and courts.

- Some state laws do not specify response time limits. Delays can be lengthy.

- Some states do not specify penalties for agencies violating their open-records laws.

State open-records laws apply not only to state government agencies and departments but also to cities, school districts and other state authorities. The law in Tennessee covers "all documents, papers, letters, maps, books, photographs, microfilms, electronic data processing files and output, films, sound recordings, or other material, regardless of physical form or characteristics made or received pursuant to law or ordinance or in connection with the transaction of official business by any governmental agency."[108]

Courts recently have considered when electronic or text messages are public records. To determine whether a retired university professor's email messages were subject to release as public records in 2021, the Supreme Court of Vermont focused on the content of messages and the circumstances under which they were created. Although the professor used University of Vermont email to correspond with people affiliated with academic journals and committees, the court reasoned the messages "were not produced or acquired in the course of public agency business." The state's open records law was designed to "shed light on government business, not on the personal endeavors of state employees."[109]

A question raised in one case was whether hidden **metadata**, a set of data that describes and gives information about data, that record the creation date, authorship and edit history of a digital file were a public record.[110] The case began when a Phoenix police officer sought the metadata because he suspected information had been altered in city records he received in response to a records request. The city argued that metadata were not part of the record and therefore not subject to the state open-records law. The Arizona Supreme Court disagreed, ruling that metadata are "part of the underlying document; [meta information] does not stand on its own."[111]

A growing number of states have ruled that government employees cannot avoid disclosure under state open-records laws by using personal accounts or devices to conduct the public's business.[112] When a nonprofit watchdog organization sought access to city officials' text and email messages relevant to lead in the Chicago Public Schools' drinking water, an Illinois appellate court found those communications via personal text and email accounts were public records.[113] To be a public record, the record "must pertain to public business" and have been prepared by or for a public body, used by a public body, received or possessed by a public body or controlled by a public body. Many officials' communications from public officials' personal accounts related to public business are prepared for or used by a public body, thus the court found such communications may be deemed "public records subject to FOIA."

Timely response and effective enforcement of open-records laws are important. In 2021, an Alabama state senate committee approved a bill to introduce a 14-day response period for agencies to provide or deny requested records and limit duplication fees.[114] In 2019, Nevada amended its public records law to include tougher fines and penalties for agencies that did not provide access to public records in a timely manner or at all.[115] Almost two-thirds of U.S. states and the District of Columbia provide civil and/or criminal sanctions for failure to comply with records requests.[116] In 2020, the Pennsylvania Supreme Court found the state had to pay more than $118,000 in legal fees for the department of corrections acting in bad faith by not acting "with diligence" in response to a request for records related to illnesses of inmates and staff.[117]

Some records requesters have fought against excessive fees or **reverse FOI lawsuits**, cases against public records requesters.[118] In 2021, the Supreme Court of Missouri declared the state's open records law allowed charging fees for time spent fulfilling records requests, but a lawyer seeking records about election contributions would not have to pay more than $3,000 for a government attorney to review and redact information from requested records.[119] After a newspaper reporter sought copies of sexual harassment complaints against a Louisiana department of justice employee in 2021, the state attorney general sought a court order declaring the requested record exempt from disclosure and requiring the requester to pay legal fees.[120] A judge determined the records must be released and required the attorney general's office to pay the journalist and her employer more than $5,000 in attorney's fees.[121]

Access to Federal and State Meetings

During meetings, government officials make important decisions that affect finances, safety and well-being of citizens. They enact laws, amend budgets, declare where structures may be constructed, consider what could protect drinking water and determine how much college students will have to pay for their education. Citizens and journalists expect to attend government meetings to learn about deliberations and decisions. The foundational law establishing public access to federal government meetings is the **Government in the Sunshine Act**—also known as the "Federal Open Meetings Law"—that was passed almost 50 years ago.[122] Because the processes of meetings as well as their results are of legitimate public interest, the act requires the 50 or so federal executive branch agencies, commissions and boards to conduct their business in public. To fall under the law, the boards or agencies must exercise independent authority and have members appointed by the president. The law requires them to give advance public notice of their meetings, to make most decisions in public and to record decisions. Their deliberations may be closed under certain circumstances, such as when addressing classified information.

Approximately 1,000 advisory boards provide expert guidance to the federal government, but are not covered by the Government in the Sunshine Act because they have no independent authority. The Federal Advisory Committee Act opens their meetings and records to the public unless the committee is "composed wholly of full-time officers or employees of the federal government."[123]

All states and the District of Columbia have laws or constitutional provisions ensuring some degree of public access to government meetings.[124] The laws vary widely, as do the penalties for violating them. In general, open-meetings laws trigger public access whenever a quorum of a decision-making body deliberates public business. The laws permit attendance but do not require public participation. Boards may meet the need for public access either through space in their meeting room or through electronic access, such as by posting a recording online.

Members of the press record a Miami, Fla., Board of Education meeting in 2021.

Jeffrey Isaac Greenberg/Alamy

Most state laws define a meeting as either a physical gathering or a videoconference that allows members to interact in real time. Most state laws require agencies to provide public notice in advance of meetings and to record minutes of their business. In 2021, the Supreme Court of Ohio found a county solid waste management board had "a duty to maintain a full and accurate record of its proceedings," which was not fulfilled when an exhibit referenced in the minutes was not attached to the minutes.[125] A few states also require boards to keep minutes of their executive (closed, nonvoting) sessions, which become available to the public if closure is improper or once the need for closure has passed.[126]

Courts and legislators recently have addressed the importance of providing citizens with clear notice about what discussions and actions are planned for public meetings. In 2021, the Supreme Court of Oklahoma found the city of Norman violated the state open meeting law by releasing a meeting agenda that did not notify the public the council would discuss and take actions on the city budget. Finding a meeting agenda "was deceptively vague and likely to mislead," the court said the city violated the state open meetings law.[127] Pennsylvania amended its open meetings law in 2021 to require meeting agendas for school district boards of directors be posted online at least a day before each meeting and available to people attending a meeting. The changes also forbid school boards from acting on business not included in public notifications, except under circumstances such as emergencies.[128]

Most state open-meetings laws are applied to allow nondisruptive audio or video recordings of public meetings.[129] For example statutes in Hawaii, Iowa and Utah allow recording that does not interfere with open meetings.[130] Attorney general advisory opinions in Kentucky and Ohio also have stated people may record public meetings in nondisruptive manners.[131] Court rulings in New York similarly recognize a right to record, but some states have no express guarantee for the right to record.[132] It is important to check local rules.

POINTS OF LAW

STATE OPEN-MEETINGS LAWS: THE WYOMING EXAMPLE

The following is excerpted from the Wyoming Open Meetings Law's section on opening meetings:

> (a) All meetings of the government body of an agency are public meetings, open to the public at all times, except as otherwise provided. No action of a government body of an agency shall be taken except during a public meeting following notice of the meeting in accordance with this act. Action taken at a meeting not in conformity with this act is null and void and not merely voidable. . . . (d) No meeting shall be conducted by electronic means or any other form of communication that does not permit the public to hear, read or otherwise discern meeting discussion contemporaneously. Communications outside a meeting, including, but not limited to, sequential communications among members of an agency, shall not be used to circumvent the purpose of this act.[133]

Several states outline provisions for the enforcement of open-meetings laws. In Michigan, any citizen may challenge in court a public body's decision to deny access. If the court determines that the closure violated the law, the court can invalidate that decision and any actions taken during the closure. In addition, a public official who intentionally breaks the law may be subject to a fine up to $1,000 as well as an award of $500 damages plus court costs and attorney fees due to a person who challenges a closure. A second deliberate violation can result in a fine up to $2,000, a jail term of up to one year or both.[134] A recent Minnesota Supreme Court opinion stated public officials who intentionally violate the state open meetings law in three separate and sequential instances may lose their right to serve the rest of their term.[135]

Under some circumstances, people may be forbidden to attend public meetings due to disruptive behavior. In 2021, the Eleventh Circuit Court of Appeals found the Atlanta Independent School System permissibly applied content-neutral policies to prevent a citizen from attending public meetings. The citizen was suspended from meetings for a year due to disruptive conduct, including directing "abusive," "hate-filled" and "racially-charged" comments toward board members during a meeting, the court said.[136] A Ninth Circuit Court of Appeals ruling, however, struck down an overbroad California city ordinance that permitted a city council to evict members of the public from its meetings for "disorderly, insolent or disruptive behavior." The court said the ordinance permitted the council to expel citizens who were "impertinent, insolent or essentially offensive" but not disruptive.[137]

Members of the public attend a Lake County, Fla., School Board meeting that addressed whether to require face masks be worn in schools in 2021.

Sipa USA via AP

Face-to-Face and Participant Recording

The record of events and conversations created by audio and video recording is a staple of much professional communication. Recording audio or video with plainly visible equipment where there is no reasonable expectation of privacy generally does not violate state or federal laws. Both federal law and the Federal Communications Commission have authority over telephone calls that cross state lines. Federal law allows recording conversations with one-participant's consent.[138]

The U.S. Congress and most states regulate recordings of telephone calls or conversations through statutes meant to prohibit eavesdropping, wiretapping and telephone interception to protect privacy interests (see Chapter 6). The federal anti-wiretapping statute prevents third-party recording of oral or electronic communication when no participant has consented.[139] Some states require notice and consent of all parties, but 38 states and the District of Columbia allow recording with one-party consent when the person doing the recording has consented and is a participant in the recorded conversation.[140] Eleven states are all-party states that require all participants in a conversation to give consent prior to starting recording.[141] In Connecticut, criminal law requires one-party consent for recording a private telephone conversation, but civil law requires all parties to consent in writing or at the start of a recording.[142]

Vermont is the only state without a law specifically addressing audio or video recording of conversations, but the state's highest court has held that hidden recordings of communications in a home violates personal privacy.[143] The court ruled in another case that recording a conversation in a parking lot "subject to the eyes and ears of passersby" is legal.[144]

In general, the law in the location of the recording device applies. Because this is not universally true, it is wise to follow the strictest of the laws that might apply. In one recent case, the

California Supreme Court held that a Georgia company that routinely recorded business calls with clients in California must comply with California's stricter statute. Georgia allows recording with one-party consent. California requires all parties to agree, and the court said application of the stricter law protected "the degree of privacy afforded to California residents" without unduly harming any Georgia interests.[145]

A recent Maryland appellate court ruling found the state wiretap statute applied to a mother's use of a smartphone app to secretly record her child discussing sexual abuse in a face-to-face conversation. The conversation occurred in a private residence and addressed an intimate topic; the recording fell under the statute's prohibition of surreptitious recording of private conversations. "The ease and popularity of cell phone recordings does not suspend the protections afforded by the statute," the court said.[146]

The FCC requires broadcasters to notify callers if the station intends to broadcast a call live or record the call for later broadcast. Consent is not necessary, only notification. There is an exception for programs that customarily air calls live or broadcast recorded calls, such as radio call-in shows. These callers have a reasonable expectation that their conversations will be aired or recorded.[147]

In *Bartnicki v. Vopper*, the U.S. Supreme Court ruled that the First Amendment allows media to use an illegal recording so long as they were not involved in its production. The case involved a third-party surreptitious recording of a phone conversation between two teachers' union negotiators about a difficult collective bargaining agreement. One negotiator said, "[W]e're gonna have to go to their, their homes . . . [t]o blow off their front porches; we'll have to do some work on some of those guys."[148] Local radio stations played the tape, and newspapers printed its contents. The negotiator sued, arguing that the media intentionally "disclosed" a private exchange they should have known was obtained in violation of the federal wiretap law. The media claimed the First Amendment allowed the use of the taped discussion of matters of significant concern because journalists were not involved in the wiretapping.[149]

The Supreme Court agreed with the media. The First Amendment protects a journalist who shares or reports on illegally intercepted private conversations when the conversation is newsworthy and the journalist was not involved in the interception. The Court said the media were protected because they (1) played no part in the illegal interception, (2) had lawful access to the information on the tapes and (3) correctly judged the conversation to be of public concern.[150]

The Court held that the ban on disclosure of illegally intercepted communications failed to serve the government's alleged compelling interest of dissuading people from intercepting private communications. The Court said the government's important interest in minimizing harm to private callers by discouraging distribution of illegally intercepted calls was outweighed by the need to inform people of matters of public interest. "[A] stranger's illegal conduct does not suffice to remove the First Amendment shield from speech about a matter of public concern,"[151] the Court concluded.

Under federal and some state laws, a recording made to commit a crime or a tort is illegal regardless of who consents. In 2020, a federal judge issued a permanent injunction against anti-abortion activists who went undercover to create gotcha videos of Planned Parenthood Federation representatives in Washington, D.C., and multiple states. Activists misrepresented their professional affiliations to attend conferences and meetings where they created secret recordings,[152] and the court determined that conduct violated federal recording laws. The court stated activists conspired to violate Maryland's recording law,[153] which says it is illegal to record communication "for the purpose of committing any criminal or tortious act,"[154] and violated a Florida law that makes it unlawful to record when a person has a reasonable expectation of privacy. Claiming an injunction would hinder journalistic efforts and attempts to oppose abortion did not provide the activists with a license to engage in illegal recording, the judge said.[155] The court awarded $2.425 million in damages for violating wiretapping, trespass, fraud and other laws.[156]

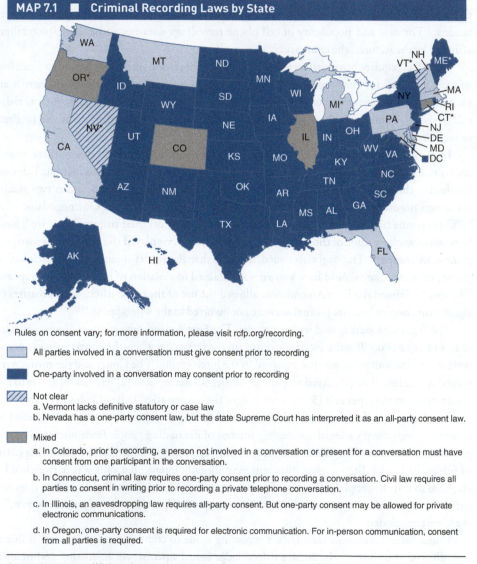

MAP 7.1 ■ Criminal Recording Laws by State

* Rules on consent vary; for more information, please visit rcfp.org/recording.

All parties involved in a conversation must give consent prior to recording

One-party involved in a conversation may consent prior to recording

Not clear
a. Vermont lacks definitive statutory or case law
b. Nevada has a one-party consent law, but the state Supreme Court has interpreted it as an all-party consent law.

Mixed

a. In Colorado, prior to recording, a person not involved in a conversation or present for a conversation must have consent from one participant in the conversation.

b. In Connecticut, criminal law requires one-party consent prior to recording a conversation. Civil law requires all parties to consent in writing prior to recording a private telephone conversation.

c. In Illinois, an eavesdropping law requires all-party consent. But one-party consent may be allowed for private electronic communications.

d. In Oregon, one-party consent is required for electronic communication. For in-person communication, consent from all parties is required.

Source: Matthiesen, Wickert & Lehrer, S.C., *Recording Conversations in All 50 States Law*, www.mwl-law.com /wp-content/uploads/2018/02/RECORDING-CONVERSATIONS-CHART.pdf.

In 2022, the Ninth Circuit Court of Appeals reversed the jury's verdict that the activists had violated the Federal Wiretap Act, but affirmed findings and awards of damages for violations of other laws. Planned Parenthood argued the activists were civilly violating the **Racketeer Influenced and Corrupt Organizations Act** (RICO),[157] a federal law that addresses patterns of serious illegal activity connected to an enterprise that affects interstate or foreign commerce,[158] by trying to harm and destroy the organization through secretly recording conferences and meetings. The court found that a civil RICO violation was not sufficient for the activists to be liable for violating the federal wiretap statute. The federal wiretap law prohibits intentionally recording oral communication in which one participates when the communication "is intercepted for the purpose of committing" any further crime or tort. The court explained that means making the recording "for the purpose of facilitating some further impropriety" that is "separate and independent" from making the recording.[159]

POINTS OF LAW
MEDIA DISTRIBUTION OF ILLEGALLY INTERCEPTED CALLS

Under the U.S. Supreme Court's ruling in *Bartnicki v. Vopper*, the First Amendment protects media from liability for truthfully distributing illegally intercepted communications when
- the media had no involvement in the interception,
- the media gained access to the intercepted calls legally and
- the content of the intercepted calls relates to matters of public concern. [160]

Some state laws on recording are complicated. In Delaware, for example, both civil and criminal statutes apply.[161] State privacy law requires all parties to consent to recording, but a federal district court applied the law years ago to find that individuals have a right to record their own conversations.[162] Delaware criminal law makes it a felony to "intercept" a call without consent from all parties unless you are a participant or have received prior permission to record. In Illinois, the state supreme court recently found the state's law was unconstitutionally overbroad because it made it a crime to record any conversation without everyone's permission. Subsequent amendments to the law distinguished recording of private and public communications and applied criminal penalties only to recording "in a surreptitious manner."[163]

STATUTORY LIMITS TO ACCESS

Statutes at the federal and state levels both guarantee and prohibit access to property, government records and meetings. Physical access to private property is circumscribed by common law, the Constitution and state statutes and rulings. Distinct rules apply to specific types of records and to the means of obtaining or recording information. Professional communicators should be familiar with this complex of laws but need to recognize that many are in nearly constant flux. Thus, when concerned about legal limits, it might be wise to seek expert legal advice.

Trespass and Ag-Gag Laws

Permission to enter private property may be given or denied only by the owner or the resident, who may not be the owner. Entering private property without permission is **trespass**.[164] The law against trespass is generally applicable to all people; no one may trespass. Law enforcement officials with a search warrant or exercising emergency control over property are authorized to enter without permission, but that authority does not extend to others.

The media **ride-along**—in which media representatives accompany government officials to various scenes—has provided material for news and entertainment as well as law enforcement public relations campaigns. When police operations occur on private property, however, residents' Fourth Amendment protection against unreasonable searches and unreasonable intrusion or trespass on their privacy comes into play. Some courts have held that the silence of the property owner implies consent, especially if the events are newsworthy; other courts disagree.[165] Rulings that balance residents' right to be free from intrusion against the media's First Amendment rights to gather information generally curtail media access to private property.

In *Hanlon v. Berger*, the U.S. Supreme Court addressed U.S. Fish and Wildlife Service agents' search of a Montana ranch while carrying CNN cameras and microphones without the residents' knowledge.[166] Officials suspected the family had shot or poisoned eagles, violating federal wildlife laws.[167] The family sued for intrusion, and the Supreme Court said a jury should decide the case. CNN was not protected by the agents' privilege because the recording was not intended to aid law enforcement, the Court said. The case was settled out of court.[168]

In *Wilson v. Layne*, the Supreme Court dealt a blow to ride-alongs. Law enforcement officers with a search warrant allowed a Washington Post photographer to accompany their early morning raid of a private home to arrest a fugitive. The photographer took pictures as officers wrestled a man to the floor and a woman emerged from the bedroom. The pair were the parents of the fugitive, who was not at home. None of the photos were published. The couple sued on the grounds that the presence of journalists violated their Fourth Amendment protection. The U.S. Supreme Court agreed.[169]

A warrant entitles officers to enter the home but does not authorize those officers to invite civilians along, the Court said. The presence of reporters was unrelated to the warrant's purpose and the limited intrusion it allowed. Any benefits ride-alongs provided to suspects or law enforcement activities were too far removed from the warrant's objective to override the residents' Fourth Amendment rights. The decision established that it generally violates the Fourth Amendment for civilians to accompany officials into a home during the execution of a warrant unless they are there to help execute the warrant.[170] Third parties, including media representatives, have greater leeway to accompany police on public property, but they are not immune from liability even in those circumstances.[171]

POINTS OF LAW

WILSON V. LAYNE[172]: THE STATE OF RIDE-ALONGS

- A search warrant entitles officers, but not reporters, to enter a home.
- The presence of reporters is unrelated to the authorized intrusion.
- The presence of reporters serves no legitimate law enforcement purposes.
- Inviting reporters for the execution of a search warrant violates the Fourth Amendment.

Following remand from the Tenth Circuit Court of Appeals, a federal district court recently reversed itself and struck down revisions to Wyoming trespass laws that made it a crime to enter private or public "open land" without permission to gather "resource data" on land and water use.[173] The laws targeted environmental and animal groups seeking to "unlawfully collect resource data," such as water samples, to test E. coli contamination from cattle waste runoff. The Tenth Circuit drew a parallel to right-to-record-in-public cases and reasoned that "collection of resource data constitutes the protected creation of speech."[174]

Certain properties also may be protected by laws specifically limiting recording. A man recently wore a body camera to city hall in Punta Gorda, Fla., to test an ordinance forbidding video and sound recording without consent of persons being recorded in city hall and the city hall annex.[175] A police officer warned him he was trespassing and could not return to either government building for a year. The man filed a complaint and sought an injunction on First and Fourteenth Amendment grounds. A federal district court in Florida found the ordinance reasonable and not viewpoint discriminatory. The court reasoned that government may "exercise control over access to the [government] workplace in order to avoid interruptions to the performance of the duties of its employees."[176]

Under some circumstances, consent to record may be revoked. For example, although a citizen-journalist initially received a property owner's permission to record a political rally on a pumpkin farm, an event organizer, property owner and law enforcement officer told her to stop filming or leave. She continued filming and remained at the rally. She was charged and convicted of misdemeanor obstruction of an officer. In 2020, an appellate court upheld her conviction.[177]

State **"ag-gag" laws** prohibit recording, photographing or entering agricultural facilities to document animal abuse or other activity without the owners' informed permission. In recent years, nonprofit animal protection and food safety organizations have challenged ag-gag laws in Arkansas, Idaho, Iowa, Kansas, North Carolina and Utah.[178] In 2020, a federal district court found unconstitutional the Kansas ag-gag law provisions forbidding any person from accessing an animal facility to take pictures with intent to damage the facility's business. "The Supreme Court has held that creation and dissemination of information are speech, and this includes videos, photographs and recordings," the court said.[179] The court enjoined Kansas from applying those content-based viewpoint-discriminatory parts of its ag-gag law that could not pass strict scrutiny.[180] In 2021, the Tenth Circuit Court of Appeals affirmed the injunction and found several sections of the Kansas law violated the First Amendment.[181]

Whereas other state ag-gag laws have allowed criminal liability for undercover investigations, North Carolina's law has allowed civil claims that seek a $5,000 per day penalty and attorneys' fees. A federal court recently found unconstitutional provisions that allowed plaintiffs to recover damages for harm resulting from recording images or data. The court reasoned that other courts had "recognized recording as either expressive conduct warranting First Amendment protection" or "conduct essentially preparatory to speech." Thus, recording may be protected by the First Amendment, and the provisions targeting recording could not survive constitutional scrutiny.[182]

In one high-profile arrest, internationally renowned photojournalist George Steinmetz was charged with trespassing after paragliding to photograph a cattle feedlot in Kansas.[183] He was on assignment for National Geographic magazine. "It was quite a surprise to me," Steinmetz said. "I've been detained in Iran and Yemen, and questioned about spying, but never arrested. And then I get thrown in jail in America."[184]

George Steinmetz's paragliding photograph of Brookover Ranch Feed Yard and adjacent crop circles in Garden City, Kan.

George Steinmetz

A 2021 Eighth Circuit Court of Appeals opinion evaluated an Iowa law that forbade using false pretenses or submitting false information on an employment application to access agricultural production facilities.[185] The court reasoned the first "provision is consistent with the First Amendment because it prohibits exclusively lies associated with a legally cognizable harm—namely, trespass to private property."[186] The court said the second provision was too broad to survive strict scrutiny. Noting that some people associate investigative journalism with using false pretenses to gain access to places, a concurring opinion stated the Supreme Court ultimately "will have to determine whether such laws can be sustained, or whether they infringe on the breathing room necessary to effectuate the promise of the First Amendment."[187] In 2022, a federal trial court temporarily enjoined the state from punishing individuals who trespassed by using deception to enter a farm to cause harm.[188]

Drone Laws

Federal Aviation Administration rules governing the use of drones allow drone flights over people or moving vehicles and at night under specific conditions. As of 2021, each drone operator must register a drone, obtain a remote pilot certificate and have proof of registration and certification available when operating a drone. To have a drone hover, fly back and forth or circle above an assembly of people, pilots must make sure their drones have remote identification capabilities, are properly maintained and are safe to fly over people. To fly over moving vehicles, the drone also must be in a closed or restricted-access area where people have been notified a drone may fly over them. For any night flight, a drone also must have operational anti-collision lighting and be operated by a pilot with night-flight training.[189]

Drones are not allowed everywhere. For instance, they are prohibited in and above national parks.[190] Drone operators must receive FAA permission to fly drones within 15 miles of the District of Columbia. They also cannot "interfere with operations and traffic patterns at any airport, heliport, or seaplane base." Operators should use the B4UFLY app, Skyvector website and FAA UAS Data to check airspace restrictions prior to launching a drone. Subject to FAA restrictions, noncommercial drone photographers and news operations generally may capture photographs and video from drones. Commercial operators—including photographers, videographers and public relations and advertising professionals—must be registered with the FAA and apply for FAA exemptions to photograph and to fly in controlled airspace.[191]

The FAA recently sought a $182,000 fine from a person without remote pilot certification accused of violating multiple FAA regulations. The pilot's YouTube videos were used as evidence that the drone was flown in controlled airspace without authorization, during times of low visibility, close to buildings and over people and moving vehicles around Philadelphia in 2019 and 2020.[192]

Many state and municipal laws impose additional limits on drone photography.[193] A 2021 national legislative roundup identified 44 states with laws addressing the use of drones.[194] These laws vary dramatically in their breadth and focus. Idaho generally prohibits using a drone to photograph or record any person or "for the purpose of publishing or otherwise publicly disseminating such photograph or recording" without an individual's permission.[195] Texas made drone photography for surveillance of any person or private property a misdemeanor,[196] but in 2022 a federal court held the Texas law's surveillance provisions were unconstitutionally overbroad and vague limitations on expression.[197]

In 2019, a national organization advocated that states revise trespass and intrusion statutes to incorporate drones.[198] Wisconsin was the first state to make it a misdemeanor to use a drone to record another person where the person has a reasonable expectation of privacy.[199] Flying a drone at a low height over private property may be considered trespassing in Oregon, Nevada and Virginia if an operator previously was notified not to fly over that property.[200] Some state trespass laws also apply to flying a drone over critical infrastructure, such as a petroleum refinery, chemical storage facility, railroad yard or portal, prison facility or drinking water treatment and storage plant.[201] Texas also deemed as a misdemeanor flying a drone at less than 400 feet over a correctional facility, detention facility or critical infrastructure facility in addition to a sports venue with seating capacity of 30,000 or more without a contract or consent from the venue.[202] In 2022, a federal court held those no-fly provisions in Texas were unconstitutionally overbroad.[203]

A drone flies over Manhattan.

Buena Vista Images

Exemptions to Open Records

Federal agencies are not compelled to hand over every record requested under the Freedom of Information Act. Although the law presumes public access to records, nine FOIA exemptions permit agencies to refuse to disclose specific types of information. The law requires agencies to interpret the exemptions narrowly and to limit withholding only those sections of records covered by an exemption. Record keepers are required to **redact**, which means to strike out, the covered portions of records rather than withhold the record in its entirety. Agencies judge what must be withheld and often exercise their discretion in favor of nondisclosure.

When an agency denies all or part of a FOIA request, the law requires the agency to explain why the record falls under one or more specific exemptions. Presidential elections and major events often trigger shifts in policies directing how agencies respond to FOIA requests. Shortly after the Sept. 11, 2001, terrorist attacks, for example, a memo from the U.S. attorney general encouraged federal agencies to withhold records whenever a "sound legal basis" might justify secrecy under one or more exemptions.[204] Another post–9/11 development was the passage of the Homeland Security Act, which provides broad exemptions from FOIA disclosure for information related to critical infrastructure, including bridges, dams and computer systems.[205]

Each of FOIA's nine exemptions and agency interpretations of them that have generated court challenges are discussed in the following section. In 2019, the U.S. Supreme Court decision in *Kisor v. Wilkie* said courts should exercise increased, independent review of executive agencies' interpretations of their own rules.[206] Observers argued that the ruling might also signal the end of deference to executive agency interpretations of applicable federal laws.[207]

POINTS OF LAW

THE FREEDOM OF INFORMATION ACT EXEMPTIONS

1. National security
2. Internal agency rules and procedures
3. Disclosures forbidden by other statutes
4. Trade secrets
5. Agency memoranda
6. Personal privacy
7. Law enforcement records
8. Financial records
9. Geological data

Exemption 1: National Security

Records fall under the exemption of national security if they are classified as confidential, secret or top secret. Members of the executive branch use each classification to reflect the rising sensitivity of the information and the potential for harm if released.[208] Records requests denied on the basis of this exemption have been the most difficult to overturn.

FOIA empowers judges to determine whether information was properly classified as a potential threat to national security. Typically, judges rule in favor of classification. The U.S. Supreme Court, for example, referred to the exemption as the "keystone of a congressional scheme that balances deference to the executive's interest in maintaining secrecy with continued judicial and congressional oversight."[209] Even when information is widely known, such as the CIA's use of waterboarding and other "enhanced interrogation techniques [of military detainees], an agency may refuse a FOIA request on the basis of national security," the Second Circuit Court of Appeals ruled.[210]

A law firm recently filed FOIA requests for military investigation records from the U.S. Central Command (CENTCOM) to confirm the types of explosives used in terrorist attacks that killed or injured U.S. servicemembers between 2004 and 2011 in Iraq. The firm sued after CENTCOM provided access to 7,749 pages of documents with redactions on almost 900 pages. A district court considered logical or plausible the CENTCOM Chief of Staff's statement that disclosing photographs revealing "penetration of armor" would disclose "vulnerabilities of American war-fighting equipment." Because the U.S. Army Central Command previously had released that precise type of detail, the court reasoned Exemption 1 had been waived, requiring CENTCOM to disclose images revealing similar information.[211]

In 2020, the Second Circuit Court of Appeals reversed the district court's opinion.[212] The court determined there was no substantial difference between information from terrorist attacks the Army previously released, but images the Army disclosed from one attack did not match images sought from other attacks. The court found logical and plausible the CENTCOM Chief of Staff's assessment that disclosing "a substantial number of images could pose significantly greater risk to national security than disclosure of just a handful." Following the court's tendency to defer to agency determinations of potential national security threats, the court found withholding more than 500 pages with images was appropriate.[213]

Exemption 2: Internal Agency Rules and Procedures

The exemption related to internal agency rules is a "housekeeping" exemption. It covers records related exclusively to the practices of the agency itself: vacation policies, lunch break rules, parking space assignments and so on. Its purpose is not so much to prevent any harm from disclosure but to eliminate the time and expense of retrieving these mundane records. The exemption also covers any internal policy that might be used inappropriately. For example, break or shift change procedures used by federal prison guards could conceivably be used to breach facility security.

This exemption cannot be used to conceal all agency practices. If an agency policy or procedure is of public concern and its disclosure would not undermine agency regulations, a court could rule that related records do not qualify for Exemption 2 and order their release. In a case seeking records related to Air Force Academy honor and ethics hearings, the U.S. Supreme Court said, "[T]he general thrust of the exemption is simply to relieve agencies of the burden of assembling and maintaining for public inspection matters in which the public could not reasonably be expected to have an interest."[214]

In another decision, the Court ruled that Exemption 2 applies only to human resource and "employee relations" records, not to other records an agency might possess. Therefore, the Court said, the U.S. Navy could not use Exemption 2 to reject a FOIA request for information about explosives at a naval base in Puget Sound, Wash. The location of the munitions is unrelated to employee records.[215]

Exemption 3: Disclosures Forbidden by Other Statutes

This exemption stipulates that FOIA cannot override other laws that forbid the disclosure of certain information. When litigation surfaces related to this exemption, courts usually require the government to show that (1) the information being sought falls within the scope of the statute being cited and (2) the statute grants no discretionary authority to the government agency holding the information (i.e., the nondisclosure is mandatory). If those standards are met, the decision to withhold records generally is upheld.

In 2021, the Court of Appeals for the District of Columbia held that Exemption 3 and the Child Victims Act applied to an agency denial of a request seeking demographics of sex trafficking defendants and victims as well as records related to a man's own sex trafficking of a minor and possession of child pornography cases.[216] The Executive Office for U.S. Attorneys released some records, but cited Exemption 3 and the Child Victims Act to withhold over 300 pages that included personally identifiable information of crime victims. That law only allows releasing such information to "persons who, by reason of the participation in the proceeding, have reason to know such information." In 2016, a federal district court granted summary judgment to the government. In 2021, a court of appeals affirmed that the information sought was properly withheld because the requester sought information as a member of the public after his conviction.[217]

Exemption 4: Trade Secrets

The private business information provided to government agencies—such as profit-and-loss statements, market-share information and secret formulas—is generally exempt from disclosure under FOIA. Agencies collect and keep the information to assist government objectives, such as enforcement of copyright law, unrelated to the recipient agency's specific duties. Trade secret information is commercially useful and confidential. Its release is likely to cause competitive harm to a business.

POINTS OF LAW
RECORDS EXEMPT AS CONFIDENTIAL TRADE SECRETS UNDER FOIA

In light of the language of Exemption 4 to the Freedom of Information Act, the U.S. Supreme Court applied the following criteria to determine whether "commercial or financial information" shared with a federal agency may be deemed confidential:

- The owner of the information "both customarily and actually" treats the information as private
- And that information is provided to a government agency "under an assurance of privacy."[218]

In 2019, the U.S. Supreme Court heard the Food Marketing Institute's challenge to a newspaper's FOIA request for the names, addresses and annual food-stamp sales of retail grocery stores participating in the U.S. Department of Agriculture's Supplemental Nutrition Assistance Program (SNAP). The majority opinion reasoned that the agency had promised to keep this information private and retailers customarily treat this information as private, thus the information "is confidential within the meaning of Exemption 4."[219] The court rejected lower courts' interpretations of Exemption 4 as requiring agencies withholding records as trade secrets to show that disclosure was almost certain to cause "substantial competitive harm."[220] Although that "substantial competitive harm" requirement was not included in the text of Exemption 4, three dissenting justices stated they would require agencies to apply that condition.

Almost four decades earlier, the Supreme Court said FOIA is a disclosure statute that does not include a mechanism for private individuals to sue to protect confidentiality.[221] In that earlier Exemption 4 case, Chrysler had turned over documents related to its affirmative-action program and workforce composition to a government agency. Chrysler challenged agency release of those records in response to a FOIA request. In *Chrysler v. Brown*, the U.S. Supreme Court remanded the case to determine whether statutory protection for trade secrets applied.[222] Courts generally have required agencies seeking to withhold material under Exemption 4 to show that the information is, in fact, a trade secret.

Exemption 5: Agency Memoranda

Sometimes referred to as the "working papers" or "discovery" exemption, Exemption 5 protects from disclosure agency memoranda, studies or drafts that are prepared and used inside agencies to create final reports or policies. One court ruled that this exemption protects both the decision-making process and the need to avoid public confusion through disclosure of preliminary decisions.[223] In 2016, Congress limited the exemption for records of "deliberative process" to 25 years.[224]

In 2014, the Sierra Club, an environmental organization, filed FOIA requests for records related to Environmental Protection Agency (EPA) consultations with the U.S. Fish and Wildlife Service and National Marine Fisheries Service regarding proposed regulations on cooling water intake structures. The EPA disclosed thousands of documents, but cited Exemption 5 to justify withholding draft biological opinions. A district court and the Ninth Circuit Court of Appeals subsequently held the opinions labeled drafts represented final opinions, thus they were subject to disclosure. In 2021, the nation's highest court, however, decided the Exemption 5 deliberative process privilege extends to the in-house drafts of an EPA proposal addressing a potential threat to an endangered species.[225]

The Court held, "The deliberative process privilege protects the draft biological opinions at issue here because they reflect a preliminary view—not a final decision—about the likely effect of the EPA's proposed rule on endangered species."[226] To determine whether the deliberative process privilege applied, Justice Amy Coney Barrett first reasoned that a draft is "a preliminary version" of a record "subject to feedback and change," and the opinions at issue were sent to decision makers for approval. Since decision makers stated more work was needed rather than approve or forward the opinions to the EPA, they were deemed "both predecisional and deliberative." Exemption 5, however, will not apply if an agency attempts to hide "a functionally final decision in draft form."[227]

Exemption 6: Personal Privacy

Privacy is at the heart of Exemptions 6 and 7. Exemption 6 allows withholding of "personnel and medical . . . and similar files, the disclosure of which would constitute a clearly unwarranted invasion of personal privacy." The phrase "similar files" has been the source of much dispute. It has generally been interpreted broadly to include lists, files, records and letters with "information that relates to identifiable individuals."[228]

Courts attempt to balance privacy concerns against the purpose of FOIA. Sometimes courts consider the purpose of the request and any public interest in disclosure. "Exemption Six overwhelmingly favors the disclosure of information relating to a violation of the public trust by a government official," one federal appeals court ruled.[229] The U.S. Supreme Court, however, favored privacy when it recognized that FOIA's purpose is allowing the activity of government—not private citizens—to be open to public scrutiny.[230]

In 2021, the U.S. Court of Appeals for the District of Columbia found the U.S. Geological Survey properly had not provided a trade association for coal tar-based sealant producers with personal information about people who participated in a 2010 study. Agreeing with a lower court's application of Exemption 6,[231] the appellate court said participants "have a greater than *de minimis* privacy interest" in "extensive personal details," including their smoking and cooking habits, recorded in study questionnaires. Disclosing the information "would constitute a clearly unwarranted invasion of personal privacy" and would not serve a public interest. The court reasoned that "pertinent scientific data" was already released and disclosing participants' personal information would not shed any additional light on agency "operations or activities."[232]

Exemption 6 also recently limited some information news organizations could receive when they sought names and addresses of borrowers and amounts borrowed from the Small Business Association's Paycheck Protection Program, also known as PPP, and Economic Injury Disaster Loans program. In 2021, a federal district court found that under Exemption 6 the Small Business Association properly did not disclose individual persons' Social Security numbers; disclosing that information "would constitute a clearly unwarranted invasion of personal privacy." Exemption 6, however, did not shield from disclosure businesses' nine-digit tax identification numbers.[233]

Exemption 7: Law Enforcement Records

Records compiled within the context of law enforcement investigations may be exempt from FOIA disclosure. There are limits, however, to the exemption. For the government to deny disclosure, release of a record must reasonably be expected to:

    a. interfere with enforcement proceedings,

    b. deprive a person of the right to a fair trial,

    c. constitute an unwarranted invasion of privacy,

    d. disclose the identity of a confidential source,

    e. disclose law enforcement techniques and procedures or

    f. endanger the life or physical safety of any individual.[234]

At one time, items such as rap sheets, arrest records, convictions records and department manuals were not exempt. In *U.S. Department of Justice v. Reporters Committee for Freedom of the Press*, excerpted at the end of this chapter, a journalist filed a FOIA request with the FBI for its criminal records on four members of a family suspected of criminal activity.[235] The FBI disclosed only the records of the three deceased family members. Challenged on the grounds that the records might disclose the survivor's involvement in political corruption, the U.S. Supreme Court said, "Disclosure of records regarding private citizens, identifiable by name, is not what the framers of FOIA had in mind." It upheld the denial of access.[236]

In 2004, the U.S. Supreme Court affirmed the authority of several federal agencies and organizations to withhold death scene photographs of the former legal counsel to President Bill Clinton.[237] Multiple independent government and private investigations concluded that the adviser committed suicide. In affirming denial of access to the photos, the Supreme Court held that the right of personal privacy under FOIA extends to surviving family members. Those seeking information that implicates personal privacy interests must demonstrate a significant public interest in the information sought. In cases of alleged government malfeasance, the Court said, "the requester must establish more than a bare suspicion . . . [and] must produce evidence that would warrant a belief by a reasonable person that the alleged government impropriety might have occurred."[238]

TOP SECRET

confinement box. The other inquiry involved claims that the SERE training caused two individuals to engage in criminal behavior, namely, felony shoplifting and downloading child pornography onto a military computer. According to this official, these claims were found to be baseless. Moreover, he has indicated that during the three and a half years he spent as ███████ ██████ of the SERE program, he trained 10,000 students. Of those students, only two dropped out of the training following the use of these techniques. Although on rare occasions some students temporarily postponed the remainder of their training and received psychological counseling, those students were able to finish the program without any indication of subsequent mental health effects.

You have informed us that you have consulted with ████████████ who has ten years of experience with SERE training ██████████████████████████████████████ ██ He stated that, during those ten years, insofar as he is aware, none of the individuals who completed the program suffered any adverse mental health effects. He informed you that there was one person who did not complete the training. That person experienced an adverse mental health reaction that lasted only two hours. After those two hours, the individual's symptoms spontaneously dissipated without requiring treatment or counseling and no other symptoms were ever reported by this individual. According to the information you have provided to us, this assessment of the use of these procedures includes the use of the waterboard.

Additionally, you received a memorandum from the ███████████████████ ████████████████████ which you supplied to us. ██████████████████ has experience with the use of all of these procedures in a course of conduct, with the exception of the insect in the confinement box and the waterboard. This memorandum confirms that the use of these procedures has not resulted in any reported instances of prolonged mental harm, and very few instances of immediate and temporary adverse psychological responses to the training. ████████ reported that a small minority of students have had temporary adverse psychological reactions during training. Of the 26,829 students trained from 1992 through 2001 in the Air Force SERE training, 4.3 percent of those students had contact with psychology services. Of those 4.3 percent, only 3.2 percent were pulled from the program for psychological reasons. Thus, out of the students trained overall, only 0.14 percent were pulled from the program for psychological reasons. Furthermore, although ████████████ indicated that surveys of students having completed this training are not done, he expressed confidence that the training did not cause any long-term psychological impact. He based his conclusion on the debriefing of students that is done after the training. More importantly, he based this assessment on the fact that although training is required to be extremely stressful in order to be effective, very few complaints have been made regarding the training. During his tenure, in which 10,000 students were trained, no congressional complaints have been made. While there was one Inspector General complaint, it was not due to psychological concerns. Moreover, he was aware of only one letter inquiring about the long-term impact of these techniques from an individual trained

TOP SECRET   5

An example of a redacted document that was released under FOIA. This is one page from a memo to the CIA's general counsel that the assistant attorney general wrote in 2002.

Memo excerpt from "Interrogation of al Qaeda operative" by Jay S. Bybee, Assistant Attorney General, OLC to John Rizzo, Acting General Counsel of the Central Intelligence Agency. Aug. 1, 2002. http://www.fas.org/irp/agency/doj/olc/zubaydah.pdf.

FOIA does not facilitate fishing expeditions into government-held information about private individuals. Its objective is to provide access to "official information that sheds light on an agency's performance of its statutory duties, . . . [which] is not fostered by disclosure of information about private citizens that . . . reveals little or nothing about an agency's own conduct."[239]

In 2011, the U.S. Supreme Court narrowed and clarified this privacy exemption. AT&T argued that, as a corporation, it qualified for Exemption 7 withholding of records to protect "personal privacy." In a unanimous decision, the Supreme Court held that Exemption 7 applies to individuals, not corporations, because the ordinary meaning of the word "personal" refers to human beings.[240] Federal agencies, then, cannot use this exemption to reject FOIA requests for information about corporations and other businesses.

Exemption 8: Financial Records

This exemption allows for nondisclosure of sensitive financial reports or audits held by government. To support nondisclosure, the government agency must show that the release of records would undermine public confidence in banks and other financial institutions. This sweeping exemption left many questions unanswered during the savings and loan collapse of the 1980s. In 2010, Congress repealed portions of the Dodd-Frank Act that had exempted the Securities and Exchange Commission from FOIA and allowed Exemption 8 to apply to the SEC.[241]

After learning Wells Fargo employees had opened fake financial accounts in 2018, a nonprofit organization that promotes government accountability and a reporter for The Daily Beast used FOIA to seek documents related to a federal agency's review of banks.[242] The agency responded in 2019 that it had located 669 pages of documents, and Exemptions 5 and 8 shielded all from disclosure. The organization and journalist sued, stating access to 34 pages that relate to the bureau's final conclusions should have been released. In 2020, a district court focused on Exemption 8 to grant the defendant's motion for summary judgment. The court said, "Exemption 8 applies to examination, operating, or condition reports prepared by or for an agency responsible for the regulation or supervision of financial institutions and any documents that are logically connected to an examination, operating, or condition report."[243]

Exemption 9: Geological Data

Exemption 9 rarely comes into play within a news media context although it is broad. It is designed to prevent oil and gas exploration companies from obtaining information from federal agencies that can provide them a competitive advantage.[244] Much like the trade secrets exemption, this exemption protects potentially profitable confidential geological information from being obtained through FOIA.

Exemptions to Open Meetings

Ten exemptions to the federal Government in the Sunshine Act allow boards to close meetings or hold closed, nonvoting executive sessions on specific topics.[245] Exemptions 1 through 9 are similar to those of the federal Freedom of Information Act detailed above.[246] Exemption 2 allows closing meetings for the board to discuss matters related to personnel rules and practices. Exemption 6 permits closures to protect personal privacy interests. Exemption 10 applies to portions of meetings addressing agency litigation or arbitration.[247]

Limits Placed on Access to Personally Identifiable Information

Federal and state laws aimed at protecting personal privacy intentionally create barriers to gathering personally identifiable information. The federal Privacy Act of 1974 limits federal agency collection of private information, allows the subject of records to review and amend their content and requires government agencies to use individual, personal information only for the reason(s) it was collected.[248]

Agencies may not release the information to anyone other than the subject of the record without the written consent of the person involved. Exceptions to the privacy provisions are for law enforcement or congressional investigations, census or labor statistics and archival of historically significant material. If FOIA mandates disclosure of information protected under the Privacy Act, FOIA prevails. Individuals may sue for "actual damages" caused by violations of the law. In a case involving interagency sharing of a pilot's HIV status, the U.S. Supreme Court ruled that damage awards are limited to financial costs and do not compensate for mental anguish or suffering.[249]

Student Records

The **Family Educational Rights and Privacy Act** of 1974 (FERPA), a federal law sometimes called the Buckley Amendment, forbids any school that receives federal funding from releasing students' academic records unless the subjects, as adults, or their parents provide consent.[250] Adult students and the parents of minor children are permitted to review and amend the records. The law shields records that contain personally identifiable information, which the Department of Education defines to include a family member's name, the student's Social Security or student ID number and personal characteristics or other information that would make it easy to determine the student's identity.[251]

Government-supported schools also are forbidden from releasing grades or information related to a student's health. In 2012, amendments to the law protected student IDs and email addresses from disclosure and clarified that "directory" information such as a student's name, address, telephone number, date and place of birth, major field of study, dates of attendance and degrees and awards received may be released. Violating the law puts an institution's government funding at risk.[252]

Such campus information is more difficult to obtain in the wake of a Sixth Circuit Court of Appeals ruling that FERPA shields student disciplinary records. After the weekly Chronicle of Higher Education and the Miami University of Ohio student newspaper sought the records of the university's internal discipline committees to examine crime trends on campus, the Sixth Circuit said the law's language made clear that disciplinary proceedings were part of student records and could not be released without consent.[253] Similarly, in 2019, the Supreme Court of Montana held a journalist could not receive copies of records pertaining to university disciplinary proceedings related to allegations of sexual assault by a student-athlete. The court reasoned that the student-athlete had a privacy interest in those records and "society is willing to recognize as reasonable" his expectation of privacy.[254]

In some instances, school records may be released after redacting personally identifying information. For example, in 2020, the Supreme Court of Pennsylvania ruled that a school bus surveillance video that showed a teacher disciplining a student is an educational record under FERPA. The court determined any images in which a student is "reasonably identifiable" must be redacted prior to disclosing the video.[255]

University of California police arrested at least 17 people during a graduate student strike in 2020.

Dan Coyro/The Santa Cruz Sentinel/Associated Press

Campus Crime

The federal Campus Security Policy and Campus Crime Statistics Act of 1990, known as the **Clery Act,** requires universities that receive federal funds to maintain up-to-date police logs and to compile and publish campus crime statistics that do not include personally identifiable information. Campus security must maintain a log of all crimes for public review and provide timely warnings of threats to safety. Campus police logs and annual statistics have uncovered significant problems on campuses.[256]

The Department of Education reviews campus compliance with the act and levies fines for noncompliance. In 2019, Michigan State University received a record $4.5 million fine for not adequately addressing a former campus sports doctor's sexual abuse of hundreds of female athletes.[257]

Medical Records

The **Health Insurance Portability and Accountability Act** (HIPAA) is a federal law that prevents health professionals and institutions from revealing individuals' personal medical information.[258] After Congress passed HIPAA in 1996, the Department of Health and Human Services crafted the first federal medical privacy regulations, called the Standards for Privacy of Individually Identifiable Health Information. These rules were designed to give patients more control over their health information and to limit the use and release of health records to third parties. Generally, the privacy standards established a federal requirement that most health care providers obtain a patient's written consent before disclosing the patient's personal health information. The rules restrict the use of such records for marketing and research purposes.[259]

Journalists seeking information related to COVID-19 often have been told they could not receive information due to the HIPAA privacy rule. That rule does not prevent every person or organization that learns health-related information from releasing that information. For example, medical information stored in public records are not exempt from disclosure under the HIPAA privacy rule. Protected health information may be released when the information is de-identified, meaning the health information is not connected to identifying characteristics, such as names or contact information.[260]

POINTS OF LAW
THE HIPAA PRIVACY RULE

The privacy rule applies to health information that

1. identifies an individual;
2. relates to an individual's health, healthcare or payment for healthcare and
3. is created or received by health plans, healthcare providers, healthcare clearinghouses or their business associates.[261]

Drivers' Information

The federal **Drivers' Privacy Protection Act of 1994 (DPPA)** prohibits states from "knowing disclosure" of information obtained from department of motor vehicle records without permission except under specific circumstances.[262] At one time, many states sold this information for millions of dollars annually. Congress stopped this practice in part to prevent stalkers from obtaining information about potential targets. The U.S. Supreme Court upheld the law against a constitutional challenge, finding that Congress's power over interstate commerce allowed it to adopt the statute.[263]

In 2019, the Ninth Circuit Court of Appeals affirmed a district court's grant of summary judgment to Sirius XM Radio Inc. in a DPPA case.[264] The plaintiff demonstrated that Sirius XM had "knowingly obtained his personal information"—his name and address—for "nonpermissible promotional purposes," promoting satellite radio. Sirius XM, however, did not obtain that information from a state department of motor vehicles' "motor vehicle records." Sirius received the plaintiff's name and address from the U.S. Postal Service's National Change of Address database and a company to which the plaintiff had shown his driver's license record and vehicle transfer form. The court reasoned that the plaintiff was the initial source of the driver's license and form; where "the initial source of personal information is a record in the possession of an individual, rather than a state DMV, then use or disclosure of that information does not violate the DPPA."[265]

The Seventh Circuit Court of Appeals, however, refused to dismiss a district court ruling that the Sun-Times newspaper of Chicago was punishable for disclosing "private information" from the driver's licenses of several police officers. The Sun-Times received photographs and physical descriptions of the officers after the state attorney general required their release under the state's freedom of information law. In criticism of the officers' participation in a homicide lineup, the newspaper included each officer's birth date, height, weight, hair and eye color, details it said were essential to demonstrate the problematic composition of a police lineup.[266] The Seventh Circuit held that the DPPA's ban on disclosure of private information applied and the newspaper enjoyed no First Amendment protection from penalty. The court reasoned that the ban was both content-neutral and rationally related to the government's legitimate interest in protecting the information from unauthorized disclosure.[267]

Covert Recording or Intercepting "Wire" Communications

Covert recording, which is unknown to some of the parties, always involves some deception; recording devices are hidden, and informed parties can shape their comments with knowledge of the recording. The ubiquity of cellphone cameras and recording increases the opportunity for covert recording. Most states have laws intended to protect against eavesdropping and unlawful surveillance.[268]

Many states have voyeurism laws that may address eavesdropping or unlawful surveillance or improper photography.[269] Maine, for example, deems a criminal invasion of privacy any intentional and nonconsensual use or installation of a recording or amplifying device to hear, record or amplify a communication in any place communication would not normally be audible.[270] New Hampshire similarly deems a misdemeanor installing or using a "device for the purpose of observing, photographing, recording, amplifying or broadcasting, or in any way transmitting images or sounds" in a public or private place without consent of any "persons entitled to privacy."[271]

Some media organizations have policies about the use of hidden recordings or recordings without consent.[272] While the use of hidden cameras by media does not always constitute an illegal intrusion, states may prohibit the secret or unauthorized use or installation of cameras in private places. Covert recording also may violate federal laws.[273]

REAL WORLD LAW
CHILLING HOSPITAL PR

Patient Approval Required

New York–Presbyterian Hospital recently agreed to pay $2.2 million in fines to federal regulators for recording patients without patient consent. The decision involved ABC's reality show "NY Med" airing the dying moments of an 83-year-old man who had been struck by a car.[274]

The U.S. Department of Health and Human Services used the fine to clarify that medical facilities violate the rights of patients if they allow media into treatment areas without patient approval. Many said the ruling would end popular television and cable shows recorded in hospitals.

"I think this will have a chilling effect on hospitals going forward," said the chairman of the ethics committee of the American College of Emergency Physicians. "Any hospital legal counsel worth his salt or any P.R. director would be committing malpractice in order to allow it to occur. It's now embodied in a federal directive."[275]

Federal laws also protect the privacy of "wire communications," which include technologies that may not be wired but transfer sounds from one point to another.[276] Landline telephones, cellphones and computer-based voice services such as Skype, Google Hangouts and FaceTime[277] all fall under this regulatory umbrella. The federal **Wiretapping and Electronic Surveillance Act** prohibits the interception (and recording, dissemination or private use) of a "wire" voice communication without a participant's permission.[278] The law allows the government to bring criminal charges, and private individuals may sue for civil damages. It does not protect messages that are stored after transmission. The data packets stored following internet calls are subject to the **Stored Communications Act**,[279] a federal law that offers "considerably less protection" than the Wiretap Act.[280] Investigative agencies may access live or stored calls with warrants and subpoenas.

The federal **Electronic Communications Privacy Act (ECPA)** also prohibits the unauthorized interception of an electronic communication while it is in transit or storage.[281] Both the ECPA and the federal **Computer Fraud and Abuse Act** (CFAA) prohibit computer and phone hacking, which violate a user's expectation of privacy.[282] All 50 states also make it illegal to hack into someone's computer or phone to obtain previously recorded conversations or messages or to gain access to another person's phone records by misrepresenting your identity.[283]

Alleged violation of the ECPA has been among the claims in suits against internet service providers who reveal the identity of anonymous communicators. Courts generally have favored ISPs that disclose identities according to the standards outlined in the act. In one case, the plaintiff posted a message on AOL (then America Online) that harassed the soon-to-be ex-wife of the plaintiff's lover. When AOL investigated, it terminated the poster's contract for violating AOL's "Rules of the Road." Under subpoena and in compliance with an exception provided by the ECPA, AOL provided the identity of the poster to the subject of the post. A federal court ruled that such disclosure did not violate the poster's privacy.[284]

In recent years, Pennsylvania courts have heard a number of wiretapping cases.[285] One recent decision established that the state law is modeled on the federal law to "emphasize[] the protection of privacy."[286] Both laws, however, expressly exempt interceptions by police and prisons that follow established procedures. In addition, the federal **Foreign Intelligence Surveillance Act** (FISA) allows government investigators to use wiretaps, surveillance and tracking of personal communications without a court order.[287] Journalists are subject to FISA, as are professional communication firms. The extent to which the government uses FISA to surveil journalists and obtain their sources is unknown, according to the Reporters Committee for Freedom of the Press.[288]

In 2021 in *Van Buren v. United States*, excerpted at the end of this chapter, the U.S. Supreme Court narrowed the scope of the CFAA provisions making it a crime to exceed authorized access to "a computer with authorization and to use such access to obtain or alter information in the computer that the accesser is not entitled so to obtain or alter." Nathan Van Buren, a police sergeant in Georgia, accepted $5,000 to search for a woman's license plate information in a law enforcement database. Using the database for non-law enforcement purposes contradicted a department policy, thus Van Buren was charged for violating the CFAA. A federal court convicted Van Buren and sentenced him to 18 months in prison. The Eleventh Circuit Court of Appeals affirmed his conviction. The Supreme Court, however, found Van Buren's conduct did not violate the CFAA.[289]

The Supreme Court focused on what is required to exceed authorized access when obtaining information. In the majority opinion, Justice Barrett wrote that the law "covers those who obtain information from particular areas in the computer—such as files, folders, or databases—to which their computer access does not extend." The law does not cover accessing information available to a user simply because a user accessed the material with "improper motives." Van Buren typically was allowed to access license plate information, thus his search did not violate the CFAA.[290]

A broader interpretation of the statute "would attach criminal penalties to a breathtaking amount of commonplace computer activity," Barrett wrote. "If the exceeds authorized access clause criminalizes every violation of a computer-use policy, then millions of otherwise law-abiding citizens are criminals."[291] Affirming the government's reading of that CFAA provision would "criminalize everything from embellishing an online-dating profile to using a pseudonym on Facebook," Barrett stated. The majority opinion alleviated some concerns that journalists might be punished for scraping data from websites and social media, but the opinion did not discuss limits addressed in contracts or policies.[292]

OTHER LIMITS TO GATHERING INFORMATION

Individuals who value their privacy or wish to avoid contact or publicity may seek protection under criminal harassment and stalking laws designed to protect crime victims.[293] The Kansas Protection From Stalking Act, for example, prohibits stalking and harassment. It defines stalking as "intentional harassment . . . that places the other person in reasonable fear for that person's safety" and harassment as a "knowing and intentional course of conduct . . . that seriously alarms, annoys, torments or terrorizes . . . that serves no legitimate purpose." Harassment may include use of a drone over a place where a person "may reasonably expect to be safe from uninvited intrusion or surveillance."[294] While prosecutors and judges tend to strike down the application of these laws to journalists who persist in asking questions, anti-harassment statutes in some states leave the door open for prosecution for repeated, aggressive and unwanted contacts to gather information.[295]

Photographers trying to photograph a celebrity lineup beside a limousine in California.

Gilles Mingason/Getty Images

Harassment and Stalking

Notable examples of aggressive newsgathering that cross the line involve "paparazzi" photographers pursuing celebrities. Decades ago, a court ordered a photographer to stay a fixed distance away from former first lady Jacqueline Kennedy Onassis, her children and their homes and schools.[296] Both Onassis and the Secret Service sued the photographer for continually interfering with the agents performing their protective duties. The court flatly rejected the photographer's claim that the First Amendment was a complete defense to his behavior.[297]

In a more recent California case, a state court upheld a law increasing penalties for reckless driving "with the intent to capture an image [or] sound recording . . . of another person for a commercial purpose."[298] A commercial photographer challenged the provision as unconstitutionally intended to infringe on the First Amendment activities of celebrity photographers. The court disagreed and said the law broadly applied to anyone engaged in the specified activities that interfere with safe driving.[299]

INTERNATIONAL LAW
HARASSMENT OF JOURNALISTS

In 2021, a journalist and founder of the Speak Up Channel in France requested police protection after she received anonymous death threats. A handwritten letter sent to her home used racist and sexist language.[300] French authorities launched an investigation and called the safe working environment for journalists a priority.[301]

Online violence against women journalists is an international problem.[302] The Center for Media Engagement recently found female journalists around the globe have faced harassment, particularly on social media.[303] Women of color are harassed more frequently on Twitter than white women, and female and nongender conforming journalists perceive online harassment as a safety concern in the U.S.[304]

Unlike attacks on or criticism of work male journalists have received, female journalists have received sexist attacks and even threats of sexual violence.[305] People have posted especially abusive comments in response to females' coverage of immigration, race, feminism, politics, vehicles and video games. Online harassment can have a chilling effect on journalists, making them less likely to cover such topics or change how they cover stories.[306]

PEN America recently published an Online Harassment Field Manual. The manual's strategies for responding to online abuse include the following:

- Document the harassment.
- Block content from users known to post abusive comments.
- Mute users known to post abusive comments.
- Restrict how people may post comments.
- Report online abuse to platforms.
- Form a community to discuss the harassment and to help moderate comments.[307]

The concept of **tortious newsgathering**, using reporting techniques that are wrongful and unlawful for which a victim may obtain damages in court, developed in response to the "ambush-and-surveillance" journalism practiced by some journalists and television programs. The tort broadly encompasses the range of problematic behaviors explored in this chapter. One case symbolizes the evolution of the law—and the media—in this area. When insurance company executives denied interviews from the television program "Inside Edition," show producers staked out the home of two executives, followed them and their child, and made recordings using hidden cameras, powerful microphones and strong telephoto lenses. The crew then followed the family to Florida and anchored a boat 50 yards offshore of the family house.[308]

A judge in Philadelphia granted the family an injunction. The "*legal* newsgathering activities" of the "Inside Edition" crew would not be "irreparably harmed by an injunction narrowly tailored to preclude them from continuing their harassing conduct" because, the judge said, the injunction targeted only illegal newsgathering tactics.[309]

Fraud and Misrepresentation

Years ago, ABC News magazine reporters used false names and fake work histories to go undercover in Food Lion grocery stores to investigate alleged unsanitary practices.[310] They wore hidden cameras and microphones.[311] Their jobs gave them access to nonpublic areas of the stores, where they filmed meat-handling practices. Food Lion denied the accusations and sued for fraud, trespass, unfair trade practices and breach of a duty of loyalty to "attack[] the methods used by defendants to gather the information ultimately aired on 'PrimeTime Live.'"[312] Because Food Lion chose not to sue for defamation, the trial court said the truth of the story was not at issue. The jury found for Food Lion, awarding the grocery chain more than $5.5 million in punitive damages. The judge reduced the award to $315,000.[313]

ABC appealed the verdict, and the Court of Appeals for the Fourth Circuit reversed on all but the trespass and breach of loyalty claims.[314] It remains a cautionary tale. Not only did the lower court call some newsgathering techniques illegal, but a dissenting judge on the federal appeals court would have sustained the fraud claim and the punitive damages against ABC.[315] Although ABC ultimately paid only $2 in damages, some factors should be kept in mind:

- First, the attorney fees were costly.[316]

- Second, those costs and the verdict should raise serious questions about newsgathering techniques that involve deception.

- Third, the jury showed animosity toward the news media, particularly toward big, powerful and seemingly well-to-do news organizations.[317]

- ABC's successful appeal relied on specific state laws. A different result might arise in a different state.

Misrepresentation also can occur when journalists disclose who they are but disguise the nature of the story they are developing. When truckers declined to participate in an NBC "Dateline" story about the trucking industry, NBC promised one truck driver and his boss that their report would be positive and would not include comments from anyone from Parents Against Tired Truckers (PATT). The "Dateline" segment was not positive. It included statements like "American highways are a trucker's killing field."[318] It also contained interviews with PATT members. The trucking company sued NBC for fraud and misrepresentation. The First Circuit Court of Appeals favored NBC on nearly every point and ruled that the network's vague promise to produce a "positive portrayal" was insufficient basis for a claim.[319] But the court said damages could be awarded based on NBC's specific and unequivocal promise not to include anyone from PATT. The parties settled for an undisclosed amount.[320]

Problems With Sources and Confidentiality

Using material from social media may be perilous. Recent research has found falsehoods are likely to spread rapidly on social media.[321] In 2021, President Biden said social media users spread of misinformation about COVID-19 vaccines was "killing people."[322] After Center for Countering Digital Hate research traced 65 percent of anti-vaccine media misinformation shared via social media to a dozen social media users, Facebook announced it had removed more of those users' accounts.[323] Many professional communication firms prohibit or caution against practitioner use of social media content. The Associated Press (AP), for example, says, "Fake accounts are rampant in the social media world. . . . [N]ever lift quotes, photos or video from social networking sites and attribute them to the name on the profile or feed where you found the material." Guidelines for AP employees say to contact the person who posted the information.[324]

When professional communicators seek sensitive information or whistleblower tips, a promise of anonymity may be the only way to gain access to key information. In exchange for information, communicators may agree to provide confidentiality for the source.[325] The promise of confidentiality is a "form of currency" used to free up tips and insights.[326] One estimate indicates that at least one-third of newspaper accounts and the vast majority of newsmagazine stories have concealed source attribution.[327] Reporters and their news organizations typically keep promises of confidentiality, even when courts ask them to break them (see Chapter 8). Keeping such promises is both ethical and practical. Individuals and organizations that break promises develop a reputation for being untrustworthy. Their sources vanish.

POINTS OF LAW
PROMISSORY ESTOPPEL

Under the doctrine of promissory estoppel, a person may seek damages for harm:
● When a clear promise is made,
● the person who received the promise relied on it,
● and breach of that promise created a harm to that person.[328]

When an organization breaks a promise and reveals the identity of a source promised anonymity, the source may sue and win. Promises, even unwritten promises, can be legally binding under the principle of **promissory estoppel**. The legal doctrine of promissory estoppel requires courts to enforce a promise if the individual who received the promise relied on it and its breach created a harm that should be remedied by law. Promissory estoppel is a generally applicable law that applies with equal force to news organizations as to anyone else.[329]

The U.S. Supreme Court ruled years ago that the First Amendment does not protect journalists from the consequences of broken promises. *Cohen v. Cowles Media Co.* involved a political campaign worker's offer of prejudicial information about a political opponent to four reporters just days before an election. On the condition that his identity be kept secret, the campaign worker disclosed that the opposing candidate had been arrested for unlawful assembly and petty theft more than a decade earlier. Two newspapers ran the stories and clearly identified the source because they said the public deserved to know who was engaged in political "dirty tricks."[330]

When the campaign worker was fired, he sued, claiming the newspapers broke a contractual agreement. At trial, the jury agreed and awarded $200,000 in compensatory damages and $500,000 in punitive damages. On review, the Minnesota Supreme Court struck down the award on the grounds that the application of promissory estoppel to newspapers would abridge First Amendment interests. On appeal, the U.S. Supreme Court reversed. The Court said the First Amendment imposed no bar to the application of promissory estoppel to the press. "Generally applicable laws do not offend the First Amendment simply because their enforcement against the press has incidental effects on its ability to gather and report the news," Justice Byron White wrote in *Cohen*.[331]

EMERGING LAW

An unprecedented number of journalists were attacked or arrested around the world in 2020.[332] In 2020 and 2021, hundreds of journalists covering protests in the United States were arrested, assaulted or confined due to crowd control measures. The U.S. Press Freedom Tracker reported 153 journalists were arrested and 415 were assaulted between May of 2020 and 2021. More than 100 reported their equipment was damaged and 21 had equipment searched or seized.[333] Before June 2022, at least 50 journalists filed lawsuits "alleging law enforcement violated their First Amendment rights" when journalists were covering protests.[334] As journalists have endured threats to their safety and First Amendment rights in recent years, news organizations have struggled economically.[335] Courts have addressed important questions about civil rights and First Amendment rights for information gatherers, and legislators have proposed laws intended to protect and preserve journalism.

New York police officers arrested independent journalist, Ashley Dorelus, covering an anti-Trump protest in 2020.
Sipa USA/Alamy Live News

Some journalists have been arrested even when they identified themselves as members of the press and attempted to follow law enforcement instructions. Almost 10 months after Des Moines Register reporter Andrea Sahouri was arrested when covering a protest in Iowa in 2020, she was acquitted of simple misdemeanor charges of failure to disperse and interference with official acts.[336] In May 2021, two journalists in North Carolina were arrested for impeding traffic while one livecasted video of a protest. One was on a sidewalk and the other was in a crosswalk. They ultimately were not charged.[337]

Journalists covering protests have been advised to be respectful of others, focus on their safety, follow police orders, identify themselves to law enforcement as members or the press, record as much as possible, stay on the periphery of crowds and stay in contact with their newsrooms.[338]

More than 125 journalists were assaulted in the U.S. alone in 2021.[339] In August 2021, a Michigan parent attacked a journalist who the parent wanted to delete photographs from a school board discussion of wearing masks in schools.[340] Videographers were punched and struck with a baton while covering protests in California less than a month earlier.[341] Research has found that 86 percent of U.S. news directors took steps, such as purchasing bullet-proof vests and sending security teams with reporters, to protect journalists in 2020.[342] Recognizing some dangers journalists have faced, Congress has introduced laws intended to protect journalists and journalism. Congress in 2018, 2019 and 2021 introduced the Journalist Protection Act to make attacks on reporters a federal crime in the United States, but the bill has not become law.[343]

Government officials sometimes use arrest or even physical assault to deter media coverage. Some believe such interference with media has increased in recent years. After facing intimidation, harassment, detention and arrest while covering protests or elections, some journalists have filed **civil rights claims**, called 1983 claims, that indicate state or local government actors deprived individuals of constitutionally guaranteed individual rights.[344] Such claims are challenging to win, in part, due to the doctrine of qualified immunity and due to *Nieves v. Bartlett*.[345]

In 2019, the U.S. Supreme Court in *Nieves v. Bartlett* determined when individuals can bring a First Amendment challenge to an arrest on the grounds that the arrest illegally restrained their protected speech. The case involved the arrest of Russell Bartlett for "aggressive" behavior at a large outdoor festival. Finding that police had probable cause to arrest Bartlett, the Supreme Court reversed the Ninth Circuit Court of Appeals ruling and barred Bartlett from pursuing a retaliatory arrest claim.[346]

Bartlett argued that the police arrested him for disorderly conduct in retaliation for his earlier comments to the officer confronting a minor suspected of underage drinking. Bartlett also had refused to respond to the officer's questions. Bartlett said the officer's comment during the arrest—"Bet you wish you would have talked to me now"—established that the arrest would not have occurred "but-for" the officer's animus.[347]

Writing for a plurality of the Court, Chief Justice John Roberts argued that causation is difficult to determine in claims of retaliatory arrest because protected speech is often "a wholly legitimate consideration" in determining whether to make an arrest.[348] A majority of the Court then concluded that "the presence of probable cause should generally defeat a First Amendment retaliatory arrest claim."[349]

Alone in dissent in the *Nieves* ruling, Justice Sonia Sotomayor said the vague decision would not adequately protect freedom of speech. She argued that the Court's logic would permit retaliatory arrests to go unpunished "unless the plaintiff can muster evidence that he was arrested when otherwise similarly situated individuals not engaged in the same sort of speech had not been."[350] Absent such comparative evidence, *Nieves* will leave plaintiffs "out of luck, even if they could offer other, unassailable proof of an officer's unconstitutional statements and motivations" for the arrest, she said.[351]

Immediately following the ruling, media advocates expressed concern that *Nieves* would have a severe chilling effect on citizens and journalists attempting to record or protest police actions. They said it would shield police officers from liability for arresting individuals out of anger prompted by protected First Amendment activities.[352]

In 2020, news organizations and journalists filed a class action suit against the City of Portland, Ore., arguing that shooting journalists with pepper balls and tear gas canisters, pepper spraying them, shoving them and preventing them from reporting on protests violated journalists' First and Fourth Amendment rights. A federal court entered a temporary restraining order preventing local authorities from using crowd-control tactics against journalists covering Black Lives Matter protests in Portland. That court subsequently entered a temporary restraining order against the Department of Homeland Security and the United States Marshals Service after journalists alleged federal agents had targeted journalists, used physical force and intimidation against journalists and deterred journalists from reporting on aggressive treatment of protesters near a federal courthouse.[353] A split Ninth Circuit Court of Appeals decision rejected the federal agencies' request to lift the injunction. "Public demonstrations and protests are clearly protected by the First Amendment, and a protest not open to the press and general public is not a public demonstration," the court said.[354]

Freelance journalists prepare for police use of force in Portland, Ore., in 2020.

Sipa USA/Alamy

In 2022, the U.S. Supreme Court made it harder to sue federal law enforcement agents for violating First and Fourth Amendment rights.[355] In *Egbert v. Boule*, the U.S. Supreme Court declined to recognize an inn-keeper's First Amendment retaliation and Fourth Amendment excessive-force claims for damages against a federal U.S. Border Patrol agent. Robert Boule, operator of a shuttle service and the "Smuggler's Inn" near the U.S.–Canadian border in Washington, alleged that Agent Erik Egbert entered Boule's driveway to check the immigration status of Boule's guest from Turkey in 2014. Boule said Agent Egbert refused to leave the property, threw Boule to the ground then checked the Turkish guest's paperwork, which was found to be in order. Boule filed a grievance complaint with the U.S. Border Patrol regarding Agent Egbert following the incident on Boule's property. Boule claimed the agent subsequently engaged in retaliation by reporting Boule's "SMUGLER" license plate to the Washington Department of Licensing and the Internal Revenue Service (IRS), and the IRS audited Boule's tax returns. Border Patrol investigated the grievance and did not discipline Egbert.[356]

In 2017, Boule sought damages under *Bivens v. Six Unknown Federal Narcotics Agents*, which determined a Fourth Amendment violation "by a federal agent acting under color of his authority gives rise to a cause of action for damages." The district court granted Agent Egbert's motion for summary judgment. The Ninth Circuit Court of Appeals reversed and found Boule's First and Fourth Amendment claims could be recognized. In a 6–3 decision, the Supreme Court held neither claim was cognizable. In the majority opinion, Justice Clarence Thomas stated the Supreme Court has held "that a court may not fashion a *Bivens* remedy if Congress already has provided, or has authorized the Executive to provide, an alternative remedial structure." And, the Court must ask whether the nation's highest court or "political branches" are "better equipped" to decide whether to create a new remedy to augment existing remedies. Thomas reasoned that Congress was better suited than the Court to provide remedies in the context of border security, and the U.S. Border Patrol had a grievance process Boule had used.[357]

Although previous Court opinions had recognized *Bivens* remedies for Fourth, Fifth and Eighth Amendment violations, the Court declined to recognize *Bivens* remedies for First Amendment retaliation claims. Thomas stated that recognizing such a cause of action would risk substantial social costs; "retaliation claims are common" and likely "to impose a significant expansion of Government liability." The judicial branch is "ill-equipped" to change frameworks political branches developed to address federal government employees' conduct, "especially so when it comes to First Amendment claims," Thomas stated.[358]

Almost a month after Justice Thomas announced the Court's decision in *Egbert v. Boule*, the Tenth Circuit Court of Appeals determined Abade Irizarry, a YouTube journalist and blogger, had demonstrated a Colorado police officer retaliated against him for exercising his First Amendment rights. In 2019, Irizarry was filming a DUI traffic stop, and an officer stood in front of him, blocking his filming. Irizarry said he objected to the officer's actions, then a police officer shone a flashlight into the journalist's camera before driving a vehicle toward the journalist. The court reversed the district court's finding that qualified immunity covered the officer because the constitutional right to film police officers was not clearly established in 2019.[359]

The Tenth Circuit found Irizarry showed he "was engaged in constitutionally protected activity." The First Amendment right to record law enforcement officers performing their official duties in public is "beyond debate" because six other federal circuit courts of appeals had recognized this right by 2019. The court reasoned that this right to film law enforcement "falls squarely within the First Amendment's core purposes to protect free and robust discussion of public affairs, hold government officials accountable, and check abuse of power." Irizarry further showed the officer's actions would chill engagement in constitutionally protected activity, and Irizarry alleged his filming motivated the officer's actions.[360]

Questions remain about what conditions under which technology may be used to record government officials. Citizens in Tennessee recently asserted a county commission policy banning livestreaming violated citizens' First and Fourteenth Amendment rights. In a 2020 motion allowing the First Amendment claim to proceed, a federal court considered whether livestreaming on Facebook is "expressive conduct that qualifies as speech." Noting a nationwide "growing trend of courts" viewing video recording as speech or expressive conduct, the court considered livestreaming expressive conduct. The court said the county had not adequately shown its policy was a reasonable time, place, and manner restriction. The county had neither articulated safety concerns to justify the policy nor provided "plausible explanation" why "a less restrictive resolution" could not address those concerns, according to the court. The equal protection claims, however, were dismissed.[361]

In 2021, the U.S. Supreme Court declined an activist group's appeal addressing rights to record public officials in public places. That case consolidated two organizations' pre-enforcement First Amendment challenges to a Massachusetts law that could be applied to punish secret nonconsensual recording of public officials discharging their duties in public. The law also could be applied to punish secret nonconsensual recording of any person who did not have a reasonable expectation of privacy. In 2020, the First Circuit Court of Appeals held that punishing secret nonconsensual recording of police officers' doing their jobs was not narrowly tailored to prevent interference with law enforcement activities or to protect personal privacy.[362]

Circuit Courts of Appeals have split in their interpretation of any extent to which the First Amendment protects making secret recordings. An amicus brief urged the Court to grant certiorari "to ensure all citizens throughout the nation enjoy the same First Amendment rights," and are able to subject government officials across the nation "to the same degree of public scrutiny and accountability."[363]

After one-fourth of the newspapers in the United States closed between 2005 and 2022, entire communities were left without local news outlets scrutinizing local officials.[364] Government officials recently proposed, but did not pass, legislation intended to help news organizations. Members of Congress drafted the Local Journalism Sustainability Act, which would provide tax credits for news outlets. State legislators in Colorado and Wisconsin considered tax credits for businesses that purchase advertising in local news outlets. U.S. senators also introduced the Journalism Competition and Preservation Act (JCPA) that would allow media organizations to collectively negotiate for payments for access to news outlets' content from large technology companies, including Google and Facebook.[365] Senator Amy Klobuchar, an author of the JCPA, stated, "Fewer local news providers translates to unchecked governmental corruption, corporate misconduct, and widespread misinformation, plus a raft of other consequences for citizens, taxpayers, and our democracy. The free and diverse press needs a level playing field to do its job."[366]

KEYTERMS

ag-gag laws

civil rights claims

Clery Act

Computer Fraud and Abuse Act

Drivers' Privacy Protection Act of 1994
   (DPPA)

Electronic Communications Privacy Act
   (ECPA)

Electronic Freedom of Information Act
   (EFOIA)

Family Educational Rights and Privacy Act
   (FERPA)

Foreign Intelligence Surveillance Act (FISA)

Freedom of Information Act (FOIA)

freedom of information law (FOIL)

"Glomar" response

Government in the Sunshine Act

Health Insurance Portability and
   Accountability Act

legislative history

metadata

promissory estoppel

Racketeer Influenced and Corrupt
   Organizations Act (RICO)

redact

reverse FOI lawsuits

ride-along

Stored Communications Act

"sunshine laws"

tortious newsgathering

trespass

Wiretapping and Electronic Surveillance Act

CASES FOR STUDY

THINKING ABOUT THEM

The two case excerpts that follow cover different subsets in the broad area of information gathering. The first case relates to the Freedom of Information Act. The second addresses using a computer for information gathering. As you read these case excerpts, keep the following questions in mind:

● Just how much information does the Freedom of Information Act provide access to? Are the limits that have been established fair?

● In the *U.S. Department of Justice v. Reporters Committee for Freedom of the Press* case, what factor does the U.S. Supreme Court identify as critical in deciding whether to disclose private information?

● The *Reporters Committee* case was decided in 1989. Has the nature of privacy changed in such a way that might change the ruling today?

● Note that in the *Van Buren v. United States* case, a communication professional is not a party to the case. How and why does this ruling affect communication professionals?

U.S. DEPARTMENT OF JUSTICE V. REPORTERS COMMITTEE FOR FREEDOM OF THE PRESS

SUPREME COURT OF THE UNITED STATES 489 U.S. 749 (1989)

JUSTICE JOHN PAUL STEVENS delivered the Court's opinion:

The Federal Bureau of Investigation (FBI) has accumulated and maintains criminal identification records, sometimes referred to as "rap sheets," on over 24 million persons. The
question presented by this case is whether the disclosure of the contents of such a file to a
third party "could reasonably be expected to constitute an unwarranted invasion of personal
privacy" within the meaning of the Freedom of Information Act (FOIA).

In 1924 Congress appropriated funds to enable the Department of Justice (Department)
to establish a program to collect and preserve fingerprints and other criminal identification records. That statute authorized the Department to exchange such information with
"officials of States, cities and other institutions." . . . Congress created the FBI's identification division, and gave it responsibility for "acquiring, collecting, classifying, and preserving criminal identification and other crime records and the exchanging of said criminal
identification records with the duly authorized officials of governmental agencies, of States,
cities, and penal institutions." Rap sheets compiled pursuant to such authority contain certain descriptive information, such as date of birth and physical characteristics, as well as a
history of arrests, charges, convictions, and incarcerations of the subject. Normally a rap
sheet is preserved until its subject attains age 80. Because of the volume of rap sheets,
they are sometimes incorrect or incomplete and sometimes contain information about other
persons with similar names.

The local, state, and federal law enforcement agencies throughout the Nation that
exchange rap-sheet data with the FBI do so on a voluntary basis. The principal use of the
information is to assist in the detection and prosecution of offenders; it is also used by courts
and corrections officials in connection with sentencing and parole decisions. As a matter of
executive policy, the Department has generally treated rap sheets as confidential and, with
certain exceptions, has restricted their use to governmental purposes. . . . Congress in 1957
amended the basic statute to provide that the FBI's exchange of rap-sheet information with
any other agency is subject to cancellation "if dissemination is made outside the receiving
departments or related agencies."

As a matter of Department policy, the FBI has made two exceptions to its general practice of prohibiting unofficial access to rap sheets. First, it allows the subject of a rap sheet
to obtain a copy, and second, it occasionally allows rap sheets to be used in the preparation
of press releases and publicity designed to assist in the apprehension of wanted persons or
fugitives. . . .

Although much rap-sheet information is a matter of public record, the availability and
dissemination of the actual rap sheet to the public is limited. Arrests, indictments, convictions, and sentences are public events that are usually documented in court records. In
addition, if a person's entire criminal history transpired in a single jurisdiction, all of the
contents of his or her rap sheet may be available upon request in that jurisdiction. That possibility, however, is present in only three States. All of the other 47 States place substantial
restrictions on the availability of criminal-history summaries even though individual events
in those summaries are matters of public record. . . .

Congress exempted nine categories of documents from FOIA's broad disclosure require-ments. Three of those exemptions are arguably relevant to this case. Exemption 3 applies to documents that are specifically exempted from disclosure by another statute. Exemption 6 protects "personnel and medical files and similar files the disclosure of which would consti-tute a clearly unwarranted invasion of personal privacy." Exemption 7(C) excludes records or information compiled for law enforcement purposes, "but only to the extent that the pro-duction of such [materials] . . . could reasonably be expected to constitute an unwarranted invasion of personal privacy."

Exemption 7(C)'s privacy language is broader than the comparable language in Exemption 6 in two respects. First, whereas Exemption 6 requires that the invasion of pri-vacy be "clearly unwarranted," the adverb "clearly" is omitted from Exemption 7(C). This omission is the product of a 1974 amendment adopted in response to concerns expressed by the President. Second, whereas Exemption 6 refers to disclosures that "would constitute" an invasion of privacy, Exemption 7(C) encompasses any disclosure that "could reasonably be expected to constitute" such an invasion. This difference is also the product of a specific amendment. Thus, the standard for evaluating a threatened invasion of privacy interests resulting from the disclosure of records compiled for law enforcement purposes is some-what broader than the standard applicable to personnel, medical, and similar files.

This case arises out of requests made by a CBS news correspondent and the Reporters Committee for Freedom of the Press (respondents) for information concerning the crimi-nal records of four members of the Medico family. The Pennsylvania Crime Commission had identified the family's company, Medico Industries, as a legitimate business dominated by organized crime figures. Moreover, the company allegedly had obtained a number of defense contracts as a result of an improper arrangement with a corrupt Congressman.

FOIA requests sought disclosure of any arrests, indictments, acquittals, convictions, and sentences of any of the four Medicos. Although the FBI originally denied the requests, it provided the requested data concerning three of the Medicos after their deaths. In their complaint in the district court, respondents sought the rap sheet for the fourth, Charles Medico (Medico), insofar as it contained "matters of public record." . . .Exemption 7(C) requires us to balance the privacy interest in maintaining, as the government puts it, the "practical obscurity" of the rap sheets against the public interest in their release.

The preliminary question is whether Medico's interest in the nondisclosure of any rap sheet the FBI might have on him is the sort of "personal privacy" interest that Congress intended Exemption 7(C) to protect. As we have pointed out before, "[t]he cases sometimes characterized as protecting 'privacy' have in fact involved at least two different kinds of inter-ests. One is the individual interest in avoiding disclosure of personal matters, and another is the interest in independence in making certain kinds of important decisions." Here, the former interest, "in avoiding disclosure of personal matters," is implicated. Because events summarized in a rap sheet have been previously disclosed to the public, respondents con-tend that Medico's privacy interest in avoiding disclosure of a federal compilation of these events approaches zero. We reject respondents' cramped notion of personal privacy.

To begin with, both the common law and the literal understandings of privacy encom-pass the individual's control of information concerning his or her person. In an organized society, there are few facts that are not at one time or another divulged to another. Thus the extent of the protection accorded a privacy right at common law rested in part on the degree of dissemination of the allegedly private fact and the extent to which the passage of time rendered it private. According to Webster's initial definition, information may be clas-sified as "private" if it is "intended for or restricted to the use of a particular person or group or class of persons: not freely available to the public." Recognition of this attribute of a privacy interest supports the distinction, in terms of personal privacy, between scattered disclosure of the bits of information contained in a rap sheet and revelation of the rap sheet as a whole. The very fact that federal funds have been spent to prepare, index, and maintain these criminal-history files demonstrates that the individual items of information in the summaries would not otherwise be "freely available" either to the officials who have access to the underlying files or to the general public. Indeed, if the summaries were "freely available," there would be no reason to invoke FOIA to obtain access to the information they contain. Granted, in many contexts the fact that information is not freely available is no reason to exempt that information from a statute generally requiring its dissemination. But the issue here is whether the compilation of otherwise hard-to-obtain information alters the privacy interest implicated by disclosure of that information. Plainly there is a vast difference between the public records that might be found after a diligent search of courthouse files, county archives, and local police stations throughout the country and a computerized summary located in a single clearinghouse of information.

This conclusion is supported by the web of federal statutory and regulatory provisions that limits the disclosure of rap-sheet information. That is, Congress has authorized rap-sheet dissemination to banks, local licensing officials, the securities industry, the nuclear-power industry, and other law enforcement agencies. Further, the FBI has permitted such disclosure to the subject of the rap sheet and, more generally, to assist in the apprehension of wanted persons or fugitives. Finally, the FBI's exchange of rap-sheet information "is subject to cancellation if dissemination is made outside the receiving departments or related agencies." This careful and limited pattern of authorized rap-sheet disclosure fits the dictionary definition of privacy as involving a restriction of information "to the use of a particular person or group or class of persons." Moreover, although perhaps not specific enough to constitute a statutory exemption under FOIA Exemption 3, these statutes and regulations, taken as a whole, evidence a congressional intent to protect the privacy of rap-sheet subjects, and a concomitant recognition of the power of compilations to affect personal privacy that outstrips the combined power of the bits of information contained within . . .

In sum, the fact that "an event is not wholly 'private' does not mean that an individual has no interest in limiting disclosure or dissemination of the information." The privacy interest in a rap sheet is substantial. The substantial character of that interest is affected by the fact that in today's society the computer can accumulate and store information that would otherwise have surely been forgotten long before a person attains age 80, when the FBI's rap sheets are discarded.

Exemption 7(C), by its terms, permits an agency to withhold a document only when revelation "could reasonably be expected to constitute an unwarranted invasion of personal privacy." We must next address what factors might warrant an invasion of the interest described in Part IV.

Our previous decisions establish that whether an invasion of privacy is warranted cannot turn on the purposes for which the request for information is made. Except for cases in which the objection to disclosure is based on a claim of privilege and the person requesting disclosure is the party protected by the privilege, the identity of the requesting party has no bearing on the merits of his or her FOIA request. . . . As we have repeatedly stated, Congress "clearly intended" FOIA "to give any member of the public as much right to disclosure as one with a special interest [in a particular document]." . . . "The Act's sole concern is with what must be made public or not made public."

Thus whether disclosure of a private document under Exemption 7(C) is warranted must turn on the nature of the requested document and its relationship to "the basic purpose of the Freedom of Information Act 'to open agency action to the light of public scrutiny'" . . . rather than on the particular purpose for which the document is being requested. In our leading case on FOIA, we declared that the Act was designed to create a broad right of access to "official information." . . .

This basic policy of "'full agency disclosure unless information is exempted under clearly delineated statutory language'" indeed focuses on the citizens' right to be informed about "what their government is up to." Official information that sheds light on an agency's performance of its statutory duties falls squarely within that statutory purpose. That purpose, however, is not fostered by disclosure of information about private citizens that is accumulated in various governmental files but that reveals little or nothing about an agency's own conduct. In this case—and presumably in the typical case in which one private citizen is seeking information about another—the requester does not intend to discover anything about the conduct of the agency that has possession of the requested records. Indeed, response to this request would not shed any light on the conduct of any Government agency or official. . . .

Finally, we note that Congress has provided that the standard fees for production of documents under FOIA shall be waived or reduced "if disclosure of the information is in the public interest because it is likely to contribute significantly to public understanding of the operations or activities of the government and is not primarily in the commercial interest of the requester." Although such a provision obviously implies that there will be requests that do not meet such a "public interest" standard, we think it relevant to today's inquiry regarding the public interest in release of rap sheets on private citizens that Congress once again expressed the core purpose of FOIA as "contribut[ing] significantly to public understanding of the operations or activities of the government."

Both the general requirement that a court "shall determine the matter de novo" and the specific reference to an "unwarranted" invasion of privacy in Exemption 7(C) indicate that a court must balance the public interest in disclosure against the interest Congress intended the Exemption to protect. Although both sides agree that such a balance must be undertaken, how such a balance should be done is in dispute. The Court of Appeals majority expressed concern about assigning federal judges the task of striking a proper case-by-case, or ad hoc, balance between individual privacy interests and the public interest in the disclosure of criminal-history information without providing those judges standards to assist in performing that task. Our cases provide support for the proposition that categorical decisions may be appropriate and individual circumstances disregarded when a case fits into a genus in which the balance characteristically tips in one direction. . . .

. . . [W]e hold as a categorical matter that a third party's request for law enforcement records or information about a private citizen can reasonably be expected to invade that citizen's privacy, and that when the request seeks no "official information" about a Government agency, but merely records that the Government happens to be storing, the invasion of privacy is "unwarranted." The judgment of the Court of Appeals is reversed.

It is so ordered.

VAN BUREN V. UNITED STATES

SUPREME COURT OF THE UNITED STATES 141 S. CT. 1648 (2021)

JUSTICE AMY CONEY BARRETT delivered the Court's opinion:

Nathan Van Buren, a former police sergeant, ran a license-plate search in a law enforcement computer database in exchange for money. Van Buren's conduct plainly flouted his department's policy, which authorized him to obtain database information only for law enforcement purposes. We must decide whether Van Buren also violated the Computer Fraud and Abuse Act of 1986, which makes it illegal "to access a computer with authorization and to use such access to obtain or alter information in the computer that the accesser is not entitled so to obtain or alter."

He did not. This provision covers those who obtain information from particular areas in the computer—such as files, folders, or databases—to which their computer access does not extend. It does not cover those who, like Van Buren, have improper motives for obtaining information that is otherwise available to them. . . .

The [CFAA] subjects to criminal liability anyone who "intentionally accesses a computer without authorization or exceeds authorized access," and thereby obtains computer information. It defines the term "exceeds authorized access" to mean "to access a computer with authorization and to use such access to obtain or alter information in the computer that the accesser is not entitled so to obtain or alter." . . .

Those who violate § 1030(a)(2) face penalties ranging from fines and misdemeanor sentences to imprisonment for up to 10 years. They also risk civil liability under the CFAA's private cause of action, which allows persons suffering "damage" or "loss" from CFAA violations to sue for money damages and equitable relief.

This case stems from Van Buren's time as a police sergeant in Georgia. In the course of his duties, Van Buren crossed paths with a man named Andrew Albo. . . . Van Buren developed a friendly relationship with Albo. Or so Van Buren thought when he went to Albo to ask for a personal loan. Unbeknownst to Van Buren, Albo secretly recorded that request and took it to the local sheriff's office, where he complained that Van Buren had sought to "shake him down" for cash.

The taped conversation made its way to the Federal Bureau of Investigation (FBI), which devised an operation to see how far Van Buren would go for money. The steps were straightforward: Albo would ask Van Buren to search the state law enforcement computer database for a license plate purportedly belonging to a woman whom Albo had met at a local strip club. Albo, no stranger to legal troubles, would tell Van Buren that he wanted to ensure that the woman was not in fact an undercover officer. In return for the search, Albo would pay Van Buren around $5,000. . . .

Van Buren used his patrol-car computer to access the law enforcement database with his valid credentials. He searched the database for the license plate that Albo had provided. After obtaining the FBI-created license-plate entry, Van Buren told Albo that he had information to share.

The Federal Government then charged Van Buren with a felony violation of the CFAA on the ground that running the license plate for Albo violated the "exceeds authorized access" clause of 18 U.S.C. § 1030(a)(2). The trial evidence showed that Van Buren had been trained not to use the law enforcement database for "an improper purpose," defined as "any personal use." . . . [T]he Government told the jury that Van Buren's access of the database "for a non[-]law[-]enforcement purpose" violated the CFAA "concept" against "using" a computer network in a way contrary to "what your job or policy prohibits." The jury convicted Van Buren, and the District Court sentenced him to 18 months in prison.

Van Buren appealed to the Eleventh Circuit, arguing that the "exceeds authorized access" clause applies only to those who obtain information to which their computer access does not extend, not to those who misuse access that they otherwise have. While several Circuits see the clause Van Buren's way, the Eleventh Circuit is among those that have taken a broader view. . . . [T]he panel held that Van Buren had violated the CFAA by accessing the law enforcement database for an "inappropriate reason." We granted certiorari to resolve the split in authority regarding the scope of liability under the CFAA's "exceeds authorized access" clause. . . .

Here, the most relevant text is the phrase "exceeds authorized access," which means "to access a computer with authorization and to use such access to obtain . . . information in the computer that the accesser is not entitled so to obtain."

The parties agree that Van Buren "access[ed] a computer with authorization" when he used his patrol-car computer and valid credentials to log into the law enforcement database. They also agree that Van Buren "obtain[ed] . . . information in the computer" when he acquired the license-plate record for Albo. The dispute is whether Van Buren was "entitled so to obtain" the record.

"Entitle" means "to give . . . a title, right, or claim to something." The parties agree that Van Buren had been given the right to acquire license-plate information—that is, he was "entitled to obtain" it—from the law enforcement computer database. But was Van Buren "entitled *so* to obtain" the license-plate information, as the statute requires?

Van Buren says yes. He notes that "so," as used in this statute, serves as a term of reference that recalls "the same manner as has been stated" or "the way or manner described." The disputed phrase "entitled so to obtain" thus asks whether one has the right, in "the same manner as has been stated," to obtain the relevant information. And the only manner of obtaining information already stated in the definitional provision is "via a computer [one] is otherwise authorized to access." Putting that together, Van Buren contends that the disputed phrase—"is not entitled *so* to obtain"—plainly refers to information one is not allowed to obtain *by using a computer that he is authorized to access*. On this reading, if a person has access to information stored in a computer—*e.g.*, in "Folder Y," from which the person could permissibly pull information—then he does not violate the CFAA by obtaining such information, regardless of whether he pulled the information for a prohibited purpose. But if the information is instead located in prohibited "Folder X," to which the person lacks access, he violates the CFAA by obtaining such information.

The Government agrees that the statute uses "so" in the word's term-of-reference sense, but it argues that "so" sweeps more broadly. It reads the phrase "is not entitled *so* to obtain" to refer to information one was not allowed to obtain *in the particular manner or circumstances in which he obtained it*. The manner or circumstances in which one has a right to obtain information, the Government says, are defined by any "specifically and explicitly" communicated limits on one's right to access information. As the Government sees it, an employee might lawfully pull information from Folder Y in the morning for a permissible purpose—say, to prepare for a business meeting—but unlawfully pull the same information from Folder Y in the afternoon for a prohibited purpose—say, to help draft a resume to submit to a competitor employer.

The Government's interpretation has surface appeal but proves to be a sleight of hand. ... Under the Government's approach, ... "so" captures *any* circumstance-based limit appearing *anywhere*—in the United States Code, a state statute, a private agreement, or anywhere else. ...

We agree with Van Buren: The phrase "is not entitled so to obtain" is best read to refer to information that a person is not entitled to obtain by using a computer that he is authorized to access. ...

As Van Buren points out, without "so," the statute would allow individuals to use their right to obtain information in nondigital form as a defense to CFAA liability. ...

This clarification is significant because it underscores that one kind of entitlement to information counts: the right to access the information by using a computer. That can expand liability, as the above example shows. But it narrows liability too. Without the word "so," the statute could be read to incorporate all kinds of limitations on one's entitlement to information. ...

The interplay between the "without authorization" and "exceeds authorized access" clauses of subsection (a)(2) is particularly probative. Those clauses specify two distinct ways of obtaining information unlawfully. *First*, an individual violates the provision when he "accesses a computer without authorization." *Second*, an individual violates the provision when he "exceeds authorized access" by accessing a computer "with authorization" and then obtaining information he is "not entitled so to obtain." Van Buren's reading places the provision's parts "into an harmonious whole."

... The "without authorization" clause, Van Buren contends, protects computers themselves by targeting so-called outside hackers—those who "acces[s] a computer without any permission at all." Van Buren reads the "exceeds authorized access" clause to provide complementary protection for certain information within computers. It does so, Van Buren asserts, by targeting so-called inside hackers—those who access a computer with permission, but then " 'exceed' the parameters of authorized access by entering an area of the computer to which [that] authorization does not extend." ...

[T]he Government's interpretation of the statute would attach criminal penalties to a breathtaking amount of commonplace computer activity. . . . If the "exceeds authorized access" clause criminalizes every violation of a computer-use policy, then millions of otherwise law-abiding citizens are criminals. Take the workplace. Employers commonly state that computers and electronic devices can be used only for business purposes. So on the Government's reading of the statute, an employee who sends a personal e-mail or reads the news using her work computer has violated the CFAA. Or consider the Internet. Many websites, services, and databases—which provide "information" from "protected computer[s]," § 1030(a)(2)(C)—authorize a user's access only upon his agreement to follow specified terms of service. If the "exceeds authorized access" clause encompasses violations of circumstance-based access restrictions on employers' computers, it is difficult to see why it would not also encompass violations of such restrictions on website providers' computers. And indeed, numerous *amici* explain why the Government's reading of subsection (a)(2) would do just that—criminalize everything from embellishing an online-dating profile to using a pseudonym on Facebook. ...

In sum, an individual "exceeds authorized access" when he accesses a computer with authorization but then obtains information located in particular areas of the computer—such as files, folders, or databases—that are off limits to him. The parties agree that Van Buren accessed the law enforcement database system with authorization. The only question is whether Van Buren could use the system to retrieve license-plate information. Both sides agree that he could. Van Buren accordingly did not "excee[d] authorized access" to the database, as the CFAA defines that phrase, even though he obtained information from the database for an improper purpose. We therefore reverse the contrary judgment of the Eleventh Circuit and remand the case for further proceedings consistent with this opinion.

It is so ordered.

JUSTICE CLARENCE THOMAS dissented, joined by CHIEF JUSTICE ROBERTS Jr. and JUSTICE ALITO:

Both the common law and statutory law have long punished those who exceed the scope of consent when using property that belongs to others. A valet, for example, may take possession of a person's car to park it, but he cannot take it for a joyride. The Computer Fraud and Abuse Act extends that principle to computers and information. The Act prohibits exceeding the scope of consent when using a computer that belongs to another person. Specifically, it punishes anyone who "intentionally accesses a computer without authorization or exceeds authorized access, and thereby obtains" information from that computer.

. . . The question here is straightforward: Would an ordinary reader of the English language understand Van Buren to have "exceed[ed] authorized access" to the database when he used it under circumstances that were expressly forbidden? In my view, the answer is yes.

. . . A person is entitled to do something only if he has a "right" to do it. Van Buren never had a "right" to use the computer to obtain the specific license-plate information. Everyone agrees that he obtained it for personal gain, not for a valid law enforcement purpose. And without a valid law enforcement purpose, he was *forbidden* to use the computer to obtain that information. . . . Because Van Buren lacked a law enforcement purpose, the "proper grounds" did not exist. He was not entitled to obtain the data when he did so. . . .

The majority offers no real response. It notes that "entitled" is modified by "so" and that courts must therefore consider whether a person is entitled to use a computer to obtain information. But if a person is not entitled to obtain information *at all*, it necessarily follows that he has no "right to access the information by using a computer." Van Buren was not entitled to obtain this information at all because the condition precedent needed to trigger an entitlement—a law enforcement purpose—was absent.

. . . In the end, the Act may or may not cover a wide array of conduct because of changes in technology that have occurred since 1984. But the text makes one thing clear: Using a police database to obtain information in circumstances where that use is expressly forbidden is a crime. I respectfully dissent.

A trial judge in Arapahoe County, Colo., sealed all court records of prosecutorial misconduct in the capital murder conviction of Sir Mario Owens. District Attorney Carol Chambers led the prosecution.[1]

Ed Endicott/Alamy Stock Photo

OVERSEEING JUSTICE

Speech and Press Freedoms In and About the Courts

CHAPTER OUTLINE

Access to Courts and Court Records
Presuming the Openness of Trials
Broadcasting and Recording Court Proceedings
Using Newer Technologies in the Courts
Accessing Court Records
Electronically Accessing Court Records

Advancing Fairness in Trials
Following *Sheppard*
Judging Impartially

Balancing Interests
Requiring Evidence
Penalizing Failure to Disclose
Protecting Juveniles
Protecting Sexual Assault Victims
Protecting State Secrets and National Security
Closing Courts
Challenging Closures

Advancing the Flow of News
Guiding Media Coverage of Courts
Protecting Confidential Information
Providing a Limited Privilege
Applying Shield Laws
Clarifying What Shield Laws Cover
Finding Other Protections for Journalists

Emerging Law

Cases for Study
- *Richmond Newspapers, Inc. v. Virginia*
- *People v. Owens*

LEARNING OBJECTIVES

8.1 Recognize how the First Amendment and common law may provide rights for the public to access court proceedings and records.

8.2 Identify steps courts and journalists may take to advance fairness in trials.

> **8.3**   Describe how courts balance constitutional fair trial rights with the public interest in learning about criminal justice.
>
> **8.4**   Compare the ways First Amendment rights and statutory rights may advance the flow of news.
>
> **8.5**   Discuss the emerging legal decisions around cameras in the Supreme Court, social media and journalists as sources for legal action.

The Sixth Amendment to the U.S. Constitution gives criminal defendants the right to a speedy public trial by an impartial jury of their peers in the locale of the crime. In the nearly 60 years since U.S. Supreme Court Justice Tom Clark suggested that courts must remedy the inherent conflict between fair trials and robust news coverage of trials and crime, we have moved to instant memes and real-time media clips of unfolding trials that circulate around the globe.[2] Trial observers describe crime scenes and evidence. Reporters interview neighbors, family, police and victims throughout investigations. Media disseminate video and audio, and public relations experts carefully craft images of crime victims.[3] Courts, at times, are called upon to determine whether such publicity provided before and during trials may prevent defendants from receiving fair trials. Judges sometimes shield privacy, reputational or security interests against threats due to public disclosure in court records or proceedings. Judges also may determine whether journalists and their sources may be called to testify during court proceedings.

Media inform; sometimes they correct the public record.[4] A 2020 Minneapolis police statement indicated a man had died after a medical incident occurred during his interaction with police officers.[5] Video recordings, however, showed a police officer kneeled on the neck of George Floyd; Floyd told officers he could not breathe, and then he died.[6] Charges ultimately were filed against four officers. Media coverage changed the public narrative.[7]

Media affect attitudes toward policing and the criminal justice system.[8] Exemplary media coverage of "unequal justice,"[9] prosecutors' discretion, the prevalence of plea bargains,[10] overcrowded and violent prisons and more do not correct public misunderstanding of the criminal justice system.[11] Studies show that most people who rely on media coverage to understand crime misunderstand the nature and frequency of crime and the identity of criminals.[12] Potential jurors read and see coverage of crime that presents the accused in overwhelmingly negative ways, focuses on community fear and outrage and contains information that may not be admissible at trial.[13] Black males and Latinos are overrepresented in media reports on crime, especially violent crime.[14] Yet, judges rarely grant defense requests to delay a trial or relocate a trial away from news coverage, despite pervasive media reporting that could influence jurors.[15] For instance, a Minnesota judge denied a request to delay the murder trial of Derek Chauvin, a former police officer charged for kneeling on Floyd's neck, because the entire state of Minnesota was "saturated with media coverage of the case" and pretrial publicity likely would continue even if the trial were delayed.[16]

ACCESS TO COURTS AND COURT RECORDS

Together the Fifth, Sixth and Seventh Amendments to the U.S. Constitution guarantee the right to a fair and open public trial.[17] Four decades ago, the U.S. Supreme Court said the public's long-standing common law right to view public trials must be balanced against protection of a fair trial. The Court's landmark ruling in *Gannett v. DePasquale* arose after Judge Daniel DePasquale granted pretrial motions to suppress evidence and confessions and to exclude the public and the press from a pretrial hearing addressing the murder of an off-duty police officer. No one at the pretrial hearing, including a Gannett reporter, objected to the court's rulings.[18]

After Gannett later objected to the court closure, the judge said the defendant's right to a fair trial outweighed the right of the press to cover the hearing. On review, the Supreme Court considered whether a criminal defendant may waive his right to a public trial regardless of whether the public, including the media, wants to attend. Because publicity could prejudice the defendant's right to a fair trial, judges may use means to protect a fair trial that are "not strictly and inescapably necessary," the Court concluded.[19] Justice Potter Stewart wrote:

> [T]here is a strong societal interest in public trials. Openness in court proceedings may improve the quality of testimony, induce unknown witnesses to come forward with relevant testimony, cause all trial participants to perform their duties more conscientiously, and generally give the public an opportunity to observe the judicial system. But there is a strong societal interest in other constitutional guarantees extended to the accused as well.[20]

While concurring with the Court's opinion to uphold closure, Justice Harry Blackmun wrote that closing a courtroom "may implicate interests beyond those of the accused," including "important social interests relating to the integrity of the trial process."[21] He said judges must weigh those competing interests fully even if no one objects to closure. Judges should presume that court processes should be open and require the party seeking closure to show convincingly (1) the probability that publicity would infringe on the right to a fair trial, (2) the inadequacy of alternatives to closure and (3) the effectiveness of closure.[22]

Presuming the Openness of Trials

In a series of cases beginning with *Gannett*, the U.S. Supreme Court largely adopted Justice Blackmun's concurring opinion that "[p]ublic confidence cannot long be maintained where important judicial decisions are made behind closed doors and then announced in conclusive terms to the public, with the record supporting the court's decision sealed, or closed, from public view."[23] These Supreme Court decisions establish a qualified First Amendment right of public access to judicial proceedings when (a) the proceeding traditionally has been open to the public and (b) openness advances the proceeding's goals. This **experience and logic test**, as it is called, is a doctrine that evaluates both the history of openness and the role it plays in ensuring the credibility of a judicial process to determine whether it is presumptively opinion. The test holds that closure of such proceedings should be a last resort used only when (a) essential (b) to avoid a substantial probability of harm (c) to some overriding interest where (d) no effective alternative exists.[24]

In *Richmond Newspapers, Inc. v. Virginia*,[25] the Supreme Court held that the Sixth Amendment right to a public trial does not belong to the defendant alone. The Court said criminal trials are presumptively open and the First Amendment prohibits their closure without a full exploration of alternatives.[26] Chief Justice Warren Burger wrote that "absent an overriding interest articulated in findings, the trial of a criminal case must be open to the public."[27] Open criminal trials serve the public interest and advance the core First Amendment goal of protecting "freedom of communications on matters relating to the functioning of government."[28] Access to the criminal process enables citizens to evaluate government performance, to maintain faith in the judicial system, and to seek catharsis for the trauma of crimes.[29]

The Supreme Court of South Dakota recently recognized a qualified First Amendment right of access to civil trials in that state. The state high court found that the presumption of openness outweighed the agreement of all trial parties and the judge to close the trial about a popular tourist attraction. In addition, the court said the desire to reduce prejudicial publicity does not justify **gag orders**, restraining orders that prohibit communication about specific material, in civil cases a judge decides.[30]

According to a 1982 U.S. Supreme Court ruling, states may not require closure of specific portions of criminal trials.[31] In *Globe Newspaper Co. v. Superior Court for Norfolk County*, the Supreme Court struck down a Virginia law that closed courtrooms during testimony of any minor who was a sexual assault victim. The Court said the automatic closure of a sexual assault trial involving testimony by a minor victim denied the defendant a fair trial because criminal trials historically have been open and "public scrutiny enhances the quality and safeguards the integrity" of trials. To justify closure of such presumptively open proceedings, the Court said, the First Amendment requires the state to provide a "weighty" showing that (1) closure is necessary (2) to protect "a compelling government interest and (3) is narrowly tailored to serve that interest."[32] The decision must be made on a case-by-case basis.[33]

In 2021, the Supreme Court of North Dakota stated that "closures of criminal trial proceedings to the public should be rare."[34] The state high court found a district court had erred excluding the public from hearing testimony of a child victim's counselor without recording findings for closing that portion of a trial. The court said not "considering obvious alternatives negatively affects the fairness, integrity, and public reputation of our criminal justice system."[35] Trial courts must consider whether closures are narrowly tailored to serve an overriding interest and alternatives to closure.

In a pair of cases involving the Press-Enterprise newspaper in California, the U.S. Supreme Court subsequently applied the experience and logic test to determine when the constitutional presumption of openness applies. In those two cases, the Court applied the qualified right of access to transcripts of trial proceedings.[36] Under the *Press-Enterprise* decisions, court procedures and their associated records are presumptively open when (1) they "have historically been open to the press and general public" and (2) "public access plays a significant positive role in the functioning of the particular process in question."[37] The Supreme Court also ruled that the presumptive public right of access applied to both jury selection and preliminary hearings, which determine whether there is sufficient evidence to proceed to trial.[38] Eleven federal courts of appeals have extended the qualified right of access to other judicial records.[39]

POINTS OF LAW

OPEN COURTS

According to the U.S. Supreme Court's rulings in two Press-Enterprise newspaper cases, court proceedings are presumptively open if experience and logic dictate openness. Accordingly, court processes are presumed to be open if

1. the proceeding traditionally has been open, and
2. openness advances the goals and functioning of the proceeding itself. [40]

The U.S. Supreme Court has held that the right of access to trials and trial records may be overcome by compelling "overriding interests." The Court has said "safeguarding the physical and psychological well-being of a minor" and protecting the right to a fair trial are overriding interests that may warrant narrowly tailored limits on public access.[41]

The Court said access to the hearings themselves, not simply to transcripts released later, is vital to ensure public confidence. Some particularly sensitive questions to potential jurors during jury selection, or voir dire, might raise privacy concerns sufficient to warrant closure. Safety concerns also might justify closure. Such closures, however, must be narrowly tailored to protect only those matters that raise serious concerns. Some courts justify closed voir dire and juror anonymity by saying that access to jury selection and juror identity erodes the candor of potential jurors and harms an integral judicial process. In 2010, the Supreme Court's decision in *Presley v. Georgia* reiterated that "the public has a right to be present whether or not any party has asserted the right."[42] The Court reaffirmed that the Sixth Amendment right to a public trial applies to **voir dire**, questioning of potential jurors as part of the jury selection process:[43] "Courts are obligated to take every reasonable measure to accommodate public attendance at criminal trials."[44]

Recent court rulings provide a glimpse into the procedures and standards by which the state of Colorado determined the openness of court proceedings related to triple murders and the capital sentence of Sir Mario Owens, excerpted at the end of the chapter.[45] Concurrent proceedings against Owens and two other defendants spanned more than a decade and presented the probability that information disclosed in one might prejudice the others.[46] For example, before the trials began and in response to defense requests to restrict pretrial publicity, the trial court found that the "nature" of the pending cases and of existing publicity demanded the court take steps to protect a fair trial process.[47]

The courts prohibited all trial participants, court personnel and others associated with trial attorneys from disclosing to the public any information or opinion that might prejudice the trial, including (1) prior criminal record, (2) defendants' statements, (3) defendants' examination results or refusal to participate in examinations, (4) identity or credibility of witnesses, (5) possibility of plea deals, (6) opinions of guilt or (7) predictions of outcomes. The order expressly forbade the release of any information not a part of the public court record, including any sealed records, **in camera** discussions, or hearings held without the public present. The limits applied for 90 days prior to trial. The court also cautioned the attorneys to seal discovery information and to consider

Journalists gather to interview family members of crime victims outside the Arapaho district court where Sir Mario Owns was sentenced to death.

Brian Brainerd/Denver Post/Getty

carefully what documents should or should not be made public. It allowed extrajudicial comment only on public records and trial proceedings to the extent they did not violate the above limits.

After the defendants were convicted and sentenced to death, they sought access to the prosecutor's files to support their claim that the prosecution had withheld evidence that might have reduced their sentences.[48] The trial court confirmed evidence of extensive prosecutorial misconduct but sealed all records relating to the motion for dismissal or disclosure because it ruled that the misconduct affected neither the verdict nor the death sentence.[49] The court sealed all transcripts, exhibits and actions in the challenge to the government's decision to execute the defendants.

In 2018, in *People v. Owens*, the Colorado Supreme Court affirmed a separate court order refusing to release witness identification and other information related to the defendants' challenge to their death-penalty sentences.[50] Some of the witnesses were in a witness protection program.[51] Without employing the two-part experience and logic test established in *Press-Enterprise*, the state supreme court held that neither the state constitution nor the First Amendment guaranteed the defendants or news organization access to sealed records in the capital murder case.[52]

The Colorado Supreme Court said that "while presumptive access to judicial proceedings is a right recognized under both the state and federal constitutions, neither the U.S. Supreme Court nor the Colorado Supreme Court has ever held that records filed with a court are treated the same way."[53] In 2019, the U.S. Supreme Court denied certiorari to review the decision.[54]

Also in 2019, in a high-profile defamation case arising from BuzzFeed reporting on Russian hacking into Democratic National Committee computers during the 2016 U.S. presidential campaign, a federal district court in Florida unsealed documents kept confidential pending the trial conclusion.[55] The judge dismissed as speculative arguments that disclosure would endanger some foreign individuals who provided evidence and taint the jury in any potential retrial.[56]

Almost two years later, a Second Circuit Court of Appeals ruling applied the experience and logic test to recognize a qualified First Amendment right to access court records and proceedings of juveniles whose cases were transferred from juvenile courts to criminal courts in Connecticut.[57] For cases addressed in regular criminal courts, "the place and process have historically been open to the public," and "public access plays a positive role in the functioning of criminal proceedings," the appeals court said.[58] A Connecticut statute that required sealing all court records and closing all court proceedings in such cases infringed those access rights. The court presumed the Connecticut law served compelling interests —protecting children against stigma and promoting public safety—but the statute was not narrowly tailored to serve those interests.[59] "A more narrowly tailored approach—with a presumption of openness but the availability of confidentiality upon a showing of necessity—would better balance the public's right of access against the dangers of stigmatizing juveniles by providing fuller protection when necessary," the court said.[60]

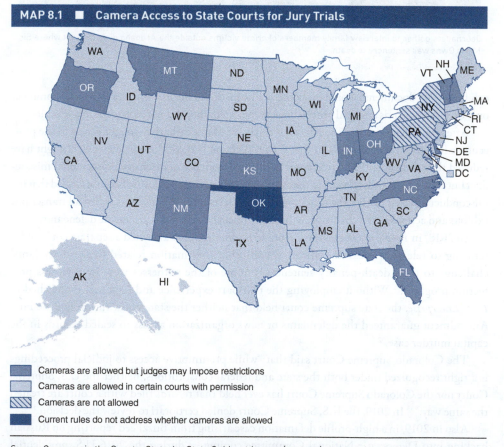

MAP 8.1 ■ Camera Access to State Courts for Jury Trials

Legend:
- Cameras are allowed but judges may impose restrictions
- Cameras are allowed in certain courts with permission
- Cameras are not allowed
- Current rules do not address whether cameras are allowed

Source: Cameras in the Courts: State-by-State Guide, rtdna.org/content/cameras_in_court

Broadcasting and Recording Court Proceedings

Although the First Amendment provides a right of access to courts, openness is not absolute. Judges may limit attendance, including the number of media present, and they may exclude recording devices to ensure decorum in their courts.[61]

In 1981 in *Chandler v. Florida*, the U.S. Supreme Court said the right of access to public trials does not include presumptive access for cameras. The Court noted that electronic coverage affects the trial process and participants in unpredictable ways. Although the Court no longer presumed cameras would be inherently prejudicial, it said individual states should determine whether to permit cameras in courtrooms; it said print coverage sufficiently protects the public interest in open trials.[62] The U.S. Supreme Court does not permit still or video cameras, laptops, tablets, cell phones or smartwatches during its oral arguments.[63]

INTERNATIONAL LAW

UNITED KINGDOM COURTS ALLOW CAMERAS IN SELECT COURT PROCEEDINGS

Cameras recently have provided greater access to some court proceedings in England and Wales. The United Kingdom Supreme Court provided virtual access to select court proceedings during the COVID-19 pandemic. In 2021, the court announced all hearings and judgments would occur via video conferencing in late April and May. Members of the public and press were allowed to view proceedings via the court's website.[64]

Those changes followed a 2020 Ministry of Justice announcement that portions of high-profile criminal cases in England and Wales would be televised for the first time. To enable the public "to hear judges explain the reasons behind their sentences for the most serious offenses," the Crown Court allowed cameras to record and broadcast judges' sentencing remarks, but not to show other trial participants.[65] That was a major shift for courts that previously did not allow filming, photographing or sketching court proceedings.[66]

The Court of Appeal (Civil Division) has livestreamed select cases via the court's YouTube channel since 2018 "to improve public access to, and understanding of, the work of the courts."[67]

The U.S. Judicial Conference recently ended a four-year national trial project[68] allowing cameras in civil proceedings in 14 federal district courts.[69] Despite majority support for cameras from participants, the national policy body continued the ban on recording in most federal trial courts.[70] Federal Rule of Criminal Procedure 53 generally prohibits cameras in federal criminal trial courts, and federal policy bans televised civil proceedings. The 13 federal circuit courts of appeal each decide whether to allow televised or other news media coverage. Judges in federal appellate courts generally permit cameras in the courtroom at least some of the time. Court rules determine the specific conditions that apply when cameras are allowed. Video coverage of some district court proceedings is allowed in the Second and Ninth Circuit. The Ninth Circuit

Judicial Council allowed three district courts to continue permitting cameras in the Northern District of California in San Francisco, District of Guam and Western District of Washington in Seattle civil proceedings (See Table 8.1.).[71]

In a narrow ruling, the U.S. Supreme Court prevented the broadcast of a federal district court trial on a California ballot measure banning same-sex marriage. The defense opposed the coverage. The Court said the trial court's decision to permit livestreaming of the proceeding failed to "follow the appropriate procedures set forth in federal law,"[72] and public viewing might cause harassment of trial participants. The trial court struck down the voter-approved same-sex marriage ban.[73]

TABLE 8.1 ■ Cameras in Federal Courts	
U.S. Supreme Court	No cameras allowed during court proceedings
U.S. Circuit Courts	Cameras permitted in select civil proceedings with parties' consent at judges' discretion; not allowed during criminal proceedings
U.S. District Courts	Cameras allowed in some civil proceedings with parties' consent at judges' discretion; barred from criminal proceedings by Federal Rule of Criminal Procedure 53

Source: Video Broadcasting from the Federal Courts: Issues for Congress, Congressional Research Service, Oct. 28, 2019, https://sgp.fas.org/crs/misc/R44514.pdf; Cameras in the Courts, RTDNA, Nov. 2022, https://www.rtdna.org/cameras-in-the-courts#Second.

Cameras are allowed in some state courtrooms some of the time.[74] In Florida, a judicially created presumption permits camera coverage of virtually all cases.[75] South Dakota allows broadcast coverage of trials with consent of the judge and all parties, except for recording of jurors or proceedings when the jury is excluded.[76] News cameras recorded closing arguments and a verdict in a South Dakota murder trial for the first time in 2011.[77] In 2020, Massachusetts courts temporarily suspended rules that banned cell phones and personal electronic devices from courthouses, yet generally forbade members of the public to use cameras or personal electronic devices to record photographs or video in courthouses.[78] The Illinois code of judicial conduct limits broadcasting of court proceedings to "the extent authorized by order of the Supreme Court"[79] and prohibits broadcasting or recording of any compelled witness testimony.[80]

Judges may limit the number and location of cameras, require pooled cameras or prohibit recording of jurors or vulnerable witnesses. States from Alabama to Utah limit camera coverage of trials when coverage could harm minors.[81] In another six states, including Pennsylvania and Louisiana, trial courts are virtually closed to cameras. Media sometimes publish sketches of court proceedings in those states.[82] To ensure they do not violate court rules, those wishing to record court proceedings must be familiar with the details of the laws in the states where they report. Journalists often must seek advance permission to record court proceedings or to have electronic devices—including mobile phones, laptops or smart watches—in courtrooms.[83] They also must check whether court rules differ for video cameras and still cameras and video recording and audio recording.[84]

A courtroom sketch shows an attorney questioning a police officer in a trial addressing the 2018 mass shooting in the Capital Gazette.

Kevin Richardson/The Baltimore Sun/Associated Press

Using Newer Technologies in the Courts

Studies of the effects on courts of accelerating news cycles, 24-hour news coverage, blogs, webcasts and other "new media" mechanisms suggest these media sensationalize rather than educate or inform the public.[85] A recent study said that the ubiquity of social media threatens the impartiality of the jury,[86] and courts concerned about their uncertain impact are not racing to embrace new media.[87] In one recent case, the Tennessee Supreme Court sent a first-degree murder conviction back for review by the trial court because the judge had failed to question a juror who had exchanged Facebook messages with one of the state's witnesses during jury deliberation.[88] Jury deliberations are sealed.

REAL WORLD LAW
MANAGING NEW MEDIA IN COURTS

U.S. Judicial Conference guidance for courts creating policies on use of electronic devices in courtrooms includes:

1. Members of the media must register with and receive approval from a clerk of court prior to requesting the presiding judge's permission to use an electronic device to communicate from a courtroom.

2. Members of the media may use electronic devices to communicate within a courtroom unless the presiding judge directs otherwise.
3. Members of the media only may send and receive text messages within a courtroom without disrupting proceedings.
4. Members of the media must not use electronic devices to create a verbatim transcript of proceedings.[89]

Led by California and Massachusetts, courts are integrating social media into their administrative offices, their courtrooms and their public outreach, but policies vary widely.[90] Some stream or have blogs that offer instant public access. Some state and federal courts allow reporters to webcast and use social media posts to provide play-by-play coverage of unfolding trials.[91] One judge—overseeing a $1 million recording industry lawsuit against a Boston University student for copyright infringement through Kazaa—echoed the *Press-Enterprise* standard and said nothing in "life or logic" prevents livestreaming of court proceedings, especially in a case involving digital technology.[92] The First Circuit Court of Appeals refused to allow webcasting of the appeal.[93] The Ninth Circuit Court of Appeals, however, began livestreaming en banc proceedings almost a decade ago.[94]

The Michigan Supreme Court became the first to ban all electronic communication by jurors during trials, and a number of courts declared mistrials because of juror use of new media during trial.[95] Similar bans have spread across the country,[96] and courts have struggled to determine whether to use new media evidence in trials. Recently proposed model jury instructions indicate jurors cannot "communicate with anyone about the case in any way, whether in writing, or through email, text messaging, blogs, or comments, or on social media websites and apps."[97]

Accessing Court Records

The public right to access court records is grounded in common law and the U.S. and state constitutions. Decisions to seal court records generally are subject to the same constitutional limits as court closure. They are strongly disfavored and must pass the stringent *Press-Enterprise* experience and logic test.[98]

In a case related to the event that ended the Nixon presidency, the U.S. Supreme Court limited the common law right of access to court records. The 1974 criminal trial of some aides to then-President Richard Nixon for the Watergate Hotel break-in and conspiracy relied on the former president's White House tape recordings as evidence. Federal law provides delayed public access to presidential records, but the district court denied media access to the tapes during the trial. It said broadcast of the tapes might prejudice defense appeals.[99]

The court of appeals reversed. In *Nixon v. Warner Communications*, the Supreme Court held that courts are not required to provide access to all records in their custody, particularly when the records are available through alternative means. The Court said the press had no First Amendment right to inspect or copy the tapes because the media have no rights of access superior to those of the general public.[100]

An attorney for the Sioux Falls Argus Leader argues before the South Dakota Supreme Court in a case seeking to unseal search warrants.

Stephen Groves/Associated Press

In 2021, the Supreme Court of Kansas recognized a qualified common law right for the public to inspect court records, including affidavits or testimony supporting an arrest warrant. Upon request, a judge may consider whether to **redact**, removing sensitive information, or seal records when necessary to minimize serious harm, including "effects of prejudicial pretrial publicity," a clearly unwarranted invasion of privacy or physical, mental or emotional harm. The court said releasing information from the probable cause affidavit in the kidnapping, murder and child endangerment case did not "inherently create any greater risk of an unfair trial than other types of pretrial publicity." Rather than restrict access to court records, the court said, "the preferred and most effective way to assure a fair trial is through voir dire."[101]

In 2019, the Eleventh Circuit Court of Appeals held that a common law right of access required the courts to release Alabama Department of Corrections records detailing the state's execution protocol.[102] The court said the state's lethal injection procedure submitted—though not formally filed—with the court during litigation was a judicial record subject to disclosure "because it was submitted to the district court to resolve disputed substantive motions, . . . was discussed and analyzed by all parties in evidentiary hearings and arguments, and was unambiguously integral to the court's resolution" of the issue. In addition, the state failed to show sufficient interests in secrecy to overcome the public's presumptive right of access. Court records that do not unduly harm due process or privacy rights should be open.[103]

Both federal and state courts tend to require government to provide a specific showing of a compelling need to maintain the secrecy of presumptively open court records. For example, the Ninth Circuit Court of Appeals recently upheld the secrecy of testimony related to a defendant's cooperation in providing information about organized drug smuggling. The appeals court found that the risk of harm to the defendant's family outweighed the qualified First Amendment right of access to the criminal court records.[104]

Although the U.S. Supreme Court has not explicitly recognized a First Amendment right to access civil court records, news outlets and First Amendment groups recently challenged courts that failed to provide timely access to court filings in Virginia, California and Vermont.[105] In 2021, the Fourth Circuit Court of Appeals addressed Virginia courts delaying journalists' access to newly filed civil complaints. The court determined those delays violated a First Amendment right for the press and public to access newly filed nonconfidential civil complaints "as expeditiously as possible."[106] In 2020, the Ninth Circuit Court of Appeals also rejected a California court's stance that there was no right for the Courthouse News Service to have timely access to nonconfidential civil court records. "Absent a showing that there is a substantial interest in retaining the private nature of a judicial record, once documents have been filed in judicial proceedings, a presumption arises that the public has the right to know the information they contain," the appeals court said.[107]

State court rules and policies generally determine the openness of state court records. To limit harms to trial fairness and privacy, rules generally seal court records of information disclosed mandatorily or under discovery unless the material is presented in open court. States may impose penalties on judicial employees who violate these rules. Four decades ago, however, the U.S. Supreme Court ruled in *Florida Star v. B.J.F* that states may not punish media for publishing truthful information obtained legally from court files unless the penalty is "narrowly tailored to a state interest of the highest order."[108] (See Chapter 6 for a discussion of this case.)

After the "Undisclosed" blog, which reports on wrongful convictions, was denied the right to copy court recordings of a murder trial, the Georgia Supreme Court held that the state law that provides public access to court records also provides a right to copy the record. The state supreme court said the public's protected right to inspect is "not complete unless it includes the right to copy." However, the court refused to release the court clerk's recording of the trial. Because the recording had not been filed with the trial court, it was not a court record. In a footnote, however, the court said a trial recording *might* be disclosable if the official transcript failed to provide a full record of what occurred in open court.[109]

Unclear judicial standards lead to wide disparities in the sealing of court records.[110] Although the U.S. Supreme Court has said access restrictions must be narrowly tailored to meet a compelling interest, few courts require detailed evidence to justify records closures. In Hawaii, the state supreme court struck down a trial court's sealing of "the entire legal file" in the prosecution of a Honolulu police officer charged with drug-related crimes. The trial court said complete secrecy was needed to protect the ongoing investigation, but the Hawaii Supreme Court said a narrower secrecy ruling would be adequate and the state must provide a specific showing of a compelling need for nondisclosure.[111]

A Pennsylvania appeals court ordered the unsealing of all trial court records connected to the sexual assault proceedings against former Pennsylvania State University assistant football coach Jerry Sandusky. The trial court refused to unseal the records that related to grand jury testimony, but the appeals court held that there was "no question" the records were covered by both a common law and First Amendment right of access.[112]

Some courts exclude sealed cases from their dockets and electronic case management systems, effectively preventing challenges to closure and minimizing knowledge that the cases exist. Where state open-records laws do apply, these rules vary. In Indiana, the open-records law covers all court records not closed by a specific exemption.[113] In contrast, Washington's broad Public Records Act excludes court records and judges' files.[114] A court said that "limit[ing] the life of a particular record" did not harm the public's right to know in Washington.[115]

Electronically Accessing Court Records

National court and judicial organizations have worked to facilitate online public access to court records while protecting important interests in privacy. Both the National Center for State Courts and the Justice Management Institute advocated for court records to be posted online and be presumptively open.[116]

The Public Access to Court Electronic Records (PACER) site (www.pacer.gov) provides online access to federal court records, often at a cost to users. In 2020, the Federal Circuit Court of Appeals recognized that "First Amendment stakes are high" when high fees prevent members of the public from accessing court records via PACER. Preventing electronic access to court records "will diminish the public's ability to participate in and serve as a check upon the judicial process—an essential component in our structure of self-government," the court said.[117] The court held that federal law allowing the judiciary to charge "reasonable fees" for access to records via PACER limits fees to the amount necessary to cover expenses for providing access to federal court electronic docketing information.[118]

Electronic access to state records varies as to which records are online, to whom they are open and for what purposes they are available.[119] Recent decisions in Maine, Oklahoma and Virginia increased public access to online court records.[120] The Supreme Court of New Mexico recently announced journalists could receive online access to court records.[121] In Florida, however, people wishing to access family court records must submit a notarized application and receive a court clerk's approval.[122]

While some states' online access systems are free and comprehensive, others provide limited information or charge fees. Most states provide some access to civil and family law case records online.[123] In Nebraska, people must subscribe and pay fees to access court documents online from the state's criminal, civil, juvenile, traffic and probate cases filed in county and district courts.[124]

Electronic access to public records has increased fears about how easily searchable data compilations alter the nature and extent of access to courts. Many states limit access to records containing sensitive information, such as financial records or addresses.[125] In 2020, almost a week after North Dakota launched a pilot program to provide public online access to court records, the state supreme court suspended the program due to concerns that documents included sensitive information that should have been redacted.[126] Information gatherers wanting detailed information on state laws on access to court records on- and offline may find it through the National Center for State Courts.[127]

In a foundational decision in 1989, long before online access to court records was common, the Supreme Court ruled in *U.S. Department of Justice v. Reporters Committee for Freedom of the Press* that federal law did not provide journalists access to an FBI electronic compilation of rap (arrest) sheets. The reporter wanted to compile information on the background of a suspected mobster, but the Court said access to the aggregated information posed an impermissible threat to individual privacy.[128]

A recent Virginia Supreme Court ruling held that the state Freedom of Information Act similarly required a newspaper to seek access to court records from each court jurisdiction rather than from the state's court-records database. The question before the court was about the source of disclosure, "not whether [the] records should be made public," because the records were unquestionably covered by the state open-records act. The court concluded, however, that access could be obtained only from the designated records custodians, which the law established to be the clerk of each court jurisdiction.[129]

State court rules may also affect electronic access. For example, the Minnesota court records committee suggests that fees be charged for court databases to make money.[130] A Washington state court rule requires people who request criminal conviction data to agree to use the information responsibly.[131] The uneven and fast-shifting pattern of electronic access to court records requires those seeking records to check federal and state rules and procedures.

ADVANCING FAIRNESS IN TRIALS

Potential jurors do not live in a vacuum. Like everyone else, they swim daily in a sea of crime coverage. The U.S. Supreme Court recognized the potential harms media publicity might cause to fair trials in the early days of television. Almost 60 years ago in *Estes v. Texas*, the Supreme Court ruled that televised coverage of the criminal trial of a Texas financier charged with a multimillion-dollar con was inherently prejudicial.[132]

Cameras were allowed in a Texas courtroom for Billie Sol Estes's fraud trial in 1962.

Bettmann/Getty

A highly publicized national investigation preceded the case, with the financier appearing on the cover of Time magazine in 1962. A Texas newspaper editor won the 1963 Pulitzer Prize for bringing the fraud "to national attention with resultant investigation, prosecution and conviction of [Billie Sol] Estes."[133] Despite defense requests to ban cumbersome television cameras from the court, cameras and reporters swarmed the trial where Estes was convicted of conspiracy and fraud.[134]

On appeal, the U.S. Supreme Court found that intensive broadcast coverage prior to the trial *automatically* altered juror perceptions of the case and created prejudice and a form of harassment of the defendant. While the media play an important role in "informing the citizenry of public events and occurrences, including court proceedings," the Court said media had no independent or greater right of access to trials than anyone else. Moreover, facts demonstrated that television crews caused sufficient disruption to the trial to undermine due process, the search for truth and a just outcome.[135]

Banning cameras did not harm press coverage because "[t]he right of the communications media to comment on court proceedings does not bring with it the right to inject themselves into the fabric of the trial process to alter the purpose of that process," wrote Justice John Marshall Harlan II in a concurring opinion.[136] The *Estes* decision did not impose a blanket ban on television coverage, especially if and when it became so commonplace that it seemed vital to the public's right to know. Instead, the Court said judges must take steps to reduce the significant potential harms of publicity on trials.[137]

The Court later rejected the assumption that all broadcast coverage of trials is inevitably prejudicial, but it continued to emphasize that judges must ensure that media publicity does not undermine trial fairness.[138] The year after *Estes*, the Supreme Court overturned a murder conviction when a judge allowed extensive pretrial and trial publicity to turn the proceedings into a "Roman holiday." The case of *Sheppard v. Maxwell* reviewed the conviction of prominent Cleveland-area physician Sam Sheppard for the beating death of his wife. Dr. Sheppard said a stranger had broken into their home, knocked him unconscious and committed the crime.[139]

The media frenzy began the day of the crime and pervaded every aspect of what was called "the trial of the century." Months before the trial, in a televised five-hour inquest, a coroner examined the defendant without counsel before hundreds of spectators, and media published juror names and addresses weeks prior to the trial. Media practically overtook the small courtroom during the trial, broadcast coverage and printed verbatim transcripts. The jury was not sequestered, and the judge said he could not restrict dissemination of prejudicial information by the media. The jury deliberated five days before handing down a conviction. The court sentenced Sheppard to life imprisonment.[140]

The U.S. Supreme Court overturned his conviction, concluding that intense and prejudicial press coverage and the failure of the judge to protect the decorum of the courtroom prevented a fair trial. The Court said judges must protect fair trials by controlling the trial process and participants, including the media. The Court acknowledged the important role of the free press in a democracy and in the administration of justice. The Court, however, said the press has no right to inflame the minds of jurors, jeopardize trial fairness or make a mockery of the judicial process.[141] After spending 10 years in jail, Sheppard was retried and found not guilty.[142]

Photographers snapped pictures of Sam Sheppard in the common pleas court in Ohio in 1954.

While some press coverage can coexist with a fair trial, the Court said "massive and pervasive" coverage that reaches the jurors and permeates the trial may be *presumed* to be prejudicial when "the totality of circumstances" presents the likelihood of prejudice.[143] The *Sheppard* Court said trial judges must supervise their courtrooms carefully and use the many narrowly tailored measures they have available to guarantee a fair trial.[144] Judges may use **admonitions**, or instructions and warnings, to tell jurors to avoid potentially prejudicial communications. Courts also may insulate witnesses, limit comments trial participants and government employees make outside the courtroom and impose rules on media behavior inside court.[145] The *Sheppard* Court recommended the following measures:

1. **Continuance**, or delay, of the trial until publicity has subsided,

2. Change of the venue, or location, of the trial to avoid areas permeated by media coverage,

3. **Sequestration**, or isolation, of the jury from the public,

4. Extensive voir dire, or questioning, of potential jurors to identify prejudice,

5. Gag orders on participants to limit discussion of the case outside the courtroom,

6. Protection of potential witnesses from outside influences,

7. Instructions, or admonitions, to the jury to avoid prejudicial influences and to set aside any preconceptions they may have,

8. Retrial if the jury or the judicial process has been contaminated by media coverage and

9. Limitations on press attendance, through measures such as pool reporting, to reduce the influence of their presence on jurors and witnesses.

REAL WORLD LAW
DOES PUBLICITY BIAS JURORS?

Recent scholarship has produced inconsistent findings as to whether and how mock jurors' exposure to pretrial publicity influenced jurors.[146] Pretrial publicity may affect verdicts when:

- jurors are exposed to heavy pretrial publicity,
- evidence in court does not point convincingly to a clear verdict,
- information provided by the media seems more convincing or reliable than the evidence in court,
- the media consistently lean toward one verdict and
- all the remedies available to the court fail at the same time.

Following *Sheppard*

The *Sheppard* ruling was applauded for its protection of defendants' rights and criticized for prompting judges to limit the openness of judicial proceedings. Judges have applied the measures suggested by the Supreme Court in *Sheppard* to prevent or correct prejudice in the jury by establishing where and how the jury is chosen, where and when the trial takes place and limiting the amount of speech freedom jury members and other trial participants have during the trial.[147]

In recent high-profile cases, judges have barred media from attending pretrial hearings or from using cameras during pretrial hearings. Despite media organizations' requests to attend Harvey Weinstein's 2019 pretrial hearing involving sexual assault charges, a New York judge prevented the media and public from attending the hearing to protect the media mogul's rights to receive a fair trial by an impartial jury.[148] A Cook County, Ill., judge did not allow cameras in preliminary court hearings for four defendants accused of attacking a man with disabilities. That case received considerable media attention after a live video of the attack was posted on Facebook. Due to concerns about prejudicing potential jurors, sketch artists were not allowed to show the defendants in jail apparel.[149]

Selecting Jurors

When a court wants to select a jury for a trial, the clerk of court selects names at random from a list, such as adult licensed drivers or registered voters, in the county where the trial will be held. The pool of jurors is called the **venire**. Each potential juror receives a **summons**, a notice asking an individual to appear in court.

Media mogul Harvey Weinstein approached a New York courtroom, where members of the media were barred from filming his trial in a sexual assault case in 2020.

RW/MediaPunch

The judge or attorneys for both sides question members of the jury pool in what is called voir dire. Public relations specialists may help identify favorable jurors. The voir dire process allows either side to pose a **for-cause challenge**, an attorney's attempt to remove a potential juror for a reason the law finds sufficient, to a potential juror if the individual's responses suggest a prejudice relevant to the case. Juror prejudice may not be assumed simply because of a juror's race or gender.[150] An impartial juror does not need to be completely uninformed about the case. **Impartial jurors** instead must persuade the court that they have no fixed opinion of the guilt or innocence of the defendant.[151] They will give the facts full and unbiased consideration and reach a verdict based solely on the evidence presented in court. A limited number of peremptory challenges enable attorneys to remove potential jurors without any explanation. The selected jurors then are **impaneled**, selected, seated and sworn in.

In the very high-profile trial that found Dzhokhar Tsarnaev guilty of the 2013 Boston Marathon bombings, Tsarnaev challenged his conviction and sentence partly on the basis "that the jurors should be presumed to have been prejudiced because of social media activity." A judge dismissed the social media threat as both "overblown" and presumptive because the defense presented no evidence of actual juror misconduct or prejudice.[152]

In 2020, the U.S. Court of Appeals for the First Circuit did not address allegations of juror misconduct related to jurors' social media content. The appeals court vacated Tsarnaev's death sentences because voir dire had not adequately addressed "the kind and degree of each prospective juror's exposure to the case."[153] Despite extensive inquiries related to degree of media exposure, nine of the 12 jurors served without specifically disclosing what they had seen. Based on exposure to pretrial publicity, four believed Tsarnaev had participated in the bombings. Although all 12 seated jurors indicated they could base their decisions on evidence, the judge erred "by not having the jurors identify what it was they already thought they knew about the case."[154]

The Supreme Court reversed the First Circuit decision in 2022. Justice Clarence Thomas wrote that a trial court has broad discretion to determine "what questions to ask prospective jurors," and refraining from asking jurors "about the content and extent" of media coverage fell within that discretion. "[A] court of appeals cannot supplant the district court's broad discretion to manage voir dire by prescribing specific lines of questioning," Thomas wrote. Other questions had addressed juror's media exposure and potential juror bias. The majority held Tsarnaev received a fair trial before an impartial jury.[155]

Instructing the Jury

Judges routinely issue admonitions to jurors to tell them to avoid potential prejudice. Typical admonitions tell jurors not to view news coverage and not to discuss the case among themselves or with others prior to jury deliberations. Recent model jury instructions also include admonitions that impartial jurors "must not communicate with anyone about this case, whether in person, in writing, or through email, text messaging, blogs, or social media websites and apps."[156] Allegations that a juror used social media during a trial, however, does not necessitate finding a trial unfair.[157]

In 2020 and 2021, the Fourth Circuit Court of Appeals affirmed a district court's choice not to hold an evidentiary hearing on potential juror bias due to a juror's use of Twitter. The juror's actions did not violate the judge's instructions "prohibit[ing] social-media usage *about the case*."[158] Prior to the mail and wire fraud trial of a former Chief Justice of the Supreme Court of Appeals of West Virginia, a juror liked or retweeted tweets related to impeachment proceedings and an ethics investigation of the defendant. That juror used Twitter during the trial to like, retweet and post tweets about football.[159]

Judges also give instructions to the jury prior to deliberation. These instructions generally outline the applicable law and remind jurors of their duty to reach a verdict based only on the evidence presented in court.

Sequestering the Jury

Sometimes, though rarely, a judge will **sequester**, or isolate, a jury during a trial and prohibit jurors from having unsupervised contact with anyone outside of court. In 2021, a judge denied a defense request to sequester jurors immediately after a police officer fatally shot a man during an arrest near Minneapolis, where a former police officer was on trial for murder. Rather, the judge instructed jurors to avoid news about the murder case. Sequestration began about a week later during deliberations. An order for some sequestration of the jury during the trial and deliberations indicated media reports during the trial likely would report evidence presented during the trial and would be "unlikely to unduly prejudice the jury."[160] Sequestration may protect trial fairness, but it may alter juror attitudes and the outcome of the trial.[161]

Relocating the Trial

Although the Sixth Amendment protects a criminal defendant's right to a trial in the location where the crime occurred, either the prosecution or the defense may request a **change of venue**, or change of location for the trial. If media coverage creates a substantial likelihood of harming a fair trial, judges may order a change of venue, but they rarely do.[162]

For example, when selection of unbiased jurors in the Boston Marathon bombing trial of Dzhokhar Tsarnaev proved difficult, the judge three times denied defense requests to move the trial out of Boston.[163] Although almost 70 percent of nearly 1,400 prospective jurors identified a personal connection to the case and belief in the defendant's guilt, the First Circuit Court of Appeals affirmed the judge's decision that the defense failed to demonstrate that irreparable harm would occur if the trial were not moved.[164]

A courtroom sketch shows Dzokhar Tsarnaev, his attorneys, a judge and potential jurors.

Jane Flavell Collins/Associated Press

Delaying the Trial

Criminal defendants may waive their Sixth Amendment right to a speedy trial. Defendants and their attorneys may seek a delay, or continuance, to try to reduce the prejudicial impact of publicity. The prosecution may oppose a continuance because postponements often reduce the availability and recall of witnesses.[165]

In 2020, the Fifth Circuit Court of Appeals found that a defendant's right to speedy trial was not violated by nearly nine years of requests for delays he filed or joined his co-defendants in filing in a double-homicide case related to human smuggling.[166] Requests for delays provided time for counsel to investigate the case and assess mitigation measures for the death penalty punishment. The appeals court previously had found that "a delay longer than five years gave rise to a presumption of prejudice" when government negligence or bad faith contributed to delays. In its 2020 opinion, the Fifth Circuit concluded the defendant's due process rights were not violated "because he failed to prove that the government acted in bad faith and caused him actual, substantial prejudice."[167] The Supreme Court declined to review this case in 2021.

In 2016, the U.S. Supreme Court ruled that the Sixth Amendment right to a speedy trial does not require speedy sentencing.[168] The case involved a man who waited in jail for more than 14 months for sentencing. He appealed his sentence of seven years in prison, arguing that the sentencing delay was unconstitutional. The Supreme Court disagreed. Its short, unanimous ruling said the "heart" of the Sixth Amendment is the desire to protect the "presumption of innocence and therefore loses force upon conviction."[169]

Making Jurors Anonymous

A tradition of openly identifying members of juries reaches back to colonial days.[170] Anonymous juries once were extremely rare and considered "a drastic measure"[171] but became more common late in the 20th century.[172] Today, the question of a constitutional or common law right of access to juror information remains unsettled. Two federal appellate courts have held that the public has a First Amendment right to timely access to juror names in a criminal proceeding.[173] Only the Tenth Circuit Court of Appeals has not approved the use of anonymous juries.[174]

Some courts refuse to release the names and identities of jurors in high-profile cases or in cases where jurors may legitimately be concerned for their personal safety or subject to intimidation or extensive media publicity.[175] In 2020, for example, a Minnesota judge ordered jurors to be anonymous in cases involving four former police officers charged with homicide-related offenses in Minneapolis. Considering protests were frequently occurring in the city and defendants and their attorneys reported being verbally harassed, the judge said, "Strong reasons exist to believe that threats to jurors' safety and impartiality exist."[176] After the first trial ended, a coalition of media organizations filed a motion for the juror names to be unsealed. The trial judge unsealed the juror's names in one trial six months after the trial ended in 2021.[177]

Members of the National Guard, law enforcement agents, fences and barricades separated protestors from a Minnesota courthouse during the murder trial of Derek Chauvin, a former police officer.

Ben Brewer/Xinhua News Agency

Other courts justify juror anonymity on grounds that release of personal information violates jurors' privacy interests. Although criminal defense attorneys argue that juror anonymity increases juror anxiety and perception that the defendant is guilty, few courts accept that anonymous juries are inherently prejudicial. In Texas, the criminal code requires anonymous juries unless there is a showing that openness serves the public good.[178]

Limiting Speech Outside of Court

Judges tend to believe that when government and court officials—police and attorneys, for example—publicly discuss ongoing trials, their speech influences jurors' perceptions of witnesses' guilt or innocence. In *Sheppard*, the Supreme Court encouraged judges to use **restraining orders**, court orders forbidding specific conduct or speech, to prevent trial participants from discussing potentially prejudicial information outside the courtroom.[179]

About 30 years ago, the U.S. Supreme Court ruled in *Mu'Min v. Virginia* that restraining attorneys' speech outside the courtroom during a trial did not violate the First Amendment.[180] The Court reasoned that insiders to a vital government process have special access to sensitive information and unique power to derail justice. Consequently, courts may control their trial-related speech when it poses a "substantial likelihood" of jeopardizing a fair trial.[181]

Gag orders on trial participants generally are upheld if (1) narrowly drawn and (2) supported by evidence that unfettered speech poses a substantial likelihood of jeopardizing a fair trial and (3) by careful consideration of alternatives. Narrowly drawn restraining orders end as soon as the threat to the trial process passes.[182] A different test applies to gag orders on the media.

In high-profile cases, judges concerned about prejudicial pretrial publicity may issue sweeping gag orders on all trial participants. In 2019, an Alabama judge in a case addressing the kidnapping and murder of a college student banned all lawyers, witnesses and potential witnesses from making statements to media outlets, participating in interviews or posting information on social media.[183]

The Supreme Court of Georgia recently lifted a gag order in a highly publicized murder case.[184] The order prevented the defendant, lawyers, law enforcement and court personnel from making extrajudicial statements publicly or via news media. The state's highest court said, "A reasonable likelihood of prejudice sufficient to justify a gag order cannot simply be inferred from the mere fact that there has been significant media interest in a case."[185] Despite significant media interest in the case, the record did not "demonstrate any likelihood" that persons the order covered "would make prejudicial statements."[186]

The U.S. Court of Appeals for the Fourth Circuit vacated[187] a West Virginia judge's ban on comments to the media about a criminal trial related to the 2010 Upper Big Branch Mine disaster that killed 29 miners.[188] The trial judge said the ban "restricting the parties and potential trial participants' statements to the press at the outset helps preserve the defendant's right to a fair and just tribunal."[189] But the Fourth Circuit required the showing set out in the *Press-Enterprise* decision that "specific findings . . . demonstrat[e] that, first, there is a substantial probability that the defendant's right to a fair trial will be prejudiced by publicity that closure would prevent and, second, reasonable alternatives to closure cannot adequately protect the defendant's fair trial rights."[190]

REAL WORLD LAW

JUDICIAL IMPARTIALITY AND "FRIENDS" OF THE COURT

In recent years, courts have disagreed on whether Facebook "friendships" pose a risk of prejudice. In 2020, the Supreme Court of Wisconsin found "extreme facts" rebutted the "presumption of judicial impartiality" when a judge did not disclose accepting a Facebook "friend" request and Facebook interactions with the mother involved in a child-custody dispute after hearing the facts of the case and before reaching a decision.[191] The court considered the timing and acceptance of the request, likelihood the judge viewed posts and comments, relevance of content to the pending proceeding and "lack of disclosure" significant.[192]

In contrast, a federal district court in Pennsylvania refused to put any weight on Facebook relationships because "'Friendships' on Facebook may be as fleeting as the flick of a delete button."[193]

Judging Impartially

Sometimes the fairness of the judge is cast into doubt. In *Sheppard*, the U.S. Supreme Court said the fact that both the judge and a prosecuting attorney were running for election during the trial posed the potential for prejudice.[194] The Supreme Court also has ruled that the Constitution requires judges to disqualify or recuse themselves from hearing a case when a risk of prejudice exists because "a person with a personal stake [in the case outcome] . . . had a significant and disproportionate influence" in the judge's election or appointment to the bench.[195] But the Supreme Court later struck down a Minnesota state law that banned judges from campaigning on issues that might come before their court.[196] The Court said the law violated the First Amendment by directly limiting speech vital to elections.[197]

BALANCING INTERESTS

Decades ago, the U.S. Supreme Court said for centuries it has been a "fundamental maxim that the public has a right to every man's evidence."[198] While law enforcement is responsible for identifying relevant evidence, judges must determine which evidence may be admitted into court. Judges may use their power to require individuals to testify or to produce relevant evidence. It is unequivocally "the obligation of all citizens to give relevant testimony with respect to criminal conduct," the Court said.[199]

Requiring Evidence

Many argue that the First Amendment's recognition of freedom for the editorial process should protect journalists from forced disclosure of information journalists have gathered. This rationale holds that a requirement to testify infringes the First Amendment guarantee of freedom of the press, which provides a **reporter's privilege**, a legal right to not divulge confidential information, such as the identity of a confidential source, in court. The U.S. Supreme Court, however, has recognized only limited constitutional protection for reporter confidentiality.[200]

REAL WORLD LAW
YOUR DATA ARE NOT SAFE FROM GOVERNMENT (SP)EYES

U.S. authorities have found ways to access data stored on smartphones and in cloud storage. A long legal battle between the U.S. Department of Justice and Apple over access to the iPhone used by one of the shooters in a terrorist attack ended when the DOJ paid hackers to break into Apple's encrypted system.[201] U.S. authorities subsequently sought and received access to device backups or iCloud content in more than 1500 cases in six months via court requests.[202]

Gag orders can make it hard to tell how frequently authorities seek and receive data access. The FBI subpoenaed and gagged Open Whisper Systems to obtain access to information in iPhones protected by the software developer's encryption system, Signal, which many people in the media use.[203] Major media and tech industry players joined a lawsuit by Microsoft that said bans on discussion of governmental snooping into customers' information violated the First Amendment. Microsoft said the government had subpoenaed its customer data 5,600 times in 18 months, with almost half of the requests accompanied by gag orders.[204]

Between January and June 2021, Twitter received 12,370 information requests from governments around the globe. Most of those requests came from the United States, India,

Japan and France, with U.S. officials submitting about one-fourth of the requests. The January 2022 Twitter Transparency Report states "Twitter may disclose account information to law enforcement officials in response to a valid emergency request."[205]

Courts provide search warrants and subpoenas to collect evidence and ensure that it is presented in court. A search warrant permits law enforcement officers to search a specified place for particular items or people. The Fourth Amendment to the U.S. Constitution requires that searches be conducted reasonably. To receive a search warrant, investigators must show probable cause that the items or people are vital to the investigation and are likely to be found in the specified location. Search warrants demand immediate compliance. There is no legal way to delay, resist or prevent a legally warranted search. Some national security mechanisms allow searches and seizures without a warrant or with a secret warrant.[206]

A search warrant implies greater urgency than a subpoena. Subpoenas do not require on-the-spot compliance. They order the person to appear at a future judicial proceeding. In the interim, the recipient can file a motion to quash, or vacate, the subpoena. Concern that evidence might be destroyed by the lapse between service of a subpoena and the date of the required court appearance is one justification for search warrants.[207]

Over 40 years ago, the U.S. Supreme Court ruled directly on the amount of protection the First Amendment provides from searches of newsrooms. Investigators with a search warrant sought unpublished photographs of a campus demonstration taken by the Stanford University student newspaper staff. The Stanford Daily sued the police, claiming the search violated the newspaper's First, Fourth and Fourteenth Amendment rights. The Fourth Amendment protects against unreasonable searches and seizures.[208]

Because no one at the newspaper was suspected of a crime, the trial judge ruled that the search warrant was unreasonable unless government could show that a subpoena was impractical. The appellate court agreed. The court reasoned that a police search of newsrooms would disrupt timely publication, dry up confidential sources, deter reporters from keeping records and chill the dissemination of news.[209]

In *Zurcher v. Stanford Daily*, the U.S. Supreme Court rejected this reasoning and ruled that newsrooms are entitled to no special treatment beyond that afforded to any citizen's property. The Court said that nothing in the Fourth Amendment restricted searches of newsrooms. Implicitly, the ruling suggested that nothing in the First Amendment did either.[210]

Penalizing Failure to Disclose

As professional collectors of news and information, journalists may be more likely than most to have information of importance to a court.[211] If reporters refuse to testify and disclose information sought under subpoena, judges may use their power of contempt to punish them.[212] A finding of criminal contempt, addressing conduct against the court, results in a fixed jail term and/or fine. Under civil contempt, addressing conduct against a private right, journalists are jailed until they comply with the order to disclose or until the matter is resolved. Contempt citations must be obeyed.[213]

When former New York Times reporter Judith Miller refused to comply with a subpoena to testify before a grand jury about her knowledge of a White House leak that outed an undercover CIA agent, she was cited with contempt and spent 85 days in jail.[214] The prosecutor argued that "journalists are not entitled to promise complete confidentiality—no one in America is."[215] The U.S. Supreme Court rejected her appeal.[216] Miller was released from jail and testified after her source relieved her of her confidentiality agreement.[217]

Aspiring crime writer Vanessa Leggett was jailed for more than five months for refusal to disclose her sources to a grand jury in 2001. Leggett later received the PEN First Amendment Award for her protection of freedom of the press.

Greg Smith/Corbis via Getty Images

In 2019, former Army intelligence analyst Chelsea Manning was jailed for contempt for refusal to testify in an ongoing grand jury investigation of WikiLeaks.[218] The Fourth Circuit Court of Appeals upheld Manning's contempt charge and denied bail for failure to comply with a subpoena to testify about her role in disclosing more than half a million classified and sensitive military and diplomatic documents to the public via WikiLeaks. Manning testified at length in 2013 during her court martial for violating the Espionage Act, and her attorneys argued that she had "no further knowledge of any relevant people or events." The court said she would remain in jail until she testified or the grand jury concluded.[219]

The Ninth Circuit Court of Appeals recently required Glassdoor, a website that addresses salaries in relation to gender and race, to respond to a federal grand jury subpoena and provide the names of anonymous users who criticized their employer, a federal contractor under investigation.[220] Glassdoor argued that the subpoena violated users' First Amendment rights and should be reviewed under strict scrutiny, but the Ninth Circuit applied the *Branzburg* standard that subpoenas issued as part of a "good faith" grand jury investigation do not warrant privilege. While the subpoenas did implicate the users' right to speak anonymously, the Ninth Circuit said that right does not cloak individuals from their duty to testify before an ongoing grand jury investigation.[221]

A federal district court recently upheld a subpoena for Twitter subscriber data on one of three anonymous users implicated in cyberharassment of an FBI agent. Applying *Branzburg*, the court said the government's compelling interest in investigating the harassment outweighed the harm to the right to speak anonymously for the one subscriber who tweeted directly with the alleged harasser. The court said this user demonstrated the "substantial relationship" to the crime needed to uphold a subpoena.[222]

POINTS OF LAW
CONTEMPT OF COURT

Judges have broad, discretionary power to cite individuals with contempt of court for failure to obey a court order or any misconduct that interferes with the court. This power is limited by some state laws and the First Amendment.[223]

- **Civil contempt** citations may compel an individual to do something, such as name a source or turn over notes. Civil contempt sometimes is called "indirect contempt" because the instigating event generally occurs outside the direct supervision of the judge.
- **Criminal contempt** is conduct in or near the court that obstructs court proceedings. Because it generally interferes directly with court proceedings, it sometimes is called "direct contempt."

Under the First Amendment, judges may issue contempt citations against negative news coverage only if the comments intimidate jurors or undermine the fairness of the trial. Individuals given lengthy jail terms for contempt have a right to a jury trial.[224]

Protecting Juveniles

Courts generally limit access to legal proceedings involving juveniles to advance the government's substantial interest in reducing trauma that might impede rehabilitation and healing of juvenile victims, defendants and witnesses. The U.S. Supreme Court has said that historically confidential juvenile processes reduce the stigmatization of minors.[225] Fifty years ago, the Supreme Court said juvenile court procedures must ensure that minors receive the full "reach of constitutional guarantees applicable to adults."[226] The Court also held that juvenile defendants have the right to counsel and notice.[227]

Federal law permits, but does not require, closure of juvenile proceedings and records on a case-by-case basis. Most federal courts do not consider juvenile proceedings to be presumptively open, and about one-fourth of the states presume that juvenile proceedings are closed while about two-fifths provide a broad right of public access to juvenile courts.[228] Juvenile proceedings are presumed open to the public in Los Angeles County.[229]

All states allow certain juveniles to be treated as adults within the justice system. Maryland, New Jersey and Wisconsin may prohibit the media from revealing the identity of a juvenile.[230] Communicators who legally obtain sealed information about juveniles, however, may publish the information without fear of punishment. A recent Massachusetts Supreme Court decision confirmed that state courts cannot ban media from releasing the legally obtained name of a minor.[231] Most states bar cameras from juvenile courts.[232]

In Massachusetts (where the law makes juvenile murder trials presumptively open, while other juvenile proceedings are presumptively closed), a trial judge denied a 14-year-old murder suspect's motion to seal the highly prejudicial video recording and transcript of his police interview.[233] The court said the records were presumptively open once entered into evidence. Police had interviewed the teen alone. He received life in prison for the rape and murder of a math teacher.[234]

MAP 8.2 ■ State-by-State Juvenile Age of Jurisdiction and Transfer to Adult Court

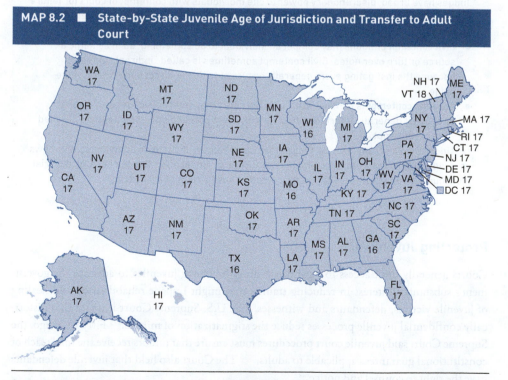

Source: National Conference of State Legislators Juvenile Age of Jurisdiction and Transfer to Adult Court: 2021 Report.

To determine the applicable right of access to juvenile proceedings, individuals should consult state laws and reports on juvenile justice from the Reporters Committee for Freedom of the Press and the National Center for Juvenile Justice.[235] In 2020, Vermont raised the age of juvenile court jurisdiction to 18.[236]

Protecting Sexual Assault Victims

In cases of sexual assault, all the states and the District of Columbia have a rape shield law to protect the alleged victim from questions that might prejudice jurors against the victim.[237] Except for Mississippi, every state has a statute excluding evidence of the complaining witness's past sexual activity.[238] Some states also shield the victim's identity and other personal information from disclosure in court and criminal investigation records.[239]

Appellate courts recently rejected challenges to two states' rape shield laws. Addressing Michigan's law, the Sixth Circuit Court of Appeals ruled that the Sixth Amendment permitted limits on the extent and nature of the defendant's cross-examination of his minor nephew, the molestation victim who experienced a nervous breakdown.[240] In 2021, the Supreme Court of Pennsylvania noted courts had found the state's rape shield law was unconstitutionally applied when restricting evidence "unrelated to impugning the complainant's character," but the shield law was properly applied to bar evidence of two complainants' prostitution arrests, which "would cast aspersions upon the moral character of the complainants."[241]

Protecting State Secrets and National Security

Almost 70 years ago, the U.S. Supreme Court granted the executive branch power to keep secret—with little judicial review—information that it said would present a "reasonable danger" to national security.[242] One study found that administrations since the Sept. 11, 2001, terrorist attack have "aggressively used the state secrets privilege, insisting that entire cases could be exempt from judicial review."[243] Another study said administrations use the power to declare "state secrets" to thwart open judicial proceedings and even prevent cases from going to trial.[244]

Over 40 years ago, the Foreign Intelligence Surveillance Act (FISA) established broad government power to conduct covert physical and electronic surveillance of foreign nationals and countries suspected of espionage.[245] Cases involving the act are heard in special FISA courts where proceedings and records are secret. National security concerns justify the secrecy of almost all FISA court actions. The courts are presumptively closed, and the court docket is "super-sealed" to hide evidence of even the existence of the case.[246] In 2015, the U.S. Supreme Court declined to review a sweeping ban on public release of information from the secret Foreign Intelligence Surveillance Court trials of alleged terrorists.[247]

In 2016, The ACLU of the Nation's Capital and the Media Freedom of Information Access Clinic requested disclosure of classified opinions and orders issued between 2001 and 2015 under the qualified First Amendment right to access court records and Foreign Intelligence Surveillance Court Rule 62.[248] Under Rule 62, a judge who wrote an opinion, order or other decision may request publication of a record, and the presiding judge may direct the record to be published. In 2020, a Foreign Intelligence Surveillance Court judge dismissed the groups' motion for the court to order releasing those opinions and orders. Congress had not empowered the court "to consider constitutional claims generally, First Amendment claims specifically, or freestanding motions filed by persons who are not authorized by FISA to invoke this Court's jurisdiction," the judge wrote.[249]

A case outside the FISA courts involved the federal government's extraordinary rendition program that covertly transferred individuals out of the United States for detention and interrogation on foreign soil. In its review of the government's asserted national security privilege, the Ninth Circuit Court of Appeals held that the privilege may (1) completely bar lawsuits in which "the very subject matter of the action" is highly threatening to national security or that (2) require the exclusion of all privileged evidence.[250] To exclude evidence rather than dismiss a trial requires courts to determine that only "some of the matters [government] seeks to protect from disclosure in th[e] litigation are valid state secrets."[251] The Ninth Circuit dismissed the case, holding that evidence about government abduction and torture was privileged and there was no way to litigate the case "without creating an unjustifiable risk of divulging state secrets."[252]

The D.C. Circuit Court of Appeals recently reversed a trial court ruling that had unsealed videotape of government treatment of a Guantanamo Bay detainee on hunger strike. The government had submitted the classified tape in the detainee's civil challenge to forced feeding. The three circuit court judges disagreed on whether any qualified First Amendment right of access applied to the videotape, but they agreed unanimously that the government's interest in secrecy outweighed any such right.[253]

Closing Courts

In *Press-Enterprise I* and *II*, the U.S. Supreme Court said, "The presumption of openness may be overcome only by an overriding interest based on findings that closure is essential to preserve higher values and is narrowly tailored to serve that interest."[254] *Press-Enterprise II* established that general privacy concerns alone do not justify closing a courtroom or voir dire. Anyone seeking to close a presumptively open hearing must show that (1) the openness has a "substantial probability" of significantly threatening the fair trial process and (2) closure is a last resort "essential" to preserving fair trial rights.[255] Before closing a courtroom, judges must determine that facts demonstrate *all* of the following:

- Openness poses a substantial threat to a fair proceeding.

- No alternative exists that would effectively eliminate the threat to fairness.

- Closure will effectively eliminate the threat.

- Closure will be narrowly tailored to protect maximum public access to the judicial process.

Before closing any or all of a trial, judges must permit interested parties and the public to raise objections. Despite this high standard, courts continue to close their doors and seal their records. Courts generally accept the commonsense notion that media coverage has an effect on the fairness of a trial.[256] Judges sometimes close trials of their own accord, called *sua sponte*, without hearings or findings of prejudice.[257] Studies, however, show that effects of media coverage appear to be highly specific and inconsistent.[258]

Courts sometimes close portions of court proceedings or records in business cases that involve trade secrets and proprietary information. In a 2021 case addressing a veterinary orthopedic implant manufacturer's alleged patent infringement, the U.S. Court of Appeals for the Federal Circuit said a party seeking to seal business information in court records must demonstrate "the existence of harm flowing from the disclosure of such information." The identity of a manufacturer was not a trade secret that could be sealed.[259]

When the parties settled the "landmark monopolization case of the 21st Century"[260] between computer industry giant Intel and its chief competitor, Advanced Micro Devices, media argued that the court's seal improperly shielded Intel business practices from public scrutiny.[261] The case was settled, ending the media request to unseal "hundreds of millions of pages of documentation" held in the court's records.[262] In a related case heard in the European Union, the U.S. Supreme Court ordered disclosure to AMD of some 600,000 pages of Intel records.[263]

POINTS OF LAW
THE PRESS-ENTERPRISE TEST FOR COURT CLOSURE

In *Press-Enterprise II v. Superior Court of California*, the U.S. Supreme Court established that an individual seeking to close open court records or proceedings, including pretrial hearings, must provide

1. specific, on-the-record findings that there is a "substantial probability" that openness will jeopardize the defendant's right to a fair trial and
2. convincing evidence that closure is "essential" to preserve the trial's fairness.[264]

The right of public access does not extend to all criminal trial proceedings. Grand jury hearings and their documents generally are sealed. The U.S. Supreme Court has not ruled directly on whether hearings to consider the suppression of evidence or plea bargains must be open. At least one federal appeals court and one state high court have ruled that judges may hold conferences in closed chambers or conduct whispered bench conferences addressing administrative matters in the courtroom during the trial.[265]

A Minnesota judge recently excluded the public from a courtroom to address administrative matters for a few minutes on the first day of a trial. Byron Smith was accused of killing two people who broke into his house, and a question arose as to whether witnesses could testify to address whether one of those people previously broke into Smith's house. Smith appealed, indicating the brief closure violated the Sixth Amendment. The state's highest court found that administrative proceedings for "routine evidentiary rulings, categorically do not implicate the Sixth Amendment right to a public trial."[266] A federal district court and the Eighth Circuit Court of Appeals denied Smith's request for habeas corpus relief. When the U.S. Supreme Court declined to hear Smith's case in 2021, Justice Sotomayor dissented. Sotomayor stated that lower courts had recognized the closure of this proceeding was "part of a broader and disturbing trend" of courtroom closure in Minnesota.[267]

Courts also protect the secrecy of jury deliberations. Although a Colorado rule of evidence protects jury deliberations from inquiry, in 2017 the U.S. Supreme Court accepted an appeal to impeach a verdict due to reports that a juror's statements demonstrated racial bias or racial animus. The Court held that a conviction should be reviewed when it is discovered that a juror reached the verdict based on racial stereotypes or racial animus toward the defendant.[268]Justice Kennedy wrote, "discrimination on the basis of race, odious in all aspects, is especially pernicious in the administration of justice."[269]

Challenging Closures

The public has a right to challenge court closures or sealed public records. Anyone may challenge a judge's order closing records or criminal proceedings. Such requests should be made in writing and/or in open court. When challenging court closures, individuals should stand, request recognition by the judge, politely state an objection to the closure and request the record include their objection. Anyone also may ask the court to delay proceedings to seek the advice of an attorney to object to the closure.[270]

ADVANCING THE FLOW OF NEWS

In the years following *Sheppard v. Maxwell*, state media, bar associations and members of the judiciary developed agreements to guide reporting on the courts. The so-called voluntary bench/bar/press guidelines aimed to limit prejudicial media coverage by restricting both the content and the tone of trial coverage. They balanced the media and public interest in information against the courts' concerns about privacy and fairness. State rules vary, but some agreements create boards able to punish media violations.[271]

Fifty years ago, a neighbor almost immediately confessed to the murder of six family members in Nebraska. National news media converged on the murder trial. The judge issued an order barring publication of specific evidence and ordering the media to follow Nebraska's bench/bar/press guidelines. The voluntary guidelines encouraged media not to disclose information about confessions, guilt or innocence, lab tests, witness credibility or statements that reasonably would be expected to influence the outcome of the trial.[272]

POINTS OF LAW

CLOSING MEDIA MOUTHS: THE NEBRASKA PRESS ASSOCIATION STANDARD

Nebraska Press Association v. Stuart established that a judge must justify gags imposed on the media with convincing evidence that

1. disclosure of the information would present a substantial threat to a fair trial,
2. there is no effective alternative to a gag on the press,

3. the gag will effectively eliminate the danger to the fair trial and
4. the gag is narrowly tailored to restrict only the information that must be kept secret.[273]

The state press association appealed. The Nebraska Supreme Court upheld the order, and in *Nebraska Press Association v. Stuart* the U.S. Supreme Court reversed. The Supreme Court said decisions about news content are the domain of editors, not judges. That remains the law.[274] The Court has never said courts may bind media to bench/bar/press guidelines.

Some courts continue to enforce the voluntary bench/bar/press guidelines on media. One state court in Washington excluded the press from a pretrial hearing after it ruled that its prior pretrial coverage violated the guidelines.[275] Another trial judge made press adherence to the guidelines a condition for media to attend a pretrial hearing open to the public. The Washington Supreme Court upheld this procedure.[276]

This screen shot from a pool video shows Hennepin County Judge Regina Chu presiding over a Minnesota trial for former police officer Kim Potter, who was convicted of first- and second-degree manslaughter for fatally shooting Daunte Wright, a 20-year-old Black man, during a traffic stop.

Court TV Pool/Associated Press

Guiding Media Coverage of Courts

The U.S. Supreme Court's landmark decision in *Nebraska Press Association* called press gags an extraordinary remedy that is presumptively unconstitutional. The Supreme Court classified gag orders on the media as the most serious and least tolerable prior restraint on First Amendment rights. Court orders that bar the media from publicizing legally obtained information about ongoing trials must meet the highest standard of review.[277]

The Supreme Court upheld a restraining order that prevented two newspapers from publicizing the confidential membership and donor list of a religious group obtained from the discovery process in a libel lawsuit. The Court unanimously found the restraining order constitutional because it did not prevent the newspapers from publishing the same information if they obtained it outside trial discovery.[278]

After *Nebraska Press Association*, courts must consider three things before imposing a media gag: (1) the quantity and content of media coverage, (2) the potential effectiveness of alternatives to a gag and (3) the likelihood that a gag would remedy the harmful publicity. Judges also must determine that the gag is a last resort that narrowly targets information that poses a clear threat to the fair trial and limits as little press freedom as possible.[279] Constitutionally valid media gag orders are rare.

Yet, courts continue to place gags on the media. An Alabama trial judge briefly forbade two newspapers from publishing information in the public record about the age and condition of gas pipes across Alabama. The judge entered the gag in response to Alabama Gas Corp.'s claim that publication of the information raised a risk to national security of sabotage and terrorism.[280]

Courts also may limit communications of participants in grand jury investigations. States, however, may not punish witnesses to secret grand jury proceedings who discuss their own testimony after the conclusion of the grand jury investigation.[281] The U.S. Supreme Court declined to review a press appeal challenging two Florida court orders directing that "no party shall further disclose the contents of the transcript of testimony before the grand jury" that had been leaked to the press.[282] In his opinion, Justice Anthony Kennedy denied certiorari "despite indications that a prior restraint may have been imposed."[283]

POINTS OF LAW
WHAT IS FAIR COVERAGE OF CRIMINAL TRIALS?

Media standards of professional and ethical performance as well as bench/bar/press guidelines establish fair reporting standards on criminal proceedings. Most guidelines say that only an overwhelming justification should lead media to report

1. the existence or content of a confession;
2. statements or opinions of guilt or innocence;
3. the results of lab tests;
4. statements or opinions on the credibility of witnesses, the evidence or the investigative process or personnel; or
5. other information reasonably likely to affect the trial verdict.[284]

The National Center for State Courts, a nonprofit clearinghouse and information resource for courts, produces several guides on court management of high-profile cases, sharing information, managing a court's image and shaping media coverage.[285] Directed primarily toward court public information and media relations officers, the center's web resources encourage court personnel to "serve as liaisons between the courts and the media," ensure fair and accurate reporting and prevent any infringement on court proceedings, especially in highly publicized and notorious trials.[286]

Florida recently launched a new plan to improve communication by and from the courts to enhance public confidence in its judiciary. Goals established by court public information officers included improving public outreach, enhancing court websites, strengthening relations with the media and increasing public educational programming.[287]

Protecting Confidential Information

Although individuals who receive subpoenas are expected to comply, recipients may move to quash the subpoena. When journalists are subpoenaed to testify about confidential information, they may use either a state reporter's privilege or state shield law in efforts to quash the subpoena.[288]

Recently, screenwriter and producer of National Public Radio's podcast "Serial" Mark Boal settled his six-month lawsuit against the government to stop a subpoena for 25 hours of unedited tapes of his interviews with accused U.S. Army deserter Bowe Bergdahl. Bergdahl was a prisoner of the Taliban in Afghanistan and Pakistan for five years. The military court trying Bergdahl had threatened Boal with a contempt citation. Military courts do not recognize a reporter's privilege, but Boal argued that federal court precedents should apply. The settlement details were not released, but the government agreed to drop the subpoena and to allow Boal to protect all confidential material from his interviews with Bergdahl.[289]

Mark Boal's interviews with U.S. Army Sgt. Bowe Bergdahl became the basis of the second season of the investigative podcast "Serial."

Providing a Limited Privilege

The concept of reporter's privilege, sometimes called "journalist's privilege," is an extension of other forms of privilege. Courts long have granted certain privileges not to testify to parties in a special relationship—lawyer–client, doctor–patient, husband–wife or clergy–parishioner, for example. Journalists argue that the reporter–source relationship is precisely one of these privileged relationships that the First Amendment protects.[290] Compelling a journalist to violate a promise of confidentiality, they say, impinges on freedom of the press and harms the flow of information. One distinction between lawyer–client and reporter–source relationships is that lawyer–client privilege "belongs" to the client, and reporter's privilege belongs to both the source and the reporter. A client may release an attorney from the agreement while a journalist may argue for privilege even after release from the promise.[291]

Reporter's privilege as we know it originated in the landmark U.S. Supreme Court case *Branzburg v. Hayes. Branzburg* consolidated four cases. Two involved Paul Branzburg's sources on illegal drug use reported in The (Louisville) Courier-Journal. Two were related to sources within the Black Panthers contacted in separate reporting by TV reporter Paul Pappas and New York Times reporter Earl Caldwell. All three reporters refused to testify before grand juries and were cited with contempt.[292]

All three reporters claimed the First Amendment provided a privilege that protected them from revealing confidential information. They argued that their ability to report news would be irreparably harmed. Sources would dry up. Mere appearance before a closed grand jury could chill their access to sources who would never know what the reporter revealed. Forced grand jury appearance alone would reduce the information available to the public in violation of the First Amendment.[293]

By a 5–4 majority, the U.S. Supreme Court disagreed.[294] The Court balanced the benefits of a reporter's privilege not to testify before a grand jury against the public interest in justice and favored the latter. Obtaining evidence is critical to justice, the Court said. The fact that the necessary evidence is held by a reporter is immaterial. Writing in concurrence, Justice Lewis Powell emphasized "the limited nature" of the Court's holding.[295] Reporter's privilege to withhold information should be determined case by case. Refusal to provide information may be permissible if the information fails to serve "a legitimate need of law enforcement."[296]

Writing in dissent, only Justice William Douglas argued that journalists have an absolute privilege to withhold information, including sources' names.[297] Three justices criticized the "Court's crabbed view of the First Amendment"[298] and said reporters have a limited First Amendment privilege to refuse to reveal sources.[299] The First Amendment guarantee is "not for the benefit of the press so much as for the benefit of all of us."[300] Writing for those three, Justice Potter Stewart said a First Amendment privilege to withhold information should exist unless officials could meet "a heavy burden of justification" to overcome the privilege.[301] He said that burden could be met only when (1) there is probable cause to believe the reporter has information clearly relevant to a specific violation of law, (2) the information being sought cannot be obtained by other means that are less intrusive of First Amendment values and (3) there is a compelling and overriding interest in the information.[302]

Many courts adopted this approach, which is called the "reporter's privilege test." Among federal appellate courts, only the Sixth Circuit Court of Appeals has not recognized some journalistic privilege to protect confidential sources.[305]

INTERNATIONAL LAW

CANADA RECOGNIZES A REPORTER'S RIGHT TO PROTECT SOURCES

Applying the Canada Evidence Act, as amended by the Journalistic Sources Protection Act of 2017, the Supreme Court of Canada recently set aside an order requiring a broadcast journalist to disclose identities of confidential sources for a story about government corruption. That Court said a court should only require a journalist to breach source confidentiality "as a last resort."[303]

Under the amended Canada Evidence Act, a journalist must show the subject of a subpoena is a journalist and the information source is a journalistic source. To overcome a presumption of non-disclosure, a party seeking disclosure must show the information sought is central in the proceeding, it cannot be produced by any other reasonable means, and "the public interest in the administration of justice outweighs the public interest in preserving confidentiality."[304]

The *Branzburg* decision is narrow, speaking only to a journalist being called before a grand jury. The various *Branzburg* opinions did not make clear how to determine privilege beyond grand juries, but an "unofficial majority" of the Court said a qualified reporter's privilege may be contemplated outside grand jury circumstances. Court application of privilege is highly fact specific. Over a decade ago, the Pennsylvania Supreme Court broke ground when it rejected the assumption that shield laws do *not* protect against grand jury subpoenas. After a newspaper reporter used a confidential source to report on a grand jury proceeding, the state high court ruled that the Pennsylvania shield law grants an absolute privilege to journalists and protects their sources in all cases.[306]

In 2016, a federal district court in Massachusetts ordered radio and television commentator Glenn Beck to provide the identities of at least two of the confidential sources he relied on to link the plaintiff, Abdulrahman Alharbi, to the 2013 Boston Marathon bombing. Alharbi sued Beck for libel for repeatedly reporting that Alharbi helped finance the bombing. Beck claimed qualified privilege from disclosure and sought summary judgment on the libel charge, asserting that the stories were accurate reports of information from confidential government sources. The court said disclosure of two of Beck's six sources was necessary due to Beck's vague and often contradictory testimony about their identities and the information they provided. Accurate reports of what they said were essential to Alharbi's case.[307]

In a highly visible case, the Justice Department investigated, questioned and subpoenaed Pulitzer Prize–winning New York Times reporter James Risen for more than six years to discover the source of classified information used in his book, "State of War: The Secret History of the CIA and the Bush Administration." The government dropped charges against Risen only after convicting former CIA agent Jeffrey Sterling for the leak.[308]

In *United States v. Sterling*, the Fourth Circuit Court of Appeals said no First Amendment or common law privilege exists for journalists.[309] The Fourth Circuit said Risen did not have protection against testifying because he could provide a "direct, firsthand account of the [alleged] criminal conduct . . . [that] cannot be obtained by alternative means, as [Risen] is without dispute the only witness who can offer this critical testimony."[310]

Recently, a New York appeals court held that reporter's privilege protected a New York Times reporter from forced disclosure of information from her jailhouse interview of a man charged with a decades-old high-profile murder. The court said Frances Robles's notes of interviews with the "Baby Hope" murder suspect were neither "critical [n]or necessary" to the prosecution.[311] An Arizona appellate court also recognized a qualified First Amendment privilege for newsgathering materials and held that the trial court should have quashed a subpoena for the interview notes of a Phoenix reporter.[312]

Relying on Delaware's Reporters' Privilege Act, a state trial court used a balancing test to let stand a subpoena against the New Journal for the unedited video of one reporter's entire interview with murder suspect Christopher Rivers. The court said the newspaper failed to show how release of the information in the interview would chill its reporting. Moreover, the information was material to the prosecution, unavailable elsewhere and intended for public display.[313]

Some lower courts have balanced *Branzburg*'s three factors (possession, alternatives and relevance) against the asserted damage to newsgathering and the First Amendment. If one factor clearly favors the journalist, the journalist may have reporter's privilege protection. For example, one federal district court ruled that reporter's privilege shielded a journalist from being questioned because there were alternative ways to obtain the information.[314] Another federal district court upheld reporter's privilege on the grounds that the information sought was not materially relevant to the charges involved in the case.[315]

When faced with subpoenas to identify those who posted anonymously on their websites, news organizations have discovered that reporter's privilege may not protect them. In Idaho, for example, a county Republican Committee official sought the source of allegedly defamatory comments about her that appeared on a blog administered by a Spokesman-Review reporter. The newspaper claimed reporter's privilege protection under the First Amendment and the state constitution. The court denied protection, reasoning that the privilege did not apply to the journalist who was "not acting as a reporter" but serving as "a facilitator of commentary."[316]

POINTS OF LAW
THE REPORTER'S PRIVILEGE TEST

A reporter's privilege to withhold information likely does not exist if the government can demonstrate all of the following:

1. **Possession:** Probable cause to believe that the reporter has information clearly connected to a specific violation of law
2. **No Alternatives:** That the information sought cannot be obtained by alternative means less destructive of First Amendment values
3. **Relevance:** That there is a compelling and overriding interest in the information.[317]

Reporter's privilege may not protect freelance journalists or filmmakers. The U.S. Court of Appeals for the Second Circuit ruled that a documentary filmmaker could not use reporter's privilege because attorneys representing the film's subjects helped with the movie's production. That meant the filmmaker was not a journalist because he did not function with journalistic independence, the court said.[318] A federal district court, however, refused to rule that documentary filmmaker Ken Burns had become an advocate and thereby lost his reporter's privilege protection when he produced "The Central Park Five," a film about five men convicted of raping a jogger in New York's Central Park.[319] The court quashed a subpoena for outtakes from the Burns film. The court rejected the argument that the filmmaker was not independent, and therefore unprotected by privilege, simply because he held an opinion about the men's guilt or innocence.[320]

Applying Shield Laws

Almost 50 years ago, the U.S. Supreme Court's opinion in *Branzburg* essentially invited legislatures to determine whether "a statutory newsman's privilege is necessary and desirable."[321] Although 17 states had enacted **shield laws**, which protect journalists from being found in contempt of court for refusing to reveal sources, prior to *Branzburg*, most others passed laws to protect journalists in some situations from contempt citations for refusing to reveal a source.[322] In eight states that lack shield laws, courts have recognized a qualified, or a limited, privilege to not have to reveal confidential sources' identities under certain conditions. Neither the Wyoming legislature nor courts have recognized a privilege for sources.[323]

The struggle to enact effective shield laws to protect confidential sources and information has been difficult and has produced what one scholar called "a haphazard system of limited protection."[324] In 2021, the Wyoming Senate Judiciary Committee did not pass a bill to protect journalists against receiving subpoenas to reveal confidential sources.[325] Hawaii's shield law expired in 2013 after legislators disagreed about who a statute should shield.[326] Recent attempts to strengthen shield laws in Colorado and Maryland failed.[327]

Efforts to pass a federal shield law have highlighted the problems inherent in broadly establishing those who would be protected and narrowly defining the conditions in which the shield would not apply. Legislators struggle when attempting to protect legitimate sources of news without shielding illegal leakers of secret government information, for example. They struggle to allow government to engage in secret surveillance and data gathering in the name of national security while prohibiting covert government fishing expeditions into the private communications of newsgatherers.[328] There is no federal shield law to protect journalists involved in federal proceedings. Journalists involved in federal proceedings have relied on the uncertain common law privilege.[329]

These problems are global, according to a recent UNESCO study. That study found most laws are outdated both in how they define "journalist" and in their failure to protect against government surveillance and data delivery laws targeting phone companies and internet service providers.[330] Montana recently became the first state in the United States to specifically protect reporters' privileged electronic communications from government intrusion. The revised law no longer permits state or local governments to request reporters' confidential information from third parties such as email providers and social networking sites.[331]

State laws vary widely. Shield statutes all grant some degree of reporter's privilege and reduce the discretion of the court about whether privilege exists and for whom. No laws protect everyone providing news to the public from every subpoena. The wording of shield laws often limits who and what they protect and in what situations, and courts tend to require compliance with a subpoena when withholding information may be seen as a threat to the Sixth Amendment right to a fair trial.[332]

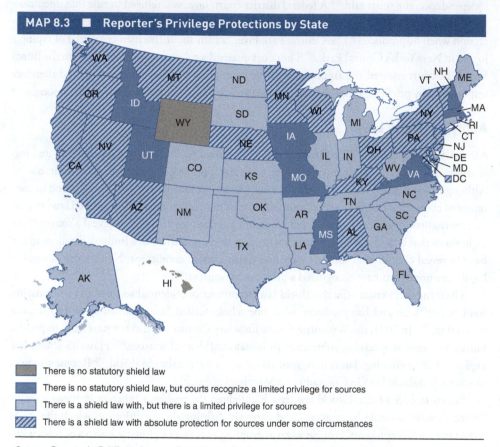

MAP 8.3   ■   Reporter's Privilege Protections by State

There is no statutory shield law

There is no statutory shield law, but courts recognize a limited privilege for sources

There is a shield law with, but there is a limited privilege for sources

There is a shield law with absolute protection for sources under some circumstances

Source: Reporter's Privilege Compendium, Reporters Committee for Freedom of the Press, www.rcfp.org/reporters-privilege/

Court rulings also are highly fact specific and do not lend themselves to broad, predictive conclusions even under a single state's well-adjudicated law. For example, a federal court did not apply California's strong shield law to a reporter's recent challenge to a subpoena to testify about her reporting on inmate deaths in San Diego County jails. The court quashed the subpoena based on the reporter's qualified First Amendment privilege because the state had not exhausted other sources for the information.[333]

In a high-profile case in Florida, BuzzFeed argued that the Florida and New York shield laws and the First Amendment protected it from forced disclosure of the source of the Christopher Steele "Trump dossier" it used in reporting on Russian hacking into Democratic National Committee computers during the 2016 presidential campaign.[334] The plaintiffs demanded disclosure of the source on the grounds that the Florida shield law did not apply to online news publications. In refusing to force disclosure of BuzzFeed's source, the federal district court wrote:

> There is nothing in the statute that limits the privilege to traditional print media. Because BuzzFeed writes stories and publishes news articles on its website, it qualifies as a news agency, news journal or news magazine. Accordingly, BuzzFeed is covered under the Florida Shield Law.[335]

The court said forced disclosure was unwarranted because the plaintiffs had failed to meet "their burden of making a clear and specific showing that the identity of the source cannot be obtained through alternative sources."[336]

REAL WORLD LAW
THE QUESTIONABLE TRUTH OF "TRUE CRIME"

Crime is big entertainment business. True crime, as the subject of podcasts like "Undisclosed" and "Serial" or documentaries like "Making a Murderer" and "Paradise Lost," has exploded in popularity, producing both greater public awareness of police or judicial misconduct and unfairness and increased desensitization to the grisly details and victims of crime.[337]

True crime "reenactments" or dramas rarely present the entire case. Prosecutors, in particular, criticize the true crime genre for producing profound misunderstandings in the minds of the general public and potential jurors about trials and the imperfect search for truth.[338] Media critics note that true crime stories tend to wrap everything up neatly, but fewer than 60 percent of real murders are actually solved.

Both "Serial" and "Making a Murderer" have been criticized for failing to provide a full view of cases and omitting incriminating evidence presented at trial.[339] In response, a producer of "Making a Murderer" said the series "hold[s] a mirror up" to the investigative and prosecutorial processes and highlights legislative reforms and advances in DNA testing that allow reinvestigation of potentially wrongful convictions.[340]

After the first season of "Serial" inspired questions about evidence prosecutors used to convict Adnan Syed on charges of strangling a high school student in 1999, prosecutors and the defense found new evidence in the case. In 2022, a judge vacated the 22-year-old conviction and ordered Syed to be released from prison.[341]

Timing also matters when considering whether a subpoena may be quashed. In a divided opinion, New York state's highest court held that the state shield law did not allow a reporter to appeal a trial court's refusal to quash a subpoena while the criminal case was proceeding. The majority criticized the state legislature for failure to act on its "repeated recommendations" to permit such appeals. The dissent said the ruling ran contrary to "our settled law and against our state's strong historical protections of journalists and the news gathering process."[342]

Some shield laws recognize the difficulty of defining "journalist" by applying protection to several categories of people. The Minnesota shield law protects anyone "directly engaged in the gathering, procuring, compiling, editing, or publishing of information . . . to the public."[343]

Some states shield those who report or write "motion picture news." Freelance writers, book authors, internet writers and many others are left out of many shield laws. Some states also exclude magazine writers.[344]

POINTS OF LAW
WHOM SHIELD LAWS PROTECT

Foundational definitions in state shield laws determine the breadth and application of the law. For example, West Virginia's law includes the following:

> Reporter means a person who regularly gathers, prepares, collects, photographs, records, writes, edits, reports or publishes news or information that concerns matters of public interest for dissemination to the public for a substantial portion of the person's livelihood, or a supervisor or employer of that person in that capacity: Provided that a student reporter at an accredited educational institution who meets all of the requirements of this definition, except that his or her reporting may not provide a portion of his or her livelihood, meets the definition of reporter for purposes of this section.[345]

> On its face, this law applies only to individuals who disseminate news for a living (including freelancers whose major income comes from news) and those working in and with campus media.[346]

In a 2021 public records case, Washington's highest court recognized that modern conceptions of news media have evolved "beyond the limits of the statutory definition" in the state shield law the legislature updated in 2007. The court said the shield law definition of news media applies to news outlets, traditional media organization and entities engaged "in the regular business of news gathering and disseminat[ing]" news. The content-creator for Libertys Champion YouTube channel was not affiliated with a traditional news organization, and the channel could not be categorized as news media, the court said.[347]

Several states have excluded bloggers from shield protection. A federal district court in Oregon said the state's shield law did not protect a self-identified investigative blogger who was a defendant in a libel suit.[348] The blog was not a "medium of communication," the court said, because it was not "affiliated with any newspaper, magazine, periodical, book, pamphlet, news service, wire service, news or feature syndicate, broadcast station or network, or cable, television system," and the blogger was not a journalist because she presented no evidence of journalistic training, affiliation or practices.[349] A Texas court similarly said its state shield law did not apply to an activist blogger with no journalism background who was not objective and did not adhere to journalistic ethics.[350]

Reporter's privileges generally are limited. For example, courts are most likely to protect source confidentiality in civil cases in which journalists are not parties to the litigation. In such cases, courts tend to assume the existence of alternative sources for the information that do not implicate the First Amendment.[351] Like other privileges, reporter's privilege can be waived. Particularly when a journalist is on the verge of going to jail, confidential sources may grant permission to the reporter to disclose their identities. Courts tend to diminish the weight of privilege once a source releases a reporter from the promise of secrecy.

Freelance videographer Joshua Wolf spent 226 days in prison after refusing to testify before a federal grand jury or to turn over his footage of an anarchist protest in 2005.

Ben Margot/Associated Press

Clarifying What Shield Laws Cover

The information protected by shield laws varies by state. Tennessee's shield law applies to any information or source of information used for publication or broadcast.[352] Most statutes do not protect journalists called to testify about events they witnessed, especially crimes. Also, the shield often crumbles when journalists are defendants—for example, in a libel case. Access to the reporter's knowledge, notes and sources may be vital to the plaintiff's effort to prove the journalist acted with negligence or actual malice.[353]

In a complex defamation and right-to-record suit involving NBC Universal's "Dateline" show, the Tenth Circuit Court of Appeals said Colorado's shield law protects confidential sources but does not prevent legitimate discovery of nonconfidential information even from journalists.[354] Courts in at least three states have ruled that their state shield laws did not prevent subpoenas for newsgathering records or confidential sources.[355]

New Hampshire's highest court did not support quashing a subpoena for a journalist to provide nonconfidential information in a voter suppression, attempted voter suppression and sending a false document case. A Concord Monitor reporter's testimony was sought regarding newsgathering for articles that said a liberal activist "had too many beers" before sending a "hoax" press release stating a Republican candidate for state representative was dropping out of the race. The court found the newsgathering privilege under the state constitution did not protect a journalist from testifying in a criminal proceeding about nonconfidential information subsequently published in a newspaper.[356]

In Virginia, however, a journalist successfully argued a qualified reporter's privilege established there by both state and federal court precedents covers both sources and unpublished information, regardless of confidentiality. A judge quashed a subpoena for the journalist to testify in the perjury trial of one of the organizers of the 2017 Unite the Right rally in Charlottesville.[357]

Finding Other Protections for Journalists

Other defenses may protect journalists from revealing information. Any subpoena in a federal criminal case must comply with Rule 17(c) of the Federal Rules of Criminal Procedure. The rule says a subpoena may be issued only for materials "admissible as evidence." The U.S. Supreme Court said that to justify a subpoena, the materials must be relevant, otherwise unavailable and necessary for the trial. The subpoena may not be a "fishing expedition."[358] Rule 26 of the Federal Rules of Civil Procedure prohibits a judge from granting a subpoena for materials in a civil trial if the materials can be obtained elsewhere or if the burden to get the materials outweighs any benefit.[359]

The Privacy Protection Act

After the *Stanford Daily* newsroom search case, Congress passed the Privacy Protection Act of 1980 that significantly limits both state and federal agencies' use of search warrants against public communicators. The law prohibits government agents from searching or seizing a journalist's "work product" or "documentary materials" in the journalist's possession as part of a criminal investigation. Work product includes notes and drafts of news stories. Documentary materials include videotapes, audiotapes and computer files. The law also protects outtakes not included in the final product.[360]

Journalists may sue government employees for violating the law and seek damages, attorney's fees and court costs. Limited exceptions under the Privacy Protection Act, however, apply if a news organization has refused an order to disclose, and all other remedies have been exhausted. Investigators may seize documentary materials to prevent their destruction or the death or other serious injury of individuals. Agents may seize certain information related to national security, child pornography or evidence that a journalist committed a crime.[361]

Visual journalists recently have filed claims that law enforcement violated the Privacy Protection Act and other laws by seizing cameras and documentary materials. In 2021, the District of Columbia Metropolitan Police Department settled a case involving the "unlawful arrest" and seizure of a documentarian's camera, phone and film. Despite telling police he was a member of the press, the documentarian was arrested while covering protests of police brutality in 2020. Authorities kept his equipment for 10 weeks, although he was released without charge.[362] In 2019, however, the Ninth Circuit Court of Appeals rejected a freelance photojournalist's Privacy Protection Act claim. A camera "documented the incidents leading to his arrest" for not abiding by a law enforcement officer's order to leave an accident scene, and there was probable cause to believe the materials related to his arrest, the court stated.[363]

In at least one case, the U.S. Department of Justice accused a reporter of a crime in an effort to circumvent the Privacy Protection Act. To justify a targeted search of a Fox News reporter's emails, the DOJ claimed the reporter conspired with a State Department analyst to obtain classified documents.[364] Subsequent rules prevented the FBI and others from using an accusation of conspiracy to obtain a search warrant for a reporter's materials.[365] In 2021 and 2022, the DOJ introduced new regulations regarding seeking information from members of the news media when they are gathering news. The regulations indicate DOJ employees may not use compulsory legal processes to secretly obtain work product materials or documentary materials from a member of the news media solely to investigate another person.[366] DOJ regulations previously required notice and notification and that subpoenas of journalists' records be narrowly tailored and used as a last resort.[367]

Facing National Security Claims

As discussed elsewhere, national security claims often trump other legal protections. The U.S. Court of Appeals for the Ninth Circuit, however, recently ruled that the Department of Homeland Security's border agents do not have unlimited power to search people's electronic devices. The case involved finding child pornography on a laptop, but the court signaled that the DHS must have "reasonable suspicion" before searching individuals' electronic devices. The Ninth Circuit, however, said, "a quick look" or "unintrusive search of a laptop," such as asking that the computer be turned on, is acceptable.[368]

A Washington Times reporter settled her lawsuit against the DHS for seizure of newsgathering materials—including information about a whistleblower. The materials were taken from her home under a warrant seeking evidence in a case unrelated to the reporter. Under a secret settlement, the DHS agreed to improve its protection of newsgathering materials in future searches.[369]

EMERGING LAW

Concerns about the spread of COVID-19 and security threats inspired courts to change procedures. Some courts used livestreaming, video conferencing or teleconferencing for hearings, oral arguments and trials in 2020, 2021 and 2022.[370] For the first time ever, in 2021, Minnesota allowed a high-profile trial to be broadcast live from a Minnesota courthouse with a metal fence, concrete barriers and National Guard troops keeping out protestors during Derek Chauvin's trial.[371] In 2021 and 2022, journalists also received some hope for greater protection against federal employees' uses of subpoenas, search warrants and court orders to seek information journalists learned through newsgathering.[372]

The Supreme Court conducted oral arguments via telephone conference and provided real-time audio access to oral arguments. The Court still followed Rule 53 of the Federal Rules of Criminal Procedure, barring photographs and broadcasting of judicial proceedings.[373] Typically, only 50 members of the public can view U.S. Supreme Court sessions in person, and everyone else receives news of the Court's oral arguments secondhand until audio recordings are published online on Fridays.[374]

In 2021, a bipartisan group of senators introduced a bill to require the nation's highest court to permit televising public court proceedings,[375] but Congress has failed many times to pass laws that would provide broadcast access to the U.S. Supreme Court unless a majority of the justices voted for closure to protect specific, enumerated interests.[376] A 2022 survey found that 65 percent of voters believe the U.S. Supreme Court should televise oral arguments; most voters believe televising the Court would increase trust in the Court and its rulings.[377]

Although Justice Amy Coney Barrett said in her Senate confirmation hearings she would be open to allowing cameras in the Court's chambers,[378] camera access is unlikely. In 2022, during

Justice Ketanji Brown Jackson's Senate confirmation hearings, Jackson said she wanted to talk with other justices and understand issues associated with allowing cameras prior to taking a position on whether to allow cameras.[379] During their Senate confirmation hearings, Justices Elena Kagan and Sonia Sotomayor expressed support, and Justice Neil Gorsuch said he had an "open mind" about broadcasts of Supreme Court sessions, but those three subsequently backed away. In 2018, Supreme Court nominee Brett Kavanaugh declined to take a stance on cameras in the Supreme Court.[380]

The future of virtual hearings and trials could be limited. Video conferenced and teleconferenced proceedings have raised concerns about distractions, technological challenges and fairness. In 2020, the Supreme Court's livestreamed teleconference hearing in a robocall case included what sounded like a toilet flushing.[381] In 2020, a Texas attorney accidentally made a virtual court appearance with a filter making him appear as a cat.[382] In another instance, a Tennessee judge lost power at her home, causing an online hearing to be delayed.[383] Research has found virtual hearings may harm defendants' rights for legal representations and virtual testimony may not convey cues used to assess credibility.[384]

In 2022, more than 300 million viewers watched livestream coverage of a defamation trial involving actors Johnny Depp and Amber Heard.[385] Due to concerns that journalists otherwise would crowd the courthouse, a Fairfax County Circuit Court judge authorized Court TV to have two pool video cameras in the courtroom during the proceedings. Allowing gavel-to-gavel coverage was criticized because portions of the trial addressed allegations of sexual violence and intimate partner violence. Critics worried that coverage could deter domestic or sexual violence victims from speaking about their experiences.[386]

Fairfax County Circuit Judge Penny Azcarate allowed two pool video cameras to cover the highly publicized Johnny Depp–Amber Heard defamation trial in 2022.

Steve Helber /Associated Press

The near ubiquity of cellphones and their associated social media platforms presents difficult questions about First and Sixth Amendment rights and new opportunities for covert juror misconduct.[387] Social media give individual jurors private access to potentially prejudicial information at the touch of a screen. The potential threat of social media interactions by jurors is a growing problem.[388] One recent study stated "there is no perfect solution to the growing risk of juror misconduct associated with social media." The study concluded that instructions to juries are effective means for mitigating risks from juror social media use.[389] A judge may sanction a juror whose actions are likely to substantially prejudice ongoing litigation, but the judge must be aware of the problem to take effective action against it.[390]

Student journalists and journalists' rights recently have been challenged as attorneys have turned to journalists for evidence in civil and criminal cases. In 2021, almost a decade after covering a murder case as a college student, a journalist's source materials and sources were subpoenaed in a civil case alleging law enforcement officials had committed "gross misconduct" in that criminal case.[391] Another student journalist received a subpoena to turn over documents as part of a civil case in which a college donor sought to have a $100 million donation returned.[392] In a criminal case, an Idaho journalist covering the disappearance and deaths of two children received a subpoena to appear as a witness in a change of venue hearing.[393]

As journalists and sources increasingly have used technology to communicate, law enforcement has sought information about those communications from technology corporations. Recent scholarship found a sharp increase in federal attempts to prosecute sources accused of leaking classified information, with investigators drawing evidence from phone, email and app records.[394] Journalists need to be aware of the pattern for investigative agencies to use electronic records to investigate journalists' sources and follow journalists' ethical obligation to educate sources on how to better protect sources' identities.[395]

Local law enforcement has sought access to electronics to seek information about journalists' confidential sources. In 2019, law enforcement officers hammered through the door of the home of Bryan Carmody, a freelance videographer in San Francisco. Seeking information about an anonymous source who provided Carmody with a police report about the death of a San Francisco public defender, officers entered his home with guns drawn, entered his office, seized his computer and attained warrants to access his call logs and text messages. The judges who had issued the warrants later quashed and deemed the warrants illegal. Police had not fully informed the judges about Carmody's status as a member of the press. In 2020, San Francisco entered a $369,000 settlement agreement with Carmody.[396]

In 2021, Amy Harris, a freelance photojournalist whose work has been published in Rolling Stone and POLITICO, filed a lawsuit to quash a subpoena issued by the House panel investigating the riot that occurred at the U.S. Capitol Building January 6, 2021. The subpoena sought Harris's cell phone provider, Verizon, to provide all information about calls, text messages and other communications associated with Harris's phone number between November 2020 and January 2021. Harris was working on a project on an extremist group known as "The Proud Boys" during that period. The lawsuit argues the subpoena violated Harris's First Amendment rights and rights under the D.C. Shield Law that protects unpublished source material.[397]

Under the Obama, Trump and Biden administrations, the Department of Justice secretly seized journalists' phone and email records when investigating leaks of government information. New York Times executives also were placed under a gag order in 2021 after they learned the DOJ was pursuing four reporters' email logs from Google.[398] Following the DOJ pursuit of reporters' phone and email records in 2021, President Biden called seizing journalists' email and phone records wrong, and declared he "won't let that happen."[399] A DOJ spokesperson said the agency would no longer "seek compulsory legal process in leak investigations to obtain source information from members of the news media doing their jobs."[400]

In 2022, the DOJ codified new rules that typically will limit DOJ uses of search warrants, subpoenas, court orders or other compulsory processes to seek information members of the news media received when gathering news. The rules also generally prohibit using compulsory processes to seek information from providers of journalists' email, phone or other digital services.[401] The DOJ, however, may seek a member of the news media's permission to access records "to authenticate already published information." The DOJ also may seek information when a person is reasonably believed to be a "foreign power or agent of a foreign power," a terrorist or terrorist organization or "[a]iding, abetting, or conspiring in illegal activity." Compulsory processes also may be used when deemed "necessary to prevent an imminent or concrete risk of death or serious bodily harm."[402]

Journalists might find some hope in the rules' recognition that "A free and independent press is vital to the functioning of our democracy." The DOJ rules describe newsgathering activities as "the process by which a member of the news media collects, pursues, or obtains information or records for purposes of producing content intended for public dissemination."[403] The rules, however, do not define member of the news media. The DOJ may use multiple factors, such as where people work and what type of content they produce, to determine who is a member of the news media.[404]

In 2022, the House of Representatives unanimously passed the Protect Reporters from Exploitative State Spying (PRESS) Act to create a federal privilege for journalists against having to reveal information that identifies sources.[405] If the bill becomes law, the law generally would provide journalists with protection against federal entities' pursuit of testimony, records or account information from journalists. The bill, however, would allow a court to compel disclosure under certain narrow circumstances, such as when necessary to prevent terrorism or "a threat of imminent violence, significant bodily harm, or death."[406] The Reporters Committee for Freedom of the Press called this bill "timely and critical," with potential to create uniformity as to how a reporter's privilege is recognized.[407]

KEYTERMS

admonitions	gag orders
change of venue	impanel
continuance	impartial jurors
experience and logic test	in camera
for-cause challenge	redact

reporter's privilege

restraining order

sequestration

shield laws

summons

venire

voir dire

CASES FOR STUDY
THINKING ABOUT THEM

The two case excerpts that follow address different aspects of access to trials. The first is the U.S. Supreme Court ruling about the right of the public, independent from the parties at trial, to attend criminal trials. The second, *People v. Owens*, is a recent decision of the Colorado Supreme Court examining whether either the state constitution or the First Amendment provides a right of access to criminal court records. As you read these case excerpts, keep the following questions in mind:

● What foundations does the U.S. Supreme Court draw upon in *Richmond Newspapers, Inc. v. Virginia* to conclude that the public has a right of access to criminal trials?

● What does the Court's decision in *Richmond Newspapers* suggest about any broader public right of access to judicial proceedings?

● How does the reasoning of the Colorado Supreme Court in *People v. Owens* compare to that of the U.S. Supreme Court in *Richmond Newspapers*?

● How do these two decisions balance a defendant's right to a fair trial against the public's right to know?

RICHMOND NEWSPAPERS, INC. V. VIRGINIA
SUPREME COURT OF THE UNITED STATES 448 U.S. 555 (1980)

Chief JUSTICE WARREN BURGER delivered the Court's opinion:

The narrow question presented in this case is whether the right of the public and press to attend criminal trials is guaranteed under the United States Constitution....

Stevenson was indicted for the murder of a hotel manager who had been found stabbed to death on December 2, 1975. Tried promptly in July 1976, Stevenson was convicted of second-degree murder in the Circuit Court of Hanover County, Va. The Virginia Supreme Court reversed the conviction in October 1977, holding that a bloodstained shirt purportedly belonging to Stevenson had been improperly admitted into evidence. Stevenson was retried in the same court. This second trial ended in a mistrial on May 30, 1978, when a juror asked to be excused after trial had begun and no alternate was available. A third trial, which began in the same court on June 6, 1978, also ended in a mistrial . . . because a prospective juror had read about Stevenson's previous trials in a newspaper and had told other prospective jurors about the case before the retrial began.

Stevenson was tried in the same court for a fourth time beginning on September 11, 1978. Present in the courtroom when the case was called were . . . reporters for appellant

Richmond Newspapers, Inc. Before the trial began, counsel for the defendant moved that it be closed to the public:

"[T]here was this woman that was with the family of the deceased when we were here before. She had sat in the Courtroom. I would like to ask that everybody be excluded from the Courtroom because I don't want any information being shuffled back and forth when we have a recess as to what—who testified to what."

The trial judge, who had presided over two of the three previous trials, asked if the prosecution had any objection to clearing the courtroom. The prosecutor stated he had no objection and . . . the trial judge . . . ordered "that the Courtroom be kept clear of all parties except the witnesses when they testify." The record does not show that any objections to the closure order were made by anyone present at the time. . . .

Later that same day, however, appellants sought a hearing on a motion to vacate the closure order. The trial judge granted the request and scheduled a hearing to follow the close of the day's proceedings. When the hearing began, the court ruled that the hearing was to be treated as part of the trial; accordingly, he again ordered the reporters to leave the courtroom, and they complied.

At the closed hearing, counsel for appellants observed that no evidentiary findings had been made by the court prior to the entry of its closure order, and pointed out that the court had failed to consider any other, less drastic measures within its power to ensure a fair trial. Counsel for appellants argued that constitutional considerations mandated that before ordering closure, the court should first decide that the rights of the defendant could be protected in no other way.

Counsel for defendant Stevenson pointed out that this was the fourth time he was standing trial. He also referred to "difficulty with information between the jurors," and stated that he "didn't want information to leak out," be published by the media, perhaps inaccurately, and then be seen by the jurors. Defense counsel argued that these things, plus the fact that "this is a small community," made this a proper case for closure.

The trial judge noted that counsel for the defendant had made similar statements at the morning hearing. The court also stated: "One of the other points that we take into consideration in this particular Courtroom is layout of the Courtroom. I think that having people in the Courtroom is distracting to the jury. Now, we have to have certain people in here and maybe that's not a very good reason. When we get into our new Court Building, people can sit in the audience so the jury can't see them. The rule of the Court may be different under those circumstances. . . ."

The prosecutor again declined comment, and the court summed up by saying: "I'm inclined to agree with [defense counsel] that, if I feel that the rights of the defendant are infringed in any way, [when] he makes the motion to do something and it doesn't completely override all rights of everyone else, then I'm inclined to go along with the defendant's motion." The court denied the motion to vacate and ordered the trial to continue the following morning "with the press and public excluded."

What transpired when the closed trial resumed the next day was disclosed in the following manner by an order of the court entered September 12, 1978:

"[In] the absence of the jury, the defendant, by counsel, made a Motion that a mistrial be declared, which motion was taken under advisement."

"At the conclusion of the Commonwealth's evidence, the attorney for the defendant moved the Court to strike the Commonwealth's evidence on grounds stated to the record, which Motion was sustained by the Court."

"And the jury having been excused, the Court doth find the accused NOT GUILTY of Murder, as charged in the Indictment, and he was allowed to depart." . . .

The Virginia Supreme Court . . . finding no reversible error, denied the petition for appeal. . . .

The criminal trial which appellants sought to attend has long since ended, and there is thus some suggestion that the case is moot. This Court has frequently recognized, however, that its jurisdiction is not necessarily defeated by the practical termination of a contest which is short-lived by nature. If the underlying dispute is "capable of repetition, yet evading review," it is not moot. . . .

In prior cases the Court has treated questions involving conflicts between publicity and a defendant's right to a fair trial. . . . But here for the first time the Court is asked to decide whether a criminal trial itself may be closed to the public upon the unopposed request of a defendant, without any demonstration that closure is required to protect the defendant's superior right to a fair trial, or that some other overriding consideration requires closure.

The origins of the proceeding which has become the modern criminal trial in Anglo-American justice can be traced back beyond reliable historical records. . . . What is significant for present purposes is that, throughout its evolution, the trial has been open to all who cared to observe. . . . From these early times, although great changes in courts and procedure took place, one thing remained constant: the public character of the trial at which guilt or innocence was decided. . . .

We have found nothing to suggest that the presumptive openness of the trial, which English courts were later to call "one of the essential qualities of a court of justice," was not also an attribute of the judicial systems of colonial America. . . . In some instances, the openness of trials was explicitly recognized as part of the fundamental law of the Colony. . . . Other contemporary writings confirm the recognition that part of the very nature of a criminal trial was its openness to those who wished to attend. . . .

As we have shown, . . . the historical evidence demonstrates conclusively that, at the time when our organic laws were adopted, criminal trials both here and in England had long been presumptively open. This is no quirk of history; rather, it has long been recognized as an indispensable attribute of an Anglo-American trial. . . . Jeremy Bentham not only recognized the therapeutic value of open justice but regarded it as the keystone:

"Without publicity, all other checks are insufficient: in comparison of publicity, all other checks are of small account. Recordation, appeal, whatever other institutions might present themselves in the character of checks, would be found to operate rather as cloaks than checks; as cloaks in reality, as checks only in appearance." . . .

. . . The early history of open trials in part reflects the widespread acknowledgment . . . that public trials had significant community therapeutic value. . . . [P]eople sensed from experience and observation that, especially in the administration of criminal justice, the means used to achieve justice must have the support derived from public acceptance of both the process and its results.

When a shocking crime occurs, a community reaction of outrage and public protest often follows. Thereafter the open processes of justice serve an important prophylactic purpose, providing an outlet for community concern, hostility, and emotion. Without an awareness that society's responses to criminal conduct are underway, natural human reactions of outrage and protest are frustrated and may manifest themselves in some form of vengeful "self-help," as indeed they did regularly in the activities of vigilante "committees" on our frontiers. . . .

Civilized societies withdraw both from the victim and the vigilante the enforcement of criminal laws, but they cannot erase from people's consciousness the fundamental, natural yearning to see justice done—or even the urge for retribution. The crucial prophylactic aspects of the administration of justice cannot function in the dark; no community catharsis can occur if justice is "done in a corner [or] in any covert manner." It is not enough to say that results alone will satiate the natural community desire for "satisfaction." A result considered untoward may undermine public confidence, and where the trial has been concealed from public view, an unexpected outcome can cause a reaction that the system at best has failed and at worst has been corrupted. To work effectively, it is important that society's criminal process "satisfy the appearance of justice," and the appearance of justice can best be provided by allowing people to observe it. . . .

People in an open society do not demand infallibility from their institutions, but it is difficult for them to accept what they are prohibited from observing. When a criminal trial is conducted in the open, there is at least an opportunity both for understanding the system in general and its workings in a particular case: "The educative effect of public attendance is a material advantage. Not only is respect for the law increased and intelligent acquaintance acquired with the methods of government, but a strong confidence in judicial remedies is secured which could never be inspired by a system of secrecy." . . .

. . . Instead of acquiring information about trials by firsthand observation or by word of mouth from those who attended, people now acquire it chiefly through the print and electronic media. In a sense, this validates the media claim of functioning as surrogates for the public. While media representatives enjoy the same right of access as the public, they often are provided special seating and priority of entry so that they may report what people in attendance have seen and heard. This "[contributes] to public understanding of the rule of law and to comprehension of the functioning of the entire criminal justice system. . . ."

From this unbroken, uncontradicted history, supported by reasons as valid today as in centuries past, we are bound to conclude that a presumption of openness inheres in the very nature of a criminal trial under our system of justice. . . .

Despite the history of criminal trials being presumptively open since long before the Constitution, the State presses its contention that neither the Constitution nor the Bill of Rights contains any provision which, by its terms, guarantees to the public the right to attend criminal trials. Standing alone, this is correct, but there remains the question whether, absent an explicit provision, the Constitution affords protection against exclusion of the public from criminal trials. . . .

The Bill of Rights was enacted against the backdrop of the long history of trials being presumptively open. Public access to trials was then regarded as an important aspect of the process itself; . . . In guaranteeing freedoms such as those of speech and press, the First Amendment can be read as protecting the right of everyone to attend trials so as to give meaning to those explicit guarantees. "The First Amendment goes beyond protection of the press and the self-expression of individuals to prohibit government from limiting the stock of information from which members of the public may draw." Free speech carries with it some freedom to listen. . . . What this means in the context of trials is that the First Amendment guarantees of speech and press, standing alone, prohibit government from summarily closing courtroom doors which had long been open to the public at the time that Amendment was adopted. . . .

. . . It is not crucial whether we describe this right to attend criminal trials to hear, see, and communicate observations concerning them as a "right of access," or a "right to gather information," for we have recognized that "without some protection for seeking out the news, freedom of the press could be eviscerated." The explicit, guaranteed rights to speak and to publish concerning what takes place at a trial would lose much meaning if access to observe the trial could, as it was here, be foreclosed arbitrarily.

The right of access to places traditionally open to the public, as criminal trials have long been, may be seen as assured by the amalgam of the First Amendment guarantees of speech and press; and their affinity to the right of assembly is not without relevance. . . . [A] trial courtroom also is a public place where the people generally—and representatives of the media—have a right to be present, and where their presence historically has been thought to enhance the integrity and quality of what takes place.

The State argues that the Constitution nowhere spells out a guarantee for the right of the public to attend trials, and that, accordingly, no such right is protected. . . . But arguments such as the State makes have not precluded recognition of important rights not enumerated. . . . We hold that the right to attend criminal trials is implicit in the guarantees of the First Amendment; without the freedom to attend such trials, which people have exercised for centuries, important aspects of freedom of speech and "of the press could be eviscerated."

Having concluded there was a guaranteed right of the public under the First and Fourteenth Amendments to attend the trial of Stevenson's case, we return to the closure order challenged by appellants. . . . Despite the fact that this was the fourth trial of the accused, the trial judge made no findings to support closure; no inquiry was made as to whether alternative solutions would have met the need to ensure fairness; there was no recognition of any right under the Constitution for the public or press to attend the trial.

There exist in the context of the trial itself various tested alternatives to satisfy the constitutional demands of fairness. . . . There was no suggestion that any problems with witnesses could not have been dealt with by their exclusion from the courtroom or their sequestration during the trial. Nor is there anything to indicate that sequestration of the jurors would not have guarded against their being subjected to any improper information. All of the alternatives admittedly present difficulties for trial courts, but none of the factors relied on here was beyond the realm of the manageable. Absent an overriding interest articulated in findings, the trial of a criminal case must be open to the public. Accordingly, the judgment under review is

Reversed. . . .

JUSTICE JOHN PAUL STEVENS concurring:

This is a watershed case. Until today, the Court has accorded virtually absolute protection to the dissemination of information or ideas, but never before has it squarely held that the acquisition of newsworthy matter is entitled to any constitutional protection whatsoever. . . .

Today, however, for the first time, the Court unequivocally holds that an arbitrary interference with access to important information is an abridgment of the freedoms of speech and of the press protected by the First Amendment. . . .

. . . I agree that the First Amendment protects the public and the press from abridgment of their rights of access to information about the operation of their government, including the Judicial Branch; given the total absence of any record justification for the closure order entered in this case, that order violated the First Amendment.

JUSTICE WILLIAM BRENNAN, with whom JUSTICE THURGOOD MARSHALL joined, concurring:

. . . I agree with those of my Brethren who hold that, without more, agreement of the trial judge and the parties cannot constitutionally close a trial to the public.

While freedom of expression is made inviolate by the First Amendment, and, with only rare and stringent exceptions, may not be suppressed, the First Amendment has not been viewed by the Court in all settings as providing an equally categorical assurance of the correlative freedom of access to information. Yet the Court has not ruled out a public access component to the First Amendment in every circumstance. Read with care and in context, our decisions must therefore be understood as holding only that any privilege of access to governmental information is subject to a degree of restraint dictated by the nature of the information and countervailing interests in security or confidentiality. These cases neither comprehensively nor absolutely deny that public access to information may at times be implied by the First Amendment and the principles which animate it.

The Court's approach in right-of-access cases simply reflects the special nature of a claim of First Amendment right to gather information. . . . [T]he First Amendment . . . has a structural role to play in securing and fostering our republican system of self-government. Implicit in this structural role is not only "the principle that debate on public issues should be uninhibited, robust, and wide-open," but also the antecedent assumption that valuable public debate—as well as other civic behavior—must be informed. The structural model links the First Amendment to that process of communication necessary for a democracy to survive, and thus entails solicitude not only for communication itself, but also for the indispensable conditions of meaningful communication. . . .

First, the case for a right of access has special force when drawn from an enduring and vital tradition of public entree to particular proceedings or information. Such a tradition commands respect, in part, because the Constitution carries the gloss of history. More importantly, a tradition of accessibility implies the favorable judgment of experience. Second, the value of access must be measured in specifics. Analysis is not advanced by rhetorical statements that all information bears upon public issues; what is crucial in individual cases is whether access to a particular government process is important in terms of that very process.

To resolve the case before us, therefore, we must consult historical and current practice with respect to open trials, and weigh the importance of public access to the trial process itself. . . . [S]ignificantly for our present purpose, [the Court has] recognized that open trials are bulwarks of our free and democratic government: public access to court proceedings is one of the numerous "checks and balances" of our system, because "contemporaneous review in the forum of public opinion is an effective restraint on possible abuse of judicial power." Indeed, the Court focused with particularity upon the public trial guarantee "as a safeguard against any attempt to employ our courts as instruments of persecution," or "for the suppression of political and religious heresies." Thus, . . . open trials are indispensable to First Amendment political and religious freedoms. . . .

Publicity serves to advance several of the particular purposes of the trial (and, indeed, the judicial) process. . . . But, as a feature of our governing system of justice, the trial process serves other, broadly political, interests, and public access advances these objectives as well. To that extent, trial access possesses specific structural significance. . . . Secrecy is profoundly inimical to this demonstrative purpose of the trial process. . . .

But the trial is more than a demonstrably just method of adjudicating disputes and protecting rights. . . . It follows that the conduct of the trial is preeminently a matter of public interest. . . .

. . . [R]esolution of First Amendment public access claims in individual cases must be strongly influenced by the weight of historical practice and by an assessment of the specific structural value of public access in the circumstances. With regard to the case at hand, our ingrained tradition of public trials and the importance of public access to the broader purposes of the trial process, tip the balance strongly toward the rule that trials be open. What countervailing interests might be sufficiently compelling to reverse this presumption of openness need not concern us now, for the statute at stake here authorizes trial closures at the unfettered discretion of the judge and parties. Accordingly, [the law] violates the First and Fourteenth Amendments, and the decision of the Virginia Supreme Court to the contrary should be reversed.

JUSTICE POTTER STEWART concurring:

. . . [The presumption of open criminal proceedings] does not mean that the First Amendment right of members of the public and representatives of the press to attend civil and criminal trials is absolute. Just as a legislature may impose reasonable time, place, and manner restrictions upon the exercise of First Amendment freedoms, so may a trial judge impose reasonable limitations upon the unrestricted occupation of a courtroom by representatives of the press and members of the public. Much more than a city street, a trial courtroom must be a quiet and orderly place. Moreover, every courtroom has a finite physical capacity, and there may be occasions when not all who wish to attend a trial may do so. And while there exist many alternative ways to satisfy the constitutional demands of a fair trial, those demands may also sometimes justify limitations upon the unrestricted presence of spectators in the courtroom.

Since, in the present case, the trial judge appears to have given no recognition to the right of representatives of the press and members of the public to be present at the Virginia murder trial over which he was presiding, the judgment under review must be reversed.

JUSTICE HARRY BLACKMUN concurring:

. . . I remain convinced that the right to a public trial is to be found where the Constitution explicitly placed it—in the Sixth Amendment.

The Court, however, has eschewed the Sixth Amendment route. The plurality turns to other possible constitutional sources and invokes a veritable potpourri of them—the Speech Clause of the First Amendment, the Press Clause, the Assembly Clause, the Ninth Amendment, and a cluster of penumbral guarantees recognized in past decisions. This course is troublesome, but it is the route that has been selected and, at least for now, we must live with it. . . .

. . . [W]ith the Sixth Amendment set to one side in this case, I am driven to conclude, as a secondary position, that the First Amendment must provide some measure of protection for public access to the trial. . . . It is clear and obvious to me, on the approach the Court has chosen to take, that, by closing this criminal trial, the trial judge abridged these First Amendment interests of the public.

I also would reverse, and I join the judgment of the Court.

JUSTICE WILLIAM REHNQUIST dissenting:

. . . I do not believe that either the First or Sixth Amendment, as made applicable to the States by the Fourteenth, requires that a State's reasons for denying public access to a trial, where both the prosecuting attorney and the defendant have consented to an order of closure approved by the judge, are subject to any additional constitutional review at our hands. . . .

The issue here is not whether the "right" to freedom of the press conferred by the First Amendment to the Constitution overrides the defendant's "right" to a fair trial conferred by other Amendments to the Constitution; it is, instead, whether any provision in the Constitution may fairly be read to prohibit what the trial judge in the Virginia state-court system did in this case. Being unable to find any such prohibition in the First, Sixth, Ninth, or any other Amendment to the United States Constitution, or in the Constitution itself, I dissent.

PEOPLE V. OWENS
SUPREME COURT OF COLORADO 420 P.3D 257 (COLO. 2018)

JUSTICE MELISSA HART delivered the court's en banc opinion:

We accepted jurisdiction in this original proceeding to consider The Colorado Independent's contention that the Arapahoe County District Court erred in refusing to grant public access to certain records maintained under seal in a capital murder case.

The Colorado Independent contends that the federal and state constitutions grant a presumptive right of access to documents filed in criminal cases. While presumptive access to judicial proceedings is a right recognized under both the state and federal constitutions, neither the United States Supreme Court nor this court has ever held that records filed with a court are treated the same way. We decline to conclude here that such unfettered access to criminal justice records is guaranteed by either the First Amendment or Article II, section 10 of the Colorado Constitution.

Defendant Sir Mario Owens was convicted of first-degree murder and sentenced to death in 2008. In 2017, the trial court denied Mr. Owens's motion for post-conviction relief ...as well as his related motion to disqualify the District Attorney's Office for the 18th Judicial District and to appoint a special prosecutor. The basis for the motion to disqualify was an allegation that the District Attorney had failed to disclose evidence that would have been favorable to Mr. Owens's defense. Over Mr. Owens's objection, the trial court issued a protective order, which remains in place today, sealing portions of the post-conviction motions practice.

In 2017, The Colorado Independent ("petitioner") filed a motion with the district court, asking the court to unseal the records, arguing that public access to the records was required by the First Amendment, Article II, section 10 of the Colorado Constitution, common law, and the Colorado Criminal Justice Records Act. The district court denied that motion, and petitioner filed for relief . . ., limiting its request for relief to the argument that presumptive access to judicial records is a constitutional guarantee.

Relief [to stay all lower court proceedings] is an extraordinary remedy limited in purpose and availability. Our exercise of original jurisdiction is discretionary. We have previously exercised our original jurisdiction to address public access to court documents. Here, we do so once again.

Because the availability of First Amendment protection presents a legal question, we review such challenges de novo. De novo review is also appropriate for alleged violations of Article II, section 10 of the Colorado Constitution.

Here, we reject petitioner's constitutional arguments for mandatory disclosure of the records sealed in this matter. We find no support in United States Supreme Court jurisprudence for petitioner's contention that the First Amendment provides the public with a constitutional right of access to any and all court records in cases involving matters of public concern. Petitioner cites none. The Tenth Circuit has more than once declined to recognize a First Amendment right of access to court records.

Moreover, we have never recognized any such constitutional right—whether under the First Amendment or Article II, section 10 of the Colorado Constitution. Petitioner's near-exclusive reliance on this court's opinion in [*Times-Call Publishing Co. v. Wingfield*] is misplaced. In *Wingfield*, we analyzed a statutory prohibition against the inspection of court records in pending cases by non-parties. We concluded that while no "absolute right to examine" court records exists, inspection may be permitted "at the discretion of the court." Contrary to petitioner's assertion, this court did not hold in *Wingfield* that limiting access to court records violates the First Amendment. We decline to do so now in the absence of any indication from the nation's high court that access to all criminal justice records is a constitutionally guaranteed right belonging to the public at large.

We also see no compelling reason to interpret our state constitution as guaranteeing such a sweeping—and previously unrecognized—right of unfettered access to criminal justice records. On the contrary, such a ruling would do violence to the comprehensive open-records laws and administrative procedures currently in place—including, but not limited to, the Colorado Criminal Justice Records Act—that are predicated upon the absence of a constitutionally guaranteed right of access to criminal justice records.

We affirm the denial of The Colorado Independent's motion to unseal the subject records.

Facebook CEO Mark Zuckerberg gives his opening statement remotely during a Senate Commerce, Science, and Transportation Committee hearing to discuss reforming Section 230 of the Communications Decency Act with big tech companies.

Credit: Greg Nash/Pool via CNP | usage worldwide

9 ELECTRONIC MEDIA REGULATION

From Radio to the Internet

CHAPTER OUTLINE

What Is Electronic Media?

History of Broadcast Regulation

Reasons to Regulate Broadcasting
Spectrum Scarcity
The Public Interest Standard

Federal Communications Commission
How Does the FCC Work?
What Does the FCC Do?
FCC Ownership Rules
Public Broadcasting

Broadcast Programming Rules
Political Broadcasting Regulations
Children's Programming Requirements

Multichannel Video Programming Distributor Regulation
History of Cable and Satellite Regulation
Must-Carry and Retransmission Consent
Public Access Channels

Internet Regulation
Section 230
The FCC's Role in Internet Regulation
Net Neutrality

Emerging Law

Cases for Study
- *Red Lion Broadcasting Co., Inc. v. Federal Communications Commission*
- *Federal Communications Commission v. Prometheus Radio Project*

LEARNING OBJECTIVES

9.1 Understand which mediums are considered electronic media and which are not.

9.2 Demonstrate how the history of broadcast regulations has shaped today's industry.

9.3 Analyze the roles of spectrum scarcity and public interest standards as justification for broadcast media regulation.

9.4 Summarize the Federal Communications Communication's various roles and responsibilities.

9.5   Apply relevant rules to questions regarding children's programming and political advertising.

9.6   Compare the regulatory framework for broadcast radio and television to rules governing MVPDs.

9.7   Describe the FCC's role in internet regulation and evaluate proposed changes to Section 230 and net neutrality.

9.8   Analyze the relationship between social media regulation and the First Amendment.

Not all media are treated the same way by the government. Certain forms of media, such as broadcast television and radio, are regulated differently than their print or digital counterparts. The Federal Communications Commission is the government agency responsible for regulating communications technologies. One of the most pressing challenges facing the FCC is how to promote diversity, localism, and competition in a media environment that is largely concentrated. The FCC is also tasked with regulating internet service, however, there are currently very few regulations or laws that apply soley to internet content. Instead, social media companies are largely left to their own devices to determine how issues such as nudity or harassment will be handled on their sites. As citizens, it is important for us to understand which forms of media are regulated by the government and the impact those rules have on public discourse, and ultimately, democracy.

WHAT IS ELECTRONIC MEDIA?

Digital technologies have transformed the distribution channels, platforms and devices through which most people consume media, news and entertainment. Today, consumers do not think about making meaningful distinctions between electronic and print media because content is so readily available in a variety of formats. Yet, the distinction between electronic and print media is still important within mass communication law.

As explained in Chapter 1, precedent is the legal principle that tells courts to stand by what they have decided previously. Because precedents are established over time, sometimes they do not quickly or easily guide new or emerging technological challenges. Throughout this book, you have read numerous examples of how courts, state legislatures, Congress and administrative agencies have adapted or changed existing laws, administrative rules and precedents to address new challenges created by emerging technologies. What is different within the context of electronic media is that the technologies themselves are interwoven into the legal and regulatory framework established over the past century. That framework does not always adapt quickly, yet technological innovation and change happen at a rapid pace.

Electronic media include all forms of media that utilize electronics or digital encoding to distribute news and entertainment. However, they do not include media that have historically been distributed through printed means, even though most print media today are created electronically and live on the internet. For example, The New York Times is considered part of the print media, even though many of its users access its content through a mobile app or on a website.

The term "electronic media" itself may seem outdated, but it acknowledges the history and evolution of media technologies and has a distinct meaning in the area of mass communication law. Within the broad category of electronic media, not all types of mass media are treated the same under the law. For example, broadcast radio and television stations must comply with more regulations designed to protect the public interest than some other forms of electronic media, such as podcasts or social media. Radio and television station licensees often tell courts there is no valid reason to regulate broadcasting because the First Amendment should apply equally to all mass media. The U.S. Supreme Court has rejected this argument, and its decisions have allowed for the different treatment of mass media under the First Amendment. Each mass medium has its own peculiarities, although each has basic free speech protection, the Court has said.

This chapter explains the distinct legal issues and regulations that govern electronic media, which include radio, television, satellite, cable, wire and broadband.

HISTORY OF BROADCAST REGULATION

The general concept of broadcasting, or the transmission of programs using the **electromagnetic spectrum**, emerged in the late 19th century after European physicists began to understand how to use the spectrum to transmit signals. The spectrum is made up of different types of energy that radiate from where they are produced—called electromagnetic radiation. Together, they form the electromagnetic spectrum, which consists of electromagnetic waves we cannot see, for example, microwaves and radio waves. In 1897, Nikola Tesla, after whom Elon Musk named his global electric car company Tesla, filed U.S. patents that explained how electrical energy could be transmitted without wires, and later realized that his patents could be used for wireless communication.[1]

At the turn of the 20th century, Italian inventor Guglielmo Marconi transmitted radio signals using radio frequencies, which are part of the electromagnetic spectrum. Often, messages interfered with each other during this early period of experimentation. In 1902, an American physicist applied his knowledge of telegraphs to advance radio tuning to try to overcome the problem of interference. A few years later, in what is hailed as the birth of public radio in the United States, the first public broadcast was transmitted in New York City in 1910. The broadcast featured the voices of the Metropolitan Opera. Members of the public and the press used earphones to listen at locations across the city.[2]

Congress passed the first federal regulation of broadcast in 1910. The Wireless Ship Act required oceangoing vessels to carry radio equipment and operators, but Congress had not considered the law's impact on the spectrum, especially given that the mandate had global implications.[3] Other nations pressured Congress to establish standards that everyone could adopt, allowing messages to reach their destinations without interference. Then tragedy struck. In

1912, the Titanic hit an iceberg, plunging thousands to their deaths. The Titanic sent a distress signal, but it did not reach authorities because of interference and because the radio operator on the nearest ship was off-duty and did not hear the message.[4]

The Titanic disaster prompted Congress to pass the Radio Act of 1912, which required oceangoing ships to have 24-hour radio operators.[5] It also gave the U.S. secretary of commerce power to grant radio station licenses, assigning each licensee a specific frequency. A **radio frequency** is any one of the electromagnetic wave frequencies that lie within a specified range that is used for communication. The intent was to prevent message interference.[6]

However, the law did not give the secretary power to refuse a license or substantially regulate radio. Anyone applying for a license would get one, as long as no two applications were for the same frequency. The commerce secretary also had no authority to limit the power used to broadcast, which allowed the most powerful stations to drown out others. Amateur radio operators began ignoring the law, changing the frequencies they used and even relocating to other cities without the secretary's approval.[7]

Because radio was playing an increasingly important role in American commerce, Congress adopted the Radio Act of 1927 to solve these growing issues.[8] The law established the **Federal Radio Commission**, a federal agency charged with issuing or denying radio licenses and assigning frequencies to prevent stations from interfering with each other. The law gave the FRC the power to regulate stations as necessary to allow radio's development.

The 1927 law included several provisions that remain in effect today. First, the act said the FRC could not censor radio content. Second, it said the public, not station licensees, owned the electromagnetic spectrum. That is, the spectrum is considered a public resource. Because of this, the law required the FRC to make decisions based on the "public interest, convenience and necessity."[9] A federal court interpreted the 1927 act to say the federal government, not the states, had exclusive control over radio broadcasting.[10]

Shortly after passing the 1927 act, Congress realized that radio needed continued oversight. In addition to the FRC, a number of different federal agencies had authority over various aspects of the radio industry. To resolve these problems, Congress rescinded the 1927 act and adopted the Communications Act of 1934.[11] The 1934 act established the **Federal Communications Commission** as a federal agency, directly responsible to Congress and charged with regulating interstate and international communications. Today, the FCC oversees radio, television, wire, satellite, cable and broadband.

REASONS TO REGULATE BROADCASTING

Congress established the FCC and began to regulate **broadcasting** because it used the spectrum—a limited, public resource. Unlike print media or even the internet today—anyone with enough money can print a newspaper or publish a website—only a select few companies in a geographical area may use the spectrum.

Broadcasting is formally defined by the Communications Act of 1934 as use of the electromagnetic spectrum to send signals to many listeners and viewers simultaneously.[12] It is not a broadcast when the CBS television network sends a signal to the CBS station in Des Moines,

Iowa. That is a private transmission from the network to the station.[13] It is a broadcast when the Des Moines station sends the signal through its transmitter to thousands of television sets and to the local cable system. CBS, then, does not broadcast; rather, the stations owned by or affiliated with CBS broadcast. The FCC's broadcast regulations apply to radio and television stations.

The Titanic.

Universal History Archive/UIG via Getty Images

Spectrum Scarcity

More than 75 years ago, the U.S. Supreme Court first established spectrum scarcity as the principal reason the government can regulate broadcasters.[14] **Spectrum scarcity** refers to the limitation on the number of segments of the broadcast spectrum that may be used for radio or television in a geographic area without causing interference. After the Communications Act of 1934 created the FCC, radio station owners expected the commission to prevent interference by carefully choosing licensees and controlling the power that stations used to broadcast. The commission took more control over the radio industry than expected. Among other decisions, the FCC adopted rules regulating the relationship between the emerging radio networks and local stations. The commission was concerned that networks exerted too much control over stations, requiring the stations to carry all network programs, for example.[15]

The networks sued the FCC, claiming that it overstepped its statutory responsibilities.[16] The U.S. Supreme Court supported the FCC. "[T]he radio spectrum simply is not large enough to accommodate everybody," the Supreme Court said.[17] The few companies using the spectrum have a special privilege, making it reasonable to regulate them, the Court decided.[18]

President Franklin D. Roosevelt signed the Communications Act of 1934.

Bettman/Getty Images

In the 1920s, the FRC also said radio stations should broadcast various views about public issues.[19] The FCC subsequently adopted regulations in 1949 stating how that policy, called the fairness doctrine, should be put into effect. The **fairness doctrine** said that television and radio stations must (1) air programs discussing public issues and (2) include a variety of views about controversial issues of public importance.[20] Different views did not have to be presented in one program, but the station's overall programming had to reflect important opinions about controversial topics. The commission justified the fairness doctrine by pointing to licensees' responsibilities to the public.[21]

The U.S. Supreme Court upheld the fairness doctrine and reinforced the spectrum scarcity rationale in *Red Lion Broadcasting Co., Inc. v. FCC* (excerpted at the end of this chapter).[22] The audience's right to hear both sides of an issue was more important than the licensee's First Amendment freedom, according to the Court.[23] The Supreme Court reiterated that the limitations of the spectrum prevent everyone who wants to broadcast from doing so and that the spectrum is a public resource. As noted in Chapter 2, the Court ruled five years later that print media do not have the same right-of-reply requirement as broadcasters.[24]

The FCC changed its rules in 1987, finding that the fairness doctrine violated broadcasters' First Amendment rights.[25] The commission said that broadcasters censored themselves under the fairness doctrine, choosing not to present discussions about important public issues rather than be forced to air a variety of opinions about those issues. Two years later, the District of Columbia Circuit Court of Appeals agreed with the broadcasters, and the fairness doctrine ended.[26]

Two features of the fairness doctrine formally remained on the books for another decade. First, the commission's personal attack rule, the *Red Lion* decision's focus, required broadcast stations to provide free reply time to any person or group whose integrity, honesty or character was attacked on the air. The rule did not apply to public officials. Second, the political editorial rule required broadcasters to give free time for a legally qualified candidate to respond to an editorial opposing the candidate or promoting any of the candidate's rivals.

In 2000, the D.C. Circuit Court said the FCC had not justified the rules and ordered their elimination.[27] Public stations still may not endorse or oppose a political candidate, although they may air editorials about public issues.[28] In 2011, the FCC formally eliminated the fairness doctrine, noting that the rule had not been enforced since the late 1980s.[29] Spectrum scarcity remains the reason courts most often give for allowing broadcast regulation. Not everyone who wants a license to operate a television or radio station may have one because the spectrum has only enough room to accommodate a limited number of stations.[30]

In continuing to use this reasoning, courts seem to ignore the development of direct broadcast satellite service, satellite radio, radio and television low-power stations (broadcasting signals available within a few miles of the transmitter), the internet and other emerging technologies. Although the U.S. Supreme Court has recognized these newer technologies, the Court said it would not alter its spectrum scarcity rationale "without some signal from Congress or the FCC that technological developments have advanced so far that some revision of the system of broadcast regulation may be required."[31]

In addition to spectrum scarcity, courts use two other rationales to justify regulating broadcast radio and television. First, broadcast media are pervasive. Without regulation, children in particular could be exposed to inappropriate content.[32] A second reason is the perception that broadcast media have a greater influence on audiences—a "special impact"—than do print media.[33] Again, this rationale is especially concerned with children.

Although broadcasting remains the most regulated mass medium, the courts have permitted the FCC to roll back many regulations during the past three decades. However, the Supreme Court has yet to clearly state that spectrum scarcity is no longer a valid rationale for regulating broadcast radio and television.

Today, 83 percent of Americans listen to radio. Additionally, almost half of Americans currently use their mobile phones to stream music. Spotify is one of the most popular music streaming services in the United States.

Andrew Harrer/Bloomberg via Getty Images

The Public Interest Standard

In both the 1927 Radio Act and the 1934 Communications Act, Congress said the public interest comes before a station's interests. Both laws say federal regulation is to be guided by the "public interest, convenience and necessity."[34] Neither law defined the term "public interest." Through its first 50 years overseeing broadcasters, the FCC justified adopting regulations by citing public interest. Then, in the 1980s, the commission said the public interest required deregulating the broadcast industry. The FCC's focus shifted more to the market to help regulate broadcasting in the public interest.[35]

Even in a market-driven model, public interest considerations persist. For example, Congress authorized the creation of the First Responder Network Authority, commonly called FirstNet, just over a decade ago. FirstNet is an independent broadband network dedicated exclusively to the public safety community. **Broadband** is a high-capacity transmission technique that uses a wide range of frequencies on the spectrum, which enables a large number of messages to be communicated simultaneously. Broadband allows for faster connection to networks, for example, the internet.

Congress allocated spectrum and provided $7 billion to construct the secure FirstNet system in all U.S. cities and rural communities. The 9/11 Commission recommended FirstNet in response to reports from police, firefighters and emergency medical personnel of communication failures because they could not access broadband networks during the 9/11 terrorist attacks. Public safety officials' access to broadband was also a problem after Hurricane Katrina in New Orleans.[36]

FirstNet's Nationwide Public Safety Broadband Network is almost complete. The network now covers more than 2.71 million square miles and provides cellular and data service to first responders across the United States.[37] At the height of the COVID-19 pandemic in 2020, FirstNet was used by emergency personnel to communicate with ambulances and first responders that had come from outside the New York City region to help with patient transfers. FirstNet also provided connectivity for the USNS Comfort, a Navy medical treatment facility sent to New York to relieve pressure on the city's overburdened hospitals.[38]

FEDERAL COMMUNICATIONS COMMISSION

The FCC "is the United States' primary authority for communications law, regulation and technological innovation."[39] The FCC adopts and enforces regulations affecting large segments of the electronic media, and it licenses spectrum users. The U.S. president selects the FCC's five commissioners, who are appointed to five-year terms. The president also designates one of the commissioners to be FCC chair—the commission's CEO. The U.S. Senate must approve commissioner nominations, including the chair. No more than three sitting commissioners may be from the same political party. Commissioners may not have financial interests in any company or industry the FCC oversees and must be U.S. citizens. The FCC operates under the Administrative Procedure Act, a law telling federal agencies how they may propose and adopt regulations and giving federal courts power to rule on challenges to those decisions. Congress gives the FCC its funding, increasing or decreasing the budget each year as Congress chooses.

How Does the FCC Work?

At the most basic level, the commissioners adopt rules and regulations. The process starts when commissioners identify a problem or receive a petition from the public that warrants attention. Problems can include an industry behavior that adversely affects consumers, difficulty in enforcing an existing rule or the need to update a rule because of changes in technology. Congress can also mandate the FCC to take action and initiate the rulemaking process.[40] FCC staff members prepare a notice of proposed rulemaking explaining what the commissioners plan to do and why. A **notice of proposed rulemaking** is a notice issued by the FCC announcing that it is considering changing certain regulations or adopting new rules. Members of the public, interested companies and industry organizations may submit comments to the commission. The FCC also provides an opportunity to submit replies that respond to the original comment submissions. FCC staff members consider all the submissions and draft a report and order. The commissioners discuss the draft, suggest changes and vote on a final version in a public meeting. Companies, organizations and individuals who object to the commission's final decision may ask the commissioners to reconsider. The FCC rarely reconsiders its decisions. The final regulations then become part of the FCC's rules. The commission's rules have the effect of law. Companies, industries and individuals must comply with the FCC's rules or face sanctions.

REAL WORLD LAW
THE FCC COMMISSIONERS

Jessica Rosenworcel became the Federal Communications Commission chairwoman in 2021.[41] Rosenworcel joined the FCC as a commissioner in 2012. The other commissioners are:
- Brendan Carr (Republican), appointed by President Trump to his first term in 2017, who prior to becoming a commissioner served as FCC general counsel.[42]
- Geoffrey Starks (Democrat), appointed by President Trump to his first term in 2019, who prior to becoming a commissioner served as assistant bureau chief in the FCC's Enforcement Bureau.[43]
- Nathan Simington (Republican), appointed by President Trump to his first term in 2020, who prior to becoming a commissioner served as senior counsel to Brightstar Corp., an international mobile device services company.[44]
  President Biden nominated Gigi Sohn to become the fifth commissioner but she withdrew her nomination in 2023 after her approval was stalled in the senate for 16 months.

A company, an industry association, or an individual affected by a commission decision may challenge the FCC policy in a federal appellate court. Usually the appeal is to the U.S. Court of Appeals for the District of Columbia Circuit, although other circuits also may hear an appeal of a commission decision. A federal court ruling overrides an FCC decision.

What Does the FCC Do?

In addition to adopting rules and regulations, another important responsibility of the FCC is to grant a license to broadcast. The FCC acts on behalf of the public in allowing a licensee to use the spectrum for the license period. The FCC's broadcast regulations apply to radio and television stations. It is unlawful to operate any broadcast station in the United States without an FCC license, which is granted for an eight-year period and may be renewed for subsequent eight-year periods. Renewal is ensured unless the licensee has not operated in the public interest, has repeatedly violated FCC rules or has shown a pattern of abusing the law. There is no limit on the number of renewals a station owner may receive; a corporate owner may retain a station license as long as the corporation exists. An FCC license is not transferable: A licensee wanting to sell a broadcast station may sell the building, equipment, transmitter and trucks—but not the license. The FCC acts on behalf of the public in allowing a licensee to use the spectrum for the license period.

FCC Chairperson Jessica Rosenworcel

Chip Somodevilla/Staff

If two or more competing applicants want a license for the frequency that is not already used for broadcasting, the FCC holds an auction.[45] The bidder offering to pay the government the most money is awarded the station license.

To obtain a license, an individual must be an American citizen.[46] A foreign corporation may not hold a license, nor may a corporation with more than 20 percent foreign ownership. A foreign government may not be a licensee, nor may a corporation controlled by another corporation with more than 25 percent foreign ownership.[47] These foreign ownership restrictions, first adopted in the 1927 law and continued in the 1934 act, were justified by national security concerns. Congress did not want U.S. media used for foreign propaganda.

The Telecommunications Act of 1996 required the FCC to review its ownership rules every two years. About 20 years ago, Congress amended the requirement. Today, the FCC conducts a review of its ownership rules every four years, called the Quadrennial Regulatory Review.[48] However, this process has been mired in legislation since the mid-2000s by legal challenges to FCC rule changes, particularly those that have impacted (or failed to impact) gender and race imbalances in broadcast media ownership.

FCC Ownership Rules

Since the Radio Act of 1927 was passed, the FCC has limited the number of stations a single licensee can own, both in one metropolitan area and nationally. The Communications Act of 1934 says that the FCC's broadcast ownership rules must promote competition, diversity and localism.[49] The broadcast and newspaper industries have long maintained that the FCC's ownership rules are overly burdensome in the fast-evolving and highly competitive modern media marketplace. Public interest groups have argued that the ownership rules are necessary to preserve the public interest in viewpoint diversity.

REAL WORLD LAW
MODERNIZATION OF THE FCC

As technology rapidly advances, how has the Federal Communications Commission adapted? The FCC website states that "[i]n its work facing economic opportunities and challenges associated with rapidly evolving advances in global communications, the agency capitalizes on its competencies in

- Promoting competition, innovation and investment in broadband services and facilities
- Supporting the nation's economy by ensuring an appropriate competitive framework for the unfolding of the communications revolution
- Encouraging the highest and best use of spectrum domestically and internationally
- Revising media regulations so that new technologies flourish alongside diversity and localism
- Providing leadership in strengthening the defense of the nation's communications infrastructure"[50]

Station owners have the power to direct the focus of news coverage and determine which entertainment and other sorts of programs are aired. These choices help set the public agenda and frame our understanding of important issues. Therefore it matters a great deal who owns our broadcast media outlets. The power of broadcast ownership was on display in 2018 when the broadcast company Sinclair, which owns 186 television stations in 87 markets,[51] required dozens of its local news anchors to read the same speech to their millions of collective viewers. The speech warned about fake news and suggested that some "media use their platforms to push their own personal bias." The "forced read" mirrored commentary by former President Donald Trump about fake news and media bias.[52] Sinclair's action demonstrates the power broadcast station owners have to influence media content.

The FCC's rationale for limiting ownership is rooted in public interest considerations. For example, when the FCC passed its first cross-ownership rule that prohibited the ownership of a newspaper and a broadcast station that served the same local community, it emphasized the need for a diversity of voices to be heard via different media outlets in each market.[53] **Cross-ownership rules** govern when one entity can own two or more companies with related interests.

Recently, through a series of reconsideration orders, reviews and amendments, the FCC has eliminated or modified many of its ownership rules that were either slightly adapted or upheld during the 2014 Quadrennial Regulatory Review process.[54] As part of its 2017 Modernization of Media Regulation Initiative, the FCC reduced or removed existing restrictions on how many and what type of media outlets a single entity could own in a given market. The FCC's 2017 Reconsideration Order impacted the national television ownership rule, the local newspaper/broadcast cross-ownership rule, the local radio/television cross-ownership rule, the local television ownership rule, the local radio ownership rule and rules that govern joint sales agreements (JSAs). JSAs allow one station to sell some or all advertising time on another station in the same market.

The FCC said at the time that its actions were a response to the "explosive growth of the number and variety of sources of local news and information in the modern marketplace."[55] Media policy scholars, on the other hand, said that the FCC's rule changes were a response to the failed Sinclair–Tribune merger,[56] which broke down when the FCC issued an order that accused Sinclair of misrepresenting its efforts to divest certain stations to stay underneath the existing limits on ownership.[57] By reducing these limits on ownership, the FCC said that it would be advancing the public interest by removing unnecessary regulations that stand in the way of fostering competition and innovation in media markets.[58] Media Activist groups disagreed with the FCC's assessment and said that the deregulation of media ownership rules would lead to greater consolidation and conglomeration of media, reduce viewpoint diversity, and set back what little progress had been achieved in addressing the lack of broadcast media ownership among women and people of color. **Media consolidation** refers to the concentration of media ownership into the hands of fewer and fewer corporations or individuals.

The 2017 Reconsideration Order brought about several changes to the broadcast ownership rules. The order recalculated how audience reach is determined for the national television ownership rule, which prohibits a single entity from owning enough stations to reach more than 39 percent of television households in the U.S. It also did away with the local newspaper/broadcast cross-ownership rule and the local radio/television cross-ownership rule. The newspaper/broadcast cross-ownership rule prohibited common ownership of a full-power broadcast station and a daily newspaper in the same market.[59] The radio/television cross-ownership rule prohibited ownership of more than two television stations and one radio station in the same market unless the market met certain size criteria that would allow for additional, proportional ownership.

These rule changes also allowed for exceptions to the Top Four Prohibition, which says that a company may own up to two television stations in the same market if at least one of the stations is not ranked among the top four stations in the market.[60] Moreover, it eliminated the Eight Voices Test, which held that at least eight independently owned television stations also had to remain in the market following the combined ownership of stations.

The JSA rule, which barred companies from using one advertising sales staff for two or more stations in the same local market, was also terminated. The rule, adopted by the FCC in 2014, limited agreements between television stations to jointly sell advertising. The 2017 order also did away with the main studio rule that required television stations to maintain at least one local studio in licensed markets.[61] The removal of this 80-year-old rule allows station owners to create centralized newsrooms with centralized distribution models. The FCC called the studio rule outdated in the digital age and burdensome on broadcasters to maintain so many physical addresses. Critics argued that the elimination of the rule would lessen stations' presence in and commitment to their local communities.[62]

The 2017 order did not substantively change the local radio ownership rule. Under the current radio ownership rule, the total number of radio stations commonly owned in a local radio market is tiered, depending on the total number of stations in the market. For example, in markets with 45 or more radio stations, a company may own up to eight commercial radio stations, as many as five of which can be in the same AM/FM service area. The 2017 order adopted a new, narrow presumption in favor of a waiver of the local radio ownership rule in certain circumstances in the New York City and Washington, D.C., markets.[63]

The 2017 order also created an incubator program to promote ownership diversity in the broadcast industry. Under the incubator program, existing operators would provide financial, operational, and technical guidance to new entities and, in return, would be granted a waiver of the current ownership limits, which could be applied to station acquisitions in other media markets. This program was the latest in a long line of initiatives enacted by the FCC to address the lack of gender and racial diversity in broadcast ownership. (see Figure 9.1 and 9.2)

TABLE 9.1 ■ Current FCC Media Ownership Rules		
FCC Rule	**Definition**	**Rule Status**
National Television Ownership Rule	Limits a single entity to reaching no more than 39 percent of all U.S. TV households.	**Reinstated** the 50 percent UHF channel discount in calculations of audience reach (called the UHF discount). No longer subject to Quadrennial Review.
Dual Television Network Ownership	Prohibits mergers between any two of the big four broadcast television networks—ABC, CBS, FOX, and NBC	**No Change**
Newspaper/Broadcast Cross-Ownership Rule	Prohibits ownership of both a broadcast station (AM, FM, TV) and a daily newspaper in the same relevant market.	**Eliminated** as "outdated considering the explosive growth of the number and variety of sources of local news and information in the modern marketplace."
Radio/Television Cross-Ownership Rule	Prohibits joint ownership of more than two television stations and one radio station in the same market (with some exceptions).	**Eliminated** because local radio and TV ownership rules continue to restrict how many radio and TV stations a single entity may own.

FCC Rule	Definition	Rule Status
Local Television Ownership Rule	Limits ownership to two TV stations in the same market, but one must not be ranked among the top four stations in the market (Top Four Prohibition) *and* at least eight independently owned TV stations must remain in the market following the combination of two TV stations in the market (Eight Voices Test).	**Modified Top Four Prohibition** by allowing for "case-by-case review . . . to account for [special] circumstances." **Eliminated Eight Voices Test** as "unsupported by the record or any reasoned basis."
Local Radio Ownership Rule	Limits (by tiers) total number of radio stations jointly owned in a local market, depending on the number of stations in the market.	**No change** except that FCC adopted a "narrow presumption" in favor of a waiver of the rule in certain circumstances in the Washington, D.C., and New York City markets.
Television JSA Attribution	Television JSAs that involve the sale of more than 15 percent of the weekly advertising time of a station are counted toward the brokering station's ownership totals.	**Eliminated** because JSAs provide "an important source of financing and tangible public interest benefits, particularly in small and medium-sized markets."

Sources: *2014 Quadrennial Regulatory Review–Review of the Commission's Broadcast Ownership Rules and Other Rules Adopted Pursuant to Section 202 of the Telecommunications Act of 1996, Order on Reconsideration,* 32 FCC Rcd. 9802 (2017). *See also* FCC, *FCC Broadcast Ownership Rules,* Jan. 17, 2020.

FIGURE 9.1 ■

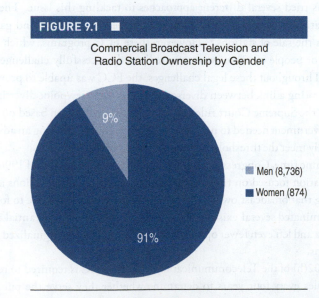

Commercial Broadcast Television and
Radio Station Ownership by Gender

9%

91%

■ Men (8,736)
■ Women (874)

Source: Third Report on Ownership of Commercial Broadcast Stations, 43 C.F.R. § 73.3615 (May 10, 2017).

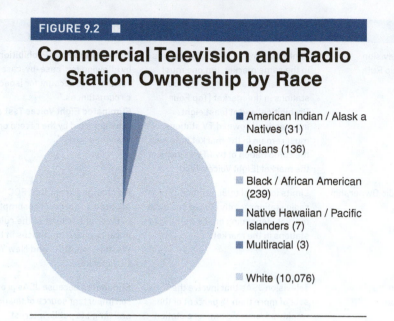

FIGURE 9.2 ◼

Commercial Television and Radio Station Ownership by Race

◼ American Indian / Alaska Natives (31)

◼ Asians (136)

▨ Black / African American (239)

◼ Native Hawaiian / Pacific Islanders (7)

◼ Multiracial (3)

▨ White (10,076)

Source: Third Report on Ownership of Commercial Broadcast Stations, 43 C.F.R. § 73.3615 (May 10, 2017).

Today, women own 9 percent of all commercial broadcast radio and television stations, and racial minorities own approximately 4 percent. After the Civil Rights Act was passed in the 1960s, the FCC began working to achieve greater racial diversity in broadcast ownership. In the late 1970s, the agency started taking steps to address the gender imbalance as well. Since then, the FCC has tried several different approaches to tackling this issue. They offered tax breaks to organizations that sold stations to women or people of color[64] and gave preference to these groups in the sale of stations.[65] However, these FCC programs, which showed preference to women or people of color, were repeatedly and successfully challenged in court as discriminatory.[66] Throughout these legal challenges, the FCC was unable to provide empirical evidence demonstrating a link between diverse ownership and viewpoint diversity in content. In the mid-1990s, the Supreme Court ruled that any legal classification based on race that was imposed by the government needed to pass strict scrutiny.[67] Rules providing an advantage based on gender need only meet the threshold of intermediate scrutiny.[68]

Around this same time, Congress passed the Telecommunications Act of 1996. At its heart, this piece of legislation focused on the deregulation of the telecommunications and broadcast industries. Fearing that broadcast ownership regulations were too restrictive to foster competition, Congress eliminated several existing rules. This brought about substantial consolidation in broadcast media and left even fewer opportunities for members of marginalized communities to purchase stations.

Under Rule 202(h) of the Telecommunications Act, the FCC is required to reassess broadcast ownership rules every four years to determine whether they serve the public and foster competition. The FCC's actions (or, in some cases, inaction) to modify these ownership rules have been repeatedly challenged in court by media activist organizations, including the Prometheus Radio Project and, eventually, the National Association of Broadcasters. In the last two decades, there have been four "Prometheus" cases, each of which has involved challenges to various rule changes, particularly as they relate to the impact those changes would have on broadcast ownership opportunities for women and people of color.

In the first Prometheus case, the FCC repealed the "Failed Station Solicitation Rule" which would have ensured that qualified minority broadcasters were able to learn that television or radio stations would soon be for sale.[69] The Third Circuit vacated the rule and remanded it back to the commission, which it said had provided no evidence regarding the effect the change would have on potential minority station owners.[70] In the second Prometheus case, the plaintiffs challenged the FCC's decision to revoke the Newspaper/Broadcast Cross-Ownership Rule and to provide advantages to companies with smaller revenues rather than give preference to racial or ethnic minorities in the sale or transfer of stations.[71] As part of its 2007 Diversity Order, the FCC said that preferences given to smaller companies would lead to greater racial and gender diversity in media ownership. The Third Circuit did not buy this argument and instead said that the FCC had failed to demonstrate how this new revenue-based approach would address the lack of diversity in broadcast ownership.[72] The Third Circuit remanded the case back to the FCC to reconsider how it defined the groups that would get preferences in the sale of stations.[73]

In 2016, the FCC was back in front of the Third Circuit again for failing to effectively reconsider how it would define the entities that were eligible to receive preferences to promote minority and female broadcast ownership.[74] Also at issue in that case was the FCC's failure to review the broadcast ownership rules for over a decade. The Third Circuit instructed the FCC to address both issues immediately. In 2017, the FCC responded with drastic action and initiated substantial rule changes (see Table 9.1). The Commission moved to eliminate several cross-ownership rules, which would leave even fewer opportunities for diverse entrants into the market. At the same time, the FCC adopted an incubator program, which asked established broadcasters to provide "training, financing and access to resources" for new entrants in exchange for even more relaxed ownership rules. "New entrants" for the Incubator Program would be determined by a company's size and revenues, not by any race or gender criteria. The FCC said that even though it wasn't considering race or gender, the new entrant requirements for the incubator program would increase ownership among women and people of color.

Fourteen entities petitioned the courts for review of the 2017 regulatory changes. In 2019, the Third Circuit heard the fourth Prometheus case, and ultimately struck down the 2017 Reconsideration Order and the Incubator Order because the FCC had not sufficiently considered the impact these changes would have on female and minority ownership.[75] The Third Circuit criticized the FCC's lack of evidence about how these changes would impact gender and racial diversity. The court remanded the case back to the FCC to find and provide evidence of the effects their proposed rule changes would have on ownership diversity.

The FCC and broadcast industry groups such as the National Association of The Third Circuit criticized Broadcasters appealed the Third Circuit's decision to the Supreme Court, which agreed to hear the case. The question before the Court was whether the Third Circuit erred in vacating the order enacting the 2017 rule changes to broadcast media ownership regulations. The FCC argued that under Section 202(h) it had the discretion to determine which rules were necessary to promote the public interest and to foster competition, even if the changes it enacted were not aimed at increasing female and minority broadcast station ownership. Prometheus Radio, along with several other public interest and consumer advocacy groups, disagreed. They argued that the FCC's mandate to consider the public interest required the agency to consider how changes to ownership regulations would impact gender and racial diversity. These groups felt that if enacted, the rule changes would lead to further media consolidation and ultimately fewer opportunities for women and people of color to own television or radio stations.

The Supreme Court ruled in favor of the FCC and the industry petitioners.[76] The Court cited the FCC's broad authority under the Administrative Procedure Act to repeal or modify broadcast ownership rules. Writing for the majority, Justice Kavanaugh cited the lack of empirical data available to demonstrate the harm the rule changes would have on ownership diversity.[77] Notably, the FCC made almost no effort to collect this data. Despite this, the Court was satisfied that the commission had adequately "considered the record evidence on competition, localism, viewpoint diversity, and minority and female ownership, and reasonably concluded that the three ownership rules no longer serve the public interest."[78]

REAL WORLD LAW
LOW POWER FM RADIO STATIONS

In addition to commercial radio stations such as Hot 97 in New York City or La Raza in Los Angeles, the FCC also operates a special class of radio stations called Low Power FM (LPFM). LPFM stations are licensed to operate with 100-watts, which allows them to reach an area with a radius of approximately three and a half miles.[79] The goal of these stations is to create opportunities for more voices to be heard on the radio. Therefore, operators of these stations must be nonprofit institutions, such as universities, community groups, public health organizations or local public safety or transportation services. Native American tribes and nations are also eligible operators.[80]

LPFM stations have grown in popularity in recent years. For example, there are 68 low power FM stations in the state of Washington, including KXSU, which is Seattle University's on-campus radio station. If your campus or university has a radio station, it is likely to be a LPFM station.

Public Broadcasting

More than 50 years ago, Congress created the Corporation for Public Broadcasting, a private, nonprofit corporation whose purpose is to ensure universal, public access to free news, information, and entertainment programming.[81] The CPB is the "steward of the federal government's investment in public broadcasting and the largest . . . source of funding for public radio, television and related online and mobile services."[82] The Public Broadcasting Act says public stations must strictly adhere to "objectivity and balance in all programs or series of programs of a controversial nature."[83] Despite this "objectivity" language, the U.S. Supreme Court has allowed public stations to air editorials favoring or opposing public and political issues.[84] Public stations have "important journalistic freedoms which the First Amendment jealously protects," the Supreme Court said.[85] The CPB supports NPR and PBS, which provide programming to public broadcast stations.

The FCC oversees public broadcasting stations, which must comply with most of the same rules commercial broadcasters follow. Public stations do not carry advertising.[86] However, corporations and individuals make financial contributions to noncommercial stations and may receive on-air acknowledgments of those contributions.[87] A federal district court decision in California upheld this advertising ban. The FCC fined a public television station in San Francisco for what the commission said amounted to paid ads. The license holder of the station, Minority Television Project, appealed the fine and also challenged the law that prohibits all advertising—both political and commercial—on public television. The Ninth Circuit Court of Appeals affirmed the lower court decision that upheld the ban on all ads on noncommercial stations.[88]

BROADCAST PROGRAMMING RULES

The FCC is not allowed to censor broadcast content.[89] But the FCC may set general programming rules, such as prohibiting hoaxes,[90] requiring children's programming and regulating politicians' radio and television appearances.

Since the FCC adopted its current ban on broadcast hoaxes over 30 years ago, it has not punished a single station for broadcasting a hoax. The FCC's definition of a hoax is knowingly broadcasting false reports of crimes or catastrophes that "directly cause" foreseeable, "immediate, substantial and actual public harm."[91]

Political Broadcasting Regulations

In both the Radio Act of 1927 and the Communications Act of 1934, Congress ensured that broadcasters could not favor one political candidate for an elective office over another. Section 315 of the 1934 act guarantees equal opportunity rather than equal time to **legally qualified candidates,** which is someone who has publicly announced a bid for office, has their name on the ballot, or is a serious write-in candidate.[92] Section 315 does not apply to ballot issues, such as referendums, state constitutional amendments, initiatives and recalls of elected officials.

"Equal opportunity" means all candidates are given the opportunity to reach approximately the same audience as an opponent. Being allowed to purchase a minute of time at midnight is not equal opportunity if the candidate's opponent purchased a minute at 9 p.m.

A few years ago, hackers broke into the Emergency Alert Systems in Montana and Michigan and sent out an emergency alert of a zombie attack. Hoaxes like this are forbidden by Federal Communications Commission rules.

iStock.com/powerofforever

Nor is being given one minute an equal opportunity if the candidate's opponent has used 30 minutes. Equal opportunity also means getting free time if a candidate's opponent appeared on a station or cable system without paying (with some exceptions). During the general election, every legally qualified candidate may use the equal opportunity rule if another candidate for the office uses a broadcast station or cable system. Equal opportunity rules do not apply to social media.

"Use" is defined as the candidate or the candidate's picture being seen or the candidate's voice being heard on a broadcast station or cable system. The broadcasting of a candidate's name without the candidate's picture or voice is not a use.

This applies to more than candidates' commercials. If candidates appear on a television station's lifestyles program to give a cooking demonstration, candidates have used the station. This is true even if the candidates do not mention that they are a candidate, discuss their platform or refer to politics in any way. Potential voters might have a more favorable impression of candidates when proving themselves a master chef instead of discussing their political platform in a commercial. Their legally qualified opponents, then, may request equal opportunity, or an equal amount of airtime for an equivalent price.

Over 60 years ago, Congress adopted four exceptions to the use rule. First, regularly scheduled news programs are exempt. This exemption was meant for local news programs. But when the commission defined this category as including "programs reporting about some area of current events, in a manner similar to more traditional newscasts,"[93] it also included such programs as "Entertainment Tonight"[94] and "Celebrity Justice."[95]

POINTS OF LAW

SECTION 315 OF THE COMMUNICATIONS ACT OF 1934

Section 315 of the Communications Act of 1934

- guarantees "equal opportunity" to "legally qualified candidates" for elective office
- to reach approximately the same audience
- when another legally qualified candidate "uses" a broadcast station or cable system
- to advertise or when they appear on any of the station's programming.
  Exceptions to "use" include
- regularly scheduled news programs,
- regularly scheduled interview programs,
- live coverage of bona fide news and debates, and
- when the legally qualified candidate's appearance is incidental to the program's topic.

Legally qualified candidates must request equal opportunity from the station or cable system within seven days of their opponent's appearance. The station or cable system is under no obligation to notify opponents of a political candidate's use of the station.

Second, regularly scheduled news interview programs are exempt. These must have been regularly scheduled for some time before the election. For example, scheduling four interview shows, one each week for a month before an election, does not qualify a program as "regularly scheduled." Although this exemption initially was for programs such as "Meet the Press" and "Face the Nation," the FCC has included "Jerry Springer"[96] and "The Howard Stern Show."[97]

Third, live coverage of bona fide news events is exempt. If a candidate's campaign speech is covered live, the candidate's on-air appearance will not be considered a use. Nor is it a use if candidates participate in a televised debate, no matter who sponsors the debate. Because debates are exempt, the debate organizers may include and exclude any candidates they want.[98]

Fourth, candidates' appearances in documentaries do not trigger Section 315 if the appearance is incidental to the program's topic. For example, if a mayoral candidate is an expert on the state's fishing industry and appears in a documentary about that topic, it will not be considered a use. Of course, if the documentary is about the candidate's childhood in a housing project, the candidate's appearance would not be incidental to the program's topic and would be use.

Candidates who want equal opportunity must request time from the station or cable system within seven days of their opponent's appearance. The station or cable system is under no obligation to notify opponents of a political candidate's use of the station.

To reduce negative political advertising, a federal law requires candidates to promise stations they will refer to their opponents in a commercial only under specific conditions. To refer to an opponent, a candidate's (1) radio commercial must include the candidate's voice approving the commercial's contents or (2) television commercial must show the candidate or the candidate's picture with a printed statement approving the commercial.[99] FCC regulations require any commercial on a broadcast station to identify who paid for the ad.[100] This rule applies to political advertisements as well. A candidate's ad, then, must say on radio or show in print for a televised ad something like "This advertisement paid for by the Pat Smith for Congress Committee."

Broadcast stations and cable systems cannot edit or censor political appearances. Because stations are not permitted to edit or censor, they also are not responsible for what candidates say. For example, if candidates libel their opponent, the opponent may sue the candidate but not the station.[101] If the first legally qualified candidate running for an office does not appear on a station, Section 315 would not be triggered for other candidates. Although this is legal under Section 315, the FCC has suggested that stations should allow candidates airtime because it is in the public interest.

Congress recognized this Section 315 loophole and closed it—at least for itself. Section 312(a)(7) of the Communications Act requires radio and television stations to provide federal candidates with reasonable access.[102] This means even the first candidate for a federal office asking to buy commercial time must be sold the advertising spot.[103] The federal elective offices are senator, representative and president. Section 312(a)(7) exempts noncommercial and cable stations from complying with the section's requirements.

Section 312(a)(7)'s requirement that commercial stations provide candidates for federal office with "reasonable access" is not clear.[104] Broadcasters must consider each federal candidate's request "on an individualized basis," and broadcasters are required to tailor their responses to accommodate, as much as reasonably possible, a candidate's stated purposes in seeking airtime. However, broadcasters also may "give weight to such factors as the amount of time previously sold to the candidate, the disruptive impact on regular programming and the likelihood of requests for time by rival candidates."[105] Broadcasters may not use these criteria as an excuse to deny federal candidates the time requested. Rather, "broadcasters must cite a realistic danger of substantial program disruption" or the likelihood of too many requests.[106] Aside from being assured they can get on the air, federal candidates are treated under Section 315 just as are candidates for state and local offices.

In 2021, the FCC issued a notice of proposed rulemaking to make minor updates to its political advertising rules.[107] The first change adds the use of social media and the creation of a campaign website as activities that may be considered when determining whether a write-in candidate qualifies as a candidate for public office.[108] The second rule change requires broadcasters to update their recordkeeping to include any request to purchase advertising that would "communicate a message related to any political matter of national importance."[109]

Children's Programming Requirements

Over 30 years ago, Congress passed the Children's Television Act.[110] The law set general requirements for children's programming on broadcast television stations. The statute required broadcast television stations to provide programming intended for children up to 17 years old that met their "educational and informational needs."[111] The law also limited commercial time before, during and after children's programs on broadcast and cable television. For children 12 years old and younger, advertising during children's programming was limited to 12 minutes per hour during the week and 10 1/2 minutes per hour on the weekends.

The FCC also has ruled that characters in children's programs cannot appear in commercials before, during or after children's programs.[112] Cartoon characters in children's programs or children's program hosts also may not sell products in commercials during or adjacent to shows in which the character or host appears.[113]

INTERNATIONAL LAW
ADVERTISING TO CHILDREN

In the United States, there are very few regulations that apply to advertising or product placement aimed at children. In contrast, many other countries have substantial rules about advertising to children. For example, Chile prohibits advertising foods and beverages high in calories, fats, sugars and salt to children under 14.[114] In Australia, the Australian Association of National Advertisers has developed a code to self-regulate. The Code for Advertising and Marketing Communication to Children prohibits the use popular personalities or celebrities (live or animated) to endorse, or advertise products in a way that obscures the distinction between commercials and program content.[115]

The FCC allowed individual stations to decide how much children's programming to carry[116] until 1996, when it adopted standards for complying with the Children's Television Act.[117] The commission ruled that broadcast television stations must carry three hours per week, averaged over a six-month period, of programming specifically intended to meet children's intellectual/cognitive and social/emotional needs. The programs must be at least 30 minutes long, regularly scheduled weekly and broadcast between 6 a.m. and 10 p.m. local time. The commission identified this as "core programming."

A station not meeting the core programming standard may substitute shorter programs, public service announcements for children and programs not scheduled weekly. The FCC may choose not to renew a station's license if it does not meet the requirements. When the core programming standard was enacted, the FCC said its children's programming rules were "reasonable, viewpoint-neutral" requirements for licensees who must operate in the public interest.[118]

Recently, Commissioner O'Rielly suggested that the 30-year-old children's television regulations are "ineffective and burdensome" to broadcasters and are no longer needed given the proliferation of children's programming across various media channels and platforms.[119]

In 2018, the FCC adopted a notice of proposed rulemaking to change the children's television rules as part of the FCC's Media Modernization Initiative. The NPRM sought comment on every aspect of the children's television rules.[120] The NPRM did not propose the elimination of the rules, but it did tentatively conclude that reporting requirements for licensees be simplified, that the core programming requirement that programs are at least 30 minutes in length be maintained and that regularly scheduled, weekly core programming requirements should be eliminated. The NPRM recognized the importance of children's programming, but it also acknowledged that broadcasters need greater flexibility and the current rules are outdated.[121]

In 2019, the FCC approved changes to the core programming requirements. Broadcasters are now allowed to begin airing children's programming at 6 a.m. (instead of 7 a.m.); stations may count some children's programming not regularly scheduled (e.g., educational specials) toward the annual core programming requirement; and stations can count some short-form programming toward the core programming requirement.[122]

The long-running, popular children's show "Sesame Street" has aired on PBS since 1969. Recently, the show moved its first-run episodes to HBO, but the show still appears on PBS.

AF archive/Alamy Stock Photo

The FCC eliminated the requirement that a station air an additional three hours of children's programming for each 24/7 multicast stream. The FCC also revised the reporting requirements for children's programming, retained rules that require program guides and eliminated the rule that required on-air notification of core programs on noncommercial stations.[123]

MULTICHANNEL VIDEO PROGRAMMING DISTRIBUTOR REGULATION

In addition to regulating broadcast media, the FCC regulates satellite and cable. As new forms of video distribution have emerged, the FCC began referring to these channels collectively as **multichannel video programming distributors** (MVPD), which are entities that provide multiple channels of video programming for purchase. The FCC defines both cable and direct broadcast satellite services as MVPDs. An MVPD is an entity that makes available for purchase multiple channels of video programming. According to the FCC, the major MVPDs today offer hundreds of linear television channels and thousands of nonlinear video-on-demand and pay-per-view programs. In addition to delivering video programming to television sets, MVPDs deliver video programming to computer screens, tablets and mobile devices. The FCC notes that MVPDs also offer internet and phone services as core elements of their business models.[124]

History of Cable and Satellite Regulation

The MVPD regulation of today has evolved from early cable regulation. Cable systems send signals through a wire—coaxial cable or fiber-optic lines—and do not use the spectrum. Cable television emerged because some people could not get a broadcast television signal, particularly in rural areas. In the 1940s, a power company employee built a large antenna in the Appalachian Mountains of Pennsylvania that received signals from Philadelphia television stations. A wire ran from the antenna to a building and from there to homes, giving birth to cable television.[125] For decades, it was called "community antenna television" or CATV.

Initially, the FCC decided it had no jurisdiction over CATV.[126] But broadcast television station owners feared CATV could take away their viewers and advertisers and urged the FCC to reconsider. In 1962, noting that some CATV operators used the spectrum to transmit signals from stations to cable system antennas, the FCC decided it had jurisdiction over at least part of the CATV business.[127] When the commission adopted several CATV rules, cable operators challenged the commission's authority to control CATV, but the U.S. Supreme Court upheld the FCC's jurisdiction.[128] The Court said that because the FCC was responsible for protecting the public's interest in broadcasting, it had the right to oversee CATV as ancillary to its responsibility toward broadcasting.

FCC rule changes in the mid-1970s allowed cable systems to move beyond delivery of local television signals to carry the signals of stations outside the local community. For example, HBO launched a pay cable service in 1975. With distant station signals and HBO, cable television could offer programming not available on local television stations.

About 40 years ago, communities wanted to regulate cable, arguing that system wires ran over public streets and sidewalks, and telephone companies wanted to offer cable services throughout the country. Cable operators did not want regulation. Trying to strike a compromise, Congress adopted the Cable Communications Policy Act of 1984.[129] The law gave local and state governments and the federal government shared authority over cable.

A few years later, critics said the 1984 law gave the cable industry monopoly power in communities and allowed cable companies to raise rates without limit, provide poor customer service and prevent competition. Congress responded by re-regulating cable in the Cable Television Consumer Protection and Competition Act of 1992.[130] The 1992 law regulated rates cable systems charged subscribers. It also required cable systems to carry local broadcast television stations and to deliver other programming, such as ESPN and MTV, to direct broadcast satellite companies and other cable competitors. The law also barred local governments from allowing one cable system to monopolize service if others wanted to compete.

When Congress adopted the Telecommunications Act of 1996, it loosened many of the cable regulations imposed in 1992.[131] Designed primarily to foster competition in the telephone industry, the 1996 law also deregulated cable subscriber rates, again allowing cable companies to raise most prices without government permission.

The 1984, 1992 and 1996 laws did not define cable's First Amendment status. The U.S. Supreme Court first decided the cable industry had protection similar to the print media,[132] then suggested it was not certain what First Amendment analysis should be applied to cable television[133] and finally applied strict scrutiny to cable content regulations.[134]

Just as the emergence of cable required the FCC to consider its role in regulation, so did the emergence of direct broadcast satellite (DBS) services to consumers. DBS uses a small dish attached to a roof or the side of a house to receive signals from a high-powered satellite. More than 34 million American households receive their television programming by subscribing to a DBS service.[135]

Years ago, the FCC encouraged DBS service to develop as a cable competitor by declining to classify satellite service as broadcasting. The commission's decision relieved DBS of the regulatory burdens that broadcasters, and to a lesser extent cable, faced. The commission instead categorized DBS as a point-to-multipoint nonbroadcast service, a ruling upheld in court.[136] Dissatisfied with the FCC's decision not to impose regulations on DBS, Congress passed the Cable Television Consumer Protection and Competition Act of 1992. The law required DBS providers to abide by the political broadcasting rules in Sections 315 and 312(a)(7), discussed earlier in this chapter.

DBS emerged as a challenger to cable's dominance when Congress allowed satellite services to offer subscribers their local television stations as well as satellite programming.[137] As DBS grew, the FCC imposed additional regulations. For example, the FCC required satellite operators to set aside 4 percent of their channel capacity for educational or informational programming.[138] The commission said carrying noncommercial or public broadcast stations would not satisfy this requirement. The FCC also required DBS systems to comply with the same advertising limits during children's programming the commission applied to broadcast television stations.[139]

REAL WORLD LAW

COVID-19 ISSUES IN AN ERA OF "CORD CUTTING"

The popularity of internet streaming services like Netflix and Hulu grew substantially during the COVID-19 pandemic. During 2020, Netflix gained 36 million new subscribers.[140] At the same time, subscriptions to MVPDs have waned as many people "cut the cord" and cancelled their cable or satellite subscriptions. Today, only about 56 percent of Americans access television content through MVPDs, down from 76 percent in 2015.[141] Those numbers are even lower among young people. Only one-third of adults 18 to 29 receive TV via cable or satellite.[142]

Must-Carry and Retransmission Consent

The Cable Television Consumer Protection and Competition Act of 1992 contained two provisions that required the carriage of broadcast stations on cable, DBS and all MVPD systems—the **must-carry rule** and **retransmission consent**. The 1992 law prohibits these providers from retransmitting a broadcast station without the broadcaster's explicit permission. The law instead gives the broadcaster the ability to negotiate with the MVPD for carriage. When the 1992 law passed, broadcast programming was the most popular content available on cable and DBS systems. One of the key concepts behind retransmission consent was the idea that broadcasters like ABC or CBS were producing popular content carried on large cable systems such as Comcast and Time Warner, but very few consumers received their broadcast programs over the air using an antenna. This meant that the broadcasters did not receive advertising revenue for their programming. The 1992 law allowed broadcasters to negotiate with cable systems to permit retransmission of their content generally for a fee and did not give the FCC authority to force broadcasters to consent to carriage.[143]

Because not all broadcast channels were popular enough to be sought after by an MVPD, the law also granted broadcasters the option to require MVPDs to carry their programming rather than negotiating for retransmission. Must-carry, also called the cable carriage requirement, means that if a broadcast station chooses must-carry status, it may not be dropped from an MVPD's channel lineup. By asserting its must-carry rights, the broadcaster cannot demand payment for its content from the MVPD.

Every three years, commercial broadcast stations choose between must-carry and retransmission consent. Noncommercial stations may not choose retransmission consent; they are carried under the must-carry provision.

In the 1990s, the cable industry fought the must-carry rule in court. Cable companies argued that a system can carry only a limited number of networks. Finding room to carry a local station's signal could force a cable system to eliminate other programming it already carried—Food Network, for example. Cable companies also said the must-carry rules were content-specific regulations, forcing cable to choose a local station over some other programming. Congress would have to show it had a compelling interest to justify imposing a content-specific rule, cable companies argued, and no such compelling interest existed.

About 30 years ago, the U.S. Supreme Court upheld the must-carry rules in *Turner Broadcasting System, Inc. v. FCC*. The Supreme Court applied the First Amendment test it uses for print media to cable: If the regulation affects speech because of its content, apply strict scrutiny; if the regulation is content neutral, apply an intermediate standard.[144] (Strict scrutiny and intermediate scrutiny are discussed in Chapter 2.)

In the second *Turner Broadcasting System, Inc. v. FCC* decision, in 1997, the U.S. Supreme Court refused to accept the cable industry's argument that the must-carry rules were content specific.[145] The must-carry rules are content neutral because they do not dictate specific programming, the Court said. To determine the rules' constitutionality, the Court applied the test it established in *United States v. O'Brien* (Chapter 2).[146] The *O'Brien* test applies to regulations incidentally affecting speech when that is not the regulation's primary purpose. The rules protect broadcast stations, which is an important objective, the Court said. In enacting them,

Congress did not intend to directly affect cable systems' speech. Rather, Congress needed to adopt the rules to achieve its purpose of ensuring consumers' access to local broadcast stations.[147]

When the cable industry again challenged the must-carry rules in 2009, the U.S. Court of Appeals for the Second Circuit rejected the argument that must-carry rules violate cable operators' First Amendment rights.[148] The U.S. Supreme Court refused to hear the case.

In 2015, the FCC implemented the requirements of the Satellite Television Extension and Localism Act Reauthorization Act of 2014, which aimed to modernize the must-carry and retransmission consent rules but maintain the basic framework of the 1992 Cable Act.[149]

Specifically, the law added a new **satellite market modification rule**, which allows a television station, satellite operator or county government to request the addition or deletion of communities from a broadcast station's local television market to better reflect current market realities. For example, in many communities, existing satellite delivery of a local broadcast television station doesn't exist because it is not technically or economically feasible.[150]

When the FCC receives a market modification request, it considers five factors that would allow a petitioner to demonstrate it provides local service to the community, including the consideration of access to television stations located in the same state. Additionally, the FCC initiated a review of the current process for evaluating whether broadcasters and MVPDs are negotiating for retransmission consent in good faith. The goal of the review of the retransmission consent rule is to ensure that negotiations are conducted fairly and "in a way that benefits consumers of video programming services."[151]

REAL WORLD LAW
ONLINE VIDEO DISTRIBUTORS

Online video distributors (OVDs) are entities that provide video programming using the internet. Currently, the Federal Communications Commission groups video content distribution into broadcast television stations, multichannel video programming distributors and online video distributors. Consumers need a broadband connection to receive video content from OVDs. The FCC recently asked for comment on whether to expand its MVPD definition to include OVDs,[152] but has not yet taken any action.

Under the FCC's current definition, an OVD is different from an MVPD.[153] OVDs are diverse and include a variety of types of distributors, such as movie companies that release their films online instead of distributing them for viewing in a movie theater. Examples of OVDs are Sling TV, Apple TV and Sony's PlayStation Vue.

The FCC noted that OVDs may "be involved in providing video storage and delivery services, content creation or aggregation (i.e., networks, studios, and sports leagues), or device manufacturing. Several technology companies, notably Amazon, Apple, Google, and Microsoft, also serve as OVDs. Each company takes a slightly different approach to integrating its online video services with storage services, apps, and devices to attract and retain customers."[154]

OVDs attempting to enter the marketplace face several challenges, including access to sufficient internet capacity to allow for a high-quality viewing experience. Recently, the FCC began an inquiry to determine whether it should address issues that independent video programmers face in gaining carriage in the current marketplace.[155]

Recently, several networks have challenged MVPD decisions about placement of their networks within subscription packages, which determine viewer access. In 2016, the D.C. Circuit Court of Appeals decided that when a network brings forward a complaint about carriage requirements, it must show that its request for carriage would provide a net benefit to the MVPD. The case involved a claim by the Tennis Channel that Comcast discriminated against it in favor of affiliated networks.[156]

Earlier, the Game Show Network alleged that Cablevision discriminated against it when the cable company repositioned the network to a premium sports tier, which meant viewers would have to pay more to access the network's programming. The Game Show Network said WE tv and Wedding Central, comparable networks, remained on a less expensive, expanded basic tier.[157] Cablevision said it moved the network because of low viewership. An administrative law judge decided in favor of the Game Show Network, citing evidence of discrimination, and ordered Cablevision to put the channel back on the expanded basic tier and pay a fine.[158] FCC commissioners reviewed the decision and reversed. They said that the Game Show Network failed to produce evidence of discrimination.[159]

In two decisions, one in 2017 and one in 2018, the FCC's Media Bureau denied two complaints filed by The Word Network, which provides original, African-American ministry programming. The FCC Media Bureau develops, recommends and administers the FCC's policy and licensing programs related to the media industry. In both complaints, The Word Network alleged that Comcast violated FCC carriage requirements by replacing The Word Network with Impact Network, which features the same kind of programming. The network also complained that when Comcast demanded exclusive digital distribution rights to The Word Network, it was asserting a financial interest in the network. The Media Bureau concluded that The Word Network did not demonstrate that Comcast had discriminated against it when it replaced The Word Network with Impact. The Media Bureau also decided that Comcast's demand for an exclusive license for digital distribution did not amount to a demand for a financial interest in the network.[160]

Public Access Channels

By the time Congress adopted the Cable Communications Policy Act of 1984, most cable franchises already included provisions for public, educational or governmental (PEG) access channels. The 1984 statute made that reality the law. Congress saw PEG access channels as a way to allow the public, various educational institutions and local governments to have access to cable systems in ways Congress does not require for newspapers, magazines, radio and television stations and other mass media. **PEG access channels** are channels that cable systems set aside for public, educational, and governmental use. The 1984 law sets aside channels for public, educational or governmental use.[161] Although the law does not require cable system operators to agree to carry PEG channels, they usually do.

Public access channels generally allow local citizens, on a first-come basis, to put on programming they choose. Many municipalities have a government official or nonprofit organization oversee public channel programming.[162] Local school boards and colleges use educational channels. Government channels often carry city council and county board meetings. The 1984 cable act prohibits cable system operators from exercising any editorial control over PEG or leased access programming.[163]

The Cable Television Consumer Protection and Competition Act of 1992 also required DBS operators to offer leased access channels for noncommercial educational purposes,[164] but a federal appellate court rejected the PEG and leased access requirements as infringing on DBS providers' First Amendment rights.[165]

In 2019, the U.S. Supreme Court considered whether a municipally licensed public access television channel's denial of access to programming it deemed offensive violated the First Amendment rights of the employees who submitted the content. The Second Circuit Court of Appeals determined that the cable public access television channel was "the electronic version of the public square," so its denial of access violated the First Amendment.[166]

The Supreme Court disagreed. In a 5–4 decision, Justice Brett Kavanaugh concluded that the First Amendment did not apply; the cable operator was not a state actor because it did not perform "a function traditionally exclusively performed by the state."[167] Both the majority and the dissent acknowledged that New York law extensively regulates cable operators, limiting their "editorial discretion and in effect requir[ing them] to operate almost like a common carrier."[168] Still, the majority said this did not make the cable company a state actor subject to the First Amendment.

INTERNET REGULATION

As new media technologies emerge, Congress, state legislatures, regulatory agencies, and courts must determine whether and how to regulate both service and content. Today, 93 percent of U.S. adults use the internet[169] but the process of regulating this medium is still evolving. In 1997 the U.S. Supreme Court held in *Reno v. American Civil Liberties Union* that the internet has complete First Amendment protection.[170] *Reno v. ACLU* decided a challenge to the Communications Decency Act, a provision of the Telecommunications Act of 1996.[171] The CDA prohibited transmitting indecent, patently offensive or obscene material to minors over the internet.

To determine the CDA's constitutionality, the Court had to decide what First Amendment protections applied to the internet. The U.S. Supreme Court has said each mass medium has its own peculiarities, so there may need to be adjustments to a medium's First Amendment rights. Broadcasting, as discussed throughout this chapter, uses public spectrum, which justifies its limited First Amendment protection. In *Reno*, the Supreme Court said that the internet did not use the spectrum and was not as invasive as broadcasting. Unlike broadcasting, the internet does not have any special characteristics that require decreasing its First Amendment rights, the *Reno* Court held. Historically, the internet has not been "subject to the type of government supervision and regulation that has attended the broadcast industry."[172]

Justice John Paul Stevens, writing for the Court majority, characterized the internet as "a unique medium" that is "a vast platform from which to address and hear from a worldwide audience of millions of readers, viewers, researchers and buyers. Any person or organization with a computer connected to the internet can 'publish' information."[173]

Having held that internet content has full First Amendment protection, the Court overturned the CDA's restrictions on transmitting indecent and patently offensive material using the internet. The Court upheld the ban on obscene content sent over the internet. The First Amendment does not protect obscene material on the internet or in any medium (see Chapter 10).[174]

Section 230

When the Supreme Court struck down the Communications Decency Act in *Reno v. ACLU*, it kept one portion of the legislation intact. Section 230 (See Chapter 5) says that ISPs and other computer services, including social media platforms, will not be treated as publishers or speakers of user-generated content.[175] The law also states that online service providers will not be held liable for good faith filtering or blocking of user generated content. Thanks to Section 230, ISPs and social media platforms are not legally responsible for what others say or do on their platforms, even if they do take steps to filter or moderate some content. Section 230 also carves out a small number of instances when immunity may not apply, such as violations of federal criminal law, intellectual property law and sex trafficking.[176]

Two cases that preceded Section 230 helped shape the legislation as we currently know it. In 1991 CompuServe, one of the country's first online service providers, was sued for libelous posts made on one of their discussion forums.[177] The court said that because CompuServe didn't review the posts before they appeared on the forum they could not be treated as the publisher of the defamatory speech.[178] In 1995 the web services company Prodigy was successfully sued for libelous posts made on the site.[179] Unlike CompuServe, Prodigy engaged in some content moderation by reviewing and filtering the posts on their site.[180] Lawmakers did not want to discourage emerging online companies from engaging in content moderation and thus, the law specifically stated that Good Samaritan efforts to regulate content would not remove liability.

Since Section 230 was written, internet use has grown exponentially. What has remained consistent, however, are courts' interpretations of Section 230. There have been several attempts to hold social media platforms and applications accountable for their behavior and in each of these, courts have said that computer services were not responsible for how their product or platform was used. For example, in *Doe v. Myspace*, the Fifth Circuit Court of Appeals barred a negligence claim brought by the parents of a 13-year-old girl who sued after their daughter pretended to be 18 on the site and was assaulted by a man she met on the platform.[181] Similarly, the Ninth Circuit Court of Appeals dismissed a failure to warn claim against Internet Brands, which ran Model Mayhem, citing Section 230 as protection from the California state law. In this instance, two perpetrators were posing as talent agents and using the site to lure models to fake photo shoots in which they were drugged, raped, and recorded.[182]

More recently, the Second Circuit Court of Appeals held that Section 230 barred the product liability claim brought against the dating app, Grindr. Matthew Herrick filed the claim against the company for failing to respond to 50 separate complaints filed to remove fake accounts which were being used by an ex-boyfriend to send men to his house and work. Over ten months, 1,400 men, as many as 23 in one day, were sent to Herrick's home or office to harass him. Herrick appealed the Second Circuit's decision but the Supreme Court denied certiorari.

Section 230 protected Grindr from liability for alleged wrong doing in Herrick v. Grindr (2019).

SOPA Images/Contributor/Getty

The Supreme Court will finally weigh in on the scope of Section 230 when it hears the *Gonzales v. Google* case. As mentioned in Chapter 5, the family of a woman killed during the 2015 ISIS attack on Paris is suing to hold YouTube's parent company, Google, liable for recommending ISIS recruiting videos.[183] This case will ask the Supreme Court to determine whether Section 230's protections extend to algorithmic recommendations of third-party content.

Congress is also considering revising the law. In the last few years, dozens of bills have been introduced to amend or even eliminate Section 230. There have been so many proposals that in 2021 researchers at American University and Duke partnered to launch the 230 Reform Legislative Tracker to help keep tabs on all of the bills that have been introduced.[184] The bills are placed into one of four categories: repeal Section 230, place limits on its scope, impose new obligations on companies in order to use Section 230 as a defense, and "Good Samaritan" bills, which would alter that specific aspect of the law in order to address perceived political bias.[185]

Unsurprisingly, Republicans' and Democrats' approaches to Section 230 reform are substantially different. Democrats are concerned with, among other things, addressing harms against vulnerable communities.[186] Republicans, on the other hand, want to limit what they see as the liberal bias that influences social media content regulation. For example, the Protecting Americans from Dangerous Algorithms Act, which was introduced by Democrats in 2021, would prevent platforms from using Section 230 as a defense in cases related to civil rights violations if the companies use algorithms to disseminate and amplify the content at issue. Republicans have introduced several bills such as the Stop Suppressing Speech Act of 2020, which would extend Section 230's liability protection only to platforms that moderate content that is illegal or involves harassment, violence or terrorism.

Some legal scholars argue that "carve outs" which remove immunity for civil rights violations are likely underinclusive and problematic given that they would need to be updated regularly.[187] Instead, reforms that exclude bad actors from protection under Section 230 are more likely to be more effective.[188] This type of approach would deny immunity to online service providers that deliberately leave up unambiguously unlawful content that clearly creates a serious harm to others.

Other scholars strongly oppose any change to the law because they believe Section 230 is responsible for creating the robust, wide-open internet we have today. These scholars fear that efforts to amend Section 230 would result in substantial censorship, as social media organizations and ISPs moved to avoid lawsuits.[189] While the exact impact of any changes to Section 230 is ultimately unknown, the law is currently in Congress' crosshairs and is likely to remain there until both parties can agree on an approach that limits harm while protecting free expression.

The FCC's Role in Internet Regulation

For the past 15 years, the FCC has considered and reconsidered its role in internet regulation. While Congress has not given the commission explicit authority over the internet, the FCC has said it had ancillary jurisdiction under the Communications Act of 1934.[190] As noted earlier in the chapter, years before Congress adopted the first cable television law in 1984, the U.S. Supreme Court held that the 1934 act's language gave the FCC jurisdiction over cable as "ancillary" to its statutory right to regulate broadcasting.[191]

Although initially the FCC took a "hands off the internet" approach, more recently it claimed ancillary jurisdiction over broadband. The FCC's claim of jurisdiction over broadband has been both upheld and rejected by courts.

About 15 years ago, the U.S. Supreme Court held that cable television systems do not have to give their customers a choice of internet service providers.[192] The case before the Supreme Court turned on determining the legal category for cable internet services. The Telecommunications Act of 1996 said telecommunications services are utilities that can be more strictly regulated than broadcast. This could include requiring them to sell access to their networks.[193] However, the FCC determined in 2002 that cable internet access is not a telecommunications service but an information service.[194] Information services, according to the FCC, provide enhanced services, like web hosting, and are more than a basic utility that provides nothing more than transmission, like a telephone wire.

One way to gain high-speed internet access is through a cable modem offered by a cable television system. An ISP provides the internet connection. Many cable systems wanted their customers to use only an ISP they owned or with which they had an agreement. But other ISPs might want to use a cable system to provide high-speed internet access through cable modems. Must cable systems allow these other ISPs to offer access?

The U.S. Supreme Court said the 1996 law was ambiguous and the FCC had a right to interpret how the law applied to ISPs. The Court's ruling affirmed the authority of the FCC to categorize cable modem service as an information service, permitting cable system operators to choose which ISPs may offer high-speed internet access through cable modems. The ruling also prevented local cable television franchising authorities from regulating high-speed internet access through cable modems.

The way the FCC categorizes internet services has an impact on how it will regulate the internet. As part of its 2015 Open Internet Order, the FCC changed the classification of internet services from an information service to a basic telecommunications service. This classification change allowed the FCC to regulate broadband providers as common carriers, meaning they were treated like landline telephone providers and other utilities.[195] As such, they must make their services available to everyone on the same terms.

In 2018, under new leadership, the FCC reversed the 2015 classification. The Restoring Internet Freedom Order reinstated the information service classification of broadband internet.[196] As a result of the classification change back to an information service, the FCC restored its earlier determination that broadband is not a commercial service subject to strict regulation. It also restored the authority of the Federal Trade Commission to provide oversight of ISPs' privacy practices.[197]

Mozilla, the company behind the web browser Firefox, challenged the FCC's decision.[198] The D.C. Circuit Court of Appeals largely upheld the FCC's Restoring Internet Freedom Order, but remanded three discrete points back to the agency for further consideration.[199] One of these focused on public safety, an issue raised to the court after Verizon accidentally throttled the internet of Santa Clara firefighters during a California wildfire. The other two issues were related to the mechanics of attaching broadband cable to telephone poles and to the agency's low-income communications access program, Lifeline. The FCC analyzed the issues outlined by the D.C. Circuit Court of Appeals and found, "no basis to alter our conclusions in the *Restoring Internet Freedom Order*."[200]

REAL WORLD LAW
AMERICA'S DIGITAL DIVIDE

When the COVID-19 pandemic forced 55 million students to attend school online and shifted the office environment online for millions of American workers, it revealed the scope of the digital divide is in the United States. While approximately 77 percent of Americans have access to low-cost broadband plans, many rural areas remain without high-speed internet access.[201] Although a 2021 Executive Order from President Biden called for a shift from a threshold from 4 MBPS to 25 MBPS, the reality is that many citizens are unable to access essential online services.[202] In western states such as Montana and New Mexico, the digital divide meant access to telehealth consultations regarding COVID-19 was limited. During the pandemic one in five teens in the U.S. had difficulty completing homework because of limited internet access.[203]

Broadband Facts

Fixed broadband consumer disclosure

Choose Your Service Data Plan for 50Mbps Service Tier

Monthly charge for month-to-month plan	**$60.00**
Monthly charge for 2 year contract plan	**$55.00**

Click here for other pricing options including promotions and options bundled with other services, like cable television and wireless services.

Other Charges and Terms

Data included with monthly charge	**300GB**
Charges for additional data usage – each additional 50GB	**$10.00**
Optional modem or gateway lease – Customers may use their own modem or gateway; click here for our policy	**$10.00/month**
Other monthly fees	**Not Applicable**
One-time fees	
Activation fee	**$50.00**
Deposit	**$50.00**
Installation fee	**$25.00**
Early termination fee	**$240.00**

Government Taxes and Other Government-Related Fees May Apply: Varies by location

Other services on network

Performance - Individual experience may vary

Typical speed downstream	**53 Mbps**
Typical speed upstream	**6 Mbps**
Typical latency	**35 milliseconds**
Typical packet loss	**0.08%**

Network Management

Application-specific network management practices?	**Yes**
Subscriber-triggered network management practices?	**Yes**

More details on network management

Privacy	See our privacy policy
Complaints or Inquiries	To contact us: online/(123)456-7890; To submit complaints to the FCC: online/(888)225-5322

Learn more about the terms used on this form and other relevant information at the FCC's website.

The FCC has proposed new rules that would require broadband providers to display easy-to-understand labels to allow consumers to comparison shop for broadband services.

United States Federal Communications Commission

Net Neutrality

The 2018 FCC order also rolled back net neutrality rules. At its core, **net neutrality** simply means that ISPs cannot charge content providers to speed up the delivery of their content. These rules also prevent ISPs from throttling or slowing down competitors' content. Supporters of net neutrality say that the concept is important for the internet to maintain its democratic status. They argue that ISPs should not favor some content providers over others simply because they can charge them more money to deliver their content, even if that content takes up a lot of broadband space (for example, video). Notable corporate supporters of net neutrality principles include Google, Microsoft, Netflix and Twitter.[204]

Opponents of net neutrality say that if ISPs cannot charge more money for different kinds of transmissions such as those required by online video distributors, then it stifles innovation and runs against the ISPs' financial interests. Opponents to net neutrality principles include Verizon, AT&T and Comcast. The net neutrality issue also tends to fall along political party lines with Democrats supporting net neutrality principles and Republicans opposing them.[205] Despite this, neutrality regulations are popular with the American public. Four out of five Americans support net neutrality rules.[206]

The FCC issued its first net neutrality order more than a decade ago.[207] In the first court challenge to that order, the D.C. Circuit Court of Appeals held that the FCC did not have jurisdiction to regulate ISP broadband services.[208] After that court decision, the FCC tried again, issuing new net neutrality rules in its 2010 Open Internet Report and Order.[209] Verizon challenged the 2010 order. In 2014, the D.C. Circuit Court struck down the FCC's new net neutrality rules.[210] The court said the FCC's Open Internet Orders failed to justify its shift away from the commission's previous decision to categorize ISPs as information services. The court's decision left open the door for the FCC to pursue new net neutrality rules if it adequately justified its reclassification of ISPs as a telecommunications service.[211] The FCC's 2015 Open Internet Order reclassified high-speed internet service as a telecommunications service under Title II of the Telecommunications Act of 1996 and effectively began treating broadband service providers like a public utility.[212]

Viewers of comedian John Oliver's weekly HBO show have twice crashed the Federal Communications Commission's system by submitting thousands of comments on net neutrality.

Gary Gershoff/Getty Images

The 2015 FCC order banned throttling, blocking and paid prioritization of content. This meant providers were not permitted to "impair or degrade" or block lawful internet traffic on the basis of content. The ban on paid prioritization cuts to the heart of net neutrality and prohibited broadband providers from creating paid "fast lanes" to favor some kinds of traffic over others.[213]

The FCC's 3–2 vote on the 2015 order divided along party lines. The three Democrats on the commission voted in favor of the order,[214] while the two Republicans on the commission voted against the order.[215] Nearly 50 organizations sued to block the rules that took effect in 2015; the D.C. Circuit Court consolidated all of the lawsuits[216] and in 2016 denied the petitions for review of the 2015 order.[217] In mid-2017, the FCC announced that it would begin the process of loosening net neutrality enforcement regulations.[218]

In 2018, the FCC adopted the Restoring Internet Freedom Order that eliminated the net neutrality rules against blocking, throttling and paid prioritization as well as the general conduct rule, which applied on a case-by-case basis to practices that harmed consumers.[219] The 3–2 vote in 2018 remained along party lines, with Republicans in the majority. The 2018 order took effect in June of that year, amid 22 state attorneys general, several companies and several public interest groups filing lawsuits in various courts to challenge the new order.[220]

In response, seven states—California, Colorado, Maine, New Jersey, Oregon, Vermont and Washington—enacted their own net neutrality laws. Several other states and the District of Columbia have introduced bills and resolutions regarding net neutrality. In 2021, President Biden issued an executive order directing the now democratically led FCC to restore Obama-era net neutrality laws.[221] The executive order instructs the FCC to reinstate the rules like those in the 2015 Open Internet Order, which prohibited "fast lanes" and "throttling."

EMERGING LAW

Since its development in the mid-2000s, social media have impacted society in a variety of ways, both positive and negative. Social media have democratized our information landscape, giving each of us the power to reach large audiences and connect with people on a global scale. However, these platforms have also emerged as a hotbed for hateful rhetoric and mis- and disinformation. During the COVID-19 pandemic, social media platforms were responsible for spreading disinformation about the virus and the vaccine. President Biden went so far as to say that Facebook's misinformation about the vaccine was killing people.[222] Before that, social media organizations were criticized for their decision to deplatform users, most notably former President Donald Trump, who was banned from Facebook and Twitter for statements made in relation to the January 6 insurrection on the nation's capitol. Social media companies have been accused of censoring content and being biased against conservative viewpoints.[223] In response to this perceived bias, Florida passed a law in 2021 that would fine social media companies for deplatforming or shadow banning political candidates or their content.[224] However in 2022, the Eleventh Circuit Court of Appeals ruled that the First Amendment prevented the government from telling a private entity what to say.[225] When social media companies moderate and curate the content they disseminate on their platforms, they are engaged in constitutionally protected expressive activity. Despite this ruling, in 2022, Texas enacted a law that prohibited social media platforms from censoring users based on viewpoint and required the company to create biannual transparency reports and better disclose their content moderation policies. Although the Fifth Circuit Court of Appeals ruled to let the law stand as the challenge to it worked its way through the lower courts, the U.S. Supreme Court ultimately decided to put the law on hold while the challenge was adjudicated.[226]

REAL WORLD LAW
SOCIAL MEDIA PLATFORMS AS PUBLIC FORUMS

In 2018, a federal district court ruled that President Donald Trump cannot block critics from his Twitter account without violating the First Amendment.[227] The court said the Twitter account was the equivalent of a public forum in which the president communicated with the public and to which the public should have access. President Trump appealed to the Supreme Court, which remanded the case back to the Second Circuit to dismiss as moot since President Trump was no longer in office.[228] Justice Thomas issued a concurrence to that decision which set forth a legal roadmap for addressing his concerns about the "concentrated control of so much speech in the hands of a few private parties."[229]

The substantial impact of social media on public discourse has led to debates among lawmakers about whether and how the government should regulate social media. Social media differ considerably from other forms of media. There is no scarcity of spectrum, as there is with broadcasting. Social media content also offers very little of the editorial oversight we see in traditional news media, and algorithms, rather than consumer choice, determines which content we have access to. As private virtual platforms, social media companies are currently free to regulate themselves essentially however they would like. The terms of service issued by social media companies and other computer services serve as a contract between the user and the platform. Users consent to follow the rules set forth by the organization to access the site. Thus, it is the company, not the government that regulates content on social media. Social media platforms' rules regarding what content is and is not allowed on the site are outlined in their community standards. Many social media platforms prohibit speech that is protected by the First Amendment, such as hate speech or nudity.[230] The companies then use a combination of artificial intelligence algorithms and community reporting to identify and remove content that violates their stated community standards.[231] Some social media organizations, such as Facebook, have even instituted their own "courts" to hear challenges to removal decisions.[232]

Despite their extensive efforts at self-regulation, problems persist, and lawmakers are actively looking for solutions on how to best regulate social media. Making changes to Section 230 is one avenue that lawmakers are exploring to reshape social media governance. Another approach utilizes existing anti-trust laws to limit the power of these large corporations. Anti-trust laws were enacted in the United States during the 19th century to promote competition and protect consumers. Existing laws give the government power to intervene to break up large businesses that have a monopoly on a particular industry.[233] In the early 1980s the government dealt with a monopoly within the telephone service industry by breaking up AT&T.

In 2020 the Federal Trade Commission (FTC) and Attorneys Generals in 48 states filed two separate suits against Facebook to stop their anti-competitive conduct.[234] The FTC argued that Facebook had established a monopoly position by purchasing several companies including Instagram and WhatsApp that would otherwise present competitive threats.[235] In June 2021, a federal judge dismissed both cases because prosecutors had failed to show enough facts to support their claim.[236] The FTC amended and refiled its claim in an effort to address the short-comings identified by the Washington D.C. District Court's opinion on the original case.[237] Facebook's initial motion to dismiss that case has been denied and the FTC's second suit against Facebook is awaiting its new day in court.[238] In addition, Congress has also introduced several bills to update antitrust laws in an effort to loosen the grip large companies like Facebook and Google have on the digital economy.[239]

Although the specific approach the government will take to regulating social media organizations and, potentially, their content remains uncertain, what we do know is that future changes are likely. Until then, social media will continue to be dominated by a handful of large corporations that have the power to shape everything from privacy to public discourse.

KEYTERMS

broadband	multichannel video programming
broadcasting	distributor
cross-ownership rule	must-carry rule
electromagnetic spectrum	net neutrality
electronic media	notice of proposed rulemaking
fairness doctrine	radio frequency
Federal Communications	retransmission consent
Commission	satellite market modification rule
Federal Radio Commission	spectrum scarcity
legally qualified candidate	

CASES FOR STUDY

THINKING ABOUT THEM

The two case excerpts that follow deal with broadcasting. As you read these case excerpts, keep the following questions in mind:

- What reasons does the U.S. Supreme Court give for the way it applies the First Amendment to broadcasting in *Red Lion v. FCC*?
- Does the Court's decision in the *Red Lion* case logically lead to the Supreme Court ruling in *Reno v. ACLU* that the internet should have full First Amendment protection? Why or why not?

- Could you imagine a modern-day Fairness Doctrine? What might that look like?
- According to *FCC v. Prometheus*, what kind of justifications or evidence is the FCC required to give for its rule changes?
- How does racial and gender diversity in broadcast ownership serve the public interest, convenience, and necessity? Do the 2017 rule changes help achieve this goal in your opinion?

RED LION BROADCASTING CO., INC. V. FEDERAL COMMUNICATIONS COMMISSION

SUPREME COURT OF THE UNITED STATES 395 U.S. 367 (1969)

JUSTICE BYRON WHITE delivered the Court's opinion:

The Federal Communications Commission has for many years imposed on radio and television broadcasters the requirement that discussion of public issues be presented on broadcast stations, and that each side of those issues must be given fair coverage. This is known as the fairness doctrine, which originated very early in the history of broadcasting and has maintained its present outlines for some time. It is an obligation whose content has been defined in a long series of FCC rulings in particular cases, and which is distinct from the statutory requirement of Section 315 of the Communications Act that equal time be allotted all qualified candidates for public office. Two aspects of the fairness doctrine, relating to personal attacks in the context of controversial public issues and to political editorializing, were codified more precisely in the form of FCC regulations in 1967. The two cases before us now, which were decided separately below, challenge the constitutional and statutory bases of the doctrine and component rules. *Red Lion* involves the application of the fairness doctrine to a particular broadcast, and *RTNDA* [*Radio and Television News Directors Association*] arises as an action to review the FCC's 1967 promulgation of the personal attack and political editorializing regulations, which were laid down after the *Red Lion* litigation had begun.

The Red Lion Broadcasting Company is licensed to operate a Pennsylvania radio station, WGCB. On November 27, 1964, WGCB carried a 15-minute broadcast by the Reverend Billy James Hargis as part of a "Christian Crusade" series. A book by Fred J. Cook entitled "Goldwater—Extremist on the Right" was discussed by Hargis, who said that Cook had been fired by a newspaper for making false charges against city officials; that Cook had then worked for a Communist-affiliated publication; that he had defended Alger Hiss and attacked J. Edgar Hoover and the Central Intelligence Agency; and that he had now written a "book to smear and destroy Barry Goldwater." When Cook heard of the broadcast he concluded that he had been personally attacked and demanded free reply time, which the station refused. After an exchange of letters among Cook, Red Lion, and the FCC, the FCC declared that the Hargis broadcast constituted a personal attack on Cook; that Red Lion had failed to meet its obligation under the fairness doctrine . . . .to send a tape, transcript, or summary of the broadcast to Cook and offer him reply time; and that the station must provide reply time whether or not Cook would pay for it. On review in the Court of Appeals for the District of Columbia Circuit, the FCC's position was upheld as constitutional and otherwise proper. . . .

Believing that the specific application of the fairness doctrine in *Red Lion*, and the promulgation of the regulations in *RTNDA*, are both authorized by Congress and enhance rather than abridge the freedoms of speech and press protected by the First Amendment, we hold them valid and constitutional, reversing the judgment below in *RTNDA* and affirming the judgment below in *Red Lion*.

The history of the emergence of the fairness doctrine and of the related legislation shows that the Commission's action in the *Red Lion* case did not exceed its authority, and that in adopting the new regulations the Commission was implementing congressional policy rather than embarking on a frolic of its own.

Before 1927, the allocation of frequencies was left entirely to the private sector, and the result was chaos. It quickly became apparent that broadcast frequencies constituted a scarce resource whose use could be regulated and rationalized only by the Government. Without government control, the medium would be of little use because of the cacophony of competing voices, none of which could be clearly and predictably heard. Consequently, the Federal Radio Commission was established to allocate frequencies among competing applicants in a manner responsive to the public "convenience, interest, or necessity."

Very shortly thereafter the Commission expressed its view that the "public interest requires ample play for the free and fair competition of opposing views, and the commission believes that the principle applies . . . to all discussions of issues of importance to the public." This doctrine was applied through denial of license renewals or construction permits, both by the FRC, and its successor FCC. After an extended period during which the licensee was obliged not only to cover and to cover fairly the views of others, but also to refrain from expressing his own personal views, the latter limitation on the licensee was abandoned and the doctrine developed into its present form.

There is a twofold duty laid down by the FCC's decisions and described by the 1949 Report on Editorializing by Broadcast Licensees. The broadcaster must give adequate coverage to public issues, and coverage must be fair in that it accurately reflects the opposing views. This must be done at the broadcaster's own expense if sponsorship is unavailable. Moreover, the duty must be met by programming obtained at the licensee's own initiative if available from no other source. . . .

When a personal attack has been made on a figure involved in a public issue, . . . [it is required] that the individual attacked himself be offered an opportunity to respond. Likewise, where one candidate is endorsed in a political editorial, the other candidates must themselves be offered reply time to use personally or through a spokesman. These obligations differ from the general fairness requirement that issues be presented, and presented with coverage of competing views, in that the broadcaster does not have the option of presenting the attacked party's side himself or choosing a third party to represent that side. But insofar as there is an obligation of the broadcaster to see that both sides are presented, and insofar as that is an affirmative obligation, the personal attack doctrine and regulations do not differ from the preceding fairness doctrine. The simple fact that the attacked men or unendorsed candidates may respond themselves or through agents is not a critical distinction, and indeed, it is not unreasonable for the FCC to conclude that the objective of adequate presentation of all sides may best be served by allowing those most closely affected to make the response, rather than leaving the response in the hands of the station which has attacked their candidacies, endorsed their opponents, or carried a personal attack upon them. . . .

The broadcasters challenge the fairness doctrine and its specific manifestations in the personal attack and political editorial rules on conventional First Amendment grounds, alleging that the rules abridge their freedom of speech and press. Their contention is that the First Amendment protects their desire to use their allotted frequencies continuously to broadcast whatever they choose, and to exclude whomever they choose from ever using that frequency. No man may be prevented from saying or publishing what he thinks, or from refusing in his speech or other utterances to give equal weight to the views of his opponents. This right, they say, applies equally to broadcasters.

Although broadcasting is clearly a medium affected by a First Amendment interest, differences in the characteristics of new media justify differences in the standards applied to them. For example, the ability of new technology to produce sounds more raucous than those of the human voice justifies restrictions on the sound level, and on the hours and places of use, of sound trucks so long as the restrictions are reasonable and applied without discrimination.

Just as the Government may limit the use of sound-amplifying equipment potentially so noisy that it drowns out civilized private speech, so may the Government limit the use of broadcast equipment. The right of free speech of a broadcaster, the user of a sound truck, or any other individual does not embrace a right to snuff out the free speech of others. . . .

It was . . . the chaos which ensued from permitting anyone to use any frequency at whatever power level he wished, which made necessary the enactment of the Radio Act of 1927 and the Communications Act of 1934. It was this reality which at the very least necessitated first the division of the radio spectrum into portions reserved respectively for public broadcasting and for other important radio uses such as amateur operation, aircraft, police, defense, and navigation; and then the subdivision of each portion, and assignment of specific frequencies to individual users or groups of users. Beyond this, however, because the frequencies reserved for public broadcasting were limited in number, it was essential for the Government to tell some applicants that they could not broadcast at all because there was room for only a few.

Where there are substantially more individuals who want to broadcast than there are frequencies to allocate, it is idle to posit an unabridgeable First Amendment right to broadcast comparable to the right of every individual to speak, write, or publish. If 100 persons want broadcast licenses but there are only 10 frequencies to allocate, all of them may have the same "right" to a license; but if there is to be any effective communication by radio, only a few can be licensed and the rest must be barred from the airwaves. It would be strange if the First Amendment, aimed at protecting and furthering communications, prevented the Government from making radio communication possible by requiring licenses to broadcast and by limiting the number of licenses so as not to overcrowd the spectrum.

This has been the consistent view of the Court. Congress unquestionably has the power to grant and deny licenses and to eliminate existing stations. No one has a First Amendment right to a license or to monopolize a radio frequency; to deny a station license because "the public interest" requires it "is not a denial of free speech."

By the same token, as far as the First Amendment is concerned those who are licensed stand no better than those to whom licenses are refused. A license permits broadcasting, but the licensee has no constitutional right to be the one who holds the license or to monopolize a radio frequency to the exclusion of his fellow citizens. There is nothing in the First Amendment which prevents the Government from requiring a licensee to share his frequency with others and to conduct himself as a proxy or fiduciary with obligations to present those views and voices which are representative of his community and which would otherwise, by necessity, be barred from the airwaves.

This is not to say that the First Amendment is irrelevant to public broadcasting. On the contrary, it has a major role to play as the Congress itself recognized in forbidding FCC interference with "the right of free speech by means of radio communication." Because of the scarcity of radio frequencies, the Government is permitted to put restraints on licensees in favor of others whose views should be expressed on this unique medium. But the people as a whole retain their interest in free speech by radio and their collective right to have the medium function consistently with the ends and purposes of the First Amendment. It is the right of the viewers and listeners, not the right of the broadcasters, which is paramount. It is the purpose of the First Amendment to preserve an uninhibited marketplace of ideas in which truth will ultimately prevail, rather than to countenance monopolization of that market, whether it be by the Government itself or a private licensee. "Speech concerning public affairs is more than self-expression; it is the essence of self-government." It is the right of the public to receive suitable access to social, political, esthetic, moral, and other ideas and experiences which is crucial here. That right may not constitutionally be abridged either by Congress or by the FCC.

Rather than confer frequency monopolies on a relatively small number of licensees, in a Nation of 200,000,000, the Government could surely have decreed that each frequency should be shared among all or some of those who wish to use it, each being assigned a portion of the broadcast day or the broadcast week. The ruling and regulations at issue here do not go quite so far. They assert that under specified circumstances, a licensee must offer to make available a reasonable amount of broadcast time to those who have a view different from that which has already been expressed on his station. The expression of a political endorsement, or of a personal attack while dealing with a controversial public issue, simply triggers this time sharing. As we have said, the *First Amendment* confers no right on licensees to prevent others from broadcasting on "their" frequencies and no right to an unconditional monopoly of a scarce resource which the Government has denied others the right to use.

In terms of constitutional principle, and as enforced sharing of a scarce resource, the personal attack and political editorial rules are indistinguishable from the equal-time provision of Section 315, a specific enactment of Congress requiring stations to set aside reply time under specified circumstances and to which the fairness doctrine and these constituent regulations are important complements. That provision, which has been part of the law since 1927, has been held valid by this Court as an obligation of the licensee relieving him of any power in any way to prevent or censor the broadcast, and thus insulating him from liability for defamation. The constitutionality of the statute under the First Amendment was unquestioned.

Nor can we say that it is inconsistent with the First Amendment goal of producing an informed public capable of conducting its own affairs to require a broadcaster to permit answers to personal attacks occurring in the course of discussing controversial issues, or to require that the political opponents of those endorsed by the station be given a chance to communicate with the public. Otherwise, station owners and a few networks would have unfettered power to make time available only to the highest bidders, to communicate only their own views on public issues, people and candidates, and to permit on the air only those with whom they agreed. There is no sanctuary in the First Amendment for unlimited private censorship operating in a medium not open to all. "Freedom of the press from governmental interference under the First Amendment does not sanction repression of that freedom by private interests."

It is strenuously argued, however, that if political editorials or personal attacks will trigger an obligation in broadcasters to afford the opportunity for expression to speakers who need not pay for time and whose views are unpalatable to the licensees, then broadcasters will be irresistibly forced to self-censorship and their coverage of controversial public issues will be eliminated or at least rendered wholly ineffective. Such a result would indeed be a serious matter, for should licensees actually eliminate their coverage of controversial issues, the purposes of the doctrine would be stifled.

At this point, however, as the Federal Communications Commission has indicated, that possibility is at best speculative. The communications industry, and in particular the networks, have taken pains to present controversial issues in the past, and even now they do not assert that they intend to abandon their efforts in this regard. It would be better if the FCC's encouragement were never necessary to induce the broadcasters to meet their responsibility. And if experience with the administration of these doctrines indicates that they have the net effect of reducing rather than enhancing the volume and quality of coverage, there will be time enough to reconsider the constitutional implications. The fairness doctrine in the past has had no such overall effect. . . .

Scarcity is not entirely a thing of the past. Advances in technology . . . have led to more efficient utilization of the frequency spectrum, but uses for that spectrum have also grown apace. Portions of the spectrum must be reserved for vital uses unconnected with human communication, such as radio-navigational aids used by aircraft and vessels. Conflicts have even emerged between such vital functions as defense preparedness and experimentation in methods of averting midair collisions through radio warning devices. . . .

The rapidity with which technological advances succeed one another to create more efficient use of spectrum space on the one hand, and to create new uses for that space by ever growing numbers of people on the other, makes it unwise to speculate on the future allocation of that space. It is enough to say that the resource is one of considerable and growing importance whose scarcity impelled its regulation by an agency authorized by Congress. . . .

In view of the scarcity of broadcast frequencies, the Government's role in allocating those frequencies, and the legitimate claims of those unable without governmental assistance to gain access to those frequencies for expression of their views, we hold the regulations and ruling at issue here are both authorized by statute and constitutional. . . .

FEDERAL COMMUNICATIONS COMMISSION V. PROMETHEUS RADIO PROJECT

SUPREME COURT OF THE UNITED STATES 141 S. CT. 1150 (2021)

JUSTICE BRETT KAVANAUGH delivered the Court's opinion:

Under the Communications Act of 1934, the Federal Communications Commission possesses broad authority to regulate broadcast media in the public interest. Exercising that statutory authority, the FCC has long maintained strict ownership rules. The rules limit the number of radio stations, television stations, and newspapers that a single entity may own in a given market. Under Section 202(h) of the Telecommunications Act of 1996, the FCC must review the ownership rules every four years, and must repeal or modify any ownership rules that the agency determines are no longer in the public interest.

In a 2017 order, the FCC concluded that three of its ownership rules no longer served the public interest. The FCC therefore repealed two of those rules—the Newspaper/Broadcast Cross-Ownership Rule and the Radio/Television Cross-Ownership Rule. And the Commission modified the third—the Local Television Ownership Rule. In conducting its public interest analysis under Section 202(h), the FCC considered the effects of the rules on competition, localism, viewpoint diversity, and minority and female ownership of broadcast media outlets. The FCC concluded that the three rules were no longer necessary to promote competition, localism, and viewpoint diversity, and that changing the rules was not likely to harm minority and female ownership.

A non-profit advocacy group known as Prometheus Radio Project, along with several other public interest and consumer advocacy groups, petitioned for review, arguing that the FCC's decision was arbitrary and capricious under the Administrative Procedure Act. In particular, Prometheus contended that the record evidence did not support the FCC's predictive judgment regarding minority and female ownership. Over Judge Scirica's dissent, the U. S. Court of Appeals for the Third Circuit agreed with Prometheus and vacated the FCC's 2017 order.

On this record, we conclude that the FCC's 2017 order was reasonable and reasonably explained for purposes of the APA's deferential arbitrary-and-capricious standard. We therefore reverse the judgment of the Third Circuit.

I

The Federal Communications Commission possesses broad statutory authority to regulate broadcast media "as public convenience, interest, or necessity requires." Exercising that authority, the FCC has historically maintained several strict ownership rules. The rules limit the number of radio stations, television stations, and newspapers that a single entity may own in a given market. The FCC has long explained that the ownership rules seek to promote competition, localism, and viewpoint diversity by ensuring that a small number of entities do not dominate a particular media market.

This case concerns three of the FCC's current ownership rules. The first is the Newspaper/Broadcast Cross-Ownership Rule. Initially adopted in 1975, that rule prohibits a single entity from owning a radio or television broadcast station and a daily print newspaper in the same media market. The second is the Radio/Television Cross-Ownership Rule. Initially adopted in 1970, that rule limits the number of combined radio stations and television stations that an entity may own in a single market. And the third is the Local Television Ownership Rule. Initially adopted in 1964, that rule restricts the number of local television stations that an entity may own in a single market.

The FCC adopted those rules in an early-cable and pre-Internet age when media sources were more limited. By the 1990s, however, the market for news and entertainment had changed dramatically. Technological advances led to a massive increase in alternative media options, such as cable television and the Internet. Those technological advances challenged the traditional dominance of daily print newspapers, local radio stations, and local television stations.

In 1996, Congress passed and President Clinton signed the Telecommunications Act. To ensure that the FCC's ownership rules do not remain in place simply through inertia, Section 202(h) of the Act directs the FCC to review its ownership rules every four years to determine whether those rules remain "necessary in the public interest as the result of competition." After conducting each quadrennial Section 202(h) review, the FCC "shall repeal or modify" any rules that it determines are "no longer in the public interest." Section 202(h) establishes an iterative process that requires the FCC to keep pace with industry developments and to regularly reassess how its rules function in the marketplace.

Soon after Section 202(h) was enacted, the FCC stated that the agency's traditional public interest goals of promoting competition, localism, and viewpoint diversity would inform its Section 202(h) analyses. The FCC has also said that, as part of its public interest analysis under Section 202(h), it would assess the effects of the ownership rules on minority and female ownership.

Since 2002, the Commission has repeatedly sought to change several of its ownership rules—including the three rules at issue here—as part of its Section 202(h) reviews. But for the last 17 years, the Third Circuit has rejected the FCC's efforts as unlawful under the APA. As a result, those three ownership rules exist in substantially the same form today as they did in 2002.

The current dispute arises out of the FCC's most recent attempt to change its ownership rules. In its quadrennial Section 202(h) order issued in 2016, the FCC concluded that the Newspaper/Broadcast Cross-Ownership, Radio/Television Cross-Ownership, and Local Television Ownership Rules remained necessary to serve the agency's public interest goals of promoting "competition and a diversity of viewpoints in local markets." The FCC therefore chose to retain the existing rules with only "minor modifications."

A number of groups sought reconsideration of the 2016 Order. In 2017, the Commission (with a new Chair) granted reconsideration. On reconsideration, the FCC performed a new public interest analysis. The agency explained that rapidly evolving technology and the rise of new media outlets—particularly cable and Internet—had transformed how Americans obtain news and entertainment, rendering some of the ownership rules obsolete. As a result of those market changes, the FCC concluded that the three ownership rules no longer served the agency's public interest goals of fostering competition, localism, and viewpoint diversity. The FCC explained that permitting efficient combinations among radio stations, television stations, and newspapers would benefit consumers.

The Commission also considered the likely impact of any changes to its ownership rules on minority and female ownership. The FCC concluded that repealing or modifying the three ownership rules was not likely to harm minority and female ownership.

Based on its analysis of the relevant factors, the FCC decided to repeal the Newspaper/Broadcast and Radio/Television Cross-Ownership Rules, and to modify the Local Television Ownership Rule.

Prometheus and several other public interest and consumer advocacy groups petitioned for review, arguing that the FCC's decision to repeal or modify those three rules was arbitrary and capricious under the APA.

The Third Circuit vacated the 2017 Reconsideration Order. The court did not dispute the FCC's conclusion that those three ownership rules no longer promoted the agency's public interest goals of competition, localism, and viewpoint diversity. But the court held that the record did not support the FCC's conclusion that the rule changes would "have minimal effect" on minority and female ownership. The court directed the Commission, on remand, to "ascertain on record evidence" the effect that any rule changes were likely to have on minority and female ownership, "whether through new empirical research or an in-depth theoretical analysis."

Judge Scirica dissented in relevant part. In his view, the FCC reasonably analyzed the record evidence and made a reasonable predictive judgment that the rule changes were not likely to harm minority and female ownership.

The FCC and a number of industry groups petitioned for certiorari. We granted certiorari.

II

In the 2017 Reconsideration Order, the FCC changed three of its ownership rules because it concluded that the rules were no longer in the public interest. In particular, the FCC concluded that the rules no longer served the agency's goals of fostering competition, localism, and viewpoint diversity, and further concluded that repealing or modifying the rules was not likely to harm minority and female ownership.

Prometheus argues that the FCC's predictive judgment regarding minority and female ownership was arbitrary and capricious under the APA. We disagree.

The APA's arbitrary-and-capricious standard requires that agency action be reasonable and reasonably explained. Judicial review under that standard is deferential, and a court may not substitute its own policy judgment for that of the agency. A court simply ensures that the agency has acted within a zone of reasonableness and, in particular, has reasonably considered the relevant issues and reasonably explained the decision.

In its 2017 Reconsideration Order, the FCC analyzed the significant record evidence of dramatic changes in the media market over the past several decades. After thoroughly examining that record evidence, the Commission determined that the Newspaper/Broadcast Cross-Ownership, Radio/Television Cross-Ownership, and Local Television Ownership Rules were no longer necessary to serve the agency's public interest goals of promoting competition, localism, and viewpoint diversity. The FCC therefore concluded that repealing the two cross-ownership rules and modifying the Local Television Ownership Rule would fulfill "the mandates of Section 202(h)" and "deliver on the Commission's promise to adopt broadcast ownership rules that reflect the present, not the past."

In analyzing whether to repeal or modify those rules, the FCC also addressed the possible impact on minority and female ownership. The Commission explained that it had sought public comment on the issue of minority and female ownership during multiple Section 202(h) reviews, but "no arguments were made" that would lead the FCC to conclude that the existing rules were "necessary to protect or promote minority and female ownership."

Indeed, the FCC stated that it had received several comments suggesting the opposite—namely, comments suggesting that eliminating the Newspaper/Broadcast Cross-Ownership Rule "potentially could increase minority ownership of newspapers and broadcast stations.". Based on the record, the Commission concluded that repealing or modifying the three rules was not likely to harm minority and female ownership.

In challenging the 2017 Reconsideration Order in this Court, Prometheus does not seriously dispute the FCC's conclusion that the existing rules no longer serve the agency's public interest goals of competition, localism, and viewpoint diversity. Rather, Prometheus targets the FCC's assessment that altering the ownership rules was not likely to harm minority and female ownership.

Prometheus asserts that the FCC relied on flawed data in assessing the likely impact of changing the rules on minority and female ownership. Prometheus further argues that the FCC ignored superior data available in the record.

Prometheus initially points to two data sets on which the FCC relied in the 2016 Order and the 2017 Reconsideration Order. Those data sets measured the number of minority-owned media outlets before and after the Local Television Ownership Rule and the Local Radio Ownership Rule were relaxed in the 1990s. Together, the data sets showed a slight decrease in the number of minority-owned media outlets immediately after the rules were relaxed, followed by an eventual increase in later years. The 2016 Order cited those data sets and explained that the number of minority-owned media outlets had increased over time. But the FCC added that there was no record evidence suggesting that past changes to the ownership rules had caused minority ownership levels to increase.

In the 2017 Reconsideration Order, the FCC referred to the 2016 Order's analysis of those data sets. The FCC stated that data in the record suggested that the previous relaxations of the Local Television Ownership and Local Radio Ownership Rules "have not resulted in reduced levels of minority and female ownership." The FCC further explained that "no party" had "presented contrary evidence or a compelling argument demonstrating why" altering the rules would have a different impact today. The FCC therefore concluded that "the record provides no information to suggest" that eliminating or modifying the existing rules would harm minority and female ownership.

Prometheus insists that the FCC's numerical comparison was overly simplistic and that the data sets were materially incomplete. But the FCC acknowledged the gaps in the data.

And despite repeatedly asking for data on the issue, the Commission received no other data on minority ownership and no data at all on female ownership levels. The FCC therefore relied on the data it had (and the absence of any countervailing evidence) to predict that changing the rules was not likely to harm minority and female ownership.

Prometheus also asserts that countervailing—and superior—evidence was in fact in the record, and that the FCC ignored that evidence. Prometheus identifies two studies submitted to the FCC by Free Press, a media reform group. Those studies purported to show that past relaxations of the ownership rules and increases in media market concentration had led to decreases in minority and female ownership levels. According to Prometheus, the Free Press studies undercut the FCC's prediction that its rule changes were unlikely to harm minority and female ownership.

The FCC did not ignore the Free Press studies. The FCC simply interpreted them differently. In particular, in the 2016 Order, the Commission explained that its data sets and the Free Press studies showed the same long-term increase in minority ownership after the Local Television Ownership and Local Radio Ownership Rules were relaxed. Moreover, as counsel for Prometheus forthrightly acknowledged at oral argument, the Free Press studies were purely backward-looking, and offered no statistical analysis of the likely future effects of the FCC's proposed rule changes on minority and female ownership.

In short, the FCC's analysis was reasonable and reasonably explained for purposes of the APA's deferential arbitrary-and-capricious standard. The FCC considered the record evidence on competition, localism, viewpoint diversity, and minority and female ownership, and reasonably concluded that the three ownership rules no longer serve the public interest. The FCC reasoned that the historical justifications for those ownership rules no longer apply in today's media market, and that permitting efficient combinations among radio stations, television stations, and newspapers would benefit consumers. The Commission further explained that its best estimate, based on the sparse record evidence, was that repealing or modifying the three rules at issue here was not likely to harm minority and female ownership. The APA requires no more.

To be sure, in assessing the effects on minority and female ownership, the FCC did not have perfect empirical or statistical data. Far from it. But that is not unusual in day-to-day agency decision making within the Executive Branch. The APA imposes no general obligation on agencies to conduct or commission their own empirical or statistical studies. And nothing in the Telecommunications Act (or any other statute) requires the FCC to conduct its own empirical or statistical studies before exercising its discretion under Section 202(h). Here, the FCC repeatedly asked commenters to submit empirical or statistical studies on the relationship between the ownership rules and minority and female ownership. Despite those requests, no commenter produced such evidence indicating that changing the rules was likely to harm minority and female ownership. In the absence of additional data from commenters, the FCC made a reasonable predictive judgment based on the evidence it had.

In light of the sparse record on minority and female ownership and the FCC's findings with respect to competition, localism, and viewpoint diversity, we cannot say that the agency's decision to repeal or modify the ownership rules fell outside the zone of reasonableness for purposes of the APA.

Demonstrators express support for The Perfect Moment, an exhibition by Robert Mapplethorpe that included nude and sexually graphic photos.

AP Photo/David Kohl

OBSCENITY AND INDECENCY

10 Social Norms and Legal Standards

CHAPTER OUTLINE

Obscenity
Comstock and *Hicklin*
Current Obscenity Definition
The *Miller* Test
Testing the *Miller* Test
Sexually Explicit Material and Children
Other Considerations

Indecency
Federal Communications Commission Regulation

Obscenity, Indecency, and the Internet

Emerging Law

Cases for Study
- *Federal Communications Commission v. Pacifica Foundation*
- *Federal Communications Commission v. Fox Television Stations, Inc.*

LEARNING OBJECTIVES

10.1   Apply the *Miller Test* to determine whether sexual expression is constitutionally protected or not.

10.2   Assess whether broadcast content violates existing indecency regulations.

10.3   Critique government and social media organizations' attempts to moderate sexual content online.

10.4   Appraise efforts to regulate deepfakes and other nonconsensual pornography.

Sexual expression is ubiquitous in contemporary societies—as it has been for centuries. It can be found in art, theater, commercials, text messages and memes; on websites like OnlyFans and on social media; in television programs and in movies. Legal experts observe that changing technology and social conventions now allow "virtually limitless" access to sexually explicit content.[1] Some believe sexually explicit material does not deserve First Amendment protection. Others argue sexual expression is just that—expression, which helps us navigate our sexuality and sexual health.[2]

The law as it applies to sexual expression comes from the U.S. Supreme Court's First Amendment decisions as well as administrative law and statutory law. Increasingly, issues surrounding sexual expression such as the distribution of nonconsensual pornography, also intersect with privacy (see Chapter 6) and other tort laws. In this chapter, we'll explore the laws that govern sexual expression broadly, and in broadcast and internet content specifically.

OBSCENITY

First Amendment decisions about sexual expression primarily focus on obscenity, a category of speech not protected by the First Amendment. The dictionary defines obscenity simply as "relating to sex in an indecent or offensive way," or "very offensive in usually a shocking way."[3] The legal definition of **obscenity** comes from *Miller v. California*, a U.S. Supreme Court case decided in 1973 and discussed in detail later in this chapter.

Administrative laws that apply to sexual expression come from the FCC (see Chapter 9) and focus on indecency. Broadly, indecency refers to content some people find offensive. It is not synonymous with obscenity. For regulatory purposes, the FCC defines indecency and determines the rules for how indecency regulation is applied to different media—most notably, broadcasting.[4]

Generally speaking, there is not agreement on what word to use in describing all offensive sexual expression. What's the difference between obscenity, pornography, and indecency? The word **pornography** is vague—not legally precise—because it encompasses both protected and unprotected sexual material. The term **indecency** has only a narrow legal meaning, referring to sexual expression and expletives inappropriate for children on broadcast radio and television. Until the mid-20th century, American courts used a broad definition of obscenity, allowing government officials to ban a wide range of materials.

Comstock and *Hicklin*

Two centuries ago, American society considered religious blasphemy and heresy to be more troublesome than sexual expression. With few exceptions, governments—state and federal— did not adopt laws or bring criminal charges related to sexual material. After the Civil War, Anthony Comstock, a store clerk, became the champion of young men's decency and launched an anti-obscenity movement.[5] He believed that "anything remotely touching upon sex was . . . obscene."[6] In 1872, Comstock convinced the Young Men's Christian Association to support his campaign against sexual content in art, newspapers, books, magazines and other media. Comstock became secretary of the New York Society for the Suppression of Vice, funded in part by prominent and wealthy businesspeople.[7]

Although federal laws already banned importing and mailing obscene material, Comstock vigorously lobbied Congress to further tighten mailing restrictions. His campaign culminated in the Comstock Act, a federal law adopted in 1873 prohibiting the mailing of "obscene, lewd, or lascivious" material.[8] Initially used only to stop mailings concerning contraception and abortion, the law was amended in 1876 to ensure that it banned the mailing of pornographic materials.[9]

After the law's adoption, Congress appointed Comstock as a special postal inspector to help enforce the statute. He held the post for 42 years. As a U.S. Postal Service special agent,

Comstock prosecuted many people for selling and mailing material that he said was lewd. Comstock would order items through the mail and then, with the illicit item as evidence, take the seller to court.[10]

In the late 1860s, when the post–Civil War United States began hearing cases involving sexually explicit material, it became clear that judges would not protect obscene publications under the First Amendment. The question was how to define obscenity. Beginning in the late 19th century and continuing for more than 60 years, federal courts applied the *Hicklin* **rule** to decide obscenity cases. The rule came from an 1868 British case, *Regina v. Hicklin*, stating that "the test of obscenity is this, whether the tendency of the matter charged as obscenity is to deprave and corrupt those whose minds are open to such immoral influences and into whose hands a publication of this sort may fall."[11]

In addition to successfully lobbying Congress to pass what became the Comstock Act, Anthony Comstock effectively pushed all states to pass obscenity laws.

Bettmann/Getty Images

In essence, the *Hicklin* rule meant adults could be exposed only to material acceptable for the most susceptible minds—children. U.S. courts commonly held that if even a portion of a publication met the *Hicklin* rule, the entire publication was obscene. The broad scope of the *Hicklin* rule gave state legislatures substantial leeway to define obscenity. As a result, much of the early obscenity doctrine in the U.S. was rooted in policies targeting members of the LGBTQ community. For example, in 1927, New York amended its obscenity law to include prohibitions on depictions of "sex, degeneracy, or perversion," terms which were common euphemisms for queer people.[12] As we'll see throughout the chapter, First Amendment law regarding obscenity has been used as both a weapon and shield in the expansion of LGBTQ rights.[13]

Although the *Hicklin* rule remained the primary test used to determine obscenity into the 1930s, it was not always applied. In a 1913 case that involved an American literary work whose publisher was prosecuted under the Comstock Act, federal Judge Learned Hand noted that the *Hicklin* standard "does not seem to me to answer to the understanding and morality of the present time" and that its application would "reduce our treatment of sex to the standard of a child's library."[14]

Judge Hand argued that courts should approach obscenity "like other kinds of conduct" and consider applying community standards that are "subject to the social sense of what is right." He added, "To put thought in leash to the average conscience of the time is perhaps tolerable, but to fetter it by the necessities of the lowest and least capable seems a fatal policy."[15] His articulation of a community standard would eventually reappear in later U.S. Supreme Court decisions about obscenity.

Deciding whether U.S. customs officials could prevent James Joyce's novel "Ulysses" from being imported, a federal district court in 1933 rejected the *Hicklin* rule and proposed a new standard for judging obscenity. The court said the test for obscenity should be the entire work's impact on an "average person." The judge noted that while the book contained four-letter profanities, it did so because that language would have been habitually used by the people the book described. The explicit sexual material in the book was not "dirt for dirt's sake." The court said "Ulysses" was literary art and was not obscene.[16]

The Second Circuit Court of Appeals upheld the decision. In writing for the court, Judge Augustus Hand (Judge Learned Hand's cousin) considered the entire work. The "Ulysses" decision suggested that courts should determine what is obscene by reviewing the material in its entirety instead of assessing isolated passages or pictures. The decision also suggested the test should ascertain a work's effect on an average person instead of on children. Despite the ruling, many federal and state courts continued to apply the *Hicklin* rule into the 1950s, reflecting the political and social climate of the times as well as the difficulty in drawing a line between obscenity and other forms of sexual expression.[17]

Current Obscenity Definition

The assumption throughout the 19th and early to mid-20th century was that the First Amendment did not protect obscene publications and materials.[18] The U.S. Supreme Court confirmed this in 1957 in *Roth v. United States*. At the same time, it definitively rejected *Hicklin* and narrowed the obscenity definition to give sexual expression more freedom. Even though the court upheld Samuel Roth's conviction for violating the Comstock Act by mailing sexually explicit literature, the decision represented the Court's first full attempt to distinguish between unprotected obscenity and protected sexual expression.[19] The Court said material was obscene if, first, an "average person, applying contemporary community standards," found the work taken as a whole appealed to **prurient interest**, meaning that it "excites lustful thoughts." Second, obscene material must be "utterly without redeeming social importance."[20] Given the antigay sentiment that permeated American attitudes in the 1950s, the inclusion of community standards was understood to be implicitly heteronormative.[21] Despite this, in 1958 the Supreme Court overturned the Los Angeles postmaster's decision to label *ONE Magazine* as obscene and prohibit its mailing.[22] *One Magazine* was the first political and news magazine in the United States created by and for the LGBTQ community.

ONE Magazine's first anniversary issue. Published by one of the first gay rights organizations in the United States, the magazine covered the interests and concerns occupying the gay community of the day.

JSTOR

The *Roth* test remained difficult for government prosecutors to meet and there were relatively few obscenity convictions after *Roth*. The Court refined the *Roth* test several times over the next two decades, but those refinements caused confusion and continued to raise questions about how to determine the social importance or social value of sexual expression.[23]

For example, in 1964, the U.S. Supreme Court overturned the conviction of a movie theater manager who showed an internationally acclaimed French film that the state of Ohio deemed obscene. The film told the story of an adulterous affair between a middle-aged woman and a young man. The six justices who voted to reverse the obscenity conviction offered five different rationales. In his concurrence in *Jacobellis v. Ohio*, Justice Potter Stewart famously expressed the challenge in creating a clear test for determining obscenity. "I shall not today attempt further to define the kinds of material I understand to be [obscene]; and perhaps I could never succeed in intelligibly doing so," he wrote. "But I know it when I see it, and the motion picture involved in this case is not that."[24] Several decades later, feminist legal scholar Catharine MacKinnon characterized Justice Stewart's now famous statement as a manifestation of his power and credibility.[25] His ability to say simply, "this is how it is" and be believed serves as a reminder of the authority the Supreme Court has to determine what sexual content will and will not be protected by the First Amendment. This was a task that Justice Black argued belonged firmly in the hands of legislators elected to represent the people and not with the judiciary.[26]

In 1973, the Court reconsidered obscenity law again in *Miller v. California* and established the definition of obscenity that remains to this day.[27] Defendant Marvin Miller mass mailed advertising brochures for four adult books and a film to people who had not requested them. The brochures included pictures, drawings and text "very explicitly depicting men and women in groups of two or more engaging in a variety of sexual activities, with genitals often prominently displayed."[28] The manager of a Newport Beach, Calif., restaurant opened the mail one morning with his mother standing at his side. Five brochures slipped out of an unmarked envelope for all to see. The manager called the police. A jury convicted Miller of violating a California statute that forbid the intentional distribution of obscene materials. Miller appealed to the U.S. Supreme Court.

In *Miller*, the justices established a complex, three-part definition of obscenity. Under the *Miller* test, to find material obscene a court must consider whether (1) "the average person, applying contemporary community standards," would find that the work, taken as a whole, appeals to prurient interests; (2) the work depicts or describes, in a patently offensive way, sexual conduct specifically defined by the applicable state law; and (3) the work, taken as a whole, lacks serious literary, artistic, political or scientific value.[29]

A work must meet every part of the test to be obscene. That is, the government must show a work, considered in its entirety, (1) arouses sexual lust, (2) is hard-core pornography and (3) has no serious social value. If the government cannot prove any part of this test, the work is not obscene, and the First Amendment protects it.

INTERNATIONAL LAW

KENYA MOVES TO BAN ALL ONLINE PORNOGRAPHY

Recently, Kenya's Parliament considered a bill that mandated severe punishments for anyone sharing pornography on the internet or via social media.[30] The additions to the existing Computer Misuse and Cybercrimes Act of 2020 would mandate a fine of 20 million Kenyan shillings or a 20-year jail sentence for anyone who shares pornographic material online or who possesses it on their phone or other computer devices.[31] The proposed law also gives the government power to block access to pornographic websites within the country. Pornography is defined here as visual or audio data that depicts people engaged in sexually explicit conduct. The law is aimed in part at addressing the problem of nonconsensual pornography in the country, after several politicians were targeted with sexually explicit content or had nude photos of themselves released publicly.[32] If passed, Kenya will join the 37 other countries that currently ban sexually explicit content online.[33]

Recognizing the limits this bill would place on Kenyans' rights to freedom of expression and access to information, which are guaranteed in Articles 33 and 35 of the Kenyan Constitution, several nongovernmental organizations (NGOs) have reached out to members of Parliament to express their concerns.[34] Article 19, Access Now, Bloggers Association of Kenya, Defenders Coalition, the Kenya ICT Action Network, and the Kenya Union of Journalists all co-signed a memo asking Parliament to reconsider the proposed amendments to the Computer Misuse and Cybercrimes Act. In the memo, the organizations argue that if passed, the bill could be used to "police *content* of a sexual nature—that should only be accessible to adults—that is legitimate and lawful, and protected under the right to free expression."[35]

The *Miller* Test

The first part of the *Miller* test requires showing that an average person would find that the work, taken in its entirety, appeals to prurient interests, or "lustful thoughts." The Court said "prurient" refers to "morbid or lascivious longings."[36] Material arousing morbid or shameful sexual thoughts meets this part of the *Miller* test.

The *Miller* case confirmed what the U.S. Supreme Court held in earlier cases: To determine whether material appeals to prurient interests, the content must be considered as a whole, not as discrete pictures or words. An assessment of whether the material appeals to prurient interests must be based on conclusions drawn by an average person in the community, not a child or a particularly sensitive person.[37] The Court has not explained how a juror can know the standards of an average person. Some courts allow survey results to help jurors understand community attitudes, but not all courts permit social science data as evidence. This ambiguity around what constitutes "prurient interests" means conventional perspectives regarding sexual expression have often been accepted as the norm, leaving judges and juries ample room to criminalize various forms of non-mainstream sexual expression such as BDSM or kink.[38]

Legislatures and courts decide what geographic area comprises the community for setting obscenity standards. The Supreme Court has said the community may be the city or county where jurors live. In the *Miller* decision, the Court allowed California to use statewide standards. Other states, such as Illinois, also have permitted statewide obscenity standards.[39] Even a "deviant sexual group, rather than the public at large," may be a community for determining appropriate standards, the Court has said.[40]

The internet has made the determination of a geographically bound community more challenging. Even so, courts have not established precedent for use of a national standard to determine a community standard.[41] For example, in a case before the Fifth Circuit Court of Appeals, a man found guilty of sharing obscene content with a minor challenged his conviction on grounds that the court improperly applied the community standard.[42] A jury found him guilty of sharing, in an internet chat room, webcam videos of himself masturbating. The recipient of the videos was an undercover police officer posing as a 14-year-old girl.

The man argued that the community standard in his case should have been defined as a national community of people who participate in internet chat rooms. The court rejected his argument, noting that no court has yet set a binding precedent for use of a national standard.[43]

About a decade ago in a case that is an outlier, the Ninth Circuit Court of Appeals suggested that jury instructions could include national community standard considerations.[44] In that case, jurors were instructed to consider contemporary community standards outside of their physical district. The appeals court said that in that instance the jury should have been allowed to apply a national community standard, but the court did not invalidate the jurors' approach of applying their own sense of what contemporary community standards should be.[45]

Several U.S. Supreme Court justices have acknowledged the challenges of applying community standards in the internet age. Where a person sends, receives or accesses content could be wide ranging and have very different community standards. Recently the U.S. Supreme Court recognized that the "national variation in community standards constitutes a particular burden on internet speech."[46] Justice Stephen Breyer said applying "the community standards of every locality in the United States would provide the most puritan of communities with a heckler's internet veto affecting the rest of the Nation."[47] Nonetheless, the U.S. Supreme Court has not adopted a national community standard in cases of internet obscenity, so local and statewide community standards still prevail.

The second part of the *Miller* test requires the government to show the material is **patently offensive** according to state law. In *Miller*, the U.S. Supreme Court provided examples of patent offensiveness: (1) "representations or descriptions of ultimate sexual acts, normal or perverted, actual or simulated" or (2) "representations or descriptions of masturbation, excretory functions and lewd exhibition of the genitals."[48] As in the first part of the *Miller* test, patent offensiveness is to be determined by contemporary community standards, the Court said.

POINTS OF LAW
THE *MILLER* TEST

To find material obscene under the *Miller* test, a court must review the work as a whole, and consider whether

1. "the average person, applying contemporary community standards," would find that the work appeals to prurient interests;
2. the work depicts or describes, in a patently offensive way, sexual conduct specifically defined by the applicable state law; and
3. the work lacks serious literary, artistic, political or scientific value (often called the SLAPS test).[49]

Patently offensive material at least has to include hard-core sexual conduct. The Supreme Court made this clear when it rejected a jury's finding that the 1971 movie "Carnal Knowledge" was obscene.[50] The award-nominated and critically acclaimed movie featured some partial nudity but had no sex scenes. An Albany, Ga., jury convicted a theater operator for showing the film. The Supreme Court said the jury had the right to use local community standards in deciding whether the film appealed to prurient interests. However, the jury could not find that the movie was patently offensive unless at a minimum it met the Supreme Court's understanding of that term, as illustrated by the Court's examples.

The Court has said the *Miller* examples of patently offensive material were not an exhaustive list. Sexually explicit material not included in the Court's list of sexual acts could be patently offensive.[51] "It would be a serious misreading of *Miller* to conclude that juries have unbridled discretion in determining what is 'patently offensive,'" the Court said.[52]

Recently, courts have found Snapchat videos that show genitalia and masturbation are patently offensive,[53] as are photographs of genitalia sent via texts.[54] In both of these cases, the intended recipients of the sexually explicit material were minors.

The third part of the *Miller* obscenity test says material cannot be found obscene if it has serious literary, artistic, political or social value. There is a wide gap between any social value and serious social value. Material falling in the space between "any social value" and "serious social value" could be found obscene if it also meets the first two parts of the *Miller* test.

In Pope v. Illinois, decided after Miller, the U.S. Supreme Court said serious social value should be decided using national standards, not local criteria.[55] The Pope decision also said a determination of serious social value should be based on what a reasonable person would decide. Because this suggests an objective, rather than a subjective, analysis of a work's social value, juries may consider testimony of expert witnesses who express their opinions about a work's social value.

Portrait of American photographer Robert Mapplethorpe.

Photo by Fred W. McDarrah/MUUS Collection via Getty Images

Expert witnesses played a key role in the case against Dennis Barrie, director of the Cincinnati Contemporary Arts Center, who along with the museum, was charged with obscenity for hosting a retrospective of photographer Robert Mapplethorpe's work. Cincinnati was the fourth city on the exhibition's tour of the country. This show was especially timely because Mapplethorpe had recently died of complications from AIDS. His death heightened the importance of his work, much of which focused on his experience as a gay man. At the center of the case were seven of the 175 photos featured in the show. These seven photos, which were displayed in an age-restricted area, documented sadomasochism in the gay community. The museum's attorney brought in art directors from institutions around the country to speak to the value of work like Mapplethorpe's art that challenged conventional values and tastes. The jury was convinced of the photos' artistic value, returning a verdict of not guilty after only two hours of deliberation.[56]

At the request of a county sheriff in Florida, a federal district court found a 2 Live Crew album, "As Nasty as They Wanna Be," to be obscene because of songs such as "Me So Horny" and "Dick Almighty." On review, the Eleventh Circuit Court of Appeals observed that 2 Live Crew presented several expert witnesses at trial who testified the album had serious social value. The sheriff played the album at trial but offered no expert witnesses to support his contention that the recording was obscene. The appellate court said simply listening to a recording was not enough to determine whether the recording possessed serious social value. Expert witnesses' testimony was required.[57]

Testing the *Miller* Test

Although the Miller Test was established in the 1970s as the legal doctrine to determine what kind of sexual content would and would not be protected by the First Amendment, the cultural debate about whether pornographic materials should be prohibited continued. This controversy was colloquially referred to as the "Porn Wars." On one side of the debate were anti-pornography feminist legal scholars like Catharine MacKinnon and Andrea Dworkin, who argued that pornography subordinates women to men and prevents equality, which ultimately leads to sexual discrimination and sexual violence.[58] On the other side were anti-censorship feminists who based their arguments not on a commitment to liberal free speech absolutism, but on a desire to protect unfettered sexual expression, resist stereotypes, and subvert existing sex roles.[59] These activists believed that efforts to censor pornography impeded a woman's right to communicate sexual desire and engage freely with depictions of sexual pleasure.[60]

Anti-pornography feminists in favor of censorship had an unlikely ally in this dispute. Social conservatives, including many Republican senators, were concerned about the increase in availability of pornographic films brought about by VHS technology. In 1986, the Attorney General established a commission to investigate the relationship between violent pornography and aggression toward women. The research focused solely on short-term rather than long-term effects and was criticized as biased. Rather than concerning themselves with women's civil rights, members of the commission sought to negate female empowerment by controlling women's bodies and sexuality.[61]

Catharine MacKinnon

REUTERS/Alamy Stock Photo

While the commission conducted its research, MacKinnon and Dworkin worked with local municipalities to craft statutes that would prohibit violent pornography on the grounds that it violated women's civil rights and created the conditions for workplace sexual harassment and date rape. **Sexual harassment** includes unwelcome sexual advances, requests for sexual favors, and other verbal or physical harassment of a sexual nature. Sexual harassment is unlawful in U.S. workplaces.

With the help of MacKinnon and Dworkin, Indianapolis passed an Antipornography Civil Rights Ordinance, which said that sexually explicit material that depicted women as sexual objects—interpreted as appearing to enjoy pain or humiliation, domination or rape—and otherwise depicted them in sexually subordinate and humiliating roles would be considered a civil rights violation.[62] The statute was ultimately struck down as unconstitutional. Writing for the court majority, Seventh Circuit Judge Frank Easterbrook said that the ordinance discriminated based on viewpoint.[63] Under the proposed law, speech treating women as equals would be considered lawful while speech depicting women as objects that enjoy humiliation would be considered unlawful. It is not the role of the government, said Judge Easterbrook, to prescribe what shall be orthodox in politics, nationalism, religion, or other matters of opinion.[64]

Sexually Explicit Material and Children

More than six decades ago, the U.S. Supreme Court held that government officials may not limit adults to seeing only material acceptable for children. In 1957, the Court struck down a Michigan law making it illegal to distribute sexual material "tending to incite minors to violent or depraved or immoral acts."[65] The Court said the law violated the First Amendment because its effect "is to reduce the adult population of Michigan to reading only what is fit for children."[66]

In 1992, a Florida county sheriff asked a court to find 2 Live Crew's "As Nasty as They Wanna Be" album obscene but did not provide any evidence.

Jeff Kravitz/FilmMagic, Inc./Getty Images

However, the opposite is not true—material not obscene for adults may be obscene if the same material is given to minors. Restricting minors' access to sexual material is sometimes called **variable obscenity**. In *Ginsberg v. New York*, the Court said minors do not have a First Amendment right to sexually explicit material acceptable for adults. Under its power to protect the well-being of minors, the Court said, a state may "adjust the definition of obscenity to social realities."[67]

Under federal law, making, selling, distributing, or possessing child pornography is illegal. Federal law defines **child pornography** as "any visual depiction . . . involving the use of a minor engaging in sexually explicit conduct . . . or such visual depiction [that] has been created . . . to appear that an identifiable minor is engaging in sexually explicit conduct."[68] The question is not whether children are appearing in videos, films, or photographs that would be obscene under the *Miller* test. Rather, the question is whether minors are being sexually exploited. In addition to the federal law, all states and the District of Columbia have child pornography laws.

Courts, Congress, and child welfare organizations have recognized the harm child pornography causes. Harm comes not only from the initial sexual act or depiction but also from the availability of the images. Today, pornographic content can be widely shared through social media. For example, some of the most popular pornography sites on the internet are "tube sites," which allow users to upload their own videos that can then be easily shared.[69]

Nearly four decades ago, in *New York v. Ferber*, the U.S. Supreme Court upheld New York's child pornography law, one of the nation's strictest.[70] Paul Ferber sold pornographic films of young boys to an undercover officer. Hearing Ferber's appeal of his conviction, the Supreme Court said child pornography laws are essential to protecting minors. Using children in sexual material harms minors' "physiological, emotional and mental health," the Court said.[71] First, the children endure psychological harm, knowing there is a permanent record of their participation in sexual activity. Second, making, selling and obtaining pornography showing children in sexual situations helps to perpetuate the sexual exploitation of children and encourages pedophilia.

Federal law is applied to visual depictions and defines child pornography as any image showing minors in "sexually explicit conduct."[72] The conduct may be actual or simulated "sexual intercourse," "masturbation" or lewd "exhibition of the genitals or pubic area."[73]

Courts strictly interpret child pornography laws. "Unlike the Court's obscenity standards, child pornography laws involve no fuzzy facts like 'community standards' or 'artistic value,' and prosecutors can make a case with little more than proof that the defendant possessed or made a visual depiction of sexual conduct by a minor," wrote a First Amendment scholar.[74] For example, a film showed preteen and teenaged girls younger than 17 years old wearing bikinis, leotards or underwear (but not nude) and gyrating to music. The "photographer would zoom in on the children's . . . genital area and display a close-up view for an extended period of time," a federal appellate court said.[75] The film was child pornography. The federal child pornography law does not require nudity, the court said, holding that this broad interpretation of federal law does not make the law unconstitutionally overbroad.[76]

More than 20 years ago, Congress adopted the Child Pornography Prevention Act, criminalizing the possession of digital images of children in sexual poses or activities, even if the images were of young-looking adults and not of real children. The U.S. Supreme Court found the law unconstitutional, noting that two provisions in the law that dealt with virtual images of children were too broad.[77]

Congress tried again and 15 years ago passed the Prosecutorial Remedies and Other Tools to End the Exploitation of Children Today (PROTECT) Act in response to the Supreme Court's decision.[78] The PROTECT Act made it a crime to offer or solicit sexually explicit images of children. The narrow focus of the new law was on pandering. If someone offers material as child pornography, they could be convicted regardless of whether the material uses or depicts real children. Under review, the Supreme Court held that the PROTECT Act was constitutional and did not violate the First Amendment because it was narrowly tailored. The Court noted that "the emergence of new technology and the repeated retransmission of picture files over the internet . . . could make it nearly impossible to prove that a particular image was produced using real children [even though] there is no substantial evidence that any of the child pornography images being trafficked today were made other than by the abuse of real children."[79]

Courts continue to hear cases about child pornography and technology. For example, in 2014, a defendant in the Eighth Circuit Court of Appeals challenged the federal definition of child pornography that includes "visual depictions . . . modified to appear" like a minor engaged in sexual conduct.[80] The defendant argued that the definition was overly broad because morphed images are not real, so sexual abuse cannot occur. The Eighth Circuit disagreed, noting that the government did not have a less restrictive means "to protect this child from the exploitation and psychological harm resulting from the distribution of the morphed image than to prevent [the defendant] from disseminating it."[81]

U.S. law allows child pornography victims to seek restitution not only from the person who created the sexually explicit images but also from those who possess them.[82] The victim may recover for physical and psychological medical services, temporary housing, childcare, lost income, attorney's fees and other expenses. The person who created the images will be liable for these damages.[83] Ten U.S. courts of appeals have ruled that the victim must show that a person who possessed or transmitted the illegal images caused specific harms.[84] The Fifth Circuit Court of Appeals is the only federal appellate court to disagree.[85] It ruled that if the victim showed that they were harmed by the fact that the image was shared, then anyone found guilty of possessing that image might be liable for damages.

In 2014, the U.S. Supreme Court took a closer look at the specific statutory language in the mandatory restitution provision of the federal law[86] and concluded in *Paroline v. United States* that Congress intended to limit restitution to only those losses proximately caused by the defendant.[87] A proximate cause is a cause that most directly produces the effect. The possession of child pornography containing a plaintiff's image, unlike the creation of that image, may not qualify as a proximate cause that entitles the victim to compensation. Or, if it does, it might not justify awarding the full amount of damages the plaintiff claims.

The Supreme Court said a victim should receive restitution only in an amount that represents the extent of loss the defendant caused the victim.[88] The court was split 5–4, with two dissenting opinions. In one, Chief Justice John G. Roberts, joined by Justices Antonin Scalia and Clarence Thomas, argued that the Court's *Paroline* ruling simply asks lower courts to pick "arbitrary" amounts for restitution. That is not "good enough for the criminal law," they said, and would ultimately result in no restitution for victims who are repeatedly victimized in cases when many offenders (sometimes thousands) possess images of the child pornography victim.[89]

In her dissent, Justice Sonia Sotomayor argued that the Court's opinion could not be reconciled with the law Congress passed, which she said requires full restitution for a victim's losses. "Given the very nature of the child pornography market—in which a large class of offenders contribute jointly to their victims' harm by trading their images—[the Court's approach leaves] victims with little hope of recovery," she wrote.[90]

One legal scholar has suggested that restitution for victims of child pornography is not as straightforward as restitution for victims of other criminal acts. She suggested, as did the dissenting justices, that Congress should revisit the law. The appellate courts that have heard these cases have also urged Congress to clarify the language in the law to provide for its consistent application.[91]

REAL WORLD LAW
SEXTING AND TEENS

A recent study assessing sexting rates among middle and high school students in the United States indicated that the practice is on the rise. Sexting is sending someone sexually explicit photographs or messages via a mobile phone. In 2019, 23 percent of middle and high schoolers said they had received a "sext" and 14 percent had sent a sext. About 5 percent said they had a sext shared without their permission.[92]

Sometimes prosecutors classify sexting involving those under 18 years old as child pornography.[93] If the act of sexting is child pornography, those who receive and retain sexually explicit images can be charged with possessing child pornography, a felony under state and federal laws. Currently, 26 states have laws that specifically target sexting.[94] Some state legislatures—including those in Arizona, Connecticut, Louisiana and Illinois—have adopted laws imposing lighter sentences on teenage sexters. Other states, for example Texas and Florida, take a rehabilitative approach to teen sexting and require education and community service as part of their accountability efforts.[95]

Other Considerations

Although courts have upheld laws against making, distributing, selling and exhibiting obscene material, the U.S. Supreme Court said the First Amendment protects possession of obscene material, except child pornography, in the privacy of one's home. More than 50 years ago, overturning a conviction for possessing obscene films, the U.S. Supreme Court in *Stanley v. Georgia* said that merely categorizing films as obscene did not justify "a drastic invasion of personal liberties guaranteed by the First Amendment."[96] Police had found the obscene films during a search of a suspected bookmaker's home. The Court said there are reasons to have obscenity statutes, but the reasons do not allow authorities to "reach into the privacy of one's own home."[97] Government may not tell people what books they may read or films they may watch, the Court said.

Authorities have tried to control obscenity using laws that target organized crime. Fifty years ago, Congress adopted the Racketeer Influenced and Corrupt Organizations Act.[98] Thirty-two states also have RICO acts. The RICO laws forbid using money earned from illegal activities—racketeering—to finance legal or illegal businesses or nonprofit enterprises engaged in interstate commerce.[99]

RICO laws implicate the First Amendment because the laws allow the government to seize all assets acquired through racketeering activity. In one case, the owner of a dozen adult theaters and bookstores was convicted of violating obscenity laws. Under the state's RICO law, authorities seized the contents of the defendant's theaters and bookstores. The defendant claimed the seizure violated his First Amendment rights. In part, he said the seizure amounted to a prior restraint because not all the seized books and his theaters' films were obscene. The Supreme Court disagreed. The seizure was for past criminal acts—selling obscene material, the Supreme Court said.[100] If the defendant wanted to open a new adult bookstore that sold sexually explicit but not obscene material, he could do so in the future. Therefore, there was no prior restraint.

INDECENCY

The U.S. Supreme Court has made clear that the First Amendment does not protect obscenity. Does the First Amendment protect indecency? Indecent speech is protected in print media, in movies, in recordings and on the internet. The Communications Act of 1934 makes it illegal to broadcast indecent material.[101] As with obscenity, the problem is defining "indecency."

According to the U.S. Supreme Court, "The normal definition of 'indecent' merely refers to nonconformance with accepted standards of morality."[102] "Indecency" is not a synonym for "obscenity," the Court said.[103] Rather, indecency is content some people find offensive. Material that is patently offensive but does not have prurient appeal is not obscene, but it may be indecent.[104] Material may also be indecent even if it has serious social value. The FCC once defined indecency as "language or material that, in context, depicts or describes in terms patently offensive as measured by contemporary community standards for the broadcast medium, sexual or excretory activities or organs."[105]

In both the Radio Act of 1927 and the Communications Act of 1934, Congress prohibited broadcasting "any obscene, indecent, or profane language."[106] Congress later eliminated this provision but inserted the ban on indecent broadcasts into the federal criminal code.[107] In 1960, Congress gave the FCC power to impose civil fines on broadcasters who violated the commission's indecency regulations.[108]

The FCC and the courts, with Congress' acquiescence, said the reason for limiting indecent programs on broadcast radio or television is to protect children.[109] For example, in fining a radio station for discussing oral sex during an afternoon program, the commission emphasized "the presence of children in the broadcast audience."[110] The First Amendment protects indecent material in other media because these media can separate children from adults in their audiences. Minors can be prevented from having access to indecent books, magazines and movies, for example. But broadcast radio and television are too pervasive; they are available everywhere, and children continually are exposed to them. Those concerned about indecency, then, had to balance potential harms to children against broadcasters' First Amendment rights.

George Carlin.
AP/Douglas C. Pizac

Federal Communications Commission Regulation

The FCC did not act against indecency until 1975. The commission responded to a father's complaint that he and his young son heard a New York City radio station playing comedian George Carlin's "Filthy Words" monologue at 2 p.m. Carlin's 12-minute live performance contained the seven "words you couldn't say on television."[111] He then said them repeatedly.[112] The FCC fined the station's operator, Pacifica Foundation, for indecency because it broadcast "language that describes, in terms patently offensive as measured by contemporary community standards for the broadcast medium, sexual or excretory activities and organs, at times of the day when there is a reasonable risk that children may be in the audience."[113]

FCC v. Pacifica Foundation (excerpted at the end of the chapter) reached the U.S. Supreme Court, which said broadcasters have First Amendment protection, but the protection is limited because of spectrum scarcity (see Chapter 9). This allows courts to restrict indecency in broadcasting but not in other media, the Court said.

In determining whether the Carlin recording was indecent, the Court said the context of the challenged material is "all-important" and that an "occasional expletive" need not lead to sanctioning a broadcaster.[114] The Court focused on the "repetitive, deliberate use" of words that refer to "excretory or sexual activities or organs" in a "patently offensive" manner.[115] This suggested that indecency applied only to a Carlin-like monologue—defining indecency as "filthy words." The Court emphasized radio and television's "uniquely pervasive presence in the lives of all Americans" and focused on children. The nature of broadcasting made it "uniquely accessible to children, even those too young to read." That concern and the specific facts of the case—Carlin's repeatedly saying the seven words—justified the FCC's fining the radio station, the Court said.[116]

For a decade after *Pacifica*, the FCC defined indecency as the intentional repetition of dirty words. The commission said, "[D]eliberate and repetitive use in a patently offensive manner is a requisite to a finding of indecency."[117] When the words were only expletives—a single swear word or exclamation—the use was not indecent.

In 1987, the FCC expressed concern that the "filthy words" indecency definition did not sufficiently protect children. The commission adopted a new, broader standard to define indecency.[118] The commission said it would consider a broadcast's context and tone as well as its language.[119] Because the *Pacifica* Court did not define "patently offensive" as measured by "community standards for the broadcast medium," broadcasters had little guidance beyond knowing the seven words Carlin used in his monologue.[120]

About 20 years ago, the FCC tried to clarify its indecency standard by adopting broadcast industry indecency guidelines. The commission again said material is indecent if it met the generic *Pacifica* test, adding that it would consider several factors in determining whether broadcast material was patently offensive: (1) how explicitly or graphically the material described sexual activities, (2) whether the material dwelt on sexual activities, and (3) whether the material was meant to shock or sexually excite the audience. The FCC said it would consider the full context in which the material appeared.[121]

U2 lead singer Bono.

Axelle/Bauer-Griffin/FilmMagic/Getty Images

Just two years after the FCC adopted the new indecency guidelines, it took action against several live broadcasts that would bring more refinement to the FCC's indecency standard. At the 2003 Golden Globes Awards, U2 lead singer Bono said, "This is really, really, fucking brilliant," in accepting an award. Viewer complaints poured in to the FCC. The FCC enforcement bureau concluded that the singer's comment was not indecent because it did not describe a sexual activity and the utterance was "fleeting and isolated."[122] The full commission reviewed and then reversed that decision.

In doing so, the FCC asserted for the first time that a "fleeting expletive"—a single, nonliteral use of a curse word—could be indecent.[123] The FCC said the "'F-Word' is one of the most vulgar, graphic and explicit descriptions of sexual activity in the English language," and therefore "inherently has a sexual connotation." The decision overruled previous decisions that did not find a fleeting expletive indecent.

Shortly after making its decision about Bono's use of a fleeting expletive at the Golden Globes, the FCC determined that two Billboard Music Awards programs were patently offensive because two celebrities uttered fleeting expletives that were shocking and gratuitous. Singer and actress Cher's unscripted exclamation in 2002—"People have been telling me I'm on the way out every year, right? So fuck 'em"—and television personality Nicole Richie's remark at the 2003 awards—"Have you ever tried to get cow shit out of a Prada purse? It's not so fucking simple"—were both found to be indecent and profane.[124]

On appeal, the Second Circuit Court of Appeals rejected the FCC's decision, saying the commission "failed to adequately explain why it had changed its nearly-30-year policy on fleeting expletives." The court noted that the FCC ruling "bore 'no rational connection to the Commission's actual policy,' because the FCC had not instituted a blanket ban on expletives."[125]

The U.S. Supreme Court overturned the Second Circuit's decision. The Supreme Court said the FCC did not act arbitrarily or capriciously and supplied sufficient reasons for its new policy. The FCC admitted it overturned a long-standing regulation that a single, fleeting expletive was not indecent. But the commission said the "F-Word" has a sexual meaning no matter how it is used, a meaning that insults and offends. That was enough justification for the Court, in a 5–4 decision, to uphold the FCC's new rule.[126]

The Supreme Court sent the case back to the Second Circuit, which on rehearing accepted a new argument from broadcasters—that the fleeting-expletives rule violated their First Amendment rights. This was a question the Supreme Court had not addressed.[127] The appellate court held that the commission's fleeting-expletives policy violated the First Amendment because it was vague, not allowing broadcasters to know what content would be found indecent and thus causing a chilling effect. The court said the chilling effect went beyond the fleeting-expletives regulation, forcing broadcasters not to take risks but rather to self-censor content that might or might not be found indecent under the FCC's definition.[128]

The FCC appealed the Second Circuit's decision to the U.S. Supreme Court. In 2012, the Supreme Court told the FCC it could not fine broadcasters for carrying the Bono, Cher and Richie utterances because the FCC adopted the fleeting-expletives rule after those programs were aired.[129] The Court also said broadcasters could not be held liable for violating a rule they did not know would change. The Supreme Court did not determine whether indecency regulations infringe broadcasters' First Amendment rights. The Court also did not define indecency, nor did it give the FCC guidance for defining indecency. Aside from telling the FCC it could not apply new rules retroactively, the Court did no more than say the FCC may modify its indecency regulations, considering the public interest and legal requirements, and courts may review the current or modified indecency rules when appropriate cases arise.[130]

While the question about whether Bono, Cher and Richie's fleeting expletives were indecent was bouncing back and forth in the courts, Justin Timberlake ever-so-briefly (for 9/16 of one second) accidentally exposed one of Janet Jackson's breasts during the 2004 Super Bowl halftime show. A frenzy ensued. Congress increased the maximum fine the FCC could impose for broadcasting indecent material "by a factor of 10."[131] Reacting to public and congressional outrage, the FCC said Jackson's partial nudity violated its indecency standard and imposed $550,000 in fines against Viacom-owned television stations that aired the Super Bowl.[132] Viacom, Inc. owns CBS, the network that carried the Super Bowl in 2004.

The Third Circuit Court of Appeals overturned the commission's decision, saying that for three decades the FCC punished broadcasters for indecent programming only when the material was "so pervasive as to amount to 'shock treatment' for the audience. . . . [T]he Commission consistently explained that isolated or fleeting material did not fall within the scope of actionable indecency."[133]

The U.S. Supreme Court told the Third Circuit to reconsider its decision in light of its 2009 ruling concerning Bono, Cher and Richie's fleeting expletives.[134] In 2011, the Third Circuit issued a new ruling that said the 2009 *Fox* decision supported its conclusion in the Super Bowl case that the FCC could not impose fines for airing a fleeting image of Jackson's breast.[135] However, both the FCC and the U.S. Supreme Court acknowledged that the commission changed the definition of indecency in its fleeting-expletives ruling, which applied to both words and images. Additionally, as with the Bono, Cher and Richie broadcasts, the Jackson incident occurred before the FCC announced its new fleeting-expletives rule, so the CBS network and stations could not have anticipated the change. On this basis, the Third Circuit affirmed its previous ruling that the FCC could not impose fines for airing a fleeting image of Jackson's breast. The Supreme Court refused to hear an appeal of the Third Circuit's 2011 decision.

The Supreme Court's 2012 *Fox Television* decision (excerpted at the end of this chapter) and the Court's refusal to review the Third Circuit's Super Bowl ruling left broadcasters with little guidance. The Court gave the FCC a suggestion, though, when it said in *Fox Television*, "[T]his opinion leaves the Commission free to modify its current indecency policy in light of its determination of the public interest and applicable legal requirements."[136] In 2013, the FCC began reconsidering its indecency regulations again. The commission sought public comment on whether the FCC should change its broadcast indecency policies but failed to take any action and has not revisited its indecency policies since the public comment period more than seven years ago.[137]

The FCC has issued few indecency rulings or fines since the Supreme Court's 2012 *Fox Television* decision. One notable fine occurred in 2015, after the FCC concluded that a local Roanoke, Va., station was liable for accidentally airing three seconds of a sexually explicit, pornographic video clip.[138] The station broadcast a news story about a porn star who volunteered with a local rescue organization. It intended to use an acceptable still image from a porn website, but instead the image came with boxes that auto-loaded pornographic films. As a result, the station accidentally aired an image of a naked man with "a hand moving up and down the length of the shaft of the erect penis."[139] The FCC fined the station the maximum $325,000.[140]

Since then, the FCC has received complaints from viewers about particular broadcasts but has been reluctant to act on these. In 2020, the FCC received over 1,300 complaints about Shakira and Jennifer Lopez's Super Bowl performance. The show included belly dancing, pole dancing, and sexually suggestive gestures some viewers felt were not appropriate for children.[141] The previous year, Adam Levine appeared without a shirt in his Super Bowl halftime show. That performance generated only 94 complaints to the FCC.[142]

In all of the U.S. Supreme Court decisions about broadcasting and indecency, the Court balanced a broadcaster's free speech rights against concerns for children. In 1993, the FCC adopted a safe harbor policy to comply with a congressional mandate. The **safe harbor policy** holds that the FCC will not punish a broadcast station that airs indecent, but not obscene, material between 10 p.m. and 6 a.m. local time.[143] With court approval, the FCC agreed not to take action against indecent broadcasts aired at a time when few children should be in the audience.[144] That decision was put to the test in 2017 when *The Late Show* host Stephen Colbert made a joke in his monologue that said the only thing then President Trump's mouth was good for was "being Vladimir Putin's cock holster."[145] Despite receiving a number of complaints, the FCC's Enforcement Bureau concluded that the incident was not actionable since it occurred after 10 p.m., which is during the safe harbor time period.

Shakira and Jennifer Lopez perform onstage during the 2020 Super Bowl Halftime Show.

Jeff Kravitz/Contributor/Getty

As noted in Chapter 9, the FCC regulates multichannel video programming distributors differently from broadcasting. Before the FCC created the current MVPD definition and framework, its indecency decisions focused on cable.

HBO's development in 1975 spurred cable's popularity. Certain movies that HBO showed offended some state legislators and local officials, and by the early 1980s they adopted laws forbidding cable indecency. Courts uniformly rejected these restrictions. For example, a Miami, Fla., ordinance prohibited cable systems from distributing "obscene or indecent" material.[146] A federal appellate court said the *Pacifica* restrictions on broadcasting indecent material did not apply to cable television. Parents could prevent their children from watching cable television by not subscribing.

REAL WORLD LAW
TECHNOLOGY AND PARENTAL CONTROL

When Congress passed the Telecommunications Act of 1996, it required all television manufacturers to include an electronic chip that would allow parents to block reception of certain programs they did not want their children to view. The V-chip, as it was commonly known, was heralded as a big step toward reducing a minor's exposure to sex, violence and vulgar language.[147]

Various studies showed that the V-chip did not work well with the Federal Communications Commission ratings system that also emerged at the time. That voluntary ratings system still exists to help parents know what audience is appropriate for a program, from TV-MA (for mature audiences) to TV-Y (for the youngest audience).[148]

Today, V-chip technology is considered a relic, and concerns about the content children consume have focused on social media channels like YouTube. After complaints that children might accidentally stumble across YouTube user-created graphic parody videos tied to popular children's programs like "Peppa Pig," YouTube introduced filters and age restrictions and created a special app for children's content called YouTube Kids.[149]

In 2019, after reports of sexual predatory behavior arose, YouTube disabled its comments function from tens of millions of videos that featured minors.[150] Investigations showed that YouTube's filter algorithm directed people to videos of young children playing once someone started searching related terms, which sent people down "a wormhole into a soft-core pedophile ring."[151]

The court also said the Miami law was overbroad because it did not allow any period when a cable system could transmit indecent material. Courts struck down several similar laws that the Utah Legislature and many Utah cities adopted to ban indecent material on cable television.[152] Congress adopted the first federal law regulating cable in 1984 but did not use the statute to limit indecent content on cable television. Rather, the law said only that cable systems could not transmit obscene material.[153] The 1984 Cable Communications Policy Act's one concession to those concerned about indecency was to require cable system operators to provide a method for subscribers to block individual cable channels.[154]

The FCC has not attempted to extend its broadcast indecency regulations to cable television.[155] However, more than 25 years ago, Congress decided that indecent cable content required its attention. A 1992 federal law included three provisions limiting indecent content on two specific types of cable channels. First, Congress allowed cable operators to ban indecent programming on the cable channels provided for community, local school and government agency use, the PEG access channels. Second, the law said cable systems could ban any programming a cable operator believed "describes or depicts sexual or excretory activities or organs in a patently offensive manner" from the cable channels individuals and companies could rent to display their own content, the leased-access channels (see Chapter 9).

In *Denver Area Educational Telecommunications Consortium, Inc. v. Federal Communications Commission*,[156] the U.S. Supreme Court upheld the leased-access provision. However, the Court said cable systems could not prohibit indecent programming on PEG access channels.[157]

The Court's *Denver Area* decision was fractious. Even when a group of justices agreed on a result, they could not agree on a reason for the outcome. Subsequently, Congress continued its efforts to limit indecency on PEG access channels. In the Telecommunications Act of 1996, Congress said cable operators could not exercise editorial control over PEG content, but they "may refuse to transmit any public access program or portion of a public access program which contains obscenity, indecency, or nudity."[158] This provision has yet to be challenged in court.

The U.S. Supreme Court overturned other sections of the 1996 act dealing with sexually explicit cable programming. Congress required cable operators to scramble the signal of any indecent programming on adult-oriented channels.[159] In part, Congress said, this was to prevent adult programming signals from bleeding into channels that children could see even in homes that did not subscribe to adult channels. Alternatively, Congress said, cable programmers could offer adult programming only during hours when children are unlikely to be watching. The FCC said the period would be 10 p.m. to 6 a.m.[160]

A unanimous Supreme Court said those provisions of the 1996 act were content-based regulations requiring a strict scrutiny analysis.[161] Protecting children from exposure to sexually explicit programming was a compelling state interest, but Congress had not adopted the least restrictive approach. Instead, the Court said, cable subscribers could ask cable companies to block channels and request the mechanism to block channels themselves. The availability of these alternatives made the 1996 act's scrambling and late-night provisions unconstitutional, the Court ruled.

Promotional Poster for the Netflix Show, Cuties

PictureLux/The Hollywood Archive / Alamy Stock Photo

Today, more Americans subscribe to digital streaming services than to paid TV subscriptions.[162] Despite the incredible popularity of platforms like Netflix, the FCC has not sought to extend indecency regulations to these streaming services.[163] The justifications that support regulating broadcast content, such as spectrum scarcity and ubiquity, simply do not apply. However, that doesn't mean that consumers have no concerns about sexually explicit content that appears on streaming services. In 2020, Netflix came under fire for hosting the award-winning French film "Cuties" on its platform. Citizens and politicians, like Texas Senator Ted Cruz, said that the film sexualized young girls. The film tells the story of an 11-year-old Senegalese girl living in Paris struggling to understand the hypersexualized portrayals of women that dominate Western culture.[164] Netflix responded to the criticism by encouraging people to watch the film before they decided whether or not to jump on the #cancelnetflix bandwagon. Netflix said that the film offered a social commentary against the sexualization of young children.[165] Despite the company's efforts, the controversy resulted in an eight-fold increase in cancellations of Netflix subscriptions in the U.S. compared to the previous year.[166] The ability to simply cancel your subscription and remove Netflix from your home demonstrates the stark differences that exist between broadcast television and streaming services.

OBSCENITY, INDECENCY AND THE INTERNET

The internet has made it easy to access sexually explicit content. For example, Pornhub, the most popular pornography video-sharing website, reported 130 million daily visits to the site annually, numbers which increased during the COVID-19 pandemic.[167] According to one legal scholar, society remains mostly concerned with protecting nonconsenting adults and children from sexually explicit content. He notes, "[T]he government can constitutionally prohibit the sale or exhibition to children of material that is obscene for minors, but only if it can do so without significantly interfering with the rights of adults." He adds that the government can prohibit the production, distribution and possession of child pornography. "Beyond that, though, there are effectively no limits on what consenting adults can see" in the internet age.[168]

Congress first attempted to regulate internet indecency with the Communications Decency Act, Title V of the Telecommunications Act of 1996.[169] The CDA made it illegal to knowingly transmit "obscene or indecent messages to any recipient under 18 years of age" or to make available "patently offensive messages" to anyone under 18 years old.

The U.S. Supreme Court rejected the indecency provision of the CDA, finding it unconstitutionally overbroad in *Reno v. American Civil Liberties Union*.[170] The Supreme Court first said that, unlike broadcasting, the internet had full First Amendment protection. The internet is not limited by spectrum scarcity, as is broadcasting. Also, the internet is not as intrusive as broadcasting. Families not wanting children to access the internet at home need not subscribe to an internet service provider, the Court said. For these reasons, the Court refused to find the internet bound by the *Pacifica* case and rejected the CDA's complete ban on indecent internet content.

Because the CDA directly restricted speech, the Court used a strict scrutiny analysis. The Court acknowledged that Congress had a compelling interest in protecting children from sexually explicit content. But the Court decided the law was too sweeping. The CDA denied adults access to protected speech as a way to prevent minors from being exposed to potentially harmful content. The Court noted that (at that time) there was no technology allowing adults to see internet material while preventing children from doing so. The Court also said the CDA was overbroad because Congress had not carefully defined the words "indecent" and "offensive."[171] The Court's decision did not apply to the CDA's restriction on sending obscene material over the internet. This limitation remains part of the federal law.

Congress enacted the Child Online Protection Act in 1998, intending to correct the CDA's constitutional problems.[172] Courts consistently have found the COPA unconstitutional. The COPA differed from the CDA in two important ways. First, the COPA banned internet distribution to children of material "harmful to minors," defined in part as being designed to pander to prurient interest, determined by applying contemporary community standards. Second, the COPA's restriction on transmitting harmful content applied only to people intending to profit from using the internet. The law also defined minors as 16 and younger, not 17 and younger.

The COPA definition of harmful to minors resembled the *Miller* obscenity definition. This meant the COPA affected a narrower range of materials than did the CDA. But the definition focused on all materials inappropriate for minors, so the COPA reduced adult access to only materials appropriate for children—just as the CDA had.

Courts consistently found the COPA unconstitutional. Challenges to the COPA stayed in the courts for a decade until it was ruled definitively unconstitutional in 2009.[173]

Even before Congress adopted the COPA, it took another, indirect route to keep sexual material off the internet. The Child Pornography Prevention Act, adopted in 1996, made it illegal to send or possess digital images of child pornography.[174] The law made it illegal to send or possess an image that "is, or appears to be, of a minor engaging in sexually explicit conduct," or if the image is advertised or distributed in a way "that conveys the impression" that a minor is "engaging in sexually explicit conduct."[175]

The U.S. Supreme Court said the CPPA abridged First Amendment rights and found it unconstitutional.[176] In *Ashcroft v. Free Speech Coalition*, the Court said the language making it illegal to send or possess images that were not obscene was overbroad. The law would prevent adults from seeing constitutionally protected content in order to block children's exposure. Because the CPPA was a content-based regulation, the Supreme Court applied strict scrutiny. It said Congress had a compelling interest in protecting children from being involved in the sex trade. However, the Court said, since computer-generated pictures of minors are outlawed, the CPPA would prohibit child pornography that does not harm an actual child. That also would be true when adults who appear to be children are pictured.

As noted earlier in the chapter, Congress adopted the PROTECT Act of 2003 in response to the Court's decision.[177] The PROTECT Act makes it illegal to provide someone with or request from someone an image that "is indistinguishable from that of a minor" in a sexual situation. This wording differs from the "appears to be" and "conveys the impression" language in the CPPA. In 2008, the Supreme Court found the PROTECT Act constitutional. The Court said the act focused not on the material but on the speech—offering or requesting child pornography—that could put the material into distribution. The First Amendment does not protect offers to engage in illegal transactions, the Court said, because offering to give or receive unlaw-ful material has no social value.[178]

In addition to the PROTECT Act, the U.S. Supreme Court found constitutional one other congressional attempt to deal with online content. Congress enacted the Children's Internet Protection Act in 2000. This law focused on schools and libraries that receive fed-eral money. The CIPA would stop federal funding from going to schools and libraries that did not install "technology protection measures" on their computers with internet access. Those schools and libraries wanting to continue receiving federal funds would have to install filtering software that blocked obscenity, child pornography or material "harmful to minors."[179]

The Supreme Court held in *United States v. American Library Association* that Congress had the right to set conditions for receipt of federal money.[180] The Court said public libraries already choose to purchase or not purchase certain books and other materials. For example, most librar-ies exclude pornographic material from their print collections, the Court said. Limiting what internet sites were available on the computers that libraries provided to the public was an equiva-lent decision. The Court also said requiring adults to ask a librarian to unblock a computer did not infringe on adults' First Amendment rights.

In 2017, Congress, state governments and the courts turned their attention to websites that feature "adult sections" through which advertisers solicit sexual services. Backpage.com and Craigslist are the two websites that have received the most attention. For example, in 2017, a Senate investigative committee concluded that Backpage was knowingly assisting human traf-fickers. Backpage called the subcommittee's findings "unconstitutional government censor-ship."[181] Soon after, however, the website said it would close its adult section while it fought several lawsuits in federal courts.[182]

Sex workers and activists stage a protest against FOSTA-SESTA legislation.

Future Publishing/Contributor/Getty

In Washington and Massachusetts, Backpage successfully argued that the First Amendment protected it from enforcement of state laws that created criminal liability for anyone who knowingly advertises "sexual abuse of a minor."[183] Backpage argued that the law would chill permissible ads and that Section 230 of the CDA (see Chapter 5) protected it from liability. Federal courts have agreed.

In 2018, former President Trump signed a bill into law that ended the protection that Section 230 provided for Backpage and others who allowed third-party users to sell sex-related services on their sites. The Allow States and Victims to Fight Online Sex Trafficking Act of 2017, known as FOSTA, allows victims to sue websites that knowingly supported sex trafficking on their sites. The law amended Section 230 by removing protection for online companies for content they host on their websites or services as it relates to the sexual exploitation of children and/or sex trafficking.[184] "Removing the unwarranted shield from legal responsibility will save countless children from horrific tragedy, both physical and emotional," one of the bill's co-sponsors said.[185]

Upon passage of the bill, Craigslist suspended its "personals" section, writing,

> US Congress just passed [a bill] seeking to subject websites to criminal and civil liability when third parties (users) misuse online personals unlawfully. Any tool or service can be misused. We can't take such risk without jeopardizing all our other services, so we are regretfully taking craigslist personals offline.[186]

While law enforcement officials praised the shutdown of adult-oriented advertising, such as what appeared on Backpage, they also said the platform had been a key tool for identifying and charging sexual predators. Sex workers said they used the sites for screening, providing them some additional protections from violence.[187] Legal experts have raised concerns about broader harms FOSTA might cause to Section 230 immunity for websites and internet service providers and also suggested the law was overbroad and violated the First Amendment.[188]

Several organizations, including anti-trafficking advocates, civil liberties groups and technology scholars, challenged the law on the grounds that it violates the First Amendment because it is overbroad. The D.C. Circuit Court of Appeals originally dismissed their suit[189] but the plaintiffs appealed and in January 2020, the D.C. Circuit Court of Appeals ruled that two of the plaintiffs had standing to pursue their constitutional challenge to the statute.[190] In the meantime, cases against social media companies who allegedly failed to remove content associated with sex trafficking are moving forward. A District Court in California allowed a claim against Twitter to move forward under the FOSTA exception. The plaintiffs in that case allege that Twitter failed to remove links to sexually explicit videos created by teens who had been solicited for sex trafficking and manipulated into participating in the videos.[191]

FOSTA represents one of the only carve outs for immunity from Section 230. Under the current regulatory framework, social media platforms and other computer services are not liable for illegal content posted to their sites by users. While these organizations must adhere to existing laws, such as those prohibiting obscenity or child pornography, as private virtual spaces they are free to regulate far more sexual content than the government can. As a result, most social media platforms such as Instagram or TikTok prohibit posting sexually explicit images or video, as well as content containing nudity. Each platform creates its own community standards and then uses a combination of artificial intelligence and community flagging to enforce those rules.[192] For example, Instagram prohibits nudity along with "photos, videos, and some digitally-created content that show sexual intercourse, genitals, and close-ups of fully-nude buttocks." It also prohibits some photos of female nipples, but photos in the context of breastfeeding, birth giving and after-birth moments, health-related situations or an act of protest are allowed. Users are also prohibited from sharing links to external pornographic websites such as OnlyFans.

Nyome Nicholas-Williams

PA Images/Alamy Stock Photo

Unlike laws, social media platforms' community standards around sexually explicit content are often vague, and their application can be biased. In 2020, Instagram repeatedly deleted and blocked content from African American plus-size model Nyome Nicholas-Williams for violating the company's policy on nudity while leaving similar content from petite, white women on the platform without penalty. This sparked a groundswell of online activism centered around the hashtag #IWantToSeeNyome and forced Instagram to address important questions about racial bias in content moderation. The company acknowledged that their policy, which prohibited "pornographic images of people 'squeezing' their breasts," had been incorrectly applied and moved to amend the policy to allow pictures of people hugging or cupping their breasts.[193]

In addition to being biased in their application, internet platforms' policies on obscene and pornographic content can also be too vague for users to understand. Research into the video game streaming platform Twitch found that the company addressed sexual content and related issues in six different public-facing policy documents but offered no concrete definition of sexual content in any of those documents.[194] Twitch's policies are also contradictory. The company allows in-game nudity to be streamed on their platform but prohibits streamers from wearing "sexually suggestive attire" on camera.[195]

EMERGING LAW

Although it doesn't necessarily violate the *Miller Test* for obscenity, the regulation of nonconsensual pornography or "revenge porn," particularly that which is created using artificial intelligence, represents the most pressing challenge within this area of law.

Nonconsensual pornography refers to the disclosure of sexually explicit images and video without consent and for no legitimate purpose.[196] According to a 2017 nationwide study, one in every eight social media users has been targets of nonconsensual pornography.[197] Research has also shown that women are one-and-a-half times more likely than men to be victims of nonconsensual pornography.[198]

The release of sexually explicit images or video without a person's consent causes social and individual harms.[199] At a societal level, the prevalence of nonconsensual pornography normalizes nonconsensual sexual activity and sexual surveillance.[200] The threat of releasing sexually explicit photos or video has been used as a tool to degrade women.

In June 2019, The Daily Caller, a right-wing news and opinion website founded by Fox News host Tucker Carlson, posted a link to a photo on Twitter, which The Daily Caller said "some people described as a nude selfie of Alexandria Ocasio-Cortez."[201] The photo, which showed a woman's feet and bare legs in a bath, was overlaid with text claiming it was posted on Instagram by Representative Ocasio-Cortez, a progressive Democrat from New York who often finds herself at odds with conservative politicians and commentators.

The photo, which had been circulated on sites like Reddit and 4chan for weeks, actually featured a woman named Sydney Leathers. Representative Ocasio-Cortez tweeted about the incident, chastising Republicans and The Daily Caller for circulating a fake nude photo of her and noting that "Women in leadership face more scrutiny. Period."[202]

Nonconsensual pornography also plays a role in intimate partner violence. In addition, victims of nonconsensual pornography are regularly threatened with sexual assault, stalked, harassed, fired from their jobs or forced to change schools.[203] Before states enacted laws criminalizing nonconsensual pornography, some individuals were able to monetize the distribution of sexually explicit images shared without consent. In 2010, Hunter Moore launched IsAnyoneUp.com, the first and arguably most notorious revenge porn site.[204] Moore solicited nonconsensual pornography for the site and along with the nude images or video, posted victims' full names, their cities of residence, and their social media account information.[205] By 2014, there were an estimated 3,000 internet sites dedicated to nonconsensual pornography.[206] Many of these sites made money not just from advertising and merchandise, but they also began to charge victims to remove the images.[207]

Recently, a group of scholars and activists including Mary Anne Franks and Danielle Citron, formed the Cyber Civil Rights Initiative. Through their work, and the work of victims' rights attorneys like Carrie Goldberg, along with victims who told their stories, states began to adopt legislation that prohibited nonconsensual pornography.

In 2021, 48 states and the District of Columbia had laws criminalizing nonconsensual pornography.[208] The laws vary from state to state. Some states designate a first offense as a misdemeanor while others consider it a felony. Many states also have exceptions for nonconsensual pornography shared in the name of the public interest. Former Congresswoman Katie Hill resigned from her post in 2019 after sexually explicit pictures of her and a staffer were leaked to the press, allegedly by her ex-husband.[209] Hill sued her ex-husband, along with the British tabloid The Daily Mail and the conservative media outlet RedState for violating California's nonconsensual pornography laws. A Los Angeles Superior Court judge ruled that the nude images could be published against her will because they were "a matter of public issue or public interest." Not only did Hill lose the case, but she was also ordered to pay $220,000 in legal fees to the media outlets she had sued.[210]

States' nonconsensual pornography laws have been challenged on First Amendment grounds. In 2019, the Illinois State Supreme Court upheld the state's law against nonconsensual pornography, ruling that prohibiting the dissemination of private sexual images without consent did not unconstitutionally restrict freedom of speech.[211] The Minnesota Supreme Court handed down a similar ruling in 2020. The court said the Minnesota nonconsensual pornography statute passed strict scrutiny and therefore did not violate the First Amendment.[212]

Given the nuances of each state's laws, the Cyber Civil Rights Initiative and other activist organizations are lobbying for a national law against nonconsensual pornography. In addition to addressing inconsistencies, a national law would help states combat the growing problem of nonconsensual pornography created using deepfake technology. Currently, only California's and Virginia's nonconsensual pornography laws address manipulated media.[213]

The term **"deepfake"** comes from a combination of the phrases deep learning and fake.[214] It refers to the fabricated but incredibly convincing images, videos and audio recordings that can be created using facial mapping and artificial intelligence technology.[215] Essentially, this software enables users to superimpose one person's face onto another person's body, manipulating the image so that the visual and audio components appear completely real.[216]

Deepfaked pornography began attracting public attention in 2017, when a Reddit user named "deepfakes," used TensorFlow, a tool created by Google to develop artificial intelligence algorithms, to transpose Gal Gadot's and other celebrities' faces onto the bodies of actors in pornographic videos. Today, there are millions of deepfaked pornographic films and images online and most of those, approximately 90 percent, feature women.[217] Some websites have taken marginal steps to prohibit and remove deepfakes created using photos of non-consenting individuals.[218] Reddit, for example, banned its deepfake subreddit and Twitter and Pornhub have both banned deep faked videos. Apps such as DeepNude, which are used to digitally "strip" the clothes off women have also been banned, but the underlying code remains available in open-source repositories.[219]

It's not just celebrities who are targeted, but also social media influencers and private individuals, including some underage girls.[220] Under the current legal framework there are very few remedies available to victims. Celebrities may be able to bring right of publicity claims (see

Chapter 6) against the creators while private individuals could potentially sue for appropriation. If a copyrighted photo or video is used in deepfaked pornographic content, intellectual property (see Chapter 11) laws may apply. If a victim can prove the deepfaked photo or video was meant to harm or blackmail them, then they may be able to bring criminal harassment or extortion charges. However, the anonymous nature of the online environment makes it almost impossible for law enforcement officials to find and charge the individuals responsible for creating and disseminating this content.[221] The fact that there are legitimate uses for this technology in filmmaking and other industries also makes it difficult to regulate. Despite this, activists are working toward a federal nonconsensual pornography law that includes punishments for deepfaked sexual content, while simultaneously addressing First Amendment concerns.

KEYTERMS

child pornography

deepfake

Hicklin rule

indecency

nonconsensual pornography

obscenity

patently offensive

pornography

prurient interest

safe harbor

safe harbor policy

serious social value

sexual harassment

variable obscenity

CASES FOR STUDY
THINKING ABOUT THEM

The two case excerpts that follow offer the U.S. Supreme Court's definition of indecency and demonstrate how the FCC has applied the concept of indecency in specific contexts over time. As you read these case excerpts, keep the following questions in mind:

- Is the rationale of protecting children and the intrusiveness of broadcasting in the home, put forth by the Court in *FCC v. Pacifica Foundation*, still relevant today? Could new technologies and different ways to deliver content such as George Carlin's monologue change the outcome in this case if it were heard by the Supreme Court today?
- Considering the different views from the justices in *Pacifica Foundation*, what are the various ways that each sees indecency as distinct from obscenity with respect to the First Amendment?
- In *FCC v. Fox Television Stations, Inc.*, does the Supreme Court clearly justify why the law forbids indecency?
- If you oversaw a broadcast channel, would you have enough specific guidance from the *Fox* decision to help you determine how to avoid getting fined for airing indecent content? Why or why not?

FEDERAL COMMUNICATIONS COMMISSION V. PACIFICA FOUNDATION

SUPREME COURT OF THE UNITED STATES 438 U.S. 726 (1978)

JUSTICE JOHN PAUL STEVENS delivered the Court's opinion:

This case requires that we decide whether the Federal Communications Commission has any power to regulate a radio broadcast that is indecent but not obscene.

A satiric humorist named George Carlin recorded a 12-minute monologue entitled "Filthy Words" before a live audience in a California theater. He began by referring to his thoughts about "the words you couldn't say on the public, ah, airwaves, um, the ones you definitely wouldn't say, ever." He proceeded to list those words and repeat them over and over again in a variety of colloquialisms. The transcript of the recording . . . indicates frequent laughter from the audience.

At about 2 o'clock in the afternoon on Tuesday, October 30, 1973, a New York radio station, owned by respondent Pacifica Foundation, broadcast the "Filthy Words" monologue. A few weeks later a man, who stated that he had heard the broadcast while driving with his young son, wrote a letter complaining to the Commission. . . .

The complaint was forwarded to the station for comment. In its response, Pacifica explained that the monologue had been played during a program about contemporary society's attitude toward language and that, immediately before its broadcast, listeners had been advised that it included "sensitive language which might be regarded as offensive to some." Pacifica characterized George Carlin as "a significant social satirist" who . . . "examines the language of ordinary people. . . . Carlin is not mouthing obscenities, he is merely using words to satirize as harmless and essentially silly our attitudes towards those words."
. . .

On February 21, 1975, the Commission issued a declaratory order granting the complaint and holding that Pacifica "could have been the subject of administrative sanctions." The Commission did not impose formal sanctions. . . .

In its memorandum opinion the Commission stated that it intended to "clarify the standards which will be utilized in considering" the growing number of complaints about indecent speech on the airwaves. Advancing several reasons for treating broadcast speech differently from other forms of expression, the Commission found a power to regulate indecent broadcasting in two statutes, [one] which forbids the use of "any obscene, indecent, or profane language by means of radio communications," and [another] which requires the Commission to "encourage the larger and more effective use of radio in the public interest."

The Commission characterized the language used in the Carlin monologue as "patently offensive," though not necessarily obscene, and expressed the opinion that it should be regulated by principles analogous to those found in the law of nuisance. . . .

Applying these considerations to the language used in the monologue as broadcast by respondent, the Commission concluded that certain words depicted sexual and excretory activities in a patently offensive manner, noted that they "were broadcast at a time when children were undoubtedly in the audience (i.e., in the early afternoon)," and that the prerecorded language, with these offensive words "repeated over and over," was "deliberately broadcast." In summary, the Commission stated: "We therefore hold that the language as broadcast was indecent and prohibited."

After the order issued, the Commission was asked to clarify its opinion by ruling that the broadcast of indecent words as part of a live newscast would not be prohibited. The Commission issued another opinion in which it pointed out that it "never intended to place an absolute prohibition on the broadcast of this type of language, but rather sought to channel it to times of day when children most likely would not be exposed to it." The Commission noted that its "declaratory order was issued in a specific factual context," and declined to comment on various hypothetical situations presented by the petition. It relied on its "long standing policy of refusing to issue interpretive rulings or advisory opinions when the critical facts are not explicitly stated or there is a possibility that subsequent events will alter them."

The United States Court of Appeals for the District of Columbia Circuit reversed, with each of the three judges on the panel writing separately. . . .

Having granted the Commission's petition for certiorari, we must decide: (1) whether the scope of judicial review encompasses more than the Commission's determination that the monologue was indecent "as broadcast"; (2) whether the Commission's order was a form of censorship . . .; (3) whether the broadcast was indecent . . .; and (4) whether the order violates the First Amendment of the United States Constitution.

. . . [A] statutory question presented by this case is whether the afternoon broadcast of the "Filthy Words" monologue was indecent. . . . Even that question is narrowly confined by the arguments of the parties. . . .

The Commission identified several words that referred to excretory or sexual activities or organs, stated that the repetitive, deliberate use of those words in an afternoon broadcast when children are in the audience was patently offensive, and held that the broadcast was indecent. Pacifica takes issue with the Commission's definition of indecency, but does not dispute the Commission's preliminary determination that each of the components of its definition was present. Specifically, Pacifica does not quarrel with the conclusion that this afternoon broadcast was patently offensive. Pacifica's claim that the broadcast was not indecent within the meaning of the statute rests entirely on the absence of prurient appeal.

The plain language of the statute does not support Pacifica's argument. The words "obscene, indecent, or profane" are written in the disjunctive, implying that each has a separate meaning. Prurient appeal is an element of the obscene, but the normal definition of "indecent" merely refers to nonconformance with accepted standards of morality.

Pacifica argues, however, that this Court has construed the term "indecent" in related statutes to mean "obscene," as that term was defined in *Miller v. California*. . . . In holding that the statute's coverage is limited to obscenity, the Court followed the lead of Mr. Justice Harlan [who] . . . thought that the phrase "obscene, lewd, lascivious, indecent, filthy or vile," taken as a whole, was clearly limited to the obscene, a reading well grounded in prior judicial constructions. . . .

. . . [T]he Commission has long interpreted [the statute] as encompassing more than the obscene. The former statute deals primarily with printed matter enclosed in sealed envelopes mailed from one individual to another; the latter deals with the content of public broadcasts. It is unrealistic to assume that Congress intended to impose precisely the same limitations on the dissemination of patently offensive matter by such different means.

Because neither our prior decisions nor the language or history of [the statute] supports the conclusion that prurient appeal is an essential component of indecent language, we reject Pacifica's construction of the statute. When that construction is put to one side, there is no basis for disagreeing with the Commission's conclusion that indecent language was used in this broadcast.

Pacifica makes two constitutional attacks on the Commission's order. First, it argues that the Commission's construction of the statutory language broadly encompasses so much constitutionally protected speech that reversal is required even if Pacifica's broadcast of the "Filthy Words" monologue is not itself protected by the First Amendment. Second, Pacifica argues that inasmuch as the recording is not obscene, the Constitution forbids any abridgment of the right to broadcast it on the radio.

The first argument fails because our review is limited to the question whether the Commission has the authority to proscribe this particular broadcast....

It is true that the Commission's order may lead some broadcasters to censor themselves. At most, however, the Commission's definition of indecency will deter only the broadcasting of patently offensive references to excretory and sexual organs and activities. While some of these references may be protected, they surely lie at the periphery of First Amendment concern.... Invalidating any rule on the basis of its hypothetical application to situations not before the Court is "strong medicine" to be applied "sparingly and only as a last resort." We decline to administer that medicine to preserve the vigor of patently offensive sexual and excretory speech.

When the issue is narrowed to the facts of this case, the question is whether the First Amendment denies government any power to restrict the public broadcast of indecent language in any circumstances....

The words of the Carlin monologue are unquestionably "speech" within the meaning of the First Amendment. It is equally clear that the Commission's objections to the broadcast were based in part on its content. The order must therefore fall if, as Pacifica argues, the First Amendment prohibits all governmental regulation that depends on the content of speech. Our past cases demonstrate, however, that no such absolute rule is mandated by the Constitution.

. . . The government may forbid speech calculated to provoke a fight. It may pay heed to the "'commonsense differences' between commercial speech and other varieties." It may treat libels against private citizens more severely than libels against public officials. Obscenity may be wholly prohibited....

The question in this case is whether a broadcast of patently offensive words dealing with sex and excretion may be regulated because of its content. Obscene materials have been denied the protection of the First Amendment because their content is so offensive to contemporary moral standards.

But the fact that society may find speech offensive is not a sufficient reason for suppressing it. Indeed, if it is the speaker's opinion that gives offense, that consequence is a reason for according it constitutional protection. For it is a central tenet of the First Amendment that the government must remain neutral in the marketplace of ideas. If there were any reason to believe that the Commission's characterization of the Carlin monologue as offensive could be traced to its political content—or even to the fact that it satirized contemporary attitudes about four-letter words—First Amendment protection might be required. But that is simply not this case. These words offend for the same reasons that obscenity offends....

Although these words ordinarily lack literary, political, or scientific value, they are not entirely outside the protection of the First Amendment. Some uses of even the most offensive words are unquestionably protected. Indeed, we may assume, *arguendo*, that this monologue would be protected in other contexts. Nonetheless, the constitutional protection accorded to a communication containing such patently offensive sexual and excretory language need not be the same in every context.... Words that are commonplace in one setting are shocking in another. To paraphrase Mr. Justice Harlan, one occasion's lyric is another's vulgarity.

In this case it is undisputed that the content of Pacifica's broadcast was "vulgar," "offensive," and "shocking." Because content of that character is not entitled to absolute constitutional protection under all circumstances, we must consider its context in order to determine whether the Commission's action was constitutionally permissible.

We have long recognized that each medium of expression presents special First Amendment problems. And of all forms of communication, it is broadcasting that has received the most limited First Amendment protection. . . . [A]lthough the First Amendment protects newspaper publishers from being required to print the replies of those whom they criticize, it affords no such protection to broadcasters; on the contrary, they must give free time to the victims of their criticism.

The reasons for these distinctions are complex, but two have relevance to the present case. First, the broadcast media have established a uniquely pervasive presence in the lives of all Americans. Patently offensive, indecent material presented over the airwaves confronts the citizen, not only in public, but also in the privacy of the home, where the individual's right to be left alone plainly outweighs the First Amendment rights of an intruder.

Because the broadcast audience is constantly tuning in and out, prior warnings cannot completely protect the listener or viewer from unexpected program content. To say that one may avoid further offense by turning off the radio when he hears indecent language is like saying that the remedy for an assault is to run away after the first blow. One may hang up on an indecent phone call, but that option does not give the caller a constitutional immunity or avoid a harm that has already taken place.

Second, broadcasting is uniquely accessible to children, even those too young to read. Although Cohen's written message might have been incomprehensible to a first grader, Pacifica's broadcast could have enlarged a child's vocabulary in an instant. Other forms of offensive expression may be withheld from the young without restricting the expression at its source. Bookstores and motion picture theaters, for example, may be prohibited from making indecent material available to children. . . . The ease with which children may obtain access to broadcast material ...amply justif[ies] special treatment of indecent broadcasting.

It is appropriate, in conclusion, to emphasize the narrowness of our holding. This case does not involve a two-way radio conversation between a cab driver and a dispatcher, or a telecast of an Elizabethan comedy. We have not decided that an occasional expletive in either setting would justify any sanction or, indeed, that this broadcast would justify a criminal prosecution. The Commission's decision rested entirely on a nuisance rationale under which context is all-important. The concept requires consideration of a host of variables. The time of day was emphasized by the Commission. The content of the program in which the language is used will also affect the composition of the audience, and differences between radio, television, and perhaps closed-circuit transmissions, may also be relevant. . . . We . . . hold that when the Commission finds that a pig has entered the parlor, the exercise of its regulatory power does not depend on proof that the pig is obscene.

The judgment of the Court of Appeals is reversed.

It is so ordered.

JUSTICE LEWIS POWELL, with whom JUSTICE HARRY BLACKMUN joined, concurring in part and concurring in the judgment:

. . . The Court today reviews only the Commission's holding that Carlin's monologue was indecent "as broadcast" at two o'clock in the afternoon, and not the broad sweep of the Commission's opinion. . . .

I also agree with much that is said in Part IV of MR. JUSTICE STEVENS' opinion, and with its conclusion that the Commission's holding in this case does not violate the First Amendment. Because I do not subscribe to all that is said in Part IV, however, I state my views separately.

It is conceded that the monologue at issue here is not obscene in the constitutional sense. . . . Some of the words used have been held protected by the First Amendment in other cases and contexts. I do not think Carlin, consistently with the First Amendment, could be punished for delivering the same monologue to a live audience composed of adults who, knowing what to expect, chose to attend his performance. And I would assume that an adult could not constitutionally be prohibited from purchasing a recording or transcript of the monologue and playing or reading it in the privacy of his own home.

But it also is true that the language employed is, to most people, vulgar and offensive. . . . The Commission did not err in characterizing the narrow category of language used here as "patently offensive" to most people regardless of age.

The issue, however, is whether the Commission may impose civil sanctions on a licensee radio station for broadcasting the monologue at two o'clock in the afternoon. The Commission's primary concern was to prevent the broadcast from reaching the ears of unsupervised children who were likely to be in the audience at that hour. . . .

In most instances, the dissemination of this kind of speech to children may be limited without also limiting willing adults' access to it. Sellers of printed and recorded matter and exhibitors of motion pictures and live performances may be required to shut their doors to children, but such a requirement has no effect on adults' access.

The difficulty is that such a physical separation of the audience cannot be accomplished in the broadcast media. During most of the broadcast hours, both adults and unsupervised children are likely to be in the broadcast audience, and the broadcaster cannot reach willing adults without also reaching children. This, as the Court emphasizes, is one of the distinctions between the broadcast and other media to which we often have adverted as justifying a different treatment of the broadcast media for First Amendment purposes.

In my view, the Commission was entitled to give substantial weight to this difference in reaching its decision in this case.

A second difference, not without relevance, is that broadcasting—unlike most other forms of communication—comes directly into the home, the one place where people ordinarily have the right not to be assaulted by uninvited and offensive sights and sounds. Although the First Amendment may require unwilling adults to absorb the first blow of offensive but protected speech when they are in public before they turn away, a different order of values obtains in the home. . . .

. . . In short, I agree that on the facts of this case, the Commission's order did not violate respondent's First Amendment rights.

. . . In my view, the result in this case does not turn on whether Carlin's monologue, viewed as a whole, or the words that constitute it, have more or less "value" than a candidate's campaign speech. This is a judgment for each person to make, not one for the judges to impose upon him.

The result turns instead on the unique characteristics of the broadcast media, combined with society's right to protect its children from speech generally agreed to be inappropriate for their years, and with the interest of unwilling adults in not being assaulted by such offensive speech in their homes. Moreover, I doubt whether today's decision will prevent any adult who wishes to receive Carlin's message in Carlin's own words from doing so, and from making for himself a value judgment as to the merit of the message and words. These are the grounds upon which I join the judgment of the Court as to Part IV.

JUSTICE WILLIAM BRENNAN and JUSTICE POTTER STEWART, with whom JUSTICE THURGOOD MARSHALL joined, dissenting:

I agree with MR. JUSTICE STEWART that . . . the word "indecent" must be construed to prohibit only obscene speech. I would, therefore, normally refrain from expressing my views on any constitutional issues implicated in this case. However, I find the Court's misapplication of fundamental First Amendment principles so patent, and its attempt to impose *its* notions of propriety on the whole of the American people so misguided, that I am unable to remain silent.

For the second time in two years, the Court refuses to embrace the notion, completely antithetical to basic First Amendment values, that the degree of protection the First Amendment affords protected speech varies with the social value ascribed to that speech by five Members of this Court. Moreover, as do all parties, all Members of the Court agree that the Carlin monologue aired by Station WBAI does not fall within one of the categories of speech, such as "fighting words," or obscenity, that is totally without First Amendment protection. This conclusion, of course, is compelled by our cases expressly holding that communications containing some of the words found condemnable here are fully protected by the First Amendment in other contexts. Yet despite the Court's refusal to create a sliding scale of First Amendment protection calibrated to this Court's perception of the worth of a communication's content, and despite our unanimous agreement that the Carlin monologue is protected speech, a majority of the Court nevertheless finds that, on the facts of this case, the FCC is not constitutionally barred from imposing sanctions on Pacifica for its airing of the Carlin monologue. This majority apparently believes that the FCC's disapproval of Pacifica's afternoon broadcast of Carlin's "Dirty Words" recording is a permissible time, place, and manner regulation. Both the opinion of my Brother STEVENS and the opinion of my Brother POWELL rely principally on two factors in reaching this conclusion: (1) the capacity of a radio broadcast to intrude into the unwilling listener's home, and (2) the presence of children in the listening audience. Dispassionate analysis, removed from individual notions as to what is proper and what is not, starkly reveals that these justifications, whether individually or together, simply do not support even the professedly moderate degree of governmental homogenization of radio communications—if, indeed, such homogenization can ever be moderate given the pre-eminent status of the right of free speech in our constitutional scheme—that the Court today permits.

Without question, the privacy interests of an individual in his home are substantial and deserving of significant protection. In finding these interests sufficient to justify the content regulation of protected speech, however, the Court commits two errors. First, it misconceives the nature of the privacy interests involved where an individual voluntarily chooses to admit radio communications into his home. Second, it ignores the constitutionally protected interests of both those who wish to transmit and those who desire to receive broadcasts that many—including the FCC and this Court—might find offensive.

. . . Even if an individual who voluntarily opens his home to radio communications retains privacy interests of sufficient moment to justify a ban on protected speech if those interests are "invaded in an essentially intolerable manner," the very fact that those interests are threatened only by a radio broadcast precludes any intolerable invasion of privacy; for unlike other intrusive modes of communication, such as sound trucks, "[the] radio can be turned off"—and with a minimum of effort.

. . . The Court's balance, of necessity, fails to accord proper weight to the interests of listeners who wish to hear broadcasts the FCC deems offensive. It permits majoritarian tastes completely to preclude a protected message from entering the homes of a receptive, unoffended minority. No decision of this Court supports such a result. . . .

...Because the Carlin monologue is obviously not an erotic appeal to the prurient interests of children, the Court, for the first time, allows the government to prevent minors from gaining access to materials that are not obscene, and are therefore protected, as to them. . . .

The opinion of my Brother POWELL acknowledges that there lurks in today's decision a potential for "'[reducing] the adult population . . . to [hearing] only what is fit for children,'" but expresses faith that the FCC will vigilantly prevent this potential from ever becoming a reality. I am far less certain than my Brother POWELL that such faith in the Commission is warranted; and even if I shared it, I could not so easily shirk the responsibility assumed by each Member of this Court jealously to guard against encroachments on First Amendment freedoms.

In concluding that the presence of children in the listening audience provides an adequate basis for the FCC to impose sanctions for Pacifica's broadcast of the Carlin monologue, the opinions of my Brother POWELL, and my Brother STEVENS, both stress the time-honored right of a parent to raise his child as he sees fit—a right this Court has consistently been vigilant to protect. Yet this principle supports a result directly contrary to that reached by the Court. [Prior decisions] hold that parents, *not* the government, have the right to make certain decisions regarding the upbringing of their children. As surprising as it may be to individual Members of this Court, some parents may actually find Mr. Carlin's unabashed attitude towards the seven "dirty words" healthy, and deem it desirable to expose their children to the manner in which Mr. Carlin defuses the taboo surrounding the words. Such parents may constitute a minority of the American public, but the absence of great numbers willing to exercise the right to raise their children in this fashion does not alter the right's nature or its existence. Only the Court's regrettable decision does that.

As demonstrated above, neither of the factors relied on by both the opinion of my Brother POWELL and the opinion of my Brother STEVENS—the intrusive nature of radio and the presence of children in the listening audience—can, when taken on its own terms, support the FCC's disapproval of the Carlin monologue. . . . Taken to their logical extreme, these rationales would support the cleansing of public radio of any "four-letter words" whatsoever, regardless of their context. The rationales could justify the banning from radio of a myriad of literary works, novels, poems, and plays by the likes of Shakespeare, Joyce, Hemingway, Ben Jonson, Henry Fielding, Robert Burns, and Chaucer; they could support the suppression of a good deal of political speech, such as the Nixon tapes; and they could even provide the basis for imposing sanctions for the broadcast of certain portions of the Bible.

In order to dispel the specter of the possibility of so unpalatable a degree of censorship, and to defuse Pacifica's overbreadth challenge, the FCC insists that it desires only the authority to reprimand a broadcaster on facts analogous to those present in this case ...For my own part, even accepting that this case is limited to its facts, I would place the responsibility and the right to weed worthless and offensive communications from the public airways where it belongs and where, until today, it resided: in a public free to choose those communications worthy of its attention from a marketplace unsullied by the censor's hand.

The absence of any hesitancy in the opinions of my Brothers POWELL and STEVENS to approve the FCC's censorship of the Carlin monologue on the basis of two demonstrably inadequate grounds is a function of their perception that the decision will result in little, if any, curtailment of communicative exchanges protected by the First Amendment. . . .

. . . [E]ven if an alternative phrasing may communicate a speaker's abstract ideas as effectively as those words he is forbidden to use, it is doubtful that the sterilized message will convey the emotion that is an essential part of so many communications.

. . . The airways are capable not only of carrying a message, but also of transforming it. A satirist's monologue may be most potent when delivered to a live audience; yet the choice whether this will in fact be the manner in which the message is delivered and received is one the First Amendment prohibits the government from making.

It is quite evident that I find the Court's attempt to unstitch the warp and woof of First Amendment law in an effort to reshape its fabric to cover the patently wrong result the Court reaches in this case dangerous as well as lamentable. Yet there runs throughout the opinions of my Brothers POWELL and STEVENS another vein I find equally disturbing: a depressing inability to appreciate that in our land of cultural pluralism, there are many who think, act, and talk differently from the Members of this Court, and who do not share their fragile sensibilities. It is only an acute ethnocentric myopia that enables the Court to approve the censorship of communications solely because of the words they contain.

. . . The words that the Court and the Commission find so unpalatable may be the stuff of everyday conversations in some, if not many, of the innumerable subcultures that compose this Nation. Academic research indicates that this is indeed the case. As one researcher concluded, "[words] generally considered obscene like 'bullshit' and 'fuck' are considered neither obscene nor derogatory in the [black] vernacular except in particular contextual situations and when used with certain intonations."

. . . In this context, the Court's decision may be seen for what, in the broader perspective, it really is: another of the dominant culture's inevitable efforts to force those groups who do not share its mores to conform to its way of thinking, acting, and speaking.

Pacifica, in response to an FCC inquiry about its broadcast of Carlin's satire on "'the words you couldn't say on the public . . . airways,'" explained that "Carlin is not mouthing obscenities, he is merely using words to satirize as harmless and essentially silly our attitudes towards those words." In confirming Carlin's prescience as a social commentator by the result it reaches today, the Court evidences an attitude toward the "seven dirty words" that many others besides Mr. Carlin and Pacifica might describe as "silly." Whether today's decision will similarly prove "harmless" remains to be seen. One can only hope that it will.

JUSTICE POTTER STEWART, with whom JUSTICE WILLIAM BRENNAN, JUSTICE BYRON WHITE and JUSTICE THURGOOD MARSHALL join, dissenting:

. . . The statute pursuant to which the Commission acted makes it a federal offense to utter "any obscene, indecent, or profane language by means of radio communication." The Commission held, and the Court today agrees, that "indecent" is a broader concept than "obscene" as the latter term was defined in *Miller v. California*, because language can be "indecent" although it has social, political, or artistic value and lacks prurient appeal. But this construction of [the statute], while perhaps plausible, is by no means compelled. To the contrary, I think that "indecent" should properly be read as meaning no more than "obscene." Since the Carlin monologue concededly was not "obscene," I believe that the Commission lacked statutory authority to ban it. Under this construction of the statute, it is unnecessary to address the difficult and important issue of the Commission's constitutional power to prohibit speech that would be constitutionally protected outside the context of electronic broadcasting.

This Court has recently decided the meaning of the term "indecent" in a closely related statutory context [and held] that "indecent" . . . has the same meaning as "obscene" as that term was defined in the *Miller* case. . . .

I would hold, therefore, that Congress intended, by using the word "indecent" in § 1464, to prohibit nothing more than obscene speech. Under that reading of the statute, the Commission's order in this case was not authorized, and on that basis I would affirm the judgment of the Court of Appeals.

FEDERAL COMMUNICATIONS COMMISSION V. FOX TELEVISION STATIONS, INC.
SUPREME COURT OF THE UNITED STATES 567 U.S. 239 (2012)

JUSTICE ANTHONY KENNEDY delivered the Court's opinion:

In FCC v. Fox Television Stations, Inc. (2009) (*Fox I*), the Court held that the Federal Communication[s] Commission's decision to modify its indecency enforcement regime to regulate so-called fleeting expletives was neither arbitrary nor capricious. The Court then declined to address the constitutionality of the policy, however, because the United States Court of Appeals for the Second Circuit had yet to do so. On remand, the Court of Appeals [in 2010] found the policy was vague and, as a result, unconstitutional. The case now returns to this Court for decision upon the constitutional question.

[The U.S. Criminal Code] provides that "[w]hoever utters any obscene, indecent, or profane language by means of radio communication shall be fined . . . or imprisoned not more than two years, or both." The Federal Communications Commission (Commission) has been instructed by Congress to enforce [that provision] between the hours of 6 a.m. and 10 p.m. And the Commission has applied its regulations to radio and television broadcasters alike.
. . .

This Court first reviewed the Commission's indecency policy in FCC v. Pacifica Foundation (1978). In *Pacifica*, the Commission determined that George Carlin's "Filthy Words" monologue was indecent. It contained "language that describes, in terms patently offensive as measured by contemporary community standards for the broadcast medium, sexual or excretory activities and organs, at times of the day when there is a reasonable risk that children may be in the audience." This Court upheld the Commission's ruling. . . .

In 1987, the Commission determined it was applying the *Pacifica* standard in too narrow a way. It stated that in later cases its definition of indecent language would "appropriately includ[e] a broader range of material than the seven specific words at issue in [the Carlin monologue]." Thus, the Commission indicated it would use the "generic definition of indecency" articulated in its 1975 *Pacifica* order and assess the full context of allegedly indecent broadcasts rather than limiting its regulation to a "comprehensive index . . . of indecent words or pictorial depictions."

Even under this context based approach, the Commission continued to note the important difference between isolated and repeated broadcasts of indecent material. In the context of expletives, the Commission determined "deliberate and repetitive use in a patently offensive manner is a requisite to a finding of indecency." For speech "involving the description or depiction of sexual or excretory functions . . . [t]he mere fact that specific words or phrases are not repeated does not mandate a finding that material that is otherwise patently offensive . . . is not indecent."

In 2001, the Commission issued a policy statement intended "to provide guidance to the broadcast industry regarding [its] caselaw interpreting [the indecency law] and [its] enforcement policies with respect to broadcast indecency." In that document the Commission restated that for material to be indecent it must depict sexual or excretory organs or activities and be patently offensive as measured by contemporary community standards for the broadcast medium. Describing the framework of what it considered patently offensive, the Commission explained that three factors had proved significant:

"(1) [T]he explicitness or graphic nature of the description or depiction of sexual or excretory organs or activities; (2) whether the material dwells on or repeats at length descriptions of sexual or excretory organs or activities; (3) whether the material appears to pander or is used to titillate, or whether the material appears to have been presented for its shock value."

As regards the second of these factors, the Commission explained that "[r]epetition of and persistent focus on sexual or excretory material have been cited consistently as factors that exacerbate the potential offensiveness of broadcasts. In contrast, where sexual or excretory references have been made once or have been passing or fleeting in nature, this characteristic has tended to weigh against a finding of indecency." The Commission then gave examples of material that was not found indecent because it was fleeting and isolated, and contrasted it with fleeting references that were found patently offensive in light of other factors.

It was against this regulatory background that the three incidents of alleged indecency at issue here took place. First, in the 2002 Billboard Music Awards, broadcast by respondent Fox Television Stations, Inc., the singer Cher exclaimed during an unscripted acceptance speech: "I've also had my critics for the last 40 years saying that I was on my way out every year. Right. So f*** 'em." Second, Fox broadcast the Billboard Music Awards again in 2003. There, a person named Nicole Richie made the following unscripted remark while presenting an award: "Have you ever tried to get cow s*** out of a Prada purse? It's not so f***ing simple." The third incident involved an episode of NYPD Blue, a regular television show broadcast by respondent ABC Television Network. The episode broadcast on February 25, 2003, showed the nude buttocks of an adult female character for approximately seven seconds and for a moment the side of her breast. During the scene, in which the character was preparing to take a shower, a child portraying her boyfriend's son entered the bathroom. A moment of awkwardness followed. The Commission received indecency complaints about all three broadcasts.

After these incidents, but before the Commission issued Notices of Apparent Liability to Fox and ABC, the Commission issued a decision sanctioning NBC for a comment made by the singer Bono during the 2003 Golden Globe Awards. Upon winning the award for Best Original Song, Bono exclaimed: "'This is really, really, f***ing brilliant. Really, really great.'" Reversing a decision by its enforcement bureau, the Commission found the use of the F-word actionably indecent. The Commission held that the word was "one of the most vulgar, graphic and explicit descriptions of sexual activity in the English language," and thus found "any use of that word or a variation, in any context, inherently has a sexual connotation." Turning to the isolated nature of the expletive, the Commission reversed prior rulings that had found fleeting expletives not indecent. The Commission held "the mere fact that specific words or phrases are not sustained or repeated does not mandate a finding that material that is otherwise patently offensive to the broadcast medium is not indecent."

Even though the incidents at issue in these cases took place before the *Golden Globes* Order, the Commission applied its new policy regarding fleeting expletives and fleeting nudity. It found the broadcasts by respondents Fox and ABC to be in violation of this standard.

As to Fox, [in 2006] the Commission found the two Billboard Awards broadcasts indecent. Numerous parties petitioned for a review of the order in the United States Court of Appeals for the Second Circuit. The Court of Appeals granted the Commission's request for a voluntary remand so that it could respond to the parties' objections. In its remand order, the Commission applied its tripartite definition of patently offensive material from its 2001 Order and found that both broadcasts fell well within its scope. As pertains to the constitutional issue in these cases, the Commission noted that under the policy clarified in the *Golden Globes* Order, "categorically requiring repeated use of expletives in order to find material indecent is inconsistent with our general approach to indecency enforcement." Though the Commission deemed Fox should have known Nicole Richie's comments were actionably indecent even prior to the *Golden Globes* Order, it declined to propose a forfeiture in light of the limited nature of the Second Circuit's remand. The Commission acknowledged that "it was not apparent that Fox could be penalized for Cher's comment at the time it was broadcast." And so, as in the Golden Globes case it imposed no penalty for that broadcast.

Fox and various intervenors returned to the United States Court of Appeals for the Second Circuit, raising administrative, statutory, and constitutional challenges to the Commission's indecency regulations. In a 2-to-1 decision, with Judge Leval dissenting, the Court of Appeals found the *Remand* Order arbitrary and capricious because "the FCC has made a 180-degree turn regarding its treatment of 'fleeting expletives' without providing a reasoned explanation justifying the about-face." While noting its skepticism as to whether the Commission's fleeting expletive regime "would pass constitutional muster," the Court of Appeals found it unnecessary to address the issue.

The case came here on certiorari. Citing the Administrative Procedure Act, this Court noted that the Judiciary may set aside agency action that is arbitrary or capricious. In the context of a change in policy (such as the Commission's determination that fleeting expletives could be indecent), the decision held an agency, in the ordinary course, should acknowledge that it is in fact changing its position and "show that there are good reasons for the new policy." There is no need, however, for an agency to provide detailed justifications for every change or to show that the reasons for the new policy are better than the reasons for the old one.

Judged under this standard, the Court in *Fox I* found the Commission's new indecency enforcement policy neither arbitrary nor capricious. The Court noted the Commission had acknowledged breaking new ground in ruling that fleeting and nonliteral expletives could be indecent under the controlling standards; the Court concluded the agency's reasons for expanding the scope of its enforcement activity were rational. Not only was it "certainly reasonable to determine that it made no sense to distinguish between literal and nonliteral uses of offensive words," but the Court agreed that the Commission's decision to "look at the patent offensiveness of even isolated uses of sexual and excretory words fits with the context-based approach [approved] . . . in *Pacifica.*" Given that "[e]ven isolated utterances can ...constitute harmful 'first blow[s]' to children," the Court held that the Commission could "decide it needed to step away from its old regime where nonrepetitive use of an expletive was *per se* nonactionable." Having found the agency's action to be neither arbitrary nor capricious, the Court remanded for the Court of Appeals to address respondents' First Amendment challenges.

On remand from *Fox I*, the Court of Appeals held the Commission's indecency policy unconstitutionally vague and invalidated it in its entirety. The Court of Appeals found the policy, as expressed in the 2001 Guidance and subsequent Commission decisions, failed to give broadcasters sufficient notice of what would be considered indecent. Surveying a number of Commission adjudications, the court found the Commission was inconsistent as to which words it deemed patently offensive. It also determined that the Commission's presumptive prohibition on the F-word and the S-word was plagued by vagueness because the Commission had on occasion found the fleeting use of those words not indecent provided they occurred during a bona fide news interview or were "demonstrably essential to the nature of an artistic or educational work." The Commission's application of these exceptions, according to the Court of Appeals, left broadcasters guessing whether an expletive would be deemed artistically integral to a program or whether a particular broadcast would be considered a bona fide news interview. The Court of Appeals found the vagueness inherent in the policy had forced broadcasters to "choose between not airing . . . controversial programs [or] risking massive fines or possibly even loss of their licenses." And the court found that there was "ample evidence in the record" that this harsh choice had led to a chill of protected speech.

The procedural history regarding ABC is more brief. On February 19, 2008, the Commission issued a forfeiture order finding the display of the woman's nude buttocks in NYPD Blue was actionably indecent. The Commission determined that, regardless of medical definitions, displays of buttocks fell within the category of displays of sexual or excretory organs because the depiction was "widely associated with sexual arousal and closely associated by most people with excretory activities." The scene was deemed patently offensive as measured by contemporary community standards, and the Commission determined that "[t]he female actor's nudity is presented in a manner that clearly panders to and titillates the audience." Unlike in the Fox case, the Commission imposed a forfeiture of $27,500 on each of the 45 ABC-affiliated stations that aired the indecent episode. In a summary order the United States Court of Appeals for the Second Circuit vacated the forfeiture order, determining that it was bound by its *Fox* decision striking down the entirety of the Commission's indecency policy.

. . . These are the cases before us.

A fundamental principle in our legal system is that laws which regulate persons or entities must give fair notice of conduct that is forbidden or required. This requirement of clarity in regulation is essential to the protections provided by the Due Process Clause of the Fifth Amendment. It requires the invalidation of laws that are impermissibly vague. A conviction or punishment fails to comply with due process if the statute or regulation under which it is obtained "fails to provide a person of ordinary intelligence fair notice of what is prohibited, or is so standardless that it authorizes or encourages seriously discriminatory enforcement." As this Court has explained, a regulation is not vague because it may at times be difficult to prove an incriminating fact but rather because it is unclear as to what fact must be proved.

Even when speech is not at issue, the void for vagueness doctrine addresses at least two connected but discrete due process concerns: first, that regulated parties should know what is required of them so they may act accordingly; second, precision and guidance are necessary so that those enforcing the law do not act in an arbitrary or discriminatory way. When speech is involved, rigorous adherence to those requirements is necessary to ensure that ambiguity does not chill protected speech.

These concerns are implicated here because, at the outset, the broadcasters claim they did not have, and do not have, sufficient notice of what is proscribed. And leaving aside any concerns about facial invalidity, they contend that the lengthy procedural history set forth above shows that the broadcasters did not have fair notice of what was forbidden. Under the

2001 Guidelines in force when the broadcasts occurred, a key consideration was "'whether the material dwell[ed] on or repeat[ed] at length'" the offending description or depiction. In the 2004 *Golden Globes* Order, issued after the broadcasts, the Commission changed course and held that fleeting expletives could be a statutory violation. In the challenged orders now under review the Commission applied the new principle promulgated in the *Golden Globes* Order and determined fleeting expletives and a brief moment of indecency were actionably indecent. This regulatory history, however, makes it apparent that the Commission policy in place at the time of the broadcasts gave no notice to Fox or ABC that a fleeting expletive or a brief shot of nudity could be actionably indecent; yet Fox and ABC were found to be in violation. The Commission's lack of notice to Fox and ABC that its interpretation had changed so the fleeting moments of indecency contained in their broadcasts were a violation of [the indecency law] as interpreted and enforced by the agency "fail[ed] to provide a person of ordinary intelligence fair notice of what is prohibited." This would be true with respect to a regulatory change this abrupt on any subject, but it is surely the case when applied to the regulations in question, regulations that touch upon "sensitive areas of basic First Amendment freedoms."

The Government raises two arguments in response, but neither is persuasive. As for the two fleeting expletives, the Government concedes that "Fox did not have reasonable notice at the time of the broadcasts that the Commission would consider non-repeated expletives indecent." The Government argues, nonetheless, that Fox "cannot establish unconstitutional vagueness on that basis . . . because the Commission did not impose a sanction where Fox lacked such notice." As the Court observed when the case was here three Terms ago, it is true that the Commission declined to impose any forfeiture on Fox, and in its order the Commission claimed that it would not consider the indecent broadcasts either when considering whether to renew stations' licenses or "in any other context." This "policy of forbearance," as the Government calls it, does not suffice to make the issue moot. Though the Commission claims it will not consider the prior indecent broadcasts "in any context," it has the statutory power to take into account "any history of prior offenses" when setting the level of a forfeiture penalty. Just as in the First Amendment context, the due process protection against vague regulations "does not leave [regulated parties] ...at the mercy of *noblesse oblige*." Given that the Commission found it was "not inequitable to hold Fox responsible for [the 2003 broadcast]," and that it has the statutory authority to use its finding to increase any future penalties, the Government's assurance it will elect not to do so is insufficient to remedy the constitutional violation.

In addition, when combined with the legal consequence described above, reputational injury provides further reason for granting relief to Fox. As respondent CBS points out, findings of wrongdoing can result in harm to a broadcaster's "reputation with viewers and advertisers." This observation is hardly surprising given that the challenged orders, which are contained in the permanent Commission record, describe in strongly disapproving terms the indecent material broadcast by Fox, and Fox's efforts to protect children from being exposed to it. Commission sanctions on broadcasters for indecent material are widely publicized. The challenged orders could have an adverse impact on Fox's reputation that audiences and advertisers alike are entitled to consider.

With respect to ABC, the Government with good reason does not argue no sanction was imposed. The fine against ABC and its network affiliates for the seven seconds of nudity was nearly $1.24 million. The Government argues instead that ABC had notice that the scene in NYPD Blue would be considered indecent in light of a 1960 decision where the Commission declared that the "televising of nudes might well raise a serious question of programming contrary to [the indecency law]." This argument does not prevail. An isolated and ambiguous statement from a 1960 Commission decision does not suffice for the fair notice required when the Government intends to impose over a $1 million fine for allegedly impermissible speech....

The Commission failed to give Fox or ABC fair notice prior to the broadcasts in question that fleeting expletives and momentary nudity could be found actionably indecent.

Therefore, the Commission's standards as applied to these broadcasts were vague, and the Commission's orders must be set aside.

It is necessary to make three observations about the scope of this decision. First, because the Court resolves these cases on fair notice grounds under the Due Process Clause, it need not address the First Amendment implications of the Commission's indecency policy. It is argued that this Court's ruling in *Pacifica* (and the less rigorous standard of scrutiny it provided for the regulation of broadcasters) should be overruled because the rationale of that case has been overtaken by technological change and the wide availability of multiple other choices for listeners and viewers. The Government for its part maintains that when it licenses a conventional broadcast spectrum, the public may assume that the Government has its own interest in setting certain standards. These arguments need not be addressed here. In light of the Court's holding that the Commission's policy failed to provide fair notice it is unnecessary to reconsider *Pacifica* at this time.

This leads to a second observation. Here, the Court rules that Fox and ABC lacked notice at the time of their broadcasts that the material they were broadcasting could be found actionably indecent under then-existing policies. Given this disposition, it is unnecessary for the Court to address the constitutionality of the current indecency policy as expressed in the *Golden Globes* Order and subsequent adjudications. The Court adheres to its normal practice of declining to decide cases not before it.

Third, this opinion leaves the Commission free to modify its current indecency policy in light of its determination of the public interest and applicable legal requirements. And it leaves the courts free to review the current policy or any modified policy in light of its content and application.

* * *

The judgments of the United States Court of Appeals for the Second Circuit are vacated, and the cases are remanded for further proceedings consistent with the principles set forth in this opinion.

It is so ordered.

Justice Sotomayor took no part in the consideration or decision of these cases.

In an intellectual property case against Disney, Marvel Studios and others, a judge ruled that the use of a specific motion-picture technology in blockbuster films like "Guardians of the Galaxy" violated the patent rights of the technology's inventors but did not violate copyright.

Photo 12/Alamy Stock Photo

11 INTELLECTUAL PROPERTY
Protecting and Using Intangible Creations

LEARNING OBJECTIVES

11.1 Understand what copyright protects and be able to identify the requirements for an infringement claim and defenses to such a claim.

11.2 Identify the requirements for federal trademark law protection and what constitutes a trademark infringement claim and defenses to such a claim.

A "Bad Lip Reading" parody of several NFL plays. Another family spoof of Disney's songs from the movie, "Frozen." Almost two million views of someone playing the video game "Minecraft."

Spend a few moments on YouTube, and most students can quickly grasp the tensions between the First Amendment and intellectual property (IP) law, a legal category that protects the investment in these works. It's hilarious to watch videos of NFL players with dubbed speech, but do those remixes violate the league's intellectual property? The Holderness family does an entertaining job infusing new lyrics into popular songs from companies like Disney on their YouTube channel, but do they pay anything to Disney for that? And while it may baffle teachers and parents, the profitable market for watching others' video game adventures recorded on YouTube may take game enthusiasts away from playing an actual game like Minecraft. Does that violate the game maker's intellectual property rights? IP law has been at the center of answering questions about the protections for and fair reuse of creative contents for decades.

Patent, trademark and copyright statutes are all characterized as intellectual property law. The study of IP law is the study of government incentives to produce new creations, whether those are creative works like film (in the case of copyright), new inventions (in the case of patent), or new labels or phrases to signal products in the market (in the case of trademark). All U.S. law in this area derives from Art. I Sec. 8 of the U.S. Constitution in which Congress is given the power "To promote the Progress of Science and useful Arts, by securing for limited Times to Authors and Inventors the exclusive Right to their respective Writings and Discoveries."[1] The aim was to incentivize citizens to create, and in return, these creators receive limited rights to control their works and remuneration.

First Amendment and free expression conflicts arise when such incentives are extended so far as to create a "walled garden" and make it difficult and costly for new creators and inventors to use existing content without permission. When that happens, the free expression environment may be affected. Courts in intellectual property cases often spend their days weighing the intellectual property rights of the creator against the freedoms of the user. This chapter explores how IP law balances these two important societal interests.

Intellectual property law is also increasingly complex because of technological advances, but as with other areas of the law, core principles still apply. Historically, the U.S. Supreme Court has decided few cases concerning intellectual property. However, over the last decade, as new inventions that facilitate new ways to create copyrightable works have brought forward new legal questions, both Congress and the U.S. Supreme Court have engaged these issues.

COPYRIGHT

A **copyright** is an exclusive legal right protecting intellectual creations from unauthorized use. U.S. copyright law protects the rights of creators of "original works of authorship" to use their creations.[2] As Justice Sandra Day O'Connor wrote, "The Framers intended copyright itself to be the engine of free expression. By establishing a marketable right to the use of one's expression, copyright supplies the economic incentive to create and disseminate ideas."[3] The work's creator—the copyright holder—determines who can use the work, for what purpose and for how long. The U.S. Constitution grants creators control over their works for a "limited time."[4] Today, copyright for many works lasts for the creator's life plus 70 years. Copyright law balances the creator's right to restrict the use of their work and society's belief that some uses should be allowed without the creator's permission. Achieving the balance has been difficult since the United States adopted its first copyright law in 1790.

The concept of protecting creators' works emerged in the 15th century, when the invention of the printing press enabled cheaper copying. In England, the monarchy held that printers would control publication and the Crown would control printers. Authors might be paid for a manuscript, but then they dropped out of the picture. Copyright's initial purpose was to prevent sedition—criticizing the king or queen. The Crown gave a group of printers, called the Stationers' Company, control over printing. Licensed printers received the right to publish a work in perpetuity.

The license requirement ended in 1694, but the Stationers' Company did not disappear. Rather, it shifted its focus from printers to authors. The first copyright law in England, the **Statute of Anne** of 1710, protected authors' works and granted authors copyright protection if they registered their works with the government.[5] Under the Statute of Anne, authors controlled their creations but often sold their rights to printers to make money. When the copyright period ended, the work entered the **public domain**, and anyone could use it without permission. The public domain concept still exists today.

The U.S. Constitution followed England's lead, allowing Congress to adopt copyright and patent laws to encourage authors to create new works.[6] Before the Constitution was ratified, 12 of the 13 states passed copyright laws. The first Congress in 1790 adopted a law giving books, maps and charts a 14-year copyright.[7] The U.S. Supreme Court later ruled that the federal law superseded state statutes and common law copyright claims.[8]

During the 19th century, Congress amended the copyright law to protect musical compositions, photographs and paintings.[9] The 1870 act established the Library of Congress, giving it the power to register copyrights and requiring creators to deposit with the library two copies of a copyrighted published work.

The copyright law passed in 1870 established the Library of Congress.

Sean Pavone/Alamy

In 1886, several countries signed the **Berne Convention** for the Protection of Literary and Artistic Works in a step toward protecting works globally. The United States did not join, although the convention spurred a major revision of U.S. copyright law in 1909.[10] Among other changes, the law extended copyright protection to 28 years, with a renewal period of another 28 years.

As the 20th century progressed, entertainment, news, technology and other industries pressured Congress to update copyright law. In response, Congress adopted the Copyright Act of 1976, which took effect Jan. 1, 1978. In 1988, Congress amended the 1976 act in ways that permitted the United States to join the Berne Convention—more than a century after the treaty's initial adoption.[11]

The 1976 Copyright Act specifies what may be protected by copyright, what rights that protection includes, any restrictions on those rights and the formalities necessary to exercise the rights. The act remains the backbone of U.S. copyright law today.

In 1998, Congress adopted the Digital Millennium Copyright Act in an attempt to integrate the internet and other digital media more squarely into copyright law.[12] The DMCA bans software and hardware that facilitate circumventing copyright protection technology, with certain exceptions.[13] For example, the act forbids software that would disable anti-copying features in software that enables the copying of digital video.[14] The DMCA also prohibits removing or changing copyright information, such as the copyright owner's name.[15]

What Does a Copyright Protect?

U.S. copyright law protects a wide variety of works. Congress provided two broad criteria, offered some examples and left it to the courts to provide more clarity. The 1976 law says that copyright protection applies to "original works of authorship" that are "fixed in any tangible medium of expression."[16] Congress used the word "authorship" to include artists, composers, journalists, sculptors and many other creators.

A work must be substantially original to be protected.[17] Copyright law does not define "original." As one court said, "originality" simply means "a work independently created by its author, one not copied from pre-existing works, and a work that comes from the exercise of the creative powers of the author's mind."[18] Explained by another court, "The *sine qua non* of copyright is originality. . . . [It] means only that the work was independently created by the author (as opposed to copied from other works), and that it possesses at least some minimal degree of creativity."[19]

POINTS OF LAW
THE 1976 COPYRIGHT ACT

Copyright protection applies to "original works of authorship" that are "fixed in any tangible medium of expression."[20]

The following works are protected by copyright:
- Literary works

- Musical works, including any accompanying words
- Dramatic works, including any accompanying music
- Pantomimes and choreographic works
- Pictorial, graphic and sculptural works
- Motion pictures and other audiovisual works
- Sound recordings
- Architectural works

The U.S. Copyright Office suggests viewing these categories broadly. For example, computer software is considered a literary work protected by copyright law.[21] In a 2017 decision, the U.S. Supreme Court said clothing design elements could receive copyright protection as pictorial, graphic and sculptural works.[22]

In addition to being original, a work must be "fixed in a tangible medium." This means a work must be capable of being seen, "reproduced, or otherwise communicated, either directly or with the aid of a machine or device"—for example, words or images on paper, software in the cloud, a quilt made of cloth, a statue made of marble or music fixed in a digital file.[23]

The 1976 Copyright Act lists eight categories of eligible works: (1) literary works; (2) musical works, including any accompanying words; (3) dramatic works, including any accompanying music; (4) pantomimes and choreographic works; (5) pictorial, graphic and sculptural works; (6) motion pictures and other audiovisual works; (7) sound recordings; and (8) architectural works.[24] These categories are more illustrative than definitive. For example, software may be copyrighted (typically it is considered a literary work because it is written code), even though it is not listed separately among the eight categories. Designs, patterns and shapes also may have copyright protection.

Design 299B
Registration No. VA 1-319-226

Design 299A
Registration No. VA 1-319-228

Two cheerleading uniforms were at the center of a U.S. Supreme Court decision to allow copyright of clothing design elements when perceived as a work of art.

https://fortunedotcom.files.wordpress.com/2016/05/screen-shot-2016-05-02-at -14-39-58.png

In 2017, the U.S. Supreme Court held that design features in clothing could be eligible for copyright protection if those features are perceived as a work of art separate from the "useful article."[25] According to the U.S. Copyright Office, a useful article is an object that has a utilitarian function "that is not merely to portray the appearance of the article or to convey information."[26] Clothing and furniture are examples of useful articles.

At issue in the case was whether stripes, zigzags and chevrons on a cheerleading uniform could receive copyright protection. Before the case reached the Supreme Court, various circuit courts of appeal had reached different conclusions on the broader issue of clothing design, resulting in nine different variability tests to determine whether copyright protection was appropriate.[27]

The U.S. Supreme Court said it accepted the case to resolve the widespread disagreement. Writing for the majority, Justice Clarence Thomas said, "[A] feature incorporated into the design of a useful article is eligible for copyright protection only if the feature (1) can be perceived as a two- or three-dimensional work of art separate from the useful article and (2) would qualify as protectable pictorial, graphic, or sculptural work—either on its own or fixed in some other tangible medium of expression—if it were imagined separately from the useful article into which it is incorporated."[28] Legal experts said the Supreme Court's decision is significant for the fashion industry, which has asserted for years that clothing not only is a useful article in that it protects the body, but also is a form of creative expression.[29]

Software is copyrightable as a literary work because it is written code.

7io/iStock.com

For many years, sound recordings—the actual recordings, as opposed to the music and lyrics—were not protected by copyright. This changed in 1971, when an update to the federal copyright law gave protection for songs recorded in 1972 or later. Songs recorded prior to 1972 have some limited protection under state laws. In 2018, the Ninth Circuit Court of Appeals considered whether digitally remastered, pre-1972 sound recordings were original enough to justify copyright protection.[30] Reversing a district court decision, the Ninth Circuit ruled that despite a sound engineer's remastering that could include aesthetic changes, these changes were not substantial enough to be considered original. "A digitally remastered sound recording made as a copy of the original analog sound recording will rarely exhibit the necessary originality to qualify for independent copyright protection," the court said.[31]

The 1976 statute protects all works eligible for copyright, both published and unpublished.[32] Before the 1976 statute was adopted, unpublished works were protected by state common law, not the federal statute. Common law protection for unpublished works and protection lasted forever.[33] The new law changed this, giving unpublished creations the same protection as published works and generally ending common law protection for copyright.

A work that is not original or is not fixed in a tangible medium cannot be copyrighted. For example, a telephone directory's contents of names, addresses and phone numbers lacked originality, the U.S. Supreme Court ruled. There was insufficient creativity in an alphabetical list.[34]

A collection of previously created works can be protected if there is substantial originality in the choice or arrangement of the works.[35] The copyright law refers to this as a "compilation."[36] An example of a compilation is a book of poetry that includes poems written by several different poets arranged around a common theme, such as love. Newspapers and magazines are also considered compilations. The statute permits a copyright of the creation of the compilation, but each work included in the collection retains its own copyright protection. Ideas, history and facts cannot be copyrighted.[37] To qualify for copyright protection, there must be originality or novelty in the compiling or organizing of facts.[38]

A news story reporting an automobile accident can receive copyright protection. But the underlying facts—the accident itself—cannot be copyrighted. A reporter's description of the accident is original and is fixed in a tangible medium when typed into a computer or smartphone. However, the reporter may not successfully claim they were first on the scene, and therefore no other journalist may write about the accident. Nor may a scholar write a book about a historical incident—even one that has not been described previously—and prevent anyone else from writing about the incident.

As technology advances, new questions arise—for example, is an individual point of interest within a GPS database copyrightable? A federal district court said "yes" because of the originality in selecting, categorizing and arranging the database.[39] In another case, a federal district court held that the HTML code and cascading style sheets (commonly called CSS) underlying an online advertiser's website were sufficiently original and creative to allow them to be copyrighted.[40] In *Google v. Oracle*, the U.S. Supreme Court assumed that an API or "application programing interface," was protected by copyright.[41] (This case is included at the end of the chapter.) An API is a type of software that allows two applications to work together. APIs can help simplify "app" development.

The law does not give copyright protection to words and phrases, including advertising slogans and titles of books, movies and television programs, because they lack sufficient originality to qualify for copyright protection. However, a trademark, discussed later in this chapter, can protect these creations. Also, works created by the U.S. government are not eligible for copyright protection.[42]

A work's creator owns the work's copyright—with some exceptions.[43] For example, if two or more people create a work, the copyright is jointly owned, and all creators share the copyright protection.

When a person creates a work as part of their employment, the law gives the copyright to the employer.[44] The copyright law calls such a creation a **work made for hire**.[45] A work may also be for hire if the creator and employer agree to that in writing and if the work is specially ordered or commissioned for use in, for example, a compilation, a motion picture, a textbook or any of several other categories the law specifies.[46]

The U.S. Supreme Court has listed a number of factors for courts to consider in determining whether a person acted as an employee.[47] These include (1) the organization's right to control how the work is accomplished, (2) who owns the equipment used to create the work, (3) where the work took place, (4) who determined the days and hours worked, (5) whether there was a long-term relationship between the two parties, (6) who hired any assistants that may have been used and several other factors. The more the company or organization controls the factors, the more the balance tips toward a work made for hire. Freelancers, today often hired as independent contractors, will own the copyrights to their works, absent a work made for hire or other agreement. It is common, however, for the employer or hiring entity to require a written agreement that establishes the employer's copyright ownership. Freelancers and independent contractors should carefully read agreements they sign to understand who owns the copyright to their work.[48]

Copyright law allows copyright ownership to be changed by contract. Creators can "assign" or "license" their rights to others. When rights are assigned, the owner sells his or her ownership rights to another party and has no control over how the third party uses those rights. When rights are licensed, the owner maintains their copyright, but allows another party (the licensee) to exercise *some* of those rights. This is regularly the case for authors who assign their rights to major publishing houses like Harper & Row, and musicians who assign all or license some portion of their copyrights to a music publisher like Sony. In return, creators receive marketing and publishing services and mass distribution of their work. However, contracts transferring copyrights in freelancer material to a newspaper or magazine do not automatically transfer control to media organizations' online publications. The copyright law calls newspapers and magazines "collective works."[49]

In *New York Times Co., Inc. v. Tasini*, the U.S. Supreme Court said online publications are reproduced and distributed individual articles. The Court said when the Times placed articles published in its paper onto the internet, it took articles out of context because the website presented individual articles rather than articles in the context of the original newspaper page. The freelance writers retained their copyrights in the individual articles, the Court said. If a contract between a freelancer and a newspaper did not specifically include online publications, the agreement covered only the initial publication.[50]

In the digital age, some individual creators have shied away from assigning their work and have chosen to license their work directly using online contracts or "terms of service" (TOS) for their work. Such TOS can detail and protect the nature of restrictions or rights given to the user. Creative Commons (CC) is one of the more popular online licensing tools; such licenses give creators a free and standardized way to grant copyright permissions for various works; ensure proper attribution; and allow others to copy, distribute, and make use of those works.[51]

Exclusive Rights and Limitations

The law specifies six exclusive rights copyright holders have in their works. This includes (1) the right to reproduce the work, (2) the right to make derivative works, (3) the right to distribute the work publicly, (4) the right to perform a work publicly, (5) the right to display a work publicly and (6) the right to transmit a sound recording through digital audio means.[52] No one may copy a work without the copyright holder's permission. There are exceptions to this copyright protection. For example, the U.S. Supreme Court allowed home recording of broadcast programming for personal use.[53] Congress amended the Copyright Act to permit making a single copy of an analog or digital recording for personal use.[54]

A **derivative work** is a work that is obtained from or created in relation to an original work. Without the copyright holder's permission, no one may use a copyrighted work to create a related work. For example, HBO reportedly paid "Game of Thrones" novelist George R. R. Martin millions of dollars for the rights to use his stories as a basis for its "Game of Thrones" series. The HBO series is a derivative work from the novels, for which Martin received compensation.[55] Derivative works can be extremely profitable and important for creators. When Disney created the film "Frozen," derivative works and merchandising included the sheet music, recordings, books derived from the movie, plus any other creative items like costumes for kids. Such sales easily reach into the billions of dollars.[56]

A federal court held that an e-book is not a derivative work because it does not recast, transform or adapt a preexisting work and it is not an original work of authorship.[57] In 2018, the Ninth Circuit Court of Appeals held that the digital remastering of pre-1972 sound recordings did not create derivative works.[58] That determination was tied to the court's reasoning, mentioned earlier, that the digital copy is not original:

> If an allegedly derivative sound recording does not add or remove any sounds from the underlying sound recording, does not change the sequence of the sounds, and does not remix or otherwise alter the sounds in sequence or character, the recording is likely to be nothing more than a copy . . . and is presumptively devoid of the original sound recording authorship required for copyright protection. . . . This presumption may, of course, be overcome, by showing that the work contains independent creative content, recognizable contributions of sound recording authorship or variations in defining aspects that give a derivative sound recording a new and different essential character and identity.[59]

In another case that involved the use of modern technology, a federal judge ruled that the creative output from a computer program is not a derivative work unless the software does the "lion's share" of the creative work.[60] The case involved a complicated mix of copyright and patent infringement claims that centered on the MOVA Contour system, software that captures the motion of the human face to create computer-generated imagery, or CGI. The software's inventor sued several major motion picture studios for alleged unauthorized use of the CGI program, cases that are still tied up in court and have broader intellectual property implications for patent owners. However, the judge rejected the software creator's argument that the software's CGI output—for example, characters in blockbuster films like "Deadpool" and "Guardians of the Galaxy"—was a derivative work of the software itself. The judge said that actors and directors substantially contributed to the facial motions shown in the films.[61]

In addition to controlling derivative works, the copyright owner also determines when a work will be publicly distributed. This includes public distribution of a work on social media. For example, a federal district court said merely posting photos on Twitter does not allow others to use them without permission.[62] Daniel Morel photographed scenes after the Haiti earthquake in 2010. He posted these photos to his Twitter account. Without Morel's permission, an employee of Agence France-Presse, an international news agency, sent eight of Morel's photos to the AFP photo desk. Morel sued AFP and several other media organizations for copyright infringement.

After this monkey selfie emerged and a copyright claim followed, a federal judge said animals do not have copyright privileges under the current law.

Wikicommons

AFP argued that when Morel posted his photos on Twitter, he accepted Twitter's terms of service, and those terms automatically granted permission to use the photos. A federal district court disagreed, holding that Twitter's terms of service do not state or mean that content posted to a Twitter account essentially falls into the public domain.[63] AFP infringed Morel's copyrights, the court ruled.[64]

The right to publicly perform a work applies to "literary, musical, dramatic and choreographic works, pantomimes, and motion pictures and other audiovisual works."[65] This restricts anyone from transmitting a movie to the public, for example, without the copyright holder's permission.

One important consideration in this area of copyright law as a result of new technology is how to apply the Transmit Clause. When Congress passed the 1976 Copyright Act, it added the **Transmit Clause** to clarify how broadcasters and cable television systems "perform" within this area of copyright law. Congress said that, under the Transmit Clause, a broadcast network is performing when it transmits content; a local broadcaster is performing when it transmits the network broadcast; and a cable television system performs when it retransmits a broadcast to its subscribers.[66]

In cable television's infancy, the U.S. Supreme Court held that cable did not infringe anyone's copyright when it retransmitted broadcast station signals to subscribers.[67] The Court said retransmitting broadcast signals was not a performance under the 1909 copyright law and did not require copyright holder permission. Congress agreed to override the Court's decisions in the 1976 law and adopted a compromise that cable system owners had reached with the producers and broadcasters.[68] That 1976 law allows cable operators to retransmit radio and television broadcast signals without obtaining permission in exchange for a compulsory fee based on a percentage of a cable system's annual revenues. The U.S. Copyright Office collects and distributes the fees to the copyright holders of the programs and other material cable broadcasts and retransmits. Multichannel video program distributors have a similar compulsory license to retransmit broadcast signals.[69] For example, direct broadcast satellite services pay royalties according to their number of subscribers.

The application of the Transmit Clause to new technology was at the heart of the U.S. Supreme Court's 2014 decision in *American Broadcasting Companies, Inc. v. Aereo, Inc.*[70] At issue was whether Aereo's innovative system of utilizing thousands of dime-sized antennas to offer its subscribers broadcast television content over the internet violated the Transmit Clause and constituted a public performance of copyrighted works. The Court held that it did, comparing Aereo's service to a cable system.[71] Immediately following the decision, Aereo suspended its video streaming service[72] and asked the Federal Communications Commission to grant it a license to retransmit broadcast material as a MVPD (see Chapter 9), which required Aereo to apply for compulsory licensing (like a cable system) under the Copyright Act.[73] The Copyright Office concluded that internet-based retransmission services are not eligible for a blanket license, like MVPDs, effectively putting them out of business.[74]

FilmOn X, a service nearly identical to Aereo, made arguments similar to Aereo's in various courts at about the same time. After the Supreme Court's *Aereo* decision, FilmOn X's appeal to the Ninth Circuit Court of Appeals ended with a full-court rehearing that resulted in the same ultimate outcome—"a service that captures copyrighted works broadcast over the air, and then retransmits them to paying subscribers over the internet without the consent of the copyright holders, is not a 'cable system' eligible for a compulsory license under the Copyright Act."[75]

In 2020, the Protecting Lawful Streaming Act (PLSA) was signed into law by former President Trump and makes unlawful streaming a felony.[76] Streaming is a method of viewing video or listening to audio content without downloading that content. In recent years, streaming has become the primary mode of music consumption in the U.S. and a growing way to watch video content.[77] The new law increases criminal penalties for those who illegally stream copyrighted content for commercial advantage or financial gain. If convicted, a defendant faces a fine and up to three years in prison for their first office and increasing penalties for additional offenses.

POINTS OF LAW
EXCLUSIVE RIGHTS IN COPYRIGHTED WORKS

The copyright holder with exclusive rights may do the following[78]:

1. Reproduce the copyrighted work
2. Prepare derivative works based upon the copyrighted work
3. Distribute copies of the copyrighted work to the public by sale or other transfer of ownership, or by rental, lease or lending (except CDs and computer software)
4. Perform the copyrighted work publicly in the case of literary, musical, dramatic and choreographic works; pantomimes; and motion pictures and other audiovisual works
5. Display the copyrighted work publicly in the case of literary, musical, dramatic and choreographic works; pantomimes; and pictorial, graphic or sculptural works, including the individual images of a motion picture or other audiovisual work
6. Perform the copyrighted work publicly by means of a digital audio transmission in the case of sound recordings

In addition to public performance rights, copyright holders have the right to publicly display a work. This applies to "literary, musical, dramatic and choreographic works [and] pantomimes," as does the right to perform a work publicly. The right to display adds protection for "pictorial, graphic, or sculptural works, including the individual images of a motion picture or other audiovisual work."[79] Under this provision, no one may display a painting, sculpture, photograph or similar work without the copyright owner's permission.

A common practice on websites today is called inline linking, or the practice of using a linked object, for example an image, that appears on one site but is hosted on another site's server. Sometimes this happens through the use of embedding tools, made available on social media platforms. Does this practice violate a copyright holder's display right? About a decade ago, the Ninth Circuit Court of Appeals created what has come to be called the "server test." The server test maintains that a copyright holder's display right for an image is not infringed when it is embedded or linked from a third-party server.[80]

More recently, at least two courts have rejected the "server test." In 2018, a federal district court chose not to apply the server test and held that Breitbart News Network violated a copyright holder's display right when it embedded a tweet featuring a photograph of New England Patriots quarterback Tom Brady on its website.[81] The candid photo of Brady and other well-known athletes was first posted to the photographer's Snapchat. The photo went viral after the image was connected to speculation that Brady might have been recruiting a free agent basketball player for Boston. The photo ended up on Reddit and then Twitter, shared without permission. Eventually, several news websites used Twitter's embed tool to display the tweets and the image in their articles about Brady and the free agent player.[82]

The court said that embedding a tweet that contains a potentially infringing copy of a photo can constitute infringement, unless it is fair use (discussed later in the chapter). In rejecting the server test, the district court noted, "The plain language of the Copyright Act . . . and subsequent Supreme Court jurisprudence [i.e., *Aereo*] provide no basis for a rule that allows the physical location or possession of an image to determine who may or may not have 'displayed'" it.[83]

The defendants argued that the server test is well-settled law and that providing HTML instructions, which is effectively what the inline linking or embedding process does, is not the same as displaying the image.[84] The Second Circuit Court of Appeals denied an appeal.[85]

In 2019, a website operator that hosts the site *Infowars*, an online conspiracy theory site, sought a declaratory judgment in federal court seeking to dismiss any claim of copyright infringement for its posting of nine photos by the defendant photographer. The photos were part of a book titled "Hungry Planet: What the World Eats" and featured weekly food purchases of families from around the world.[86]

The operator argued that the posts only "pointed" to images hosted at the photographer's own server and that the website "did not itself store any of the photographs at issue."[87] In *Free Speech Systems, LLC v. Menzel*, the court allowed for the direct infringement claim to proceed and left open the possibility of a fair use defense. The court, however, "refused to apply the *Perfect 10* server test outside of that context."[88]

The final exclusive right maintained by a copyright holder is the right to transmit a sound recording through digital audio means.[89] This provision requires obtaining permission from a recording company to play one of its recordings via the internet, satellite radio or other digital media, including interactive services. Permission is not required to play a recording over a broadcasting station or in a live performance, but permission is required to play the composition embedded within the recording (unless its copyright protection has expired).

Some protections are not absolute under U.S. copyright law. For example, libraries open to the public have a limited right to make photocopies for certain purposes.[90] Though not part of the law, Congress provided guidelines for teachers in not-for-profit educational institutions. A teacher may, no more than twice per term, copy one chapter from a book for the teacher's own use or copy an excerpt of no more than 1,000 words or 10 percent of a book to distribute to a class. The guidelines do not allow students to copy materials.[91]

Copyright owners do not have the right to control individual copies of their works after distribution—with a few exceptions. A person who buys a copy of a novel may give away that book, sell it, rent it or throw it away.[92] The author has no right to stop the purchaser from taking any of those actions. This is called the **first-sale doctrine**.[93] The copyright law says that once creators have distributed copies of a work, they no longer can regulate what happens to those copies. However, when copyright holders agree to transfer the physical object containing the copyrighted work—the printed book containing a novel, for example—they do not transfer any rights in the copyrighted content. For example, the law still restricts copying the novel or making derivative works. The first-sale doctrine distinguishes between the physical object and the intellectual creation itself. The doctrine does not change the copyright holder's control of the creation; it changes only control of the object containing the creation. The U.S. Supreme Court has said the first-sale doctrine also allowed the purchase of foreign-manufactured books and the sale of them in the United States.[94]

The first-sale doctrine, like some other parts of the copyright law, was meant for a pre-digital world. When a digital copy is sent from one computer to another, the receiving computer makes an additional copy of the document, something the law does not allow.

Concerns about people making cheap copies of computer software, music or movies prompted Congress to limit the first-sale doctrine by restricting the ability to share digital copies without the copyright holder's permission.[95] The U.S. Court of Appeals for the Second Circuit ruled that a company called ReDigi infringed Capitol Records' copyrights in its sound recordings. ReDigi allowed people to "sell their legally acquired digital music files and buy used digital music from others at a fraction of the price currently available on iTunes." Essentially, ReDigi acted as a used digital music store. The Second Circuit held that when a digital music file moves from one person's computer to another computer, the file is reproduced. Because reproduction is one of the rights guaranteed to a copyright owner, ReDigi infringed Capitol's rights under the copyright law, the court said.[96]

REAL WORLD LAW
UNDERSTANDING NFTS

The rise of the NFT—or non-fungible token—has presented both hype and hypotheses about its impact on and connection to questions of intellectual property. Understanding what an NFT is can confound even the most expert digital minds. As a result, NFTs have presented some market confusion, especially about IP rights attached to NFTs.

As a part of blockchain technology, an NFT is "a programmable digital unit of value that is recorded on a digital ledger."[97] Fungible token goods are exchangeable (like gold or silver), but non-fungible token goods are not because they are one of a kind (like custom-made gold earrings or a painting). NFTs use a particular token programming standard known as ERC-721. Any digital work, including physical goods, that can be found in digital form, such as a photo, video, or a scan, can become a non-fungible token.[98]

The most common NFT "is a metadata file containing information encoded with a digital version of the work that is being tokenized."[99] As the World Intellectual Property Organization (WIPO) points out, there is a lot of confusion about what NFTs mean to copyright law. Many works that are traded as NFTs, such as works of art, are protected by copyright, and it is often unclear about what buyers are getting when they buy an NFT. Some buyers *think* they acquire the underlying work of art when they buy an NFT, in addition to other rights. But buyers are usually buying *only the metadata* associated with the work and not the work itself, although some sellers can also offer to turn the token into an actual transfer of rights. Each NFT sale is unique in terms of the exact rights offered. It is also possible that some NFTs may be infringing. In 2022, Nike filed a lawsuit against StockX, a clothing and sneaker reseller.[100] The complaint charges StockX with trademark infringement and unfair competition for selling nearly 500 Nike brand sneaker NFTs without Nike's permission.

An NFT of Nike sneakers is sold by StockX. StockX has been sued by Nike for selling nearly 500 Nike brand sneaker NFTs without Nike's permission.

(https://heitnerlegal.com/wp-content/uploads/Nike-v-StockX.pdf)

Duration, Licensing and Scope

A copyright is a property right. Just like a car, a copyright can be given away, sold or leased.

Rights protected by copyright can be thought of as a bundle that includes a number of rights. For example, an author writes a novel and has the right, among others, to prevent unauthorized copying. If the author sells the right to reproduce the novel as a hardback book, the author still holds all the other copying rights. The author may sell the paperback copying rights to another publisher. The author may sell to a film studio one of the rights to a derivative work—the right to make a movie from the novel. That still leaves the author with many other rights. Or the author may choose to sell all of their rights to one person or company. Each time the author sells a right, they receive a lump sum payment or, often, a percentage of revenue from sales.

Whoever buys a right from the author then owns that right unless a contract between the author and the buyer says otherwise. If the buyer wants to sell the right to a third person, the author cannot refuse to allow the sale unless the author has a contractual right to do so. A copyright does not disappear when the copyright holder dies. The copyright holder may transfer the right to someone else through a will.

As mentioned previously, not only may copyright holders completely transfer their rights; they may license or lease rights. A license is a contract giving limited permission for use. The 1976 copyright law recognizes that creators often do not have equal bargaining rights with the large corporations purchasing creators' copyrights. To strike a more equal balance, the law gives creators a termination right.[101] This allows creators, or their heirs, to require that the transferred rights be returned 35 to 40 years after the original transfer. This does not apply to works made for hire.

Licensing music in the age of streaming has challenged existing laws and norms. In 2018, Congress passed the Music Modernization Act (MMA) to update music licensing and royalty rules and address royalty problems.[102] The new law, the first major update of copyright law since the DMCA in 1998, ensures that songwriters and artists receive royalties for songs recorded before 1972 and creates a new, independent entity, called the Mechanical Licensing Collective (MLC), to help streaming services, like Apple Music and Spotify, pay copyright holders.[103]

The MMA created a new blanket license for streaming music, managed by the new MLC. This new blanket license will cover activities related to making permanent and limited downloads and interactive streams of "musical works embodied in sound recordings."[104] The MLC is required to:

(i) collect, distribute and audit the royalties generated from these licenses to and for the respective musical work owners; (ii) create and maintain a public database that identifies musical works with their owners along with ownership share information; (iii) provide information to help with and engage in matching musical works with their respective sound recordings; and (iv) hold unclaimed royalties for at least 3 years before distributing them on a market-share basis to copyright owners.[105]

In addition, the MMA improves royalty compensation to songwriters and provides royalties for record producers and sound engineers. Music creators, artists, the recording industry and the tech industry all supported the MMA as an important first step to fix many of the challenges that evolved as the digital music revolution took shape over the past decade.[106]

The U.S. Constitution gives Congress the right to adopt copyright and patent laws "for limited times."[107] The 1976 copyright law gave copyright protection for the creator's lifetime plus 50 years after the creator's death with no renewal. The Sonny Bono Copyright Term Extension Act of 1998 extended all copyright periods by 20 years. Sonny Bono, formerly an entertainer and singer—actress Cher's first husband, was a member of the U.S. House of Representatives when he died. Congress named the copyright extension act in Bono's honor because Bono believed copyrights should last forever.[108]

Mickey Mouse's copyright protection would have expired in 2003 if Congress had not passed the Bono Act.[109] The copyright originally was granted in 1928 when Mickey's first cartoon, "Steamboat Willie," was shown. After the Bono Act took effect, the copyright period for works created on or after Jan. 1, 1978, became the author's lifetime plus 70 years.[110] The Bono Act protects Steamboat Willie's copyright until 2024.

Works made for hire are protected for 95 years from publication or 120 years from creation, whichever is shorter.[111] Copyright protection's duration depends on several factors. First, the current law did not affect works created in the United States that were in the public domain on Jan. 1, 1978. When the current copyright statute took effect, the public domain included many works because their copyrights had expired—such as Herman Melville's "Moby-Dick." Also, some works copyrighted under the 1909 law lost protection because their creators failed to renew copyrights.

Mickey Mouse as Steamboat Willie in the first Mickey cartoon.

AF archive/Alamy Stock Photo

The U.S. Supreme Court upheld the Bono Act against claims that it violates the constitutional copyright clause and the First Amendment.[112] In *Eldred v. Ashcroft*, the Supreme Court said extending the copyright period is constitutional. Congress has the right to determine what "limited" means as long as the copyright period is not forever, the Court said. Congress could justify extending the copyright period because people live longer now. Also, technological changes make copyrighted works last longer.

The creator's life plus 70 years is a limited time within the meaning of the Constitution's copyright clause, the Court said.[113] The phrase "limited time" does not mean a fixed time. The copyright period may be flexible. However, the Court did not define "limited time," nor did it offer a test for determining what period might go beyond "limited."

The Court also rejected First Amendment arguments against the Bono Act. The Constitution's adopters found no tension between the First Amendment and the copyright clause, according to the Court. The current law balances free speech and copyright protection concerns. And the fair use defense, discussed later in this chapter, allows the public to use portions of copyrighted works under certain circumstances, the Court said.

When the United States joined the Berne Convention, many works created in other countries had fallen into the public domain in the United States but not in their creators' countries.[114] That allowed orchestras on limited budgets and school programs, for example, to perform compositions by 20th-century composers such as Dmitri Shostakovich and Igor Stravinsky without paying a royalty fee. Films Alfred Hitchcock directed in England and Pablo Picasso's paintings also were freely available. In 1994, Congress gave copyright protection to these foreign works.[115]

Works affected generally were those produced between 1923 and 1989 that remained under copyright in the country where they were created.[116]

Groups directly affected by losing free access to these works sued, arguing Congress' action was unconstitutional. In *Golan v. Holder*, the U.S. Supreme Court disagreed.[117] The Court said the Constitution's language allows Congress to give copyright protection to works that once were in the public domain. Congress' action did no more than put the United States in the same position as other countries that are parties to the Berne Convention.

The Court also said Congress might reasonably assert that the comportment of U.S. copyright law with the laws of other Berne members would help create a well-functioning international system and thus inspire new works. The Court rejected the plaintiffs' argument that their First Amendment rights were abridged because they no longer could perform the newly protected works. The Court said any work Congress brought under copyright protection remained available, just for a fee. The Court also emphasized Congress' freedom to broadly interpret the Constitution's copyright clause.[118]

Copyright Infringement

Using any part of a copyrighted work without permission is **infringement** unless there is an applicable defense. The copyright statute allows a court to award **statutory damages** even if the infringer does not make a profit from the creator's work.[119]

In addition to statutory damages, the successful party in a copyright infringement lawsuit may recover some of its legal costs. In 2019, the U.S. Supreme Court held unanimously that Section 505 of the Copyright Act allows the prevailing party in copyright litigation to recover only the costs of the legal action that are specifically listed in the six categories in Section 505.[120] In *Rimini Street v. Oracle USA*, Oracle had argued that it was entitled to the "full costs" of its legal action, which the lower courts awarded as $29 million in attorney's fees, $3.4 million in taxable costs and $13 million in additional nontaxable costs, such as covering expert witness costs or jury consultation costs. Justice Brett Kavanaugh wrote for the Court that the $13 million in nontaxable costs was not allowed under Section 505.[121]

Copyright automatically begins for an original work the moment it is created and fixed in a tangible medium. However, if an entity infringes upon the copyright, the copyright holder cannot sue under the law unless the copyright has been registered. To sue for copyright infringement, the plaintiff first must show proof of a valid, registered copyright prior to bringing a lawsuit. After several circuit court decisions left unclear the point in the copyright application process at which an infringement claim may begin, the U.S. Supreme Court weighed in. In 2019, the Supreme Court unanimously held that a copyright claimant may only commence a copyright infringement lawsuit after the copyright is registered by the U.S. Copyright Office. Copyright owners may recover for infringements that occurred before and after the copyright's registration, but they may not bring an infringement claim until the Register of Copyrights has approved a properly filed application and registered the copyright.[122]

Nearly 70 years ago, a landmark decision in the Second Circuit Court of Appeals defined the basic structure of most copyright infringement claims.[123] Called the *Arnstein* test, it first requires a determination of whether a plaintiff's work was actually copied. Without proof of copying, there is no infringement. To prove that something was copied, juries and judges consider whether a defendant had access to the work and whether the works are substantially similar. Today, expert witness testimony is allowed as part of the process to help better understand differences in various contexts. For example, the context of a copyright infringement claim about music sampling could be different than a claim about software. It is common for courts to recognize the need for expert testimony in cases that are highly technical.[124]

POINTS OF LAW
INFRINGING COPYRIGHT

A copyright plaintiff must prove

1. the work used is protected by a valid copyright—meaning it is an original work fixed in a tangible medium;
2. the plaintiff owns the copyright;
3. the valid copyright is registered with the Copyright Office; *and*
4. there is evidence that the defendant directly copied the copyrighted work *or* the infringer had access to the copyrighted work, and the two works are substantially similar.

Over the years, courts have created several different tests to help refine the definition of substantial similarity.[125] Regardless of the test applied, the keys to determining infringement are access and substantial similarity. Legal experts note that the *Arnstein* decision deliberately empowered juries to play a central role in determining the answer to both questions. The question of access to a copyrighted work always comes before consideration of substantial similarity.

Robin Thicke and Pharrell Williams perform in 2013. Their song, "Blurred Lines," was the target of a copyright infringement lawsuit by the estate of Motown legend Marvin Gaye.

In a well-publicized infringement case, a Los Angeles jury in 2015 awarded the estate of Motown legend Marvin Gaye $7.3 million for copyright infringement. At issue was substantial similarity between the 2013 smash hit "Blurred Lines," written and performed by Robin Thicke, Pharrell Williams and Clifford Harris (better known as rapper T.I.), and Gaye's 1977 classic "Got to Give It Up."[126] The judgment was later reduced to $5.3 by the district court, which found insufficient evidence the artists had acted in bad faith.[127]

Thicke, Williams and Harris ended months of arguing with Gaye's family by filing a lawsuit asking the federal court to declare that their song did not infringe "Got to Give It Up." The three argued that what they were trying to capture with "Blurred Lines" was a specific "feel," paying tribute to an era and a genre. Gaye's estate filed a counterclaim, arguing that the two songs contained eight similarities that infringed, including a signature phrase in the main vocal melodies, hooks with similar notes and backup vocals and similarity of the core themes of the songs, among other similarities.[128] The case wound up before a jury.

Because Gaye's estate owned only the composition (the sheet music), not the sound recording, the court allowed the jury only to hear a stripped-down version of Gaye's recording of "Got to Give It Up." The jury sided with Gaye's estate, deciding that Thicke and Williams had infringed but Harris had not, nor had the distributors of the song (Universal Music Group, Interscope Records and Williams' Star Trak Entertainment).[129]

Experts argue that copyright law today has become so complex that jury decisions create ad hoc and arbitrary results. The U.S. Supreme Court has never weighed in on copyright infringement analyses, which is why courts differ in their approach to determining infringement.

A plaintiff does not have to prove that a copyright infringement was deliberate. Accidental infringement violates the law. A court may reduce statutory damages imposed on a person who unintentionally infringed on another person's copyright and waive statutory damages completely if the innocent infringer works for a nonprofit library or public broadcaster.[130]

In addition to direct copyright infringement, other forms of infringement can occur. Showing that the defendant knowingly aided or contributed to copyright infringement is sufficient for **contributory infringement**. Although contributory infringement is not specifically banned in the copyright law, the statute implies that contributory infringement violates the law, and courts long have held it actionable.[131]

Contributory infringement may be difficult to prove. Several television program producers sued Sony for making VCRs that allowed viewers to tape copyrighted programs without permission. The producers claimed the VCRs enabled unauthorized copying. In *Sony Corp. of America v. Universal City Studios, Inc.*, the U.S. Supreme Court said Sony might have known that viewers used VCRs to record television programs, but it could be fair use (discussed later in this chapter) to record programs to watch later—time shifting.[132] Sony was not liable because the VCRs could be used for noninfringing purposes, the Court ruled.[133]

A quarter-century later, Cablevision Systems faced a similar challenge to its digital video recorder system. A group of movie studios and broadcast and cable networks argued that Cablevision's DVRs directly infringed on program copyrights by making unauthorized copies on computers and publicly performing the programs when customers later watched them. The U.S. Court of Appeals for the Second Circuit ruled that the cable customer, rather than Cablevision, copied the program. Cablevision's computers acted as a modern VCR. Because only one customer at a time viewed the program, the program was not publicly performed, "public" being a group larger than just one customer.[134]

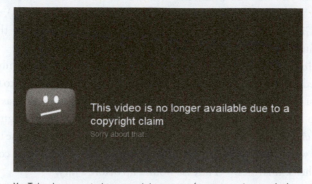

YouTube has created a copyright center (www.youtube.com/yt/copyright/) to teach users about copyright infringement and avoid video removals.

YouTube

Another form of infringement is **vicarious infringement**, based on a common law principle that holds companies responsible for the acts of employees if the acts are within the nature and scope of the employment. To establish liability, direct infringement must occur. In cases of vicarious infringement, the company has a financial interest in the infringement and the ability to control it even if the company does not have direct knowledge of the infringement.

Early digital music file-sharing services are examples of vicarious and contributory infringement. Napster, one of the first music file-sharing services, allowed users to reach into each other's computers to retrieve files containing copyrighted music. Before the Ninth Circuit Court of Appeals ruled that Napster's operation violated copyright law, millions of people used this peer-to-peer network to make unauthorized copies of sound recordings.[135] Napster's sole purpose was to aid copyright infringement by allowing users to share copyrighted music, according to the court.

More than 15 years ago, the recording and movie industries filed a copyright infringement lawsuit against two peer-to-peer networks, Grokster and Morpheus, claiming they contributed to copyright infringement by allowing network users to illegally download copyrighted songs and movies. In the *Metro-Goldwyn-Mayer Studios, Inc. v. Grokster, Ltd.* decision, the U.S. Supreme Court held that Grokster infringed on MGM's copyright because it knew people used its software to download music files. The Supreme Court said it did not matter that the software could be used for legal purposes because Grokster induced, or encouraged, users to infringe on copyrights.[136] Courts call this **infringement by inducement**. Infringement by inducement is when a person or entity who does not directly infringe induces others to do so and can be held liable for that infringement.[137]

Websites allowing users to illegally download movies violate the *Grokster* decision's inducement rule, the Ninth Circuit Court of Appeals held in 2013.[138] Seven major movie studios showed that the defendant's peer-to-peer file-sharing sites directly helped site users locate specific movies and television programs to upload copyrighted works and burn copyrighted material onto DVDs to play on television sets. The court said this and other evidence showed the defendant induced site users to infringe the movie studio's copyrights.

REAL WORLD LAW

THE COPYRIGHT ALTERNATIVE IN SMALL-CLAIMS ENFORCEMENT ACT OF 2020

The Copyright Alternative in Small-Claims Enforcement Act, or CASE Act, was passed by Congress in 2020 to help streamline copyright infringement claims for matters less than $30,000.[139] The Act established a Copyright Claims Board as a low-cost alternative to litigation in federal court. The Board will hear cases for $100, with or without a lawyer. Organizations supporting the law included the Professional Photographers of America and the Society of Composers & Lyricists supported the legislation.

"Images are infringed just at this exponential number and short of going to federal court, which is really expensive, there's no real other alternative," said National Press Photographers Association general counsel Mickey Osterreicher told Bloomberg Law. "Hopefully through the review board, you're not going to have those kinds of costs."[140]

Fair Use Defense

A person sued for copyright infringement might claim that the plaintiff did not file within the law's three-year statute of limitations (or five years for criminal charges).[141] Or a defendant may argue that the copyright holder knowingly has abandoned the copyright, placing the work in the public domain.[142] The most common defense, however, is **fair use**.

Courts recognized the fair use defense long before Congress wrote it into the 1976 copyright law.[143] Courts understood that the copyright statutes—from 1790 to the present—give copyright holders the right to forbid any use of their works without permission. But what if an English teacher copies a few paragraphs from a novel for a class discussion? Or a movie reviewer shows 15 seconds of a film on television to illustrate a point about the movie? Or a comedian sings a portion of a song's lyrics in a parody? Courts have decided that these and similar uses could be fair to the copyright holder and to society. The 1976 Copyright Act included fair use as a defense.[144]

Fair use is difficult to define. One judge has said that to be fair "the use must be of a character that serves the copyright objective of stimulating productive thought and public instruction without excessively diminishing the incentives for creativity."[145] The 1976 law set out four criteria courts use in balancing the plaintiff's rights to forbid any use of a work without permission and the defendant's right to use a portion of the work under certain circumstances: (1) the purpose and character of the use, (2) the nature of the copyrighted work, (3) the amount and substantiality of the portion used, and (4) the effect on the plaintiff's potential market.

1. The Purpose and Character of the Use

In determining the purpose and character of the defendant's use of the copyrighted material, courts consider several factors, including whether the use is for commercial or nonprofit purposes. The law gives examples of uses that would tilt the balance toward a fair use: criticism, comment, news reporting, teaching (including multiple copies for classroom use), scholarship, parody, searchable databases and research.[146]

POINTS OF LAW
FAIR USE DEFENSE

1. For what purpose was the copyrighted work used without permission?
2. What was the nature of the copyrighted work that was used without permission?
3. How much and what portion of the copyrighted work was used without permission?
4. What effect did the unauthorized use have on the copyrighted work's market value?

News reporting may be a purpose considered to be a fair use, but this is not clear. For example, more than 30 years ago, The Nation magazine used 300 to 400 words from President Gerald R. Ford's memoirs without the book publisher's permission. The publisher had sold Time magazine the exclusive right to run excerpts. The U.S. Supreme Court acknowledged that Ford's thoughts were news, but that alone was not sufficient to qualify The Nation's copying as fair use.[147] The Supreme Court said it was not.

In a case involving a cover version of a popular song, the U.S. Supreme Court considered whether a parody changes the work it mocks or merely repeats without permission the copyrighted material.[148] In its decision, the Supreme Court made **transformative use** a key part of fair use's first element (the concept of transformative use is also discussed in Chapter 6, related to the right of publicity). The more the parody transforms the work it mimics, the more likely it is that the nature of the use is fair.

The Court said fair use is more likely if the new work "adds something new, with a further purpose or different character, altering the [copyrighted work] with new expression, meaning, or message."[149] A 2 Live Crew parody of Roy Orbison's song "Oh, Pretty Woman" might be fair use because it did transform the original, the Supreme Court said.[150] The Court emphasized the importance of 2 Live Crew's transformation of the original but said the district court must reconsider whether the other fair use elements established fair use. The parties settled the case.[151] The reach of the transformative use test was under review by the U.S. Supreme Court in 2022 in *Andy Warhol Foundation for the Visual Arts v. Goldsmith*.[152] In that case, the justices considered whether a Warhol screen print of the artist Prince, which was heavily based on a photograph of Prince taken by Lynn Goldsmith, qualified as a transformative use. The Second Circuit had ruled that the screen print was not transformative because while the Warhol piece had added a new aesthetic, it was not enough activity to qualify as transformative.[153]

The Seventh Circuit Court of Appeals ruled that a parody by the animated television program "South Park" of a viral video, "What What (In the Butt)," was fair use because the program's intent was "to comment on and critique the social phenomenon that is the 'viral video.'"[154] In 2015, the Second Circuit held that an unauthorized derivative work of the film "Point Break" was also fair use and could itself be copyrighted because the parody added sufficient originality.[155]

Arguments for transformative use go beyond parodies, and they do not always succeed. For example, in a bench trial in federal court in New York, the judge found that a celebrity gossip website infringed on the copyrights of the owners of celebrity photos it used. The website argued that its unauthorized use of the paparazzi images in website banners and as thumbnail images along with "clickbait" headlines was transformative, but the court disagreed.[156]

A federal court of appeals found a "South Park" parody to be fair use.

AF archive/Alamy Stock Photo

A federal judge held that the legal databases Lexis and Westlaw did not violate copyright law when they copied legal briefs in their entirety to create an interactive legal research tool. Although the use of the legal briefs was commercial (or for profit), the judge said the transformative nature of the database carried greater weight.[157]

A federal district court in New York held that a service that monitors and records television and radio broadcasts to turn them into a searchable database for its users amounts to fair use because the database is transformative.[158] On appeal, however, the Second Circuit Court of Appeals reversed.[159] The court said that while the service was developed and offered for transformative purposes, the service's watch function, which allowed viewers to watch the recorded video clips, was not fair use.[160]

Transformative use is one of the primary defenses used today when arguing fair use. Transformative use is generally fair use if the answer to two questions is "yes":

1. Has the material you have taken from the original work been transformed by adding new expression or meaning?

2. Was value added to the original by creating new information, new aesthetics or new insights and understandings?

Courts must also apply the other fair use factors (discussed in this section) to transformative use, but frequently it is the transformative use determination that carries the most weight.

In 2015, the Second Circuit Court of Appeals held that Google's mass digitization of millions of books, in connection with providing brief excerpts of books used in Google's search function, was a transformative fair use.[161] Several book publishers and the Authors Guild, which represents authors whose works were made into digital books without their permission, sued Google, claiming copyright infringement. A federal district judge ruled that scanning the books amounted to fair use for purposes of preserving the works, making the books available to those with sight impairment and enabling the works to be searched.[162] The Second Circuit agreed and noted that Google's "snippet" view of the books added value and context to the basic transformative search function.[163]

More recently, the U.S. Supreme Court decided that Google's use of Oracle's API (application programming interface) for their Google smartphone to be transformative. In *Google LLC v Oracle America, Inc.*, the Court said Google's objective was to create " a new collection of tasks operating in a distinct and different computing environment."[164] (See more about this case at the end of the chapter.)

2. The Nature of the Copyrighted Work. This factor examines whether the copyrighted work is largely creative, such as a feature film, or more informational or functional, like a compilation of court decisions.[165] Courts often find more copyright protection for creative works. Copying portions of factually based materials may tilt the balance toward a fair use.

The question of whether unpublished materials should have special protection against a fair use defense arose when a court allowed J. D. Salinger, the author of "The Catcher in the Rye," to stop distribution of an unauthorized biography including excerpts from his letters.[166] A federal appellate court held that unpublished materials are entitled to more protection than published works. Congress later amended the Copyright Act to clarify that while unpublished materials are afforded more protection than published materials, fair use is still an appropriate defense if a person can meet all four factors.[167]

3. The Amount and Substantiality of the Portion Used. Courts ask two questions with regard to the amount and substantiality factor. First, how much of the copyrighted work was used without permission? Courts may count how many lines of code from a computer program, words from a story or seconds from a movie were used. A court may also consider what percentage of the original was used. Second, what particular portion of the copyrighted work was used, and how important was it to the copyrighted work? If the most important portion of a work is used without permission, the balance tips toward infringement.

Copying the entirety of a copyrighted work does not necessarily mean the use was not fair. A group of students sued the company that owns Turnitin, a plagiarism detection service, because Turnitin archived their work in the company's computers. The students claimed the archiving effectively copied their work, thus infringing their copyrights. The Fourth Circuit Court of Appeals disagreed.[168] Although the company copied each student paper in its entirety, the court found Turnitin's archiving to be fair use. In general, the court said, "as the amount of the copyrighted material that is used increases, the likelihood that the use will constitute a 'fair use' decreases."[169] However, the court balanced the amount used against other fair use factors, particularly the purpose of the use. Turnitin uses each student paper for a limited purpose, that is, to enable students and teachers to expose plagiarism. In the database-related transformative use cases noted earlier, courts reinforced the idea that fair use can apply even if works are copied in their entirety.[170]

Similarly, a federal appellate court said reprinting full pictures of Grateful Dead posters and concert tickets did not preclude finding fair use when the images were scattered throughout a book in collages of images, text and graphic art. The court said the use was transformative because images were shown in reduced size and only a few unauthorized copyrighted works were published among 2,000 images.[171]

4. The Effect on the Plaintiff's Potential Market. Many courts consider the extent to which the unauthorized copying diminished the copyright holder's likely profits from their creation. Historically, this was the most important of the four fair use factors. Today, it is typically the second most important factor behind transformative use. When a Kinko's store responded to professors' requests to make course packets by copying chapters from numerous books without permission, several publishers sued for copyright infringement. A court rejected Kinko's fair use defense, finding the fourth factor the "single most important" part of the fair use test in that particular case.[172] If students purchased the professor's course packet, they were not purchasing the textbook from which the chapters came.

The U.S. Supreme Court has said copying a substantial portion of a copyrighted work without permission may prove a "greater likelihood of market harm under the fourth" element of the fair use test.[173] That is, typically, the more of a work that someone copies, the less likely it is someone else will purchase the original. This would cause market harm to the copyright holder. With the increase in the application of transformative use in the first part of the fair use test (purpose and character of the use), some courts have acknowledged that under the fourth part of the test the transformative use of the work actually expands the market for the original work.[174] That is, copying the entire work for a searchable database, as Google has done, can make the full work more widely available in the marketplace, and that enhances the value of the copyrighted work.

Sec. 512 and the DMCA Safe Harbor Protections

As noted earlier in this chapter, the Digital Millennium Copyright Act was an attempt to bring the internet and other digital media under copyright law.[175] One of the concerns the DMCA addresses is whether internet service providers can lose copyright suits based on content their users post.

Section 512 of the DMCA shields internet service providers (ISPs) and platforms from copyright infringement claims if they remove material that a copyright holder tells them is posted without permission.[176] This is called "notice and takedown." This protection is available if a website names an agent to receive takedown requests, lets site users know of the site's copyright infringement policy and complies with takedown requests it receives. Users also have the ability to engage in counter-notification and challenge the notice and takedown process. Platforms must comply with takedown requests that clearly identify the work claimed to infringe copyright and provide the URL of the infringing work.[177] A customer cannot sue the platform for removing material even if the customer later shows the material did not violate a copyright holder's rights. Platforms that knowingly transmit material that violates copyright are not protected.

The DMCA offers other protection to video-sharing websites such as YouTube and Vimeo. It protects video-sharing websites from monetary damages when a user, rather than the site, posts copyrighted material without permission. The copyright holder cannot successfully sue the site operator if the operator (1) did not know the content infringed someone's copyright, (2) did not earn money directly from the posted material, and (3) promptly complied with a takedown notice. These takedown protections, also known as **safe harbor**, limit video-sharing sites' liability.

The DMCA's safe harbor saved Veoh Networks, an internet-based video-sharing service, from losing a copyright infringement suit. Universal Music Group, one of the world's largest recording companies, sued Veoh over user-uploaded videos that included UMG-copyrighted songs. Veoh had implemented a copyright infringement policy and taken down videos when notified of violations but was not able to prevent all infringements. Despite failure to notify Veoh of all infringing videos, UMG said Veoh should have known some of its videos infringed copyright. The Ninth Circuit Court of Appeals said the DMCA requires specific notification to Veoh of videos that need to be removed.[178] Absent such notification, Veoh had neither the right nor the ability to prevent users from posting videos that infringed copyright, the court said.

The DMCA's safe harbor provision also kept Google-owned YouTube from losing a $1 billion suit filed by Viacom in 2013. A district judge in 2013 held that YouTube's removal of 100,000 videos that Viacom said infringed its copyrights did not show that YouTube knew it carried Viacom's copyrighted material.[179] Without that knowledge, the safe harbor protected YouTube.

In 2016, the Second Circuit Court of Appeals ruled that the DMCA safe harbor did not protect a handful of infringing videos that Vimeo employees viewed and did not flag for possible infringement.[180] This is sometimes called **red-flag knowledge**. The phrase refers to a platform that is "subjectively aware of facts that would have made the specific infringement 'objectively' obvious to a reasonable person."[181] If a website or platform has red-flag knowledge of infringing material and does not remove it, then a court could find it responsible for infringement. Vimeo argued that the videos reviewed by the employees did not contain "objectively obvious" infringement and should be protected by the safe harbor provision, but the court disagreed.[182]

The DMCA safe harbor does not offer protection if an ISP or sharing service does not implement its policies for enforcement. For example, in 2018, the Fourth Circuit Court of Appeals rejected Cox Communications' safe harbor defense in a case that involved its subscribers' use of BitTorrent, a peer-to-peer file sharing system used mostly for the sharing of copyrighted material without permission. While the ISP had a policy for terminating repeat infringers, evidence showed it did not act to actually terminate users who received multiple notices of infringing behavior.[183]

In the context of a news website, the Tenth Circuit Court of Appeals held in 2016 that Examiner.com was protected under the DMCA safe harbor provision after individuals contributing to the website posted photographs without permission. The court's decision was based on the fact that the site's contributors are considered users under the DMCA and that the infringing photos were posted at their discretion. The website did not have red-flag knowledge.[184]

TRADEMARKS

Trademarks help businesses protect their brands and identity. A **trademark** is a word, name, symbol or design used to identify a company's goods and distinguish them from similar products other companies make.[185] A service mark accomplishes the same purpose for services a firm provides. A trade name identifies a particular company rather than the company's product or service. Federal law also protects trade dress, which describes a product's total look, including size, shape, color, texture and graphics. The word "trademark" may be used generally to include all four of these categories. However, the law does not protect trade names or trade dress as completely as it protects trademarks and service marks. Marks must be in use and remain in use to retain federal trademark law protection.

Trademarks may be brand names or logos designed to identify a company's product. The Nike "swoosh" is a well-known logo. But the list of what can be trademarked is lengthy: letters (CBS), numbers (VO5), domain names (Amazon.com), slogans ("Just do it"), shapes (Coke bottle), colors (Corning fiberglass pink insulation),[186] sounds (quacking noise made by guides and participants in duck boat tours)[187] and smells ("fresh cut grass" for tennis balls).[188]

When a company filed to register "The Krusty Krab" as a trademark for a future restaurant chain, Viacom, the owner of "SpongeBob SquarePants" trademarks, sued for trademark infringement and won.

Photo 12/Alamy Stock Photo

Trademarks are valuable. For example, consider the importance of McDonald's, Google, Nike, Amazon, Kleenex, Starbucks and Coke as trademarks. Companies use trademarks to advertise their products and services. Customers use trademarks to ensure they are getting the goods or services from a particular company. The federal Lanham Act protects trademarks that are eligible for registration with the U.S. Patent and Trademark Office (USPTO).[189] The law ensures that if a company complies with certain requirements, no other company may use the trademarked word, symbol, slogan or other such item that will confuse consumers about who supplies a particular product or service. The Lanham Act also prevents using a mark to falsely suggest a product's source even if the mark is not registered.[190]

Distinctiveness Requirement

Distinctive words, designs or other indicators of a product or service's origin are eligible for trademark registration.[191] A trademark will be protected only if it is distinctive. A trademark is distinctive if it distinguishes one company's goods from another's.

There is a spectrum of distinctiveness in trademark law. The less unique—that is, the more broadly descriptive—a mark is, the less likely it is to be eligible for trademark registration. The most distinctive category is **fanciful marks**. These are invented marks, including made-up words. Lexus, Xerox and Exxon are examples of fanciful marks. A court found that Peterbilt and Kenworth are fanciful marks applied to trucks.[192] The trucks' manufacturer sued a website operator who used the words "Peterbilt" and "Kenworth" in the site's address without permission. Because fanciful marks are the strongest and most distinctive trademarks possible, the greatest trademark protection should be applied to fanciful marks, the court said. When a strong mark is infringed, it is more likely consumers will be confused, the court concluded.

Arbitrary marks, the next most distinctive category, are words that have ordinary meanings unrelated to the product or service. For example, an apple is a fruit, but Apple is a trademark for computers and other products manufactured by Apple, Inc. A dictionary will define the word "apple" as a fruit, but not as a computer. Numbers and letters arranged in a distinctive order may be arbitrary marks, such as bebe for clothes[193] or V8 for vegetable juice.[194]

Suggestive marks suggest a product's qualities or a manufacturer's business but do not describe either. A suggestive mark requires consumers to use their imaginations to discern the company's exact business.[195] One court said Coppertone, Orange Crush and Playboy are good examples of suggestive marks "because they conjure images of the associated products without directly describing those products."[196] A court held that the word "CarMax" is a suggestive mark for a used car dealership.[197] The word suggests that CarMax is involved in the automobile business but does not say the company sells used cars.

A **descriptive mark** leaves little to a consumer's imagination. The mark describes the product or service and may or may not suggest what company provided it. Generally, commonly used descriptive terms cannot be trademarked. For example, many soft drink companies may use the word "refreshing" to describe their products. However, a descriptive mark may be a trademark if it has acquired a distinctive connection to the product for which it is used. Courts call this a **secondary meaning** beyond the word's common meaning. Distinctive, arbitrary and suggestive marks do not require a secondary meaning.

To obtain a secondary meaning, the public must associate a word with a product's source or producer, not the product. Courts do not agree on a test for finding a secondary meaning, but the Ninth Circuit Court of Appeals' approach is illustrative. It considers "(1) whether actual purchasers of the product bearing the claimed trademark associate the trademark with the producer; (2) the degree and manner of advertising under the claimed trademark; (3) the length and manner of use of the claimed trademark; and (4) whether use of the claimed trademark has been exclusive."[198]

In 2018, the Fifth Circuit Court of Appeals held that Viacom held the common law trademark to "The Krusty Krab," the name of the restaurant central to the Viacom-owned animated show "SpongeBob SquarePants."[199] Viacom had sued a corporation that sought to register the trademark "The Krusty Krab" for its planned chain of restaurants. The court said that "The Krusty Krab" was distinctive and had acquired secondary meaning. The public associates "The Krusty Krab" with "SpongeBob SquarePants" because it is a significant element in the show that has aired for 18 years, it is depicted in advertisements that promote franchise sales and it is used on social media platforms by the "SpongeBob" franchise, as well as in mobile apps and games, the court said. The court rejected the argument from the restaurant owner that the public would find the cartoon distinct from the restaurant.[200]

POINTS OF LAW
TYPES OF MARKS

A trademark is only protected if it is distinctive. The more distinct or unique a mark, the more likely it will be eligible for trademark registration.
- **Fanciful marks**—invented marks, including made-up words (for example, "Lexus") most likely to receive trademark protection
- **Arbitrary marks**—words that have ordinary meanings unrelated to the product or service (for example, "Apple")
- **Suggestive marks**—marks that suggest a product's source or manufacturer's business but do not describe what the product is (for example, "Playboy")
- **Descriptive marks**—marks that describe the product or service and leave little to a consumer's imagination and that must attach a distinctive meaning to the product or service (called secondary meaning) to be trademarked

Certain groups of descriptive words, such as geographic terms, rarely acquire the secondary meaning needed to be a registered trademark if they only describe where the goods or services are made or offered.

For example, a court refused to find that the word "Boston" had a secondary meaning in the phrase "Boston Beer."[201] Although the beer is manufactured in Boston, "Boston" means the Massachusetts city and is not connected in the public's mind with that brand of beer, the court said. The court did not allow "Boston Beer" to become a trademark. A geographic term also cannot be a registered trademark if it is deceptive. For example, a ham processor located in Nebraska cannot use the term "Danish ham" as a trademark for its product.

Similarly, people's names must acquire a secondary meaning to be protected. In one case, Fabrikant & Sons, a jewelry company, trademarked the word "Fabrikant." Several years later, Fabrikant Fine Diamonds began business as a buyer and seller of jewelry. Both companies are located in New York City, and both are owned by individuals named Fabrikant. A court ruled that Fabrikant Fine Diamonds had to either stop using the name Fabrikant or use a first name in front of the word to distinguish it from Fabrikant & Sons.[202] Otherwise the public would be confused, the court said. Courts often consider three factors to rule in competing name cases. As one court put it, the factors are "(a) the interest of the plaintiff in protecting the good will which has attached to his personal name trademark, (b) the interest of the defendant in using his own name in his business activities and (c) the interest of the public in being free from confusion and deception."[203]

Finally, **generic words** will not be given trademark protection. A graham cracker manufacturer cannot use the word "cracker" as a trademark, for example. A manufacturer is not allowed to take a word commonly used to describe a product category and use it exclusively for the company's own purpose. For instance, Harley-Davidson could not use the word "hog" as a mark for its motorcycles,[204] nor could a concert promoter obtain a trademark for the term "summer jam" to advertise its summer concerts.[205]

Some marks that once were protected became generic when the public used the mark to mean a category of goods rather than a particular manufacturer's product. "Thermos," "cellophane," "brassiere," "aspirin," "shredded wheat" and "monopoly" (the board game) all once were protected copyrights that became generic words.[206] Courts ask what a word's primary significance is to the public. If the public thinks of a word as describing a class of goods—a vacuum bottle is a thermos—the word is generic and cannot be a protected mark. If the word primarily means a particular manufacturer—Xerox makes Xerox copying machines—the word will remain a trademark.[207]

Companies often take several steps to prevent a trademark from becoming generic. Among other actions, a company may select a distinctive mark, advertise the goods using both the trademark and the product's generic word (Kleenex facial tissue), use advertisements to educate the public that the product's trademark is not a generic word and use the trademark on several different products.[208]

Registering a Trademark

A history of using a distinctive mark to identify a product can give the mark protection even if it is not registered. The first person or company to use the mark owns it. State courts recognize common law rights in marks within the geographic area where the mark is used. It is not necessary to register a mark to give it common law protection. An owner of a mark protected by common law may use the symbols ™ (trademark) or ˢᴹ (service mark), but these are not recognized by statute.

A mark must be registered with the U.S. Patent and Trademark Office to have statutory protection under the Lanham Act.[209] Registering a mark requires submitting an application form, a drawing of the mark and a filing fee to the USPTO. Trademark law's complexity means a trademark attorney needs to be involved in registering a mark. Trademark registration excludes marks with a flag or other insignia of any country or U.S. state or city, marks with a name or other identification of a living person without the individual's consent or marks that are only descriptive without secondary meaning.[210] Nor will the USPTO register a mark identical to or similar to an existing mark.[211]

Congress recently passed the Trademark Modernization Act of 2020 to combat an increase in fraudulent trademark filings (many coming from China) and to improve the overall efficiency of the registry.[212] The new act allows third parties to petition for reexamination or expungement of marks from the registry in an effort to clear unused or "deadwood" marks. The new act also provides for shorter examination periods to clear a trademark and faster movement to remove trademarks that are not in use.

Federal registration provides more protection for a mark than does common law. Registration establishes the date of the mark's first use, protects nationwide use and lets competitors know that a company owns the mark.[213] A company may use the statutory symbol for registered marks. The symbol ® or the phrase "Registered U.S. Patent and Trademark Office" is acceptable. If a registered mark is infringed, its owner may sue in federal court. After five years of use, the mark gains nearly complete protection.[214] During the sixth year after registration, a mark owner must file an affidavit confirming the mark has been in continued use.[215] Marks registered after Nov. 16, 1989, have a 10-year term. Registrations may be renewed indefinitely.[216]

Section 2(a) of the Lanham Act has been the focus of several lawsuits in recent years, two of which have been heard by the U.S. Supreme Court. Part of Section 2(a) prevented the USPTO from registering a mark that was considered immoral, disparaging or deceptive.[217] These kinds of trademarks are often referred to as **disparaging marks**. In 2017, the U.S. Supreme Court considered whether the Lanham Act's ban on disparaging trademarks violated the First Amendment.[218] Simon Tam and his Asian-American band the Slants applied for a trademark to protect the band name. The band said it used the name to reappropriate the slur sometimes applied to Asians. The USPTO refused to register the trademark because it was disparaging. Sitting en banc, the D.C. Circuit Court of Appeals reversed and held that the USPTO's ban on disparaging marks was an unconstitutional viewpoint-based restriction on speech.[219] "Courts have been slow to appreciate the expressive power of trademarks," the D.C. Circuit Court wrote. "The government cannot refuse to register disparaging marks because it disapproves of the expressive messages conveyed by the marks."[220]

The government argued that trademarks, like license plates, are a form of government speech. Government's power to operate the trademark program includes the power to reject the disparaging mark. In *Matal v. Tam*, excerpted at the end of the chapter, the U.S. Supreme Court held that the disparagement clause violates the First Amendment. "Contrary to the Government's contention, trademarks are private, not government speech," Justice Samuel Alito wrote for the Court. "Because the "Free Speech Clause . . . does not regulate government speech," the government is not required to maintain viewpoint neutrality on its own speech. This Court exercises great caution in extending its government-speech precedents, for if private speech could be passed off as government speech by simply affixing a government seal of approval, government could silence or muffle the expression of disfavored viewpoints."[221]

While the Court's decision in *Matal v. Tam* addressed disparaging trademarks, Section 2(a) of the Lanham Act also prevented the USPTO from registering a mark that was considered immoral. In 2019, the U.S. Supreme Court considered whether the registration of "immoral" or "scandalous" marks violates the First Amendment. The case involved the USPTO's rejection of the trademark "FUCT" under Section 2(a). Los Angeles artist Erik Brunetti founded the FUCT clothing brand in 1991. Brunetti sought trademark protection in 2011. The PTO rejected the trademark because it viewed the mark as a scandalous, four-letter word.[222]

In addition to raising First Amendment concerns, the Oregon-based band the Slants said it needed its name trademarked to land a record label deal.

Anthony Pidgeon/Redferns/Getty Images

After the Supreme Court's ruling in *Matal*, the D.C. Circuit Court of Appeals ruled in Brunetti's favor, finding that Section 2(a)'s ban on immoral trademarks violated the First Amendment because it was a content-based restriction that should be subject to strict scrutiny.[223] In oral arguments before the Supreme Court, the government argued that registering a trademark is a government benefit that does not prevent Brunetti from selling his clothes with the FUCT brand. By not registering his trademark, the government is placing a valid condition on participation in a federal program, the government argued.[224]

The Supreme Court disagreed. Justice Elena Kagan, writing for the majority, said that the Lanham Act's ban was viewpoint based, overly broad and violated the First Amendment. She highlighted the USPTO's inconsistent application of the ban—for example, the USPTO's rejection of a mark that promoted the use of medical marijuana, but approval of a mark used to discourage drug use; or, the approval of a mark with the words "War on Terrorism Memorial," but the rejection of a mark that reflected support for the terrorist group al-Qaeda. "These decisions are understandable. The rejected marks express opinions that are, at the least, offensive to many Americans," Kagan wrote. "But as the Court made clear in *Tam*, a law disfavoring 'ideas that offend' discriminates based on viewpoint, in violation of the First Amendment."[225]

All of the justices agreed that the Lanham Act's provision violated the First Amendment. Three justices concurred in part and dissented in part, writing separate opinions. Chief Justice John Roberts and Justices Stephen Breyer and Sonia Sotomayor all said the Court should have accepted the government's argument that a narrow construction of the definition of "scandalous" would not violate the First Amendment—it would only regulate marks that are obscene, vulgar or profane.[226] "Freedom of speech is a cornerstone of our society and the First Amendment protects Brunetti's right to use words like the one at issue here," wrote Justice Sotomayor. "The Government need not, however, be forced to confer on Brunetti's trademark . . . when 'scandalous' can reasonably be read to bar the registration of only those marks that are obscene, vulgar, or profane."[227]

Domain Names, Keywords and Hashtags

Congress adapted trademark law to the internet, but website addresses, or domain names, have been a particular problem for trademark law. Domain names may be trademarked and protected against infringement, although the domain name suffixes, such as .com or .org, are not considered part of a trademarked domain name.

Cybersquatters claim domain names that include trademarks or famous people's names. Before Congress passed the Anticybersquatting Consumer Protection Act (ACPA), trademark owners often sued cybersquatters, frequently successfully, to try to stop the practice.[228] The ACPA provides civil and criminal remedies for registering a domain name with the intention of selling it to the trademark owner. The law applies to a domain name identical or confusingly similar to a trademark or that disparages or injures a well-known trademark. A defendant must have acted in bad faith to be liable under the statute.

In one ACPA case, a company named Spider Webs registered hundreds of domain names, including ErnestandJulioGallo.com. The Gallo winery sued. A federal appellate court held the ACPA constitutional and said the unauthorized domain name could injure Gallo's trademark.[229] Spider Webs admitted it registered the domain name hoping the ACPA would be found unconstitutional. That showed bad faith, the appellate court said, and it upheld a $25,000 damage award and a court order preventing Spider Webs from registering any domain name that used "Gallo" or "Ernest and Julio."

If two companies have identical or similar trademarks for two different products, the companies' domain names might be the same—chip.com for a computer chip company or for a potato chip company. In such a case, one court said trademark law takes precedence over domain registration. The court gave a disputed domain name—moviebuff—to the company that first used the mark.[230] However, if two domain names are similar and both describe the companies' products, courts may allow the firms to continue using the names. For example, the manufacturer of Beanie Babies sued a company using bargainbeanies.com as a domain name. The bargain beanies company sold used beanbag animals. A federal appellate court said preventing a firm from using a domain name describing its business would be like "forbidding a used car dealer who specializes in selling Chevrolets to mention" the car's name in the dealer's advertising.[231] The court allowed both companies to use their domain names.

More recently, lawsuits have arisen around trademarks and keywords used for internet searches. A federal court in California held that use of a competitor's trademark as an advertising keyword in a search is not likely to cause consumer confusion and is not a trademark infringement.[232] For example, in 2018, a court held that the Alzheimer's Foundation of America's purchase of the Alzheimer's Disease and Related Disorders Association trademarks as search engine keywords, as well as purchasing the two-word phrase "Alzheimer's Foundation" as search engine keywords, did not violate the Lanham Act.[233]

Companies have also been permitted to register hashtags as trademarks. The USPTO's Trademark Manual of Examining Procedures allows a hashtag to be registered as a trademark "only if it functions as an identifier of the source of the applicant's goods or services."[234] Generally, hashtags do not provide any source-indicating function, because they merely facilitate categorization and searching within online social media. Examples of registered hashtag trademarks include: #smilewithacoke and #cokecanpics (The Coca-Cola Company), #McDstories (McDonalds), and #makeitcount (Nike).[235]

Trademark Infringement

Anyone may use a protected trademark in a way that is not confusing. The Lanham Act says trademark infringement occurs when a mark "is likely to cause confusion, or to cause a mistake, or to deceive as to the affiliation, connection, or association of such person with another person, or as to the origin, sponsorship, or approval of his or her goods, services, or commercial activities by another person."[236] Including the words "Starbucks," "Prada" and "Chipotle" in this paragraph is not a trademark infringement. Using marks for informational purposes is a fair use.

The First Amendment protects using a competitor's trademark in comparative advertising, courts have ruled.[237] However, a competitor may not alter a mark in a comparative ad. In one case, a competitor to John Deere's lawn tractor business aired a comparative ad that distorted and animated Deere's trademarked deer logo, showing the deer jumping through a hoop that breaks apart, for instance. The ad diminished Deere's logo in consumers' minds, a court ruled.[238]

Facebook claimed likelihood of confusion and won a trademark infringement lawsuit against a social networking site named Teachbook. Teachbook marketed to teachers, stating that many schools forbid teachers from using Facebook because students might learn teachers' personal information. A federal district court found a likelihood of confusion between the two marks because the "Teachbook mark is highly similar to the registered Facebook mark in appearance, sound, meaning, and commercial impression."[239]

Similar—even identical—marks may not cause confusion if the goods for which the marks are used are not the same. Wendy's automobile parts may coexist with Wendy's restaurants if a court says consumers would not think the restaurant company also owns the auto parts store.

Companies may redesign or refresh logos and retain the original trademark. Trademark **tacking** allows a trademark owner to slightly alter a trademark without abandoning ownership of the original mark. In order to "tack" a trademark, the owner must show that "the two trademarks create the same, continuing commercial impression, and the later mark should not materially differ from or alter the character of the mark attempted to be tacked."[240] Courts review tacking claims with a higher likelihood of confusion standard. That is, rather than establishing the likelihood of confusion in the marketplace, when a trademark owner is arguing for tacking, that owner must show that consumers believe both trademarks represent the same company or product and that there is no marketplace confusion. A business owner can show tacking by demonstrating that the new trademark is basically the same as the original in the eyes of consumers.

The evolution of the Pepsi logo would likely qualify as tacking.

famouslogos.us

For example, "Pepsi-Cola" was trademarked in 1903. Since then, the company's logo has evolved from the soda's name appearing in cursive font to a circle-shaped logo with "Pepsi" in the center. Since the 1940s, the logos have incorporated red, white and blue as part of the circle.[241] Pepsi would likely be able to "tack" its logos since changes always incorporate previous, recognizable logo elements. The logo the company uses today combines the colors it started using in the 1940s with a font that contains a modern look but incorporates elements of the original logo.[242]

In 2015, the U.S. Supreme Court ruled unanimously that a jury should decide questions of tacking because it involves a question of fact—whether the two marks create the same commercial impression to consumers.[243] As one trademark expert observed, "This makes sense: A jury is comprised of 12 ordinary people, and questions about trademarks usually revolve around whether ordinary consumers would be confused."[244] In 2020, the U.S. Supreme Court decided that the Lanham Act does not require a plaintiff in a trademark infringement suit to show that a defendant willfully infringed the plaintiff's trademark as a precondition to an award of profits.[245]

Courts use a variety of criteria to determine whether consumers likely will be confused by similar marks used by different products or services. These include the marks' similarities, the similarities of products or services for which the marks are used, how consumers purchase the goods (impulse buying or careful consideration), how well known the first-used mark is, actual confusion that can be proved and how long both marks have been used without confusion.[246]

Using a famous trademark in a way that disparages or diminishes the mark's effectiveness is known as **dilution**. Dilution may happen in two ways.[247] First, a product name similar to a well-known trademark could make the famous mark less distinctive. What the law calls

blurring whittles away a trademark's selling power. Second, a poorly made or unsavory product using a name similar to a famous trademark could cause consumers to think less of the well-known mark. This is **tarnishment**.[248]

Congress revised federal anti-dilution law in response to a U.S. Supreme Court decision involving an "adult novelties" store in Elizabethtown, Ky., called Victor's Secret. After the Victoria's Secret franchise asked the store's owners not to use the name Victor's Secret, the owners called it Victor's Little Secret. Victoria's Secret sued for trademark dilution based on tarnishment. Victoria's Secret argued that Victor's Little Secret associated the famous brand with lewd, sexual products. The Supreme Court said Victoria's Secret had to show *actual* dilution of its trademark, which might be difficult for the large corporation to do.[249] The Court said there is "a complete absence of evidence of any lessening of the capacity of the Victoria's Secret mark to identify . . . goods . . . sold in Victoria's Secret stores or advertised in its catalogs."[250]

Congress rejected that approach. It revised anti-dilution law to require companies with famous trademarks to show only a *likelihood* of dilution, not actual dilution of trademark effectiveness. But the core of the anti-dilution law remains the same: A company does not have to prove it is likely consumers will be confused between a famous trademark and a similar product or service name. Rather, the company has to show only that another firm's similar mark has diminished the well-known mark's distinctiveness or injured its reputation.

Nearly half the states have anti-dilution statutes. These laws protect dilution of all marks used in the state, not just the famous marks the federal anti-dilution law protects.

Defenses

The Lanham Act lists nine defenses to a trademark infringement action.[251] Most turn on disputed facts. For example, a defendant might argue that the registered trademark was obtained fraudulently, that the trademark has been abandoned and no longer is in use or that the mark misrepresents a product's origin. A defendant also might claim to have used and registered the mark first.

The Lanham Act also provides a variety of fair use defenses.[252] This allows one company's trademark to describe another company's product. Courts will accept the fair use defense if the defendant used the mark to describe its goods and not as a trademark. Also, the use cannot cause customer confusion. This is understood as **descriptive fair use**. For example, a federal court in Utah held that NoMoreRack.com's use of the word "overstock" in its advertisements was a fair use and did not infringe on Overstock.com's trademark. The court said that use of such a general term, even though the websites directly compete with each other, did not create a likelihood of confusion.[253]

The Ninth Circuit Court of Appeals held that use of the phrase "web celeb" as part of an entertainment website and as a television award show category was fair use even though "web-celeb" is a trademark attached to a website that provides a marketplace for independent musicians and fans to buy music. The court held that the phrase "web celeb" was merely a common descriptive phrase for internet celebrities.[254]

Referring to the defendant's own product or service by using the plaintiff's mark without permission also may be a fair use. This type of **nominative fair use** may be done in comparative advertising, or in other contexts. In one case, two newspapers used the trademarked name of a band, New Kids on the Block, to promote the newspapers' telephone polls about the band. The papers used the band's name to describe the papers' own product: the telephone poll. A court found this a fair use because the band could not be identified without using its trademarked name and the papers did not suggest that the band endorsed the poll.[255]

VIP Products was sued for trademark dilution, among other claims, by Jack Daniels, the maker of the famous whiskey. (Legal papers filed by Jack Daniels.)

Some claims of fair use relate more directly to First Amendment interests. The landmark case *Rogers v. Grimaldi* established one of the most widely applied tests for protecting the fair use of trademarks. In that case, the famous dancer and actress Ginger Rogers brought suit against producers and distributors of a film titled "Ginger and Fred," alleging that the film's title violated the Lanham Act by creating a false impression that the film was about her. The Second Circuit established a two-part test to determine whether the title of an artistic work is entitled to First Amendment protection in such cases. Under the *Rogers* test, a defendant must show that (a) the title of the work has some artistic relevance to the underlying work; and (b) that the title is not explicitly misleading as to the source or content of the work.[256] In addition, the *Rogers* test may only be applied to noncommercial uses of a mark.

In 2020, the Ninth Circuit relied on the *Rogers* test to decide, in part, for VIP Products for it sales of its Bad Spaniels Silly Squeaker dog chew toy. When Jack Daniels, the maker of the famous whiskey, sued VIP for trade dress infringement and dilution, the Ninth Circuit ruled that the chew toy was an expressive work and protected by the First Amendment; it remanded the case for further proceedings on the basis of the test.[257] The U.S. Supreme Court granted certiorari in the case and heard oral arguments in 2023. A decision is pending.

The Ninth Circuit had relied on an older Fourth Circuit case, *Louis Vuitton Malletier S.A. v. Haute Diggity Dog, LLC*, to make its decision.[258] In that case, dog toys which "loosely resemble[d]" small Louis Vuitton handbags were "successful parodies of LVM handbags and the LVM marks and trade dress" and therefore did not infringe the LVM trademark.[259] The Fourth Circuit wrote that although "[t]he dog toy is shaped roughly like a handbag; its name 'Chewy Vuiton' sounds like and rhymes with LOUIS VUITTON; its monogram CV mimics LVM's LV mark; the repetitious design clearly imitates the design on the LVM handbag; and the coloring is similar," "no one can doubt . . . that the 'Chewy Vuiton' dog toy is not the 'idealized image' of the mark created by LVM."[260]

The anti-dilution law also provides a fair use exception. Using a famous trademark for comparative advertising, parody or all forms of news reporting and commentary is not an infringement.[261]

EMERGING LAW

The growth of sites like Etsy and Spoonflower have contributed to the growth of e-commerce, particularly during and after the COVID-19 pandemic. With the increase in homemade products for the retail market, platforms hosting such sellers have found themselves in trouble with trademark holders. While protections from secondary liability exist under the DMCA for copyright holders, no similar protections exist for platforms that host sellers of products that infringe on registered trademarks. In most cases, it is incumbent upon those platforms to police their sites for those sellers who may be infringing others' trademarks.[262]

In *Ohio State University v. Redbubble*, The Ohio State University (OSU) sued Redbubble, a site for independent artists to host and sell their work.[263] OSU alleged direct trademark infringement by Redbubble for the sale of apparel, stickers, phone cases and other products.

Artists on the site used the "OSU" and "O" insignias and Brutus Buckeye mascot without permission. The district court ruled for Redbubble, holding that Redbubble acted as only a "transactional intermediary" among buyers and sellers.[264] The Sixth Circuit reversed, finding that a "use in commerce" may be found not just through sales but also through other activity, such as selling, distributing or advertising a product.[265] The court remanded the case for reconsideration in light of its ruling. In a similar case in California, a jury found that Redbubble did not infringe any of gamemaker Atari's intellectual property for goods on its site. But in another California case involving a teen's fashion brand, a court ruled that Redbubble knew of the infringing activity on its platform and found the company liable for contributory infringement.[266] This remains an unsettled and developing area of trademark law.

KEYTERMS

arbitrary marks

Berne Convention

blurring

copyright

contributory infringement

descriptive fair use

descriptive marks

fanciful marks

fair use

derivative work

dilution

disparaging marks

first-sale doctrine

generic marks

infringement

infringement by inducement

nominative fair use

public domain

red-flag knowledge

safe harbor

secondary meaning

Statute of Anne

statutory damages

suggestive marks

tacking

tarnishment

trademark

transformative use

Transmit Clause

vicarious infringement

work made for hire

CASES FOR STUDY
THINKING ABOUT THEM

Historically, the U.S. Supreme Court has decided few cases concerning intellectual property, but as technology advances rapidly, the Supreme Court has heard multiple cases in the past few terms. Both of these case excerpts are recent decisions. As you read them, keep the following questions in mind:

● How does the Supreme Court's ruling about disparaging trademarks in *Matal v. Tam* address the issue of viewpoint discrimination?

● Do you agree with the Supreme Court's fair use reasoning in *Google v. Oracle*? What makes a fair use determination involving advanced technology so challenging?

MATAL V. TAM

SUPREME COURT OF THE UNITED STATES, 137 S. CT. 1744 (2017)

JUSTICE SAMUEL ALITO (joined by CHIEF JUSTICE JOHN ROBERTS, JUSTICE CLARENCE THOMAS and JUSTICE STEPHEN BREYER) delivered the Court's opinion:

This case concerns a dance-rock band's application for federal trademark registration of the band's name, "The Slants." "Slants" is a derogatory term for persons of Asian descent, and members of the band are Asian-Americans. But the band members believe that by taking that slur as the name of their group, they will help to "reclaim" the term and drain its denigrating force.

The Patent and Trademark Office (PTO) denied the application based on a provision of federal law prohibiting the registration of trademarks that may "disparage . . . or bring . . . into contemp[t] or disrepute" any "persons, living or dead." We now hold that this provision violates the Free Speech Clause of the First Amendment. It offends a bedrock First Amendment principle: Speech may not be banned on the ground that it expresses ideas that offend.

"The principle underlying trademark protection is that distinctive marks—words, names, symbols, and the like—can help distinguish a particular artisan's goods from those of others."

"[F]ederal law does not create trademarks." Trademarks and their precursors have ancient origins, and trademarks were protected at common law and in equity at the time of the founding of our country. . . . The foundation of current federal trademark law is the Lanham Act, enacted in 1946. By that time, trademark had expanded far beyond phrases that do no more than identify a good or service. Then, as now, trademarks often consisted of catchy phrases that convey a message.

Under the Lanham Act, trademarks that are "used in commerce" may be placed on the "principal register," that is, they may be federally registered. . . . "[N]ational protection of trademarks is desirable," we have explained, "because trademarks foster competition and the maintenance of quality by securing to the producer the benefits of good reputation." . . .

The Lanham Act contains provisions that bar certain trademarks from the principal register. . . .

At issue in this case is one such provision, which we will call "the disparagement clause." This provision prohibits the registration of a trademark "which may disparage ...persons, living or dead, institutions, beliefs, or national symbols, or bring them into contempt, or disrepute." This clause appeared in the original Lanham Act and has remained the same to this day.

When deciding whether a trademark is disparaging, an examiner at the PTO generally applies a "two-part test." The examiner first considers "the likely meaning of the matter in question, taking into account not only dictionary definitions, but also the relationship of the matter to the other elements in the mark, the nature of the goods or services, and the manner in which the mark is used in the marketplace in connection with the goods or services." "If that meaning is found to refer to identifiable persons, institutions, beliefs or national symbols," the examiner moves to the second step, asking "whether that meaning may be disparaging to a substantial composite of the referenced group." If the examiner finds that a "substantial composite, although not necessarily a majority, of the referenced group would find the proposed mark ...to be disparaging in the context of contemporary attitudes," a prima facie case of disparagement is made out, and the burden shifts to the applicant to prove that the trademark is not disparaging. What is more, the PTO has specified that "[t]he fact that an applicant may be a member of that group or has good intentions underlying its use of a term does not obviate the fact that a substantial composite of the referenced group would find the term objectionable."

Simon Tam is the lead singer of "The Slants." He chose this moniker in order to "reclaim" and "take ownership" of stereotypes about people of Asian ethnicity. The group "draws inspiration for its lyrics from childhood slurs and mocking nursery rhymes" and has given its albums names such as "The Yellow Album" and "Slanted Eyes, Slanted Hearts."

Tam sought federal registration of "THE SLANTS," on the principal register, but an examining attorney at the PTO rejected the request, applying the PTO's two-part framework and finding that "there is . . . a substantial composite of persons who find the term in the applied-for mark offensive." The examining attorney relied in part on the fact that "numerous dictionaries define 'slants' or 'slant-eyes' as a derogatory or offensive term." The examining attorney also relied on a finding that "the band's name has been found offensive numerous times"—citing a performance that was canceled because of the band's moniker and the fact that "several bloggers and commenters to articles on the band have indicated that they find the term and the applied-for mark offensive."

Tam contested the denial of registration before the examining attorney and before the PTO's Trademark Trial and Appeal Board (TTAB) but to no avail. Eventually, he took the case to federal court, where the en banc Federal Circuit ultimately found the disparagement clause facially unconstitutional under the First Amendment's Free Speech Clause. The majority found that the clause engages in viewpoint-based discrimination, that the clause regulates the expressive component of trademarks and consequently cannot be treated as commercial speech, and that the clause is subject to and cannot satisfy strict scrutiny. The majority also rejected the Government's argument that registered trademarks constitute government speech, as well as the Government's contention that federal registration is a form of government subsidy. And the majority opined that even if the disparagement clause were analyzed under this Court's commercial speech cases, the clause would fail the "intermediate scrutiny" that those cases prescribe. . . .

The Government filed a petition for certiorari, which we granted in order to decide whether the disparagement clause "is facially invalid under the Free Speech Clause of the First Amendment." . . .

Because the disparagement clause applies to marks that disparage the members of a racial or ethnic group, we must decide whether the clause violates the Free Speech Clause of the First Amendment. And at the outset, we must consider three arguments that would either eliminate any First Amendment protection or result in highly permissive rational-basis review. Specifically, the Government contends (1) that trademarks are government speech, not private speech, (2) that trademarks are a form of government subsidy, and (3) that the constitutionality of the disparagement clause should be tested under a new "government-program" doctrine. We address each of these arguments below.

The First Amendment prohibits Congress and other government entities and actors from "abridging the freedom of speech"; the First Amendment does not say that Congress and other government entities must abridge their own ability to speak freely. . . .

As we have said, "it is not easy to imagine how government could function" if it were subject to the restrictions that the First Amendment imposes on private speech. "'[T]he First Amendment forbids the government to regulate speech in ways that favor some viewpoints or ideas at the expense of others,'" but imposing a requirement of viewpoint-neutrality on government speech would be paralyzing. When a government entity embarks on a course of action, it necessarily takes a particular viewpoint and rejects others. . . .

But while the government-speech doctrine is important—indeed, essential—it is a doctrine that is susceptible to dangerous misuse. If private speech could be passed off as government speech by simply affixing a government seal of approval, government could silence or muffle the expression of disfavored viewpoints. For this reason, we must exercise great caution before extending our government-speech precedents.

At issue here is the content of trademarks that are registered by the PTO, an arm of the Federal Government. The Federal Government does not dream up these marks, and it does not edit marks submitted for registration. Except as required by the statute involved here, an examiner may not reject a mark based on the viewpoint that it appears to express. Thus, unless that section is thought to apply, an examiner does not inquire whether any viewpoint conveyed by a mark is consistent with Government policy or whether any such viewpoint is consistent with that expressed by other marks already on the principal register. Instead, if the mark meets the Lanham Act's viewpoint-neutral requirements, registration is mandatory. And if an examiner finds that a mark is eligible for placement on the principal register, that decision is not reviewed by any higher official unless the registration is challenged. Moreover, once a mark is registered, the PTO is not authorized to remove it from the register unless a party moves for cancellation, the registration expires, or the Federal Trade Commission initiates proceedings based on certain grounds.

In light of all this, it is far-fetched to suggest that the content of a registered mark is government speech. If the federal registration of a trademark makes the mark government speech, the Federal Government is babbling prodigiously and incoherently. It is saying many unseemly things. It is expressing contradictory views. It is unashamedly endorsing a vast array of commercial products and services. And it is providing Delphic advice to the consuming public.

For example, if trademarks represent government speech, what does the Government have in mind when it advises Americans to "make.believe" (Sony), "Think different" (Apple), "Just do it" (Nike), or "Have it your way" (Burger King)? Was the Government warning about a coming disaster when it registered the mark "EndTime Ministries"?

The PTO has made it clear that registration does not constitute approval of a mark. And it is unlikely that more than a tiny fraction of the public has any idea what federal registration of a trademark means. None of our government speech cases even remotely supports the idea that registered trademarks are government speech. . . .

Trademarks have not traditionally been used to convey a Government message. With the exception of the enforcement of 15 U.S.C. § 1052(a), the viewpoint expressed by a mark has not played a role in the decision whether to place it on the principal register. And there is no evidence that the public associates the contents of trademarks with the Federal Government.

This brings us to the case on which the Government relies most heavily, *Walker*, which likely marks the outer bounds of the government-speech doctrine. Holding that the messages on Texas specialty license plates are government speech, the *Walker* Court cited three factors. . . . First, license plates have long been used by the States to convey state messages. Second, license plates "are often closely identified in the public mind" with the State, since they are manufactured and owned by the State, generally designed by the State, and serve as a form of "government ID." Third, Texas "maintain[ed] direct control over the messages conveyed on its specialty plates." . . . [N]one of these factors are present in this case. . . .

Perhaps the most worrisome implication of the Government's argument concerns the system of copyright registration. If federal registration makes a trademark government speech and thus eliminates all First Amendment protection, would the registration of the copyright for a book produce a similar transformation?

The Government attempts to distinguish copyright on the ground that it is "'the engine of free expression,'" but as this case illustrates, trademarks often have an expressive content. Companies spend huge amounts to create and publicize trademarks that convey a message. It is true that the necessary brevity of trademarks limits what they can say. But powerful messages can sometimes be conveyed in just a few words.

Trademarks are private, not government, speech.

We next address the Government's argument that this case is governed by cases in which this Court has upheld the constitutionality of government programs that subsidized speech expressing a particular viewpoint. These cases implicate a notoriously tricky question of constitutional law. "[W]e have held that the Government 'may not deny a benefit to a person on a basis that infringes his constitutionally protected . . . freedom of speech even if he has no entitlement to that benefit.'" But at the same time, government is not required to subsidize activities that it does not wish to promote. Determining which of these principles applies in a particular case "is not always self-evident," but no difficult question is presented here.

Unlike the present case, the decisions on which the Government relies all involved cash subsidies or their equivalent. . . . In other cases, we have regarded tax benefits as comparable to cash subsidies.

The federal registration of a trademark is nothing like the programs at issue in these cases. The PTO does not pay money to parties seeking registration of a mark. Quite the contrary is true: An applicant for registration must pay the PTO a filing fee of $225–$600. And to maintain federal registration, the holder of a mark must pay a fee of $300–$500 every 10 years. The Federal Circuit concluded that these fees have fully supported the registration system for the past 27 years. . . .

Finally, the Government urges us to sustain the disparagement clause under a new doctrine that would apply to "government-program" cases. For the most part, this argument simply merges our government-speech cases and the . . . subsidy cases in an attempt to construct a broader doctrine that can be applied to the registration of trademarks. The only new element in this construct consists of two cases involving a public employer's collection of union dues from its employees. But those cases occupy a special area of First Amendment case law, and they are far removed from the registration of trademarks. . . .

Potentially more analogous are cases in which a unit of government creates a limited public forum for private speech. When government creates such a forum, in either a literal or "metaphysical" sense, some content- and speaker-based restrictions may be allowed. However, even in such cases, what we have termed "viewpoint discrimination" is forbidden.

Our cases use the term "viewpoint" discrimination in a broad sense, and in that sense, the disparagement clause discriminates on the bases of "viewpoint." To be sure, the clause evenhandedly prohibits disparagement of all groups. It applies equally to marks that damn Democrats and Republicans, capitalists and socialists, and those arrayed on both sides of every possible issue. It denies registration to any mark that is offensive to a substantial percentage of the members of any group. But in the sense relevant here, that is viewpoint discrimination: Giving offense is a viewpoint.

We have said time and again that "the public expression of ideas may not be prohibited merely because the ideas are themselves offensive to some of their hearers." For this reason, the disparagement clause cannot be saved by analyzing it as a type of government program in which some content- and speaker-based restrictions are permitted.

Having concluded that the disparagement clause cannot be sustained under our government-speech or subsidy cases or under the Government's proposed "government-program" doctrine, we must confront a dispute between the parties on the question whether trademarks are commercial speech. . . . The Government and *amici* supporting its position argue that all trademarks are commercial speech. They note that the central purposes of trademarks are commercial and that federal law regulates trademarks to promote fair and orderly interstate commerce. Tam and his *amici*, on the other hand, contend that many, if not all, trademarks have an expressive component. In other words, these trademarks do not simply identify the source of a product or service but go on to say something more, either about the product or service or some broader issue. The trademark in this case illustrates this point. The name "The Slants" not only identifies the band but expresses a view about social issues.

We need not resolve this debate between the parties because the disparagement clause cannot withstand even *Central Hudson* review. Under *Central Hudson*, a restriction of speech must serve "a substantial interest," and it must be "narrowly drawn." The disparagement clause fails this requirement.

It is claimed that the disparagement clause serves two interests. The first is phrased in a variety of ways in the briefs. Echoing language in one of the opinions below, the Government asserts an interest in preventing "'underrepresented groups'" from being "'bombarded with demeaning messages in commercial advertising.'" An *amicus* supporting the Government refers to "encouraging racial tolerance and protecting the privacy and welfare of individuals." But no matter how the point is phrased, its unmistakable thrust is this: The Government has an interest in preventing speech expressing ideas that offend. And, as we have explained, that idea strikes at the heart of the First Amendment. Speech that demeans on the basis of race, ethnicity, gender, religion, age, disability, or any other similar ground is hateful; but the proudest boast of our free speech jurisprudence is that we protect the freedom to express "the thought that we hate."

The second interest asserted is protecting the orderly flow of commerce. Commerce, we are told, is disrupted by trademarks that "involv[e] disparagement of race, gender, ethnicity, national origin, religion, sexual orientation, and similar demographic classification." Such trademarks are analogized to discriminatory conduct, which has been recognized to have an adverse effect on commerce.

A simple answer to this argument is that the disparagement clause is not "narrowly drawn" to drive out trademarks that support invidious discrimination. The clause reaches any trademark that disparages *any person, group, or institution*. It applies to trademarks like the following: "Down with racists," "Down with sexists," "Down with homophobes." It is not an anti-discrimination clause; it is a happy-talk clause. In this way, it goes much further than is necessary to serve the interest asserted.

The clause is far too broad in other ways as well. The clause protects every person living or dead as well as every institution. Is it conceivable that commerce would be disrupted by a trademark saying: "James Buchanan was a disastrous president" or "Slavery is an evil institution"?

There is also a deeper problem with the argument that commercial speech may be cleansed of any expression likely to cause offense. The commercial market is well stocked with merchandise that disparages prominent figures and groups, and the line between commercial and non-commercial speech is not always clear, as this case illustrates. If affixing the commercial label permits the suppression of any speech that may lead to political or social "volatility," free speech would be endangered.

***

For these reasons, we hold that the disparagement clause violates the Free Speech Clause of the First Amendment. The judgment of the Federal Circuit is affirmed.

It is so ordered.

JUSTICE ANTHONY KENNEDY and JUSTICE CLARENCE THOMAS, with whom JUSTICE RUTH BADER GINSBURG, JUSTICE SONIA SOTOMAYOR, and JUSTICE ELENA KEGAN join, concurring in part and concurring in the judgment:

The Patent and Trademark Office (PTO) has denied the substantial benefits of federal trademark registration to the mark THE SLANTS. The PTO did so under the mandate of the disparagement clause. . . .

As the Court is correct to hold, § 1052(a) constitutes viewpoint discrimination—a form of speech suppression so potent that it must be subject to rigorous constitutional scrutiny. The Government's action and the statute on which it is based cannot survive this scrutiny.

The Court is correct in its judgment, and I join Parts I, II, and III-A of its opinion. This separate writing explains in greater detail why the First Amendment's protections against viewpoint discrimination apply to the trademark here. . . .

Those few categories of speech that the government can regulate or punish—for instance, fraud, defamation, or incitement—are well established within our constitutional tradition. Aside from these and a few other narrow exceptions, it is a fundamental principle of the First Amendment that the government may not punish or suppress speech based on disapproval of the ideas or perspectives the speech conveys.

The First Amendment guards against laws "targeted at specific subject matter," a form of speech suppression known as content based discrimination. This category includes a subtype of laws that go further, aimed at the suppression of "particular views . . . on a subject." A law found to discriminate based on viewpoint is an "egregious form of content discrimination," which is "presumptively unconstitutional."

At its most basic, the test for viewpoint discrimination is whether—within the relevant subject category—the government has singled out a subset of messages for disfavor based on the views expressed. In the instant case, the disparagement clause the Government now seeks to implement and enforce identifies the relevant subject as "persons, living or dead, institutions, beliefs, or national symbols." Within that category, an applicant may register a positive or benign mark but not a derogatory one. The law thus reflects the Government's disapproval of a subset of messages it finds offensive. This is the essence of viewpoint discrimination.

The Government disputes this conclusion. It argues, to begin with, that the law is viewpoint neutral because it applies in equal measure to any trademark that demeans or offends. This misses the point. A subject that is first defined by content and then regulated or censored by mandating only one sort of comment is not viewpoint neutral. To prohibit all sides from criticizing their opponents makes a law more viewpoint based, not less so. The logic of the Government's rule is that a law would be viewpoint neutral even if it provided that public officials could be praised but not condemned. The First Amendment's viewpoint neutrality principle protects more than the right to identify with a particular side. It protects the right to create and present arguments for particular positions in particular ways, as the speaker chooses. By mandating positivity, the law here might silence dissent and distort the marketplace of ideas.

The Government next suggests that the statute is viewpoint neutral because the disparagement clause applies to trademarks regardless of the applicant's personal views or reasons for using the mark. Instead, registration is denied based on the expected reaction of the applicant's audience. In this way, the argument goes, it cannot be said that Government is acting with hostility toward a particular point of view. For example, the Government does not dispute that respondent seeks to use his mark in a positive way. Indeed, respondent endeavors to use The Slants to supplant a racial epithet, using new insights, musical talents, and wry humor to make it a badge of pride. Respondent's application was denied not because the Government thought his object was to demean or offend but because the Government thought his trademark would have that effect on at least some Asian-Americans.

The Government may not insulate a law from charges of viewpoint discrimination by tying censorship to the reaction of the speaker's audience. The Court has suggested that viewpoint discrimination occurs when the government intends to suppress a speaker's beliefs, but viewpoint discrimination need not take that form in every instance. The danger of viewpoint discrimination is that the government is attempting to remove certain ideas or perspectives from a broader debate. That danger is all the greater if the ideas or perspectives are ones a particular audience might think offensive, at least at first hearing. An initial reaction may prompt further reflection, leading to a more reasoned, more tolerant position.

Indeed, a speech burden based on audience reactions is simply government hostility and intervention in a different guise. The speech is targeted, after all, based on the government's disapproval of the speaker's choice of message. And it is the government itself that is attempting in this case to decide whether the relevant audience would find the speech offensive. For reasons like these, the Court's cases have long prohibited the government from justifying a First Amendment burden by pointing to the offensiveness of the speech to be suppressed.

The Government's argument in defense of the statute assumes that respondent's mark is a negative comment. In addressing that argument on its own terms, this opinion is not intended to imply that the Government's interpretation is accurate. From respondent's submissions, it is evident he would disagree that his mark means what the Government says it does. The trademark will have the effect, respondent urges, of reclaiming an offensive term for the positive purpose of celebrating all that Asian-Americans can and do contribute to our diverse Nation. While thoughtful persons can agree or disagree with this approach, the dissonance between the trademark's potential to teach and the Government's insistence on its own, opposite, and negative interpretation confirms the constitutional vice of the statute.

. . . To the extent trademarks qualify as commercial speech, they are an example of why that term or category does not serve as a blanket exemption from the First Amendment's requirement of viewpoint neutrality. Justice Holmes' reference to the "free trade in ideas" and the "power of . . . thought to get itself accepted in the competition of the market," was a metaphor. In the realm of trademarks, the metaphorical marketplace of ideas becomes a tangible, powerful reality. Here that real marketplace exists as a matter of state law and our common-law tradition, quite without regard to the Federal Government. These marks make up part of the expression of everyday life, as with the names of entertainment groups, broadcast networks, designer clothing, newspapers, automobiles, candy bars, toys, and so on. Nonprofit organizations—ranging from medical-research charities and other humanitarian causes to political advocacy groups—also have trademarks, which they use to compete in a real economic sense for funding and other resources as they seek to persuade others to join their cause. To permit viewpoint discrimination in this context is to permit Government censorship.

. . . It is telling that the Court's precedents have recognized just one narrow situation in which viewpoint discrimination is permissible: where the government itself is speaking or recruiting others to communicate a message on its behalf. The exception is necessary to allow the government to stake out positions and pursue policies. But it is also narrow, to prevent the government from claiming that every government program is exempt from the First Amendment. These cases have identified a number of factors that, if present, suggest the government is speaking on its own behalf; but none are present here.

There may be situations where private speakers are selected for a government program to assist the government in advancing a particular message. That is not this case either. The central purpose of trademark registration is to facilitate source identification. To serve that broad purpose, the Government has provided the benefits of federal registration to millions of marks identifying every type of product and cause. Registered trademarks do so by means of a wide diversity of words, symbols, and messages. Whether a mark is disparaging bears no plausible relation to that goal. While defining the purpose and scope of a federal program for these purposes can be complex, our cases are clear that viewpoint discrimination is not permitted where, as here, the Government "expends funds to encourage a diversity of views from private speakers."

***

A law that can be directed against speech found offensive to some portion of the public can be turned against minority and dissenting views to the detriment of all. The First Amendment does not entrust that power to the government's benevolence. Instead, our reliance must be on the substantial safeguards of free and open discussion in a democratic society.

For these reasons, I join the Court's opinion in part and concur in the judgment.

GOOGLE LLC, PETITIONER V. ORACLE AMERICA, INC.
SUPREME COURT OF THE UNITED STATES (2021)

JUSTICE BREYER delivered the Court's opinion:

Oracle America, Inc., is the current owner of a copyright in Java SE, a computer program that uses the popular Java computer programming language. Google, without permission, has copied a portion of that program, a portion that enables a programmer to call up prewritten software that, together with the computer's hardware, will carry out a large number of specific tasks. The lower courts have considered (1) whether Java SE's owner could copyright the portion that Google copied, and (2) if so, whether Google's copying nonetheless constituted a "fair use" of that material, thereby freeing Google from copyright liability. The Federal Circuit held in Oracle's favor (*i.e.*, that the portion is copyrightable and Google's copying did not constitute a "fair use"). In reviewing that decision, we assume, for argument's sake, that the material was copyrightable. But we hold that the copying here at issue nonetheless constituted a fair use. Hence, Google's copying did not violate the copyright law.

I

In 2005, Google acquired Android, Inc., a startup firm that hoped to become involved in smartphone software. Google sought, through Android, to develop a software platform for mobile devices like smartphones. A platform provides the necessary infrastructure for computer programmers to develop new programs and applications. One might think of a software platform as a kind of factory floor where computer programmers (analogous to autoworkers, designers, or manufacturers) might come, use sets of tools found there, and create new applications for use in, say, smartphones.

Google envisioned an Android platform that was free and open, such that software developers could use the tools found there free of charge. Its idea was that more and more developers using its Android platform would develop ever more Android-based applications, all of which would make Google's Android-based smartphones more attractive to ultimate consumers. Consumers would then buy and use ever more of those phones. That vision required attracting a sizeable number of skilled programmers.

At that time, many software developers understood and wrote programs using the Java programming language, a language invented by Sun Microsystems (Oracle's predecessor). About six million programmers had spent considerable time learning, and then using, the Java language. Many of those programmers used Sun's own popular Java SE platform to develop new programs primarily for use in desktop and laptop computers. That platform allowed developers using the Java language to write programs that were able to run on any desktop or laptop computer, regardless of the underlying hardware (*i.e.*, the programs were in large part "interoperable"). Indeed, one of Sun's slogans was "'write once, run anywhere.'"

Shortly after acquiring the Android firm, Google began talks with Sun about the possibility of licensing the entire Java platform for its new smartphone technology. But Google did not want to insist that all programs written on the Android platform be interoperable. As Android's founder explained, "[t]he whole idea about [an] open source [platform] is to have very, very few restrictions on what people can do with it," and Sun's interoperability policy would have undermined that free and open business model. Apparently, for reasons related to this disagreement, Google's negotiations with Sun broke down. Google then built its own platform.

The record indicates that roughly 100 Google engineers worked for more than three years to create Google's Android platform software. In doing so, Google tailored the Android platform to smartphone technology, which differs from desktop and laptop computers in important ways. A smartphone, for instance, may run on a more limited battery or take advantage of GPS technology. The Android platform offered programmers the ability to program for that environment. To build the platform, Google wrote millions of lines of new code. Because Google wanted millions of programmers, familiar with Java, to be able easily to work with its new Android platform, it also copied roughly 11,500 lines of code from the Java SE program. The copied lines of code are part of a tool called an Application Programming Interface, or API.

What is an API? The Federal Circuit described an API as a tool that "allow[s] programmers to use . . . prewritten code to build certain functions into their own programs, rather than write their own code to perform those functions from scratch." Through an API, a programmer can draw upon a vast library of prewritten code to carry out complex tasks. For lay persons, including judges, juries, and many others, some elaboration of this description may prove useful.

Consider in more detail just what an API does. A computer can perform thousands, perhaps millions, of different tasks that a programmer may wish to use. These tasks range from the most basic to the enormously complex. Ask the computer, for example, to tell you which of two numbers is the higher number or to sort one thousand numbers in ascending order, and it will instantly give you the right answer. An API divides and organizes the world of computing tasks in a particular way. Programmers can then use the API to select the particular task that they need for their programs. In Sun's API (which we refer to as the Sun Java API), each individual task is known as a "method." The API groups somewhat similar methods into larger "classes," and groups somewhat similar classes into larger "packages." This method-class-package organizational structure is referred to as the Sun Java API's "structure, sequence, and organization," or SSO.

For each task, there is computer code, known as "implementing code," that in effect tells the computer how to execute the particular task you have asked it to perform (such as telling you, of two numbers, which is the higher). The implementing code (which Google independently wrote) is not at issue here. For a single task, the implementing code may be hundreds of lines long. It would be difficult, perhaps impossible, for a programmer to create complex software programs without drawing on prewritten task-implementing programs to execute discrete tasks.

But how do you as the programmer tell the computer which of the implementing code programs it should choose, *i.e.*, which task it should carry out? You do so by entering into your own program a command that corresponds to the specific task and calls it up. Those commands, known as "method calls," help you carry out the task by choosing those programs written in implementing code that will do the trick, *i.e.*, that will instruct the computer so that your program will find the higher of two numbers. If a particular computer might perform, say, a million different tasks, different method calls will tell the computer which of those tasks to choose. Those familiar with the Java language already know countless method calls that allow them to invoke countless tasks.

And how does the method call (which a programmer types) actually locate and invoke the particular implementing code that it needs to instruct the computer how to carry out a particular task? It does so through another type of code, which the parties have labeled "declaring code." Declaring code is part of the API. For each task, the specific command entered by the programmer matches up with specific declaring code inside the API. That declaring code provides both the name for each task and the location of each task within the API's overall organizational system (*i.e.*, the placement of a method within a particular class and the placement of a class within a particular package). In this sense, the declaring code and the method call form a link, allowing the programmer to draw upon the thousands of prewritten tasks, written in implementing code. Without that declaring code, the method calls entered by the programmer would not call up the implementing code.

The declaring code therefore performs at least two important functions in the Sun Java API. The first, more obvious, function is that the declaring code enables a set of shortcuts for programmers. By connecting complex implementing code with method calls, it allows a programmer to pick out from the API's task library a particular task without having to learn anything more than a simple command. For example, a programmer building a new application for personal banking may wish to use various tasks to, say, calculate a user's balance or authenticate a password. To do so, she need only learn the method calls associated with those tasks. In this way, the declaring code's shortcut function is similar to a gas pedal in a car that tells the car to move faster or the QWERTY keyboard on a typewriter that calls up a certain letter when you press a particular key. As those analogies demonstrate, one can think of the declaring code as part of an *interface* between human beings and a machine.

The second, less obvious, function is to reflect the way in which Java's creators have divided the potential world of different tasks into an actual world, *i.e.*, precisely which set of potentially millions of different tasks we want to have our Java-based computer systems perform and how we want those tasks arranged and grouped. In this sense, the declaring code performs an organizational function. It determines the structure of the task library that Java's creators have decided to build. To understand this organizational system, think of the Dewey Decimal System that categorizes books into an accessible system or a travel guide that arranges a city's attractions into different categories. Language itself provides a rough analogy to the declaring code's organizational feature, for language itself divides into sets of concepts a world that in certain respects other languages might have divided differently. The developers of Java, for example, decided to place a method called "draw image" inside of a class called "graphics."

Consider a comprehensive, albeit farfetched, analogy that illustrates how the API is actually used by a programmer. Imagine that you can, via certain keystrokes, instruct a robot to move to a particular file cabinet, to open a certain drawer, and to pick out a specific recipe. With the proper recipe in hand, the robot then moves to your kitchen and gives it to a cook to prepare the dish. This example mirrors the API's task-related organizational system. Through your simple command, the robot locates the right recipe and hands it off to the cook. In the same way, typing in a method call prompts the API to locate the correct implementing code and hand it off to your computer. And importantly, to select the dish that you want for your meal, you do not need to know the recipe's contents, just as a programmer using an API does not need to learn the implementing code. In both situations, learning the simple command is enough.

. . .

Now we can return to the copying at issue in this case. Google did not copy the task-implementing programs, or implementing code, from the Sun Java API. It wrote its own task-implementing programs, such as those that would determine which of two integers is the greater or carry out any other desired (normally far more complex) task. This implementing code constitutes the vast majority of both the Sun Java API and the API that Google created for Android. For most of the packages in its new API, Google also wrote its own declaring code. For 37 packages, however, Google copied the declaring code from the Sun Java API. As just explained, that means that, for those 37 packages, Google necessarily copied both the names given to particular tasks and the grouping of those tasks into classes and packages.

In doing so, Google copied that portion of the Sun Java API that allowed programmers expert in the Java programming language to use the "task calling" system that they had already learned. As Google saw it, the 37 packages at issue included those tasks that were likely to prove most useful to programmers working on applications for mobile devices. In fact, "three of these packages were . . . fundamental to being able to use the Java language at all." *Oracle*, 872 F. Supp. 2d, at 982. By using the same declaring code for those packages, programmers using the Android platform can rely on the method calls that they are already familiar with to call up particular tasks (*e.g.*, determining which of two integers is the greater); but Google's own implementing programs carry out those tasks. Without that copying, programmers would need to learn an entirely new system to call up the same tasks.

We add that the Android platform has been successful. Within five years of its release in 2007, Android-based devices claimed a large share of the United States market. As of 2015, Android sales produced more than $42 billion in revenue.

In 2010 Oracle Corporation bought Sun. Soon thereafter Oracle brought this lawsuit in the United States District Court for the Northern District of California.

. . .

III

A

Copyright and patents, the Constitution says, are to "promote the Progress of Science and useful Arts, by securing for limited Times to Authors and Inventors the exclusive Right to their respective Writings and Discoveries." Art. I, §8, cl. 8. Copyright statutes and case law have made clear that copyright has practical objectives. It grants an author an exclusive right to produce his work (sometimes for a hundred years or more), not as a special reward, but in order to encourage the production of works that others might reproduce more cheaply. At the same time, copyright has negative features. Protection can raise prices to consumers. It can impose special costs, such as the cost of contacting owners to obtain reproduction permission. And the exclusive rights it awards can sometimes stand in the way of others exercising their own creative powers.

. . .

Four provisions of the current Copyright Act are of particular relevance in this case. First, a definitional provision sets forth three basic conditions for obtaining a copyright. There must be a "wor[k] of authorship," that work must be "original," and the work must be "fixed in any tangible medium of expression."

Second, the statute lists certain kinds of works that copyright can protect. They include "literary," "musical," "dramatic," "motion pictur[e]," "architectural," and certain other works. In 1980, Congress expanded the reach of the Copyright Act to include computer programs. And it defined "computer program" as " 'a set of statements or instructions to be used directly or indirectly in a computer in order to bring about a certain result.'"

Third, the statute sets forth limitations on the works that can be copyrighted, including works that the definitional provisions might otherwise include. It says, for example, that copyright protection cannot be extended to "any idea, procedure, process, system, method of operation, concept, principle, or discovery . . . ." These limitations, along with the need to "fix" a work in a "tangible medium of expression," have often led courts to say, in shorthand form, that, unlike patents, which protect novel and useful ideas, copyrights protect "expression" but not the "ideas" that lie behind it.

Fourth, Congress, together with the courts, has imposed limitations upon the scope of copyright protection even in respect to works that are entitled to a copyright. For example, the Copyright Act limits an author's exclusive rights in performances and displays, or to performances of sound recordings. And directly relevant here, a copyright holder cannot prevent another person from making a "fair use" of copyrighted material.

We have described the "fair use" doctrine, originating in the courts, as an "equitable rule of reason" that "permits courts to avoid rigid application of the copyright statute when, on occasion, it would stifle the very creativity which that law is designed to foster." The statutory provision that embodies the doctrine indicates, rather than dictates, how courts should apply it. The provision says:

"[T]he fair use of a copyrighted work, . . . for purposes such as criticism, comment, news reporting, teaching . . . scholarship, or research, is not an infringement of copyright. In determining whether the use made of a work in any particular case is a fair use the factors to be considered shall include—

"(1) the purpose and character of the use, including whether such use is of a commercial nature or is for nonprofit educational purposes;

"(2) the nature of the copyrighted work;

"(3) the amount and substantiality of the portion used in relation to the copyrighted work as a whole; and

"(4) the effect of the use upon the potential market for or value of the copyrighted work."

In applying this provision, we, like other courts, have understood that the provision's list of factors is not exhaustive (note the words "include" and "including"), that the examples it sets forth do not exclude other examples (note the words "such as"), and that some factors may prove more important in some contexts than in others. In a word, we have understood the provision to set forth general principles, the application of which requires judicial balancing, depending upon relevant circumstances, including "significant changes in technology."

B

Google's petition for certiorari poses two questions. The first asks whether Java's API is copyrightable. It asks us to examine two of the statutory provisions just mentioned, one that permits copyrighting computer programs and the other that forbids copyrighting, *e.g.*, "process[es]," "system[s]," and "method[s] of operation." Google believes that the API's declaring code and organization fall into these latter categories and are expressly excluded from copyright protection. The second question asks us to determine whether Google's use of the API was a "fair use." Google believes that it was.

A holding for Google on either question presented would dispense with Oracle's copyright claims. Given the rapidly changing technological, economic, and business-related circumstances, we believe we should not answer more than is necessary to resolve the parties' dispute. We shall assume, but purely for argument's sake, that the entire Sun Java API falls within the definition of that which can be copyrighted. We shall ask instead whether Google's use of part of that API was a "fair use." Unlike the Federal Circuit, we conclude that it was.

IV

The language of the "fair use" provision, reflects its judge-made origins. That background, as well as modern courts' use of the doctrine, makes clear that the concept is flexible, that courts must apply it in light of the sometimes conflicting aims of copyright law, and that its application may well vary depending upon context. Thus, copyright's protection may be stronger where the copyrighted material is fiction, not fact, where it consists of a motion picture rather than a news broadcast, or where it serves an artistic rather than a utilitarian function. Similarly, courts have held that in some circumstances, say, where copyrightable material is bound up with uncopyrightable material, copyright protection is "thin."

Generically speaking, computer programs differ from books, films, and many other "literary works" in that such programs almost always serve functional purposes. These and other differences have led at least some judges to complain that "applying copyright law to computer programs is like assembling a jigsaw puzzle whose pieces do not quite fit."

These differences also led Congress to think long and hard about whether to grant computer programs copyright protection. In 1974, Congress established a National Commission on New Technological Uses of Copyrighted Works (CONTU) to look into the matter. After several years of research, CONTU concluded that the "availability of copyright protection for computer programs is desirable." At the same time, it recognized that computer programs had unique features. Mindful of not "unduly burdening users of programs and the general public," it wrote that copyright "should not grant anyone more economic power than is necessary to achieve the incentive to create." And it believed that copyright's existing doctrines (*e.g.*, fair use), applied by courts on a case-by-case basis, could prevent holders from using copyright to stifle innovation. Congress then wrote computer program protection into the law.

The upshot, in our view, is that fair use can play an important role in determining the lawful scope of a computer program copyright, such as the copyright at issue here. It can help to distinguish among technologies. It can distinguish between expressive and functional features of computer code where those features are mixed. It can focus on the legitimate need to provide incentives to produce copyrighted material while examining the extent to which yet further protection creates unrelated or illegitimate harms in other markets or to the development of other products. In a word, it can carry out its basic purpose of providing a context-based check that can help to keep a copyright monopoly within its lawful bounds. . . .

VI

We turn now to the basic legal question before us: Was Google's copying of the Sun Java API, specifically its use of the declaring code and organizational structure for 37 packages of that API, a "fair use." In answering this question, we shall consider the four factors set forth in the fair use statute as we find them applicable to the kind of computer programs before us. . . .

A. "The Nature of the Copyrighted Work"

The Sun Java API is a "user interface." It provides a way through which users (here the programmers) can "manipulate and control" task-performing computer programs "via a series of menu commands." The API reflects Sun's division of possible tasks that a computer might perform into a set of actual tasks that certain kinds of computers actually will perform. Sun decided, for example, that its API would call up a task that compares one integer with another to see which is the larger. Sun's API (to our knowledge) will not call up the task of determining which great Arabic scholar decided to use Arabic numerals (rather than Roman numerals) to perform that "larger integer" task. No one claims that the decisions about what counts as a task are themselves copyrightable—although one might argue about decisions as to how to label and organize such tasks.

As discussed above, we can think of the technology as having three essential parts. First, the API includes "implementing code," which actually instructs the computer on the steps to follow to carry out each task. Google wrote its own programs (implementing programs) that would perform each one of the tasks that its API calls up.

Second, the Sun Java API associates a particular command, called a "method call," with the calling up of each task. The symbols **java.lang.**, for example, are part of the command that will call up the program (whether written by Sun or, as here, by Google) that instructs the computer to carry out the "larger number" operation. Oracle does not here argue that the use of these commands by programmers itself violates its copyrights.

Third, the Sun Java API contains computer code that will associate the writing of a method call with particular "places" in the computer that contain the needed implementing code. This is the declaring code. The declaring code both labels the particular tasks in the API and organizes those tasks, or "methods," into "packages" and "classes." We have referred to this organization, by way of rough analogy, as file cabinets, drawers, and files. Oracle does claim that Google's use of the Sun Java API's declaring code violates its copyrights.

The declaring code at issue here resembles other copyrighted works in that it is part of a computer program. Congress has specified that computer programs are subjects of copyright. It differs, however, from many other kinds of copyrightable computer code. It is inextricably bound together with a general system, the division of computing tasks, that no one claims is a proper subject of copyright. It is inextricably bound up with the idea of organizing tasks into what we have called cabinets, drawers, and files, an idea that is also not copyrightable. It is inextricably bound up with the use of specific commands known to programmers, known here as method calls (such as **java.lang.Math.max**, etc.), that Oracle does not here contest. And it is inextricably bound up with implementing code, which is copyrightable but was not copied.

Moreover, the copied declaring code and the uncopied implementing programs call for, and reflect, different kinds of capabilities. A single implementation may walk a computer through dozens of different steps. To write implementing programs, witnesses told the jury, requires balancing such considerations as how quickly a computer can execute a task or the likely size of the computer's memory. One witness described that creativity as "magic" practiced by an API developer when he or she worries "about things like power management" for devices that "run on a battery." This is the very creativity that was needed to develop the Android software for use not in laptops or desktops but in the very different context of smartphones.

The declaring code (inseparable from the programmer's method calls) embodies a different kind of creativity. Sun Java's creators, for example, tried to find declaring code names that would prove intuitively easy to remember. They wanted to attract programmers who would learn the system, help to develop it further, and prove reluctant to use another. Sun's business strategy originally emphasized the importance of using the API to attract programmers. It sought to make the API "open" and "then . . . compete on implementations." The testimony at trial was replete with examples of witnesses drawing this critical line between the user-centered declaratory code and the innovative implementing code.

These features mean that, as part of a user interface, the declaring code differs to some degree from the mine run of computer programs. Like other computer programs, it is functional in nature. But unlike many other programs, its use is inherently bound together with uncopyrightable ideas (general task division and organization) and new creative expression (Android's implementing code). Unlike many other programs, its value in significant part derives from the value that those who do not hold copyrights, namely, computer programmers, invest of their own time and effort to learn the API's system. And unlike many other programs, its value lies in its efforts to encourage programmers to learn and to use that system so that they will use (and continue to use) Sun-related implementing programs that Google did not copy.

Although copyrights protect many different kinds of writing, we have emphasized the need to "recogni[ze] that some works are closer to the core of [copyright] than others," In our view, for the reasons just described, the declaring code is, if copyrightable at all, further than are most computer programs (such as the implementing code) from the core of copyright. That fact diminishes the fear, expressed by both the dissent and the Federal Circuit, that application of "fair use" here would seriously undermine the general copyright protection that Congress provided for computer programs. And it means that this factor, "the nature of the copyrighted work," points in the direction of fair use.

B. "The Purpose and Character of the Use"

In the context of fair use, we have considered whether the copier's use "adds something new, with a further purpose or different character, altering" the copyrighted work "with new expression, meaning or message." Commentators have put the matter more broadly, asking whether the copier's use "fulfill[s] the objective of copyright law to stimulate creativity for public illumination." In answering this question, we have used the word "transformative" to describe a copying use that adds something new and important. An " 'artistic painting' " might, for example, fall within the scope of fair use even though it precisely replicates a copyrighted " 'advertising logo to make a comment about consumerism.' " Or, as we held in *Campbell*, a parody can be transformative because it comments on the original or criticizes it, for "[p]arody needs to mimic an original to make its point."

Google copied portions of the Sun Java API precisely, and it did so in part for the same reason that Sun created those portions, namely, to enable programmers to call up implementing programs that would accomplish particular tasks. But since virtually any unauthorized use of a copyrighted computer program (say, for teaching or research) would do the same, to stop here would severely limit the scope of fair use in the functional context of computer programs. Rather, in determining whether a use is "transformative," we must go further and examine the copying's more specifically described "purpose[s]" and "character."

Here Google's use of the Sun Java API seeks to create new products. It seeks to expand the use and usefulness of Android-based smartphones. Its new product offers programmers a highly creative and innovative tool for a smartphone environment. To the extent that Google used parts of the Sun Java API to create a new platform that could be readily used by programmers, its use was consistent with that creative "progress" that is the basic constitutional objective of copyright itself.

The jury heard that Google limited its use of the Sun Java API to tasks and specific programming demands related to Android. It copied the API (which Sun created for use in desktop and laptop computers) only insofar as needed to include tasks that would be useful in smartphone programs. And it did so only insofar as needed to allow programmers to call upon those tasks without discarding a portion of a familiar programming language and learning a new one. To repeat, Google, through Android, provided a new collection of tasks operating in a distinct and different computing environment. Those tasks were carried out through the use of new implementing code (that Google wrote) designed to operate within that new environment. Some of the *amici* refer to what Google did as "reimplementation," defined as the "building of a system . . . that repurposes the same words and syntaxes" of an existing system—in this case so that programmers who had learned an existing system could put their basic skills to use in a new one.

The record here demonstrates the numerous ways in which reimplementing an interface can further the development of computer programs. The jury heard that shared interfaces are necessary for different programs to speak to each other. It heard that the reimplementation of interfaces is necessary if programmers are to be able to use their acquired skills. It heard that the reuse of APIs is common in the industry. It heard that Sun itself had used pre-existing interfaces in creating Java. And it heard that Sun executives thought that widespread use of the Java programming language, including use on a smartphone platform, would benefit the company. . . .

These and related facts convince us that the "purpose and character" of Google's copying was transformative—to the point where this factor too weighs in favor of fair use.

There are two other considerations that are often taken up under the first factor: commerciality and good faith. The text of §107 includes various noncommercial uses, such as teaching and scholarship, as paradigmatic examples of privileged copying. There is no doubt that a finding that copying was not commercial in nature tips the scales in favor of fair use. But the inverse is not necessarily true, as many common fair uses are indisputably commercial. For instance, the text of §107 includes examples like "news reporting," which is often done for commercial profit. So even though Google's use was a commercial endeavor—a fact no party disputed—that is not dispositive of the first factor, particularly in light of the inherently transformative role that the reimplementation played in the new Android system. . . .

C. "The Amount and Substantiality of the Portion Used"

If one considers the declaring code in isolation, the quantitative amount of what Google copied was large. Google copied the declaring code for 37 packages of the Sun Java API, totaling approximately 11,500 lines of code. Those lines of code amount to virtually all the declaring code needed to call up hundreds of different tasks. On the other hand, if one considers the entire set of software material in the Sun Java API, the quantitative amount copied was small. The total set of Sun Java API computer code, including implementing code, amounted to 2.86 million lines, of which the copied 11,500 lines were only 0.4 percent.

The question here is whether those 11,500 lines of code should be viewed in isolation or as one part of the considerably greater whole. We have said that even a small amount of copying may fall outside of the scope of fair use where the excerpt copied consists of the " 'heart' " of the original work's creative expression. On the other hand, copying a larger amount of material can fall within the scope of fair use where the material copied captures little of the material's creative expression or is central to a copier's valid purpose. If a defendant had copied one sentence in a novel, that copying may well be insubstantial. But if that single sentence set forth one of the world's shortest short stories—"When he awoke, the dinosaur was still there."—the question looks much different, as the copied material constitutes a small part of the novel but the entire short story. See A. Monterroso, El Dinosaurio, in Complete Works & Other Stories 42 (E. Grossman transl. 1995). (In the original Spanish, the story reads: "Cuando despertó, el dinosaurio todavía estaba allí.")

Several features of Google's copying suggest that the better way to look at the numbers is to take into account the several million lines that Google did not copy. For one thing, the Sun Java API is inseparably bound to those task-implementing lines. Its purpose is to call them up. For another, Google copied those lines not because of their creativity, their beauty, or even (in a sense) because of their purpose. It copied them because programmers had already learned to work with the Sun Java API's system, and it would have been difficult, perhaps prohibitively so, to attract programmers to build its Android smartphone system without them. Further, Google's basic purpose was to create a different task-related system for a different computing environment (smartphones) and to create a platform—the Android platform—that would help achieve and popularize that objective. The "substantiality" factor will generally weigh in favor of fair use where, as here, the amount of copying was tethered to a valid, and transformative, purpose.

We do not agree with the Federal Circuit's conclusion that Google could have achieved its Java-compatibility objective by copying only the 170 lines of code that are "necessary to write in the Java language." In our view, that conclusion views Google's legitimate objectives too narrowly. Google's basic objective was not simply to make the Java programming language usable on its Android systems. It was to permit programmers to make use of their knowledge and experience using the Sun Java API when they wrote new programs for smartphones with the Android platform. In principle, Google might have created its own, different system of declaring code. But the jury could have found that its doing so would not have achieved that basic objective. In a sense, the declaring code was the key that it needed to unlock the programmers' creative energies. And it needed those energies to create and to improve its own innovative Android systems.

We consequently believe that this "substantiality" factor weighs in favor of fair use.

D. Market Effects

The fourth statutory factor focuses upon the "effect" of the copying in the "market for or value of the copyrighted work." Consideration of this factor, at least where computer programs are at issue, can prove more complex than at first it may seem. It can require a court to consider the amount of money that the copyright owner might lose. As we pointed out in *Campbell*, "verbatim copying of the original in its entirety for commercial purposes" may well produce a market substitute for an author's work. Making a film of an author's book may similarly mean potential or presumed losses to the copyright owner. Those losses normally conflict with copyright's basic objective: providing authors with exclusive rights that will spur creative expression.

But a potential loss of revenue is not the whole story. We here must consider not just the amount but also the source of the loss. As we pointed out in *Campbell*, a "lethal parody, like a scathing theatre review," may "kil[l] demand for the original." Yet this kind of harm, even if directly translated into foregone dollars, is not "cognizable under the Copyright Act."

Further, we must take into account the public benefits the copying will likely produce. Are those benefits, for example, related to copyright's concern for the creative production of new expression? Are they comparatively important, or unimportant, when compared with dollar amounts likely lost (taking into account as well the nature of the source of the loss)?

We do not say that these questions are always relevant to the application of fair use, not even in the world of computer programs. Nor do we say that these questions are the only questions a court might ask. But we do find them relevant here in helping to determine the likely market effects of Google's reimplementation.

As to the likely amount of loss, the jury could have found that Android did not harm the actual or potential markets for Java SE. And it could have found that Sun itself (now Oracle) would not have been able to enter those markets successfully whether Google did, or did not, copy a part of its API. First, evidence at trial demonstrated that, regardless of Android's smartphone technology, Sun was poorly positioned to succeed in the mobile phone market. The jury heard ample evidence that Java SE's primary market was laptops and desktops. It also heard that Sun's many efforts to move into the mobile phone market had proved unsuccessful. As far back as 2006, prior to Android's release, Sun's executives projected declining revenue for mobile phones because of emerging smartphone technology. When Sun's former CEO was asked directly whether Sun's failure to build a smartphone was attributable to Google's development of Android, he answered that it was not. Given the evidence showing that Sun was beset by business challenges in developing a mobile phone product, the jury was entitled to agree with that assessment.

Second, the jury was repeatedly told that devices using Google's Android platform were different in kind from those that licensed Sun's technology. For instance, witnesses explained that the broader industry distinguished between smartphones and simpler "feature phones." As to the specific devices that used Sun-created software, the jury heard that one of these phones lacked a touchscreen, while another did not have a QWERTY keyboard. For other mobile devices, the evidence showed that simpler products, like the Kindle, used Java software, while more advanced technology, like the Kindle Fire, were built on the Android operating system. This record evidence demonstrates that, rather than just "repurposing [Sun's] code from larger computers to smaller computers," Google's Android platform was part of a distinct (and more advanced) market than Java software.

Looking to these important differences, Google's economic expert told the jury that Android was not a market substitute for Java's software. As he explained, "the two products are on very different devices," and the Android platform, which offers "an entire mobile operating stack," is a "very different typ[e] of produc[t]" than Java SE, which is "just an applications programming framework." Taken together, the evidence showed that Sun's mobile phone business was declining, while the market increasingly demanded a new form of smartphone technology that Sun was never able to offer.

Finally, the jury also heard evidence that Sun foresaw a benefit from the broader use of the Java programming language in a new platform like Android, as it would further expand the network of Java-trained programmers. In other words, the jury could have understood Android and Java SE as operating in two distinct markets. And because there are two markets at issue, programmers learning the Java language to work in one market (smartphones) are then able to bring those talents to the other market (laptops).

Sun presented evidence to the contrary. Indeed, the Federal Circuit held that the "market effects" factor militated against fair use in part because Sun had tried to enter the

Android market. But those licensing negotiations concerned much more than 37 packages of declaring code, covering topics like "the implementation of [Java's] code" and "branding and cooperation" between the firms. In any event, the jury's fair use determination means that neither Sun's effort to obtain a license nor Oracle's conflicting evidence can overcome evidence indicating that, at a minimum, it would have been difficult for Sun to enter the smartphone market, even had Google not used portions of the Sun Java API.

On the other hand, Google's copying helped Google make a vast amount of money from its Android platform. And enforcement of the Sun Java API copyright might give Oracle a significant share of these funds. It is important, however, to consider why and how Oracle might have become entitled to this money. When a new interface, like an API or a spreadsheet program, first comes on the market, it may attract new users because of its expressive qualities, such as a better visual screen or because of its superior functionality. As time passes, however, it may be valuable for a different reason, namely, because users, including programmers, are just used to it. They have already learned how to work with it.

The record here is filled with evidence that this factor accounts for Google's desire to use the Sun Java API. This source of Android's profitability has much to do with third parties' (say, programmers') investment in Sun Java programs. It has correspondingly less to do with Sun's investment in creating the Sun Java API. We have no reason to believe that the Copyright Act seeks to protect third parties' investment in learning how to operate a created work.

Finally, given programmers' investment in learning the Sun Java API, to allow enforcement of Oracle's copyright here would risk harm to the public. Given the costs and difficulties of producing alternative APIs with similar appeal to programmers, allowing enforcement here would make of the Sun Java API's declaring code a lock limiting the future creativity of new programs. Oracle alone would hold the key. The result could well prove highly profitable to Oracle (or other firms holding a copyright in computer interfaces). But those profits could well flow from creative improvements, new applications, and new uses developed by users who have learned to work with that interface. To that extent, the lock would interfere with, not further, copyright's basic creativity objectives. After all, "copyright supplies the economic incentive to [both] create and disseminate ideas," and the reimplementation of a user interface allows creative new computer code to more easily enter the market.

The uncertain nature of Sun's ability to compete in Android's marketplace, the sources of its lost revenue, and the risk of creativity-related harms to the public, when taken together, convince that this fourth factor—market effects—also weighs in favor of fair use.

   ***

The fact that computer programs are primarily functional makes it difficult to apply traditional copyright concepts in that technological world. In doing so here, we have not changed the nature of those concepts. We do not overturn or modify our earlier cases involving fair use—cases, for example, that involve "knockoff" products, journalistic writings, and parodies. Rather, we here recognize that application of a copyright doctrine such as fair use has long proved a cooperative effort of Legislatures and courts, and that Congress, in our view, intended that it so continue. As such, we have looked to the principles set forth in the fair use statute, and set forth in our earlier cases, and applied them to this different kind of copyrighted work.

We reach the conclusion that in this case, where Google reimplemented a user interface, taking only what was needed to allow users to put their accrued talents to work in a new and transformative program, Google's copying of the Sun Java API was a fair use of that material as a matter of law. The Federal Circuit's contrary judgment is reversed, and the case is remanded for further proceedings in conformity with this opinion.

It is so ordered.

Justice Barrett took no part in the consideration or decision of this case.

In 2022, legal and advertising battles continued between traditional meat and dairy producers and the substitutes rapidly gaining market share.

Michael Thomas/Getty Images

12 ADVERTISING

When Speech and Commerce Converge

CHAPTER OUTLINE

Commercial Speech
  Early Case Law
  Difficulties Defining Commercial Speech
  Testing Commercial Speech Protection
  Compelling Commercial Speech
  Regulating Vice Products
      Tobacco
      Gambling
      Alcohol
      Prescription Drugs
      Guns
  Regulating Ads on Government Property
  False or Misleading Speech
  The Lanham Act
  State Law Claims
  Confusion and Doctrinal Pressures

Consumer Protection and the Federal Trade Commission (FTC)
  Deception Authority
  Unfairness Authority
  Enforcement

Other Executive Agencies
  Federal Communications Commission (FCC)
  Federal Election Commission (FEC)
  Food and Drug Administration (FDA)
  Securities and Exchange Commission (SEC)

Corporate Political Speech
  Consumer Activism and Corporate Speech
  Professional Speech

Emerging Law

Cases for Study
  • *Central Hudson Gas & Electric Corp. v. Public Service Commission of New York*
  • *Sorrell v. IMS Health, Inc.*

LEARNING OBJECTIVES

12.1 Understand how the Supreme Court came to protect commercial speech and the development of judicial doctrine for it.

12.2   Identify the powers of the FTC to protect consumers.

12.3   Learn about the role of other executive agencies in protecting consumers.

12.4   Describe and define the development of judicial doctrine for corporate speech.

Advertising is the lifeblood of the U.S. economy, and more than ever, business efforts to find and narrowly target consumers through digital media offer unprecedented marketing opportunities. Need a new pair of boots? Your online search for just the perfect pair will find ads for boots following you on your smartphone for days. Tracking your running or walking habits with a new app? Not only will that app flood your email with promotions, but ads for related exercise products will find their way into your social media, your newsfeeds, your billing statements, and even your snail mail, and you'll be incentivized to change your overall habits toward exercise.

The United States is the largest advertising market in the world, with estimated total ad spending of $276 billion in 2021—approximately $191 billion on digital advertising alone.[1] Record growth of the digital economy has created extraordinary advertising capabilities by tracking the habits, purchases and location of U.S. consumers. Years ago, marketers would simply create print and television advertising, target their audiences using the demographics of the particular newspaper or TV show, and hope such ads resulted in sales. Today, advertisers find consumers by tracking their online lives and purchases in ways that offer both consumer convenience and speed, but which also produce precise and voluminous data about consumers and their habits. Such data not only drive sales, but also fuel a thriving, if troubled, social media and platform economy. Digital tracking can also significantly influence our personal behaviors. The algorithms that drive consumer behaviors become part of what Harvard Business Professor Shoshana Zuboff describes as "behavioral surplus," the raw data of our actions online that result from such intense tracking. This "surplus" is then monetized—what she labels "surveillance capitalism."[2]

Such dramatic shifts in advertising raise new questions about the scope of the government's role. If it is easier than ever to reach and track consumers, how does the First Amendment protect advertisers looking to use such technologies, and what is the government's role in situations where consumer privacy harms may lurk? Does the First Amendment protect companies that want to speak in the public interest in the same way as it protects ordinary citizens? Should it? Striking the balance between protecting the rights of advertisers and corporations in the digital era and protecting consumers from deceptive and unfair advertising practices lies at the heart of studying the law of advertising—or what courts refer to as the law of "commercial speech."

COMMERCIAL SPEECH

The law of commercial speech is rooted both in the First Amendment and in the Commerce Clause—Article 1, Section 8 of the U.S. Constitution—which enumerates Congress' power "to regulate commerce with foreign nations, and among the several states."[3] Commerce generally is defined as the provision of goods or services in exchange for compensation, usually payment. While advertising certainly existed long before the 19th and 20th centuries, it was the Industrial Revolution, the rise of consumer culture, and the advent of broadcast media that ignited the consumer landscape and grew the U.S. advertising market from one that created anxieties about advertising speech to one that would be the envy of the world.[4]

With that growth, however, came an increase in unfair and monopolistic business practices. Business "trusts" at that time combined several large companies to control production and distribution of goods for mutual advantage. But such trusts also created abusive market powers—monopolies—that often prohibited others from entering the same business. In the most well-known example, Standard Oil, John D. Rockefeller's company that existed from 1870 to 1911, controlled almost all oil production, processing, marketing and transportation in the U.S. with the help of trust agreements and mergers.[5] Congress responded to such market power by passing the Sherman Antitrust Act in 1890, and the company was ultimately ordered to divest its major holdings.

But Congress also decided federal laws were not enough. When judicial interpretation of such laws continued to favor large business interests and the costs of litigating such disputes increased, Congress began discussing a new commission to regularly check such powerful interests.[6] The **Federal Trade Commission** (FTC) was established in 1914 and its powers were expanded under the Lanham Act. Today, the primary function of the FTC is to prohibit "unfair or deceptive acts or practices in or affecting commerce."[7] The FTC protects consumers by ensuring that advertisers have evidence to support their claims, but it also helps to ensure a fair and competitive marketplace for businesses.[8] The FTC's powers will be discussed in greater detail later in the chapter.

Early Case Law

As commercial advertising took hold of the U.S. economy in the 20th century, the U.S. Supreme Court also reluctantly began crafting a speech category to help define the boundaries between the constitutionally approved regulation of commerce under the Commerce Clause and the constitutionally protected freedom of speech under the First Amendment.

In *Valentine v. Chrestensen*, the U.S. Supreme Court's first ruling to suggest the category of commercial speech 80 years ago, the Court only mentioned the term "speech" once.[9] The case involved distribution of a handbill encouraging people on the streets of New York to pay to tour a decommissioned U.S. Navy submarine docked at a city pier. City law prohibited commercial handbill distribution except when "solely devoted to information or a public protest," so the promoter printed a protest to that law on the flip side of the ad.[10] Lower courts ruled that the inclusion of this "political speech" immunized him from prosecution, but the U.S. Supreme Court reversed.

In its six-paragraph opinion, the Supreme Court described the handbill as "commercial advertising" and "soliciting," as prohibited by the law, and emphasized the public's right to be free of interference on public thoroughfares.[11] By "attempting to use the streets of New York by distributing commercial advertising, the prohibition of the code provision was lawfully invoked against [the respondent's] *conduct*," the Court said.[12] Moreover, because "affixing of the protest against official conduct to the advertising circular was with the intent, and for the purpose, of evading" the law, the Court said the city could legally prevent its distribution.[13]

Many interpreted *Chrestensen* to mean that a message whose primary purpose was to promote commerce did not receive First Amendment protection. Then, in *Breard v. Alexandria*, the Supreme Court upheld a law banning unsolicited door-to-door sales of magazines.[14] The Court acknowledged the First Amendment value of magazines but reasoned that the "primary purpose" of the activity was commercial and, therefore, regulable.[15]

New York Times Co. v. Sullivan, which involved a paid ad promoting the civil rights movement in the midst of violent, national upheaval (see Chapter 5), presented the question of whether the payment for the ad or the nature of the message established its primary purpose.[16] In its landmark ruling in *Sullivan*, the U.S. Supreme Court distinguished the civil rights ad from *Chrestensen*'s overt "commercial advertising." The Court described the *Sullivan* ad as communicating information and opinions and seeking support "on behalf of a movement whose existence and objectives are matters of the highest public interest and concern."[17] The fact "that the Times was paid for publishing the advertisement is as immaterial in this connection as is the fact that newspapers and books are sold," the Court concluded.[18] While recognizing the often multiple and complicated nature of paid messages, the Court in *Sullivan* affirmed the notion that government could regulate commercial messages more readily than noncommercial messages.

In a subsequent case, the Supreme Court said the holding in *Chrestensen* was limited and established only that government could regulate "the *manner* in which commercial advertising could be distributed."[19] In *Bigelow v. Virginia*, as in *Sullivan*, the Court looked beyond commercial motivation to the political nature and public interest in advertising about legal abortions in New York state to determine that neither payment for nor the format of such commercial speech deprived it of First Amendment protection.[20] The *Bigelow* decision used the commercial purpose of the ad as a factor to be balanced against the public interest in the speech and "clearly establish[ed] that speech is not stripped of First Amendment protection merely because it appears in [the] form" of paid commercial advertisements.[21] The Court said *Chrestensen* had never been intended to permit any and all government regulation of commercial advertising.[22]

DIFFICULTIES DEFINING COMMERCIAL SPEECH

The Supreme Court overturned *Chrestensen* and provided commercial speech explicit First Amendment protection in *Virginia State Board of Pharmacy v. Virginia Citizens Consumer Council*.[23] Reviewing a Virginia state ban on pharmacists' advertising of prescription drug prices, the Court said the ban violated the public's **right to receive information** about the prices and the need for a free flow of commercial information to aid intelligent consumer decisions.[24] The Court clarified that commercial speech does not fall "wholly outside the protection" of the First Amendment.[25] Commercial speech has value within the economic marketplace and as a venue for debate.[26] The Court wrote,

> As to the particular consumer's interest in the free flow of commercial information, that interest may be as keen, if not keener by far, than his interest in the day's most urgent political debate. . . . Advertising, however tasteless and excessive it sometimes may seem, is nonetheless dissemination of information as to who is producing and selling what product, for what reason, and at what price. So long as we preserve a predominantly

free enterprise economy, the allocation of our resources in large measure will be made through numerous private economic decisions. It is a matter of public interest that those decisions, in the aggregate, be intelligent and well informed. To this end, the free flow of commercial information is indispensable.[27]

In a test that looked something like intermediate scrutiny, the U.S. Supreme Court found the government's asserted interest in fostering high professional standards among pharmacists insufficient to support a ban on price advertising and found the law overbroad in achieving its stated goal. The Court added that its ruling allowed the government to continue to regulate false, deceptive or misleading speech that was "*purely* commercial."[28]

Applying this reasoning, the Court then struck down laws prohibiting "for sale" signs on lawns, ads for contraceptives and lawyer advertising.[29] In the last of these, however, the Supreme Court said that "there are commonsense differences between commercial speech and other varieties" of speech that make commercial speech more resilient in the face of government regulation.[30] In another case involving attorney solicitation of clients, the Court said that it "afforded commercial speech a limited measure of protection, commensurate with its subordinate position in the scale of First Amendment values."[31]

POINTS OF LAW

THE 1976 U.S. SUPREME COURT DEFINITION OF COMMERCIAL SPEECH

More than half a century ago, the U.S. Supreme Court decision in *Virginia State Board of Pharmacy v. Virginia Citizens Consumer Council* said the purely commercial speech that warranted reduced First Amendment protection

1. did nothing more than propose a commercial transaction and
2. was unrelated to the exploration of ideas, truth, science and the arts.[32]

Some 40 years after its initial foray into commercial speech, the U.S. Supreme Court had failed to define the category clearly. In *Central Hudson Gas & Electric Corp. v. Public Service Commission*, the decision widely touted as the cornerstone of modern commercial speech law, the Court said commercial speech was "expression related *solely* to the economic interests of the speaker and its audience" and/or "speech proposing a commercial transaction."[33] The Supreme Court generally described commercial speech as an advertisement for the sale of goods and services.[34] That ambiguous definition remains to this day. (This important case is discussed in more detail in the next section.)

Scholars generally define advertising or commercial speech as "paid, mass-mediated attempts to persuade."[35] That persuasion increasingly comes in digital form, and it is growing: Spending in digital advertising was forecast to grow more than 25 percent in 2021 to more than $190 billion.[36]

The terms to describe this explosive growth are somewhat confusing and often contested. But the terms are likely to be hugely important as courts begin to wrestle with what and how to protect these new forms of advertising and marketing. **Native advertising**, which represented the greatest share of the roughly $53 billion digital advertising market in 2020,[37] disguises commercial advertising content by mirroring the tone, style and design of the nonadvertising copy in which it is embedded. It is usually hosted by established publishers. The Wall Street Journal, BuzzFeed, HuffPost and others have employees or third parties dedicated to generating this paid content.[38] It can also include promoted tweets, suggested Facebook posts, and editorial-based content recommendations.[39]

Content marketing, sponsored content, branded content or brand promotion are similar terms for the same idea—brands are themselves becoming publishers, creating their own platforms and posting content directly to consumers.[40] This kind of advertising often takes the form of video shorts, brand documentaries or brand podcasts. **Celebrity marketing** of brands has long been a hallmark of advertising and remains popular. But the extraordinary growth of **influencer marketing**, generally less famous fans of brands who develop expertise and a significant social media following, is changing the advertising landscape. Some forecasts predicted that influencer marketing would reach $4.14 billion in 2022.[41] Some advertising scholars call the combination of these old and new techniques "integrated brand promotion."

Influencer marketing is on the rise in the United States. Some forecasts predicted that influencer marketing would reach $4.14 billion in 2022.

Getty

Advertising is often difficult to define and identify today for another reason. Advertisers are increasingly addressing social issues like "toxic masculinity," teen suicide and gun control.[42] Some publicists argue that the resulting public controversy strategically fuels both the viewing and the impact of ads, even if it requires public relations teams to step in to smooth ruffled feathers.[43] This mingling of commerce with public issues and political speech also moves the speech away from being *purely* commercial," which the U.S. Supreme Court has said may be regulated.

Lower courts struggle to define what is, and is not, commercial speech. In one case, the Fifth Circuit Court of Appeals ruled that one company's claim that the chief employee of another firm was a "deadbeat dad" was commercial speech because the individual "made [the posted comment] with the economic interest of harming" the other's business.[44] The court held that the First Amendment permitted legal action against the commenter.[45]

In another case, former Chicago Bulls star Michael Jordan sued a grocery store for printing his photograph and a message congratulating him for being inducted into the Basketball Hall of Fame in a magazine ad bearing the store's logo and marketing slogan.[46] Without determining the store's liability, the Seventh Circuit Court of Appeals found that the paid content was commercial speech even though it did not "propose a commercial transaction."[47] On remand, the trial court found for the store.[48]

When Army Sgt. Jeffrey Sarver sued the producers of the Oscar-winning film "The Hurt Locker" for appropriating his image as a lead character, he categorized the film as commercial speech that deserved reduced First Amendment protection. The Ninth Circuit Court of Appeals disagreed. It said the film was not commercial speech because it did not propose a commercial transaction.[49]

When the Enigma Software Group sued Bleeping Computer for false advertising through its online forum discussing software firms and products, Bleeping moved for dismissal, claiming that user comments were not commercial speech.[50] The federal district court, however, said a "hybrid" combination of commercial and noncommercial speech could be regulated under commercial speech standards if the (1) advertisement (2) referenced a specific product or service (3) to advance the speaker's economic interests.[51] Because the user comments "lambasted" Enigma and recommended "a trustworthy alternative," the court said the false advertising claim could proceed to trial.[52]

TESTING COMMERCIAL SPEECH PROTECTION

In the 1970s, the U.S. Supreme Court established that when truthful commercial speech is of core public interest, the First Amendment protection for the speech outweighs the government's interest in regulating advertising.[53] But the Court did not make clear exactly what level of First Amendment protection such nondeceptive advertising enjoys.

In the 1980 Supreme Court case *Central Hudson Gas & Electric v. Public Service Commission of New York*, the Court designed a new test. The case involved an order from the Public Service Commission of New York to ban advertising that promoted the use of electricity because of concerns related to the supply of power and fuel shortages during winter of 1973 and 1974. Central Hudson Gas & Electric challenged the regulation on First Amendment grounds.

The Court's decision in *Central Hudson* established that regulation of (1) nondeceptive advertising for legal products and services is constitutional *only* if (2) government demonstrates a "substantial" state interest in the regulation, (3) the regulation "directly advance[s]" that interest and (4) the regulation is "no more extensive than necessary to serve that interest."[54] Applying the new test, which bears a striking resemblance to the *O'Brien* test for content-neutral regulations of speech (see Chapter 2),[55] the Court found a New York state ban on energy-use advertising unconstitutional. The court said that although the state had a substantial interest in energy conservation, the commission's order was more extensive than necessary, among other findings.

In *Posadas de Puerto Rico Associates v. Tourism Co. of Puerto Rico*, the U.S. Supreme Court walked through the steps it set out in *Central Hudson*. It first reaffirmed that "commercial speech receives a limited form of First Amendment protection so long as it concerns a lawful activity and is not misleading or fraudulent."[56] The advertising at issue in *Posadas* was for casino gambling, a lawful activity for the targeted residents of Puerto Rico, and the ad was neither misleading nor fraudulent. Such commercial speech "may be restricted only if the government's interest in doing so is substantial, the restrictions directly advance the government's asserted interest, and the restrictions are no more extensive than necessary to serve that interest," the Court said.[57]

The government interest in regulating casino advertising was to reduce demand from Puerto Rico residents for casino gambling, and the Supreme Court said this "interest in the health, safety and welfare of its citizens constitutes a 'substantial' governmental interest" as required under *Central Hudson*.[58] The remainder of the test examines

the "fit" between the legislature's *ends* and the *means* chosen to accomplish those ends. Step three asks . . . whether the challenged restrictions on commercial speech "directly advance" the government's asserted interest. . . . [T]he restrictions on advertising of casino gambling "directly advance" the legislature's interest in reducing demand for games of chance. . . . [T]he legislature felt that for Puerto Ricans the risks associated with casino gambling were significantly greater than those associated with the more traditional kinds of gambling in Puerto Rico. In our view, the legislature's separate classification of casino gambling, for purposes of the advertising ban, satisfies the third step of the *Central Hudson* analysis.[59]

The Court said the regulation certainly passed the final step of the test as "no more extensive than necessary" because the law was aimed only at residents, not tourists, and because the Puerto Rico Legislature surely could have prohibited casino gambling by the residents of Puerto Rico altogether. "In our view, the greater power to completely ban casino gambling necessarily includes the lesser power to ban advertising of casino gambling."[60]

POINTS OF LAW

THE CENTRAL HUDSON COMMERCIAL SPEECH TEST

- The government may regulate advertising that is false, misleading or deceptive.
- The government may regulate advertising for unlawful goods and services.

Even accurate advertising for legal goods and services may be regulated if the government demonstrates the following:

- There is a substantial state interest behind the regulation.
- The regulation directly advances the state's interest.
- The regulation is not more extensive than is necessary to serve that interest.[61]

The U.S. Supreme Court has tinkered with, clarified or altered the "fit," or "no more extensive than necessary," requirement of the *Central Hudson* test almost since its adoption. In *Board of Trustees of the State University of New York v. Fox*, the Court attempted to clarify that element of the test.[62] In *Fox*, the Court said advertising regulation did not need to employ the "least restrictive means" available.[63] Instead, regulation must demonstrate a "reasonable fit" to the state interest. Citing *Posadas*, the Court explained, "What our decisions require is a 'fit' between the legislature's ends and the means chosen to accomplish those ends—a fit that is not necessarily perfect, but reasonable."[64] This revision displayed deference to legislative judgments and made it easier for advertising regulations to be found constitutional.

In subsequent commercial speech rulings, the U.S. Supreme Court tried to help lower courts grapple with the determination. It said a law does not "fit" its objective when alternatives are available "which could advance the government's asserted interest in a manner less intrusive to . . . First Amendment rights."[65] Alternately, "the scope of the restriction on speech must be reasonably, though it need not be perfectly, targeted to address the harm intended to be regulated."[66] Or the required match between the law and its goals must be one of "narrow tailoring" where courts "carefully calculate the costs and benefits associated with the burden on speech."[67] It's a matter of "proportionality," some justices said.[68] And in the case of *Sorrell v. IMS Health, Inc.* (discussed again later and excerpted at the end of the chapter), the Court sidestepped the definition of fit to explain its objective: The proper "fit" ensures "not only that the State's interests are proportional to the resulting burdens placed on speech but also that the law does not seek to suppress a disfavored message."[69]

Lower courts and scholars criticized the Supreme Court's shifting definition of *Central Hudson*'s required "fit" because it made consistent decisions difficult and altered the level of First Amendment protection given to truthful commercial speech about legal products.

The U.S. Supreme Court further increased confusion about the protection of commercial speech in cases where it considered the nature of the advertised product. In *44 Liquormart, Inc. v. Rhode Island*, a case about the state's ban on price advertising for alcohol, the Supreme Court emphasized that government could not ban advertising even for dangerous or disfavored "vice" products, such as alcohol, "to keep people in the dark for what the government perceives to be their own good."[70] The Court said advertising bans were the most egregious regulatory approach and courts should use "special care" in review of their use to achieve government goals unrelated to the speech involved.[71] Justice Clarence Thomas went further; he said all regulations that prohibit truthful advertising for legal products are per se unconstitutional.[72]

Then, in *Sorrell v. IMS Health, Inc.*, the Supreme Court said strict scrutiny applies to government attempts to prohibit dissemination of truthful, nonmisleading information about a lawful product even when the speech is commercial.[73] The Vermont law at issue placed a ban on the sale, disclosure and use of the prescribing patterns of physicians. The law specifically sought to prevent drug marketers from using information gathered by pharmacists about which drugs specific doctors prescribed to tailor their marketing and promotional efforts.[74] Both the marketers for pharmaceutical companies and the data-mining firms that collected and sold the prescribing information challenged the law as a First Amendment violation.

The Supreme Court identified the law as both a content- and a speaker-based restriction on speech as well as an attempt to prohibit certain uses of truthful information. After acknowledging *Central Hudson*'s intermediate-level scrutiny as the standard test for review of restrictions on commercial speech, the Court said that "commercial speech, including advertising, has an informational function and is not valueless in the marketplace of ideas."[75] The Court then said that "strict" or "heightened" scrutiny was the appropriate standard to review "a specific, content-based burden on protected expression."[76] Strict scrutiny was justified, the Court said, because the government was trying to suppress the flow of information "out of disagreement with the message it conveys."[77]

Examining the law as a content-based regulation, the Court found the law unconstitutional without relying on its commercial speech precedents.[78] In passing, at the end of its lengthy decision, the Court dismissed its commercial speech decisions as relevant only to laws with a "neutral justification" intended to prevent "commercial harms" or false, deceptive or misleading advertising.[79] In broad disagreement, the dissent said the law was an economic regulation that should be upheld if it used a reasonable means to achieve the government's objective.[80]

Scholars have called *Sorrell* "incoherent," arguing that it introduced "a new rationale so jarring"[81] that it "pinched the already-narrow space between the First Amendment protection accorded commercial and non-commercial speech."[82] Some said the decision eviscerated well-developed precedent that speech intended solely to generate profits and sales should not receive the full constitutional protection afforded to political, artistic or scientific speech.[83] Only a year after it was handed down, observers said the *Sorrell* decision led courts to heighten the scrutiny applied to laws that regulated truthful, nondeceptive advertising, twisting the outcomes in cases on both advertising and product labeling.[84]

Circuit courts seemed uncertain when to apply *Sorrell* and when to rely on *Central Hudson*. For example, the Ninth Circuit Court of Appeals remanded a case with guidance to review a California restriction on alcohol advertising under *Sorrell*'s heightened scrutiny.[85] A year earlier, the Ninth Circuit said the *Central Hudson* test should apply to consideration of whether an ordinance restricting in-window alcohol advertising by stores along a pedestrian mall "fit" the city's stated goals.[86]

Ruling after *Sorrell*, an en banc D.C. Circuit Court of Appeals also applied the *Central Hudson* test, ignoring its "directly advances" element, to affirm the constitutionality of U.S. Department of Agriculture meat-labeling requirements.[87] The court said the merchants' minimal First Amendment interest in refusing to disclose factual information was easily overcome by the consumer benefits of the information.[88]

POINTS OF LAW
THE CENTRAL HUDSON TEST AFTER SORRELL

In *Sorrell v. IMS Health, Inc.*,[89] the U.S. Supreme Court instructed courts ruling on the constitutionality of a commercial speech regulation to ask:

1. Is the commercial speech false or related to an illegal activity?
   a. If yes, the speech may be banned or strictly regulated.
   b. If no, proceed with the test.
2. Is the regulation of commercial speech based on its content?

      a. If yes, the court must apply heightened, or strict, scrutiny and presume that the regulation is unconstitutional.

      b. If no, proceed with the test.

  3. Is the regulation of commercial speech content neutral?

      a. If yes, the court must apply the *Central Hudson*[90] test and strike down the regulation unless the answer to all of the following is yes.

         i. Does the rule relate to a significant government interest?

        ii. Does the rule directly advance that government interest?

      iii. Is the regulation unrelated to the suppression of speech?

      iv. Does the regulation "fit" the government interest without unduly infringing on speech?

This new standard makes it very difficult for regulations of truthful commercial speech to survive First Amendment review unless the speech promotes an illegal activity.

COMPELLING COMMERCIAL SPEECH

For more than 30 years, the U.S. Supreme Court has held that government efforts to compel speech and government efforts to silence speech are equally suspect. The freedom of speech "necessarily compris[es] the decision of both what to say and what not to say," the Supreme Court said.[91]

Government-mandated disclosures—such as loyalty oaths, safety recall notifications or cigarette warning labels—threaten First Amendment freedoms in two ways. First, they alter the speaker's coherent message. "For instance, by compelling newspaper editors or parade organizers to include certain material," they "unduly intrude" on the editors' or organizers' ability to communicate their chosen message.[92] Second, they force a speaker to declare something as fact that the speaker disputes.[93] Mandated speech also prevents silence by those who prefer not to speak at all. The U.S. Supreme Court has said that speech mandates are content-based regulations subject to strict scrutiny review.[94]

REAL WORLD LAW
UNCERTAIN TRUTHS, LABELS AND LAWSUITS

Monsanto's multimillion-dollar 2019 advertising campaign defended its popular weed killer, Roundup, against lawsuits that the product causes cancer.[95] Roundup product labels also stated that the active ingredient, "glyphosate, targets an enzyme found in plants but not in people or pets."[96]

California was the first state to list glyphosate as an agent that may cause cancer, requiring product warning labels.[97] A federal judge in 2018 blocked the required labeling because Monsanto likely would win its First Amendment argument that the label was controversial and could mislead consumers.[98]

In 2019, a California jury ordered Monsanto to pay $2 billion to a couple who said using Roundup according to label instructions caused their cancer.[99] Soon after, Monsanto sought to relocate Roundup trials outside the reach of California's "liberal" consumer-protection laws.[100]

However, for the past three-plus decades, the Supreme Court has applied a relaxed standard of review to government mandates for "purely factual and uncontroversial" commercial disclosures.[101] In *Zauderer v. Office of Disciplinary Counsel of Supreme Court of Ohio*, the Court established that

> [b]ecause the extension of First Amendment protection to commercial speech is justified principally by the value to consumers of the information such speech provides . . . [and the advertiser's] protected interest in *not* providing any particular factual information in his advertising is minimal, [the government has some freedom] to prescribe what shall be orthodox in commercial advertising.[102]

When government requires only truthful, uncontroversial commercial information intended to assist informed consumer choice, courts should defer to the government's judgment, the Supreme Court held. Required factual disclosures infringe "much more narrowly" on the First Amendment interests of commercial speakers than other forms of compelled speech, the Court said, so the government may require warnings or disclaimers that are "reasonably related to the state's interest in preventing deception of consumers."[103]

Lower courts struggled to distinguish *Zauderer*'s purely factual disclosures needing only rational review from government mandates that imposed intrusive or ideological messages that triggered strict scrutiny review.[104] The courts did not agree on how to apply *Zauderer*'s lesser review for an "uncontroversial" disclosure that (1) was factually accurate or (2) reflected a commonly accepted understanding.[105] Some limited *Zauderer* review to disclosures intended to prevent deception.[106] Others applied *Zauderer* to disclosures that informed consumers of basic information, such as product origin.[107]

In 2018, in *National Institute of Family and Life Advocates v. Becerra*, the U.S. Supreme Court suggested that *Zauderer*'s departure from strict scrutiny review of government-compelled commercial disclosures should apply narrowly and only to disclosures that were unrelated to a subject of disagreement.[108] In *NIFLA*, the Supreme Court struck down a California law requiring commercial, pregnancy-crisis centers to provide factual information about public abortion services without deciding what standard of review applied.[109] The Court explained that compelled disclosures must "remedy a harm that is *potentially real* not purely hypothetical" and be "no broader than reasonably necessary" to survive constitutional review.[110] California could not require pro-life centers to inform women of low-cost abortions, the Court said, because the state had failed to draft a narrow law that served a substantial state interest.

In 2018, the Supreme Court's one-sentence opinion in *CTIA—The Wireless Association v. City of Berkeley* instructed the U.S. Court of Appeals for the Ninth Circuit to reconsider a Berkeley city commercial speech mandate and to use *NIFLA* rather than *Zauderer* to guide the outcome. The Ninth Circuit upheld its original decision on remand, relying on *Zauderer* to uphold the city ordinance. That ordinance required cellphone retailers to tell customers that carrying a cellphone in certain ways could expose them to radiation beyond Federal Communications Commission recommended limits.[111] The Ninth Circuit reasoned that the disclosure was purely factual and not unduly burdensome.

The Ninth Circuit had relied on the *Zauderer* test even though the required disclosure was not justified by the need to prevent consumer deception.[112] The circuit court reasoned that both the FCC and the city had found a substantial interest "in this compelled disclosure [that] is reasonably related to protection of the health and safety of consumers."[113] The court said the purpose of the forced disclosure did not need to be prevention of consumer deception. "Any governmental interest will suffice so long as it is substantial, . . . given that the purpose of the compelled disclosure is to provide accurate factual information to the consumer."[114]

Prior to the Supreme Court's *NIFLA* and *CTIA* opinions, the Ninth Circuit had relied on *Zauderer* to find that the First Amendment challenge to a San Francisco ordinance requiring health warnings on sugar-sweetened beverage products and their fixed advertising (billboards) was likely to succeed because the ordinance "was unjustified or unduly burdensome."[115] A three-judge panel of the Ninth Circuit found that a health warning on soda pop and other sweetened beverages but not on other sugar-laden food products was neither an "uncontroversial" nor a "purely factual" disclosure, as *Zauderer* requires.[116] In 2019, the court reheard the case en banc and decided the beverage industry plaintiffs were likely to prevail in the case because the restrictions placed an undue burden on the industry.[117] In 2020, the city passed a revised ordinance with a scaled-down warning on beverage labels; industry groups sued again.[118]

REGULATING VICE PRODUCTS

Controversial commercial speech—such as advertising for **vice products** or advertising to susceptible audiences—is a prime arena for testing the limits of constitutional protection for commercial speech. The U.S. Supreme Court must often determine the limits of permissible regulation of advertising for alcohol, tobacco, drugs, gambling, guns and, more recently, marijuana.

Tobacco

The Lorillard brothers began advertising their tobacco products in a New York daily newspaper in 1789. Nearly two centuries later, a district court in Washington, D.C., ruled that the federal Public Health Cigarette Smoking Act's ban on broadcast TV and radio ads for cigarettes did not violate the free speech rights of tobacco companies because other outlets existed for their advertising.[119] The court said the government had the power to regulate tobacco advertising to protect minors and others from the lure of tobacco. Tobacco producers responded by increasing advertising via print media, billboards and other means.

In 2001, Lorillard Tobacco Co. challenged a Massachusetts law that limited point-of-sale tobacco ads and banned outdoor tobacco ads within 1,000 feet of schools or playgrounds. The U.S. Supreme Court reviewed the law under *Central Hudson* and held that the limits on ads at the point of purchase advanced a legitimate state interest in preventing minors from accessing tobacco products that were illegal for them to consume. In *Lorillard Tobacco Co. v. Reilly*, the Court said the restrictions addressed a state interest "unrelated to the communication of ideas."[120] However, the ban on outdoor advertising was unconstitutional because it did not reasonably fit the state's interest.

In 2017, one federal district court upheld the authority of the Food and Drug Administration (discussed later in this chapter) to regulate all tobacco products, including cigars, e-cigarettes and vaping materials.[121] That same year, a district court in West Virginia ruled that an e-cigarette consumer could pursue his First Amendment claim against the FDA and its new rules, which he

In 2013, a quarter century after federal law prohibited cigarette ads on TV, R. J. Reynolds Tobacco Co. launched a campaign for its e-cigarette, Vuse.

Justin Sullivan/Getty Images

claimed prohibited him from receiving truthful and non-misleading information about vaping products and from receiving other forms of protected expression, including free samples of vaping devices or e-liquids from manufacturers.[122]

Initially, the Trump administration blocked enforcement of new FDA rules that prohibited the sale of cigars, e-cigarettes and vaping materials to anyone under 18 and required the products to provide ingredient labels, addictiveness warnings and proof of claims that they were "light" or "mild."[123] Later, the Trump administration raised the federal legal age for purchasing tobacco from 18 to 21, a new rule that also encompassed e-cigarettes and vaping.[124] In 2020, the Trump administration proposed legislation blocking the FDA's authority to regulate tobacco.[125] Under the Biden administration, the FDA continues its regulation of tobacco and tobacco products, but remains under scrutiny for banning fruity flavored e-cigs and vapes while it allows for menthol varieties.[126] At the same time, the FDA has also allowed the sale of some e-cigarette and vaping products that have demonstrated their use is less toxic and have helped smokers to move away from smoking.[127] If this all sounds confusing, it is. Uncertainty in this area of law has led some experts to call it a "regulatory muddle."[128]

Gambling

The case of *Posadas* discussed earlier involved casino advertising in Puerto Rico, where gambling is legal.[129] But a few years later, the U.S. Supreme Court reviewed the constitutionality of a federal law that banned a radio station in North Carolina, where gambling was illegal, from advertising lotteries even when most of the station's listeners lived in Virginia, where lotteries were legal. The station was only three miles from Virginia.

The U.S. Supreme Court upheld the ban, finding that the state power to ban gambling provided a legitimate government interest in discouraging gambling promotion.[130] The Court said that

> Congress surely knew that stations in one state could often be heard in another but expressly prevented each and every North Carolina station, including Edge, from carrying lottery ads . . . [because] each North Carolina station would have an audience in that state, even if its signal reached elsewhere.[131]

In addition to finding that the state's greater power to ban gambling encompassed the lesser power to ban its promotion, the Court said that the radio station's audience-based argument "has no logical stopping point once state boundaries are ignored." The Court declined "to start down that road."[132]

Alcohol

When Coors Brewing Co. wanted to advertise and label its beer with the percentage of alcohol content, a federal law stood in the way. Coors challenged the law on First Amendment grounds, and the federal government said the law was a reasonable means to prevent "strength wars" that might increase beer potency and harm society. In *Rubin v. Coors Brewing Co.*, the U.S. Supreme Court held for Coors.[133] The Court said that while combating "strength wars" might be a substantial interest, a ban on alcohol content advertising or labeling did not "fit" that goal as well as would alternatives "less intrusive to the First Amendment's protections for commercial speech."[134]

In the case of *44 Liquormart, Inc. v. Rhode Island* mentioned earlier, Rhode Island fined a liquor store owner who tried to evade a state ban on ads that made "reference to the price" of liquor by placing the exclamation "Wow" instead of prices next to bargain products in newspaper ads. The owner raised a First Amendment challenge to the law, and the state argued that the ban advanced the government's substantial interest in promoting temperance by preventing bargain-priced alcohol promotions designed to increase consumption.

REAL WORLD LAW
DOES ADVERTISING INCREASE PRODUCT DEMAND?

A key justification for government regulation of advertising is that it alters consumer choices and increases product demand. Policy and empirical studies find mixed results. One study suggested that advertising increases demand for cigarettes. Another found that alcohol advertising instead shifts consumption among brands.[135] The Food and Drug Administration found a correlation between advertising and increased product demand, but other federal agencies were "not convinced."[136]

Nonetheless, U.S. Supreme Court's rulings have reasoned that

- companies "believe that promotion would increase sales"[137];
- legislatures have a "reasonable" belief that advertising "would serve to increase the demand for the product advertised"[138]; and

- "[p]roduct advertising stimulates demand for products, while suppressed advertising may have the opposite effect."[139]

The U.S. Supreme Court favored the liquor store.[140] The Court first surveyed "the role commercial speech has long played" in American culture,[141] noted the Court's own long-standing hostility to commercial speech regulation of this type and "decline[d] to give force to [the] highly deferential approach" the Court utilized in *Posadas*.[142] It concluded that the state's "paternalistic assumption that the public will use truthful, non-misleading commercial information unwisely cannot justify a decision to suppress it."[143] The Supreme Court ruled the law unconstitutional because it did "not agree with the assertion that the price advertising ban [would] significantly advance the state's interest in promoting temperance."[144]

Almost 25 years later, the Fourth Circuit Court of Appeals held that Virginia's ban on alcohol ads in college newspapers violated the First Amendment because it was not narrowly tailored to the state's interest in reducing alcohol abuse on college campuses.[145] The same court earlier held that the ban was facially constitutional.[146] The later decision found the regulation was unconstitutional as applied because most readers of the Virginia Tech newspaper were 21 or older. Both the newspaper and its readers "have a protected interest" in "truthful, non-misleading" alcohol advertising, the court ruled.

More recently, a federal court in North Carolina struck down a state regulation that prohibited alcohol advertising that "contain[s] any statement, design, device, or representation that depicts the use of alcoholic beverages in a scene that is determined by the (Alcoholic Beverage Control) Commission to be undignified, immodest, or in bad taste."[147] Flying Dog brewery sued the state when the Commission refused to certify the label for its beer, which included a cartoon of a naked male figure. Using the Central Hudson test, the court ruled the regulation failed the fourth part of the test, finding that the regulation, as written, was overbroad.

A North Carolina federal court struck down an alcoholic beverage control regulation that prohibited any label that was "undignified, immodest, or in bad taste." The court said the regulation failed the *Central Hudson* test and was overbroad.

Court record

Prescription Drugs

The U.S. Supreme Court applied strict scrutiny in its review of a Vermont law that prohibited only certain marketers from buying doctors' prescription records from pharmacies.[148] The state law limited access to specific brand-name drug sales data to protect doctors' privacy and prevent drug marketing designed to quash demand for cheaper generic drugs.[149] In *Sorrell v. IMS Health, Inc.* (discussed earlier and excerpted at the end of this chapter), the Supreme Court found that "the state has burdened a form of protected expression that it found too persuasive. At the same time, the state has left unburdened those speakers whose messages are in accord with its own views. This the state cannot do."[150]

Guns

Mass shootings in the United States have focused attention on the manufacturers of guns and ammunition and on gun safety laws. Federal law shields the gun industry from nearly all civil liability for the dangers their products pose.[151] But some lawmakers and activists have attempted to address the problem by regulating gun advertising. To date, those efforts have been largely unsuccessful.

In 2018, a California law established that "[n]o handgun or imitation handgun, or placard advertising the sale or other transfer thereof, shall be displayed in any part of [commercial] premises where it can readily be seen from the outside."[152] When two gun stores were forced to remove in-store signs, the owners sued. Applying *Central Hudson*, a federal trial court in California said the advertising at issue was lawful and nonmisleading and the state's interest in reducing handgun suicide was substantial.[153] However, the court found "paternalistic" and "highly speculative" the government's theory

> that an impulsive person will see a handgun sign outside a store, will impulsively buy the gun (although the Government does not identify a specific purpose for the purchase), and then, at some unspecified future time likely years later, the person's impulsive temperament will lead him to impulsively misuse the handgun that he bought in response to seeing the sign.[154]

The law was unconstitutional, the court concluded, because it did not substantially advance the state's legitimate interest and was intended to suppress truthful speech that the government found too persuasive. In an earlier ruling, the court said the First Amendment challenge to the law would likely succeed because the state's goals of dampening demand and reducing violence were tenuous and only indirectly advanced by limiting the merchants' speech.[155]

But gun safety advocates have continued to sue advertisers. In 2022, the families of nine Sandy Hook Elementary School shooting victims agreed to a $73 million settlement with gun-maker Remington, producer of an AR-15-style rifle like the one used to kill 20 children and six educators in Newton, Conn., in 2012. The families claimed the gun maker used ads with macho, military themes that appealed to troubled youths, like the shooter in Sandy Hook.[156] In 2020, attorneys for Fred Guttenberg, father of Jaime Guttenberg, a student who was killed in the 2018 Stoneman Douglas High School shooting in Parkland, Fla., filed a complaint with the Federal Trade Commission alleging that gun manufacturer Smith & Wesson used unfair and deceptive practices to market rifles to young, male consumers.[157] The complaint alleges that Smith & Wesson sought to grow the civilian market for its assault rifles by deceptively marketing them as associated with the U.S. military, a strategy intended to enhance the credibility of its firearms. That complaint is still pending, and more about filing complaints with the FTC is covered below.

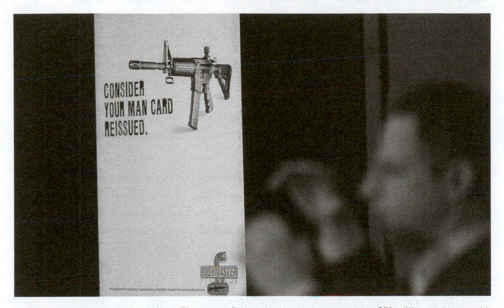

In 2022, the families of nine Sandy Hook Elementary School shooting victims agreed to a $73 million settlement with gun-maker Remington. The families claimed the gun maker used ads with macho, military themes that appealed to troubled youths, like the shooter in Sandy Hook.

AP

REGULATING ADS ON GOVERNMENT PROPERTY

A number of cases address the rights of individuals, especially proponents of controversial positions, to advertise in space offered by the government, especially on public transit. Case outcomes vary with those favoring advertisers often determined by the nature of speech involved and those favoring government focused on the nature of the forum.

For example, a divided Ninth Circuit Court of Appeals upheld the authority of Seattle Metro Transit to prohibit ads on its buses that criticized Israeli policies toward Palestinians.[158] In rejecting ads that read "ISRAELI WAR CRIMES . . . YOUR TAX DOLLARS AT WORK," the court said the county applied viewpoint-neutral, content-based review of speech in a limited public forum. The SMT ruling responded to "real and substantial" fears that the ads' display "presented a reasonably foreseeable threat of disruption" to transit passengers.[159]

The First Circuit Court of Appeals also affirmed a Massachusetts ban on ads that "demean or disparage" individuals or groups from its transit vehicles.[160] One banned ad read "IN ANY WAR BETWEEN THE CIVILIZED MAN AND THE SAVAGE, SUPPORT THE CIVILIZED MAN. SUPPORT ISRAEL. DEFEAT JIHAD." The court said the ad space was a nonpublic forum and the ban a constitutional application of "reasonable, viewpoint-neutral limits."

In contrast, a federal district court ruled that the Philadelphia public transit authority's refusal to display ads that read "Islamic Jew-Hatred: It's in the Quran. Two Thirds of All US Aid Goes to Islamic Countries" violated the First Amendment.[161] The court reasoned that the ad was "exactly the sort of political expression that lies at the heart of the First Amendment . . . regardless of its alleged falsity."[162] The court then enjoined the city's ban on the ads.[163]

FALSE OR MISLEADING COMMERCIAL SPEECH

Neither the definition of the category nor the precise test applied to government constraints on commercial speech is clear and stable, but the U.S. Supreme Court has steadfastly held that the Constitution does not protect false or **deceptive advertising**.[164] In addition to giving commercial speech First Amendment protection for the first time in *Virginia State Board of Pharmacy*, the Supreme Court also established that government could regulate commercial lies and deceptions because

> the advertiser's access to the truth about his product and its price substantially eliminates any danger that governmental regulation of false or misleading price or product advertising will chill accurate and nondeceptive commercial expression. There is, therefore, little need to sanction some falsehood in order to protect speech that matters.[165]

INTERNATIONAL LAW
MISLEADING ADVERTISING IN EUROPE

According to the European Commission, anyone advertising, marketing, promoting or selling goods and services is required to provide consumers with enough accurate information to make an informed purchase.[166] The European Union identifies "bait advertising, phony 'free' offers, manipulation of children, false claims of cures, hidden [native] advertisements in media, . . . [and] false offers of prizes" as among the most prominent misleading or aggressive practices that are prohibited.[167]

Recent EU regulations bar "unfair commercial practices" in advertising and marketing that are likely to materially distort the purchase decisions of a reasonable consumer.[168] The EC found that earlier policies failed to prevent deceptive online practices such as misleading internet offers, false product and price comparisons, fake internet domain name sales, use of competitors' trademarks and other internet-based fraud.[169]

The Court developed this thought further in *Lorillard Tobacco Co.* when it wrote,

> [I]n the context of commercial speech, it is less necessary to tolerate inaccurate statements for fear of silencing the speaker, and also . . . it is more appropriate to require that a commercial message appear in such a form, or include such additional information, warnings and disclaimers, as are necessary to prevent its being deceptive.[170]

For decades, U.S. Supreme Court opinions have flatly stated that commercial speech loses its First Amendment protection if it is misleading, fraudulent, false, deceptive or coercive. In reviewing a city ordinance that prohibited the distribution of "commercial handbills," but not newspapers, on public property, the Court discussed the expanse of permitted government regulation.

> Obviously, much commercial speech is not provably false, or even wholly false, but only deceptive or misleading. We foresee no obstacle to a state's dealing effectively with this problem. The First Amendment, as we construe it today, does not prohibit the state from insuring that the stream of commercial information flow[s] cleanly as well as freely.[171]

In *Zauderer*, the Court said government could justify regulation if an ad had a "tendency to mislead" consumers.[172] Then *Cincinnati v. Discovery Network* seemed to suggest that regulation of a "literally true but misleading disclosure [that] creates the *possibility* of consumer deception" might also be permitted.[173]

The Supreme Court rarely attempted to define when advertising became impermissibly deceptive or misleading. Circuit Courts of Appeal have wrestled to decide when advertising "is inherently likely to deceive or where the record indicates that a particular form or method . . . of advertising has in fact been deceptive."[174] Determining the truth or falsity of an ad involves a relatively straightforward, fact-based inquiry. For example, in 2018, the makers of Canada Dry Ginger Ale faced a number of lawsuits because of the label and advertising claim that the carbonated soft drink is "Made from Real Ginger." Independent tests showed no "detectable" amount of ginger in the beverage.[175]

Identifying deceptive advertising that misleads potential customers requires the difficult determination of probable audience response. The courts do not provide consistent guidance.

THE LANHAM ACT

More than half a century before the U.S. Supreme Court established that the First Amendment protected truthful, nonmisleading commercial speech about legal products and services in *Virginia State Board of Pharmacy*, Congress began enacting laws to protect consumers from unscrupulous business practices.[176] Because commercial speech often crosses state lines and falls under the U.S. Constitution's Commerce Clause, the federal government generally preempts state regulation of advertising and other commercial speech.[177] Congress has enacted scores of laws to ensure that companies provide consumers with essential and accurate information. Competing firms initiate lawsuits when they believe they have been harmed or treated unfairly contrary to the provisions of these laws.

In 1946, Congress passed the **Lanham Act** to prohibit any false or misleading description or promotion of goods, services or commercial activities.[178] The law was amended in 1988. At the outset, the law was seldom used to curtail advertising practices, but it became the foundation for lawsuits, especially over ads using price or product comparisons. Today, the Act applies to competitors, not consumers. Courts have formulated five elements for a successful claim under the Act: (1) The defendant must have made a false or misleading statement of fact in advertising; (2) The statement must have actually deceived or had the capacity to deceive a substantial segment of the audience; (3) The deception must have been material, in that it was likely to influence the purchasing decision; (4) The defendant must have caused its goods to enter interstate commerce; and (5) The plaintiff must have been or is likely to be injured as a result.[179]

POINTS OF LAW

UNDERSTANDING THE LANHAM ACT

A. The Lanham Act is federal law. The false advertising section of the Lanham Act provides that:

Any person who, on or in connection with any goods or services, or any container for goods, uses in commerce any word, term, name, symbol, or device, or any combination thereof, or any false designation of origin, false or misleading description of fact, or false or misleading representation of fact, which—

1. is likely to cause confusion, or to cause mistake, or to deceive as to the affiliation, connection, or association of such person with another person, or as to the origin, sponsorship, or approval of his or her goods, services, or commercial activities by another person, or

2. in commercial advertising or promotion, misrepresents the nature, characteristics, qualities, or geographic origin of his or her or another person's goods, services, or commercial activities, shall be liable in a civil action by any person who believes that he or she is or is likely to be damaged by such act.[180]

B. Courts have generally identified five elements for a successful Lanham Act claim:

1. The defendant must have made a false or misleading statement of fact in advertising. Two types of claims of claims are actionable here:
   a. statements that are literally false; and
   b. statements that are literally true, but are likely to mislead, confuse, or deceive. Statements of opinion or claims of superiority, known as "puffery," are usually not actionable.

2. The statement must have actually deceived or had the capacity to deceive a substantial segment of the audience.

3. The deception must have been material, in that it was likely to influence the purchasing decision. Here, courts will assume a literally false ad deceives in a material way, but a claim for misleading but true statements must demonstrate the misleading effect of the ad. Often extrinsic evidence, such as a survey, is presented.

4. The defendant must have caused its goods to enter interstate commerce; and

5. The plaintiff must have been or is likely to be injured as a result. Plaintiffs need only show threatened injury, not actual injury.[181]

The U.S. Supreme Court has determined that the Lanham Act does not require a party to be either a direct corporate competitor or a consumer of the product to sue under the law.[182] In a case that involved printer toner cartridges, the Supreme Court said a plaintiff has standing to sue when the defendant allegedly caused an injury to the plaintiff's commercial interest that lies in the law's "zone of interest."[183] The Court did not define "zone of interest," but suggested it is roughly equivalent to legislative intent. The intent of the Lanham Act is broadly to prevent commercial deception.

In a recent Lanham Act case, a California district court ruled for a restaurant who said DoorDash, the online delivery food service, deceptively directed customers away from its business. The restaurant said though it never partnered with DoorDash, DoorDash had created a landing page for the restaurant and deceptively led consumers to believe the restaurant was closed during the COVID-19 pandemic, which was untrue. DoorDash argued that the restaurant was unable to show specific consumers were deceived and that DoorDash did not directly compete with the restaurant. The court did not agree, writing that DoorDash had created "obvious, significant and unfair impact upon the competitive landscape within the restaurant industry," which was particularly troubling for restaurants trying to survive during the pandemic.[184] Furthermore, the court said the U.S. Supreme Court made clear that the parties' need not be direct competitors for plaintiffs to claim relief.

DoorDash

In a recent Lanham Act case, a California district court ruled for a restaurant who said DoorDash, the online delivery food service, deceptively directed customers away from its business.

Getty

Courts continually wrestle with the scope of the Lanham Act. The U.S. Supreme Court interpreted the federal Food, Drug and Cosmetic Act[185] (FDCA) to complement the goals and mechanisms of the Lanham Act and allowed POM Wonderful to sue Coca-Cola over the labeling of its Minute Maid pomegranate blueberry juice.[186] The FDCA allowed the product, which contained only 0.3 percent pomegranate and 0.2 percent blueberry juice, to be labeled "a flavored blend of five juices."[187] But the Court said the law did not prevent POM Wonderful from pursuing a claim that the label violated the Lanham Act ban on deceptive and misleading advertising.

The Supreme Court said Coca-Cola was incorrect in arguing "that because food and beverage labeling is involved, it has no Lanham Act liability here for practices that allegedly mislead and trick customers, all to the injury of the competitor."[188] The Court went further. It said the Lanham Act did not require the false advertising to directly cause the injury at the heart of the suit. Rather, the injury must be "proximately caused" by the false advertising.[189] Consumer response to a defendant's false advertising that harms a company's sales or reputation is sufficient to establish the "injury in fact" necessary to bring suit.

STATE LAW CLAIMS

While the Lanham Act and other federal law in this area generally preempts state law, states are not entirely powerless in regulating against false and deceptive advertising. Many states have laws prohibiting unfair competition and false and deceptive advertising. For example, North Carolina's law prohibits "unfair methods of competition in or affecting commerce and unfair or deceptive acts or practices in or affecting commerce."[190] Some states, like Minnesota, specifically legislate against ads that contain "any material assertion, representation, or statement of fact which is untrue, deceptive or misleading."[191] Commercial speech cases can involve a variety of federal and state law claims, which courts and lawyers often spend significant time arguing and sorting out.

States obviously regulate within their own borders, particularly in areas where the federal government has not claimed jurisdiction. In recent years, plaintiffs have tried to sue under state law on the basis of advertising claims made on a product's labels. In 2020, plaintiffs were unsuccessful in a series of "white" non-chocolate claims, with lawsuits against several candy companies alleging their "white"-labeled products deceived reasonable consumers into thinking the products contain white chocolate, when they did not. To date, several class action lawsuits have been dismissed against Nestle, Ghirardelli, and Hershey. In *Prescott v. Nestle USA, Inc.*, a district court in California held that "[n]o reasonable consumer could believe that a package of baking chips contains white chocolate simply because the product includes the word 'white' in its name or label."[192]

CONFUSION AND DOCTRINAL PRESSURES

The regulation of commercial speech has attempted to balance the rights of commercial speakers against concerns for the public welfare and the state's interest in protecting its citizenry and encouraging fair and robust competition. Since the 1970s, the U.S. Supreme Court has provided increasing First Amendment protection for commercial speakers. But as the previous sections demonstrate, both courts and lawmakers have struggled with defining the boundaries of commercial speech under the First Amendment. Whereas the courts have allowed wide room for false political speech under the First Amendment (see *U.S. v. Alvarez*, Ch. 2), the U.S. Supreme Court has consistently held that false or deceptive commercial speech receives no protection under the First Amendment. But precisely defining those boundaries has proved challenging, as this chapter has so far illustrated.

One way that courts have justified the separation between political and commercial speech doctrines is by arguing that commercial speech is hardier and less likely to be chilled when regulated, unlike political speech. But given all the confusion in this area of law, some members of the U.S. Supreme Court have begun expressing interest in eliminating the separation between political and commercial speech doctrines altogether—most notably, Justice Thomas, who has long favored increased protection for commercial speech in several opinions. In *44 Liquormart Inc. v. Rhode Island*, the Court struck down two Rhode Island laws that prohibited advertising the prices of alcoholic beverages.[193] In his concurrence in that case, Justice Thomas wrote: "I do not see a philosophical or historical basis for asserting that 'commercial speech' is of 'lower value' than noncommercial speech. Indeed some historical materials suggest to the contrary."[194] Nonetheless, for the time being, the doctrinal separations between political speech and commercial speech remain—and the intricacies of commercial speech law continue. But given doctrinal confusion, commentators see a U.S. Supreme Court moving in Justice Thomas' direction.[195]

CONSUMER PROTECTION AND THE FEDERAL TRADE COMMISSION (FTC)

The Progressive Era of the early 20th century saw the birth of concerns for consumer protection, but increased interest in safeguarding consumers has been a century-long, if sometimes challenging project that continues today. As the Industrial Revolution gave rise to consumer culture, the progressives of that era fought for social and political reforms to counter problems caused by industrialization. The formation of the Federal Trade Commission in 1914 by Congress was part of several federal laws to address everything from the safety of food and drugs to changes in the banking system. It was part of a push to hold manufacturers accountable and to protect citizens from the harms caused by a changing and booming U.S. economy. Initially, the FTC was formed to address the growth of the business trusts that created monopolistic environments (see above). Today, the FTC handles a variety of antitrust and consumer protection laws.

The Federal Trade Commission has two key commercial speech powers, both derived from Section 5(a) of the FTC Act. The agency is empowered to investigate and prevent (1) unfair or deceptive acts or practices affecting commerce and (2) unfair methods of competition.[196] It oversees nearly all parts of commerce and targets its enforcement efforts at practices that cause the greatest harm to consumers.[197] The first power is used in cases against advertisers; the second power is one that the FTC increasingly relies on to monitor competitive harms caused by businesses generally, especially those businesses more recently engaged in the digital economy. For example, the FTC has used its "unfairness authority" to regulate digital platforms like Facebook, which has repeatedly deceived users about its ability to control the privacy of user personal information.

The statute also gives the FTC authority to seek relief for consumers, and in some instances to seek civil penalties from wrongdoers. In 2021, a unanimous U.S. Supreme Court ruled that the FTC can no longer grant monetary relief from companies engaged in deceptive practices under Section 13(b) of the FTC Act.[198] As of 2022, the FTC was voting to update its rules and seek more authority to collect penalties under other provisions of the FTC Act. In addition, the FTC has lobbied Congress to revise the law to make clearer its ability to collect civil penalties. President Biden's Build Back Better bill also provides for expanded FTC powers.[199] In addition to fines, the FTC can implement rules for advertisers that define acts or practices that are unfair or deceptive. It publishes reports, monitors compliance, and makes legislative recommendations to Congress about issues affecting the economy.[200]

The FTC is led by five commissioners, who are nominated by the President and confirmed by the U.S. Senate. No more than three commissioners can be of the same political party, and the president chooses one to be chair. The FTC has several bureaus that carry out its work: the Bureau of Consumer Protection, the Bureau of Competition and the Bureau of Economics.

Deception Authority

The FTC's 1983 Policy Statement on Deception is aligned with numerous decisions the agency and courts have made in interpreting the agency's authority, and it still serves as the agency's guide for all false, deceptive and misleading advertising cases. The statement identifies three elements that comprise deception cases. First, there must be a "representation, omission or practice that is likely to mislead the consumer." Second, the case must be examined "from the perspective of a consumer acting reasonably in the circumstances." Finally, the "representation, omission or practice must be a 'material' one."[201] The FTC in 2009 also updated its rule on endorsements so that consumers are not deceived or misled.

Likely to Mislead. An ad is misleading when it is *likely* to mislead; the FTC does not require it to be *actually* misleading. Here, the FTC will look at both express claims and implied claims in advertising. **Express claims** make explicit representations without the need for additional evidence. For example, "ABC Nasal Spray prevents COVID-19" is an express claim that the product will prevent COVID. **Implied claims** will be based on a reasonable consumer "take away," where the FTC will consider factors such as the layout, wording of claims, and phrasing. An implied claim is one made indirectly or by inference. "ABC Nasal Spray kills the virus that causes COVID-19" contains an implied claim that the product will prevent COVID. Although the ad doesn't literally say that the product prevents COVID, it would be reasonable for a consumer to conclude from the statement that the product will kill the COVID virus.[202] Here, extrinsic evidence, such as consumer surveys, may be considered, but the FTC will largely step into the shoes of the reasonable consumer to make its determination. In 2021, the FTC took action against several manufacturers who claimed their products helped to prevent, mitigate or kill the COVID-19 virus.

REAL WORLD LAW
COVID-19 AND THE FTC

In 2021, Congress passed the COVID-19 Consumer Protection Act, which made it illegal for "any person, partnership, or corporation to engage in a deceptive act or practice in or affecting commerce associated with the treatment, cure, prevention, mitigation, or diagnosis of COVID–19 or a government benefit related to COVID–19."[203] The Act provides that such violations be treated as an unfair or deceptive act or practice under the FTC Act.

The FTC subsequently targeted many marketers who claimed their products could prevent or treat COVID-19. Some of the actions involved bogus treatments such as intravenous (IV) Vitamin C infusions, ozone therapy, peptide therapy, nasal sprays, saunas and supplements.[204] The FTC warned advertisers that one or more of the efficacy claims made by these marketers were unsubstantiated because they were not supported by scientific evidence, and therefore violated the law.[205]

In a 2021 report, the FTC also announced it had filed 13 enforcement actions against companies that, among other things, failed to deliver personal protective equipment or made deceptive health or earnings claims.[206] It required hundreds of companies to remove deceptive claims related to COVID-19 treatments, potential earnings, and financial relief for small business and students. It warned companies that it is illegal to assist and facilitate deceptive COVID-19 calls.[207] It also addressed privacy enforcement actions related to remote or online work, healthcare, and schooling.

Between January 2020 and April 2021, it collected and tracked more than 436,000 reports associated with COVID-19 and issued consumer and business alerts.[208] Consumers can report false and deceptive advertising problems and other fraud to the FTC at https://www.ftc.gov/.

A Reasonable Consumer and Disclosures. The FTC considers the perspective of the reasonable consumer acting under reasonable circumstances and the average target audience member for the ad. For instance, an ad for a toy would be considered differently than an ad for a supplement that claims to improve memory. Children and seniors will evaluate targeted ads differently and will evaluate ad disclosures differently. If an ad makes express or implied claims that might be misleading without additional information, that information must be disclosed. According to the FTC, a "**disclosure** can only qualify or limit a claim to avoid a misleading impression"—a disclosure "cannot cure a false claim," and it must not contradict a material claim.[209] An example of a disclosure might be an ad for imitation pearl earrings. The FTC requires such a disclosure that the earrings are "imitation," and it must be "**clear and conspicuous**." The commission will look at the ad's performance, how consumers perceive and understand the disclosure, and its overall "net impression."[210]

The FTC has used the pneumonic called "**The 4 Ps**" to help guide advertisers with disclosures. Much of this instruction is directed at the graphic designers of print, broadcast, and online advertising:

Prominence: Is the disclosure large enough for consumers to read? Small type can be easy to overlook as can quickly moving text or narration. The FTC has challenged advertisers who engage in fine print and quickly moving audio disclosures.

Presentation: Can consumers understand the disclosure? Using confusing language or burying important information will attract FTC scrutiny. The FTC more recently is investigating what is referred to as **dark patterns or "negative options" practices**.[211] These are tactics used by companies and individuals to trick consumers into making certain choices, such as purchasing a good, subscribing to a service, or agreeing to a contract. An example of a dark pattern would be a box that is already checked that says to continue a subscription to an app beyond the initial subscription period. The new "Enforcement Policy Statement Regarding Negative Option Marketing" from the FTC warns companies they will face legal action if they engage in such tactics.[212]

Placement: Is the disclosure in a place where consumers are likely to look? Small type and buried links, away from the main advertising copy, might also draw the FTC's scrutiny.

Proximity: Is the disclosure close to the claim it modifies? The further a disclosure is from the main advertising text, the more it will draw attention from regulators. An asterisk may not be suitable if it is difficult to locate the qualifying language.[213]

Ads that contain **puffery** are obviously exaggerated claims or statements, and the FTC assumes that reasonable consumers would not take them seriously. These are statements intended to brag or amuse and create memorable associations with the advertised product. They are not objective representations of fact. Examples of puffery include GEICO's "Switching to Geico is so easy a caveman could do it" or Starbuck's "The Best Coffee for the Best You."[214]

When the FTC told Ellen DeGeneres and Nicki Minaj, among almost two dozen celebrities, that they needed to be transparent about all "material connections" to the products they promote through their social media, publicists scrambled to reshape Instagram and Facebook posts to comply with disclosure requirements.[215] A year later, an FTC report found that only one-fourth of celebrities were following its regulations that require clear notification of compensation for content on social media.[216] (The growing role of influencers is addressed in more detail in the section on endorsements below.)

In 2015, the FTC announced that its disclosure requirements applied to native advertising in which ads resemble the editorial content of the medium in which they appear. The FTC said native ads are deceptive when their overall impression so closely mimics nonpaid content as to be likely to confuse consumers.[217]

POINTS OF LAW
FALSE AND MISLEADING ADVERTISING

A Federal Trade Commission policy statement establishes the three-part federal definition of false and misleading advertising:

A representation, omission or practice that is likely to mislead . . .	. . . a reasonable consumer . . .	. . . who is influenced to buy.
Practices that have been found misleading or false include false oral or written representations, misleading price claims, sales of hazardous defective products or services without disclosures, failure to perform services, among other actions.	The case must be examined from the perspective of a consumer acting reasonably in the circumstances.	The representation, omission or practice must be a "material" one. That is, it must affect a consumer's decision to buy.

Materiality. A **material decision** is one that is likely to affect a consumer's choice or conduct regarding a product or service. Both express and implied claims can be material, and material claims in advertising can be ones regarding health and safety; a product's performance or features; or a product's purpose and effectiveness. Advertisers must have proof—or what the FTC calls **substantiation**—to back up express <u>and</u> implied claims that advertisers make.

The FTC's Statement on Regarding Advertising Substantiation requires that advertisers and ad agencies have a **reasonable basis** for advertising claims before they are disseminated.[218] Scientific or engineering tests, in addition to primary evidence such as user surveys, are considered the best types of substantiation.[219] In a case against Pfizer, Inc., the FTC said Pfizer had no prior substantiation for claims regarding the pain-relieving qualities of a sunburn product called "Un-Burn." The FTC ruled that Pfizer's statements required prior substantiation and identified several factors to help determine the appropriate level of substantiation an advertiser must have for **efficacy claims**—those claims for products that perform the advertised function or yield the advertised benefit, but which do not suggest scientific proof of the product's effectiveness. The Pfizer factors include:

1. the type and specificity of the claim made—e.g., safety, efficacy, dietary, health, medical;

2. the type of product—e.g., food, drug, potentially hazardous consumer product, other consumer product;

3. the possible consequences of a false claim—e.g, personal injury, property damage;

4. the degree of reliance by consumers on the claims;

5. the type, and accessibility, of evidence adequate to form a reasonable basis for making the particular claims.[220]

In the 2013 case *POM Wonderful v. FTC,* an appeals court agreed with the FTC's finding that in 19 different ads, the marketers of the POM Wonderful 100% Pomegranate Juice and POM supplements deceptively advertised that the products could treat, prevent, or reduce the risk of heart disease, prostate cancer, and erectile dysfunction, and were clinically proven to have such benefits.[221] The POM advertisements made a type of **establishment claim,** a claim that suggests effectiveness or superiority of the product is established by scientific proof. The court stated that at least one randomized, controlled, human clinical trial study was required before POM could claim a relationship between its products and the treatment or prevention of any disease. While POM had sponsored several studies, the court said the findings of those studies were either inflated or the limitations ignored.[222]

Endorsements. The FTC's 2009 revisions to its guide on endorsements and testimonials in advertising reflects the changing nature of advertising in the digital world. The FTC defines an **endorsement** as "any advertising message (including verbal statements, demonstrations, or depictions of the name, signature, likeness or other identifying personal characteristics of an individual or the name or seal of an organization) that consumers are likely to believe reflects the opinions, beliefs, findings or experiences of a party other than the sponsoring advertiser, even if the views expressed by that party are identical to those of the sponsoring advertiser."[223]

Here, the main goal of the FTC is to make sure audiences fully understand the relationship between the advertiser and the endorser.

Sometimes, experts can be used as endorsers, often the case for health products. The FTC defines an **expert** as an "individual, group, or institution possessing, as a result of experience, study, or training, knowledge of a particular subject, which knowledge is superior to what ordinary individuals generally acquire."[224] Expert endorsers must have the relevant expertise and any claims of expected results or superior performance must be substantiated. Their endorsements must be truthful, nondeceptive and substantiated, and any advertiser who presents endorsements by "actual consumers" should use actual consumers or disclose they are not actual consumers if that is the case.[225] Finally, all material connections must be disclosed. That is, if payment or consideration was given for an endorsement, that must be disclosed to the reader or viewer.[226]

More recently, the FTC issued a guide for social media influencers. The guide requires influencers to disclose financial, employment, personal or family relationship with a brand. A financial relationship may include free or discounted products or other perks. Tags, likes, and pins can be endorsements if influencers have a relationship with the brand. Influencers should also follow the "4 Ps" (see above) with disclosures and use simple and clear language.

In its first enforcement against native ads and influencers, the FTC in 2016 issued a complaint against clothing retailer Lord & Taylor.[227] Lord & Taylor's marketing of a new women's clothing line included blog posts, digital photos, video uploads, native ads in online fashion magazines and a team of online "fashion influencers recruited for their fashion style and extensive base of followers on social media platforms."[228] The FTC said the influencers received undisclosed payment and free clothing to send preapproved Lord & Taylor posts and hashtags that reached an estimated 11.4 million Instagram users. Lord & Taylor also preapproved at least one online article and an Instagram photo without disclosing that the content was paid.

In settling the case, the FTC prohibited Lord & Taylor from making any representations that suggest that paid content is independent or objective. The FTC required Lord & Taylor to ensure that all endorsers disclosed their paid relationship with the retailer.[229] The settlement punished only Lord & Taylor (the advertiser), not the influencers or the publishers, although FTC policy allows liability for all of these parties.[230]

In another case involving paid influencers, an FTC order required Machinima, a multichannel YouTube network about video games and gaming culture, to ensure its ad campaigns carried proper disclosure. Microsoft and its advertising agency paid influencers to promote Microsoft's Xbox One through a Machinima video campaign. The FTC said that many influencers "gave the impression that their videos were independently produced and that their comments reflected the influencer's personal views."[231] The FTC's settlement punished the publisher, Machinima, not Microsoft, the ad agency or the influencers.[232]

A study conducted in 2016 found that 40 percent of publishers were not complying with FTC rules requiring labeling of native ads.[233] In 2017, the FTC sent out more than 90 warning letters in one week to remind broadcasters, advertisers, marketers and "influencers" of their obligation to disclose all sponsored promotions and endorsements they distribute through social media. In 2018, an FTC study found that "a significant percentage" of consumers could not identify some native advertising as advertising even with prominent labeling.[234]

REAL WORLD LAW
STUDENT INFLUENCERS AND DISCLOSURES

Many college students have been recruited to be social media influencers for everything from makeup and bras to restaurants and vitamins. Influencers, including students, are required to be honest about their appraisals and disclose their relationships. Not disclosing these relationships can lead to warnings and/or fines from the FTC.

Disclosures can take several forms. These include[235]:

- Thanking the manufacturers for the free product.
- Using terms like "advertisement," "ad" and "sponsored."
- Using words like "partner" or "ambassador" along with the brand name.
- Posting hashtags (i.e., #ad, #sponsored).
- Avoiding vague or confusing terms like "sp" or "spon" for "sponsored" or other abbreviations that might be misunderstood.
- Not assuming a platform's disclosure tool is enough.

Unfairness Authority

In the 1970s, the FTC faced criticism as it used its unfairness powers to legislate against perceived violations of "public policy." The most prominent example of overreach occurred when the FTC tried to ban all advertising directed to children on the grounds that it was "immoral, unscrupulous, and unethical" and based on generalized public policies to protect children.[236] Gradually, the Commission moved away from an emphasis on public policy and toward a focus on consumer injury and consumer sovereignty. Today, a three-part definition guides what constitutes the FTC's unfairness authority:

> An act or practice that (1) causes or is likely to cause substantial injury to consumers; (2) which is not reasonably avoidable by consumers themselves; and (3) not outweighed by countervailing benefits to consumers or competition.[237]

Examples of unfairness actions vary, but can include coercion or fraud (in which companies exercise undue influence in some way); withholding of information from consumers; targeting of vulnerable consumers (such as children or the elderly); and/or a lack of "privity," in which obligations or conditions are imposed on consumers in excess of a contract or agreement.[238] In recent years, the FTC has used its unfairness authority to especially protect online consumer fraud.

In *FTC v. Wyndham Worldwide Corp.* the FTC filed suit against the hotel chain for a series of data breaches in which online hackers accessed more than 619,000 consumer accounts, resulting in approximately $10.6 million in fraud.[239] The FTC made both deception and unfairness claims against Wyndham. The hotel chain made two arguments in its defense: that the FTC lacked authority to regulate data security under its unfairness authority and that the commission had not given the chain fair notice about its cybersecurity rules. In 2015, the U.S. Circuit of Appeals for the Third Circuit rejected Wyndham's arguments, ruling that the FTC indeed had such authority to regulate data security under its unfairness powers and that the agency had given businesses fair warning about new cybersecurity rules. The court wrote that the hotel had been hacked three times, and the chain's alleged security practices were counseled against by FTC guidance and complaints.[240] In 2016, the FTC published a new guide for businesses that experience a data breach, warning companies to move swiftly and remove hacking vulnerabilities.[241]

More recently, the FTC has fined Facebook for decisions regarding its users' privacy. In 2012, the FTC issued an order against Facebook which required it to correct its privacy settings. That order prohibited Facebook from making misrepresentations about the privacy or security of consumers' personal information, including names and dates of birth, with third parties. It also required Facebook to maintain a program that safeguarded the privacy and confidentiality of user information.[242] In 2019, the FTC alleged that Facebook violated the 2012 order by sharing the data of users' Facebook friends with third-party app developers, even when those friends had set more restrictive privacy settings.[243] Facebook paid a record-breaking $5 billion penalty, and agreed to new restrictions and a modified corporate structure to hold the company accountable. The penalty was the largest ever imposed on any company for violating consumer privacy. In 2021, whistleblower Frances Haugen revealed information that Facebook understood its platform impacted teens' mental health and understood the extent of misinformation on its platforms without failing to act, accusations Facebook denies. As of 2022, a complaint by Haugen had been filed with the Securities and Exchange Commission (SEC). This case is covered in more detail in the SEC section below.

Enforcement

While complaints, congressional inquiries or publicity often alert the FTC to potentially problematic advertisements, the commission also initiates inquiries into products, services or advertising practices. Some issues arise directly from advertisers seeking advice to avoid problems. FTC inquiries and fact-findings, like grand jury investigations, generally are closed to protect the privacy of those investigated. FTC powers range from rulemaking to investigation to enforcement, and their enforcements run from quite informal letters to serious, official legal actions. The FTC acts both preventatively and correctively.

The least formal FTC preventive action is a nonbinding opinion letter sent to an advertiser seeking advice about advertising and promotions. The next step up is an official FTC advisory opinion that is part of the public record. Advisory opinions inform individuals beyond those directly involved about various trade-related issues, and they often require advertisers to adhere to the opinion or face potential legal liability.

FTC industry guides suggest policies about particular products or services. FTC trade regulation rules target an entire trade to mandate a particular practice. The FTC industry guide on advertising testimonials and endorsements established that endorsers, especially celebrity endorsers, may be personally liable for false claims.[244] Other guides, like the ones on cybersecurity and influencers and disclosures, also offer companies direction and instruction.

The FTC generally seeks voluntary compliance with its actions and asks advertisers to provide evidence of their own corrective steps before initiating investigations or corrective measures. If an advertiser fails to comply voluntarily, the FTC may initiate corrections and sanctions through a consent order or decree. Consent orders are typically an FTC contract with a private party and are not filed in court. A decree is filed with and sanctioned by a court.

For example, the FTC ordered American Nationwide Mortgage Co. to cease and desist its direct mail ad campaign that stated, "30-Year Fixed. 1.95%." In a virtually illegible footnote on the ad's reverse side, the text stated, "4.981% Annual Percentage Rate."[245] Under the FTC order, the mortgage company agreed to discontinue the advertisement.

A consent decree is for settlement purposes only. It does not constitute an admission of guilt by the advertiser. The FTC issued its first consent decree for deceptive online advertising after a service placed advertisements on the internet advising consumers to take illegal steps to repair their credit records.[246] The FTC required the advertiser to provide consumer compensation, to cease misrepresentations and to cooperate in FTC investigations of the sellers of the credit program materials.

In 2017, Uber signed an FTC consent order and agreed to establish strict privacy practices to settle FTC charges that it had deceived customers about Uber drivers' access to customers' private information.[247] In 2018, after Uber failed to inform the FTC of a major breach of customer data, Uber signed an expanded agreement that included possible penalties for failure to maintain customer privacy and inform the FTC of security breaches.[248]

Later in 2018, the FTC found that Uber had failed to comply with the agreements and ordered Uber to implement a privacy program.[249] The order mandated specific corrective provisions, including Uber recordkeeping and reporting, FTC monitoring and independent external assessment of Uber compliance for up to 20 years. The FTC also filed a formal complaint against Uber for false or misleading claims about the security of customer information.[250] In an earlier FTC action, Uber paid $20 million to settle claims that its online advertising for drivers falsely inflated their hourly earnings.[251]

The FTC sued Volkswagen for false and deceptive "clean diesel" vehicle advertising and promotions.[252] The action followed public disclosure that the car manufacturer falsified its vehicle emission-test results for years.[253]

FTC actions like these produce negative publicity for the companies involved and may result in court- or FTC-imposed fines, which the FTC often publicizes. For example, when the FTC concluded that Rite Aid pharmacies failed to provide their advertised protection for the privacy of individuals' prescription drug information, the resulting consent order mandated specific corrective measures by Rite Aid and fined the company $1 million.[254]

If advertisers refuse to sign a consent order, the FTC may issue a litigated order. The FTC files litigated orders in an administrative court. If the court affirms the order, the advertiser may appeal to a federal court. Failure to follow a litigated order upheld by the courts may result in fines of up to $10,000 per day. In one litigated action, the promoters of two dietary supplements advertised for weight loss and disease prevention agreed to pay the FTC $4.5 million for their false or unsubstantiated product claims and deceptively formatted infomercials.[255]

The FTC's substantiation requirements demand that advertisers prove their claims with "competent and reliable evidence."[256] The FTC's demand to "prove it" was central to its case against Tropicana's Healthy Heart orange juice. Through both television and print, Tropicana advertised that drinking its product increased "good" cholesterol and lowered blood pressure.

The FTC said the clinical study Tropicana used to substantiate its claims was inadequate.[257] The FTC said the ads were false or misleading and ordered Tropicana to stop making the claims.

If an advertiser fails to substantiate its advertised claims, the FTC may impose fines, initiate court action and/or order **corrective advertising** that requires the advertiser to correct the misleading claims through new ads or other means.

Decades ago, the FTC used corrective advertising against a then-famous Listerine mouthwash ad campaign. The FTC found that Listerine misled the public for more than half a century with ad claims that the mouthwash killed germs and helped prevent colds and sore throats. A federal appeals court ruled that the FTC-ordered corrective advertising did not violate the First Amendment because "Listerine's advertisements play[ed] a substantial role in creating or reinforcing in the public's mind a false belief about the product . . . [that would] linger on after the false advertising ceases."[258] Nearly a year of required corrective advertising was not "an unreasonably long time in which to correct a hundred years of cold claims," the court ruled.[259] The company spent $10 million on those ads.

The FTC issued a litigated corrective advertising order for unsubstantiated superiority claims in advertisements and packaging claims for Doan's analgesic products.[260] The commission said substantial evidence supported its finding that the ads' deceptive claims were material, affected consumer beliefs and created lingering effects that required remedy.[261] The order required Doan's to spend its average annual advertising budget on corrective ads for a minimum of one year.

The FTC also may seek court injunctions or restraining orders to stop advertising that is false or misleading and may cause immediate harm. These orders generally stop the advertising until a full hearing takes place. The FTC, however, sought permanent injunctions to stop companies from making unsubstantiated claims that required consumers to pay thousands of dollars in up-front fees to receive promised reductions in credit card debt.[262]

POINTS OF LAW
FEDERAL TRADE COMMISSION MECHANISMS

Preventive Measures	Corrective Measures
● Opinion letters	● Cease and desist orders
● Advisory opinions	● Consent orders
● Industry guides	● Substantiation
● Trade rules	● Litigated orders
● Voluntary compliance	● Corrective advertising
	● Injunctions

More than 40 years ago, government attempts to protect susceptible people, especially children, from tobacco promotions targeted Camel's use of the cartoon character Joe Camel.[263] The

FTC asked an administrative law judge to issue a cease and desist order to stop R. J. Reynolds Tobacco Co. from using Joe Camel in any way that "would have a substantial appeal to children … below the age of 18."[264] Critics said Joe Camel prompted smoking by minors, for whom smoking was illegal. In fact, Camel cigarettes' share of the youth market rose from 4 percent to 13 percent after the introduction of Joe Camel.[265] The tobacco industry settled, agreeing to end all use of cartoon characters and all billboard and transit ads promoting tobacco products in all 50 states.

Vintage Camel cigarette advertising featuring Joe Camel.

Viviane Moos/Getty Images

Online Advertising

The internet provides fertile ground for fraud and unwanted ads, and the cost-effectiveness of online advertising is attractive to companies. Internet ads can reach an enormous audience of consumers targeted because their online behavior indicates interest in relevant activities or products. Clicking on online ads also provides advertisers with marketable user data and a back door to illegal snooping.

In one example, the FTC settled its action against the Canadian dating site Ashley Madison (AM) after it created fake profiles of members to lure others—including 19 million Americans—to pay to initiate or end memberships. The FTC settled, with AM paying $1.6 million and agreeing to correct its "lax" data security.[266]

In 2015, the FTC settled a complaint that app developers violated the Children's Online Privacy Protection Act[267] by enabling advertisers to use "persistent identifiers," or trackers, to target ads toward children.[268] The FTC's rules under COPPA classify persistent identifiers as personal information and prohibit their collection from children under 13 without parental notice and consent.[269]

The FTC has asked internet platforms and their advertisers voluntarily to give consumers "effective and meaningful privacy protection" via an easy, internet-wide "Do Not Track" option.[270] The FTC has said that because mechanisms targeting advertising to consumers are invisible, consumers should have an easy way to opt out.[271] The FTC promised Congress a simple, global solution for consumers, but its proposed rules allowed Facebook, Google and other "internet publishers with a direct relationship with consumers" to collect a wide array of data.[272]

In 2019, the FTC completed its first review of the opt-out, labeling and identification requirements it imposed on commercial senders of unsolicited email, or spam advertising.[273] The review found that the rules that implemented the 2004 federal Controlling the Assault of Non-Solicited Pornography and Marketing Act [274] were effective and did not need to be modified.[275] The CAN-SPAM law prohibits "the transmission . . . of a commercial electronic mail message . . . that contains, or is accompanied by, header information that is materially false or materially misleading."[276] The law also empowers internet service providers and the government to sue spammers and requires unsolicited messages to include opt-out instructions.

Penalties for violations include up to five years' imprisonment and fines of up to $6 million.[277] In addition, the FTC requires employees who send out personal messages about company products to disclose their conflict of interest and make clear that they are not speaking on behalf of the employer.[278]

Most states have their own anti-spam laws.[279] In Virginia, where laws target unsolicited commercial bulk emails,[280] Jeremy Jaynes, a man once considered one of the world's most prolific spammers,[281] was charged with violating the law after he sent more than 55,000 unsolicited emails to subscribers of AOL (then America Online). The Virginia Supreme Court overturned Jaynes' conviction, finding the law's prohibition on false labeling of routing information overbroad and facially unconstitutional because it infringed the First Amendment right to engage in anonymous speech and targeted not only unsolicited commercial bulk emails but "the anonymous transmission of all unsolicited bulk e-mails including those containing political, religious or other speech protected by the First Amendment to the United States Constitution."[282]

For almost two decades, Congress and the Federal Trade Commission have worked to implement a simple, global way to eliminate unwanted commercial email and social media spam.

REAL WORLD LAW

THE GREAT RECESSION AND THE CONSUMER FINANCIAL PROTECTION BUREAU (CFPB)

The Great Recession of 2008 was the result of many factors, but especially a market that permitted high-risk housing loans and credit. The downturn began in December 2007 and lasted 18 months, with the nation's gross domestic product dropping 4.3 percent, the largest decline in 60 years. Unemployment reached 10 percent, and rates were higher for Black and Hispanic households. In addition, nearly three million homes went into foreclosure.[283]

The marketing and promotion of high-risk subprime mortgages targeted home buyers who were told they could borrow money even with low credit ratings and with no income, job, or assets. When interest rates started to rise, defaults on these loans increased, and providers of these mortgages began to declare bankruptcy. Citizens were forced out of their homes, and whole neighborhoods went dark.

In July 2010, Congress passed the Dodd-Frank Wall Street Reform and Consumer Protection Act, which was signed into law by President Barack Obama. The law created the Consumer Financial Protection Bureau (CFPB).[284] While the FTC had oversight advertisers, it did not have over control over banking promotion. The CFPB became the agency to initiate consumer protection in banking. The act also gave the CFPB jurisdiction over any company, not just banks and credit unions, that offers financial services. Today the CFPB, which works collaboratively with the FTC, is responsible for[285]:

- Rooting out unfair, deceptive, or abusive acts or practices by writing rules, supervising companies, and enforcing the law
- Enforcing laws that outlaw discrimination in consumer finance
- Taking consumer complaints
- Enhancing financial education
- Researching the consumer experience of using financial products
- Monitoring financial markets for new risks to consumers

The CFPB's website educates consumers about all kinds of financial instruments and can help consumers freeze their credit reports in instances of fraud or hacking. Consumers can also file complaints against financial institutions. See more at: www.consumerfinance.gov.

OTHER EXECUTIVE AGENCIES

While consumer protection and unfair competition are primarily the jurisdiction of the FTC, other agencies within the executive branch are also charged with protecting U.S. citizens from deceptive and unfair practices by advertisers and corporations. These agencies usually receive their mandates through specific acts of the U.S. Congress. The agencies below regulate particular kinds of broadcast advertising, political advertising, food and drug advertising, and investor communications.

The Federal Communications Commission (FCC)

The Federal Communications Commission is among the numerous other federal agencies that impose requirements on advertisers to prevent consumer deception. The FCC's oversight of broadcast television includes regulation of certain types of advertising, marketing and promotional content to serve the public interest (see Chapter 9).

FCC rules prohibit paid, for-profit business and campaign advertising on public television stations.[286] The U.S. Supreme Court denied certiorari to review the Ninth Circuit Court of Appeals' summary judgment upholding the FCC ban against a public television station's First Amendment challenge. The Ninth Circuit found that substantial evidence supported the FCC's conclusion that commercial and political advertising posed a legitimate threat to the noncommercial, educational "essence" of public television.[287] The court accepted the decades-old rationale that the scarcity of broadcast airwaves supports government's increased regulation of television.

The FCC also regulates offensive broadcast advertising, but no federal agency or law controls offensive nonbroadcast ads or advertising of disfavored activities, such as violence or pornography. FCC guidelines suggest that offensiveness can arise from the nature of the product, the time at which the ad appears or the manner in which it is presented.[288] In recent years, the FCC has reported no enforcement actions against offensive broadcast ads.

FCC rules banned broadcasters in Louisiana from airing ads for private casino gambling because the ads reached states where such gambling was illegal. In a case brought by an association of broadcasters, a unanimous U.S. Supreme Court held that although the state had a substantial interest in reducing the social costs of gambling, the rules failed the *Central Hudson* test because they did not advance that interest.[289] The rules were underinclusive because they prohibited only advertising for private casinos (not for casinos operated by Native American tribes and not advertising of other forms of gambling). The rules simply directed gamblers to favored outlets, the Court said. Moreover, the rules were not as narrowly tailored as they could be.[290]

The Federal Election Commission (FEC)

The U.S. Court of Appeals for the D.C. Circuit affirmed Federal Election Commission rules requiring disclosure of corporate and union funding, but not other types of funding, for broadcast "electioneering communications." The court said Congress had "spoke[n] plainly" about its intentions, and the FEC rules were not "capricious" or "arbitrary" or unsupported by a substantial government interest.[291]

In its opinion, the court focused significant attention on the tension between unfettered free speech and forced disclosures, whose "deleterious effects . . . have been ably catalogued."[292] The opinion opens by declaring that

> [d]isclosure chills speech. Speech without disclosure risks corruption [or deception]. And the Supreme Court's track record of expanding who may speak while simultaneously blessing robust disclosure rules has set these two values on an ineluctable collision course.[293]

The D.C. Circuit Court suggested that the U.S. Supreme Court has failed to provide clear guidance to lower courts on when the First Amendment does and does not permit government-compelled disclosures.

The problem of disinformation in online political advertising is a growing issue, contributing to concerns about the overall health of U.S. democracy. At least eight states now have statutes regulating online political advertising in which regulators require the disclosure of sources of online ads.[294] In Maryland, a federal appeals court struck down their law as unconstitutional because although the state had significant interests in preventing disinformation, the law's disclosure requirements were a type of compelled speech and could not pass either strict or exacting scrutiny.[295] Congress has proposed an "Honest Ads Act" to regulate the problem at the federal level, but it has not yet passed.

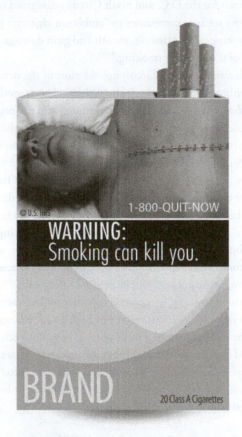

One of the proposed cigarette-package images abandoned by the Food and Drug Administration.

FDA via Getty Images

The Food and Drug Administration (FDA)

While the FTC has the authority to regulate advertising more broadly, the Food and Drug Administration (FDA) has jurisdiction over labels and labeling. Because issues of advertising, labeling and consumer harm can and do overlap, the FDA and FTC often regularly work together to regulate and prosecute offenders.

When the Food and Drug Administration initiated rules "designed to stop sales and marketing of cigarettes and smokeless tobacco to children," a federal district court in North Carolina said the FDA had authority to impose only some of the rules.[296] The court said the FDA could regulate access and labeling of tobacco products as part of its authority over sales and use, but FDA authority "cannot be so broadly construed as to encompass conditions on advertising and promotion."[297]

A decade later, as regulators struggled to balance consumer protection and tobacco company speech rights, Congress enacted the Family Smoking Prevention and Tobacco Control Act.[298] Under the new law, the FDA adopted graphic labeling requirements for cigarettes.[299] The U.S. Courts of Appeals for the D.C. and Sixth Circuits disagreed on the constitutionality of the FDA rules requiring tobacco companies to "emblazon cigarette packaging with images of people dying from smoking-related disease, mouth and gum damage linked to smoking and other graphic portrayals of the harms of smoking."[300]

Applying *Central Hudson*, the Sixth Circuit upheld most of the new labeling requirements because they regulated only commercial speech about risky tobacco products. The D.C. Circuit also applied *Central Hudson*, but decided that the government did not provide evidence showing that graphic images would directly advance its interest in lessening the number of Americans who smoke.[301] Both courts said the rules required speech that was neither purely factual nor uncontroversial.[302] The Supreme Court declined review of both cases.[303]

As mentioned earlier, the FDA in 2016 applied its tobacco label rules to all "e-cigarettes, vaping devices and other electronic nicotine delivery systems," including hookahs.[304] In 2017 and 2018, two federal district court decisions upheld the FDA's inclusion of vaping devices under "tobacco products" subject to its disclosure and other advertising requirements.[305] One applied *Zauderer* and found that the FDA had made the necessary showing to support its required factual and uncontroversial disclosures that reasonably advanced the government's significant interest in informing the public about health and safety risks.[306]

In 2021, the FDA issued warning letters to companies selling vaping product containing vitamins or essential oils who made various unproven health and wellness claims. In the letters, the FDA claimed that the companies sold new drugs that have not been approved by the FDA. In addition, the FDA said that the use of the companies' products "raises safety concerns for the agency because the ingredients and/or impurities in oral inhalation products may trigger laryngospasm or bronchospasm, may be toxic to the tissues in the upper or lower airways, or may be absorbed and exert undesirable systemic effects or organ toxicity."[307]

The Securities and Exchange Commission (SEC)

The mission of the Securities and Exchange Commission (SEC) is to protect investors; maintain fair, orderly, and efficient markets; and facilitate capital formation.[308] Before the creation of the SEC in 1934, the oversight of trade in stocks, bonds and other securities did not exist. Fraud and abuse contributed to the effects of the Great Depression after the 1929 Stock Market Crash. Hearings about the crash led to the formation of the SEC and the passage of the 1933 Securities Act and the 1934 Securities Exchange Act, which created the SEC, giving it power to regulate the securities industry, including the New York Stock Exchange.

While the SEC's role is to help regulate markets, the information required to do so falls within discussions about commercial and corporate speech. The SEC's policy on the disclosure of such information is that investors should be treated fairly and have access to certain facts about investments and those who sell them. Toward that end, the SEC requires "public companies, fund and asset managers, investment professionals, and other market participants to regularly disclose significant financial and other information so investors have the timely, accurate, and complete information they need to make confident and informed decisions about when or where to invest."[309] Those who don't disclose are subject to fines and other penalties.

Sec. 5(c) of the Securities Act of 1933 prohibits promotion of an initial public offering (IPO) before registration is filed with SEC and declared effective. As such, the SEC requires the time between an intention to file and IPO and the registration to be a quiet period. During this period, advertising and promotion of the IPO is prohibited; Legitimate company news and other typical corporate communications are still permitted.

Additionally, the Securities Exchange Act of 1934 prohibits fraudulent or misleading statements by publicly traded corporations. These include statements found in annual reports, proxy statements, required disclosures, press releases, speeches by management, among other communications. Corporate executives as well as hired public relations firms may be held accountable. Together Sec. 10 (b) and Rule 10b-5 of the Securities Exchange Act prohibit fraudulent statements that are deliberate and misleading. A fraudulent statement is an untrue statement of material fact or a material fact by omission made in connection with the purchase or sale of securities. Other parts of the Act regulate **insider trading**, the trading of a company's stocks or other securities by those with access to non-public information about the company.

In 2021, Frances Haugen made headlines when, as a former Facebook employee, she disclosed tens of thousands of pages to Congress and the SEC about harms to users on Facebook, including harms to the mental health of teens and what Facebook understood about the spread of mis- and disinformation on its service. Haugen and her lawyers filed at least eight complaints with the SEC, alleging that the platform lied to investors by "making material misrepresentations and omissions in statements to investors and prospective investors through filings with the SEC, testimony to Congress, online statements and media stories."[310] As of 2022, the complaints were pending.

CORPORATE POLITICAL SPEECH

The U.S. Supreme Court has distinguished the First Amendment right of a business to communicate political messages from its commercial speech. In 1977, when the First National Bank of Boston wanted to spend money to oppose a ballot initiative that would allow Massachusetts to institute a graduated income tax, the Supreme Court affirmed the bank's constitutional right to speak out.[311] The bank challenged state restrictions on political contributions by corporations to influence the outcome of the vote. Relying on the public's right to free-flowing information and the nearly impossible differentiation of media companies from others, the Court provided businesses' noncommercial speech with greater protection than afforded under the commercial speech doctrine.[312] The Court concluded that the bank's speech was "at the heart of the First Amendment's protection."[313]

The Supreme Court's 2010 decision in *Citizens United v. Federal Election Commission* (see Chapter 2) also increased First Amendment protection for corporate and nonprofit funding of political speech.[314] That landmark case involved "Hillary: The Movie," a film produced by

Frances Haugen and her lawyers filed at least eight complaints with the SEC, alleging Facebook lied to investors about what it understood about disinformation on the site and harms to teen mental health.

AP

Citizens United, a conservative nonprofit group, that was highly critical of Democratic presidential candidate Hillary Clinton's experience and ability to hold the office. A federal law called the Bipartisan Campaign Reform Act of 2001, an attempt to regulate "big money" campaign contributions, placed restrictions on corporations and labor unions from funding such communication—what is often referred to as "independent expenditures." Citizens United challenged provisions in that law on First Amendment grounds. Overturning more than 100 years of precedent, the U.S. Supreme Court held that such independent political spending did not present a threat of corruption, as long as it was not coordinated with a candidate's campaign. As a result, corporations can now spend unlimited funds on campaign advertising as long as they are independent and not formally associated with a candidate for office or a political party. The Court held that political speech does not lose First Amendment protection "simply because its source is a corporation."[315]

The 5–4 decision in *Citizens United* remains highly controversial. Free speech advocates heralded the opinion as a win for corporations and an open, unfettered marketplace of ideas. Critics have lamented that the opinion has hurt the country, ushering in "massive increases in political spending from outside groups" and "dramatically expanding the already outsized political influence of wealthy donors, corporation and special interest groups."[316] The case has fueled the growth of so-called Super PACs—outside groups, separate from official political campaigns where there are more regulations on contributions. Super PACs are not constrained by what they can spend on candidates. Since 2010, they have spent almost $3 billion on federal elections.[317]

Consumer Activism and Corporate Speech

In recent decades, corporate and professional self-promotion and branding have grown in economic and social importance, and businesses have stepped increasingly into public debates on social issues like climate change, teen suicide and gun safety.[318] If such advertising goes awry, it may or may not land companies in court, but some publicists argue that the public attention and even legal controversy effectively increase both the viewing and the impact of their commercial messages.[319] Consumer activists argue that some corporate messaging goes too far and should be more regularly challenged.

Marc Kasky is a longtime consumer activist and lawyer who has advocated for increased corporate accountability and responsibility. In the early 2000s, he and others argued that Nike made multiple misrepresentations regarding its overseas labor practices. In the midst of the large public controversy about Nike's offshore factories, Nike issued press releases and letters to newspapers and university athletic directors in an attempt to place itself in a positive light. In *Nike, Inc. v. Kasky*, the U.S. Supreme Court was asked to determine whether Nike's published communications responding to accusations of illegal, unsafe and abusive conditions in its overseas plants could be punished as false advertising.[320]

The trial court dismissed the case, but the California Supreme Court ruled that the speech contained statements of fact that might be punishable under the state's false advertising and unfair competition laws. The court said Nike's published statements to potential customers were commercial speech intended to maintain or increase sales.[321] Nike appealed to the U.S. Supreme Court and argued that, even if false, its speech was political and protected by the First Amendment. The Supreme Court dismissed the case without addressing the core question. Nike reportedly settled and paid $1.5 million to the Fair Labor Association.

More recently, environmental activists have both pressured and faced pressure from the fossil fuel industry. In 2015, an environmental journalism organization called Inside Climate News published a report titled "Exxon: The Road Not Taken," an award-winning series and a finalist for the Pulitzer Prize. The report revealed that ExxonMobil's own scientists had known about the existence of climate change caused by fossil fuel, and its effects on the planet. The report also revealed that ExxonMobil had spent millions of dollars over the past 35 years funding climate denial organizations and politicians who produced misleading advertisements designed to promote uncertainty and skepticism about climate change. In *People of New York v. Exxon Mobil Corp.*, however, the Supreme Court of New York ruled that Exxon had not violated securities law by misleading investors regarding what the company understood about climate change.[322] The court said the state had failed to prove by a preponderance of evidence that Exxon Mobil made any misrepresentations that would significantly alter the investment choices of ordinary investors.

Professional Speech

Corporate, business and professional ads designed to enhance sales and revenue generally are commercial speech. When state bar associations of lawyers and judges prohibited advertising by lawyers, the U.S. Supreme Court struck down the ban.[323] The Court said the absolute prohibition on truthful advertising was unconstitutional, although "[r]easonable restrictions—such as those pertaining to false advertising—might survive First Amendment scrutiny."[324] The Court did not indicate how it would review professional association limits on advertising by professionals in other fields, such as public relations or marketing.

When a dentist with a specialty in endodontics was denied permission to list both "dentist" and "endodontist" on his signs, he raised a First Amendment challenge to the Ohio law that prohibited dentists from advertising both general and specialized practices. The trial court dismissed the claim, but the Sixth Circuit Court of Appeals reversed. It instructed the trial court to apply the *Central Hudson* test, which it said must place the burden on the government to justify the law's restraint of speech.[325]

The professional speech of doctors has been the special focus of several cases in the last two decades. In 2002, patients and physicians brought a class action lawsuit to stop enforcement of a government policy that threatened to punish physicians for communicating with their patients about the medical use of marijuana. The U.S. Court of Appeals for the Ninth Circuit held that a doctor's recommendation of medical use of marijuana was protected by the First Amendment. The court wrote:

> Being a member of a regulated profession does not, as the government suggests, result in a surrender of First Amendment rights. . . . To the contrary, professional speech may be entitled to "the strongest protection our Constitution has to offer." . . . Even commercial speech by professionals is entitled to First Amendment protection.[326]

In 2011, Florida legislators passed the Firearm Owner's Privacy Act, which prevented doctors from asking about patients' or family members' ownership of firearms. Doctors who violated the law faced fines and revocation of their medical license. The law contained specific provisions against "anti-harassment, inquiry, record keeping and anti-discrimination" by doctors who questioned their patients about gun ownership.[327] Physicians challenged the law. Employing strict scrutiny, the U.S. Court of Appeals for the Eleventh Circuit ruled that the record-keeping, inquiry and anti-harassment provisions constituted unconstitutional speaker-focused and content-based restrictions on speech. The Court said that the state had not demonstrated an actual problem with physicians taking firearms away from families nor evidence of patient concern about the questions. The Court wrote that the state might believe that doctors "should not ask about nor express views hostile to firearm ownership, but it may not burden the speech of others in order to tilt public debate in a preferred direction."[328]

In *NIFLA v Becerra*, a 2017 U.S. Supreme Court case discussed earlier in the chapter, the Court said it has never recognized "professional speech" as a separate category despite its use by lower courts; it did not find a reason to extend such a category to health officials in *NIFLA*. The Court wrote that "speech is not unprotected merely because it is uttered by 'professionals.'"[329] The Court's ruling puts the future of speech protections for professionals in doubt.

EMERGING LAW

Some scholars suggest that changes in the U.S. Supreme Court's rulings, including in *Sorrell* and *NIFLA*, undermine the constitutional protection of advertising regulation.[330] They see a Court shift away from relaxed, deferential review of commercial speech regulations[331] toward the application of a strict content-neutrality rule to the commercial and compelled speech categories, which, "almost by definition, [are] content- and speaker-focused."[332] Simply put, they see a Court giving greater protections to commercial speakers and striking down state and federal regulation.

Many scholars believe the Supreme Court has moved toward much more rigorous oversight of the restrictions on commercial speech that long have been viewed as "reasonable social and economic regulations."[333] Stricter review of commercial speech regulations would require stronger government justification to support regulation and likely mean that fewer government regulations would survive court First Amendment scrutiny. One scholar concluded that "some aspects of the compelled speech doctrine . . . seem hard to wrestle into a fully coherent pattern."[334]

At the same time that courts are relaxing scrutiny of commercial speech regulation, regulators themselves have been pressured to adopt more rules to avoid deception in the sale of new products. In 2021, The New York Times reported a "mounting wave of legal activism" to "convince federal regulators to increase their oversight over the nation's food supply—or even to provide definitions for words like 'healthy' or 'all natural.'"[335] The Times wrote that the new fight over food labeling represents efforts by environmental and animal welfare groups to increase transparency, force humane animal practices, and attack "greenwashing."[336] **Greenwashing** refers to efforts to deceptively capture consumer interest in sustainability.

In 2021, the FDA announced it will soon issue guidance on the labeling of plant-based milk alternatives, including soy milk, almond milk, oat milk, and other beverages based on legumes, nuts, grains, and other plants.[337] The agency is developing new rules to prevent consumer deception when plant-based products use "milk" or "cheese" in their labeling. One FDA commissioner joked that almond milk should not be called milk because "an almond doesn't lactate."[338] Between 2012 and 2017, sales of nondairy milks—like almond, coconut and soy—grew more than 60 percent while dairy milk sales fell.[339] Dairy farmers led the movement to call such products nut juice.[340]

Similar concerns have arisen in the meat industry. Arguing that labeling alternately sourced protein products "meat" was misleading, the U.S. Cattlemen's Association asked the U.S. Department of Agriculture to prohibit the "meat" label on "plant-based" substitutes.[341]

In 2021, the USDA began to solicit comments in advance of proposed rulemaking regarding the issue. At least 10 states have passed laws prohibiting the use of meat terminology for products not derived from harvested livestock.[342] The U.S. Court of Appeals for the Eighth Circuit affirmed a district court decision that denied an injunction in a case challenging a Missouri law which criminalized "mispresenting a product as meat that is not derived from harvested production livestock or poultry."[343] The challengers in the case were producers of Tofurky, a vegan food brand, and they raised a First Amendment claim, arguing that they must be able to compare their products to conventional meat products in their labeling. While the Court supported Tofurky's challenge on the basis of the First Amendment, they agreed with the lower court that at this early stage in the case, the vegan producers failed to show irreparable harm.

The labeling of genetically engineered food or seed has also raised concerns. In 2016, the USDA's National Bioengineered Food Disclosure Standard preempted state authority for such labeling.[344] The law was a compromise between those who wanted explicit labels on all products containing genetically modified organisms and those who argued that such labels increased consumers' misperceptions of GMOs. The new standards, which were introduced in 2022, allow for four types of bioengineered food disclosures: labeling text, a symbol, an electronic/digital link (QR code), or a text-messaging phone number, each with its own specific requirements. The disclosure must be of "sufficient size and clarity to appear prominently and conspicuously on the label, making it likely to be read and understood by the consumer under ordinary shopping conditions."[345]

In 2020, the Alcohol and Tobacco Tax and Trade Bureau modernized labeling and advertising regulations for wine, distilled spirits and malt beverages. The new rules give companies more flexibility on the placement of brand name, class and type of spirit, alcohol content and net contents to appear anywhere on the label as long as all of it can be viewed at the same time, without having to turn the container.[346] The new rules also will allow strength claims on beer labels and in beer ads, with words like "strong," "full strength," and "extra strength," now allowed.[347] The new rules treat all alcoholic beverages similarly and modify existing limits on strength claims on beer that were struck down by the U.S. Supreme Court more than 20 years ago in *Rubin v. Coors Brewing Co.*[348]

KEY TERMS

celebrity marketing	Federal Trade Commission
content marketing	greenwashing
clear and conspicuous	implied claims
corrective advertising	influencer marketing
dark patterns or "negative options"	insider trading
practices	Lanham Act
deceptive advertising	material
disclosure	native advertising
efficacy claim	reasonable basis
endorsement	right to receive information
establishment claim	substantiation
expert	vice products
express claims	

CASES FOR STUDY

THINKING ABOUT THEM

The two case excerpts that follow address the regulation of commercial speech and whether specific regulations are consistent with the First Amendment. The first is the U.S. Supreme Court case that established the test for answering that question. In the second case, the U.S. Supreme Court declines to apply that test and shifts toward the scrutiny it employs in "pure" speech cases. As you read these case excerpts, keep the following questions in mind:

- What are the circumstances surrounding each case?
- Specifically, what type of speech is involved, and in what ways is it intermingled with commerce?
- What is the nature of the regulations being challenged?
- What is the state interest in each case? Are those interests legitimate?
- How does the Court's review in Sorrell differ from the test established by Central Hudson? What implications does this difference have for First Amendment protection of commercial speech?

CENTRAL HUDSON GAS & ELECTRIC CORP. V. PUBLIC SERVICE COMMISSION OF NEW YORK

SUPREME COURT OF THE UNITED STATES 447 U.S. 557 (1980)

JUSTICE LEWIS POWELL delivered the Court's opinion:

This case presents the question whether a regulation of the Public Service Commission of the State of New York violates the First and Fourteenth Amendments because it completely bans promotional advertising by an electrical utility.

In December, 1973, the Commission, appellee here, ordered electric utilities in New York State to cease all advertising that "promot[es] the use of electricity." The order was based on the Commission's finding that "the interconnected utility system in New York State does not have sufficient fuel stocks or sources of supply to continue furnishing all customer demands for the 1973–1974 winter."

Three years later, when the fuel shortage had eased, the Commission requested comments from the public on its proposal to continue the ban on promotional advertising. Central Hudson Gas & Electric Corp., the appellant in this case, opposed the ban on First Amendment grounds. After reviewing the public comments, the Commission extended the prohibition in a Policy Statement issued on February 25, 1977.

The Policy Statement divided advertising expenses "into two broad categories: promotional—advertising intended to stimulate the purchase of utility services . . . and institutional and informational, a broad category inclusive of all advertising not clearly intended to promote sales." The Commission declared all promotional advertising contrary to the national policy of conserving energy. It acknowledged that the ban is not a perfect vehicle for conserving energy. For example, the Commission's order prohibits promotional advertising to develop consumption during periods when demand for electricity is low. By limiting growth in "off-peak" consumption, the ban limits the "beneficial side effects" of such growth in terms of more efficient use of existing powerplants. And since oil dealers are not under the Commission's jurisdiction and thus remain free to advertise, it was recognized that the ban can achieve only "piecemeal conservationism." Still, the Commission adopted the restriction because it was deemed likely to "result in some dampening of unnecessary growth" in energy consumption.

The Commission's order explicitly permitted "informational" advertising designed to encourage "shifts of consumption" from peak demand times to periods of low electricity demand. Informational advertising would not seek to increase aggregate consumption, but would invite a leveling of demand throughout any given 24-hour period. The agency offered to review "specific proposals by the companies for specifically described [advertising] programs that meet these criteria."

When it rejected requests for rehearing on the Policy Statement, the Commission supplemented its rationale for the advertising ban. The agency observed that additional electricity probably would be more expensive to produce than existing output. Because electricity rates in New York were not then based on marginal cost, the Commission feared that additional power would be priced below the actual cost of generation. The additional electricity would be subsidized by all consumers through generally higher rates. The state agency also thought that promotional advertising would give "misleading signals" to the public by appearing to encourage energy consumption at a time when conservation is needed. . . .

The Commission's order restricts only commercial speech, that is, expression related solely to the economic interests of the speaker and its audience. The First Amendment, as applied to the States through the Fourteenth Amendment, protects commercial speech from unwarranted governmental regulation. Commercial expression not only serves the economic interest of the speaker, but also assists consumers and furthers the societal interest in the fullest possible dissemination of information. In applying the First Amendment to this area, we have rejected the "highly paternalistic" view that government has complete power to suppress or regulate commercial speech. . . .

Nevertheless, our decisions have recognized "the 'commonsense' distinction between speech proposing a commercial transaction, which occurs in an area traditionally subject to government regulation, and other varieties of speech." . . . The Constitution therefore accords a lesser protection to commercial speech than to other constitutionally guaranteed expression. The protection available for particular commercial expression turns on the nature both of the expression and of the governmental interests served by its regulation.

The First Amendment's concern for commercial speech is based on the informational function of advertising. Consequently, there can be no constitutional objection to the suppression of commercial messages that do not accurately inform the public about lawful activity. The government may ban forms of communication more likely to deceive the public than to inform it, or commercial speech related to illegal activity.

If the communication is neither misleading nor related to unlawful activity, the government's power is more circumscribed. The State must assert a substantial interest to be achieved by restrictions on commercial speech. Moreover, the regulatory technique must be in proportion to that interest. The limitation on expression must be designed carefully to achieve the State's goal. Compliance with this requirement may be measured by two criteria. First, the restriction must directly advance the state interest involved; the regulation may not be sustained if it provides only ineffective or remote support for the government's purpose. Second, if the governmental interest could be served as well by a more limited restriction on commercial speech, the excessive restrictions cannot survive. . . .

The second criterion recognizes that the First Amendment mandates that speech restrictions be "narrowly drawn." The regulatory technique may extend only as far as the interest it serves. The State cannot regulate speech that poses no danger to the asserted state interest, nor can it completely suppress information when narrower restrictions on expression would serve its interest as well. . . .

In this case, the Commission's prohibition acts directly against the promotional activities of Central Hudson, and, to the extent the limitations are unnecessary to serve the State's interest, they are invalid. . . .

In commercial speech cases, then, a four-part analysis has developed. At the outset, we must determine whether the expression is protected by the First Amendment. For commercial speech to come within that provision, it at least must concern lawful activity and not be misleading. Next, we ask whether the asserted governmental interest is substantial. If both inquiries yield positive answers, we must determine whether the regulation directly advances the governmental interest asserted, and whether it is not more extensive than is necessary to serve that interest.

We now apply this four-step analysis for commercial speech to the Commission's arguments in support of its ban on promotional advertising.

The Commission does not claim that the expression at issue either is inaccurate or relates to unlawful activity. Yet the New York Court of Appeals questioned whether Central Hudson's advertising is protected commercial speech. Because appellant holds a monopoly over the sale of electricity in its service area, the state court suggested that the Commission's order restricts no commercial speech of any worth. The court stated that advertising in a "noncompetitive market" could not improve the decision making of consumers. The court saw no constitutional problem with barring commercial speech that it viewed as conveying little useful information.

This reasoning falls short of establishing that appellant's advertising is not commercial speech protected by the First Amendment. Monopoly over the supply of a product provides no protection from competition with substitutes for that product. . . .

Even in monopoly markets, the suppression of advertising reduces the information available for consumer decisions and thereby defeats the purpose of the First Amendment. The New York court's argument appears to assume that the providers of a monopoly service or product are willing to pay for wholly ineffective advertising. Most businesses—even regulated monopolies—are unlikely to underwrite promotional advertising that is of no interest or use to consumers. Indeed, a monopoly enterprise legitimately may wish to inform the public that it has developed new services or terms of doing business. A consumer may need information to aid his decision whether or not to use the monopoly service at all, or how much of the service he should purchase. In the absence of factors that would distort the decision to advertise, we may assume that the willingness of a business to promote its products reflects a belief that consumers are interested in the advertising. Since no such extraordinary conditions have been identified in this case, appellant's monopoly position does not alter the First Amendment's protection for its commercial speech.

The Commission offers two state interests as justifications for the ban on promotional advertising. The first concerns energy conservation. Any increase in demand for electricity—during peak or off-peak periods—means greater consumption of energy. The Commission argues, and the New York court agreed, that the State's interest in conserving energy is sufficient to support suppression of advertising designed to increase consumption of electricity. In view of our country's dependence on energy resources beyond our control, no one can doubt the importance of energy conservation. Plainly, therefore, the state interest asserted is substantial.

The Commission also argues that promotional advertising will aggravate inequities caused by the failure to base the utilities' rates on marginal cost. The utilities argued to the Commission that if they could promote the use of electricity in periods of low demand, they would improve their utilization of generating capacity. The Commission responded that promotion of off-peak consumption also would increase consumption during peak periods. If peak demand were to rise, the absence of marginal cost rates would mean that the rates charged for the additional power would not reflect the true costs of expanding production.

Instead, the extra costs would be borne by all consumers through higher overall rates. Without promotional advertising, the Commission stated, this inequitable turn of events would be less likely to occur. The choice among rate structures involves difficult and important questions of economic supply and distributional fairness. The State's concern that rates be fair and efficient represents a clear and substantial governmental interest.

Next, we focus on the relationship between the State's interests and the advertising ban. Under this criterion, the Commission's laudable concern over the equity and efficiency of appellant's rates does not provide a constitutionally adequate reason for restricting protected speech. The link between the advertising prohibition and appellant's rate structure is, at most, tenuous. The impact of promotional advertising on the equity of appellant's rates is highly speculative. Advertising to increase off-peak usage would have to increase peak usage, while other factors that directly affect the fairness and efficiency of appellant's rates remained constant. Such conditional and remote eventualities simply cannot justify silencing appellant's promotional advertising.

In contrast, the State's interest in energy conservation is directly advanced by the Commission order at issue here. There is an immediate connection between advertising and demand for electricity. Central Hudson would not contest the advertising ban unless it believed that promotion would increase its sales. Thus, we find a direct link between the state interest in conservation and the Commission's order.

We come finally to the critical inquiry in this case: whether the Commission's complete suppression of speech ordinarily protected by the First Amendment is no more extensive than necessary to further the State's interest in energy conservation. The Commission's order reaches all promotional advertising, regardless of the impact of the touted service on overall energy use. But the energy conservation rationale, as important as it is, cannot justify suppressing information about electric devices or services that would cause no net increase in total energy use. In addition, no showing has been made that a more limited restriction on the content of promotional advertising would not serve adequately the State's interests.

Appellant insists that, but for the ban, it would advertise products and services that use energy efficiently. These include the "heat pump," which both parties acknowledge to be a major improvement in electric heating, and the use of electric heat as a "backup" to solar and other heat sources. Although the Commission has questioned the efficiency of electric heating before this Court, neither the Commission's Policy Statement nor its order denying rehearing made findings on this issue. In the absence of authoritative findings to the contrary, we must credit as within the realm of possibility the claim that electric heat can be an efficient alternative in some circumstances.

The Commission's order prevents appellant from promoting electric services that would reduce energy use by diverting demand from less efficient sources, or that would consume roughly the same amount of energy as do alternative sources. In neither situation would the utility's advertising endanger conservation or mislead the public. To the extent that the Commission's order suppresses speech that in no way impairs the State's interest in energy conservation, the Commission's order violates the First and Fourteenth Amendments, and must be invalidated.

The Commission also has not demonstrated that its interest in conservation cannot be protected adequately by more limited regulation of appellant's commercial expression. To further its policy of conservation, the Commission could attempt to restrict the format and content of Central Hudson's advertising. It might, for example, require that the advertisements include information about the relative efficiency and expense of the offered service, both under current conditions and for the foreseeable future. In the absence of a showing that more limited speech regulation would be ineffective, we cannot approve the complete suppression of Central Hudson's advertising.

Our decision today in no way disparages the national interest in energy conservation. We accept without reservation the argument that conservation, as well as the development of alternative energy sources, is an imperative national goal. Administrative bodies empowered to regulate electric utilities have the authority—and indeed the duty—to take appropriate action to further this goal. When, however, such action involves the suppression of speech, the First and Fourteenth Amendments require that the restriction be no more extensive than is necessary to serve the state interest. In this case, the record before us fails to show that the total ban on promotional advertising meets this requirement.

Accordingly, the judgment of the New York Court of Appeals is
Reversed. . . .

JUSTICE WILLIAM REHNQUIST, dissenting:

The Court today invalidates an order issued by the New York Public Service Commission designed to promote a policy that has been declared to be of critical national concern. The order was issued by the Commission in 1973 in response to the Mideastern oil embargo crisis. It prohibits electric corporations "from promoting the use of electricity through the use of advertising, subsidy payments . . . or employee incentives." Although the immediate crisis created by the oil embargo has subsided, the ban on promotional advertising remains in effect. The regulation was re-examined by the New York Public Service Commission in 1977. Its constitutionality was subsequently upheld by the New York Court of Appeals, which concluded that the paramount national interest in energy conservation justified its retention.

The Court's asserted justification for invalidating the New York law is the public interest discerned by the Court to underlie the First Amendment in the free flow of commercial information. Prior to this Court's recent decision in *Virginia Pharmacy Board v. Virginia Citizens Consumer Council,* however, commercial speech was afforded no protection under the First Amendment whatsoever. Given what seems to me full recognition of the holding of *Virginia Pharmacy Board* that commercial speech is entitled to some degree of First Amendment protection, I think the Court is nonetheless incorrect in invalidating the carefully considered state ban on promotional advertising in light of pressing national and state energy needs. . . .

This Court has previously recognized that, although commercial speech may be entitled to First Amendment protection, that protection is not as extensive as that accorded to the advocacy of ideas. . . . "We have not discarded the 'common-sense' distinction between speech proposing a commercial transaction, which occurs in an area traditionally subject to government regulation, and other varieties of speech. To require a parity of constitutional protection for commercial and noncommercial speech alike could invite dilution, simply by a leveling process, of the force of the Amendment's guarantee with respect to the latter kind of speech. Rather than subject the First Amendment to such a devitalization, we instead have afforded commercial speech a limited measure of protection, commensurate with its subordinate position in the scale of First Amendment values, while allowing modes of regulation that might be impermissible in the realm of noncommercial expression."

The Court's decision today fails to give due deference to this subordinate position of commercial speech. The Court in so doing returns to the bygone era . . . in which it was common practice for this Court to strike down economic regulations adopted by a State based on the Court's own notions of the most appropriate means for the State to implement its considered policies.

I had thought by now it had become well established that a State has broad discretion in imposing economic regulations. . . . The State of New York has determined here that economic realities require the grant of monopoly status to public utilities in order to distribute efficiently the services they provide, and in granting utilities such status it has made them subject to an extensive regulatory scheme. When the State adopted this scheme and when its Public Service Commission issued its initial ban on promotional advertising in 1973, commercial speech had not been held to fall within the scope of the First Amendment at all. . . .

The Court today holds not only that commercial speech is entitled to First Amendment protection, but also that when it is protected a State may not regulate it unless its reason for doing so amounts to a "substantial" governmental interest, its regulation "directly advances" that interest, and its manner of regulation is "not more extensive than necessary" to serve the interest. The test adopted by the Court thus elevates the protection accorded commercial speech that falls within the scope of the First Amendment to a level that is virtually indistinguishable from that of noncommercial speech. . . .

An ostensible justification for striking down New York's ban on promotional advertising is that this Court has previously "rejected the 'highly paternalistic' view that government has complete power to suppress or regulate commercial speech. '[P]eople will perceive their own best interests if only they are well enough informed and . . . the best means to that end is to open the channels of communication, rather than to close them. . . .'" Whatever the merits of this view, I think the Court has carried its logic too far here. . . .

While it is true that an important objective of the First Amendment is to foster the free flow of information, identification of speech that falls within its protection is not aided by the metaphorical reference to a "marketplace of ideas." There is no reason for believing that the marketplace of ideas is free from market imperfections any more than there is to believe that the invisible hand will always lead to optimum economic decisions in the commercial market. . . . Indeed, many types of speech have been held to fall outside the scope of the First Amendment, thereby subject to governmental regulation, despite this Court's references to a marketplace of ideas. . . .

I remain of the view that the Court unlocked a Pandora's Box when it "elevated" commercial speech to the level of traditional political speech by according it First Amendment protection in *Virginia Pharmacy Board v. Virginia Citizens Consumer Council*. The line between "commercial speech," and the kind of speech that those who drafted the First Amendment had in mind, may not be a technically or intellectually easy one to draw, but it surely produced far fewer problems than has the development of judicial doctrine in this area since *Virginia Pharmacy Board*. . . .

The notion that more speech is the remedy to expose falsehood and fallacies is wholly out of place in the commercial bazaar, where if applied logically the remedy of one who was defrauded would be merely a statement, available upon request, reciting the Latin maxim "*caveat emptor*." But since "fraudulent speech" in this area is to be remediable under *Virginia Pharmacy Board*, the remedy of one defrauded is a lawsuit or an agency proceeding based on common-law notions of fraud that are separated by a world of difference from the realm of politics and government. What time, legal decisions, and common sense have so widely severed, I declined to join in *Virginia Pharmacy Board*, and regret now to see the Court reaping the seeds that it there sowed. For in a democracy, the economic is subordinate to the political, a lesson that our ancestors learned long ago, and that our descendants will undoubtedly have to relearn many years hence.

The Court concedes that the state interest in energy conservation is plainly substantial, as is the State's concern that its rates be fair and efficient. It also concedes that there is a direct link between the Commission's ban on promotional advertising and the State's interest in conservation. The Court nonetheless strikes down the ban on promotional advertising because the Commission has failed to demonstrate, under the final part of the Court's four-part test, that its regulation is no more extensive than necessary to serve the State's interest. In reaching this conclusion, the Court conjures up potential advertisements that a utility might make that conceivably would result in net energy savings. The Court does not indicate that the New York Public Service Commission has in fact construed its ban on "promotional" advertising to preclude the dissemination of information that clearly would result in a net energy savings, nor does it even suggest that the Commission has been confronted with and rejected such an advertising proposal. The final part of the Court's test thus leaves room for so many hypothetical "better" ways that any ingenious lawyer will surely seize on one of them to secure the invalidation of what the state agency actually did. . . .

Ordinarily it is the role of the State Public Service Commission to make factual determinations concerning whether a device or service will result in a net energy savings and, if so, whether and to what extent state law permits dissemination of information about the device or service. Otherwise, as here, this Court will have no factual basis for its assertions. And the State will never have an opportunity to consider the issue and thus to construe its law in a manner consistent with the Federal Constitution. . . .

It is, in my view, inappropriate for the Court to invalidate the State's ban on commercial advertising here, based on its speculation that in some cases the advertising may result in a net savings in electrical energy use, and in the cases in which it is clear a net energy savings would result from utility advertising, the Public Service Commission would apply its ban so as to proscribe such advertising. Even assuming that the Court's speculation is correct, I do not think it follows that facial invalidation of the ban is the appropriate course. . . .

For the foregoing reasons, I would affirm the judgment of the New York Court of Appeals.

SORRELL V. IMS HEALTH, INC.

SUPREME COURT OF THE UNITED STATES 131 S. CT. 2653 (2011)

JUSTICE ANTHONY KENNEDY delivered the Court's opinion:

. . . Pharmaceutical manufacturers promote their drugs to doctors through a process called "detailing." This often involves a scheduled visit to a doctor's office to persuade the doctor to prescribe a particular pharmaceutical. Detailers bring drug samples as well as medical studies that explain the "details" and potential advantages of various prescription drugs. Interested physicians listen, ask questions, and receive follow-up data. Salespersons can be more effective when they know the background and purchasing preferences of their clientele, and pharmaceutical salespersons are no exception. Knowledge of a physician's prescription practices—called "prescriber-identifying information"—enables a detailer better to ascertain which doctors are likely to be interested in a particular drug and how best to present a particular sales message. Detailing is an expensive undertaking, so pharmaceutical companies most often use it to promote high-profit brand-name drugs protected by patent. Once a brand-name drug's patent expires, less expensive bioequivalent generic alternatives are manufactured and sold.

Pharmacies, as a matter of business routine and federal law, receive prescriber-identifying information when processing prescriptions. Many pharmacies sell this information to "data miners," firms that analyze prescriber-identifying information and produce reports on prescriber behavior. Data miners lease these reports to pharmaceutical manufacturers subject to nondisclosure agreements. Detailers, who represent the manufacturers, then use the reports to refine their marketing tactics and increase sales.

In 2007, Vermont enacted the Prescription Confidentiality Law. The measure is also referred to as Act 80. It has several components. The central provision of the present case is § 4631(d).

> A health insurer, a self-insured employer, an electronic transmission intermediary, a pharmacy, or other similar entity shall not sell, license, or exchange for value regulated records containing prescriber-identifiable information, nor permit the use of regulated records containing prescriber-identifiable information for marketing or promoting a prescription drug, unless the prescriber consents. . . . Pharmaceutical manufacturers and pharmaceutical marketers shall not use prescriber-identifiable information for marketing or promoting a prescription drug unless the prescriber consents. . . .

The quoted provision has three component parts. The provision begins by prohibiting pharmacies, health insurers, and similar entities from selling prescriber-identifying information, absent the prescriber's consent. The parties here dispute whether this clause applies to all sales or only to sales for marketing. The provision then goes on to prohibit pharmacies, health insurers, and similar entities from allowing prescriber-identifying information to be used for marketing, unless the prescriber consents. This prohibition in effect bars pharmacies from disclosing the information for marketing purposes. Finally, the provision's second sentence bars pharmaceutical manufacturers and pharmaceutical marketers from using prescriber-identifying information for marketing, again absent the prescriber's consent. The Vermont attorney general may pursue civil remedies against violators.

Separate statutory provisions elaborate the scope of the prohibitions. . . . "Marketing" is defined to include "advertising, promotion, or any activity" that is "used to influence sales or the market share of a prescription drug." § 4631(d) further provides that Vermont's Department of Health must allow "a prescriber to give consent for his or her identifying information to be used for the purposes" identified. . . . Finally, the Act's prohibitions on sale, disclosure, and use are subject to a list of exceptions. For example, prescriber-identifying information may be disseminated or used for "health care research"; to enforce "compliance" with health insurance formularies, or preferred drug lists; for "care management educational communications provided to" patients on such matters as "treatment options"; for law enforcement operations; and for purposes "otherwise provided by law."

Act 80 also authorized funds for an "evidence-based prescription drug education program" designed to provide doctors and others with "information and education on the therapeutic and cost-effective utilization of prescription drugs." An express aim of the program is to advise prescribers "about commonly used brand-name drugs for which the patent has expired" or will soon expire. Similar efforts to promote the use of generic pharmaceuticals are sometimes referred to as "counter-detailing." The counter-detailer's recommended substitute may be an older, less expensive drug and not a bioequivalent of the brand-name drug the physician might otherwise prescribe. Like the pharmaceutical manufacturers whose efforts they hope to resist, counter-detailers in some states use prescriber-identifying information to increase their effectiveness. States themselves may supply the prescriber-identifying information used in these programs. . . .

Act 80 was accompanied by legislative findings. Vermont found, for example, that the "goals of marketing programs are often in conflict with the goals of the state" and that the "marketplace for ideas on medicine safety and effectiveness is frequently one-sided in that brand-name companies invest in expensive pharmaceutical marketing campaigns to doctors." Detailing, in the legislature's view, caused doctors to make decisions based on "incomplete and biased information." Because they "are unable to take the time to research the quickly changing pharmaceutical market," Vermont doctors "rely on information provided by pharmaceutical representatives." The legislature further found that detailing increases the cost of health care and health insurance; encourages hasty and excessive reliance on brand-name drugs, before the profession has observed their effectiveness as compared with older and less expensive generic alternatives; and fosters disruptive and repeated marketing visits tantamount to harassment. . . . Use of prescriber-identifying data also helps detailers shape their messages by "tailoring" their "presentations to individual prescriber styles, preferences, and attitudes."

The present case involves two consolidated suits. One was brought by three Vermont data miners, the other by an association of pharmaceutical manufacturers that produce brand-name drugs.... Contending that § 4631(d) violates their First Amendment rights as incorporated by the Fourteenth Amendment, the respondents sought declaratory and injunctive relief. . . .

After a bench trial, the United States District Court for the District of Vermont denied relief. The District Court found that "[p]harmaceutical manufacturers are essentially the only paying customers of the data vendor industry" and that, because detailing unpatented generic drugs is not "cost-effective," pharmaceutical sales representatives "detail only branded drugs." . . . The United States Court of Appeals for the Second Circuit reversed and remanded. It held that § 4631(d) violates the First Amendment by burdening the speech of pharmaceutical marketers and data miners without an adequate justification. . . . The decision of the Second Circuit is in conflict with decisions of the United States Court of Appeals for the First Circuit concerning similar legislation enacted by Maine and New Hampshire. Recognizing a division of authority regarding the constitutionality of state statutes, this Court granted certiorari.

The beginning point is the text of § 4631(d). In the proceedings below, Vermont stated that the first sentence . . . prohibits pharmacies and other regulated entities from selling or disseminating prescriber-identifying information for marketing. The information, in other words, could be sold or given away for purposes other than marketing. . . . At oral argument in this Court, however, the state for the first time advanced an alternative reading . . . namely, that pharmacies, health insurers, and similar entities may not sell prescriber-identifying information for any purpose, subject to the statutory exceptions set out [in the law]. It might be argued that the state's newfound interpretation comes too late in the day. . . . For the state to change its position is particularly troubling in a First Amendment case, where plaintiffs have a special interest in obtaining a prompt adjudication of their rights, despite potential ambiguities of state law.

In any event, § 4631(d) cannot be sustained even under the interpretation the state now adopts. As a consequence this Court can assume that the opening clause . . . prohibits pharmacies, health insurers, and similar entities from selling prescriber-identifying information, subject to the statutory exceptions set out ...Under that reading, pharmacies may sell the information to private or academic researchers, but not, for example, to pharmaceutical marketers. There is no dispute as to the remainder of § 4631. It prohibits pharmacies, health insurers, and similar entities from disclosing or otherwise allowing prescriber-identifying information to be used for marketing. And it bars pharmaceutical manufacturers and detailers from using the information for marketing. The questions now are whether § 4631(d) must be tested by heightened judicial scrutiny and, if so, whether the state can justify the law.

On its face, Vermont's law enacts content- and speaker-based restrictions on the sale, disclosure, and use of prescriber-identifying information. The provision first forbids sale subject to exceptions based in large part on the content of a purchaser's speech. For example, those who wish to engage in certain "educational communications" may purchase the information. The measure then bars any disclosure when recipient speakers will use the information for marketing. Finally, the provision's second sentence prohibits pharmaceutical manufacturers from using the information for marketing. The statute thus disfavors marketing, that is, speech with a particular content. More than that, the statute disfavors specific speakers, namely pharmaceutical manufacturers. As a result of these content- and speaker-based rules, detailers cannot obtain prescriber-identifying information, even though the information may be purchased or acquired by other speakers with diverse purposes and viewpoints. Detailers are likewise barred from using the information for marketing, even though the information may be used by a wide range of other speakers. For example, it appears that Vermont could supply academic organizations with prescriber-identifying information to use in countering the messages of brand-name pharmaceutical manufacturers and in promoting the prescription of generic drugs. But § 4631(d) leaves detailers no means of purchasing, acquiring, or using prescriber-identifying information. The law on its face burdens disfavored speech by disfavored speakers.

Any doubt that § 4631(d) imposes an aimed, content-based burden on detailers is dispelled by the record and by formal legislative findings. As the District Court noted, "[p]harmaceutical manufacturers are essentially the only paying customers of the data vendor industry"; and the almost invariable rule is that detailing by pharmaceutical manufacturers is in support of brand-name drugs. Vermont's law thus has the effect of preventing detailers—and only detailers—from communicating with physicians in an effective and informative manner. Formal legislative findings accompanying § 4631(d) confirm that the law's express purpose and practical effect are to diminish the effectiveness of marketing by manufacturers of brand-name drugs.... The legislature designed § 4631(d) to target those speakers and their messages for disfavored treatment. "In its practical operation," Vermont's law "goes even beyond mere content discrimination, to actual viewpoint discrimination." Given the legislature's expressed statement of purpose, it is apparent that § 4631(d) imposes burdens that are based on the content of speech and that are aimed at a particular viewpoint.

Act 80 is designed to impose a specific, content-based burden on protected expression. It follows that heightened judicial scrutiny is warranted. The Court has recognized that the "distinction between laws burdening and laws banning speech is but a matter of degree" and that the "Government's content-based burdens must satisfy the same rigorous scrutiny as its content-based bans."

The First Amendment requires heightened scrutiny whenever the government creates "a regulation of speech because of disagreement with the message it conveys." . . . Even if the hypothetical measure on its face appeared neutral as to content and speaker, its purpose to suppress speech and its unjustified burdens on expression would render it unconstitutional. Commercial speech is no exception. A "consumer's concern for the free flow of commercial speech often may be far keener than his concern for urgent political dialogue." That reality has great relevance in the fields of medicine and public health, where information can save lives.

The State argues that heightened judicial scrutiny is unwarranted because its law is a mere commercial regulation. It is true that restrictions on protected expression are distinct from restrictions on economic activity or, more generally, on nonexpressive conduct. It is also true that the First Amendment does not prevent restrictions directed at commerce or conduct from imposing incidental burdens on speech. . . . But § 4631(d) imposes more than an incidental burden on protected expression. Both on its face and in its practical operation, Vermont's law imposes a burden based on the content of speech and the identity of the speaker. While the burdened speech results from an economic motive, so too does a great deal of vital expression. Vermont's law does not simply have an effect on speech, but is directed at certain content and is aimed at particular speakers. . . .

Vermont further argues that § 4631(d) regulates not speech but simply access to information. Prescriber-identifying information was generated in compliance with a legal mandate, the state argues, and so could be considered a kind of governmental information. . . . An individual's right to speak is implicated when information he or she possesses is subjected to "restraints on the way in which the information might be used" or disseminated. . . . It is true that the respondents here . . . do not themselves possess information whose disclosure has been curtailed. That information, however, is in the hands of pharmacies and other private entities. There is no question that the "threat of prosecution . . . hangs over their heads." . . . [R]estrictions on the disclosure of government-held information can facilitate or burden the expression of potential recipients and so transgress the First Amendment. Vermont's law imposes a content- and speaker-based burden on respondents' own speech. That consideration . . . requires heightened judicial scrutiny.

The state also contends that heightened judicial scrutiny is unwarranted in this case because sales, transfer, and use of prescriber-identifying information are conduct, not speech. Consistent with that submission, the United States Court of Appeals for the First Circuit has characterized prescriber-identifying information as a mere "commodity" with no greater entitlement to First Amendment protection than "beef jerky." In contrast the courts below concluded that a prohibition on the sale of prescriber-identifying information is a content-based rule akin to a ban on the sale of cookbooks, laboratory results, or train schedules.

This Court has held that the creation and dissemination of information are speech within the meaning of the First Amendment. Facts, after all, are the beginning point for much of the speech that is most essential to advance human knowledge and to conduct human affairs. There is thus a strong argument that prescriber-identifying information is speech for First Amendment purposes.

The state asks for an exception to the rule that information is speech, but there is no need to consider that request in this case. The state has imposed content- and speaker-based restrictions on the availability and use of prescriber-identifying information. So long as they do not engage in marketing, many speakers can obtain and use the information. But detailers cannot. Vermont's statute could be compared with a law prohibiting trade magazines from purchasing or using ink. Like that hypothetical law, § 4631(d) imposes a speaker- and content-based burden on protected expression, and that circumstance is sufficient to justify application of heightened scrutiny. As a consequence, this case can be resolved even assuming, as the state argues, that prescriber-identifying information is a mere commodity.

In the ordinary case it is all but dispositive to conclude that a law is content-based and, in practice, viewpoint-discriminatory. The state argues that a different analysis applies here because, assuming § 4631(d) burdens speech at all, it at most burdens only commercial speech. As in previous cases, however, the outcome is the same whether a special commercial speech inquiry or a stricter form of judicial scrutiny is applied. For the same reason there is no need to determine whether all speech hampered by § 4631(d) is commercial, as our cases have used that term.

Under a commercial speech inquiry, it is the state's burden to justify its content-based law as consistent with the First Amendment. To sustain the targeted, content-based burden

§ 4631(d) imposes on protected expression, the state must show at least that the statute directly advances a substantial governmental interest and that the measure is drawn to achieve that interest. There must be a "fit between the legislature's ends and the means chosen to accomplish those ends." As in other contexts, these standards ensure not only that the state's interests are proportional to the resulting burdens placed on speech but also that the law does not seek to suppress a disfavored message.

The state's asserted justifications for § 4631(d) come under two general headings. First, the state contends that its law is necessary to protect medical privacy, including physician confidentiality, avoidance of harassment, and the integrity of the doctor-patient relationship. Second, the state argues that § 4631(d) is integral to the achievement of policy objectives—namely, improved public health and reduced healthcare costs. Neither justification withstands scrutiny.

Vermont argues that its physicians have a "reasonable expectation" that their prescriber-identifying information "will not be used for purposes other than . . . filling and processing" prescriptions. It may be assumed that, for many reasons, physicians have an interest in keeping their prescription decisions confidential. But § 4631(d) is not drawn to serve that interest. Under Vermont's law, pharmacies may share prescriber-identifying information with anyone for any reason save one: They must not allow the information to be used for marketing. Exceptions further allow pharmacies to sell prescriber-identifying information for certain purposes, including "health care research." § 4631(e). And the measure permits insurers, researchers, journalists, the state itself, and others to use the information. . . .

Perhaps the state could have addressed physician confidentiality through "a more coherent policy." . . . But the state did not enact a statute with that purpose or design. Instead, Vermont made prescriber-identifying information available to an almost limitless audience. The explicit structure of the statute allows the information to be studied and used by all but a narrow class of disfavored speakers. Given the information's widespread availability and many permissible uses, the state's asserted interest in physician confidentiality does not justify the burden that § 4631(d) places on protected expression.

The State points out that it allows doctors to forgo the advantages of § 4631(d) by consenting to the sale, disclosure, and use of their prescriber-identifying information. See § 4631(c)(1). . . . Vermont has given its doctors a contrived choice: Either consent, which will allow your prescriber-identifying information to be disseminated and used without constraint; or, withhold consent, which will allow your information to be used by those speakers whose message the state supports. Section 4631(d) may offer a limited degree of privacy, but only on terms favorable to the speech the state prefers. . . . [T]he state has conditioned privacy on acceptance of a content-based rule that is not drawn to serve the state's asserted interest. To obtain the limited privacy allowed by § 4631(d), Vermont physicians are forced to acquiesce in the state's goal of burdening disfavored speech by disfavored speakers.

. . . Rules that burden protected expression may not be sustained when the options provided by the state are too narrow to advance legitimate interests or too broad to protect speech. As already explained, § 4631(d) permits extensive use of prescriber-identifying information and so does not advance the state's asserted interest in physician confidentiality. The limited range of available privacy options instead reflects the state's impermissible purpose to burden disfavored speech.

The state also contends that § 4631(d) protects doctors from "harassing sales behaviors." "Some doctors in Vermont are experiencing an undesired increase in the aggressiveness of pharmaceutical sales representatives," the Vermont Legislature found, "and a few have reported that they felt coerced and harassed." It is doubtful that concern for "a few" physicians who may have "felt coerced and harassed" by pharmaceutical market-ers can sustain a broad content-based rule like § 4631(d). Many are those who must endure speech they do not like, but that is a necessary cost of freedom. In any event the State offers no explanation why remedies other than content-based rules would be inadequate. Physicians can, and often do, simply decline to meet with detailers, including detailers who use prescriber-identifying information. Doctors who wish to forgo detailing altogether are free to give "No Solicitation" or "No Detailing" instructions to their office managers or to receptionists at their places of work. . . .

Vermont argues that detailers' use of prescriber-identifying information undermines the doctor-patient relationship by allowing detailers to influence treatment decisions. According to the state, "unwanted pressure occurs" when doctors learn that their prescrip-tion decisions are being "monitored" by detailers. Some physicians accuse detailers of "spy-ing" or of engaging in "underhanded" conduct in order to "subvert" prescription decisions. And Vermont claims that detailing makes people "anxious" about whether doctors have their patients' best interests at heart. But the state does not explain why detailers' use of prescriber-identifying information is more likely to prompt these objections than many other uses permitted by § 4631(d). In any event, this asserted interest is contrary to basic First Amendment principles. Speech remains protected even when it may "stir people to action," "move them to tears," or "inflict great pain." The more benign and, many would say, beneficial speech of pharmaceutical marketing is also entitled to the protection of the First Amendment. If pharmaceutical marketing affects treatment decisions, it does so because doctors find it persuasive. Absent circumstances far from those presented here, the fear that speech might persuade provides no lawful basis for quieting it.

The state contends that § 4631(d) advances important public policy goals by lowering the costs of medical services and promoting public health. If prescriber-identifying information were available for use by detailers, the state contends, then detailing would be effective in promoting brand-name drugs that are more expensive and less safe than generic alterna-tives. This logic is set out at length in the legislative findings accompanying § 4631(d). Yet at oral argument here, the state declined to acknowledge that § 4631(d)'s objective purpose and practical effect were to inhibit detailing and alter doctors' prescription decisions. The state's reluctance to embrace its own legislature's rationale reflects the vulnerability of its position.

While Vermont's stated policy goals may be proper, § 4631(d) does not advance them in a permissible way. As the Court of Appeals noted, the "state's own explanation of how" § 4631(d) "advances its interests cannot be said to be direct." The state seeks to achieve its policy objectives through the indirect means of restraining certain speech by certain speak-ers—that is, by diminishing detailers' ability to influence prescription decisions. Those who seek to censor or burden free expression often assert that disfavored speech has adverse effects. But the "fear that people would make bad decisions if given truthful information" cannot justify content-based burdens on speech. These precepts apply with full force when the audience, in this case prescribing physicians, consists of "sophisticated and experi-enced" consumers.

As Vermont's legislative findings acknowledge, the premise of § 4631(d) is that the force of speech can justify the government's attempts to stifle it. Indeed the state defends the law by insisting that "pharmaceutical marketing has a strong influence on doctors' prescrib-ing practices." This reasoning is incompatible with the First Amendment. In an attempt to reverse a disfavored trend in public opinion, a state could not ban campaigning with slo-gans, picketing with signs, or marching during the daytime. Likewise the state may not seek to remove a popular but disfavored product from the marketplace by prohibiting truthful, nonmisleading advertisements that contain impressive endorsements or catchy jingles. That the state finds expression too persuasive does not permit it to quiet the speech or to burden its messengers.

The defect in Vermont's law is made clear by the fact that many listeners find detailing instructive. Indeed the record demonstrates that some Vermont doctors view targeted detailing based on prescriber-identifying information as "very helpful" because it allows detailers to shape their messages to each doctor's practice. Even the United States, which appeared here in support of Vermont, took care to dispute the state's "unwarranted view that the dangers of [n]ew drugs outweigh their benefits to patients." There are divergent views regarding detailing and the prescription of brand-name drugs. Under the Constitution, resolution of that debate must result from free and uninhibited speech. . . . The choice "between the dangers of suppressing information, and the dangers of its misuse if it is freely available," is one that "the First Amendment makes for us."

Vermont may be displeased that detailers who use prescriber-identifying information are effective in promoting brand-name drugs. The state can express that view through its own speech. But a state's failure to persuade does not allow it to hamstring the opposition. The state may not burden the speech of others in order to tilt public debate in a preferred direction. "The commercial marketplace, like other spheres of our social and cultural life, provides a forum where ideas and information flourish. Some of the ideas and information are vital, some of slight worth. But the general rule is that the speaker and the audience, not the government, assess the value of the information presented."

It is true that content-based restrictions on protected expression are sometimes permissible, and that principle applies to commercial speech. Indeed the government's legitimate interest in protecting consumers from "commercial harms" explains "why commercial speech can be subject to greater governmental regulation than noncommercial speech." Here, however, Vermont has not shown that its law has a neutral justification. The state nowhere contends that detailing is false or misleading within the meaning of this Court's First Amendment precedents. Nor does the state argue that the provision challenged here will prevent false or misleading speech. The state's interest in burdening the speech of detailers instead turns on nothing more than a difference of opinion.

* * *

The capacity of technology to find and publish personal information, including records required by the government, presents serious and unresolved issues with respect to personal privacy and the dignity it seeks to secure. In considering how to protect those interests, however, the state cannot engage in content-based discrimination to advance its own side of a debate.

If Vermont's statute provided that prescriber-identifying information could not be sold or disclosed except in narrow circumstances then the state might have a stronger position. Here, however, the state gives possessors of the information broad discretion and wide latitude in disclosing the information, while at the same time restricting the information's use by some speakers and for some purposes, even while the state itself can use the information to counter the speech it seeks to suppress. Privacy is a concept too integral to the person and a right too essential to freedom to allow its manipulation to support just those ideas the government prefers.

When it enacted § 4631(d), the Vermont Legislature found that the "marketplace for ideas on medicine safety and effectiveness is frequently one-sided in that brand name companies invest in expensive pharmaceutical marketing campaigns to doctors." "The goals of marketing programs," the legislature said, "are often in conflict with the goals of the state." The text of § 4631(d), associated legislative findings, and the record developed in the

District Court establish that Vermont enacted its law for this end. The state has burdened a form of protected expression that it found too persuasive. At the same time, the state has left unburdened those speakers whose messages are in accord with its own views. This the state cannot do.

The judgment of the Court of Appeals is affirmed.

It is so ordered.

JUSTICE STEPHEN BREYER, with whom JUSTICE RUTH BADER GINSBURG and JUSTICE ELENA KAGAN join, dissenting:

The Vermont statute before us adversely affects expression in one, and only one, way. It deprives pharmaceutical and data-mining companies of data, collected pursuant to the government's regulatory mandate, that could help pharmaceutical companies create better sales messages. In my view, this effect on expression is inextricably related to a lawful governmental effort to regulate a commercial enterprise. The First Amendment does not require courts to apply a special "heightened" standard of review when reviewing such an effort. And, in any event, the statute meets the First Amendment standard this Court has previously applied when the government seeks to regulate commercial speech. For any or all of these reasons, the Court should uphold the statute as constitutional.

GLOSSARY

absolute privilege: A complete exemption from liability for defamation because the statement was made within the performance of official government duties.

actual malice: A statement made knowing it is false or with reckless disregard for its truth. As a general rule, public officials and public figures must prove actual malice as a standard of fault, and private individuals must prove negligence.

ad hoc balancing: Making decisions according to the specific facts of the case under review rather than more general principles.

administrative law: The orders, rules and regulations promulgated by executive branch administrative agencies to carry out their delegated duties.

admonitions: Judges' instructions to jurors warning them to avoid potentially prejudicial communications.

affirm: To ratify, uphold or approve a lower court ruling.

ag-gag laws: State laws that prohibit recording, photographing or entering farms or agricultural facilities to document animal abuse or other activity without permission.

all-purpose public figures: A person who occupies a position of such persuasive power and influence as to be deemed a public figure for all purposes. All-purpose public figure libel plaintiffs are required to prove actual malice.

amicus brief: A submission to the court from amicus curiae, or "friends of the court," which are interested individuals or organizations that are parties in the case.

anti-SLAPP laws: State laws meant to provide a remedy for a SLAPP. Plaintiffs have the burden to show that they will prevail in the lawsuit; otherwise, the suit is dismissed.

appellant: The party making the appeal; also called the petitioner.

appellee: The party against whom an appeal is made.

appropriation: Using a person's name, picture, likeness, voice or identity for commercial or trade purposes without permission.

arbitrary marks: Words that have ordinary meanings unrelated to the product or service that may be trademarked.

artistic relevance test: A test to determine whether the commercial use of a celebrity's name, picture, likeness, voice or identity is relevant to a disputed work's artistic purpose.

as applied: A legal phrase referring to interpretation of a statute on the basis of actual effects on the parties in the present case.

assertion of fact: A statement of information perceived as being capable of being proven true or false.

avatar: An icon or image that represents a person in a video game or other computer-generated content.

Berne Convention: The primary international copyright treaty adopted by many countries in 1886 and by the United States in 1988.

biometric data: This type of information relates to personal characteristics, such as fingerprints or unique facial features, that may be used to identify an individual.

black-letter law: Formally enacted, written law that is available in legal reporters or other documents.

blurring: A famous mark's distinctiveness is injured because it becomes or is likely to become associated with a similar mark or trade name.

bootstrapping: In libel law, the forbidden practice of a defendant claiming that the plaintiff is a public figure solely on the basis of the statement that is the reason for the lawsuit.

broadband: A high-capacity transmission technique using a wide range of spectrum frequencies to enable a large number of messages to be communicated simultaneously.

broadcasting: Defined by the Communications Act of 1934 as use of the electromagnetic spectrum to send signals to many listeners and viewers simultaneously.

burden of proof: The requirement for a party to a case to demonstrate one or more claims by the presentation of evidence.

categorical balancing: Legal reasoning that weighs different broad categories, such as political speech, against other interests, such as privacy, to create general rules that may be applied in later cases with similar facts.

celebrity marketing: Contracted celebrities who endorse brands and create interest in the brand through advertising.

change of venue: Altering the location of a trial to avoid areas permeated by media coverage.

child pornography: Any image showing children in sexual or sexually explicit situations.

chilling effect: The discouragement of a constitutional right, especially free speech, by any government practice that creates uncertainty about the proper exercise of that right.

civil contempt: orders generally respond to something that occurred outside the direct supervision of a judge. Civil contempt orders may compel an individual to do something.

civil rights claims: Federal 1983 claims that indicate state or local government actors deprived individuals of constitutionally guaranteed individual rights.

class action lawsuit: A lawsuit in which a group of people with similar injuries caused by the same product or action sue a defendant as a group.

clear and conspicuous: A requirement from the FTC for ads with disclosures. Any disclosures must be seen by the reader.

clear and present danger: Doctrine establishing that restrictions on First Amendment rights will be upheld if they are necessary to prevent an extremely serious and imminent harm.

Clery Act: A federal law, the Campus Security Policy and Campus Crime Statistics Act of 1990, that requires universities that receive federal funds to maintain up-to-date police logs and to compile and publish statistics on campus crime each year.

commercialization: The appropriation tort used to protect people who want privacy; prohibits using another person's name or likeness for commercial purposes without permission.

common law: Judge-made law composed of the principles and traditions established through court rulings; precedent-based law.

Communications Decency Act: Part of the 1996 Telecommunications Act that largely attempted to regulate internet content.

compelled speech: A legal doctrine in First Amendment law that generally prevents the government from punishing citizens for refusing to express ideas that the government might require.

compelling interest: A government interest of the highest order, an interest the government is required to protect.

Computer Fraud and Abuse Act: A federal law that prohibits computer and phone hacking that violate a user's expectation of privacy.

concurring opinion: A separate opinion of a minority of the court or a single judge or justice agreeing with the majority opinion but applying different reasoning or legal principles.

constitutional law: The set of laws that establish the nature, functions and limits of government.

construction: The process by which courts and administrative agencies determine the proper meaning and application of laws, rules and regulations.

content based: A term used to describe government actions prompted by the ideas, subject matter or position of the message.

content marketing: Advertising content shared directly from a brand's platform.

content neutral: A term used to describe government actions that incidentally and unintentionally affect speech as they advance other important government interests unrelated to the content of speech.

continuance: Postponement of a trial to a later time.

contributory infringement: The participation in, or contribution to, the infringing acts of another person.

copyright: An exclusive legal right used to protect intellectual creations from unauthorized use.

corrective advertising: The Federal Trade Commission power to require an advertiser to advertise or otherwise distribute information to correct false or misleading advertisement claims.

cross-ownership rule: A Federal Communications Commission rule that governs when one entity can own two or more companies with related interests.

Criminal contempt orders may impose fines or imprisonment as punishment for behavior that directly interferes with court proceedings.

damages: Compensation that may be recovered in court by any person who has suffered loss or injury. Damages may be compensatory for actual loss or punitive as punishment for outrageous conduct.

dark patterns or "negative options" practices: Design tactics that trick consumers into making certain choices, such as purchasing a good, subscribing to a service or agreeing to a contract. "Negative option marketing" broadly refers to transactions containing terms or conditions under which the seller may interpret a consumer's silence or failure to reject or cancel a product as acceptance. Common examples include automatic renewal subscriptions, continuity plans, free programs and prenotification plans.

data broker: An entity that collects and stores personal information about consumers, then sells that information to other organizations.

deceptive advertising: Material claims made in the promotion, advertising or marketing of products or services that are likely to deceive consumers.

decisional privacy: An individual's interest in having independence to make important decisions, particularly decisions related to one's intimate life.

deepfake: A video of a person in which their face or body has been digitally altered so that they appear to be someone else. Typically used maliciously or to spread false information.

defamation: A false communication that harms another's reputation and subjects them to ridicule and scorn; incorporates both libel and slander.

defamation plaintiff's case: A plaintiff must prove a false and defamatory statement of fact of and concerning the plaintiff was published with fault and caused harm to the plaintiff.

defamatory: A statement that is harmful to reputation.

defendant: The party accused of violating a law, or the party being sued in a civil lawsuit.

deference: The judicial practice of interpreting statutes and rules by relying heavily on the judgments and intentions of the administrative experts and legislative agencies that enacted the laws.

demurrer: A request that a court dismiss a case on the grounds that although the claims are true, they are insufficient to warrant a judgment against the defendant.

de novo: Literally, "new" or "over again." On appeal, the court may review the facts de novo rather than simply reviewing the legal posture and process of the case.

derivative work: A work that is obtained from or created in relation to an original work.

descriptive fair use: This allows one company's trademark to describe another company's product.

descriptive marks: Marks that describe the product or service and leave little to a consumer's imagination and that must attach a distinctive meaning to the product or service (called secondary meaning) to be trademarked.

designated or limited public forum: Government spaces or buildings that are available for public use (within limits).

dicta: Statements in a court opinion that are not central or essential to its reasoning or holding. These statements are technically not part of the law but often influence and contextualize legal doctrine.

dilution: Using a famous trademark in a way that disparages or diminishes the mark's effectiveness in the market. Can happen from blurring or tarnishment.

disclosure: Part of an ad that qualifies or limits a claim to avoid a misleading impression—a disclosure cannot cure a false claim, and it must not contradict a material claim.

disclosure of private facts: Publicizing highly offensive, true private information that is not newsworthy or lawfully obtained from a public record.

discovery: The pretrial process of gathering evidence and facts. The word also may refer to the specific items of evidence that are uncovered.

discretion: The authority to determine the proper outcome.

disparaging marks: Derogatory trademarks with matter that can bring certain groups into contempt or disrepute. Recently, the U.S. Supreme Court has ruled that the First Amendment protects immoral and disparaging marks.

dissenting opinion: A separate opinion of a minority of the court or a single judge or justice disagreeing with the result reached by the majority and challenging the majority's reasoning or the legal basis of the decision.

distinguish from precedent: To justify an outcome in a case by asserting that differences between that case and preceding cases outweigh any similarities.

doctrines: Principles or theories of law that shape judicial decision making (e.g., the doctrine of content neutrality).

Drivers' Privacy Protection Act of 1994 (DPPA): A federal law that prohibits states from "knowing disclosure" of information obtained from department of motor vehicle records without permission except under specific circumstances.

due process: Fair legal proceedings. Due process is guaranteed by the Fifth and Fourteenth Amendments to the U.S. Constitution.

duty of care: A standard applied in civil cases that means defendants should have foreseen negligence could cause harm to the person or people to whom they owed a duty.

efficacy claim: A claim for products that perform the advertised function or yield the advertised benefit, but which do not suggest scientific proof of the product's effectiveness.

electromagnetic spectrum: The range of wavelengths or frequencies over which electromagnetic radiation extends. It is used to send both analog and digital signals.

Electronic Communications Privacy Act (ECPA): A federal law that prohibits the unauthorized interception of an electronic communication while it is in transit or storage.

Electronic Freedom of Information Act (EFOIA): A 1996 amendment to FOIA that applies the law to electronically stored information and extends FOIA to computer records.

electronic media: All forms of media that utilize electronics or digital encoding to distribute news and entertainment.

emotional distress: Serious mental or emotional pain and suffering or mental anguish.

en banc: Literally, "on the bench" but now meaning "in full court." The judges of a circuit court of appeals will sit en banc to decide important or controversial cases.

endorsement: Any advertising message (including verbal statements, demonstrations or depictions of the name, signature, likeness or other identifying personal characteristics of an individual or the name or seal of an organization) that consumers are likely to believe reflects the opinions, beliefs, findings or experiences of a party other than the sponsoring advertiser, even if the views expressed by that party are identical to those of the sponsoring advertisers.

equity law: Law created by judges to decide cases based on fairness and ethics and also to determine the proper remedy.

establishment claim: A claim that suggests effectiveness or superiority of the product is established by scientific proof.

executive orders: Orders from a government executive, such as the president, a governor or a mayor, that have the force of law.

experience and logic test: A doctrine that evaluates both the history of openness and the role it plays in ensuring the credibility of a judicial process to determine whether it is presumptively open.

expert: An individual, group, or institution possessing, as a result of experience, study, or training, knowledge of a particular subject, which knowledge is superior to what ordinary individuals generally acquire.

express claims: Ads that make explicit representations without the need for additional evidence.

facial meaning: The plain and straightforward meaning.

fact finder: In a trial, a judge or the jury determining which facts presented in evidence are accurate.

Fair Credit Reporting Act: A federal law that addresses the accuracy, fairness and privacy of information stored in consumer reporting agency files.

fairness doctrine: The Federal Communications Commission rule requiring broadcast stations to air programs discussing public issues and include a variety of views about controversial issues of public importance.

fair report privilege: A privilege for accurate and fair reports on the content of official records and proceedings. Sometimes called "conditional privilege."

fair use: A test courts use to determine whether using another's copyrighted material without permission is legal or an infringement. Also used in trademark infringement cases.

false light: A privacy tort, not recognized in all states, that involves making persons seem in the public eye to be persons they are not.

falsity: A statement perceived as fact that is not true.

Family Educational Rights and Privacy Act (FERPA): A federal law that forbids any school that receives federal funding from releasing students' academic records unless the students, as adults, or their parents provide consent.

fanciful marks: Invented marks, including made-up words. Most likely to receive trademark protection.

fault: Liability or responsibility for making public an allegedly false and defamatory statement of fact.

Federal Communications Commission: A U.S. government agency, directly responsible to Congress and charged with regulating interstate and international communications by radio, television, wire, satellite, cable and broadband.

federalism: A principle according to which the states are related to yet independent of each other and are related to yet independent of the federal government.

Federal Radio Commission: A federal agency established by the Radio Act of 1927 to oversee radio broadcasting. The Federal Communications Commission succeeded the FRC in 1934.

Federal Rules of Civil Procedure: General rules that govern all civil proceedings in the U.S. district courts.

Federal Trade Commission: A federal agency created in 1914. Its purpose is to promote free and fair competition in interstate commerce; this includes preventing false and misleading advertising.

fighting words: Words not protected by the First Amendment because they are directed at an individual and cause immediate harm or trigger violent response.

first-sale doctrine: Once a copyright owner sells a copy of a work, the new owner may possess, transfer or otherwise dispose of that copy without the copyright owner's permission.

for-cause challenge: In the context of jury selection, the ability of attorneys to remove a potential juror for a reason the law finds sufficient, as opposed to a peremptory challenge.

Foreign Intelligence Surveillance Act (FISA): A federal law that allows government investigators to use wiretaps, surveillance and tracking of personal communications without a court order.

forum shopping: A practice whereby the plaintiff chooses a court in which to sue because they believe the court will rule in the plaintiff's favor.

Fourth Estate: A label given to the traditional press in its role as a watchdog of the other three branches of government in the U.S.

Freedom of Information Act (FOIA): A federal law that requires records held by federal government agencies be made available to the public.

freedom of information law (FOIL): A law that provides access to records held by non-federal government agencies.

gag orders: A nonlegal term used to describe court restraining orders that prohibit publication or discussion of specific materials.

generic marks: Marks that are understood as a common term for something. Some former trademarks can become generic when they pass into common usage and lose their distinctiveness or have been abandoned.

gerrymandering: A practice in which electoral districts are drawn to favor one political party over another. Both Republicans and Democrats have engaged in the practice of gerrymandering throughout history.

"Glomar" response: A nonreply response that indicates government agents don't have to tell if they have requested documents.

Government in the Sunshine Act: The Federal Open Meetings Law.

grand jury: A group summoned to hear the state's evidence in criminal cases and decide whether a crime was committed and whether charges should be filed; grand juries do not determine guilt.

greenwashing: Marketing efforts that deceptively capture consumer interest in sustainability.

hate speech: A category of speech that includes name-calling and pointed criticism that demeans others on the basis of race, color, gender, ethnicity, religion, national origin, disability, intellect or the like.

Health Insurance Portability and Accountability Act: A federal law that prevents health professionals and institutions from revealing individuals' personal information stored in medical records.

Hicklin **rule:** Taken from a mid-19th-century English case and used in the United States until the mid-20th century, a rule that defines material as obscene if it tends to corrupt children.

highly offensive to a reasonable person: Something that would outrage community notions of decency.

holding: The decision or ruling of a court.

identification: Being of and concerning a plaintiff.

impanel: To select and seat a jury.

impartial jurors: Jurors who persuade the court that they have no fixed opinion of the guilt or innocence of the defendant.

implied claims: Ads based on a reasonable consumer "take away," where the FTC will consider factors such the layout, wording of claims and phrasing.

important government interest: An interest of the government that is substantial or significant (i.e., more than merely convenient or reasonable) but not compelling.

in camera: Discussions or hearings held without the public present.

incorporation doctrine: The Fourteenth Amendment concept that most of the Bill of Rights applies equally to the states.

indecency: A narrow legal term referring to sexual expression and expletives inappropriate for children on broadcast radio and television.

influencer marketing: Contracted brand fans and experts with a significant online following who help to create sales and positive discussions about brands.

informational privacy: An individual's interest in avoiding having personal matters disclosed.

infringement: The unauthorized manufacture, sale or distribution of an item protected by copyright, patent or trademark law.

infringement by inducement: Sometimes just called inducement. When a person or entity who does not directly infringe can be held liable for inducing others to infringe.

injunction: A court order prohibiting a person or organization from doing some specified act.

insider trading: The trading of a company's stocks or other securities by those with access to non-public information about the company.

intentional infliction of emotional distress: Extreme and outrageous intentional or reckless conduct causing plaintiffs' severe emotional harm; public official and public figure plaintiffs must show actual malice on the defendant's part.

intermediate scrutiny: A standard applied by the courts to review laws that implicate but do not directly regulate core constitutional values; also called heightened review.

intrusion upon seclusion: Physically or technologically disturbing another's reasonable expectation of privacy.

involuntary public figure: A person who is involuntarily drawn into a given issue, or was drawn in without their intentional involvement. This category of plaintiff is rare.

judicial review: The power of the courts to determine the meaning of the Constitution and to decide whether laws violate the Constitution.

jurisdiction: The geographic or topical area of responsibility and authority of a court.

knowledge of falsity: Awareness that information is inaccurate.

Lanham Act: A federal law that regulates the trademark registration process but also contains a section permitting business competitors to sue one another for false advertising.

laws of general application: Laws such as tax and equal employment laws that fall within the express power of government. Laws of general application are generally reviewed under minimum scrutiny.

legal doctrine: A long-established rule or set of rules followed by the courts based on precedent. These rules are part of the law.

legally qualified candidate: Someone who has publicly announced a bid for office, has their name on the ballot or is a serious write-in candidate.

The candidate also must be legally qualified to hold the office.

legislative history: Congressional reports and records of deliberations about proposed legislation.

libel by implication: Individual statements that may be factually accurate, but taken together they paint a different picture. Through implication or innuendo, one can create libelous messages.

libel per quod: A statement actionable as defamation only when the plaintiff introduces additional facts to show defamation.

libel per se: A statement whose injurious nature is apparent and requires no further proof.

libel-proof plaintiff: A plaintiff whose reputation is deemed to be so damaged that additional false statements of and concerning them cannot cause further harm.

limited-purpose public figure: In libel law, a plaintiff who has attained public figure status within a narrow set of circumstances by thrusting themself to the forefront of particular public controversies in order to influence the resolution of the issues involved, this kind of public figure is more common than the all-purpose public figure.

marketplace of ideas: In Milton's time, the open competition of ideas in society that led to the discovery of Truth in the religious sense. Today, the marketplace of ideas represents a competition free from government interference, and that leads to the best ideas or

outcomes for the welfare of a democratic society.

material: When a claim in an ad is likely to affect a consumer's choice or conduct regarding a product or service.

memorandum order: An order announcing the vote of the Supreme Court without providing an opinion.

metadata: A set of data that describes and gives information about data.

modify precedent: To change rather than follow or reject precedent.

moot: Term used to describe a case in which the issues presented are no longer "live" or in which the matter in dispute has already been resolved; a case is not moot if it is susceptible to repetition but evades review.

motion to dismiss: A request to a court to reject a complaint because it does not state a claim that can be remedied by law or is legally lacking in some other way.

motion to dismiss: A formal request to the court to dismiss a case.

mug shot: The law enforcement photograph of an arrested person's face.

multichannel video programming distributor: An entity, including cable or direct broadcast satellite services, that provides multiple channels of video programming for purchase.

must-carry rule: Regulations enacted under the federal cable law that require multichannel video programming distributors to transmit local broadcast television stations.

Also called the cable carriage requirement.

native advertising: Ads designed to resemble the editorial content of the medium where they appear.

negligence: Generally, the failure to exercise reasonable or ordinary care.

negligence: Acting with a failure to exercise due care or a failure to follow professional standards.

negligent: An act or statement made by mistake or without anticipating the possible harm the act or statement could cause.

negligent infliction of emotional distress: Careless breach of a duty that causes the plaintiff severe emotional harm.

net neutrality: The principle that holds that internet service providers cannot charge content providers to speed up the delivery of their goods—all internet traffic is treated equally.

neutral reportage: In libel law, a defense accepted in some jurisdictions that provides First Amendment protection for reporting of an accusation made by a responsible and prominent organization, even when it turns out the accusation was false and libelous.

newsworthy: Matters that are of legitimate public concern or interest.

nominative fair use: Referring to the defendant's own product or service by using the plaintiff's mark without permission.

nonconsensual pornography: The disclosure of sexually explicit images or video without consent.

nonpublic forum: Government-held property that is not available for public speech and assembly purposes.

notice of proposed rulemaking: A notice issued by the Federal Communications Commission announcing that it is considering changing certain of its regulations or adopting new rules.

O'Brien **test:** A three-part test used to determine whether a content-neutral law is constitutional.

obscenity: The dictionary defines it as relating to sex in an indecent, very offensive or shocking way. The legal definition of obscenity comes from *Miller v. California*—material is determined to be obscene if it passes the *Miller* test.

original intent: The perceived intent of the Framers of the Constitution that guides some First Amendment application and interpretation.

originalists: Supreme Court justices who interpret the Constitution according to the perceived intent of its framers.

original jurisdiction: The authority to consider a case at its inception, as contrasted with appellate jurisdiction.

outrageous and extreme conduct: Conduct that a reasonable person would consider beyond the scope of all possible bounds for decency.

overbroad laws: A principle that directs courts to find laws unconstitutional if they restrict more legal activity than necessary.

overrule: To reverse the ruling of a lower court.

overturn precedent: To reject the fundamental premise of a precedent.

patently offensive: Term describing material with hard-core sexual conduct.

per curiam opinion: An unsigned opinion issued by the Court as a whole, rather than by individual judges.

peremptory challenge: During jury selection, a challenge in which an attorney rejects a juror without showing a reason. Attorneys have the right to eliminate a limited number of jurors through peremptory challenges.

plaintiff: The party who files a complaint; the one who sues.

political questions: Questions not subject to judicial review because they fall into areas properly handled by another branch of government.

pornography: A vague—not legally precise—term for sexually oriented material.

post-mortem (After death): Post-mortem right of publicity generally refers to famous persons' ability to control the commercial use of their name, picture, likeness, voice and identity after death.

precedent: The outcome of a previous case that establishes a rule of law for courts within the same jurisdiction to follow to determine cases with similar issues.

predominant use test: In a right of publicity lawsuit, a test to determine whether the defendant used the plaintiff's name or picture more for commercial purposes or protected expression.

prima facie: Latin for "at first look" or "on its face"; evidence before a trial that is sufficient to prove the case unless substantial contradictory evidence is presented.

prior restraint: Action taken by the government to prohibit publication of a specific document or text before it is distributed to the public; a policy that requires government approval before publication.

private facts: Information that is asserted as a true statement and is not newsworthy or of legitimate public concern.

private figure: A plaintiff who cannot be categorized as either a public figure or a public official. Generally, in order to recover damages, a private figure is required to prove negligence on the part of the defendant.

probable cause: The standard of evidence needed for an arrest or to issue a search warrant. More than mere suspicion, it is a showing through reasonably trustworthy information that a crime has been or is being committed.

probable cause: Sufficient information and facts to think a crime was committed based on reliable information and facts.

promissory estoppel: A legal doctrine that requires courts to enforce a promise if the individual who received the promise relied on it and its

breach created a harm that should be remedied by law.

proximate cause: The legal determination of whether it is reasonable to conclude that the defendant's actions led to the plaintiff's injury.

prurient interest: Lustful thoughts or sexual desires.

publication: Making a statement to more than the plaintiff and defendant.

public domain: Refers to creative materials that are not protected by intellectual property laws. The public can use public domain work without permission.

public figures: In libel law, a plaintiff who is in the public spotlight, usually voluntarily, and must prove the defendant acted with actual malice in order to win damages.

public forum: Government property held for use by the public, usually for purposes of exercising rights of speech and assembly.

public record: A government record, particularly one that is available for people to inspect.

purposeful avoidance of the truth: Publishing information when there are obvious doubts about the accuracy of information and not taking obvious steps to check its accuracy.

quash: To void or nullify a legal procedure or action; a motion often made in response to subpoenas for confidential information.

Racketeer Influenced and Corrupt Organizations Act (RICO): A federal law that addresses

patterns of serious illegal activity connected to an enterprise that affects interstate or foreign commerce.

radio frequency: Any one of the electromagnetic wave frequencies that lie in the range extending from around 3 kHz to 300 GHz, which includes those frequencies used for communications or radio signals.

rational review: A standard of judicial review that assumes the constitutionality of reasonable legislative or administrative enactments and applies minimum scrutiny to their review.

reasonable basis: The FTC requires that advertisers and agencies have competent and reliable evidence for ad claims.

reasonable person: The law's version of an average person.

reckless: An action taken with no consideration of the legal harms that might result.

reckless disregard for the truth: Publishing information with serious doubts about whether information is accurate or purposefully avoiding the truth.

redact: Strike out information so it cannot be read or perceived; removing sensitive information, when necessary to minimize serious harm.

red-flag knowledge: When an internet service provider or website is aware of facts that would make infringement obvious to a reasonable person.

remand: To send back to the lower court for further action.

reporter's privilege: The concept that reporters may keep information such as source identity confidential. The rationale is that the reporter-source relationship is similar to doctor–patient and lawyer–client relationships.

republication: Repeating libelous information.

restraining order: A court order forbidding an individual or group of individuals from doing a specified act until a hearing can be conducted.

retraction statutes: In libel law, state laws that limit the damages a plaintiff may receive if the defendant has issued a retraction of the material at issue. Retraction statutes are meant to discourage the punishment of any good-faith effort of admitting a mistake.

retransmission consent: Part of the federal cable law allowing broadcast stations to negotiate a fee for retransmission of their programs.

reverse FOI lawsuits: Cases against public records requesters.

ride-along: A process through which representatives accompany government officials to various scenes.

right of publicity: The appropriation tort protecting celebrities' rights to have their name, picture, likeness, voice and identity used for commercial or trade purposes only with permission.

right to receive information: A right to send or disseminate information, important to the public interest.

rule of law: The legal standards that guide the proper and consistent creation and application of the law.

safe harbor: The takedown notification provision of the Digital Millennium Copyright Act that protects internet service providers and video-sharing websites from claims of infringement when they do not know about or profit from the infringement and promptly comply with a takedown notice.

safe harbor policy: A Federal Communications Commission policy designating 10 p.m. to 6 a.m. as a time when broadcast radio and television stations may air indecent material without violating federal law or FCC regulations.

satellite market modification rule: Part of the Satellite Television Extension and Localism Act Reauthorization Act of 2014 that allows a television station, satellite operator or county government to request the addition or deletion of communities from a broadcast station's local television market.

search warrant: A legal order by a judge to authorize law enforcement to search locations and seize items. Only issued with probable cause.

secondary meaning: Meaning beyond a word's common meaning. To obtain secondary meaning, the public must associate a word with a product's source or producer, not the product.

Sedition Act of 1798: Federal legislation under which anyone "opposing or resisting any law of the United States, or any act of the President of the United States," could be imprisoned for up to two years. The act also made it illegal to "write, print, utter, or publish" anything that criticized the president or Congress.

seditious libel: Communication meant to incite people to change the government; criticism of the government.

sequestration: The isolation of jurors to avoid prejudice from publicity in a sensational trial.

serious social value: Material cannot be found obscene if it has serious literary, artistic, political or scientific value determined using national, not local/community, standards.

sexual harassment: This can include unwelcome sexual advances, requests for sexual favors and other verbal or physical harassment of a sexual nature. Sexual harassment also refers to offensive remarks about a person's sex.

shadow docket: A nickname for the U.S. Supreme Court's use of emergency orders that do not follow the customary briefings, arguments and opinions issued by the Court. The practice has come under increasing criticism in recent years.

shield laws: State laws that protect journalists from being found in contempt of court for refusing to reveal sources.

single-publication rule: A rule that limits libel victims to only one cause of action even with republications of the libel in the same outlet; common in the mass media and on websites.

SLAPP (strategic lawsuit against public participation): A lawsuit whose purpose is to harass critics into silence, often to suppress those critics' First Amendment rights.

sound-alike: Someone whose voice sounds like another person's voice. Sound-alikes require permission or a disclaimer for commercial use.

spectrum scarcity: The limitation to the number of segments of the broadcast spectrum that may be used for radio or television in a specific geographical area without causing interference.

stare decisis: The doctrine that courts follow precedent; the basis of common law, it literally means to stand by the previous decision.

state action: The requirement that the government (local, state or federal) is responsible for the regulation or censorship of speech. There must be state action for a plaintiff to file a First Amendment lawsuit.

Statute of Anne: The first copyright law, adopted in England in 1710, protected authors' works if the authors registered them with the government.

statutory damages: Damages specified in certain laws. Under these laws, copyright being an example, a judge may award statutory damages even if a plaintiff is unable to prove actual damages.

statutory law: Written law formally enacted by city, county, state and federal legislative bodies.

Stored Communications Act: A federal law that protects data packets stored following internet calls.

strict construction: Courts' narrow interpretation and application of a law based on the literal meaning of its language. Especially applied in interpreting the Constitution.

strict liability: Liability without fault; liability for any and all harms, foreseeable or unforeseen, which result from a product or an action.

strict scrutiny: A court test for determining the constitutionality of laws aimed at speech content, under which the government must show it is using the least restrictive means available to directly advance its compelling interest.

subpoena: A command for someone to appear or testify in court or to turn over evidence, such as notes or recordings, with penalties for noncompliance.

substantial truth: A statement that is primarily accurate in substance related to the sting of a defamatory statement despite having minor inaccuracies.

substantiation: Support of a claim with objective data or evidence.

suggestive marks: Marks that may be trademarked and suggest a product's source or manufacturer's business but do not describe what the product is.

summary judgment: The resolution of a legal dispute without a full trial when a judge determines that undisputed evidence is legally sufficient to render judgment.

summons: A notice asking an individual to appear at a court. Potential jurors receive such a summons.

"sunshine laws": Laws for access to government information and meetings.

Supremacy Clause: Article IV, Part 2 of the U.S. Constitution establishes that federal law takes precedence over, or supersedes, state laws.

symbolic expression: Action that warrants some First Amendment protection because its primary purpose is to express ideas.

tacking: Allows a trademark owner to slightly alter a trademark without abandoning ownership of the original mark.

tarnishment: A poorly made or unsavory product using a mark similar to a famous trademark that could cause consumers to think less of the well-known product.

textualists: Judges—in particular, Supreme Court justices—who rely exclusively on a careful reading of legal texts to determine the meaning of the law.

third-party doctrine: A legal concept that holds that people who voluntarily give information to third parties, such as banks or phone companies, forfeit any reasonable expectation of privacy in that information.

time/place/manner laws: A First Amendment concept that laws regulating the conditions of speech are more acceptable than those regulating content; also, the laws that regulate these conditions.

tort: A private or civil wrong for which a court can provide remedy in the form of damages.

tortious newsgathering: Using reporting techniques that are wrongful and unlawful for which a victim may obtain damages in court.

trademark: A word, name, symbol or design used to identify a company's goods and distinguish them from similar products other companies make.

traditional public forum: Lands designed for public use and historically used for public gathering, discussion and association (e.g., public streets, sidewalks and parks). Free speech is protected in these areas.

transformative use: When the reuse of an original copyrighted work has transformed the work's appearance or nature to such a degree that the use is not infringing.

transformative use test: A test to determine whether the First Amendment protects a work that uses a person's name, picture, likeness, voice or identity for artistic purposes. Changing the original to give it new meaning or a different message justifies First Amendment protection.

Transmit Clause: Part of the 1976 Copyright Act that says broadcast networks, local broadcasters and cable television systems perform a work when they transmit content to viewers.

trespass: Entering private property without permission.

true threat: Speech directed toward an individual or historically identified group with the intent of causing fear of harm.

underinclusive: A First Amendment doctrine that disfavors narrow laws that target a subset of a recognized category for discriminatory treatment.

vague laws: Laws that fail to define their terms or use language so general that it fails to inform citizens or judges with certainty what the laws permit or punish.

variable obscenity: The concept that sexually oriented material not obscene for adults may be obscene if distributed to minors.

venire: Literally, "to come" or "to appear"; the term used for the location from which a court draws its pool of potential jurors, who must then appear in court for voir dire; a change of venire means a change of the location from which potential jurors are drawn, the pool of jurors.

venue: The locality of a lawsuit and of the court hearing the suit. Thus, a change of venue means a relocation of a trial.

vicarious infringement: Under common law principles, companies are responsible for the acts of employees if the acts are within the nature and scope of their employment and the company has a financial interest in the infringement and the ability to control it.

vice products: Products related to activities generally considered unhealthy or immoral or whose use is restricted by age or other condition. The category includes alcohol, tobacco, firearms, sexually explicit materials and drugs.

viewpoint-based discrimination: Government censorship or punishment of expression based on the ideas or attitudes expressed. Courts will apply a strict scrutiny test to determine whether the government acted constitutionally.

voir dire: Literally, "to speak the truth"; the questioning of prospective jurors to assess their suitability.

voir dire: Questioning of potential jurors as part of the selection process.

widespread publicity: Making material available to a lot of people or the general public.

Wiretapping and Electronic Surveillance Act: A federal law that prohibits the interception (and recording, dissemination or private use) of a voice communication without a participant's permission.

work made for hire: Work created when working for another person or company. The copyright in a work made for hire belongs to the employer, not the creator.

writ of certiorari: A petition for review by the Supreme Court of the United States; *certiorari* means "to be informed of."

ENDNOTES

CHAPTER 1

1. Ankhush Khardori, *When the Rule of Law Turns into Rule by Law*, THE NEW YORK REVIEW OF BOOKS, Sept. 25, 2020, https://www.nybooks.com/daily/2020/09/25/when-the-rule-of-law-turns-into-rule-by-law/.

2. Spencer S. Hsu, *Judge blasts Barr, Justice Dept. for 'Disingenuous' Handling of Secret Trump Obstruction Memo*, WASH. POST, May 5, 2021, https://www.washingtonpost.com/local/legal-issues/barr-memo-russia-investigation/2021/05/05/c5d0c286-ada8-11eb-ab4c-986555a1c511_story.html.

3. Alex Jokich, *Parents of Daunte Wright Call for Accountability After Killing of Their Son*, KSTP.COM, April 15, 2021, https://kstp.com/news/daunte-wright-family-calls-for-stiffer-charge-against-ex-cop/6076592/?cat=1&utm_medium=social&utm_source=facebook_KSTP-TV&fbclid=IwAR27tE9hj8WgjUgl74mk54Kymxy5alcZxeSJDg4zUDRFb9oZ1tk9fyiTrGQ.

4. Jeremy Waldron, *Rule By Law: A Much Maligned Preposition*, (NYU School of Law Public Law & Legal Theory Research Paper Series), June 2019, https://papers.ssrn.com/sol3/papers.cfm?abstract_id=3378167.

5. *See* DR. SEUSS, THE LORAX (1971). (Dr. Seuss is Theodor Seuss Geisel's pseudonym.)

6. Kenneth Grady, *The Election, the Rule of Law, and the Role of Lawyers*, SEYTLINES, Nov. 17, 2016, www.seytlines.com/2016/11/the-election-the-rule-of-law-and-the-role-of-lawyers.

7. Marbury v. Madison, 5 U.S. 137, 163 (1803).

8. FREIDRICH A. HAYEK, THE ROAD TO SERFDOM 54 (1944).

9. *Public Trust in Government: 1958–2021*, PEW RESEARCH CENTER, May 17, 2021, https://www.pewresearch.org/politics/2021/05/17/public-trust-in-government-1958-2021/.

10. Richard Wike, Laura Silver, Shannon Schumacher & Aidan Connaughton, *Many in the U.S., Western Europe Say Their Political System Needs Major Reform*, PEW RESEARCH CENTER, March 31, 2021, https://www.pewresearch.org/global/2021/03/31/many-in-us-western-europe-say-their-political-system-needs-major-reform/.

11. Martha Kinsella, Daniel Weiner & Tim Lau, *Why We Need to Protect the Rule of Law in the Federal Government*, BRENNAN CENTER FOR JUSTICE, Oct. 7, 2020, https://www.brennancenter.org/our-work/research-reports/why-we-need-protect-rule-law-federal-government.

12. LARRY LESSIG, CODE AND OTHER LAWS OF CYBERSPACE, 88 (1999).

13. *See, e.g.,* John Gardner, *The Supposed Formality of the Rule of Law, in* LAW AS A LEAP OF FAITH 205 (2012).

14. Moeen H. Chema, *The Politics of the Rule of Law*, 24 MICH. ST. J. INT'L L. 449, 492 (2015).

15. Kimberlé Crenshaw, *Twenty Years of Critical Race Theory: Looking Back to Move Forward Commentary: Critical Race Theory: A Commemoration: Lead Article*, 43 CONN. L. REV. 1253 (2011).

16. *What Is the Rule of Law?* WORLD JUSTICE PROJECT, worldjusticeproject.org/about-us/overview/what-rule-law.

17. Rosa Ehrenreich Brooks, *The New Imperialism: Violence, Norms, and the "Rule of Law,"* MICH. L. REV. 101 (2003); *but see* David Pimental, *Rule of Law Reform Without*

Cultural Imperialism? HAGUE JOURNAL ON THE RULE OF LAW 2 (2010).

18. 18 U.S.C. § 16(b).

19. Sessions v. Dimaya, 138 S. Ct. 1204 (2018).

20. *Id.* at 1222–3.

21. *Id.* at 1225.

22. *Rule of Law Index 2021*, WORLD JUSTICE PROJECT, data.worldjusticeproject. org.

23. Chief Rabbi Lord Sacks, *Passover Tells Us: Teach Your Children Well*, HUFF POST BLOG, April 17, 2011, www.huffingtonpost.co m/chief-rabbi-lord-sack s/passover-message-for -huff_b_849623.html.

24. Planned Parenthood of Southeastern Pa. v. Casey, 505 U.S. 833, 854 (1992).

25. American Bar Association, *With Roe Overturned, Legal Precedent Moves to Center Stage*, June 24, 2022, https://www.amer icanbar.org/news/abane ws/aba-news-archives/2 022/06/stare-decisis-ta kes-centerstage/.

26. Brandon J. Murrill, *The Supreme Court's Overruling of Constitutional Precedent*, CONG. RES. SERV., Sept. 24, 2018, fas.org/ sgp/crs/misc/R45319. pdf.

27. Grady, *supra* note 6.

28. Johnson v. Department of Justice, 341 P.3d 1075, 1082 (Cal. 2015).

29. Lisa McElroy, *Citizens United v. FEC in Plain English*, SCOTUS BLOG, Jan.

22, 2010, www.scotusbl og.com/2010/01/citizens -united-v-fec-in-plain-e nglish/.

30. Adam Liptak, *Justices, 5–4, Reject Corporate Spending Limit*, N.Y. TIMES, Jan. 21, 2010, www.nytim es.com/2010/01/22/us/p olitics/22scotus.html.

31. Glenn Greenwald, *What the Supreme Court Got Right*, SALON, Jan. 22, 2010, www.salon.com/20 10/01/22/citizens_uni ted/.

32. H.R.J. Res. 4, 62nd Cong., 1st Sess., 47 Cong. Rec. 4 (1911).

33. Aktepe v. United States, 105 F.3d 1400, 1402 (11th Cir. 1997) (citing Japan Whaling Ass'n v. American Cetacean Soc., 478 U.S. 221, 230 (1986)).

34. Jon C. Rogowski & Andrew R. Stone, *How Political Contestation Over Judicial Nominations Polarizes Americans' Attitudes Toward the Supreme Court*, BRIT. J. POL. SCI., June 25, 2019, https://sch olar.harvard.edu/files/ro gowski/files/rogowski_a nd_stone_bjps.pdf.

35. Vincent Cannato, *Our Evolving Immigration Policy*, NAT'L AFF., Fall 2012, h ttps://www.nationalaffai rs.com/publications/det ail/our-evolving-immigr ation-policy.

36. Brendan Farrington, *Florida Sued Over Law to Ban Social Media Content Blocking*, ASSOCIATED PRESS, May 27, 2021, https ://apnews.com/article/d

onald-trump-florida-soc ial-media-media-busine ss-7202f424f2cbdf71df8f e97c2e8cb61d.

37. ROBERT SPITZER, THE POLITICS OF GUN CONTROL (2020).

38. Stephanie Condon, *After 148 Years, Mississippi Finally Ratifies 13th Amendment*, CBS NEWS, Feb. 18, 2013, www.cbsn ews.com/8301-250_162- 57569880/after-148-year s-mississippi-finally-rat ifies-13th-amendment-w hich-banned-slavery/.

39. Wash. St. Const. art. 1, § 7.

40. U.S. Const. art. 1, § 8, cl. 11; *id.* art. II, § 2.

41. *Id.* art. VI, cl. 2.

42. Anthony Bellia Jr. & B. R. Clark, *Why Federal Courts Apply the Law of Nations Even Though It Is Not the Supreme Law of the Land*, 106 GEO L.J. 1815–1960 (2017–18), www.law.geor getown.edu/georgetown -law-journal/wp-conten t/uploads/sites/26/2018 /10/Why-Federal-Court s-Apply-the-Law-of-Nat ions.pdf.

43. U.S. Const. art. III.

44. David Moore, *The Supremacy Clause and International Law*, JURIST, July 1, 2012, www.jur ist.org/commentary/ 2012/07/david-moore -international-law/; *but see* John Harrison, *The Constitution, and the Law of Nations*, 106 GEO L. J. 1659 (2018).

45. 5 U.S. 137, 177 (1803).

46. Reno v. American Civil Liberties Union, 521 U.S. 844 (1997).

47. PAUL W. KAHN, THE REIGN OF LAW: MARBURY V. MADISON AND THE CONSTRUCTION OF AMERICA 4 (1997).

48. 5 U.S. 137 (1803).

49. KAHN, *supra* note 47.

50. Janus v. AFSCME, 138 S. Ct. 2448, 2497 (2018) (Kagan, J., dissenting) (internal citations omitted).

51. See, e.g., Miller v. Alabama, 567 U.S. 460, 469 (2012) ("The cases before us implicate two strands of precedent reflecting our concern with proportionate punishment").

52. Dept. of Justice v. Rep. Committee for Freedom of the Press, 489 U.S. 749 (1989).

53. See, e.g., Red Lion Broadcasting Co. v. FCC, 395 U.S. 367 (1969); Miami Herald Pub. Co. v. Tornillo, 418 U.S. 241 (1974).

54. See Bolger v. Youngs Drug Products Corp., 463 U.S. 60 (1983); Central Hudson Gas & Electric Corp. v. Public Service Commission of New York, 447 U.S. 557, 562–63 (1980); Ohralik v. Ohio State Bar Assn., 436 U.S. 447, 455–56 (1978); Virginia Pharmacy Bd. v. Virginia Citizens Consumer Council, Inc., 425 U.S. 748, 771–72, n. 24 (1976).

55. Janus v. Am. Fed. of State, County, and Mun. Employees, 138 S. Ct. 2448 (2018) (rev'g Abood v. Detroit Bd. of Ed., 431 U.S. 209 (1997)).

56. King v. Burwell, 135 S. Ct. 2480, 2488 (2015) (rejecting Chevron v. Natural Resource Defense Council, 467 U.S. 837, 842–43 (1984), two-stage process of (1) finding ambiguity and (2) deferring to reasonable administrative interpretations).

57. *Id.* at 2489.

58. *Id.* at 2492.

59. *Id.* at 2496.

60. 142 S. Ct. 2587 (2022).

61. Richard J. Pierce Jr., *The Future of Deference*, 84 GEO. WASH. L. REV. 1293 (2016).

62. See, e.g, Panama Refining Co. v. Ryan, 293 U.S. 388, 431–34 (1935) (tying ambiguous presidential authority to explicit findings of fact and substantive due process).

63. Youngstown v. Sawyer, 343 U.S. 579, 637 (1952) (Jackson, J., concurring).

64. KENNETH MAYER, WITH THE STROKE OF A PEN: EXECUTIVE ORDERS AND PRESIDENTIAL POWER (2001).

65. Dartunorro Clark, *ACLU Sues Trump Over His National Emergency for Border Wall*, NBC NEWS, Feb. 19, 2019, www.nbcnews.com/politics/politics-news/aclu-sues-trump-over-his-national-emergency-border-wall-n973306.

66. Sierra Club v. Trump, No. 19-16102 (9th Cir. 2020), https://cdn.ca9.uscourts.gov/datastore/opinions/2020/10/09/19-17501.pdf.

67. *Proclamation on the Termination of Emergency With Respect to the Southern Border of the United States and Redirection of Funds Diverted to Border Wall Construction*, Jan. 20, 2021, https://www.whitehouse.gov/briefing-room/presidential-actions/2021/01/20/proclamation-termination-of-emergency-with-respect-to-southern-border-of-united-states-and-redirection-of-funds-diverted-to-border-wall-construction/.

68. Protecting the Nation from Foreign Terrorist Entry in the United States, 82 FR 8977 (2017), available at https://www.federalregister.gov/documents/2017/02/01/2017-02281/protecting-the-nation-from-foreign-terrorist-entry-into-the-united-states.

69. State of Washington and State of Minnesota v. Trump, 847 F.3d 1151 (9th Cir. 2017).

70. Trump v. Hawaii, 201 L. Ed. 2d 775, 138 S. Ct. 2392 (2018).

71. Bristol-Myers Squibb Co. v. Superior Court, 137 S. Ct. 1773 (2017).

72. See, e.g., Keeton v. Hustler Magazine, Inc., 465 U.S. 770 (1984) (overturning lower court ruling dismissing libel suit filed by resident of New

York against Ohio corporation in New Hampshire court). *See also* New York Times Co. v. Sullivan, 376 U.S. 254 (1964) (in which trial and first appeal were heard in Alabama courts).

73. *Tribal Court Systems*, U.S. Dept. of the Interior Indian Affairs, https://www.bia.gov/CFRCourts/tribal-justice-support-directorate.

74. McGirt v. Oklahoma, 207 L. Ed. 2d 985, 140 S. Ct. 2452 (2020).

75. Oklahoma v. Castro-Huerta, 213 L. Ed. 2d 847, 142 S. Ct. 2486 (2022).

76. Rich Samp & Bauman v. Daimler Chrysler, *High Court May Have Put Brakes on Forum Shopping*, Forbes, Feb. 4, 2014, www.forbes.com/sites/wlf/2014/02/04/with-bauman-v-daimlerchrysler-high-court-may-have-put-brakes-on-forum-shopping.

77. Daimler AG v. Bauman, 571 U.S. 117 (2014).

78. Dashiell Bennett, *Obama: The Internet Is a Utility*, Atlantic, Nov. 10, 2014, www.theatlantic.com/technology/archive/2014/11/obama-internet-utility-fcc-regulation-net-neutrality/382561.

79. Matthew Chivvis, *Reexamining the Yahoo! Litigations: Toward an Effects Test for Determining International Cyberspace Jurisdiction*, 41 U.S.F.L. Rev. 699 (2007).

80. Calder v. Jones, 465 U.S. 783, 789 (1983).

81. *Id.* at 783, 789.

82. Silva Mathema, *Assessing the Economic Impacts of Granting Deferred Action Through DACA and DAPA*, Ctr. for Am. Progress, June 15, 2016, us-legalsolutions.com/wp-content/uploads/2016/06/Assessing-the-Economic-Impacts-of-Granting-Deferred-Action-Through-DACA-and-DAPA-_-Center-for-American-Progress1.pdf.

83. 28 U.S.C. § 1292(a)(1).

84. U.S. Const. art. III, § 1.

85. Brakkton Booker, *What Justice Kentanji Brown Jackson Means for the Country*, Politico, April 7, 2022, https://www.politico.com/news/2022/04/07/ketanji-brown-jackson-supreme-court-impact-00023961.

86. *Rule of Law Talk: Professor Jack Knight on Judicial Selection*, World Justice Project, Sept. 5, 2018, worldjusticeproject.org/about-us/connect/podcast/rule-law-talk-episode-1-judicial-selection.

87. Mark Tushnet, *Opinions: Five Myths About the Roberts Court*, Wash. Post, Oct. 11, 2013, www.washingtonpost.com/opinions/five-myths-about-the-roberts-court/2013/10/11/69924370-30f4-11e3-8627-c5d7de0a046b_story.html.

88. Alicia Parlapiano & Karen Yourish, *Where Neil Gorsuch Would Fit on the Supreme Court*, N.Y. Times, Feb. 1, 2017, www.nytimes.com/interactive/2017/01/31/us/politics/trump-supreme-court-nominee.html?_r=0.

89. David Masci & Gregory A. Smith, *Seven Facts About U.S. Catholics*, Pew Research Center, Oct. 10, 2018, www.pewresearch.org/fact-tank/2018/10/10/7-facts-about-american-catholics/.

90. John G. Roberts Jr., *Statement by Chief Justice John G. Roberts Jr.*, Feb. 13, 2016, www.supremecourt.gov/publicinfo/press/pressreleases/pr_02-13-16. (William O. Douglas, the longest-serving justice, served 36 and a half years.) *See also* Supreme Court of the United States, *Frequently Asked Questions*, Mar.14, 2016, www.supremecourt.gov/about/faq_justices.aspx.

91. Antonin Scalia, *Originalism: The Lesser Evil*, 57 U. Cin. L. Rev. 849, 862–64 (1989).

92. Antonin Scalia & Bryan A. Garner, Reading Law: The Interpretation of Legal Texts (2012).

93. Antonin Scalia, *The Rule of Law as a Law of Rules*, U. Chi. L. Rev. 56 (1989).

94. Alex Kozinski, *My Pizza With Nino*, 12 Cardozo L. Rev. 1583 (1991).

95. Richard Wolf, *About 2,000 Petitions Await Supreme*

Court's Return, USA Today, Sept. 23, 2013, www.usatoday.com/story/news/nation/2013/09/23/supreme-court-petitions-prisoners-clerks/2843401/.

96. Samantha O'Connell, *Supreme Court "Shadow Docket" Under Review by U.S. House of Representatives*, ABA Blog, April 14, 2021, https://www.americanbar.org/groups/committees/death_penalty_representation/publications/project_blog/scotus-shadow-docket-under-review-by-house-reps/.

97. *See, e.g.,* Gregory A. Caldeira & John R. Wright, *The Discuss List: Agenda Building in the Supreme Court*, 24 Law & Society Rev. 807 (1990).

98. Gabe Del Valle, *Most Criminal Cases End in Plea Bargains, Not Trials*, Outline, Aug. 7, 2017, theoutline.com/post/2066/most-criminal-cases-end-in-plea-bargains-not-trials?zd=1&zi=nxl77iqo.

99. Matt Vautour, *Colin Kaepernick, Eric Reid and NFL Reach Confidential Settlement in Collusion Case*, Mass. Live, Feb. 15, 2019, masslive.com/patriots/2019/02/colin-kaepernick-nfl-reach-confidential-settlement-in-collusion-case.html.

100. *Government Survey Shows 97 Percent of Civil Cases Settled*, Phoenix Bus. J., May 27, 2004, www.bizjournals.com/phoenix/stories/2004/05/31/newscolumn5.html?page=all.

101. Fed. R. Civ. P. 56(a).

102. Mourning v. Family Publishing Service, 411 U.S. 356, 382 (1973). *See also* Adickes v. Kress & Co., 398 U.S. 144, 157 (1970); United States v. Diebold, Inc., 369 U.S. 654, 655 (1962).

103. *See* Anderson v. Liberty Lobby, Inc., 477 U.S. 242 (1986).

104. Washington Post Co. v. Keogh, 365 F.2d 965, 968 (D.C. Cir. 1966).

105. Conley v. Gibson, 355 U.S. 41 (1957).

106. 550 U.S. 544 (2007).

107. 556 U.S. 662 (2009).

108. Joseph A. Seiner, *After Iqbal*, 45 Wake Forest L. Rev. 179, 180–81 (2010).

109. *See* New York Times Co. v. Sullivan, 376 U.S. 254 (1964).

110. *See, e.g.,* 44 Liquormart v. Rhode Island, 517 U.S. 484 (1996).

111. See New York Times Co., 376 U.S. 254.

CHAPTER 2

1. Deena Zaru, *Trump Twitter Ban Raises Concerns Over "Unchecked" Power of Big Tech*, ABC News, Jan. 13, 2021, https://abcnews.go.com/US/trump-twitter-ban-raises-concerns-unchecked-power-big/story?id=75150689.

2. Nandita Bose & Jarrett Renshaw, *Exclusive: Big Tech's Democratic Critics Discuss Ways to Strike Back with White House*, Reuters, Feb. 17, 2021, https://www.reuters.com/article/us-usa-tech-white-house-exclusive/exclusive-big-techs-democratic-critics-discuss-ways-to-strike-back-with-white-house-idUSKBN2AH1A4.

3. *See* Cass R. Sunstein, Can it Happen Here? Authoritarianism in America (2018). *See also* Daniel Ziblatt and Steven Levitsky, How Democracies Die (2018).

4. Daniel Kreiss & Shannon McGregor, *The Arbiters of What Our Voters See: Facebook and Google's Struggle with Policy, Process and Enforcement Around Political Advertising*, 36 Political Communication 499 (2019).

5. Palko v. Connecticut, 302 U.S. 319 (1937).

6. Gitlow v. New York, 268 U.S. 652 (1925).

7. *See, e.g.,* Schenck v. United States, 249 U.S. 47 (1919); Brandenburg v. Ohio, 395 U.S. 444 (1969); Miller v. California, 413 U.S. 15 (1973); Nat'l Endowment for the Arts v. Finley, 524 U.S. 569 (1998). Note that even Justice Hugo Black, viewed as nearly a First Amendment absolutist, acknowledged that the authors of the First Amendment accepted some restraints on speech.

8. John Milton, Areopagitica (1st ed. n.p. 1644), *in* Great Books of the Western World 409 (1952).

9. JOHN STUART MILL, ON LIB-ERTY 63-67 (1956).

10. *Id.*

11. 250 U.S. 616, 630 (1919).

12. *See* Eugene Cerruti, *Dancing in the Court-house: The First Amendment Right of Access Opens a New Round*, 29 U. RICH. L. REV. 237 (1994–95); Steven G. Gey, *The First Amendment and the Dissemination of Socially Worthless Untruths*, 36 FLA. ST. U. L. REV. 1 (2008); Steven G. Gey, *Procedural Annihilation of Structural Rights*, 61 HASTINGS L.J. 1 (2009); Helen Norton, *Lies and the Constitution*, 2012 SUP. CT. REV. 161 (2012); Philip M. Napoli, *What If More Speech Is No Longer the Solution: First Amendment Theory Meets Fake News and the Filter Bubble*, 70 FED. COMM. L.J. 55 (2018); Clay Calvert et al., *Fake News and the First Amendment: Reconciling a Disconnect Between Theory and Doc-trine*, 86 U. CINN. L. REV. 99 (2018).

13. Steven G. Gey, *The First Amendment and the Dis-semination of Socially Worthless Untruths*, 36 FLA. ST. U. L. REV. 1 (2008); Toni M. Massaro et al., *SIRI-OUSLY 2.0: What Artificial Intelligence Reveals About the First Amendment*, 101 MINN. L. REV. 2481 (2017). *But see* Bruce E. H. Johnson et al., *Panel 1: Robotic Speech and the First Amendment*, 41 SEATTLE U. L. REV. 1075 (2018), digitalcommons.law.

seattleu.edu/sulr/vol41/iss4/4/ (arguing that whether viewed nega-tively or positively, the First Amendment pro-tection is for listeners, not for speakers).

14. West Virginia State Bd. of Educ. v. Barnette, 319 U.S. 624, 642 (1943).

15. James Madison, *Report on the Virginia Resolution*, January 1800, https://founders.archives.gov/documents/Madison/01-17-02-0202#.

16. *Id.*

17. JEAN-JACQUES ROUSSEAU, THE SOCIAL CONTRACT (1762).

18. ALEXANDER MEIKLEJOHN, FREE SPEECH AND ITS RELA-TION TO SELF-GOVERNMENT 45 (1948).

19. WILLIAM BLACKSTONE, COM-MENTARIES 151-52 (1769).

20. *Id.*

21. FREDERICK S. SIEBERT, FREE-DOM OF THE PRESS IN ENGLAND 1476-1776, 10 (1952); LEONARD LEVY, LEGACY OF SUPPRESSION (1960).

22. *See, e.g.,* Leonard Levy, LEGACY OF SUPPRESSION (1960); Leonard Levy, EMERGENCE OF A FREE PRESS (1985). *But see* ZECHARIAH CHAFEE, FREE SPEECH IN THE UNITED STATES 2 (1941) (arguing the First Amendment was designed to eliminate law of sedition forever).

23. JARED SCHROEDER, THE PRESS CLAUSE AND DIGITAL TECHNOLOGY'S FOURTH WAVE: MEDIA LAW AND THE SYMBIOTIC WEB 11 (2018).

24. *See* JAMES MORTON SMITH, FREEDOM'S FETTERS (1956).

25. *See* New York Times Co. v. Sullivan, 376 U.S. 254 (1964).

26. Vincent Blasi, *The Check-ing Value in First Amend-ment Theory*, 2 AM. B. FOUND. RES. J. 521, 533 (1977).

27. *Id.*

28. C. EDWIN BAKER, HUMAN LIBERTY AND FREEDOM OF SPEECH 47 (1989)

29. *Id.* at 5.

30. Thomas Emerson, *Toward a General Theory of the First Amendment*, 72 YALE L.J. P. 877, 885 (1962-1963).

31. Barbara Pfeffer Billauer, *When Public Health is Eroded by Junk Science: Muzzling Anti-Vaxxer FEAR Speech – and the First Amendment*, March 6, 2020, https://papers.ssrn.com/sol3/papers.cfm?abstract_id=3550670.

32. KIMBERLÉ CRENSHAW ET AL., CRITICAL RACE THEORY: THE KEY WRITINGS THAT FORMED THE MOVEMENT (1995).

33. *Critical Race Theory Fre-quently Asked Questions*, LEGAL DEFENSE FUND (n.d.), https://www.naacpldf.org/critical-race-theory-faq/.

34. *Id.*

35. MARI J. MATSUDA ET AL. WORDS THAT WOUND: CRITI-CAL RACE THEORY, ASSAUL-TIVE SPEECH, AND THE FIRST AMENDMENT 7 (1993).

36. *See* NADINE STROSSEN, HATE: WHY WE SHOULD RESIST IT

with Free Speech, Not Censorship (2018).

37. Matsuda et al., *supra* note 35.

38. *Universal Declaration of Human Rights*, G.A. Res. 217A, U.N. GAOR, 3d Sess., 1st plen. Mtg. U.N. A/810 (December 12, 1948), https://www.un.org/en/about-us/universal-declaration-of-human-rights.

39. Sara Fischer, *U.S. Ranks Third Among G20 Nations in Google Censorship Requests*, Axios, March 5, 2019, www.axios.com/google-government-censorship-requests-1dac73c4-0f94-455d-9245-ea2d36cbd10d.html.

40. *The Global Expression Report*, Article 19, July 2021, https://www.article19.org/gxr-2021/.

41. Bland v. Roberts, 730 F.3d 368, 386 (4th Cir. 2013).

42. *Id.*

43. *See, e.g.*, City of Ladue v. Gilleo, 512 U.S. 43 (1994).

44. Nicholas Rapp & Aric Jenkins, *These 6 Companies Control Much of U.S. Media*, Fortune, July 24, 2018, fortune.com/longform/media-company-ownership-consolidation.

45. *See* Robert W. McChesney, Digital Disconnect: How Capitalism is Turning the Internet Against Democracy (2013).

46. *See* Deen Freelon, Charlton D. McIlwain &

Meredith Clark, *Beyond the Hashtags: #Ferguson, #Blacklivesmatter, and the Online Struggle for Offline Justice*, Center for Media & Social Impact, Feb. 29, 2016, https://cmsimpact.org/resource/beyond-hashtags-ferguson-blacklivesmatter-online-struggle-offline-justice/.

47. *Overview: The State of the News Media 2005, An Annual Report on American Journalism*, Project for Excellence in Journalism, www.journalism.org.

48. Siva Vaidhyanathan, *The New Nightmare Scenario for the Media*, Slate, May 21, 2021, https://slate.com/business/2021/05/att-warnermedia-discovery-hbo-media-concentration-facebook-google.html.

49. *Id.*

50. *Id.*

51. *See* Lovell v. Griffin, 303 U.S. 444, 452 (1938); Burstyn v. Wilson, 343 U.S. 495 (1952).

52. Kovacs v. Cooper, 336 U.S. 77, 97 (1949) (Jackson, J., concurring).

53. Minneapolis Star & Tribune Co. v. Minnesota Comm'r of Revenue, 460 U.S. 575, 585 (1983).

54. *See, e.g.*, Red Lion Broadcasting Co. v. FCC, 395 U.S. 367 (1969).

55. *See, e.g.*, Turner Broadcasting Sys., Inc. v. FCC, 512 U.S. 622 (1994); Turner Broadcasting Sys., Inc. v. FCC, 520 U.S. 180 (1997).

56. 137 S.Ct. 1730, 1737 (2017).

57. *Id.*

58. *See* Haleigh Jones, *Public Officials' Facebook "Likes": The Case for Leaving Regulation of Official "Likes" to the Torches and Pitchforks of Constituents*, 18 SMU Sci. & Tech. L. Rev. 263 (2015); Jonathan Peters, *WikiLeaks, the First Amendment, and the Press*, Harv. L. & Pol'y Rev., Apr. 18, 2011, hlpronline.com; Bland v. Roberts, 857 F. Supp. 2d 599 (E.D. Va. 2012).

59. *See, e.g.*, Angela Rulffes, *The First Amendment in Times of Crisis: An Analysis of Free Press Issues in Ferguson, Missouri*, 68 Syracuse L. Rev. 607 (2018); Katlyn E. DeBoer, *Clash of the First and Second Amendments: Proposed Regulation of Armed Protests*, 45 Hastings Const. L.Q. 333 (2017–18).

60. 315 U.S. 568, 571–72 (1942).

61. *See, e.g.*, United States v. Williams, 553 U.S. 285 (2008).

62. 573 U.S. 228 (2014).

63. *Id.* at 228, 224 (quoting Garcetti v. Ceballos, 547 U.S. 410, 421 (2006)).

64. United States v. Alvarez, 567 U.S. 709 (2012).

65. 18 U.S.C. § 704(b).

66. United States v. Swisher, 771 F.3d 514 (9th Cir. 2014).

67. Susan B. Anthony List v. Driehaus, 814 F.3d 466, 472 (6th Cir. 2016).

68. West Virginia State Bd. of Educ. v. Barnette, 319 U.S. 624, 642 (1943).

69. 283 U.S. 697 (1931).

70. *Id.*

71. *Id.*

72. *Id.* at 708, 720.

73. *Id.* at 716.

74. 403 U.S. 713 (1971).

75. Janie Lorber, *Early Word: WikiLeaked*, N.Y. TIMES, July 30, 2010, thecaucus.blogs.nytimes.com.

76. Adam Kirsch, *Why Wikileaks Still Needs "The New York Times*," NEW REPUBLIC, July 25, 2010, newrepublic.com/article/76562/why-wikileaks-still-needs-the-new-york-times.

77. WIKILEAKS, wikileaks.org.

78. 403 U.S. at 731.

79. *Id.* at 714.

80. Nebraska Press Ass'n v. Stuart, 427 U.S. 539, 559 (1976).

81. New York Times Co. v. Jascalevich, 439 U.S. 1317 (1978); Nebraska Press Ass'n v. Stuart, 427 U.S. 539 (1976).

82. *See National Writers Union, Who Will Rid Me of This Troublesome Reporter?*, TRENTONIAN, Feb. 20, 2019, www.trentonian.com/news/local/national-writers-union-who-will-rid-me-of-this-troublesome/article_5e810062-3534-11e9-a c48-03a151496542.html ; Kathryn Foxhall, *When Censorship Becomes a Cultural Norm*, EDITOR & PUBLISHER, May 16, 2014, www.editorandpublisher.com/feature/when-censorship-becomes-a-cultural-norm2014-05-15t11-11-19.

83. CBS v. Davis, 510 U.S. 1315 (1994) (Blackmun, J., Circuit Justice).

84. Miami Herald Publ'g Co. v. McIntosh, 340 So. 2d 904, 910 (Fla. 1977).

85. Charlie Savage, *Judge Rejects Trump Request for Order Blocking Bolton's Memoir*, N.Y. TIMES, June 20, 2020, https://www.nytimes.com/2020/06/20/us/politics/john-bolton-book-ruling.html.

86. U.S. v. Bolton, Case No. 1:20-cv-01580 (D.D.C. 2020) (Mem. at 9), https://pacer-documents.s3.amazonaws.com/36/219024/04517891261.pdf.

87. *Id.* (Stipulation of Dismissal), https://int.nyt.com/data/documenttools/justice-department-dismissal-of-john-bolton-lawsuit/5598d063bf52c996/full.pdf.

88. Nebraska Press Ass'n v. Stuart, 427 U.S. 539, 559 (1976).

89. CBS v. Davis, 510 U.S. 1315, 1320 (1994).

90. Jack Balkin, *Old-School New-School Speech Regulation*, 127 HARV. L. REV. 2296, 2299 (2014).

91. *See* Machovec et al., *Palm Beach County*, *Order Denying Plaintiffs' Verified Emergency Motion for Temporary Injunction*, Case No. 2020CA006920AXX, July 27, 2020, https://www.documentcloud.org/documents/7007471-Circuit-Judge-John-Kastrenakes-denies-Palm-Beach ; Minnesota Voters Alliance v. Walz, Case No. 20-CV-1688 (PJS/ECW) (D. Minn. Oct. 2, 2020), https://storage.courtlistener.com/recap/gov.uscourts.mnd.189156/gov.uscourts.mnd.189156.51.0.pdf.

92. Daniel R. Karon & Gillian E. Karon, *To Mask Or Not To Mask? It's Not a Constitutional Question*, CLS BLUE AND SKY BLOG, October 29, 2020, https://clsbluesky.law.columbia.edu/2020/10/29/to-mask-or-not-to-mask-its-not-a-constitutional-question/.

93. Jacobson v. Massachusetts, 197 U.S. 11, 26 (1905).

94. Machovec et al., *supra* note 91, at 11.

95. Minnesota Voters Alliance, *supra* note 91, at 31.

96. U.S. Const. art. I, § 8 (giving Congress authority "to regulate Commerce with foreign nations, and among the several states, and with the Indian Tribes").

97. Texas v. Johnson, 491 U.S. 397 (1989).

98. 502 U.S. 105 (1991).

99. *Id.*

100. Grayned v. City of Rockford, 408 U.S. 104 (1972).

101. United States v. O'Brien, 391 U.S. 367 (1968).

102. *Id.*

103. Ward v. Rock Against Racism, 491 U.S. 781 (1989). *See also* Matthew D. Bunker & Emily Erickson, *The Jurisprudence of Precision: Contrast Space and Narrow Tailoring in First Amendment Doctrine*, 6 COMM. L. & POL'Y 259 (2001).

104. Forsyth County v. The Nationalist Movement, 505 U.S. 123 (1992).

105. Ward v. Rock Against Racism, 491 U.S. 781 (1989).

106. 530 U.S. 703 (2000).

107. 573 U.S. 464 (2014).

108. Brown v. Town of Cary, 706 F.3d 294 (4th Cir. 2013).

109. 135 S. Ct. 2218 (2015).

110. *Id.* at 2227.

111. *Id.*

112. United States v. O'Brien, 391 U.S. 367 (1968).

113. *Id.*

114. Genevieve Lakier, *Reed v. Town of Gilbert, Arizona, and the Rise of the Anticlassificatory First Amendment*, 1 SUP. CT. REV. 2016, www.journals.uchicago.edu/doi/full/10.1086/691625. *See also* Adam Liptak, *Court's Free-Speech Expansion Has Far-Reaching Consequences*, N.Y. TIMES, Aug. 17, 2015, www.nytimes.com/2015/08/18/us/politics/courts-free-speech-expansion-has-far-reaching-consequences.html.

115. *See* Free Speech Coalition, Inc. v. Attorney Gen. United States, 825 F.3d 149 (3rd Cir. 2016); Sarver v. Chartier, 813 F.3d 891, 905–06 (9th Cir. 2016); Central Radio Co. v. City of Norfolk, 811 F.3d 625, 631 (4th Cir. 2016); Norton v. City of Springfield, Ill., 806 F.3d 411 (7th Cir. 2015).

116. Norton v. City of Springfield, Ill., 806 F.3d 411 (7th Cir. 2015).

117. https://www.tandfonline.com/doi/abs/10.1080/10811680.2019.1586406.

118. 596 U.S. _____ (2022).

119. *Id.* at 8.

120. 135 S. Ct. 2218 (2015).

121. Virginia v. Black, 538 U.S. 343, 365 (2003).

122. Meyer v. Grant, 486 U.S. 414 (1988).

123. *See, e.g.,* Buckley v. Valeo, 424 U.S. 1 (1976).

124. Minnesota Voters Alliance v. Mansky, 138 S. Ct. 1876, 1885–92 (2018).

125. *Id.* at 1891. *See also* Michael R. Dimino, *Minnesota Voters Alliance v. Mansky Strikes Down a Vague Ban on Speech in Polling Places, But Future Bans May Be Upheld*, 19 FED. SOCIETY REV. 2018 (9 Widener L. Commonwealth Res. Paper No. 18–16), poseidon01.ssrn.com.

126. Susan B. Anthony List v. Driehaus, 779 F.3d 628 (6th Cir. 2015).

127. Susan B. Anthony List v. Driehaus, 525 Fed. App'x 415 (6th Cir. 2013); rev'd, 573 U.S. 616 (2014).

128. Susan B. Anthony List v. Driehaus, 814 F.3d 466 (6th Cir. 2016).

129. David Ardia, Evan Ringel & Allysan Scatterday, *State Regulation of Election-Related Speech in the U.S.: An Overview and Comparative Analysis*, Aug. 9, 2021, https://papers.ssrn.com/sol3/papers.cfm?abstract_id=3899542.

130. Nelson v. McClatchy, 936 P.2d 1123 (Wash. 1997).

131. *See, e.g.,* Perry v. Sindermann, 408 U.S. 593 (1972). For discussion of parallel treatment of public school students, see Chapter 3 and Tinker v. Des Moines Independent Community School Dist., 393 U.S. 503 (1969).

132. *See, e.g.,* Pickering v. Bd. of Educ., 391 U.S. 563 (1968); Snepp v. United States, 444 U.S. 507 (1980); Toni M. Massaro, *Significant Silences: Freedom of Speech in the Public Sector Workplace*, 61 S. CAL. L. REV. 1 (1987). *But see* DANIEL N. HOFFMAN, GOVERNMENTAL SECRECY AND THE FOUNDING FATHERS: A STUDY IN CONSTITUTIONAL CONTROLS (1981); Kermit L. Hall, *The Virulence of the National Appetite for Bogus Revelation*, 56 MD. L. REV. 1 (1997).

133. Agency for Int'l Dev. v. Alliance for Open Society Int'l, Inc., 570 U.S. 205 (2013).

134. *Id.*

135. *Id.*

136. 547 U.S. 410 (2006).

137. *Id.* at 422.

138. Heffernan v. City of Paterson, 136 S. Ct. 1412 (2016).

139. Borough of Duryea v. Guarnieri, 131 S.Ct. 2488 (2011).

140. *Id.*

141. Harris v. Quinn, 573 U.S. 616 (2014).

142. Friedrichs v. California Teachers Ass'n, 135 S. Ct. 2993 (2016).

143. Matal v. Tam, 137 S. Ct. 1744, 1758 (2017).

144. Wandering Dago v. Destito, 879 F.3d 20 (2d Cir. 2018). *See* Matal v. Tam, 137 S. Ct. 1744 (2017).

145. Eric Sundin, *Note: To Alito, or Not to Alito: An Analysis of Government Speech in a Post-Walker World*, 8 HOUSTON L. REV. 31, 42 (2017).

146. Matal v. Tam, 137 S. Ct. 1744, 1760 (2017) (characterizing Walker v. Texas Div., Sons of Confed. Veterans, 135 S. Ct. 2239 (2015)).

147. *Walker*, 135 S. Ct. at 2245.

148. Pleasant Grove City v. Summum, 555 U.S. 460 (2009).

149. *Id.*

150. *Id.* at 481.

151. *Walker*, 135 S. Ct. at 2255 (Alito, J., dissenting).

152. Manhattan Cmty. Access Corp. v. Halleck, 2019 U.S. LEXIS 4178 (2019).

153. 882 F.3d 300, 304 (2d Cir. 2018).

154. *Id.*

155. *Halleck*, 2019 U.S. LEXIS 4178.

156. *Id.* at *5.

157. *Id.*

158. *Id.* at *18.

159. *Id.* at *19.

160. *Id.* at *40, *39.

161. *Id.* at *46.

162. Charles Fain Lehman, *SCOTUS: Private Firms Not Bound by First Amendment*, WASHINGTON FREE BEACON, June 17, 2019, freebeacon.com/issues/scotus-private-firms-not-bound-by-first-amendment/.

163. Elliot Mincbert, *Kavanaugh and Gorsuch Cast Deciding Votes to Allow Public Access Cable TV Censorship, Confirmed Judges, Confirmed Fears*, June 17, 2019, www.pfaw.org/blog-posts/confirmed-judges-confirmed-fears-kavanaugh-and-gorsuch-cast-deciding-votes-to-allow-public-access-cable-tv-censorship/.

164. Tony Mauro, *SCOTUS Ruling Could Let Tech Platforms Avoid First Amendment Constraints*, NAT'L L. J., June 17, 2019, www.law.com/nationallawjournal/2019/06/17/scotus-ruling-could-let-tech-platforms-avoid-first-amendment-constraints/.

165. Wooley v. Maynard, 430 U.S. 705, 714 (1977).

166. David Hudson, *Compelled Speech*, THE FIRST AMENDMENT ENCYCLOPEDIA, https://www.mtsu.edu/first-amendment/article/933/compelled-speech.

167. West Virginia State Bd. of Educ. v. Barnette, 319 U.S. 624 (1943).

168. Ambach v. Norwick, 441 U.S. 68 (1979).

169. *See, e.g.,* Epperson v. Arkansas, 393 U.S. 97 (1968); Edwards v. Aguillard, 482 U.S. 578 (1987); Pickering v. Bd. of Educ., 391 U.S. 563 (1968).

170. West Virginia State Bd. of Educ. v. Barnette, 319 U.S. 624, 642 (1943).

171. Wooley v. Maynard, 430 U.S. 705, 714 (1977).

172. Nat'l Instit. of Family & Life Advocates v. Becerra, 138 S. Ct. 2361 (2018).

173. 138 S. Ct. 1719 (2018).

174. *See* Scott W. Gaylord, *Is a Cake Worth a Thousand Words? Masterpiece Cakeshop and the Impact of Antidiscrimination Laws on the Marketplace of Ideas*, 85 TENN. L. REV. 361 (2018); John G. Culhane, *The Right to Say, But Not to Do: Balancing First Amendment Freedom of Expression With the Anti-Discrimination Imperative*, 24 WIDENER L. REV. 235 (2018).

175. 558 U.S. 310 (2010).

176. *See, e.g.,* Am. Tradition Partnership v. Bullock, 132 S. Ct. 2490 (2012) (per curiam); Texans for Free Enter. v. Tex. Ethics Comm'n, 732 F.3d 535 (5th Cir. 2013); Wis. Right to Life v. Barland, 751 F.3d 804 (7th Cir. 2014); c.f. Bluman v. FEC, 132 S. Ct. 1087 (2012) (summary judgment upholding ban on foreign political contributions); Republican Party v. King, 741 F.3d 1089 (10th Cir. 2013).

177. McCutcheon v. FEC, 572 U.S. 185 (2014).

178. *Id.* at 224.

179. 558 U.S. 310 (2010).

180. Zachary Albert, *Trends in Campaign Financing, 1980–2016, Campaign Finance Task Force*, October 12, 2017, bipartisanpolicy.org/wp-content/ uploads/2018/01/ Trends-in-Campaign-Financing-1980-2016.-Zachary-Albert.pdf.

181. *Statistical Summary of 24-Month Campaign Activity of the 2019-2020 Election Cycle*, April 2, 2021, Federal Election Commission, https://www.fec.gov /updates/statistical-summary-24-month-campaign-activity-2019-2020-election-cycle/.

182. Nour Abdul-Razzak et al., *After Citizens United: How Outside Spending Shapes American Democracy*, April 17, 2018, papers.ssrn.com/sol3/ papers.cfm?abstract_ id=2823778.

183. *See* Lawrence Lessig, Republic Lost: How Money Corrupts Congress – and a Plan to Stop It (2012).

184. Citizens United v. Gessler, 773 F.3d 200 (10th Cir. 2014).

185. *Id.*

186. Ysursa v. Pocatello Educ. Ass'n, 555 U.S. 353 (2009).

187. McIntyre v. Ohio Election Comm'n, 514 U.S. 334, 357 (1995).

188. *Id.* at 342.

189. *See* Talley v. California, 362 U.S. 60 (1960); Buckley v. Am. Const. L. F., 525 U.S. 182 (1999); Watchtower v. Stratton, 536 U.S. 150 (2002).

190. Doe v. Reed, 561 U.S. 186 (2010).

191. Doe v. Reed, 823 F. Supp. 2d 1195 (W.D. Wash. 2011).

192. *In re* Grand Jury Subpoena, 875 F.3d 1179 (9th Cir. 2017).

193. 18 U.S.C. § 2703. *But see* 47 U.S.C. § 551(c) (potentially establishing a higher standard for forced disclosure of identifying information on cable subscribers).

194. Branzburg v. Hayes, 408 U.S. 665 (1972).

195. *In re* Grand Jury Subpoena Issued to Twitter, Inc., 2017 WL 9485553 (N.D. Tex. Nov. 7, 2017); *see also* Music Grp. Macao Commercial Offshore, Ltd. v. Does, 82 F. Supp. 3d 979, 983 (N.D. Cal. 2015) (denying motion to compel Twitter to disclose anonymous website posters).

196. Matt Binder, *U.S. Government Requests for Google User Data Up 510% Since 2010, Report Says*, Mashable, June 16, 2020, https ://mashable.com/article /google-facebook-gover nment-user-data-study.

197. Ben Lovejoy, *Secure Chat App Could Prove Key to Unmasking Charlottesville White Supremacists*, 9To5Mac, August 8, 2018, 9to5mac. com/2018/08/08/ discord-app-charlottes-ville.

198. Sines v. Kessler, 2018 WL 3730434 (N.D. Cal. Aug. 6, 2018).

199. Hague v. Comm. for Industrial Org., 307 U.S. 496, 515 (1939).

200. *See, e.g.,* Susan Dente Ross, *An Apologia to Radical Dissent and a Supreme Court Test to Protect It*, 7 Comm. L. & Pol'y 401 (2002); Ronald J. Krotoszynski Jr., *Essay: Celebrating Selma: The Importance of Context in Public Forum Analysis*, 104 Yale L.J. 1411 (1995).

201. *See, e.g.,* Skokie v. Nat'l Socialist Party of America, 439 U.S. 916 (1978); Hess v. Indiana, 414 U.S. 105 (1973); Brown v. Louisiana, 383 U.S. 131 (1966); Edwards v. South Carolina, 371 U.S. 229 (1963); NAACP v. Claiborne Hardware Co., 458 U.S. 886 (1982); Gregory v. City of Chicago, 394 U.S. 111 (1969); Grayned

v. Rockford, 408 U.S. 104 (1972).

202. 562 U.S. 443 (2011).

203. Grayned v. Rockford, 408 U.S. 104, 116 (1972); Perry Educ. Ass'n v. Perry Local Educators' Ass'n, 460 U.S. 37 (1983).

204. *See, e.g.,* Hague v. Comm. for Industrial Org., 307 U.S. 496 (1939).

205. Speet v. Schuette, 726 F.3d 867, 879 (2013).

206. Coe v. Town of Blooming Grove, 429 F. App'x 55 (2d Cir. 2011).

207. Bell v. Keating, 697 F.3d 445 (7th Cir. 2012).

208. *See, e.g.,* Frisby v. Schultz, 487 U.S. 474 (1988); Madsen v. Women's Health Center, Inc., 512 U.S. 753 (1994). *But see* Scheidler v. Nat'l Org. for Women, 537 U.S. 393 (2003) (removing civil injunction on anti-abortion protesters and rejecting claim that their protests constituted illegal extortion and racketeering).

209. *See, e.g.,* Greer v. Spock, 424 U.S. 828 (1976).

210. *See, e.g.,* Smith v. Exec. Dir. of the Indiana War Memorials Comm'n, 742 F.3d 282 (7th Cir. 2014); Miller v. City of Cincinnati, 622 F.3d 524 (6th Cir. 2010), *cert. denied,* 536 U.S. 974 (2011).

211. Zeran v. America Online, 129 F.3d 327, 330 (4th Cir. 1997).

212. Packingham v. North Carolina, 137 S. Ct. 1730 (2017).

213. *Id.* at 1732.

214. Davison v. Randall, 912 F.3d 666 (4th Cir. 2019).

215. Knight First Amend. Institute v. Trump, 928 F.3d 226 (2d Cir. 2019).

216. *Id.* at 237.

217. Biden v. Knight First Amend. Institute, 141 S.Ct. 1220 (Mem) (2021).

218. Special Regulations, Areas of the National Park System, National Capital Region, Special Events and Demonstrations, 83 Fed. Reg. 40, 460 (proposed Aug. 15, 2018) (to be codified at 36 C.F.R. 7). *See* Olivia Paschal, *The Backlash to New Rules on Protests in D.C.,* ATLANTIC, October 13, 2018, www.theatlantic.com/politics/archive/2018/10/new-rules-could-curb-protests-dc/572944.

219. Kriston Capps, *White House to Protesters: "Get Off My Lawn?"* CITYLAB, October 16, 2018, www.citylab.com/design/2018/10/white-house-to-protesters-get-off-my-lawn/573040.

220. Black Lives Matter v. Trump, 2021 WL 2530722 (2021).

221. *See, e.g.,* United States v. Albertini, 472 U.S. 675 (1985); Los Angeles City Council v. Taxpayers for Vincent, 466 U.S. 789 (1984); United States v. Kokinda, 497 U.S. 720 (1990).

222. *See, e.g.,* Adderley v. Florida, 385 U.S. 39 (1966).

223. *See, e.g.,* Amalgamated Food Employees Union v. Logan Valley Plaza, Inc., 391 U.S. 308 (1968); Hudgens v. Nat'l Labor Relations Bd., 424 U.S. 507 (1976); PruneYard Shopping Center v. Robins, 447 U.S. 74 (1980). *But see* Lloyd Corp., Ltd. v. Tanner, 407 U.S. 551 (1972).

224. Thornhill v. Alabama, 310 U.S. 88, 101–02 (1940) (emphasis added).

225. *See, e.g.,* Madsen v. Women's Health Ctr., 512 U.S. 753 (1994); United States v. Kokinda, 497 U.S. 720 (1990); Frisby v. Schultz, 487 U.S. 474 (1988); United States v. Grace, 461 U.S. 171 (1983); Cox v. Louisiana, 379 U.S. 536 (1965); Schneider v. New Jersey, 308 U.S. 147 (1939).

226. *See, e.g.,* Bd. of Regents of the Univ. of Wis. v. Southworth, 529 U.S. 217 (2000); Rosenberger v. Rector & Visitors of the Univ. of Virginia, 515 U.S. 819 (1995).

227. *See, e.g.,* Grosjean v. Am. Press Co., 297 U.S. 233 (1936); Minneapolis Star & Tribune Co. v. Minnesota Comm'r of Revenue, 460 U.S. 575 (1983); Arkansas Writers' Project v. Ragland, 481 U.S. 221 (1987). *But see* Leathers v. Medlock, 499 U.S. 439 (1991).

228. Legal Services Corp. v. Velasquez, 532 U.S. 533 (2001).

229. NEA v. Finley, 524 U.S. 569 (1998).

230. Island Trees Union Free School Dist. Bd. of Ed. v. Pico, 457 U.S. 853 (1982).

231. Brandon T. Metroka, *The Roberts Court Constitution of Freedom of Speech: Preferences, Principles, and the Study of Supreme Court Decision-Making*, Surface 268 no. 1 (2017) (Ph.D. dissertation, Syracuse University), surface.syr. edu/cgi/viewcontent. cgi?referer=https://scholar.google.com/scholar ?hl=en&as_sdt=0%2C4 8&as_ylo=2015&q=SCO TUS+%22freedom+of+a ssociation%22+underde veloped&btnG=&httpsre dir=1&article=1695&con text=etd.

232. Margaret M. Russell (ed.), Freedom of Assembly and Petition 21 (2010). *See also* Tabatha Abu El-Haj, *The Neglected Right of Assembly*, 56 UCLA L. Rev. 543 (2009).

233. *See, e.g.*, Boy Scouts of America v. Dale, 530 U.S. 640 (2000).

234. Hurley v. Irish-American Gay, Lesbian and Bisexual Group of Boston, 515 U.S. 557, 575 (1995).

235. Brian MacQuarrie & Laura Krantz, *Strife Forgotten Amid Inclusive St. Patrick's Day Parade*, Boston Globe, Mar. 18, 2015, www.bostonglobe.com/ metro/2015/03/15/prepa rations-under-way-for-t his-afternoon-patrick-d ay-parade/XBloZY1z2vTe 9SZnev8qyN/story.html.

236. *Gerrymander*, Legal Information Institute (Cornell Law School), https://ww w.law.cornell.edu/wex/g errymander.

237. Abbott v. Perez, 138 S. Ct. 1916 (2018); Gill v. Whitford, 138 S. Ct. 2305 (2018).

238. Abigail Aguilera, *Drawing the Line: Whitford v. Gill and the Search for Manageable Partisan Gerrymandering Standards*, 86 U. Cinn. L. Rev. 775 (2018).

239. Gill v. Whitford, 138 S. Ct. at 1934 (Kagan, J., dissenting).

240. *Id.* at 1939.

241. 139 S.Ct. 2484, 2505 (2019).

CHAPTER 3

1. Chaplinsky v. New Hampshire, 315 U.S. 568, 572 (1942).

2. *Schenck*, 249 U.S. 47, 52 (1919).

3. *Id.*

4. *Id.*

5. Frohwerk v. United States, 249 U.S. 204 (1919).

6. *Id.* at 208–09.

7. Debs v. United States, 249 U.S. 211 (1919).

8. Abrams v. United States, 250 U.S. 616 (1919).

9. *Id.* at 628 (Holmes, J., dissenting).

10. *Id.* at 630.

11. Dennis v. United States, 341 U.S. 494 (1951); Scales v. United States, 367 U.S. 203 (1961). *See also* Whitney v. California, 274 U.S. 357 (1927).

12. Gitlow v. New York, 268 U.S. 652 (1925).

13. *Id.* at 669.

14. *Id.* at 667.

15. *Id.* at 673 (Holmes, J., dissenting).

16. *Id.* at 666.

17. Whitney v. California, 274 U.S. 357 (1927).

18. *Id.* at 377–78 (Brandeis, J., concurring).

19. *Id.* at 379 (emphasis added).

20. Am. Commc'n Ass'n v. Douds, 339 U.S. 382 (1950).

21. *Id.* at 448–49 (Black, J., dissenting).

22. Dennis v. United States, 341 U.S. 494 (1951); Kunz v. New York, 340 U.S. 290, 300 (1951); Yates v. United States, 354 U.S. 298 (1957).

23. *See* Liezl Irene Pangilinan, *When a Nation Is at War: A Context-Dependent Theory of Free Speech for the Regulation of Weapon Recipes*, 22 Cardozo Arts & Ent. L.J. 683 (2004).

24. 395 U.S. 444 (1969).

25. *Id.* at 447.

26. *Id.* at 448.

27. *Id.* at 444.

28. Richard A. Wilson & Jordan Kiper, *Brandenburg in an Era of Populism: Risk Analysis in the First Amendment*, 5 U. OF PA. J.L. & PUB. AFF. 57, 80 (2020).

29. 414 U.S. 105 (1973) (per curiam).

30. Bell Atl. Corp. v. Twombly, 550 U.S. 544 (2007); Ashcroft v. Iqbal, 556 U.S. 662 (2009).

31. Brandenburg v. Ohio, 395 U.S. 444, 447 (1969).

32. *Bell Atl. Corp.*, 550 U.S. at 544; *Ashcroft*, 556 U.S. at 662.

33. Nwanguma v. Trump, 903 F.3d 604 (6th Cir. 2018), *rehearing en banc denied*, 2018 U.S. App. LEXIS 33603 (6th Cir., Nov. 29, 2018).

34. *Bell Atl. Corp.*, 550 U.S. at 555.

35. *Ashcroft*, 556 U.S. at 678.

36. Impeaching Donald John Trump, President of the United States, for high crimes and misdemeanors, H.R. 24, 117th Cong. (2021–2022).

37. Virginia v. Black, 538 U.S. 343 (2003).

38. *Id.* at 394.

39. *See* Watts v. United States, 394 U.S. 705 (1969).

40. Elonis v. United States, 135 S. Ct. 2001 (2015).

41. Two representative posts read: "There's one way to love you/but a thousand ways to kill you./I'm not going to rest/until your body is a mess,/soaked in blood and dying from all the little cuts." And: "That's it, I've had about enough/I'm checking out and making a name for myself/Enough elementary schools in a ten mile radius to initiate the most heinous school shooting ever imagined/And hell hath no fury like a crazy man in a Kindergarten class/The only question is . . . which one?"

42. United States v. Elonis, 730 F.3d 321 (3d Cir. 2013).

43. *Elonis*, 135 S. Ct. 2001.

44. *Id.* at 2012.

45. *Id.* at 2009.

46. United States v. Elonis, 841 F.3d 589 (3rd Cir. 2016).

47. 538 U.S. 343 (2003).

48. United States v. Elonis, 841 F.3d 589 (3d Cir. 2016), *cert. denied*, 138 S. Ct. 67 (2017).

49. *See* United States v. Wheeler, 776 F.3d 736 (10th Cir. 2015).

50. *See* United States v. Magleby, 241 F.3d 1306 (10th Cir. 2001).

51. Eric P. Robinson & Morgan B. Hill, *The Trouble with "True Threats,"* 8 U. BALT. J. MEDIA L. & ETHICS 37 (2020).

52. State v. Boettger, 450 P.3d 818 (Kan. 2019).

53. *Id.*

54. Kansas v. Boettger, 140 S. Ct. 1956 (2020).

55. Commonwealth v. Knox, 190 A.3d 1146 (Pa. 2018).

56. Veronica Stracqualursi, *Killer Mike, Chance the Rapper, Meek Mill to Supreme Court: Pittsburgh Rapper's Lyrics Are Not "a True Threat of Violence,"* CNNPOLITICS, March 7, 2019, *available at* www.cnn.com/2019/03/07/politics/supreme-court-first-amendment-rappers/index.html.

57. Pennsylvania v. Knox, 190 A.3d 1146 (Pa. 2018), *petition for cert. filed*, No. 18-949 (U.S. Jan. 18, 2019), *cert. denied*, Knox v. Pennsylvania, 203 L. Ed. 2d 746 (2019).

58. *People ex rel. R.D.*, 2020 CO 44, 464 P.3d 717.

59. *Id.*

60. *See* Alice E. Warwick & Ross Miller, *Online Harassment, Defamation, and Hateful Speech: A Primer of the Legal Landscape,* FORDHAM CENTER ON LAW AND INFORMATION POLICY REPORT, June 10, 2014, *available at* https://www.fordham.edu/info/23830/research/5915/a_primer_of_the_legal_landscape; *see also* Viktorya Vilk, *You're Not Powerless in the Face of Online Harassment*, HARV. BUS. REV., June 3, 2020, *available at* https://hbr.org/2020/06/youre-not-powerless-in-the-face-of-online-harassment.

61. *Online Harassment and Cyberstalking*, PRIVACY RIGHTS CLEARINGHOUSE, https://privacyrights.org/consumer-guides/online

-harassment-cyberstalking (last visited Feb. 16, 2022).

62. *See* State v. Calvert, No. 15-0195, 2016 WL 3179968, at *2 (W. Va. June 3, 2016); *see also* Welfare of A. J. B., 929 N.W.2d 840, 844 (Minn. 2019).

63. Eugene Volokh, *One-to-One Speech vs. One-to-Many Speech, Criminal Harassment Laws, and Cyberstalking*, 107 Nw. U. L. Rev. 731, (2013).

64. *Id.*

65. Sameer Hinduja & Justin W. Patchin, *State Cyberbullying Laws: A Brief Review of State Cyberbullying Laws and Policies*, Cyberbullying Research Center, 2018, https://cyberbullying.org/Bullying-and-Cyberbullying-Laws.pdf.

66. *See Online Harassment Field Manual*, Pen America, https://onlineharassmentfieldmanual.pen.org/. (last visited Dec. 28, 2020).

67. Chaplinsky v. New Hampshire, 315 U.S. 568 (1942).

68. *Id.* at 571–72.

69. Terminiello v. Chicago, 337 U.S. 1, 3 (1949).

70. *Id.* at 4 (emphasis added).

71. *Id.*

72. *Id.*

73. *See, e.g.,* Gooding v. Wilson, 405 U.S. 518 (1972).

74. Wood v. Eubanks, No. 20-3599, 2022 U.S. App.

LEXIS 3427 (6th Cir. Feb. 8, 2022).

75. *Id.*

76. Barnes v. Wright, 449 F.3d 709, 718 (6th Cir. 2006) (quoting Greene v. Barber, 310 F.3d 889, 896 (6th Cir. 2002)).

77. D.D. v. Scheeler, 645 F. App'x 418, 425 (6th Cir. 2016).

78. United States v. Bartow, 997 F.3d 203 (4th Cir. 2021).

79. State v. Liebenguth, No. 20145, 336 Conn. 685, 250 A.3d 1, 2020 Conn. LEXIS 194, 2020 WL 5094669 (Conn. Aug. 27, 2020).

80. *Id.* at 2-9.

81. *Id.* at 8-9.

82. Greene v. Barber, 310 F.3d 889, 896 (6th Cir. 2002) (quoting Sandul v. Larion, 119 F.3d 1250, 1255 (6th Cir. 1997)).

83. Nadine Strossen, *The Interdependence of Racial Justice and Free Speech of Racists*, 1 J. of Free Speech L. 51 (2020).

84. Commonwealth v. Love, No. 3529 EDA 2014, 2015 Pa. Super. Unpub. LEXIS 4348 (Nov. 23, 2015).

85. R.A.V. v. City of St. Paul, 505 U.S. 377 (1992).

86. *Id.* at 384–85, 386.

87. *Walker v. Tex. Div., Sons of Confederate Veterans, Inc.*, 576 U.S. 200, 135 S. Ct. 2239 (2015).

88. Transparency Report, Facebook, https://transparency.fb.com/data/com

munity-standards-enforcement/hate-speech/facebook/ (last visited Feb. 27, 2022).

89. Bobbu Allyn, *Here Are 4 Key Points From the Facebook Whistleblower's Testimony on Capitol Hill*, NPR, Oct. 5, 2021, *available at* https://www.npr.org/2021/10/05/1043377310/facebook-whistleblower-frances-haugen-congress.

90. Strafgesetzbuch [StGB] [Network Enforcement Act], Nov. 19, 1998, BGBl. I at 3322, last amended by Gasetz [G], June 19, 2019, BGBl. I at 844, art. 2.

91. Natasha Lomas, *Germany Tightens Online Hate Speech Rules to Make Platforms Send Reports Straight to the Feds*, TechCrunch, June 19, 2020, *available at* https://techcrunch.com/2020/06/19/germany-tightens-online-hate-speech-rules-to-make-platforms-send-reports-straight-to-the-feds/.

92. Hadas Gold, *French Parliament Passes Law Requiring Social Media Companies Delete Certain Content Within an Hour*, CNN, May 14, 2020, *available at* https://www.cnn.com/2020/05/13/tech/french-hate-speech-social-media-law/index.html.

93. Robert Gorwa, Dia Kayyali, & Sonja Solomun, *Two Years After Christchurch Call What's Changed?* Center for International Governance

INNOVATION, May 7, 2021, *available at* https://www.cigionline.org/articles/two-years-after-adoption-christchurch-call-what-has-changed/.

94. Anna Pingen, *Commission: 6th Evaluation of Code of Conduct on Countering Illegal Hate Speech Online*, EUROPEAN CRIMINAL LAW ASSOCIATION FORUM, Nov. 17, 2021, *available at* https://eucrim.eu/news/commission-6th-evaluation-of-code-of-conduct-on-countering-illegal-hate-speech-online/.

95. Cohen v. California, 403 U.S. 15 (1971).

96. *Id.* at 25.

97. United States v. O'Brien, 391 U.S. 367, 376 (1968).

98. Tinker v. Des Moines Indep. Cmty. Sch. Dist., 393 U.S. 503, 505 (1969).

99. *O'Brien*, 391 U.S. at 367.

100. Texas v. Johnson, 491 U.S. 397 (1989). The Supreme Court has said symbolic speech exists and warrants First Amendment protection when (1) speech and action combine, (2) there is an intent to convey a message and (3) witnesses are likely to understand that message.

101. *Id.* at 414.

102. Hess v. Indiana, 414 U.S. 105 (1973).

103. *See Marketing Violent Entertainment to Children: A Sixth Follow-up Review of Industry Practices in the Motion Picture, Music Recording & Electronic Game Industries*, FEDERAL TRADE COMMISSION, Dec. 2009, www.ftc.gov/sites/default/files/documents/reports/marketing-violent-entertainment-children-sixth-follow-review-industry-practices-motion-picture-music/p994511violententertainment.pdf.

104. *Sunday Dialogue: Mayhem on Our Screens*, N.Y. TIMES, Jan. 27, 2013, at SR2; Tracy Reilly, *The "Spiritual Temperature" of Contemporary Popular Music: An Alternative to the Legal Regulation of Death-Metal and Gangsta-Rap Lyrics*, 11 VAND. J. ENT. & TECH. L. 335 (2009).

105. *See, e.g.*, Ty Burr, *An Uncertain Line Between Fantasy's Lure, Nightmare*, BOSTON GLOBE, July 21, 2012, at A1; Nolan Finley, *Missing the Real Lessons From Arizona*, DETROIT NEWS, Jan. 20, 2011, at B1; Marc Fisher et al., *Lanza's Isolated Life Stymies Investigators*, WASH. POST, Dec. 23, 2012, at A1.

106. *See generally* John Charles Kunich, *Shock Torts Reloaded*, 6 APPALACHIAN J.L. 1 (2006); John Charles Kunich, *Natural Born Copycat Killers and the Law of Shock Torts*, 78 WASH. U. L. Q. 1157 (2000).

107. Zamora v. Columbia Broadcasting System, 480 F. Supp. 199, 200 (S.D. Fla. 1979).

108. *Id.* at 201, 205.

109. Herceg v. Hustler Magazine, 814 F.2d 1017 (5th Cir. 1987), *cert. denied*, 485 U.S. 959 (1988).

110. Yakubowicz v. Paramount Pictures Corp., 536 N.E.2d 1067 (Mass. 1989).

111. Rice v. Paladin Enterprises, Inc., 128 F.3d 233 (4th Cir. 1997), *cert. denied*, 523 U.S. 1074 (1998).

112. *Id.* at 244.

113. Martin Garbus, *State of the Union for the Law of the New Millennium, the Internet, and the First Amendment*, 1999 ANN, SURV, AM. L. 169 (1999).

114. Timothy D. Reeves, *Tort Liability for Manufacturers of Violent Video Games*, 60 ALA. L. REV. 519 (2009); Jonathan M. Proman, *Liability of Media Companies for the Violent Content of Their Products Marketed to Children*, 78 ST. JOHN'S L. REV. 427 (2004).

115. Olivia N. v. Nat'l Broad. Co., 126 Cal. App. 3d 488 (1981).

116. Norwood v. Soldier of Fortune Magazine, Inc., 651 F. Supp. 1397 (W.D. Ark. 1987).

117. *Id.* at 1403.

118. Eimann v. Soldier of Fortune Magazine, Inc., 880 F.2d 830, 834 (5th Cir. 1989), *cert. denied*, 493 U.S. 1024 (1990).

119. *Id.*

120. Braun v. Soldier of Fortune Magazine, Inc., 968 F.2d 1110 (11th Cir. 1992),

cert. denied, 506 U.S. 1071 (1993).

121. James v. Meow Media, Inc., 300 F.3d 683 (6th Cir. 2002), *cert. denied*, 537 U.S. 1159 (2003).

122. *Id.*

123. *Id.* at 693.

124. Watters v. TSR, Inc., 904 F.2d 378 (6th Cir. 1990).

125. *See* April M. Perry, *Comment: Guilt by Saturation: Media Liability for Third-Party Violence and the Availability Heuristic*, 97 Nw. U. L. Rev. 1045 (2003).

126. Brown v. Ent. Merchants Ass'n, 564 U.S. 786 (2011).

127. *Id.*

128. *Id.*

129. *Id.* at 794.

130. *Id.* at 790.

131. *Id.* at 806.

132. Dana Beyerle, *"Grand Theft Auto" Killer's Sentence Upheld*, Gadsden Times, Feb. 17, 2012, *available at* www.gadsdentimes.com/news/20120217/grand-theft-auto-killers-sentence-upheld.

133. *Alabama Top Court Denies Industry Motion to Dismiss GTA Killer Suit*, Game Politics, March 29, 2006, *available at* gamepolitics.livejournal.com/244744.html.

134. *In re* Facebook, Inc., 625 S.W.3d 80 (Tex. 2021).

135. *Id.* at 9.

136. *Doe v. Twitter, Inc.*, No. 21-cv-00485-JCS, 2021

137. Animal Crush Video Prohibition Act, 18 U.S.C. § 48.

138. 559 U.S. 460 (2010).

139. *Id.* at 472.

140. *Id.*

141. Wildmon v. Berwick Universal Pictures, 803 F. Supp. 1167 (D. Miss. 1992), *aff'd without opinion*, 979 F.2d 21 (5th Cir. 1992).

142. Scott W. Gaylord, *Is a Cake Worth a Thousand Words? Masterpiece Cakeshop and the Impact of Antidiscrimination Laws on the Marketplace of Ideas*, 85 Tenn. L. Rev. 361 (2018); John G. Culhane, *The Right to Say, But Not to Do: Balancing First Amendment Freedom of Expression With the Anti-Discrimination Imperative*, 24 Widener L. Rev. 235 (2018).

143. Masterpiece Cakeshop v. Colorado Civil Rights Comm'n, 138 S. Ct. 1719, 1728 (2018).

144. 303 Creative LLC v. Elenis, No. 21-476, 2022 U.S. LEXIS 840 (Feb. 22, 2022).

145. Packingham v. North Carolina, 137 S. Ct. 1730 (2017).

146. Wooley v. Maynard, 430 U.S. 705, 714 (1977) (Burger, C.J.).

147. West Virginia State Bd. of Educ. v. Barnette, 319 U.S. 624 (1943).

U.S. Dist. LEXIS 157158 (N.D. Cal. Aug. 19, 2021).

148. Ambach v. Norwick, 441 U.S. 68 (1979).

149. *See, e.g.*, Epperson v. Arkansas, 393 U.S. 97 (1968); Edwards v. Aguillard, 482 U.S. 578 (1987); Pickering v. Bd. of Educ., 391 U.S. 563 (1968).

150. *Barnette*, 319 U.S. at 642.

151. Mark C. Rahdert, *Point of View: The Roberts Court and Academic Freedom*, Chronicle Higher Educ., July 27, 2007, *available at* eric.ed.gov/?q=retraction&pg=2&id=EJ773860.

152. *Policy Map*, GLSEN, https://www.glsen.org/policy-maps (last visited Sept. 12, 2021).

153. *Fact Sheet on U.S. Department of Education Policy Letter on Transgender Students*, National Center for Transgender Equality, https://transequality.org/sites/default/files/ED-DCL-Fact-Sheet.pdf (last visited Dec. 15, 2021).

154. Kluge v. Brownsburg Cmty. Sch. Corp., 432 F. Supp. 3d 823, 837 (S.D. Ind. 2020); Vlaming v. W. Point Sch. Bd., 480 F. Supp. 3d 711, 716, 720 (E.D. Va. 2020); Loudoun Cnty. Sch. Bd. v. Cross, No. 210584, at 3 (Va. Aug. 30, 2021) (order affirming preliminary injunction), https://adfmedialegalfiles.blob.core.windows.net/files/CrossOrderVSC.pdf.

155. *Kluge*, 432 F. Supp. 3d at 837; *Vlaming*, 480 F. Supp. 3d at 716, 720; Loudoun Cnty. Sch. Bd. v. Cross, No. 210584, at 3 (Va. Aug. 30, 2021), https

://adfmedialegalfiles.blo
b.core.windows.net/files
/CrossOrderVSC.pdf.

156. Loudoun Cnty. Sch. Bd.
v. Cross, No. 210584, at 3
(Va. Aug. 30, 2021).

157. Kluge v. Brownsburg
Cmty. Sch. Corp., 432 F.
Supp. 3d 823, 837 (S.D.
Ind. 2020);

158. Caitlin Ring Carlson &
Emma Hansen, *Pronoun
Policies in Public Schools:
The Case Against First
Amendment Exceptions
for K-12 Teachers*, 32 GEO.
Mason U. C.R. L.J. 261
(2022).

159. Tinker v. Des Moines
Indep. Cmty. Sch. Dist.,
393 U.S. 503 (1969).

160. Erwin Chemerinsky,
*Students Do Leave Their
First Amendment Rights
at the Schoolhouse Gates:
What's Left of Tinker?* 48
DRAKE L. REV. 527 (2000).

161. Tinker v. Des Moines
Indep. Cmty. Sch. Dist.,
393 U.S. 503, 508 (1969).

162. *Id.*

163. *Id.* at 506.

164. *Id.* at 509.

165. Grayned v. Rockford, 408
U.S. 104 (1972).

166. Morse v. Frederick, 551
U.S. 393 (2007).

167. *Id.* at 410.

168. *Mahanoy Area Sch. Dist.
V. B.L.*, 141 S. Ct. 2038
(2021).

169. *Id.* At 2043.

170. *Id.* At 2044-45.

171. *Id.* At 2047.

172. *Id.* At 2058.

173. *Id.* At 2059.

174. *Id.*

175. Bethel Sch. Dist. V. Fraser, 478 U.S. 675 (1986).

176. *Id.*

177. Hazelwood Sch. Dist. V.
Kuhlmeier, 484 U.S. 260
(1988).

178. *Id.* at 271.

179. *Id.* at 270.

180. *Id.* at 273 n.7.

181. New Voices FAQ, STUDENT
PRESS LAW CENTER, https
://splc.org/new-voices
-faqs/#what-is-nv (last
visited Feb. 27, 2022),

182. Tinker v. Des Moines
Indep. Cmty. Sch. Dist.,
393 U.S. 503, 509 (1969).

183. Bethel Sch. Dist. v. Fraser, 478 U.S. 675 (1986);
Hazelwood Sch. Dist. v.
Kuhlmeier, 484 U.S. 260
(1988).

184. *Hazelwood*, 484 U.S. 260;
Lemon v. Kurtzman, 403
U.S. 602 (1971); Bd. Of
Regents of Univ. of Wis.
System v. Southworth,
529 U.S. 217 (2000).

185. A.M. v. Taconic Hills
Cent. Sch. Dist., 510 F.
App'x 3 (2d Cir. 2013),
cert. denied, 571 U.S. 828
(2013).

186. K.A. *ex. rel.* Ayers v.
Pocono Mt. Sch. Dist.,
710 F. 3d 99 (3d Cir. 2013).

187. B.H. *ex rel.* Hawk v.
Easton Area Sch. Dist.,
725 F.3d 293 (3d Cir.
2013), *cert. denied*, 572
U.S. 1002 (2014).

188. Taylor v. Roswell Ind.
Sch. Dist., 713 F.3d 25
(10th Cir. 2013).

189. Hardwick v. Heyward,
711 F.3d 426 (4th Cir.),
cert. denied, 571 U.S. 829
(2013).

190. Bd. Of Regents of Univ.
of Wis. System v. South-
worth, 529 U.S. 217, 234
n.7 (2000).

191. Widmar v. Vincent, 454
U.S. 263, 274 (1981).

192. Bethel Sch. Dist. v. Fraser, 478 U.S. 675, 683
(1986). *See also* Edwards
v. Aguillard, 482 U.S. 578,
583 (1987).

193. *See, e.g.,* Bd. Of Regents,
529 U.S. 217 (2000);
Rosenberger v. Rector
and Visitors of the Univ.
of Va., 515 U.S. 819 (1995).

194. Papish v. Bd. Of Curators
of the Univ. of Missouri,
410 U.S. 667, 670 (1973).

195. *Id.; see also* Bd. Of
Regents, 529 U.S. at 233.

196. *Bd. Of Regents*, 529 U.S.
at 242–43 (Souter, J.,
dissenting). Note that
the Court said this public
forum also enhanced
the university's cur-
ricular goals, but public
forum analysis typically
protects precisely those
types of speech that
would not be embraced
by the government
agency providing the
forum.

197. *Id.*

198. CAITLIN RING CARLSON, HATE
SPEECH 101 (2021).

199. *The 2021 College Free
Speech Rankings*, FIRE,

https://www.thefire.org/the-2021-college-free-speech-rankings/ (last visited Feb. 27, 2022).

200. *Id.*

201. *Id.*

202. Alexander Tsesis, *Campus Speech and Harassment*, 101 Minn. L. Rev. 1863 (2017).

203. Rosenberger v. Rector and Visitors of the Univ. of Va., 515 U.S. 819 (1995).

204. *Id.* at 833.

205. *Southworth*, 529 U.S. at 239 (Souter, J., concurring).

206. See, *e.g.*, *Southworth*, 529 U. S. at 217; *Rosenberger*, 515 U.S. at 819.

207. *Id.*

208. *Id.*

209. *Id.*

210. *Id.*

211. Greg Lukianoff, *Feigning Free Speech on Campus*, N. Y. Times, Oct. 25, 2012, *available at* www.nytimes.com/2012/10/25/opinion/feigning-free-speech-on-campus.html.

212. Kincaid v. Gibson, 236 F.3d 342 (6th Cir. 2001) (en banc).

213. *Id.* at 346.

214. Hosty v. Carter, 412 F.3d 731 (7th Cir. 2005), *cert. denied*, 546 U.S. 1169 (2006).

215. OSU Student Alliance v. Ray, 699 F.3d 1053 (9th Cir. 2012), *cert denied*, 571 U.S. 819 (2013).

216. Richard Pérez-Peña, *Student Paper Editors Quit at University of Georgia*, N. Y. Times, Aug. 16, 2012, *available at* www.nytimes.com/2012/08/17/us/georgia-student-newspaper-editors-quit-over-interference.html.

217. Alexis Steven, *Editors Rejoin UGA Student Newspaper*, Atlanta J. Const., Aug. 20, 2012, *available at* https://www.ajc.com/news/local/editors-rejoin-uga-student-newspaper/VnqJbXx9PbFVhdXzQ0xC1M/.

218. Michele Nagar, *Fired for Diversity's Sake*, Accuracy in Academia (July 22, 2004), www.academia.org/fired-for-diversitys-sake/.

219. *SPJ Members Issue Resolution Condemning Kansas Adviser's Firing*, Student Press L. Ctr. (Oct. 6, 2004), www.splc.org/2004/10/spj-members-issue-resolution-condemning-kan-advisers-firing/?id=877; *SPLC Condemns Censorship at Kansas State*, Student Press L. Ctr. (Aug. 1, 2004), splc.org/2004/08/splc-condemns-censorship-at-kansas-state/.

220. Marnette Federis, *Court to Review Kansas State Adviser Dismissal Case*, Student Press L. Ctr., Sept. 29, 2006, *available at* splc.org/2006/09/court-to-review-kansas-state-adviser-dismissal-case.

221. *See* Lane v. Simon, 2005 U.S. Dist. LEXIS 11330 (D. Kan. 2005), *vacated and remanded*, 2007 U.S. App. LEXIS 17814 (10th Cir., July 26, 2007).

222. Tatro v. Univ. of Minn., 816 N.W.2d 509 (Minn. 2012).

223. *Id.* at 517.

224. *Id.* at 513.

225. *Id.* at 521.

226. *Id.* at 511–12.

227. *Id.* at 521.

228. *See* Oyama v. Univ. of Hawaii, 813 F.3d 850 (9th Cir. 2015), *cert. denied*, 136 S. Ct. 2520 (2016); Keefe v. Adams, 840 F.3d 523 (8th Cir. 2016), *cert. denied*, 137 S. Ct. 1448 (2017).

229. Hazelwood Sch. Dist. v. Kuhlmeier, 484 U.S. 260 (1988).

230. *Compare, e.g., Keefe*, 840 F.3d at 532 (relying on *Hazelwood* to affirm the authority of the university to expel a student for unprofessional off-campus Facebook posts about classmates that were reasonably related to and materially disrupted the graduate nursing program), *with Oyama*, 813 F.3d at 863 (not relying on *Hazelwood* and creating a new test to affirm the authority of the university to deny student teacher placement for a student's inappropriate remarks). *See also* Ward v. Polite, 667 F.3d 727, 733–34 (6th Cir. 2012) (applying *Hazelwood* to establish authority of

the university to impose regulations on speech that are "reasonably related to legitimate pedagogical concerns. . . . Nothing in *Hazelwood* suggests a stop-go distinction between student speech at the high school and university levels, and we decline to create one"); Keeton v. Anderson-Wiley, 664 F.3d 865, 875–76 (11th Cir. 2011) (relying on *Hazelwood* to reject graduate student claim to affirm university authority to control of graduate student speech within a "school-sponsored expressive activity" because graduate program standards constitute a nonpublic forum for government speech); Flint v. Dennison, 488 F.3d 816, 829 n.9 (9th Cir. 2007) (applying *Hazelwood* to college student campaign spending); Hosty v. Carter, 412 F.3d 731, 735 (7th Cir. 2005) (en banc) ("We hold . . . that *Hazelwood*'s framework applies to subsidized student newspapers at colleges as well as elementary and secondary schools"); Axson-Flynn v. Johnson, 356 F.3d 1277, 1285, 1289–93 (10th Cir. 2004) (concluding that a graduate student's speech "constitutes 'school-sponsored speech' and is thus governed by *Hazelwood*"); Student Gov't Ass'n v. Bd. Of Trs. Of Univ. of Mass., 868 F.2d 473, 480 n.6 (1st Cir. 1989) ("*Hazelwood* . . . is

not applicable to college newspapers").

231. *Oyama*, 813 F.3d at 862.

232. *Id.* at 863.

233. *Id.* at 855, 860.

234. *Keefe*, 840 F.3d at 532 (8th Cir. 2016), *cert denied*, 137 S. Ct. 1448 (2017).

235. *Id.* at 526, 528.

236. *Id.* at 531.

237. *Id.*

238. *Id. See also* Conner Mitchell, *Supreme Court Declines to Hear Free Speech Case*, Student Press L. Ctr. (April 4, 2017), splc.org/2017/04/keefe-certiorari-denied/.

239. Roxann Elliott, *Court of Appeals Rules in Favor of Community College That Removed Nursing Student Over Facebook Posts*, Student Press L. Ctr. (Nov. 3, 2016), www.splc.org/blog/splc/2016/11/keefe-eighth-circuit; Frank LoMonte, *Appeals Court Won't Apply Hazelwood to Teacher Trainee's Case, Instead Creates New "Professional Standards" Exception*, Student Press L. Ctr. (Dec. 29, 2015), www.splc.org/blog/splc/2015/12/oyama-hawaii-ninth-circuit-college-hazelwood-ruling.

240. *See, e.g.,* Dinesh D'Souza, Illiberal Education: The Politics of Race and Sex on Campus (1992).

241. *See, e.g.,* Laura Lederer & Richard Delgado eds., The Price We Pay: The Case Against Racist Speech,

Hate Propaganda, and Pornography (1994).

242. *See, e.g.,* Andrew Altman, *Liberalism and Campus Hate Speech*, in Campus Wars: Multiculturalism and the Politics of Difference, ed. John Arthur & Amy Shapiro (1993).

243. *See, e.g.,* Doe v. Univ. of Mich., 721 F. Supp. 852 (E.D. Mich. 1989); UWM Post v. Bd. of Regents of Univ. of Wis., 774 F. Supp. 1163 (E.D. Wis. 1991); Dambrot v. Central Mich. Univ., 839 F. Supp. 477 (E.D. Mich. 1993).

244. *Doe*, 721 F. Supp. 852, 864 (E.D. Mich. 1989).

245. Arati R. Korwar, War of Words: Speech Codes at Public Colleges and Universities (1994); Jon B. Gould, *The Precedent That Wasn't: College Hate Speech Codes and the Two Faces of Legal Compliance*, 35 Law & Soc'y Rev. 345 (2001).

246. *See, e.g.,* Jeremy Bauer-Wolf, *A University's New Rules on Rape*, Inside Higher Ed, Oct. 18, 2017, *available at* www.insidehighered.com/news/2017/10/18/university-minnesota-revises-sexual-harassment-policies; Exec. Pol. 15 Prohibiting Discrimination, Sexual Harassment and Sexual Misconduct, Wash. State Univ., policies.wsu.edu/prf/index/manuals/executive-policy-manual-contents/ep15-discrimination-sexual-harassment-sexual-misconduct (last visited Nov. 22, 2022).

247. Civil Rights Act of 1964, 42 U.S.C. § 2000e-2(a)(1). *See* Vance v. Ball State Univ., 570 U.S. 421 (2013).

248. *See* Johnson v. Univ. of Cincinnati, 215 F. 3d 561 (6th Cir. 2000) (finding noncompliance with affirmative-action requirements a matter of public interest but that effective hiring procedures outweighed plaintiff's free speech interests).

249. UWM Post v. Bd. Of Regents of Univ. of Wis., 774 F. Supp. 1163 (1991).

250. *See* Katarina I. Chavez, *The Problems with the Solutions: Examining the Response from Universities, President Trump, and State Legislatures to Campus Free Speech Issues*, 19 Ave. Maria L. Rev. 146 (2021).

251. Sarah Brown, *When Professors Stir Outrage, What's a University to Do?* Chronicle of Higher Ed. (June 26, 2018), *available at* www.chronicle.com/article/When-Professors -Stir-Outrage/243764.

252. Hailie Higgins, *Professor Suspended for Saying N-Word in Class*, Campus Times, Dec. 5, 2021, *available at* http://www.campustimes.org/2021/12/05/professor-suspended -after-saying-n-word-in -class/.

253. Selim Algar, *Columbia Declines to Punish Professor for Using N-word While Quoting "8 Mile,"* N.Y. Post, Dec. 6, 2021, *available at* https://nypo

st.com/2021/12/06/columbia-declines-to-punish-professor-for-using-n -word-in-8-mile-quote/.

254. Randall Kennedy & Eugene Volokh, *The New Taboo: Quoting Epithets in the Classroom and Beyond*, 49 Cap. U. L. Rev. 1 (2021).

255. Richard Thompson Ford, *Racial Epithets and Racial Etiquette*, 49 Cap. U. L. Rev. 527 (2021).

256. Bd. of Educ., Island Trees Union Free Sch. Dist. v. Pico 457 U.S. 853 (1982).

257. *Id.* at 857.

258. *Id.* at 868.

259. *Id.* at 870.

260. Jenny Gross, *School Board in Tennessee Bans Teaching of Holocaust Novel "Maus,"* N. Y. Times, Jan. 27, 2022, *available at* https://www.nytimes.com/2022/01/27/us/maus -banned-holocaust-tennessee.html.

261. Mirna Alsharif & Liam Reilly, *Pennsylvania School District Reverses Ban on Books by Authors of Color After Students Fought Back*, CNN, Sept. 23, 2021, *available at* https://www.cnn.com/2021/09/23/us/pennsylvania-school-book-ban-reversed/index.html.

262. Evan Ringel, Deborah Dwyer & Victoria Smith Eckstrand, Public Education, Moral Panics, and the First Amendment: A Case Study of Anti-Critical Race Theory Legislation (Media

Law and Policy Scholars Conference, 2023).

263. Jeffery Solochek, *Florida House Approves CRT, "Don't Say Gay" Bills*, Tampa Bay Times, Feb. 24, 2022, *available at* https://www.tampabay.com/news/florida-politics/2022/02/24/florida-house-approves-crt-dont-say-gay-bills/.

CHAPTER 4

1. *See, e.g.*, Paul Farhi, *Washington Post Settles Lawsuit with Family of Kentucky Teenager*, Wash. Post, July 4, 2020, washingtonpost.com/lifestyle/style/washington-post-settles-lawsuit-with-family-of-kentucky-teenager/2020/07/24/ae42144c-cdbd-11ea-b0e3-d55bda07d66a_story.html; Oliver Darcy, *CNN Settles Lawsuit with Nick Sandmann Stemming from Viral Video Controversy*, CNN, Jan. 7, 2020, cnn.com/2020/01/07/media/cnn-settles-lawsuit-viral-video/index.html; Quinlan Bentley, *Covington Catholic Graduate Nicholas Sandmann Reaches Settlement in Lawsuit against NBC*, Cincinnati Enquirer, Dec. 17, 2021, cincinnati.com/story/news/2021/12/17/covington-catholic-grad-nick-sandmann-reaches-settlement-nbc/8946470002/.

2. Sandmann v. New York Times Co., No. 2:20CV23, 2022 WL 2960763, at *8 (E.D. Ky., July 26, 2022).

3. Alison Durkee, *After Lawsuits Against Newsmax and OANN, Here's Who Dominion and Smartmatic Have Sued So Far—And Who Could Be Next*, Forbes, Nov. 3, 2021, forbes.com/sites/alisondurkee/2021/11/03/after-lawsuits-against-newsmax-and-oann-heres-who-dominion-and-smartmatic-have-sued-so-far-and-who-could-be-next/?sh=38ce8af9b291.

4. Coral Ridge Ministries Media, Inc. v. Amazon.com, Inc., 6 F.4th 1247, 1253 (11th Cir. 2021), *cert denied*, Coral Ridge Ministries Media, Inc. v. Southern Poverty Law Ctr., 142 S.Ct. 2453 (2022) (Thomas, J., dissenting); Berisha v. Lawson, 973 F.3d 1304 (11th Cir.) *cert. denied*, 594 U.S. (2021) (Gorsuch, J., dissenting); McKee v. Cosby, 874 F.3d 54 (1st Cir. 2017), *cert. denied*, 139 S. Ct. 675 (Thomas, J., concurring).

5. *See, e.g.*, Diane Leenheer Zimmerman, *Real People in Fiction: Cautionary Words About Troublesome Old Torts Poured Into New Jugs*, 51 Brook. L. Rev. 355 (1985).

6. Milkovich v. Lorain Journal Co., 497 U.S. 1, 22 (1990).

7. Rosenblatt v. Baer, 383 U.S. 75, 86 (1966).

8. Dun & Bradstreet, Inc. v. Greenmoss Builders, Inc., 472 U.S. 749, 757 (1985).

9. *See, e.g.*, Philadelphia Newspapers, Inc. v. Hepps, 475 U.S. 767, 777 (1986).

10. *See* Gavin Clark, Famous Libel and Slander Cases of History (1950).

11. Van Vechten Veeder, *The History and Theory of the Law of Defamation I*, 3 Colum. L. Rev. 546 (1903) (citing *De Libellis Famosis*, 5 Rep. 125a (1609)).

12. *Id.*

13. J. H. Baker, An Introduction to English Legal History 506 (3d ed. 1990).

14. William Blackstone, Commentaries 152 (1799).

15. *Id.*

16. Milkovich v. Lorain Journal Co., 497 U.S. 1, 12 (1990).

17. Sedition Act of 1798, ch. 74, 1 Stat. 596 (1798).

18. John Marshall, *Report of the Minority on the Virginia Resolutions*, 6 J. House of Delegates (Va.) 93–95 (Jan. 22, 1799), *in* 5 The Founders' Constitution 136–38 (Philip B. Kurland & Ralph Lerner eds., 1987).

19. *Id.* at 138.

20. James Madison, *The Virginia Report of 1799–1800, Touching the Alien and Sedition Laws*, *in* The Founders' Constitution 141–42 (Philip B. Kurland & Ralph Lerner eds., 1987).

21. Janet Boeth Jones, *Validity of Criminal Defamation Statutes*, 68 Am. L. Rep.4th

1014 (Originally published in 1989).

22. Freese v. Formella, No. 21-1068 *2 (1st Cir. Nov. 8, 2022).

23. *Id.* at *3-4.

24. *Id.* at *4-5.

25. *Id.* at *2 (citing Garrison v. Louisiana, 379 U.S. 63, 75 (1964).

26. *Id.* at *5-13.

27. *Id.* at *20-27 (Thompson, J., concurring).

28. *See, e.g.*, Whitney v. California, 274 U.S. 357, 374–77 (1927) (Brandeis, J., concurring) (stating, "The best answer for bad speech is more speech.").

29. *See, e.g.*, David Folkenflik, *Could Libel Lawsuits Squash Misinformation?"* NPR, March 12, 2022, npr.org/2022/03/12/1086274333/libel-suits-and-disinfo.

30. Philadelphia Newspapers, Inc. v. Hepps, 475 U.S. 767, 777 (1986).

31. Vivek H. Murthy, *Confronting Health Misinformation: The U.S. Surgeon General's Advisory on Building a Healthy Information Environment*, 2021, hhs.gov/sites/default/files/surgeon-general-misinformation-advisory.pdf.

32. Fact, Merriam-Webster (last visited Nov. 24, 2022), merriam-webster.com/dictionary/fact.

33. *Opinion*, Merriam-Webster (last visited Nov. 24,

2022), merriam-webster.
com/dictionary/opinion.

34. Evanger's Cat & Dog
Food Co., Inc. v. Thix-
ton, 412 F. Supp. 3d 889,
897–900 (N.D. Ill. 2019).

35. Wolsfelt v. Gloucester
Times, 98 Mass. App.
Ct. 155 N.E.3d 737, 745
(2020).

36. Nunes v. Lizza, 12 F.4th
890, 900 (8th Cir. 2021)
(citing RESTATEMENT (SEC-
OND) OF TORTS § 577A(3)
(1977).

37. Clark v. Viacom Int'l Inc.,
617 F. App'x 495, 505 (6th
Cir. 2015).

38. *Nunes*, 12 F.4th at 900;
Lokhova v. Halper, 995
F.3d 134, 152 (4th Cir.
2021) (Quattlebaum, J.,
concurring in part & dis-
senting in part).

39. *Lokhova*, 995 F.3d at 144.

40. *Id.* at 143.

41. *Id.* at 152 (4th Cir. 2021)
(Quattlebaum, J., con-
curring in part & dissenting in part).

42. Lindberg v. Dow Jones &
Co., Inc., No. 20-CV-8231
(LAK), 2021 WL 3605621,
at *6 (S.D.N.Y. Aug. 11,
2021) (quoting Enigma
Software Grp. USA, LLC
v. Bleeping Computer
LLC, 194 F. Supp. 3d 263,
277 (S.D.N.Y. 2016) (internal quotation marks
omitted).

43. Nunes v. Lizza, 12 F.4th
890, 900-01 (8th Cir.
2021).

44. Nunes v. Lizza, No.
20-2719 (8th Cir. Nov. 23,
2021).

45. Stratton Oakmont v.
Prodigy Servs. Co., 1995
N.Y. Misc. LEXIS 229 (N.Y.
Sup. Ct., May 24, 1995)
(holding that because
Prodigy claimed to moni-
tor its content, the ISP
is placed in the role of
publisher).

46. Cubby, Inc. v. Com-
puServe, Inc., 776 F.
Supp. 135 (S.D.N.Y. 1991)
(holding that the ISP is
not responsible for con-
tent posted).

47. Zeran v. America Online,
Inc., 129 F.3d 327, 330
(4th Cir. 1997).

48. *Id.* at 330.

49. *Id.*

50. *Id.* at 331.

51. Universal Commc'n
Systems, Inc. v. Lycos,
Inc., 478 F.3d 413 (1st Cir.
2007).

52. *Id.* at 418–19.

53. La Liberte v. Reid, 966
F.3d 79, 83-85 (2d Cir.
2020).

54. *Id.* at 89 (2d Cir. 2020)
(quoting 47 U.S.C.
§ 230(c)(1)(emphasis in
original)(internal quota-
tion marks removed).

55. Josh Taylor, *Lawyers Use
Voller Defamation Case
to Demand Facebook
Group Admins Remove
Posts*, THE GUARDIAN, Oct.
21, 2021, theguardian.
com/law/2021/oct/29/
lawyers-use-voller-
defamation-case-to-
demand-facebook-
group-admins-remove-
posts.

56. Elizabeth Byrne, *High
Court Finds Media Out-
lets Are Responsible For
Facebook Comments in
Dylan Voller Defama-
tion Case*, ABC NEWS,
Sept. 7, 2021, abc.net.
au/news/2021-09-08/
high-court-rules-on-
media-responsibility-
over-facebook-com-
ments/100442626.

57. Order, Fairfax Media
Publications Pty Ltd. v.
Voller, Nationwide News
Pty Ltd v. Voller, Austra-
lian News Channel Pty
Ltd. v. Voller, S236/2020
and S238/2020[2021]
HCA 27 (Sept. 8, 2021), in
JEREMY FEIBGELSON & KELLI
L. SAGER, COMMC'N L. IN
THE DIGITAL AGE 961-1059
(2021).

58. *Id.*

59. *Id.* (citing Webb v. Bloch,
41 CLR 331, 363-64
(1928).

60. *Id.*

61. *Id.* (citing 263 CLR 149,
163 (2018).

62. *Australia To Introduce
New Laws To Force Media
Platforms To Unmask
Online Trolls*, REUTERS,
Nov. 28, 2021, reuters.
com/world/asia-pacific/
australia-introduce-
new-laws-force-media-
platforms-unmask-on-
line-trolls-2021-11-28/.

63. McIntyre v. Ohio Elections Comm'n, 514 U.S.
334, 357 (1995).

64. Nathaniel Plemons,
*Weeding Out Wolves:
Protecting Speakers
and Punishing Pirates in
Unmasking Analyses*, 22

Vand. J. Ent. & Tech. L. 181, 196 (2019).

65. Dendrite Int'l, Inc. v. Doe No. 3, 342 N.J. Super. 134 (July 11, 2001).

66. Yelp, Inc. v. Superior Court, 224 Ca. Rptr. 3d 887 (Cal. Ct. App. 2017), *review denied* (Feb. 14, 2018).

67. *Id.*

68. ZL Techs., Inc. v. Does 1–7, 220 Cal. Rptr. 3d 569 (Ct. App. 2017).

69. *Id.*

70. Kevin T. Baine, *Defamation Law Case Summaries (September 2017–August 2018)*, 6 Commc'n L. in the Digital Age 445 (2018).

71. Plemons, *supra* note 64, at 198-99,

72. Doe v. Cahill, 884 A.2d 451, 457 (Del. 2005) (internal quotation marks omitted).

73. Farmland Partners Inc. v. Fortunae, No. 18-CV-02351-KLM, 2020 WL 12575073, at *2 (D. Colo. May 18, 2020).

74. *Id.* at *4.

75. Ashley I. Kissinger, Katharine Larsen, & Matthew E. Kelley, *Protections for Anonymous Online Speech*, 2 Commc'n L. in the Digital Age 532 (2012) (stating good faith is only applied in the state of Virginia.)

76. Emerito Estrada Rivera-Isuzu de P.R., Inc. v. Consumers of U.S., Inc., 233 F.3d 24, 26 (1st Cir. 2000).

77. Miller v. Sawant, 18 F.4th 328 (9th Cir. 2021).

78. *Id.*

79. Restatement (Second) of Torts § 564A cmt. b (1976).

80. Neiman-Marcus v. Lait, 13 F.R.D. 311, 316 (S.D.N.Y. 1952).

81. JB & Assocs., Inc. v. Neb. Cancer Coal., 932 N.W.2d 71, 79 (Neb. 2019).

82. Sandmann v. WP Co. LLC, 401 F. Supp. 3d 781, 788-96 (E.D. Ky. 2019).

83. *See* Restatement (Second) of Torts § 559 (1997).

84. *See* Kristina E. Music Biro et al., *Publications that Are Libelous Per Se and Libelous Per Quod— Rules of Construction*, 50 Am. Jur. 2d. *Libel and Slander* § 150 (2022).

85. *See id.* at § 165.

86. Balla v. Hall, 59 Cal. App. 5th 652, 686–87 (2021), *review denied* (April 14, 2021).

87. Yanong v. Coleman, 317 So.3d 905, 905-16 (La. App. 2 Cir. 2021), *reh'g denied* (La. App. 2 Cir. June 24, 2021), *writ denied*, 326 So. 3d 1249 (La. Nov. 11, 2021).

88. Olson v. City of N. Liberty, 451 F. Supp. 3d 1010, 1027–28 (S.D. Iowa 2020).

89. Nolan v. State of New York, 158 A.D.3d 186 (N.Y. App. Div. 2018).

90. *See* Restatement (Second) of Torts § 559 (1997).

91. *See* W. Page Keeton et al., Prosser and Keeton on the Law of Torts § 111, at 773–78 (5th ed. 1984).

92. *See* Restatement (Second) of Torts § 559 cmt. e.

93. *See, e.g.,* Kimmerle v. New York Evening Journal, Inc., 262 N.Y. 99 (1933).

94. Turntine v. Peterson, 959 F.3d 873, 878-86, (8th Cir. 2020).

95. Virginia Citizens Def. League v. Couric, 910 F.3d 780 (4th Cir. 2018).

96. Zervos v. Trump, 171 A.D.3d 110, 114 (2019), *appeal dismissed*, 36 N.Y.3d 1083, 166 N.E.3d 1059 (2021).

97. Zervos v. Trump, 74 N.Y.S.3d 442 (Sup. Ct. 2018).

98. *Id.*

99. *See* Clinton v. Jones, 520 U.S. 681 (1997).

100. Kevin McCoy, *NY Appeals Court Rules President Donald Trump Must Face Summer Zervos' Defamation Lawsuit*, USA Today, March 14, 2019, usatoday.com/story/news/2019/03/14/president-donald-trump-must-face-summer-zervos-defamation-case-ny-court-rules/3162078002/.

101. *Zervos*, 74 N.Y.S.3d 442.

102. Zervos v. Trump, 166 N.E. 3d 1059, 1059 (N.Y. 2021).

103. Zervos v. Trump, No. 0150522/2017 (N.Y.Sup. Ct., Oct. 18, 2021). *See* Josh Russell,

Trump Accuser Settles Defamation Case Without Compensation, Courthouse News Service, April. 10, 2022, courthousenews.com/ trump-accuser-settles-defamation-case-without-compensation/.

104. *Id.*

105. Carroll v. Trump, No. 20-CV-7311 (LAK), 2022 WL 748128 (S.D.N.Y. March 11 2022).

106. Clifford v. Trump, 339 F.Supp.3d 915 (C.D. Cal. 2018), *aff'd*, 818 Fed. Appx. 746 (9th Cir. 2020), *cert. denied*, 141 S.Ct. 1374 (2021).

107. Jonathan Stempel, *Harvard Professor Lessig Sues NY Times for 'Clickbait Defamation' Over Jeffrey Epstein Story*, Reuters, Jan. 13, 2020, reuters.com/article/us-people-jeffrey-epstein-new-york-times/ harvard-professor-lessig-sues-ny-times-for-clickbait-defamation-over-jeffrey-epstein-story-idUSKBN1ZC2IJ.

108. Hudik v. Fox News Network, LLC, 512 F. Supp. 3d 816, 834 (M.D. Tenn. 2021).

109. Knutt v. Metro Int'l, 938 N.Y.S.2d 134 (N.Y. App. Div. 2012).

110. *See* Kristina E. Music Biro et al., *Definitions of Libel Per Se and Libel Per Quod*, 50 Am. Jur. 2d *Libel & Slander* § 148 (2022).

111. Cochran v. NYP Holdings, Inc., 58 F. Supp. 2d 1113, 1121 (C.D. Cal. 1998).

112. J.A. Bryant, Jr., *Libel and Slander: Actionability of Defamatory Statements as to Business Conduct, Relating to a Single Transaction or Occurrence*, 51 Am. L. Rep.3d 1300 § 2a (Originally published in 1973).

113. Texas Beef Group v. Oprah Winfrey, 11 F. Supp. 2d 858, 862 (N.D. Tex. 1998) (indicating the program had been tape recorded on April 11, 1996).

114. *Id.*

115. *Id.*

116. *Id.* The ruling was also based on the failure of the plaintiffs to prove that cattle are perishable food, a requirement under the Texas False Disparagement of Perishable Food Products Act. The plaintiffs sued for the alleged violation of this provision of the act.

117. *Trade Libel Basics: The Pink Slime Case*, Kelly/ Warner Law, July 16, 2013, kellywarnerlaw.com/ trade-libel-basics/.

118. Amanda Radke, *Update on BPI Lawsuit Against ABC*, Beef Daily, Oct. 12, 2016, beefmagazine. com/blog/update-bpi-lawsuit-against-abc.

119. Beef Prods., Inc. v. ABC, No. CIV12292, 2014 WL 1245307 (S.D. Cir. March 27, 2014) (internal quotation marks omitted).

120. Daniel Victor, *ABC Settles With Meat Producer in "Pink Slime" Defamation Case*, N.Y. Times, June 28, 2017, nytimes. com/2017/06/28/business/media/pink-slime-abc-lawsuit-settlement. html?_r=0.

121. Next Techs. Inc. v. Beyond the Off. Door, LLC, 992 F.3d 589, 593 (7th Cir. 2021).

122. *See, e.g.*, Deen Freelon & Chris Wells, *Disinformation as Political Communication*, 37 Political Commc'n 145 (2020).

123. *Words We're Watching: The Real Story on Fake News*, Merriam-Webster (last visited Nov. 24, 2022), merriam-webster. com/words-at-play/ the-real-story-of-fake-news.

124. *Id.*

125. Jane E. Kirtley, *Getting to the Truth: Fake News, Libel Laws, and "Enemies of the American People,"* 43 A.B.A., March 1, 2019, americanbar.org/ groups/crsj/publications/human_rights_ magazine_home/the-ongoing-challenge-to-define-free-speech/ getting-to-the-truth/.

126. *See, e.g., New Research Shows Facebook Making Strides Against False News*, Facebook Newsroom (last visited Nov. 24, 2022), newsroom. fb.com/news/2018/10/ inside-feed-michigan-lemonde/.

127. *See, e.g.*, Madeline de Cock Bunning, *A Multi-Dimensional Approach to Disinformation,*

INDEPENDENT HIGH LEVEL GROUP ON FAKE NEWS AND ONLINE DISINFORMATION, 2018, ecsite.eu/sites/default/files/amulti-dimensionalapproachtodisinformation-reportoftheindependenthighlevelgrouponfakenewsandonlinedisinformation.pdf.

128. *See, e.g.* Jonah E. Bromwich & Ben Smith, *Fox News Is Sued by Election Technology Company for Over $2.7 Billion*, N.Y. TIMES, Feb. 4, 2021, nytimes.com/2021/02/04/business/media/smartmatic-fox-news-lawsuit.html.

129. Letter from J. Erik Connolly to Lily Fu Claffee, FOX NEWS NETWORK (Dec. 10, 2020), documentcloud.org/documents/20423795-legal-notice-and-retraction-demand-from-smartmatic-usa-corp-to-fox-news.

130. *Lou Dobbs Tonight*, FOX NEWS, DEC. 19, 2020, video.foxbusiness.com/v/6217257237001#sp=show-clips.

131. Jonah E. Bromwich & Michael M. Grynbaum, *Smartmatic Sues Newsmax and One America News Network, Claiming Defamation*, N.Y. TIMES, Nov. 3, 2021, nytimes.com/2021/11/03/business/media/smartmatic-newsmax-oan.html.

132. *See, e.g.*, Katie Robertson & Jonah E. Bromwich,

A Judge Rejects Fox News's Request to Dismiss Dominion's Defamation Suit, N.Y. TIMES, Dec. 17, 2021, nytimes.com/2021/12/17/business/fox-news-dominion-lawsuit.html.

133. 475 U.S. 767, 776–77 (1986).

134. Masson v. New Yorker Magazine, Inc., 501 U.S. 496, 516–17 (1991).

135. Harvey v. Cable News Network, Inc., 520 F. Supp. 3d 693, 704-15 (D. Md. 2021). (quoting Nanji v. Nat'l Geographic Soc'y, 403 F. Supp. 2d 425, 431 (D. Md. 2005) (internal quotation marks omitted).

136. Yeakey v. Hearst Commc'ns, Inc., 234 P.3d 332 (Wash. App. 2010).

137. Stevens v. Iowa Newspapers, Inc., 728 N.W.2d 823 (Iowa 2007).

138. Nunes v. Lizza, 12 F.4th 890, 896-900 (8th Cir. 2021), *reh'g and reh'g en banc denied* (Nov. 23, 2022).

139. Cheney v. Daily News, LP, 654 Fed. Appx. 578 (3d Cir. July 19, 2016).

140. Manzari v. Assoc. Newspapers, Ltd., 830 F.3d 881 (9th Cir. 2016).

141. 376 U.S. 254 (1964).

142. *Id.*

143. *See, e.g.*, Harry Kalven Jr., *The New York Times Case: A Note on "The Central Meaning of the First Amendment*,*"* 1964 SUP. CT. REV. 191.

144. Coral Ridge Ministries Media, Inc. v. Amazon.com, Inc., 6 F.4th 1247, 1253 (11th Cir. 2021), *cert denied*, Coral Ridge Ministries Media, Inc. v. Southern Poverty Law Ctr., 142 S.Ct. 2453 (2022) (Thomas, J., dissenting); Berisha v. Lawson, 973 F.3d 1304 (11th Cir.), *cert denied*, 141 S.Ct. 2424 (2021) (Gorsuch, J., dissenting); McKee v. Cosby, 874 F.3d 54 (1st Cir. 2017), *cert. denied*, 139 S. Ct. 675 (2019)(Thomas, J., dissenting).

145. 142 S.Ct. at 2454-55 (Thomas, J., dissenting).

146. *Id.* (quoting *Tah v. Global Witness Publ'g, Inc.*, 991 F.3d 231, 254 (C.A.D.C. 2021) (internal quotation marks omitted).

147. *Berisha*, 141 S.Ct. at 2424 (Thomas, J., dissenting).

148. *Id.* at 2425-30 (Gorsuch, J., dissenting)(citing New York Times Co. v. Sullivan, 376 U.S. 254, 272 (1964).

149. *Id* at 2428.

150. *Id.* at 2424-25 (2021) (Thomas, J., dissenting).

151. *Id.* (citing Merrit Kennedy, *'Pizzagate' Gunman Sentenced to 4 Years in Prison*, NPR, June 22, 2017, https://www.npr.org/sections/thetwo-way/2017/06/22/533941689/pizzagate-gunman-sentenced-to-4-years-in-prison; McKee v. Cosby, 139 S. Ct. 675 (Thomas, J., concurring).

152. McKee v. Cosby, 139 S. Ct. 675 (2019)(Thomas, J., concurring).

153. *Id.*

154. *Id.*

155. New York Times Co. v. Sullivan, 376 U.S. 254, 272 (1964).

156. *Id.* at 270.

157. *Id.* at 266.

158. *Id.* at 279.

159. *Id.* at 270.

160. *Id.*

161. *Id.* at 278.

162. *See, e.g.,* LAWRENCE FRIEDMAN, AM. LAW IN THE 20TH CENTURY 341 (2002).

163. Goldwater v. Ginzburg, 414 F.2d 324 (2d Cir. 1969), *cert. denied*, 396 U.S. 1049 (1970).

164. Masson v. New Yorker Magazine, Inc., 501 U.S. 496, 517 (1991).

165. Air Wis. Airlines Corp. v. Hoeper, 571 U.S. 237 (2014).

166. *Id.* at 253–54.

167. *Id.* at 864.

168. Curtis Publ'g Co. v. Butts, 388 U.S. 130, 158 (1967).

169. Associated Press v. Walker, 388 U.S. 130, 140 (1967).

170. *Id.* at 157–59.

171. St. Amant v. Thompson, 390 U.S. 727, 731 (1968).

172. Herbert v. Lando, 441 U.S. 153 (1979).

173. Harte-Hanks Commc'ns, Inc. v. Connaughton, 491 U.S. 657 (1989).

174. Desmond v. News and Observer Pub'g Co., 848 S.E. 2d 647, 673 (N.C. 2020), *reh'g denied*, 848 S.E.2d 487 (N.C. 2020).

175. *Id.* at 652-74.

176. 653-74.

177. *Id.*

178. *Id.*

179. *Id.* at 664-74.

180. Rosenblatt v. Baer, 383 U.S. 75, 85 (1966) (internal quotation marks omitted).

181. *Id.* at 86.

182. Am. C.L. Union, Inc. v. Zeh, 864 S.E.2d 422, 436-38 (Ga. 2021).

183. *Id.* at 87.

184. 388 U.S. 130, 163 (1967) (Warren, C.J., concurring) (internal quotation marks omitted).

185. *Id.* at 163–64 (internal quotation marks omitted).

186. 418 U.S. 323, 345 (1974).

187. *Id.* at 344.

188. *Id.* at 345.

189. *Id.*

190. Renner v. Donsbach, 749 F. Supp. 987 (W.D. Mo. 1990).

191. Fridman v. Orbis Bus. Intl. Ltd., 229 A.3d 499, 509 (D.C. 2020), *cert. denied* 141 S. Ct. 1074 (2021).

192. Curtis Publ'g Co. v. Butts and Associated Press v. Walker, 388 U.S. 130, 163 (1967).

193. Wolston v. Reader's Digest Ass'n, 443 U.S. 157 (1979).

194. Time, Inc. v. Firestone, 424 U.S. 448 (1976).

195. Hutchinson v. Proxmire, 443 U.S. 111 (1979).

196. Involuntary public figures are not included in the table because these cases are rare. The standard of fault for these plaintiffs generally is actual malice. *See, e.g.,* George L. Blum, *Who Is "Involuntary Public Figure" for Purposes of Defamation Action*, 17 AM. L. REP. art. 1 §§ 3-6 (originally published in 2016).

197. *Id.* at 135.

198. Chuy v. Philadelphia Eagles Football Club, 431 F. Supp. 254, 276 (E.D. Pa. 1977).

199. McKee v. Cosby, 874 F.3d 54, 61 (1st Cir. 2017).

200. McKee v. Cosby, 236 F. Supp. 3d 427 (D. Mass 2017).

201. *McKee*, 874 F.3d 54, 61 (internal quotation marks omitted).

202. McKee v. Cosby, 874 F.3d 54 (1st Cir. 2017), *cert. denied*, 139 S. Ct. 675 (2019)(Thomas, J., dissenting).

203. Gertz v. Robert Welch, Inc., 418 U.S. 323, 351 (1974).

204. *Id.* at 345.

205. Tillman v. Freedom of Info. Comm'n, 2008 Conn. Super. LEXIS 2120, *25 (Aug. 15, 2008).

206. MediaOne, L.L.C. v. Henderson, 592 S.W.3d 933, 937-42 (Tex. Ct. App. 2019) (citing Zerangue v. TSP Newspapers, Inc., 814 F.2d 1066, 1069 (5th Cir. 1987).

207. Anderson v. WBNS-TV, Inc., 165 N.E.3d 790, 793–99 (Ohio Ct. App. 2020), *appeal not allowed*, 168 N.E.3d 1201 (Ohio 2021).

208. Dun & Bradstreet, Inc. v. Greenmoss Builders, Inc., 472 U.S. 749 (1985).

209. *Id.* at 783.

210. *Id.* at 772.

211. Michael K. Cantwell, *Exploring the Issue of "Strict Liability" for Defamation*, MLRC Bulletin, Dec. 2012, at 3.

212. *Id.*

213. Obsidian Finance Group, LLC v. Cox, 812 F. Supp. 2d 1220 (D. Ore. 2011).

214. Obsidian Finance Group, LLC v. Cox, 740 F.3d 1284 (9th Cir. 2014).

215. *Id.* at 1290–91 (quoting Citizens United v. Federal Election Comm'n, 558 U.S. 310, 352 (2010).

216. Bryan A. Garner, Black's Law Dictionary (11th ed. 2019).

217. Restatement (Second) of Torts § 46 (1965) cmt. j.

218. *See, e.g.*, Gouin v. Gouin, 249 F. Supp. 2d 62 (D. Mass. 2003).

219. *See* Charles E. Cantu, *An Essay on the Tort of Negligent Infliction of Emotional Distress in Texas: Stop Saying It Does Not Exist*, 33 St. Mary's L.J. 455, 458 (2002).

220. Restatement (Second) of Torts § 46 (1965).

221. *Id.* cmt. d.

222. Restatement (Second) of Torts § 46(1) (1965).

223. Bozemon v. Elite Media, LLC, 2021 WL 4843976 (Oct. 18, 2021).

224. Bozeman v. Elite Media, LLC, No. 21-CV-345-JDP, 2022 WL 3576194, at *1 (W.D. Wis. Aug. 19, 2022).

225. Rich v. Fox News Network, LLC, 939 F.3d 112, 124-25 (2d Cir. 2019).

226. Snyder v. Phelps, 562 U.S. 443, 465, 131 S. Ct. 1207, 1223, 179 L. Ed. 2d 172 (2011) (citing Restatement (Second) of Torts § 46, cmt. d).

227. Restatement (Second) of Torts § 46 (1965).

228. Marshall Cty. Coal Co. v. Oliver, No. 17-C-124, 2018 WL 1082525 (W.Va. Cir. Ct. Feb. 22, 2018).

229. *Id.*

230. Mullane v. Breaking Media, Inc., 433 F.Supp.3d 102, 107-14 (D. Mass. 2020).

231. Katie Robertson, *Fox News Reaches Settlement With Parents of Seth Rich*, N.Y. Times, Nov. 24, 2020, nytimes.com/2020/11/24/business/media/fox-news-seth-rich.html.

232. Rich v. Fox News Network, LLC, 939 F.3d 112, 122-23 (2d Cir. 2019).

233. *Id.* at 117-25

234. *Id.* at 121-23.

235. *Statement on Coverage of Seth Rich Murder Investigation*, Fox News, May 23, 2017, foxnews.com/politics/statement-on-coverage-of-seth-rich-murder-investigation.

236. *Rich*, 939 F.3d at 123-25.

237. Gilmore v. Jones, 370 F. Supp.3d 630 (W.D. Va., 2019).

238. Doe v. Roe, 864 S.E.2d 206, 215 (Ga. Ct. App. 2021), *reconsideration denied* (Nov. 17, 2021).

239. Hustler Magazine, Inc. v. Falwell, 485 U.S. 46 (1988).

240. New York Times Co. v. Sullivan, 376 U.S. 254 (1964).

241. *Hustler Magazine*, 485 U.S. at 46.

242. *See* Rodney Smolla, Smolla and Nimmer on Freedom of Speech § 24.10 (2012). *See also* Rodney A. Smolla, Jerry Falwell v. Larry Flynt: The First Amendment on Trial (1988).

243. Falwell v. Flynt, 797 F.2d 1270 (4th Cir.), *reh'g en banc denied*, 805 F.2d 484 (4th Cir. 1986).

244. *Hustler Magazine*, 485 U.S. at 46 (1988).

245. *Id.*

246. *Id.*

247. *Id.*

248. Snyder v. Phelps, 562 U.S. 443, 444 (2011).

249. *Id.* at 448.

250. *Id.*

251. Snyder v. Phelps, 580 F.3d 206 (4th Cir. Md. 2009).

252. *Snyder*, 562 U.S. at 452.

253. Honoring America's Veterans and Caring for Camp Lejeune Families Act, 38 U.S.C. § 101.

254. *Snyder*, 562 U.S. at 454.

255. Lawrence v. Altice USA, 841 F. App'x 273, 277 (2d Cir. 2021) (unpub.), *cert. denied*, 142 S. Ct. 487 (2021).

256. *See, e.g.,* Neilson v. Union Bank of Cal., N.A., 290 F. Supp. 2d 1101, 1142 (C.D. Calif. 2003).

257. Wright v. Penguin Random House, 783 F. App'x 578, 584 (6th Cir. 2019) (unpub.).

258. *See, e.g.,* Dowty v. Riggs, 385 S.W.3d 117 (Ark. 2010).

259. *See, e.g.,* Nelson v. Harrah's Entm't, Inc., 2008 U.S. Dist. LEXIS 46524 (N.D. Ill., June 13, 2008).

260. *See* Camper v. Minor, 915 S.W.2d 437, 440 (Tenn. 1996). *See also* K.G. by Next Friend Ruch v. Smith, No. 21S-CT-561, 2021 WL 6063878, at *1–4 (Ind. Dec. 22, 2021).

261. Camper v. Minor, 915 S.W.2d 437, 440 (Tenn. 1996).

262. Colon v. Twitter, Inc., 14 F.4th 1213, 1213–27 (11th Cir. 2021).

263. *Id.*

264. Hyde v. City of Columbia, 637 S.W.2d 251 (Mo. Ct. App. 1982).

265. Ann C. Motto, *First Amendment: "Equity Will Not Enjoin a Libel": Well, Actually, Yes, It Will*, 11 SEVENTH CIR. REV. 271 (Spring 2016).

266. Michael M. Grynbaum, *Judge Upholds His Block on New York Times Coverage of Project Veritas*, N.Y. TIMES, Dec. 24, 2021, nytimes.com/2021/12/24/business/media/new-york-times-project-veritas.html.

267. Michael M. Grynbaum, *Judge Says New York Times Can Retain Project Veritas Memos, for Now*, N.Y. TIMES, Dec. 28, 2021, nytimes.com/2021/12/28/business/media/nyt-project-veritas.html.

268. Nina Pullano, *NY Times Gets Green Light to Publish Veritas Attorney Memos*, COURTHOUSE NEWS SERVICE, Feb. 10, 2022, courthousenews.com/ny-times-gets-green-light-to-publish-veritas-attorney-memos/.

269. Sindi v. El-Moslimany, 896 F.3d 1, 3 (1st Cir. 2018).

270. *Id.*

271. *Id.* at 33.

272. Stipulated Order Granting Permanent Injunction. Signed by Judge William M. Ray, II, Almanzar v. Kebe, No. 1:19CV-01301 (N.D.Ga. April 4, 2022).

273. *See, e.g.,* Paul Meara, *YouTuber Tasha K Ordered by Judge to Pay Cardi B $4M or Secure Bond for the Amount*, BET, Oct. 14, 2022, https://www.bet.com/article/2bxemh/tasha-k-ordered-judge-cardi-b-pay-4-million.

274. Almanzar v. Kebe, 2022 U.S. App. LEXIS 19656 *1 (11th Cir. July 15, 2022).

275. Notice of Appeal filed in Almanzar v. Kebe, 1:19-cv-01301-WMR *1-2 (July 29, 2022), https://storage.courtlistener.com/recap/gov.uscourts.gand.261932/gov.uscourts.gand.261932.242.0.pdf.

276. Coral Ridge Ministries Media, Inc. v. Amazon.com, Inc., 6 F.4th 1247, 1253 (11th Cir. 2021), *cert denied*, Coral Ridge Ministries Media, Inc. v. Southern Poverty Law Ctr., 142 S.Ct. 2453 (2022) (Thomas, J., dissenting).

277. Coral Ridge Ministries Media, Inc. v. Southern Poverty Law Center, SCOTUSBLOG, scotusblog.com/case-files/cases/coral-ridge-ministries-media-inc-v-southern-poverty-law-center/.

278. Coral Ridge Ministries Media, Inc. v. Amazon.com, Inc., 6 F.4th 1247, 1253 (11th Cir. 2021), *cert denied*, Coral Ridge Ministries Media, Inc. v. Southern Poverty

Law Ctr., 142 S.Ct. 2453 (2022) (Thomas, J., dissenting).

279. Tah v. Global Witness Publishing, Inc., 991 F.3d 231, 242 (D.C. Cir. 2020), *cert. denied* 142 S.Ct. 427 (2021).

280. *Id.* at 257-60.

281. Berisha v. Lawson, 973 F.3d 1304 (11th Cir.) *cert. denied*, 141 S.Ct. 2424 (2021)(Gorsuch, J., dissenting)(Thomas, J., dissenting). *See also* McKee v. Cosby, 874 F.3d 54 (1st Cir. 2017), *cert. denied*, 139 S. Ct. 675 (Thomas, J., concurring).

282. Matthew Schafer, *Actual Malice: The Bit That Justice Thomas Left Out*, MEDIUM, Jan. 26, 2021, matthewschafer.medium.com/actual-malice-the-bit-that-justice-thomas-left-out-1a464f82f693.

283. Adam Liptak, *By Turns Cautious and Confident, Judge Jackson Takes the Stage*, N.Y. TIMES, March 23, 2022, nytimes.com/2022/03/22/us/ketanji-brown-jackson-judicial-philosophy.html.

284. Matthew Schafer, *In Defense: New York Times v. Sullivan*, 82 LA. L. REV. 1, 70 (2022).

285. *See*, *e.g.*, Nunes v. Lizza, 12 F.4th 890, 900-01 (8th Cir. 2021), *reh'g denied* (8th Cir. Nov. 23, 2021); Desmond v. News and Observer Publishing Co., 848 S.E. 2d 647, 673 (N.C. 2020), *reh'g denied*, 848 S.E.2d 487 (N.C. 2020).

286. *Nunes*, 12 F.4th at 900-01.

287. Nunes v. Lizza, No. 20-2719 (8th Cir. Nov. 23, 2021).

288. Henry v. Media Gen. Operations, Inc., 254 A.3d 822, 827-43 (R.I. 2021).

289. *Id.*

290. *Id.*

291. *Id.* at 844 (citing Edwards v. National Audubon Society, 556 F.2d 113, 121 (2d Cir. 1977).

292. *Id.* at 847-48 (R.I. 2021) (citing Trainor v. The Standard Times, 924 A.2d 766, 769 n.1 (R.I. 2007).

293. Miller v. Target Corp., 854 Fed. Appx. 567, 569-70 (5th Cir. 2021) (per curium) (unpub.).

294. Rich v. Fox News Network, LLC, 939 F.3d 112, 122 (2d Cir. 2019) (citing Salmon v. Blesser, 802 F.3d 249, 256 (2d Cir. 2015).

295. Mullane v. Breaking Media, Inc., 433 F.Supp. 3d 102, 114 (D.Mass. 2020) (quoting Shay v. Aalters, 702 F.3d 76, 83 (1st Cir. 2012) (internal quotation marks omitted).

CHAPTER 5

1. The expression "SLAPP" was initially coined by two University of Denver professors. *See* Penelope Canan & George W. Pring, *Studying Strategic Lawsuits Against Public Participation: Mixing Quantitative and Qualitative Approaches*, 22 Law & SOC'Y REV. 385 (1988).

2. *See*, *e.g.*, Cal. Code Civ. Proc. § 425.16 (stating, in part, "The Legislature finds and declares that there has been a disturbing increase in lawsuits brought primarily to chill the valid exercise of the constitutional rights of freedom of speech and petition for the redress of grievances. The Legislature finds and declares that it is in the public interest to encourage continued participation in matters of public significance, and that this participation should not be chilled through abuse of the judicial process. . . . A cause of action against a person arising from any act of that person in furtherance of the person's right of petition or free speech under the United States or California Constitution in connection with a public issue shall be subject to a special motion to strike, unless the court determines that the plaintiff has established that there is a probability that the plaintiff will prevail on the claim").

3. Davis v. Cox, 351 P.3d 862 (2015); Leiendecker v. Asian Women United of Minn., 895 N.W.2d 623 (2017).

4. Wash. Rev. Code § 4.24.525 (2021).

5. N.Y. Civ. Rights § 70-a (2020).

6. Coleman v. Grand, E.D.N.Y. No. 18-cv-5663 (ENV) (RLM).

7. Palin v. N.Y. Times Co., No. 17-cv-4853 (JSR), 2022 U.S. Dist. LEXIS 36035 (S.D.N.Y. Mar. 1, 2022).

8. *Id.*

9. *Id.*

10. Typically, these cases end up in federal court because of diversity jurisdiction, which has two requirements— jurisdictional amount exceeds $75,000, and no plaintiff shares a state of citizenship with any defendant. *See* 28 U.S.C. § 1332 (a).

11. William James Seidleck, *Comment: Anti-SLAPP Statutes and the Federal Rules: Why Preemption Analysis Shows They Should Apply in Federal Diversity Suits*, 166 U. Pa. L. Rev. 547 (Jan. 2018).

12. Clifford v. Trump , 818 F. App'x 746 (9th Cir. 2020).

13. Cal. Civ. Proc. Code § 425.16 (2019).

14. La Liberte v. Reid, 966 F.3d 79, 87-88 (2d Cir. 2020).

15. Abbas v. Foreign Policy Group, LLC, 783 F.3d 1328, 1332 (2015).

16. *Id.* at 1338.

17. *Defamation and Related Claims*, Comm. L. in the Digital Age 2016 (Nov. 10, 2016).

18. *See, e.g.,* Yagman v. Edmondson, 723 Fed. App'x 463 (9th Cir. 2018), *cert. denied,* 139 S. Ct. 823 (2019); Planned Parenthood Federation of America, Inc. v. Center for Medical Progress, 897 F.3d 1224 (9th Cir. 2018), *cert denied,* 139 S. Ct. 1446 (2019).

19. Los Lobos Renewable Power, LLC v. AmeriCulture, Inc., 885 F.3d 659 (10th Cir.), *cert. denied*, 1139 S. Ct. 591 (2018).

20. Citizen Participation Act, H.R. 7771, 116th Cong. (2020).

21. *But see, e.g.,* Lee v. Dong-A Ilbo, 849 F.2d 876 (4th Cir. 1988) (ruling that the privilege does not extend to official reports issued by governments other than those in the United States).

22. Allen v. Ray, 87 A.3d 890 (Pa. Super. Ct. 2013) (table).

23. Tacopina v. O'Keeffe, 2015 U.S. Dist. LEXIS 118546 (S.D.N.Y. Sept. 4, 2015), *aff'd,* 645 Fed. Appx. 7 (2d Cir. 2016).

24. Hurst v. Capital Cities Media, Inc., 754 N.E.2d 429 (Ill. App. 2001).

25. Wiemer v. Rankin, 790 P.2d 347 (Idaho 1990).

26. DMC Plumbing and Remodeling v. Fox News Network, 2012 U.S. Dist. LEXIS 167318 (E.D. Mich. Nov. 26, 2012); *New Developments 2012*, MLRC Bulletin, Dec. 2012, at 60–61.

27. Milligan v. United States, 670 F. 3d 686, 698 (6th Cir. 2012).

28. Kevin T. Baine et al., *Defamation Law Case Summaries for PLI*, 2 Comm. L. in the Digital Age 15 (2014); Barhoum v. NYP Holdings, Inc., 2014 Mass. Super. LEXIS 52 (Mass. Super. Ct. 2014).

29. *Barhoum*, 2014 Mass. Super. LEXIS 52.

30. Lee v. TMZ Prods., Inc., 2015 U.S. Dist. LEXIS 104387 (D.N.J. 2015).

31. Lee v. TMZ Prods., Inc., 710 Fed. Appx. 551 (3d Cir. 2017).

32. Kinsey v. The N.Y. Times Co., 991 F.3d 171 (2d Cir. 2021).

33. Neiman Nix v. ESPN, Inc., 772 F. App'x 807 (11th Cir. 2019).

34. Landry's, Inc. v. Animal Legal Def. Fund, 631 S.W.3d 40 (Tex. 2021).

35. *Id.* at 25.

36. *Defamation and Related Claims*, Comm. L. in the Digital Age (2018).

37. Adelson v. Harris, 876 F.3d 413, 414 (2d Cir. 2017).

38. *Id.*

39. *Defamation and Related Claims, supra* note 36.

40. *New Developments 2012*, MLRC Bulletin, Dec. 2012, at 61.

41. To see if the fair report privilege applies in your state, you can read your state's defamation law or search for state cases

that have ruled on the fair report privilege. See Chapter 1 for more information on finding cases and statutes.

42. Whitney v. California, 274 U.S. 357, 375 (1927) (Brandeis, J., concurring).

43. Fowler v. Harper & Fleming James Jr., Law of Torts § 5.28, at 456 (1956).

44. *See* Gertz v. Robert Welch, Inc., 418 U.S. 323, 339–40 (1974).

45. Ollman v. Evans, 750 F.2d 970 (D.C. Cir. 1984).

46. Fowler v. Harper & Fleming James Jr., Law of Torts § 5.28, at 456 (1956).

47. *See* RESTATEMENT OF TORTS § 606 (1938).

48. RESTATEMENT (SECOND) OF TORTS § 566 (1977) cmt. a.

49. Milkovich v. Lorain Journal Co., 497 U.S. 1, 14 (1990).

50. Gertz v. Robert Welch, Inc., 418 U.S. 323, 351 (1974).

51. Milkovich v. Lorain Journal Co., 497 U.S. 1 (1990).

52. *Id.*

53. Janklow v. Newsweek, 788 F.2d 1300, 1305 (8th Cir. 1986).

54. Spelson v. CBS, Inc., 581 F.Supp. 1195 (N.D. Ill. 1984); Liberty Lobby, Inc. v. Anderson, 746 F.2d 1563 (D.C. Cir. 1984), *vacated on other grounds*, 477 U.S. 242 (1986); Henderson v. Times Mirror

Co., 669 F.Supp. 356 (D. Colo. 1987); Dow v. New Haven Indep., Inc., 549 A.2d 683 (Conn. 1987).

55. Milkovich v. Lorain Journal Co., 497 U.S. 1, 4 (1990).

56. *Id.* at 1.

57. *Id.* at 18.

58. *Id.*

59. *Id.* at 21.

60. *Id.* at 17.

61. Dallas Morning News v. Tatum, 554 S.W.3d 614 (Tex. 2018), *cert. denied*, 139 S. Ct. 1216 (Feb. 19, 2019).

62. *Id.*

63. Donald J. Trump for President v. CNN, 500 F. Supp. 3d 1349 (N.D. Ga. Nov. 12, 2020).

64. *Id.* at 2.

65. Milkovich v. Lorain Journal Co., 497 U.S. 1, 4 (1990).

66. McCafferty v. Newsweek Media Grp., Ltd., 955 F.3d 352 (3d Cir. 2020).

67. Madsen v. Buie, 454 So. 2d 727, 729 (Fla. Dist. Ct. App. 1984).

68. Unsworth v. Musk, No. 2:18-cv-08048-SVW-JC, 2019 U.S. Dist. LEXIS 229076 (C.D. Cal. Nov. 18, 2019).

69. *Id.* at 29.

70. *New Developments 2012*, MLRC BULLETIN, Dec. 2012, at 52.

71. Redmond v. Gawker Media, LLC, 2012 Cal. App. Unpub. LEXIS 5879

(Cal. App. Aug. 10, 2012) (unpublished).

72. Hustler Magazine, Inc. v. Falwell, 485 U.S. 46 (1988).

73. Greenbelt Cooperative Publ'g Ass'n, Inc. v. Bressler, 398 U.S. 6, 7–8 (1970).

74. Seaton v. TripAdvisor LLC, 728 F.3d 592 (6th Cir. 2013).

75. Herring Networks, Inc. v. Maddow, 8 F.4th 1148 (9th Cir. 2021).

76. *Id.* at 6-7.

77. *Id.* at 26.

78. Moore v. Cohen, 548 F. Supp. 3d 330 (S.D.N.Y. 2021).

79. *Id.* at 14-15.

80. 47 U.S.C. §§ 230 (c)(1), (e)(3).

81. RonNell Andersen Jones, *Developments in the Law of Social Media*, COMM. L. IN THE DIGITAL AGE (2016).

82. *Legal Guide for Bloggers*, *Section 230 Protections*, ELECTRONIC FRONTIER FOUND., www.eff.org/iss ues/bloggers/legal/liabi lity/230 (last visited Nov. 22, 2022).

83. *Id.*

84. Although this was not a libel case (the underlying right of publicity is discussed in Chapter 6), the court's ruling broadly applied to how Section 230 is used by services like Facebook to defend libel and privacy claims.

85. Fraley v. Facebook, Inc., 830 F.Supp. 2d 801–02 (N.D. Cal. 2011).

86. Jones v. Dirty World Entm't Recordings, 755 F.3d 398, 401 (6th Cir. 2014).

87. *Id.* at 417.

88. *Id.*

89. Doe No. 14 v. Internet Brands, Inc., 824 F. 3d 846, 850 (9th Cir. 2016).

90. *Id.* at 851.

91. Gonzalez v. Google LLC, 214 L.Ed.2d 12 (U.S. 2022).

92. Gonzalez v. Google LLC, 2 F.4th 871 (9th Cir. 2021).

93. 47 U.S.C. §§ 230 (c)(1), (e)(3).

94. Edwards v. National Audubon Society, 556 F.2d 113 (2d Cir. 1977) (ruling that "when a responsible, prominent organization . . . makes serious charges against a public figure, the First Amendment protects the accurate and disinterested reporting of those charges, regardless of the reporter's private views of their validity. . . . We do not believe that the press may be required under the First Amendment to suppress newsworthy statements merely because it has serious doubts regarding their truth"). *Id.* at 120.

95. Dan Laidman, *When the Slander Is the Story: The Neutral Report Privilege in Theory and Practice*, 17 UCLA Ent. L. Rev. 74, 76 (2010).

96. Eli Segal & Michael E. Baughman, *#MeToo and the Media*, Pepper Hamilton, LLC, May 2018, www.pepperlaw.com/publications/metoo-and-the-media-2018-06-05/.

97. Smartmatic Corp. USA v. Fox Corp., No. 151136/2021 (N.Y. Sup. Ct. filed Feb. 3, 2021).

98. Memorandum in Support of Defendant's Motion to Dismiss, Smartmatic Corp. USA v. Fox Corp., No. 151136/2021 (N.Y. Sup. Ct. motion to dismiss filed Feb. 8, 2021).

99. McKinney v. Avery Journal, Inc., 393 S.E.2d 295 (N.C. 1990).

100. Auvil v. CBS, 140 F.R.D. 450 (E.D. Wash. 1991).

101. See Firth v. State of New York, 775 N.E.2d 463 (N.Y. 2002), which outlines the principles of applying the single-publication rule to the internet and is often used as a precedent to support similar cases in other states and in the federal court system.

102. Masson v. New Yorker Magazine, Inc., 501 U.S. 496, 523 (1991).

103. Cardillo v. Doubleday & Co., Inc., 518 F.2d 638 (2d Cir. 1975) (ruling that the passages of a book whose authors wrote that a habitual criminal was involved in various other criminal activities did not constitute actual malice).

104. Dykstra v. St. Martin's Press Llc, No. 153676/2019, 2020 N.Y.

Misc. LEXIS 7819 (Sup. Ct. May 29, 2020).

105. *Id.* at 29.

106. Liberty Lobby, Inc. v. Anderson, 746 F.2d 1563, 1568 (D.C. Cir. 1984), *vacated on other grounds*, 477 U.S. 242 (1986).

107. *Id.*

108. 28 U.S.C. §§ 4101–4105 (2012).

109. TV Azteca v. Ruiz, 490 S.W. 3d 29 (Tex. 2016), *cert. denied*, 137 S.Ct. 2290 (2017).

110. Logan v. District of Columbia, 447 F.Supp. 1328 (D.D.C. 1978).

111. Mourning v. Family Publ'ns. Serv., 411 U.S. 356, 382 (1973). *See also* Adickes v. Kress & Co., 398 U.S. 144, 157 (1970); United States v. Diebold, Inc., 369 U.S. 654, 655 (1962).

112. *See* Anderson v. Liberty Lobby, Inc., 477 U.S. 242 (1986).

113. Washington Post Co. v. Keogh, 365 F.2d 965, 968 (D.C. Cir. 1966).

114. Hutchinson v. Proxmire, 443 U.S. 111, 120 n.9 (1979).

115. Anderson v. Liberty Lobby, Inc., 477 U.S. at 244, 256.

116. Bell Atlantic Corp. v. Twombly, 550 U.S. 544 (2007).

117. Ashcroft v. Iqbal, 556 U.S. 662 (2009).

118. Suja A. Thomas, *The New Summary Judgment Motion: The Motion to*

Dismiss Under Iqbal and Twombly, Ill. Pub. L. and Legal Theory Res. Papers Series (Oct. 27, 2009), papers.ssrn.com/sol3/papers .cfm?abstract_id=1494683.

119. Schatz v. Republican State Leadership Committee, 669 F.3d 50, 57 (1st Cir. 2012).

120. Mayfield v. NASCAR, 674 F. 3d 369 (4th Cir. 2012).

121. Michel v. NYP Holdings, Inc., 816 F. 3d 686 (11th Cir. 2016).

122. William H. J. Hubbard, *The Empirical Effects of Twombly and Iqbal*, 14 J. Empirical Legal Stud. 474 (2017).

123. McDougal v. Fox News Network, LLC , 489 F. Supp. 3d 174 (S.D.N.Y. 2020).

124. *See, e.g.,* Keeton v. Hustler Magazine, Inc., 465 U.S. 770 (1984) (overturning a lower court ruling dismissing a libel suit filed by a resident of New York against an Ohio corporation in a New Hampshire court). *See also* New York Times Co. v. Sullivan, 376 U.S. 254 (1964) (where the trial and first appeal were heard in Alabama courts).

125. Young v. New Haven Advocate, 315 F.3d 256, 261 (4th Cir. 2002), *cert. denied*, 538 U.S. 1035 (2003).

126. *Id.* at 263.

127. *Id.*

128. *See, e.g.,* Baines v. Daily News 2018 WL 1546555 (table) (N.Y. Sup. Ct. Mar. 28, 2018); Hearst Newspapers, LLC v. Status Lounge, Inc., 541 S.W.3d 881 (Tex. App. 2017).

129. John C. Martin, *The Role of Retraction in Defamation Suits*, 1993 U. Chi. Legal F. 293, 294 (1993).

130. Two states' retraction statutes apply only to newspapers. *See* Minn. Stat. Ann. 548.06 (1987); S.D. Codified Laws 20–11–7 (1995). Two others include media other than newspapers but exclude radio and television. *See* Wis. Stat. 895.05 (1998); Okla. Stat. tit. 12, § 1446a.

131. Dennis Hale, *The Impact of State Prohibitions of Punitive Damages on Libel Litigation: An Empirical Analysis*, 5 Vand. J. Ent. L. & Prac. 96, 100 (2003).

132. Boswell v. Phoenix Newspapers, Inc., 730 P.2d 186 (Ariz. 1986).

133. Ariz. Rev. Stat. §§ 12–653.02 and 12.653.03.

134. Ariz. Const., art. 18, § 6.

135. RonNell Andersen Jones, *Developments in the Law of Social Media*, Comm. L. in the Digital Age (2016).

136. Hassell v. Bird, 203 Cal. Rptr. 3d 203 (Ct. App. 2016).

137. Hassell v. Bird, 420 P.3d 776, 882 (Cal. 2018), *cert. denied*, 139 S. Ct. 940 (2019).

138. Eric Goldman, *The California Supreme Court Didn't Ruin Section 230 (Today)—Hassell v. Bird*, Technology & Marketing Law Blog, July 2, 2018, blog.ericgoldman.org/archives/2018/07/the-california-supreme-court-didnt-ruin-section-230-today-hassell-v-bird.htm.

139. Lokhova v. Halper, 995 F.3d 134 (4th Cir. 2021).

140. *Id.* at 143.

141. Nunes v. Lizza, No. 20-2710, 2021 U.S. App. LEXIS 27630 (8th Cir. Sep. 15, 2021).

142. *Id.* at 19.

143. *Id.* at 21.

144. In its entirety, the column reads as follows:

Yesterday in the Franklin County Common Pleas Court, Judge Paul Martin overturned an Ohio High School Athletic Assn. decision to suspend the Maple Heights wrestling team from this year's state tournament.

It's not final yet—the judge granted Maple only a temporary injunction against the ruling—but unless the judge acts much more quickly than he did in this decision (he has been deliberating since a Nov. 8 hearing) the temporary injunction will allow Maple to compete in the tournament and make any further discussion meaningless.

But there is something much more important involved here than whether Maple was denied due process by the OHSAA, the basis of the temporary injunction. When a person takes on a job in a school, whether it be as a teacher, coach, administrator or even maintenance w rker, it is well to remember that his primary job is that of educator.

There is scarcely a person concerned with school who doesn't leave his mark in some way on the young people who pass his way—many are the lessons taken away from school by students which weren't learned from a lesson plan or out of a book. They come from personal experiences with and observations of their superiors and peers, from watching actions and reactions. Such a lesson was learned (or relearned) yesterday by the student body of Maple Heights High School, and by anyone who attended the Maple-Mentor wrestling meet of last Feb. 8. A lesson which, sadly, in view of the events of the past year, is well they learned early.

It is simply this: If you get in a jam, lie your way out.

If you're successful enough, and powerful enough, and can sound sincere enough, you stand an excellent chance of making the lie stand up,

regardless of what really happened.

The teachers responsible were mainly head Maple wrestling coach, Mike Milkovich, and former superintendent of schools H. Donald Scott.

Last winter they were faced with a difficult situation. Milkovich's ranting from the side of the mat and egging the crowd on against the meet official and the opposing team backfired during a meet with Greater Cleveland Conference rival Metor [sic], and resulted in first the Maple Heights team, then many of the partisan crowd attacking the Mentor squad in a brawl which sent four Mentor wrestlers to the hospital.

Naturally, when Mentor protested to the governing body of high school sports, the OHSAA, the two men were called on the carpet to account for the incident.

But they declined to walk into the hearing and face up to their responsibilities, as one would hope a coach of Milkovich's accomplishments and reputation would do, and one would certainly expect from a man with the responsible poisition [sic] of superintendent of schools.

Instead they chose to come to the hearing and misrepresent the things that happened to the OHSAA Board of Control, attempting not only to

convince the board of their own innocence, but, incredibly, shift the blame of the affair to Mentor.

I was among the 2,000-plus witnesses of the meet at which the trouble broke out, and I also attended the hearing before the OHSAA, so I was in a unique position of being the only non-involved party to observe both the meet itself and the Milkovich-Scott version presented to the board. Any resemblance between the two occurrances [sic] is purely coincidental.

To anyone who was at the meet, it need only be said that the Maple coach's wild gestures during the events leading up to the brawl were passed off by the two as "shrugs," and that Milkovich claimed he was "Powerless to control the crowd" before the melee.

Fortunately, it seemed at the time, the Milkovich-Scott version of the incident presented to the board of control had enough contradictions and obvious untruths so that the six board members were able to see through it.

Probably as much in distasteful reaction to the chicanery of the two officials as in displeasure over the actual incident, the board then voted to suspend Maple from this year's tournament and to put Maple Heights, and both Milkovich and his son, Mike Jr. (the Maple Jaycee coach), on two-year probation.

But unfortunately, by the time the hearing before Judge Martin rolled around, Milkovich and Scott apparently had their version of the incident polished and reconstructed, and the judge apparently believed them.

"I can say that some of the stories told to the judge sounded pretty darned unfamiliar," said Dr. Harold Meyer, commissioner of the OHSAA, who attended the hearing. "It certainly sounded different from what they told us."

Nevertheless, the judge bought their story, and ruled in their favor.

Anyone who attended the meet, whether he be from Maple Heights, Mentor, or impartial observer, knows in his heart that Milkovich and Scott lied at the hearing after each having given his solemn oath to tell the truth.

But they got away with it. Is that the kind of lesson we want our young people learning from their high school administrators and coaches? I think not.

145. In its entirety, the column reads as follows:

So I guess we're down to just one form of death still considered worthy of deception.

I'm told there was a time when the word "cancer" was never mentioned. Oddly, it was considered an embarrassing way to die.

It took a while for honesty to come to the AIDS epidemic. Ironically, the first person I knew to die of AIDS was said to have cancer.

We're open these days with just about every form of death except one—suicide.

When art expert Ted Pillsbury died in March, his company said he suffered an apparent heart attack on a country road in Kaufman County.

But what was apparent to every witness on the scene that day was that Pillsbury had walked a few paces from his car and shot himself.

Naturally, with such a well-known figure, the truth quickly came out.

More recently, a paid obituary in this newspaper reported that a popular local high school student died "as a result of injuries sustained in an automobile accident."

When one of my colleagues began to inquire, thinking the death deserved news coverage, it turned out to have been a suicide.

There was a car crash, all right, but death came from a self-inflicted gunshot wound [page break] in a time of remorse afterward.

And for us, there the matter ended. Newspapers

don't write about suicides unless they involve a public figure or happen in a very public way.

But is that always best?

I'm troubled that we, as a society, allow suicide to remain cloaked in such secrecy, if not outright deception.

Some obituary readers tell me they feel guilty for having such curiosity about how people died. They're frustrated when obits don't say. "Morbid curiosity," they call it apologetically.

But I don't think we should feel embarrassment at all. I think the need to know is wired deeply in us. I think it's part of our survival mechanism.

Like a cat putting its nose to the wind, that curiosity is part of how we gauge the danger out there for ourselves and our loved ones.

And the secrecy surrounding suicide leaves us greatly underestimating the danger there.

Did you know that almost twice as many people die each year from suicide as from homicide?

Think of how much more attention we pay to the latter. We're nearly obsessed with crime. Yet we're nearly blind to the greater threat of self-inflicted violence.

Suicide is the third-leading cause of death among

young people (ages 15 to 24) in this country.

Do you think that might be important for parents to understand?

In part, we don't talk about suicide because we don't talk about the illness that often underlies it—mental illness.

I'm a big admirer of Julie Hersh. The Dallas woman first went public with her story of depression and suicide attempts in my column three years ago.

She has since written a book, Struck by Living. Through honesty, she's trying to erase some of the shame and stigma that compounds and prolongs mental illness.

Julie recently wrote a blog item titled "Don't omit from the obit," urging more openness about suicide as a cause of death.

"I understand why people don't include it," she told me. "But it's such a missed opportunity to educate."

And she's so right.

Listen, the last thing I want to do is put guilt on the family of suicide victims. They already face a grief more intense than most of us will ever know.

But averting our eyes from the reality of suicide only puts more lives at risk.

Awareness, frank discussion, timely intervention, treatment—those are

the things that save lives. Honesty is the first step.

CHAPTER 6

1. Riley v. California, 573 U.S. 373, 385 (2014).

2. Jeffery A. Smith, *Moral Guardians and the Origins of the Right to Privacy*, 10 Journalism & Comm. Monographs 65 (2008).

3. Samuel D. Warren & Louis D. Brandeis, *The Right to Privacy*, 4 Harv. L. Rev. 193 (1890).

4. Warren and Brandeis rested their contention on an English case, Prince Albert v. Strange, 64 Eng. Rep. 293 (V.C. 1848), *on appeal*, 64 Eng. Rep. 293 (1849). But not until 2001 did English courts explicitly recognize a right to privacy. *See* Douglas v. Hello! Ltd., [2001] W.L.R. 992, 1033, ¶ 110 ("We have reached a point at which it can be said with confidence that the law recognizes and will appropriately protect a right of personal privacy") (per Sedley, L.J.).

5. Warren & Brandeis, *supra* note 3, at 197; *See also* Dorothy J. Glancy, *The Invention of the Right to Privacy*, 21 Ariz. L. Rev. 1 (1979).

6. *See* Don R. Pember, Privacy and the Press (1972).

7. *FTC Explores Rules Cracking Down on Commercial Surveillance and Lax Data Security Practices*, Federal Trade Commission, August 11, 2022, ftc.gov/news-events/news/press-releases/2022/08/ftc-explores-rules-cracking-down-commercial-surveillance-lax-data-security-practices.

8. *State Laws Related to Digital Privacy*, National Conference of State Legislators, June 7, 2022, ncsl.org/research/telecommunications-and-information-technology/state-laws-related-to-internet-privacy.aspx.

9. Carpenter v. United States, 138 S. Ct. 2206, 2213 (2018).

10. U.S. Const. amend. IV.

11. U.S. Const. amend. III, V.

12. Griswold v. Connecticut, 381 U.S. 479, 481 (1965).

13. *Id.* at 483.

14. Roe v. Wade, 410 U.S. 113 (1973).

15. *Id.* at 153.

16. *Id.*

17. 429 U.S. 589, 589-600 (1977).

18. *Id.* at 605.

19. Planned Parenthood of Southeastern Pennsylvania v. Casey, 505 U.S. 833, 852-53 (1992).

20. *Id.* at 851.

21. Olmstead v. United States, 277 U.S. 438 (1928).

22. *Id.* at 478 (Brandeis, J., dissenting).

23. Silverman v. United States, 365 U.S. 505 (1961).

24. Katz v. United States, 389 U.S. 347 (1967) (Harlan, J., concurring).

25. Daniel T. Pesciotta, *I'm Not Dead Yet: Katz, Jones, and the Fourth Amendment in the 21st Century*, 63 Case W. Res. 187, 198 (2012).

26. Carpenter v. United States, 138 S. Ct. 2206, 2237 (2018).

27. Griswold v. Connecticut, 381 U.S. 479, 481 (1965).

28. Katz v. United States, 389 U.S. 347 (1967) (Harlan, J., concurring).

29. O'Connor v. Ortega, 480 U.S. 709 (1987).

30. Ray Lewis, *Comment: Employee E-mail Privacy Still Unemployed: What the United States Can Learn From the United Kingdom*, 67 La. L. Rev. 959 (2007): 959; *see also* Smyth v. Pillsbury Co., 914 F. Supp. 97, 101 (E.D. Pa. 1996).

31. City of Ontario v. Quon, 560 U.S. 746 (2010).

32. *See* Comsys, Inc. v. Pacetti, 893 F. 3d 468 (7th Cir. 2018).

33. Kyllo v. United States, 533 U.S. 27 (2001).

34. United States v. Jones, 565 U.S. 400 (2012).

35. Riley v. California, 573 U.S. 373, 393 (2014).

36. Carpenter v. United States, 138 S. Ct. 2206 (2018).

37. *Id.* at 2219.

38. *Id.* at 2206.

39. *Id.* at 36.

40. *Id.*

41. *Carpenter*, 138 S. Ct. at 2217–18 (internal quotation marks omitted).

42. *Id.* at 2223 (Kennedy, J., dissenting), 2246 (Alito, J., dissenting).

43. *Id.* at 2235 (Thomas, J., dissenting).

44. *Id.* at 2261 (Gorsuch, J., dissenting).

45. *Privacy*, Merriam-Webster, Mar. 31, 2019, merriam-webster.com/dictionary/privacy.

46. William L. Prosser, *Privacy*, 48 Cal. L. Rev. 383 (1960).

47. Restatement (Second) of Torts § 652I.

48. *See, e.g.*, Restatement (Third) of Unfair Competition § 46 cmt. d (right of publicity limited to "natural persons").

49. Restatement (Second) of Torts § 652B.

50. Media L. Resource Ctr., Media Privacy and Related Law 50-State Survey 2016–2017 (2017).

51. *Id.* at cmt. b.

52. *See, e.g.*, Restatement (Second) of Torts § 652B cmt. a.

53. *In re* Facebook, Inc. Internet Tracking Litig., 956 F.3d 589, 602–06 (9th Cir. 2020), *cert. denied sub nom.* Facebook, Inc. v. Davis, 141 S. Ct. 1684, 209 L. Ed. 2d 464 (2021).

54. *See, e.g.*, Eli A. Meltz, Note, *No Harm, No Foul? "Attempted" Invasion of Privacy and the Tort of Intrusion Upon Seclusion*, 83 Fordham L. Rev. 3431, 3452–53 (2015).

55. Boring v. Google, Inc., 362 F. App'x 273 (3d Cir.), *cert. denied*, 562 U.S. 836 (2010).

56. Hill v. Colorado, 530 U.S. 703 (2000).

57. Shulman v. Group W Prods., Inc., 74 Cal. Rptr. 2d 843, *opinion modified*, 1998 Cal. LEXIS 4846 (Cal. 1998).

58. United States v. Maldonado-Norat, 122 F. Supp. 2d 264 (D.P.R. 2000).

59. *See, e.g.*, Broughton v. McClatchy Newspapers, Inc., 588 S.E.2d 20 (N.C. App. 2003); Livingstone v. Hugo Boss Store, At. City, NJ, No. CV101971RB-KAMD, 2021 WL 3910149, at *6 (D.N.J. Sept. 1, 2021).

60. *Current Unmanned Aircraft State Law Landscape*, Nat'l Conference of State Legislatures, Aug. 3, 2021, ncsl.org/research/transportation/current-unmanned-aircraft-state-law-landscape.aspx#overview.

61. Simmons v. Bauer Media Grp. USA, LLC, 263 Cal. Rptr. 3d 903 (2020).

62. Broidy Cap. Mgmt. LLC v. Muzin, No. 19-CV-0150 (DLF), 2020 WL 1536350, at *19 (D.D.C. Mar. 31, 2020), *aff'd*, 12 F.4th 789 (D.C. Cir. 2021).

63. Webb v. CBS Broad., Inc., 2009 U.S. Dist. LEXIS 38597, at *9 (N.D. Ill., May 7, 2009).

64. Jackman v. Cebrink-Swartz, No. 2D20-2384, 2021 WL 2171745, at *3 (Fla. Dist. Ct. App. May 28, 2021), *review denied*, No. SC21-913, 2021 WL 4240567 (Fla. Sept. 17, 2021).

65. Mezger v. Bick, 280 Cal. Rptr. 3d 720 (2021), *reh'g denied* (July 19, 2021), *review denied* (Oct. 13, 2021).

66. *In re* Facebook, Inc. Internet Tracking Litig., 956 F.3d 589, 606 (9th Cir. 2020), *cert. denied sub nom.* Facebook, Inc. v. Davis, 141 S. Ct. 1684, 209 L. Ed. 2d 464 (2021).

67. Medical Laboratory Mgmt. Consultants v. Am. Broad. Cos., Inc., 306 F.3d 806, 819 (9th Cir. 2002).

68. Belluomo v. KAKE TV & Radio, Inc., 596 P.2d 832 (Kan. App. 1979).

69. Machleder v. Diaz, 538 F. Supp. 1364 (S.D.N.Y. 1982).

70. Desnick v. Am. Broad. Cos., Inc., 44 F.3d 1345 (7th Cir. 1995).

71. Carter v. Superior Court of San Diego Cty., 2002 Cal. App. Unpub. LEXIS 5017 (Ct. App. 2002).

72. Dietemann v. Time, Inc., 449 F.2d 245, 249 (9th Cir. 1971).

73. *Id.*

74. *See, e.g., Criminal Liability for False Personation During Stop for Traffic Infraction*, 26 A.L.R. 5th 378 (Originally published in 1995).

75. *See, e.g.,* Restatement (Second) of Torts § 652E cmt. b, illus. 1.

76. Solano v. Playgirl, Inc., 292 F.3d 1078, 1082 (9th Cir.), *cert. denied*, 537 U.S. 1029 (2002).

77. *False Light Invasion of Privacy—Cognizability and Elements*, 57 A.L.R.4th 22 (Originally published in 1987).

78. Gaprindashvili v. Netflix, Inc., No. 221CV07408VAPSKX, 2022 WL 363537, at *2-10. (C.D. Cal. Jan. 27, 2022).

79. Brian Bushard, *Netflix Settles 'Queen's Gambit' Defamation Lawsuit With Georgian Chess Master*, Forbes, Sept. 6, 2022, forbes.com/sites/brianbushard/2022/09/06/netflix-settles-queens-gambit-defamation-lawsuit-with-georgian-chess-master/?sh=92bc51f1ee1f.

80. *See* Restatement (Second) of Torts § 652E.

81. *Id.* at § 652I cmt. c.

82. *Id.* at § 652D cmt. a.

83. *Solano*, 292 F.3d 1078, 1082 (9th Cir.), *cert. denied*, 537 U.S. 1029 (2002).

84. *See, e.g., id.*

85. *See, e.g.,* Austin Eberhardt Donaldson Corp. v. Morgan Stanley Dean Witter Trust FSB, 2001 U.S. Dist. LEXIS 1090 (N.D. Ill. 2001).

86. Howard v. Antilla, 294 F.3d 244 (1st Cir. 2002).

87. Longoria v. Kodiak Concepts LLC, 527 F.Supp.3d 1085, 1102 (D. Ariz. 2021).

88. Michael Sewell, *Note and Comment: Invasion of Privacy in Texas: Public Disclosure of Embarrassing Private Facts*, 2 Tex. Wesleyan L. Rev. 411 (1995).

89. Moriarty v. Greene, 732 N.E.2d 730 (Ill. App. Ct. 2000).

90. Balla v. Hall, 59 Cal. App. 5th 652, 687 (2021), *review denied* (Apr. 14, 2021).

91. Peoples Bank & Trust Co. v. Globe Int'l, 978 F.2d 1065 (8th Cir. 1992), *on remand*, Mitchell v. Globe Int'l Publ'g, Inc., 817 F. Supp. 72 (W.D. Ark.), *cert. denied*, 510 U.S. 931 (1993).

92. Time, Inc. v. Hill, 385 U.S. 374 (1967).

93. *Id.*

94. Cantrell v. Forest City Pub. Co., 419 U.S. 245 (1974).

95. State courts or federal courts applying state law to follow *Gertz* rather than *Hill* and *Cantrell*, thus not requiring private false light plaintiffs to prove actual malice, include Alabama, Delaware, Kansas, Utah, West Virginia and the District of Columbia, Media L. Resource Ctr.,

Media Privacy and Related Law 50-State Survey 2018–2019 (2019).

96. State courts or federal courts applying state law to follow *Hill* and *Cantrell* rather than *Gertz*, thus requiring private false light plaintiffs to prove actual malice, include Arkansas, California, Connecticut, Florida, Georgia, Illinois, Indiana, Iowa, Kentucky, Maine, Michigan, Mississippi, Montana, Nebraska, Nevada, New Jersey, Oklahoma, Oregon, Pennsylvania, Tennessee and Washington. *See, e.g.,* Lohrenz v. Donnelly, 223 F. Supp. 2d, 25 (2002).

97. Talley v. Time, Inc., 923 F.3d 878 (10th Cir. 2019).

98. *Id.*

99. State courts or federal courts applying state law to follow *Gertz* rather than *Hill* and *Cantrell*, thus not requiring private false light plaintiffs to prove actual malice, include Alabama, Delaware, Kansas, Utah, West Virginia and the District of Columbia. Media L. Resource Ctr., Media Privacy and Related Law 50-State Survey 2016–2017 (2017).

100. Santoni v. Mueller, No. 3:20-CV-00975, 2022 WL 97049, at *13 (M.D. Tenn. Jan. 10, 2022).

101. *See* Harvey L. Zuckman et al., Modern Commc'ns L. 357–61 (1999).

102. *See id.* at 360–61 (1999).

103. *E.g.,* Dudee v. Philpot, 133 N.E.3d 590 (Ohio Ct. App. 2019) (stating "If a statement is true, then there is no false light.").

104. *E.g.,* Veilleux v. NBC, 206 F.3d 92, 134 (1st Cir. 2000), said opinion could be a false light defense, while Boese v. Paramount Pictures Corp., 952 F. Supp. 550, 558–59 (N.D. Ill. 1996), said opinion is not a false light defense.

105. *See Application of Anti-SLAPP ("Strategic Lawsuit Against Public Participation") Statutes to Invasion of Privacy Claims,* 85 A.L.R.6th 475 (Originally published in 2013).

106. Abrams v. Sanson, 458 P.3d 1062 (Nev. 2020).

107. *Id.*

108. Restatement (Third) of Unfair Competition §§ 46-47.

109. 433 U.S. 562 (1977).

110. *See* Kelli L. Sager & Karen A. Henry, *Developments in Misappropriation and Right of Publicity Law—2014,* Comm. L. in the Digital Age 2 (2014).

111. Media L. Resource Ctr., Media Privacy and Related Law 50-State Survey 2018–2019 (2019).

112. Restatement (Third) of Unfair Competition § 46.

113. N.Y. Civil Rights Law §§ 50–51.

114. Haelan Labs., Inc. v. Topps Chewing Gum, Inc., 202 F.2d 866 (2d Cir. 1953).

115. *See* J. Thomas McCarthy, The Rights of Publicity and Privacy, 2d §§ 1:27, 4:7 (2018).

116. By statute: California, Florida, Illinois, Indiana, Kentucky, Nebraska, Nevada, Ohio, Oklahoma, Pennsylvania, Tennessee, Texas, Virginia and Washington. By common law: Connecticut, Georgia, Michigan, New Jersey and Utah. *Id.* New York also has recognized statutory post-mortem publicity rights since 2021. N.Y. Civ. Rights Law § 50-f (McKinney 2021).

117. Some states, such as Georgia, New Jersey and Utah, and the U.S. Court of Appeals for the Second Circuit have decided by common law that the right of publicity survives after death. Statutes in 10 states say the same. Some states, such as Illinois and Ohio, and the U.S. Courts of Appeals for the Sixth and Seventh Circuits say by common law that the right of publicity ends when a person dies. Five states agree by statute: Arizona, Massachusetts, New York, Rhode Island and Wisconsin. J. Thomas McCarthy, The Rights of Publicity and Privacy, 2d §§ 1:27, 4:7 (2018).

118. N.Y. Civ. Rights Law § 50-f (McKinney 2021).

119. For example, Virginia limits the right of publicity to 20 years after a person's death, and Indiana and Oklahoma allow

the right to last 100 years after a person's death.

120. Neb. Rev. Stat. § 20-202.

121. *New Developments 2012*, MLRC Bulletin, Dec. 2012, at 68–71.

122. Est. of Jackson v. Comm'r of Internal Revenue, 121 T.C.M. (CCH) 1320 (T.C. 2021).

123. Hebrew Univ. of Jerusalem v. General Motors, LLC, 903 F. Supp. 2d 932 (C.D. Cal 2012).

124. *Louisiana House Bill 377*, The Media Coalition, Oct. 3, 2019, mediacoalition. org/louisiana-house-bill-0377/.

125. Louisiana H.B. 377 (2019).

126. *See, e.g.,* Dalbec v. Gentleman's Companion, Inc., 828 F.2d 921 (2d Cir. 1987).

127. Jennifer Rothman, *Harris Faulkner Hamster Case Settles*, Rothman's Roadmap to the Right of Publicity, Oct. 7, 2016, rightofpublicityroadmap. com/news-commentary/harris-faulkner-hamster-case-settles.

128. *See* J. Thomas McCarthy, The Rights of Publicity and Privacy, 2d § 3:7 (2018).

129. Jackson v. Odenat, 9 F. Supp. 3d 342 (S.D.N.Y. March 24, 2014).

130. Martin v. Wendy's Int'l, Inc., 2017 WL 1545684 (N.D. Ill. April 28, 2017), *aff'd*, 714 F. App'x 590 (7th Cir.), *cert. denied*, 139 S. Ct. 104 (2018).

131. Martin v. Wendy's Int'l, Inc., 714 F. App'x 590 (7th Cir. 2018).

132. C.B.C. Distribution and Mktg., Inc. v. Major League Baseball Advanced Media, LP, 505 F.3d 818 (8th Cir. 2007), *cert. denied*, 553 U.S. 1090 (2008).

133. Dobrowolski v. Intelius, Inc., 2017 WL 3720170 (N.D. Ill. Aug. 29, 2017).

134. Midler v. Ford Motor Co., 849 F.2d 460 (9th Cir. 1988). A federal district court denied Midler punitive damages, but the jury awarded $400,000 in compensatory damages. The Ninth Circuit affirmed. Midler v. Young & Rubicam, Inc., 944 F.2d 909 (9th Cir. 1991), *cert. denied*, 503 U.S. 951 (1992).

135. White v. Samsung Elec. Am., Inc., 971 F.2d 1395 (9th Cir. 1992), *cert. denied*, 508 U.S. 951 (1993).

136. *See, e.g.,* Cardtoons, L.C. v. Major League Baseball Players Ass'n, 95 F.3d 959 (10th Cir. 1996).

137. *White*, 971 F.2d at 1401.

138. Jennifer E. Rothman, *Sacha Baron Cohen sues Over Unauthorized Ad Campaign*, Rothman's Roadmap to the Right of Publicity, July 14, 2021, rightofpublicityroadmap. com/news_commentary/sacha-baron-cohen-sues-over-unauthorized-ad-campaign/.

139. *Baron Cohen Drops Lawsuit Over Cannabis Dispensary Billboard*, AP, May 18, 2022, apnews. com/article/borat-cannabis-billboard-82f3d34abd8e861a9f-703837c09ef7bd.

140. Kolebuck-Utz v. Whitepages Inc., No. C21-0053-JCC,2021 WL 1575219 (W.D. Wash. Apr. 22, 2021).

141. Brooks v. Thomson Reuters, No. 21CV01418EMC, 2021 WL 3621837 (Aug. 16, 2021).

142. *Id.*

143. Ohio Rev. Code § 2741.01.

144. Pinder v. 4716 Inc., 494 F. Supp. 3d 618 (D. Ariz. 2020).

145. Electra v. 59 Murray Enterprises, Inc., 987 F.3d 233 (2d Cir. 2021).

146. ETW Corp. v. Jireh Publ'g, Inc., 332 F.3d 915, 924 (6th Cir. 2003).

147. Zacchini v. Scripps-Howard Broad. Co., 433 U.S. 562, 578 (1977).

148. *Id.*

149. *Id.*

150. Porco v. Lifetime Entertainment Services, LLC, 195 A.D.3d 1351 (2021).

151. *Id.*

152. *Id.*

153. *Id.* at 383.

154. *Id.*

155. *Id.*

156. *See* Mark S. Lee, *Agents of Chaos: Judicial Confusion in Defining the Right of Publicity-Free Speech Interface*, 23 Loy. L. A.

ENT. L. REV. 471, 488 (2003).

157. Hoang v. Tran, 60 Cal. App.5th 513 (2021).

158. Paulsen v. Personality Posters, Inc., 299 N.Y.S.2d 501 (Sup. Ct. 1968); Montana v. San Jose Mercury News, Inc., 40 Cal. Rptr. 2d 639 (Ct. App. 1995).

159. Factors Etc., Inc. v. Pro Arts, Inc., 579 F.2d 215 (2d Cir. 1978); Titan Sports, Inc. v. Comics World Corp., 870 F.2d 85 (2d Cir. 1989).

160. Eriq Gardner, *Lindsay Lohan Loses Lawsuit Against Pitbull Over Hit Song*, HOLLYWOOD REP., Feb. 21, 2013, hollywood-reporter.com/thr-esq/lindsay-lohan-loses-lawsuit-pitbull-423228.

161. *See* Campbell v. Acuff-Rose Music, Inc., 510 U.S. 569 (1994); Pierre N. Leval, *Toward a Fair Use Standard*, 103 HARV. L. REV. 1105, 1111 (1990).

162. For a thorough and critical discussion of the Three Stooges decision, see F. Jay Daugherty, *All the World's Not a Stooge: The "Transformativeness" Test for Analyzing a First Amendment Defense to a Right of Publicity Claim Against Distribution of a Work of Art*, 27 COL. J. L. & ARTS 1 (2003).

163. Comedy III Prods., Inc. v. Gary Saderup, Inc., 106 Cal. Rptr. 2d 126, 140 (2001), *cert. denied*, 534 U.S. 1078 (2002).

164. Brophy v. Almanzar, No. SACV1701885CJCJPRX, 2020 WL 8175605 (C.D.Cal. Dec. 4, 2020).

165. Jennifer E. Rothman, *Cardi B Wins Jury Verdict Against Tattooed Plaintiff*, ROTHMAN'S ROADMAP TO THE RIGHT OF PUBLICITY, Nov. 1, 2022, rightof-publicityroadmap.com/news_commentary/cardi-b-wins-jury-verdict-against-tattooed-plaintiff/.

166. Steve Berkowitz, *Payouts for College Athletes From EA Sports Distributed Soon*, USA TODAY, Nov. 7, 2015, usatoday.com/story/sports/college/2015/11/07/ncaa-college-ea-sports-lawsuit-payouts/75367410/.

167. Keller v. Elec. Arts, Inc., 2010 U.S. Dist. LEXIS 10719 (N.D. Calif. Feb. 8, 2010), *aff'd*, 724 F.3d 1268 (9th Cir. 2013), *cert. dismissed*, 573 U.S. 589 (2014).

168. Hart v. Elec. Arts, Inc., 808 F. Supp. 2d 757 (D.N.J. 2011).

169. *Id.* at 787.

170. Hart v. Elec. Arts, Inc., 717 F.3d 141 (3d Cir. 2013), *cert. dismissed*, 573 U.S. 989 (2014).

171. Anne Bucher, *EA, NCAA Video Game Likeness Class Action Settlement*, TOP CLASS ACTIONS, Oct. 24, 2014, topclassactions.com/lawsuit-settlements/open-lawsuit-settlements/42811-ea-ncaa-video-game-likeness-class-action-settlement/.

172. Derek Svendsen, *Former Student-Athletes File Lawsuit to Protect Their Rights of Publicity: Recap of Marshall v. ESPN* (filed 10/3/14), SPORT IN LAW, Oct. 15, 2014, heitner-legal.com/2014/10/15/former-student-athletes-file-lawsuit-to-protect-their-rights-of-publicity-recap-of-marshall-v-espn-filed-10314/.

173. Marshall v. ESPN, 668 F. App'x 155 (Mem.) (6th Cir. 2016).

174. Steve Berkowitz, *Judges Who Ruled Against EA Sports Set to Hear NCAA Appeal in O'Bannon*, USA TODAY, Jan. 23, 2015, usa-today.com/story/sports/college/2015/01/23/obannon-class-action-lawsuit-ncaa-appeal-keller-case/22242583/.

175. Hamilton v. Speight, 413 F.Supp.3d 423 (E.D. Pa. 2019).

176. Pelligrino v. Epic Games, Inc., 451 F.Supp.3d 373 (E.D. Pa. 2020).

177. K and K Prods, Inc. v. Walt Disney Studios Motion Pictures, No. 220CV1753JCMNJK, 2021 WL 4394787, at *5-7 (D. Nev. Sept. 23, 2021).

178. *Id.*

179. Winter v. DC Comics, 69 P.3d 473 (Cal. 2003).

180. *Id.* at 478 (*quoting* Comedy III Prods., Inc. v. Gary Saderup, Inc., 106 Cal. Rptr. 2d 126, 140 (2001))

(internal quotation marks omitted).

181. Doe v. TCI Cablevision, 110 S.W.3d 363 (Mo. 2003), *on remand*, Doe v. McFarlane, 207 S.W.3d 52 (Mo. Ct. App. 2006).

182. Seale v. Gramercy Pictures, 949 F. Supp. 331 (E.D. Pa. 1996), *aff'd without opinion*, 156 F.3d 1225 (3d Cir. 1998).

183. Booth v. Curtis Publ'g Co., 223 N.Y.S.2d 737 (Sup. Ct.), *aff'd*, 228 N.Y.S.2d 468 (1962).

184. Jordan v. Jewel Food Stores, Inc., 743 F.3d 509 (7th Cir. 2014).

185. *See Invasion of Privacy by Use of Plaintiff's Name or Likeness in Advertising— Consent and Waiver*, 13 A.L.R.7th Art. 4 (Originally published in 2016).

186. Pratt v. Everalbum, Inc., 283 F. Supp. 3d 664 (N.D. Ill 2017).

187. Netzer v. Continuity Graphic Assoc., Inc., 963 F. Supp. 1308 (S.D.N.Y. 1997).

188. Roe v. Amazon.com, 170 F. Supp. 3d 1028 (S.D. Ohio 2016).

189. *Id.* at 1035.

190. Roe v. Amazon.com, 714 F. App'x 565 (6th Cir. 2017).

191. Brents v. Morgan, 299 S.W. 967 (Ky. Ct. App. 1927).

192. Community Health Network, Inc. v. McKenzie, 185 N.E.3d 368, 381 (Indiana 2022) (citing Abby DeMare, Note, *The Disclosure Tort in Indiana: How a Contemporary Twist Could Revive a Dormant Remedy*, 54 Ind. L. Rev 661, 670 n.95 (2021).

193. Michaels v. Internet Entm't Grp., 5 F. Supp. 2d 823, 842 (C.D. Cal. 1998).

194. Media L. Resource Ctr., Media Privacy and Related Law 50-State Survey 2016–2017 (2017). Four states have rejected the tort—Nebraska, New York, North Carolina and Virginia.

195. Restatement (Second) of Torts § 652D.

196. Restatement (Second) of Torts § 652D requires the private facts to be disseminated "to the public at large, or to so many persons that the matter must be regarded as substantially certain to become one of public knowledge."

197. *See* Patrick J. McNulty, *The Public Disclosure of Private Facts: There Is Life After Florida Star*, 50 Drake L. Rev, 93, 100 (2001).

198. See Beaumont v. Brown, 257 N.W.2d 522, 531 (Mich. 1977), *overruled in part on other grounds*, Bradley v. Saranac Board of Education, 565 N.W.2d 650 (1997).

199. *See, e.g.*, Jones v. U.S. Child Support Recovery, 961 F. Supp. 1518 (D. Utah 1997). A debt collection agency sent a "wanted" poster to the employer of a divorced parent who was behind on child support payments.

200. *See, e.g.*, Y.G. v. Jewish Hosp. of St. Louis, 795 S.W.2d 488 (Mo. Ct. App. 1990). A couple, pregnant with triplets after an in vitro fertilization process, were invited to and attended a social gathering for couples who were part of a hospital's in vitro program. The hospital promised there would be no publicity. However, a television station reporting team was at the gathering, photographing and trying to interview the couple. The couple's pictures were part of the station's television report. The couple had not told anyone they were part of the in vitro program.

201. *See, e.g.*, Baugh v. CBS, Inc., 828 F. Supp. 745 (N.D. Cal. 1993). Without permission, a television program taped and showed the aftermath of a domestic violence incident.

202. *See, e.g.*, Michaels v. Internet Entm't Grp., 5 F. Supp. 2d 823, 842 (C.D. Cal. 1998). Musician Bret Michaels brought a private facts suit against an internet adult entertainment company for distributing a videotape showing Michaels and actress Pamela Anderson Lee having sex. Michaels and Lee made the tape, which an unknown person apparently stole and sold to the internet company.

203. *See* M.G. v. Time Warner, Inc., 107 Cal. Rptr. 2d 504, 511 (Cal. App. 2001).

204. Grimes v. Cty. of Cook, 455 F.Supp.3d 630 (N.D. Ill. 2020).

205. Sandler v. Calcagni, 565 F. Supp. 2d 184 (D. Me. 2008).

206. *Id.* at 198.

207. Woodrow Hartzog, *How to Fight Revenge Porn*, Atlantic, May 10, 2013, theatlantic.com/technology/archive/2013/05/how-to-fight-revenge-porn/275759/.

208. *48 States + DC + Two Territories Have Revenge Porn Laws*, Cyber Civil Rights Initiative, cybercivilrights.org/nonconsensual-pornography-laws/. The states without revenge porn laws are Massachusetts and South Carolina. *Id.*

209. Restatement (Second) of Torts § 652D cmt. c.

210. Community Health Network, Inc. v. McKenzie, 185 N.E. 3d 368 (Indiana 2022).

211. Restatement (Second) of Torts § 652D cmts. g, h.

212. Grayson v. No Labels, Inc., No. 6:20-CV-1824-PGB-LRH, 2021 WL 2871243, at *6 (M.D. Fla. Apr. 7, 2021).

213. Michaels v. Internet Entm't Grp., Inc., 5 F. Supp. 2d 823 (C.D. Cal. 1998).

214. Tina Gehres, *Gehres Law Group Reviews the Constitutional Issues in Hulk Hogan v. Gawker*, Gehres L. Grp., March 22, 2016.

215. Gawker Media, LLC v. Bollea, 129 So. 3d 1196 (Fla. Dist. Ct. App. 2014).

216. Thomas S. Leatherbury, *2015–16 Developments in Newsgathering and Privacy Liability*, Comm. L. in the Digital Age, Nov. 10, 2016.

217. Thomas S. Leatherbury, Marc A. Fuller, Ethan Nutter, & Bobbye Pyke, *Developments in the Law of Newsgathering and Privacy Liability (August 2020-August 2021)*, Comm. L. in the Digital Age, (2021).

218. Max Kennerly, *Hulk Hogan v. Gawker Legal FAQ—In Their Lawyers' Words*, Litigation & Trial, May 26, 2016, litigation-andtrial.com/2016/05/articles/attorney/hogan-v-gawker-legal-faq/.

219. Diaz v. Oakland Tribune, 188 Cal. Rptr. 762 (1983).

220. *Id.*

221. David Kravets, *Shamed by Mugshot Sites, Arrestees Try Novel Lawsuit*, Wired, Dec. 12, 2012, wired.com/2012/12/mugshot-industry-legal-attack/.

222. Kearston L. Wesner, *A Reputation Held Hostage? Commercial Mug Shot Web Sites and the Trade in Digital Shame*, 22 Commc'n L. & Pol'y 459 (2017).

223. *See* Taha v. Bucks Cty., 9 F. Supp. 3d 490 (E.D. Pa. 2014).

224. Gabiola v. Sarid, 2017 U.S. Dist. LEXIS 157699 (N.D. Ill. Sept. 26, 2017).

225. Sidis v. F-R Publ'g Corp., 113 F.2d 806 (2d Cir.), *cert. denied*, 311 U.S. 711 (1940).

226. Florida Star v. B.J.F., 491 U.S. 524, 541 (1989).

227. *Id.* at 524.

228. *Id.*

229. *Id.*

230. *See* Green v. Chicago Tribune Co., 675 N.E.2d 249 (Ill. App. Ct. 1996), *appeal denied*, 679 N.E.2d 379 (Ill. 1997).

231. Cox Broad. Corp. v. Cohn, 420 U.S. 469 (1975).

232. Oklahoma Publ'g Co. v. Dist. Court, 430 U.S. 308 (1977).

233. Smith v. Daily Mail, 443 U.S. 97 (1979).

234. Bartnicki v. Vopper, 532 U.S. 514 (2001).

235. *Id.*

236. Fed. Trade Comm'n, *Data Brokers: A Call for Transparency and Accountability* (May 2014), ftc.gov/system/files/documents/reports/data-brokers-call-transparency-account-ability-report-federal-trade-commission-may-2014/140527data brokerreport.pdf.

237. Geoffrey A. Fowler, *It's the Middle of the Night. Do You Know Who Your iPhone Is Talking To?* Wash. Post, May 28, 2019, washingtonpost.com/technology/2019/05/28/

its-middle-night-do-you-know-who-your-iphone-is-talking/?utm_term=.b8e8ea31da8d.

238. *See, e.g., In re* Double-Click, Inc. PRIVACY LITIGA-TION, 154 F. Supp. 2d 497 (S.D.N.Y. 2001).

239. *See* Woodrow Hartzog, *Massachusetts Has a Chance to Clean up Our National Privacy Disaster*, BOSTON GLOBE, Oct. 7, 2021, bostonglobe.com/2021/10/07/opinion/massachusetts-has-chance-clean-up-our-national-privacy-disaster./

240. Daisuke Wakabayashi, *California Passes Sweeping Law to Protect Online Privacy*, N. Y. TIMES, June 28, 2018, nytimes.com/2018/06/28/technology/california-online-privacy-law.html.

241. CAL. CIV. CODE § 1798.100.

242. Frances Floriano Goins & Michael Hoenig, *Colorado Passes New Comprehensive Data Protection Act*, JD SUPRA, Aug. 12, 2021, jdsupra.com/legalnews/colorado-passes-new-comprehensive-8862065/#:~:text=Colorado%20Passes%20New%20Comprehensive%20Consumer%20Data%20Protection%20Act,-Frances%20Floriano%20Goins&text=Earlier%20this%20month%2C%20the%20governor,and%20Virginia%20in%20March%202021.

243. CO. STAT. § 6-1-1306.

244. Taylor Kay Lively, *Connecticut Enacts Comprehensive Consumer Data Privacy Law*, THE PRIVACY ADVISOR, May 11, 2022, iapp.org/news/a/Connecticut-enacts-comprehensive-consumer-data-privacy-law/.

245. VA. CODE § 59.1-578.

246. 2022 Virginia H.B. No. 1259, Virginia 2022 Reg. Sess.

247. Kate Berry, Nancy Libin, & John D. Seiver, *And Utah Makes 4—Beehive State Passes Consumer Privacy Law*, PRIVACY & SECURITY LAW BLOG, March 31, 2022, dwt.com/blogs/privacy-security-law-blog/2022/03/Utah-consumer-privacy-act.

248. NEV. STAT. § 603A.300-360.

249. Jane Kirtley, *Privacy and Data Protection*, COMM. L. IN THE DIGITAL AGE (2021): 131–32.

250. Hartzog, *supra note 239.*

251. *Opt In or Opt Out? Active Comprehensive State Privacy Bills*, IAPP, iapp.org/media/pdf/resource_center/opt_in_vs_opt_out_state_privacy_bills_introduced_2021.pdf.

252. 740 Ill. Comp. Stat. Ann. 14/15.

253. 15 U.S.C.A. §§ 1681 et seq.

254. Spokeo, Inc. v. Robins, 136 S. Ct. 1540 (2016); TransUnion LLC v. Ramirez, 141 S.Ct. 2190 (2021).

255. *Robins*, 136 S. Ct. at 1540.

256. *Id.*

257. Jane Kirtley, *Private Data Collection: Global Privacy and Data Protection*, COMM. L. IN THE DIGITAL AGE (2016).

258. *Ramirez*, 141 S.Ct. at 2190-25.

259. *Id.*

260. *Id.* at 2214-25 (Thomas, J. dissenting).

261. *Id.* at 2226 (Kagan, J. dissenting)

262. Fed. Trade Comm'n, *FTC Issues Final Commission Report on Protecting Consumer Privacy* (March 26, 2012), ftc.gov/opa/2012/03/privacy-framework.shtm.

263. Declan McCullagh, *FTC Says Current Privacy Laws Aren't Working*, CNET NEWS, June 22, 2010, cnet.com/news/ftc-says-current-privacy-laws-arent-working/.

264. Fed. Trade Comm'n, *supra* note 262.

265. *Id.*

266. Fed. Trade Comm'n, *FTC Gives Final Approval to Settlement with Zoom over Allegations the Company Misled Consumers About Its Data Security Practices*, Feb. 1, 2021, ftc.gov/news-events/press-releases/2021/02/ftc-gives-final-approval-settlement-zoom-over-allegations-company. *In re* Zoom Video Comm. Inc., No. C-4731 (Jan. 19, 2021).

267. Jane Kirtley, *Privacy and Data Protection 2018*, COMM. L. IN THE DIGITAL AGE (2018).

268. Case C-131/12, Google Spain SL v. Agencia Española de Protección de Datos (Court of Justice of European Union, 2014), curia.europa .eu/juris/document/document.jsf?docid=152065&doclang=en.; *see also* Jeffrey Toobin, *The Solace of Oblivion*, NEW YORKER, September 29, 2014, newyorker.com/magazine/2014/09/29/solace-oblivion.

269. *Search Removals Under European Privacy Law*, GOOGLE, March 31, 2019, google.com/transparencyreport/removals/europeprivacy/.

270. Elizabeth Harding & L. Hannah Ji-Otto, *Five Immediate Steps to Take in Preparation for China's New Comprehensive Privacy Law*, JDSUPRA, Nov. 2, 2021, jdsupra.com/legalnews/five-immediate-steps-to-take-in-3088812/.

271. Josh Gerstein & Alexander Ward, *Supreme Court Has Voted to Overturn Abortion Rights, Draft Opinion Shows,* POLITICO, May 3, 2022, politico.com/news/2022/05/02/supreme-court-abortion-draft-opinion-00029473.

272. Dobbs v. Jackson Women's Health Organization, 142 S.Ct. 2228, 2242-2267 (2022).

273. *Id.* at 2243 (internal quotation marks omitted).

274. *Id.* at 2243 (quoting Washington v. Glucksberg, 521 U.S. 702, 721 (1997) (internal quotation marks omitted).

275. *Id.* at 2243–57.

276. Organization of American Historians and American Historical Association, *Joint OAH-AHA Statement in* Dobbs v. Jackson *Decision*, July 2022.

277. Alasaad v. Mayorkas, 988 F.3d 8, 18 (1st Cir.), *cert. denied sub nom.* Merch. v. Mayorkas,. 141 S. Ct. 2858, 210 L. Ed. 2d 964 (2021) (quoting United States v. Flores-Montano, 541 U.S. 149, 152 (2004))(internal quotation marks omitted).

278. Facebook, Inc. v. Duguid, 141 S. Ct. 1163 (2021).

279. *Id.* at 1170-73.

280. Cynthia J. Larose & Natalie A. Prescott, *Facebook to Pay $90 Million to Settle Data Privacy Lawsuit*, NAT'L L. REV., Feb. 18, 2022, natlawreview.com/article/facebook-to-pay-90-million-to-settle-data-privacy-lawsuit#:~:text=Facebook's%20parent%20company%20Meta%20has,of%20the%20social%20media%20platform.

281. Kristin L. Bryan, *Federal Court Gives Preliminary Approval of $92 Million TikTok MDL Settlement Over Objections*, NAT'L L. REV., Oct. 5, 2021, natlawreview.com/article/federal-court-gives-preliminary-approval-92-million-tiktok-mdl-settlement-over.

282. The states are Arkansas, California, Illinois, New York, Texas and Washington. Natalie A. Prescott, *The Anatomy of Biometric Laws: What U.S. Companies Need to Know in 2020*, NAT. L. REV., Jan. 15, 2020, natlawreview.com/article/anatomy-biometric-laws-what-us-companies-need-to-know-2020.

283. Fed. Trade Comm'n, *FTC Explores Rules Cracking Down on Commercial Surveillance and Lax Data Security Practices*, August 11, 2022, ftc.gov/news-events/news/press-releases/2022/08/ftc-explores-rules-cracking-down-commercial-surveillance-lax-data-security-practices.

284. Joseph Duball, *US Lawmakers Unveil Bipartisan American Data Privacy and Protection Act*, THE PRIVACY ADVISOR, June 6, 2022, iapp.org/news/congress-unveils-american-data-privacy-and-protection-act/.

285. 2021 Hawaii Laws Act 59 (S.B. 309).

286. N.Y. Civ. Rights Law § 52-c.

287. N.Y. Civ. Rights Law § 50-f.

288. Hepp v. Facebook, 14 F.4th 204 (3d Cir. 2021).

289. *Id.* at 206-14.

290. NCAA, *Interim NIL Policy*, ncaaorg.s3.amazonaws.com/ncaa/NIL/NIL_InterimPolicy.pdf.

291. Kristi Dosh, *Tracker: Name, Image and Likeness Legislation by State*, Business of College Sports, Feb. 25, 2022, businessofcollegesports.com/tracker-name-image-and-likeness-legislation-by-state/. The states with bills signed into law are Arizona, Arkansas, California, Colorado, Connecticut, Florida, Georgia, Illinois, Kentucky, Louisiana, Maryland, Michigan, Mississippi, Missouri, Montana, Nebraska, Nevada, New Jersey, New Mexico, Oklahoma, Oregon, South Carolina, Tennessee, Texas and Virginia. Ohio included NIL language in its state budget. The governors of Kentucky, Ohio, and North Carolina signed executive orders.

292. Justices Kennedy, Thomas, Alito, and Gorsuch all wrote dissenting opinions in this case. Justice Kennedy's dissent, joined by Justices Thomas and Alito, is the only one excerpted for this chapter in the interest of space. While not entirely inclusive, it captures most of the arguments and positions made in the other individual dissents.

CHAPTER 7

1. *2020 World Press Freedom Index: Entering a Decisive Decade for Journalism, Exacerbated by Coronavirus*, Reporters Without Borders, 2021, rsf.org/en/2020-world-press-freedom-index-entering-decisive-decade-journalism-exacerbated-coronavirus.

2. Fed. Housekeeping Statute, 5 U.S.C. § 301.

3. Harold C. Relyea, *Access to Government Information in the United States*, Report for Congress, Jan. 7, 2005, fas.org/sgp/crs/97-71.pdf.

4. 5 U.S.C. ch. 5, subch. I § 500 *et seq.*

5. *See, e.g.*, Erin K. Coyle, *Press Freedom and Citizens' Right to Know in the 1960s*, 43 Jour. History (2017); Derigan Silver, *The News Media & the FOIA*, 21 Comm. L. & Pol'y (2016); Emily Erickson, *The Watchdog Joins the Fray: The Press, Records Audits, and State Access Reform*, 16 Journalism & Comm'n Monographs 104 (2014); Shannon Martin & Kamilla Benko, *Forming FOIA: The Influence of Editors and Publishers on the Freedom of Information Act*, 14 Media Hist. Monographs (2011).

6. Zemel v. Rusk, 381 U.S. 1 (1965).

7. 5 U.S.C. § 552.

8. Federal Advisory Committee Act, 5 U.S.C. app. §§ 1–15, Pub. L. 92–463, 86 Stat. 770 (1972).

9. Government in the Sunshine Act, 5 U.S.C. § 552b (1976).

10. Privacy Act, 5 U.S.C. § 552a (1974).

11. Branzburg v. Hayes, 408 U.S. 665 (1972).

12. Houchins v. KQED, 438 U.S. 1, 14 (1978).

13. The earliest adopters likely were Utah (1898) and Florida (1905). *See also* Joseph W. Little & Thomas Tompkins, *Open Government Laws: An Insider's View*, 53 N.C. L. Rev. 451 (1974–1975).

14. Electronic Freedom of Information Act, Pub. L. No. 104–231, 110 Stat. 3048, §§ 1–12 (1996) (codified as amended in various sections of 5 U.S.C. § 552).

15. OPEN FOIA Act, Pub. L. 111–83 § 564, 123 Stat. 2184 (2009) (establishing criteria for new exemptions to FOIA).

16. *Issue Brief: State Freedom of Information Laws*, Society of Am. Archivists, Sept. 2015, archivists.org/statements/issue-brief-state-freedom-of-information-laws.

17. Dep't. of Corrections v. Porche, 485 P.3d 1010 (Alaska 2021) (citing U.S. Dep't of Justice v. Reporters Comm. For Freedom of the Press, 489 U.S. 749 (1989)).

18. U.S. Dep't of Justice v. Reporters Comm. For

Freedom of the Press, 489 U.S. at 749.

19. Michael Roffe, *Post-9/11 Info Access*, Freedom F. Inst., July 2010, freedomforuminstitute.org/first-amendment-center/topics/freedom-of-the-press/freedom-of-information-overview/post-911-info-access.

20. Nicholas Kusnetz, *State Integrity Investigation Spurs Proposals for Reform*, Center for Public Integrity, January 20, 2016, publicintegrity.org/state-politics/state-integrity-investigation-spurs-proposals-for-reform.

21. Vt. tit. 1 § 317 (2021-22); Caitlin Ginley, *The State of Open Records Laws: Access Denied*, Center for Public Integrity, June 1, 2012, publicintegrity.org/politics/state-politics/the-state-of-open-records-laws-access-denied/.

22. H.R. 2048, Pub. L. 114–23 (2015).

23. *See, e.g.,* Erwin Chemerinsky, *Protect the Press: A First Amendment Standard for Safeguarding Aggressive Newsgathering*, 33 Univ. Richmond L. Rev. 1143 (2000).

24. Branzburg v. Hayes, 408 U.S. 665 (1972).

25. Project Veritas Action Fund v. Rollins, 982 F.3d 813 (1st Cir. 2020), *cert. denied*, 142 S.Ct. 560 (2021).

26. *Id.*

27. *See* N.Y. Civil Liberties Union v. N.Y. City Transit Auth., 684 F.3d 286 (2d Cir. 2011) (access right applies to administrative hearing on violation of transit rules); Detroit Free Press v. Ashcroft, 303 F.3d 681 (6th Cir. 2002) (access right applies to executive branch deportation proceeding); N.J. Media Grp., Inc. v. Ashcroft, 308 F.3d 198 (3d Cir. 2003) (access right applies to deportation hearings).

28. First Amendment Coal. of Ariz., Inc. v. Ryan, 938 F.3d 1069 (9th Cir. 2019).

29. *Id.*

30. Pizzuto v. Tewalt, 997 F.3d 893 (9th Cir. 2021).

31. Ala. Dep't of Corrections v. Advance Local Media, 918 F.3d 1161 (11th Cir. 2019).

32. *See, e.g,* John K. MacIver Inst. for Pub. Policy, Inc. v. Evers, 994 F.3d 602 (7th Cir. 2021).

33. *Id.*

34. *See, e.g.,* Nation Magazine v. U.S. Dep't of Defense, 762 F. Supp. 1558 (S.D.N.Y. 1991); Flynt v. Rumsfeld, 180 F. Supp. 2d 174 (2002).

35. James Mooney, *Comment: The Power of Police to Give Lawful Orders*, 129 Yale L.J. 1568, 1574–75 (2019–2020).

36. *See* Askins v. U.S. Dep't of Homeland Sec., 899 F.3d 1035 (9th Cir. 2018).

37. *Id.*

38. Picard v. Clark, 475 F.Supp.3d 198, 202-08 (S.D.N.Y. 2020), *appeal filed sub nom.* (1st Cir. Sept. 15, 2020).

39. Picard v. Magliano, 42 F.4th 89, 108 (2d Cir. 2022).

40. PG Publ'g Co. v. Aichele, 705 F.3d 91 (3d Cir.), *cert. denied*, 569 U.S. 1018 (2013).

41. Ketcham v. U.S. Nat'l Park Serv., 2016 U.S. Dist. LEXIS 178823 (D. Wyo., May 5, 2016).

42. City of Oak Creek v. Ah King, 436 N.W.2d 285 (Wis. 1989).

43. Sherrill v. Knight, 569 F.2d 124 (D.C. Cir. 1977).

44. Mathew Ingram, *White House Revokes Press Passes for Dozens of Journalists*, Colum. Journalism Rev., May 9, 2019, cjr.org/the_media_today/white-house-press-passes.php.

45. Karem v. Trump, 960 F.3d 656 (D.C. Cir. 2020).

46. Price v. Barr, 514 F. Supp. 3d 171, 177-87 (D.D.C. 2021), *rev'd and remanded sub nom.* Price v. Garland, 45 F. 4th 1059 (D.C. Cir. 2022).

47. Price v. Garland, 45 F. 4th 1059, 1064–75 (D.C. Cir. 2022).

48. *Id.* at 1075.

49. Bryan Anderson, *Judge Jails Editor over Reporter's Use of Recorder in Court*, ABC News, July 7, 2021, abcnews.go.com/Lifestyle/wireStory/

judge-jails-editor-reporters-recorder-court-78703062.

50. Whiteland Woods, L.P. v. Township of West Whiteland, 193 F.3d 177 (3rd Cir. 1999).

51. Sigma Delta Chi v. Speaker, Md. House of Delegates, 310 A.2d 156 (Md. 1973).

52. *Id.*

53. *See also* RONALD L. GOLDFARB, TV OR NOT TV: TELEVISION, JUSTICE, AND THE COURTS 56–95 (1998).

54. *See* Fields v. City of Philadelphia, 862 F.3d 353 (3d Cir. 2017); Turner v. Lieutenant Driver, 848 F.3d 678 (5th Cir. 2017); Gericke v. Begin, 753 F.3d 1 (1st Cir. 2014); Am. Civil Liberties Union of Ill. v. Alvarez, 679 F.3d 583 (7th Cir. 2012); Glik v. Cunniffe, 655 F.3d 78 (1st Cir. 2011); Smith v. City of Cumming, 212 F.3d 1332 (11th Cir. 2000); Fordyce v. City of Seattle, 55 F.3d 436 (9th Cir. 1995).

55. Frasier v. Evans, 992 F.3d 1003 (10th Cir. 2021), *cert. denied*, 142 S.Ct. 427 (2021).

56. *Id.*

57. Project Veritas Action Fund v. Rollins, 982 F.3d 813 (1st Cir. 2020), *cert. denied*, 142 S.Ct. 560 (2021).

58. *Gericke*, 753 F.3d 1.

59. *Glik*, 655 F.3d 78.

60. Buehler v. City of Austin, 824 F.3d 548 (5th Cir. 2016), *cert. denied*, 137 S. Ct. 1579 (2017); Spoor v. Hamoui, 2017 U.S. Dist. LEXIS 2546 (M.D. Fla., Jan. 9, 2017).

61. State v. Russo, 407 P.3d 137 (Haw., Dec. 14, 2017).

62. Patrick v. Andrews, 849 S.E.2d 241 (Ga. Ct. App. 2020).

63. *See, e.g.*, Fields v. City of Philadelphia, 862 F.3d 353 (3rd Cir. 2020).

64. Commonwealth v. Bradley, 232 A.3d 747 (2020).

65. Letter from James Madison to W. T. Barry (Aug. 4, 1822), in THE WRITINGS OF JAMES MADISON, 1819–1836, at 103 (Galliard Hunt ed. 1910).

66. *See, e.g.*, SHANNON E. MARTIN, FREEDOM OF INFORMATION: THE NEWS THE MEDIA USE (2008).

67. 5 U.S.C. § 522 (1966).

68. Dep't of the Air Force v. Rose, 425 U.S. 352, 361 (1976).

69. Amended in 1976.

70. Electronic Freedom of Information Act of 1996, Pub. L. No. 104–231, 110 Stat. 3048, §§ 1–12 (1996) (codified as amended in various sections of 5 U.S.C. § 552).

71. Honest Leadership and Open Government Act of 2007, Pub. L. No. 110–81, 121 Stat. 735 (2007).

72. FOIA Improvement Act, Pub. L. No. 114–85 (2016).

73. Am. Oversight v. Gen. Serv. Admin., 311 F. Supp. 3d 327 (D.D.C. 2018).

74. 5 U.S.C. § 552(f)(1).

75. *See, e.g.*, Kissinger v. Reporters Comm. for Freedom of the Press, 445 U.S. 136 (1980). *But cf.* United States v. Clarridge, 811 F. Supp. 697 (D.D.C. 1992) (holding that the Tower Commission was an "agency" for purposes of 18 U.S.C. § 1001); Nat'l Sec. Archive v. Archivist of the U.S., 909 F.2d 541 (D.C. Cir. 1990) (holding that FOIA does not reach Office of Counsel to the President). The Sunshine Act incorporates FOIA's definition of "agency."

76. Goland v. CIA, 607 F.2d 339 (D.C. Cir. 1978). In Forsham v. Harris, 445 U.S. 169 (1980), the Supreme Court declared that Congress "did not provide any definition of 'agency records.'"

77. *Note: A Control Test for Determining "Agency Record" Status Under the Freedom of Information Act*, 85 COLUM. L. REV. 611 (1985).

78. *See, e.g.*, *Note: The Definition of "Agency Records" Under the Freedom of Information Act*, 31 STAN. L. REV. 1093, 1093 (1979); *Note: What Is a Record? Two Approaches to the Freedom of Information Act's Threshold Requirement*, 1978 B.Y.U. L. REV. 408, 408; Nichols v. United States, 325 F. Supp. 130 (D. Kan. 1971), *aff'd on other grounds*, 460 F.2d 671 (10th Cir. 1972), *cert. denied*, 409 U.S. 966 (1972).

79. *Forsham*, 445 U.S. at 178.

80. *Id.* at 184.

81. *Goland*, 607 F.2d 339.

82. *Id.*

83. *See, e.g.,* Mark Carreau, *Another Shuttle, Another Breach*, Houston Chron., July 9, 2003, A1; Lee Hockstader, *Release of Challenger Tape Ordered*, Wash. Post, July 30, 1988, A8; John Schwartz & Matthew L. Wald, *Earlier Shuttle Flight Had Gas Enter Wing on Return*, N. Y. Times, July 9, 2003, A14; Ralph Vartabedian, *E-Mail to Columbia Discounted Danger*, L. A. Times, July 1, 2003, A12.

84. *See, e.g.,* Jake Lucas, *How Times Reporters Use the Freedom of Information Act*, N. Y. Times, July 21, 2018, nytimes.com/2018/07/21/insider/information-freedom-reporters-pruitt.html.

85. David Cuillier & Charles N. Davis, The Art of Access: Strategies for Acquiring Public Records (2010). *See also* theartofaccess.com.

86. *How to Use the Federal FOIA Act*, Reporters Comm. for Freedom of the Press, n.d., rcfp.org/open-government-guide/.

87. *FOIA Letter Generator*, Reporters Comm. for Freedom of the Press, n.d., rcfp.org/foia-letter-generator/.

88. Citizens for Responsibility and Ethics in Washington v. Fed. Election Comm., 711 F.3d 180 (D.C. Cir. 2013).

89. *FOIA Suits Rise Because Agencies Don't Respond Even as Requesters Wait Longer to File Suit*, FOIA Project, Dec. 15, 2019, foiaproject.org/2019/12/15/foia-suits-rise-because-agencies-dont-respond-even-as-requesters-wait-longer-to-file-suit/.

90. *25-Year-Old FOIA Request Confirms FOIA Delays Continue Unabated*, Nat'l Security Archive, March 8, 2019, nsarchive.gwu.edu/foia-audit/foia/2019-03-08/25-year-old-foia-request-confirms-foia-delays-continue-unabated.

91. *See, e.g., Appeals*, U.S. Dept. of State, Aug. 10, 2020, foia.state.gov/Request/Appeals.aspx.

92. *When FOIA Goes to Court: 20 Years of Freedom of Information Act Litigation by News Organizations and Reporters*, FOIA Project, Jan. 13, 2021, foiaproject.org/2021/01/13/foialitigators2020/.

93. Porup v. CIA, 997 F.3d 1224 (D.C. Cir. 2021). *See* also J.M. Porup, jmporup.com.

94. Porup, 997 F.3d at 1224-39.

95. *Id.* (quoting *In re* Clinton, 973 F.3d 106 (D.C. Cir. 2020) (en banc), *cert. denied*, 141 S. Ct. 1740 (2021).

96. *Id.* at 1235 (citing CIA v. Sims, 471 U.S. 159 (1985) (internal quotes omitted).

97. *Id.* at 1239.

98. A. Jay Wagner, *Controlling Discourse, Foreclosing Recourse: The Creep of the Glomar Response*, 21 Comm. L. & Pol'y 539 (2016).

99. Leopold v. CIA, 987 F.3d 163 (D.C. Cir. 2021).

100. Electronic Freedom of Information Act Amendments of 1996, Pub. L. No. 104–231, 110 Stat. 3048, §§ 1–12 (1996) (codified as amended in various sections of 5 U.S.C. § 552).

101. TPS, Inc. v. Dep't of Def., 330 F.3d 1191 (9th Cir. 2003).

102. *See, e.g.,* Humane Society of the United States v. U.S. Fish & Wildlife Serv., 838 Fed.Appx. 721 (4th Cir. 2020).

103. *Id.* at 732.

104. *See, e.g.,* Richard Matthews et al., *State-by-State Report on Permanent Public Access to Electronic Government Information*, U. Ga. Sch. L., 2003, digitalcommons.law.uga.edu/cgi/viewcontent.cgi?article=1009&context=law_lib_artchop.

105. *Sample FOIA Request Letters*, Nat'l Freedom of Info. Coalition, www.nfoic.org/sample-foia-request-letters.

106. Freedom of Info. Found. of Texas, *Texas Pub. Info. Act*, n.d., foift.org/resources/texas-public-information-act.

107. 5 Ill. Comp. Stat. 140/1–1.

108. Tennessee Public Records Act, T.C.A. § 10–7–301 (6).

109. U.S. Right to Know v. Univ. of Vermont, 2021 WL 1940551 (Vt. May 14, 2021).

110. *Id.*

111. *Id.*

112. Better Gov't Ass'n v. City of Chicago, 169 N.E.3d 1066 (Ill. App. 2020); Toensing v. Attorney General, 178 A.3d 1000 (Vt. 2017); City of San Jose v. Superior Court, 389 P.3d 848 (Cal. 2017); Associated Press v. Canterbury, 688 S.E.2d 317 (W. Va. 2009); Howell Educ. Assoc. v. Howell Bd. of Educ., 789 N.W.2d 495 (Mich. App. 2010); Convertino v. U.S. Dep't of Justice, 674 F. Supp. 2d 97 (D.D.C. 2009).

113. Better Gov't Ass'n v. City of Chicago, 169 N.E.3d 1066 (Ill. App. 2020).

114. Brian Lyman, *Alabama's Public-Records Law Could Improve after Senate Committee Gives Bill Qualified Approval*, Montgomery Advertiser, March 31, 2021, montgomeryadvertiser. com/story/news/ politics/2021/03/31/ alabama-public-records-law-senate-committee-qualified-approval/4817900001/.

115. Bill Dentzer, *Sisolak Signs Public Records Reform Bill into Law*, Las Vegas Review-Journal, June 13, 2019, reviewjournal. com/news/politics-and-government/2019-legislature/ sisolak-signs-public-records-reform-bill-into-law-1686669/.

116. Daxton R. "Chip" Stewart, *Let the Sunshine In, or Else: An Examination of the "Teeth" of State and Federal Open Meetings and Open Records Laws*, 15 Comm. L. & Pol'y 265 (2010).

117. Uniontown Newspapers, Inc. v. Pennsylvania, 243 A.3d 19 (Pa. 2020).

118. *See, e.g.*, Jonathan Peters, *When Governments Sue Public-Records Requesters*, Colum. Journalism Rev., June 30, 2015, cjr.org/ united_states_project/ when_governments_ sue_public_record_ requesters.php.

119. *See, e.g.*, Gross v. Parson, 624 S.W.3d 877 (Mo. 2021) (en banc); Dan Margolies, *Missouri Supreme Court Shuts Down Governor Over 'Exorbitant' Fees for Public Records*, KCUR, June 30, 2021, kcur. org/news/2021-06-30/ missouri-supreme-court-shuts-down-governor-over-exorbitant-fees-for-public-records.

120. *See, e.g.*, Jordan Williams, *Louisiana AG Sues Reporter over FOIA Request*, Hill, Feb. 6, 2021, thehill. com/homenews/ media/537648-louisiana-ag-sues-reporter-over-foia-request; Landry v. Gallo, *petition for declaratory motion*, Feb. 5, 2021, bloximages. newyork1.vip.townnews. com/theadvocate.com/ content/tncms/assets/ v3/editorial/3/ 6e/36e986e4-6982-11eb-8d85-b3762bda7b4d/ 60204c47057a2.pdf.pdf.

121. *See, e.g.*, Gordon Russell, *Jeff Landry Must Release Records on Aide, as Judge Rules in Favor of Advocate Reporter*, Advocate, March 4, 2021, theadvocate. com/baton_rouge/ news/article_8929eaac-7d14-11eb-b84b-a3ff205810e7.html; *Louisiana AG Loses in Suit Against Reporter over Records*, Associated Press, March 4, 20201, apnews. com/article/media-lawsuits-jeff-landry-baton-rouge-louisiana-6743c3cd4c532bebdd 2160d745c62fbb.

122. Government in the Sunshine Act, 5 U.S.C. § 552b (1976).

123. Federal Advisory Committee Act, 5 U.S.C. App. §§ 1–15 (1972).

124. Seven states provide access to government meetings and records in one law. They are Arkansas, Connecticut, Maine, Missouri, North Dakota, South Carolina and Virginia.

125. State ex rel. Ames v. Portage Cty. Bd. of Commissioners, 2021 WL 2944137 (Ohio 2021).

126. Susan Dente Ross, *Break Down or Breakthrough in Participatory Government? How State Open Meetings Laws Apply to*

Virtual Meetings, 19 News-PAPER Res. J. 31 (1998).

127. Fraternal Ord. of Police, Bratcher/Miner Mem'l Lodge, Lodge No. 122 v. City of Norman, 489 P.3d 20 (Okla. 2021).

128. *Sunshine Law Amendments to Require Prior Public Notice of Official Actions at Board Meetings*, JDSupra, July 4, 2021, jdsupra.com/ legalnews/sunshine-law-amendments-to-require-7912516/.

129. *See, e.g., Sound Recordings Allowed*, Reporters Committee for Freedom of the Press, n.d., rcfp. org/open-government-sections/1-sound-recordings-allowed/.

130. Haw. Rev. Stat. § 92-9(c); Iowa Code Ann. § 21.7; Utah Code § 52-4-203(5).

131. *See, e.g., Sound Recordings Allowed, supra* note 129.

132. *See, e.g., id.*

133. Wyoming Open Meetings Law, Wy. Stat. § 16-4-403 (2022).

134. Mich. Comp. Laws § 15.272-15.273; Michigan Open Meetings Act and Freedom of Information Act, 1976 PA 267, MCL 15.261 *et seq.* (1976), legislature.mi.gov/docu-ments/Publications/OpenMtgsFreedom.pdf.

135. Funk v. O'Connor, 916 N.W.2d 319 (Minn. 2018); Minn. Stat. § 13D.06.

136. Dyer v. Atlanta Indep. Sch. Sys., 852 Fed.Appx. 397 (11th Cir. 2021),

petition for cert. denied, 142 S.Ct. 484 (Nov. 15, 2021).

137. Acosta v. City of Costa Mesa, 718 F.3d 800 (9th Cir. 2013).

138. 18 U.S.C. § 2511(2)(d).

139. *Id.*

140. *Laws on Recording Conversations in All 50 States*, MWL, Feb. 14, 2022, mwl-law.com/wp-con-tent/uploads/2018/02/RECORDING-CONVER-SATIONS-CHART.pdf. Nevada has a one-party consent law, but the state's highest court has interpreted the law as requiring consent from all parties. *Id.*

141. The 11 states are California, Delaware, Florida, Illinois, Maryland, Massachusetts, Montana, Nevada, New Hampshire, Pennsylvania and Washington. *See id.*

142. C.G.S.A. §§ 53a-187, -89; C.G.S.A. § 52-570d.

143. Vermont v. Geraw, 795 A.2d 1219 (Vt. 2002).

144. Vermont v. Brooks, 601 A.2d 963 (Vt. 1991).

145. Kearney v. Salomon Smith Barney, 137 P.3d 914 (Cal. 2006).

146. Holmes v. State, 182 A.3d 341 (Md. 2018), *cert. denied*, 188 A.3d 924 (2018).

147. 47 C.F.R. § 73.1206.

148. Bartnicki v. Vopper, 532 U.S. 514 (2001).

149. 18 U.S.C. § 2511(1)(c).

150. *Bartnicki*, 532 U.S. at 525.

151. *Id.* at 534, 535.

152. Planned Parenthood Fed'n of Am., Inc. v. Center for Medical Progress, 2020 WL 2065700 (N.D. Cal. Apr. 20, 2020), *appeal filed*, No. 20-16820 (9th Cir. Sept. 21, 2020).

153. *Id.*

154. Md. Code Ann., Cts. & Jud. Proc. § 10-402.

155. Planned Parenthood Fed'n of Am., Inc., 2020 WL 2065700 (April 29, 2020), *appeal filed*, No. 20-16820 (9th Cir. Sept. 21, 2020).

156. Planned Parenthood Fed'n of Am., Inc. v. Newman, 51 F.4th 1125, 1132 (9th Cir. 2022).

157. *Id.* at 1135-36.

158. 18 U.S.C.A. § 1962.

159. *Planned Parenthood Fed'n of Am., Inc.*, 51 F.4th at 1135–36.

160. 532 U.S. 514, 518–19 (2001).

161. For a useful summary of state wiretapping laws, see *Laws on Recording Conversations in All 50 States*, MWL, Feb. 14, 2022, mwl-law. com/wp-content/uploads/2018/02/RECORDING-CONVER-SATIONS-CHART.pdf.

162. United States v. Vespe, 389 F. Supp. 1359 (D. Del. 1975).

163. People v. Melongo, 6 N.E. 3d 120 (Ill. 2014).

164. *See, e.g.*, Miller v. NBC, 232 Cal. Rptr. 668 (Cal. Ct. App. 1986) (stating

"The essence of the cause of action for trespass is an 'unauthorized entry' onto the land of another.").

165. Fla. Publ'g Co. v. Fletcher, 340 So.2d 914 (Fla. 1976) (finding owner's silence during unauthorized intrusion is implied consent); *but see* Ayeni v. Mottola, 35 F.3d 680 (2d Cir. 1994) (finding a "clearly established" right to be free from intrusion of unauthorized persons).

166. Hanlon v. Berger, 526 U.S. 808 (1999).

167. Nancy L. Trueblood, *Comment: Curbing the Media: Should Reporters Pay When Police Ride-Alongs Violate Privacy?*, 84 Marq. L. Rev. 541, 560 no. 131 (2000). ("At trial, Paul Berger was acquitted of federal charges of violating laws protecting eagles and found guilty of misdemeanor use of a pesticide.")

168. *Obituaries*, St. Petersburg (Fla.) Times, April 20, 2003, at 21A.

169. Wilson v. Layne, 526 U.S. 603, 607 (1999).

170. *Id.* at 611-14 (1999).

171. *See, e.g.,* Shulman v. Grp. W Prods., Inc., 955 P.2d 469 (Cal. 1998) (ruling that outfitting a nurse with a wireless microphone, then videotaping her rescue of two people in an overturned automobile at the bottom of an embankment, then

broadcasting the tape, constituted intrusion).

172. Wilson v. Layne, 526 U.S. 603, 607 (1999).

173. Shane Anderson, *Federal Judge Rules Against Wyoming's "Date Trespass" Laws on First Amendment Grounds*, Star Tribune, Oct. 30, 2018, trib.com/news/local/crime-and-courts/federal-judge-rules-against-wyomings-data-trespass-laws-on/article_6c736e53-4e12-5cca-bfbc-2bdd71e3ac92.html. *See* W. Watersheds Project v. Michael, 869 F.3d 1189 (10th Cir. 2017).

174. *W. Watersheds Project*, 869 F.3d at 1195-96.

175. Sheets v. City of Punta Gorda, Fla., 415 F. Supp. 3d 1115, 1123 (M.D. Fla. 2019) (quoting Cornelius v. NAACP Legal Defense & Educ. Fund, Inc., 473 U.S. 788, 805-06 (1985).

176. *Id.*

177. Tisdale v. State, 841 S.E.2d 82 (Ga. Ct. App. 2020), *cert denied* (Ga. App. Feb. 1, 2021).

178. *See, e.g., Ag-Gag Laws*, Animal Defense Fund, June 12, 2021, aldf.org/issue/ag-gag/.

179. Animal Legal Def. Fund v. Kelly, 434 F.Supp.3d 974 (D. Kan. 2020), *aff'd*, 2021 WL 3671122 (10th Cir. Aug. 19, 2021).

180. *Id., amended by* 2020 WL 1659855 (D.Kan. Apr. 3, 2020).

181. Animal Legal Defense Fund v. Kelly, 2021 WL 3671122 (10th Cir. 2021), *appeal docketed*, No. 21-760 (U.S. Nov. 21, 2021).

182. People for the Ethical Treatment of Animals, Inc. v. Stein, 466 F.Supp.3d 547 (M.D.N.C. Jun. 12, 2020), *appeal filed, No.* 20-1807 (4th Cir. July 24, 2020).

183. Heff Zalesin, *Paragliding Journalist Arrested After Photographing Kansas Feedlot*, Reporters Comm. for Freedom of the Press, July 15, 2013, rcfp.org/paragliding-journalist-arrested-after-photographing-kansas-feedlot/.

184. *George Steinmetz Wonders: Was It Worth Getting Arrested for National Geographic Cover Story Photos?*, Photo District News, May 1, 2014, pdnpulse.pdnonline.com/2014/05/george-steinmetz-wonders-worth-getting-arrested-national-geographic-cover-story-photos.html.

185. Animal Legal Def. Fund v. Reynolds, No. 19-1364, 2021 WL 3504493 (8th Cir. Aug. 10, 2021).

186. *Id.*

187. *Id.* (Gatz, J., concurring).

188. David Pitt, *Federal Judge Finds Another Iowa Ag-Gag Law Unconstitutional*, U.S. News & World Report, March 17, 2022, usnews.com/news/us/articles/2022-03-17/federal-judge-finds-

another-iowa-ag-gag-law-unconstitutional.

189. *Executive Summary—Final Rule on Operation of Small Unmanned Aircraft Systems Over People*, Fed. Aviation Admin., Dec. 28, 2020, faa.gov/news/media/attachments/OOP_Executive_Summary.pdf.

190. *DC Area Prohibited & Restricted Airspace*, Fed. Aviation Admin., Aug. 7, 2019, faa.gov/uas/resources/community_engagement/no_drone_zone/dc/.

191. John Reinhardt, *FAA Safety Briefing—Drone Operations Near Air/Heliports in Class G Airspace*, Medium, March 1, 2021, medium.com/faa/drone-operations-near-air-heliports-in-class-g-airspace-15bfbdc5592a.

192. *FAA Fines Drone Pilot $182,000*, Nat'l L. Rev., Dec. 24, 2020, natlawreview.com/article/faa-fines-drone-pilot-182000.

193. *Aerial Photographers: Drone Laws You Need to Know Before Flying*, SLR Lounge, March 12, 2016, slrlounge.com/aerial-photographers-drone-laws-need-know-flying-infographic. *See also* Alissa M. Dolan & Richard M. Thompson II, Integration of Drones Into Airspace: Selected Legal Issues (2013) R42940. *See* Fla. Stat. § 934.50 (2021); Idaho Code Ann. § 21-213 (2021); Tex. Gov't Code § 423.003 (2021); Utah

Code § 72-14-304 (2021); 2013 Va. Code 18.2-324.2 (2021); Wis. Stat. § 942.10 (2021).

194. *Current Unmanned Aircraft State Law Landscape*, Nat'l Conf. of State Legislatures, Aug. 3, 2021, ncsl.org/research/transportation/current-unmanned-aircraft-state-law-landscape.aspx.

195. Idaho Code § 21-213 (2)(b).

196. Tex. Gov't Code § 423.003.

197. Nat'l Press Photographers Assoc. v. McCraw, No. 1:19-CV-946-RP, 2022 WL 939517, at * 11 (W.D. Tex. Mar. 28, 2022).

198. Isabella Lee, *Uniform Law Commission Offers Revised Approach to Trespass and Privacy Laws Relating to Drones*, UAV Coach, Feb. 28, 2019, uavcoach.com/ulc-drone-tort-law/.

199. Wis. Stat. § 942.10 (2015).

200. *See, e.g.*, Or. Rev. Stat. § 837.380 (1)(a&b); Nev. Rev. Stat. § 493.103 (1)(a&b): Va. Stat. § 18.2-121.3(A).

201. *See, e.g.*, Ark. Stat. § 5-60-103; Ky. Stat § 511.100.

202. Tex. Gov't Code § 423.0046.

203. Nat'l Press Photographers Assoc. v. McCraw, No. 1:19-CV-946-RP, 2022 WL 939517, at * 11 (W.D. Tex. March 28, 2022).

204. *See* John Ashcroft, *Memorandum for Heads of All Federal Departments and Agencies*, U.S. Dep't of Justice, Oct. 12, 2001, justice.gov/archive/oip/011012.htm.

205. *See, e.g.,* Brett Strohs, *Protecting the Homeland by Exemption: Why the Critical Infrastructure Information Act of 2002 Will Degrade the Freedom of Information Act*, 2002 Duke L. & Tech. Rev. 18 (2002).

206. Steven D. Schwinn, *Auer Deference, Limited, Hangs On (But Chevron May Soon Go)*, Con. L. Prof. Blog, June 26, 2019, lawprofessors.typepad.com/conlaw/2019/06/auer-deference-limited-hangs-on-but-chevron-may-go.html.

207. *Id.*

208. *See* Exec. Order No. 12958, § 4.2 (b), fas.org/sgp/bush/drafteo.html.

209. CIA v. Sims, 471 U.S. 159, 183 (1985).

210. Am. Civil Liberties Union v. U.S. Dep't of Defense, 681 F.3d 61 (2d Cir. 2012).

211. Osen LLC v. U.S. Cent. Command, 375 F.Supp. 409 (S.D.N.Y. 2019), *rev'd in part, vacated in part*, 969 F.3d 102 (2d Cir. 2020).

212. *Id.*

213. *Id.*

214. Dep't of the Air Force v. Rose, 425 U.S. 352 (1976).

215. Milner v. Dep't of the Navy, 562 U.S. 562 (2011).

216. Corley v. Dep't of Justice, 998 F.3d 981 (D.C. Cir. 2021).

217. *Id.*

218. Food Mktg. Inst. v. Argus Media Leader, 139 S. Ct. 2356, 2366 (2019).

219. *Id.*

220. Argus Leader Media v. Food Mktg. Inst., 889 F.3d 914 (8th Cir. 2018).

221. Chrysler v. Brown, 441 U.S. 281, 316 (1979).

222. *Id.* at 292.

223. Russell v. Dep't of the Air Force, 682 F.2d 1045 (D.C. Cir. 1982).

224. FOIA Improvement Act of 2016, Pub. L. No. 114–85 (2016).

225. U.S. Fish & Wildlife Serv. v. Sierra Club, Inc., 141 S. Ct. 777 (2021).

226. *Id.*

227. *Id.*

228. Matthew Bunker & Stephen Perry, *Privacy Exemptions and the Press under the FOIA*, 16 Newspaper Research J. 84, 88 (1995).

229. Cochran v. United States, 770 F.2d 949 (11th Cir. 1985).

230. *See* Dep't of Justice v. Reporters Comm. for Freedom of the Press, 489 U.S. 749 (1989).

231. Pavement Coatings Tech. Council v. U.S. Geological Surv., 995 F.3d 1014 (D.C. Cir. 2021).

232. *Id.* (internal quotes omitted).

233. WP Co. LLC v. U.S. Small Business Admin., 2021 WL 2982173 (Jul. 15, 2021) (memorandum).

234. Dep't of Justice, *Exemption 7 (C) (2014)*, justice. gov/sites/default/files/ oip/legacy/2014/07/23/ exemption7c_0.pdf.

235. Dep't of Justice v. Reporters Comm. for Freedom of the Press, 489 U.S. 749 (1989).

236. *Id.*

237. Nat'l Archives and Records Admin. v. Favish, 541 U.S. 157 (2004).

238. *Id.*

239. *Reporters Comm. for Freedom of the Press*, 489 U.S. at 773.

240. FCC v. AT&T, 562 U.S. 397 (2011).

241. Dodd-Frank Wall St. Reform and Consumer Protection Act, Pub. L. No. 111–201, July 21, 2010, govinfo.gov/ content/pkg/PLAW-111publ203/pdf/PLAW-111publ203.pdf.

242. James Madison Project v. Dep't of the Treasury, 478 F. Supp. 3d 8 (D.D.C. 2020).

243. *Id.* at 14 (quoting Pub. Inv'rs Arbitration Bar Ass'n v. SEC, 930 F. Supp. 2d 55 (D.D.C. 2013) (internal quotes omitted).

244. Dep't of Justice, *Exemption 9* (2009), justice. gov/archive/oip/foia_ guide09/exemption9.pdf.

245. Government in the Sunshine Act, 5 U.S.C. § 552b (1976).

246. Freedom of Information Act, 5 U.S.C. § 552 (1966).

247. Government in the Sunshine Act, 5 U.S.C. § 552b (1976).

248. Privacy Act, 5 U.S.C. § 552a (1974).

249. Fed. Aviation Admin. v. Cooper, 566 U.S. 284 (2012).

250. Family Educational Rights and Privacy Act, 20 U.S.C. § 1232g. (The nickname "Buckley Amendment" refers to U.S. Sen. James Buckley, who introduced the bill.)

251. *See* 34 C.F.R. § 99.3.

252. *Id.*

253. United States v. Miami Univ., 294 F.3d 797 (6th Cir. 2002).

254. Krakauer v. State by & through Comm'r of Higher Educ., 445 P.3d 201, 205-10 (Mont. 2019), *cert. denied*, 140 S. Ct. 1107 (2020).

255. Easton Area Sch. Dist. v. Miller, 232 A.3d 716 (Pa. 2020).

256. Clery Act, 20 U.S.C. § 1092(f) (1990).

257. Collin Binkley & Carole Feldman, *Michigan State University fined $4.5 million in Nassar Case*, Associated Press, Sept. 5, 2019, apnews.com/article/ sports-politics-education-michigan-larry-nassar-b651cba13cf-74c3ba85645ea3a-d702a9.

258. Health Insurance Portability & Accountability

Act, P. L. 104–191, 110 Stat. 1936 (1996).

259. *Id.*

260. Adam A. Marshall & Gunita Singh, *Journalists Guide to HIPAA During the COVID-19 Health Crisis*, REPORTERS COMM. FOR FREEDOM OF THE PRESS, April 28, 2020, rcfp.org/covid-19-journalists-hipaa-guide/.

261. *Id.*

262. Driver's Privacy Protection Act, 18 U.S.C. §§ 2721–2725 (1994).

263. Reno v. Condon, 528 U.S. 141 (2000).

264. Andrews v. Sirius XM Radio Inc., 932 F.3d 1253 (9th Cir. 2019).

265. *Id.*

266. Dahlstrom v. Sun-Times Media, LLC, 777 F.3d 937 (7th Cir. 2015), *cert. denied*, 136 S. Ct. 689 (2015).

267. *Id.*

268. Matthiesen, Wickert & Lehrer, S .C., *Laws on Recording Conversations in All 50 States*, Feb. 4, 2022, https://www.mwl-law.com/wp-content/uploads/2018/02/RECORDING-CONVERSATIONS-CHART.pdf.

269. *See, e.g., Wiretapping and Surveillance at the State Level (Which May Be Illegal Just FYI)*, MEDIUM, n.d., medium.com/golden-data/wiretapping-and-surveillance-at-the-state-level-which-may-be-illegal-just-fyi-e6b3b8a090ba.

270. Me. Rev. Stat. tit. 17-A, § 511(1)(C).

271. N.H. Rev. Stat. § 644:9 (1) (a-b).

272. *See, e.g., Guidelines for Hidden Cameras*, RTDNA, rtdna.org/content/hidden_cameras.

273. *See Reporter's Recording Guide*, REPORTERS COMM. FOR FREEDOM OF THE PRESS, Summer 2012, rcfp.org/wp-content/uploads/imported/RECORDING.pdf.

274. Charles Ornstein, *NY Hospital to Pay $2.2 Million Over Unauthorized Filming of 2 Patients*, N. Y. TIMES, April 21, 2016, www.nytimes.com/2016/04/22/nyregion/new-york-hospital-to-pay-fine-over-unauthorized-filming-of-2-patients.html.

275. *Id.*

276. 18 U.S.C. § 2510(1).

277. *See, e.g.,* Robert Valdes & Dave Roos, *How VoIP Works*, HOWSTUFFWORKS, May 9, 2001, computer.howstuffworks.com/ip-telephony.htm; Ruby Carlino, *Internet Phones: The Cheaper Alternative to Calling Home*, DATABASE SYSTEMS CORP., n.d., database systemscorp.com/tech-cti-softphone_55.htm.

278. Wiretap Act, 18 U.S.C. § 2510 (2002) (defining the "aural transfer" that occurs in wire communication as "a transfer containing the human voice at any point between and including the point

of origin and the point of reception").

279. Stored Communications Act, 18 U.S.C. §§ 2701–2711.

280. Eric Koester, *VoIP Goes the Bad Guy: Understanding the Legal Impact of the Use of Voice Over IP Communications in Cases of NSA Warrantless Eavesdropping*, 24 J. MARSHALL J. COMPUTER & INFO. L. 227, 234 (2006).

281. Electronic Communications Privacy Act, 18 U.S.C. § 2511.

282. Computer Fraud and Abuse Act, Pub. L. No. 99–508, 100 Stat. 1848 (1986) and 18 U.S.C. § 1030.

283. Pam Greenberg, *Computer Crime Statutes*, NAT'L CONF. OF STATE LEGISLATURES, June 14, 2018, ncsl.org/research/telecommunications-and-information-technology/computer-hacking-and-unauthorized-access-laws.aspx.

284. Jessup-Morgan v. America Online, Inc., 20 F. Supp. 2d 1105 (E.D. Mich. 1998).

285. *See, e.g.,* Pennsylvania v. Cline, 177 A.3d 922 (Pa. Super. Ct. 2017); Pennsylvania v. Byrd, 185 A.3d 1015 (Pa. Super. Ct. 2018).

286. Pennsylvania v. Patterson, 180 A.3d 1217, 1234 (Pa. Super. Ct. 2018), *appeal denied*, 229 A.3d 562 (Pa. 2020).

287. Foreign Intelligence Surveillance Act, 50 U.S.C. § 1802.

288. Gabe Rottman & Linda Moon, *How Foreign Intelligence Surveillance Law Applies to the News Media*, REPORTERS COMM. FOR FREEDOM OF THE PRESS, Nov. 9, 2018, rcfp.org/how-foreign-intelligence-surveillance-law-applies-news-media.

289. Van Buren v. United States, 141 S. Ct. 1648, 1652 (2021).

290. *Id.*

291. *Id.* at 1661 (internal quotation marks omitted).

292. *See, e.g.,* Soraya Ferdman, *SCOTUS Ruling in Van Buren a Win for Data Journalists and Security Researchers*, FIRST AM. WATCH, June 4, 2021, first-amendmentwatch.org/scotus-ruling-in-van-buren-a-win-for-data-journalists-and-security-researchers/.

293. Erin K. Coyle & Eric Robinson, *Chilling Journalism: Can Newsgathering Be Harassment or Stalking?*, 22 COMM. L. & POL'Y 65 (2017).

294. K.S.A. 2016 Supp. 60-31a01 *et seq.*

295. Coyle & Robinson, *supra* note 293, n.422–423. The states are Colorado, Delaware, Idaho, Illinois, Louisiana, Maine, New Jersey, Ohio and Vermont.

296. Galella v. Onassis, 353 F. Supp. 196 (S.D.N.Y. 1972).

297. Galella v. Onassis, 487 F.2d 986 (2d Cir. 1973).

298. Raef v. App. Div. of Sup. Ct. of Los Angeles, 240 Cal. App. 4th 1112 (Cal. App. Dep't Super. Ct. 2015).

299. *Id.*

300. *Journalist Nadiya Lazzouni Threatened with Death*, COUNCIL OF EUROPE, July 29, 2021, coe.int/en/web/media-freedom/detail-alert?p_p_id=sojdashboard_WAR_coesojportlet&p_p_lifecycle=0&p_p_col_id=column-3&p_p_col_pos=1&p_p_col_count=10&_sojdashboard_WAR_coesojportlet_alertPK=104524983#block-member-replies.

301. *Réponse des Autorités Françaises*, April 11, 2021, rm.coe.int/france-reply-fr-la-journaliste-nadiya-lazzouni-menacee-de-mort-22juill/1680a34d2f.

302. *International Day to End Impunity for Crimes against Journalists*, U.N., Nov. 2, 2021, un.org/en/observances/end-impunity-crimes-against-journalists.

303. Gina M. Masullo et al., *Women Journalists and Online Harassment*, CENTER FOR MEDIA ENGAGEMENT, April 2018, mediaengagement.org/wp-content/uploads/2018/04/Women-Journalists-and-Online-Harassment-1.pdf.

304. Caitlin Ring Carlson & Haley Witt, *Online Harassment of U.S. Women Journalists and Its Impact on Press Freedom*, FIRST MONDAY, 2020, firstmonday.org/ojs/index.php/fm/article/view/11071/9995.

305. *See* Masullo et al., *supra* note 303.

306. *See* Carlson & Witt, *supra* note 304.

307. *Online Harassment Field Manual*, PEN AMERICA, onlineharassmentfieldmanual.pen.org.

308. Wolfson v. Lewis, 924 F. Supp. 1413 (E.D. Pa. 1996).

309. *Id.*

310. Food Lion, Inc. v. Capital Cities, Inc./ABC, 964 F. Supp. 956, 959 (M.D. N.C. 1997).

311. *See generally* Jane Kirtley, *It's the Process, Stupid: Newsgathering Is the New Target*, COLUM. JOURNALISM REV., Sept./Oct., 2000.

312. *Id.*

313. *Id.*

314. *Food Lion, Inc.*, 964 F. Supp. at 959.

315. *Food Lion*, Inc. v. Capital Cities/ABC, Inc., 194 F.3d 505, 526 (4th Cir. 1999) (Niemeyer, J., dissenting).

316. According to one of the attorneys involved, ABC's bill from one of the law firms handling the appeal only was in the "six figures" (personal communication on file with authors).

317. *Hidden Cameras, Hard Choices*, PRIMETIME LIVE, Feb. 12, 1997. After the trial portion of the case, ABC's "Primetime Live" broadcast interviews with members of the jury. One juror said that on a scale of 1 to 10, with 10 being the worst, ABC's wrongdoing was a 10. "Because the—the girls were telling stories to get into a man's personal business, and they even made up stories to get in." This same juror said she wanted the punitive damages levied against ABC to be $1 billion. *Id.*

318. Veilleux v. NBC, 8 F. Supp. 2d 23 (D. Me. 1998).

319. Veilleux v. NBC, 206 F.3d 92 (1st Cir. 2000).

320. Nancy Garland, *Settlement Reached in "Dateline" Suit*, BANGOR DAILY NEWS, Sept. 1, 2000.

321. Sara Brown, *MIT Sloan Research About Social Media, Misinformation, and Elections*, MIT MANAGEMENT SLOAN SCHOOL, Oct. 5, 2020, mitsloan.mit.edu/ideas-made-to-matter/mit-sloan-research-about-social-media-misinformation-and-elections.

322. Tarini Part & Sarah E. Needleman, *Biden Blasts Covid-19 Vaccine Misinformation on Social Media*, WALL ST. J., July 16, 2021, wsj.com/articles/biden-blasts-covid-19-vaccine-misinformation-on-social-media-11626464163.

323. Shannon Bond, *Just 12 People Are Behind Most Vaccine Hoaxes on Social Media, Research Shows*, NPR, May 14, 2021, npr.org/2021/05/13/996570855/disinformation-dozen-test-facebooks-twitters-ability-to-curb-vaccine-hoaxes.

324. *Social Media Guidelines*, ASSOCIATED PRESS, May 2013, ap.org/assets/documents/social-media-guidelines_tcm28-9832.pdf. *See also* RonNell Anderson Jones & Lyrissa Barnett Lidsky, *Recent Developments in the Law of Social Media Communications*, 3 COMM. L. IN THE DIGITAL AGE 75, 85 (2012).

325. Record at 1279, Cohen v. Cowles Media Co. (No. 90–634) (testimony of Bernard Casserly, characterizing the use of confidential sources as "a way of life in the profession of journalism").

326. Record at 694, Cohen v. Cowles Media Co., 501 U.S. 663 (testimony of Arnold Ismach).

327. *See, e.g.,* Brief of Petitioner, Cohen v. Cowles Media Co., 501 U.S. 663 (1990). One of the best known examples of investigative journalism, The Washington Post's uncovering of the Watergate scandal, was driven by a confidential source the reporters dubbed "Deep Throat." *See* BOB WOODWARD, THE SECRET MAN: THE STORY OF WATERGATE'S DEEP THROAT (2005).

328. *See* Mendez v. Bank of Am. Home Loans Servicing, LP, 840 F. Supp. 2d 639, 654 (E.D.N.Y. 2012) (explaining promissory estoppel under New York law).

329. Cohen v. Cowles Media Co., 501 U.S. 663 (1991).

330. *Id.*

331. *Id.*

332. *See, e.g.,* Andrew Marquardt, *These 11 Journalists Were Attacked for Reporting on Democracy*, FORBES, Feb. 1, 2021, fortune.com/2021/02/01/most-urgent-cases-journalists-killed-ranked-february-2021/.

333. *1 Year of Unprecedented Violence Against Journalists*, U.S. PRESS FREEDOM TRACKER, May 26, 2020–May 25, 2021, pressfreedomtracker.us/1-year-blm/.

334. *Accountability Two Years Later: Tracking Journalists' Lawsuits*, U.S. PRESS FREEDOM TRACKER, May 31, 2022, pressfreedomtracker.us/blog/accountability-two-years-later-tracking-journalists-lawsuits/.

335. Penny Abernathy, *The State of Local News : The 2022 Report*, June 29, 2022, localnews-initiative.northwestern.edu/research/state-of-local-news/report/.

336. William Morris, *The Jury Made the Right Decision*, DES MOINES REGISTER, March 11, 2021, desmoinesregister.com/

story/news/2021/03/10/
andrea-sahouri-trial-
des-moines-register-
reporter-acquitted-
george-floyd-protest-
arrest/6933780002/.

337. Paul Woolverton, *No
Charges for Reporters
Arrested Wednesday
While Covering Elizabeth
City Protests*, FAYETTE-
VILLE OBSERVER, May 20,
2021, fayobserver.com/
story/news/2021/05/20/
reporters-arrested-
covering-elizabeth-city-
protests-andrew-brown-
jr-no-charges-filed-
police/5184491001/.

338. Al Tompkins, *23 Guidelines for Journalists to
Safely Cover Protests*,
POYNTER, June 1, 2020,
poynter.org/reporting-
editing/2020/23-guide-
lines-for-journalists-to-
safely-cover-protests-
this-weekend/.

339. *2021 Quick Facts*, U.S.
PRESS FREEDOM TRACKER,
n.d., pressfreedom-
tracker.us.

340. *Parent Accosts Mich.
Journalist after School
Bd. Meeting*, U.S. PRESS
FREEDOM TRACKER, Aug. 2,
2021, pressfreedom-
tracker.us/all-incidents/
parent-accosts-mich-
igan-journalist-after-
school-board-meeting/.

341. *Independent Videog-
rapher Punched While
Covering Anti-Vaccine
Protest in LA*, U.S. PRESS
FREEDOM TRACKER, July 29,
2021, pressfreedom-
tracker.us/all-incidents/
independent-videog-
rapher-punched-

while-covering-anti-
vaccine-protest-in-la/;
*Independent Videographer
Struck with Baton Dur-
ing Protest at LA's Wi
Spa*, U.S. PRESS FREEDOM
TRACKER, July 17, 2021,
pressfreedomtracker.
us/all-incidents/
independent-videogra-
pher-struck-with-baton-
during-protest-at-las-
wi-spa/.

342. *2021 Newsrooms by the
Numbers: Data From a
Dangerous Year in Jour-
nalism*, RTDNA, April
28, 2021, rtdna.org/
article/2021_news-
rooms_by_numbers.

343. Joe Concha, *Dem Lawmakers Unveil Journal-
ist Protection Act Amid
Trump Attacks on Media*,
HILL, March 12, 2019,
thehill.com/homenews/
media/433709-dem-
lawmakers-unveil-
journalist-protection-
act-amid-trump-
attacks-on-media.

344. *See, e.g.,* Kristen Rasmussen, *After an Arrest*,
REPORTERS COMM. FOR FREE-
DOM OF THE PRESS, Winter
2012, rcfp.org/wp-con-
tent/uploads/imported/
PPTP.pdf.

345. Nieves v. Bartlett, 139 S.
Ct. 1715 (2019).

346. *Id.*

347. *Id.*

348. *Id.*

349. *Id.*

350. *Id.* at 1736 (Sotomayor, J.,
dissenting).

351. *Id.*

352. Frank LoMonte, *Supreme
Court Puts Journalists at
Greater Risk When Cover-
ing Crime Scenes, Pro-
tests*, BRECHNER REPORT,
June 4, 2019, medium.
com/@frankbrechner/
supreme-court-puts-
journalists-at-greater-
risk-when-covering-
crime-scenes-protests-
feb70110c553.

353. Index Newspapers LLC v.
United States Marshals
Service, 977 F.3d 817
(2020).

354. *Id.*

355. Damon Root, *SCOTUS
Just Made it Even Harder
to Sue an Abusive Fed-
eral Agent*, REASON,
June 8, 2022, reason.
com/2022/06/08/
scotus-just-made-it-
even-harder-to-sue-an-
abusive-federal-agent/.

356. Egbert v. Boule, 2022
U.S. LEXIS 2829 (Jun. 8,
2022).

357. *Id.*

358. *Id.*

359. The First, Third, Fifth,
Seventh, Ninth, and
Eleventh Circuits have
recognized this First
Amendment right.
Irizarry v. Yehia, 38
F.4th 1282, 1294 (10th
Cir. 2022)(quoting Cum-
mings v. Dean, 931 F.3d
1227, 1239 (10th Cir.
2019)(internal quotation
marks removed).

360. *Id.* at 1282–94.

361. Knight v. Montgomery
Cty., Tennessee, 470 F.
Supp. 3d 760 (M.D. Tenn.
2020).

362. Project Veritas Action Fund v. Rollins, 982 F.3d 813 (1st Cir. 2020), *cert. denied* 142 S.Ct. 560 (Nov. 22, 2021).

363. *Project Veritas Action Fund v. Rollins*, AMICUS BRIEF OF ACCURACY IN MEDIA, 2021, supremecourt.gov/DocketPDF/20/20-1598/181908/202106161 44636476_20-1598%20Amicus%20Brief%20of%20Accuracy%20In%20Media.pdf.

364. Penny Abernathy, *The State of Local News : The 2022 Report*, June 29, 2022, localnews-initiative.northwestern.edu/research/state-of-local-news/report/.

365. Rick Edmonds, *Reeling in a Federal Boost for Local Journalism Remains Elusive*, POYNTER, March 29, 2022, poynter.org/business-work/2022/local-journalism-sustainability-act-status-federal-funding-journalism/.

366. *Klobuchar, Kennedy, Cicilline, Buck, Durbin, Nadler Release Updated Bipartisan Journalism Bill*, Aug. 22, 2022, klobuchar.senate.gov/public/index.cfm/2022/8/klobuchar-kennedy-cicilline-buck-durbin-nadler-release-updated-bipartisan-journalism-bill.

CHAPTER 8

1. *Court Finds Prosecutorial Misconduct But Allows Death Sentence to Stand*, DEATH PENALTY INFO. CTR., Sept. 21, 2017, deathpenaltyinfo.org/node/6875.

2. Sheppard v. Maxwell, 384 U.S. 333. *See, e.g.*, Peter Suciu, *Guilty Verdict in Derek Chauvin Trial Blows up Twitter*, FORBES, April 20, 2021, forbes.com/sites/petersuciu/2021/04/20/guilty-verdict-in-derek-chauvin-trial-blows-up-twitter/?sh=44dc84c69c06.

3. *See, e.g., 'I Can't Breathe!': Video of Fatal Arrest Shows Minneapolis Officer Kneeling on George Floyd's Neck for Several Minutes*, CBS MINN., May 26, 2020, minnesota.cbslocal.com/2020/05/26/george-floyd-man-dies-after-being-arrested-by-minneapolis-police-fbi-called-to-investigate/; *CNN Special Report: Married to a Murderer: The Drew Peterson Story*, CNN, June 25, 2015, cnn.com/videos/tv/2015/06/25/exp-cnn-creative-marketing-cnn-special-report-married-to-a-murderer.cnn/video/playlists/drew-peterson/.

4. Mark Wilson, *Adnan Syed, Subject of "Serial," Asks for Another Appeal*, FINDLAW, Jan. 14, 2015, blogs.findlaw .com/celebrity_justice/2015/01/adnan-syed-subject-of-serial-asks-for-another-appeal.html. *See also* Brian Witte, *Adnan Syed, Subject of 'Serial' Podcast, to Be Released from Prison*, PBS NEWS HOUR, Sept. 19, 2022, pbs.org/newshour/nation/adnan-syed-subject-of-serial-podcast-to-be-released-from-prison.

5. Minneapolis Police, *Investigative Update on Critical Incident*, May 26, 2020, web.archive.org/web/20200526183652/https://www.insidempd.com/2020/05/26/man-dies-after-medical-incident-during-police-interaction/.

6. *See, e.g.*, Evan Hill et al., *How George Floyd Was Killed in Police Custody*, N.Y. TIMES, May 31, 2020, nytimes.com/video/us/100000007159353/george-floyd-arrest-death-video.html.

7. Amy Forliti & Michael Balsamo, *4 Ex-cops Indicted on US Civil Rights Charges in Floyd Death*, AP, May 7, 2021, apnews.com/article/george-floyd-officers-charged-6d87b905692ddfa9594b-36c876366f4b.

8. Zsoit Boda & Gabriella Szabó, *The Media and Attitudes Towards Crime and the Justice System*, EUR. J. CRIM., July 20, 2011, doi.org/10.1177/147737 0811411455.

9. Jim Redden, *Criminal Justice Series Wins Award*, PORTLAND TRIB., June 26, 2018, pamplinmedia.com/

pt/9-news/399236-293995-criminal-justice-series-wins-award.

10. *See, e.g.,* Terry Gross, *"Charged" Explains How Prosecutors and Plea Bargains Drive Mass Incarceration,* NPR FRESH AIR, April 10, 2019, npr.org/2019/04/10/711654831/charged-explains-how-prosecutors-and-plea-bargains-drive-mass-incarceration.

11. Michael McLaughlin, *Overcrowding in Federal Prisons Harms Inmates, Guards: GAO Report,* HUFFPOST, Sept. 14, 2012, huffpost.com/entry/prison-overcrowding-report_n_1883919.

12. *See, e.g., Why the Public Perception of Crime Exceeds the Reality,* NPR, July 36, 2016, npr.org/2016/07/26/487522807/why-the-public-perception-of-crime-exceeds-the-reality; Daniel Romer et al., *Television News and the Cultivation of Fear of Crime,* 53 J. COMMC'N. 88 (2003).

13. Romeo Vitelli, *New Research Explores How Media Bias Impacts the Right to a Fair Trial,* PSYCHOL. TODAY, Aug. 22, 2018, psychology today.com/us/blog/media-spotlight/201808/how-trial-media-can-undermine-the-court-room.

14. Elizabeth Sun, *The Dangerous Racialization of Crime in U.S.*

News Media, CTR. FOR AM. PROGRESS, Aug. 29, 2018, americanprogress.org/issues/criminal-justice/news/2018/08/29/455313/dangerous-racialization-crime-u-s-news-media/.

15. *See, e.g.,* Joran Gross, *If Skilling Can't Get a Change of Venue, Who Can? Salvaging Common Law Implied Bias Principles from the Wreckage of the Constitutional Pretrial Publicity Standard,* 85 TEMPLE L. REV. 575, 578 (2013); Romeo Vitelli, *How 'Trial by Media' Can Undermine the Courtroom,* PSYCHOL. TODAY, Aug. 22, 2018, psychologytoday.com/us/blog/media-spotlight/201808/how-trial-media-can-undermine-the-court-room.

16. Tim Arango, *Judge Denies Motion to Delay Derek Chauvin Trial,* N.Y. TIMES, Mar. 19, 2021, nytimes.com/2021/03/19/us/derek-chauvin-trial-judge-george-floyd.html.

17. The Fifth Amendment provides rules for indictment and due process and prohibits double jeopardy and self-incrimination. The Sixth protects criminal defendants' rights to counsel, to confront evidence and witnesses and to a speedy, local, public trial. The Seventh ensures trial by jury in civil cases.

18. Gannett v. DePasquale, 433 U.S. 368 (1979).

19. *Id.* at 378.

20. *Id.* at 383.

21. *Id.* at 415, 423.

22. *Id.* at 441-42.

23. *Id.* at 429.

24. *Id.*

25. Richmond Newspapers, Inc. v. Virginia, 448 U.S. 555 (1980).

26. *Id.* at 569.

27. *Id.* at 581.

28. *Id.* at 575.

29. *Id.* at 556; *see also, e.g., Tsarnaev Convicted on All Counts,* HERE & NOW, April 8, 2015, hereandnow.wbur.org/2015/04/08/tsarnaev-trial-verdict.

30. Rapid City Journal v. Delaney, 804 N.W.2d 388 (S.D. 2011).

31. Globe Newspaper Co. v. Super. Ct. for Norfolk Cty., 457 U.S. 596 (1982).

32. *Id.*

33. *Id.* at 606.

34. State v. Martinez, 956 N.W.2d 772, 779 (N.D. 2021).

35. *Id.* at 791. The court also noted the defendant had not voluntarily waived his public trial rights.

36. Press-Enterprise (I) v. Super. Ct. of Calif., 464 U.S. 501 (1984); Press-Enterprise (II) v. Super. Ct. of Calif., 478 U.S. 1 (1986).

37. *Press-Enterprise II,* 478 U.S. at 11.

38. *Id.*

39. Eugene Volokh, *Does the First Amendment Protect a Presumptive Right to Access Criminal Court Records*, Volokh Conspiracy, Oct. 25, 2018, reason.com/volokh/2018/10/25/does-the-first-amendment-protect-a-presu.

40. Press-Enterprise (I) v. Super. Ct. of Calif., 464 U.S. 501 (1984); Press-Enterprise (II) v. Super. Ct. of Calif., 478 U.S. 1 (1986).

41. Globe Newspaper Co. v. Super. Ct. for Norfolk Cty., 457 U.S. 596, 607 (1982); *Press-Enterprise I*, 464 U.S. at 510.

42. Presley v. Georgia, 558 U.S. 209, 214 (2010).

43. *Id.*

44. *Id.* at 215.

45. *See, e.g.*, People v. Ray, 2006 WL 6924824 (Colo. Dist. Ct. 2006); People v. Ray, 252 P.3d 1042 (Colo. 2011); People v. Owens, 2012 WL 2488070 (Colo. Dist. Ct. 2012); People v. Ray, 417 P.3d 939 (Colo. App. 2018); People v. Ray, 420 P.3d 257 (Colo. 2018).

46. *Id.*

47. *Ray*, 2006 WL 6924824.

48. *Owens*, 2012 WL 2488070.

49. *In re* People v. Owens, Case. No. 06CR705, Petition for Original Proceeding and Issuance of Rule to Show Cause Under C.A.R. 21, June 21, 2013, scribd .com/document/150184019/Sir-Mario-Owens-Ruling; *see Colo. Supreme Court Denies Motion to Open Files of Death-Row Inmates*, Colo. Freedom of Info. Coalition, Sept. 19, 2013, coloradofoic.org/cfoic-joins-call-open-files-death-row-inmates/.

50. *Ray*, 420 P.3d 257.

51. *Ray*, 252 P.3d 1042.

52. *Owens*, 420 P.3d 257.

53. People v. Owens, 420 P.3d 257, 258 (Colo. 2018).

54. Colo. Indep. v. Dist. Ct. for Eighteenth Judicial Dist., 139 S. Ct. 1165 (2019)(mem.).

55. Gubarev v. BuzzFeed, 365 F. Supp. 3d 1250 (S.D. Fla. 2019).

56. *Id.* at 1260. *See also* Gubarev v. BuzzFeed, 340 F. Supp. 3d 1304 (S.D. Fla. 2018).

57. Hartford Courant Co. v. Carroll, 986 F.3d 211 (2d Cir. 2021).

58. *Id.* at 221.

59. *Id.* at 221-23.

60. *Id.* at 223.

61. *See, e.g.*, FL ST 17 J CIR 2021-74-GEN (2022); Minn. R. Crim. Proc. 26.03 (2022).

62. Chandler v. Florida, 449 U.S. 560 (1981).

63. *Entering the Building & Prohibited Items*, Sup. Ct. of the U.S., supremecourt.gov/visiting/prohibited-items.aspx (last visited Nov. 19, 2022).

64. *Arrangements during the Coronavirus (COVID-19) Pandemic*, The Sup. Ct. of the U.S., March 29, 2021, supremecourt.uk/news/arrangements-during-the-coronavirus-pandemic.html.

65. *Cameras to Broadcast from the Crown for First Time*, Ministry Just. & HM Cts & Tribunals Serv., Jan. 16, 2020, gov.uk/government/news/cameras-to-broadcast-from-the-crown-court-for-first-time.

66. Elian Peltier, *TV Cameras Coming to English Criminal Courts*, N. Y. Times, Jan. 16, 2020, nytimes.com/2020/01/16/world/europe/cameras-british-courts.html.

67. *The Court of Appeal (Civil Division)—Live Streaming of Court Hearings*, Cts & Tribunals Judiciary, judiciary.uk/you-and-the-judiciary/going-to-court/court-of-appeal-home/the-court-of-appeal-civil-division-live-streaming-of-court-hearings/.

68. *Courtroom Camera Pilot Program Grounded*, Reporters Comm. for Freedom of the Press, 2015, rcfp.org/journals/news-media-and-law-spring-2016/courtroom-camera-pilot-prog/.

69. *Judicial Conference Says "No" to Expanding Cameras Pilot Program*, Fix the Ct., Mar. 15, 2016, fixthecourt.com/2016/03/judicial-conference-says-no-to-expanding-cameras-pilot-program/.

70. Michael Lambert, *Courtroom Camera Pilot*

Program Grounded, Reporters Comm. for Freedom of the Press, Spring 2016, rcfp.org/browse-media-law-resources/news-media-law/news-media-and-law-spring-2016/courtroom-camera-pilot-prog.

71. *Video Broadcasting from the Federal Courts: Issues for Congress*, Cong. Res. Serv., Oct. 28, 2019, fas.org/sgp/crs/misc/R44514.pdf.

72. Hollingsworth v. Perry, 558 U.S. 183 (2010).

73. Lisa Leff, *Court Won't Order California Officials to Appeal Ruling That Struck Down Gay Marriage Ban*, L.A. Times, Sept. 8, 2010.

74. Kathy Kirby, *Cameras in the Court: A State-by-State Guide*, RTDNA, Summer 2012, rtdna.org/article/cameras_in_the_court_a_state_by_state_guide_updated.

75. *See* Rule 2.450, Rules of Judicial Administration, Florida Rules of Ct. (2008); Florida v. Palm Beach Newspapers, 395 So. 2d 544 (1981).

76. Sup. Ct. Rule 10–8 & 10–9 (S.D. 2011).

77. *Cameras Document Murder Trial for First Time in South Dakota*, Mitchell Republic, July 2, 2011, mitchellrepublic.com/news/1535999-cameras-document-murder-trial-first-time-south-dakota.

78. Paula M. Carey, *Trial Court Emergency Administrative Order 20-10:* *Order Concerning Trial Court Policy on Possession & Use of Cell Phones & Personal Electronic Devices*, Mass.gov, June 24, 2020, mass.gov/doc/trial-court-emergency-administrative-order-20-10-order-concerning-trial-court-policy-on/download. *See* Electronic Access to the Courts, Sup. Ct. Rule 1:19 (Mass. 2012), mass.gov/courts/case-legal-res/rules-of-court/sjc/sjc119.html.

79. Ill. Code of Judicial Conduct, Rule 63(A)(7).

80. 735 Ill. Code Civil Procedure 5/Art. VII, Part 7, § 8–701, Broadcast or Televised Testimony.

81. *Managing the Media in High Profile Cases*, BBA Bench and Bar Retreat, 2018, cdn.ymaws.com/birminghambar.site-ym.com/resource/resmgr/member_benefits/cle_materials/media_-_managing_the_media_-.pdf; Utah Code of Judicial Administration, Rule 4-401.01 (2) (B) (iii) Electronic Media Coverage of Court Proceedings.

82. *Cameras in the Courts: State* by *State Guide*, RTDNA, 2021, rtdna.org/content/cameras_in_court.

83. *See, e.g., Model Policy for the Use of Portable Electronic Devices in Courthouses and Courtrooms*, Sup. Ct. of Va., Dec. 5, 2018, vacourts.gov/news/items/2018_1214_scv_press_release_electronic_devices.pdf.

84. *See, e.g.*, Barbara Allen & Al Tompkins, *How the Pandemic Forced the Chauvin Trial to Open to Cameras*, Poynter, April 21, 2021, poynter.org/ethics-trust/2021/how-the-pandemic-forced-the-chauvin-trial-to-open-to-cameras/.

85. C. Danielle Vinson & John S. Ertter, *Entertainment or Education: How Do Media Cover the Courts?* 7 Harv. Int'l J. Press/Pol. 80 (2002).

86. Leslie Y. Garfield Tenzer, *Social Media, Venue and the Right to a Fair Trial*, SSRN, Feb. 4, 2019, papers.ssrn.com/sol3/papers.cfm?abstract_id=3328959.

87. James Podgers, *Social Media Is New Norm, but Courts Still Grappling With Whether to Let Cameras In*, A.B.A. J., Aug. 8, 2010, abajournal.com/news/article/social_media_is_norm_but_courts_still_grappling_with_whether_to_let_cameras/.

88. State v. Smith, No. M2010–01384–SC–R11–CD (2013).

89. *Portable Communication Devices in Courthouses*, U.S. Cts, June 2017, uscourts.gov/sites/default/files/portable_comm_devices_policy.3.12.17.pdf.

90. *See, e.g., Juror Use of Social Media: A State-by-State Guide*, Blog L. Online, Sept. 13, 2010, bloglawonline.blogspot.com/2010/02/

juror-use-of-social-media-state-by.html.

91. *See, e.g., Kan. Reporter Gets OK to Use Twitter to Cover Federal Gang Trial*, AP, March 6, 2009.

92. Nate Anderson, *Appeals Court: No Webcast for Joel Tenenbaum*, ARS TECHNICA, April 16, 2009, arstech nica.com/tech-policy/2009/04/appeals-court-no-webcast-for-joel-tenenbaum/.

93. Jaikumar Vijayan, *Appeals Court Blocks Internet Streaming Order in RIAA Music Piracy Case*, COMPUTERWORLD, April 16, 2009, computerworld.com/ article/2523464/appeals-court-blocks-internet-streaming-order-in-riaa-music-piracy-case.html.

94. *Ninth Circuit Begins Live Video Streaming En Banc Proceedings*, REPORTERS COMM. FOR FREEDOM OF THE PRESS, 2014, rcfp.org/journals/news-media-and-law-winter-2014/ninth-circuit-begins-live-v/.

95. Hilary Hylton, *Tweeting in the Jury Box: A Danger to Fair Trials?*, TIME, Dec. 29, 2009, content.time.com/time/nation/article/0,8599,1948971,00.html.

96. Meghan Dunn, *Jurors' Use of Social Media During Trials and Deliberations*, FED. JUDICIAL CTR., Nov. 22, 2011, fjc.gov/sites/default/files/2012/DunnJuror.pdf.

97. *Proposed Model Jury Instructions: The Use of Electronic Technology to Learn or Communicate about a Case*, JUDICIAL CONF. COMM. ON CT. ADMINISTRATION AND CASE MANAGEMENT, June 2020, uscourts.gov/sites/default/files/proposed_model_jury_instructions.pdf.

98. Press-Enterprise (I) v. Super. Ct. of Calif., 464 U.S. 501 (1984); Press-Enterprise (II) v. Super. Ct. of Calif., 478 U.S. 1 (1986).

99. Nixon v. Warner Comm., 435 U.S. 589 (1978).

100. *Id.* at 608–11.

101. State v. Bodine, 2021 WL 1826987 (Kan. May 7, 2021).

102. Ala. Dep't of Corrections *v. Advance Local Media*, 918 F.3d 1161 (11th Cir. 2019); Steven D. Schwinn, *Eleventh Circuit Orders Release of Alabama's Execution Protocol Under Common Law Right to Access*, Conlawprof, March 20, 2019.

103. *Ala. Dep't of Corrections*, 918 F.3d at 1167.

104. United States v. Doe, 870 F.3d 991 (9th Cir. 2017).

105. *See, e.g.*, Alan J. Keays, *News Outlets, First Amendment Groups Bring Suit over Access to Court Records*, VTDIGGER, May 23, 2021, vtdigger.org/2021/05/23/news-outlets-first-amendment-groups-bring-suit-over-access-to-court-records/;

106. Courthouse News Serv. v. Planet, 947 F.3d 581, 591-92 (9th Cir. 2020).

106. Courthouse News Serv. v. Schaefer, 2 F.4th 318 (4th Cir. June 24, 2021).

107. Courthouse News Serv. v. Planet, 947 F.3d 581, 591-92 (9th Cir. 2020).

108. Florida Star v. B.J.F., 491 U.S. 524, 540 (1989).

109. Undisclosed, LLC v. State, 807 S.E. 2d 393 (Ga. 2017); Colin Miller, *The Supreme Court of Georgia's Ruling in Undisclosed, LLC v. The State*, EVIDENCEPROF BLOG, Nov. 2, 2017, lawprofessors.typepad.com/evidence prof/2017/11/on-monday-the-supreme-court-of-georgia-ruled-against-undisclosed-in-our-attempt-to-get-the-court-reporters-recording-of-the.html.

110. Robert Timothy Reagan et al., *Sealed Settlement Agreements in Federal District Court*, FED. JUDICIAL CTR. (2009).

111. Grube v. Trader, 420 P.3d 343 (Haw. 2018).

112. Pennsylvania v. Curley, 189 A.3d 467 (Pa. Super. Ct. 2018).

113. Ind. Code § 5–15–3–3, § 5–14–3–4.

114. Wash. Admin. Code 44-14-01001.

115. *See* Nast v. Michels, 730 P.2d 54 (Wash. 1986).

116. *Privacy Policy for Electronic Case Files*, U.S. Cts, Mar. 2008, privacy.

uscourts.gov/b4amend. htm; Alan Carlson & Martha Wade Steketee, *Public Access to Court Records: Implementing the CCJ/COSCA Guidelines Final Project Report*, St. Just. Inst., Oct. 15, 2005, it.ojp.gov/documents/d/2005-10-15%20Final%20Report.pdf; Martha Wade Steketee & Alan Carlson, *Developing CCJ/COSCA Guidelines for Public Access to Court Records: A National Project to Assist State Courts*, St. Just. Inst., Oct. 18, 2002, ncsc.contentdm.oclc.org/digital/collection/accessfair/id/210/.

117. Nat'l Veterans Legal Services Program v. U.S., 968 F.3d 1340, 1357 (Fed. Cir. 2020).

118. *Id.*

119. *See, e.g.*, D.R. Jones, *Protecting the Treasure: An Assessment of State Court Rules and Policies for Access to Online Civil Court Records*, 61 Drake L Rev. 375, 389-422 (2012). *See also A Quiet Revolution in the Courts: Electronic Access to State Court Records,* Center for Democracy & Tech., Aug. 2002, cdt.org/publications/020821 courtrecords.shtml.

120. *A Boon for Transparency in Maine's Court System*, Bangor Daily News, June 21, 2018, bangordailynews.com/2018/06/21/opinion/editorials/a-boon-for-transparency-in-maines-court-system/; L. Dieringer, *Okla.*

Supreme Court Issues Rule Allowing Greater Public Access to Online Court Records, Republic, Dec. 14, 2011; Carmen Forman, *Virginia Supreme Court Announces Plans for Public Records, Statewide Case Search*, Roanoke Times, Jan. 25, 2018, roanoke.com/news/politics/general_assembly/virginia-supreme-court-announces-plans-for-public-records-statewide-case/article_67e30a88-60a1-5512-9c9a-6af586d189eb.html.

121. Andrew Oxford, *State Court Records Go Online*, Santa Fe New Mexican, Jan. 7, 2017.

122. Mike Schneider, *Access to Florida Online Court Records Varies by Hierarchy*, Miami Herald, March 16, 2015.

123. Oonagh Doherty & Sara Tonneson, *How to Look Up Court Records on the Internet*, Mass. Justice Project, March 30, 2010, masslegalservices.org/content/how-look-court-records-internet-links-online-access-records-other-states.

124. *JUSTICE Search*, Neb. Judicial Branch, nebraska.gov/justicecc/ccname.cgi.

125. Final Report Minn. Sup. Ct. Advisory Comm. and Order on Rules of Pub. Access to Records of the Judicial Branch. Minn. Ct. Rules: Record Access Rules Order

No. C4–85–1848, Minn. Statutes; Martha Wade Steketee & Alan Carlson, *Developing CCJ/COSCA Guidelines for Public Access to Court Records: A National Project to Assist State Courts*, St. Just. Inst., Oct. 18, 2002, ncsc.contentdm.oclc.org/digital/collection/accessfair/id/210/.

126. Jack Dura, *North Dakota Supreme Court Suspends Expanded Access to Online Documents due to Privacy Concerns*, Bismarck Trib., Jan. 7, 2020.

127. *Privacy/Public Access to Court Records*, Nat'l Ctr. for St. Cts, ncsc.org/topics/access-and-fairness/privacy-public-access-to-court-records/state-links.aspx.

128. U.S. Dep't of Justice v. Reporters Comm. for Freedom of the Press, 489 U.S. 749 (1989).

129. Daily Press v. Office of Exec. Sec'y, 800 S.E.2d 822 (Va. 2017).

130. *Court Fees*, Minn. Judicial Branch, July 1, 2017, mncourts.gov/Help-Topics/Court-Fees.aspx.

131. General Rule 31, adopted Oct. 7, 2004, by the Washington Supreme Court. *See* courts.wa.gov/newsinfo/?fa=newsinfo.pressdetail&newsid=484.

132. Estes v. Texas, 381 U.S. 532 (1965).

133. *1963 Pulitzer Prizes: Journalism*, The Pulitzer

PRIZES, pulitzer.org/awards/1963.

134. *Estes*, 381 U.S. at 577-78.

135. *Id.* at 539-40.

136. *Id.* at 585 (Harlan, J., concurring).

137. *Id.* at 595.

138. Patton v. Yount, 467 U.S. 1025 (1984).

139. Sheppard v. Maxwell, 384 U.S. 333 (1966).

140. *Id.* at 340.

141. *Id.* at 349 *et seq.*

142. Allen Pusey, *Sam Sheppard Seeks a New Trial*, 104 ABA J. 72 (2018).

143. Sheppard, 384 U.S. at 384.

144. *Id.* at 358.

145. *Id.* at 358–62.

146. Christine L. Ruva & Anthony E. Coy, *Your Bias is Rubbing Off on Me: The Impact of Pretrial Publicity and Jury Type on Guilt Decisions, Trial Evidence Interpretation, and Impression Formation*, 26 PSYCHOL., PUB. POL'Y, & L. 22 (2020); Jon Bruschke et al., *The Influence of Heterogeneous Exposure and Pre-deliberation Queries on Pretrial Publicity Effects*, 83 COMMC'N MONOGRAPHS 521 (2016); JON BRUSCHKE & WILLIAM E. LOGES, FREE PRESS VS. FAIR TRIALS: EXAMINING PUBLICITY'S ROLE IN TRIAL OUTCOMES 134–137 (2004).

147. *See, e.g.*, Erin K. Coyle, *Turning Point: Balancing Free Press & Fair Trial Rights After* Sheppard v. Maxwell, 44 JOURNALISM HIST. 150 (Fall 2018); Erin K. Coyle, *Press Freedom & Citizens Right to Know in the 1960s*, 43 JOURNALISM HIST. 44 (Spring 2017).

148. *See, e.g.*, Gene Maddaus, *Media Organizations Seek Access to Key Harvey Weinstein Hearing*, VARIETY, Apr. 22, 2019; Shayna Jacobs & Larry McShane, *Judge Rules Details of Session Would Ruin Defense Chances of Selecting Impartial Jury*, N.U. DAILY NEWS, April 26, 2019.

149. *See, e.g.*, Elyssa Cherney, *Cameras Barred from Pretrial Hearings for 4 Accused in Facebook Live Attack*, CHICAGO TRIB., Jan. 27, 2017.

150. Batson v. Kentucky, 476 U.S. 79 (1986); J.E.B. v. Alabama, 511 U.S. 127 (1994).

151. Mu'Min v. Virginia, 500 U.S. 415 (1991).

152. United States v. Tsarnaev, 157 F. Supp. 3d 57, 66 (D. Mass. 2016).

153. United States v. Tsarnaev, 968 F.3d 24, 53-58 (1st Cir. 2020).

154. *Id.* at 59.

155. United States v. Tsarnaev, 2022 U.S. LEXIS 1327, at *12-24 (Mar. 4, 2022).

156. *Proposed Model Jury Instructions: The Use of Electronic Technology to Learn or Communicate about a Case*, JUDICIAL CONF. COMM. ON CT. ADMIN. & CASE MGMT., June 2020, uscourts.gov/sites/default/files/proposed_model_jury_instructions.pdf.

157. People v. Tanubagijo, 2017 WL 526485 (1st D. Cal. App., Feb. 9, 2017). *See* leagle.com/decision/incaco20170209030.

158. *Id.*

159. United States v. Loughry, 2021 WL 2005932 (4th Cir. May 20, 2021)(per curiam), *Aff'd by an equally divided court*, United States v. Loughry, 983 F.3d. 698 (4th Cir. 2020).

160. State v. Chauvin, Order for Jury Sequestration and Anonymity (27-CR-20-12951), Nov. 4, 2020, mncourts.gov/mncourtsgov/media/High-Profile-Cases/27-CR-20-12951-TKL/27-CR-20-12951_Order-RE-Jurors_11-4.pdf.

161. *See, e.g.*, Jenni Fink, *What Is Sequestering a Jury? Lawyer Looks to Isolate George Floyd Jurors After Daunte Wright Shooting*, NEWSWEEK, April 12, 2021. *See* also Amy Forliti, *Explainer: How Will Jury Deliberations Work in Chauvin Case?* ABC NEWS, April 19, 2021, abcnews.go.com/US/wireStory/explainer-jury-deliberations-work-chauvin-case-77174630.

162. *See, e.g.*, Jordan Gross, *If Skilling Can't Get a Change of Venue, Who Can? Salvaging Common Law Implied Bias Principles from the Wreckage of the Constitutional Pretrial*

Publicity Standard, 85 Temple L. Rev. 578 (2013).

163. Katharine Q. Seelye, *Surveys Show Bias of Potential Jurors in Boston Bombing Trial*, Int'l N.Y. Times, Jan. 23, 2015, nytimes.com/2015/01/23/us/boston-marathon-case-surveys-tell-of-troubles-in-selection-of-a-jury.html.

164. *Id.*

165. U.S. v. Velarde, 606 F. App'x 434 (10th Cir. 2015) (finding failure to file necessary pretrial motion for dismissal under Speedy Trial Act or to show delay caused prejudice).

166. United States v. Duran-Gomez, 984 F.3d 366 (5th Cir. 2020), *cert. denied*, 142 S. Ct. 133 (2021).

167. *Id.* at 379-81.

168. Betterman v. Montana, 136 S. Ct. 1609 (2016).

169. *Id.* at 1614.

170. *See* Abraham Abramovsky & Jonathan I. Edelstein, *Anonymous Juries: In Exigent Circumstances Only*, 13 St. John's J. Legal Comment. 457 (1999).

171. United States v. Ross, 33 F.3d 1507, 1519 (11th Cir. 1994).

172. *See* Christopher Keleher, *The Repercussions of Anonymous Juries*, 44 U.S.F. L. Rev. 531 (2010).

173. United States v. Wecht, 537 F.3d 222 (3d Cir. 2008); United States v. Blagojevich, 612 F.3d 558 (7th Cir. 2010).

174. *The Right of Access to Juror Names and Addresses*, Reporters Comm. for Freedom of the Press, 2016, rcfp.org/journals/news-media-and-law-summer-2016/right-access-juror-names-an/#_ftn6.

175. *See, e.g.*, United States v. Shryock, 342 F.3d 948 (9th Cir. 2003), *cert. denied*, 541 U.S. 965 (2004).

176. State v. Chauvin, Order for Jury Sequestration and Anonymity (27-CR-20-12951), Nov. 4, 2020, mncourts.gov/mncourtsgov/media/High-Profile-Cases/27-CR-20-12951-TKL/27-CR-20-12951_Order-RE-Jurors_11-4.pdf.

177. Nicholas Bogel-Burroughs, *Jurors Who Convicted Derek Chauvin Are Identified for First Time*, N.Y. Times, Nov. 1, 2021, nytimes.com/2021/11/01/us/derek-chauvin-trial-jury.html.

178. Tex. Crim. Proc. Code Ann. § 35.29 (1994).

179. Sheppard v. Maxwell, 384 U.S. 333 (1966).

180. Mu'Min v. Virginia, 500 U.S. 415 (1991).

181. *Id.*

182. Butterworth v. Smith, 494 U.S. 624 (1990).

183. State v. Yazeed, Order that Defendant Be Held Without Bond and Gag Order (WR-2019-2466), Nov. 8, 2019, rtdna.org/uploads/files/YAZEED%20GAG%20ORDER.pdf. *See also Man Held in Custody in Connection to Death of Teen-Stepchild of UFC Fighter*, Legal Monitor Worldwide, Dec. 6, 2019.

184. WXIA-TV v. State, 811 S.E.2d 378 (2018).

185. *Id.* at 387.

186. *Id.*

187. *In re* Wall St. J., 601 F. App'x 215 (4th Cir. 2015).

188. Ruthann Robson, *West Virginia District Judge's Extensive "Gag" and Sealing Order in Blankenship Trial*, Conlawprof, Jan. 8, 2015, lawprofessors.typepad.com/conlaw/2015/01/west-virginia-district-judges-extensive-gag-order-in-blankenship-trial .html.

189. United States v. Blankenship, 79 F. Supp. 3d 613, 618 (S.D. W. Va. 2015).

190. *Wall St. J.*, 601 F. App'x at 218.

191. *In re* Paternity of B.J.M., 944 N.W.2d 542, 552-53 (Wis. 2020).

192. *Id.* at 550-53.

193. Quigley Corp. v. Karkus, 2009 U.S. Dist. LEXIS 41296 at *16 (E.D. Pa., May 19, 2009).

194. Sheppard v. Maxwell, 384 U.S. 333, 342 (1966).

195. Caperton v. Massey, 556 U.S. 868, 870 (2009).

196. Republican Party of Minn. v. White, 536 U.S. 765 (2002).

197. *Id.* at 787.

198. United States v. Bryan, 339 U.S. 323, 331 (1950).

199. Branzburg v. Hayes, 408 U.S. 665, 710 (1972) (Powell, J., concurring).

200. *Introduction to the Reporter's Privilege Compendium*, REPORTERS COMM. FOR FREEDOM OF THE PRESS, Nov. 5, 2021, rcfp. org/introduction-to-the-reporters-privilege-compendium/.

201. Ellen Nakashima, *FBI Paid Professional Hackers One-Time Fee to Crack San Bernardino iPhone*," WASH. POST, April 12, 2016, www.washingtonpost.co m/world/national-secur ity/fbi-paid-professiona l-hackers-one-time-fee -to-crack-san-bernardi no-iphone/2016/04/12/5 397814a-00de-11e6-9d3 6-33d198ea26c5_story. html?utm_term=.33d99 2d3b0c7.

202. Joseph Menn, *Apple Dropped Plan for Encrypting Backups after FBI Complained – Sources*, REUTERS, Jan. 21, 2020, reuters.com/article/ us-apple-fbi-icloud-exclusive/exclusive-apple-dropped-plan-for-encrypting-backups-after-fbi-complained-sources-idUSKBN1Z-K1CT.

203. Nicole Perlroth & Katie Benner, *Subpoenas and Gag Orders Show Government Overreach, Tech Companies Argue*, N. Y. TIMES, Oct. 4, 2016, nytime s.com/2016/10/05/tech nology/subpoenas-and -gag-orders-show-gove rnment-overreach-tech -companies-argue.htm l?_r=0.

204. Nick Wingfield, *Microsoft's Challenge to Government Secrecy Wins Dozens of Supporters*, N.Y. TIMES, Sept. 2, 2016, nytim es.com/2016/09/03/tech nology/microsofts-chall enge-to-government-se crecy-wins-dozens-of-s upporters.html.

205. *Twitter Transparency Report*, TWITTER, Jan. 25, 2022, transparency, twit-ter.com.

206. *See, e.g., National Security Letters*, Electronic Privacy Info. Ctr., epic. org/privacy/nsl/. *See also* Daniel J. Malooly, *Searches Under FISA: A Constitutional Analysis*, 35 AM. CRIM. L. REV. 411 (1997–1998).

207. *See, e.g.,* Guidelines on Methods of Obtaining Documentary Materials Held by Third Parties, 28 C.F.R. § 59.4 (2022).

208. Zurcher v. Stanford Daily, 436 U.S. 547 (1978).

209. *Id.*

210. *Id.* at 563–67.

211. Report of the Committee of the Judiciary: Free Flow of Info. Act, S. Rep. No. 113–118, at § B (2013).

212. *See Paying the Price: A Recent Census of Reporters Jailed or Fined for Refusing to Testify*, REPORTERS COMM. FOR FREEDOM OF THE PRESS, rcfp. org/jailed-journalists/. *See also* Edmond J. Bartnett, *Columnist Loses in Contempt Case*, N.Y. TIMES, Oct. 1, 1958, at 30 (explaining the jailing of reporter Marie Torre for refusing to disclose a source of information); Ross E. Milloy, *Writer Who Was Jailed in Notes Dispute Is Freed*, N.Y. TIMES, Jan. 5, 2002, at A8 (detailing Vanessa Leggett's incarceration and release).

213. Lonnie E. Grifith, Jr, & Sonja Larsen, *Classifications & Distinctions*, 17 AM. JUR. 2d CONTEMPT § 5, November 2022.

214. *In re* Grand Jury Subpoena (Miller), 397 F.3d 964 (D.C. Cir. 2005).

215. *New York Times Reporter Jailed*, CNN, Oct. 28, 2005, cnn.com/2005/ LAW/07/06/reporters. contempt.

216. Miller v. United States, 545 U.S. 1150 (2005).

217. Carol D. Leonnig, *N.Y. Times Reporter Jailed*, WASH. POST, July 7, 2005, at A1.

218. Kevin Gosztola, *Chelsea Manning Believes Subpoena from WikiLeaks Grand Jury May Be "Perjury Trap," According to Unsealed Documents*, COMMON DREAMS, Mar. 22, 2019, commondreams. org/views/2019/03/22/ chelsea-manning-believes-subpoena-wikileaks-grand-jury-

may-be-perjury-trap; Matthew Barakat, *Chelsea Manning Continues to Fight Grand Jury Subpoena*, AP, March 5, 2019, apnews.com/966c33f56 0564678a8d0df58f9003 34f.

219. Sarah N. Lynch, *U.S. Appeals Court Denies Manning's Bail Request, Upholds Contempt Finding*, REUTERS, April 22, 2019, reuters.com/ article/usa-manning/ update-1-u-s-appeals-court-denies-mannings-bail-request-upholds-contempt-finding-idUSL1N2240Z5.

220. *In re* Grand Jury Subpoena, 875 F.3d 1179 (9th Cir. 2017).

221. Branzburg v. Hayes, 408 U.S. 665, 708 (1972).

222. *In re* Grand Jury Subpoena Issued to Twitter, Inc., 2017 WL 9485553 (N.D. Tex. Nov. 7, 2017), *report and recommendation adopted*, 2018 WL 2421867 (N.D. Tex. Dec. 11, 2017).S. 665, 708 (1972).

223. Pennekamp v. Florida, 328 U.S. 331 (1946).

224. *See, e.g.*, Bloom v. Illinois, 391 U.S. 194, 203 n.6 (1968).

225. Smith v. Daily Mail, 443 U.S. 97, 107 (1979).

226. Kent v. United States, 383 U.S. 541, 556 (1966).

227. *In re* Gault, 387 U.S. 1, 33, 36–37 (1967).

228. States that presumptively close juvenile proceedings are Alabama, Alaska, Hawaii, Kentucky, Mississippi, New Jersey, Rhode Island, South Carolina, Vermont, West Virginia, Wisconsin and Wyoming. States with presumptively open proceedings are Arizona, Arkansas, Colorado, Connecticut, Florida, Georgia, Illinois, Iowa, Michigan, Minnesota, Montana, Nevada, New Mexico, New York, North Carolina, North Dakota, Ohio, Oregon, Tennessee and Washington. States with open proceedings for children over a certain age or charged with certain offenses are California, Delaware, Idaho, Indiana, Kansas, Louisiana, Maine, Maryland, Massachusetts, Missouri, Oklahoma, Pennsylvania, South Dakota, Texas, Utah and Virginia. Kristen Rasmussen, *Access to Juvenile Justice*, REPORTERS COMM. FOR FREEDOM OF THE PRESS, Spring 2012, rcfp.org/rcfp/orders/ docs/SJAJJ.pdf. *See also* Kristin N. Henning, *Eroding Confidentiality in Delinquency Proceedings: Should Schools and Public Housing Authorities Be Notified?* 79 N.Y.U. L. REV. 520 (2004).

229. Garrett Therolf, *L.A. Judge Orders Juvenile Courts Opened to Press*, L.A. TIMES, Feb. 1, 2012, articles.latimes. com/2012/feb/01/ local/la-me-open-courts-20120131.

230. HOWARD N. SNYDER, JUVENILE OFFENDERS & VICTIMS: NATIONAL REPORT 109 (2006).

231. Commonwealth v. Barnes, 963 N.E.2d 1156 (Mass. 2012).

232. *Rasmussen, supra* note 228.

233. Commonwealth v. Chism, 2015 Mass. Super. LEXIS 14 (Mass. Super. Ct., Mar. 3, 2015); 23 Mass. L. Rep. 423 (Mass. Super. Ct., Jan. 23, 2015).

234. Ralph Ellis & Jason Hanna, *Teen Sentenced to at Least 40 Years in Massachusetts Teacher Killing*, CNN, Feb. 26, 2016, cnn.com/2016/02/26/us/ massachusetts-teacher-killing-sentence/.

235. *Rassmussen, supra* note 232.pdf.; *see* Howard Snyder & Melissa Sickmund, *Juvenile Offenders and Victims: 2006 National Report*, NCJJ & U.S. DOJ, OFFICE OF JUV. JUST. & DELINQ. PREVENTION, March 2006, ojjdp. ncjrs.gov/ojstatbb/ nr2006/DOWNLOADS/ NR2006.PDF.

236. Anne Teigen, *Juvenile Age of Jurisdiction and Transfer to Adult Court Laws*, NAT'L CONF. OF ST. LEGISLATURES, Apr. 8, 2021, ncsl.org/research/civil-and-criminal-justice/ juvenile-age-of-jurisdiction-and-transfer-to-adult-court-laws. aspx#:~:text=State%20 juvenile%20 courts%20with%20 delinquency,court%20 jurisdiction%20is%20 age%2017.

237. For a summary of these statutes, see *Rape Shield Statutes*, Am. Prosecutors Research Inst., May 1, 2003, arte-sana. com/articles/rape_shield_laws_us.pdf.

238. *Rape Shield Statutes*, Nat'l Dist. Attorneys Ass'n, March 2011, ndaa.org/wp-content/uploads/NCPCA-Rape-Shield-2011.pdf. s

239. *See, e.g.,* Nev. Rev. Stat. Ann. § 200.3771 (2021) and Erin K. Coyle, *Evaluating Methods to Protect Sex Crime Victims Privacy: A Legal Analysis of States' Attempts to Protect Victims' Identities*, 27 Commc'n L. & Pol'y 102 (2022).

240. Batey v. Haas, 573 F. App'x 590 (6th Cir. 2014), *cert. denied*, 575 U.S. 1010 (2015).

241. Commonwealth v. Rogers, 2021 WL 1975272 (Pa. May 18, 2021).

242. United States v. Reynolds, 345 U.S. 1 (1953).

243. *State Secrets Privilege*, Electronic Frontier Found., Dec. 4, 2012, eff. org/nsa-spying/state-secrets-privilege; *see* Rory Eastburg, *Behind Closed Courtroom Doors: From Criminal Cases to Civil, the Bush Administration Sought Unprecedented Levels of Secrecy in the Courts*, News Media & The L., Oct. 1, 2008 (internal quotation marks omitted).

244. Patrice McDermott & Amy Fuller, *Secrecy Report Card 2008*, Open the Government, 2008, open thegovernment. org/wp-content/uploads/other-files/otg/SecrecyReportCard08. pdf.

245. Pub. L. 95–511, 92 Stat. 1783, 50 U.S.C. ch. 36.

246. Ginnie Graham, *Courts Keeping Cases Secret*, Tulsa World, Aug. 10, 2008, tulsaworld.com/news/local/courts-keeping-cases-secret/article_e6f0b2ad-a19c-5f75-89ab-0551a6bd2951.html.

247. United States v. Daoud, 755 F.3d 479 (7th Cir. 2014), *cert. denied*, 135 S. Ct. 1456 (2015).

248. *In re* Opinions and Orders of This Court Containing Novel or Significant Interpretations of Law, 2020 WL 5637419, Sept. 15, 2020.

249. *Id.*

250. Mohamed v. Jeppesen Dataplan, 614 F.3d 1070 (9th Cir. 2010) (en banc).

251. *Id.* at 1086.

252. *Id.* at 1087.

253. Dhiab v. Trump, 852 F.3d 1087 (D.C. Cir. 2017).

254. Press-Enterprise (I) v. Super. Ct., 464 U.S. 501, 510 (1984).

255. *See, e.g., In re* Globe Newspaper Co., 920 F.2d 88 (1st Cir. 1990).

256. *See, e.g.,* Don J. DeBenedictis, *The National Verdict*, A.B.A. J., Oct. 1994, at 52, 54 (citing poll finding 86 percent of those people questioned thought media had some effect on trial fairness); Edith Greene, *Media Effects on Jurors*, 14 L. & Human Behavior 439, 448 (1990).

257. *In re* Charlotte Observer, 882 F.2d 850 (4th Cir. 1989).

258. Claire S.H. Lim, *Media Influence on Courts: Evidence From Civil Case Adjudication*, 17 Am. L. & Econ. Rev. 87 (2015), pdfs.semanticscholar.org/8b06/55851fb15f178af482bd53513f64935bd2ad.pdf; Jon Bruschke & William Loges, Free Press vs. Fair Trials: Examining Publicity's Role in Trial Outcomes (2004); Vincent Carroll, *Overreacting to Pretrial Publicity*, Denv. Post, Aug. 19, 2012, denverpost.com/ci_21331048/overreacting-pretrial-publicity?IADID=.

259. DePuy Synthes Products, Inc. v. Veterinary Orthopedic Implants, Inc., 990 F.3d 1364, 1372 (Fed. Cir. 2021).

260. *AMD v. Intel Antitrust Case*, are.berkeley.edu/~sberto/AMDIntel.pdf.

261. AMD v. Intel Corp., 2006 U.S. Dist. LEXIS 72722 (D. Del. Sept. 26, 2006).

262. *In re* Intel Corp. Microprocessor Antitrust Litigation, Consolidated Action: Motion to Intervene for Purpose of Unsealing Judicial Records and for Partial Reassignment, C.A. No.

05–441-JJF (D. Del. Aug. 21, 2008).

263. Intel Corp. v. AMD, 524 U.S. 241 (2004).

264. Press-Enterprise (II) v. Super. Ct. of California, 478 U.S. 1 (1986).

265. *See, e.g.*, State v. Smith, 876 N.W.2d 310, 330 (Minn. 2016)(stating "In this case, the district court's nonpublic proceeding was administrative in nature and did not constitute a closure implicating Smith's Sixth Amendment right to a public trial."); United States v. Valenti, 987 F.2d 708, 714 (11th Cir. 1993)(stating, however, that "Even where a court properly denies the public and the press access to portions of a criminal trial, the transcripts of properly closed proceedings must be released when the danger of prejudice has passed.").

266. Smith v. Titus, 141 S. Ct. 982, 982-88 (2021) (Sotomayor, J., dissenting)(quoting State v. Smtih, 876 N.W.2d 310, 329 (Minn. 2016) (internal quotation marks omitted).

267. *Id.* (quoting Smith v. Smith, 2018 WL 3696601, *11 (Aug. 3, 2018) and State v. Silvernail, 831 N.W.2d 594, 609 (2013)) (internal quotation marks omitted).

268. Peña Rodriguez v. Colorado, 137 S.Ct. 855 (2017) (finding that juror reliance on racial animus jeopardizes a fair trial and overcomes the Rules of Evidence that preclude admission of testimony into the deliberative process of the jury).

269. *Id.* at 868.

270. *Remedies if You Are Denied Access to Court Proceedings*, Digital Media Law Project, Jan. 22, 2021, dmlp.org/legal-guide/remedies-if-you-are-denied-access-court-proceedings.

271. *See, e.g.*, *Oregon State Bar – Press – Broadcasters Joint Statement of Principles*, pages. uoregon.edu/tgleason/j385/BBPGuide.htm; *Bench-Bar-Press-Committee of Washington Statement of Principles*, courts.wa.gov/court_rules/?fa=court_rules.rulesPDF&ruleId=ambbpstate&pdf=1.

272. Nebraska Press Ass'n v. Stuart, 427 U.S. 539 (1976).

273. *Id.* at 562.

274. *Id.*

275. Federated Publications, Inc. v. Kurtz, 615 P.2d 440 (Wash. 1980).

276. Federated Publications, Inc. v. Swedberg, 633 P.2d 74 (Wash. 1981), *cert. denied*, 456 U.S. 984 (1982).

277. *Nebraska Press Ass'n*, 427 U.S. at 539.

278. Seattle Times v. Rhinehart, 467 U.S. 20 (1984).

279. *Nebraska Press Ass'n*, 427 U.S. at 562.

280. Alabama Gas Corp. v. Advertiser Co., CV-2014-000488.00 (Ala. Cir. Ct., Sept. 23, 2014), s3.documentcloud.org/documents/1303999/filing.pdf.

281. Butterworth v. Smith, 494 U.S. 624 (1990).

282. Multimedia Holdings Corp. v. Circuit Court of Fla., 544 U.S. 1301 (2005). *See Justice Kennedy Denies Application for Stay in Prior Restraint Case, First Coast News v. Circuit Court of Florida, St. Johns County*, Media L. Prof Blog, Apr. 25, 2005, lawprofessors.typepad.com/media_law_prof_blog/2005/04/justice_kennedy.html.

283. Multimedia Holdings Corp., 544 U.S. at 1304.

284. *See, e.g.*, *Oregon State Bar – Press – Broadcasters Joint Statement of Principles*, *supra* note 271 and Society of Professional Journalists, *SPJ Code of Ethics*, 2014, spj.org/ethicscode.asp.

285. *See, e.g.*, Greg Hurley, *Managing High Profile Cases*, Nat'l Ctr. for St. Cts., 2017, ncsc.org/sitecore/content/microsites/trends/home/Monthly-Trends-Articles/2017/Managing-High-Profile-Cases.aspx.

286. *Media Relations Resource Guide*, Nat'l Ctr. for St. Cts., ncsc.org/Topics/Media/Media-Relations/Resource-Guide.aspx.

287. *The Supreme Court of Florida: Florida State Courts Annual Report, July 1, 2016–June 30, 2017*, OFFICE OF THE ST. CTS. ADMIN., 2018, flcourts.org/content/download/218125/1974696/florida-courts-annual-report-2016-17.pdf.

288. *Reporter's Privilege Compendium*, REPORTERS COMM. FOR FREEDOM OF THE PRESS, rcfp.org/reporters-privilege/.

289. Maane Khatchatourian, *Mark Boal Settles Bowe Bergdahl Lawsuit, Won't Turn Over Tapes*, VARIETY, Dec. 13, 2016, variety.com/2016/film/news/mark-boal-bowe-bergdahl-lawsuit-settled-1201941202.

290. *See, e.g.*, Nathan Swinton, *Privileging a Privilege: Should the Reporter's Privilege Enjoy the Same Respect as the Attorney-Client Privilege?*, 19 GEO. J. LEGAL ETHICS 979 (2006).

291. *See generally* David Rudenstine, *A Reporter Keeping Confidences: More Important Than Ever*, 29 CARDOZO L. REV. 1431 (2008).

292. Branzburg v. Hayes, 408 U.S. 665, 710 (1972).

293. *Id.*

294. *Id.*

295. *Id.* at 709.

296. *Id.* at 710.

297. *Id.* at 712.

298. *Id.* at 725.

299. *Id.*

300. *Id.* (quoting Time, Inc. v. Hill, 385 U.S. 374, 389 (1967)).

301. *Id.* at 739.

302. *Id.* at 743.

303. *See, e.g.*, Denis v. Côté, 2019 S.C.C. 44, scc-csc.lexum.com/scc-csc/scc-csc/en/17946/1/document.do.

304. *Id.*

305. *See, e.g.*, United States v. Lloyd, 71 F.3d 1256 (7th Cir. 1995) (finding that a district court did not abuse discretion in quashing a subpoena in a criminal case); LaRouche v. NBC, 780 F.2d 1134 (4th Cir. 1986) (finding that a lower court correctly applied privilege when it quashed subpoenas for journalists in a libel case); United States v. Caporale, 806 F.2d 1487 (11th Cir. 1986) (recognizing qualified privilege in a criminal case); Zerilli v. Smith, 656 F.2d 705 (D.C. Cir. 1981) (recognizing existence of federal privilege in a civil case in which journalists were not parties); Miller v. Transamerican Press, Inc., 621 F.2d 721 (5th Cir. 1980) (finding that journalists have a First Amendment privilege, although it is not absolute); United States v. Cuthbertson, 630 F.2d 139 (3d Cir. 1980) (stating that federal privilege exists in both civil and criminal cases); Silkwood v. Kerr-McGee, 563 F.2d 433 (10th Cir. 1977) (recognizing privilege and finding that a documentary filmmaker could assert it); Cervantes v. Time, Inc., 464 F.2d 986 (8th Cir. 1972) (determining that a magazine could assert privilege in a libel case); Bursey v. United States, 466 F.2d 1059 (9th Cir. 1972) (finding that newspaper employees could assert privilege to quash grand jury subpoenas); Baker v. F & F Investment Co., 470 F.2d 778 (2d Cir. 1972) (recognizing privilege in a civil case).

306. Castellani v. Scranton Times, 956 A.2d 937 (Pa. 2008).

307. Alharbi v. The Blaze, Inc., 199 F. Supp. 3d 334 (D. Mass. 2016).

308. *Eric Holder Says Putting Reporter James Risen Through Hell is a Good "Example" of DOJ Process for Leak Investigations*, TECHDIRT, Feb. 19, 2015, techdirt.com/articles/20150218/17531730067/.

309. United States v. Sterling, 724 F.3d 482 (4th Cir. 2013), *cert. denied*, 572 U.S. 1149 (2014).

310. *Id.; see also* Charlie Savage, *Court Tells Reporter to Testify in Case of Leaked C.I.A. Data*, N.Y. TIMES, July 19, 2013, at A1.

311. Alan Feuer, *Times Reporter Can't Be Compelled to Testify in Baby Hope Case, Court Rules*, N.Y. TIMES, Oct. 20, 2016, nytimes.com/2016/10/21/nyregion/

times-reporter-baby-hope-case.html.

312. Phoenix Newspapers, Inc. v. Arizona, No. 1 CA–SA 16–0096 (Ariz. Ct. App., Aug. 11, 2016).

313. State v. Benson, 44 Media L. Rep. 2094 (Del. Super. Ct. 2016).

314. Peck v. City of Boston (*In re* Slack), 768 F. Supp. 2d 189 (D.D.C. 2011).

315. Keefe v. City of Minneapolis v. Star Tribune Media Co., 2012 U.S. Dist. LEXIS 187017, at *12–*13 (D. Minn. May 25, 2012).

316. Amended Memo. Op. and Order Re: Cowles Publishing Motion to Quash Subpoena Duces Tecum, Jacobson v. John Doe, Case No. CV-12-2098 (Idaho Dist. Ct., July 10, 2012).

317. Branzburg v. Hayes, 408 U.S. 665, 710 (1972).

318. Chevron Corp. v. Berlinger, 629 F.3d 297 (2d Cir. 2011).

319. *In re* McCray, 928 F. Supp. 2d 748 (S.D.N.Y. 2013), *aff'd*, 991 F. Supp. 2d 464 (S.D.N.Y. 2013).

320. *In re* McCray, 928 F. Supp. 2d 748 (S.D.N.Y. 2013).

321. *Branzburg*, 408 U.S. at 706.

322. Bill Kensworthy, *State Shield Laws and Leading Cases*, Freedom Forum Inst., Apr. 2011, freedomforuminstitute.org/first-amendment-center/topics/freedom-of-the-press/state-shield-statutes-leading-cases/.

323. *Reporter's Privilege Compendium*, Reporters Comm. for Freedom of the Press, rcfp.org/reporters-privilege/.

324. Anthony L. Fargo, *A Federal Shield Law That Works*, 8 J. Int'l Media and Ent. L. 35 (2018–19).

325. Catherine Wheeler, *Senate Judiciary Committee Votes Down Shield Law Bill*, Wyo. Pub. Radio, March 22, 2021.

326. *Reporter's Privilege Compendium*, Reporters Comm. for Freedom of the Press, rcfp.org/reporters-privilege/. *See also* Marina Riker, *Media Shield Law 2015: Who's Really A Journalist?*, (Honolulu) Civil Beat, Feb. 20, 2015, civilbeat.org/2015/02/media-shield-law-2015-whos-really-a-journalist/.

327. Cindy Gierhart, *Colorado Considers Bill to Bolster Reporter Shield Law*, Reporters Comm. for Freedom of the Press, Jan. 16, 2014, rcfp.org/colorado-considers-bill-bolster-reporter-shield-law/; Nate Rabner, *Journalists Urge Expansion of Media Shield Law in Maryland to Protect Against Out-of-State Subpoenas*, Fox News, Feb. 3, 2015, foxnews.com/politics/journalists-urge-expansion-of-media-shield-law-in-maryland-to-protect-against-out-of-state-subpoenas; Marina Riker, *Media Shield Law 2015: Who's Really a Journalist?*, (Honolulu) Civil Beat, Feb. 20, 2015,

civilbeat.org/2015/02/media-shield-law-2015-whos-really-a-journalist/.

328. Anthony L. Fargo, *A Federal Shield Law That Works*, 8 J. Int'l Media and Ent. L. 35 (2018–19).

329. *See, e.g., Reporter's Privilege Compendium*, Reporters Comm. for Freedom of the Press, rcfp.org/reporters-privilege/.

330. *See* Julie Posetti, *Protecting Journalism Sources in the Digital Age*, UNESCO Series on Internet Freedom, 2017, unesdoc.unesco.org/images/0024/002480/248054E.pdf. *See also* Fargo, *supra* note 328, 36; New York Times Co. v. Gonzales, 459 F. 3d 160 (2d Cir. 2006) and Reporters Comm. for Freedom of the Press v. AT&T, 593 F. 2d 1030 (D.C. Cir. 1978).

331. James Warren, *Guess Which State Passed a Landmark Shield Law to Protect Reporters?*, Poynter, Oct. 1, 2015, danielzolnikov.com/press-release-governor-signs-bill-protecting-freedom-of-the-press/.

332. *See, e.g., Reporter's Privilege Compendium*, Reporters Comm. for Freedom of the Press, rcfp.org/reporters-privilege/.

333. Abby Hamblin, *Dozens of San Diego Inmates Dead, A Journalist Subpoenaed After Reporting On It*, San Diego Union-Trib., May 28, 2018, sandiegouniontribune.com/opinion/the-conversa

tion/sd-kelly-davis-san-diego-county-jail-deaths-20180209-html-story.html.

334. Gubarev v. BuzzFeed, Inc., 2017 U.S. Dist. LEXIS 209697 (S.D. Fla. Dec. 21, 2017).

335. *Id.*, 2017 U.S. Dist. LEXIS 209697, at *10 (internal quotation marks removed).

336. *Id.* at *11–12.

337. Becca Gmerek, *Society's Obsession With True Crime*, RED SUMMIT PRODUCTIONS, July 30, 2018, medium.com/@RedSummitProductions/societys-obsession-with-true-crime-4f5e51cfd05c.

338. Adam Banner, *What Happens When Hollywood Gets "True Crime" Wrong?* ABA J., Sept. 27, 2017, abajournal.com/news/article/what_happens_when_hollywood_gets_true_crime_wrong.

339. *"Making a Murderer" Filmmakers Address Criticisms of Docuseries Ahead of New Season*, CBS NEWS, Oct. 18, 2018, cbsnews.com/news/making-a-murderer-part-two-filmmakers-address-criticisms-of-netflix-docuseries/.

340. *Id.*

341. Witte, *supra* note 4.

342. People v. Juarez, 80 N.Y.S.3d 913 (App. Div. 2018).

343. Minn. Stat. Ann. § 595.023.

344. *See, e.g., Reporter's Privilege Compendium*, REPORTERS COMM. FOR FREEDOM OF THE PRESS, rcfp.org/reporters-privilege/.

345. W.Va. Code § 57-3-10 (internal quotation marks omitted).

346. *Id.*

347. Green v. Pierce Cty., 2021 WL 2149389 (Wash. May 27, 2021).

348. Obsidian Finance Grp. v. Cox, 2011 U.S. Dist. LEXIS 137548 (D. Ore. Nov. 30, 2011).

349. *Id.*, 2011 U.S. Dist. LEXIS 137548, at *13.

350. Lipsky v. Durant, 2012 WL 11953251 (Tex. Dist. Ct. Feb. 16, 2012).

351. *See, e.g., Reporter's Privilege*, ELECTRONIC FRONTIER FOUND., eff.org/issues/bloggers/legal/journalists/privilege and Ken Schmetterer & Joe Roselius, *Reporter's Privilege*, EDITOR & PUBLISHER, March 16, 2015, editorandpublisher.com/Features/Article/Reporter-s-Privilege.

352. Tenn. Stat. Ann. § 24-1-208.

353. *See, e.g., Reporter's Privilege Compendium*, REPORTERS COMM. FOR FREEDOM OF THE PRESS, rcfp.org/reporters-privilege/.

354. Brokers' Choice of America v. NBCUniversal, 757 F.3d 1125 (10th Cir. 2014).

355. The states are Delaware, Minnesota and New York.

356. State v. Gibson, 172 A.3d 529 (N.H. 2017).

357. Lisa Provence, *Kessler Subpoenaed C-VILLE Reporter*, C-VILLE WKLY., May 22, 2018, c-ville.com/kessler-subpoenaed-c-ville-reporter/#.WwyBiakh1E5.

358. United States v. Nixon, 418 U.S. 683 (1974).

359. Rule 26 of the Federal Rules of Civil Procedure.

360. 42 U.S.C. § 2000aa.

361. *Id.*

362. *District of Columbia Metropolitan Police Department Agrees to Settle Civil Rights Lawsuit Brought by NPPA Member*, NPPA, April 22, 2021, nppa.org/news/district-columbia-metropolitan-police-department-agrees-settle-civil-rights-lawsuit-brought.

363. American News & Information Services, Inc. v. Gore, 778 Fed.Appx. 429 (9th Circ. 2019).

364. *Id.*

365. *Id.*

366. Jessica Schneider & Hannah Rabinowitz, *DOJ Codifies Rule Barring Secret Subpoenas of Journalists' Records*, CNN, Oct. 26, 2022, cnn.com/2022/10/26/media/doj-journalists-records-biden.

367. *See, e.g., New Guidelines Issued for US News Media Leak Investigations*, AP, Jan. 14, 2015, ap.org/ap-in-the-news/2015/new-guidelines-issued-for-us-news-media-leak-investigations.

368. United States v. Cotterman, 709 F.3d 952 (9th Cir. 2013), *cert. denied*, 571 U.S. 1156 (2014).

369. *Audrey Hudson Wins Settlement in Reporter Privacy Rights Case*, HARRIS, WILTSHIRE & GRANNIS, LLP, Sept. 30, 2014, hwglaw.com/audrey-hudson-wins-settlement-in-reporter-privacy-rights-case.

370. *See, e.g., As Pandemic Lingers, Courts Lean Into Virtual Technology*, U.S. CTS, Feb. 18, 2020, uscourts.gov/news/2021/02/18/pandemic-lingers-courts-lean-virtual-technology; *Guide to Virtual Hearings*, MASS.GOV, mass.gov/info-details/guide-to-virtual-hearings.

371. Haley Miller, et al., *Scenes Outside Courthouse Where Derek Chauvin is on Trial for George Floyd's Death*, HUFFINGTON POST, March 29, 2021.

372. *See, e.g.,* Emily Hockett, *A Big Week for Press Freedom in Congress*, REPORTERS COMM. FOR FREEDOM OF THE PRESS, Oct. 3, 2022, rcfp.org/house-passes-press-act/; Adam Shaw, *DOJ Pledges to No Longer Seize Reporters' Records*, FOX NEWS , June 5, 2021, foxnews.com/politics/doj-pledges-reporters-records-white-house-unaware-nyt-gag-order; 28 CFR § 50.10

373. Edith Roberts, *Courtroom Access: Legislative Efforts to Allow Cameras in Supreme Court Chamber*, SCOTUS-BLOG, April 27, 2020, scotusblog.com/2020/04/courtroom-access-legislative-efforts-to-allow-cameras-in-supreme-court-chamber/.

374. La Monica Everett-Haynes, *Experts Evaluate the "New Media" and Courts*, UNIV. ARIZ. NEWS, Sept. 9, 2008, uanews.org/node/21471. *See also Oral Arguments*, SUP. CT. OF THE U.S., supremecourt.gov/oral_arguments/oral_arguments.aspx.

375. Caroline Kelly, *Senators Introduce Bipartisan Bill to Televise Supreme Court Proceedings*, CNN POLITICS, March 18, 2021, cnn.com/2021/03/18/politics/bill-televise-supreme-court-proceedings/index.html.

376. Mike Cavender, *SCOTUS Camera Bill Resurfaces*, RTDNA, Jan. 16, 2017, rtdna.org/article/scotus_camera_bill_resurfaces; *see, e.g.,* Anthony E. Mauro, *Let the Cameras Roll: Cameras in the Court and the Myth of Supreme Court Exceptionalism*, 1 REYNOLDS CTS. & MEDIA L.J. 259 (2011).

377. *C-SPAN/PierrepontSupreme Court Survey 2022*, Mar. 15, 2022, c-span.org/scotussurvey2022//.

378. *See, e.g.,* Patricia Zengerle, *Supreme Court TV? Trump Nominee Has Open Mind on Cameras*, REUTERS, Oct. 14, 2020, reuters.com/article/us-usa-court-barrett-cameras/supreme-court-tv-trump-nominee-has-open-mind-on-cameras-idUSKBN26Z29J; Sam Baker, *Justice Sotomayor No Longer Backs Television Cameras in Supreme Court*, HILL, Feb. 7, 2013, thehill.com/homenews/news/281765-sotomayor-no-longer-backs-cameras-in-supreme-court; and *Battles to Gain Camera/Audio Access to State and Federal Courtrooms Continue*, SILHA CTR. BULL., Fall 2011, silha.umn.edu/news/Fall2011/battles-togain.html.

379. *Judge Ketanji Brown Jackson on Cameras in the Court*, C-SPAN, March 22, 2022, youtube.com/watch?v=QzzsRRV3IOU.

380. Caroline Kelly, *Senators Introduce Bipartisan Bill to Televise Supreme Court Proceedings*, CNN POLITICS, March 18, 2021, cnn.com/2021/03/18/politics/bill-televise-supreme-court-proceedings/index.html; Ashley Killough, *Neil Gorsuch Says He Has an "Open Mind" on Cameras in the Supreme Court*, CNN POLITICS, March 21, 2017, cnn.com/2017/03/21/politics/gorsuch-cameras-supreme-court; Baker, *supra* note 378; *Battles to Gain, supra* note 378.

381. Fred Barbash, *Oyez. Oy Vey. Was That a Toilet Flush in the Middle of*

a Supreme Court Live-Streamed Hearing?, Wash. Post, May 20, 2020, washingtonpost.com/nation/2020/05/07/toilet-flush-supreme-court/.

382. Connor Perrett, *Jury Trials Conducted by Zoom Can Lead to Biased Juries, Distractions, and Other Dangers, Lawyers Say*, Insider.com, March 20, 2021, insider.com/virtual-trials-can-lead-to-biased-juries-distractions-lawyers-say-2021-3.

383. *Judges Discuss Pros and Cons of Virtual Litigation*, Tenn. Cts, Jan. 19, 2021, tncourts.gov/news/2021/01/19/judges-discuss-pros-and-cons-virtual-litigation.

384. *See The Legal and Technical Danger in Moving Criminal Courts Online*, TechStream, Aug. 6, 2020, brookings.edu/techstream/the-legal-and-technical-in-moving-criminal-courts-online/.

385. *Law&Crime Network Hits Record 330 Million Viewers on* Depp v. Heard *Coverage*, Law&Crime, May 2, 2022, lawandcrime.com/live-trials/live-trials-current/depp-v-heard/lawcrime-network-hits-record-330-million-viewers-on-depp-v-heard-coverage/.

386. Gene Maddaus, *Why Was Depp-Heard Trial Televised? Critics Call It 'Single Worst Decision' for Sexual Violence Victims*, Variety, May 27, 2022, Variety.com/2022/film/news/john-depp-heard-cameras-courtroom-penny-azcarate-1235280060/.

387. *See* Gustavo A. Gelpi Jr. & Valeria M. Pelet del Toro, *Trial by Google: Juror Misconduct in the Age of Social Media*, Fed. Lawyer (Jan./Feb. 2018), fedbar.org/Resources_1/Federal-Lawyer-Magazine/2018/JanuaryFebruary/Trial-by-Google-Juror-Misconduct-in-the-Age-of-Social-Media.aspx?FT=.pdf.

388. *See* Joshua Dubin, *Juror Misconduct in the Age of Social Technology*, Champion, March 2017; Robin H. Jones & Eli Lightner II, *Combating Jurors' Improper Internet Usage and Winning*, A.B.A., Nov. 3, 2011, apps.americanbar.org/litigation/committees/ commercial/articles/fall2011-jurors-improper-internet-usage.html; and Thaddeus Hoffmeister, *Google, Gadgets, and Guilt: Juror Misconduct in the Digital Age*, 83 U. Colo. L. Rev. 410 (2012).

389. Amy J. St. Eve et al., *More From the #Jury Box: The Latest on Juries and Social Media*, 12 Duke L. & Tech. Rev. 64, 90 (2014).

390. *See* Amy J. St. Eve & Michael A. Zuckerman, *Ensuring an Impartial Jury in the Age of Social Media*, 11 Duke L. & Tech. Rev. 1, 2 (2012) and Katie L. Dysart & Camalla M. Kimbrough, *#Justice? Social Media's Impact on the U.S. Jury System*, A.B.A., Aug. 22, 2013, apps.americanbar.org/litigation/committees/trialevidence/articles/summer2013-0813-justice-social-media-impact-us-jury-system.html.

391. Kate Kortepeter, *Nine Years After Covering a Murder Trial, Former Student Journalist's Rights Jeopardized by Subpoena*, The Fire, May 12, 2021, thefire.org/nine-years-after-covering-a-murder-trial-former-student-journalists-rights-jeapardized-by-subpoena.

392. Jamie Ehrlich, *Student Journalist Subpoenaed by a Wealthy Family over Documents Allegedly Found in a Trash Can*, CNN, May 25, 2019, cnn.com/2019/05/25/media/eurim-choi-university-of-chicago-pearsons-index.html.

393. Kade Garner, *Reporter Nate Eaton Ordered to Testify in Daybell Case*, ABC4, May 14, 2021, abc4.com/news/national/reporter-nate-eaton-ordered-to-testify-in-daybell-case/.

394. Anthony L. Fargo, *The End of the Affair: Can the Relationship Between Journalists and Sources Survive Mass Surveillance and Aggressive Leak Prosecutions*, 26 Commc'n L. & Pol'y 185, 198–221 (2021).

395. *Id.* at 221.

396. Nicholas Iovino, *San Francisco Oks $369,000 Settlement for Journalist Targeted by Police*, Courthouse News Service, Mar. 31, 2020, courthousenews.com/san-francisco-oks-369000-settlement-for-journalist-targetd-by-police/.

397. *CPJ Urges U.S. House Committee to Drop Subpoena of Journalist Amy Harris's Phone Records*, Comm. to Protect Journalists, Dec. 16, 2021, cpj.org/2021/12/cpj-urges-us-house-committee-to-drop=subpoena-of-journalist-amy-harriss-phone-records/.

398. *See, e.g.*, Charlie Savage & Katie Benner, *Trump Administration Secretly Seized Phone Records of Times Reporters*, N.Y. Times, June 2, 2021, nytimes.com/2021/06/02/us/trump-administration-phone-records-times-reporters.html.

399. *Biden Won't Allow Justice Dept. to Seize Reporters' Records*, AP, May 21, 2021, apnews.com/article/arts-and-entertainment-government-and-politics-27a0ab87662217be-1989a2d5a7465610.

400. *See, e.g.*, Shaw, *supra* note 372.

401. 28 CFR § 50.10. *See also* Lynn Oberlander and Charles Tobin, *New DOJ Rules and Press Act Are a Win for Journalists*, Ballard Spahr, Nov. 15, 2022, ballardspahr.com/Insights/News/2022/11/New-DOJ-Rule-and-PRESS-Act-Are-a-Win-for-Journalists.

402. 28 CFR § 50.10.

403. *Id.*

404. Anna Diakun, *New DOJ Regulations Are a Victory for Press Freedom, But More Work Remains*, Just Sec., Nov. 18, 2022, justsecurity.org/84171/new-doj-regulations-are-a-victory-for-press-freedom-but-more-work-remains/.

405. Hockett, *supra* note 372.

406. Protect Reporters from Exploitative State Spying Act, H.R. 4330, 117th Congress (2021-2022).

407. Hockett, *supra* note 372.

CHAPTER 9

1. Joseph Turow, Media Today: Mass Communication in a Converging World 334 (6th ed. 2017).

2. *Id.*

3. Wireless Ship Act of 1910, Pub. L. 262, 36 Stat. 629.

4. See Thomas G. Krattenmaker, Telecommunications Law and Policy 3 -4 (1994).

5. Radio Act of 1912, Pub. L. 264, 37 Stat. 302.

6. *Id.*

7. United States v. Zenith Radio Corp., 12 F.2d 614 (N.D. Ill. 1926).

8. Radio Act of 1927, Pub. L. 69–632, ch. 169, 44 Stat. 1162.

9. FRC v. Nelson Bros., 289 U.S. 266 (1933).

10. *Id.*

11. Communications Act of 1934, Ch. 652, 48 Stat. 1064.

12. 47 U.S.C. § 153(6).

13. 47 U.S.C. § 605.

14. Nat'l Broad. Co. v. United States, 319 U.S. 190 (1943).

15. *Id.*

16. *Id.*

17. *Id.* at 213.

18. *Id.*

19. Great Lakes Broad., 3 F.R.C. Ann. Rep. 34 (1929).

20. Editorializing by Broad. Licensees, 13 F.C.C. 1246 (1949).

21. *Id.* at 1257–58.

22. Red Lion Broad. Co., Inc. v. FCC, 395 U.S. 367, 391 (1969).

23. *Id.* at 367.

24. Miami Herald Publ'g Co. v. Tornillo, 418 U.S. 241 (1974).

25. Syracuse Peace Council, 2 F.C.C.Rcd. 5043 (1987).

26. Syracuse Peace Council v. FCC, 867 F.2d 654 (D.C. Cir. 1989), *cert. denied*, 493 U.S. 1019 (1990).

27. Radio-Television News Dirs. Ass'n v. FCC, 229 F.3d 269 (D.C. Cir. 2000).

28. 47 U.S.C. § 399; FCC v. League of Women Voters

of California, 468 U.S. 364 (1984).

29. Dylan Matthews, *Everything You Need to Know About the Fairness Doctrine in One Post*, Wash. Post, Aug. 23, 2011, *available at* www.washingtonpost.com/blogs/ezra-klein/post/everything-you-need-to-know-about-the-fairness-doctrine-in-one-post/2011/08/23/gIQAN8CXZJ_blog.html.

30. *League of Women Voters*, 468 U.S. at 376 n.11.

31. *Id.*

32. FCC v. Pacifica Found., 438 U.S. 726 (1978).

33. *See* Robinson v. Am. Broad. Co., 441 F.2d 1396, 1399 (6th Cir. 1971).

34. *See, e.g.*, 47 U.S.C. §§ 302(a), 307(d), 309(a) and 316(a).

35. Peter J. Boyer, *Under Fowler, F.C.C. Treated TV as Commerce*, N.Y. Times, Jan. 19, 1987, *available at* www.nytimes.com/1987/01/19/arts/under-fowler-fcc-treated-tv-as-commerce.html.

36. *Guiding Principles*, First-net, https://www.ntia.doc.gov/files/ntia/attachment_a_icert_firstnet_guiding_principles.pdf (last visited Aug. 11, 2021).

37. *FirstNet Surpasses 2.71 Million Square Miles Supporting More Than 2 Million Connections*, Firstnet, https://www.firstnet.gov/newsroom/press-releases/expanding-serve-firstnet-surpasses-271-million-square-miles-supp

orting-more (last visited Aug. 11, 2021).

38. Press Release, AT&T, *FirstNet: Supporting New York City's COVID-19 Emergency Response*, (April 06, 2020), https://about.att.com/innovationblog/2020/04/fn_nyc_covid_19.html.

39. *What We Do*, FCC, www.fcc.gov/about-fcc/what-we-do (last visited Nov. 21, 2022).

40. *Rulemaking Process*, FCC, www.fcc.gov/about-fcc/rulemaking-process (last visited Nov. 21, 2022).

41. Jessica Rosenworcel Bio, FCC, https://www.fcc.gov/about/leadership/jessica-rosenworcel (last visited Nov. 21, 2022).

42. Brendan Carr Bio, FCC, www.fcc.gov/about/leadership/brendan-carr (last visited Nov. 21, 2022).

43. Geoffrey Starks Bio, FCC, www.fcc.gov/about/leadership/geoffrey-starks#bio (last visited Nov. 21, 2022).

44. Nathan Simington *Bio*, FCC, https://www.fcc.gov/about/leadership/nathan-simington (last visited Nov. 21, 2022).

45. 47 U.S.C. § 309(j); 47 C.F.R. §§ 73.5000–73.5009; Competitive Bidding Order, 13 F.C.C.Rcd. 15920 (1998).

46. 47 U.S.C. §§ 308(b), 319(a).

47. 47 U.S.C. § 310(b).

48. Telecommunications Act of 1996, Pub. L. No. 104–104, § 202(h), 110 Stat. 56, 111–12 (1996); Consolidated Appropriations Act of 2004, Pub. L. No. 108–99, § 629, 118 Stat. 3, 99–100 (2004) (Appropriations Act) (amending Sections 202(c) and 202(h) of the 1996 act). In 2004, Congress revised the then-biennial review requirement to require such reviews quadrennially. *See* Appropriations Act § 629, 118 Stat. at 100.

49. 47 U.S.C. § 303

50. *What We Do*, FCC, www.fcc.gov/about-fcc/what-we-do (last visited Nov. 21, 2022).

51. *About Sinclair Broadcast Group*, Sinclair, https://sbgi.net/ (last visited Aug. 11, 2021).

52. *Id.*

53. See Jonathan Obar, *Beyond Cynicism: A Review of the FCC's Reasoning for Modifying the Newspaper/Broadcast Cross-ownership Rule*, 14 Comm. L. Pol'y 479, 485 (2009).

54. *2014 Quadrennial Regulatory Review—Review of the Commission's Broadcast Ownership Rules and Other Rules Adopted Pursuant to Section 202 of the Telecommunications Act of 1996*, Order on Reconsideration, 32 FCC Rcd. 9802 (2017).

55. *Id.*

56. Chris Terry, Stephen Schmitz, Lee Joseph

Silberg, *The Score Is 4-0: FCC Media Ownership Policy, Prometheus Radio Project, and Judicial Review*, 73 FED. COMM. L.J 101, 110 (2021).

57. *Applications of Tribune Media Company and Sinclair Broadcast Group*, Hearing Designation Order, 33 FCC Rcd. 6830 (11) (2018).

58. *Id.*

59. *2014 Quadrennial Regulatory Review—Review of the Commission's Broadcast Ownership Rules and Other Rules Adopted Pursuant to Section 202 of the Telecommunications Act of 1996,* Order on Reconsideration, 32 FCC Rcd. 9802 (2017).

60. *Id.*

61. *Id.*

62. John Eggerton, *Divided FCC Eliminates Main Studio Rule*, BROADCASTING & CABLE, Mar. 16, 2018, *available at* www.broadcastingcable.com/news/divided-fcc-eliminates-main-studio-rule-169598.

63. *Id.*

64. W. LaNelle Owens, *Inequities on the Air: The FCC Media Ownership Rules - Encouraging Economic Efficiency and Disregarding the Needs of Minorities*, 47 HOWARD L.J. 1037 (2004).

65. Promoting Diversification of Ownership in the Broadcasting Services,

Report and Order and Third Further Notice of Proposed Rule Making, 23 FCC Rcd. 5922 (2008).

66. *See* Steele v. FCC, 770 F 2d 1192 (D.C. Cir. 1985); *See also* Metro Broadcasting, Inc. v. FCC, 97 U.S. 547 (1990), *See also* Lamprecht v. FCC, 958 F.2d 382, 391 (D.C. Cir. 1992).

67. Adarand Constructors, Inc. v. Peña, 515 U.S. 200 (1995).

68. Lamprecht v. FCC, 958 F.2d 382, 391 (D.C. Cir. 1992).

69. Prometheus Radio Project v. FCC, 373 F.3d 372, 383 (3d Cir. 2004).

70. *Id.* at 94.

71. Prometheus Radio Project v. FCC, 652 F.3d 431, 437 (3d Cir. 2011).

72. *Id.*

73. *Id.* at 15.

74. Prometheus Radio Project v. FCC, 824 F.3d 33, 37 (3d Cir. 2016).

75. Prometheus IV, 939 F.3d 567 (3d Cir. 2019).

76. FCC v. Prometheus Radio Project, 592 U. S. ___ (2021).

77. *Id.* at 12.

78. *Id.* at 9.

79. *FCC*, LOW POWER FM Radio, www.fcc.gov/consumers/guides/low-power-fm-lpfm-radio (last visited Nov. 22, 2022).

80. *Id.*

81. 47 U.S.C. § 396(g)(1)(D).

82. *About CPB*, CORP. FOR PUBLIC BROAD., www.cpb.org/aboutcpb (last visited Nov. 21, 2022).

83. 47 U.S.C. § 396(g)(1)(A).

84. FCC v. League of Women Voters of California, 468 U.S. 364 (1984).

85. *Id.* at 402.

86. 47 U.S.C. § 399B.

87. 47 U.S.C. § 399b(A).

88. Minority TV Project, Inc. v. FCC, 649 F. Supp. 2d 1025 (N.D. Cal. 2009), *aff'd*, 736 F.3d 1192 (9th Cir. 2013), *cert. denied*, 573 U.S. 946 (2014).

89. 47 U.S.C. § 326.

90. *See* Justin Levine, *A History and Analysis of the Federal Communications Commission's Response to Radio Broadcast Hoaxes*, 52 FED. COMM. L.J. 273, 277 -79 (2000); HADLEY CANTRIL, THE INVASION FROM MARS (1940).

91. 47 C.F.R. § 73.1217.

92. *See, e.g.,* 47 C.F.R. § 73.1940.

93. Paramount Pictures Corp., 3 F.C.C.Rcd. 245, 246 (Mass Media Bureau 1988).

94. *Id.*

95. Time-Telepictures Television, 17 F.C.C.Rcd. 16273 (2002).

96. Multimedia Entm't, Inc., 9 F.C.C.Rcd. 2811 (Political Programming Branch 1994).

97. Infinity Broad., 18 F.C.C.Rcd. 18603 (Media Bureau 2003).

98. Arkansas Educ. Television Comm'n v. Forbes, 523 U.S. 666 (1998).

99. 47 U.S.C. § 315(b).

100. 47 U.S.C. §§ 317, 507.

101. Farmers Educ. and Coop. Union v. WDAY, Inc., 360 U.S. 525 (1959).

102. 47 U.S.C. § 312(a)(7).

103. CBS v. FCC, 453 U.S. 367 (1981).

104. *Id.*

105. *Id.* at 387.

106. *Id.* at 387–88.

107. Revisions to Political Programming and Record-Keeping Rules, 87 F.C.C.R. at 7748.

108. *Id.*

109. *Id.*

110. Children's Television Act of 1990, Pub. L. 101–437, 104 Stat. 996.

111. 47 C.F.R. §§ 73.520, 73.671.

112. Children's Television Programming, 6 F.C.C.Rcd. 7199 (1990).

113. Children's Television Report and Policy Statement, 50 F.C.C.2d 1, 13–14 (1974). The commission's current rules also prevent displaying a website address during a children's show if the website uses the show's characters to sell products or the site offers products featuring the show's characters.

114. Francesca Dillman Carpentier, Teresa Correa, Marcela Reyes & Lindsey Smith Tallie, *Evaluating the Impact of Chile's Marketing Regulation of Unhealthy Foods and Beverages: Preschool and Adolescent Children's Changes in Exposure to Food Advertising on Television*, 23 PUB. HEALTH NUTRITION 747, 747-749 (2020).

115. Australian Association of National Advertisers, *Advertising to Children - Codes and Initiatives*, AD STANDARDS (March 2017), https://adstandards.com.au/issues/advertising-children.

116. Children's Television Programming, 6 F.C.C.Rcd. 2111 (1991); Children's Television Programming, 6 F.C.C.R. 5093 (1991).

117. *In re* Policies & Rules Concerning Children's Television Programming, 11 FCC Rcd. 10660, 10660 (1996).

118. *Id.* at 10730.

119. Michael O'Rielly, *It's Time to Reexamine the FCC's Kid Vid Requirements*, FCC (Jan. 26, 2018), www.fcc.gov/news-events/blog/2018/01/26/its-time-reexamine-fccs-kid-vid-requirements.

120. *Children's Television Programming Rules, Notice of Proposed Rulemaking*, FCC 18–93 (rel. July 13, 2018).

121. *Id.*

122. *FCC Releases Draft Order Modifying Children's Programming Rules*, WILEYREIN (June 20, 2019), www.wileyrein.com/newsroom-articles- FCC-Releases-Draft-Order-Modifying-Childrens-Programming-Rules.html.

123. Dade Hayes, *FCC's Vote to Ease "Kid Vid" Rules Draws Pushback And Democrats' Dissent*, DEADLINE (July 10, 2019), deadline.com/2019/07/fcc-vote-to-ease-kid-vid-rules-draws-pushback-and-democrats-dissent-1202644411/.

124. FCC Annual Assessment of the Status of Competition in the Market for the Delivery of Video Programming, 16 FCC Rcd 6005 (9) (2001).

125. *See* James C. Goodale & Rob Frieden, ALL ABOUT CABLE & BROADBAND § 1.02 (2019).

126. Frontier Broad. Co., 24 F.C.C. 251 (1959).

127. Carter Mountain Transmission Corp., 32 F.C.C. 459 (1962), *aff'd*, 321 F.2d 359 (D.C. Cir. 1963), *cert. denied*, 375 U.S. 951 (1963).

128. United States v. Sw. Cable Co., 392 U.S. 157 (1968).

129. Cable Communications Policy Act of 1984, Pub. L. No. 98–549, 98 Stat. 2779.

130. Cable Television Consumer Protection and Competition Act of 1992,

Pub. L. No. 102–385, 106 Stat. 1460.

131. Telecommunications Act of 1996, Pub. L. No. 104–104, 110 Stat. 56.

132. Turner Broad. Sys., Inc. v. FCC, 512 U.S. 622 (1994).

133. Denver Area Educ. Telecomm. Consortium, Inc. v. FCC, 518 U.S. 727 (1996) (plurality opinion).

134. *See* United States v. Playboy Entm't Grp., Inc., 529 U.S. 803 (2000).

135. *Major Pay-TV Providers Lost About 1,325,000 Subscribers in 1Q 2019*, Leichtman Res. Group, www.leichtmanresearch.com/major-pay-tv-providers-lost-about-1325000-subscribers-in-1q-2019/ (last visited Nov. 22, 2022).

136. Nat'l Ass'n of Broads. v. FCC, 740 F.2d 1190 (D.C. Cir. 1984).

137. Satellite Home Viewer Improvement Act of 1999, Pub. L. No. 106–13, § 1001–12, 113 Stat. 1501. The act was upheld in Satellite Broad. and Comm'n Ass'n v. FCC, 275 F.3d 337 (4th Cir. 2001), *cert. denied*, 536 U.S. 922 (2002).

138. Direct Broadcast Satellite Public Interest Obligations, 13 F.C.C.Rcd. 23254 (1998); 47 C.F.R. § 100.5.

139. Direct Broadcast Satellite Public Interest Obligations, 19 F.C.C.Rcd. 5647 (2004).

140. Natalie Jarvey, *Netflix Tops 200 Million Subscribers Amid Pandemic*, Hollywood Reporter, Jan. 19, 2021, *available at* https://www.hollywoodreporter.com/business/digital/netflix-tops-200-million-subscribers-amid-pandemic-4118251/.

141. Lee Raine, *Cable and Satellite Use has Dropped Dramatically in the U.S. since 2015*, Pew Research (March 17, 2021), https://www.pewresearch.org/fact-tank/2021/03/17/cable-and-satellite-tv-use-has-dropped-dramatically-in-the-u-s-since-2015/.

142. *Id.*

143. 47 U.S.C. §§ 534 (commercial stations), 535 (noncommercial stations).

144. 512 U.S. 622 (1994).

145. Turner Broad. Sys., Inc. v. FCC, 520 U.S. 180 (1997).

146. United States v. O'Brien, 391 U.S. 367 (1968).

147. *Turner Broad. Sys., Inc.*, 520 U.S. at 180.

148. Cablevision Sys. Corp. v. FCC, 570 F.3d 83 (2d Cir. 2009), *cert. denied*, 560 U.S. 918 (2010).

149. *In re* Implementation of Section 103 of the STELA Reauthorization Act of 2014, Totality of the Circumstances Test, Notice of Proposed Rulemaking, MB Docket No. 15–216 (rel. Sep. 2, 2015).

150. *Id.*

151. *Id.*

152. FCC Annual Assessment of the Status of Competition in the Market for the Delivery of Video Programming, 16 FCC Rcd. 6005 (9) (2001). *See also* Applications of Comcast Corp., General Electric Co., and NBC Universal, Inc. for Consent to Assign Licenses and Transfer Control of Licenses, MB Docket No. 10–56, Memorandum Opinion and Order, 26 FCC Rcd. 4238, 4357, App. A (2011).

153. *Id.*

154. Press Release, FCC, *FCC Proposes to Modernize MVPD Definition* (Dec. 19, 2014) https://www.fcc.gov/document/fcc-proposes-modernize-mvpd-definition.

155. FCC Independent Programming Notice of Inquiry, 31 FCC Rcd. 1610 (2) (Feb.18 2016) www.fcc.gov/document/independent-programming-noi.

156. Tennis Channel, Inc. v. FCC, 827 F.3d 137 (2016).

157. Game Show Network, LLC v. Cablevision Sys. Corp., 27 FCC Rcd. 5113 (2012).

158. *In re* Game Show Network, LLC v. Cablevision Systems Corp., Initial Decision of Chief Administrative Law Judge Richard L. Sippel, 31 FCC Rcd. 13841 (2016).

159. *In re* Game Show Network, LLC v. Cablevision Systems Corp., 32 FCC Rcd. 6160 (2017).

160. *In re Word Network Operating Company d/b/a The Word Network v. Comcast Corp. and Comcast Cable Comm., LLC,* Memorandum Opinion and Orders, 32 FCC Rcd. 7704 (2017); 33 FCC Rcd. 5041 (2018).

161. 47 U.S.C. § 531.

162. *See, e.g.,* Denver Area Educ. Telecomm. Consortium, Inc. v. FCC, 518 U.S. 727, 761–62 (1996).

163. 47 U.S.C. §§ 531(e) (public access), 532(c)(2) (leased access).

164. Cable Television Consumer Protection and Competition Act of 1992, Pub. L. No. 102–385, § 25, 106 Stat. 1460.

165. Daniels Cablevision, Inc. v. United States, 835 F. Supp. 1 (D.D.C. 1993).

166. Halleck v. Manhattan Cmty. Access Corp., 882 F.3d 300, 304 (2d Cir. 2018).

167. Manhattan Cmty. Access Corp. v. Halleck, 139 S. Ct. 1921, 1928 (2019).

168. *Id.* at 1932.

169. *Internet Broadband Fact Sheet,* Pew Research, https://www.pewresearch.org/internet/fact-sheet/internet-broadband/ (last visited Nov. 22, 2022).

170. Reno v. ACLU, 521 U.S. 844 (1997).

171. Telecommunications Act of 1996, Pub. L. No. 104–104, Title V, §§ 501–61, 110 Stat. 56, 133–43 (codified at 18 U.S.C. §§ 1462, 1465, 2422 and at scattered sections of 47 U.S.C.).

172. *Reno,* 521 U.S. at 869.

173. *Id.* at 853.

174. Miller v. California, 413 U.S. 15 (1973).

175. 47 U.S.C. § 230

176. *Id.*

177. Cubby, Inc. v. CompuServe Inc., 776 F. Supp. 135 (S.D.N.Y. 1991).

178. *Id.*

179. Stratton Oakmont, Inc. v. Prodigy Services Co., 23 Media L. Rep. 1794 (N.Y. Sup. Ct. 1995).

180. Id.

181. Doe v. MySpace, Inc., 528 F.3d 413 (5th Cir. 2008), *cert. denied,* 129 S. Ct. 600 (2008).

182. Doe v. Internet Brands, Inc., 824 F. 3d 846, 848–49 (9th Cir. 2016).

183. Gonzalez v. Google LLC, 214 L.Ed.2d 12 (U.S. 2022).

184. Kiran Jeevanjee et al., *All the Ways Congress Wants to Change Section 230,* Slate, March 23, 2021, https://slate.com/technology/2021/03/section-230-reform-legislative-tracker.html

185. *Id.*

186. *Id.*

187. Danielle Keats Citron & Mary Anne Franks, *The Internet as a Speech Machine and Other Myths Confounding Section 230 Reform,* 2020 U. Chi. Legal F. 45 (2020).

188. *Id.* at 70.

189. Jeff Kosseff, The Twenty-Six Words That Created the Internet 239-251 (2019).

190. Appropriate Framework for Broadband Access to the Internet Over Wireline Facilities, 20 F.C.C.Rcd. 148653 (2005).

191. United States v. Sw. Cable Co., 392 U.S. 157 (1968); United States v. Midwest Video Corp., 406 U.S. 649 (1972) (*Midwest I*); United States v. Midwest Video Corp., 440 U.S. 689 (1979) (*Midwest II*).

192. NCTA v. Brand X Internet Servs., 545 U.S. 967 (2005).

193. Telecommunications Act of 1996, 47 U.S.C. §§ 201–09, 251(a)(1).

194. High-Speed Access to the Internet Over Cable and Other Facilities, 17 F.C.C.Rcd. 4798 (2002).

195. *In re* Protecting and Promoting the Open Internet, Report and Order on Remand, Declaratory Ruling, and Order, 30 FCC Rcd. 5601 (2015).

196. *In re* Restoring Internet Freedom, Declaratory Ruling, Report and Order, 33 FCC Rcd. 311 (2018).

197. *Id.*

198. Mozilla v. FCC, 940 F.3d 1 (D.C. Cir. 2019).

199. *Id.* at 10.

200. FCC Restoring Internet Freedom; Bridging the Digital Divide for

Low-Income Consumers; Lifeline and Link Up Reform and Modernization Final Rule, 47 C.F.R. §54 (2021).

201. Tyler Cooper & Julia Tanberk, *Broadband Now Report,* Broadband Now, July 30, 2021, *available at* https://broadbandnow.com/research/q1-broadband-report-2021.

202. Exec. Order No. EO 14036, 86 Fed. Reg. 36987 (July 9, 2021).

203. Bhaskar Chakavorti, *How to Close the Digital Divide in the U. S,* Harv. Bus. Rev., July 20, 2021, *available at* https://hbr.org/2021/07/how-to-close-the-digital-divide-in-the-u-s.

204. *Id.*

205. *Id.*

206. Emily Birnbaum, *4 Out of 5 Americans Say They Support Net Neutrality,* The Hill March 20, 2019, *available at* https://thehill.com/policy/technology/435009-4-in-5-americans-say-they-support-net-neutrality-poll.

207. Broadband Industry Practices, 223 F.C.C.Rcd. 13028 (2008).

208. Comcast Corp. v. FCC, 600 F.3d 642, 644 (D.C. Cir. 2010).

209. *In re* Preserving the Open Internet, 25 F.C.C.Rcd. 17905 (2010).

210. Verizon v. FCC, 740 F.3d 623, 628 (D.C. Cir., 2014).

211. *Telecommunications Law, Internet Regulation: D.C. Circuit Holds That Federal Communication Commission Violated Communications Act in Adopting Open Internet Rules,* 127 Harv. L. Rev. 2565, 2574 (2014).

212. 47 C.F.R. Title II, § 20.15.

213. Protecting and Promoting the Open Internet, 80 Fed. Reg. 19737 (Apr. 13, 2015).

214. Protecting and Promoting the Open Internet, 2015 FCC LEXIS 1008 (Mar. 12, 2015) (Wheeler, Chair, concurring).

215. *Id.* (Pai, dissenting).

216. List of Pending Appellate Cases, FCC, Feb. 24, 2016, transition.fcc.gov/Daily_Releases/Daily_Business/2016/db0224/DOC-337898A1.pdf.

217. U.S. Telecomm. Ass'n v. FCC, 825 F.3d 674 (D.C. Cir. 2016).

218. Alina Selyukh & David Greene, *Tackling Net Neutrality Violations "After the Fact,"* NPR, May 5, 2017, *available at* www.npr.org/sections/alltechconsidered/2017/05/05/526916610/fcc-chief-net-neutrality-rules-treating-internet-as-utility-stifle-growth.

219. *In re* Restoring Internet Freedom, Declaratory Ruling, Report and Order, 33 FCC Rcd. 311 (2018).

220. Brian Heater, *Lawsuit Filed by 22 State Attorneys General Seeks to Block Net Neutrality Repeal,* TechCrunch, Jan. 16, 2018, *available at* techcrunch.com/2018/01/16/lawsuit-filed-by-22-state-attorneys-general-seeks-to-block-net-neutrality-repeal/; *see also* Jordan Crook, *Internet Association Wants in on the Lawsuit Challenging Net Neutrality Repeal,* TechCrunch, March 22, 2018, *available at* techcrunch.com/2018/03/22/internet-association-wants-in-on-the-lawsuit-challenging-net-neutrality-repeal/.

221. Exec. Order No. EO 14036, 86 Fed. Reg. 36987 (July 9, 2021).

222. *See* James Clayton, *COVID Misinformation on Facebook is Killing People— Biden,* BBC, July 17, 2021, *available at* https://www.bbc.com/news/world-us-canada-57870778.

223. *See* Emily Vogels et al., *Most Americans Think Social Media Sites Censor Political Viewpoints,* Pew Research Ctr. (Aug. 19, 2020); *see also* Paul Barret & J. Grant Sims, *False Accusation: The Unfounded Claim that Social Media Companies Censor Conservatives,* NYU Stern Ctr. for Bus. & Human Rights (Jan. 29, 2021), https://bhr.stern.nyu.edu/blogs/2021/1/29/report-false-accusation-the-unfounded-claim-that-social-media-companies-censor-conservatives.

224. Netchoice, LLC v. Moody, No. 4:21cv220-RH-MA, 2021 WL 2690876 (N.D. Fla. July 13, 2021).

225. NetChoice, LLC v. AG, Fla., No. 21-12355, 2022 U.S. App. LEXIS 13852 (11th Cir. May 23, 2022).

226. NetChoice, LLC v. Paxton, No. 21A720, 2022 U.S. LEXIS 2669 (May 31, 2022).

227. Knight First Amendment Inst. v. Trump, 302 F. Supp. 3d 541 (S.D.N.Y. 2018).

228. Biden v. Knight First Amendment Inst. at Columbia Univ., 141 S. Ct. 1220 (2021).

229. *Id.* at 1221.

230. *See Community Standards*, Facebook, https://www.facebook.com/communitystandards/ (last visited Aug. 11, 2021). *See also The Twitter Rules*, Twitter, https://help.twitter.com/en/rules-and-policies/twitter-rules (last visited Aug. 11, 2021).

231. Tarleton Gillespie, Custodians of the Internet 75 -97 (2018).

232. Kate Klonick, *Inside the Making of Facebook's Supreme Court*, New Yorker, Feb. 12, 2021, *available at* https://www.newyorker.com/tech/annals-of-technology/inside-the-making-of-facebooks-supreme-court.

233. 15 U.S.C. § 1; 15 U.S.C. §§ 12–27; 15 U.S.C. §§ 41-58.

234. FTC v. Facebook, Inc., 560 F. Supp. 3d 1 (D.D.C. 2021); New York v. Facebook, Inc., 549 F. Supp. 3d 6 (D.D.C. 2021).

235. *Id.*

236. *Id.*

237. FTC v. Facebook, Inc., 581 F. Supp. 3d 34 (D.D.C. 2022).

238. *Id.*

239. Cecilia Kang & David McCabe, *Antitrust Overhaul Passes its First Tests. Now the Hard Part*, N.Y. Times, June 29, 2021, *available at* https://www.nytimes.com/2021/06/24/technology/antitrust-overhaul-congress.html.

CHAPTER 10

1. Geoffrey R. Stone, Sex and the Constitution: Sex, Religion, and Law from America's Origins to the Twenty-First Century 310 (2017).

2. Jacobellis v. Ohio, 378 U.S. 184, 191 (1964) (Stewart, P., concurring).

3. *Obscene*, Merriam-Webster, www.merriam-webster.com/dictionary/obscene (last visited Nov. 22, 2022).

4. Martin Cogan, *In the Beginning, There Was a Nipple*, ESPN, Jan. 28, 2014, espn.go.com/espn/feature/story/_/id/10333439/wardrobe-malfunction-beginning-there-was-nipple.

5. *See* Margaret A. Blanchard, Revolutionary Sparks: Freedom of Expression in Modern America (1992). *See also* Margaret A. Blanchard & John E. Semonche, *Anthony Comstock and His Adversaries: The Mixed Legacy of This Battle for Free Speech*, 11 Comm. L. & Pol'y 317 (2006).

6. Heywood Broun & Margaret Leech, Anthony Comstock 265 (1927).

7. Robert Corn-Revere, *New Age Comstockery*, 4 CommLaw Conspectus 173, 173 (1996).

8. An Act for the Suppression of Trade in, and Circulation of, Obscene Literature and Articles of Immoral Use, Ch. 258, § 2, 17 Stat. 598, 599 (1873).

9. Amendment to the Comstock Act, ch. 186, § 1, 19 Stat. 90.

10. Margaret A. Blanchard, *The American Urge to Censor*, 33 Wm. & Mary L. Rev. 741, 749 (1992).

11. L.R. 3 Q.B. 360, 371 (1868).

12. Whitney Strub, *Lavendar, Menaced: Lesbianism, Obscenity Law, and the Feminist Antipornography Movement*, 22, J. Women's Hist., 83, 86 (2010).

13. Jason M. Shepard, *The First Amendment, and the Roots of LGBT Rights Law: Censorship in the Early Homophile Era, 1958-1962*, 26 Wm. & Mary J. Women & L. 599 (2020).

14. United States v. Kennerley, 209 F. 119, 120–21 (S.D.N.Y. 1913).

15. *Id.* at 121.

16. United States v. One Book Called "Ulysses," 5 F. Supp. 182, 184, 185 (S.D.N.Y. 1933), *aff'd sub nom.* United States v. One Book Entitled Ulysses, 72 F.2d 705 (2d Cir. 1934).

17. Geoffrey R. Stone, Sex and the Constitution: Sex, Religion, and Law from America's Origins to the Twenty-First Century 268 (2017).

18. *Id.*

19. Roth v. United States, 354 U.S. 476, 484, 485, 497 (1957); *see also* Chaplinsky v. New Hampshire, 315 U.S. 568, 571–72 (1942).

20. *Roth*, 354 U.S. at 489.

21. Whitney Strub, *Lavendar, Menaced: Lesbianism, Obscenity Law, and the Feminist Antipornography Movement*, 22, J. Women's Hist., 83, 84 (2010).

22. 355 U.S. at 371; One, Inc. v. Oleson, 2241 F.2d 773 (9th Cir. 1957), *rev'd*, 355 U.S. 371 (1958).

23. Geoffrey R. Stone, Sex and the Constitution: Sex, Religion, and Law from America's Origins to the Twenty-First Century 341 (2017).

24. Jacobellis v. Ohio, 378 U.S. 184, 197 (1964) (Stewart, J., concurring).

25. Catharine A. MacKinnon, *Pornography, Civil Rights, and Speech*, 20 Harv. C.R.-C.L. L. Rev. 1, 3 (1985).

26. Mishkin v. New York, 383 U.S. 502, 516 (1966).

27. Miller v. California, 413 U.S. 15 (1973).

28. *Id.* at 18.

29. *Id.* at 22.

30. Victor Oluwole, *Kenya Is Reviewing a New Bill That Would Land Anyone Sharing Porn on Social Media 20 Years in Jail*, Bus. Insider Africa, March 2, 2021, *available at* https:// africa.businessinsider.c om/local/lifestyle/kenya -is-reviewing-a-new-bil l-that-would-land-anyon e-sharing-porn-on-soci al-media-20/x0j1we8.

31. *Id.*

32. Ogheneruemu Oneyibo, *What You Need to Know, As Kenya Moves to Outlaw Pornography*, TechPoint Africa, May 27, 2021, *available at* https://techp oint.africa/2021/05/27/ kenya-outlaws-pornog raphy/.

33. Paul Bischoff, *2020 Global Map of Internet Restrictions*, Comparitech, Jan. 15, 2020, *available at* http s://www.comparitech.co m/blog/vpn-privacy/inte rnet-censorship-map/In ternetCensorship.

34. *Kenya: Withdraw proposed amendments to cyber-crimes law*, Article 19 (July 7, 2021), https://ww w.article19.org/resource s/kenya-withdraw-propo sed-amendments-to-cy bercrimes-law/.

35. *Id.*

36. Roth v. United States, 354 U.S. 476, 487 n.20 (1957).

37. Smith v. United States, 431 U.S. 291, 305 (1977); Hamling v. United States, 418 U.S. 87, 104–05 (1974); United States v. Salcedo, 2019 U.S. App. LEXIS 14069 (5th Cir. May 10, 2019).

38. Brooks P. Fuller et al., *Porn Wars: Serious Value, Social Harm, and the Burdens of Modern Obscenity Doctrine*, 28 Am. U. J. Gender Soc. Pol'y & L. 121, 159 (2020).

39. Ward v. Illinois, 431 U.S. 767 (1977).

40. Mishkin v. New York, 383 U.S. 502, 508–09 (1966).

41. United States v. Thomas, 74 F.3d 701 (6th Cir.), *cert. denied*, 519 U.S. 820 (1996).

42. United States v. Kirkpatrick, 663 F. App'x 237 (2016).

43. *Id.*

44. United States v. Kilbride, 584 F.3d 1240 (9th Cir. 2009).

45. *Id.*

46. Ashcroft v. ACLU, 535 U.S. 564, 597 (2002) (Kennedy, J., concurring in the judgment).

47. *Id.* at 590 (Breyer, J., concurring in part and concurring in the judgment).

48. Miller v. California, 413 U.S. 15, 25 (1973).

49. *Id.*

50. Jenkins v. Georgia, 418 U.S. 153 (1974).

51. Ward v. Illinois, 431 U.S. 767 (1977).

52. *Jenkins*, 418 U.S. at 160.

53. United States v. Guthrie, 720 F. App'x. 199 (2018).

54. United States v. Salcedo, 2019 U.S. App. LEXIS 14069 (5th Cir. May 10, 2019).

55. Pope v. Illinois, 481 U.S. 497 (1987).

56. City of Cincinnati v. Contemporary Arts Center, 566 N.E.2d 214 (Ohio Misc. 2d 1990).

57. Luke Records, Inc. v. Navarro, 960 F.2d 134 (11th Cir.), *cert. denied*, 506 U.S. 1022 (1992).

58. Catharine MacKinnon & Andrea Dworkin, Pornography and Civil Rights: A New Day for Women's Equality (1988).

59. Brooks P. Fuller et al., *Porn Wars: Serious Value, Social Harm, and the Burdens of Modern Obscenity Doctrine*, 28 Am. U. J. Gender Soc. Pol'y & L. 121, 142 (2020).

60. Nadine Strossen, Defending Pornography: Free Speech, Sex, and the Fight for Women's Rights (1995).

61. Fuller et al., *supra* note 59.

62. Catharine A. MacKinnon, *Pornography, Civil Rights, and Speech*, 20 Harv. C.R.-C.L. L. Rev. 1, 23 (1985).

63. American Booksellers v. Hudnut, 771 F. 2d 323 (7th Cir 1987).

64. *Id.*

65. Butler v. Michigan, 352 U.S. 380, 383 (1957).

66. *Id.*

67. Ginsberg v. New York, 390 U.S. 629 (1968).

68. 18 U.S.C. § 2256(8).

69. John Herrman, *How the U.K. Won't Keep Porn Away From Teens*, N.Y. Times, May 3, 2019, www.nytimes.com/2019/05/03/style/britain-age-porn-law.html.

70. New York v. Ferber, 458 U.S. 747 (1982).

71. *Id.* at 758.

72. 18 U.S.C. §§ 2251(a), 2252(b)(4), 2256(8).

73. 18 U.S.C. § 2256(2)(A).

74. John A. Humbach, *"Sexting" and the First Amendment*, 37 Hastings Const. L.Q. 433, 446 (2010).

75. United States v. Knox, 32 F.3d 733, 737 (3d Cir. 1994), *cert. denied*, 513 U.S. 1109 (1995).

76. *Id.*

77. Ashcroft v. Free Speech Coal., 535 U.S. 234 (2002).

78. *Id.*

79. United States v. Williams, 553 U.S. 285 (2008).

80. United States v. Anderson, 759 F. 3d 891 (8th Cir. 2014).

81. *Id.* at 896.

82. 18 U.S.C. § 2259.

83. *See* Emily Bazelon, *Money Is No Cure*, N.Y. Times, Jan. 27, 2013, § 8 (Magazine), at 22.

84. United States v. Monzel, 641 F.3d 528 (D.C. Cir.), *cert. denied*, 565 U.S. 1072 (2011); United States v. Kearney, 672 F.3d 81 (1st Cir. 2012), *cert. dismissed*, 568 U.S. 1223 (2013); United States v. Aumais, 656 F.3d 147 (2d Cir. 2011); United States v. Crandon, 173 F.3d 122 (3d Cir.), *cert. denied*, 528 U.S. 855 (1999); United States v. Burgess, 684 F.3d 445 (4th Cir.), *cert. denied*, 568 U.S. 968 (2012); United States v. Evers, 669 F.3d 645 (6th Cir. 2012); United States v. Laraneta, 700 F.3d 983 (7th Cir. 2012), *cert. denied*, 571 U.S. 898 (2013); United States v. Fast, 709 F.3d 712 (8th Cir. 2013); United States v. Kennedy, 643 F.3d 1251 (9th Cir. 2011); United States v. McGarity, 669 F.3d 1218 (11th Cir.), *cert. denied*, 568 U.S. 921 (2012).

85. *In re* Amy Unknown, 701 F.3d 749 (5th Cir. 2012) (*en* banc), *vacated and remanded sub nom.* Paroline v. United States, 572 U.S. 434 (2014).

86. 18 U.S.C. § 3663A (2012).

87. Paroline v. United States, 572 U.S. 434 (2014).

88. *Id.*

89. *Id.* at 454 (Roberts, C.J., dissenting).

90. *Id.* at 461 (Sotomayor, J., dissenting).

91. Mary Margaret Giannini, *Continuous Contamination: How Traditional Criminal Restitution Principles and §2259 Undermine Cleaning Up the Toxic Waste of Child Pornography Possession*, 40 New. Eng. J. on Crim. & Civ. Confinement 21, 25–26 (2014).

92. Sameer Hinduja & Justin W. Patchin, *Sexting Among Middle and High School Students 2020*, Cyberbullying Res. Center (July 14, 2020), https://cyberbullying.org/teen-sexting-research-2016-2019.

93. *See, e.g.*, A.H. v. State, 949 So. 2d 234 (Fla. Dist. Ct. App. 2007).

94. *State Sexting Laws*, Cyberbullying Research Ctr., https://cyberbullying.org/sexting-laws (last visited Nov. 22, 2022).

95. Ronak Patel, *Taking It Easy on Teen Pornographers: States Respond to Minors' Sexting*, 13 J. of High Tech. L. 574 (2013).

96. Stanley v. Georgia, 394 U.S. 557 (1969).

97. *Id.* at 568.

98. Pub. L. No. 91–452, 84 Stat. 922 (1970), codified at 18 U.S.C. §§ 1961–1968 (as amended by USA PATRIOT Act of 2001, Pub. L. No. 107–56, § 813, 115 Stat. 272, 382).

99. *See* Teresa Bryan et al., *Racketeer Influenced and Corrupt Organizations*, 40 Am. Crim. L. Rev. 987 (2003).

100. Alexander v. United States, 509 U.S. 544 (1993).

101. 18 U.S.C. § 1464.

102. FCC v. Pacifica Found., 438 U.S. 726, 739 (1978).

103. *Id.* at 740.

104. *Id.* at 727.

105. Enforcement of Prohibitions Against Broad. Indecency, 8 F.C.C.R. 704, 705 n.10 (1993).

106. Pub. L. 69–632, ch. 169, § 29, 44 Stat. 1162 (1927); ch. 652, § 326, 48 Stat. 1064 (1934).

107. 18 U.S.C. § 1464.

108. 47 U.S.C. § 503(b)(1)(D).

109. *See, e.g., Application of The Jack Straw Memorial Foundation for Renewal of the License of Station KRAB-FM, Seattle, Wash.*, 21 Rad. Reg. 2d (P&F) 505 (1971).

110. Sonderling Broad. Corp., 41 F.C.C.2d 777, 782 (1973), *aff'd*, Illinois Citizens Comm. for Broad. v. FCC, 515 F.2d 397 (D.C. Cir. 1974).

111. *FCC Transcript: Filthy Words*, UMCK, law2.umkc.edu/faculty/projects/ftrials/conlaw/filthywords.html (last visited May 18, 2019).

112. Pacifica Found., 56 F.C.C.2d 94 (1975) (the words, as listed in the FCC's decision, are "shit, piss, fuck, cunt, cocksucker, motherfucker, and tits").

113. Citizen's Complaint Against Pacifica Found.

Station WBAI (FM), N.Y., N.Y., 56 F.C.C.2d 94 (1975).

114. FCC v. Pacifica Found., 438 U.S. 726, 750 (1978).

115. *Id.*

116. *Id.*

117. Pacifica Found., 2 F.C.C.R. 2698, 2699 (1987).

118. *In re* Infinity Broad. Corp. of Pa., 2 F.C.C.R. 2705 (1987); *In re* Pacifica Found., 2 F.C.C.R. 2698 (1987); *In re* Regents of the Univ. of Calif., 2 F.C.C.R. 2703 (1987); New Indecency Enforcement Standards to Be Applied to All Broad. & Amateur Radio Licensees, 2 F.C.C.R. 2726 (1987).

119. 2 F.C.C.R. 2726 (1987). The D.C. Circuit upheld the FCC's more expansive indecency definition. Action for Children's Television v. FCC, 852 F.2d 1332 (D.C. Cir. 1988) (*ACT I*).

120. FCC v. Pacifica Found., 438 U.S. 726, 772 (1978).

121. *In re* Indus. Guidance on the Comm'n's Case Law Interpreting 18 U.S.C. § 1464 & Enforcement Policies Regarding Broad. Indecency, 16 F.C.C.R. 7999, 8002–03 (2001).

122. *In re* Complaints Against Various Broad. Licensees Regarding Their Airing of the "Golden Globe Awards" Program, 19 F.C.C.R. 4975, 4976 (2004).

123. *Id.*

124. *In re* Complaints Regarding Various Television Broad. Between Feb. 2, 2002 & Mar. 8, 2005, 21 F.C.C.R. 2664 (2006).

125. *See* Fox Television Stations, Inc. v. FCC, 613 F.3d 317, 324 (2d Cir. 2010), *vacated by, remanded by* FCC v. Fox Television Stations, Inc., 567 U.S. 239 (2012).

126. FCC v. Fox Television Stations, Inc., 556 U.S. 502 (2009).

127. Fox Television Stations, Inc., 613 F.3d at 324.

128. *Id.*

129. *Fox Television Stations, Inc.*, 556 U.S. 502.

130. *Id.*

131. *Fox Television Stations, Inc.*, 613 F.3d at 323.

132. Complaints Against Various Television Licensees Concerning Their Feb. 1, 2004, Broad. of the Super Bowl XXXVIII, 19 F.C.C.R. 19230 (2004).

133. CBS Corp. v. FCC, 535 F.3d 167, 174 (3d Cir. 2008), *vacated and remanded*, 556 U.S. 1218 (2009).

134. *CBS Corp.*, 556 U.S. 1218.

135. CBS Corp. v. FCC, 663 F.3d 122 (3d Cir. 2011), *cert. denied*, 567 U.S. 953 (2012).

136. FCC v. Fox Television Stations, Inc., 567 U.S. 239, 258 (2012).

137. *FCC Reduces Backlog of Indecency Cases*, 28 FCC Rcd. 4082 (6) (2013) https://www.fcc.gov/documen

t/fcc-cuts-indecency-complaints-1-million-seeks-comment-policy.

138. *Issued a Notice of Apparent Liability for Forfeiture Proposing a $325,000 Penalty Against WDBJ Television, Inc. for Its Willful Violation of Federal Indecency Restrictions*, Notice of Apparent Liability for Forfeiture, 30 FCC Rcd. 3024 (4) (2015).

139. Clay Calvert et al., *Indecency Four Years After Fox Television Stations: From Big Papi to a Porn Star, An Egregious Mess at the FCC Continues*, 51 U. Rich. L. Rev. 329, 329–330 (2017).

140. *Id.*

141. Alaa Elassar, *Over 1, Complaints 300 Were Sent to the FCC About Shakira and J.Lo's Super Bowl Halftime Show*, CNN, Feb. 26, 2020, *available at* https://www.cnn.com/2020/02/25/us/shakira-jlo-super-bowl-halftime-show-fcc-complaints-trnd/index.html.

142. Janelle Griffith, *FCC Gets 1300 Complaints over Jennifer Lopez, Shakira Halftime Show*, NBC News, Feb. 26, 2020, *available at* https://www.nbcnews.com/news/us-news/fcc-gets-1-300-complaints-over-jennifer-lopez-shakira-super-n1143506.

143. 47 C.F.R. § 73.3999.

144. Action for Children's Television v. FCC, 58 F.3d 654 (D.C. Cir. 1995) (*en banc*), *cert. denied*, 516 U.S. 1043 (1996) (*ACT III*).

145. Jon Blistein, *Stephen Colbert Avoids FCC Penalties for Controversial Trump Joke*, Rolling Stone, May 24, 2017, https://www.rollingstone.com/tv/tv-news/stephen-colbert-avoids-fcc-penalties-for-controversial-trump-joke-129148/.

146. Cruz v. Ferre, 755 F.2d 1415 (11th Cir. 1985), citing FCC v. Pacifica Found., 438 U.S. 726 (1978).

147. David Grossman, *Whatever Happened to the V-Chip? Long Irrelevant, the Small Piece of Hardware Was Once Seen as a Generational Savior*, Popular Mechanics, March 12, 2018, *available at* www.popularmechanics.com/culture/tv/a19408909/20-years-ago-v-chip/.

148. Implementation of Section 551 of the Telecommunications Act of 1996; Video Programming Ratings, 13 Fixed Charge Coverage Ratio 13 (1998): 8232–37.

149. Grossman, *supra note* 147.

150. YouTube, *More Updates on Our Actions Related to the Safety of Minors on YouTube*, Creator Blog (Feb. 28, 2019), youtube-creators.googleblog.com/2019/02/more-updates-on-our-actions-related-to.html.

151. Chavie Lieber, *YouTube Has a Pedophilia Problem, and Its Advertisers Are Jumping Ship*, Vox, March 1, 2019, *available at* www.vox.com/the-goods/20

19/2/27/18241961/youtube-pedophile-ring-child-safety-advertisers-pulling-ads.

152. *See, e.g.,* Cmty. Television of Utah, Inc. v. Roy City, 555 F. Supp. 1164 (D. Utah 1982); HBO, Inc. v. Wilkinson, 531 F. Supp. 987 (D. Utah 1982).

153. 47 U.S.C. § 532(h) (franchising authorities may prohibit leased access programming that is "obscene or is in conflict with community standards in that it is lewd, lascivious, filthy or indecent, or is otherwise unprotected by the Constitution of the United States"); 47 U.S.C. § 544(d)(i) (franchising authorities may require a franchise to prohibit obscene or "otherwise unprotected" programming); 47 U.S.C. § 558 (franchising authorities may enforce state or local laws forbidding obscenity and "other similar laws").

154. 47 U.S.C. § 544(d)(2).

155. Various Complaints Against the Cable/Satellite Television Program "Nip/Tuck," 20 F.C.C.R. 4255, 4255 (2005), quoting Violent Television Programming and Its Impact on Children, Notice of Inquiry, 19 F.C.C.R. 14394, 14403 (2004).

156. Denver Area Educ. Telecomm. Consortium, Inc. v. FCC, 518 U.S. 727 (1996) (ruling on Pub. L.

No. 102–385, § 10, 106 Stat. 1486).

157. *Id.*

158. 47 U.S.C. § 531.

159. Telecommunications Act of 1996, Pub. L. 104–104, §§ 504, 505, 110 Stat. 136.

160. Implementation of Section 505 of the Telecommunications Act of 1996, 12 F.C.C.R. 5212 (1997).

161. United States v. Playboy Entm't Grp., Inc., 529 U.S. 803 (2000).

162. Kevin Westcott et al., *Digital Media Trends, 5th Edition: Courting the Consumer,* Deloitte Insights (April 16, 2021), https://www2.deloitte.com/us/en/insights/industry/technology/digital-media-trends-consumption-habits-survey/summary.html.

163. Michael O'Rielly, FCC Regulatory Free Arena. (June 1, 2018), https://www.fcc.gov/news-events/blog/2018/06/01/fcc-regulatory-free-arena.

164. Todd Spangler, *Cuties Controversies: Surge in Netflix Cancellations Was Short Lived, Data Shows,* Variety, Sept. 25, 2020, available at https://variety.com/2020/digital/news/cuties-cancel-netflix-account-surge-data-1234783460/.

165. *Id.*

166. *Id.*

167. *2021 Tech Review,* Pornhub Insights (April 8, 2021), https://www.pornhub.com/insights/tech-review#devices.

168. Geoffrey R. Stone, *Sexual Expression and Free Speech: How Our Values Have (D)evolved,* 43 A.B.A. Hum. Rts. Mag., May 14, 2019, *available at* www.americanbar.org/groups/crsj/publications/human_rights_magazine_home/the-ongoing-challenge-to-define-free-speech/sexual-expression-and-free-speech/.

169. Pub. L. No. 104–104, § 502, 110 Stat. 56 (1996) (codified at 47 U.S.C. §§ 223(a)(1)(B)(ii), 223(d)).

170. Reno v. ACLU, 521 U.S. 844 (1997).

171. *Id.* at 877.

172. Pub. L. No. 105–277, §§ 1401–1406, 112 Stat. 1681 (codified at 47 U.S.C. § 231).

173. Mukasey v. ACLU, 555 U.S. 1137 (2009).

174. Pub. L. 104–208, 110 Stat. 3009.

175. 18 U.S.C. § 2256(8)(B), (D).

176. Ashcroft v. Free Speech Coalition, 535 U.S. 234 (2002).

177. Pub. L. 108–21, §§ 102–601, 117 Stat. 650.

178. United States v. Williams, 553 U.S. 285 (2008).

179. Pub. L. No. 106–554, 114 Stat. 2763A-335 (2000).

180. United States v. Am. Library Ass'n, 539 U.S. 194 (2003).

181. Derek Hawkins, *Backpage.com Shuts Down Adult Services Ads After Relentless Pressure From*

Authorities, Wash. Post, Jan. 10, 2017, *available at* www.washingtonpost.com/news/morning-mix/wp/2017/01/10/backpage-com-shuts-down-adult-services-ads-after-relentless-pressure-from-authorities/?utm_term=.227390c60d61.

182. Steven Koff, *Backpage. com Still Appears to Be Running Ads for Prostitutes, Sexual Services*, Cleveland.com, Jan. 12, 2017, *available at* www.cleveland.com/metro/index.ssf/2017/01/backpagecom_might_not_have_act.html.

183. Doe v. Backpage.com, LLC, 817 F.3d 12 (1st Cir. 2016), *cert. denied*, 137 S. Ct. 622 (2017); Backpage.com, LLC v. McKenna, 881 F. Supp. 2d 1262 (W.D. Wash. 2012).

184. Pub. L. No. 115–164, 132 Stat. 1253 (2018) (codified as amended at 18 U.S.C. §§ 1591, 2421A and 47 U.S.C. §230).

185. Cecilia Kang, *In Reversal, Tech Companies Back Sex Trafficking Bill*, N.Y. Times, Nov. 3, 2017, *available at* www.nytimes.com/2017/11/03/technology/sex-trafficking-bill.html.

186. Aja Romano, *A New Law Intended to Curb Sex Trafficking Threatens the Future of the Internet as We Know It*, July 2, 2018, Vox, *available at* www.vox.com/culture/2018/4/13/17172762/fosta-sest

a-backpage-230-internet-freedom.

187. Ryan Tarinelli, *Online Sex Ads Rebound, Months After Shutdown of Backpage*, AP, Nov. 29, 2018, *available at* www.apnews.com/159434f052eb40dd87b9dd9b65da53f5.

188. *See e.g.,* Lura Chamberlain, *Note: FOSTA: A Hostile Law With a Human Cost*, 87 Fordham L. Rev. 2171 (2019).

189. Woodhull Freedom Found. v. United States, 334 F. Supp. 3d 185 (D.D.C. 2018); *see also* Alex F. Levy, *Constitutional Challenge to FOSTA Dismissed for Lack of Standing* (Guest Blog Post), Tech. & Marketing Blog (Oct. 8, 2018), blog.ericgoldman.org/archives/2018/10/constitutional-challenge-to-fosta-dismissed-for-lack-of-standing-guest-blog-post.htm. (The appeal was filed Oct. 12, 2018.)

190. Woodhull Freedom Foundation v. United States, No. 18-5298 (D.C. Cir. 2020).

191. *Doe v. Twitter, Inc.,* 555 F. Supp. 3d 889 (N.D. Cal. 2021).

192. Tarleton Gillespie, Custodians of the Internet 75–97 (2018).

193. Igor Bonifacic, *Instagram Changes Nudity Policy After Controversy with Black, Plus-Sized Model*, Engaget, Oct. 26, 2020,

available at https://www.engadget.com/instagram-nudity-policy-change-204903089.html.

194. Bonnie Ruberg, *Obscene, Pornographic, or Otherwise Objectionable: Biased Definitions of Sexual Content in Video Game Live Streaming*, 23 New Media & Soc'y 1, 15 (2020).

195. *Id.*

196. Mary Anne Franks, Cult of the Constitution 128 (2020).

197. Asia A. Eaton et al., *Cyber Civil Rights Initiative Report: Nationwide Online Study of Nonconsensual Porn and Victimization and Perpetration, Cyber Civil Rights Initiative* (June 2017), https://www.cybercivilrights.org/research/.

198. Id.

199. Franks, *supra* note 196, at 128–129.

200. *Id.*

201. Michael Gold, *The Latest Smear Against Ocasio-Cortez: A Fake Nude Photo*, N.Y. Times, Jan. 10, 2019, *available at* https://www.nytimes.com/2019/01/10/nyregion/ocasio-cortez-fake-nude-photo.html.

202. *Id.*

203. Franks, *supra* note 199.

204. Carrie Goldberg, Nobody's Victim: Fighting Psychos, Stalkers, Pervs, and Trolls 119 (2019).

205. *Id.* at 120.

206. *Id.* at 121.

207. *Id.*

208. *48 States + DC + One Territory Now Have Revenge Porn Laws*, Cyber Civil Rights Initiative, June 4 , 2021, https://www.cybercivilrights.org/revenge-porn-laws/. Massachusetts and South Carolina do not have nonconsensual pornography laws.

209. Seema Mehta, *Katie Hill Ordered to Pay Attorneys' Fees in Revenge Porn Case*, L.A. Times Tech. Rev., June 3, 2021, *available at* https://www.latimes.com/politics/story/2021-06-02/katie-hill-attorneys-fees-revenge-porn.

210. *Id.*

211. State of Illinois v. Austin, 2019 IL 123910, *cert. denied*, 141 S. Ct. 233 (2020).

212. *State v. Casillas*, 952 N.W.2d 629, 634 (Minn. 2020).

213. Karen Hao, *Deepfake Porn Is Ruining Women's Lives. Now the Law May Finally Ban It*, MIT Tech. Rev., Feb. 12, 2021, *available at* https://www.technologyreview.com/2021/02/12/1018222/deepfake-revenge-porn-coming-ban/.

214. Prajakta Pradhan, *AI Deepfakes: The Goose is Cooked*, U. Ill. L. Rev. Blog (Oct. 4, 2020), https://www.illinoislawreview.org/blog/ai-deepfakes/

215. *Id.*

216. Douglas Harris, *Deepfakes: False Pornography Is Here and the Law Cannot Protect You*, 17 Duke Tech. L. Rev. 99–127 (2019).

217. Hao, *supra* note 213.

218. Harris, *supra* note 216, at 101.

219. Hao, *supra* note 213.

220. *Id.*

221. *Id.*

CHAPTER 11

1. U.S. Const. art. I, § 8, cl. 8.

2. 17 U.S.C. § 102(a).

3. Harper v. Nation Enterprises, 471 U.S. 539 (1985).

4. U.S. Const. art. I, § 8, cl. 8.

5. 8 Anne, C. 19 (1710).

6. U.S. Const. art. I, § 8, cl. 8.

7. Act of May 31, 1790, ch. 15, 1 Stat. 124.

8. Wheaton v. Peters, 33 U.S. 591 (1834).

9. Act of Feb. 3, 1831, 4 Stat. 436 (musical compositions); Copyright Act of 1865, 13 Stat. 540 (photographs); Act of July 8, 1870, 16 Stat. 212 (paintings).

10. Pub. L. No. 60–349, 35 Stat. 1075.

11. Berne Convention Implementation Act of 1988, Pub. L. 100–568, 102 Stat. 2853.

12. Digital Millennium Copyright Act of 1998, Pub. L. 105–304, 112 Stat. 2860.

13. 17 U.S.C. § 1201.

14. *See, e.g.*, 321 Studios v. MGM Studios, Inc., 307 F. Supp. 2d 1085 (N.D. Cal. 2004).

15. 17 U.S.C. § 1202.

16. 18 U.S.C. § 102(a).

17. *See* Burrow-Giles Lithographic Co. v. Sarony, 111 U.S. 53 (1884).

18. Boisson v. Banian, Ltd., 273 F.3d 262, 268 (2d Cir. 2001).

19. ABS Entm't, Inc. v. CBS Corp., 908 F.3d 405, 414 (5th Cir. 2018).

20. 18 U.S.C. § 102(a).

21. U.S. Copyright Off., Copyright Basics, May 23, 2019, www.copyright.gov/circs/circ01.pdf.

22. Star Athletica, LLC v. Varsity Brands, Inc., 137 S. Ct. 1002 (2017).

23. 17 U.S.C. § 102(a).

24. *Id.*

25. Star Athletica, L.L.C. v. Varsity Brands, Inc., 137 S. Ct. 1002 (2017).

26. U.S. Copyright Off., *Useful Articles*, www.copyright.gov/register/va-useful.html.

27. Gene Quinn & Steve Brachmann, *Copyrights at the Supreme Court: Star Athletica v. Varsity Brands*, IPWatchdog, March 22, 2017, www.ipwatchdog.com/2017/03/22/copyrights-supreme-court-sta

r-athletica-v-varsity-bra nds/id=79767/.

28. *Star Athletica*, 137 S. Ct. at 1007.

29. Bruce Keller, *Communications Law in the Digital Age: Intellectual Property*, Comm. L. in the Digital Age (2016).

30. ABS Entm't, Inc. v. CBS Corp., 908 F.3d 405 (9th Cir. 2018).

31. *Id.* at 423.

32. 17 U.S.C. § 301.

33. *See* Wheaton v. Peters, 33 U.S. 591 (1834).

34. Feist Publ'ns, Inc. v. Rural Tel. Serv. Co., Inc., 499 U.S. 340 (1991).

35. *See, e.g.,* Am. Dental Ass'n v. Delta Dental Plans Ass'n, 126 F.3d 977 (7th Cir. 1997).

36. 17 U.S.C. § 103.

37. *See* 17 U.S.C. § 102(b).

38. *Feist Publ'ns*, 499 U.S. 340.

39. PhantomALERT, Inc. v. Google, Inc., No. 15-cv-03986-JCS (N.D. Cal., Mar. 8, 2016).

40. Media.net Advert., FZ-LLC v. NetSeer, Inc., 156 F. Supp. 3d 1052 (N.D. Cal. 2016).

41. 593 U.S. ___ (2021).

42. 17 U.S.C. § 105.

43. 17 U.S.C. § 201(a).

44. 17 U.S.C. § 201(b).

45. 17 U.S.C. §§ 101, 201.

46. 17 U.S.C. § 101.

47. Cmty. for Creative Non-Violence v. Reid, 490 U.S. 730 (1989).

48. *Who Owns the Intellectual Property Developed by an Independent Contractor?*, HG, May 23, 2019, www.hg.org/legal-articles/who-owns-the-intellectual-property-developed-by-an-independent-contractor-7502.

49. 17 U.S.C. § 201(c).

50. N.Y. Times Co., Inc. v. Tasini, 533 U.S. 483 (2001).

51. *What We Do*, Creative Commons, https://creativecommons.org/about/.

52. 17 U.S.C. § 106.

53. Sony Corp. of Am. v. Universal City Studios, Inc., 464 U.S. 417 (1984).

54. Audio Home Recording Act of 1992, Pub. L. No. 102–563, 106 Stat. 4244 (codified at 17 U.S.C. §§ 1001–1010).

55. Tom Huddleston, Jr., *"Game of Thrones" Creator George R.R. Martin Almost Quit Writing for Real Estate*, CNBC, April 14, 2019, www.cnbc.com/2019/04/12/how-game-of-thrones-creator-george-rr-martin-overcame-failure.html.

56. Natalie Robehmed, *The 'Frozen' Effect: When Disney's Movie Merchandising is Too Much*, Forbes, July 28, 2015, https://www.forbes.com/sites/natalierobehmed/2015/07/28/the-frozen-effect-when-disneys-movie-merch

andising-is-too-much/?sh=e894c4b22ca8.

57. Peter Mayer Publishers, Inc. v. Shilovskaya, 11 F. Supp. 3d 421 (S.D.N.Y. 2014).

58. ABS Entm't, Inc. v. CBS Corp., 908 F.3d 405 (2018).

59. *Id.* at 418.

60. Rearden, LLC v. Walt Disney Co., 293 F. Supp. 3d 963 (N.D. Cal. 2018).

61. *Id.*

62. Agence France Presse v. Morel, 934 F. Supp. 2d 547 (S.D.N.Y. 2013).

63. *Id.*

64. Joseph Ax, *Photographer Wins $1.2 Million From Companies That Took Pictures Off Twitter*, Reuters, Nov. 22, 2013, www.reuters.com/article/2013/11/22/us-media-copyright-twitter-idUSBRE9AL16F20131122.

65. 17 U.S.C. § 106(4).

66. WNET, Thirteen v. Aereo, Inc., 712 F. 3d 676, 685 (2d Cir. 2013), *rev'd and remanded sub nom.* ABC, Inc. v. Aereo, Inc., 573 U.S. 431 (2014).

67. Teleprompter Corp. v. CBS, 415 U.S. 394 (1974); Fortnightly Corp. v. United Artists Television, Inc., 392 U.S. 390 (1968).

68. 17 U.S.C. § 111.

69. 17 U.S.C. § 119; Satellite Home Viewer Improvement Act of 1999, Pub. L. No. 106–113, §§ 1001–1012, 113 Stat. 1501.

70. *ABC, Inc.*, 573 U.S. 431.

71. *Id.*

72. Corinee Lestch, *Aereo Suspends Video Streaming After Supreme Court Decision*, N.Y. DAILY NEWS, June 29, 2014, www.nydailyne ws.com/news/national/a ereo-suspends-streami ng-service-supreme-co urt-decision-article-1.1 847702.

73. Matthew Syrkin, *U.S. Television on the Internet and the New "MVPDs,"* HUGHES, HUBBARD & REED, March 18, 2015, www.hu gheshubbard.com/news/ u-s-television-on-the-in ternet-and-the-new-mv pds-updated.

74. John Eggerton, *Ninth Circuit Reverses FilmOn X Decision*, BROADCASTING & CABLE, March 16, 2018, w ww.broadcastingcable.c om/news/ninth-circuit-r everses-filmon-x-decisi on-164275.

75. Fox TV Stations, Inc. v. Aereokiller, LLC, 851 F.3d 1002, 1006 (2017).

76. 18 U.S.C. § 2139C.

77. Matthew Strauss, *Streaming Now Officially the Number One Way We Listen to Music in America*, PITCHFORK, Jan. 6, 2017, https://pitchfork.co m/news/70724-streami ng-now-officially-the-nu mber-one-way-we-liste n-to-music-in-america/.

78. 17 U.S.C. § 106.

79. 17 U.S.C. § 106.

80. Perfect 10, Inc. v. Ama-zon.com, Inc., 508 F.3d 1146 (9th Cir. 2007).

81. Goldman v. Breitbart News Network, LLC, 302 F. Supp. 3d 585 (S.D.N.Y. 2018).

82. Jeffrey Neuburger, *New York Court Rebuffs Ninth Circuits' Copyright "Server Test," Finds Embedded Tweet Display-ing Copyrighted Image to be Infringement*, NEW MEDIA AND TECH. L. BLOG, March 2, 2018, new-medialaw.proskauer. com/2018/03/02/ new-york-court-rebuffs-ninth-circuits-copyright-server-test-finds-embedded-tweet-displaying-copyrighted-image-to-be-infringe-ment/.

83. *Goldman*, 508 F.3d at 593.

84. *Id.*

85. Jeffrey P. Cunard et al., *Intellectual Property 2018: Select Developments*, COMM. L. IN THE DIGITAL AGE (2018).

86. Free Speech Sys., LLC v. Menzel, 390 F. Supp. 3d 1162, 1166 (N.D. Cal. 2019)

87. *Id.* at 1172.

88. *Id.*

89. Digital Performance Right in Sound Record-ings Act, Pub. L. No. 104–39, 109 Stat. 336, as amended by DMCA, Pub. L. 105–304, 112 Stat. 2860.

90. 17 U.S.C. § 108.

91. U.S. Copyright Off., Reproduction of Copy-right Works by Educators and Librarians (June 2, 2019), www.copyright.go v/circs/circ21.pdf.

92. 17 U.S.C. § 109(a).

93. The Supreme Court provides a brief history and interpretation of the first-sale doctrine in Quality King Distribs., Inc. v. L'Anza Research Int'l, Inc., 523 U.S. 135 (1998).

94. Kirtsaeng v. John Wiley & Sons, Inc., 568 U.S. 519 (2013).

95. 17 U.S.C. § 109(b)(1)(A); Computer Software Rental Amendments, Pub. L. No. 101–650, tit. viii, 104 Stat. 5089, 5134–35; Record Rental Amendment of 1984, Pub. L. No. 98–450, 98 Stat. 1727.

96. Capitol Records, LLC v. ReDigi, Inc., 934 F. Supp. 2d 640 (S.D.N.Y. 2013), aff'd, 910 F.3d 649 (2d Cir. 2018), *cert. denied*, 2019 WL 2124143 (June 24, 2019).

97. Andes Guadamuz, *Non-fungible tokens (NFTs) and copyright*, WIPO MAGAZINE, Dec. 2021, https://www. wipo.int/wipo_magazin e/en/2021/04/article_00 07.html.

98. *Id.*

99. *Id.*

100. Nike Inc. v. StockX LLC, No. 22-cv-983, (S.D.N.Y. Feb. 3, 2022), https://heit

nerlegal.com/wp-content/uploads/Nike-v-StockX.pdf.

101. 17 U.S.C. §§ 203(a), 304(c).

102. Amy X. Wang, *Trump Signs Landmark Music Bill Into Law*, Rolling Stone, Oct. 11, 2018, www.rollingstone.com/music/music-news/trump-signs-music-modernization-act-736185/.

103. The Orrin G. Hatch-Bob Goodlatte Music Modernization Act (MMA), Pub. L. 115–264, 132 Stat. 3676 (Oct. 11, 2018).

104. *Summary of H.R. 1551, the Music Modernization Act*, Copyright Alliance, May 24, 2019, copyrightalliance.org/wp-content/uploads/2018/10/CA-MMA-2018-senate-summary_CLEAN.pdf.

105. *Id.*

106. Mitch Glazier, *Creators and Tech Companies: Let's Fix the DMCA Together* (Guest Column), Variety, May 6, 2019, variety.com/2019/music/news/digital-copyright-act-creators-tech-lets-fix-dmca-together-riaa-1203205595/.

107. U.S. Const. art I, § 8, cl. 8.

108. *See* 3 Melville B. Nimmer & David Nimmer, Nimmer on Copyright § 9.01 (2012).

109. Laurie Richter, *Reproductive Freedom: Striking a Fair Balance Between Copyright and Other Intellectual Property Protections in Cartoon Characters*, 21 St. Thomas L. Rev. 441, 451–52 (2009).

110. 17 U.S.C. § 302(a).

111. 17 U.S.C. § 302(c).

112. Eldred v. Ashcroft, 537 U.S. 186 (2003).

113. *Id.*

114. This was "due to (i) failure to comply with copyright formalities, (ii) lack of subject matter protection, or (iii) lack of national eligibility due to the absence of copyright relations with the" United States. Dan Laidman, *Golan v. Holder and the Controversial New Efforts to Update IP Law for the Internet Age*, Davis Wright Tremaine, March 12, 2012, www.lexology.com/library/detail.aspx?g=2d5e85f7-9b48-4c6a-beff-c63c25335859.

115. 17 U.S.C. § 104A.

116. Laidman, *supra* note 114.

117. Golan v. Holder, 565 U.S. 302 (2012).

118. *Id.* at 311.

119. 17 U.S.C. § 401(c).

120. Rimini Street, Inc. v. Oracle USA, Inc., 139 S. Ct. 873 (2019).

121. *Id.*

122. Fourth Estate Pub. Benefit Corp. v. Wall-Street.com, LLC, 139 S. Ct. 881 (2019).

123. Arnstein v. Porter, 154 F.2d 464 (2d Cir. 1946).

124. Shyamkrishna Balganesh, *The Questionable Origins of the Copyright Infringement Analysis*, 68 Stan. L. Rev. 791 (April 2016).

125. *See, e.g.,* Sid & Marty Krofft Television Prods., Inc. v. McDonald's Corp., 562 F.2d 1157 (9th Cir. 1977); Comput. Assocs. Int'l v. Altai, Inc., 982 F.2d 693, 713 (2d Cir. 1992).

126. Kory Grow, *Robin Thicke, Pharrell Lose Multi-Million Dollar "Blurred Lines" Lawsuit*, Rolling Stone, March 10, 2015, www.rollingstone.com/music/news/robin-thicke-and-pharrell-lose-blurred-lines-lawsuit-20150310.

127. *Williams v. Bridgeport Music, Inc.*, Loeb & Loeb, April 12, 2016, https://www.loeb.com/en/insights/publications/2016/04/williams-v-bridgeport-music-inc.

128. Josh H. Escovedo, *The Blurred Lines of an Infringement Action*, IP L. Blog, March 6, 2015, www.theiplawblog.com/2015/03/articles/copyright-law/the-blurred-lines-of-an-infringement-action/.

129. *Id.*

130. 17 U.S.C. § 504(c).

131. *See, e.g.,* Kalem Co. v. Harper Bros., 222 U.S. 55 (1911) (producer of infringing film violated copyright law although movie theaters, not producer, showed film to public); 17 U.S.C. §§ 106, 501(a).

132. Sony Corp. of Am. v. Universal City Studios, Inc., 464 U.S. 417 (1984).

133. *Id.*

134. Cartoon Network, LP v. CSC Holdings, Inc., 536 F.3d 121 (2d Cir. 2008), *cert. denied*, 557 U.S. 946 (2009).

135. A&M Records, Inc. v. Napster, Inc., 239 F.3d 1004 (9th Cir. 2001).

136. MGM Studios, Inc. v. Grokster, Ltd., 545 U.S. 913 (2005).

137. *See* 35 U.S.C. § 271(b).

138. Columbia Pictures Indus., Inc. v. Fung, 710 F.3d 1020 (9th Cir.), cert. dismissed, 571 U.S. 1007 (2013).

139. *Congress Passes CASE Act of 2020 and Law Regarding Unauthorized Streaming Services*, U.S. COPYRIGHT OFFICE, Dec. 22, 2020, https://www.copyright.gov/newsnet/2020/866.html.

140. Samantha Handler, *Opt-Out Option Threatens Fledging Small Claims Copyright Board*, BLOOMBERG LAW, March 1, 2022, https://news.bloomberglaw.com/ip-law/opt-out-option-threatens-fledgling-small-claims-copyright-board.

141. 17 U.S.C. § 507.

142. *See, e.g.*, Dam Things From Denmark v. Russ Barrie & Co., 290 F.3d 548, 560 (3d Cir. 2002).

143. *See* Pierre N. Leval, *Toward a Fair Use Standard*, 103 HARV. L. REV. 1105, 1105 (1990).

144. 17 U.S.C. § 107.

145. Leval, *supra* note 143, at 1110.

146. Campbell v. Acuff-Rose Music, Inc., 510 U.S. 569, 578 (1994).

147. Harper & Row Publishers, Inc. v. Nation Enters., 471 U.S. 539 (1985).

148. *See* 4 Melville Nimmer & David Nimmer, NIMMER ON COPYRIGHT § 13.05[A][1] (2012).

149. *Campbell*, 510 U.S. at 579.

150. *Id.* at 569.

151. *See* Nimmer & Nimmer, *supra* note 148, at § 13.05[C][1].

152. 992 F.3d 99 (2021).

153. *Id.*

154. Brownmark Films, LLC v. Comedy Partners, 682 F.3d 687 (7th Cir. 2012).

155. Keeling v. Hars, 809 F.3d 43 (2d Cir. 2015), *cert. denied*, 136 S. Ct. 2519 (2016).

156. Barcroft Media, Ltd. V. Coed Media Grp., LLC, 297 F. Supp. 3d 339 (S.D.N.Y. 2017).

157. White v. West Publ'g Corp., 29 F. Supp. 3d 396 (S.D.N.Y. 2014).

158. Fox News Network, LLC v. TVEyes, Inc., 43 F. Supp. 3d 379 (S.D.N.Y. 2014).

159. Fox News Network, LLC v. TVEyes, Inc., 883 F.3d 169 (2d Cir.), *cert. denied*, 139 S. Ct. 595 (2018).

160. *Id.*

161. Authors Guild v. Google, Inc., 804 F.3d 202 (2d Cir.

2015), *cert. denied*, 136 S. Ct. 1658 (2016).

162. Authors Guild v. HathiTrust, 902 F. Supp. 445 (S.D.N.Y. 2012).

163. *Authors Guild*, 804 F.3d 202.

164. 593 U.S. ____ (2021).

165. *See* 4 Melville Nimmer & David Nimmer, NIMMER ON COPYRIGHT § 13.05[A][2] (2012).

166. Salinger v. Random House, Inc., 811 F.2d 90 (2d Cir. 1987), cert. denied, 484 U.S. 890 (1988).

167. 17 U.S.C. § 107; Pub. L. No. 102–492, 106 Stat. 3145.

168. A.V. v. iParadigms, LLC, 562 F.3d 630 (4th Cir. 2009).

169. *Id.* at 642.

170. *See* Fox News Network, LLC v. TVEyes, Inc., 43 F. Supp. 3d 379 (S.D.N.Y. 2014); White v. West Publ'g Corp., 29 F. Supp. 3d 396 (S.D.N.Y. 2014).

171. Bill Graham Archives v. Dorling Kindersley, Ltd., 448 F.3d 605 (2d Cir. 2006).

172. Basic Books, Inc. v. Kinko's Graphics Corp., 758 F. Supp. 1522, 1534 (S.D.N.Y. 1991).

173. Campbell v. Acuff-Rose Music, Inc., 510 U.S. 569, 587 (1994).

174. *See, e.g.*, Authors Guild, Inc. v. Google, Inc., 954 F. Supp. 2d 282 (S.D.N.Y. 2013), aff'd, 804 F.3d 202 (2d Cir. 2015), *cert.*

denied, 136 S. Ct. 1658 (2016); Authors Guild, Inc. v. HathiTrust, 755 F.3d 87 (2d Cir. 2014).

175. Pub. L. 105–304, 112 Stat. 2860.

176. 17 U.S.C. § 512(c).

177. Perfect 10, Inc. v. Google, Inc., 2010 U.S. Dist. LEXIS 75071 (C.D. Cal., July 26, 2010), *aff'd,* 653 F.3d 976 (9th Cir. 2011), *cert. denied,* 565 U.S. 1245 (2012).

178. UMG Recordings, Inc. v. Veoh Networks, Inc., 718 F.3d 1006 (9th Cir. 2013); *see also* Io Group, Inc. v. Veoh Networks, Inc., 586 F. Supp. 2d 1132 (N.D. Cal. 2008).

179. Viacom Int'l, Inc. v. YouTube, Inc., 940 F. Supp. 2d 110 (S.D.N.Y. 2013), on remand from Viacom Int'l, Inc. v. YouTube, Inc., 676 F.3d 19 (2d Cir. 2012); *see* Meg James, *YouTube Prevails in Viacom Copyright Suit,* L.A. TIMES, April 19, 2013, at B3.

180. Capitol Records, LLC v. Vimeo, LLC, 972 F. Supp. 2d 537 (S.D.N.Y. 2014), aff'd in part, vacated in part, 826 F.3d (2d Cir. 2016), *cert. denied,* 137 S. Ct. 1374 (2017).

181. Evan Sheres, *Disabling the "Red Flag" Doctrine: Missed Opportunity to Establish Reasonable Precedent in Capitol Records v. Vimeo,* COPYRIGHT ALL., Sept. 25, 2013.

182. Capitol Records, 972 F. Supp. 2d 537.

183. BMG Rights Mgmt. (US), LLC v. Cox Commc'ns, Inc., 881 F.3d 293 (4th Cir. 2018).

184. BWP Media USA, Inc. v. Clarity Digital Grp., LLC, 820 F. 3d 1175 (10th Cir. 2016).

185. 15 U.S.C. § 1127.

186. Qualitex Co. v. Jacobson Prods. Co., Inc., 514 U.S. 159 (1995).

187. Ride the Ducks, LLC v. Duck Boat Tours, Inc., 2005 U.S. Dist. LEXIS 4422 (E.D. Pa. Mar. 21, 2005), *aff'd,* 138 F. App'x. 431 (3d Cir. Pa. 2005).

188. *See* Anne Gilson LaLonde, GILSON ON TRADEMARKS § 10A.09[5] (2019).

189. 15 U.S.C. § 1051 et seq.

190. 15 U.S.C. § 1125(a).

191. 15 U.S.C. § 1052.

192. PACCAR, Inc. v. TeleScanTechnologies, LLC, 319 F.3d 243 (6th Cir. 2003).

193. Bebe Stores, Inc. v. May Dep't Stores Int'l, 313 F.3d 1056 (8th Cir. 2002) (per curiam).

194. Standard Brands, Inc. v. Smidler, 151 F.2d 34 (2d Cir. 1945).

195. *See* Anne Gilson LaLonde & Jerome Gilson, GILSON ON TRADEMARKS § 2.04[1] (2019).

196. Sara Lee Corp. v. Kayser-Roth Corp., 81 F.3d 455, 464 (4th Cir. 1996).

197. Circuit City Stores, Inc. v. CarMax, Inc., 165 F.3d 1047 (6th Cir. 1999).

198. Japan Telecom, Inc. v. Japan Telecom Am., Inc., 287 F.3d 866, 873 (9th Cir. 2002).

199. Viacom Int'l, Inc. v. IJR Capital Invs., LLC, 891 F.3d 178 (5th Cir. 2018).

200. *Id.*

201. Boston Beer Co., LP v. Slesar Bros. Brewing Co., Inc., 9 F.3d 175 (1st Cir. 1993).

202. M. Fabrikant & Sons, Ltd. v. Fabrikant Fine Diamonds, Inc., 17 F. Supp. 2d 249 (S.D.N.Y. 1998).

203. Anne Gilson LaLonde & Jerome Gilson, GILSON ON TRADEMARKS § 2.08[1] (2019).

204. Harley-Davidson, Inc. v. Grottanelli, 164 F.3d 806 (2d Cir. 1999).

205. Small Bus. Assistance Corp. v. Clear Channel Broad., Inc., 210 F.3d 278 (5th Cir. 2000).

206. *See* Sung In, *Note: Death of a Trademark: Genericide in the Digital Age,* 21 REV. LITIG. 159 (2002).

207. *See, e.g.,* George K. Chamberlin, *Annotation: When Does Product Mark Become Generic Term or "Common Descriptive Name" So as to Warrant Cancellation of Registration of Mark,* 55 A.L.R. FED. 241 (2004).

208. *See* Anne Gilson LaLonde & Jerome Gilson, GILSON ON TRADEMARKS § 2.02[6] (2019).

209. 15 U.S.C. § 1051.

210. 15 U.S.C. § 1052 (b), (c), (d), (e).

211. 15 U.S.C. § 1091.

212. *Expungement and Reexamination and Shorter Trademark Office Action Response Periods, Oh My!,* JDSupra, Feb. 4, 2022, https://www.jdsupra.com/legalnews/expungement-and-reexamination-and-2143508/.

213. 15 U.S.C. §§ 1052, 1072, 1115.

214. 15 U.S.C. § 1115(a), (b).

215. 15 U.S.C. § 1058.

216. 15 U.S.C. § 1059.

217. 15 U.S.C. § 1052(a).

218. *In re* Tam, 808 F.3d 1321 (D.C. Cir. 2015), aff'd sub nom., Matal v. Tam, 137 S. Ct. 1744 (2017).

219. *Id.*

220. *Id.* at 1327–28.

221. *Matal*, 137 S. Ct. at 1748.

222. *In re* Brunetti, 877 F.3d 1330 (D.C. Cir., 2017), cert. granted, 139 S. Ct. 782 (2019).

223. *Id.*

224. David G. Savage, *Supreme Court Debates Whether FUCT Clothing Line Can Trademark Its Name,* L.A. Times, April 15, 2019, www.latimes.com/politics/la-na-pol-supreme-court-trademark-free-speech-dispute-fuct-20190415-story.html.

225. Iancu v. Brunetti, 2019 U.S. LEXIS 4201, 13 (2019).

226. *Id.* at 32 (Sotomayor, J., dissenting).

227. *Id.* at 54 (Sotomayor, J., dissenting).

228. Pub. L. 106–113, 113 Stat. 1536.

229. E. & J. Gallo Winery v. Spider Webs, Ltd., 286 F.3d 270 (5th Cir. 2002).

230. Brookfield Commc'ns, Inc. v. West Coast Entm't Corp., 174 F.3d 1036 (9th Cir. 1999).

231. Ty, Inc. v. Perryman, 306 F.3d 509, 513 (7th Cir. 2002), *cert. denied,* 538 U.S. 971 (2003).

232. Infostream Grp., Inc. v. Avid Life Media, Inc., 2013 U.S. Dist. LEXIS 161940 (C.D. Cal., 2013).

233. Alzheimer's Disease and Related Disorders Ass'n v. Alzheimer's Found. of Am., Inc., 307 F. Supp. 3d 260 (S.D.N.Y. 2018).

234. TMEP §1202.18 (July 2021), https://tmep.uspto.gov/RDMS/TMEP/current#/current/ch1200_d1ff5e_1b5ad_3bc.html.

235. Claire Jones, *Hashtag Trademarks: What Can be Protected?* WIPO Magazine, Oct. 2017, https://www.wipo.int/wipo_magazine/en/2017/05/article_0009.html.

236. 15 U.S.C. § 1125(a)(1) (Lanham Act—U.S. trademark law).

237. *See, e.g.,* Triangle Publ'ns v. Knight-Ridder Newspapers, Inc., 626 F.2d 1171 (5th Cir. 1978).

238. Deere & Co. v. MTD Prods., Inc., 41 F.3d 39 (2d Cir. 1994).

239. Facebook, Inc. v. Teachbook.com, LLC, 819 F. Supp. 2d 764, 781 (N.D. Ill. 2011).

240. *Tacking,* MarkLaw, www.marklaw.com/index.php/trademark-terms-t/308-tacking.

241. *Pepsi Logo Timeline: The Evolution of the Company's Brand,* Huff. Post, Dec. 18, 2014, www.huffingtonpost.com/2012/12/28/pepsi-logo-timeline_n_2279676.html.

242. *Id.*

243. Hana Fin., Inc. v. Hana Bank, 135 S. Ct. 907 (2015).

244. Mark Wilson, *What Is Trademark Tacking,* FindLaw, Jan. 21, 2015, blogs.findlaw.com/free_enterprise/2015/01/what-is-trademark-tacking.html.

245. Romag Fasteners, Inc. v. Fossil Group, Inc., 590 U.S.____(2020).

246. *See* Application of E.I. DuPont de Nemours & Co., 476 F.2d 1357, 1361 (C.C.P.A. 1973).

247. 15 U.S.C. §§ 1125(c), 1127.

248. Anne Gilson LaLonde & Jerome Gilson, Gilson on Trademarks § 5A.01[5], [6] (2019).

249. Moseley v. V Secret Catalogue, Inc., 537 U.S. 418 (2003).

250. *Id.* at 434.

251. 15 U.S.C. § 1115(b).

252. 15 U.S.C. § 115(b)(4).

253. Overstock.com v. NoMoreRack.com, 2014 U.S. Dist. LEXIS 89620 (2014).

254. Webceleb, Inc. v. Procter & Gamble Co., 554 F. App'x 606 (9th Cir. 2014).

255. New Kids on the Block v. News Am. Publ'g, Inc., 971 F.2d 302 (9th Cir. 1992).

256. 875 F.2d 994, 999 (2d Cir. 1989).

257. VIP Prods. LLC v. Jack Daniel's Props. Inc., 953 F.3d 1170 (9th Cir. 2020).

258. Megan Bannigan & Jared Kagan, *Trademarks in 2021: Recounting the Most High-Profile Trademark Developments of the Year*, IP Watchdog, Dec. 16, 2021, https://www.ipwat chdog.com/2021/12/16/ trademarks-2021-recou nting-high-profile-trade mark-developments-yea r/id=140998/.

259. Daniel Jacob Wright, *Explicitly Explicit: The Rogers Test and the Ninth Circuit*, 21 J. INTELL. PROP. L. 193, 203 (2013).

260. 507 F.3d 252 (4th Cir. 2007).

261. *Id.* at 258, 260, 263.

262. *Id.* at 260.

263. 15 U.S.C. § 1125(c)(3).

264. Megan Bannigan & Jared Kagan, *Trademarks in 2021: Recounting the Most High-Profile Trademark Developments of the Year*, IP Watchdog, Dec. 16, 2021, https://www.ipwat chdog.com/2021/12/16/ trademarks-2021-recou nting-high-profile-trade mark-developments-yea r/id=140998/.

265. 989 F.3d 435 (6th Cir. 2021).

266. Ohio State Univ. v. Red-bubble, Inc., 369 F. Supp. 3d 840, 844 (S.D. Ohio 2019).

267. *Ohio State Univ. v. Red-bubble, supra* note 265, 989 F.3d 435, at 448.

268. Y.Y.G.M. SA d.b.a. Brandy Melville v. Redbubble, Inc., 2020 WL 3984528 (C.D. Cal. Jul. 10, 2020)."

CHAPTER 12

1. *Advertising Market in the U.S.*, STATISTA, 2021, https ://www.statista.com/stu dy/11706/advertising-ma rket-in-the-united-state s--statista-dossier/.

2. "The competitive dynamics of these new markets drive surveillance capitalists to acquire ever-more-predictive sources of behavioral surplus: our voices, personalities, and emotions ... surveillance capitalists discovered that the most predictive behavioral data come from intervening in the state of play in order to nudge, coax, tune and herd behavior toward profitable outcomes." *See* SHOSHANA ZUBOFF, THE AGE OF SURVEILLANCE CAPITALISM: THE FIGHT FOR A HUMAN FUTURE AT THE NEW FRONTIER OF POWER (2020), 8.

3. U.S. Const. art. 1, § 8.

4. THOMAS C. O'GUINN, ADVERTISING AND INTEGRATED BANK PROMOTION (2019).

5. *Standard Oil*, BRITANNICA, h ttps://www.britannica.co m/topic/Standard-Oil.

6. *See generally* Neil W. Averitt, *The Meaning of 'Unfair Methods of Competition' in Section 5 of the Federal Trade Commission Act*, 21 B.C.L. REV. 227 (1980).

7. 15 U.S.C. § 1125.

8. Roscoe B. Starek III, Myths and Half-Truths About Deceptive Advertising, Address to the Nat'l Infomercial Marketing Ass'n (Oct. 15, 1996), www.ftc.gov/spee ches/starek/nima96d4 .htm.

9. Valentine v. Chrestensen, 316 U.S. 52, 53 (1942).

10. *Id.* at 53.

11. *Id.* at 53, 55.

12. *Id.* (emphasis added).

13. *Id.* at 55.

14. Breard v. Alexandria, 341 U.S. 622 (1951).

15. *Id.* at 645.

16. N.Y. Times Co. v. Sullivan, 376 U.S. 254 (1964).

17. *Id.* at 266.

18. *Id.*

19. Bigelow v. Virginia, 421 U.S. 809, 819 (1975) (emphasis added).

20. *Id.*

21. *Id.* at 817.

22. *Id.* at 820.

23. Va. State Bd. of Pharmacy v. Va. Citizens Consumer Council, 425 U.S. 748 (1976).

24. *Id.* at 755.

25. *Id.* at 761.

26. *Id.* at 772 n. 24.

27. *Id.* at 764–765.

28. *Id.* at 772 n. 24, 776.

29. Linmark Assocs. v. Twp. of Willingboro, 431 U.S. 85 (1977); Carey v. Population Servs. Int'l, 431 U.S. 678 (1977); Bates v. State Bar, 433 U.S. 350 (1977).

30. *Bates*, 433 U.S. at 380–81.

31. Ohralik v. Ohio State Bar Ass'n, 436 U.S. 447, 456 (1978).

32. Va. State Bd. of Pharmacy v. Va. Citizens Consumer Council, 425 U.S. 748, 771–72 (1976).

33. Cent. Hudson Gas & Elec. Corp. v. Pub. Serv. Comm'n, 447 U.S. 557, 561 (1980) (emphasis added).

34. *Id.* at 561.

35. THOMAS O'GUINN, ET AL., ADVERTISING AND INTEGRATED BRAND PROMOTION 8 (2019).

36. *Advertising Market in the U.S.*, *supra* note 1.

37. *Native Digital Display Advertising Spending in the United States from 2016 to 2020*, STATISTA, Jan. 14, 2021, https://www.statista.com/statistics/369886/native-ad-spend-usa/; Jayson DeMers, *Is Native Advertising Sustainable for the Long Haul?*, FORBES, March 1, 2018, www.forbes.com/sites/jaysondemers/2018/03/01/is-native-advertising-sustainable-for-the-long-haul/.

38. L. Moses, *The Wall Street Journal Launches Native Ad Studio*, ADWEEK, March 10, 2014, www.adweek.com/news/press/wall-street-journal-launches-native-ad-studio-156212.

39. Olle Pettersson, *Content Marketing or Native Advertising?*, PULSE, May 12, 2017, https://www.linkedin.com/pulse/content-marketing-native-advertising-olle-pettersson/.

40. Olle Pettersson, *What's the Difference Between Branded and Sponsored Content?*, PULSE, June 12, 2017, https://www.linkedin.com/pulse/branded-content-vs-sponsored-whats-difference-olle-pettersson/.

41. Insider Intelligence, *US Influencer Marketing Spending Will Surpass $4 Billion in 2022*, INSIDER INTELLIGENCE, Jan. 13, 2022, https://www.insiderintelligence.com/insights/us-influencer-marketing-spending/.

42. Peter Horst, *Gillette's Controversial "Toxic Masculinity" Ad and the Opportunity It Missed*, FORBES, Jan. 18, 2019, www.forbes.com/sites/peterhorst/2019/01/18/gillettes-controversial-toxic-mascul inity-ad-and-the-opportunity-it-missed/#57aef3ff5506.

43. Carl Jones, *Getting Ads Banned Is a Planned PR and Advertising Strategy*, DRUM, Nov. 21, 2018, www.thedrum.com/opinion/2018/11/21/getting-ads-banned-planned-pr-and-advertising-strateg y; Sam Pudwell, *Gillette Ad: What's Wrong With Controversy in PR?*, RED LORRY YELLOW LORRY, Jan. 16, 2019, www.rlyl.com/us/gillette-ad-pr-controversy-2/. *See also* ANNE M. CRONIN, PUBLIC RELATIONS CAPITALISM 105–16 (2018).

44. Test Masters Educ. Servs., Inc. v. Robin Singh Educ. Servs., Inc., 799 F.3d 437, 453 (5th Cir. 2015), *cert. denied*, 137 S. Ct. 499 (2016).

45. 16 C.F.R. § 255.5.

46. Jordan v. Jewel Food Stores, Inc., 743 F.3d 509 (7th Cir. 2014).

47. Va. State Bd. of Pharmacy v. Va. Citizens Consumer Council, Inc., 425 U. S. 748, 762 (1976).

48. Jordan v. Jewel Food Stores, Inc., 83 F. Supp. 3d 761 (N.D. Ill. 2015).

49. Sarver v. Chartier, 813 F.3d 891 (9th Cir. 2016) (citing Va. State Bd. of Pharmacy, 425 U.S. at 762).

50. Enigma Software Grp., LLC v. Bleeping Comput., LLC, 194 F. Supp. 3d 263 (S.D.N.Y. 2016).

51. *Id.* at 294.

52. *Id.*

53. Pittsburgh Press Co. v. Pittsburgh Comm'n on Human Relations, 413 U.S. 376, 389 (1973).

54. Cent. Hudson Gas & Elec. Corp. v. Pub. Serv. Comm'n of N.Y., 447 U.S. 557, 569–70 (1980) (emphasis added).

55. *See* United States v. O'Brien, 391 U.S. 367 (1968).

56. Posadas de Puerto Rico Assocs. v. Tourism Co. of Puerto Rico, 478 U.S. 328, 340 (1986).

57. *Cent. Hudson*, 447 U.S. at 566.

58. *Posadas*, 478 U.S. at 341.

59. *Id.* at 341–43.

60. *Id.* at 345–46.

61. *Cent. Hudson* Gas & Elec. Corp. v. Pub. Serv. Comm'n of N.Y., 447 U.S. 557, 569–70 (1980).

62. Bd. of Trs. of the State Univ. of N.Y. v. Fox, 492 U.S. 469 (1989).

63. *Id.* at 477.

64. *Id.* at 480.

65. Rubin v. Coors Brewing Co., 514 U.S. 476, 491 (1995).

66. 44 Liquormart, Inc. v. Rhode Island, 517 U.S. 484, 529 (1996) (Thomas, J., concurring in Parts I, II, VI and VII, and in judgment).

67. Lorillard Tobacco Co. v. Reilly, 533 U.S. 525, 536, 561 (2001).

68. Thompson v. Western States Medical Center, 535 U.S. 357 (2002) (Breyer, J., dissenting).

69. Sorrell v. IMS Health, Inc., 564 U.S. 552, 572 (2011).

70. *44 Liquormart*, 517 U.S. at 503.

71. *Id.* at 500.

72. *Id.* at 518.

73. *Sorrell*, 564 U.S. at 552.

74. Vt. Stat. Ann., Tit. 18, § 4631(d).

75. *Sorrell*, 564 U.S. at 583.

76. *Id.* at 565.

77. *Id.* at 566.

78. *Id.* at 565–57.

79. *Id.* at 579.

80. *Id.* at 585–86.

81. Robert L. Kerr, *Desperately Seeking Coherence: The Lower Courts Struggle to Determine the Meaning of Sorrell for the Commercial Speech Doctrine*, 7 U. Balt. J. Media L. & Ethics 1 (2019).

82. Hunter B. Thomson, *Whither Central Hudson? Commercial Speech in the Wake of Sorrell v. IMS Health*, 47 Columbia J.L. & Soc. Probs. 171 (2013–14).

83. *One Year Later: The Consequences of Sorrell v. IMS Health Inc.*, Justice Watch, July 2, 2012, afjjustice watch.blogspot.com//2012/07/one-year-later-consequences-of-sorrell.html.

84. *Id.*

85. Retail Dig. Network, LLC v. Appelsmith, 810 F.3d 638 (9th Cir. 2016), *aff'd* 861 F.3d 839 (9th Cir. 2017).

86. Crazy Ely W. Vill., LLC v. City of Las Vegas, 618 F. App'x 904 (9th Cir. 2015).

87. Am. Meat Inst. v. USDA, 760 F.3d 18, 26 (D.C. Cir. 2014).

88. *Id.*

89. Sorrell v. IMS Health, Inc., 564 U.S. 552 (2011).

90. Cent. Hudson Gas & Elec. Corp. v. Pub. Serv. Comm'n of New York, 447 U.S. 557, 561 (1980).

91. Riley v. Nat'l Fed'n of the Blind of N.C., Inc., 487 U.S. 781, 796–97 (1988).

92. Eugene Volokh, *The Law of Compelled Speech*, 97 Tex. L. Rev. 355 (2018).

93. *Id.*

94. Wieman v. Updegraff, 344 U.S. 183 (1952). *See also* Shelton v. Tucker, 364 U.S. 479 (1960) (disclosure of memberships and contributions); Keyishian v. Bd. of Regents of Univ. of State of N.Y., 385 U.S. 589 (1967) (subversive speech).

95. Jacob Bunge, *Roundup Sellers Boost Advertising as Lawsuits Mount for Weedkiller*, The Wall Street Journal, May 1, 2019, www.wsj.com/articles/roundup-sellers-boost-advertising-as-lawsuits-mount-for-weedkiller-11556738038.

96. *Monsanto Sued for False Advertising*, Matthews & Assocs., n.d., www.dmlawfirm.com/monsanto-sued-for-false-advertising/.

97. *Jury Awards Groundskeeper $289.2 Million in Landmark Monsanto Roundup Verdict*, Baum, Hedlund, Aristei, Goldman, July 7, 2017, www.baumhedlundlaw.com/toxic-tort-law/monsanto-roundup-lawsuit/california-glyphosate-warning/.

98. Malcolm C. Weiss & Shannon Oldenburg, *Judge Halts Monsanto Warning Label on First Amendment Grounds*, Nickel Rep., March 7, 2018, www.huntonnickelreportblog.com/2018/03/judge-halts-monsanto-warning-label-on-first-amendment-grounds/.

99. Carey Gillam, *Monsanto Ordered to Pay $2 Billion to Cancer Victims*, U.S. Right to Know, May 13, 2019, usrtk.org/monsanto-roundup-trial-tacker/monsanto-ordered-to-pay-2-billion-to-cancer-victims/; *But see In re* Monsanto Co. v. Office of Envtl. Health Hazard Assessment, Case No. 16 CE CG 00183, Tentative Ruling for Dept. 403, Fresno Super. Ct. Cal., Jan. 26, 2017 (dismissing suit against Monsanto).

100. *See, e.g.,* Bob Egelko, *Monsanto Wants Roundup Cancer Lawsuits Moved Out of California*, S.F.

Chron., May 30, 2019, www.sfchronicle.com/bayarea/article/Monsanto-wants-Roundup-cancer-lawsuits-moved-out-1390 7970.php.

101. Zauderer v. Office of Disciplinary Counsel of Sup. Ct. of Ohio, 471 U.S. 626, 651 (1985).

102. *Id.*

103. *Id.*

104. Sarah C. Haan, *Facebook's Alternative Facts*, 105 Va. L. Rev. Online 18 (2019).

105. *See* Sarah C. Haan, *The Post-Truth First Amendment*, 94 Indiana L.J. (2019), papers.ssrn.com/sol3/papers.cfm?abstract_id=3209366 (arguing that the application of a common ideology approach embroils courts in the current "post-truth" controversy in which "facts are a matter of perspective").

106. *See, e.g.,* Dwyer v. Cappell, 762 F.3d 275, 282–85 (3d Cir. 2014); *see also* Entm't Software Ass'n v. Blagojevich, 469 F.3d 641, 652 (7th Cir. 2006) (quoting Zauderer as authorizing disclaimers aimed at preventing deception without further analysis); United States v. Wenger, 427 F.3d 840, 849 (10th Cir. 2005).

107. *See, e.g.,* Am. Meat Inst. v. USDA, 760 F.3d 18, 20 (D.C. Cir. 2014); Disc.

Tobacco City & Lottery, Inc. v. United States, 674 F.3d 509, 559 n.8 (6th Cir. 2012); Pharm. Care Mgmt. Ass'n v. Rowe, 429 F.3d 294, 310 n.8 (1st Cir. 2005); Nat'l Elec. Mfrs. Ass'n v. Sorrell, 272 F.3d 104, 115 (2d Cir. 2001).

108. Nat'l Inst. of Family and Life Advocates v. Becerra, 138 S. Ct. 2361 (2018).

109. *Id.* at 2377.

110. *Id.* (emphasis added).

111. CTIA—The Wireless Ass'n v. City of Berkeley, 138 S. Ct. 2708 (2018).

112. CTIA—The Wireless Ass'n v. City of Berkeley, 854 F.3d 1105 (9th Cir. 2017).

113. *Id.* at 1119.

114. *Id.* at 1117.

115. Am. Beverage Ass'n v. City & Cty. of San Francisco, 871 F.3d 884, 887 (9th Cir. 2017).

116. *Id.* at 895.

117. Am. Beverage Ass'n v. City & Cty. of San Francisco, 916 F.3d 749, 757 (9th Cir. 2019).

118. Mital Patel, *American Beverage Association v. City and County of San Francisco*, FDLI, https://www.fdli.org/2020/10/american-beverage-association-v-city-and-county-of-san-francisco/.

119. Capital Broad. Co. v. Mitchell, 333 F. Supp. 582 (D.D.C. 1971).

120. Lorillard Tobacco Co. v. Reilly, 533 U.S. 525, 569 (2001).

121. Nicopure Labs v. FDA, 266 F. Supp. 3d 360 (D.D.C. 2017). *See also Effective and Compliance Dates Applicable to Retailers, Manufacturers, Importers and Distributors of Deemed Tobacco Products*, FDA, Aug. 9, 2018, www.fda.gov/tobacco-products/compliance-enforcement-training/effective-and-compliance-dates-applicable-retailers-manufacturers-importers-and-distributors-deemed.

122. Faircloth v. Food & Drug Admin., No. 2:16-CV-5267, 2017 WL 4319495, at *6 (S.D.W. Va. Sept. 28, 2017).

123. Juliet Eilperin, *FDA Delays Enforcement of Stricter Standards for E-cigarette, Cigar Industry*, WASH. POST., May 2, 2017, www.washingtonpost.com/politics/fda-suspends-enforcement-of-stricter-standards-for-e-cigarette-cigar-industry/2017/05/02/be7e557a-2ed6-11e7-9534-00e4656c22aa_story.html?utm_term=.86eaa43eec2a.

124. Madeleine Carlisle, *Federal Legal Age to Buy Tobacco Products Officially Raised to 21*, TIME, Dec. 23, 2019, https://time.com/5754266/trump-tobacco-age-21/.

125. Michael Nedelman & Jen Christensen, *Trump Budget Plan Could Push Tobacco Oversight Out of the FDA*, CNN, Feb. 10, 2020, https://www.cnn.com/2020/02/10/health/tobacco-regulation-fda-trump/index.html.

126. Katherine Ellen Foley, *Tobacco Lawsuits Could Upend Biden's Plan for Historic Menthol Ban*, POLITICO, Nov. 14, 2021, https://www.politico.com/news/2021/11/14/tobacco-lawsuits-biden-menthol-ban-521174.

127. Kim Tingley, *Vaping is Risky. Why is the FDA Authorizing E-Cigarettes?* N. Y. TIMES MAG., Nov. 23, 2021, https://www.nytimes.com/2021/11/23/magazine/vaping-fda.html.

128. *Id.*

129. Posadas de Puerto Rico Assocs. v. Tourism Co. of Puerto Rico, 478 U.S. 328, 340 (1986).

130. United States v. Edge Broad., 509 U.S. 418 (1993).

131. *Id.* at 428.

132. *Id.* at 435.

133. Rubin v. Coors Brewing Co., 514 U.S. 476 (1995).

134. *Id.* at 490.

135. Barry J. Seldon & Khosrow Doroodian, *A Simultaneous Model of Cigarette Advertising: Effects on Demand and Industry Response to Public Policy*, THE REV. OF ECON. & STAT. 71 (1989): 673; Jon P. Nelson & John R. Moran, *Advertising and U.S. Alcoholic Beverage Demand: System-Wide Estimates*, APPLIED ECON. 27 (1995): 1225.

136. *See, e.g.,* Rosalind M. Kendellen, *The Food and Drug Administration Retreats From Patient Package Inserts for Prescription Drugs*, FOOD & DRUG L.J. 40 (1985): 172. (showing the FDA's motivation for establishing a package insert plan for consumers). *But see* 1 Antitrust & Trade Reg. Rep. (BNA) No. 1277, 199 (Aug. 7, 1986).

137. Cent. Hudson Gas & Elec. Corp. v. Pub. Serv. Comm'n, 447 U.S. 557, 569 (1980).

138. Posadas de Puerto Rico Assocs. v. Tourism Co. of Puerto Rico, 478 U.S. 328, 342 (1986).

139. Lorillard Tobacco Co. v. Reilly, 533 U.S. 525, 557 (2001).

140. 44 Liquormart, Inc. v. Rhode Island, 517 U.S. 484, 507 (1996).

141. *Id.* at 496.

142. *Id.* at 509.

143. *Id.* at 497.

144. *Id.* at 505.

145. Educ. Media Co. at Va. Tech., Inc. v. Insley, 731 F.3d 291 (4th Cir. 2013).

146. Educ. Media Co. at Va. Tech. v. Swecker, 2008 U.S. Dist. LEXIS 124685 (E.D. Va., June 19, 2008), vacated, 602 F.3d 583 (4th Cir. 2010).

147. Flying Dog Brewery, LLC v. N. Carolina Alcoholic Beverage Control Comm'n, No. 5:21-CV-343-BO, 2022 WL

148. Sorrell v. IMS Health, Inc., 564 U.S. 552 (2011).

149. Vt. Stat. Ann., Tit. 18, § 4631 (Supp. 2010).

150. *Sorrell*, 564 U.S. at 580.

151. 15 U.S.C. §§7901-7903. *See alsoGun Industry Immunity*, Giffords Law Center, https://giffords.org/lawcenter/gun-laws/policy-areas/other-laws-policies/gun-industry-immunity/.

152. Calif. Penal Code § 26820.

153. Tracy Rifle & Pistol, LLC v. Harris, 339 F. Supp. 3d 1007, 1012-13 (E.D. Cal. 2018).

154. *Id.* at 1014.

155. Tracy Rifle & Pistol, LLC v. Harris, 118 F. Supp. 3d 1182 (E.D. Cal. 2015).

156. Dave Collins, *After $73 million win, Sandy Hook Families Zero in on Gun Marketing*, ABC News via AP, Feb. 19, 2022, https://abcnews.go.com/US/wireStory/73m-win-sandy-hook-families-gun-marketing-82999674.

157. *Complaint and Request for Investigation of Smith & Wesson Brands, Inc.*, Everytown Law, May 31, 2020, https://everytownlaw.org/wp-content/uploads/sites/5/2020/06/ftc-letter.pdf.

158. Seattle Mideast Awareness Campaign v. King Cty., 781 F.3d 489 (9th Cir. 2015).

159. *Id.* at 503.

160. Am. Freedom Def. Initiative v. Mass. Bay Transp. Auth., 781 F.3d 571 (1st Cir. 2015), *cert. denied*, 136 S. Ct. 793 (2016).

161. Am. Freedom Def. Initiative v. Se. Penn. Transp. Auth., 92 F. Supp. 3d 314 (E.D. Pa. 2015).

162. *Id.* at 321.

163. *Id.*

164. Va. State Bd. of Pharmacy v. Va. Citizens Consumer Council, 425 U.S. 748, 771-72 (1976); Cent. Hudson Gas & Elec. Corp., v. Pub. Serv. Comm'n, 447 U.S. 557, 564, 566 (1980); Zauderer v. Office of Disciplinary Counsel, 471 U.S. 626, 652-53 (1985); Cincinnati v. Discovery Network, 507 U.S. 410, 434 (1993); Lorillard Tobacco Co. v. Reilly, 533 U.S. 535, 576 (2001).

165. *Va. State Bd. of Pharmacy*, 425 U.S. at 777-78 (Stewart, J. concurring).

166. *Unfair Commercial Practices*, Your Europe, Dec. 14, 2022, europa.eu/youreurope/citizens/consumers/unfair-treatment/unfair-commercial-practices/index_en.htm.

167. *Id.*

168. *Consumer Rights Directive*, European Commission, https://commission.europa.eu/law/law-topic/consumer-protection-law/consumer-contract-law

/consumer-rights-directive_en.

169. Council Directive 2005/29.

170. Lorillard Tobacco Co. v. Reilly, 533 U.S. 535, 576 (2001).

171. Va. State Bd. of Pharmacy v. Va. Citizens Consumer Council, 425 U.S. 748, 771-72 (1976).

172. Zauderer v. Office of Disciplinary Counsel, 471 U.S. 626, 652-53 (1985).

173. Cincinnati v. Discovery Network, 507 U.S. 410, 434 (1993) (emphasis added).

174. Pub. Citizen v. La. Attorney Disciplinary, 632 F.3d 212, 218 (5th Cir. 2011). *See also* Am. Beverage Ass'n v. San Francisco, 871 F.3d 884, 893 (9th Cir. 2017); Ocheesee Creamery v. Putnam, 851 F.3d 1228, 1235-36 (11th Cir. 2017); Dwyer v. Cappell, 762 F.3d 275, 281-83 (3d Cir. 2014); Greater Baltimore Ctr. for Pregnancy Concerns v. Mayor of Baltimore, 721 F.3d 264, 283 (4th Cir. 2013).

175. Karlene Lukovitz, *Canada Dry Maker Faces False Advertising Lawsuits*, Marketing Daily, July 5, 2018, www.mediapost.com/publications/article/321742/canada-dry-maker-faces-false-advertising-lawsuits.html.

176. *See* Cent. Hudson Gas & Elec. Corp. v. Pub. Serv. Comm'n, 447 U.S. 557 (1980); FTC Act of

1914; Everette MacIntyre (FTC member), *Statement on Fair Advertising Landmarks*, Before N.Y. Bar Ass'n, Jan. 22, 1963 (marking the 25th anniversary of the Wheeler-Lea amendment to the FTC Act that "so greatly strengthened the authority of the FTC to protect businessmen and the public from false advertising and other deceptive and unfair acts"), www.ftc.gov/system/files/documents/public_statements/683461/19620122_macintyre_fair_advertising_landmarks.pdf.

177. *See, e.g.*, Lorillard Tobacco Co. v. Reilly, 533 U.S. 525, 540–41 (2001) (reading the U.S. Constitution's Article VI Supremacy Clause and express language of federal statutes to preempt contravening state or local actions).

178. 15 U.S.C. 1125, § 43 (a)(1)(A)(B).

179. United Industries Corp. v. Clorox Co., 140 F.3d 1175, 1180 (8th Cir. 1998).

180. 41 U.S.C. § 1125(a)(1).

181. Clorox Co., 140 F.3d at 1175, 1180.

182. Lexmark v. Static Control, 572 U.S. 118 (2014).

183. *Id.* at 131–32.

184. Lona's Lil Eats, LLC v. DoorDash, Inc., Jan. 18, 2021, N.D. Cal. Case No. 20-cv-06703-TSH, https://www.courthousenews.com/wp-content/upload

s/2021/01/Lonas_DoorDash-mtdORDER.pdf .

185. 21 U.S.C.S. § 301 et seq.

186. Aaron Taube, *Coca-Cola Loses Huge False-Advertising Case in Supreme Court*, Bus. Insider, Jun. 12, 2014, www.businessinsider.com/scotus-revives-false-ad-claims-against-coke-2014-6.

187. POM Wonderful, LLC v. Coca-Cola Co., 573 U.S. 102, 119 (2014).

188. *Lexmark*, 572 U.S. at 188.

189. Eric Goldman, *Supreme Court Changes False Advertising Law Across the Country*, Forbes, Mar. 26, 2014, www.forbes.com/sites/ericgoldman/2014/03/26/supreme-court-changes-false-advertising-law-across-the-country/#782612674671.

190. N.C. Gen. Stat. Ann. § 75-1.1

191. Minn. Stat. Ann. § 325F.67 (West).

192. No. 19-CV-07471-BLF (N.D. Cal. June 4, 2020), https://www.proskaueronadvertising.com/wp-content/uploads/sites/16/2020/07/Prescott-v.-Nestle.pdf.

193. 517 U.S. 484 (1996).

194. *Id.* at 522 (Thomas, J. concurring).

195. *Commercial Speech and the First Amendment(2020)*, Information Society Project at Yale Law School, June 2, 2020, https://law.yale.edu/isp/initiatives/floyd-abrams-in

stitute-freedom-expression/commercial-speech-and-first-amendment/commercial-speech-and-first-amendment-2020.

196. 15 U.S.C. Sec. 45 (a)(1).

197. *What the FTC Does*, FTC, https://www.ftc.gov/news-events/media-resources/what-ftc-does.

198. AMG Capital Management LLC v. FTC, slip op. 593 U.S. ___ (2021).

199. *FTC Issues Notice Contemplating Rulemaking for Security, Privacy and AI in 2022*, The Nat'l L. Rev., Dec. 1, 2021, https://www.natlawreview.com/article/ftc-issues-notice-contemplating-rulemaking-security-privacy-and-ai-2022.

200. *Id.*

201. James C. Miller III, *FTC Policy Statement on Deception*, FTC, Oct. 1, 1983, https://www.ftc.gov/system/files/documents/public_statements/410531/831014deceptionstmt.pdf.

202. *Advertising FAQ's, Guide for Small Businesses*, FTC, April 2001, https://www.ftc.gov/tips-advice/business-center/guidance/advertising-faqs-guide-small-business.

203. COVID-19 Consumer Protection Act of the 2021 Consolidated Appropriations Act, Pub. L. No. 116-260, 134 Stat. 1182, Division FF, Title XIV, § 1401, https://www.congress.gov/116/bills

/hr133/BILLS-116hr133enr.pdf.

204. Mitchell Katz, *The FTC Directed 30 More Marketers to Stop Making Unsupported Claims That Their Products and Therapies Can Effectively Prevent or Treat COVID-19*, FTC, April 29, 2021, https://www.ftc.gov/news-events/press-releases/2021/04/ftc-directed-30-more-marketers-stop-making-unsupported-claims.

205. *Id.*

206. *Protecting Consumers During the COVID-19 Pandemic: A Year in Review, Staff Report of the Federal Trade Commission*, FTC, April 2021, https://www.ftc.gov/reports/protecting-consumers-during-covid-19-pandemic-year-review.

207. *Id.*

208. *Id.*

209. *.com Disclosures: how to Make Effective Disclosures in Digital Advertising*, FTC, March 2013, https://www.ftc.gov/sites/default/files/attachments/press-releases/ftc-staff-revises-online-advertising-disclosure-guidelines/130312dotcomdisclosures.pdf.

210. *Id.*

211. *FTC to Ramp up Enforcement against Illegal Dark patterns that Trick or Trap Consumers into Subscriptions*, FTC, Oct. 28, 2021, https://www.ftc.gov/news-events/press-release

s/2021/10/ftc-ramp-enforcement-against-illegal-dark-patterns-trick-or-trap.

212. *Enforcement Policy Statement Regarding Negative Option Marketing*, FTC, Oct. 28, 2021, https://www.ftc.gov/system/files/documents/public_statements/1598063/negative_option_policy_statement-10-22-2021-tobureau.pdf.

213. Lesley Fair, *Full Disclosure*, FTC Business Blog, Sept. 23, 2014, https://www.ftc.gov/news-events/blogs/business-blog/2014/09/full-disclosure

214. Roger Colaizzi, et al., *The Best Explanation and Update on Puffery You Will Ever Read*, Antitrust 31 (Summer 2017), https://www.venable.com/files/Publication/073d0951-9fa6-4977-9e68-4deb21a819d8/Presentation/PublicationAttachment/c245d881-6fd8-434e-b068-52959159e864/Best-Explanation-and-Update-on-Puffery-You-Will-Ever-Read-Antitrust-Summer-2017.pdf.

215. Sam Sabin, *DeGeneres, Minaj Among Celebrities Whose Social Posts Drew FTC Interest in Past Year*, Morning Consult, Oct. 5, 2018, morningconsult.com/2018/10/05/degeneres-minaj-among-celebrities-whose-social-posts-drew-ftc-interest-in-past-year/.

216. Sam Sabin, *A Year After Major Actions,*

FTS's Influencer Marketing Guidelines Still Overlooked, Morning Consult, Oct. 4, 2018, morningconsult.com/2018/10/04/a-year-later-ftcs-influencer-marketing-guidelines-still-largely-ignored/.

217. *Enforcement Policy Statement on Deceptively Formatted Advertisements*, FTC, 2015, www.ftc.gov/system/files/documents/public_statements/896923/151222deceptiveenforcement.pdf; *Native Advertising: A Guide for Businesses*, FTC, Dec. 2015, www.ftc.gov/tips-advice/business-center/guidance/native-advertising-guide-businesses.

218. *FTC Policy Statement Regarding Advertising Substantiation*, FTC, Nov. 23, 1984, https://www.ftc.gov/public-statements/1984/11/ftc-policy-statement-regarding-advertising-substantiation.

219. Stephanie W. Kanwit, 2 Fed. Trade Comm'n. § 22:10 (2021-2022).

220. Pfizer, Inc., 81 F.T.C. 23, 62-64 (1972).

221. No. 13-1060 (D.C. Cir. 2015)

222. *Id.* at 45.

223. *Guides Concerning the Use of Endorsements and Testimonials in Advertising*, 16 CFR 255, https://www.ftc.gov/sites/default/files/attachments/press-releases/ftc-publishes-final-guides-governing-endorsements-testim

onials/091005revisedendorsementguides.pdf.

224. *Id.* at Sec. 255.

225. *Id* at Sec. 255.2 (c).

226. *Id.* at Sec. 255.5.

227. *Lord & Taylor Settles FTC Charges It Deceived Consumers Through Paid Article in an Online Fashion Magazine and Paid Instagram Posts by 50 "Fashion Influencers,"* FTC, March 15, 2016, www.ftc.gov/news-events/press-releases/2016/03/lord-taylor-settles-ftc-charges-it-deceived-consumers-through.

228. Complaint *in re* Lord & Taylor, LLC, Docket No. C-4576, FTC, March 15, 2016, www.ftc.gov/system/files/documents/cases/160523lordtaylorcmpt.pdf.

229. *FTC Approves Final Lord & Taylor Order Prohibiting Deceptive Advertising Techniques*, FTC, May 23, 2016, www.ftc.gov/news-events/press-releases/2016/05/ftc-approves-final-lord-taylor-order-prohibiting-deceptive.

230. Patrick Coffee, *FTC Slams Lord & Taylor for Not Disclosing Paid Social Posts and Native Ads*, AdWeek, Mar. 15, 2016, www.adweek.com/news/advertising-branding/ftc-slamslord-taylor-deceiving-customers-not-disclosing-its-native-ads-170229.

231. Agreement Containing Consent Order, *in re* Machinima, Inc., File No. 1423090, FTC, March 17, 2016.

232. *See* Closing Letter, Microsoft/Starcom, File No. 142-3090, FTC, Aug. 26, 2015, www.ftc.gov/system/files/documents/closing_letters/nid/150902machinima_letter.pdf.

233. Paul Fletcher, *Report: Nearly 40% of Publishers Ignore FTC's Native Advertising Rule*, Forbes, March 19, 2017, www.forbes.com/sites/paulfletcher/2017/03/19/nearly-40-percent-of-publishers-ignore-ftcs-native-advertising-rules/#67d0ed2967db.

234. Tracy P. Marshall & Sheila A. Millar, *FTC Issues Staff Report on Native Advertising*, Nat'l L. Rev., Jan. 3, 2018, www.natlawreview.com/article/ftc-issues-staff-report-native-advertising.

235. *Disclosures 101 for Social Media Influencers*, FTC, Nov. 2019, https://www.ftc.gov/system/files/documents/plain-language/1001a-influencer-guide-508_1.pdf.

236. J. Howard Beales, *The FTC's Use of Unfairness Authority: Its Rise, Fall, and Resurrection*, May 30, 2003, https://www.ftc.gov/public-statements/2003/05/ftcs-use-unfairness-authority-its-rise-f

all-and-resurrection#N_14_.

237. 15 U.S.C. Sec. 45(n).

238. Thomas B. Leary, *Unfairness and the Internet*, April 30, 2000, https://www.ftc.gov/public-statements/2000/04/unfairness-and-internet.

239. 799 F.3d 236 (3rd Cir. 2015).

240. *Id.* at 256.

241. *Data Breach Response: A Guide for Business*, FTC, May 2019, https://www.ftc.gov/system/files/documents/plain-language/pdf-0154_data-breach-response-guide-for-business-042519-508.pdf.

242. *FTC Imposes $5 Billion Penalty and Sweeping New Privacy Restrictions on Facebook*, FTC, July 24, 2019, https://www.ftc.gov/news-events/press-releases/2019/07/ftc-imposes-5-billion-penalty-sweeping-new-privacy-restrictions.

243. *Id.*

244. *Three Home Loan Advertisers Settle FTC Charges; Failed to Disclose Key Loan Terms in Ads*, FTC, Jan. 8, 2009, www.ftc.gov/opa/2009/01/anm.shtm.

245. Decision and Order: Am. Nationwide Mortgage Co., Docket No. C-2429, FTC, Feb. 17, 2009, www.ftc.gov/sites/default/files/documents/cases/2009/01/090108americancmpt.pdf.

246. FTC v. Corzine, No. Civ.-S-94–1446 (E.D. Cal. 1994).

247. *Uber Settles FTC Allegations That It Made Deceptive Privacy and Data Security Claims*, FTC, Aug. 15, 2017, www.ftc.gov/news-events/press-releases/2017/08/uber-settles-ftc-allegations-it-made-deceptive-privacy-data.

248. *Uber Agrees to Expanded Settlement With FTC Related to Privacy, Security Claims*, FTC, Apr. 12, 2018, www.ftc.gov/news-events/press-releases/2018/04/uber-agrees-expanded-settlement-ftc-related-privacy-security.

249. Decision and Order *in re* Uber Techs., Docket No. C-4662, FTC, Oct. 25, 2018, www.ftc.gov/system/files/documents/cases/152_3054_c-4662_uber_technologies_revised_decision_and_order.pdf.

250. Complaint *in re* Uber Techs., Docket No. C-4662, FTC, Oct. 26, 2018, www.ftc.gov/system/files/documents/cases/152_3054_c-4662_uber_technologies_revised_complaint.pdf. *See also in re* Uber Techs., 304 F. Supp. 3d 1351 (Apr. 4, 2018).

251. *Uber to Pay $20 Million Over Claims It Misled Drivers Over How Much They Would Earn*, GUARDIAN, Jan. 19, 2017, www.theguardian.com/technology/2017/jan/19/uber-settlement-ftc-driver-earnings-car-leases.

252. *In re* Volkswagen "Clean Diesel" Mktg., 328 F. Supp. 3d 963 (N.D. Cal. 2018).

253. *FTC Charges Volkswagen Deceived Consumers With Its "Clean Diesel" Campaign*, FTC, Mar. 29, 2016, www.ftc.gov/news-events/press-releases/2016/03/ftc-charges-volkswagen-deceived-consumers-its-clean-diesel.

254. *Rite Aid Settles FTC Charges That It Failed to Protect Medical and Financial Privacy of Customers and Employees*, FTC, July 27, 2010, www.ftc.gov/opa/2010/07/riteaid.shtm.

255. *Three CortiSlim Defendants to Give Up $4.5 Million in Cash and Other Assets*, FTC, Sept. 21, 2005, www.ftc.gov/news-events/press-releases/2005/09/three-cortislim-defendants-give-45-million-cash-and-other-assets.

256. Lesley Fair, *Substantiation: The Science of Compliance*, FTC, Dec. 15, 2011, www.ftc.gov/news-events/blogs/business-blog/2011/12/science-reliance-compliance.

257. Complaint *in re* Tropicana Products, Inc., Docket No. C-4145, FTC, 2005, www.ftc.gov/os/caselist/0423154/050825comp0423154.pdf.

258. Warner-Lambert Co. v. FTC, 562 F.2d 749 (1977), *cert. denied*, 435 U.S. 950 (1978).

259. *Id.* at 762, 764.

260. Michael B. Mazis, *FTC v. Novartis: The Return of Corrective Advertising?*, 20 J. PUB. POL'Y & MKTG. 114 (2001).

261. *Id.*

262. *FTC Charges Marketers With Making Unsubstantiated Claims That They Could Eliminate Consumers' Debt*, FTC, Dec. 2, 2010, www.ftc.gov/opa/2010/12/ffdc.shtm.

263. Sam Fulwood III & Henry Weinstein, *"Joe Camel" Ads Illegally Target Youths, FTC Says*, L.A. TIMES, May 29, 1997, www.latimes.com/archives/la-xpm-1997-05-29-mn-63716-story.html.

264. *Id.*

265. Stuart Elliott, *Joe Camel, A Giant in Tobacco Marketing, Is Dead at 23*, N.Y. TIMES, July 11, 1997, www.nytimes.com/1997/07/11/business/joe-camel-a-giant-in-tobacco-marketing-is-dead-at-23.html.

266. *Operators of AshleyMadison.com Settle FTC, State Charges Resulting from 2015 Data Breach That Exposed 36 Million Users' Profile Information*, FTC, Dec. 14, 2016, https://www.ftc.gov/news-events/news/press-releases/2016/12/operators-ashleymadisoncom-settle-ftc-st

ate-charges-resulting-2 015-data-breach-expose d-36-million.

267. 15 U.S.C. § 6501 et seq.

268. *Two App Developers Settle FTC Charges They Violated Children's Online Privacy Protection Act*, FTC, Dec. 17, 2016, www.ftc.gov/ne ws-events/press-relea ses/2015/12/two-app-d evelopers-settle-ftc-ch arges-they-violated-ch ildrens.

269. 16 C.F.R. § 312 et seq.; *see also* Seena Gressin, *COPPA: When Persistence Doesn't Pay*, Bus. Blog, Dec. 17, 2015, www.ftc.go v/news-events/blogs/bu siness-blog/2015/12/cop pa-when-persistence-d oesnt-pay.

270. Jessica Guynn, *FTC Calls on Online Ad Industry to Agree on Do-Not-Track Standard*, L.A. Times, Apr. 17, 2013, www.latimes.c om/business/la-xpm-20 13-apr-17-la-fi-tn-ftc-o nline-ad-industry-do-n ot-track-20130417-stor y.html.

271. *FTC Testifies on Do Not Track Legislation*, FTC, Dec. 2, 2010, www.ftc.go v/opa/2010/12/dnttestim ony.shtm.

272. Dawn Chmielewski, *How "Do Not Track" Ended Up Going Nowhere*, Vox, Jan. 4, 2016, www.vox.com/2 016/1/4/11588418/how-d o-not-track-ended-up-g oing-nowhere.

273. *FTC Completes Review of CAN-SPAM Rule*, FTC,

Feb. 12, 2019, www.ftc.g ov/news-events/press-r eleases/2019/02/ftc-co mpletes-review-can-sp am-rule.

274. 15 U.S.C. §§ 7701–7713 (2004).

275. *Id.*

276. 15 U.S.C. § 7704(a)(1).

277. *FTC Approves New Rule Provision Under the CAN-SPAM Act*, FTC, May 12, 2008, www.ftc.govopa/2 008/05/canspam.shtm.

278. 16 C.F.R. § 255.5.

279. These states are Alaska, Arizona, Arkansas, California, Colorado, Connecticut, Delaware, Florida, Georgia, Idaho, Illinois, Indiana, Iowa, Kansas, Louisiana, Maine, Maryland, Michigan, Minnesota, Missouri, Nevada, New Mexico, North Carolina, North Dakota, Ohio, Oklahoma, Pennsylvania, Rhode Island, South Dakota, Tennessee, Texas, Utah, Virginia, Washington, West Virginia, Wisconsin and Wyoming.

280. Va. Code Ann. § 18.2–152.3:1.

281. *SeeVirginia: Spam Law Struck Down on Grounds of Free Speech*, N.Y. Times, Sept. 13, 2008, at A17.

282. Jaynes v. Virginia, 666 S.E.2d 303, 314 (Va. 2008), *cert. denied*, 556 U.S. 1152 (2009).

283. Anne Field, *What Factors Cause the Great Recession? Understanding the Key Factors that Led to One of the Worst Economic Downturns in US History*, Insider, July 8, 2021, https ://www.businessinsider. com/what-caused-the-g reat-recession.

284. *Building the CFPB*, Consumer Financial Protection Bureau, https://www.con sumerfinance.gov/data-r esearch/research-repor ts/building-the-cfpb/.

285. *The Bureau*, Consumer Financial Protection Bureau, https://www.con sumerfinance.gov/abou t-us/the-bureau/.

286. Minority TV Project v. FCC, 573 U.S. 946 (2014).

287. Minority TV Project v. FCC, 736 F.3d 1192, 1204 (9th Cir. 2013).

288. *The Public and Broadcasting: Offensive Advertising*, FCC, Dec. 2018, www.fc c.gov/media/radio/publi c-and-broadcasting#OF FENSIVE.

289. Greater New Orleans Broad. Ass'n, Inc. v. United States, 527 U.S. 173 (1999).

290. *Id.*

291. Van Hollen v. FEC, 811 F.3d 486 (D.C. Cir. 2016).

292. *Id.* at 500.

293. *Id.* at 488.

294. The states are Colorado, Vermont, Wyoming, California, New Jersey, Washington and

Maryland. *See* Victoria Smith Ekstrand and Ashley Fox, *Regulating the Political Wild West: State Efforts to Disclose Sources of Online Political Advertising*, 47 J. Legis. 81 (2021).

295. Wash. Post v. McManus, 944 F.3d 506 (4th Cir. 2019).

296. Coyne Beahm, Inc. v. FDA, 966 F. Supp. 1374 (M.D.N.C. 1997).

297. *Id.* at 1399.

298. Family Smoking Prevention and Tobacco Control Act (FSPTCA), Pub. L. No. 111–31, 123 Stat. 1776 (2009).

299. Steven Reinberg, *U.S. Abandons Effort to Place Graphic Labeling on Cigarettes*, HealthDay, March 20, 2013, consumer. healthday.com/cancer-information-5/lung-cancer-news-100/u-s-abandons-effort-to-place-graphic-labeling-on-cigarettes-674641. html.

300. Discount Tobacco City & Lottery Co. v. United States, 674 F.3d 509 (6th Cir. 2012), *cert. denied*, 569 U.S. 946 (2013); R.J. Reynolds Tobacco Co. v. FDA, 696 F.3d 1205 (D.C. Cir. 2012).

301. *R.J. Reynolds Tobacco Co.*, 696 F.3d at 1219.

302. *See, e.g.*, Discount Tobacco City, 674 F.3d 524–25.

303. *Discount Tobacco City*, 674 F.3d at 509; R.J. *Reynolds*

Tobacco Co., 696 F.3d at 1205.

304. *The Facts on the FDA's New Tobacco Rule*, FDA, Apr. 8, 2017, www.fda.go v/ForConsumers/Cons umerUpdates/ucm5066 76.htm

305. Nicopure Labs v. FDA, 266 F. Supp. 3d 360 (D.D.C. 2017); Cigar Ass'n of Am. v. FDA, 315 F. Supp. 3d 143 (D.D.C. 2018).

306. Cigar Ass'n of Am., 315 F. Supp. 3d at 164–67.

307. Jeffrey A. Greenbaum, *United States: FDA Issues Warning Letters to Vaping Companies*, mondaq, Dec. 14, 2021, https://www.m ondaq.com/unitedstates /media-telecoms-it-ente rtainment/1141266/fda-i ssues-warning-letters-t o-vaping-companies.

308. *What We Do*, SEC, Nov. 22, 2021, https://www.sec.g ov/about/what-we-do.

309. *Id.*

310. *Anonymous Whistleblower Disclosure*, WhistleBlower Aid, https://drive.google. com/file/d/1_HXsokitiJ5 b_5jOTvhvITlmQHAt3M9 m/viewt.

311. First Nat'l Bank of Boston v. Bellotti, 435 U.S. 765 (1978).

312. *See, e.g.*, FEC v. Nat'l Right to Work Comm., 459 U.S. 197 (1982); FEC v. Nat'l Conservative Political Action Comm., 470 U.S. 480 (1985); FEC v. Mass. Citizens for Life, Inc., 479 U.S. 238 (1986);

Austin v. Mich. State Chamber of Commerce, 494 U.S. 652 (1990).

313. *First Nat'l Bank*, 435 U.S. at 776.

314. Citizens United v. FEC, 558 U.S. 310 (2010).

315. *Id.* at 342. *See also* Tim Lau, *Citizens United Explained*, The Brennan Center, Dec. 12, 2019, htt ps://www.brennancente r.org/our-work/researc h-reports/citizens-unite d-explained.

316. Lau, *supra* note 315.

317. Ian Vandewalker, *Since Citizens United a Decade of Super PACs*, The Brennan Center, Jan. 14, 2020, https://www.brennance nter.org/our-work/anal ysis-opinion/citizens-un ited-decade-super-pacs.

318. Peter Horst, *Gillette's Controversial "Toxic Masculinity" Ad and the Opportunity It Missed*, Forbes, Jan. 18, 2019, www.forbe s.com/sites/peterhorst/ 2019/01/18/gillettes-con troversial-toxic-mascul inity-ad-and-the-oppor tunity-it-missed/#57aef 3ff5506.

319. Carl Jones, *Getting Ads Banned Is a Planned PR and Advertising Strategy*, Drum, Nov. 21, 2018, ww w.thedrum.com/opinion /2018/11/21/getting-ad s-banned-planned-pr-a nd-advertising-strateg y; Sam Pudwell, *Gillette Ad: What's Wrong With Controversy in PR?*, Red Lorry Yellow Lorry, Jan. 16, 2019, www.rlyl.com/u

s/gillette-ad-pr-controversy-2/. *See also* ANNE M. CRONIN, PUBLIC RELATIONS CAPITALISM 105–16 (2018).

320. Nike, Inc. v. Kasky, 539 U.S. 654 (2003).

321. Kasky v. Nike, Inc., 45 P.3d 243, 258 (Cal. 2002).

322. People of New York v. Exxon Mobil Corp., Dec. 10, 2019, https://int.nyt.com/data/documenthelper/6569-new-york-vs-exxonmobil/eb27e49cb4cdbb4add80/optimized/full.pdf#page=1.

323. *See, e.g.*, Bates v. State Bar of Ariz., 433 U.S. 350 (1977).

324. *Id.*

325. Kiser v. Kamdar, 831 F.3d 784 (6th Cir. 2016).

326. Conant v. Walters, 309 F.3d 629, 637 (9th Cir. 2002).

327. Wollschlaeger v. Governor, Fla., 848 F.3d 1293 (11th Cir. 2017).

328. *Id.* at 1313–14.

329. 585 U.S. ___ (2018).

330. *See, e.g.*, William D. Araiza, *Invasion of the Content Neutrality Rule*, 2019 BYU L. REV. 875 (2020).

331. *See, e.g.*, Mark Robertson, *Proposed Federal Alcohol Labeling Revisions Retain Constitutionally Suspect Review Standards*, FORBES, Apr. 8, 2019, www.forbes.com/sites/wlf/2019/04/08/proposed-federal-alcohol-labeling-revisions-retain-constitutionally-susp

ect-review-standards/#4e40048323c2; Sarah C. Haan, *The Post-Truth First Amendment*, 94 INDIANA L.J. 1351 (2019); Valerie C. Brannon, *Assessing Commercial Disclosure Requirements Under the First Amendment*, CONG. RES. SERV., Apr. 23, 2019, fas.org/sgp/crs/misc/R45700.pdf.

332. Mark Robertson, *Proposed Federal Alcohol Labeling Revisions Retain Constitutionally Suspect Review Standards*, FORBES, Apr. 8, 2019, www.forbes.com/sites/wlf/2019/04/08/proposed-federal-alcohol-labeling-revisions-retain-constitutionally-suspect-review-standards/#4e40048323c2.

333. *Id.*

334. Eugene Volokh, *The Law of Compelled Speech*, 97 TEX. L. REV. 355, 395 (2018–19). *See also* R. Randall Kelso, *Clarifying Viewpoint Discrimination in Free Speech Doctrine*, 52 IND. L. REV. 355 (2019) (arguing that the Court's review of compelled speech cases has caused "unnecessary confusion" among lower courts).

335. Andrew Jacobs, *Lawsuits Over 'Misleading' Food Labels Surge as Groups Cite Lax U.S. Oversight*, N.Y. TIMES, Sept. 7, 2021, https://www.nytimes.com/2021/09/07/science/food-labels-lawsuits.html.

336. *Id.*

337. Reed Mangels, *US Food and Drug Administration Plans to Develop Guidelines for Labeling Plant Milks*, THE VEGETARIAN RESOURCE GROUP BLOG, July 30, 2021, https://www.vrg.org/blog/2021/07/30/us-food-and-drug-administration-plans-to-develop-guidelines-for-labeling-plant-milks/.

338. Nick Sibilla, *FDA Crackdown on Calling Almond Milk "Milk" Could Violate the First Amendment*, FORBES, Jan. 31, 2019, www.forbes.com/sites/nicksibilla/2019/01/31/fda-crackdown-on-calling-almond-milk-milk-could-violate-the-first-amendment/#743f3ccc7b70.

339. *U.S. Non-Dairy Milk Sales Grow 61% Over the Last Five Years*, MINTEL, Jan. 4, 2018, www.mintel.com/press-centre/food-and-drink/us-non-dairy-milk-sales-grow-61-over-the-last-five-years.

340. Allison Shoemaker, *Some Dairy Farmers Would Rather You Call It "Nut Juice" Than Almond Milk*, TAKEOUT, Feb. 19, 2019, thetakeout.com/dairy-farmers-rather-you-call-it-nut-juice-almond-milk-1832732529.

341. Kevin Pang, *Meat Association Would Like Fake Meat Companies to Not Use the Word Meat*, TAKEOUT, Feb. 26, 2018, thetakeout.com/meat-association-would-like-

fake-meat-companies-to-not-1823344442.

342. *Scope of the Meat Labeling Law Issue Tracker*, Penn State Law Center for Agricultural and Shale Law, https://aglaw.psu.edu/wp-content/uploads/2021/04/Turtle-Island-Foods-v.-Richardson-Opinion-3.29.21.pdf

343. Turtle Island Foods, SPC v. Thompson, 992 F.3d 694 (8th Cir. 2021).

344. 7 U.S.C.S. § 1639i (2019). Dan Charles, *Congress Just Passed a GMO Labeling Bill. Nobody's Super Happy About It*, NPR: All Things Considered, July 14, 2016, www.npr.org/sections/thesalt/2016/07/14/486060866/congress-just-passed-a-gmo-labeling-bill-nobodys-super-happy-about-it.

345. 7 C.F.R. § 66.100(c), https://www.federalregister.gov/documents/2018/12/21/2018-27283/national-bioengineered-food-disclosure-standard.

346. Jan de Beer and Chanhee Han, *Modernization of Labeling and Advertising Regulations on Alcoholic Beverages*, FrostBrownTodd, June 16, 2020, https://frostbrowntodd.com/modernization-of-labeling-and-advertising-regulations-on-alcoholic-beverages/.

347. *Id.*

348. 514 U.S. 476 (1995).

NAME INDEX

SUBJECT INDEX